Huxford's
OLD BOOK
Value Guide

Third Edition

25,000 Listings of Old Books with Current Values

COLLECTOR BOOKS
A Division of Schroeder Publishing Co., Inc.

The current values in this book should be used only as a guide. They are not intended to set prices, which vary from one section of the country to another. Auction prices as well as dealer prices vary greatly and are affected by condition as well as demand. Neither the Editors nor the Publisher assumes responsibility for any losses that might be incurred as a result of consulting this guide.

On the cover:

Alger, Horatio. *Risen From the Ranks*. New York Book Co.
Braden, James A. *The Auto Boys' Quest*. Saalfield Pub. Co., 1927.
Rockwood, Roy. *Bomba the Jungle Boy on Jaguar Island*. Cupples & Leon, New York, 1927.
Reade, Charles. *A Simpleton*. P.F. Collier & Son, New York.
Fox, John, Jr. *The Trail of the Lonesome Pine*. Grosset & Dunlap, New York, 1908.
Defoe, Daniel. *Robinson Crusoe*. Doubleday, & Co., Garden City, New York, 1946.
Duffield, J.W. *Bert Wilson's Twin Cylinder Race*. Sully and Kleinteich, 1914.
Cobb, Irvin S. *Fibble D.D*. George H. Doran Co., New York, 1916.
Cohen, Lester. *Coming Home*. Viking Press, New York, 1945.
Alcott, L.M. *Rose in Bloom*. Saalfield Pub. Co., 1932.
Hobson, Laura. *Gentleman's Agreement*. Simon & Schuster, New York, 1947.
Grey, Zane. *The Lone Star Ranger*. Grosset & Dunlap, New York, 1915.
Connor, Ralph. *The Prospector*. Fleming H. Revell Co., New York. 1904.
Dumas, Alexandre. *The Three Musketeers*. Doubleday & Co., Garden City, New York, 1952.

Additional copies of this book may be ordered from:

Collector Books
P.O. Box 3009
Paducah, KY 42002-3009

@$19.95. Add $2.00 for postage and handling.

Copyright: Schroeder Publishing Co., Inc. 1991

Introduction

This book was compiled to help the owner of old books evaluate his holdings and find a buyer for them. Most of us have a box, trunk, stack, or bookcase of old books. Chances are they are not rare books, but they may have value. Two questions that we are asked most frequently are 'Can you tell me the value of my old books?' and 'Where can I sell them?' *Huxford's Old Book Value Guide* will help answer both of these questions. Not only does this book place retail values on over 25,000 old books, it also lists scores of buyers along with the type of material each is interested in purchasing. Note that we list retail values (values that an interested party would be willing to pay to obtain possession of the book). These prices are taken from recent dealer's selling lists. Some of the listings are coded (A1, S7, etc.) before the price. This coding refers to a specific dealer's listing for that book. Please refer to the section titled 'Book Sellers' for information.

If you were to sell your books to a dealer, you would expect to receive no more than 50% of the values listed in this book unless the dealer had a specific buyer in mind for some of your material. In many cases, a dealer will pay less than 50% of retail for a book to stock.

Do not ask a dealer to evaluate your old books unless you intend to sell your books to him. Most Antiquarian book dealers in the larger cities will appraise your books and ephemera for a fee that ranges from a low of $10.00 per hour to $50.00 per hour. If you were to have an extensive library of rare books, the $50.00-an-hour figure would be money well spent (assuming, of course, the appraiser to be qualified and honest).

Huxford's Old Book Value Guide places values on the more common holdings that many seem to accumulate. You will notice that many of the books listed are in the $5.00 to $20.00 range. Many such guides list only the rare, almost non-existent books that the average person will never see. The format is very simple: the listings are alphabetized first by the name of the author, translator, editor, or illustrator; if more than one book is listed for a particular author, each title is listed alphabetically under his or her name. Also dust jackets or wrappers are noted when present, and sizes when given are approximate.

In the back of the book, we have listed buyers of books and book-related material. When you correspond with these dealers, be sure to enclose a self-addressed, stamped envelope if you want a reply. Please do not send lists of books for an appraisal. If you wish to sell your books, quote the price that you want or negotiate price only on the items the buyer is interested in purchasing. When you list your books, do so by author, full title, publisher and place, date, and edition. Indicate condition, noting any defects on cover or contents.

When shipping your books, first wrap each book in paper such as brown kraft or a similar type of material. Never use newspaper for the inner wrap, since newsprint tends to rub off. (It may, however be used as a cushioning material within the outer carton.) Place your books in a sturdy corrugated box, and use a good shipping tape to seal it. Tape impregnated with nylon string is preferable, as it will not tear.

Books shipped by parcel post may be sent at a special fourth class book rate, which is much lower than regular parcel post zone rates.

Listing of Standard Abbreviations

Am........American	Intro........introduction	TEG........top edge gilt
AEG........all edge gilt	lg........large	Trans........translated
/........and	Lib........library	U........University
AP........Advance Proof	Ltd........limited	VG........very good
ARC........Advance Reading Copy	M........minted	W........west, western
bdg........binding, bound	MIT........MA Institute of Technology	wraps........wrappers
BOMC........Book of the Month Club	MOMA........Museum of Modern Art	xl........ex-library
c........circa	N........north, northern	#d........numbered
dj........dust jacket	nd........no date	12mo........about 7" tall
dtd........dated	np........no place	16mo........6 to 7" tall
E........east, eastern	orig........original	24mo........5 to 6" tall
ed........edition	p........page, pages	32mo........4 to 5" tall
Eng........English	pb........paperback	48mo........less than 4" tall
ep........end pages	pl........plate	64mo........about 3" tall
ES........errata slip	Pr........press	sm 8vo........7½ to 8" tall
EX........excellent	Pub........publisher	8vo........8 to 9" tall
fld........folded	RS........review slip	sm 4to........about 10" tall
G........good	S........south, southern	4to........between 11 to 13" tall
GPO........Government Printing Office	s/wrap........shrink wrap	folio........13" or larger
HrdCvr........hard cover	SF........Science Fiction	elephant folio........23" or larger
Ils........illustrated	SftCvr........soft cover	atlas folio........25"
imp........impression	sgn........signature, signed	double elephant folio........larger than 25"
inscr........inscribed	sm........small	
Internat........international	TB........textbook	

A'BECKETT, G.A. *Comic History of England.* c 1880. London. Ils Leech. AEG. green bdg. VG. $130.00

A'BECKETT, G.A. *Comic History of England.* nd. London. Ils Leech. 4to. 304 p. 2 vols in 1. $145.00

A'BECKETT, G.A. *Comic History of Rome.* Bradbury Agnew. Ils John Leech. 8vo. VG. $350.00

A'KEMPIS, Thomas. *Of the Imitation of Christ.* 1878. London. Ils. 8vo. AEG. gilt leather. VG. T1. $40.00

AARON, J. *Second Sight.* 1982. NY. UCP. VG. $25.00

AARONSON, S.D. *Law of Israel.* 1897. 3 vols. red bdg. fair. $75.00

ABBEY, Edward. *Desert Solitaire.* 1968. NY. 1st ed. dj. VG. $50.00

ABBEY, Edward. *Hayduke Lives!* Boston. UCP. yellow wraps. EX. $75.00

ABBEY, Edward. *Jonathan Troy.* 1954. NY. Dodd Mead. 1st Am ed. dj. $200.00

ABBEY, Edward. *Monkey Wrench Gang.* 1975. Phil. 1st ed. dj. M. $150.00

ABBEY, Edward. *Vox Clamantis in Deserto.* 1989. Santa Fe. 1/250. slipcase. EX. $125.00

ABBOTT, A.O. *Prison Life in the S...* 1865. Ils. 374 p. G. J4. $15.00

ABBOTT, Berenice. *Berenice Abbott, American Photographer.* 1982. McGraw Hill. Ils. folio. dj. $75.00

ABBOTT, Berenice. *Guide to Better Photography.* 1941. NY. Crown. Ils. 4to. 182 p. dj. $75.00

ABBOTT, Berenice. *World of Atget.* 1964. NY. Horizon. 1st ed. 4to. dj. EX. $65.00

ABBOTT, C.C. *Wasteland Wanderings.* 1887. Harper. 1st ed. VG. $25.00

ABBOTT, John. *History of Civil War in America.* 1863. NY. Ils. 2 vols. $70.00

ABBOTT, John. *History of Hortense.* 1870. Harper. Ils. VG. $25.00

ABBOTT, John. *History of the Civil War in America.* 1863. Ils. 2 vols. original leather. K1. $32.50

ABBOTT, John. *Life of General Ulysses S. Grant.* 1868. Ils. 309 p. K1. $13.50

ABBOTT, R.J. *American Seashells.* 1954. Van Nostrand. 40 pls. 541 p. dj. VG. M2. $35.00

ABBOTT, S. *NH Volunteers.* 1890. NY. Ils 1st ed. orig cloth. EX. R1. $125.00

ABBOTT, Wilbur. *NY in the American Revolution.* 1929. Scribner. 1st ed. VG. J2. $12.50

ABBOTT & HENNING *S African Butterflies.* 1984. S Africa. Macmillan. Ils 1st ed. dj. M2. $22.00

ABDILL, G.B. *Civil War Railroads: Pictorial History 1861-1865.* Bonanza. reprint. 192 p. dj. EX. M2. $20.00

ABDILL, G.B. *This Was Railroading.* 1958. Seattle. Ils. folio. dj. VG. $12.00

ABE, Kobo. *Secret Rendezvous.* 1979. NY. 1st ed. dj. VG. $25.00

ABERCONWAY, Christabel. *Story of Mr. Korah.* 1954. London. Ils Whistler. dj. EX. $20.00

ABERCROMBIE, John. *Inquiries Concerning Intellectual Powers.* 1832. Harper. reprint 2nd Edinburgh ed. $27.50

ABERCROMBIE, W.R. *Copper River Exploring Expedition.* 1890. WA. 168 photos. 169 p. M2. $65.00

ABERLE, S.D. *Pueblo Indians of NM: Their Land, Economy & Organization.* 1940. Am Antho Assn. Ils. map. 93 p. wraps. A3. $35.00

ABERNATHY, Byron. *Private Elisha Stockwell, Jr. Sees the Civil War.* 1958. Norman. OK U. 1st ed. 8vo. dj. VG. $35.00

ABERNATHY, T.P. *Burr Conspiracy.* 1954. NY. Ils 1st ed. 301 p. dj. B2. $22.50

ABERNATHY, T.P. *Burr Conspiracy.* 1954. NY. 1st ed. 301 p. dj. T5. $22.50

ABERT, J.W. *Through Country of Comanche Indian in Fall of 1845.* 1970. San Francisco. 1/5000. pls. dj. EX. $95.00

ABERT, J.W. *W America in 1846-1847.* 1966. San Francisco. 4to. EX. $60.00

ABINGDON & SEU. *More Boners.* 1931. 2nd print. VG. $80.00

ABLES, E.D. *Axis Deer in TX.* 1977. A&M U. photos. 86 p. M. M2. $10.00

ABLES, Robert. *Antique Firearms & Edged-Weapons Catalogs.* c 1960. EX. $7.00

ABLES, Robert. *Classic Bowie Knives.* 1968. NY. 1st ed. dj. EX. $35.00

ABRAMS, Alan. *Special Treatment.* 1985. NY. 1st ed. dj. VG. $7.50

ABRAMS, H.D. *Medora Field Perkerson.* nd. np. Ils. 24 p. printed wraps. $6.50

ABRAMS, Leroy. *Illustrated Flora of Pacific States.* 1955. Stanford. EX. $100.00

ABRAMSKY, Chimen. *Jews in Poland.* 1986. NY. 1st ed. dj. VG. $10.00

ACEE BLUE EAGLE. *OK Indian Painting & Poetry.* 1959. Tulsa. dj. VG. $12.00

ACHESON, Arthur. *Mistress Davenant: Dark Lady of Shakespeare's Sonnets.* 1913. London. EX. $55.00

ACHESON, D. *Present at the Creation.* 1969. NY. N Pub. 789 p. dj. EX. $10.00

ACKERMAN, I.C. *Complete Fox Terrier.* 1938. Orange Judd. 312 p. dj. VG. $18.00

ACKERMAN, W.K. *Historical Sketch of IL Central Railroad.* 1890. 153 p. rebound. $35.00

ACKROYD, Peter. *Hawksmore.* 1985. Harper. 1st Am ed. dj. EX. $17.00

ACKROYD, Peter. *Last Testament of Oscar Wilde.* 1983. London. Hamilton. 1st ed. dj. M. $35.00

ACOSTA, O. *Autobiography of Brown Buffalo.* 1972. Straight Arrow. dj. M. $35.00

ACTON, Harold. *Prince Isidore.* 1950. London. Methuen. 1st ed. dj. EX. $75.00

ACWORTH, Bernard. *Butterfly Miracles & Mysteries.* 1947. Eyre Spottiswoode. 1st ed. dj. J2. $17.50

ACWORTH, Bernard. *Cuckoo & Other Bird Mysteries.* 1946. Eyre Spottiswoode. 202 p. VG. M2. $10.00

ADAIR, Douglas. *Fame & the Founding Fathers.* NY. Norton. dj. VG. $30.00

ADAIR, J. *Adair's History of American Indians.* 1973. Promontory. reprint. 508 p. dj. M2. $18.00

ADAIR, J. *Adair History & Genealogy.* 1924. Los Angeles. Ils. G. $15.00

ADAMIC, Louis. *My America.* 1938. NY. Harper. 1st ed. sgn. dj. $30.00

ADAMIC, Louis. *Native's Return.* 1934. Harper. 1st ed. $12.00

ADAMS, A.B. *Eternal Quest: Story of the Great Naturalists.* 1986. Putnam. Ils. 509 p. dj. EX. M2. $16.00

ADAMS, Andy. *Outlet.* 1905. Boston/NY. Ils. $80.00

ADAMS, Andy. *TX Matchmaker.* 1904. Boston. Ils 1st ed. 355 p. G. T5. $22.50

ADAMS, Ansel. *Images 1923-1974.* 1974. NY Graphic. 1st ed. sgn. dj. boxed. VG. B2. $200.00

ADAMS, Ansel. *My Camera in the National Parks.* Houghton. 1st ed. sgn. spiral bdg. dj. VG. $215.00

ADAMS, Ansel. *Photographs of the SW.* 1976. NY Graphic Soc. 1st ed. inscr. dj. EX. $75.00

ADAMS, Ansel. *Photographs of the SW.* 1984. NY. oblong 4to. 128 p. wraps. VG. $15.00

ADAMS, Ansel. *Yosemite & the Range of Light.* 1979. NY Graphic Soc. Special ed. 1st print. wraps. EX. $65.00

ADAMS, Ansel. *Yosemite & the Range of Light.* 1980. Time Life. Special ed. sgn. dj. EX. $100.00

ADAMS, Ansel. *Yosemite & the Range of Light.* 1981. 4th print. dj. VG. $50.00

ADAMS, Brooks. *Emancipation of MA.* 1919. Houghton. Revised Enlarged 1st ed. VG. J2. $12.50

ADAMS, C.B. *Old Cabin Home Minstrels.* 1921. Lorenz, NY. 40 p. paper wraps. G. $7.50

ADAMS, C.F. *Studies of Military & Diplomatic America 1775-1865.* 1911. Macmillan. 1st ed. J2. $12.50

ADAMS, Charles. *Home Bodies.* 1954. Simon Schuster. 1st ed. dj. VG. $25.00

ADAMS, Clinton. *Fritz Scholder Lithographs.* 1975. Boston. NY Graphic Soc. dj. EX. $25.00

ADAMS, Douglas. *Dirk Gently's Holistic Detective Agency.* Simon Schuster. 1st ed. dj. M. $12.50

ADAMS, E.C.L. *Congaree Sketches, Scenes From Negro Life...* 1927. Chapel Hill. 1st ed. 116 p. $27.50

ADAMS, E.C.L. *Nigger to Nigger.* 1928. Scribner. 12mo. 270 p. VG. $47.50

ADAMS, E.L. *Pirates of the Air.* 1929. Grosset Dunlap. 12mo. VG. $15.00

ADAMS, Evangeline. *Bowl of Heaven.* 1926. NY. $60.00

ADAMS, F.C. *Story of a Trooper.* 1865. NY. 1st ed. 616 p. B2. $60.00

ADAMS, G.W. *Doctors in Blue: Medical History of Union Army.* 1952. NY. 1st ed. sgn. dj. EX. $28.00

ADAMS, George. *Roxbury Directory.* 1856. Roxbury. 24mo. cloth bdg. xl. T5. $12.50

ADAMS, H.C. *Traveler's Tales. A Book of Marvels.* 1927. NY. Ils Siegel. 334 p. VG. T5. $22.50

ADAMS, H.G. *Language & Poetry of Flowers.* 1868. Phil. 4 pls. 272 p. G. M2. $18.00

ADAMS, Henry. *History of US During the Administration of Jefferson.* 1930. Boni. 4 vols. VG. J2. $60.00

ADAMS, Henry. *Letters to a Niece & Prayer to the Virgin of Chartres.* 1920. Boston. 1st ed. EX. $20.00

ADAMS, Henry. *Mont-Saint-Michel & Chartres.* 1913. Boston/NY. orig bdg. VG. J2. $45.00

ADAMS, J.Q. *Oration on Life & Character of Gilbert Mottier de Lafayette.* 1835. NY. Minor. 32 p. wraps. rebound. VG. $90.00

ADAMS, James T. *Adams' New Musical Dictionary. Vol. I.* 1865. NY. Gordon. Ils. 8vo. 271 p. VG. $25.00

ADAMS, James T. *America's Tragedy.* 1934. 414 p. K1. $12.50

ADAMS, James T. *Dictionary of American History.* 1940. NY. Revised 2nd ed. 7 vols. xl. VG. $20.00

ADAMS, Joey. *Cindy & I: Real Life Adventures of Mr. & Mrs. Joey Adams.* 1957. Crown. sgn. $8.50

ADAMS, John. *Reminiscences of the 19th MA Regiment.* 1899. 186 p. K1. $55.00

ADAMS, R.F. *Best of the American Cowboy.* 1957. Norman. Ils. sgn. dj. EX. $50.00

ADAMS, R.F. *Cowman & His Philosophy.* 1967. Austin. 1/750. sgn. EX. $60.00

ADAMS, R.F. *Fitting Death for Billy the Kid.* 1960. Norman. Ils. dj. EX. $30.00

ADAMS, R.F. *From the Pecos to the Powder: Cowboy's Autobiography...* 1965. Norman. Ils. dj. EX. $50.00

ADAMS, R.F. *Language of the Railroader.* 1977. 180 p. RS. $14.50

ADAMS, R.F. *Old-Time Cowhand.* 1961. NY. 1st ed. G. $25.00

ADAMS, R.F. *Old-Time Cowhand.* 1961. NY. 1st ed. 354 p. dj. EX. $35.00

ADAMS, R.F. *Prose & Poetry of the Livestock Industry.* 1959. Antiquarian. facsmilie ed. slipcase. EX. T6. $275.00

ADAMS, R.F. *Six-Guns & Saddle Leather.* 1954. OK. 1st ed. sgn. 426 p. dj. VG. $125.00

ADAMS, R.G. *About Books: Gathering of Essays.* 1941. Berkeley. 1/450. G. $29.50

ADAMS, Rachael. *On the Other Hand: Life in the Upper Reaches of Government.* 1963. Harper Row. 1st ed. dj. EX. $10.00

ADAMS, Richard. *Shardik.* 1974. Simon Schuster. 1st Am ed. sgn. dj. $30.00

ADAMS, Robert. *Alternatives.* 1989. Baen. 1st ed. pb. M. C1. $4.50

ADAMS, Robert. *Bili the Axe.* 1985. Orbit 8133. sgn. EX. P1. $5.00

ADAMS, Robert. *Narrative of Robert Adams Wrecked on W Coast of Africa...* 1816. London. 4to. VG. $200.00

ADAMS, Robert. *Woman of the Horse Clans.* 1985. Orbit 8135. sgn. EX. P1. $5.00

ADAMS, S.H. *A. Woollcott: His Life & His World.* 1945. Ils. dj. VG. $10.00

ADAMS, W.H.D. *Land of Incas; or, Story of Francisco Pizarro...* c 1890. London. Book Soc. Ils. VG. $25.00

ADAMS, W.I. *Sunlight & Shadow: Book for Photographers...* 1897. NY. Ils Stieglitz. AEG. EX. scarce. T5. $350.00

ADAMS, W.L. *Exploits & Adventures of a Soldier Ashore & Afloat.* 1911. Lippincott. G. $15.00

ADAMS & JOESTING. *Introduction to HI.* 1964. San Francisco. VG. P3. $35.00

ADAMS & NEWHALL. *This Is the American Earth.* 1960. San Francisco. Sierra Club. 1st ed. folio. dj. VG. $85.00

ADAMS & NEWHALL. *This Is the American Earth.* 1960. Sierra Club. 2nd ed. dj. EX. $75.00

ADAMSON, Joy. *Born Free.* 1960. Pantheon. 1st ed. dj. M. $12.00

ADAMSON, Joy. *Spotted Sphinx.* 1969. Harcourt Brace. Ils 1st Am ed. 313 p. dj. EX. M2. $11.00

ADAMSON, Joy. *Spotted Sphinx.* 1969. Harcourt Brace. 1st Am ed. dj. M. $12.00

ADDAMS, Charles. *Homebodies.* 1954. NY. 1st ed. 4to. VG. $29.00

ADDAMS, Charles. *Monster Rally.* 1950. NY. 1st ed. dj. VG. $25.00

ADDINGTON, J.E. *Hidden Mystery of the Bible.* 1969. NY. $12.50

ADDINGTON, L.F. *Story of Wise Co., VA.* 1956. HrdCvr. reprint. 294 p. J4. $24.00

ADDINGTON, R.M. *History of Scott Co., VA.* 1932. private print. VG. $60.00

ADDISON, Joseph. *Works of Joseph Addison.* 1855. NY. 3 vols in 1. full calf. $75.00

ADDISON & STEELE. *Spectator.* 1832. Phil. 2 vols in 1. G. $15.00

ADELER, Max. *In Happy Hollow.* 1903. Coates. Ils Dwiggins. 1st ed. $12.00

ADELSON, Alan. *Lodz Ghetto.* 1989. NY. 1st ed. dj. $15.00

ADES, Dawn. *20th-C Poster.* 1984. Abbeville. 216 p. dj. xl. VG. $12.00

ADHEMAR, Jean. *Toulousse-Lautrec: Complete Lithographs & Drypoints.* nd. Abrams. dj. VG. $85.00

ADLEMAN, R. *Devil's Brigade.* 1966. Phil. 1st ed. 259 p. dj. VG. $15.00

ADLER, Bill. *Dear President Johnson.* 1964. NY. Ils Shulz. 1st ed. dj. G. $15.00

ADLER, Edward. *Notes From a Dark Street.* 1962. NY. 1st ed. dj. VG. $25.00

ADLER, H.L.M. *Mencken Bibliography.* 1961. Baltimore. 1st ed. $50.00

ADLER, Jacques. *Jews of Paris & the Final Solution.* 1987. NY. 1st ed. dj. EX. $20.00

ADLER, Mortimer. *How To Read a Book.* 1972. Simon Schuster. $12.00

ADLER, Mortimer. *Idea of Freedom.* 1958. NY. VG. $22.50

ADLER & MARGALITH. *With Firmness in the Right: American Diplomatic Action...* 1946. NY. EX. $12.50

ADNEY & CHAPELLE. *Bark Canoes & Skin Boats of N America.* 1964. WA. Ils. photos. 4to. EX. $50.00

ADRICH, T.B. *Course of True Love Never Did Run Smooth.* 1858. NY. 1st ed. 1st state. $20.00

AGARD, Walter. *Classical Myths in Sculpture.* 1951. WI U. 1st ed. dj. J2. $25.00

AGASSIZ, G.R. *Letters & Recollections of Alexander Agassiz.* 1913. Houghton Mifflin. Ils 1st ed. M2. $35.00

AGASSIZ, Louis. *Contributions to the Natural History of the USA.* 1857-1860. Boston. 3 vols. rebound. M2. $350.00

AGASSIZ, Louis. *Geological Sketches.* 1876. Osgood. 229 p. EX. M2. $25.00

AGASSIZ, Louis. *Journey in Brazil.* 1871. Boston. 8th ed. VG. $25.00

AGEE, James. *Collected Short Prose of James Agee.* 1968. Houghton Mifflin. 1st ed. dj. $20.00

AGEE, James. *Death in the Family.* 1957. Obolensky. 1st ed. dj. $27.50

AGEE, James. *Letters to Father Flye.* 1962. NY. 1st ed. dj. VG. B2. $17.50

AGEE, James. *Obolensky.* 1957. 2nd ed. dj. VG. $20.00

AGEE, James. *On Film.* 1958. NY. McDowell Obolensky. 1st ed. VG. $12.00

AGEE & EVANS. *Let Us Now Praise Famous Men.* 2nd ed. dj. EX. S2. $50.00

AGEE & EVANS. *Let Us Now Praise Famous Men.* 1941. Boston. Houghton. 1st ed. VG. $135.00

AGEE & EVANS. *Let Us Now Praise Famous Men.* 1941. Boston. 1st ed. sgn. dj. M. $175.00

AGEE & EVANS. *Let Us Now Praise Famous Men.* 1960. Boston. Revised 1st ed. dj. VG. B2. $25.00

AGEMATSU, Yuji. *Rudolf Steiner.* 1985. Parco Ltd. Ils. photos. 180 p. dj. D2. $65.00

AGNEW, Brad. *Ft. Gibson: Terminal of the Trail of Tears.* 1981. OK U. photos. maps. 274 p. dj. EX. M2. $15.00

AGRICOLA, G. *De Re Metallica.* 1950. Dover. Trans Hoover. dj. EX. M2. $25.00

AI. *Killing Floor.* 1979. Boston. UCP. VG. $30.00

AI. *Sin.* 1986. Houghton. ARC. wraps. EX. $25.00

AIKEN, Conrad. *Clerk's Journal.* 1971. NY. Eakins. Ltd ed. 1/300. sgn. dj. boxed. $75.00

AIKEN, Conrad. *In the Human Heart.* 1940. NY. 1st ed. dj. EX. $40.00

AIKEN, Conrad. *John Deth & Other Poems.* 1930. NY. 140 p. dj. VG. $45.00

AIKEN, Conrad. *Selected Poems.* 1982. NY. UCP. VG. $20.00

AIKEN, Conrad. *Thee.* 1967. Braziller. Ils Baskin. 1st ed. dj. VG. $25.00

AIKEN, Conrad. *Ushant.* 1952. NY. 1st ed. 365 p. dj. EX. $35.00

AIKEN, G.D. *Pioneering With Wild Flowers.* 1946. NY. Daye. 48 pls. 132 p. dj. EX. $35.00

AIKEN, Joan. *Stolen Lake.* 1981. 1st Am ed. dj. EX. C1. $11.00

AIKIN, J. *Select Works of British Poets From S to Croly.* 1845. Phil. gilt bdg. $20.00

AIKIN, J. *Woodland Companion; or, Brief Description of British Trees.* 1802. London. 1st ed. 28 pls. $150.00

AIKMAN, L. *Nature's Healing Arts: From Folk Medicine to Modern Drugs.* 1977. Nat Geog Soc. photos. 199 p. dj. EX. M2. $15.00

AIKMAN, W. *Life at Home; or, Family & Its Members.* 1870. NY. with sgn letter/photo. G. $50.00

AINSWORTH, W.H. *Tower of London.* nd. Routledge. Ils Cruikshank. rebound. VG. $75.00

AINSWORTH, W.H. *Tower of London.* 1841. Phil. Ils Cruikshank. 8vo. 210 p. $35.00

AIRD, Catherine. *Harm's Way.* 1984. London. 1st ed. sgn. dj. EX. $27.00

AITKEN, Jane. *Constitution of Presbyterian Church in USA.* 1806. Phil. Aiken. 1st ed. 8vo. leather. $150.00

AKED, Charles. *Wells & Palm Trees.* 1908. Dodge Pub. 8vo. G. $5.00

AKELEY, M.L.J. *Congo Eden.* 1950. Dodd Mead. photos. map. 356 p. dj. EX. M2. $20.00

AKELEY, M.L.J. *Congo Eden.* 1950. Dodd Mead. photos. 356 p. G. M2. $10.00

AKELEY, M.L.J. *Wilderness Lives Again: Carl Akeley & the Great Adventure.* 1940. Dodd Mead. photos. maps. 411 p. dj. EX. M2. $30.00

AKENSON, Donald. *Beind-Had Historians, Evidence & the Irish in N America.* 1985. Meany. 1st ed. dj. VG. J2. $15.00

ALBACETE, M.J. *Architecture in Canton, 1805-1976.* 1976. Canton, OH. 91 p. wraps. VG. T5. $25.00

ALBAUGH, W.A. *Confederate Arms.* 1957. Harrisburg. Stackpole. 1st ed. sm folio. dj. $35.00

ALBAUGH, W.A. *Confederate Arms.* 1957. Harrisburg. 1st ed. VG. $50.00

ALBAUGH, W.A. *Confederate Handguns.* nd. Bonanza. Ils. dj. $15.00

ALBAUGH, W.A. *More Confederate Faces: Pictorial Review.* 1972. Ils. 233 p. EX. J4. $65.00

ALBAUGH, W.A. *Photographic Supplement of Confederate Swords.* 1963. Ils. 205 p. M. J4. $40.00

ALBAUGH, W.A. *Photographic Supplement of Confederate Swords.* 1979. VA. 2nd ed. dj. EX. $35.00

ALBERT, A.D. *History of 45th Regiment PA Infantry.* 1912. Williamsport. 1st ed. EX. $55.00

ALBERT & MELVIN. *New England Diesels.* 1975. Ltd 1st ed. 1/4000. 232 p. $35.00

ALBION, Robert. *Rise of NY Port, 1815-1860.* 1939. Scribner. 1st ed. dj. VG. J2. $20.00

ALBRIGHT, CASH & SANDSTRUM. *Seven Firefights in Vietnam.* 1970. WA. Ils 1st ed. 159 p. wraps. T5. $12.50

ALBRIGHT & TAYLOR. *Oh, Ranger!* 1928. Stanford. 2nd print. photos. G. $35.00

ALBRIGHT & TAYLOR. *Oh, Ranger! A Book About National Parks.* 1946. Dodd Mead. Ils Revised ed. 299 p. VG. M2. $9.00

ALCAREZ, Ramon. *Other Side; or, Mexican History of War in Mexico.* 1850. NY. pls. 24 maps. 458 p. VG. B1. $125.00

ALCOHOLICS ANONYMOUS. *Works of Alcoholics Anonymous.* 1951. NY. 14th print. dj. $210.00

ALCOTT, L.M. *Aunt Jo's Scrap Bag.* 1872. Boston. 1st ed. VG. $45.00

ALCOTT, L.M. *Jo's Boys.* 1886. Boston. 1st ed. EX. $60.00

ALCOTT, L.M. *Jo's Boys.* 1933. Little Brown. Ils Burd. $25.00

ALCOTT, L.M. *Life, Letters & Journals.* 1889. Boston. 1st ed. VG. $30.00

ALCOTT, L.M. *Little Men.* 1871. Boston. 1st ed. 1st issue. $125.00

ALCOTT, L.M. *Little Men.* 1901. Little Brown. Orchard House ed. Ils Birch. B4. $20.00

ALCOTT, L.M. *Little Men.* 1947. Grosset Dunlap. 8vo. dj. EX. $7.50

ALCOTT, L.M. *Little Men.* 1955. Racine. Whitman. 283 p. pb. $3.00

ALCOTT, L.M. *Little Women.* nd. Orchard House. Ils Smith. dj. EX. $25.00

ALCOTT, L.M. *Rose in Bloom.* 1933. Winston. Ils Burd. VG. $12.00

ALCOTT, L.M. *Spinning Wheel Stories.* 1884. Boston. 1st Am ed. gilt bdg. $35.00

ALCOTT, L.M. *Under the Lilacs.* 1928. Boston. Ils Davis. VG. J2. $20.00

ALCOTT, W.A. *House I Live In; or, The Human Body.* 1849. Boston. Ils. fair. $25.00

ALCOTT, W.A. *Housekeeper; or, Thoughts on Food & Cookery.* 1838. 4th ed. 16mo. G. $50.00

ALCOTT, William. *Essay on Construction of School Houses.* 1832. Boston. 8vo. 66 p. self wraps. $125.00

ALDEN, H.M. *Study of Death.* 1895. NY. 1st ed. sm 8vo. green bdg. xl. B1. $95.00

ALDEN, J.B. *Alden's Home Atlas of the World.* 1887. NY. 95 maps. lg quarto. A3. $60.00

ALDIN, Cecil. *Hunting Scenes.* 1936. Scribner. $90.00

ALDIN, Cecil. *Right Royal, John Masefield.* 1922. Macmillan. Ils 1st ed. VG. $20.00

ALDIN, Cecil. *Romance of the Road.* 1927. London. Eyre Spottiswoode. folio. TEG. $150.00

ALDIN, Cecil. *Romance of the Road.* 1928. London. Ils. map. dj. EX. $75.00

ALDIN, Cecil. *Time I Was Dead.* 1934. NY. 1st ed. 8vo. 389 p. VG. $125.00

ALDINGTON, Richard. *Complete Poems.* 1948. London. 1st ed. dj. VG. $35.00

ALDINGTON, Richard. *Portrait of a Genius.* 1951. London. Heinemann. Ils. VG. $10.00

ALDISS, Brian. *Frankenstein Unbound.* 1973. London. 1st ed. dj. EX. $20.00

ALDISS, Brian. *Malacia Tapestry.* 1977. NY. Harper. 1st Am ed. dj. M. $10.00

ALDRICH, B.S. *Drum Goes Dead.* 1941. NY. 1st ed. dj. VG. $17.50

ALDRICH, Lorenzo. *Journal Overland Route to CA Gold Mines.* 1950. Plantin Pr. map. dj. VG. $40.00

ALDRICH, Mildred. *On the Edge of the War Zone.* 1918. London. Constable. 2nd imp. M1. $10.50

ALDRICH, T.B. *Story of a Bad Boy.* 1927. Phil. Ils Prittie. J2. $20.00

ALDRICH, T.B. *Story of a Bad Boy.* 1927. Winston. Ils Prittie. dj. VG. B4. $30.00

ALDRIDGE, James. *Sea Eagle.* 1944. Boston. 1st ed. inscr. VG. $15.00

ALEMAN, M. *Rogue.* 1623. London. 1st ed. 2nd issue. rebound. $175.00

ALEXANDER, E.P. *Civil War Railroads & Models.* 1977. Potter. Ils. 256 p. dj. EX. M2. $35.00

ALEXANDER, E.P. *Down at the Depot.* 1970. NY. Ils 1st ed. 4to. 320 p. dj. VG. T5. $27.50

ALEXANDER, E.P. *Military Memoirs of a Confederate.* 1912. NY. G. $55.00

ALEXANDER, F.L. *S African Bookplates From Percival J.G. Bishop Collection.* 1955. Balkeman. 1st ed. 1/500. VG. $100.00

ALEXANDER, J. *Jews: Their Past, Present & Future.* 1870. London. 218 p. EX. $150.00

ALEXANDER, J.B. *Biographical Sketches of Early Settlers of Hopewell Section.* 1897. Charlotte. VG. $75.00

ALEXANDER, Karl. *Time After Time.* 1979. NY. 1st ed. dj. VG. $15.00

ALEXANDER, Kent. *Colors Aloft!* 1986. NY. 1st Am ed. dj. EX. $25.00

ALEXANDER, Lloyd. *Taran Wanderer.* 1967. Holt Rinehart. 1st ed. dj. $30.00

ALEXANDER, Shana. *Nutcracker.* nd. Doubleday. 1st ed. dj. VG. $10.00

ALEXANDER, William. *Costume of China.* 1805. London. Miller. Ils 1st ed. folio. full morocco. $950.00

ALEXANDER. *Striptease.* 1938. NY. Ils. VG. C4. $39.00

ALEXANDRE-BISSON, Juliette. *Phenomenes Dits de Materialisation.* 1914. Paris. $150.00

ALFAU, Felipe. *Locos.* 1956. Farrar Rinehart. 1st ed. sgn. VG. $65.00

ALGER, Horatio. *Facing the World.* 1893. Phil. 1st ed. pls. 318 p. VG. T5. $45.00

ALGER, Horatio. *Frank's Campaign.* nd. Cleveland. World. $10.00

ALGER, Horatio. *Herbert Carter's Legacy.* 1875. Boston. 1st ed. G. $20.00

ALGER, Horatio. *Young Bank Messenger.* 1898. Phil. Coates. Ils 1st ed. 325 p. fair. scarce. $25.00

ALGREN, Nelson. *Chicago: City on the Make.* 1951. NY. 1st ed. dj. M. $30.00

ALGREN, Nelson. *Chicago: City on the Make.* 1951. NY. 1st ed. dj. VG. B2. $35.00

ALGREN, Nelson. *Jungle.* 1935. Avon. 1st pb ed. wraps. EX. $15.00

ALGREN, Nelson. *Last Carousel.* 1973. NY. 1st ed. dj. VG. $12.50

ALGREN, Nelson. *Last Carousel.* 1973. Putnam. 1st ed. dj. EX. $20.00

ALGREN, Nelson. *Man With the Golden Arm.* 1949. Doubleday. 1st ed. dj. EX. $65.00

ALGREN, Nelson. *Man With the Golden Arm.* 1949. Doubleday. 1st ed. dj. VG. $45.00

ALGREN, Nelson. *Man With the Golden Arm.* 1951. Cardinal. dj. EX. P1. $75.00

ALGREN, Nelson. *Man With the Golden Arm.* 1951. Cardinal. dj. VG. P1. $35.00

ALGREN, Nelson. *Nelson Algren's Own Book of Lonesome Monsters.* 1962. NY. Lancer. 1st ed. pb. EX. $10.00

ALGREN, Nelson. *Neon Wilderness.* 1965. London. Deutsch. 1st ed. dj. VG. $30.00

ALGREN, Nelson. *Notes From a Sea Diary: Hemingway All the Way.* 1965. NY. 1st ed. sgn. dj. EX. $50.00

ALGREN, Nelson. *Walk on the Wild Side.* 1956. NY. 1st ed. dj. $35.00

ALGREN, Nelson. *Who Lost an American?* 1963. Macmillan. dj. EX. $25.00

ALI, S. *Book of Indian Birds.* 1955. Bombay. Ils 5th ed. 142 p. dj. G. M2. $10.00

ALIBERT, M. *Precis Theorique et Pratique sur les Maladies de la Peau.* 1810 & 1818. Paris. 1st ed. 2 vols. wraps. VG. $260.00

ALIREZA, Marianne. *At the Drop of a Veil: Story of CA Girl's Years in Harem.* 1971. Houghton Mifflin. inscr. dj. EX. $35.00

ALLAN, Donald. *Off the Wall, Interviews With Philip Whalen.* 1978. Four Seasons. wraps. $10.00

ALLAN, P.B.M. *Book-Hunter at Home.* 1922. NY. Revised Enlarged 2nd ed. 1/500. $37.50

ALLAN, Tony. *Americans in Paris.* 1977. 1st Am ed. dj. M. $27.50

ALLAND & RISENBERG. *Portrait of NY.* 1939. Macmillan. 1st ed. 4to. dj. EX. $45.00

ALLBEURY, Ted. *Mission Berlin.* 1986. NY. 1st ed. dj. EX. $15.00

ALLBUT, R. *Tourist Handbook to Switzerland.* 1884. np. 1st ed. 24 maps. 344 p. VG. $35.00

ALLBUTT, T.C. *Science & Medieval Thought.* 1901. London. Cambridge. VG. $25.00

ALLEN, A.A. *Golden Plover & Other Birds.* 1939. Comstock. Ils 324 p. dj. VG. M2. $19.00

ALLEN, A.A. *Stalking Birds With Color Camera.* 1951. Nat Geog Soc. Ils 1st ed. 328 p. EX. M2. $25.00

ALLEN, A.A. *Stalking Birds With Color Camera.* 1963. Nat Geog Soc. Revised 2nd ed. dj. EX. M2. $25.00

ALLEN, A.D. *Official View Book of Century of Progress Exposition.* 1933. Chicago. Ils. dj. T5. $25.00

ALLEN, Bryan. *Print Collection.* 1970. London. Muller. Ils. 127 p. D2. $15.00

ALLEN, D. *N.C. Wyeth.* nd. NY. Bonanza. Ils. 4to. 335 p. EX. $18.00

ALLEN, D.L. *Pheasants in N America.* 1956. Stackpole. Ils. 490 p. dj. EX. M2. $55.00

ALLEN, D.L. *Wolves of Minong: Their Vital Role in a Wild Community.* 1979. Houghton. Ils 1st ed. map. 499 p. dj. EX. M2. $20.00

ALLEN, E.S. *Arctic Odyssey: Life of Rear Admiral Donald B. Macmillan.* 1962. Dodd Mead. photos. map. 340 p. dj. EX. M2. $17.00

ALLEN, E.S. *Arctic Odyssey: Life of Rear Admiral Donald B. Macmillan.* 1962. NY. Ils. sgn Macmillan. dj. VG. B2. $27.50

ALLEN, E.S. *Children of the Light: Rise & Fall of New Bedford Whaling...* 1973. Little Brown. Ils. maps. sgn. 302 p. EX. M2. $6.00

ALLEN, Ethan. *Narrative of Col. Ethan Allen's Captivity.* 1845. 126 p. $60.00

ALLEN, Ethan. *Narrative of Col. Ethan Allen's Captivity.* 1930. NY. Ltd ed. 1/540. 8vo. 134 p. VG. $20.00

ALLEN, F.L. *Great Pierpont Morgan.* 1949. 306 p. $20.00

ALLEN, F.M. *Diabetes & Its Treatment.* 1928. Funk Wagnalls. dj. VG. P1. $10.00

ALLEN, G.C. *Tales From Tennyson.* c 1910. juvenile. VG. C1. $6.50

ALLEN, George. *Inside Football.* 1970. Ils. photos. 4to. 421 p. dj. EX. $6.00

ALLEN, Glover. *Birds & Their Attributes.* 1948. Jones. Ils. 338 p. VG. $13.00

ALLEN, Hervey. *Action at Aquila.* 1938. NY. Farrar Rinehart. 1st ed. dj. $15.00

ALLEN, Hervey. *Action at Aquila.* 1938. NY. 1st ed. inscr/sgn. dj. M. $45.00

ALLEN, Hervey. *Anthony Adverse.* 1934. Farrar Rinehart. 2 vols. VG. $65.00

ALLEN, Hervey. *Israefel: Life & Time of Edgar A. Poe.* 1936. NY. 2 vols. djs. EX. $40.00

ALLEN, Hervey. *Israfel: Life & Times of Edgar A. Poe.* 1936. Doran. 1/250. sgn. 8vo. TEG. green cloth. VG. D1. $125.00

ALLEN, Hervey. *Toward the Morning.* 1948. Rinehart. 1st ed. sgn. dj. VG. $10.00

ALLEN, Hugh. *House of Goodyear.* 1949. np. Ils Revised ed. 691 p. dj. VG. T5. $12.50

ALLEN, Hugh. *Rubber's Home Town: Real-Life Story of Akron.* 1949. NY. Ils 1st ed. 265 p. dj. VG. T5. $19.50

ALLEN, Ivan. *Atlanta From the Ashes.* 1928. Athens. Ils 1st ed. 144 p. G. $15.00

ALLEN, J.A. *History of N American Pinnipeds.* 1880. WA. Ils. 785 p. xl. EX. M2. $115.00

ALLEN, J.A. *On the Coatis.* 1879. WA. 180 p. disbound. A3. $30.00

ALLEN, J.A. *On the Species of the Genus Bassaris.* 1879. WA. 190 p. disbound. A3. $30.00

ALLEN, J.L. *KY Cardinal & Aftermath.* 1900. NY. Ils. 8vo. G. $20.00

ALLEN, J.L. *Passage Through the Garden.* 1975. IL U. 412 p. dj. EX. $30.00

ALLEN, J.R. *Heat Engines: Steam, Gas, Steam Turbines & Auxiliaries.* 1910. Ils. 422 p. VG. $12.00

ALLEN, Joel. *Geographical Distribution of Mammilia.* 1878. WA. 234 p. wraps. A3. $35.00

ALLEN, Joel. *Preliminary List of Works...Relating to...Orders of Cete...* 1881. WA. 210 p. wraps. A3. $30.00

ALLEN, L.D. *SF Reader's Guide.* 1974. Centennial Pr. VG. P1. $4.00

ALLEN, Louis. *Singapore, 1941-1942.* 1979. DE U. 1st Am ed. dj. EX. $15.00

ALLEN, M. *Falconry in Arabia.* 1984. London. Orbis. photos. 143 p. EX. M2. $20.00

ALLEN, Paul. *Writings & Lectures of Rudolf Steiner, a Bibliography.* 1956. NY. Whittier. 1st ed. 140 p. stiff wraps. J2. $25.00

ALLEN, Philip S. *King Arthur & His Knights.* 1930. Ils Schaeffer/Neill. VG. C1. $9.50

ALLEN, R.P. *Birds of the Caribbean.* 1961. NY. 1st ed. dj. VG. B2. $45.00

ALLEN, R.P. *On the Trail of Vanishing Birds.* 1957. McGraw Hill. photos. 251 p. dj. EX. M2. $11.00

ALLEN, R.S. *Our Fair City.* 1947. NY. 387 p. dj. G. T5. $17.50

ALLEN, Ruth. *E TX Lumber Workers.* 1961. TX U. 1st ed. dj. EX. J2. $15.00

ALLEN, Stanton. *Down in Dixie: 4th MA Cavalry.* 1893. Boston. Ils Lothrop. VG. $140.00

ALLEN, Steve. *Ripoff.* 1979. NY. with 2 sgn photos. EX. $20.00

ALLEN, T. *Vanishing Wildlife of N America.* 1974. Nat Geog Soc. Ils. 207 p. dj. EX. M2. $18.00

ALLEN, V.C. *Rhea & Meigs Co. (TN) in the Confederate War.* 1908. 126 p. VG. scarce. $35.00

ALLEN, Woody. *Side Effects.* 1980. NY. 1st ed. dj. EX. $15.00

ALLEN, Woody. *Side Effects.* 1981. London. 1st ed. dj. EX. $20.00

ALLEN, Woody. *Without Feathers.* 1976. NY. 1st ed. dj. with sgn photo. EX. $50.00

ALLEN & DAVIS. *Walt Whitman's Poems.* 1955. NY U. 1st ed. dj. VG. $15.00

ALLEN. *Gold, Men & Dogs.* 1931. NY. Ils. dj. VG. $15.00

ALLEN. *Rural Architecture.* 1873. NY. Ils. VG. C4. $65.00

ALLHANDS, J.L. *Boll Weevil: Recollections of Trinity/Brazos Valley Railway.* 1946. Ltd ed. 1/250. sgn. 279 p. $37.50

ALLHANDS, J.L. *Gringo Builders.* 1931. np. sgn. M. $110.00

ALLINGHAM, Margery. *Death of a Ghost.* 1946. Penguin. 4th print. dj. VG. P1. $50.00

ALLISON, Susan. *Fantasy Sampler.* 1985. Berkeley. proof. EX. P1. $20.00

ALLSOPP, F.W. *Folklore of Romantic AR.* 1931. Grolier. 2 vols. EX. M2. $95.00

ALLSOPP, F.W. *History of AR Press for a Hundred Years & More.* 1922. Parke Harper. Ils. photos. 684 p. EX. M2. $35.00

ALLYN, R. *Dictionary of Fishes.* 1963. Great Outdoors. Ills. 4to. 126 p. G. M2. $5.00

ALMAZAN. *Historia de la Monteria en Espana.* 1934. Madrid. 1/400. folio. 471 p. slipcase. EX. $950.00

ALPERS, A. *Katherine Mansfield.* 1953. Knopf. 1st ed. dj. VG. $9.00

ALTHER, Lisa. *Other Women.* 1984. NY. 1st ed. dj. VG. $8.00

ALTMAN, L.C. *Oligochaeta of WA.* 1936. WA U. 16 pls. 137 p. M2. $10.00

ALTMAN & ALTMAN. *Book of Buffalo Pottery.* 1969. Crown. 1st ed. dj. VG. $25.00

ALTON, John. *Painting With Light.* 1949. Macmillan. Rudy Vallee xl. dj. scarce. D2. $200.00

ALVORD, H.B. *Report of Special Commissioners To Visit Kiowas & Comanches.* 1872. GOP. 22 p. wraps. VG. A3. $60.00

ALVORD, T.G. *Paul Bunyan.* 1934. Derrydale. 1/332. sgn. 8vo. glassine dj. EX. $160.00

ALWALL. *Proceedings 4th International Congress of Nephrology.* 1969. Stockholm. 3 vols. boxed. M. $55.00

AMADO, Jorge. *Gabriela: Clove & Cinnamon.* 1962. Knopf. Trans Taylor/Grossman. 1st Am ed. $16.00

AMADO, Jorge. *Miracle of the Birds.* 1983. NY. Targ. 1/250. sgn. glassine dj. EX. $40.00

AMADO, Jorge. *Show Down.* 1988. NY. Bantam. AP. 1st ed. wraps. EX. $20.00

AMADO, Jorge. *Tent of Miracles.* 1971. Knopf. Ils Shelby. 1st Am ed. dj. EX. $15.00

AMAN, Theodor. *Masters of Rumanian Painting.* 1954. Bucharest. Ils. fair. $25.00

AMBLER, C.H. *WV Stories & Biographies.* 1942. NY. Ils. maps. 600 p. T5. $12.50

AMBLER, Charles. *Reports in High Court of Chancery.* 1790. London. sm folio. full leather. $50.00

AMBLER, Eric. *Care of Time.* 1981. NY. 1st ed. dj. VG. $20.00

AMBLER, Eric. *Judgement on Deltchev.* 1st ed. G. $125.00

AMBLER, Eric. *Light of Day.* 1963. Knopf. 1st ed. dj. $7.00

AMBLER, Eric. *Passage of Arms.* 1960. NY. 1st ed. 2 djs. EX. $50.00

AMBLER, Eric. *Schirmer Inheritance.* 1953. Knopf. 1st Am ed. dj. VG. $15.00

AMBROSE, S.E. *Struggle for Vicksburg.* 1967. 65 Ils. 15 maps. 66 p. EX. J4. $12.50

AMENDOLA, Joseph. *Ice Carving Made Easy.* 1965. Stamford. 2nd print. VG. J2. $20.00

AMERICAN RED CROSS. *First Aid TB.* 1940. sm 8vo. 256 p. EX. $2.00

AMERICAN RED CROSS. *First Aid TB.* 1945. 8vo. 254 p. EX. $3.00

AMERICAN TRACT SOCIETY. *Proceedings of First Ten Years of American Tract Society.* 1824. Boston. 1st ed. VG. $75.00

AMES, C.E. *Pioneering the Union Pacific.* 1969. 591 p. $35.00

AMES, E. *Glimpse of Eden.* 1967. Houghton Mifflin. Ils. dj. EX. M2. $13.00

AMES, J.S. *Constitution of Matter.* 1913. Cambridge. Riverside Pr. VG. $22.00

AMES, Nathanel. *Astronomical Diary; or, Almanac for 1749.* Boston. Draper. G. $60.00

AMES & AMES. *Japan & Zen.* 1961. Cincinnati. $10.00

AMICHAL, Yehuda. *Not of This Time, Not of This Place.* 1968. Harper. 1st ed. dj. VG. $25.00

AMIEL. *Homage to Chagall: Special Issue of XXe Siecle Review.* 1982. NY. folio. blue bdg. dj. VG. G2. $50.00

AMIS, Kingsley. *Anti-Death League.* London. 1st ed. sgn. dj. EX. $50.00

AMIS, Kingsley. *Colonel Sun.* 1968. NY. Harper. dj. VG. $20.00

AMIS, Kingsley. *Jake's Thing.* 1978. London. 1st ed. dj. EX. $45.00

AMIS, Kingsley. *New Maps of Hell.* 1966. Harcourt Brace. 4th print. dj. xl. P1. $10.00

AMIS, Kingsley. *Old Devils.* 1986. London. Hutchinson. 1/250. sgn/#d. M. $95.00

AMIS, Kingsley. *On Drink.* 1972. London. Ils 1st ed. $25.00

AMIS, Kingsley. *Riverside Villas Murder.* 1973. NY. Harcourt. dj. EX. $15.00

AMIS, Martin. *Einstein's Monsters.* 1987. NY. Harmony. 1st Am ed. dj. M. $10.00

AMIS, Martin. *Money.* 1985. NY. 1st Am ed. M. $15.00

AMMONS, A.R. *Six-Piece Suite.* 1978. Palaemon. 1/230. sgn/#d. wraps. EX. $45.00

AMON, A. *Talking Hands: How To Use Indian Sign Language.* 1973. Young Readers Pr. 80 p. VG. M2. $4.00

AMORY, Cleveland. *Who Killed Society?* 1960. Harper. dj. G. $20.00

AMORY, T.C. *Our English Ancestors.* 1872. Boston. Clapp. orig purple wraps. EX. $35.00

AMOS, J.M. *City Directory, Cambridge, OH, for 1893.* 1893. Cambridge. 59 p. G. T5. $42.50

AMPERE & AMPERE. *Correspondance et Souvenirs.* 1875. Paris. 12mo. 2 vols. $125.00

AMSDEN, C.A. *Navaho Weaving.* 1934. SW Mus. Fine Arts Pr. Ils Lea. xl. VG. $100.00

AMUCHASTEQUI. *Studies of Birds & Mammals of S America.* 1967. NY. Van Nostrand. dj. EX. $30.00

ANAND, Valerie. *Norman Pretender.* 1979. 1st Am ed. dj. M. C1. $9.00

ANASTASIA. *I Am Anastasia.* 1959. NY. 1st ed. dj. VG. B2. $22.50

ANASTOASOFF, Christ. *Tragic Peninsula: History of Macedonian Movement...* 1938. St. Louis. Ils. 369 p. VG. T5. $22.50

ANATI. *Camonica Valley.* 1961. NY. 1st Am ed. dj. VG. $12.50

ANDER, O. *American Origin of the Augustana Synod.* 1942. Augustana Hist Soc. 1st ed. J2. $12.50

ANDER, O. *Cultural Heritage of the Swedish Immigrant.* 1956. Augustana Lib. 1st ed. VG. J2. $12.50

ANDERS, Curt. *Fighting Airmen.* 1966. NY. 1st ed. 287 p. dj. VG. T5. $12.50

ANDERS, F. *Custer Trail 1876.* 1983. Clark. Ltd ed. 1/350. sgn editor. EX. $75.00

ANDERS, Leslie. *18th MO.* 1968. Bobbs Merrill. dj. EX. $25.00

ANDERS, Leslie. *21st MO: Home Guard to Union Regiment.* 1975. Greenwood Pr. M. $33.00

ANDERS, Leslie. *21st MO: Home Guard to Union Regiment.* 1975. Wesport. 1st ed. maps. dj. EX. $20.00

ANDERSCH BROS. *Hunters' & Trapers' Guide.* 1906. Revised 2nd ed. G. $65.00

ANDERSEN, H.C. *Fairy Tales From Andersen Arranged for Little Readers.* 1920. Flanagan. Ils. G. $15.00

ANDERSEN, H.C. *Fairy Tales.* 1924. NY. Ils Nielsen. VG. J2. $90.00

ANDERSEN, H.C. *Fairy Tales.* 1942. Ltd Ed Club. sgn Hersholt/Kredel. 2 vols. boxed. $175.00

ANDERSEN, H.C. *Fairy Tales.* 1981. Viking. Ils Nielsen. 1st ed. dj. $15.00

ANDERSEN, H.C. *Kate Greenaway's Original Drawings for Snow Queen.* 1981. NY. Schocken. 1st ed. 58 p. EX. $6.50

ANDERSEN, H.C. *Stories From Hans Christian Andersen.* 1911. NY. Ils Dulac. disbound. $45.00

ANDERSON, Anne. *Ali Baba & the 40 Thieves.* 1928. NY. Nelson. Ils. 40 p. G. $14.00

ANDERSON, Anne. *Fairy Tale Book.* c 1920s. NY. Ils. color pls. G. $30.00

ANDERSON, B.C. *Life Line to the Yukon: History of Yukon River Navigation.* 1983. Superior. VG. $15.00

ANDERSON, C. *Historical Sketches of Ancient Irish...* 1828. Edinburgh. 1st ed. 8vo. 266 p. $125.00

ANDERSON, C.W. *Big Red.* 1943. NY. 1st ed. VG. B2. $27.50

ANDERSON, C.W. *Deep Through the Heart.* nd. Macmillan. Ils. VG. $12.00

ANDERSON, Erasmus. *Norroena, Anglo-Saxon Classic.* 1907. London. 1/350. 10 vols. VG. $350.00

ANDERSON, F. *Treasury of Orchids.* 1979. NY. dj. VG. $10.00

ANDERSON, F.J. *Geography & Travels.* 1970. Wofford College Lib. spiral bdg. $25.00

ANDERSON, Frank Maloy. *Mystery of a Public Man.* 1948. Minneapolis. 1st ed. 256 p. dj. fair. T5. $19.50

ANDERSON, Isabel. *Great Sea Horse.* 1909. Little Brown. Ils Ellot. inscr/sgn. VG. $65.00

ANDERSON, J. *Unknown Turner.* 1926. NY. Ils. 4to. 151 p. dj. EX. J2. $150.00

ANDERSON, J.D. *Making the American Thoroughbred, Especially TN, 1800-1845.* 1916. Norwood. VG. $125.00

ANDERSON, J.R.L. *Death in the Greenhouse.* 1983. Scribner. proof. VG. P1. $12.50

ANDERSON, J.W. *Diesel Engines.* 1949. McGraw Hill. Ils. 2 vols. VG. $17.00

ANDERSON, John. *American Theatre, Motion Picture in America.* 1938. NY. Miller. 1st ed. 4to. 430 p. boxed. EX. B1. $50.00

ANDERSON, M. *Key Largo.* 1939. WA. 1st ed. dj. VG. B2. $22.50

ANDERSON, M.D. *Misericords: Medieval Life in English Woodcarving.* 1954. 1st ed. dj. VG. C1. $9.50

ANDERSON, M.L. *Proverbs in Scots.* 1957. Edinburgh. 1st ed. dj. VG. J2. $15.00

ANDERSON, Nels. *Right To Work.* 1938. Modern Age. dj. G. P1. $10.00

ANDERSON, Paul. *Agent of the Terran Empire.* nd. NY. 1st ed. dj. VG. $30.00

ANDERSON, Paul. *Ensign Flandry.* NY. 1st ed. dj. VG. $30.00

ANDERSON, Paul. *Midsummer Tempest.* 1974. 1st ed. xl. VG. C1. $7.50

ANDERSON, Paul. *Star Ways.* 1963. Ace #D-568. sgn. VG. P1. $10.00

ANDERSON, Paul. *Three Hearts & Three Lions.* c 1962. Book Club. 1st ed. dj. VG. C1. $5.00

ANDERSON, Paul. *Trouble Twisters.* 1966. Doubleday. 1st ed. dj. VG. $35.00

ANDERSON, R.E. *Liberia: America's African Friend.* 1952. Chapel Hill. Ils 1st ed. 305 p. dj. G. T5. $25.00

ANDERSON, R.W. *Romance of Air Fighting.* 1917. NY. 31 p. wraps. VG. T5. $12.50

ANDERSON, Robert. *Getting Up & Going Home.* 1978. NY. 1st ed. sgn. dj. M. $15.00

ANDERSON, Rufus. *HI Islands: Progress & Condition Under Missionary Labors.* 1864. Boston. 2nd ed. pls. fld map. $125.00

ANDERSON, Sherwood. *Beyond Desire.* 1932. NY. Ltd ed. 1/165. sgn. EX. $125.00

ANDERSON, Sherwood. *Dark Laughter.* 1925. NY. 1/350. sgn. boxed. VG. $90.00

ANDERSON, Sherwood. *Death in the Woods.* 1933. NY. 1st ed. B2. $45.00

ANDERSON, Sherwood. *Hello Towns.* 1929. NY. 1st ed. inscr. $85.00

ANDERSON, Sherwood. *Home Town.* 1940. NY. Alliance. 1st ed. EX. $55.00

ANDERSON, Sherwood. *Many Marriages: A Novel.* 1923. NY. 1st ed. sgn. dj. EX. scarce. $225.00

ANDERSON, Sherwood. *New Testament.* 1927. Boni Liveright. 1/265. sgn. $90.00

ANDERSON, Sherwood. *Plays: Winesburg & Others.* 1937. NY. dj. EX. $65.00

ANDERSON, Sherwood. *Tar, a Midwest Childhood.* 1926. NY. 1st ed. 1/350. sgn. boxed. EX. $100.00

ANDERSON, W.H. *Vanishing Roadside America.* 1981. Ltd 1st ed. 1/300. sgn. EX. $15.00

ANDERSON, W.R. *Nautilus 90 N.* 1959. Cleveland. 1st ed. sgn. dj. VG. $45.00

ANDERSON, William. *Scottish Nation; or, Surnames, Families, Literature...* 1865. London. 2 vols. G. $65.00

ANDERSON & BRACTON. *Tale of 1812.* 1882. London. 1st ed. 257 p. fair. T5. $15.00

ANDERSON & JONES. *Recent Mammals of the World: Synopsis of Families.* 1967. Ronald. Ils. 453 p. xl. VG. M2. $20.00

ANDERSON & REGLI. *Alec Majors.* 1953. Wheeler. 204 p. EX. $3.00

ANDERSON. *American Country Fair.* 1930. NY. Ltd ed. 1/857. wraps. VG. $35.00

ANDERSON. *Black Panther of Sivanipalli.* 1960. NY. dj. EX. $18.00

ANDERSON. *By Sea & River: Naval History of Civil War.* 1962. NY. 1st ed. dj. $23.00

ANDERSON. *Dog Team Doctor.* 1940. Caldwell. Ils 1st ed. EX. $20.00

ANDERSON. *How To Hypnotize.* 1896. Science Inst. Ils 2nd ed. photos. G. $24.00

ANDRAL, Gabriel. *Clinique Medicale.* 1829-1833. Paris. 2nd ed. 5 vols. fair. $200.00

ANDRAL, Gabriel. *Diseases of the Chest.* 1843. Phil. wraps. VG. $75.00

ANDRAL, Gabriel. *Medicinal Clinic.* 1838. Phil. VG. leather. $100.00

ANDREE. *Andree's Story: Complete Record of His Polar Flight, 1897.* 1930. Blue Ribbon. Boys' ed. 250 p. M1. $15.00

ANDREW, R.W. *Photographers of Frontier W: Their Lives & Works, 1875-1915.* nd. Bonanza. 100 photos. 4to. 182 p. dj. $35.00

ANDREWARTHA, H.G. *Introduction to the Study of Animal Populations.* 1966. London. Methuen. Ils. 281 p. EX. M2. $18.00

ANDREWS, Bart. *From the Blob to Star Wars.* 1977. Signet. pb. VG. P1. $3.25

ANDREWS, Bart. *Star Trek Quiz Book.* Signet. 1st ed. wraps. EX. $10.00

ANDREWS, C.W. *John Crerar Library, 1894-1901.* 1902. Chicago. $15.00

ANDREWS, C.W. *John Crerar Library, 1894-1905.* MI U. reprint of 1905 ed. $12.50

ANDREWS, Christopher. *Lives of Wasps & Bees.* 1971. Am Elsevier. 1st ed. dj. VG. J2. $17.50

ANDREWS, E. *People Called Shakers.* 1953. NY. 1st ed. dj. VG. B2. $17.50

ANDREWS, Lancelot. *Manual of Private Devotions With Manual of Directions...* 1682. London. Black Swan. 24mo. G. scarce. G2. $90.00

ANDREWS, M. *Flight of the Condor: Wildlife Exploration in the Andes.* 1982. Little Brown. 1st Am ed. 157 p. dj. EX. M2. $18.00

ANDREWS, M.P. *Dixie Book of Days.* 1912. Phil. 1st ed. 12mo. gilt red bdg. $20.00

ANDREWS, M.P. *Women of the S in War Times.* 1922. 2nd print. EX. J4. $25.00

ANDREWS, M.P. *Women of the S in War Times.* 1923. Baltimore. 465 p. K1. $18.50

ANDREWS, R.C. *Across Mongolian Plains: Naturalist's Account of China.* 1921. Blue Ribbon. reprint. 276 p. G. M2. $13.00

ANDREWS, R.C. *Ends of the Earth.* 1929. NY. 1st ed. dj. M. $20.00

ANDREWS, R.C. *Ends of the Earth.* 1929. Garden City. photos. 293 p. VG. M2. $10.00

ANDREWS, R.C. *Explorer Comes Home.* 1947. Doubleday. 276 p. EX. $6.00

ANDREWS, R.C. *Nature's Ways: How Nature Takes Care of Its Own.* 1951. Crown. Ils. 206 p. dj. VG. M2. $10.00

ANDREWS, R.C. *On the Trail of Ancient Man.* 1926. Garden City. reprint. 375 p. G. M2. $8.00

ANDREWS, Raymond. *Appalachee Red.* 1978. NY. Ils 1st ed. dj. VG. $45.00

ANDREWS, Raymond. *Baby Sweet's.* 1983. NY. Ils 1st ed. dj. EX. $25.00

ANDREWS, Raymond. *Rosiebelle Lee Wildcat TN.* 1980. NY. Ils 1st ed. inscr. dj. EX. $35.00

ANDREWS, Sidney. *S Since the War.* 1971. Boston. EX. $20.00

ANDREWS & SOLOMON. *Cocoa Leaf & Cocaine Papers.* 1975. NY. 1st ed. dj. VG. $18.00

ANDREWS. *Air Marshals.* 1970. NY. Morrow. 1st ed. dj. VG. $10.00

ANDREWS. *Dirigibles.* 1931. NY. Burt. Ils. dj. G. $10.00

ANDRIST, R.K. *Long Death: Last Days of Plains Indian.* 1964. NY. Macmillan. 1st ed. dj. EX. $28.00

ANET, Claude. *End of a World.* 1927. Knopf. Ils. $5.00

ANGEBERT. *Occult & 3rd Reich.* 1974. NY. Macmillan. 1st ed. dj. EX. $25.00

ANGEL, Harriet. *Recipes by Ladies of St. Paul's P.E. Church, Akron, OH.* nd. Arkon. facsimile of 1887 ed. wraps. T5. $19.50

ANGEL, P.M. *Chicago Historical Society 1856-1956.* 1956. NY. Ils 1st ed. dj. slipcase. VG. T1. $25.00

ANGEL, S.B. *History of the 13th Regiment, TN Volunteer Cavalry.* 1903. Knoxville. reprint. J4. $29.00

ANGELL, James. *From VT to MI: Correspondence of James B. Angell: 1869-1871.* 1936. MI U. 1st ed. VG. J2. $15.00

ANGELL, Norman. *Great Illusion Now.* 1938. Penguin. dj. VG. P1. $7.50

ANGELL, Norman. *Money Game.* nd. Dent. G. rare. $100.00

ANGELOU, Maya. *Gather Together in My Name.* 1974. Random House. 1st ed. dj. EX. $25.00

ANGELOU, Maya. *I Know Why the Caged Bird Sings.* 1969. NY. 1st ed. inscr. dj. M. $35.00

ANGELOU, Maya. *I Know Why the Caged Bird Sings.* 1969. Random House. 1st ed. black cloth. dj. VG. $20.00

ANGELOU, Maya. *Singin' & Swingin'.* 1976. NY. 1st ed. presentation. sgn. dj. VG. B2. $47.50

ANGIER, Bradford. *At Home in the Woods.* 1951. Sheridan House. photos. 255 p. dj. EX. M2. $13.00

ANGIER, Bradford. *Wilderness Skills & Outdoor Know-How.* 1983. Stackpole. Ils. 358 p. dj. EX. M2. $16.00

ANGLE, P.M. *Chicago Historical Society: 1856-1956.* c 1956. NY/Chicago/San Francisco. boxed. $10.00

ANGLE, P.M. *Great Chicago Fire.* 1946. Chicago. Ils 1st ed. 85 p. dj. VG. T5. $12.50

ANGLE, P.M. *Pictorial History of Civil War Years.* 1967. Ils. 242 p. J4. $6.50

ANGLE, Paul. *Abraham Lincoln by Men Who Knew Him.* 1950. Chicago. Am House. 1/650. slipcase. M. $16.00

ANGLE, Paul. *Abraham Lincoln by Men Who Knew Him.* 1950. Chicago. 1st ed. 1/650. slipcase. VG. $10.00

ANGLE, Paul. *100 Years of Law: Account of Law Office of J.T. Stuart...* 1928. Springfield. 1st ed. VG. $38.00

ANGLE & MIERS. *Ballad of N & S.* 1959. Kingsport. private print. 1/1250. slipcase. $25.00

ANGLE & MIERS. *Prose & Poetry by Lincoln.* 1956. Kingsport. 1/1500. slipcase. M. $15.00

ANGLUND, J.W. *Christmas Is a Time of Giving.* 1961. Harcourt World. 1st ed. dj. VG. $10.00

ANGLUND, J.W. *Friend Is Something Who Likes You.* 1958. Harcourt. Ils 1st ed. dj. VG. B4. $15.00

ANGLUND, J.W. *Look Out the Window.* 1959. NY. VG. $15.00

ANGLUND, J.W. *Pocketful of Proverbs.* 1964. NY. dj. slipcase. EX. $15.00

ANGLUND, J.W. *Slice of Snow.* 1970. NY. Ils 1st ed. dj. EX. $15.00

ANGLUND, J.W. *What Color Is Love?* 1966. NY. dj. VG. $15.00

ANGUS, W. *Seats of Nobility & Gentry in Great Britain & Wales.* 1787. Islington. modern buckram. VG. J2. $300.00

ANKER & ANDERSON. *Art of Scandinavia.* 1970. London. 1st ed. 2 vols. djs. VG. B2. $35.00

ANNABEL, Russell. *Hunting & Fishing in AK.* 1948. Knopf. 1st ed. dj. EX. $40.00

ANNABEL, Russell. *Tales of Big Game Guide.* 1938. Derrydale. 1/950. VG. B2. $275.00

ANONYMOUS. *Adventure in Service.* 1949. Chicago. $12.50

ANONYMOUS. *Adventures of Baron Von Munchausen.* nd. London. Ils Dore. 3rd ed. G. $50.00

ANONYMOUS. *Affecting History of Captivity & Sufferings of Mary Velnet.* c 1804. Boston. 1st ed. VG. rare. $175.00

ANONYMOUS. *Album von Palastina.* 1899. Palestine. photos. pls. 4to. scarce. $350.00

ANONYMOUS. *Alexander Melville Bell: Some Memories With Fragments...* 1906. Boston. School of Expression. EX. $60.00

ANONYMOUS. *American Shooter's Manual. By a Gentleman of Phil.* 1928. Derrydale. 1/375. 8vo. gray/green bdg. EX. $200.00

ANONYMOUS. *Book of Ballads.* 1938. London. Chatto Windus. dj. VG. C1. $9.00

ANONYMOUS. *Boy: Photographic Essay.* 1964. Horizon. 1st ed. dj. EX. $65.00

ANONYMOUS. *Face of Lincoln.* 1979. Viking. 1st ed. dj. VG. $75.00

ANONYMOUS. *Godly Women of the Bible (by Ungodly Woman of 19th C).* c 1881. EX. $75.00

ANONYMOUS. *Guide to Subjects & Concepts in Picture Book Format.* 1979. Dobbs Ferry. Oceana. green bdg. xl. VG. $15.00

ANONYMOUS. *Happy Transformation: History of a London Apprentice.* 1866. Sheldon. VG. B4. $25.00

ANONYMOUS. *Historic Toronto.* 1953. Toronto Civic. dj. EX. P1. $20.00

ANONYMOUS. *Jews of Czechoslovakia.* 1968. NY. 1st ed. dj. EX. $40.00

ANONYMOUS. *Leaders & Leading Men of Indian (Choctaw) Territory.* 1891. Chicago. G. B1. $60.00

ANONYMOUS. *Leisure Hour 1869.* 1869. pls. 4to. 800 p. K1. $18.50

ANONYMOUS. *Life & Tragic Death of Jesse James.* 1966. Steck. reprint of 1883 ed. slipcase. EX. $20.00

ANONYMOUS. *Life of Stonewall Jackson.* 1863. NY. reprint of Richmond ed. K1. $24.50

ANONYMOUS. *Little Puzzle Book.* 1955. Peter Pauper. 62 p. dj. VG. $12.00

ANONYMOUS. *Manual de Terceros.* 1874. Puebla. VG. $50.00

ANONYMOUS. *My Cave Life in Vicksburg.* 1864. NY. Ils. 196 p. very scarce. K1. $110.00

ANONYMOUS. *Old Capitol & Its Inmates.* 1867. NY. 226 p. K1. $18.50

ANONYMOUS. *Pioneer Citizens' History of Atlanta, 1833-1902.* 1902. Atlanta. Ils. 400 p. VG. B1. $150.00

ANONYMOUS. *Planet of the Apes Annual.* 1976. Brown Watson. VG. P1. $25.00

ANONYMOUS. *Saint Annual.* 1968. World. VG. P1. $30.00

ANONYMOUS. *Shadow of the War: Story of S in Reconstruction Times.* 1884. Chicago. McClurg. 1st ed. 378 p. $46.00

ANONYMOUS. *Six Million Dollar Man Annual 1977.* 1976. Stafford. VG. P1. $22.50

ANONYMOUS. *Space 1999 Annual.* 1976. World. VG. P1. $25.00

ANONYMOUS. *Star Trek Annual 1972.* 1971. World. HrdCvr. VG. P1. $30.00

ANONYMOUS. *Star Trek Annual 1974.* 1973. World. HrdCvr. VG. P1. $22.50

ANONYMOUS. *Star Trek Annual 1980.* 1979. World. HrdCvr. EX. P1. $25.00

ANONYMOUS. *Thirteen Months in the Rebel Army.* 1862. NY. 232 p. cloth bdg. K1. $20.00

ANONYMOUS. *Those War Women: By One of Them.* 1929. NY. 1st ed. 283 p. dj. VG. T5. $27.50

ANONYMOUS. *Victory Cookbook.* 1943. Wartime ed. VG. $15.00

ANONYMOUS. *Vision Shared: Portrait of America & People, 1935-1943.* 1976. St. Martin. dj. VG. $40.00

ANONYMOUS. *Visit to the Seaside.* 1828. Boston. possible 1st ed. juvenile. G. rare. $85.00

ANSON, P.F. *Churches: Their Plan & Furnishing.* 1948. Milwaukee. Ils 1st Am ed. 242 p. dj. VG. T5. $19.50

ANSON, W.S.W. *Three Foolish Little Gnomes.* c 1880. London. Ils. VG. $40.00

ANSPACHER, H.H. *Alice in Wonderland Rhymes, Done in Poster Stamps.* 1915. NY. United Art Pub. EX. $175.00

ANSTRUTHER, Ian. *Knight & the Umbrella: Account of Eglinton Tournament, 1839.* 1986. 1st pb ed. C1. $9.50

ANTHOLOGY. *American Ballet Theatre.* 1978. NY. sm folio. 380 p. dj. EX. $50.00

ANTHOLOGY. *Americana Esoterica.* 1927. Macy Masius. Ils Kent. 1/3000. G. $35.00

ANTHOLOGY. *Beat Coast.* 1960. NY. 1st ed. wraps. EX. $25.00

ANTHOLOGY. *Beat Road.* 1984. CA. 1st ed. wraps. EX. $20.00

ANTHOLOGY. *Chinese Art.* c 1930s. London. Ils. red cloth. EX. $35.00

ANTHOLOGY. *Collected Studies on Dionne Quintuplets.* 1937. Toronto. VG. B1. $35.00

ANTHOLOGY. *Collection of Memorials Concerning Quakers in PA, NJ...* 1787. Phil. 8vo. full leather. VG. $150.00

ANTHOLOGY. *Contact 1.* 1958. San Francisco. 1st ed. wraps. VG. $15.00

ANTHOLOGY. *Death Valley.* 1954. San Francisco. 1st ed. photos. 4to. 59 p. wraps. $75.00

ANTHOLOGY. *Declaration.* 1958. NY. $20.00

ANTHOLOGY. *Ellery Queen's Awards 10th Series.* 1955. Little Brown. 1st ed. dj. EX. $12.00

ANTHOLOGY. *Evergreen No. 1.* 1957. Grove. wraps. EX. $25.00

ANTHOLOGY. *Evergreen No. 15.* 1960. Grove. $20.00

ANTHOLOGY. *Letters to Master Jeremy Gaige From His Uncles.* 1930. private print. 1/50. $60.00

ANTHOLOGY. *Library of Wit & Humor.* nd. Thompson & Thomas. EX. $30.00

ANTHOLOGY. *Murder Cavalcade.* 1953. Hammond. 1st Eng ed. dj. EX. $17.50

ANTHOLOGY. *Out of the W: Poems...* 1979. Lord John. 1st ed. 1/350. plastic wraps. EX. $95.00

ANTHOLOGY. *Poems of the Old S.* 1877. Boston. Ils 1st ed. square 12mo. AEG. T1. $30.00

ANTHOLOGY. *S Winter-Wreath, Culled for the Motherless.* 1866. Riverside. 101 p. AEG. $75.00

ANTHOLOGY. *Song Folio.* 1883. Hunter. Ils. G. $26.00

ANTHOLOGY. *Transformation Four.* 1946. Britain. dj. EX. $20.00

ANTHOLOGY. *Transformation Two.* 1944. Britain. dj. EX. $20.00

ANTHOLOGY. *Transition Stories.* 1929. NY. McKee. 1st ed. dj. VG. $110.00

ANTHOLOGY. *View of Edinburgh.* nd. Edinburgh. Grant. 20 photos. 8vo. $10.00

ANTHOLOGY. *View of Trianon's Hungary.* 1928. Budapest. Ils. inscr/sgn 8 Hungarians. B1. $40.00

ANTHONY, Gordon. *Camera at the Ballet.* 1975. London. Crown. 8vo. dj. $25.00

ANTHONY, Gordon. *Sadler's Wells Ballet.* 1942. London. $20.00

ANTHONY, Irvin. *Revolt at Sea.* 1937. NY. Ils. 296 p. dj. T5. $15.00

ANTHONY, Piers. *Out of Phaze.* nd. Putnam. 1st ed. EX. $15.00

ANTHONY. *Company of Saints.* 1984. NY. 1st ed. dj. VG. $7.50

ANTIN, Mary. *They Who Knock at Our Gates.* 1914. Boston. 1st ed. inscr. with sgn letter. VG. $45.00

ANTON, Charles. *Classical Dictionary.* 1851. Harper. 1451 p. M1. $20.00

ANTON, F. *Art of Ancient Peru.* 1972. NY. Ils. pls. 4to. dj. EX. J2. $50.00

ANTRAM, Charles. *Butterflies of India.* 1924. Calcutta. 1st ed. wraps. VG. $65.00

APENSZLAK. *Black Book of Polish Jewry.* 1943. Roy Pub. 343 p. black cloth. VG. $38.00

APPEL, Benjamin. *Fantastic Mirror.* 1969. Pantheon. VG. P1. $15.00

APPEL, J.H. *Business Biography of John Wanamaker.* 1930. Macmillan. VG. $10.00

APPEL, Willi. *Harvard Dictionary of Music.* 1973. 2nd ed. dj. M. $27.00

APPERLEY. *Nimrod's Hunting Tours.* 1903. NY. 18 pls. VG. $165.00

APPLEMAN-JURMAN, Alicia. *Alicia: My Story.* 1988. NY. 1st ed. dj. EX. $8.50

APPLER, A.C. *Thrilling Story of Adventures & Exploits of James Brothers.* 1882. Chicago. Ils. 285 p. scarce. A3. $90.00

APPLETON, J.H. *Appleton's Cyclopaedia of American Biography.* 1888. NY. 6 vols. djs. VG. B1. $250.00

APPLETON, J.H. *Appleton's Journal.* 1878. Appleton. 4to. wraps. VG. D1. $25.00

APPLETON, J.H. *Appleton's Physical Geography.* 1887. NY. large 4to. $22.00

APPLETON, J.H. *Appleton's Quantitative Analysis.* 1893. 8vo. 182 p. TB. EX. $2.00

APPLETON, J.H. *Beginners Handbook of Chemistry.* 1888. NY. 14 pls. 254 p. VG. $35.00

APPLETON, Victor. *Tom Swift & His Airship.* 1910. Grosset Dunlap. 1st ed. VG. $9.00

APPLETON, Victor. *Tom Swift & His Giant Telescope.* 1939. Racine. Ils. 424 p. fair. very scarce. T5. $42.50

APPLETON, Victor. *Tom Swift & His Submarine Boat.* 1910. Grosset Dunlap. 1st ed. EX. $9.00

APPLETON, Victor. *Tom Swift & His Undersea Search.* 1920. Grosset Dunlap. tan cloth. dj. VG. $9.50

APPLETON, Victor. *Tom Swift & His War Tank.* 1918. Grosset Dunlap. 1st ed. $8.00

APPLETON, Victor. *Tom Swift Among the Diamond Makers.* 1911. Grosset Dunlap. tan cloth. VG. $8.00

APPONYI, Sandor. *Rariora et Curiosa.* 1925. Budapest. 1/100. pls. $50.00

APTED & GILYARD-BEER. *Ancient Monuments & Their Intrepretation.* 1977. London. dj. EX. $35.00

APULEIUS, Lucius. *Marriage of Cupid & Psyche. Retold by Walter Pater.* 1951. NY. Heritage. Ils Dulac. slipcase. J2. $15.00

ARABIAN HORSE ASSOCIATION. *Arabian Horse Yearbook.* 1972. Ils. 710 p. EX. $12.50

ARACRO, Eddie. *I Ride To Win.* 1951. NY. 1st ed. dj. VG. B2. $25.00

ARAKI, Chiyo. *Origami for Christmas.* 1987. Tokyo. Ils. tall 4to. pb. wraps. $30.00

ARAM, Eugene. *Trial & Life of Eugene Aram.* 1842. Richmond. 12mo. VG. $50.00

ARBER, Agnes. *Herbals: Their Origin & Evolution...* 1912. Cambridge. 1st ed. VG. J2. $50.00

ARBER. *Travels & Works of Captain John Smith.* 1910. Edinburgh. 2 vols. VG. B1. $50.00

ARBUTHNOT, Thomas. *African Hunt.* 1954. NY. 1st ed. dj. VG. $25.00

ARCHER, Jeffrey. *Twist in the Tale.* Simon Schuster. 3rd ed. dj. EX. $7.50

ARDOIN, John. *Stages of Menotti.* 1985. NY. Ils Gerald Fitzgerald. dj. VG. $25.00

ARENDT, Hannah. *Eichmann in Jerusalem.* 1963. NY. 1st ed. dj. M. $50.00

ARENDT, Hannah. *Eichmann in Jerusalem.* 1963. NY. 1st ed. G. $10.00

AREVALO, J.J. *Shark & the Sardines.* 1961. Lyle Stuart. dj. G. $20.00

ARIEL. *Progress in Clinical Cancer. Vol. 1.* 1965. NY. 789 p. $44.00

ARIEL. *Progress in Clinical Cancer. Vol. 3.* 1967. NY. 369 p. $37.00

ARISTO. *Orlando Furiso.* 1973. Ballantine. 1st ed. VG. C1. $3.50

ARISTOPHANES. *Comoediae.* 1676. Ravesteinium. 1087 p. $275.00

ARISTOPHANES. *Lysistrata.* 1962. Heritage. Ils Picasso. Trans Seldes. EX. C1. $12.50

ARISTOTLE. *Politics & Poetics.* 1964. Lunenburg, VT. Ltd Ed Club. Ils Baskin. dj. EX. $100.00

ARLEN, Michael. *Exiles.* 1970. NY. 1st ed. dj. EX. $12.00

ARLEN, Michael. *Lily Christine.* 1928. Doubleday. 1st ed. dj. VG. $35.00

ARMITAGE, Merle. *Railroads of America.* 1952. Ils. maps. diagrams. 319 p. $30.00

ARMITAGE, T. *History of Baptists.* 1887. Ils. 4to. 978 p. G. $22.00

ARMOUR, Richard. *Drug Store Days.* 1959. NY. 1st ed. dj. VG. $6.00

ARMOUR, Tom. *Round of Golf.* 1959. NY. 1st ed. dj. VG. $15.00

ARMS, J.T. *American Etchings.* 1930. NY. VG. $20.00

ARMSTRONG, E.A. *Bird Display & Behavior: Study of Bird Psychology.* 1965. Dover. 32 photos. 431 p. VG. M2. $10.00

ARMSTRONG, E.A. *Life & Lore of the Bird in Nature, Art, Myth, & Literature.* 1975. Crown. 1st ed. 4to. 250 p. dj. EX. M2. $17.00

ARMSTRONG, John. *Notices of the War of 1812. Vol. I.* 1836. NY. 1st ed. 263 p. orig cloth. T5. $65.00

ARMSTRONG, John. *Young Woman's Guide to Virtue, Economy & Happiness...* c 1810s. Newcastle. Mackenzie Dent. EX. $50.00

ARMSTRONG, L.E. *Literature Reader, 7th Year, CA State Series.* 1916. sm 8vo. 400 p. TB. EX. $2.50

ARMSTRONG, R.C. *Light From the E.* 1914. Toronto. VG. $60.00

ARMSTRONG, R.H. *Guide to the Birds of AK.* 1984. AK NW. Ils Revised ed. 332 p. EX. M2. $16.00

ARMSTRONG, W.C. *Life & Adventures of Captain John Smith...* 1855. Andrus. G. $22.50

ARMSTRONG & MURPHY. *Natural History of America.* 1979. KS U. 43 photos. maps. 88 p. EX. M2. $10.00

ARMSTRONG. *Railroad: What It Is, What It Does.* 1978. Simmons Boardman. EX. $15.00

ARMSTRONG. *Torpedoes & Torpedo Vessels.* 1901. London. Revised 2nd ed. VG. $55.00

ARNAC, Marcel. *Private Memoirs of Profiteer.* 1939. NY. dj. with sgn cartoon. $50.00

ARNHEIM, Rudolf. *Visual Thinking.* 1969. London. 1st ed. dj. VG. $15.00

ARNOLD, A.F. *Sea-Beach at Ebb Tide.* 1901. Century. Ils 1st ed. VG. $35.00

ARNOLD, CAPE & DAVIDSON. *Fifties Photographs of America.* 1985. NY. Pantheon. Ils. 4to. 150 p. wraps. $12.50

ARNOLD, E. *Japonica.* 1892. NY. tall 8vo. 128 p. TEG. VG. $15.00

ARNOLD, Edwin. *Light of Asia.* 1932. Phil. Ils Pogany. VG. J2. $25.00

ARNOLD, H.H. *Army Flyer.* 1942. NY. 1st ed. 299 p. T5. $12.50

ARNOLD, H.H. *Global Mission.* 1949. NY. Ils. 626 p. dj. VG. T5. $15.00

ARNOLD, L.R. *Hemingway High on the Wild.* 1977. NY. Grosset. Ils. lg 4to. 163 p. dj. $37.50

ARNOLD, Matthew. *Literature & Dogma.* 1873. London. 1st ed. VG. $95.00

ARNOLD, W. *Shadowland.* 1978. NY. 1st ed. dj. VG. B2. $17.50

ARNOLD & HALE. *Hot Irons: Heraldry of the Range.* 1940. 2nd print. 241 p. dj. B1. $25.00

ARNOLD & HALE. *Hot Irons: Heraldry of the Range.* 1940. NY. 1st ed. sgn. 8vo. dj. M. $85.00

ARNOLD. *Scholar, Gypsy & Thyrsis.* 1910. Warner. Ils Flint. 4to. brown cloth. G2. $75.00

ARNOLD-BERNARD, P. *Vir Sadhana-Sanskrit Studies.* 1919. NY. $20.00

ARNSTEIN. *Legacy of Hours.* 1927. Grabhorn. 1/250. 12mo. EX. $35.00

ARONOWITZ & HAMILL. *Hemingway: Life & Death of a Man.* 1961. Lancer. VG. P1. $3.75

ARONSON, Joseph. *Book of Furniture & Decoration.* 1941. NY. Crown. Revised ed. 358 p. D2. $65.00

ARROWSMITH, Nancy. *Field Guide to Little People.* 1977. NY. Ils. 292 p. dj. EX. $7.50

ARROWSMITH, Nancy. *Field Guide to Little People.* 1978. pb. VG. C1. $6.00

ARROWSMITH & WICHER. *First Latin Readings.* 1894. Ils. 344 p. EX. $6.00

ARSLAN, Edoardo. *Gothic Architecture in Venice.* 1972. NY. orig bdg. dj. VG. J2. $40.00

ARTHUR, Eric. *Barn.* 1972. Boston. Galahad. 1st ed. dj. EX. $25.00

ARTHUR, S.C. *Old Families of LA.* 1971. Baton Rouge. Ils. 8vo. 432 p. EX. T1. $35.00

ARTHUR, T.S. *Heiress.* 1842. Anners. VG. $30.00

ARTHUR, William. *Mission to the Mysore.* 1902. London. G. $25.00

ARTMAN & HALL. *Beauties & Achievements of the Blind.* 1857. Auburn. orange cloth. $40.00

ARTZIBASHEV, Michael. *Sanine.* 1932. Three Sirens. Ils Wright. 328 p. VG. $12.00

ARWAS, Victor. *Art Deco.* 1980. Abrams. Ils 1st ed. 316 p. dj. EX. $55.00

ASBURY, Herbert. *Barbary Coast: San Francisco Underworld.* 1933. NY. Ils. G. $12.00

ASBURY, Herbert. *Carry Nation.* 1929. NY. 1/150. sgn. P3. $25.00

ASBURY, Herbert. *French Quarter: Informal History of New Orleans' Underworld.* 1936. NY. G. $12.00

ASCHMANN, Homer. *Central Desert of Baja CA: Demography & Ecology.* 1959. CA U. 1st ed. 282 p. stiff wraps. J2. $15.00

ASHBERY, John. *Houseboat Days.* 1977. NY. Penguin. 1st ed. sgn. VG. $18.00

ASHBERY, John. *Some Trees.* 1970. NY. Corinth. not 1st ed. dj. VG. $23.00

ASHBERY, John. *Three Madrigals.* 1968. Poet Pr. 1/150. sgn/#d. wraps. EX. $50.00

ASHBERY, John. *Three Plays.* 1978. Z Pr. 1/500. sgn/#d. EX. $35.00

ASHBURN, T.Q. *History of the 324th Field Artillery, US Army.* 1919. NY. Ils. 141 p. dj. VG. T5. $32.50

ASHE, Geoffrey. *Miracles.* 1978. London. 1st ed. dj. M. C1. $19.00

ASHE, Geoffrey. *Quest for Arthur's Britain.* 1972. Book Club. VG. C1. $14.00

ASHLEY, Clifford. *Yankee Whaler.* 1938. Boston. Popular ed. 4to. VG. $75.00

ASHLEY, Michael. *Fantasy Readers` Guide 1.* 1979. Cosmos. EX. P1. $4.50

ASHMAN, Charles. *Nazi Hunters.* 1988. NY. 1st ed. dj. VG. $9.00

ASHTON, Dore. *Reading of Modern Art.* 1969. Cleveland. 1st ed. presentation. sgn. dj. D2. $60.00

ASHTON, Helen. *Dr. Serocold.* 1930. Doubleday. G. $5.00

ASHTON, John. *Romances of Chivalry.* 1890. London. Ils. VG. scarce. C1. $44.00

ASHTON & GRAY. *Chinese Art.* 1953. Beechurst. 1st ed. VG. J2. $20.00

ASIMOV, Isaac. *Fantastic Voyage II.* 1987. Ltd ed. 1/450. sgn. VG. $100.00

ASIMOV, Isaac. *Foundation's Edge.* 1982. Garden City. 1st ed. dj. VG. $18.00

ASIMOV, Isaac. *Foundation's Edge.* 1982. Whispers. Ltd ed. sgn. $100.00

ASIMOV, Isaac. *Masters Library.* 1984. Amaranth Pr. TEG. gilt leather. VG. $15.00

ASIMOV, Isaac. *Robots & Empire.* 1985. Phantasia. Ltd 1st ed. 1/650. boxed. EX. $75.00

ASIMOV, Isaac. *SF Weight-Loss Book.* 1982. Crown. 1st ed. dj. VG. P1. $15.00

ASIMOV, Isaac. *Stars & Their Courses.* 1971. Garden City. 1st ed. dj. VG. $20.00

ASIMOV, Isaac. *Witches.* Signet. 1st ed. pb. VG. C1. $4.00

ASIMOV, Issac. *Gods Themselves.* 1972. Doubleday. 1st ed. dj. EX. $80.00

ASKINS, Charles. *African Hunt.* 1958. Harrisburg. Ils 1st ed. 189 p. dj. VG. B2. $50.00

ASKINS, Charles. *Wing & Trap Shooting.* 1948. Macmillan. Ils 1st ed. 205 p. dj. EX. $12.50

ASPINALL, James. *William Roscoe's Library; or, Old Books & Old Times.* 1853. London. 1st ed. $59.50

ASQUITH, Cynthia. *King's Daughters.* 1938. NY. Ils 1st ed. photos. dj. EX. $35.00

ASQUITH, Cynthia. *This Mortal Coil.* 1947. Arkham House. 1st ed. EX. $30.00

ASTOR, Brooke. *Last Blossom on the Plum Tree.* 1986. NY. 1st ed. M. $10.00

ASTOR, J.J. *Journey in Other Worlds: Romance of the Future.* 1894. Appleton. 1st ed. G. $110.00

ATEN, Marion. *Last Train Over Rostov Bridge.* 1961. NY. 1st ed. 340 p. dj. VG. T5. $17.50

ATGET, Eugene. *Paris du Temps Perdu.* 1963. Paris. Lausanne. 1st ed. 1/1000. EX. $225.00

ATGET, Eugene. *Photographs...From Collection of Berenice Abbott.* 1967. TX U. Ils. wraps. $20.00

ATGET & PROUST. *Vision of Paris.* 1963. Macmillan. 1st ed. folio. dj. EX. $135.00

ATGET & PROUST. *Vision of Paris.* 1963. Macmillan. 1st ed. folio. gilt bdg. VG. $95.00

ATHEARN, R.G. *Soldier in the W: Civil War Letters of A.L. Hough.* 1957. PA U. photos. 250 p. dj. EX. M2. $25.00

ATHEARN, Robert. *Westward the Briton.* 1953. Scribner. 1st ed. VG. J2. $15.00

ATHELING, William. *More Issues at Hand.* 1970. Advent. 1st ed. dj. VG. P1. $35.00

ATHERTON, Gertrude. *Conqueror.* 1902. NY. 1st ed. 8vo. VG. $35.00

ATHERTON, Gertrude. *Gorgeous Isle.* 1908. NY. Ils Phillips. 8vo. G. $45.00

ATHERTON, Gertrude. *Life in the War Zone.* 1916. NY. sgn. $25.00

ATHERTON, Gertrude. *Mrs. Pendleton's Four-in-Hand.* 1903. NY. 1st ed. 8vo. VG. $15.00

ATHERTON, Gertrude. *Rezanov.* 1906. Authors/Newspapers Assn. $12.00

ATHERTON, Gertrude. *White Moring.* 1918. 1st ed. VG. S2. $75.00

ATHERTON, Lewis. *Cattle Kings.* 1961. Bloomington. 1st ed. dj. VG. $25.00

ATHILL, Diana. *Instead of a Letter.* 1969. London. Chatto Windus. 1st ed. dj. $60.00

ATKINSON, D.T. *Magic, Myth & Medicine.* 1956. NY. 320 p. dj. EX. $22.00

ATKINSON, G.F. *Studies of American Fungi, Mushrooms, Edible, Poisonous...* 1901. Andrus Church. Ils 2nd ed. inscr/sgn. 322 p. M2. $70.00

ATMAN & HALL. *Beauties & Achievements of the Blind.* 1879. Rochester. G. $17.50

ATREYA, B.L. *Moral & Spiritual Foundations of Peace.* 1952. India. $16.00

ATTENBOROUGH, David. *Journeys to the Past.* 1981. Lutterworth. 384 p. dj. EX. M2. $24.00

ATTENBOROUGH, David. *Living Planet.* 1984. Little Brown. photos. map. 320 p. dj. EX. M2. $16.00

ATTENBOROUGH, David. *Zoo Quest to Guiana.* 1957. Crowell. Ils. map. dj. EX. M2. $15.00

ATWATER, Richard. *Mr. Popper's Penguins.* 1935. Little Brown. Ils Muth. VG. B4. $25.00

ATWOOD, Margaret. *Bluebeard's Egg: Stories.* 1983. Toronto. 1st ed. sgn. dj. EX. $65.00

ATWOOD, Margaret. *Bodily Harm.* 1982. NY. 1st ed. sgn. dj. EX. $35.00

ATWOOD, Margaret. *Cat's Eye: A Novel.* 1988. Toronto. 1st ed. sgn. M. $45.00

ATWOOD, Margaret. *Handmaid's Tale.* 1986. Boston. ARC. 1st Am ed. wraps. EX. $35.00

ATWOOD, Margaret. *Handmaid's Tale.* 1986. Boston. 1st Am ed. dj. EX. T6. $20.00

ATWOOD, Margaret. *Journals of Susanna Moodie.* 1970. Toronto. 1st ed. wraps. EX. $30.00

ATWOOD, Margaret. *Surfacing.* 1972. Toronto. 1st ed. dj. VG. $75.00

ATWOOD & BARKHOUSE. *Anna's Pet.* 1980. Toronto. Ils 1st ed. sgn. EX. scarce. $65.00

ATWOOD & MC CURDY. *Encounters With the Element Man.* NH. Deluxe ed. 1/60. sgns. M. $100.00

ATWOOD & MC CURDY. *Encounters With the Element Man.* 1982. NH. Ils/sgn McCurdy. 1/100. wraps. M. $45.00

AUBEL & AUBEL. *Der Kunstlerische Tanz Unserer Zeit.* 1928. Leipzig. German text. 4to. wraps. $75.00

AUBERT, E. *Tresor de l'Abbaye de St. Maurice d'Agaune.* 1872. 45 pls. xl. VG. $175.00

AUBERT, Marcel. *French Cathedral Windows.* 1947. NY. VG. P3. $35.00

AUBIN, J.H. *Register of the Military Order of the Loyal Legion of US.* 1906. Legion of US. 253 p. EX. M2. $45.00

AUCHINCLOSS, Louis. *Dark Lady.* 1977. Boston. 1st ed. dj. EX. $20.00

AUCHINCLOSS, Louis. *Exit Lady Masham.* 1983. NY. 1st ed. sgn. dj. EX. $12.50

AUCHINCLOSS, Louis. *Partners.* 1974. Boston. 1st ed. dj. $17.50

AUCHINCLOSS, Louis. *Pioneers & Caretakers: Nine American Women Novelists.* 1965. MN U. 1st ed. dj. EX. $25.00

AUCHINCLOSS, Louis. *Tales of Manhattan.* 1967. Boston. dj. EX. P3. $22.00

AUCHINCLOSS, Louis. *Watchfires, Novel of the Civil War.* 1982. Boston. Houghton Mifflin. Book Club ed. dj. $4.50

AUCHINCLOSS, Louis. *World of Profit.* 1968. Boston. 1st ed. dj. $20.00

AUDEN, W.H. *About the House.* nd. Faber. 1st ed. dj. EX. $25.00

AUDEN, W.H. *Age of Anxiety.* 1947. NY. 1st Am ed. dj. EX. $45.00

AUDEN, W.H. *Collected Poetry.* 1945. NY. 1st ed. 1st print. dj. M. $125.00

AUDEN, W.H. *Double Man.* 1941. NY. 1st ed. EX. $30.00

AUDEN, W.H. *Good-Bye to Mezzogiorno.* 1958. Milan. Ltd ed. 16 p. wraps. EX. $20.00

AUDEN, W.H. *Homage to Clio.* 1960. London. 1st ed. dj. VG. $20.00

AUDEN, W.H. *Homage to Clio.* 1960. NY. 1st ed. dj. EX. $35.00

AUDEN, W.H. *On This Island.* 1937. NY. 2nd ed. EX. $35.00

AUDEN, W.H. *Poems.* 1930. London. 1st ed. blue wraps. $350.00

AUDEN, W.H. *Shield of Achilles.* 1955. London. 1st ed. dj. EX. $30.00

AUDEN, W.H. *Spain.* 1937. London. 1st ed. wraps. VG. $60.00

AUDEN, W.H. *Thank You, Fog.* 1974. NY. 1st ed. dj. EX. $35.00

AUDEN, W.H. *Three Songs for St. Cecilia's Day.* 1941. NY. private print. 1/250. blue wraps. $400.00

AUDEN, W.H. *Two Songs.* 1948. Phoenix. 1/26. sgn/lettered. EX. $250.00

AUDEN & ISHERWOOD. *On the Frontier.* 1938. London. 1st ed. EX. $85.00

AUDSLEY & AUDSLEY. *Guide to Art of Illuminating & Missal Painting.* 1862. London. Ils. EX. $75.00

AUDSLEY & AUDSLEY. *Polychromatic Decorations As Applied to Buildings...* 1882. London. 1st ed. 36 pls. later buckram. xl. VG. $275.00

AUDUBON, J.J. *American Wildlife Heritage.* Vol. 4. nd. Volair. EX. $30.00

AUDUBON, J.J. *Birds of America.* 1937. NY. 1st ed. 500 color pls. slipcase. T5. $125.00

AUDUBON, J.J. *Birds of America.* 1941. Macmillan. Ils 2nd ed. $40.00

AUDUBON, J.J. *Delineations of American Scenery & Character.* 1926. Baker. 349 p. VG. M2. $36.00

AUDUBON, J.J. *Original Watercolor Paintings for Birds of America.* 1966. NY/London. 2 vols. boxed. VG. $100.00

AUDUBON, J.J. *1826 Journal of John James Audubon.* 1967. Norman. 1st ed. dj. EX. $40.00

AUDUBON SOCIETY. *Field Guide to N American Trees: W Region.* 1987. Knopf. 540 photos. 639 p. M. M2. $12.00

AUDUBON SOCIETY. *Field Guide to N American Wild Flowers: W Region.* 1987. Knopf. 666 photos. 862 p. M. M2. $12.00

AUEL, J.M. *Clan of the Cave Bear.* 1980. NY. 1st ed. dj. VG. $45.00

AUEL, J.M. *Clan of the Cave Bear.* 1980. NY. 1st ed. presentation. sgn. dj. VG. B2. $62.50

AUEL, J.M. *Mammoth Hunters.* nd. Crown. Ltd ed. sgn. $40.00

AUEL, J.M. *Mammoth Hunters.* nd. Crown. 1st ed. dj. VG. $15.00

AUEL, J.M. *Valley of Horses.* 1982. NY. 1st ed. dj. EX. $30.00

AUEL, J.M. *Valley of the Horses.* 1982. nd. Crown. 1st ed. dj. VG. $20.00

AUGERVILLE, R.D. *Philobiblon of Richard de Bury.* 1933. Berkeley. 1/174. dj. $35.00

AUGUSTA, J. *Prehistoric Reptiles & Birds.* 1961. Hamlyn. Ils Burian. 4to. 104 p. dj. EX. M2. $25.00

AULD, Joseph. *Picturesque Burlington: Handbook of Burlington, VT...* 1893. Burlington. Ils. 180 p. G. T5. $15.00

AUMENT, Shary. *Unforgettable Faces.* 1972. Kalamazoo. Ils 1st ed. sgn. 4to. 216 p. T5. $25.00

AUROBINDO, Sri. *Last Poems.* 1952. India. $16.50

AUROUSSEAU, M. *Letters of F.W. Leichhardt.* 1968. Hakluyt Soc. 3 vols. djs. M. $165.00

AURTHUR & COHLMIA. *Third Marine Division.* 1948. WA. Ils 1st ed. 385 p. VG. T5. $65.00

AUSLANDER, Joseph. *Letters to Women.* 1929. NY. Harper. Ils Leighton. dj. EX. $15.00

AUSLANDER, Joseph. *No Traveler Returns.* 1925. 1st ed. dj. M. C1. $16.50

AUSLANDER, Joseph. *Yseult.* 1924. NY. 1st ed. VG. C1. $11.00

AUSLANDER & WURDEMANN. *Islanders.* 1951. Longman Green. 1st ed. sgns. 8vo. dj. VG. $35.00

AUSTEN, Jane. *Complete Works of Jane Austen.* 1927. London. 5 vols. djs. G. $75.00

AUSTEN, Jane. *Everyman & Other Plays.* 1925. London. Chapman Hall. Ils. 8vo. EX. $50.00

AUSTEN, Jane. *Friendly Persuasion.* Ltd Ed Club. slipcase. M. B3. $40.00

AUSTEN, Jane. *Love & Friendship & Other Early Works.* 1922. London. Intro Chesterton. 1st ed. VG. $54.00

AUSTEN, Jane. *Novels & Letters of Jane Austen.* 1913. NY. Winchester. brown cloth. VG. $250.00

AUSTEN, John. *Collected Tales of Pierre Louys.* 1930. Ltd ed. 1/2000. VG. $60.00

AUSTEN, John. *Shakespeare's Hamlet.* nd. London. 4to. VG. $35.00

AUSTIN, G. *Practical Magic With Popular Patter.* 1919. London. 1st ed. VG. $20.00

AUSTIN, J.G. *Nantucket Scraps.* 1895. Boston. G. $10.00

AUSTIN, L. *Around the World in San Francisco.* 1940. Grabhorn. Ltd ed. 1/500. dj. EX. $250.00

AUSTIN, Mary. *Flock.* 1906. Houghton Mifflin. 1st ed. G. $60.00

AUSTIN, Mary. *Land of Little Rain.* 1903. 1st ed. xl. G. $68.00

AUSTIN, Mary. *Land of Little Rain.* 1950. Boston. Ils Ansel Adams. 4to. dj. VG. $100.00

AUSTIN, O.L. *Birds of the World.* 1961. Golden Pr. Ils Arthur Singer. 4to. dj. EX. M2. $24.00

AUSTIN, O.L. *Water & Marsh Birds of the World.* 1967. Golden Pr. Ils. 223 p. EX. M2. $5.00

AUSTIN, R.B. *Early American Medical Imprints.* 1977. Arlington, MA. reprint. 240 p. wraps. EX. $25.00

AUSTIN & SHORT. *Reproduction in Mammals: Evolution of Reproduction.* 1975. Cambridge. 189 p. dj. EX. M2. $18.00

AUSTIN. *Labor Story, 1786-1949.* 1949. 3rd print. dj. VG. $15.00

AUSTING, R. *I Went to the Woods: Adventures of a Bird Photographer.* 1964. Coward McCann. Ils 1st Am ed. 144 p. dj. EX. M2. $8.00

AUSTURIAS, M.A. *Mulata.* 1967. Delacorte. Trans Rabassa. dj. EX. $14.00

AUTIER, Albert. *Italian Peasant Rugs.* 1923. Valcarenghi. fair. $25.00

AUTRY, Gene. *Back in the Saddle Again.* 1978. Doubleday. dj. VG. $20.00

AVARY, M.L. *Dixie After the War.* 1937. Boston. Houghton. 1st ed. dj. RS. $35.00

AVEBURY, Lord. *Ants, Bees & Wasps.* 1903. Appleton. Ils. 448 p. VG. M2. $16.00

AVEDON, Richard. *Nothing Personal.* 1964. Penguin. sgns. glassine dj. $425.00

AVEDON, Richard. *Photographs, 1947-1977.* 1978. Farrar. 1st ed. sgn. glassine wraps. $200.00

AVEDON, Richard. *Photographs, 1947-1977.* 1978. NY. Farrar. 1st ed. folio. VG. $115.00

AVEDON & CAPOTE. *Observations.* 1959. NY. 1st ed. glassine dj. EX. B2. $125.00

AVERY, E.M. *History of Cleveland & Its Environs, Heart of New CT.* 1918. Chicago. 3 vols. T5. $75.00

AVIRETT, J.B. *Memoirs of General Ashby.* 1867. Baltimore. Selby & Dunlany. 408 p. xl. $165.00

AVIRETT, J.B. *Old Plantation: How We Lived in Great House & Cabin...* 1901. NY. Neely. inscr. 12mo. VG. $55.00

AXELROD, George. *Seven-Year Itch.* 1952. NY. 1st ed. inscr/sgn. EX. $25.00

AYDEN, Erje. *From Hauptbahnhof I Took a Train.* 1966. Candy Stripe. 1st ed. wraps. $35.00

AYENSU, E.S. *Life & Mysteries of the Jungle.* 1980. Crescent. Ils 1st ed. 4to. 200 p. dj. EX. M2. $20.00

AYERS & BIRD. *Missing Men.* 1932. Garden City. Intro Alfred Smith. 293 p. G. $8.00

AYERS & FRANKLIN. *Diary of James T. Ayers.* 1947. Springfield. IL Hist Soc. Ils. VG. $25.00

AYMAR, Brandt. *Young Male Figure in Paintings, Sculpture & Drawings.* 1972. NY. Crown. 2nd print. 247 p. dj. D2. $38.50

AYRTON, Michael. *Distraction of Wits Nurtured in Elizabethan England.* 1958. Cambridge. Ils Ltd 1st ed. 1/500. VG. $50.00

AYSCOUGH, Anthony. *Country House Baroque: Photographs of 18th-C Ornaments.* 1940. London. dj. VG. J2. $20.00

AYTOUN, W.E. *Lays of the Scottish Cavaliers.* 1863. Edinburgh. Ils Paton. full red leather. $275.00

AZEMA, M.A. *Conquest of Fitzroy.* 1957. London. 1st ed. dj. VG. $45.00

AZUELA, A. *La Casa de las Mil Virgenes.* 1984. Plaza y Janes. Spanish text. pb. EX. $7.50

B

BABB, Sanora. *Owl on Every Post.* 1970. NY. 1st ed. dj. VG. B2. $17.50

BABCOCK, Bernie. *Halleroogy's Ride With Santa Claus.* 1943. Perryville, AR. Rice Print Shop. 48 p. wraps. $50.00

BABCOCK, Bernie. *Little Abe Lincoln.* 1926. Lippincott. G. $20.00

BABCOCK, Havilah. *Best of Babcock.* 1974. NY. dj. EX. $30.00

BABCOCK, Havilah. *I Don't Want To Shoot an Elephant.* 1958. NY. Holt. 1st ed. dj. EX. $60.00

BABCOCK, Philip. *Falling Leaves.* 1937. Derrydale. 1/950. EX. $125.00

BABINGTON-SMITH, Constance. *Air Spy: Story of Photo Intelligence in WWII.* 1957. NY. Ils 1st ed. 266 p. VG. T5. $17.50

BABSON, W.A. *Modern Wilderness.* 1940. Doubleday Doran. 1st ed. dj. M2. $10.00

BACH, Marcus. *Strange Alters.* 1952. Indianapolis. $22.50

BACH, Richard. *Bridge Across Forever.* 1984. NY. 1st ed. dj. EX. $12.00

BACH, Richard. *Stranger to the Ground.* 1963. NY. 1st ed. dj. EX. $18.00

BACHELDER, Ernest A. *Principles of Design.* 1904. Chicago. Inland Printer. 171 p. scarce. D2. $75.00

BACHELLER, Irving. *Candle in the Wilderness.* 1930. Bobbs Merrill. 1st ed. $12.00

BACHELLER, Irving. *Eben Holden.* 1st ed. 1st state. $85.00

BACHELLER, Irving. *Turning of Griggsby.* 1913. Harper. Ils Birch. 1st ed. $12.00

BACHMAN, Richard. *Long Walk.* nd. Signet. 3rd ed. EX. P1. $25.00

BACHMAN, Richard. *Long Walk.* 1979. Signet. VG. P1. $60.00

BACHMAN, Richard. *Roadwork.* 1981. Signet E9668. 2nd ed. VG. P1. $40.00

BACHMAN, Richard. *Running Man.* 1982. Signet AE1508. 1st Canadian ed. VG. P1. $40.00

BACHMAN, Richard. *Thinner.* 1985. Signet AE3796. VG. P1. $3.50

BACHMAN, Richard. *Thinner.* 1986. Hall Large Print ed. dj. EX. P1. $20.00

BACKSCHEIDER, P.R. *Restoration & 18th-C Dramatists.* 1989. Gale Research. 397 p. VG. T5. $35.00

BACKUS, A. *Genealogical Memoir of Backus Family.* 1890. CT. 374 p. VG. $50.00

BACKUS, J.L. *Letters From Amelia: 1901-1937.* 1982. Boston. Ils 1st ed. 253 p. dj. EX. $20.00

BACON, Francis. *Advancement of Learning.* 1902. Collier. 431 p. VG. M2. $10.00

BACON, Francis. *Tragedy of Francis Bacon.* 1940. LA. $37.50

BACON, R.L. *Secrets of Professional Turf Betting.* 1968. NY. Am Pub. 8th print. 282 p. dj. VG. $20.00

BACOU, Roseline. *Drawings in the Louvre: Italian Drawings.* 1968. London. Cassell. 100 pls. 223 p. dj. D2. $50.00

BACOU, Roseline. *Great Drawings in Louvre Museum: German, Flemish, Dutch.* 1968. Braziller. 100 pls. 223 p. dj. D2. $75.00

BACOU, Roseline. *Piranesi: Etchings & Engravings.* 1975. Boston. 1st Am ed. dj. EX. $30.00

BACOU & SERULLAY. *Great Drawings of the Louvre Museum.* 1968. Braziller. 4to. 3 vols. djs. EX. $50.00

BADINO, G. *Big Cats of the World.* 1975. Bounty. photos. 4to. 128 p. dj. EX. M2. $20.00

BAEDEKER, Karl. *Austria.* 1929. 86 maps. 518 p. EX. $65.00

BAEDEKER, Karl. *Belgium & Holland.* 1910. Leipzig. maps. VG. $20.00

BAEDEKER, Karl. *Berlin & Its Environs.* 1912. Leipzig. 5th ed. maps. plans. VG. $35.00

BAEDEKER, Karl. *Deutsches Reich.* 1936. 524 p. VG. B1. $20.00

BAEDEKER, Karl. *Egypt.* 1898. Leipsic. 4th ed. VG. B2. $60.00

BAEDEKER, Karl. *Germany.* 1914. Ils 1st ed. VG. $18.00

BAEDEKER, Karl. *Great Britain Handbook for Travelers.* 1897. 4th ed. G. $12.00

BAEDEKER, Karl. *Mediterranean.* 1911. 1st ed. VG. $95.00

BAEDEKER, Karl. *N France.* 1899. 3rd ed. G. $12.00

BAEDEKER, Karl. *N France.* 1909. 16 maps. 55 plans. 454 p. VG. $25.00

BAEDEKER, Karl. *Palestine & Syria.* 1912. 1st ed. VG. $110.00

BAEDEKER, Karl. *Paris.* 1913. 18th ed. G. $12.00

BAEDEKER, Karl. *Rhine.* 1911. 1st ed. VG. $30.00

BAEDEKER, Karl. *S Germany.* 1914. Ils 1st ed. VG. $18.00

BAEDEKER, Karl. *S Germany.* 1929. 118 maps. 547 p. G. $15.00

BAEDEKER, Karl. *Switzerland.* 1883. 32 maps. 466 p. VG. $35.00

BAER, Morley. *Room & Time Enough: Land of Mary Austin.* 1979. Northland. dj. VG. $15.00

BAER & LEIDECKER. *Secret of Recognition.* 1938. Adyar. $50.00

BAGGS, M.L. *CO.* 1920. Boston. 2nd imp. map. TEG. EX. $25.00

BAGNALL, W.R. *Samuel Slater & Early Development of Cotton Manufacturing.* 1890. Middletown. inscr. EX. $45.00

BAGNOLD, Enid. *National Velvet.* 1935. Morrow. 1st ed. dj. VG. $15.00

BAHR, Fritz. *Commerical Floriculture.* 1941. NY. Revised 4th ed. EX. $18.00

BAHR, Hermann. *Expressionismus.* 1919. Munich. Delphin. 3rd ed. 152 p. VG. D2. $40.00

BAIGELL, Matthew. *Dictionary of American Art.* 1979. NY. Ils. 390 p. dj. $25.00

BAIGENT, Leigh & Lincoln. *Holy Blood, Holy Grail.* 1981. 1st Am ed. dj. M. C1. $14.00

BAILES, Frederick. *Hidden Power for Human Problems.* 1957. NJ. $18.50

BAILEY, A.A. *Unfinished Autobiography.* 1951. NY. 304 p. VG. $20.00

BAILEY, A.W. *Flower Fancies.* 1889. Boston. Prang. sm folio. VG. $85.00

BAILEY, Alice. *Between War & Peace.* 1942. NY. $125.00

BAILEY, Alice. *Skating Gander.* 1927. Volland. Ils Myers. VG. $15.00

BAILEY, Brian. *Great Romantic Ruins of England & Wales.* 1984. Crown. 1st ed. dj. M. $10.00

BAILEY, C.S. *Finnegan II: His Nine Lives.* 1953. Viking. Ils cloth bdg. $12.00

BAILEY, C.S. *Little Rabbit Who Wanted Red Wings.* 1945. Platt Munk. Ils Grider. VG. B4. $20.00

BAILEY, Carolyn. *Stories From an Indian Cave.* 1924. Whitman. Ils. EX. $15.00

BAILEY, David. *Good-Bye Baby & Amen: Saraband for the Sixties.* 1969. Conde Nast. dj. VG. $75.00

BAILEY, F. *Early MA Marriages.* 1800. Worcester City. $16.00

BAILEY, F.M. *Birds of NM.* 1928. NM Fish/Game. Ils 1st ed. maps. 807 p. VG. M2. $100.00

BAILEY, F.M. *Handbook of Birds of the W US.* 1902. Houghton. Ils Fuertes. 1st ed. 512 p. VG. M2. $70.00

BAILEY, G.W. *Private Chapter of the War.* 1880. St. Louis. EX. K1. $45.00

BAILEY, G.W. *Private Chapter of the War.* 1880. St. Louis. Jones. 1st ed. inscr/sgn. VG. $65.00

BAILEY, H.C. *Meet Mr. Fortune.* 1942. Doubleday. dj. VG. $20.00

BAILEY, H.C. *Mr. Fortune Please.* 1938. Penguin. 4th print. dj. VG. P1. $20.00

BAILEY, J.C. *Studies of Some Famous Letters.* 1899. London. Burleigh. 12mo. brown cloth. $21.50

BAILEY, K.K. *S White Protestantism in 20th C.* 1964. Harper. 1st ed. 180 p. dj. $6.50

BAILEY, L.H. *Cultivated Conifers in N America: Pine Family & Taxads.* 1960. Macmillan. 40 photos. 404 p. VG. M2. $20.00

BAILEY, L.H. *Garden of Gourds.* 1937. NY. VG. scarce. $25.00

BAILEY, L.H. *Garden of Larkspurs.* 1939. NY. 1st print. VG. $25.00

BAILEY, N. *Universal Etymological English Dictionary.* 1784. London. full old calf. fair. T5. $75.00

BAILEY, Paul. *Armies of God: Mormon Militia on the Frontier.* 1968. Doubleday. 1st ed. dj. EX. $18.00

BAILEY, Paul. *City in the Sun.* 1971. Los Angeles. Ils 222 p. dj. EX. $27.50

BAILEY, Pearl. *Raw Pearl.* 1968. 1st ed. sgn. dj. VG. $25.00

BAILEY, Pearl. *Talking to Myself.* 1971. NY. 1st ed. dj. VG. B2. $15.00

BAILEY, Philip. *J. Festus: A Poem.* 1838. NY. Miller. 1st Am ed. EX. $75.00

BAILEY, R.F. *Pre-Revolutioary Dutch Houses & Families.* 1936. NY. Holland Soc. Ils. 4to. G. $75.00

BAILEY, R.G. *Hells Canyon.* 1943. Lewiston. Ils 1st ed. sgn. 575 p. G. B2. $80.00

BAILEY, V.H. *Skyscrapers of NY.* 1927. Rudge. Ils Bailey. folio. VG. G2. $65.00

BAILEY, Vernon. *Animal Life of Carlsbad Cavern.* 1928. Williams Wilkins. 195 p. VG. M2. $16.00

BAILEY, Vernon. *Cave Life of KY, Mainly in the Mammoth Cave Region.* 1933. Notre Dame. Ils. 256 p. EX. M2. $18.00

BAILEY, Vernon. *Mammals of NM.* 1931. USDA. pls. wraps. EX. $20.00

BAILEY & BAILEY. *Concise Dictionary of Gardening.* 1930. NY. Ils 1st ed. 4to. VG. T1. $35.00

BAILEY & NIEDRACH. *Birds of CO.* 1965. Denver. Ils 1st ed. 4to. 2 vols. EX. $125.00

BAILEY & NIEDRACH. *Pictorial Check List of CO Birds.* 1967. Denver. sm folio. dj. EX. $60.00

BAILLIE-GROHMAN. *15 Years' Sport & Life.* 1900. London. fld maps. VG. $225.00

BAILLIETT, Whitney. *Ecstasy at the Onion.* 1971. Bobbs Merrill. 1st ed. dj. EX. $22.50

BAINBRIDGE, Beryl. *Young Adolf.* 1979. NY. 1st ed. dj. VG. $8.00

BAINBRIDGE, Henry Charles. *Peter Carl Faberge: Goldsmith & Jeweler to Russian Court.* 1972. London/NY. Spring Books. 4th imp. dj. D2. $65.00

BAINBRIDGE-HOFF, William. *Elementary Naval Tactics.* 1901. NY. Wiley. 15 fld pls. 110 p. G. $35.00

BAIR, Clay Jr. *Beyond Courage.* 1955. NY. photos. 247 p. dj. VG. T5. $12.50

BAIR, D. *Samuel Beckett.* 1978. Harcourt Brace. dj. EX. $37.00

BAIRD, B.M. *Roses for S Gardens.* 1948. Chapel Hill. color pls. sgn. 96 p. boxed. VG. $30.00

BAIRD, BREWER & RIDGEWAY. *Water Birds of N America.* 1884. Little Brown. Ils 1st ed. 2 vols. $200.00

BAIRD, C.W. *History of Rye, Westchester City, NY, 1660-1870.* 1871. Randolph. fld map. 570 p. VG. $75.00

BAIRD, R. *Visit to N Europe.* 1841. NY. Ils 2 vols. G. $95.00

BAIRD, S.F. *Birds.* 1858. WA. 4to. 1005 p. rebound. EX. M2. $175.00

BAIRD. *Dome & the Rock.* 1968. Baltimore. 1st ed. dj. VG. $17.50

BAKER, A.B. *Spiral Road to God.* 1933. Boston. $15.00

BAKER, Bill. *Faces We See.* 1939. S Yarn Spinners Assn. VG. $37.50

BAKER, Bobby. *Wheeling & Dealing: Confessions of Capitol Hill Operator.* 1978. NY. 1st ed. dj. $11.00

BAKER, C.A. *Epitaphs in Old Burying Ground at Deerfield, MA.* 1924. 49 p. VG. $25.00

BAKER, C.A. *True Stories of New England Captives.* 1897. Cambridge. Ils 1st ed. inscr. $65.00

BAKER, C.H. *Gentleman's Companion Cookbook.* Derrydale. as issued. VG. B2. $115.00

BAKER, C.H. *Gentleman's Companion: Exotic Cookery.* 1946. Crown. 2 vols. boxed. G. $12.00

BAKER, Carlos. *Year & a Day.* 1963. Nashville. 1st ed. sgn. dj. VG. $15.00

BAKER, D.W. *T'ai Shan.* 1925. Shanghai. 1st ed. xl. VG. $20.00

BAKER, Denys. *Face in the Mirror.* Sauk City. 1st ed. dj. EX. $20.00

BAKER, Dorothy. *Cassandra at the Wedding.* 1962. Boston. 1st ed. dj. VG. $10.00

BAKER, E.C.S. *Zoology of Indian Parasitic Cuckoos.* 1906-1908. Bombay. Nat Hist Soc. $20.00

BAKER, E.L. *Gunman's Territory.* 1969. Naylor. Ils 1st ed. 339 p. dj. M2. $35.00

BAKER, Elliott. *When Dogs Barked Trees.* 1946. Albuquerque. Ils 1st ed. sgn. 209 p. B2. $37.50

BAKER, J.A. *Peregrine.* 1967. Harper Row. 1st Am ed. 191 p. dj. EX. M2. $25.00

BAKER, Lafayette. *Spies, Traitors & Conspirators of the Late Civil War.* 1894. Phil. Potter. Ils. 398 p. dj. $100.00

BAKER, Leonard. *Days of Sorrow & Pain.* 1978. NY. 1st ed. dj. VG. $8.50

BAKER, Lily. *Sewanee, TN, 1932.* Sewanee, TN. 156 p. purple wraps. $35.00

BAKER, M.N. *Quest for Pure Water.* 1949. Am Water Works. 2nd print. VG. J2. $35.00

BAKER, Michael. *Doyle Diary: Last Great Conan Doyle Mystery.* 1978. NY. Ils 1st ed. oblong 4to. white cloth. dj. T1. $40.00

BAKER, R.S.B. *Men of the Trees.* 1931. NY. $20.00

BAKER, Russell. *So This Is Depravity.* 1980. NY. 1st ed. 1/500. sgn. slipcase. EX. $45.00

BAKER, S.W. *Nile Tributaries of Abyssinia.* 1896. Phil. 4th ed. EX. $50.00

BAKER, Z. *Modern House Builder From Log Cabin & Cottage to Mansion.* 1857. Boston. Ils. plans. 208 p. D2. $65.00

BALANENKO. *Moscow.* 1975. dj. slipcase. M. S2. $85.00

BALCH, Thomas. *Al Arbitration.* 1900. Phil. Allen Lane Scott. inscr. VG. $35.00

BALDWIN, Christopher. *Diary of Christopher Columbus Baldwin.* 1901. Am Antiq Soc. 1st ed. VG. J2. $35.00

BALDWIN, J.G. *Flush Times of AL & MS.* 1858. San Francisco. Whitney. Ils. 330 p. $55.00

BALDWIN, James. *Baldwin's Readers, 7th Year.* 1897. sm 8vo. 240 p. TB. EX. $2.50

BALDWIN, James. *Devil Finds Work.* 1976. NY. 1st ed. dj. EX. B2. $17.50

BALDWIN, James. *No-Name Street.* 1972. NY. 1st ed. dj. EX. $25.00

BALDWIN, James. *Rhyming Alphabets in English.* 1972. Ils. 4to. 296 p. dj. EX. $20.00

BALDWIN, James. *Story of Roland.* 1930. Scribner. Ils Peter Hurd. VG. $15.00

BALDWIN, James. *Tell Me How Long the Train's Been Gone.* 1968. NY. 1st ed. dj. M. $20.00

BALDWIN, T. *Picture Making for Pleasure & Profit.* 1903. VG. $20.00

BALDWIN & MEAD. *Rap on Race.* 1971. NY. 1st ed. dj. VG. $14.00

BALDWINN, W.W. *Chicago, Burlington & Quincy Railroad Co. History.* 1928. 2 vols. $145.00

BALE, Florence Gratiot. *Galena's Yesterdays.* 1931. Waukegon. Ils. 31 p. wraps. VG. T5. $25.00

BALL, Charles. *History of Indian Mutiny: Giving Detailed Account...* c 1860. NY. Brain. Ils. 823 p. leather. M1. $175.00

BALL, Don. *America's Colorful Railroads.* 1980. Ils 1st ed. 210 p. $30.00

BALL, Don. *America's Railroads: 2nd Generation.* 1980. Review 1st ed. 216 p. $35.00

BALL, Don. *Portraits of the Rails From Steam to Diesel.* 1972. 1st ed. 95 p. $27.50

BALL, Don. *Rails.* 1981. 1st ed. photos. $19.50

BALL, John. *Arctic Showdown.* 1966. NY. 1st ed. dj. EX. $15.00

BALL, John. *Chief Tallon & the S.O.B.* 1984. NY. 1st ed. dj. EX. $10.00

BALL, John. *Cool Cottontail.* 1966. NY. 1st ed. dj. EX. $30.00

BALL, John. *Eyes of Buddha.* 1975. Boston. 1st ed. dj. EX. $15.00

BALL, John. *Eyes of Buddha.* 1976. London. 1st ed. dj. EX. $15.00

BALL, John. *First Team.* 1971. Boston. 1st ed. dj. EX. $25.00

BALL, John. *Five Pieces of Jade.* 1971. London. 1st ed. dj. EX. $15.00

BALL, John. *Judo Boy.* 1968. London. 1st ed. dj. EX. $15.00

BALL, John. *Mark One: The Dummy.* 1974. Boston. 1st ed. dj. EX. $10.00

BALL, John. *Phase Three Alert.* 1977. Boston. 1st ed. dj. EX. $12.50

BALL, John. *Singapore.* 1986. Dodd Mead. 1st ed. dj. M. $10.00

BALL, John. *Then Came Violence.* 1980. NY. 1st ed. dj. EX. $15.00

BALL, John. *Trouble for Tallon.* 1981. NY. 1st ed. dj. EX. $10.00

BALL, John. *Winds of Mitamura.* 1975. Boston. 1st ed. dj. EX. $20.00

BALL, Phyllis. *Photographic History of U of AZ, 1885-1985.* 1986. private print. photos. oblong folio. dj. G. $25.00

BALL, W. *State That Forgot: SC Surrender to Democracy.* 1932. Bobbs Merrill. 1st ed. G. $15.00

BALL, W. *Sussex.* 1906. London. 1st ed. 75 pls. VG. B2. $42.50

BALL & WHITAKER. *Decade of the Trains.* 1977. 1st ed. 277 p. $35.00

BALLANTINE, Bill. *Wild Tigers & Tame Fleas.* 1958. NY. Ils. 344 p. dj. VG. T5. $12.50

BALLANTYNE, R.M. *Blown to Bits; or, Lonely Man of Rakata.* 1889. NY. 6 pls. blue-gray cloth. $15.00

BALLANTYNE, R.M. *Hot Swamp.* 1887. NY. 1st ed. VG. $18.00

BALLANTYNE, R.M. *Hudson Bay.* 1890. London/NY. Ils. G. $5.00

BALLARD, Bobby. *How To Build a Soap Box Racer.* 1938. Racine. Ils. 46 p. wraps. VG. T5. $25.00

BALLARD, J.G. *Atrocity Exhibition.* 1970. London. 1st ed. dj. VG. $100.00

BALLARD, J.G. *Crash.* 1973. Farrar Straus. 1st Am ed. dj. EX. $65.00

BALLARD, J.G. *Empire of the Sun.* 1984. London. 1st ed. dj. EX. $45.00

BALLENTINE, George. *Autobiography of English Solider in US Army.* 1986. Chicago. Lakeside Classic. 354 p. G. T5. $15.00

BALLOU, J. *Period Piece.* 1940. Houghton. VG. $40.00

BALMER & WYLIE. *When World's Collide.* c 1932. Boston. Lippincott. 341 p. dj. EX. $20.00

BALOKOVIC, J.B. *From the Center.* 1966. ME. $27.50

BALOKOVIC, J.B. *Towards the Center.* 1956. NY. $24.00

BALSTAD, L. *N of the Desolate Sea.* 1958. Souvenir. 1st Eng ed. 223 p. EX. M2. $14.00

BANCROFT, Aaron. *Life of George WA.* 1848. Boston. Phillips Sampson. 2 vols. VG. $35.00

BANCROFT, Frederic. *Slave Trading in the Old S.* 1959. NY. Ungar. Ils. 415 p. dj. $35.00

BANCROFT, G. *Flight of Least Petrel.* 1932. Putnam. 1st ed. VG. $50.00

BANCROFT, George. *History of Battle of Lake Erie.* 1891. NY. Ils. 264 p. G. T5. $35.00

BANCROFT, H.H. *American Antiquities.* c 1891. NY. Bancroft. Ils. maps. 807 p. VG. A3. $80.00

BANCROFT, H.H. *History of AK, 1730-1885.* 1960. Antiquarian Pr. fld map. 775 p. dj. EX. M2. $45.00

BANCROFT, H.H. *History of Mexico.* 1883. Bancroft. Ils. maps. 6 vols. new cloth. M2. $145.00

BANCROFT, H.H. *History of NW Coast.* 1884. San Francisco. 1st ed. 2 vols. VG. $175.00

BANCROFT, H.H. *History of the US.* 1883-1885. NY. Revised last ed. VG. $45.00

BANCROFT, H.H. *History of UT, 1540-1886.* 1889. Hist Co. maps. 808 p. new cloth. M2. $45.00

BANCROFT. *Games for Playground, Home, School & Gym.* 1922. Macmillan. photos. G. $5.00

BANDELIER, Adolph. *Islands of Titicaca & Koati.* 1916. NY. 1st ed. 84 pls. 358 p. rebound. VG. B2. $100.00

BANDINI, R. *Veiled Horizons: Stories of Big Game Fish of the Sea.* 1939. Derrydale. 1/950. 8vo. acetate dj. EX. $160.00

BANDY, M.C. *Geology & Petrology of Easter Island.* 1937. Geol Soc Am. Ils. EX. M2. $10.00

BANGS, J.K. *Bicyclers & Three Other Farces.* 1896. Ils Penfield. 1st ed. G. $25.00

BANGS, J.K. *Booming of Acre Hill.* 1900. Ils Gibson. 1st ed. VG. $45.00

BANGS, J.K. *Uncle Sam Trustee.* 1902. Autograph ed. 1/100. sgn. 342 p. TEG. VG. $85.00

BANKO, W.E. *Trumpeter Swan.* 1980. NE U. photos. maps. 214 p. EX. M2. $7.00

BANKS, C.E. *Winthrop Fleet of 1630.* 1976. Baltimore. 8vo. 119 p. EX. T1. $25.00

BANKS, Edgar. *Bismya: Lost City of Adab.* 1912. Putnam. Ils 1st ed. photos. G. $65.00

BANKS, Iain. *Wasp Factory.* 1984. NY. 1st Am ed. sgn. dj. EX. $45.00

BANKS, N. *Treatise on the Acarina or Mites.* 1905. US Nat Mus. Ils. M2. $10.00

BANNERMAN, D.A. *Birds of the W & Equatorial Africa.* 1953. Edinburgh. Oliver Boyd. 1st ed. 2 vol set. M2. $195.00

BANNERMAN & BECK. *Little Black Sambo Storybook.* 1943. Platt Munk. 110 Ils. 63 p. EX. $125.00

BANNING, M.C. *Mesabi.* 1969. NY. 1st ed. sgn. dj. EX. $15.00

BANNING, W.P. *Commercial Broadcasting Pioneer. WEAF Experiment, 1925-1926.* 1946. Harvard. 1st ed. 308 p. dj. VG. $35.00

BANNING & BANNING. *Six Horses.* 1928. Century. Ils. map. 410 p. VG. M2. $19.00

BANRING, Kendall. *Pirates! Or, Cruise of the Black Revenge...* 1916. Boston. Ils Baumann. unbound in folder. VG. $45.00

BANTA, R.E. *Hoosier Caravan.* 1951. IN U. presentation. dj. G. $50.00

BAR-ZOHAR, Michel. *Spies in the Promised Land.* 1972. London. dj. EX. $10.00

BARADA, B. *Underwater Hunting: Its Techniques & Adventures.* 1969. Doubleday. Ils 1st ed. 237 p. dj. EX. M2. $14.00

BARBASH, Jack. *Practice of Unionism.* 1956. NY. VG. $12.00

BARBASH, Jack. *Universities & Unions of Workers' Education.* 1955. NY. VG. $20.00

BARBER, E.A. *Anglo-American Views.* 1899. Indianapolis. 1st ed. index. 159 p. VG. B2. $50.00

BARBER, E.A. *Comparative Vocabulary of UT Dialects.* 1877. WA. maps. 200 p. disbound. A3. $45.00

BARBER, G.M. *People's OH Handbook.* 1851. Sandusky City. 1st ed. 122 p. VG. T5. $42.50

BARBER, H.C. *Tony Tompkins, the Lion Tamer.* 1908. Reilly Britton. Ils Newman. G. $25.00

BARBER, J.W. *Historical American Scenes.* 1852. New Haven. 12mo. 337 p. gilt bdg. VG. G2. $29.00

BARBER, J.W. *Historical Collections of Every Town in MA.* 1839. Worcester. 1st ed. pls. fld map. $45.00

BARBER, J.W. *Interesting Events in History of US.* 1820. New Haven. 15 pls. fld map. 8vo. gilt bdg. $75.00

BARBER, Joel. *Wildfowl Decoys.* 1934. NY. 4to. 156 p. red leather. EX. $75.00

BARBER, L. *Heyday of Natural History: 1820-1870.* 1980. Doubleday. Ils 1st Am ed. dj. EX. M2. $15.00

BARBER, Richard. *Arthurian Legends: Illustrated Anthology.* 1985. Ils. dj. M. C1. $20.00

BARBER, Richard. *Arthurian Literature IV.* 1985. dj. VG. C1. $39.00

BARBER, Richard. *Reign of Chivalry.* 1980. 1st Am ed. dj. M. C1. $22.00

BARBER, Richard. *Tournaments.* 1978. Ils Dalton. 1st Eng ed. M. C1. $10.00

BARBOUR, Frances. *Proverbs & Proverbial Phrases of IL.* 1965. S IL U. 1st ed. dj. VG. J2. $17.50

BARBOUR, R.H. *Cupid in Love.* 1912. Boston. Ils 1st ed. EX. $12.00

BARBOUR, T. *Naturalist at Large.* 1945. Little Brown. photos. 314 p. VG. M2. $14.00

BARBOUR, T. *Naturalist's Scrapbook.* 1946. Harvard. photos. 218 p. EX. M2. $14.00

BARBOUR & DAVIS. *Mammals of KY.* 1974. KY U. Ils. maps. 322 p. dj. EX. M2. $18.00

BARCLAY, John. *Euphormio's Satyricon.* 1954. London. Golden Cockerel. 1/260. EX. $115.00

BARD, F.C. *Horse Wrangler: Sixty Years in Saddle in WY & MT.* 1960. Norman. Ils. dj. EX. $30.00

BARD, N.P. *Hoodlebug Valley Stories.* 1979. Solon, OH. 1st ed. 360 p. dj. VG. T5. $17.50

BARDOF & BALL. *Elements of Sugar Refining.* 1925. Easton. G. $18.00

BARE, J.E. *Wild Flowers & Weeds of KS.* 1979. Regents Pr. Ils. 4to. 509 p. dj. M. M2. $38.00

BARETTI, Joseph. *Dictionary of Spanish/English-English/Spanish.* 1800. London. full leather. rebound. VG. $85.00

BARGAINNIER, Earl. *Gentle Art of Murder.* 1980. OH. 232 p. dj. EX. $12.50

BARHAM, R.H. *Ingoldsby Legends.* 1912. London. Ils Rackham. 4to. G. $115.00

BARING-GOULD, W.S. *Annotated Sherlock Holmes.* 1967. 2nd ed. 4to. 2 vols. djs. M. $50.00

BARING-GOULD, W.S. *Curiosities of Olden Times.* 1896. NY. 1st Am ed. EX. $18.00

BARING-GOULD, W.S. *Nero Wolfe of W 35th St.* 1969. NY. 1st ed. dj. EX. $35.00

BARKER, Alan. *Civil War in America.* 1961. Doubleday. 1st ed. maps. EX. $10.00

BARKER, Clive. *Books of Blood. Vols. I, II, III.* 1984. London. sgn. 3 vols. djs. EX. $150.00

BARKER, Clive. *Books of Blood. Vols. I, II, III.* 1984. London. 1st ed. djs. EX. $100.00

BARKER, Clive. *Books of Blood. Vols. I-VI.* Ltd Am ed. 1/250. sgns. djs. EX. $200.00

BARKER, Clive. *Books of Blood. Vols. I-VI.* 1st Am trade ed. sgns. djs. EX. $100.00

BARKER, Clive. *Cabal.* 1988. NY. 1st ed. 1/750. sgn. boxed. EX. $125.00

BARKER, Clive. *Damnation Game.* 1st Am ed. sgn. dj. EX. $65.00

BARKER, Clive. *Damnation Game.* 1985. London. 1st ed. 1/250. inscr/sgn. slipcase. $325.00

BARKER, Clive. *Weaveworld.* London. Ltd 1st ed. 1/500. sgn. boxed. M. $200.00

BARKER, Clive. *Weaveworld.* nd. 1st Canadian ed. dj. M. $65.00

BARKER, Clive. *Weaveworld*. 1987. Collins. ARC. sgn. VG. P1. $75.00

BARKER, Clive. *Weaveworld*. 1987. NY. 1st Am ed. 1/500. sgn. acetate dj. boxed. EX. $150.00

BARKER, Nicolas. *Bibliotheca Lindesiana*. 1977. London. pls. 4to. EX. $75.00

BARKER, Pat. *Blow Your House Down*. 1984. NY. Putnam. 1st Am ed. dj. EX. $10.00

BARKER, Pat. *Union Street*. 1983. NY. Putnam. 1st Am ed. inscr. dj. EX. $10.00

BARKER, R.C. *Treat Yourself to Life*. 1956. NY. $12.50

BARKER, R.C. *You Are Invisible*. 1973. NY. $10.00

BARKER, S.O. *Born To Battle: Collection of Animal Stories*. 1951. NM U. Ils. 187 p. dj. VG. M2. $12.00

BARKIN. *International Labor*. 1967. NY. 1st ed. dj. $25.00

BARLOW, Ronald. *How To Be Successful in Antique Business: Survival Handbook*. 1979. CA. trade ed. pb. EX. $3.00

BARLOW, W.P. *Felicities of Book Collecting*. 1958. Piedmont. Ltd ed. $59.50

BARNARD, Henry. *Report on Condition & Improvement of Public Schools of RI*. 1846. Providence. 8vo. 252 p. wraps. G. $50.00

BARNARD, J.G. *CSA & the Battle of Bull Run*. 1862. 1st ed. fld maps. 124 p. scarce. J4. $60.00

BARNARD, J.L. *Abyssal Crustacea*. 1962. Columbia U. Ils. 4to. 223 p. dj. EX. M2. $25.00

BARNARD, J.L. *Bathyal & Abyssal Gammaridean Amphipoda of Cedros Trench*. 1967. US Nat Mus. Ils. M2. $12.00

BARNARD, Robert. *Bodies*. 1986. NY. 1st Am ed. dj. EX. $12.50

BARNARD, Robert. *Bodies*. 1986. NY. 1st Am ed. inscr. dj. EX. $20.00

BARNARD, Robert. *Corpse in a Gilded Cage*. 1984. London. 1st ed. dj. EX. $27.00

BARNARD, Robert. *Death & the Princess*. 1982. NY. 1st Am ed. dj. EX. $15.00

BARNARD, Robert. *Death in a Cold Climate*. 1981. NY. 1st Am ed. dj. EX. $15.00

BARNARD, Robert. *Death in Purple Prose*. 1987. London. 1st ed. sgn. dj. EX. $30.00

BARNARD, Robert. *Out of the Blackout*. 1984. NY. Review 1st ed. dj. EX. $17.00

BARNES, A.S. *One Hundred Years of American Independence*. 1876. NY. Ils. 664 p. xl. $65.00

BARNES, Djuna. *Greenwich Village As It Is*. 1978. Phoenix. 1/300. $40.00

BARNES, Djuna. *Ryder*. 1928. Liveright. Ltd 1st ed. VG. M1. $45.00

BARNES, J. *Wilkie*. 1952. Simon Schuster. 405 p. dj. EX. $9.00

BARNES, James. *Naval Actions of War of 1912*. 1896. NY. Ils 1st ed. TEG. 263 p. VG. $20.00

BARNES, James. *Ships & Sailors*. 1898. NY. 1st ed. 12 pls. VG. T5. $250.00

BARNES, Joshua. *Euripidis*. 1811. Oroni. 32mo. VG. $95.00

BARNES, Linda. *Trouble of Fools*. 1987. St. Martin. 1st ed. dj. M. $10.00

BARNES, M. *Mountain World: 1956-1957*. nd. Harper. Ils. 200 p. dj. EX. M2. $15.00

BARNES, Margaret. *Brief Gaudy Hour: Novel of Anne Boleyn*. 1959. Book Club. dj. VG. C1. $5.00

BARNES, Melvyn. *Dick Francis: Biography*. 1986. NY. 1st ed. dj. EX. $25.00

BARNES, W.C. *Tales From the X-Bar Horse Camp*. 1920. Chicago. Breeders Gazette. 1st ed. EX. $175.00

BARNES & BURR. *Thirteen Months in the Rebel Army*. 1862. 232 p. EX. scarce. J4. $25.00

BARNETT, P.N. *Pictorial Bookplates: Their Origins & Use in Australia*. 1931. Sydney. 1st ed. 1/300. presentation. sgn. VG. J2. $150.00

BARNEY, Maginel. *Valley of Gode Almighty Joneses*. 1965. Appleton. 1st ed. dj. VG. J2. $15.00

BARNHART & CARMONY. *IN From Frontier to Industrial Commonwealth*. 1954. Lewis Pub. Ils. maps. 4to. 4 vols. VG. M2. $85.00

BARNOUW, E. *Radio Drama in Action: 25 Plays of a Changing World*. 1945. NY/Toronto. 1st ed. VG. $37.50

BARNOUW, E. *Tower in Babel*. 1966. NY. Ils 1st ed. dj. VG. B2. $17.50

BARNUM, P.T. *Struggles & Triumphs; or, Life of P.T. Barnum*. 1927. Knopf. 1st ed. 2 vols. VG. J2. $45.00

BAROJA, Pio. *La Vie Adventureuse de Juan Van Halen*. 1943. Brussells. 1/420. slipcase. J2. $35.00

BARR, A.E. *Preacher's Daughter*. 1892. Bradley Woodruff. 1st ed. $12.00

BARR, A.E. *Remember the Alamo*. 1888. Dodd Mead. 431 p. VG. scarce. A3. $50.00

BARR, Alfred H. *Cubism & Abstract Art*. 1936. MOMA. 1/3000. 249 p. D2. $85.00

BARR, Alfred H. *Matisse*. 1951. MOMA. G. $22.00

BARR, M.S. *Medardo Rosso*. 1963. NY. Ils. 92 p. dj. $20.00

BARR & BOLAND. *Camelot 3000*. 1988. stiff wraps. M. C1. $16.00

BARRATT, Raven. *Coronets & Buckskin*. 1957. Boston. 1st ed. dj. VG. $30.00

BARRETT, E.B. *Magnificent Illusion*. 1930. NY. $25.00

BARRETT, H.B. *19th-C Journals & Paintings of William Pope*. 1976. Toronto. VG. $15.00

BARRETT, Peter. *In Search of Trout*. 1973. Prentice Hall. 1st ed. 223 p. dj. VG. $10.00

BARRIE, J.M. *Entrancing Life*. 1930. London. 1st ed. dj. EX. $25.00

BARRIE, J.M. *Half Hours. Der Tag*. 1921. Scribner. VG. $7.50

BARRIE, J.M. *Little Minister*. 1891. London. Cassell. 1st ed. 3 vols. $100.00

BARRIE, J.M. *Little White Bird; or, Adventures in Kensington Gardens*. 1902. NY. VG. $25.00

BARRIE, J.M. *Peter Pan & Wendy*. 1940. Scribner. Ils Blampied. 1st ed. VG. J2. $35.00

BARRIE, J.M. *Peter Pan in Kensington Gardens*. 1906. London. Hodder. Ils Rackham. 1st ed. EX. $295.00

BARRIE, J.M. *Peter Pan in Kensington Gardens*. 1916. London. EX. $85.00

BARRIE, J.M. *Sentimental Tommy*. 1896. Scribner. Ils Armstrong. 1st ed. VG. $15.00

BARRIE, J.M. *Tommy & Grizel*. 1900. Scribner. Ils Partridge. 1st ed. VG. $15.00

BARRIE, J.M. *Works of J.M. Barrie*. 1929-1931. NY. Peter Pan Ltd ed. 14 vols. djs. $575.00

BARRINGTON, R. *Joys of a Garden for Your Birds*. 1971. Grosset Dunlap. Ils. 123 p. dj. EX. M2. $7.00

BARRIO-GARAY, J.L. *Jose Gutierrez Solana: His Paintings & Writings.* 1976. London. 1st ed. folio. dj. VG. $30.00

BARROW, G.W.S. *Feudal Britain.* 1956. London. 451 p. VG. $26.00

BARROW, George. *Lavengro.* 1936. Curwen. Ils/sgn Bagnett Freedman. boxed. $80.00

BARROW, J. *Captain Cook's Voyages of Discovery.* 1944. Dent. 479 p. EX. M2. $10.00

BARROW, Sarah F. *Medieval Society Romances.* 1924. Columbia U. 1st ed. xl. C1. $22.00

BARROWS, W.B. *MI Bird Life.* 1912. MI Agric Coll. Ils 1st ed. sgn. 822 p. G. M2. $45.00

BARRUS, Clara. *Life & Letters of John Burroughs.* 1925. Boston. 2 vols. djs. EX. $75.00

BARRUS, Clara. *Whitman & Burroughs: Comrads.* 1931. Houghton. Deluxe 1st ed. 1/250. VG. J2. $35.00

BARRY, F.V. *Century of Children's Books.* c 1920s. NY. $45.00

BARRY, Julian. *Lenny, a Play: Life & Words of Lenny Bruce.* 1971. NY. 1st print. dj. VG. $10.00

BARRY, T. *San Francisco in Spring of '50.* 1973. 1st ed. G. $150.00

BARRY, Wendell. *Place on Earth.* 1967. NY. 1st ed. sgn. EX. $35.00

BARRY. *Railway Appliances.* 1876. NY. Ils. 294 p. VG. C4. $40.00

BARSLEY, M. *Orient Express.* 1966. photos. 204 p. $14.00

BARSNESS, L. *Heads, Hides & Horns: Complete Buffalo Book.* 1985. TX Christ U. Ils. 4to. 233 p. dj. EX. M2. $40.00

BARTH, Gunther. *City People.* 1980. NY. 1st ed. dj. EX. $15.00

BARTH, John. *Chimera.* 1972. NY. 1st Am ed. dj. VG. $20.00

BARTH, John. *Giles Goat Boy.* 1966. Doubleday. 1st ed. 1/250. dj. boxed. EX. $120.00

BARTH, John. *Letters of John Barth.* 1979. Putnam. Ltd 1st ed. sgn. slipcase. EX. $60.00

BARTH, John. *Lost in the Funhouse.* 1958. Doubleday. 1st ed. 201 p. dj. EX. T5. $25.00

BARTH, John. *Lost in the Funhouse.* 1979. Putnam. 1st ed. dj. VG. $50.00

BARTH, John. *Sabbatical.* 1982. Putnam. 1st ed. dj. VG. $20.00

BARTH, John. *Sot Weed Factor.* 1960. Doubleday. 1st ed. VG. $50.00

BARTH, John. *Todd Andrews to the Author.* 1979. Lord John. 1/50. sgn. slipcase. M. $125.00

BARTHELME, Donald. *Amateurs.* 1976. NY. 1st ed. dj. EX. $15.00

BARTHELME, Donald. *Amateurs.* 1977. London. 1st ed. dj. EX. $14.00

BARTHELME, Donald. *Come Back, Dr. Caligari.* 1964. Boston. 1st ed. EX. $100.00

BARTHELME, Donald. *Come Back, Dr. Caligari.* 1966. London. 1st ed. 8vo. dj. EX. $110.00

BARTHELME, Donald. *Dead Father.* 1975. NY. 1st ed. sgn. dj. $45.00

BARTHELME, Donald. *Emerald.* 1980. Los Angeles. 1/330. sgn. M. $75.00

BARTHELME, Donald. *Guilty Pleasures.* 1974. NY. 1st ed. dj. EX. $20.00

BARTHELME, Donald. *Here in the Village.* 1978. Lord John. 1st ed. 1/275. sgn. dj. VG. $50.00

BARTHELME, Donald. *Sadness.* 1972. NY. Stated 1st ed. 8vo. dj. VG. $30.00

BARTHELME, Donald. *Second Marriage.* 1984. Simon Schuster. 1st ed. dj. EX. $20.00

BARTHELME, Donald. *Slightly Irregular Fire Engine.* 1971. NY. 1st ed. dj. VG. $30.00

BARTHELME, Donald. *Snow White.* 1967. Atheneum. 1st ed. 8vo. white cloth. dj. EX. $75.00

BARTHELME, Donald. *Unspeakable Practices, Unnatural Acts.* 1968. NY. 1st ed. 8vo. dj. EX. $45.00

BARTHELME, Frederick. *Moon Deluxe.* 1983. Simon Schuster. 1st ed. dj. $25.00

BARTHOLOMEW, E. *Wild Bill Longley: TX Hardcase.* 1953. TX. wraps. VG. $40.00

BARTHOLOMEW, E. *1,200 Old Medicine Bottles With Current Prices.* 1971. Ft. Davis. Ils. 8vo. 120 p. $15.00

BARTLET, R.A. *Last Voyage of Karluck Flag Ship of Stefansson's Expedition.* 1916. Boston. 1st ed. VG. $35.00

BARTLETT, A.E. *Least-Known America.* 1925. NY. Revell. Ils. 286 p. dj. scarce. A3. $65.00

BARTLETT, R.A. *Log of the Bob Bartlett.* 1928. Putnam. Ils. 352 p. VG. M2. $18.00

BARTLETT, R.A. *Sails Over Ice.* 1934. NY/London. Ils. photos. fair. $50.00

BARTLETT, W.H. *History of the US of N America.* 1856. NY. Virtue. 87 pls. 3 vols. morocco. AEG. J2. $250.00

BARTLETT, William. *Pilgrim Fathers; or, Founders of New England.* 1854. London. Revised 2nd ed. pls. G. $65.00

BARTLETT & BARTLETT. *Flight of the Snow Geese.* 1975. Stein Day. Ils 1st ed. 189 p. dj. EX. M2. $9.00

BARTLETT & BARTLETT. *Nature's Paradise: Africa.* 1967. Houghton. 1st ed. dj. VG. $30.00

BARTLETT. *History, Diagnosis, Treatment of Typhoid & Typhus Fever.* 1842. 1st ed. VG. $260.00

BARTLEY, E.R. *Ridelands Oil Controversy.* 1953. Austin. 1st ed. 312 p. dj. VG. B2. $32.50

BARTLEY, N.V. *From Thurmond to Wallace: Political Tendencies in GA...* 1970. Baltimore. Johns Hopkins. 117 p. dj. $450.00

BARTON, Clara. *Story of the Red Cross.* 1904. NY. 1st ed. 199 p. fair. T5. $17.50

BARTON, Don. *Carolina-Clemson Game, 1896-1966.* 1967. Columbia. State Print Co. 1st ed. 367 p. $25.00

BARTON, F. *Horses & Practical Horsekeeping.* 1912. NY. Ils. 643 p. VG. $32.00

BARTON, G.A. *Sketch of Semitic Origins: Social & Religious.* 1902. Macmillan. 342 p. green cloth. VG. $30.00

BARTON, John. *Rural Artists of WI.* 1948. WI U. 1st ed. VG. J2. $25.00

BARTON, William. *Abraham Lincoln & Walt Whitman.* 1928. Indianapolis. 1st ed. dj. EX. $75.00

BARTON, William. *Life of Abraham Lincoln.* 1925. Bobbs Merrill. 2 vols. $40.00

BARTON, William. *Women Lincoln Loved.* 1927. Bobbs Merrill. Ils. G. $40.00

BARTSCH, P. *Monograph of the American Shipworms.* 1922. US Nat Mus. 37 pl. 51 p. M2. $9.00

BARTTER, M.A. *Way to Ground Zero.* 1988. Greenwood. EX. P1. $39.95

BARWLOW, Edward. *Barlow's Journal of His Life at Sea in King's Ships...* 1934. Hurst Blackett. Trans Lubbock. 1st ed. 2 vols. J2. $100.00

BARZIN, L. *Paris to Peking.* 1973. NY. ARC. dj. VG. $15.00

BARZUN, Jacques. *Catalog of Crime.* 1971. Harper. 1st ed. 831 p. dj. VG. $25.00

BARZUN & VIKING PRESS. *Birthday Tribute to Rex Stout.* 1965. NY. 16 p. pb. printed wraps. EX. $35.00

BASEDOW, H. *Australian Aboriginal Adelaide.* 1929. Ils. photos. maps. G. $20.00

BASHO, Matsuo. *Back Roads to Far Towns.* 1968. NY. 1st ed. dj. boxed. VG. B2. $45.00

BASILE, G. *Stories From Pentamerone.* 1911. London. Ils Goble. G. $60.00

BASKERVILLE. *Big Show.* 1938. Rand McNally. Ils McKee. G. $20.00

BASKIN, Esther. *Creatures of Darkness.* 1962. Boston. Little Brown. 1st ed. dj. EX. $25.00

BASKIN, Leonard. *Ars Anatomica: Medical Fantasia.* 1972. NY. Ltd ed. 13 pls. sgn. folio. EX. $125.00

BASKIN, Leonard. *Caprices & Grotesques.* 1965. Northampton. Gehenna Pr. 1/500. slipcase. $150.00

BASKIN, Leonard. *Passover Haggadah.* 1974. Ltd ed. 1/500. 4to. EX. $100.00

BASS, R.D. *Swamp Fox: Life & Campaigns of General Francis Marion.* 1959. NY. Holt. 1st ed. 275 p. dj. $35.00

BASSETT, John. *William Faulkner: Annotated Check List of Criticism.* 1972. NY. 1st ed. dj. EX. $45.00

BASSHAM, A. *Memories of an American Impressionsist.* 1980. Kent State. EX. $18.50

BASTIN, E.S. *College Botany.* 1889. Ils. 451 p. VG. $10.00

BATCHELLOR, I. *Story of a Passion.* 1901. Roycroft. green suede. VG. D1. $45.00

BATEMAN, E. *Horse Breaker: TX Style.* 1947. Ils Thompson. 1st ed. 4to. dj. EX. $40.00

BATEMAN, Gregory. *Fresh-Water Aquaria: Construction, Arrangement, Management.* 1902. London. 12mo. 352 p. green bdg. $35.00

BATEMAN, J. *Animal Traps & Trapping.* 1971. Stackpole. photos. 286 p. dj. EX. M2. $10.00

BATES, E.S. *Touring in 1600.* 1911. Boston. 1st ed. pls. VG. $12.50

BATES, H.E. *Love for Lydia.* 1952. London. 1st ed. dj. VG. $35.00

BATES, H.W. *Naturalist on the Amazons.* 1930. London. Dent. Ils. map. 407 p. EX. M2. $20.00

BATES, Joe. *Streamer Fly Tying & Fishing.* 1966. Stackpole. Ils 1st ed. dj. EX. $17.50

BATES, M. *Forest & the Sea.* 1980. Time Life. 272 p. EX. M2. $10.00

BATES, M. *Where Winter Never Comes.* 1942. Scribner. Ils 1st ed. 310 p. dj. VG. M2. $10.00

BATES, N.W. *Genealogy of Descendants of John Whitmarsh of Weymouth, MA.* 1916. Ashtabula. 85 p. fair. T5. $10.00

BATES, Ralph. *Olive Field.* 1936. NY. Dutton. 3rd ed. sgn. EX. $15.00

BATES & HUMPHREY. *Darwin Reader.* 1956. Scribner. Ils. 470 p. dj. EX. M2. $17.00

BATES. *Through the Woods.* 1936. London. Ils Agnes Parker. dj. EX. $12.00

BATESON, W. *Mendel's Principles of Heredity.* 1909. Cambridge. 2nd print. VG. J2. $100.00

BATHKE, E.A. *Denver Westerners' Brand Book.* 1973. 1/700. photos. 421 p. EX. M2. $22.00

BATTELL, Joseph. *Ellen; or, Whisperings of an Old Pine.* 1901. VT. 1st ed. EX. $20.00

BATTEN, J.M. *Reminiscences of Two Years in US Navy.* 1881. Lancaster. 1st ed. presentation. sgn. VG. $125.00

BATTEY, Thomas C. *Life & Adventures of a Quaker Among the Indians.* 1875. Boston. Lee Shepard. 1st ed. T6. $45.00

BATTLES & COLT. *Fifty Blooming Years, 1913-1963.* Garden Club of Am. 1/3000. G. $20.00

BAUDELAIRE, Charles. *Flowers of Evil.* 1936. NY. Trans Dillon/Millay. 1st ed. T5. $95.00

BAUDELAIRE, Charles. *Flowers of Evil.* 1947. Sylvan Pr. Ils Beardsley. VG. C1. $17.50

BAUDINO, Gael. *Strands of Starlight.* 1989. 1st pb ed. EX. C1. $3.50

BAUDOUIN, Frans. *Pietro Pauolo Rubens.* 1977. Abrams. Ils. 407 p. dj. D2. $175.00

BAUDRILLARD, Jean. *Enrico Baj.* 1980. Paris. Filipacchi. French/Eng text. D2. $25.00

BAUER, C.M. *Yellowstone Geysers.* 1947. Haynes. Ils Revised ed. 125 p. VG. M2. $15.00

BAUER, E.A. *Bass Fisherman's Bible.* 1961. Doubleday. 1st ed. wraps. VG. $12.50

BAUER, E.A. *Treasury of Big Game Animals.* 1975. Outdoor Life. clr photos. 398 p. dj. EX. M2. $10.00

BAUER, Johann. *Kafka & Prague.* 1971. NY. 1st ed. dj. EX. $25.00

BAUERMAN, Theodore. *Treatise on Metallury of Iron.* 1868. NY. Ils 1st Am ed. 406 p. VG. C4. $55.00

BAUGHMAN, Harold. *Baughman's Aviation Dictionary & Reference Guide.* 1942. Aero Pub. VG. $17.50

BAUGHMAN, R.W. *KS in Maps.* 1961. KS Hist Soc. 90 maps. 104 p. dj. M. A3. $20.00

BAUGHMAN, Theodore. *OK Scout.* nd. Chicago. VG. $40.00

BAULAU, A.E. *Footprints of Assurance.* 1953. NY. 1st ed. 319 p. xl. T5. $45.00

BAUM, L.F. *American Fairy Tales.* reprint of 1901 ed. wraps. M. $10.00

BAUM, L.F. *Annabel.* 1912. Chicago. 2nd ed. EX. B2. $125.00

BAUM, L.F. *Army Alphabet.* 1900. Chicago. Hill. Ils Kennedy/Costello. VG. T1. $375.00

BAUM, L.F. *Boy Fortune Hunters in Yucatan.* 1910. Chicago. 1st ed. G. $90.00

BAUM, L.F. *Cowardly Lion & Hungry Tiger.* 1913. Chicago. Little Wizard Series. 1st ed. $65.00

BAUM, L.F. *Dorothy & the Wizard in Oz.* c 1960s. reprint of 1908 ed. 226 p. M. $12.50

BAUM, L.F. *Dorothy & the Wizard in Oz.* 1940. reprint of 1908 ed. 226 p. dj. VG. $35.00

BAUM, L.F. *Dorothy & the Wizard of Oz.* 1917. Reilly Lee. Ils Neill. 312 p. G. $175.00

BAUM, L.F. *Emerald City of Oz.* c 1960s. reprint of 1910 ed. 296 p. M. $12.50

BAUM, L.F. *Emerald City of Oz.* 1940. Reilly Lee. dj. $40.00

BAUM, L.F. *Father Goose's Yearbook.* 1907. Reilly Britton. 1st ed. $100.00

BAUM, L.F. *Glinda of Oz.* c 1970s. reprint of 1920 ed. 279 p. M. $10.00

BAUM, L.F. *Glinda of Oz.* 1920. Reilly Lee. 1st ed. EX. $150.00

BAUM, L.F. *John Dough & the Cherub.* Reilly Britton. Ils Neill. 1st ed. 3rd state. G. $95.00

BAUM, L.F. *John Dough & the Cherub.* 1906. Reilly Britton. Ils Neill. 1st ed. EX. $150.00

BAUM, L.F. *John Dough & the Cherub.* 1974. Dover. rerpint of 1906 ed. 315 p. dj. M. $25.00

BAUM, L.F. *Land of Oz.* c 1960s. reprint of 1904 ed. 288 p. M. $12.50

BAUM, L.F. *Life & Adventures of Santa Claus.* 1902. Bowen Merrill. 1st state. fair. scarce. $100.00

BAUM, L.F. *Little Dorothy & Tots of Oz.* 1939. Rand McNally. VG. $35.00

BAUM, L.F. *Lost Princess of Oz.* 1939. Rand McNally. VG. $20.00

BAUM, L.F. *Magical Monarch of Mo.* 1968. Dover. reprint of 1903 ed. 237 p. wraps. $15.00

BAUM, L.F. *Master Key.* 1901. Indianapolis. Ils Cory. 1st issue. 1st state. G. $125.00

BAUM, L.F. *Master Key.* 1901. Indianapolis. 1st ed. 1st state. EX. B2. $185.00

BAUM, L.F. *Navy Alphabet.* 1900. Chicago. Hill. Ils Kennedy/Costello. VG. T1. $375.00

BAUM, L.F. *Patchwork Girl of Oz.* 1913. Chicago. 1st ed. 1st state. EX. T5. $150.00

BAUM, L.F. *Queen Zixi of Ix.* 1905. NY. Century. 1st ed. 1st state. $125.00

BAUM, L.F. *Queen Zixi of Ix.* 1971. Dover. reprint of 1905 ed. 231 p. wraps. $12.50

BAUM, L.F. *Road to Oz.* c 1930s. reprint of 1909 ed. 261 p. G. $10.00

BAUM, L.F. *Road to Oz.* c 1940s. reprint of 1909 ed. 261 p. M. $35.00

BAUM, L.F. *Road to Oz.* c 1960s. reprint of 1909 ed. 261 p. M. $12.50

BAUM, L.F. *Runaway Shadows & Other Stories.* 1980. Escanaba, MI. Ils Eubank. 40 p. wraps. M. $35.00

BAUM, L.F. *Tik-Tok of Oz.* c 1960s. reprint of 1914 ed. 292 p. EX. $10.00

BAUM, L.F. *Tik-Tok of Oz.* 1940. Ils Neill. reprint of 1914 ed. M. $25.00

BAUM, L.F. *Tin Woodsman of Oz.* 1940. Popular ed. Ils Neill. 288 p. VG. $35.00

BAUM, L.F. *Visitors From Oz.* 1960. Chicago. Ils Dick Martin. 96 p. dj. EX. $45.00

BAUM, L.F. *Wizard of Oz.* 1939. Movie ed. Ils Denslow. 308 p. VG. $50.00

BAUM, L.F. *Wizard of Oz.* 1944. Ils Copelman. reprint of 1899 ed. 209 p. dj. VG. $40.00

BAUM, L.F. *Wizard of Oz.* 1982. NY. Ils/sgn Hague. 4to. slipcase. G2. $95.00

BAUM, L.F. *Wizard of Oz. 1939 Cocomalt Giveaway.* 1939. Ils Henry Vallely. 48 p. wraps. EX. $50.00

BAUME, M. *Elements de Pharmacie.* 1740. Paris. 2 copper pls. 8vo. 894 p. $540.00

BAUR, John I. *George Grosz.* 1954. Macmillan. Ils. dj. VG. D2. $45.00

BAUSCH, Edward. *Manipulation of the Microscope.* 1885. Rochester. 1st ed. VG. M1. $35.00

BAWLEY, B. *Paul Laurence Dunbar, Poet of His People.* 1936. Chapel Hill. xl. G. $35.00

BAXLEY, H.W. *What I Saw on the W Coast of N & S America at HI Islands.* 1865. Appleton. Ils 1st ed. 632 p. A3. $180.00

BAYES, H.E. *Hessian Prisoner.* 1930. London. Ils Austen. 1/550. sgn. 8vo. VG. $50.00

BAYLEY, C. *Complete Photographer.* 1932. Stokes. 10th print. VG. $20.00

BAYLISS. *Bolivar.* Derrydale. as issued. VG. B2. $50.00

BAYNE, Samuel. *Derricks of Destiny.* 1942. NY. $10.00

BAYNE, Spencer. *Agent Extraordinary.* 1942. Dutton. 1st ed. dj. $15.00

BAYNES. *Polaris: Story of Eskimo Dog.* 1922. NY. Ils 1st ed. inscr. dj. EX. $25.00

BAZIN, Germain. *Museum Age.* 1967. NY. Universe. Ils. 304 p. dj. D2. $45.00

BEACH, C.A. *Centennial Celebration of State of NY.* 1879. Albany. pls. xl. G. $12.50

BEACH, J.P. *Log of Apollo: Joseph Perkins Beach's Journal of Voyage...* 1986. San Francisco. Arion Pr. Book Club CA. 1/550. EX. $115.00

BEACH, Rex. *Iron Trail.* 1913. Harper. $12.00

BEACH, Rex. *Ne'er Do Well.* 1911. Harper. Ils Christy. 1st ed. $12.00

BEACH, W.M. *In the Shadow of Mt. McKinley.* 1931. Derrydale. 1/750. dj. slipcase. $225.00

BEADLE, J.H. *Life in UT; or, Mysteries & Crimes of Mormonism.* 1870. Phil. 1st ed. EX. $70.00

BEAGLE, P.S. *I See by My Outfit.* 1965. NY. 1st ed. dj. VG. B2. $30.00

BEAGLE, P.S. *I See by My Outfit.* 1965. Viking. 1st ed. dj. EX. $35.00

BEAGLE, P.S. *Last Unicorn.* 1968. Viking. 1st ed. dj. VG. $20.00

BEAGLEHOLE, J.C. *Life of Capt. James Cook.* 1974. Stanford. 1st Am ed. dj. VG. $30.00

BEALE, H. *Diary of Edward Bates, 1859-1866.* 1933. WA. VG. $25.00

BEALE, James. *Battle Flags of the Army of the Potomac at Gettysburg.* 1885. 1/125. pls. 4to. sgn. with pamphlet. K1. $450.00

BEALER, Alex. *Only the Names Remain: Cherokees & the Trail of Tears.* 1972. Boston. Ils Bock. 88 p. dj. VG. $10.00

BEALS, Carlton. *Crime of Cuba.* 1933. Phil. Ils Evans. 1st ed. VG. B2. $47.50

BEALS, Carlton. *Crime of Cuba.* 1933. Phil. Ils Walker Evans. sgns. dj. scarce. $75.00

BEALS, Carlton. *Passaconaway.* 1916. Boston. $12.00

BEAN, G.B. *Charles Boettcher: Study in Pioneer W Enterprise.* 1976. Boulder. Ils 1st ed. 8vo. dj. EX. T1. $35.00

BEAN, L.L. *Hunting, Fishing & Camping.* 1942. 3rd ed. red bdg. G. $12.00

BEAN, L.L. *Hunting, Fishing & Camping.* 1944. np. Bean. 4th ed. G. $8.00

BEAN, W.G. *Sandie Pendleton: Stonewall's Man.* 1959. Chapel Hill. 1st ed. dj. EX. $20.00

BEAN, W.L. *Twenty Years of Electrical Operation on NYNH&H Railroad.* 1927. c 1950s. Ils. photos. 145 p. $40.00

BEARD, Dan C. *American Boys' Book of Signs, Signals & Symbols.* 1918. Phil. 3rd print. 250 p. G. $20.00

BEARD, Dan C. *American Boys' Handy Book: What To Do & How To Do It.* 1885. NY. Ils. 391 p. fair. T5. $25.00

BEARD, Henry. *Miss Piggy's Guide to Life, As Told to Henry Beard.* NY. Muppet Pr. 8th print. dj. EX. $8.00

BEARD, James. *Cook's Catalog.* 1975. NY. Ils. folio. dj. EX. $16.00

BEARD, Peter. *End of the Game.* 1965. London. 1st ed. 256 p. dj. VG. B2. $87.50

BEARD & BEARD. *America in Mid-Passage.* 1939. NY. 2 vols. slipcase. G. $20.00

BEARDEN, C.M. *Common Marine Fishes of SC.* 1961. Wadmalaw Island. Ils. 47 p. wraps. $20.00

BEARDSLEY, Aubrey. *Early Work of Beardsley.* 1899. London. 4to. TEG. cloth. VG. J2. $165.00

BEARDSLEY, Aubrey. *Letters to Smithers.* 1937. Chiswick Pr. 1st Ed Club. gilt black bdg. EX. $105.00

BEARDSLEY, Aubrey. *Poems of Ernest Dowson.* 1905. London. Ils 1st ed. VG. $75.00

BEARDSLEY, Aubrey. *Selected Drawings.* 1967. Grove. 1st ed. dj. EX. $30.00

BEARDSLEY, Aubrey. *Selected Works of Aubrey Beardsley.* 1987. London. Ills. 4to. 311 p. dj. EX. $70.00

BEARDSLEY, Aubrey. *Story of Venus & Tannhauser.* 1974. St. Martin. Ils. 4to. 80 p. EX. $6.00

BEARDSLEY, Aubrey. *Under the Hill.* 1959. NY. Grove. 1st ed. dj. VG. $20.00

BEARDSLEY, Aubrey. *Yellow Book. Vol. I.* April, 1894. VG. $55.00

BEARSS, E.C. *LA Confederate, Diary of Felix Pierre Poche.* 1972. NW State U. Trans Watson. 352 p. $35.00

BEASLEY, B. *Little River Co.* 1975. Little River Co Hist Soc. M2. $32.00

BEASLEY, Norman. *Men Working: Story of Goodyear Tire & Rubber Co.* 1931. NY. 1st ed. 296 p. dj. VG. T5. $22.50

BEATON, Cecil. *Glass of Fashion.* 1954. Doubleday. 1st ed. dj. EX. $55.00

BEATON, Cecil. *Japanese.* 1959. NY. VG. $25.00

BEATON, Cecil. *Memoirs of the '40s.* 1972. NY. 310 p. dj. EX. $20.00

BEATON, Cecil. *Photobiography.* 1951. Garden City. 1st Am ed. 4to. 255 p. dj. VG. T5. $37.50

BEATON, Cecil. *Royal Portraits.* 1963. dj. EX. S2. $45.00

BEATON, Cecil. *Time Exposure.* 1946. London. Batsford. dj. EX. $35.00

BEATTIE, Ann. *Burning House.* 1982. NY. 1st Am ed. dj. $25.00

BEATTIE, Ann. *Chilly Scenes of Winter.* 1976. Garden City. 1st ed. dj. VG. $20.00

BEATTIE, Ann. *Jacklighting.* 1981. Metacom. 1st ed. 1/250. sgn. wraps. VG. $32.50

BEATTIE, James. *Essay on Nature & Immutability of Truth.* 1809. Wieatt. 1st Am ed. full calf. G. J3. $100.00

BEATTIE, William. *Scotland.* 1838. London. 118 pls. fld maps. 4to. 2 vols. VG. $150.00

BEATTY, J.W. *Relation of Art to Nature.* 1922. NY. Rudge. G. $25.00

BEATTY, John. *Memoirs of a Volunteer, 1861-1863.* 1946. 1st ed. rebound. xl. G. J4. $8.50

BEATTY, R.C. *William Byrd of Westover.* 1932. Boston. dj. EX. $14.00

BEAUCLERK, H. *Green Lacquer Pavilion.* c 1925. Doran. Ils Dulac. $20.00

BEAUMONT, Francis. *Salmacis & Hermaphroditus.* 1951. London. Golden Cockerel. 1/380. 4to. EX. $115.00

BEAUREGARD, Nettie H. *Illustrations of Lindbergh's Decorations & Trophies.* 1935. St. Louis. Ils. color wraps. VG. T5. $15.00

BEBBE, I. *True Life Story of Swiftwater Bill Gates.* 1908. 1st ed. G. $150.00

BECATTI, Giovanni. *Art of Ancient Greece & Rome.* 1967. NY. Abrams. Trans John Ross. 441 p. D2. $85.00

BECERRA, Francisco. *Alamo & San Jacinto.* 1980. Austin. Jenkins. 1st ed. sgn. dj. EX. T6. $20.00

BECH, BERTOLE & CHILD. *Mastering the Art of French Cooking.* 1961. NY. 1st ed. dj. VG. $35.00

BECHER, H.C.R. *Trip to Mexico, Being Notes of Journey From Lake Erie...* 1880. Toronto. Wiling Williamson. presentation. $650.00

BECHTEL, L.S. *Books in Search of Children.* 1969. Macmillan. 1st print. gilt red bdg. dj. VG. $15.00

BECK, Carl. *Fractures.* 1900. Phil. Ils 1st ed. orig blue bdg. VG. $55.00

BECKER, A.C. *Waterfowl in the Marshes.* 1976. Barnes. Ils 2nd print. dj. EX. M2. $16.00

BECKER, P. *Dingane: King of the Zulu 1828-1840.* 1965. Crowell. Ils 1st Am ed. 283 p. dj. EX. M2. $17.00

BECKETT, G.A. *Comic Blackstone.* 1869. Chicago. Ils Cruikshank. EX. P3. $75.00

BECKETT, Samuel. *All That Fall: Play for Radio.* 1957. London. 1st ed. wraps. EX. $75.00

BECKETT, Samuel. *First Love.* 1973. London. 1st Eng ed. dj. EX. $30.00

BECKETT, Samuel. *From an Abandoned Work.* 1958. London. 1st ed. wraps. VG. $65.00

BECKETT, Samuel. *Ill Seen Ill Said.* 1982. CA. 1st ed. 1/299. sgn. M. $100.00

BECKETT, Samuel. *Molloy.* 1955. Paris. 1st ed. dj. with sgn card. VG. $200.00

BECKFORD, Peter. *Thoughts on Hunting.* 1820. London. Ils Bewick. 8vo. gilt green bdg. $200.00

BECKFORD, William. *Hamilton Palace Libraries. Catalog of Beckford Library.* 1882. London. $350.00

BECKFORD, William. *Vathek.* 1929. Nonesuch. 1/1050. $100.00

BECKFORD, William. *Vathek.* 1945. Ltd Ed Club. Ils/sgn Angelo. 12mo. dj. EX. $85.00

BEDA. *Historica Ecclesiastica Gentis Anglorum.* 1838. London. 424 p. $175.00

BEDDALL, B.G. *Wallace & Bates in the Tropics.* 1969. Macmillan. Ils 1st print. dj. EX. M2. $14.00

BEDFORD, John. *Pewter: Collector's Pieces, Vol. 6.* 1968. London. Walker. 3rd ed. $4.50

BEDFORD. *Mauser Self-Loading Pistol.* Alhambra. 1st ed. dj. EX. $30.00

BEDICHECK, R. *Adventures With a TX Naturalist.* 1984. TX U. Ils. 330 p. EX. M2. $9.00

BEDIER, Joseph. *Romance of Tristan & Iseult.* 1904. Mosher. 1/925. Trans Belloc. 1st Am ed. EX. C1. $17.50

BEDIER & HAZARD. *Historie de la Literature Francaise Illustree.* 1923. Paris. 2 vols. TEG. EX. $65.00

BEDLORD, G.R. *Some Early Recollections.* 1917. presentation. 110 p. later buckram wraps. VG. B1. $30.00

BEE, J.W. *Mammals in KS.* 1981. KS U. Ils. maps. table. 300 p. EX. M2. $18.00

BEEBE, Lucius. *Big Spenders.* 1966. Doubleday. 1st ed. dj. VG. $12.50

BEEBE, Lucius. *Cable Car Carnival.* 1951. Ltd 1st ed. sgn. dj. EX. $90.00

BEEBE, Lucius. *Highball.* 1945. 1st ed. 224 p. $25.00

BEEBE, Lucius. *Highliners.* 1960. NY. reprint. dj. VG. $20.00

BEEBE, Lucius. *Mansions on Rails.* 1959. Ils. photos. 382 p. $45.00

BEEBE, Lucius. *Mixed Train Daily: Book of Short-Line Railroads.* 1961. Berkeley. Ils. 367 p. dj. VG. T5. $22.50

BEEBE, Lucius. *Overland Limited.* 1963. Berkeley. Ils. 157 p. dj. VG. T5. $19.50

BEEBE, Lucius. *Saga of Wells Fargo.* nd. Bonanza. reprint. dj. EX. $20.00

BEEBE, William. *Arcturus Adventure.* 1926. np. Ils 1st ed. 439 p. EX. M2. $25.00

BEEBE, William. *Arcturus Adventure.* 1926. NY Putnam. Author ed. 1/50. EX. $400.00

BEEBE, William. *Beneath Tropic Seas: Diving Among the Coral Reefs of Haiti.* 1937. Halcyon House. G. M2. $8.00

BEEBE, William. *Galapagos: World's End.* 1925. Putnam. Ils. 4to. TEG. 443 p. VG. M2. $33.00

BEEBE, William. *Half Mile Down.* 1957. NY. Ils. 344 p. VG. $15.00

BEEBE, William. *Jungle Days.* 1925. NY. Ils. dj. fair. $10.00

BEEBE, William. *Jungle Days.* 1925. Putnam. photos. 201 p. VG. M2. $16.00

BEEBE, William. *Log of the Sun.* 1906. NY. Ils Stone. 1st ed. 4to. AEG. EX. $65.00

BEEBE, William. *Pheasant Jungles.* 1932. Blue Ribbon. Ils. 248 p. dj. EX. M2. $22.00

BEEBE, William. *Pheasants: Their Lives & Homes.* 1926. 1st trade ed. 2 vols. TEG. VG. $110.00

BEEBE, William. *Pheasants: Their Lives & Homes.* 1936. Doubleday. 4to. 2 vol in 1. EX. M2. $95.00

BEEBE, William. *Zaca Venture.* 1938. Harcourt Brace. 1st ed. photos. G. $25.00

BEEBE & CLEGG. *Age of Steam.* 1957. 304 p. $45.00

BEEBE & CLEGG. *American W.* 1955. NY. dj. VG. $25.00

BEEBE & CLEGG. *Hear That Train Blow.* 1952. Dutton. 1st ed. dj. EX. $35.00

BEEBE & CLEGG. *Narrow Gauge in the Rockies.* 1958. Berkeley. Ils. 224 p. dj. VG. T5. $25.00

BEEBE & CLEGG. *Sage of Wells Fargo.* 1949. Bonanza. reprint. 320 p. dj. EX. M2. $10.00

BEEBE & CLEGG. *When Beauty Rode the Rails.* 1962. NY. Ils 1st ed. 222 p. dj. VG. T5. $25.00

BEEBE & WEBSTER. *N American Falconry & Hunting Hawks.* 1976. Denver. private print. 4to. dj. EX. M2. $25.00

BEECHER, H.H. *Record of 114th Regiment NYSV.* 1866. NY. VG. $55.00

BEECHER, John. *Here I Stand.* 1941. NY. 1/100. sgn. dj. EX. $35.00

BEECHER, John. *Here I Stand.* 1941. NY. 1/400. dj. EX. $20.00

BEECHER, John. *I Will Be Heard.* 1940. NY. 1st ed. EX. $25.00

BEECHER, Lyman. *Plea for the W.* 1835. Cincinnati. gilt floral cloth. VG. T1. $40.00

BEECHER, Lyman. *Six Sermons on Nature, Occasions, Signs...of Intemperance.* 1827. Boston. Marvin. 2nd ed. orig bdg. EX. $150.00

BEECHER, Mrs. H.W. *Home.* 1885. index. 597 p. K1. $13.50

BEECHER & SCOVILLE. *Biography of Rev. Henry Ward Beecher.* 1888. 713 p. EX. J4. $10.00

BEECHER & STOWE. *American Woman's Home; or, Principles of Domestic Science.* 1869. NY. Ils 1st ed. 500 p. G. $35.00

BEEDING, Francis. *Death Walks in Eastrepps.* c 1931. NY. Mystery League. 1st ed. VG. $10.00

BEEHLER, B.M. *Birds of New Guinea.* 1986. Princeton. Ils. maps. dj. EX. M2. $65.00

BEELER, Joe. *Cowboys & Indians.* 1967. Norman. 1st ed. dj. EX. $20.00

BEELER, John. *Warfare in England, 1066-1189.* 1966. Ithaca. 1st ed. 493 p. dj. VG. T5. $19.50

BEER, Thomas. *George Bellows: His Lithographs.* 1927. NY. 195 pls. 4to. buckram bdg. VG. J2. $125.00

BEER, Thomas. *Stephen Crane: Study in American Letters.* 1924. London. 1st ed. dj. EX. $40.00

BEERBOHM, Max. *Christmas Garland.* 1912. London. 1st ed. sgn. EX. $115.00

BEERBOHM, Max. *Dreadful Dragon of Hay Hill.* 1928. London. Ils 1st ed. dj. VG. C1. $19.50

BEERBOHM, Max. *Happy Hypocrite.* 1914. Bodley Head. Lane. Ils Sheringham. VG. B4. $245.00

BEERBOHM, Max. *Happy Hypocrite.* 1915. London. Lane. 24 color pls. EX. $145.00

BEERBOHM, Max. *Mainly on the Air.* 1946. London. 1st ed. dj. EX. $30.00

BEERBOHM, Max. *Survey.* 1921. London. Heinemann. red bdg. $50.00

BEERBOHM, Max. *Works of Max Beerbohm.* 1922. London. Heinemann. 1/750. sgn. 8 vols. VG. $150.00

BEERBOHM, Max. *Zuleika Dobson.* 1911. Heinemann. 1st ed. 8vo. brown cloth. $100.00

BEERS, C.W. *Mind That Found Itself.* 1908. Longman. 1st print. VG. $45.00

BEERS, H.P. *Guide to the Archives of the Government of the CSA.* 1968. WA. VG. T5. $27.50

BEERY, Jesse. *Practical System of Colt Training & Subduing Wild Horses.* 1896. WA, D.C. Ils 1st ed. 272 p. G. B2. $32.50

BEESON, L.S. *One Hundred Years of the Old Govenor's Mansion.* 1938. Macon. 1st ed. 1/1000. sgn. 81 p. G. $40.00

BEGEMAN, Louis. *Principles of Physics.* 1904. sm 8vo. 267 p. EX. $2.00

BEHAN, Brendan. *Borstal Boy.* 1958. London. 1st ed. dj. EX. $40.00

BEHAN, Brendan. *Brendan Behan's Island: Irish Sketchbook.* 1962. NY. Ils Hogarth. 1st Am ed. dj. $35.00

BEHAN, Brendan. *Hold Your Hour & Have Another.* 1963. London. 1st ed. dj. VG. $25.00

BEHAN, Brendan. *Quare Fellow: A Commedy-Drama.* 1956. NY. 1st Am ed. 1/100. 86 p. VG. T5. $125.00

BEHLER & KING. *Field Guide to N American Reptiles & Amphibians.* 1979. Knopf. Ils. 719 p. EX. M2. $12.00

BEHR, H.H. *Hoot of the Owl.* 1904. San Francisco. 1st ed. VG. $29.50

BEHRENDT, W.C. *Modern Building: Its Nature, Problems & Forms.* 1937. NY. Ils 1st ed. 8vo. 241 p. EX. $35.00

BEHRMAN, S.N. *Conversation With Max.* 1960. London. 1st ed. dj. G. $17.50

BEHRMAN, S.N. *Duveen.* 1972. London. Hamish Hamilton. 232 p. dj. D2. $45.00

BEHRMAN, S.N. *Portrait of Max.* nd. BOMC. dj. VG. P1. $5.00

BEIGHLE, Nellie. *Book of Knowledge: Psychic Facts.* 1903. np. $60.00

BEINHART, Larry. *No One Rides for Free.* 1986. NY. Morrow. 1st ed. dj. M. $15.00

BEINHART, Larry. *You Get What You Pay For*. 1988. NY. Morrow. 1st ed. dj. M. $12.00

BEIRCE & KNEPPER. *Travels in the Southland: 1822-1823*. 1966. Columbus. 1st ed. sgn Knepper. 139 p. dj. T5. $25.00

BEIRNE, F.F. *War of 1812*. 1949. NY. 1st ed. 410 p. dj. VG. T5. $15.00

BELASCO, David. *Plays Produced Under Stage Direction of David Belasco*. 1925. NY. inscr. G. M1. $35.00

BELASCO & BYRNE. *Fairy Tales Told by Seven Travelers*. 1906. Benesch Pub. Ils. blue cloth. $15.00

BELGIOJOSO, Christine. *Oriental Harems & Scenery*. 1862. NY. 442 p. G. T5. $17.50

BELGRAVE, C.D. *Siwa: Oasis of Jupiter Ammon*. 1922. NY. Ils. photos. fld map. 275 p. G. T5. $22.50

BELISLE, J.G. *History of Sabine Parish, LA*. 1912. Sabin Banner. G. $25.00

BELKNAP, Jeremy. *Sacred Poetry Consisting of Psalms & Hymns...* 1795. Boston. Apollo/Beklnap. 1st ed. EX. $350.00

BELL, A. *Sunset Canada: British Columbia & Beyond*. 1918. Page. 1st ed. presentation. 320 p. VG. M2. $10.00

BELL, A.G. *Nuremberg*. 1905. London. Black. 1st ed. pls. G. $50.00

BELL, A.G. *Sander's Reader*. nd. Alex Bell Assn for Deaf. Ils. VG. $32.50

BELL, Charles. *Hand Mechanism & Vital Endowments*. 1835. Phil. Ils. VG. $95.00

BELL, E.T. *Search for Truth*. 1934. Baltimore. 1st ed. dj. VG. B2. $15.00

BELL, Helen. *Winning the King's Cup*. 1928. NY. 1st ed. 10 fld charts. VG. $20.00

BELL, Jessica LaForge. *Wards' Land: Story of Wards in KS in Days of Civil War*. 1967. San Antonio. Ltd ed. 272 p. VG. T5. $9.50

BELL, M. *Edward Burne-Jones: Record & Review*. 1892. 1/390. VG. $225.00

BELL, M.S. *Waiting for the End of the World*. 1985. NY. 1st Am ed. dj. VG. $35.00

BELL, Mrs. N. *Bay Colony: Pathways of the Puritans*. 1930. Old Am Books. 1st ed. xl. VG. R1. $15.00

BELL, R.A. *Rubaiyat of Omar Khayyam*. nd. Boston. Bartlett. gilt gray bdg. EX. $125.00

BELL, Vanessa. *Notes on VA's Childhood*. 1974. NY. 1/300. $35.00

BELL, W.E. *Art & Science of Carpentry Made Easy*. 1875. Phil. Challen. Revised 2nd ed. 44 pls. G. $60.00

BELLAMY, Edward. *Equality*. 1897. NY. 1st ed. blue cloth. VG. $50.00

BELLARD, Alfred. *Gone for a Soldier*. 1975. Ils. 4to. 298 p. dj. K1. $14.50

BELLOC, Hilaire. *Cautionary Tales for Children*. 1922. Knopf. Ils. VG. B4. $25.00

BELLOC, Hilaire. *Cruise of the Nona*. 1925. Boston. 1st ed. VG. T1. $25.00

BELLOC, Hilaire. *Missing Masterpiece With 41 Drawings by G.K. Chesterton*. 1929. London. 1st ed. dj. EX. $75.00

BELLOC, Hilaire. *More Beasts (for Worse Children)*. nd. London. Arnold. Ils. VG. B4. $40.00

BELLOC, Hilaire. *Sonnets & Verses*. 1924. NY. 1/525. dj. EX. B1. $50.00

BELLOCQU. *Storyville Portraits*. 1970. NY. MOMA. dj. EX. $35.00

BELLOSTE, Augustin. *Esperienze Medicine ed Osservationi Sopra il Mercurio*. 1734. Venedig. 8vo. 123 p. $180.00

BELLOW, Saul. *Dean's December*. 1982. NY. 1st ed. dj. VG. B2. $12.50

BELLOW, Saul. *Dean's December*. 1982. NY. Ltd 1st ed. 1/500. sgn. boxed. EX. $65.00

BELLOW, Saul. *Henderson, the Rain King*. 1959. NY. 1st ed. 1st issue. dj. VG. $85.00

BELLOW, Saul. *Herzog*. 1964. Viking. 1st ed. dj. VG. $25.00

BELLOW, Saul. *More Die of Heartbreak*. 1987. NY. 1st ed. dj. VG. $8.00

BELLOW, Saul. *Nobel Lecture*. 1979. Targ. 1st ed. 1/350. sgn. $65.00

BELLOW, Saul. *Seize the Day*. 1956. Viking. 1st ed. dj. VG. B2. $60.00

BELOE, C.H. *On the Construction of Catch-Water Reservoirs in Mountain...* 1872. London. fld plts. VG. P3. $25.00

BEMELMANS, Ludwig. *Best of Times*. 1948. NY. Ils 1st ed. VG. $30.00

BEMELMANS, Ludwig. *Blue Danube*. 1945. Viking. Ils 1st ed. EX. $50.00

BEMELMANS, Ludwig. *Father, Dear Father*. 1953. NY. Ltd ed. 1/150. sgn. EX. $45.00

BEMELMANS, Ludwig. *Madeline's Rescue*. 1953. Viking. Ils. VG. B4. $25.00

BEMELMANS, Ludwig. *Now I Lay Me Down To Sleep*. 1943. NY. Ils 1st ed. 1/400. sgn. boxed. EX. $100.00

BEMELMANS, Ludwig. *To the One I Love Best*. 1955. Viking. 1st ed. dj. EX. $30.00

BEMELMANS, Ludwig. *Woman of My Life*. 1957. NY. 1st ed. dj. EX. $12.00

BEN-GURION, David. *Israel: Personal History*. 1971. Ils 1st ed. 862 p. dj. VG. $13.00

BENARDETTE, Doris. *Civil War Humor*. 1963. 62 p. J4. $3.50

BENAVENTE, Jacinto. *Cartas de Mujeres*. 1923. Madrid. Spanish text. 12mo. VG. $40.00

BENCH, Johnny. *Catch You Later*. 1979. NY. Ils 1st ed. 245 p. dj. VG. B2. $40.00

BENCHLEY, N. *Off Islanders*. 1961. NY. 1st ed. dj. VG. B2. $15.00

BENCHLEY, Peter. *Jaws*. 1974. London. 1st ed. dj. EX. $7.00

BENCHLEY, Peter. *Treasurer's Report & Other Aspects of Community Singing*. 1930. NY. 1st ed. 8vo. VG. $35.00

BENCHLEY, R.C. *Of All Things*. 1921. NY. Holt. 1st ed. 8vo. blue cloth. $50.00

BENDERSKY, J.W. *History of Nazi Germany*. 1985. Chicago. 1st ed. dj. VG. $6.50

BENDINER, A. *Music to My Eyes*. 1952. PA U. 2nd ed. inscr/sgn. dj. $18.00

BENEDICT, Elsie & Ralph. *Our Trip Around the World*. 1926. Roycroft. 8vo. 592 p. purple suede. VG. D1. $30.00

BENEDICT, G.G. *VT in the Civil War*. Ils. maps. 2 vols. scarce. J4. $65.00

BENEDICT, G.G. *VT in the Civil War*. 1886. Ils. 2 vols. K1. $35.00

BENEDICT, J.D. *Muskogee & NE OK*. 1922. Chicago. Ils 1st ed. 2 vols. VG. $150.00

BENESCH, Otto. *Artistic & Intellectual Trends From Rubens to Daumier...* 1969. Harvard Lib. 2nd print. glassine wraps. VG. $20.00

BENESCH, Otto. *Master Drawings in the Albertina*. 1967. London. Ils. 379 p. D2. $85.00

BENET, S.V. *John Brown's Body*. 1930. Garden City. Ils Daugherty. 376 p. dj. G. $20.00

BENET, S.V. *John Brown's Body*. 1954. 368 p. VG. J4. $9.50

BENEZIT, Emmanuel. *Dictionnaire Critique & Documentaire des Peintres...* 1966. Paris. Grund. 8 vols. maroon cloth. EX. D2. $300.00

BENGTSSON, F.G. *Long Ships.* 1954. NY. 1st ed. dj. VG. $17.50

BENHOTE, J.L. *Birds of Britain.* 1907. London. Black. Ils. 8vo. 399 p. EX. $50.00

BENJAMIN, Park. *Age of Electricity From Amber-Soul to Telephone.* 1886. Scribner. VG. $50.00

BENJAMIN, Rupert. *Seed of Avalon.* 1986. 1st ed. pb. M. C1. $5.50

BENJAMIN, S.C.W. *Art in America: Critical & Historical Sketch.* 1880. Harper. Ils. black cloth. TEG. scarce. D2. $90.00

BENKARD, E. *Undying Faces: Collection of Death Masks.* 1929. London. Ils. 8vo. 118 p. VG. J2. $50.00

BENNETT, Alan. *Beyond the Fringe.* c 1963. Random House. 1st ed. dj. EX. $35.00

BENNETT, Arnold. *Journals of Arnold Bennett.* 1932. London. 1st ed. 2 vols. djs. EX. $75.00

BENNETT, Arnold. *Old Wives' Tale.* NY. Hodder Stoughton. rebound. VG. P3. $165.00

BENNETT, Arnold. *Paris Nights & Other Impressions of Places & People.* 1913. NY. Ils 1st Am ed. 8vo. $60.00

BENNETT, C.E. *Latin Grammar.* 1899. 272 p. TB. G. $3.00

BENNETT, C.E. *Preparatory Latin Writer.* 1907. 194 p. EX. $5.00

BENNETT, Emerson. *Forest Rose: Tale of OH Frontier.* 1959. Lancaster, OH. reprint of 1848 ed. 301 p. G. T5. $22.50

BENNETT, Emerson. *Prairie Flower; or, Adventures in Far W.* 1881. Carleton. New ed. G. $24.00

BENNETT, H.S. *English Books & Readers, 1475-1557.* 1952. Cambridge. $39.50

BENNETT, I. *Complete Illustrated Rugs & Carpets of the World.* 1977. NY. dj. $37.50

BENNETT, J.C. *History of Saints; or, Expose of Joseph Smith & Mormonism.* 1842. Boston. 344 p. 1 pl missing. $150.00

BENNETT, J.G. *Memoirs of J.G. Bennett.* 1855. NY. VG. $15.00

BENNETT, J.J. *French Quarter Interviews.* 1969. Vagabond. Ils. 96 p. wraps. $15.00

BENNETT, J.R. *Control of Information in the US: Annotated Bibliography.* 1987. Meckler. 487 p. VG. T5. $17.50

BENNETT, James. *Much-Loved Books.* 1927. NY. 1st ed. inscr. EX. $20.00

BENNETT, John. *Madam Margot, Grotesque Legend of Old Charleston.* 1921. NY. Century. 1st trade ed. 110 p. $12.50

BENNETT, Joseph. *Billiards by Joseph Bennett.* 1884. London. Ils 4th ed. 483 p. G. C4. $55.00

BENNETT, P.A. *Books & Printing. Treasury for Typophiles.* 1951. World. 1st ed. gray linen. dj. VG. $30.00

BENNETT, Tiny. *Art of Angling.* 1970. Prentice Hall. Ils 1st ed. dj. EX. $12.50

BENNETT, W.W. *Narrative of Great Revival Which Prevailed in S Armies...* 1877. Phil. Claxton. 1st ed. 427 p. xl. $50.00

BENSELL, Royal. *All Quiet on the Yamhill.* 1959. Eugene, OR. dj. VG. $25.00

BENSON, A.L. *Daniel Webster.* 1929. NY. 1st ed. 402 p. dj. $17.50

BENSON, L. *Cacti of the US & Canada.* 1983. Stanford. photos. maps. 4to. dj. EX. M2. $95.00

BENSON, M. *Martha Maxwell: Rocky Mountain Naturalist.* 1986. NE U. Ils 1st ed. 335 p. dj. EX. M2. $23.00

BENSON, Raymond. *James Bond Bedside Companion.* 1984. Dodd Mead. AP. VG. P1. $25.00

BENSON, S.B. *Concealing Coloration Among Desert Rodents of SW US.* 1933. CA U. Ils. map. 68 p. M2. $7.00

BENSON, Sally. *Meet Me in St. Louis.* 1942. Random House. 1st ed. dj. EX. $20.00

BENSON & HEDGES. *Book of Racing Colors.* 1973. Weather Oak. 1st ed. leather. EX. $90.00

BENT, A.C. *Life Histories of N American Blackbirds, Orioles...* 1965. Dover. photos. 549 p. EX. M2. $11.00

BENT, A.C. *Life Histories of N American Diving Birds.* 1963. Dover. photos. 239 p. EX. M2. $7.00

BENT, A.C. *Life Histories of N American Gallinaceous Birds.* 1963. Dover. photos. 490 p. EX. M2. $11.00

BENT, A.C. *Life Histories of N American Gulls & Terns.* 1963. Dover. photos. 337 p. EX. M2. $8.00

BENT, A.C. *Life Histories of N American Jays, Crows & Titmice.* 1964. Dover. photos. 2 vols. EX. M2. $13.00

BENT, A.C. *Life Histories of N American Marsh Birds.* 1963. Dover. photos. 392 p. EX. M2. $10.00

BENT, A.C. *Life Histories of N American Petrels & Pelicans...* 1964. Dover. photos. 335 p. EX. M2. $9.00

BENT, A.C. *Life Histories of N American Thrushes, Kinglets...* 1964. Dover. photos. 452 p. EX. M2. $10.00

BENT, A.C. *Life Histories of N American Wagtails, Shrikes...* 1965. Dover. photos. 411 p. EX. M2. $9.00

BENT, A.C. *Life Histories of N American Wildfowl: Ducks, Geese...* 1951. Dover. Ils. 2 vols. EX. M2. $45.00

BENT, A.C. *Life Histories of N American Woodpeckers.* 1939. US Nat Mus. Ils. 334 p. EX. M2. $28.00

BENT, A.C. *Life Histories of N American Woodwarblers.* 1963. Dover. photos. 2 vols. EX. M2. $15.00

BENTLEY, E.C. *Elephant's Work.* 1950. NY. 1st ed. dj. VG. $35.00

BENTLEY. *Blake Books.* 1977. Oxford U. dj. EX. $125.00

BENTON, C.E. *As Seen From Ranks: Boy in Civil War.* 1902. NY. 1st ed. G. $35.00

BENTON, Frank. *Cowboy Life on the Sidetrack.* 1903. Denver. Ils. 207 p. scarce. A3. $30.00

BENTON, T.H. *Artist in America.* MO Ed. 1st ed. sgn. dj. $325.00

BENTON, T.H. *Thirty Years' View.* 1893. NY. 2 vols. VG. $55.00

BENTON, T.H. *Thirty Years in the US Senate.* 1854. Appleton. 2 vols. $90.00

BENY, Roloff. *Pleasure of Ruins.* 1964. dj. EX. S2. $50.00

BENY, Roloff. *Pleasure of Ruins.* 1977. NY. 1st ed. dj. VG. $20.00

BENY, Roloff. *To Everything There Is a Season.* 1969. London. later ed. folio. dj. EX. $50.00

BENZAQUIN, Paul. *Fire in Boston's Coconut Grove Holocaust!* 1967. Boston. New ed. 248 p. dj. G. $20.00

BERARD, C. *Lecons Francaises.* 1833. NY. 302 p. full leather. fair. T5. $27.50

BERENS, S.L. *Fram Expedition.* 1897. Phil. 1st ed. VG. $65.00

BERENSON, Bernard. *Drawings of Florentine Painters.* 1938. Chicago. 2nd ed. 2nd print. 3 vols. D2. $185.00

BERENSON, Bernard. *Italian Pictures of the Renaissance: Venetian School.* 1957. NY. Ils. 4to. 2 vols. djs. slipcase. J2. $250.00

BERENSON, Bernard. *Study & Criticism of Italian Art.* 1930. London. 8vo. green cloth. VG. J2. $75.00

BERENSON, Bernard. *Three Essays in Method.* 1926. Oxford. 1st ed. $100.00

BERG. *Encyclopedia of Continental Army Units.* 1972. Stackpole. dj. EX. $20.00

BERG. *Warsaw Ghetto: Diary.* 1945. NY. Special ed. 253 p. dj. VG. $45.00

BERGE, Carol. *Tituals & Gargoyles.* 1976. Black Book. sgn. wraps. EX. $15.00

BERGENGRUEN. *Rome Remembered.* 1969. NY. 1st ed. dj. EX. $22.00

BERGER, Alwin. *Crassulacea.* 1930. Leipzig. wraps. G. $15.00

BERGER, Arthur. *Aaron Copland.* 1953. Oxford. 1st ed. sgn. dj. $60.00

BERGER, J.G. *Physiologia Medica Sive de Natura Humana.* 1602. Vitembergae. 4to. $410.00

BERGER, J.G. *Physiologia Medica Sive de Natura Humana.* 1737. Frankfurt. 4to. full calf. xl. $300.00

BERGER, Klaus. *Odilon Redon: Fantasy & Color.* 1965. McGraw Hill. Ils 244 pls. photos. dj. D2. $250.00

BERGER, Ludwig. *Theatermenschen, so Sah Ich Sie.* 1962. Hannover. square 8vo. 107 p. $20.00

BERGER, Thomas. *Arthur Rex.* 1978. 1st ed. regular book-sized pb. VG. C1. $7.00

BERGER, Thomas. *Little Big Man.* 1964. NY. 1st Am ed. sgn. dj. EX. $65.00

BERGER, Thomas. *Nowhere.* 1985. NY. 1st Am ed. dj. VG. $20.00

BERGER, Thomas. *Reinhart's Women.* 1981. Delacorte. 1st ed. dj. EX. $20.00

BERGMAN, I. *Scenes From a Marriage.* 1974. NY. 1st Am ed. photos. 199 p. G. $22.50

BERGMAN, J. *Peafowl of the World.* 1980. Saiga, England. Ils. 4to. 99 p. dj. EX. M2. $19.00

BERGMAN, Ray. *Trout.* Feb., 1940. Ils Burke. VG. $25.00

BERGNER, Herz. *Between Sky & Sea.* 1946. Dolphin. dj. VG. P1. $12.50

BERINGER, R.E. *Elements of Confederate Defeat.* 1988. GA U. map. 244 p. M. M2. $10.00

BERKELEY, Anthony. *Piccadilly Murder.* 1938. Penguin. 2nd ed. dj. VG. P1. $15.00

BERKELEY, Anthony. *Trial & Error.* 1945. Pocket. 2nd ed. dj. VG. P1. $35.00

BERKELEY & BERKELEY. *John Clayton: Pioneer of American Botany.* 1963. Chapel Hill. 236 p. dj. EX. $15.00

BERKHOFER, R.F. *White Man's Indian: Images of American Indian...* 1978. Knopf. 1st ed. 261 p. dj. EX. M2. $13.00

BERLANT & KAHLENBERG. *Walk in Beauty.* 1977. Boston. 1st ed. dj. EX. $38.00

BERLITZ, Charles. *Bermuda Triangle.* 1974. NY. $6.00

BERLYN, A. *Sunrise Land.* 1894. London. Ils. 8vo. VG. scarce. G2. $70.00

BERMAN & LOEB. *Laws & Men: Challenge of American Politics.* 1970. Riverside. Macmillan. 1st ed. dj. $8.00

BERNANOS. *Diary of a Country Priest.* Lt Ed Club. slipcase. M. B3. $225.00

BERNARD, Brianchon. *L'Art du Ballet des Origines a Nos Jours.* 1952. Paris. Ils. 345 p. wraps. VG. $30.00

BERNAYS, E.L. *Biography of an Idea.* 1965. Simon Schuster. 1st print. dj. EX. $55.00

BERNHARDT, C. *Indian Raids in Lincoln Co., KS, 1864 & 1869.* 1971. Lincoln Co. reprint of 1910 ed. 62 p. EX. M2. $18.00

BERNHEIMER, C.L. *Rainbow Bridge.* 1924. Doubleday Page. 1st ed. 192 p. A3. $60.00

BERNSTEIN, Aline. *Three Blue Suits.* 1933. NYC. 1/600. sgn. 74 p. VG. T5. $125.00

BERNSTEIN, Burton. *Last Act.* 1963. World. Ils Stevenson. 1st ed. EX. $25.00

BERNSTEIN, Hillel. *L'Affaire Jones.* 1934. NY. Stokes. inscr. 8vo. VG. $30.00

BERNSTEIN, Leonard. *Joy of Music.* nd. np. sgn. pb. $25.00

BERQUIN. *Children's Friend.* 1845. Ils. 2 vols. K1. $12.50

BERRA, T.M. *William Beebe: An Annotated Bibliography.* 1977. Archon. Ils 1st ed. 157 p. dj. EX. M2. $22.00

BERRALL, J.S. *Flowers & Table Settings.* 1951. Crowell. photos. folio. 92 p. dj. EX. $30.00

BERRALL, Julia. *Garden.* 1966. NY. 1st ed. 8vo. dj. VG. $35.00

BERRIGAN, Daniel. *Love, Love at the End.* 1968. Macmillan. 1st ed. dj. VG. $20.00

BERRIGAN, Daniel. *Time Without Numbers.* 1957. NY. dj. EX. $40.00

BERRIGAN, Ted. *Many Happy Returns.* 1969. Corinth. 1/1500. inscr. wraps. $25.00

BERRY, C.D. *Loss of the Sultana.* 1892. Lansing, MI. Ils 1st ed. 426 p. xl. G. T5. $85.00

BERRY, Wendell. *Henry's Fate & Other Poems.* 1977. NY. dj. EX. $50.00

BERRY, Wendell. *November 26, 1963.* 1964. NY. Ils Shahn. slipcase. EX. P3. $25.00

BERRY. *Henry Cavendish: His Life & Scientific Work.* 1960. London. 1st ed. dj. EX. $16.00

BERRYMAN, John. *Love & Fame.* 1970. NY. 1st ed. 1/250. sgn. boxed. EX. $150.00

BERRYMAN, John. *Poems.* 1942. New Directions. 1st ed. wraps. EX. $90.00

BERRYMAN, John. *Recovery.* 1973. NY. 1st ed. dj. EX. $20.00

BERRYMAN, John. *Stephen Crane.* 1950. Sloane. 1st ed. dj. VG. J2. $85.00

BERRYMAN, John. *Stephen Crane.* 1950. Sloane. 2nd print. dj. VG. J2. $35.00

BERTARELLI, Achille. *Il Biglietto di Visita Italiano.* 1911. Bergamo. folio. 215 p. T5. $150.00

BERTELSON, David. *Lazy S.* 1967. NY. Oxford. 1st ed. dj. EX. $15.00

BERTHEL, M.W. *Horns of Thunder: Life & Times of James M. Goodhue...* 1948. MN Hist Soc. Ils 1st ed. 276 p. dj. EX. M2. $18.00

BERTHRONG, D.J. *S Cheyennes.* 1963. Norman. Ils. dj. $35.00

BERTOLT, Brecht. *Helene Weigel, Actress.* 1961. Leipzig. Ils Goedhart. 1st ed. $50.00

BERTON, Pierre. *Klondike Fever.* 1958. Knopf. 1st ed. dj. EX. $30.00

BERTON, Pierre. *Klondike Fever.* 1960. London. 1st ed. dj. EX. $20.00

BERTON, R. *Remembering Bix.* 1974. NY. 1st ed. dj. VG. B2. $22.50

BERY, R.P. *Bridge of Turquoise.* 1975. NY. 1st ed. dj. EX. $75.00

BERZELIUS, J.J. *Lehrbuch der Chemie.* 1831. Dresden. 7 fld pls. VG. $110.00

BESANT, Annie. *Dharma.* 1899. Benares. VG. $25.00

BESANT, W. *London City.* 1910. London. VG. $55.00

BESHOAR. *Out of the Depths: Story of John Lawson.* 1942. 2nd ed. dj. $35.00

BESSET, Maurice. *Who Was Le Corbusier?* 1968. Geneva. Ils 1st ed. 228 p. G. T5. $65.00

BEST, Herbert. *Twenty-Fifth Hour.* 1940. NY. 1st ed. dj. EX. $30.00

BESTERMAN, T. *Mrs. Annie Besant: A Modern Prophet.* 1934. London. 274 p. dj. $25.00

BESTETTI, Carlo. *Volti del Cinema Italiano.* 1952. Rome. 30 photo portraits. folio. $35.00

BESTON, Henry. *American Memory.* 1937. NY. inscr/sgn. dj. VG. $25.00

BESTON, Henry. *Book of Gallant Vagabonds.* 1925. NY. Ils. sgn. VG. $35.00

BESTON, Henry. *N Farm.* 1948. NY. Ils Thoreau MacDonald. inscr. dj. $35.00

BESTON, Henry. *Outermost House.* 1929. NY. dj. VG. $30.00

BETJEMAN, John. *Collected Poems.* nd. London. $18.00

BETJEMAN, John. *English Cities & Small Towns.* 1943. London. Collins. dj. EX. $22.50

BETT, Henry. *English Legends.* 1952. Ils Fraser. 2nd ed. dj. VG. C1. $10.00

BETTEN, H.L. *Upland Game Shooting.* 1940. Phil. 1st ed. VG. B2. $50.00

BETTERSWORTH & SILVER. *MS in the Confederacy.* 1961. Baton Rouge. 2 vols. djs. slipcase. EX. $50.00

BETTEX, Albert. *Discovery of the World.* 1960. Simon Schuster. Ils. 4to. 379 p. dj. VG. $37.50

BETTMAN, O. *Pictorial History of Medicine.* 1956. Springfield. Ils 1st ed. 318 p. dj. VG. B2. $27.50

BETTS, Doris. *Heading W.* 1981. NY. Knopf. dj. $10.00

BETTS, Doris. *River to Pickle Beach.* 1972. Harper. 1st ed. dj. EX. $30.00

BEURDELEY, Michel. *Chinese Erotic Art.* Ils Chartwell. dj. EX. E2. $25.00

BEVERIDGE, A.J. *Abraham Lincoln, 1809-1858.* 1928. Houghton. 4th print. 2 vols. $37.50

BEVERIDGE, A.J. *Abraham Lincoln: 1809-1858 & 1858-1865.* 1928. 1st ed. 2 vols. K1. $18.50

BEVERIDGE, A.J. *Life of John Marshall.* 1916 & 1919. Boston. 4 vols. VG. $45.00

BEWICK, Thomas. *General History of Quadrupeds.* 1980. Windward. Ils. 525 p. dj. EX. M2. $25.00

BEWICK, Thomas. *History of British Birds.* 1805. Newcastle. 8vo. 2 vols. EX. $350.00

BEWLEY, E.T. *Family of Poe.* 1906. Ireland. Ponsonby Gibbs. 1/200. 4to. G. D1. $180.00

BEY, R. *Vanishing Depot.* 1973. Livingston. 1st ed. 4to. 113 p. dj. VG. $20.00

BEZUCHA, R.D. *Golden Anniversary Book of Scouting.* 1959. Golden. Ils Rockwell. 2nd print. $20.00

BIANCHI, M.D. *Unpublished Poems of Emily Dickinson.* 1936. Boston. 1st ed. 157 p. dj. VG. $30.00

BIANCO, M.W. *Apple Tree.* 1926. NY. Ils Artzybasheff. 1st ed. dj. J2. $30.00

BIANCO, M.W. *Candlestick.* 1929. Doubleday. 1st ed. VG. $35.00

BIANCO, M.W. *Hurdy-Gurdy Man.* 1938. Oxford U. Ils Lawson. 5th print. VG. B4. $30.00

BIBBY, G. *Four-Thousand Years Ago: World Panorama of Life.* 1961. Knopf. Ils 1st d. 398 p. dj. EX. M2. $11.00

BIBERMAN, Herbert. *Salt of the Earth: Story of a Film.* 1965. Boston. 1st ed. sgn. dj. VG. $25.00

BIBLE. *American Bible.* 1912. Roycroft. full leather. VG. $35.00

BIBLE. *Ecclesiasticus.* 1927. London. Lane. Ils Brunton. TEG. VG. $50.00

BIBLE. *Holy Bible.* c 1850. Carlton Porter. 4to. full leather. $68.00

BIBLE. *Holy Bible.* 1806. Phil. Woodward. AEG. full red leather. $55.00

BIBLE. *Holy Bible.* 1845. Am Bible Soc. 12mo. full leather. G. $28.00

BIBLE. *Holy Bible.* 1861. pocket size. leather bdg with clasps. K1. $18.50

BIBLE. *Holy Bible.* 1867. Cobbin. Ils. 4to. full leather. VG. $88.00

BIBLE. *Holy Bible. King James Version.* 1935. New Haven. Ltd Ed Club. 1/1500. 8vo. slipcase. $125.00

BIBLE. *Holy Scriptures.* 1917. Jewish Pub Soc. 8vo. black cloth. G. $7.50

BIBLE. *New Testament.* 1853. Am Bible Soc. with Psalms. gilt bdg. K1. $12.50

BIBLIOPHILE SOCIETY. *Odes & Epodes of Horace.* 1901. Boston. 1/467. 9 vols. djs. slipcase. VG. $250.00

BICKELL, N. *Ducks, Geese & Swans of Africa & Its Outlying Islands.* 1988. Frandsen. Ils 1st ed. 228 p. dj. M. M2. $32.00

BIDDLE, George. *Indian Impressions.* 1960. NY. Orion Pr. dj. VG. $20.00

BIDDLE, J.B. *Materia Medica for Use of Students.* 1865. Phil. Ils. 359 p. VG. $100.00

BIDDLE, Owen. *Young Carpenter's Assistant.* 1810. Phil. 2nd ed. 44 pls. fld pls. $325.00

BIDERMAN, Bob. *Strange Inheritance.* 1985. London. Pluto. 1st ed. dj. M. $10.00

BIDWELL, F.D. *Life of General Daniel Davidson Bidwell.* c 1900. Albany. Ils 1st ed. inscr. 223 p. T5. $45.00

BIDWELL, George. *Forging His Own Chains.* 1891. Hartford, CT. G. $20.00

BIEDL, A. *Innere Sekretion.* 1916. Berlin. 3rd ed. 2 vols. G. $65.00

BIERCE, A. *Devil's Dictionary.* 1972. Ltd Ed Club. Ils Kredel. 1st ed. sgn. EX. $80.00

BIERCE, A. *Three Tales.* 1920. San Francisco. 1/400. $135.00

BIERCE, L.V. *Asaph Whittlesey.* 1872. Cleveland. 14 p. wraps. VG. T5. $12.50

BIERCE, L.V. *Historical Reminiscences of Summit Co., OH.* 1854. Akron. 1st ed. 157 p. slipcase. G. T5. $175.00

BIGELOW, H.E. *Mushroom Pocket Field Guide.* 1974. Macmillan. Ils 1st ed. 117 p. VG. M2. $7.00

BIGELOW, Horatio. *Gunnerman.* 1939. Derrydale. 1/950. sgn. EX. $150.00

BIGELOW, Horatio. *Gunnerman's Gold.* 1943. Huntington. 1/1000. VG. B2. $70.00

BIGELOW, Mrs. Marion. *Songs From the St. Lawrence.* 1851. NY. VG. $40.00

BIGELOW, Poultney. *Seventy Summers.* 1925. Longman Green. 1st ed. dj. VG. $18.00

BIGGERS, E.D. *Behind That Curtain.* 1928. Grosset Dunlap. reprint. dj. VG. $10.00

BIGGERS, E.D. *Black Camel.* 1926. Indianapolis. $30.00

BIGGERS, E.D. *Chinese Parrot.* 1926. Bobbs Merrill. 1st ed. EX. $60.00

BIGGERS, E.D. *Keeper of the Keys.* 1932. Indianapolis. 1st ed. EX. $20.00

BIGGERS, E.D. *50 Candles.* 1926. Indianapolis. dj. VG. $35.00

BIGGERS, E.D. *7 Keys to Baldpate.* Grosset Dunlap. Movie ed. dj. VG. $25.00

BIGGERS & SCHUETZ. *Ogenesis.* 1972. U Park. Ils 543 p. EX. M2. $22.00

BIGGS, J.R. *Approach To Type.* 1952. NY. Ils. 152 p. dj. VG. T5. $19.50

BIGLAND, John. *Geographical & Historical View of World.* 1812. Phil. 8vo. 5 vols. full leather. G2. $76.00

BIGLAND, John. *Natural History of Birds & Fishes & Reptiles & Insects.* 1831. Phil. 12 pls. 179 p. $100.00

BILET, Mrs. *Family Pictures From Bible.* 1849. London. gilt embossed leather. G. $50.00

BILL, A.H. *Beleagured City: Richmond 1861-1865.* 1946. Knopf. Ils 1st ed. maps. 313 p. EX. M2. $11.00

BILLE, S.C. *Le Grand Tourment.* 1951. Lausanne. Ils Edmond Bille. wraps. VG. $35.00

BILLIG & LOEWENDAHL. *Mobilization of the Human Body.* 1949. Stanford. $20.00

BILLING, G. *Forebush & the Penguins.* 1965. Holt Rinehart Winston. dj. EX. M2. $22.00

BILLINGS, J.D. *Hardtack & Coffee.* 1960. Donnelley. Lakeside Classic. A3. $40.00

BILLINGS, J.D. *Hardtack & Coffee.* 1982. Time Life. reprint of 1887 ed. 408 p. EX. M2. $35.00

BILLINGS, J.D. *History of the 10th MA Battery.* 1881. Boston. Ils 400 p. K1. $55.00

BILLINGTON, Ray. *Words That Won the W, 1830-1850.* 1963. San Francisco. 1st ed. 20 p. wraps. EX. $6.00

BILYEU, Richard. *Tanelorn Archives.* 1981. Pandora. 1/250. sgn/#d. EX. P1. $20.00

BILYEU, Richard. *Tanelorn Archives.* 1981. Pandora. 1/350. sgn/#d. EX. P1. $15.95

BILYEU, Richard. *Tanelorn Archives.* 1981. Pandora. 1/900. pb. EX. P1. $7.95

BINDING, P. *Separate Country: Literary Journey Through American S.* 1979. Paddington. 224 p. dj. EX. $25.00

BING, S. *Artistic America: Tiffany Glass & Art Nouveau.* 1970. EX. $15.00

BINGHAM, Hiram. *Across S America.* 1911. Boston/NY. Houghton Mifflin. 1st ed. EX. $60.00

BINGHAM, Hiram. *Explorer in the Air Service.* 1920. New Haven. Ils 1st ed. maps. 260 p. T5. $47.50

BINGHAM, Hiram. *Lost City of the Incas: Story of Machu Picchu.* 1948. Duell Sloan. Ils 1st ed. 263 p. M2. $20.00

BINGHAM, Hiram. *Lost City of the Incas: Story of Machu Picchu.* 1948. NY. Ils 1st ed. dj. B2. $45.00

BINGHAM, John. *Trial of Conspirators for Assassination of Lincoln.* 1965. WA. 122 p. printed wraps. xl. $75.00

BINGHAM, M.T. *Ancestor's Brocades: Literary Debut of Emily Dickinson.* 1945. NY. Ils 1st ed. 8vo. 464 p. gilt bdg. dj. T1. $150.00

BINNS, Archie. *Roaring Land.* 1942. Ils 1st ed. EX. $10.00

BINYON, Laurence. *Followers of William Blake: Cavert, Palmer, Richmond...* 1925. London. Halton Smith. 8vo. VG. J2. $175.00

BINYON, Laurence. *N Star & Other Poems.* 1941. London. 1st ed. dj. EX. $15.00

BINYON, Laurence. *Painting in Far E.* 1934. London. Revised 4th ed. 41 pls. 304 p. VG. $40.00

BIRBECK, Morris. *Notes on Journey in America to Territory of IL.* 1818. Dublin. fld map. boxed. VG. $350.00

BIRCH, Reginald. *Reginald Birch: His Book.* 1939. Harcourt. 1st ed. sgn. dj. EX. $65.00

BIRCH, Samuel. *Ancient Pottery & Porcelain.* 1858. 1st ed. 2 vols. VG. $100.00

BIRCH & JENNER. *Early Drawings & Illuminations.* 1879. London. Ils 8vo. $75.00

BIRD, Brandon. *Downbeat for a Dirge.* 1952. Dodd Mead. 1st ed. dj. EX. $50.00

BIRD, H.E. *Chess Masterpieces: Collection of 150 Choice Games.* 1875. London. gilt blue bdg. $65.00

BIRD, I.L. *Lady's Life in the Rocky Mountains.* 1962. OK U. Ils. 249 p. EX. M2. $10.00

BIRENBAUM, Halina. *Hipe Is the Last To Die.* 1971. NY. 1st ed. dj. VG. $7.50

BIRKBECK, M. *Letters From IL.* 1818. London. 8vo. 114 p. scarce. G2. $79.00

BIRKHIMER, W.E. *Historical Sketch of Organization, Administration...* 1881. WA. Chapman. 402 p. $87.50

BIRMINGHAM, Stephen. *Grand Dames.* 1982. Simon Schuster. 1st ed. dj. EX. $25.00

BIRMINGHAM, Stephen. *Life at the Dakota.* 1979. NY. 1st ed. dj. VG. B2. $15.00

BIRNIE, J.E. *Earles & the Birnies.* 1974. Richmond. private print. 235 p. $55.00

BIRRELL, Augustine. *Among My Books: Papers on Literary Subjects.* 1898. NY. 1st Am ed. $35.00

BIRREN, Faber. *Monument to Color.* 1938. NY. 1st ed. dj. VG. J2. $40.00

BIRREN, Faber. *Story of Color.* 1941. Westport. 1st ed. VG. J2. $40.00

BISCHOFF, David. *Star Spring.* 1st ed. pb. VG. C1. $4.50

BISHOP, Elizabeth. *Collected Prose.* 1984. London. 1st ed. dj. EX. $11.00

BISHOP, Elizabeth. *Collected Prose.* 1984. NY. 1st ed. dj. EX. $25.00

BISHOP, Elizabeth. *Geography III.* 1976. NY. 1st ed. dj. EX. $40.00

BISHOP, Isabel. *Isabel Bishop.* 1974. Tucson. 1/2500. dj. EX. $25.00

BISHOP, J.P. *Collected Poems.* 1948. Scribner. 1st ed. dj. EX. $20.00

BISHOP, Jim. *Day Lincoln Was Shot.* 1955. Ils 1st ed. 304 p. K1. $9.50

BISHOP, Morris. *Bowl of Bishop.* 1954. NY. Dial. 1st ed. G. $5.00

BISHOP, Morris. *Odyssey of Cabeza da Vaca.* 1933. Century. Ils. 395 p. dj. scarce. G. A3. $40.00

BISHOP, R.E. *Bishop's Birds: Etchings of Waterfowl & Upland Game Birds.* 1936. Lippincott. 1/1000. 73 pls. 4to. EX. M2. $225.00

BISHOP, R.E. *Bishop's Wildfowl.* 1948. St. Paul. Ltd ed. G. $125.00

BISHOP, R.E. *Bishop's Wildfowl.* 1948. St. Paul. 1st ed. folio. EX. $150.00

BISHOP, R.E. *Ways of Wildfowl.* 1971. Ferguson. 1/3000. 4to. 260 p. slipcase. M2. $135.00

BISHOP, Robert. *Folk Painters of America.* 1979. Dutton. 1st ed. dj. VG. J2. $25.00

BISHOP, Robert. *Gallery of Amish Quilts.* 1976. NY. Dutton. Ils. 96 p. wraps. $30.00

BISHOP, Zealia. *Curse of Yig.* 1953. Arkham House. 1st ed. dj. EX. $70.00

BISSETT, Robert. *Life of Edmund Burke.* 1800. London. 2 vols. xl. VG. $27.50

BITTING. *Gastronomic Bibliography.* 1981. London. 1/500. dj. EX. $60.00

BITTNER, Herbert. *George Grosz.* 1960. NY. Arts. Ils. dj. D2. $50.00

BIUNDEN, Edmund. *To Nature.* 1923. Westminister. Beaumont. 1/310. EX. $60.00

BIXBY, W. *Track of the Bear.* 1965. McKay. photos. maps. 309 p. dj. EX. M2. $15.00

BIXBY-SMITH, S. *Adobe Days.* 1925. Torch. 1st ed. sgn. VG. $85.00

BLACHON. *Nature Library of Birds.* 1926. Doubleday Page. Ils. 8vo. $75.00

BLACK, A. *Transport Aviation.* 1926. Simmons Boardman. Ils. 245 p. G. $10.00

BLACK, A.P. *End of the Long-Horn Trail.* 1936. Selfridge, ND. Ils. 59 p. wraps. A3. $60.00

BLACK, Alexander. *Richard Gordon.* 1902. Lathrop. Ils Fuhr. $12.00

BLACK, C.V. *History of Jamaica.* 1958. London. Collins. 1st ed. 250 p. VG. $23.00

BLACK, Campbell. *Asterisk's Destiny.* 1978. Knopf. 1st ed. dj. EX. $12.50

BLACK, Campbell. *Letters From the Dead.* 1985. Villard Books. 1st ed. dj. M. $9.50

BLACK, Clemengina. *Princess Desiree.* 1896. Longman. Ils Williamson. 1st ed. $12.00

BLACK, George. *Narrative of Arctic Land Expedition.* 1836. Phil. 1st Am ed. fld map. $350.00

BLACK, Hugh. *Work.* 1904. Revell. G. $20.00

BLACK, J.L. *Crumbling Defenses; or, Memoirs & Reminiscences.* 1960. Macon. 1st ed. EX. $65.00

BLACK, Neal. *Mantons: Gunmakers.* 1967. NY. 1st Am ed. dj. M. $35.00

BLACK, Robert. *Art of Jacob Epstein.* 1942. World. Ils. index. D2. $75.00

BLACKBURN, William. *One & Twenty.* 1945. Durham. 1st ed. dj. EX. $45.00

BLACKHALL & GRIEVE. *How To Know the Australian Wild Flowers, Part II.* 1956. W Australia U. 1st ed. VG. $25.00

BLACKHALL & GRIEVE. *How To Know the W Australian Wild Flowers, Part III.* 1965. W Australia U. dj. VG. $25.00

BLACKHURST, Hector. *Africa Bibliography, 1987.* 1988. Manchester U. 303 p. wraps. VG. T5. $12.50

BLACKIE, J.S. *Language & Literature of Scottish Highlands.* 1876. Edinburgh. Edmonston Douglas. 331 p. VG. $40.00

BLACKMORE, H.L. *Guns & Rifles of the World.* 1965. 1st ed. dj. M. $28.00

BLACKMORE, R.D. *Slain by the Doones.* 1895. NY. 1st ed. EX. $45.00

BLACKWELL & MAY. *This Is S Africa.* 1947. Pietermaritzburg. Ils. dj. $20.00

BLACKWOOD, Algernon. *Doll & One Other.* 1946. Arkham House. 1st ed. EX. $30.00

BLACKWOOD, Algernon. *Incredible Adventures.* 1914. London. Macmillan. 1st ed. EX. $65.00

BLACKWOOD, Algernon. *Prisoner in Fairyland.* 1913. London. 1st ed. VG. $45.00

BLAGDEN, Cyprian. *Stationers' Co.: A History, 1403-1959.* 1960. Harvard. VG. $15.00

BLAINE, G. *Falconry.* 1974. Branford. reprint. 253 p. dj. EX. M2. $25.00

BLAINE, James G. *Thirty Years of Congress.* 1884. Ils 1st ed. index. 2 vols. scarce. K1. $23.50

BLAINE, James G. *Twenty Years in Congress.* 1886. 2 vols. xl. G. $5.00

BLAIR, C.D. *Potters & Potteries of Summit Co., OH.* 1965. Akron. Ils. photos. 59 p. G. T5. $15.00

BLAIR, Charles F. *Red Ball in the Sky.* 1969. NY. photos. 203 p. dj. VG. T5. $17.50

BLAIR, Claude. *European & American Arms, 1100-1850.* 1962. NY. Crown. 1st ed. dj. EX. $20.00

BLAIR, Claude. *History of Silver.* 1987. London. Macdonald Orbis. 256 p. dj. D2. $55.00

BLAIR, Claude. *Pistols of the World.* 1968. 1st ed. dj. M. $28.00

BLAIR, Maria. *Matthew Fontaine Maury.* 1918. Richmond. 1st ed. wraps. VG. $15.00

BLAIR, W. *Native American Humor: 1800-1900.* 1937. Am Book Co. Ils. 573 p. VG. M2. $10.00

BLAIR, W. *Tall-Tale America: Legendary History of Our Humorous Heroes.* 1944. Coward McCann. Ils. 262 p. dj. VG. M2. $10.00

BLAIR, W.F. *Vertebrates of the US.* 1957. McGraw Hill. photos. 819 p. EX. M2. $25.00

BLAIR, W.T. *Michael Shoemaker (Schumaker) Book.* 1924. Scranton. Internat TB Pr. 1st ed. VG. $25.00

BLAIR & HILL. *America's Humor From Poor Richard to Doonesbury.* 1978. Oxford U. Ils. inscr/sgn/cartoon. 559 p. dj. M2. $15.00

BLAKE, E.R. *Birds of Mexico: Guide for Field Identification.* 1963. Chicago U. Ils. map. 644 p. EX. M2. $30.00

BLAKE, F.E. *History of Town of Princeton... Vol. II, Genealogies.* 1915. Princeton. 331 p. g. T5. $17.50

BLAKE, Peter. *Master Builders: Le Corbusier, Van Der Rohe & F.L. Wright.* 1965. Knopf. 1st ed. dj. J2. $25.00

BLAKE, William *Auguries of Innocence.* 1968. NY. Ils Baskin. facsimile of Gehenna ed. slipcase. $20.00

BLAKE, William. *Book of Thel.* 1928. London. facsimile 1st ed. dj. G. $50.00

BLAKE, William. *Europe: Prophecy.* 1969. London. facsimile of 1795 ed. slipcase. EX. $150.00

BLAKE, William. *Europe: Prophecy.* 1969. Paris. Trianon Pr. 1/526. slipcase. $150.00

BLAKE, William. *Jerusalem.* nd. Trianon Pr. 1/516. 100 pls. folio. boxed. EX. $850.00

BLAKE, William. *Pencil Drawings.* 1927. London. Chiswick. 1/1550. 4to. VG. $100.00

BLAKE, William. *Prophetic Writings of William Blake.* 1926. Oxford. 1st ed. 2 vols. VG. J2. $60.00

BLAKE, William. *Report Upon the Precious Metals.* 1869. charts. 360 p. EX. K1. $18.50

BLAKE, William. *Watercolor Designs for Poems of Thomas Gray.* 1972. Paris. Trianon Pr. 1/518. 3 vols. boxed. $750.00

BLAKELY, R.L. *King Site.* 1988. GA U. Ils. map. 170 p. dj. M. M2. $15.00

BLAKER, A.A. *Photography for Scientific Publication.* 1965. Freeman. Ils. 158 p. dj. EX. M2. $13.00

BLAKEY, Robert. *Angling.* 1857. London. 16mo. $55.00

BLAMIRES, Harry. *Bloomsday Book: Guide Through Joyce's Ulysses.* 1983. London. Methuen. pb. $7.50

BLANC, C. *Grammar of Painting & Engraving*. 1874. NY. Trans Doggett. 8vo. VG. J2. $75.00

BLANCH, H.J. *Century of Guns*. 1909. London. EX. $150.00

BLANCH, Lesley. *Journey Into the Mind's Eye*. 1969. NY. 1st ed. dj. VG. $15.00

BLANCH, Lesley. *Sabres of Paradise*. 1960. NY. 1st ed. 495 p. dj. VG. B2. $17.50

BLANCHAN, Neltje. *American Flower Garden*. 1909. NY. 1/1050. 4to. 368 p. TEG. VG. T5. $75.00

BLANCHAN, Neltje. *American Flower Garden*. 1913. Garden City. color pls. 4to. VG. C4. $32.00

BLANCHE, Jacques Emile. *Cahiers d'un Artiste*. 1917. Paris. Freres. orig wraps. D2. $50.00

BLANCK, Jacob. *Merle Johnson's American 1st Editions*. 1942. NY. 4th ed. inscr. EX. $175.00

BLANCK, Jacob. *Peter Parley to Penrod*. 1974. MA. Mark Pr. 4th print. $50.00

BLANCO, Fierro. *Journey of the Flame*. 1933. Boston. 1st ed. dj. VG. B2. $20.00

BLAND, J. *Forests of Lilliput: Realm of Mosses & Lichens*. 1971. Prentice Hall. Ils. 210 p. dj. EX. M2. $17.00

BLANDEN, Charles. *Bale of Gossamer*. 1927. San Diego. Artemisia. 1st ed. 1/250. EX. C1. $19.50

BLANDING, Don. *Hula Moons*. 1933. NY. 4th print. sgn. dj. VG. $12.00

BLANDING, Don. *Let Us Dream*. 1935. NY. 3rd print. sgn. reprint dj. EX. $12.00

BLANDING, Don. *Pictures of Paradise: Moods & Moments in HI Poems*. nd. np. Ils Frank Warren. slipcase. VG. $45.00

BLANDING, Don. *Pilot Bails Out*. 1943. NY. 1st ed. dj. EX. $16.00

BLANDING, Don. *Rest of the Road*. 1946. NY. Ils. VG. $15.00

BLANDING, Don. *Stowaways in Paradise: Two Boys' Adventures in HI*. 1931. NY. 1st ed. dj. VG. $45.00

BLANDING, Don. *Today Is Here*. 1946. NY. 1st ed. sgn. dj. EX. $20.00

BLANDING, Don. *Vagabond House*. 1928. Dodd Mead. 2nd print. sgn. dj. $15.00

BLANDING, Don. *Vagabond House*. 1935. NY. 16th print. sgn. dj. $10.00

BLANDING, Don. *Vagabond's House*. 1943. NY. G. $8.50

BLANKENSTEN, G.I. *Peron's Argentina*. 1953. Chicago Pr. 478 p. dj. G. $7.50

BLANSHARD, Brand. *On Philosophical Style*. 1969. NY. reprint. 69 p. EX. $20.00

BLANSHARD, Brand. *Reason & Belief*. 1974. London. 1st ed. 620 p. dj. EX. $40.00

BLANSHARD, Brand. *Reason & Goodness*. 1975. NY. reprint. 451 p. EX. $25.00

BLASDALE, Walter. *Cultivated Species of Primula*. 1948. Berkeley. green cloth. VG. $45.00

BLASER, Robin. *Collected Books of Jack Spicer*. 1975. Black Sparrow. 1/100. sgn/#d. slipcase. EX. $37.50

BLASSINGAME, W. *Wonders of Racoons*. 1977. Dodd Mead. Ils 1st ed. 80 p. dj. EX. M2. $9.00

BLATTY, W.P. *Exorcist*. 1971. NY. 1st ed. dj. EX. $20.00

BLAVATSKY, H.P. *Secret Doctrine*. 1962. Adyar. 5th ed. 6 vols. djs. EX. G1. $60.00

BLAY, John S. *Civil War: A Pictorial Profile*. 1958. Ils. 16 maps. 342 p. dj. J4. $9.50

BLAYLOCK, James. *Last Coin*. 1988. 1st ed. sgn. dj. M. C1. $27.00

BLEEK, W.H.I. *Reynard the Fox in S Africa; or, Hottentot Fables & Tales*. 1864. London. 1st ed. 94 p. VG. scarce. T5. $225.00

BLEGEN, T.C. *Book Collecting & Scholarship*. 1954. Mineapolis. 1/750 $25.00

BLEGEN, Theodore. *Lincoln's Imagery: Study in Word Power*. 1954. La Crosse. 1/780. EX. $25.00

BLEILER. *Treasure of Victorian Ghost Stories*. 1981. NY. dj. G. $15.00

BLESER, Carol. *Hammonds of Redcliffe*. 1981. NY. Oxford. Ils. 421 p. dj. $27.50

BLEVINS, W. *Give Your Heart to the Hawks: Tribute to Mountain Men*. 1973. Nash. Ils. 1st print. maps. EX. M2. $19.00

BLEW. *Brighton & Its Coaches: History of London & Brighton Road*. 1894. London. 20 pls. VG. $150.00

BLINDLOSS, Harold. *Gold Trail*. 1910. NY. Stokes. Ils Megarger. 1st ed. EX. $35.00

BLISH, James. *Earthman Come Home*. 1955. Putnam. 1st ed. dj. VG. $40.00

BLISH, James. *Nebula Award*. 1970. NY. 1st ed. dj. VG. $10.00

BLISH, James. *Star Trek Reader II*. nd. Book Club. dj. VG. P1. $7.50

BLISH, James. *Star Trek 3*. 1969. Bantam. 1st ed. orig wraps. EX. $15.00

BLIVEN, Bruce. *Battle for Manhattan*. 1956. NY. Ils 1st ed. 128 p. dj. VG. T5. $27.50

BLIVEN, Bruce. *This Wonderful Writing Machine*. 1954. Random House. dj. EX. $20.00

BLOCH, E. Maurice. *George Caleb Bingham: Catalog Raisonne*. 1967. Berkeley. dj. D2. $95.00

BLOCH, E. Maurice. *Paintings of George Caleb Bingham: Catalog Raisonne*. 1986. Columbia. MO U. 23 pls. dj. D2. $65.00

BLOCH, G. *Pablo Picasso. Vol. II*. 1971. Berne. Kornfeld Klipstein. Ils. 348 p. D2. $150.00

BLOCH, G. *Pablo Picasso: Catalogue de l'Euvre Grave et Lithographie...* 1971. Berne. 4to. dj. EX. J2. $200.00

BLOCH, Robert. *American Gothic*. 1975. Crest. sgn. VG. P1. $12.50

BLOCH, Robert. *Atoms & Evil*. 1962. Gold Medal. sgn. G. P1. $10.00

BLOCH, Robert. *Bogey Men*. 1963. Pyramid. sgn. VG. P1. $20.00

BLOCH, Robert. *Dead Beat*. 1961. Popular. sgn. VG. P1. $25.00

BLOCH, Robert. *Dragons & Nightmares*. 1969. Belmont. sgn. VG. P1. $12.50

BLOCH, Robert. *Fear Today, Gone Tomorrow*. 1971. Award. sgn. G. P1. $10.00

BLOCH, Robert. *More Nightmares*. 1962. Belmont. sgn. G. P1. $22.50

BLOCH, Robert. *Opener of the Way*. 1945. Sauk City. 1st ed. dj. EX. $100.00

BLOCH, Robert. *Scarf*. 1947. Dial. 1st ed. sgn. dj. VG. $75.00

BLOCH, Robert. *Scarf*. 1966. Gold Medal. sgn. VG. P1. $20.00

BLOCH, Robert. *Skull of the Marquis de Sade*. 1965. Pyramid. sgn. G. P1. $17.50

BLOCH, Robert. *Unholy Trinity*. 1986. Scream Pr. Ils Morris. 1st ed. sgn. dj. EX. $40.00

BLOCK, Herbert. *Herblock on All Fronts*. 1980. New Am Lib. 1st ed. sgn. 280 p. dj. VG. M1. $17.00

BLOCK, Lawrence. *Like a Lamb to Slaughter*. 1984. NY. 1st ed. sgn. dj. EX. $20.00

BLOCK, Lawrence. *When the Sacret Ginmill Closes.* 1986. NY. 1st ed. sgn. dj. EX. $20.00

BLODGETT, H.W. *Best of Walt Whitman.* 1953. NY. Ronald Pr. dj. VG. $10.00

BLOETSCHER, V.C. *Indians of the Cuyahoga Valley.* 1987. Akron. Ils 3rd print. sgn. wraps. T5. $15.00

BLOM, Eric. *Grove's Dictionary of Music.* 1955. NY. 5th ed. 8 vols. xl. VG. $80.00

BLOME, Richard. *Hawking & Falconry.* 1929. London. Cresset. Ils. 1/650. dj. EX. M2. $125.00

BLOME, Richard. *Hawking & Falconry.* 1929. London. 1/50. square 8vo. slipcase. VG. $275.00

BLOMFIELD, Reginald. *History of French Architecture From Reign of Charles VIII...* 1911. London. Bell. Orig ed. 2 vols. D2. $185.00

BLOOM, Vera. *Empress Eugenie 1920.* 1923. NY. Ils/sgn Bernhardt Wall. 1/50. EX. $250.00

BLOOM. *English Seals.* 1906. London. 1st ed. VG. $40.00

BLOOMFIELD, Rob. *Vengeance Street.* 1952. Crime Club. 1st ed. dj. VG. $12.00

BLOOMSTER, Edgar. *Sailing & Small Craft Down the Ages.* 1940. Annapolis. Ils. $35.00

BLOSS, R.S. *Pony Express: Great Gamble.* 1959. CA. Howell. 159 p. dj. VG. $18.50

BLOUT, Berniece & Henry. *French Cameo Glass.* 1968. Des Moines. Wallace Homestead. 160 p. dj. D2. $65.00

BLOUT & MOE. *Milwaukee Brace.* 1973. 8vo. 198 p. cloth. VG. $25.00

BLOWER, A.H. *Akron at the Turn of the Century, 1890-1913.* 1962. Akron. 2nd ed. 63 p. VG. T5. $8.50

BLUE, H.T.O. *History of Stark Co., OH, From Prehistoric Man to Present.* 1927. Chicago. 3 vols. VG. T5. $75.00

BLUEM, A.W. *Documentary in American Televison: Form, Function, Method.* 1968. Hastings House. 2nd print. dj. VG. J2. $12.50

BLUM, A. *Vermeer et Thor-Burger.* 1946. Mont-Blac. 2nd ed. wraps. EX. $60.00

BLUM, H.F. *Time's Arrow & Evolution.* 1951. Princeton. 222 p. dj. EX. M2. $10.00

BLUM, Ralph. *Book of Runes: Handbook for Use of an Ancient Oracle.* 1982. 1st ed. VG. C1. $14.00

BLUMENKRANZ, Bernard. *Bibliographie des Juifs en France.* 1974. Paris. 1/1500. 4to. $50.00

BLUMENSON, Martin. *Bloody River: Real Tragedy of the Rapido.* 1970. Boston. Ils 1st ed. 150 p. dj. VG. T5. $15.00

BLUMENSON, Martin. *Patton Papers, 1940-1945. Vol. 2.* 1974. Boston. 1st ed. maps. 889 p. dj. VG. T5. $35.00

BLUNDEN, Edmund. *De Bello Germanico: Fragment of Trench History Written 1918.* 1930. Hawstead. 1/250. inscr. EX. $185.00

BLUNDEN, Edmund. *Near & Far: New Poems.* 1929. London. Cobden-Sanderson. 1/150. sgn. $35.00

BLUNT, Wilfrid. *Secret of History of English Occupation of Egypt.* 1922. Knopf. 1st ed. VG. J2. $17.50

BLY, Robert. *Light Around the Body.* 1967. NY. Grove. 1st ed. dj. M. $45.00

BLY, Robert. *Morning-Glory: Twelve Prose Poems.* 1969. Kayak Pr. Ils Tomie De Paola. 1/850. wraps. $75.00

BLY, Robert. *Visiting Emily Dickinson's Grave & Other Poems.* 1979. Red Ozier. 1/200. sgn/#d. EX. $35.00

BOAG, D. *Kingfisher.* 1988. Blanford. Ils. 120 p. M. M2. $14.00

BOAG & ALEXANDER. *Atlantic Puffin.* 1986. Blanford. Ils 1st ed. 128 p. dj. EX. M2. $19.00

BOALCH. *Makers of Harpsichord & Clavicord, 1440-1840.* 1974. Oxford. 2nd ed. dj. EX. $50.00

BOARDMAN, E.A. *Wings in the Blue.* 1936. Christopher. Ils Frank Benson. 75 p. dj. EX. M2. $28.00

BOARDMAN, E.A. *Yacht Racing.* 1931. Boston. Little Brown. 218 p. G. $15.00

BOARDMAN, F.W. *America & the Rober Barons, 1865-1913.* 1979. 152 p. $16.50

BOARDMAN, John. *Greek Gems & Finger Rings: Early Bronze Age to Classical.* nd. (1972?) Abrams. photos. 458 p. dj. D2. $150.00

BOAS, Nancy. *Society of Six: CA Colorists.* 1988. San Francisco. Ils. 224 p. dj. M. D2. $59.95

BOAS, Nancy. *Tsimshian Texts.* 1902. WA. xl. VG. $65.00

BOBRICK, Benson. *Labyrinths of Iron.* 1981. 352 p. $20.00

BOCCACCIO, Giovanni. *Decameron.* 1896. London. 1/100. 4 vols. black cloth. EX. $50.00

BOCCACCIO, Giovanni. *Life of Dante.* 1904. Boston. Riverside. Ltd ed. 1/265. EX. $70.00

BOCCACCIO, Giovanni. *Pasquerella & Madonna Babetta.* 1927. NY. private print. 1/300. 4to. VG. $60.00

BODE, F.A. *Protestanitism & the New S.* 1975. VA U Pr. 171 p. VG. $12.50

BODEA & CANDEA. *Transylvania in History of Romanians.* 1982. EX. $23.00

BODIN, Ed. *Scare Me.* 1940. NY. $15.00

BODINE, A.A. *My MD.* 1952. Baltimore. Camera Magazine. 4to. EX. $35.00

BODIO, S. *Rage for Falcons.* 1984. Lyons Schocken. Ils 1st ed. 135 p. dj. EX. M2. $25.00

BODSWORTH, F. *Last of the Curlews.* 1955. Dodd Mead. Ils. 128 p. dj. VG. M2. $8.00

BOECK & SABARTES. *Picasso.* 1955. NY. Abrams. 1st ed. dj. EX. $100.00

BOESEN & BOJE. *Old Danish Silver.* 1949. Copenhagen. Hassing. dj. xl. G. M1. $75.00

BOESKY, I.F. *Merger Mania.* 1985. NY. Holt. 1st ed. dj. M. $15.00

BOEWE, Charles. *Prairie Albion: English Settlement in Pioneer IL.* 1962. Carbondale. Ils 1st ed. dj. VG. T5. $22.50

BOGGS, J. *Degas.* 1988. NY. Ils. 49 pls. 8vo. 420 p. TEG. EX. J2. $100.00

BOGGS, R.F. *Captain Frank Mundus: Shark Man, Master of the Deep.* 1977. Lorenz. Ils. 202 p. EX. M2. $14.00

BOGGS, S.S. *Eighteen Months a Prisoner Under the Rebel Flag.* 1887. Lovington, IL. Ils. 96 p. wraps. scarce. $65.00

BOGGS, W.R. *Military Reminiscences of General William R. Boggs, CSA.* 1913. Durham. 1st ed. $125.00

BOGNER, Norman. *Madonna Complex.* 1968. Coward McCann. sgn. 377 p. dj. VG. M1. $12.00

BOHAN & HAMMERSLOUGH. *Early CT Silver: 1700-1840.* 1970. Wesleyan U. 1st ed. 288 p. dj. VG. M1. $35.00

BOHR, Niels. *Atomic Physics & Human Knowledge.* 1958. NY. Ils 1st ed. 101 p. dj. VG. C4. $22.00

BOHROD, Aaron. *Decade of Still Life.* 1966. WI U. Ils. 298 p. EX. $20.00

BOILEAU, Ethel. *Clansmen.* 1936. NY. AP. Ltd ed. 448 p. color wraps. VG. T1. $75.00

BOISSEAU, F.G. *Anatomie Pathologique. Dernier Cours de Xavier Bichat.* 1825. Paris. 8vo. 335 p. xl. $150.00

BOL, L.J. *Bosschaert Dynasty: Painters of Flowers & Fruit.* 1980. Lewis. Ils. 108 p. dj. D2. $115.00

BOLAND, John. *Shakespeare Curse.* 1969. NY. Walker. 1st Am ed. dj. EX. $30.00

BOLITHO, William. *Twelve Against the Gods.* 1937. Modern Age. dj. G. P1. $15.00

BOLL, Heinrich. *Irish Journal.* 1967. McGraw Hill. 1st ed. dj. VG. $22.50

BOLL, Heinrich. *Soldier's Legacy.* 1985. Knopf. 1st Am ed. dj. VG. $10.00

BOLLANDIANI, S. *Bibliotheca Hagiographica Latina.* 1898-1899. 2 vols. xl. G1. $60.00

BOLLIGER, H. *Picasso for Vollard.* nd. NY. 4to. boxed. EX. J2. $75.00

BOLLINGER, E.T. *Rails That Climb.* 1950. Ils 2nd ed. photos. 402 p. $32.50

BOLLINGER & BAUER. *Moffat Road.* 1962. Denver. Sage. 1/2000. sgn. 357 p. scarce. dj. A3. $60.00

BOLOGNA, G. *Birds of the World.* 1978. Simon Schuster. 420 photos. 511 p. EX. M2. $8.00

BOLOGNA, G. *Illuminated Manuscripts.* 1988. NY. Weidenfeld. Ils. 4to. 199 p. $28.00

BOLTON, A.H. *Arabian Nights.* 1925. Winston. Ils Bolton. VG. B4. $25.00

BOLTON, C.K. *Elizabeth Whitman Mystery.* 1912. Peabody. 1st ed. 1/300. pls. VG. $22.50

BOLTON, E.S. *American Samplers.* 1973. reprint of 1921 ed. 416 p. wraps. $20.00

BOLTON, H. *Outpost of Empire.* 1939. dj. EX. $45.00

BOLTON, H.E. *Coronado: Knight of Pueblos & Plains.* 1949. NM U. 1st ed. 491 p. dj. $45.00

BOLTON, H.E. *Coronado: Knight of Pueblos & Plains.* 1949. Whittesey. 1st ed. dj. VG. J2. $20.00

BOLTON, H.E. *Outpost of Empire: Founding San Francisco.* 1931. NY. Ils. 11 maps. EX. $45.00

BOLTON, H.E. *Rim of Christendom.* 1936. Macmillan. 1st ed. VG. J2. $45.00

BOLTON, H.E. *Rim of Christendom.* 1936. NY. 1st ed. G. $30.00

BOLTON, H.W. *Our Fallen Heroes & Other Addresses.* 1892. 204 p. G. J4. $25.00

BOLUS, Jim. *Run for the Roses.* 1974. NY. 1st ed. 209 p. dj. VG. B2. $40.00

BONANNI, P.P. *Numismata Summorum Pontificum Templi Vaticani...* 1696. Rome. Ils. pls. folio. vellum bdg. VG. $900.00

BONAR. *Narrative of Mission of Inquiry to Jews From Scotland, 1839.* c 1843. Phil. Ils. maps. EX. $250.00

BOND, F.B. *Gospel of Philip the Deacon.* 1932. NY. $20.00

BOND, Francis. *Gothic Architecture in England.* 1906. London. Ils 1st ed. 4to. VG. G1. $50.00

BOND, G.B. *Mystery at Far Reach.* 1968. Alelard Schuman. AP. dj. VG. P1. $15.00

BOND, James. *America's No. 1 Trophy.* 1951. Portland. sgn. wraps. VG. $45.00

BOND, James. *Birds of the W Indies.* 1960. London. Collins. Ils. map. 256 p. VG. M2. $15.00

BOND, James. *Birds of the W Indies.* 1961. Houghton. Ils 1st Am ed. 256 p. dj. EX. M2. $20.00

BOND, James. *Field Guide to Birds of the W Indies.* 1947. Macmillan. Ils 1st print. 257 p. dj. EX. M2. $10.00

BOND, James. *From Out of the Yukon.* 5th print. sgn. wraps. $25.00

BOND, M.W. *To James Bond With Love.* 1980. Lititz, PA. 1st ed. dj. VG. B2. $15.00

BONE, Gertrude. *Came to Oxford.* Ils Muirhead. 4to. dj. EX. $40.00

BONE, James. *Preambulator in Edinburgh.* 1926. NY. Ils Lumsden. 1st Am ed. EX. $35.00

BONEHILL, Ralph. *Four Boy Hunters.* 1906. Cupples Leon. 1st ed. $8.00

BONEHILL, Ralph. *Guns & Snowshoes.* 1907. Cupples Leon. 1st ed. $8.00

BONEHILL, Ralph. *Out With Gun & Camera.* 1910. Cupples Leon. 1st ed. $9.00

BONEHILL, Ralph. *With Custer in the Black Hills.* 1902. Rahway. tan cloth. EX. $16.00

BONEHILL, Ralph. *Young Hunters of the Lake.* 1908. Cupples Leon. 1st ed. $9.00

BONET, Honore. *Tree of Battles of English Version With Intro by Coopland.* 1949. Liverpool. 1st ed. 4to. 316 p. dj. EX. T5. $95.00

BONEY, F.M. *Pictorial History of U of GA.* 1984. Athens. 262 p. dj. EX. $25.00

BONHAM, Jeriah. *Fifty Years' Recollections.* 1883. Peoria. 1st ed. G. $45.00

BONHOTE, J.L. *Birds of Britain.* 1907. London. 1st ed. VG. $30.00

BONI, Bradford. *Songs of the Gilded Age.* 1960. NY. Golden Pr. 1st ed. dj. EX. $15.00

BONNARDOT, Alfred. *Mirror of Parisian Bibliophile.* 1931. Chicago. 1/500. Trans/sgn Koch. slipcase. $40.00

BONNELL, J.S. *Pastoral Psychiatry.* 1938. NY. $16.50

BONNER, J.T. *Cels & Societies.* 1957. Princeton. photos. 234 p. dj. EX. M2. $10.00

BONNER, J.T. *Ideas of Biology.* 1962. Harper. Ils 1st ed. 180 p. EX. M2. $14.00

BONNER, T.D. *Life & Adventures of James P. Beckwourth...* 1856. Harper. Ils 1st ed. 538 p. VG. scarce. A3. $250.00

BONNEY, T.G. *Cathedrals, Abbeys & Churches of England & Wales. Vol. 2.* 1896. Cassell. VG. $40.00

BONOMI, Joseph. *Nineveh & Its Palaces.* Revised 3rd ed. 537 p. gilt full leather. VG. T5. $35.00

BOOKS INCORPORATED. *New American Encyclopedia.* 1942. Boston. Ils. 1496 p. VG. $5.00

BOOLE, Mary. *Collected Works.* 1931. London. Daniel. 1st ed. 4 vols. VG. J2. $100.00

BOON, K.G. *Rembrandt: Complete Etchings.* 1963. Abrams. Ils. dj. D2. $150.00

BOONE & CROCKETT CLUB. *N American Big Game Records 1939.* 1939. 1st ed. dj. VG. B2. $325.00

BOONE & CROCKETT CLUB. *N American Big Game Records 1939.* 1939. Scribner. 1st ed. EX. $345.00

BOONE & CROCKETT CLUB. *N American Big Game Records 1952.* 1st ed. EX. $300.00

BOONE & CROCKETT CLUB. *N American Big Game Records 1958.* 1st ed. dj. EX. $250.00

BOONE & CROCKETT CLUB. *N American Big Game Records 1964.* 1964. dj. EX. $95.00

BOONE & CROCKETT CLUB. *N American Big Game Records 1973.* 1st ed. dj. VG. $50.00

BOONE & CROCKETT CLUB. *N American Big Game Records 1977.* 1st ed. dj. VG. $40.00

BOOR, Ella. *We Are Many.* 1940. presentation. VG. $45.00

BOORSTIN, Daniel. *Discoverers.* 1983. NY. dj. EX. $15.00

BOOTH, E.S. *Birds of the W.* 1960. Outdoor Pictures. 3rd ed. G. M2. $14.00

BOOTH, Evangeline. *Woman.* 1930. Fleming. sgn. 12mo. EX. $40.00

BOOTH, Mary L. *Uprising of a Great People.* 1861. NY. 1st ed. 263 p. VG. K1. $21.00

BOOTH, William. *Orders & Regulations for Field Officers of Salvation Army.* 1891. London. 8vo. orig red cloth. VG. J2. $75.00

BOOTH. *Sleepy-Time Stories.* 1900. NY. Ils Maud Humphrey. EX. $10.00

BORAH, WOODROW & COOK. *Aboriginal Population of Central Mexico on Eve...Conquest.* 1963. CA U. 1st ed. 157 p. stiff wraps. VG. J2. $15.00

BORAH, WOODROW & COOK. *Early Colonial Trade & Navigation Between Mexico & Peru.* 1954. CA U. 1st ed. 170 p. stiff wraps. VG. J2. $15.00

BORAH, WOODROW & COOK. *Population of Central Mexico in 1548.* 1960. CA U. 1st ed. 215 p. stiff wraps. VG. J2. $15.00

BORAH, WOODROW & COOK. *Price Trends of Some Basic Commodities in Central Mexico...* 1958. CA U. 1st ed. 89 p. stiff wraps. VG. J2. $12.50

BORG, B. *My Life & Game.* 1980. Simon Schuster. 1st print. dj. M. $30.00

BORGE, Victor. *My Favorite Comedies in Music.* 1980. Watts. sgn. VG. $10.00

BORGES. *Ficciones.* Ltd Ed Club. slipcase. M. B3. $350.00

BORGESON, G. *Golden Age of the American Racing Car.* 1966. Bonanza. dj. VG. $15.00

BORGHESE, Paolo. *Catalogue de la Bibliotheque de Borghese.* 1892. Rome. Ils. pls. wraps. $69.50

BORGMANN, Dmitri. *Language on Vacation. Olio of Orthographic Oddities.* 1965. NY. dj. EX. $20.00

BORK & MAIER. *Historical Dictionary of Ecuador.* 1973. Scarecrow. M. $18.00

BORLAND, Hal. *Twelve Moons of the Year.* 1979. Knopf. Ils 1st ed. 369 p. dj. M2. $14.00

BORLAND, Hal. *Twelve Moons of the Year.* 1979. NY. 1st ed. dj. B2. $20.00

BORN, Wolfgang. *American Landscape Painting.* 1948. New Haven. 142 pls. EX. D2. $75.00

BORN, Wolfgang. *Still-Life Painting in America.* 1947. Oxford. 1st ed. dj. VG. J2. $25.00

BORNEMAN, Henry. *PA German Bookplates: A Study.* 1953. German Soc. 1st ed. VG. J2. $50.00

BORROR & DELONG. *Introduction to the Study of Insects.* 1954. Rinehart. Ils. 1030 p. VG. M2. $8.00

BORROW, George. *Zincale: Account of Gypsies of Spain.* 1907. London. Ils. 433 p. TEG. G. T5. $17.50

BORUP, George. *Tender Foot With Perry.* 1911. Stokes. Souvenir ed. 8vo. 317 p. VG. $25.00

BORYCZKA, Raymond. *No Strength Without Union: History of OH Workers, 1803-1980.* 1982. Columbus. Ils. 4to. 328 p. dj. xl. VG. T5. $11.50

BOSANQUET, M. *Life & Death of Dietrich Bonhoeffer.* 1968. Hodder Stoughton. dj. M. $38.00

BOSCH, R. *Introduction to Biological Control.* 1982. Plenum. photos. 247 p. EX. M2. $14.00

BOSKER, B.Z. *Legacy of Maimonides.* 1950. NY. $8.50

BOSO, Charles M. *View of WA Bottom: Glance at Blennerhassett Island.* 1984. Parsons, WV. Ils. sgn. 121 p. T5. $8.50

BOSWELL, James. *Boswell's Life of Johnson.* nd. NY. 1st ed. 6 vols. G. $45.00

BOSWELL, James. *Life of Samuel Johnson.* 1791. 1st ed. 1st issue. 2 vols. boxed. $3200.00

BOSWELL, James. *Life of Samuel Johnson.* 1901. Dent. Ils. EX. $100.00

BOSWELL, Jeanetta. *Edwin Arlington Robinson & the Critics.* Scarecrow Pr. 285 p. VG. T5. $12.50

BOSWELL, Jeanetta. *Past Ruined Ilion.* 1982. Scarecrow Pr. 321 p. VG. T5. $9.50

BOSWELL, Jeanetta. *Spokesmen for the Minority...* Scarecrow Pr. 296 p. VG. T5. $12.50

BOSWELL, Jeanetta. *Theodore Dreiser & the Critics, 1911-1982.* Scarecrow Pr. 305 p. VG. T5. $9.50

BOSWORTH, P. *Biography of Montgomery Clift.* 1978. Harcourt Brace. dj. EX. $38.00

BOTELER. *Boteler's Dialogues.* 1929. Navy Records Soc. 1st ed. J2. $20.00

BOTHA, C.G. *Our S Africa: Past & Present.* 1938. Cape Town. United Tobacco Co. Ils. $45.00

BOTKIN, B.A. *MS River Folklore.* 1955. Crown. Ltd ed. sgn. dj. VG. B2. $15.00

BOTZUM, J.A. *Summit County Looks Back Through 100 Years, 1840-1940.* 1940. Akron. Souvenir ed. 4to. 61 p. wraps. T5. $15.00

BOUCHARD, Charles. *Lectures on Auto-Intoxication in Disease.* 1894. Phil. VG. $10.00

BOUDAILLE, Georges. *Expressionists.* 1981. NY. Alpine. Ils. 170 p. dj. D2. $35.00

BOUDINOT, Elias. *Journey to Boston in 1809.* 1955. Princeton. VG. $7.50

BOUDREAUX, H.B. *Arthropod Pylogeny With Special Reference to Insects.* 1979. Wiley. Ils 1st ed. 320 p. dj. EX. M2. $22.00

BOUHOURS, P. *Vie de St. Francois Xavier Apotre des Indes et du Japon.* 1852. Bruxelles. fair. $55.00

BOULDTON, Rudyerd. *Traveling With the Birds.* 1933. Chicago. Ils Weber. VG. $25.00

BOULLE, P. *Planet of the Apes.* 1963. NY. 1st Am ed. sgn. dj. EX. $125.00

BOULTON, Harold. *Prince Charlie in Song: Short Selection of Jacobite Songs.* 1933. London. 56 p. VG. $35.00

BOULTON, W.B. *Amusements of Old London.* 1901. London. 1st ed. 8vo. 2 vols. TEG. gilt cloth. T1. $85.00

BOURJAILY, V. *End of My Life.* 1947. NY. 1st ed. dj. VG. B2. $12.50

BOURJAILY, V. *Unnatural Enemy: Essays on Hunting.* 1963. Dial. Ils. 182 p. dj. EX. M2. $15.00

BOURKE, J.G. *Apache Campaign.* 1958. NY. reprint of 1886 ed. dj. EX. $15.00

BOURKE, J.G. *Urine Dance of Zuni Indians of NM.* 1903. np. private print. 7 p. wraps. A3. $45.00

BOURKE-WHITE, Margaret. *Dear Fatherland Rest Quietly.* 1946. Simon Schuster. 1st ed. inscr. 8vo. dj. M. $85.00

BOURKE-WHITE, Margaret. *Dear Fatherland Rest Quietly.* 1946. Simon Schuster. 1st ed. VG. $35.00

BOURKE-WHITE, Margaret. *Eyes on Russia.* 1931. 1st ed. dj. VG. S2. $250.00

BOURKE-WHITE, Margaret. *Eyes on Russia.* 1931. NY. 1st ed. sgn. 4to. 135 p. dj. T5. $350.00

BOURKE-WHITE, Margaret. *Eyes on Russia.* 1931. Simon Schuster. 1st ed. inscr. 4to. G. $175.00

BOURKE-WHITE, Margaret. *One Thing Leads to Another. Growth of an Industry.* 1936. Boston. 1st ed. 104 p. dj. $65.00

BOURKE-WHITE, Margaret. *Portrait of Myself.* 1963. Simon Schuster. 1st ed. dj. EX. $25.00

BOURKE-WHITE, Margaret. *Shooting the Russian War.* 1942. Simon Schuster. 1st ed. 4to. dj. $65.00

BOURKE-WHITE, Margaret. *They Call It Purple Heart Valley.* 1944. Simon Schuster. 1st ed. dj. VG. $25.00

BOURKE-WHITE & CALDWELL. *You Have Seen Their Faces.* 1937. NY. Modern Age Books. 1st ed. dj. $40.00

BOURKE-WHITE & CALDWELL. *You Have Seen Their Faces.* 1937. Viking. 1st ed. 4to. VG. $65.00

BOURLIERE, F. *Natural History of Mammals.* 1970. Knopf. Ils Revised ed. dj. EX. M2. $13.00

BOURNE, George. *Life of Rev. John Wesley...* 1807. Baltimore. 8vo. 352 p. VG. $65.00

BOURNE. *World Review Nutrition & Dietetics.* 1972. Basel. $47.00

BOUTELL, R. *First Editions of Today & How To Tell Them.* 1937. Phil. Revised 2nd ed. dj. VG. $20.00

BOUVET. *Child of Tuscany.* 1895. McClurg. Ils Hooper. G. $12.00

BOUVIER, Jacqueline. *One Special Summer.* 1974. NY. 1st ed. dj. VG. $10.00

BOWAN, I. *Desert Trails of Atacama.* 1924. Am Geog Soc. photos. maps. 362 p. EX. M2. $27.00

BOWDITCH, H.I. *Address on Life & Character of James Deane.* 1845. Greenfield. 8vo. wraps. $50.00

BOWDITCH, Nathaniel. *New American Practical Navigator.* 1807. Newburyport. Ils Hooker. 2nd ed. 679 p. VG. $900.00

BOWEN, E. *High Sierra.* 1972. Time Life. photos. map. 184 p. EX. M2. $8.00

BOWEN, Elizabeth. *Eva Trout.* 1968. NY. 1st ed. dj. VG. $15.00

BOWEN, Elizabeth. *Eva Trout.* 1969. London. 1st ed. dj. EX. $30.00

BOWEN, F.C. *American Sails the Seas.* 1938. NY. 411 p. VG. $35.00

BOWEN, R.L. *RI Colonial Money & Its Counterfeiting, 1647-1726.* 1942. Providence. Ils 1st ed. 112 p. dj. EX. $125.00

BOWEN, Richard. *Early Arabian Necropolis of Ain Jawan.* 1950. Schools of Oriental Research. J2. $15.00

BOWER, K. *Song for Satawal.* 1983. Harper Row. 1st ed. 218 p. dj. EX. M2. $16.00

BOWER, Kenneth. *Guale: Golden Coast of GA.* nd. San Francisco. 143 p. dj. EX. $55.00

BOWER, Tom. *Klaus Barbie: Butcher of Lyons.* 1984. NY. 1st ed. dj. VG. $9.50

BOWERS, C.G. *Tragic Era: Revolution After Lincoln.* 1929. 567 p. VG. J4. $6.50

BOWERS, G.M. *Proceedings of Fourth International Fishery Congress...* 1910. US Fisheries. Ils. pls. 2 vols. xl. VG. A3. $180.00

BOWLES, Paul. *Delicate Prey.* 1950. NY. 1st ed. dj. G. $45.00

BOWLES, Paul. *Let It Come Down.* 1952. Random House. 1st ed. dj. EX. $50.00

BOWLES, Paul. *Next to Nothing: Collected Poems, 1926-1977.* 1981. Santa Barbara. 1st ed. 1/26. sgn. acetate dj. EX. $150.00

BOWLES, Paul. *Spider's House.* 1957. London. 1st ed. dj. EX. $35.00

BOWLES, Paul. *Up Above the World.* 1966. NY. 1st print. 223 p. dj. VG. T5. $25.00

BOWLES, Samuel. *Across the Continent: Summer's Journey to Rocky Mountains.* 1866. Springfield. Ils. map. 452 p. G. A3. $70.00

BOWLES, Samuel. *Summer Vacation in Parks & Mountains of CO.* 1869. NY. Bowles. 1st ed. 166 p. VG. A3. $50.00

BOWLES & HAEBERLIN. *Yallah.* 1957. NY. Ils 1st ed. 4to. dj. EX. $150.00

BOWLES & MILLER. *Paul Bowles: Descriptive Bibliography.* 1986. Santa Barbara. 1st ed. 1/200. sgns. acetate dj. $85.00

BOWMAN, S.M. *Sherman & His Campaigns.* 1865. NY. Ils 1st ed. 8vo. 512 p. VG. G2. $42.00

BOWMAN & IRWIN. *Sherman & His Campaigns.* 1865. NY. xl. fair. $30.00

BOWMAN. *Famous Guns From the Winchester Collection.* 1969. NY. 2nd print. photo. dj. VG. $10.00

BOXER, C.R. *Jan Compagnie in Japan, 1600-1817.* 1936. Hague. pls. EX. $250.00

BOYCE, B.S. *Dear Dad: Letters From New Guinea.* 1928. Chicago. Ils. VG. $30.00

BOYCE, J.C. *New Weapons for Air Warfare.* 1947. Boston. 1st ed. 292 p. T5. $19.50

BOYD, James. *Long Hunt.* 1930. Scribner. 1st ed. dj. EX. $40.00

BOYD, James. *Marching On.* 1927. Scribner. 1st ed. gilt green bdg. $22.00

BOYD, Jason. *Recent Indian Wars Under Lead of Sitting Bull & Others.* 1891. Pub Union. Ils. $35.00

BOYD, L.A. *Fiord Region of E Greenland.* 1924. Am Geog Soc. photos. maps. 369 p. slipcase. M2. $20.00

BOYD, R.J. *Elk of the White River Plateau, CO.* 1970. CO Fish/Game. photos. 126 p. EX. M2. $9.00

BOYD, William. *Good Man in Africa.* 1982. NY. ARC. 1st ed. dj. M. $40.00

BOYD, William. *Good Man in Africa.* 1982. NY. Morrow. 1st Am ed. dj. $15.00

BOYD, William. *New Confessions.* 1988. NY. Morrow. ARC. wraps. M. $15.00

BOYD, William. *School Ties.* 1985. NY. 1st Am ed. dj. VG. $25.00

BOYDSTON & HARWELL. *TX Big Game Investigations: White-Tailed Deer Harvest.* 1981. TX Parks/Wildlife. 121 p. G. M2. $7.00

BOYER, R.O. *Legend of John Brown: Biography & History.* 1973. Knopf. Ils 1st ed. 627 p. dj. EX. M2. $20.00

BOYER, Rick. *Whale's Footprints.* 1988. Boston. Houghton Mifflin. 1st ed. dj. M. $10.00

BOYER & BURTON. *Vanishing Eagles.* 1983. Dodd Mead. Ils 1st ed. 4to. dj. EX. M2. $25.00

BOYERS, Bettina & Audrey. *Murder by Proxy.* 1945. NY. 1st ed. dj. VG. T1. $35.00

BOYKIN, B.A. *Civil War Treasury of Tales, Legends & Folklore.* 1960. Random House. Ils. dj. EX. $25.00

BOYKIN, B.A. *Ghost Ship of the Confederacy.* 1957. NY. dj. VG. $20.00

BOYKIN, Edward. *Congress & the Civil War.* 1955. 352 p. dj. VG. $12.50

BOYKIN, Edward. *Wisdom of Thomas Jefferson.* 1941. 1st ed. dj. $18.00

BOYLE, E.V. *Days & Hours in a Garden.* 1898. London. VG. P3. $25.00

BOYLE, Kay. *Autobiography of Emmanuel Carnevali.* nd. Horizon. Ils. sgn. dj. $35.00

BOYLE, T.C. *Greasy Lake & Other Stories.* 1985. NY. 1st Am ed. dj. VG. $20.00

BOYLES, C.A. *Acoustic Wave Guides.* 1984. Wiley. dj. M. $30.00

BOYN. *Glacier Bay.* 1967. dj. EX. S2. $45.00

BOYNE, W.J. *Phantom in Combat.* 1985. WA. photos. 176 p. dj. EX. T5. $15.00

BRACE, C.L. *Dangerous Classes of NY.* 1880. NY. EX. $22.50

BRACK & KELLEY. *Early Biographies of Samuel Johnson.* 1973. IA U. s/wrap. M. $30.00

BRACKETT, Albert. *History of the US Cavalry.* 1865. NY. EX. scarce. K1. $45.00

BRADBURY, Ray. *Dandelion Wine.* 1957. Garden City. 1st ed. dj. M. $125.00

BRADBURY, Ray. *Dark Carnival.* 1947. Arkham House. 1/3000. inscr/sgn. dj. M. $650.00

BRADBURY, Ray. *Dark Carnival.* 1948. Hamilton. 1st Eng ed. dj. $250.00

BRADBURY, Ray. *Death Is Lonely Business.* 1984. Franklin M. 1st ed. sgn. s/wrap. EX. $50.00

BRADBURY, Ray. *Fahrenheit 451.* Ltd Ed Club. slipcase. M. B3. $150.00

BRADBURY, Ray. *Fahrenheit 451.* 1953. Ballantine. sgn. pb. VG. P1. $35.00

BRADBURY, Ray. *Forever & the Earth.* 1984. Croissant. 1st ed. dj. VG. $55.00

BRADBURY, Ray. *Ghosts of Forever.* 1980. Rizzoli. 1st ed. folio. dj. EX. $55.00

BRADBURY, Ray. *Golden Apples of the Sun.* 1953. Doubleday. Ils Mugnaini. 1st ed. dj. EX. $85.00

BRADBURY, Ray. *Golden Apples of the Sun.* 1953. Doubleday. 1st ed. VG. $55.00

BRADBURY, Ray. *Halloween Tree.* 1972. NY. 1st ed. dj. VG. $30.00

BRADBURY, Ray. *I Sing the Body Electric.* 1969. Knopf. 1st ed. inscr/sgn. dj. M. $95.00

BRADBURY, Ray. *Last Circus & Electrocution.* Arkham House. 1st ed. 1/100. sgn. boxed. EX. $100.00

BRADBURY, Ray. *Last Circus & Electrocution.* 1980. Northridge. 1/300. sgn. slipcase. EX. $65.00

BRADBURY, Ray. *Last Circus.* Lord John. sgn. dj. EX. $50.00

BRADBURY, Ray. *Long After Midnight.* 1976. NY. 1st ed. dj. EX. $20.00

BRADBURY, Ray. *Martian Chronicles.* 1950. Garden City. 1st ed. dj. VG. $85.00

BRADBURY, Ray. *Mummies of Guanajuato.* 1978. NY. Ils Lieberman. 1st ed. sgn. dj. EX. $100.00

BRADBURY, Ray. *R Is for Rocket.* 1962. Garden City. 1st ed. dj. VG. $45.00

BRADBURY, Ray. *S Is for Space.* 1966. Doubleday. 1st ed. inscr. dj. EX. $95.00

BRADBURY, Ray. *Switch on the Night.* 1955. Pantheon. Ils Gekiere. VG. $95.00

BRADBURY, Ray. *Toynbee Convector.* 1988. NY. AP. EX. $40.00

BRADBURY, Ray. *Toynbee Convector.* 1988. NY. 1st ed. sgn. dj. EX. $30.00

BRADBURY, Ray. *Twin Hieroglyphs.* 1978. Lord John. Ltd ed. sgn. EX. $80.00

BRADBURY, Ray. *Zen & the Art of Writing.* 1973. Capra Pr. 1/250. inscr/sgn. EX. $100.00

BRADDON. *Cheshire VC.* 1954. London. 1st ed. dj. VG. $15.00

BRADDY, H. *Pancho Villa at Columbus: Raid of 1916.* 1965. TX W College. photos. map. 43 p. EX. M2. $10.00

BRADEN, J.A. *Centennial History of Akron, 1825-1925.* 666 p. rebound. G. T5. $27.50

BRADEN, Waldo. *Oratory in the New S.* 1979. Baton Rouge. 286 p. dj. EX. $15.00

BRADFORD, G. *Confederate Portraits.* 1914. Houghton. Ils. 291 p. EX. M2. $23.00

BRADFORD, Roark. *John Henry.* 1931. Harper. Ils Lankes. 1st ed. $30.00

BRADFORD, Roark. *John Henry.* 1931. NY. Literary Guild. 1st ed. VG. $25.00

BRADLEY, A.G. *Captain John Smith.* 1909. Macmillan. fld map. VG. R1. $11.50

BRADLEY, B. *Life on the Run.* 1976. Quadrangle. dj. VG. $35.00

BRADLEY, D. *Expert Skiing.* 1960. NY. Ils 1st ed. photos. $50.00

BRADLEY, D. *No Place To Hide.* 1948. Little Brown. dj. VG. $8.00

BRADLEY, G.S. *Star Corps.* 1865. Milwaukee. xl. $60.00

BRADLEY, M.H. *On the Gorilla Trail.* 1923. Appleton. photos. map. 270 p. G. M2. $30.00

BRADLEY, M.Z. *Black Trillium.* 1980. Doubleday. AP. EX. P1. $45.00

BRADLEY, M.Z. *House Between the Worlds.* pb. VG. C1. $3.00

BRADLEY, M.Z. *House Between the Worlds.* 1st ed. sgn. pb. M. C1. $12.50

BRADLEY, M.Z. *Mists of Avalon.* full book-sized pb. VG. C1. $6.00

BRADLEY, M.Z. *Ruins of Isis.* pb. VG. C1. $3.50

BRADLEY, M.Z. *Ruins of Isis.* 1978. Starblaze. 1st print. M. C1. $24.50

BRADLEY, Mario. *In the Steps of the Master.* 1973. Tempo. VG. P1. $12.50

BRADLEY, Omar. *Soldier's Story.* 1951. Book Club. Ils. maps. inscr. 618 p. VG. T5. $35.00

BRADLEY, Omar. *Soldier's Story.* 1951. Holt. 1st ed. dj. VG. $36.00

BRADLEY, Richard. *New Improvements of Planting & Gardening.* 1739. London. VG. P3. $135.00

BRADLEY, S.S. *Aircraft Yearbook 1928.* 1928. NY. Ils. 551 p. G. T5. $42.50

BRADLEY, V.A. *Handbook of Values.* 1972. NY. 3rd imp. dj. VG. $45.00

BRADLEY, V.A. *More Gold in Your Attic.* 1961. NY. Fleet Pub. 1st ed. dj. VG. $50.00

BRADLEY, V.A. *Music for Millions: Kimball Piano & Organ Story.* 1957. Regnery. dj. G. $10.00

BRADLEY & BRADLEY. *Psychic Phenomena: Revelations & Experiences.* 1967. W Nyack. $15.00

BRADNA, Fred. *Big Top.* 1952. 3rd print. 333 p. dj. VG. $15.00

BRADNER, Enos. *NW Angling.* 1950. 1st ed. inscr/sgn. VG. $25.00

BRADSHAW, Gillian. *Hawk of May.* 1st ed. pb. VG. C1. $3.00

BRADSHAW, Gillian. *Hawk of May.* 1980. 1st ed. dj. EX. C1. $12.50

BRADSHAW, Gillian. *In Winter's Shadow.* 1st ed. dj. VG. C1. $14.50

BRADSHAW, Gillian. *Kingdom of Summer.* 1st Am ed. dj. EX. C1. $12.50

BRADSHAW, M.J. *Nature of ME.* 1945. Bangor. 3rd print. 177 photos. sgn. VG. $35.00

BRADY, C.T. *American Fights & Fighters Series.* 1909-1913. Doubleday Page. 6 vols. VG. $30.00

BRADY, C.T. *Recollections of Missionary in W.* 1900. NY. 1st ed. xl. VG. $15.00

BRADY, C.T. *When Blades Are Out & Love's Afield.* 1901. Lippincott. 1st ed. VG. $15.00

BRADY, G.S. *Harry Housel Everhard.* nd. (c 1970) Canton. Ils. 49 p. G. T5. $12.50

BRADY, W.Y. *Brady Annals.* 1923. WA. photos. 132 p. G. T5. $17.50

BRADY & TATE. *New Version of Psalms of David Fitted to Tunes...* 1788. Worcester. 1st ed. 358 p. G. $250.00

BRAGDON, Claude. *Episodes From an Unwritten History.* 1910. NY. $50.00

BRAGDON, Claude. *Four-Dimensional Vistas.* 1941. NY. $45.00

BRAGDON, Claude. *Introduction to Yoga.* 1933. NY. $50.00

BRAGDON & BRAGDON. *Oracle.* 1941. NY. $60.00

BRAGG, Clara. *Poe Material in Columbia University Library.* 1909. Columbia Lib. 16mo. 18 p. wraps. VG. D1. $8.00

BRAGG, Melvyn. *Richard Burton, a Life.* 1988. Boston. Book Club. 1st Am ed. dj. EX. $6.50

BRAGG, W.H. *John Brown's Army Mercer Macon.* 1987. dj. EX. $25.00

BRAGGS. *X Rays & Crystal Structure.* 1924. London. Revised Enlarged 4th ed. EX. $50.00

BRAIDER. *George Bellows & the Aschan School of Painting.* 1971. Doubleday. 1st ed. black cloth. dj. D2. $30.00

BRAIN, Belle. *Transformation of HI.* 1898. Revell. photos. G. $24.00

BRAIN, W.R. *Diseases of Nervous System.* 1951. Oxford. 4th ed. G. $5.00

BRAINARD, Joe. *I Remember.* 1975. Full Court Pr. 1st ed. sgn. dj. VG. $20.00

BRAINE, John. *Room at the Top.* 1957. London. 1st ed. presentation. sgn. dj. VG. $75.00

BRAITHWAITE, W. *Retrospect of Practical Medicine & Surgery.* 1857. NY. index. 350 p. orig bdg. K1. $21.00

BRAITHWAITE, W. *Retrospect of Practical Medicine & Surgery.* 1868. NY. Ils. 600 p. K1. $23.50

BRAMAH, Ernest. *Kai Lung's Golden Hours.* 1923. Doran. 1st ed. EX. $47.50

BRAMAH, Ernest. *Mirror of Kong Ho.* 1930. Doubleday. 1st Am ed. dj. VG. $75.00

BRAMAH, Ernest. *Wallet of Kai Lung.* 1900. London. 1st ed. G. $90.00

BRAND, Max. *Dionysus in Hades.* 1931. Shakespeare Head. VG. $80.00

BRAND, Max. *Thunderer.* 1933. Derrydale. Ils Paul Brown. 1/950. VG. $70.00

BRANDE. *Encyclopedia of Science, Literature & Art: A Dictionary.* 1848. Harper. 1352 p. full leather. G. $65.00

BRANDEIS, L.D. *Curse of Bigness.* 1934. NY. 1st ed. 339 p. VG. B2. $35.00

BRANDENBURG, J. *White Wolf: Living With an Arctic Legend.* 1988. Northword. 160 photos. oblong 4to. dj. EX. M2. $36.00

BRANDES, George. *Main Currents in 19th-C Literature.* 1906. NY/London. Macmillan/Heinemann. 6 vols. VG. $110.00

BRANDES, George. *William Shakespeare: Critical Study.* 1898. NY. 2 vols. VG. $35.00

BRANDI, Cesare. *Burri.* 1963. Rome. Editalia. Ils. 235 p. dj. D2. $100.00

BRANDON, Wilfred. *Incarnation.* 1936. NY. $20.00

BRANDON, Wilfred. *Open the Door!* 1935. NY. $18.00

BRANDOW, H.J. *Story of Old Saratoga: Burgoyne Campaign.* 1919. NY. Albany. 2nd ed. 528 p. dj. T5. $17.50

BRANDT, Bill. *Nudes, 1945-1980.* 1980. Boston. 1st ed. 100 pls. dj. VG. B2. $60.00

BRANDT, Bill. *Portraits.* 1982. TX U. Intro Alan Ross. 1st ed. dj. $50.00

BRANDT, Herbert. *AK Bird Trails.* 9143. Cleveland. 1st ed. dj. VG. J2. $100.00

BRANNER. *Casper Branner of VA & His Descendants.* 1913. Stanford. private print. Ils. 469 p. VG. C4. $85.00

BRANNON, Peter. *Organization of Confederate Post Office Dept. at Montgomery.* 1960. Ils. sgn. 164 p. dj. M. J4. $25.00

BRAQUE, Georges. *Colors of Masters.* 1946. NY. Tudor. Intro Stanislas Fumet. G. $25.00

BRASHER, T.L. *Early Poems & Fiction of Walt Whitman.* 1963. NY U. dj. EX. $15.00

BRASHLER, William. *City Dogs.* 1976. NY. 1st ed. dj. EX. $20.00

BRASSAI. *Histoire de Marie.* 1949. Paris. Les Eds du Point du Jour. wraps. $175.00

BRASSAI. *Paris by Night.* 1987. Pantheon. 1st ed. square 4to. 64 p. EX. $20.00

BRASWELL, O.K. *History of Carrol Co., AR.* nd. reprint of 1889 ed. M2. $7.00

BRATTON, S.T. *Geography of the St. Francis Basin.* 1926. MO U. Ils. maps. 54 p. EX. M2. $10.00

BRAUN, E. *Grand Canyon of the Living CO.* 1970. Sierra Club. photos. 144 p. dj. EX. M2. $10.00

BRAUN, H. *Die Lokalanasthesie.* 1907. Leipzig. 2nd ed. G. $45.00

BRAUN, M. *Naturgeschichte der Tierischen Parasiten des Denschen.* 1915. Wurzburg. Ils. German text. 559 p. G. M2. $10.00

BRAUND, S.R. *Skin Boats of St. Lawrence Island, AK.* 1988. WA U. 67 photos. 141 p. dj. M. M2. $20.00

BRAUNE, Anna. *Honey Chile.* 1937. Doubleday. Ils 1st ed. 4to. juvenile. $27.50

BRAUNTON, Ernest. *Garden Beautiful in CA.* 1915. Los Angeles. G. P3. $20.00

BRAUTIGAN, Richard. *Confederate General.* 1964. Castle. dj. VG. $50.00

BRAUTIGAN, Richard. *Hawkline Monster.* 1974. NY. 1st ed. dj. VG. $25.00

BRAUTIGAN, Richard. *Revenge of the Lawn.* 1971. NY. 1st ed. dj. EX. $55.00

BRAUTIGAN, Richard. *Sombrero Fallout.* 1976. NY. 1st ed. dj. VG. $14.00

BRAUTIGAN, Richard. *Tokyo-MT Express: Stories.* 1979. NY. 1st ed. 1/350. sgn. dj. EX. $50.00

BRAUTIGAN, Richard. *Willard & His Bowling Trophies.* 1975. NY. 1st ed. dj. EX. $25.00

BRAZELTON. *Neonatal Behavioral Assessment Scale.* 1973. 8vo. 66 p. VG. $20.00

BREASTED, J.H. *Oriental Forerunners of Byzantine Painting.* 1924. 23 pls. VG. $30.00

BRECHT. *Three Penny Opera.* Ltd Ed Club. slipcase. M. B3. $60.00

BRECKINRIDGE, Myra. *Myra Breckinridge Cookbook.* 1970. 1st ed. wraps. VG. $15.00

BREDON, Juliet. *Peking.* 1922. Shanghai. 2nd ed. 523 p. VG. B1. $35.00

BREE & BREE. *Life That Is Waiting.* 1940. England. $4.00

BREEN, J.L. *Hair of the Sleuthhound: Parodies of Mystery Fiction.* 1982. Metuchen. Scarecrow. EX. $10.00

BREESE. *Some Unwritten Laws of Fox Hunting in America.* 1909. np. VG. $35.00

BREIDENBAUGH, E.S. *PA College Book, 1832-1882.* 1882. Phil. 21 photos. 475 p. xl. $150.00

BREIHAN, C.W. *Complete & Authentic Life of Jesse James.* 1953. Fell. photos. 287 p. G. M2. $18.00

BREIHAN, C.W. *Great Gunfighter of the W.* 1962. Naylor. photos. 175 p. dj. EX. M2. $25.00

BREIHAN, C.W. *Killer Legions of Quantrill.* 1971. Superior. 1st ed. photos. 144 p. EX. M2. $20.00

BREIHAN, C.W. *Younger Brothers.* 1961. Naylor. photos. 260 p. dj. M2. $22.00

BREIHAN, Carl. *Day Jesse James Was Killed.* 1961. NY. Ils 1st ed. sgn. dj. VG. B2. $20.00

BREKHOVSKIKH & LYSANOV. *Fundamentals of Ocean Acoustics.* 1982. Berlin. Verlag. EX. $30.00

BREMER, F. *Homes of the New World. Vol. II.* 1853. NY. G. $24.00

BREMMER, R.H. *Public Good: Philanthropy & Welfare in Civil War Era.* 1980. 234 p. dj. M. J4. $10.00

BREMSER, Ray. *Madness.* 1965. Pb Book Gallery. inscr. wraps. VG. $75.00

BRENGLE, Richard. *Arthur: King of Britian.* 1964. Corner Stone. 1st/only ed. pb. VG. C1. $14.50

BRENNAN, J.P. *Sixty Selected Poems.* 1985. New Establishment Pr. dj. EX. P1. $5.00

BRENNAN, Louis. *Beginner's Guide to Archaeology.* 1973. PA. $20.00

BRENNECKE. *Life & Art of Thomas Hardy.* 1976. NY. dj. EX. $15.00

BRESLER, Fenton. *Mystery of Georges Simenon.* 1983. Beaufort. 1st ed. dj. EX. $18.95

BRESLIN, Howard. *Hundred Hills.* 1960. NY. Crowell. Book Club ed. dj. $4.50

BRESLIN, Jimmy. *World Without End, Amen.* 1973. NY. 1st ed. inscr. dj. VG. $30.00

BRETON, Andre. *Le Cadavre Exquis Son Exaltation.* 1948. Paris. 1/515. wraps. D2. $55.00

BRETT, David. *My Dear Wife: Civil War Letters of David Brett.* 1964. Pioneer Pr. photos. map. 137 p. dj. EX. $15.00

BRETT, W.H. *Indian Tribes of Guiana.* 1861. Carter. G. $80.00

BRETTELL, Richard. *Art of Paul Gauguin.* 1988. AT&T. Ils. 4to. 519 p. wraps. EX. $18.00

BRETZ, J.H. *Caves of MO.* 1956. Rolla. Ils 1st ed. 490 p. VG. $40.00

BREUIL & LANTIER. *Men of the Old Stone Age.* 1965. St. Martin. Ils 272 p. dj. EX. M2. $15.00

BREWER, A.T. *PA Volunteers, 1861-1865: 61st Regiment.* 1911. Ils. 234 p. gilt bdg. J4. $50.00

BREWER, Jo. *Wings in the Meadow.* 1967. Houghton. Ils 1st print. 187 p. dj. EX. M2. $7.00

BREWER, S. *Chimps of Mount Asserik.* 1978. Knopf. Ils 1st Am ed. 302 p. dj. EX. M2. $12.00

BREWSTER, David. *Life of Sir Isaac Newton.* 1833. NY. Harper. 1st Am ed. 323 p. EX. $95.00

BREWSTER, William. *Concord River.* 1937. Cambridge. 1st ed. 259 p. dj. VG. B2. $40.00

BREWSTER, William. *October Farm.* 1936. Cambridge. 1st ed. dj. EX. $30.00

BRIAND, P. *Daughter of the Sky.* 1960. NY. 1st ed. 230 p. dj. VG. $25.00

BRICK, John. *Richmond Raid.* 1963. Garden City. Doubleday. Book Club ed. dj. $7.50

BRICKER, F.E. *Audel's Automobile Guide.* 1966. 1st ed. 723 p. EX. $12.50

BRICKER, W.P. *Complete Book of Collecting Hobbies.* c 1951. NY. Ils. 12mo. 316 p. xl. G2. $9.00

BRIDENBAUGH, Carl. *Cities in the Wilderness.* 1960. NY. 500 p. dj. VG. T5. $15.00

BRIDGE, Ann. *And Then You Came.* 1949. NY. 2nd print. dj. VG. C1. $15.00

BRIDGE, J.H. *Inside History of Carnegie Steel Co.* 1903. NY. Ills. EX. T1. $35.00

BRIDGES, E.C. *GA Signers & Declaration of Independence.* 1981. Cherokee Pub. Ils. tall 8vo. dj. $15.00

BRIDGES, E.L. *Uttermost Part of the Earth.* 1949. Dutton. 97 photos. 5 maps. dj. EX. M2. $25.00

BRIDGES, Hal. *Lee's Maverick General, Daniel Harvey Hill.* 1961. Ils 1st ed. 323 p. EX. J4. $24.50

BRIDGES, Robert. *Eros & Psyche.* 1885. London. Bell. 1st ed. VG. $40.00

BRIDGES, Robert. *Testament of Beauty.* 1930. NY. 1st ed after Oxford U ed. G. $12.50

BRIDGES, W. *Zoo Expeditions.* 1954. Morrow. Ils. inscr/sgn. 191 p. VG. M2. $11.00

BRIDGMAN, P.W. *Logic of Modern Physics.* 1927. NY. 1st ed. VG. $55.00

BRIFFAULT, R. *Mothers.* 1927. NY. 1st ed. 3 vols. VG. B2. $95.00

BRIGGS, L.V. *History of Shipbuilding of N River, Plymouth Co., MA...* 1981. Norwell, MA. reprint. slipcase. M. T1. $45.00

BRIGGS & ROBBINS. *Where Birds Live: Habitats in the Middle Atlantic States.* 1951. Audubon Soc. photos. 58 p. M2. $5.00

BRIGHT, M.C. *Early GA Portraits 1715-1870.* 1975. Athens. Ils. 338 p. dj. EX. $40.00

BRIMLOW, G.F. *Harney Co., OR.* 1951. Portland. dj. VG. $30.00

BRIN, David. *Startide Rising.* 1985. Phantasia. 1/1200. sgn. dj. EX. $100.00

BRININSTOOL, E.A. *Trail Dust of a Maverick.* 1914. NY. Ils 1st ed. VG. $35.00

BRININSTOOL, E.A. *Trooper With Custer.* 1925. Columbus. 1st ed. presentation. VG. A3. $65.00

BRINK, Andre. *Looking on Darkness.* 1975. Morrow. 1st ed. dj. VG. $30.00

BRINNIN, J.M. *No Arch, No Triumph.* 1945. Knopf. 1st ed. inscr. $75.00

BRINNIN, J.M. *Third Rose: Gertrude Stein & Her World.* 1959. Little Brown. 1st ed. dj. VG. $16.00

BRINTON, J.H. *Personal Memoirs of John H. Brinton.* 1914. NY. Neale. VG. $70.00

BRION, Marcel. *Masterpieces of the Louvre.* 1974. Abrams. sm folio. dj. VG. $36.00

BRIQUET, Charles Moise. *Les Filigranes: Dictionnaire Historiques des Marques...* 1968. Amsterdam. facsimile of 1907. 4 vols. D2. $650.00

BRISBIN, L. *Bibliography of the American Alligator.* 1986. Savannah River 4to. 310 p. EX. M2. $50.00

BRISTOL, F.M. *Life of Chaplain McCabe.* 1908. Revell. Ils. 416 p. VG. $13.00

BRISTOW & MANNING. *Gutenberg Murders.* 1931. Mystery League. 1st ed. dj. EX. $17.00

BRITANNICA. *Encyclopedia Britannica.* 1910-1936. 32 vols in 16. green cloth. $175.00

BRITANNICA. *Encyclopedia Britannica.* 1909. 30 vols. leather. $115.00

BRITISH MUSEUM. *Guide to Exhibition in King's Library.* 1901. London. Ils. $25.00

BRITTEN, E.H. *Electric Physician; or, Self-Cure Through Electricity.* 1875. Boston/NY. HrdCvr. 59 p. red bdg. VG. $25.00

BRITTEN, Evelyn. *Chronicles of Saratoga.* 1959. 1st ed. sgn. VG. $20.00

BRITTON, Nan. *President's Daughter.* 1927. NY. 439 p. G. $7.50

BRITTON & BROWN. *Illustrated Flora of N US & Canada...* 1896-1898. 1st ed. 2 vols. VG. $120.00

BRITTON & HAYASHIDA. *Japanese Crane: Bird of Happiness.* 1981. Kodansha. Ils. 4to. 63 p. dj. EX. M2. $15.00

BROADFOOT, Tom. *Civil War Books: A Check List.* 1978. 501 p. M. J4. $28.50

BROCH, Theodore. *Mountains Wait.* 1942. St. Paul. Ils Kent. dj. VG. $45.00

BROCH, Theodore. *Mountains Wait.* 1943. Webb Books. Ils Kent. VG. $10.00

BROCK, S.E. *More About Leemo: Adventures of a Puma.* 1968. Taplinger. Ils 1st ed. dj. EX. M2. $10.00

BROCKETT, L.P. *Life & Times of Abraham Lincoln.* 1865. 750 p. full leather bdg. EX. K1. $14.50

BROCKETT, L.P. *Woman: Rights, Wrongs, Priviledges, Responsibilites.* 1869. Hartford. 1st ed. VG. $54.00

BROCKETT, L.P. *Woman's Work in the Civil War.* 1867. Phil. 1st ed. 16 engravings. 799 p. VG. $50.00

BROCKMAN, C.F. *Trees of N America.* 1969. Golden Pr. Ils. maps. 280 p. G. M2. $6.00

BROCQ, L. *Traite Elementaire de Dermatologie Pratique Comprenant...* 1907. Paris. 4to. 2 vols. $160.00

BRODER, Patricia J. *Dean Cornwell: Dean of Illustrators.* 1978. Watson Guptill. Ils 239 p. dj. D2. $100.00

BRODIE, F.M. *Thomas Jefferson: Intimate History.* 1974. 1st ed. dj. $15.00

BRODIE, Fawn. *Devil Drives: Life of Sir Richard Burton.* 1967. NY. 1st ed. dj. VG. B2. $20.00

BRODIE, H.J. *Fungi: Delight of Curiosity.* 1978. Toronto. photos. 131 p. EX. M2. $9.00

BRODIE, John. *Open Field.* 1974. Boston. 2nd ed. EX. $12.50

BRODISH. *Brain-Pituitary Interrelationships.* 1973. Basel. 340 p. $48.00

BRODRICK. *N Africa.* 1943. Oxford. Ils. xl. VG. $4.50

BROEMEL, L. *Sheet Metal Worker's Manual.* 1942. 550 p. EX. $4.00

BROER, L.R. *Sanity Plea Novels of Vonnegut.* 1989. UMI Research. dj. EX. P1. $35.00

BROKE-SMITH, P.W.L. *History of Early British Military Aeronautics.* 1968. Bath. Ils 56 p. dj. T5. $12.50

BROM, J.L. *Pitiless Jungle.* 1955. McKay. Ils. 309 p. dj. EX. $15.00

BROMFIELD, Louis. *Animals & Other People.* 1955. Harper. Ils 272 p. M2. $5.00

BROMFIELD, Louis. *Awake & Rehearse.* 1929. NY. 1st trade ed. 349 p. VG. T5. $37.50

BROMFIELD, Louis. *From My Experience: Pleasures & Miseries of Life on Farm.* 1955. NY. Book Club. Ils. 355 p. dj. VG. T5. $9.50

BROMFIELD, Louis. *Malabar Farm.* 1948. NY. Ils Kate Lord. 1st ed. dj. T5. $22.50

BROMFIELD, Louis. *Modern Hero.* 1932. NY. 1/250. sgn/#d. 450 p. dj. EX. T5. $125.00

BROMFIELD, Louis. *Out of the Earth.* 1950. NY. Ils 1st ed. 305 p. dj. VG. T5. $19.50

BROMFIELD, Louis. *Rains Came.* 1937. NY. Harper. 1st ed. fair. $8.00

BROMFIELD, Louis. *Wild Country.* 1948. NY. Harper. 1st ed. sgn. 274 p. dj. M1. $18.00

BROMFIELD, Louis. *Wild Is the River.* 1941. NY. 1st ed. dj. EX. $12.00

BROMFIELD, Louis. *World We Live In.* 1944. NY. 1st ed. 339 p. dj. VG. T5. $22.50

BROMLEY, Joseph. *Clear the Tracks.* 1943. NY. 288 p. VG. $50.00

BROMLEY & MAY. *Fifty Years of Progressive Transit.* 1973. Ils. 176 p. $25.00

BROMWELL, William. *Locomotive Sketches With Pen & Pencil...* 1854. Phil. Ils 1st ed. map. 192 p. G. T5. $150.00

BRONGERSMA & VENEMA. *To the Mountains of the Stars.* 1963. Doubleday. Ils 1st Am ed. 318 p. dj. EX. M2. $20.00

BRONSON, Wilfrid. *Children of the Sea.* 1940. NY. Harcourt. Ils. VG. $40.00

BRONTE, Charlotte. *Bell, Currer.* 1861. NY. Harper. 12mo. blue cloth. G. $15.00

BRONTE, Charlotte. *Legends of Angria.* 1933. Yale. 1st ed. dj. M. $70.00

BRONTE, Charlotte. *Professor.* 1860. Smith Elder. 1st ed. 8vo. orange cloth. $115.00

BRONTE, Charlotte. *Search After Happiness.* 1969. London. 1st ed. dj. VG. $40.00

BRONTE, Emily. *Poems.* 1947. London. Curwen. 1st ed. dj. VG. $27.00

BROOK, J.M. *Dictionary of Literary Biography Yearbook: 1988.* Gale Research. 312 p. VG. T5. $45.00

BROOKE, Rupert. *Five Previously Unpublished Poems.* 1914. Gloucester. Ryton Dymock. wraps. $125.00

BROOKE, Rupert. *John Webster & Elizabethan Drama.* 1916. London. 1st ed. VG. $50.00

BROOKE, Rupert. *Letters to His Publisher.* 1975. Octagon Books. 1/400. slipcase. EX. $19.00

BROOKES, Owen. *Inheritance.* 1980. Holt Rinehart. AP. VG. P1. $20.00

BROOKHAUSER, Frank. *Our Phil.* 1957. NY. 1st ed. sgn. dj. EX. $22.50

BROOKNER, Anita. *Family & Friends.* 1985. London. 1st ed. dj. EX. $40.00

BROOKS, A.H. *Blasing AK's Trails.* 1953. AK U. photos. maps. 528 p. dj. EX. M2. $35.00

BROOKS, Amy. *Dorothy Dainty at Foam Ridge.* 1918. Boston. 1st ed. EX. $12.50

BROOKS, Charles. *English Spring.* 1932. NY. 1st ed. VG. C1. $9.50

BROOKS, Edward. *Wonder Stories From the Mabinogion.* 1925. Ils. C1. $12.50

BROOKS, G. *Street in Bronzeville.* 1945. NY. Harper. 1st ed. dj. VG. $175.00

BROOKS, G.R. *This Was Joanna.* 1949. News Stand Lib. dj. VG. P1. $40.00

BROOKS, Jennie. *Under Oxford Trees.* 1911. Cincinnati. VG. $20.00

BROOKS, Joe. *Trout Fishing.* 1972. NY. 1st ed. dj. VG. $15.00

BROOKS, John. *American Syndicalism: WWI.* 1913. NY. VG. $30.00

BROOKS, John. *Labors' Challenge to the Social Order.* 1920. NY. VG. $30.00

BROOKS, John. *Room Outside.* 1970. NY. dj. VG. $15.00

BROOKS, Juanita. *Mountain Meadows Massacre.* 1962. Norman. Ils. dj. EX. $30.00

BROOKS, Louise. *Lulu in Hollywood.* 1982. NY. 1st ed. dj. EX. $20.00

BROOKS, V.W. *John Sloan: Painter's Life.* 1955. NY. Ils. 246 p. EX. $30.00

BROOKS, V.W. *Pilgrimage of Henry James.* 1925. Dutton. VG. $15.00

BROOKS & HERRICK. *Embryology & Metamorphosis of the Macroura.* 1891. NAS. 57 pl. 4to. new cloth. EX. M2. $57.00

BROOME, H. *Faces of the Wilderness.* 1972. Mountain Pr. Ils 1st ed. 271 p. dj. VG $12.00

BROSSARD, Chandler. *Who Walk in Darkness.* 1952. NY. 1st ed. dj. EX. $45.00

BROSSE, J. *Great Voyages of Discovery: Circumnavigators & Scientists.* 1983. Facts on File. Ils. 4to. 228 p. dj. EX. M2. $35.00

BROTHERHEAD, William. *Forty Years Among Booksellers of Phil.* 1891. Phil. 1st ed. $75.00

BROUGHTON, James. *Ecstasies Poems, 1975-1983.* 1983. Syzygy. 1/200. EX. $25.00

BROUN, Heywood. *Junior Great Books.* 1984. pb. EX. C1. $5.00

BROUN, Heywood. *Pieces of Hate.* 1922. NY. 1st ed. 8vo. G. $22.00

BROWER, C.D. *Fifty Years Below Zero.* 1942. NY. 3rd ed. sgn. 310 p. VG. $35.00

BROWER, C.D. *Fifty Years Below Zero.* 1948. Dodd Mead. photos. 310 p. VG. M2. $5.00

BROWER, David. *Manual of Ski Mountaineering.* 1962. Sierra Club. Ils. 224 p. VG. M2. $10.00

BROWER, David. *Meaning of Wilderness to Science.* 1960. Sierra Club. photos. map of AK. 129 p. dj. M2. $8.00

BROWER, K. *Wake of the Whale.* 1979. Friends of the Earth. dj. EX. M2. $19.00

BROWER. *Headlands.* 1976. Ltd ed. 1/800. sgn. M. S2. $275.00

BROWER. *With Their Islands Around Them.* 1974. NY. 1st ed. dj. EX. $10.00

BROWN, Alec. *Voyage of the Chelyuskin.* 1934. Macmillan. photos. maps. 325 p. EX. M2. $30.00

BROWN, Alexander. *Cabells & Their Kin.* 1895. Boston. Ils. 641 p. VG. C4. $125.00

BROWN, C.H. *Insurrection at Magellan: Narrative of Imprisonment...* 1854. Boston. rebound. $50.00

BROWN, C.J. *OH Roster of Township & Municipal Officers & Members...* 1930. Springfield. inscr. 512 p. wraps. G. T5. $4.50

BROWN, Christy. *Background Music.* 1973. NY. 1st ed. VG. B2. $17.50

BROWN, Clara. *Cloth Construction.* 1927. Boston. Ginn. 236 p. cloth bdg. VG. $10.00

BROWN, Claude. *Manchild in Promised Land.* 1965. NY. 1st Am ed. dj. VG. $30.00

BROWN, D.A. *Bold Cavaliers: Morgan's 2nd KY Cavalry Raiders.* 1959. Phil. Ils 1st ed. 353 p. dj. VG. T5. $49.50

BROWN, D.E. *Grizzly in the SW: Documentary of an Extinction.* 1985. OK U. Ils 1st ed. maps. 274 p. dj. M. M2. $19.00

BROWN, D.E. *Wolf in the SW: Making of an Engangered Species.* 1988. AZ U. photos. 195 p. M. M2. $13.00

BROWN, E.K. *Willa Cather, Critical Biography.* 1953. Knopf. 8vo. dj. VG. G2. $18.00

BROWN, E.K. *Willa Cather, Critical Biography.* 1953. NY. 1st ed. dj. M. $45.00

BROWN, Edward. *Wadsworth Memorial.* 1875. Wadsworth, OH. inscr. 232 p. G. T5. $125.00

BROWN, F.A. *Selected Invertebrate Types.* 1950. Wiley. Ils. 597 p. EX. M2. $18.00

BROWN, Fredric. *Here Comes a Candle.* 1950. NY. Dutton. 1st ed. dj. VG. $75.00

BROWN, G. *Child's First Book: New Primer for Families & Schools.* 1829. Providence. Brown. Ils. 36 p. G. rare. $250.00

BROWN, H.T. *Five Hundred & Seven Mechanical Movements...* 1868. NY. Ils 1st ed. 131 p. EX. T5. $55.00

BROWN, Henry. *Cotton Fields & Cotton Factories.* c 1840. London. Darton Clark. Ils Graf. 166 p. VG. $350.00

BROWN, Irving. *Gypsy Fires in America.* 1924. Harper. photos. $15.00

BROWN, J. *Early Days of San Francisco.* 1949. Bio Books. Ltd ed. 1/500. EX. $75.00

BROWN, J.C. *Calabazas: Amusing Recollections of AZ City.* 1961. AZ Silhouettes. 1/1500. 251 p. dj. EX. M2. $15.00

BROWN, J.D. *Manual of Practical Bibliography.* c 1910. London. Rutledge. 16mo. 175 p. VG. $30.00

BROWN, J.E. *John Brown & His Wife, Mary Ann Longstreth, a Supplement.* 1956. Columbus. 36 p. wraps. G. T5. $6.50

BROWN, J.J. *American Angler's Guide.* 1857. NY. 4th ed. 12mo. $90.00

BROWN, John. *Short Catechism.* 1822. Pittsburgh. Andrews. 80 p. wraps. fair. T5. $27.50

BROWN, Kenneth. *Medchester Club.* Derrydale. as issued. VG. B2. $50.00

BROWN, L. *African Birds of Prey.* 1971. Houghton. Ils 1st ed. 320 p. dj. EX. M2. $50.00

BROWN, L. *I Married a Dinosaur.* 1950. Dodd Mead. photos. 268 p. dj. VG. M2. $16.00

BROWN, L.F. *Apostle of Democracy: Life of Lucy Maynard Salmon.* 1943. NY. 1st ed. 315 p. dj. VG. $20.00

BROWN, L.W. *Aunty Brown's Story: Token of Love & Friendship.* 1908. Akron. Ils. 60 p. G. T5. $22.50

BROWN, Leonard. *American Patriotism.* 1869. Des Moines. 1st ed. 574 p. EX. $65.00

BROWN, M. *Louis Bromfield & His Books.* 1957. Fairlawn, NJ. 1st ed. dj. VG. B2. $15.00

BROWN, M.L. *Firearms in Colonial America.* 1980. Ils 1st ed. 4to. 449 p. dj. M. $40.00

BROWN, M.L. *Firearms in Colonial America.* 1980. Ils. 448 p. K1. $27.50

BROWN, M.W. *Baby Animals.* 1941. NY. Ils Cameron. dj. EX. $20.00

BROWN, M.W. *Golden Egg Book.* Ils Weisgard. Big Golden Book. VG. B4. $25.00

BROWN, M.W. *Little Pig's Picnic.* 1838. Boston. Heath. EX. C4. $30.00

BROWN, Marion. *S Cookbook.* 1951. Chapel Hill. Revised 2nd ed. 388 p. dj. VG. $25.00

BROWN, Mark. *Before Barbed Wire.* 1956. NY. 1st ed. dj. EX. $27.50

BROWN, Paul. *Silver Heels.* 1951. Scribner. 1st ed. dj. EX. $32.50

BROWN, Peter. *Book of Kells.* 1981. Thames Hudson. 1st ed. dj. EX. T6. $25.00

BROWN, R.M. *Bingo.* 1988. NY. Bantam. ARC. wraps. M. $10.00

BROWN, R.M. *In Her Day.* 1976. Plainfield. 1st ed. wraps. $15.00

BROWN, R.M. *Six of One.* 1978. NY. Harper. 1st ed. dj. M. $10.00

BROWN, Rosemary. *Immortals by My Side.* 1975. Chicago. 1st ed. dj. EX. $10.00

BROWN, T.W. *Sharks: Silent Savages.* 1973. Little Brown. Ils. 134 p. dj. EX. M2. $12.00

BROWN, Tom. *Amusements Serious & Comical.* 1927. NY. Ils Hayward. dj. VG. J2. $50.00

BROWN, Walter. *Laughing Death.* 1932. Phil. 1st ed. dj. VG. $30.00

BROWN, William. *Horse of the Desert.* 1929. Derrydale. 1/750. folio. blue cloth. EX. $200.00

BROWN, William. *Retriever Gun Dogs.* 1945. np. 2nd print. dj. VG. $20.00

BROWN, Z. *Charles Olson Reading at Berkeley.* 1966. Coyote. 1st ed. pb. VG. $22.00

BROWN & AMADON. *Eagles, Hawks & Falcons of the World.* 1968. McGraw Hill. Ils 1st ed. 2 vols. slipcase. M2. $195.00

BROWN & FELTON. *Before the Barbed Wire.* 1956. NY. 1st ed. $42.00

BROWN & GORDON. *S & E African Yearbook & Guide.* 1928. London. Ltd 34th ed. atlas. maps. 128 p. $35.00

BROWN. *Brown's Nautical Almanac.* 1949. Glasgow. 8vo. 744 p. G. G2. $8.00

BROWN. *Hebrew English Lexicon Old Text.* 1974. Oxford. VG. G1. $15.00

BROWN. *Pastoral From Walt Disney's Fantasia.* 1940. NY. Standard 1st ed. dj. VG. C4. $65.00

BROWNE, C.F. *Artemus Ward: His Book.* 1862. Ils. 262 p. J4. $7.50

BROWNE, G.B. *Unknown Indian.* 1930. 1st ed. 299 p. $25.00

BROWNE, G.W. *Franconian Gateway & Region of Lost River.* 1925. Standard Book. Ils. 155 p. VG. $12.00

BROWNE, G.W. *St. Lawrence River.* 1905. NY. Ils 1st ed. 365 p. VG. B2. $55.00

BROWNE, G.W. *Story of NH.* 1925. Standard Book. Ils. 276 p. VG. $12.00

BROWNE, H.C. *Glimpses of Old NY.* 1917. NY. Anderson Galleries. 4to. VG. $135.00

BROWNE, Howard. *Warrior of the Dawn.* 1943. Chicago. 1st ed. dj. EX. $75.00

BROWNE, Irving. *Ballads of a Bookworm.* 1899. Roycroft. 1/850. 8vo. boxed. EX. D1. $250.00

BROWNE, J. *Indians of CA.* 1944. Colt. Ltd ed. 1/500. dj. EX. $75.00

BROWNE, J. *Washoe Revisited.* 1957. Bio Books. Ltd ed. 1/500. EX. $75.00

BROWNE, Thomas. *Works of Sir Thomas Browne.* 1928. Faber. 1st ed. 6 vols. boxed. VG. J2. $150.00

BROWNELL, C.D. *Indian Races of N & S America.* 1864. Hartford. Hurlburt. 745 p. xl. A3. $80.00

BROWNELL, C.D. *Indian Races of N & S America.* 1865. Hartford. Hurlburt Scranton. pls. 760 p. EX. $175.00

BROWNELL, E.B. *Really Babies.* 1908. Chicago/NY. 1st ed. VG. G1. $20.00

BROWNELL, H.H. *Pioneer Heroes of the New World.* 1856. Cincinnati. Ils. 736 p. rebound. G. T5. $25.00

BROWNELL, L.W. *Photography for Sportsman Naturalist.* 1904. Macmillan. 1st ed. 84 photos. 311 p. gilt bdg. $35.00

BROWNING, E.B. *Drama of Exile.* 1845. NY. 1st Am ed. 2 vols. VG. $165.00

BROWNING, E.B. *Poet's Enchiridion.* 1914. Boston. Bibliophile Soc. VG. $75.00

BROWNING, E.B. *Poetical Works.* 1880. London. 12th ed. 5 vols. full calf. EX. $300.00

BROWNING, E.B. *Sonnets From the Portuguese.* 1898. Roycroft. 1/480. 4to. VG. D1. $100.00

BROWNING, E.B. *Sonnets From the Portuguese.* 1948. Ltd Ed Club. sgn. folio. boxed. $125.00

BROWNING, Robert. *Aristophanes' Apology.* 1875. London. 1st ed. $110.00

BROWNING, Robert. *Christmas Eve.* 1899. Roycroft. 8vo. green suede. VG. D1. $50.00

BROWNING, Robert. *History of Golf.* 1955. NY. dj. VG. $25.00

BROWNING, Robert. *Last Ride.* 1900. Roycroft. 8vo. vellum bdg with ties. VG. D1. $250.00

BROWNING, Robert. *Men & Women.* 1855. London. 1st ed. 1st state bdg. 2 vols. $125.00

BROWNING, Robert. *Pied Piper of Hamelin.* nd. London. Ils Greenaway. 4to. G. $125.00

BROWNING, Robert. *Pied Piper of Hamelin.* 1910. Chicago. Ils Hope Dunlap. VG. $27.50

BROWNING, Robert. *Pied Piper of Hamelin.* 1986. Lathrop. Ils Ivanov. 1st ed. 4to. EX. $7.00

BROWNING, Robert. *Poems by Robert Browning.* 1907. London. Ils Byam Shaw. Art Nouveau bdg. $85.00

BROWNING, Robert. *Ring & the Book.* 1868. London. 1st ed. 1st state bdg. 4 vols. EX. $250.00

BROWNING, Robert. *Selections From Poetical Works of Robert Browning.* 1901. London. 1st ed. leather. $160.00

BROWNING, Robert. *Selections From Poetical Works of Robert Browning.* 1901. London. 1st ed. with sgn tipped in. $200.00

BROWNLOW, Kevin. *Parades Gone By.* 1968. Knopf. 1st ed. 577 p. dj. VG. $20.00

BROWNLOW, W.G. *Great Iron Wheel Examined; or, Its False Spokes Extracted...* 1856. Nashville. 1st ed. 331 p. $75.00

BROWNLOW, W.G. *Sketches of Rise, Progress & Decline of Secession.* 1862. Phil. 1st ed. 12mo. 458 p. brown cloth. G. G2. $35.00

BRUCCOLI, Matthew J. *Fortunes of Mitchell Kennerley Bookman.* 1986. Harcourt Brace. 1st ed. dj. EX. T6. $15.00

BRUCCOLI, Matthew J. *Romantic Egoists.* 1974. Scribner. 1st trade ed. T6. $125.00

BRUCE, A.G. *Highway Design & Construction.* 1937. Scranton. Ils. 646 p. EX. $20.00

BRUCE, A.W. *Steam Locomotive in America.* 1952. Bonanza. 443 p. $30.00

BRUCE, D. *Bird of Jove.* 1973. Ballantine. photos. 283 p. M2. $12.00

BRUCE, J.C. *Cougar Killer.* 1953. NY. presentation. dj. VG. $25.00

BRUCE, Lenny. *How To Talk Dirty & Influence People.* 1965. Chicago. 1st ed. dj. VG. $55.00

BRUCE, P.A. *Brave Deeds of Confederate Soldiers.* 1916. Phil. Ils 1st ed. 350 p. dj. M. $60.00

BRUCE, R.V. *Lincoln & the Tools of War.* 1956. Bobbs Merrill. Special Ordnance ed. 368 p. M2. $21.00

BRUCE, Robert. *Lincoln Highway in PA.* 1920. WA. M1. $25.00

BRUCE. *City Laid Waste: Tornado Devastation at Gainesville, GA.* 1936. Gainsville. photos. 127 p. scarce. B1. $75.00

BRUEHL, Anton. *Mexico.* 1933. Delphic Studio. 1/1000. slipcase. VG. $200.00

BRUEHL, Anton. *Tropical Patterns.* 1970. Hollywood, FL. Dukane. 1st ed. dj. EX. $25.00

BRUETTE, William. *American Duck, Goose & Brant Shooting.* 1929. NY. 1st ed. color pls. VG. $35.00

BRUETTE, William. *American Duck, Goose & Brant Shooting.* 1945. NY. color pls. dj. VG. $25.00

BRUGIONI, D.A. *Civil War in MO As Seen From the Capital City.* 1987. Summers. photos. 168 p. EX. M2. $19.00

BRUGUIERE, Francis. *San Francisco.* 1918. San Francisco. Crocker. Ils 1st ed. dj. EX. $135.00

BRULLER, Jean. *Visions Intimes et Ressurantes de la Guerre.* 1936. Paris. 1/1000. wraps. $35.00

BRUMAGH, R.S. *Most Mysterious Manuscript.* 1978. S IL U. 1st ed. dj. EX. $30.00

BRUN, Christian. *Guide to Manuscript Maps in William Clement Library.* 1959. MI U. M. $35.00

BRUNDSON, J. *Technique of Etching & Engraving.* 1965. 1st ed. dj. VG. $5.00

BRUNEFILLE. *Topo.* 1881. London. Ils Greenaway. VG. $110.00

BRUNHAMMER, Yvonne. *Meubles et Ensembles: Anglais.* nd. Paris. Ils. 4to. dj. VG. $17.50

BRUNNER, C. *Wings Upon the Heavens.* 1976. Ideals. Ils R Sloan. 4to. 78 p. EX. M2. $10.00

BRUNNER, J. *Crucible of Time.* 1983. NY. 1st ed. dj. VG. $15.00

BRUNNER, J. *Track & Tracking.* 1908. Outing Pub. 1st ed. G. $18.00

BRUNTON, Violet. *Ecclesiasticus.* 1927. NY. Ils. VG. J2. $35.00

BRUSH, D.H. *Growing Up in S IL, 1820-1861: Memoirs of D.H. Brush.* 1944. Chicago. Lakeside Classic. 265 p. T5. $30.00

BRUSH, D.H. *Growing Up in S IL, 1820-1861: Memoirs of D.H. Brush.* 1944. Donnelley. Lakeside Classic. A3. $45.00

BRUTON, Eric. *Clocks & Watches.* 1968. Italy. dj. VG. $20.00

BRUUN, A.F. *Galathea Deep Sea Expedition 1950-1952.* 1956. Allen Unwin. Ils 1st ed. fld map. dj. EX. M2. $20.00

BRUUN, A.F. *List of Danish Vertebrates.* 1950. Copenhagen. fld map. EX. M2. $15.00

BRUUN, B. *Birds of Europe.* 1971. Golden Pr. Ils Arthur Singer. 4to. dj. EX. M2. $25.00

BRYAN, E.H. *Insects of HI: Johnston Island & Wake Island.* 1926. Bishop Mus. Ils. 94 p. M2. $11.00

BRYAN, Julian. *Siege.* 1940. NY. photos. presentation. sgn. VG. $35.00

BRYAN, T.C. *Confederate GA.* 1953. GA U. inscr/sgn. 299 p. VG. M2. $19.00

BRYANT, Arthur. *Unfinished Victory.* 1940. Macmillan. 1st ed. red cloth. VG. D1. $40.00

BRYANT, Billy. *Children of Ol' Man River & Times of Showboat Trooper.* c 1936. NY. pls. sgn. VG. $15.00

BRYANT, Helen. *Royston, Historical Novel.* 1986. NY. Vantage. 1st ed. dj. $15.00

BRYANT, Sara. *Epaminondas & His Auntie.* 1938. Houghton. Ils Inez Hogan. G. $28.00

BRYANT, T. *Practice of Surgery.* 1873. Phil. Ils. inscr. 4to. 984 p. $90.00

BRYANT, W.C. *New Library of Poetry.* 1877. Howard Hulbert. AEG. VG. $65.00

BRYANT, W.C. *Picturesque America.* 1894. Appleton. Revised ed. G. $95.00

BRYANT, W.C. *Picturesque America; or, Land We Live In.* 1872-1874. NY. Appleton. 2 vols. morocco. AEG. J2. $175.00

BRYANT, W.C. *Story of the Fountain.* 1872. Appleton. Ils. gilt bdg. EX. $75.00

BRYHER. *Ruan.* 1960. 1st Am ed. dj. EX. C1. $12.00

BUBER-NEUMANN, Margarete. *Milena.* 1988. NY. 1st ed. dj. EX. $7.50

BUCHAN, John. *History of Great War.* 1922. NY. 1st ed. 1/500. sgn. 8 vols. $250.00

BUCHAN, John. *Three Hostages.* 1949. Zephyr. dj. VG. P1. $21.25

BUCHANAN, James. *Sketches of N American Indians.* 1824. NY. 1st ed. 2 vols. boxed. B2. $200.00

BUCHANAN, Lamont. *Pictorial History of the Confederacy.* 1951. Crown. Ils. dj. EX. $28.00

BUCHANAN, Lamont. *Steel Trails & Iron Horses.* 1955. Ils. 159 p. $17.50

BUCHANAN, T. *Who Killed Kennedy?* 1964. London. Secker Warburg. VG. $35.00

BUCHENHOLZ, Bruce. *Doctor in the Zoo.* 1974. David Charles. Ils 1st Eng ed. dj. EX. M2. $13.00

BUCHHEIM, Lothar-Gunther. *Max Beckmann: Holzschnitte, Radierungen, Lithographien.* 1954. Feldafing. Ils. D2. $18.50

BUCHNER, A. *Mechanical Musical Instruments.* nd. London. Batchworth. 4to. dj. EX. $40.00

BUCHSBAUM, Ann. *Practical Guide to Print Collecting.* 1975. Van Nostrand. Ils. dj. D2. $18.50

BUCK, Albert. *Diagnosis & Treatment of Ear Diseases.* 1880. NY. Ils. green cloth. VG. $40.00

BUCK, Albert. *Treatise on Hygiene & Public Health.* 1879. NY. Wood. 2 vols. xl. G. $55.00

BUCK, Frank. *Animals Are Like That!* 1939. McBride. photos. 240 p. EX. M2. $26.00

BUCK, Pearl. *All Under Heaven.* 1972. NY. Ltd 1st ed. 1/1000. sgn. VG. B2. $32.50

BUCK, Pearl. *China As I See It.* 1970. NY. 1st ed. 1/3000. sgn. dj. EX. $37.00

BUCK, Pearl. *Good Earth.* nd. Grosset Dunlap. dj. VG. $6.50

BUCK, Pearl. *Kennedy Women.* 1970. NY. 1st ed. later print. sgn. dj. EX. $23.00

BUCK, Pearl. *One Bright Day.* 1950. NY. inscr/sgn. VG. $45.00

BUCK, Pearl. *Pearl Buck's America.* 1971. np. 1/5000. photos. sgn. dj. EX. $50.00

BUCK, Pearl. *Sons.* 1972. NY. John Day. 1/1000. sgn. 8vo. EX. $50.00

BUCK & ANTHONY. *Bring 'Em Back Alive.* 1930. NY. 1st ed. 291 p. gilt cloth. G. T5. $17.50

BUCK & ANTHONY. *Wild Cargo.* 1932. Simon Schuster. photos. 244 p. EX. M2. $15.00

BUCKBEE, E. *Pioneer Days of Angels Camp.* 1932. 1st ed. wraps. EX. $100.00

BUCKERIDGE, J.O. *Lincoln's Choice: Civil War Repeating Rifle.* 1956. Harrisburg. Ils 1st ed. 254 p. dj. B2. $60.00

BUCKINGHAM, J.E. *Reminiscences & Souvenirs of Assassination of Lincoln.* reprint of 1894 ed. HrdCvr. J4. $22.50

BUCKINGHAM, Nash. *Blood Lines: Tales of Shooting & Fishing.* 1938. Derrydale. 1/1250. presentation. sgn. EX. $375.00

BUCKINGHAM, Nash. *De Shootin'est Gent'man.* 1934. Derrydale. 1/950. presentation. sgn. EX. $625.00

BUCKINGHAM, Nash. *De Shootin'est Gent'man.* 1934. Derrydale. 1/950. VG. $425.00

BUCKINGHAM, Nash. *De Shootin'est Gent'man.* 1941. Scribner. 1st ed. dj. EX. $65.00

BUCKINGHAM, Nash. *Game Bag: Tales of Shooting & Fishing.* Derrydale. 1/1250. sgn/#d. EX. $300.00

BUCKINGHAM, Nash. *Game Bag: Tales of Shooting & Fishing.* 1945. Putnam. 1/1250. sgn. EX. $175.00

BUCKINGHAM, Nash. *Hallowed Years.* 1953. Stackpole. dj. EX. $50.00

BUCKINGHAM, Nash. *Mark Right! Tales of Shooting & Fishing.* 1936. Derrydale. 1/1250. EX. $250.00

BUCKINGHAM, Nash. *Ole Miss'.* 1937. Derrydale. 1/1250. EX. $275.00

BUCKINGHAM, Nash. *Ole Miss'.* 1937. Derrydale. 1/1250. VG. B2. $195.00

BUCKINGHAM, Nash. *Ole Miss'.* 1946. NY. Ils 1st trade ed. 178 p. dj. G. T5. $22.50

BUCKINGHAM, Nash. *Tattered Coat.* 1944. Putnam. 1/995. presentation. sgn. EX. $225.00

BUCKLEY, Christopher. *Steaming to Bamboola.* 1982. NY. 1st ed. 8vo. dj. EX. $15.00

BUCKLEY, W.F. *Quotations From Chairman Bill.* 1970. New Rochelle. Arlington House. VG. $16.00

BUCKLEY. *PT Boats in the US Navy.* 1962. GPO. VG. $12.00

BUCKLEY. *Story of Henri Tod.* 1984. Garden City. 1st ed. dj. VG. $10.00

BUCKMASTER, Henrietta. *Freedom Bound.* 1965. NY. Macmillan. 1st ed. dj. EX. $10.00

BUDGE, E.A.W. *By Nile & Tigris.* 1920. London. Murray. 2 vols. $450.00

BUDGE, E.A.W. *Rosetta Stone.* 1929. London. dj. VG. $60.00

BUDKER, P. *Life of Sharks.* 1971. Columbia. Ils. 222 p. M2. $9.00

BUECHNER, Frederick. *Brendan.* 1st pb ed. VG. C1. $9.50

BUECHNER, Frederick. *Brendan.* 1988. 1st pb ed. M. $11.00

BUEL, J.W. *Cannoneer: Recollections of Service in Army of Potomac.* 1890. WA. EX. $90.00

BUEL, J.W. *Glimpses of America: Pictorial & Descriptive History...* 1894. Phil. oblong folio. $25.00

BUEL, J.W. *Heroes of the Plains.* 1881. St. Louis. Moffat. Ils. 548 p. scarce. A3. $180.00

BUEL, J.W. *Heroes of the Plains.* 1882. Cincinatti. Ils. G. $45.00

BUELER, L.E. *Wild Dogs of the World.* 1973. Stein Day. Ils 1st ed. map. 274 p. dj. EX. M2. $18.00

BUELER, L.E. *Wild Dogs of the World.* 1980. Stein Day. Ils. maps. 274 p. EX. M2. $13.00

BUETTNER, Alex. *Menschenflug (Human Flight).* 1924. Stuttgart. Ils 1st ed. 4to. 115 p. scarce. T5. $175.00

BUFF, Mary & Conrad. *Dancing Cloud.* 1937. NY. 80 p. cloth. G. T5. $15.00

BUGLIOSI, Vincent. *Helter Skelter.* 1974. NY. 1st ed. dj. EX. $15.00

BUKOWSKI, Charles. *Barfly: A Screenplay.* 1984. Paget/Sutton W. 1/20. acetate dj. with sgn Ils. EX. $450.00

BUKOWSKI, Charles. *Bring Me Your Love.* 1983. Black Sparrow. 1/376. sgn author/Crumb. M. $75.00

BUKOWSKI, Charles. *Bukowski-Purdy Letters, 1964-1974.* 1983. Black Sparrow. 1/200. sgns. acetate dj. M. $75.00

BUKOWSKI, Charles. *Crucifix in the Deathland.* 1965. NY. Ltd ed. sgn. VG. P3. $85.00

BUKOWSKI, Charles. *Day It Snowed in LA.* 1986. Black Sparrow. Ils Deluxe ed. 1/200. sgn. M. $60.00

BUKOWSKI, Charles. *Day It Snowed in LA.* 1986. Black Sparrow. Ils 1st ed. EX. $50.00

BUKOWSKI, Charles. *Day It Snowed in LA.* 1986. Santa Barbara. Ils 1st ed. wraps. VG. $30.00

BUKOWSKI, Charles. *Days Run Away Like Wild Horses.* nd. Black Sparrow. 1st ed. pb. VG. $15.00

BUKOWSKI, Charles. *Days Run Away Like Wild Horses.* 1969. LA. 1st ed. 1/250. sgn/#d. dj. VG. $150.00

BUKOWSKI, Charles. *Factotum.* 1975. Black Sparrow. 1st ed. wraps. EX. $15.00

BUKOWSKI, Charles. *Hot Water Music.* 1983. Black Sparrow. 1st ed. 1/400. sgn. M. $75.00

BUKOWSKI, Charles. *No Business.* 1983. Black Sparrow. 1/376. sgn author/Crumb. M. $75.00

BUKOWSKI, Charles. *Shakespeare Never Did This.* 1979. San Francisco. HrdCvr ed. dj. VG. $45.00

BUKOWSKI, Charles. *War All the Time.* 1981. Black Sparrow. 1/400. sgn/#d. M. $65.00

BUKOWSKI, Charles. *Women.* 1981. London. Allen. 1st ed. dj. M. $30.00

BUKOWSKI & MONTFORT. *Horse Meat.* 1982. LA. 1/125. sgns. folio. acetate dj. scarce. $650.00

BULAU, A.E. *Footprints of Assurance.* 1953. 1st ed. 4to. dj. B1. $30.00

BULAU, A.E. *Footprints of Assurance.* 1953. Macmillan. 319 p. M1. $39.50

BULFINCH, Thomas. *Age of Chivalry or Legends of King Arthur.* 1874. Ils. C1. $22.50

BULFINCH, Thomas. *Age of Chivalry or Legends of King Arthur.* 1884. Revised ed. VG. C1. $19.50

BULL, John. *Birds of NY State.* 1974. Garden City. 1st ed. 4to. dj. M. $30.00

BULL, Peter. *Teddy Bear Book.* 1970. NY. 1st ed. dj. VG. B2. $45.00

BULL, R.C. *Civil War Diary.* 1977. NY. 1st ed. dj. EX. $38.00

BULLA, Clyde. *Sword in the Tree.* Ils Galdone. 11th print. VG. C1. $10.00

BULLA, Clyde. *Viking Adventure.* c 1963. Childrens Book Club. Ils Corsline. $5.00

BULLARD & COLLINS. *Who's Who in Sherlock Holmes.* 1980. NY. Stated 1st ed. 251 p. dj. M. $45.00

BULLEN, F.T. *Cruise of the Cachalot.* 1899. NY. 1st Am ed. VG. $25.00

BULLOCH, J.D. *Secret Service of Confederate States in Europe. Vol. 1.* 1959. NY. New ed. 460 p. VG. T5. $17.50

BULLOCK, Barbara. *Wynn Bullock.* 1971. 1st ed. sgn. M. $35.00

BULLOUGH, G. *Narrative & Dramatic Sources of Shakespeare.* 1957-1975. London. 8 vols. djs. $125.00

BULLUCK & HOFFMAN. *Art of the Empire Strikes Back.* 1980. NY. Ils. tall 4to. $40.00

BUMP, Gardiner. *Ruffed Grouse: Life History, Propagation, Management.* 1947. Albany. Ils Everitt. 1st ed. 4to. VG. $85.00

BUMP, Gardiner. *Ruffed Grouse: Life History, Propagation, Management.* 1947. NY. Ils 1st ed. 915 p. EX. scarce. M2. $115.00

BUMPER, J.I. *Gettysburg: Historic Views of Gettysburg.* 1904. Bumber Miller. Ils. 54 p. EX. J4. $10.00

BUNIN, Ivan. *Memories & Portraits.* 1951. London. dj. EX. $20.00

BUNNELL, L.H. *Discovery of Yosemite & Indian War of 1851...* 1911. Los Angeles. Gerrlicher. 4th ed. 355 p. VG. A3. $90.00

BUNTON, M.T. *Bride on Old Chisholm Trail in 1886.* 1939. San Antonio. 1st ed. inscr. dj. EX. $30.00

BUNYAN, John. *Pilgrim's Progress.* nd. London. Ils Byam Shaw. J2. $35.00

BUNYAN, John. *Pilgrim's Progress.* 1879. NY. Ils Barnard. 1st ed. VG. J2. $35.00

BUNYAN, John. *Pilgrim's Progress.* 1880. London. Ltd Deluxe ed. $125.00

BUNYAN, John. *Pilgrim's Progress.* 1890. Altemus. square 4to. gilt blue cloth. $35.00

BUNYAN, John. *Pilgrim's Progress.* 1898. NY. Ils Rhead. J2. $35.00

BUNYAN, John. *Pilgrim's Progress.* 1918. London. Nister. Ils Paget. AEG. $35.00

BUNYAN, John. *Pilgrim's Progress. Retold & Shortened for Modern Readers...* 1939. Stokes. Ils Lawson. 1st ed. VG. B4. $40.00

BUNZL, George. *Face of the Sun Kingdoms: Indians of Mexico, Guatemala...* 1969. NY. Ils. 116 p. dj. EX. T5. $22.50

BURACK, A.S. *Television Plays for Writers: 8 Plays With Comment...* 1957. Boston. 1st ed. dj. VG. $27.50

BURBANK, Luther. *His Methods & Discoveries & Practical Application.* 1914-1915. NY. 14 vols. orig bdg. VG. $300.00

BURBANK, Luther. *Training of the Human Plant.* 1922. NY. G. $20.00

BURBANK, Luther. *Works of Luther Burbank.* 1914. NY. Ils. 8vo. 12 vols. VG. $175.00

BURCH, J.P. *True Story of Charles W. Quantrell & His Guerilla Band.* 1923. Ils. 265 p. EX. J4. $20.00

BURDEN, D.W. *Look to Wilderness.* Stated 1st ed. dj. VG. $12.00

BURDER, Samuel. *Memoirs of Eminently Pious Women.* 1834. Phil. New ed. full leather. VG. $35.00

BURDETT, Charles. *Life & Adventures of Christopher Carson...* 1860. Phil. Evans. Ils 1st ed. 374 p. scarce. A3. $140.00

BURDETTE, Robert. *Rise & Fall of Mustache & Other Hawk-Eyetems.* 1877. Ils Wallis. G. $25.00

BURDICK, Eugene. *Ninth Wave.* 1956. Boston. 1st ed. sgn. 8vo. dj. VG. $35.00

BURFORD, Lolah. *Vision of Stephen.* 1977. 1st ed. xl. C1. $6.00

BURGER, Carl. *All About Dogs.* 1962. Random House. Ils. G. $15.00

BURGER, Carl. *All About Dogs.* 1962. Random House. Ils. VG. B4. $20.00

BURGESS, Anthony. *Beds in the E.* 1959. London. dj. G. $45.00

BURGESS, Anthony. *Coaching Days of England.* 1966. London. Elke. Ils. dj. VG. $75.00

BURGESS, Anthony. *Hemingway & His World.* 1978. London. 1st ed. dj. EX. $25.00

BURGESS, Anthony. *Moses (a Narrative).* 1976. NY. 1st Am ed. dj. VG. $20.00

BURGESS, Anthony. *One-Hand Clapping.* 1972. NY. 1st ed. inscr. G. $35.00

BURGESS, Anthony. *Piano Players.* 1986. London. 1st ed. dj. EX. $20.00

BURGESS, Anthony. *Piano Players.* 1986. NY. Review ed. dj. RS. EX. $25.00

BURGESS, Anthony. *Vision of Battlements.* 1965. NY. 1st ed. dj. VG. $18.00

BURGESS, F.W. *Old Prints & Engravings.* 1948. NY. Tudor. Ils. 281 p. D2. $40.00

BURGESS, Gelett. *Little Sister of Destiny.* 1906. Houghton Mifflin. 1st ed. G. $12.00

BURGESS, Gelett. *Little Sister of Destiny.* 1906. Boston. 1st ed. dj. EX. $40.00

BURGESS, Gelett. *Look Eleven Years Younger.* 1942. 1st ed. 8vo. dj. G. $18.00

BURGESS, Gelett. *Purple Cow.* 1895. San Francisco. 1st issue. 1st state. VG. $100.00

BURGESS, Gelett. *Vivette; or, Memoirs of Romance Association.* 1897. Boston. Copeland Day. 152 p. G. $50.00

BURGESS, J. *Rock Temples of Elephanta.* 1871. 13 mounted photos. VG. $325.00

BURGESS, R.F. *Sharks.* 1970. Doubleday. photos. dj. EX. M2. $10.00

BURGESS, T.W. *Birds You Should Know.* 1933. Little Brown. Ils Fuertes. 1st ed. 256 p. dj. M2. $15.00

BURGESS, T.W. *Burgess Animal Book for Children.* 1931. Little Brown. VG. $15.00

BURGESS, T.W. *Burgess Seashore Book for Children.* 1948. Boston. dj. B2. $40.00

BURGESS, T.W. *Happy Jack.* 1920. Boston. 8 color pls. VG. $28.00

BURGESS, T.W. *Mother W Wind's Neighbors.* Sept., 1913. Boston. Little Brown. 1st ed. EX. $55.00

BURGESS, T.W. *Now I Remember.* 1960. Boston. 1st ed. 338 p. dj. VG. $25.00

BURGESS, Tristam. *Oration, Pronounced Before Citizens of Providence...* 1831. Providence. Marshall. 32 p. EX. $45.00

BURK, B. *Waterfowl Studies.* 1976. Winchester. photos. 4to. 254 p. dj. EX. M2. $20.00

BURK, D. *Black Bear in Modern N America.* 1973. Boone/Crockett Club. photos. 299 p. M. M2. $12.00

BURKE, J.L. *Heaven's Prisoners.* 1988. NY. 1st ed. dj. EX. $15.00

BURKE, J.L. *Lay Down My Sword & Shield.* 1971. NY. Crowell. 1st ed. dj. EX. $50.00

BURKE, J.L. *Neon Rain.* 1987. NY. 1st ed. dj. M. $30.00

BURKE, J.R. *Let Us In.* 1931. NY. 1st ed. dj. VG. $15.00

BURKE, John. *Roman England.* 1984. Ils 1st Am ed. dj. M. C1. $7.50

BURKE, Paul. *Adventures of a Farm Boy.* 1942. private print. 1/500. sgn. dj. EX. $30.00

BURKE & CALDWELL. *Hogarth: Complete Engravings.* c 1968. Abrams. Ils. pls. D2. $95.00

BURKERT, Nancy. *Art of Nancy Burkert.* 1977. Harper. 1st Am ed. dj. VG. $20.00

BURKHARDT, Jacob. *Civilization of Renaissance in Italy: Essay.* 1951. Phaidon. 4th ed. dj. D2. $25.00

BURLAND, Brian. *Surprise.* 1974. NY. Harper. 1st ed. presentation. sgn. $20.00

BURLEIGH, T.D. *Birds of ID.* 1972. Caxton. photos. 467 p. dj. xl. EX. M2. $45.00

BURLEND, Rebecca. *True Picture of Emigration.* 1936. Chicago. Lakeside Classic. 167 p. T5. $30.00

BURLEND, Rebecca. *True Picture of Emigration.* 1936. Donnelley. Lakeside Classic. A3. $45.00

BURLINGAME, Roger. *Endless Frontiers: Story of McGraw Hill.* 1959. NY. Ils 1st ed. slipcase. $25.00

BURNE, A.H. *Lee, Grant & Sherman: Study in Leadership...* 1939. Scribner. Ils 1st ed. 216 p. dj. M2. $42.00

BURNE, R. *McGorrty: Story of Billia Bum.* 1972. Stuart. dj. M. $40.00

BURNETT, F.H. *Cozy Lion.* 1927. Century. Ils Cady. 1st ed. VG. B4. $40.00

BURNETT, F.H. *Dawn of a Tomorrow.* 1906. NY. Ils 1st ed. VG. $20.00

BURNETT, F.H. *Edith's Burglar.* 1906. Caldwell. Ils Sandhorn. New ed. G. $15.00

BURNETT, F.H. *Editha's Burglar.* 1988. Marsh. Jordan. Ils Sandham. 1st ed. VG. B4. $60.00

BURNETT, F.H. *In the Closed Room.* 1904. NY. Ils Smith. 1st ed. EX. $50.00

BURNETT, F.H. *In the Closed Room.* 1904. NY. McClure Phillips. Ils Smith. M. $65.00

BURNETT, F.H. *Little Lord Fauntleroy.* c 1886. NY. Scribner. 1st ed. with sgn letter. $250.00

BURNETT, F.H. *Little Lord Fauntleroy.* c 1886. NY. Scribner. 1st ed. 1st print. M. $150.00

BURNETT, F.H. *Piccino & Other Child Stories.* 1894. Scribner. Ils Birch. 1st ed. G. $40.00

BURNETT, F.H. *Secret Garden.* 1911. Grosset Dunlap. dj. G. $22.50

BURNETT, F.H. *Secret Garden.* 1911. Stokes. 1st ed. EX. $47.50

BURNETT, F.H. *Shuttle.* 1907. NY. 1st ed. EX. $30.00

BURNEY, James. *History of Buccaneers of America.* 1891. London. fair. $25.00

BURNFORD, S. *One Woman's Arctic.* 1973. Little Brown. 1st Am ed. 234 p. dj. M1. $12.50

BURNHAM, Alan. *NY Landmarks.* 1963. Middletown, CT. 1st ed. sgn. dj. VG. J2. $30.00

BURNHAM, Bonnie. *Art Crisis.* 1975. St. Martin. 256 p. dj. D2. $27.50

BURNS, E. *Angler's Anthology.* 1952. Harris. 1st ed. dj. VG. $20.00

BURNS, George. *How To Live To Be 100 or More.* 1983. NY. 1st ed. dj. EX. $10.00

BURNS, George. *I Love Her, That's Why!* 1955. NY. 1st ed. dj. B2. $25.00

BURNS, George. *I Love Her, That's Why!* 1955. Simon Schuster. 2nd print. dj. G. $12.00

BURNS, Robert. *Burns' Merry Muses.* 1886. Edinburgh. 1st ed. 1/200. gray cloth. G. $30.00

BURNS, Robert. *Poems Chiefly in Scottish Dialect (Posthumous Poems).* 1896. Kilmarnock. facsimile. 1/600. VG. $75.00

BURNS, W.N. *Saga of Billy the Kid.* 1926. Garden City. reprint. 322 p. G. M2. $13.00

BURNS, W.N. *Saga of Billy the Kid.* 1926. NY. tan cloth. VG. $15.00

BURNS, W.N. *Tombstone: Iliad of the SW.* 1927. Doubleday Page. 1st ed. 388 p. scarce. M2. $22.00

BURNS, W.N. *Tombstone: Iliad of the SW.* 1927. Garden City. 1st ed. C4. $25.00

BURNS, Z. *Confederate Forts.* 1977. Natchez. 4to. dj. EX. $25.00

BURNSIDE, W. *Maynard Dixon.* 1974. Provo. 1/250. sgn. boxed. EX. $55.00

BURPEE, L. *Among the Canadian Alps.* 1914. NY. VG. $65.00

BURR, Fearing. *Field & Garden: Vegetables of America.* 1865. Boston. Tilton. Ils. 642 p. G. $25.00

BURR & HINTON. *Life of General Philip H. Sheridan.* 1888. Providence. Ils. 8vo. 445 p. G. G2. $30.00

BURRETT, W.R. *Pale Moon: Novel of SW.* 1957. London. dj. VG. $12.00

BURROUGH, H.E. *Tales of Vanished Land.* 1930. Boston/NY. Ils Simon. 1/1000. sgn. $47.50

BURROUGHS, Alan. *Limners & Likenesses: Three Centuries of American Painting.* 1936. Cambridge, MA. Ils 1st ed. 4to. 246 p. dj. T5. $95.00

BURROUGHS, E.R. *Apache Devil.* 1933. Grosset Dunlap. Ils Studley Burroughs. dj. VG. T5. $32.50

BURROUGHS, E.R. *Bandit of Hell's Bend.* nd. Grosset Dunlap. fair. $15.00

BURROUGHS, E.R. *Bandit of Hell's Bend.* 1925. Grosset Dunlap. EX. $25.00

BURROUGHS, E.R. *Bandit of Hell's Bend.* 1925. NY. dj. VG. T5. $22.50

BURROUGHS, E.R. *Beasts of Tarzan.* 1916. Chicago. 1st ed. VG. B2. $47.50

BURROUGHS, E.R. *Beasts of Tarzan.* 1916. NY. Burt. dj. VG. $27.00

BURROUGHS, E.R. *Carson of Venus.* 1939. Tarzana. 1st ed. dj. $150.00

BURROUGHS, E.R. *Cave Girl.* 1974. Canaveral Pr. dj. M. $25.00

BURROUGHS, E.R. *Escape on Venus.* 1946. Tarzana. Ils 1st ed. 347 p. dj. T5. $95.00

BURROUGHS, E.R. *Escape on Venus.* 1974. Canaveral Pr. dj. M. $25.00

BURROUGHS, E.R. *Eternal Lover.* 1925. Chicago. 1st ed. G. $40.00

BURROUGHS, E.R. *Fighting Man of Mars.* 1974. Canaveral Pr. dj. M. $27.00

BURROUGHS, E.R. *Girl From Hollywood.* 1923. Macauley. G. $35.00

BURROUGHS, E.R. *Girl From Hollywood.* 1923. NY. 1st ed. EX. $65.00

BURROUGHS, E.R. *Gods of Mars.* 1974. Canaveral Pr. dj. M. $30.00

BURROUGHS, E.R. *I Am a Barbarian.* 1967. Tarzana. 1st ed. dj. EX. $60.00

BURROUGHS, E.R. *Jungle Girl.* 1933. London. 1st ed. dj. G. $40.00

BURROUGHS, E.R. *Jungle Girl.* 1933. London. 1st ed. dj. VG. $85.00

BURROUGHS, E.R. *Jungle Tales of Tarzan.* 1919. Chicago. 1st ed. orange cloth. G. T1. $85.00

BURROUGHS, E.R. *Jungle Tales of Tarzan.* 1919. London. 1st ed. VG. $80.00

BURROUGHS, E.R. *Lad & the Lion.* 1938. Tarzana. 1st ed. G. $175.00

BURROUGHS, E.R. *Land of Terror.* 1944. Tarzana. 1st ed. 319 p. dj. G. scarce. T5. $150.00

BURROUGHS, E.R. *Land of Terror.* 1963. Canaveral Pr. Ils Krenkel. 1st ed. $40.00

BURROUGHS, E.R. *Land That Time Forgot.* 1924. Chicago. 1st ed. VG. $45.00

BURROUGHS, E.R. *Land That Time Forgot.* 1946. Doubleday. dj. EX. $12.50

BURROUGHS, E.R. *Llana of Gathol.* 1948. Tarzana. Ils 1st ed. dj. EX. scarce. $125.00

BURROUGHS, E.R. *Llana of Gathol.* 1948. Tarzana. Ils 1st ed. 317 p. dj. VG. T5. $75.00

BURROUGHS, E.R. *Lost on Venus.* 1935. Tarzana. 318 p. dj. $45.00

BURROUGHS, E.R. *Mad King.* 1926. McClurg. 1st ed. G. $35.00

BURROUGHS, E.R. *Mastermind of Mars.* 1928. McClurg. G. $32.50

BURROUGHS, E.R. *Monster Men.* 1929. Chicago. 1st ed. VG. $60.00

BURROUGHS, E.R. *Moon Men.* 1975. Canaveral Pr. dj. M. $25.00

BURROUGHS, E.R. *Mucher.* Grosset Dunlap. reprint. VG. $15.00

BURROUGHS, E.R. *Oakdale Affair & the Rider.* 1937. Tarzana. 1st ed. VG. $75.00

BURROUGHS, E.R. *Odhams.* 1933. London. 1st ed. dj. $95.00

BURROUGHS, E.R. *Pellicidar.* 1923. Chicago. 1st ed. VG. $70.00

BURROUGHS, E.R. *Pirates of Venus.* 1934. Tarzana. Ils. 314 p. dj. VG. $225.00

BURROUGHS, E.R. *Pirates of Venus.* 1974. Canaveral Pr. dj. M. $25.00

BURROUGHS, E.R. *Princess of Mars.* 1952. London. Methuen. dj. VG. $12.50

BURROUGHS, E.R. *Return of Tarzan.* 1915. Chicago. 1st ed. VG. $150.00

BURROUGHS, E.R. *Return of Tarzan.* 1915. McClurg. 1st ed. G. $75.00

BURROUGHS, E.R. *Return of Tarzan.* 1967. Ballantine. 3rd ed. pb. G. P1. $3.25

BURROUGHS, E.R. *Savage Pellucidar.* 1963. Canaveral Pr. 1st ed. dj. EX. $50.00

BURROUGHS, E.R. *Son of Tarzan.* 1917. Grosset Dunlap. dj. G. $35.00

BURROUGHS, E.R. *Son of Tarzan.* 1941. Grosset Dunlap. dj. VG. $25.00

BURROUGHS, E.R. *Swords of Mars.* 1936. Tarzana. dj. VG. $25.00

BURROUGHS, E.R. *Tales of Three Planets.* 1974. Canaveral Pr. dj. M. $95.00

BURROUGHS, E.R. *Tarzan & Golden Lion.* 1923. Grosset Dunlap. dj. $35.00

BURROUGHS, E.R. *Tarzan & Jewels of Opar.* 1918. Chicago. McClurg. 1st ed. VG. $85.00

BURROUGHS, E.R. *Tarzan & the Castaways.* 1975. Canaveral Pr. Ils Frazetta. dj. M. $50.00

BURROUGHS, E.R. *Tarzan & the City of Gold.* 1954. Racine. Whitman. 282 p. pb. $4.00

BURROUGHS, E.R. *Tarzan & the Forbidden City.* 1938. Tarzana. Ils John Burroughs. 315 p. dj. $175.00

BURROUGHS, E.R. *Tarzan & the Foreign Legion.* 1947. Tarzana. Ils 1st ed. dj. EX. $75.00

BURROUGHS, E.R. *Tarzan & the Foreign Legion.* 1947. Tarzana. Ils 1st ed. 314 p. dj. VG. T5. $65.00

BURROUGHS, E.R. *Tarzan & the Jewels of Opar.* nd. Grosset Dunlap. dj. VG. $30.00

BURROUGHS, E.R. *Tarzan & the Jewels of Opar.* 1918. Chicago. 1st ed. EX. $100.00

BURROUGHS, E.R. *Tarzan & the Leopard Men.* 1935. Tarzana. frontis by St. John. 332 p. dj. $350.00

BURROUGHS, E.R. *Tarzan & the Leopard Men.* 1935. Tarzana. 1st ed. Grosset Dunlap dj. VG. $90.00

BURROUGHS, E.R. *Tarzan & the Lion Man.* 1934. Tarzana. 318 p. dj. $22.50

BURROUGHS, E.R. *Tarzan & the Lost Empire.* 1929. NY. 1st ed. orange A bdg. $65.00

BURROUGHS, E.R. *Tarzan & the Madman.* 1964. Canaveral Pr. 1st ed. dj. EX. $100.00

BURROUGHS, E.R. *Tarzan & the Madman.* 1974. Canaveral Pr. dj. M. $50.00

BURROUGHS, E.R. *Tarzan at the Earth's Core.* 1922. Chicago. 277 p. $200.00

BURROUGHS, E.R. *Tarzan at the Earth's Core.* 1929. Tarzana. 301 p. dj. $225.00

BURROUGHS, E.R. *Tarzan at the Earth's Core.* 1962. Canaveral Pr. Ils Frazetta. 1st ed. dj. M. $100.00

BURROUGHS, E.R. *Tarzan of the Apes.* 1964. Racine. Whitman. 285 p. pb. $3.50

BURROUGHS, E.R. *Tarzan of the Apes.* 1966. Ballantine. 3rd ed. pb. VG. P1. $6.00

BURROUGHS, E.R. *Tarzan the Invincible.* c 1930. Tarzana. 1st ed. VG. $50.00

BURROUGHS, E.R. *Tarzan the Untamed.* 1920. Chicago. 1st ed. VG. $50.00

BURROUGHS, E.R. *Tarzan the Untamed.* 1920. McClurg. 1st ed. EX. $75.00

BURROUGHS, E.R. *Tarzan Triumphant.* 1932. Tarzana. Ils. 318 p. dj. VG. $175.00

BURROUGHS, E.R. *Tarzan's Quest.* 1936. Tarzana. 318 p. dj. VG. $110.00

BURROUGHS, E.R. *Thurvia, Maid of Mars.* 1920. Chicago. 1st ed. 256 p. recased. G. T5. $22.50

BURROUGHS, E.R. *Thurvia, Maid of Mars.* 1920. Grosset Dunlap. Ils. brown cloth. $30.00

BURROUGHS, E.R. *Thurvia, Maid of Mars.* 1951. London. Methuen. dj. VG. $12.50

BURROUGHS, E.R. *Thurvia, Maid of Mars.* 1969. Ballantine. pb. $10.00

BURROUGHS, E.R. *Thurvia, Maid of Mars.* 1969. Ballantine. 3rd print. VG. $10.00

BURROUGHS, E.R. *Warlord of Mars.* Sept., 1919. McClurg. fair. $25.00

BURROUGHS, E.R. *Warlord of Mars.* 1919. McClurg. 1st ed. 1st issue. 296 p. VG. $50.00

BURROUGHS, John. *Burrough's Complete Works.* 1921. Houghton. 12 vols. EX. M2. $75.00

BURROUGHS, John. *In the Catskills.* 1910. Houghton. 1st ed. VG. $25.00

BURROUGHS, John. *Pepacton.* 1881. Boston. 1st ed. VG. $55.00

BURROUGHS, John. *Wake-Robin.* 1871. Hurd Houghton. 1st ed. 1st issue. EX. $75.00

BURROUGHS, John. *Winter Sunshine.* 1917. Houghton. 241 p. M2. $5.00

BURROUGHS, John. *Writings of John Burroughs.* 1966. NY. 23 vols. green bdg. $95.00

BURROUGHS, Marie. *Marie Burroughs' Art Portfolio of Stage Celebrities.* 1894. Chicago. Marquis. 20 portrait photos. wraps. $40.00

BURROUGHS, W.S. *Book of Breething.* 1975. Blue Wind. 1st ed. sgn. wraps. $30.00

BURROUGHS, W.S. *Book of Breething.* 1980. Blue Wind. 1/175. sgn/#d. M. $65.00

BURROUGHS, W.S. *Cities of the Red Night.* 1981. NY. 1st Am ed. dj. VG. $25.00

BURROUGHS, W.S. *Early Routines.* 1981. Cadmus. Ils Hockney. 1/26. sgns. EX. $175.00

BURROUGHS, W.S. *Junkie.* 1964. Ace. 1st Separate ed. wraps. EX. $25.00

BURROUGHS, W.S. *Naked Lunch.* 1959. Paris. 1st ed. wraps. M. $125.00

BURROUGHS, W.S. *Nova Express.* 1964. Grove. dj. EX. $25.00

BURROUGHS, W.S. *Place of Dead Roads.* 1984. NY. 1/300. sgn. slipcase. M. $100.00

BURROUGHS, W.S. *Queer.* 1985. Viking. 1st ed. M1. $25.00

BURROUGHS, W.S. *Soft Machine.* 1966. NY. 1st Am ed. dj. EX. $40.00

BURROUGHS, W.S. *Soft Machine.* 1966. NY. 1st Am ed. dj. VG. $25.00

BURROUGHS, W.S. *Soft Machine.* 1967. NY. Evergreen. 1st ed. wraps. EX. $15.00

BURROUGHS, W.S. *Speed.* 1981. NY. 1st HrdCvr ed. dj. EX. $25.00

BURROUGHS, W.S. *Ticket That Exploded.* 1962. Paris. 1st ed. sgn. dj. wraps. M. $250.00

BURROUGHS, W.S. *Ticket That Exploded.* 1967. NY. 1st ed. dj. EX. $35.00

BURROUGHS, W.S. *Tornado Alley.* 1989. Ils Wilson. 1/100. sgn. black bdg. dj. M. $75.00

BURROUGHS, W.S. *Wild Boys.* 1971. NY. Grove. 1st ed. dj. EX. $12.00

BURROUGHS & GATEWOOD. *Sidetripping.* 1975. NY. photos. sgns. wraps. EX. $90.00

BURROUGHS & GYSIN. *Third Mind.* 1978. NY. dj. EX. $35.00

BURROW, J.A. *Reading of Sir Gawain & the Green Knight.* 1966. London. 2nd imp. dj. VG. C1. $6.00

BURROWS, Abe. *Honest Abe.* 1980. Boston. 1st ed. sgn. dj. $10.00

BURROWS, Larry. *Compassionate Photographer.* 1972. Time Life. slipcase. boxed. EX. $50.00

BURSIL, Henry. *Hand Shadows To Be Thrown Upon the Wall.* 1859. London. Ils 2nd ed. EX. $150.00

BURT, Struthers. *Diary of Dude Wrangler.* 1924. Scribner. G. $35.00

BURT, Struthers. *Powder River.* 1938. Ils 1st ed. index. 389 p. dj. M. K1. $14.50

BURT, W.H. *Field Guide to Mammals.* 1961. Houghton. Ils. maps. 200 p. VG. M2. $6.00

BURTIS, Thomson. *Rex Lee's Mysterious Flight.* 1930. Grosset Dunlap. 12mo. 247 p. VG. $15.00

BURTON, Clarence. *When Detroit Was Young.* nd. Detroit. Burton Abstract Tile Co. fair. $6.00

BURTON, E.M. *Charleston Furniture, 1700-1825.* 1955. Charleston. 1st ed. VG. $18.00

BURTON, J. *Black Jack Christian: Outlaw.* 1967. Pr of Territorian. 42 p. EX. M2. $25.00

BURTON, J.A. *Birds of the Tropics.* 1973. Bounty. Ils. 128 p. dj. EX. M2. $5.00

BURTON, J.A. *Rare Mammals of the World.* 1988. Greene. Ils 1st Am ed. 240 p. dj. M. M2. $25.00

BURTON, J.H. *Book Hunter.* 1862. NY. Sheldon. 411 p. VG. $55.00

BURTON, M. & R. *Encyclopedia of Insects & Arachnids.* 1984. Finsbury. photos. 4to. 252 p. dj. EX. M2. $24.00

BURTON, Maurice. *Animal Legends.* 1957. Coward McCann. Ils 1st Am ed. 318 p. dj. VG. M2. $5.00

BURTON, Maurice. *Encyclopedia of Animal Life.* 1986. Bonanza. Ils Revised ed. 4to. 640 p. dj. M2. $40.00

BURTON, Maurice. *Encyclopedia of Reptiles, Amphibians & Cold-Blooded Animals.* 1984. Finsbury. photos. 4to. 252 p. dj. EX. M2. $24.00

BURTON, Maurice. *Just Like an Animal.* 1978. NY. Scribner. Ils. 215 p. dj. VG. $8.00

BURTON, Maurice. *Systematic Dictionary of Mammals of the World.* 1962. Crowell. Ils. 307 p. dj. EX. M2. $12.00

BURTON, Miles. *Secret of High Eldersham.* c 1931. NY. Mystery League. 1st ed. VG. $8.00

BURTON, R. *Carnivores of Europe.* 1979. Batsford. Ils 1st ed. maps. dj. EX. M2. $20.00

BURTON, R. *Life & Death of Whales.* 1980. London. Deutsch. 185 p. dj. EX. M2. $5.00

BURTON, R.F. *Book of Thousand Nights & a Night.* nd. Burton Club. Ltd ed. VG. $250.00

BURTON, R.F. *City of the Saints.* 1963. NY. VG. $32.00

BURTON, R.F. *Kasidah of Haji Abdu El-Yezdi.* 1931. Phil. Ils Pogany. VG. J2. $25.00

BURTON, R.F. *Kasidah of Haji Abdu El-Yezdi.* 1937. Ltd Ed club. Ils/sgn Angelo. 12mo. slipcase. EX. $95.00

BURTON, Richard. *Historical Remarks on Cities of London & Westminister.* 1810. Westminister. New ed. 4to. $85.00

BURTON, Robert. *Anatomy of Melancholy.* 1821. London. 8vo. 2 vols. VG. G2. $79.00

BURTON, William. *General History of Porcelain.* 1921. NY. 32 color pls. 2 vols. VG. $50.00

BURTS, R.M. *Richard Irvine Manning & Progressive Movement in SC.* 1974. Columbia. SC U. 1st ed. dj. M. $15.00

BURWELL, Basil. *Our Brother the Sun.* 1954. NY. Hermitage House. 1st ed. 8vo. dj. $12.00

BUSBY, Roger. *Main Line Kill.* 1968. Walker. 1st ed. dj. EX. $7.00

BUSCH, Frederick. *Hawkes: Guide to His Fictions.* 1973. Syracuse. 1st ed. dj. EX. $15.00

BUSCH, Moritz. *Travels Between the Hudson & the MS, 1851-1852.* Lexington. reprint. dj. M. $15.00

BUSCH, Moritz. *Travels Between the Hudson & the MS, 1851-1852.* 1971. Lexington. 1st ed. 295 p. dj. VG. T5. $9.50

BUSCH, Niven. *Duel in the Sun.* 1947. Allen. dj. VG. $10.00

BUSH, Christopher. *Dead Man Twice.* 1930. Crime Club. 1st ed. VG. $20.00

BUSHNELL, A.S. *Report of the US Olympic Committee.* 1948. NY. photos. 387 p. G. T5. $22.50

BUSSON & LEROY. *Last Secrets of the Earth.* 1956. NY. 1st Am ed. dj. VG. $12.00

BUSTARD, R. *Sea Turtles: Their Natural History & Conservation.* 1972. London. Collins. Ils 1st ed. dj. EX. M2. $30.00

BUSWELL, Leslie. *Ambulance No. 10: Personal Letters From the Front.* 1916. Boston. Ils. 155 p. G. T5. $25.00

BUTIKOV, G. *St. Isaac's Cathedral.* 1974. Leningrad. dj. EX. J2. $25.00

BUTLER, B.F. *Butler's Book.* 1892. Boston. Ils 1st ed. 1154 p. T5. $15.00

BUTLER, B.F. *Butler's Book.* 1892. Ils. 1154 p. K1. $14.50

BUTLER, E.M. *Myth of the Magus.* 1948. Cambridge. dj. VG. C1. $12.50

BUTLER, Ivan. *Horror in the Cinema.* 1970. Zwemmer Barnes. 2nd ed. VG. P1. $7.50

BUTLER, Joseph. *Candle Holders in America, 1650-1900.* 1967. Crown. 1st ed. dj. VG. J2. $20.00

BUTLER, M.M. *Lakewood Story.* 1949. NY. Ils 1st ed. sgn. EX. $20.00

BUTLER, Octavia. *Dawn.* 1987. NY. Warner. UCP. wraps. M. $15.00

BUTLER, R.G. *On Distant Ground.* 1985. Knopf. 1st ed. dj. M. $10.00

BUTLER, R.O. *Wabash.* 1987. Knopf. 1st ed. dj. VG. $15.00

BUTLER, Samuel. *Hudibras.* 1744. Cambridge. Ils Hogarth. 8vo. 2 vols. VG. $150.00

BUTLER, W.F. *Wild N Land.* 1905. NY. Ltd ed. 1/210. VG. B2. $50.00

BUTLIN, M. *Paintings of J.M.W. Turner.* 1977. New Haven/London. 2 vols. djs. J2. $100.00

BUTRES, Julia. *Rhythm of the Redman.* 1930. NY. Ils 1st ed. dj. EX. $35.00

BUTTERFIELD, M.D. *First Lady: My Thirty Days Upstairs in White House.* 1964. Morrow. 1st ed. dj. xl. VG. M1. $15.00

BUTTERICK & OLSON. *Muthologos.* 1978. Four Seasons. 2 vols. $35.00

BUTTERWORTH, Elizabeth. *Parrots, Macaws & Cockatoos: Art of Elizabeth Butterworth.* 1988. Abrams. 29 pls. folio. EX. M2. $20.00

BUTTERWORTH, Hezekiah. *In Boyhood of Lincoln.* 1893. Appleton. 3rd ed. G. $12.00

BUTTITTA, Tony. *After the Good Gay Times.* 1974. Viking. 1st ed. dj. EX. T6. $15.00

BUTTLE, Myra. *Bitches Brew; or, Plot Against Bertrand Russell.* 1960. London. dj. EX. $10.00

BUTTRE, L.C. *American Portrait Gallery.* 1877. Buttre Pub. 2 vols. green leather. VG. $120.00

BUTTREE, J.M. *Rhythm of Redman in Song, Dance & Decoration.* 1930. NY. Ils Seton. 1st ed. EX. $85.00

BUTTREE, J.M. *Rhythm of Redman in Song, Dance & Decoration.* 1930. NY. Ils 1st ed. 280 p. dj. VG. B2. $47.50

BUTTS, Mary. *Imaginary Letters.* 1928. Paris. Ils/inscr Cocteau. 1/250. $200.00

BUXTON, A. *Traveling Naturalist.* 1948. London. Collins. Ils. 224 p. dj. EX. M2. $20.00

BUXTON, D. *Travels in Ethiopia.* 1957. Benn. Ils 2nd ed. 176 p. dj. VG. M2. $23.00

BUXTORFFII, P.J. *Chaldaicum Talmudicum et Rabbinicum.* 1875. London/Phil. lg 8vo. 2 vols in 1. G. $135.00

BUYUKMIHCI, H.S. *Unexpected Treasure.* 1968. Evans. Ils 1st ed. 190 p. dj. EX. M2. $6.00

BYARS, William. *American Commoner: Life & Times of Richard Parks Bland.* 1900. St. Louis. photos. G. $50.00

BYCHOWSKY, B.E. *Monogenetic Trematodes: Their Systematics & Phylogeny.* 1961. Am Inst Biol. Ils. 4to. 627 p. EX. M2. $45.00

BYERS, Arley. *Bent, Zigzag & Crooked.* 1974. Sycamore Valley, OH. 1st ed. T5. $65.00

BYINGTON, M.F. *Homestead: Households of a Mill Town.* 1910. NY. Russell Sage. 1st ed. 8vo. VG. $75.00

BYNE, M.S. *Forgotten Shrines of Spain.* 1926. Phil. Ils. map. TEG. VG. $65.00

BYRD, Armanda. *Reveries of a Homesteader.* 1916. Denver. Smith Brooks. Ils. 20 p. wraps. A3. $40.00

BYRD, Cecil. *Bibliography of IL Imprints, 1814-1858.* 1966. Chicago. VG. $28.00

BYRD, Donn. *Little America.* 1930. Putnam. 1st ed. VG. $25.00

BYRD, R.E. *Alone.* 1938. NY. Putnam. 1st ed. VG. $15.00

BYRD, R.E. *Discovery.* 1935. NY. 1st ed. VG. $15.00

BYRD, R.E. *Skyward.* 1928. NY. Ils 1st ed. 359 p. dj. VG. T5. $32.50

BYRD, R.E. *Skyward.* 1981. Chicago. Lakeside Classic. 382 p. EX. M2. $22.00

BYRNE. *Field of Honor.* 1929. NY/London. 1/500. sgn Dorothea Byrne. EX. $35.00

BYRNES, J.F. *All in One Lifetime.* 1958. NY. Harper. 1st ed. inscr/sgn. VG. $15.00

BYRNES, J.F. *Speaking Frankly.* 1947. Harper. 1st ed. presentation. dj. $45.00

BYRNES, James B. *Artist As a Collector.* 1975. 96 p. stiff paper wraps. D2. $28.50

BYRNES, Thomas. *Professional Criminals of America.* 1895. NY. Ils. photos. 402 p. G. $85.00

BYRON, Donn. *Gun Marks.* 1979. Crowell. 1st ed. dj. VG. $28.00

BYRON, Lord. *Childe Harold's Pilgrimage.* 1841. London. Ils. with proof set pls. $355.00

BYRON, Lord. *Don Juan.* 1929. NY. Ils Austen. 4th print. dj. EX. J2. $30.00

BYRON, Lord. *Don Juan: Campion Edition.* 1924. London. Philpot. 1/25. TEG. VG. $125.00

BYRON, Lord. *Mazeppa: A Poem.* 1819. London. 1st ed. 2nd issue. G. $35.00

BYRON, Lord. *Sardanapolus; Two Foscari; Cain.* 1821. 1st ed. VG. $150.00

BYRON, Lord. *Siege of Corinth & Parisina.* 1816. London. orig wraps. scarce. $150.00

BYRON, Lord. *Works of Byron.* 1898-1904. London. Murray. 13 vols. TEG. VG. $150.00

C

CABARET-DUPATY, M. *Ovide, Les Metamorphoses Traduction Francaise de Gros.* 1862. Paris. $20.00

CABELL, J.B. *Eagle's Shadow: A Comedy.* 1923. NY. Review 1st ed. dj. EX. $55.00

CABELL, J.B. *Figures of Earth.* 1925. NY. Ils Frank Pape. dj. EX. $45.00

CABELL, J.B. *Jurgen: Comedy of Justice.* 1921. London. Ils Pape. 1/3000. gilt black bdg. $65.00

CABELL, J.B. *Ladies & Gentlemen.* 1934. 2nd print. VG. scarce. C1. $19.50

CABELL, J.B. *Lineage of Lichfield: Essay.* 1922. NY. 1st ed. 1/365. sgn. $75.00

CABELL, J.B. *Silver Stallion.* 1928. NY. Ils 1st ed. EX. $30.00

CABELL, J.B. *Silver Stallion.* 1928. NY. McBride. Ils Pape. 1st ed. M1. $45.00

CABELL, J.B. *Smirt.* 1934. NY. McBride. Ltd 1st ed. 1/153. sgn. EX. $100.00

CABELL, J.B. *Some of Us.* 1930. NY. 1/1295. sgn. VG. G1. $35.00

CABELL, J.B. *Something About Eve.* 1927. London. Bodley Head. Ils Pape. EX. $75.00

CABELL, J.B. *Something About Eve.* 1927. NY. 1st trade ed. 1/850. dj. EX. $50.00

CABELL, J.B. *Something About Eve.* 1929. NY. Ils 1st ed. EX. G1. $30.00

CABELL, J.B. *There Were Two Pirates.* 1946. NY. 1st Am ed. dj. VG. $25.00

CABELL, J.B. *There Were Two Pirates.* 1946. NY. 1st ed. sgn. dj. EX. $30.00

CABELL, J.B. *These Restless Heads: A Trilogy.* 1932. NY. 1st ed. 1/410. sgn. dj. slipcase. EX. $95.00

CABELL, J.B. *Way of Ecben.* 1929. NY. 1st ed. slipcase. G1. $35.00

CABELL, J.B. *Works of J.B. Cabell.* 1927. Storisende. 1/1590. 16 vols. green cloth. EX. $200.00

CABLE, G.W. *Creoles of LA.* 1884. Scribner. Ils 1st ed. 320 p. $125.00

CABLE, G.W. *Old Creole Days.* 1897. Scribner. 1st ed. VG. $50.00

CABLE, G.W. *Old Creole Days.* 1943. Heritage. Ils Cosgrove. EX. $17.50

CABLE, G.W. *Posson Jone & Pere Raphael.* 1900. Scribner. Ils Armstrong. 1st ed. VG. $15.00

CABOT, R.C. *Differential Diagnosis.* 1911. Phil. Saunders. 1st ed. VG. $50.00

CACKLER, Christian. *Recollections of an Old Settler.* 1964. Ravenna, OH. Ils 3rd ed. 60 p. wraps. VG. T5. $15.00

CACUTT, L. *British Fresh-Water Fishes: Story of Their Evolution.* 1979. Croom Helm. 25 photos. 202 p. EX. M2. $16.00

CADFRYN-ROBERTS, J. *Four Seasons of Sport.* 1960. London. 12 color pls. folio. $70.00

CADIEUX, C.L. *Coyotes: Predators & Survivors.* 1983. Stone Wall. photos. 233 p. dj. EX. M2. $19.00

CADILLAC & LIETTE. *W Country in the 17th C.* 1947. Donnelley. Lakeside Classic. A3. $40.00

CADIOT. *Exercises in Equine Surgery.* 1893. NY. Ils. EX. $18.00

CADWALLADER, Sylvanus. *Three Years With Grant.* 1955. 353 p. EX. J4. $10.00

CADWALLADER, Sylvanus. *Three Years With Grant.* 1955. Knopf. 1st ed. sgn Thomas. dj. EX. $28.00

CADY, Jack. *McDowell's Ghost.* 1982. Arbor House. 1st ed. dj. EX. $17.50

CAEN, Herb. *One Man's San Francisco.* 1976. Garden City. 1st ed. 8vo. 232 p. VG. $10.00

CAESAR, Julius. *Gallic Wars.* 1983. Heritage. sm quarto. slipcase. EX. $15.00

CAFKY, Morris. *Rails Around Gold Hill.* 1955. Denver. Ils 1st ed. map. 463 p. B2. $125.00

CAFKY, Morris. *Rails Around Gold Hill.* 1955. Ltd ed. 1/2750. sgn. 4to. 463 p. VG. $75.00

CAGE, John. *X: Writings 1979-1982.* 1983. CT. UCP. wraps. $35.00

CAGLE & MANSON. *Sea War in Korea.* 1957. Annapolis. Ils 1st ed. 555 p. dj. G. T5. $22.50

CAHALANE, V.H. *Mammals of N America.* 1964. Macmillan. Ils Jaques. 682 p. dj. EX. M2. $13.00

CAHN, William. *Good Night, Mrs. Calabash: Secret of Jimmy Durante.* 1963. Duell. 1st ed. dj. VG. J2. $10.00

CAHOON, Ida M. *History of the Cahoon Family.* nd. Cleveland. Ils. 47 p. G. T5. $35.00

CAIN, J.M. *Career in C Major.* 1986. NY. 1st ed. dj. EX. $15.00

CAIN, J.M. *Enchanted Isle.* 1985. NY. 1st ed. dj. EX. $15.00

CAIN, J.M. *Love's Lovely Counterfeit.* 1945. Tower. VG. $10.00

CAIN, Julien. *Lithographs of Chagall: 1962-1968. Vol. III.* 1969. Paris. Ils. 179 p. dj. D2. $550.00

CAINE, L.S. *Game Fish of the S & How To Catch Them.* 1935. Boston. Ils Lloyd. inscr. dj. EX. $50.00

CALBURN & KEMP. *Owls of S Africa.* 1987. Cape Town. Struik. 1st ed. dj. slipcase. M2. $80.00

CALDECOTT, Moyra. *Etheldreda.* 1987. 1st ed. pb. EX. C1. $8.00

CALDECOTT, Moyra. *Shadow on the Stones.* 1979. 1st Am ed. dj. EX. C1. $7.50

CALDECOTT, Randolph. *Bracebridge Hall.* 1887. London. AEG. G. $30.00

CALDECOTT, Randolph. *Caldecott's Picture Book.* c 1890s. London. EX. $75.00

CALDECOTT, Randolph. *Caldecott's Picture Book.* 1880. London. pls. 4to. VG. $50.00

CALDECOTT, Randolph. *Complete Collection of Randolph Caldecott's Contributions...* 1888. London. Evans. 1/1250. sgns. folio. dj. VG. $225.00

CALDECOTT, Randolph. *Fox Jumps Over the Parson's Gate.* nd. London. $25.00

CALDECOTT, Randolph. *Hey Diddle Picture Book.* c 1890s. London. VG. $75.00

CALDECOTT, Randolph. *Panjandrum Picture Book.* 1885. London. VG. $75.00

CALDECOTT, Randolph. *Randolph Caldecott's Graphic Pictures.* 1891. London. Complete ed. 1/1250. oblong 4to. G. $70.00

CALDECOTT, Randolph. *Some Aesop's Fables With Modern Instances.* 1883. London. Ils. 4to. VG. $55.00

CALDWELL, B.D. *Founders & Builders of Greensboro: 1808-1808.* 1925. Greensboro. xl. VG. $15.00

CALDWELL, Erskine. *All Out on the Road to Smolensk.* 1942. NY. 1st ed. dj. EX. $70.00

CALDWELL, Erskine. *Claudelle.* 1959. London. 1st ed. dj. VG. $40.00

CALDWELL, Erskine. *Close to Home.* 1962. NY. 1st ed. dj. EX. $25.00

CALDWELL, Erskine. *Courting of Susie Brown.* 1952. NY. 1st ed. dj. EX. $25.00

CALDWELL, Erskine. *God's Little Acre.* 1933. Viking. 1st ed. VG. $18.00

CALDWELL, Erskine. *House in Uplands.* 1946. NY. 1st ed. 238 p. dj. VG. T5. $32.50

CALDWELL, Erskine. *House in Uplands.* 1947. London. 1st ed. dj. VG. $50.00

CALDWELL, Erskine. *Jenny by Nature.* 1961. NY. 1st ed. dj. EX. $25.00

CALDWELL, Erskine. *Love & Money.* 1954. NY/Boston. 1st ed. dj. EX. $30.00

CALDWELL, Erskine. *Negro in the Well.* Oct., 1935. printed wraps. $10.00

CALDWELL, Erskine. *Poor Fool.* 1930. NY. Rariora. Ils Couard. 1/1000. dj. VG. $70.00

CALDWELL, Erskine. *Some American People.* 1935. NY. 1st ed. dj. VG. $55.00

CALDWELL, Erskine. *Southways.* 1938. NY. 1st ed. dj. EX. $55.00

CALDWELL, Erskine. *Sure Hand of God.* 1947. NY. 1st ed. dj. VG. $35.00

CALDWELL, Erskine. *Tenant Farmer.* 1935. Phalanx. 32 p. green wraps. VG. scarce. G2. $85.00

CALDWELL, Erskine. *Tobacco Road.* 1947. Modern Lib. 1st ed. dj. G. $25.00

CALDWELL, Erskine. *We Are the Living.* c 1953. NY/Boston. reprint. dj. EX. $20.00

CALDWELL, Steven. *Aliens in Space.* 1979. Crescent. dj. EX. $7.50

CALDWELL, Steven. *Worlds at War.* 1980. Crescent. VG. $5.00

CALDWELL & BOURKE-WHITE. *Say Is This the USA?* 1941. NY. VG. S2. $95.00

CALDWELL & BOURKE-WHITE. *Say Is This the USA?* 1941. NY. 1st ed. dj. VG. B2. $95.00

CALDWELL & LUNDEEN. *Do You Believe It?* 1934. NY. $17.50

CALEF, George. *Caribou & the Barren Lands.* 1981. Firefly. Ils. square 4to. 176 p. dj. EX. M2. $28.00

CALEF, George. *Caribou & the Barren Lands.* 1981. Ottawa. G. $20.00

CALHOON, R.M. *Loyalists in Revolutionary America: 1760-1781.* 1973. Harcourt Brace. 1st ed. 580 p. dj. EX. M2. $18.00

CALHOUN, F.B. *Miss Minerva & William Green Hill.* 1915. Chicago. Reilly Britton. 3rd Popular ed. $12.50

CALHOUN, F.B. *Miss Minerva & William Green Hill.* 1922. Reilly Lee. Ils. G. $12.00

CALHOUN, Ferdinand. *Pinzy Family in America.* nd. Atlanta. 176 p. xl. G. B1. $40.00

CALIC, Edouard. *Reinhard Heydrich.* 1982. NY. 1st ed. dj. VG. $10.00

CALISHER, Hortense. *Extreme Magic.* 1964. Little Brown. 1st ed. dj. EX. $25.00

CALISHER, Hortense. *Textures of Life.* 1963. Little Brown. 1st ed. dj. EX. $25.00

CALKINS, F. *Rocky Mountain Warden.* 1971. Knopf. 1st ed. 365 p. dj. EX. M2. $16.00

CALKINS & CURRAN. *In Canada's Wonderful N Land.* 1917. Putnam. Ils 2nd ed. maps. G. $35.00

CALLAGHAN, E.B. *Documentary History of State of NY.* 1849. Albany. Ils. maps. 4 vols. G. $250.00

CALLAGHAN, Morley. *Fine & Private Place.* 1975. Toronto. 1st ed. presentation. dj. EX. $45.00

CALLAGHAN, Morley. *More Joy in Heaven.* 1937. NY. 1st ed. dj. VG. B2. $22.50

CALLAGHAN, Morley. *That Summer in Paris.* 1963. NY. 1st ed. dj. VG. B2. $22.50

CALLAHAN, Harry. *Water's Edge.* 1980. Viking. dj. EX. $35.00

CALLANDER, C.L. *Surgical Anatomy.* 1933. Saunders. Ils. 1115 p. VG. $135.00

CALLAWAY, Nicholas. *GA O'Keeffe: One Hundred Flowers.* 1987. NY. Knopf. 1st ed. 100 pls. photos. dj. D2. $100.00

CALLAWAY. *Event-Related Brain Potential in Man.* 1978. 631 p. $55.00

CALLENDER, J.T. *Political Progress of Britain; or, Impartial History...* 1795. Phil. 3rd ed. $85.00

CALLOWAY, Cab. *Minnie the Moocher & Me.* 1976. Crowell. 1st ed. inscr. dj. VG. $20.00

CALMAN, W.T. *Life of Crustacea.* 1911. Methuen. Ils 1st ed. 289 p. VG. M2. $30.00

CALTHROP, D.C. *Diary of an 18th-C Garden.* c 1927. NY. 12mo. dj. VG. $16.00

CALTHROP, D.C. *English Costume.* 1907. London. Black. Ils author/Hollar/Dighton. EX. $150.00

CALVERT, Jesse. *History of Jonesville.* c 1970. nd. 1st ed. 39 p. wraps. $20.00

CALVINO, Italo. *Baron in the Trees.* 1959. Random House. 1st Am ed. dj. VG. $35.00

CALVINO, Italo. *Mr. Palomar.* 1985. Harcourt. 1st Am ed. dj. VG. $15.00

CALVINO, Italo. *Silent Mr. Palomar.* 1981. NY. Targ. 1/250. sgn. glassine dj. EX. $40.00

CALVOCORESSI, Richard. *Magritte.* 1979. Oxford. Phaidon. Ils. D2. $18.95

CAMBIAIRE, C.P. *Influence of Poe in France.* 1927. Stechert, NY. 1st ed. 8vo. VG. D1. $55.00

CAMDEN, Charles. *Autobiography of Charles Camden.* 1916. Philopolis. 1/50. VG. scarce. $150.00

CAMERON, Anne. *Stubby Amberchuck & the Holy Grail.* 1987. 1st ed. dj. M. C1. $9.50

CAMERON, Berl. *Cosmic Echelon.* 1952. Curtis. dj. VG. $8.50

CAMERON, Frank J. *Hungry Tiger.* 1964. NY. Ils 1st ed. 277 p. dj. VG. T5. $22.50

CAMERON, J.M. *Victorian Photographs of Famous Men & Fair Women.* 1973. Godine. reprint of 1926 ed. folio. dj. EX. $35.00

CAMERON, Kenneth. *Emerson the Essayist.* 1945. Raleigh. 1st ed. 1/150. 2 vols. VG. J2. $75.00

CAMERON, W.B. *War Trail of Big Bear.* 1927. Boston. photos. VG. $26.50

CAMERON & PARNALL. *Night Watchers.* 1978. Four Winds. Ils. 4to. 111 p. dj. EX. M2. $25.00

CAMFIELD, W.A. *Francis Picabia.* 1970. NY. 1st ed. wraps. EX. $25.00

CAMMELL, C.R. *Aleister Crowley.* 1951. London. 1st ed. 230 p. EX. $45.00

CAMP, Raymond. *Hunter's Encyclopedia.* 1948. Stackpole. 1st ed. EX. $40.00

CAMP, Raymond. *Hunting Trails.* 1961. Appleton. 1st ed. dj. VG. $15.00

CAMP, W.E. *World in Your Garden.* 1959. Nat Geog Soc. 2nd ed. dj. EX. $8.00

CAMPBELL, A.C. *Coral Reef.* 1976. Putnam. Ils. 4to. 128 p. dj. EX. M2. $14.00

CAMPBELL, Albert. *Report Upon the Pacific Wagon Roads.* 1859. 6 fld maps. 125 p. scarce. A3. $225.00

CAMPBELL, Arthur. *Siege*. 1956. London. 1st ed. 4th imp. dj. $10.00

CAMPBELL, D.J. *American Military Insignia, 1800-1851*. 1963. Ils. 124 p. EX. J4. $28.50

CAMPBELL, H.J. *Case for Mrs. Surratt*. 1943. Putnam. 272 p. EX. M2. $13.00

CAMPBELL, H.J. *Red Planet*. 1953. London. Panther Book. 1st ed. dj. VG. $12.50

CAMPBELL, J.W. *Cloak of Aesir*. 1952. Shasta. 1st ed. dj. VG. $35.00

CAMPBELL, J.W. *Incredible Planet*. 1949. Reading. 1st trade ed. dj. EX. $35.00

CAMPBELL, J.W. *Mightiest Machine*. 1947. Providence. 1st ed. dj. EX. $75.00

CAMPBELL, J.W. *Who Goes There?* 1948. Chicago. 1st ed. sgn. dj. VG. $65.00

CAMPBELL, John. *Superstitions of Highlands & Islands of Scotland*. 1900. MacLehose. 1st ed. VG. J2. $35.00

CAMPBELL, John. *Witchcraft & 2nd Sight in Highlands & Islands of Scotland*. 1902. MacLehose. 1st ed. VG. J2. $35.00

CAMPBELL, Joseph. *Masks of God*. 1959-1968. Viking. 1st ed. 4 vols. djs. J2. $100.00

CAMPBELL, Julie. *Rin Tin Tin's Rinty*. 1954. Whitman. EX. P1. $15.00

CAMPBELL, Marjorie. *McGillivray: Lord of the NW*. 1962. Clark Irwin. 1st ed. dj. J2. $15.00

CAMPBELL, N.R. *Modern Electrical Theory*. 1907. Cambridge. 1st ed. G. $35.00

CAMPBELL, Ramsey. *Ancient Images*. London. 1st ed. sgn. $50.00

CAMPBELL, Ramsey. *Dark Feast*. London. 1st ed. sgn. $50.00

CAMPBELL, Ramsey. *Demons by Daylight*. 1973. Arkham House. 1st ed. dj. EX. $22.50

CAMPBELL, Ramsey. *Scared Stiff*. 1987. Scream Pr. Ils Potter. 1st ed. sgn. $75.00

CAMPBELL, Sam. *How's Inky?* 1943. Bobbs Merrill. G. $4.00

CAMPBELL, Sandy. *Mrs. Joyce of Zurich & Mr. Forster of Kings*. 1989. Verona. 1/20. sgn Windham. slipcase. $50.00

CAMPBELL, Sheldon. *Lifeboats to Ararat*. 1978. Times. Ils. 240 p. VG. M2. $8.00

CAMPBELL, W.W. *Historical Sketch of Robin Hood & Captain Kidd*. 1853. NY. fair. $25.00

CAMPBELL & ROBINSON. *Skeleton Key to Finnegans' Wake*. 1944. NY. 1st ed. 1st issue dj. M. $35.00

CAMPBELL. *Campbell's Operative Orthopedics*. 1956. St. Louis. 2124 p. $75.00

CAMPEN, R.N. *Architecture of the W Reserve, 1800-1900*. 1971. Cleveland. Ils. 260 p. dj. VG. T5. $45.00

CAMPEN, R.N. *Outdoor Sculpture in OH*. 1980. Chagrin Falls. Ils 1st ed. 4to. 175 p. dj. VG. T5. $27.50

CAMPOS, Jules. *Sculpture of Jose de Creeft*. 1972. NY. Kennedy. Ils. 227 p. xl. D2. $65.00

CAMUS, Albert. *Collected Fiction of Albert Camus*. London. Hamilton. 1st ed. 2 djs. EX. $20.00

CAMUS, Albert. *Fall*. 1957. Knopf. 1st ed. dj. EX. $25.00

CANADY, John. *Lives of the Painters*. 1969. NY. Ils. 4 vols. slipcase. T1. $35.00

CANADY, John. *Lives of the Painters*. 1969. NY. Norton. 4 vols. D2. $45.00

CANBY, C. *Lincoln & Civil War: Profile & History*. 1960. Braziller. 416 p. dj. EX. M2. $10.00

CANDLER, A.D. *Revolutionary War Records of the State of GA*. 1908. Atlanta. 1st ed. 883 p. xl. G. $65.00

CANE, M. *Eloquent April*. 1971. NY. 1st ed. sgn. dj. EX. $15.00

CANFIELD, C. *Iron Will of Jefferson Davis*. 1981. Fairfax. Ils. maps. dj. M2. $10.00

CANFIELD, C. *Iron Will of Jefferson Davis*. 1981. Fairfax. Ils. 146 p. K1. $12.50

CANFIELD, Dorothy. *Seasoned Timber*. 1939. NY. Ils Honore. 1st ed. EX. $12.00

CANFIELD, E.B. *Notes on Naval Ordnance of American Civil War 1861-1865*. 1960. Am Ordnance Assn. 4to. 23 p. M2. $10.00

CANFIELD, E.B. *Notes on Naval Ordnance of American Civil War 1861-1865*. 1960. WA. Ils. 24 p. wraps. VG. T5. $17.50

CANFIELD, Mary C. *Lackeys of the Moon: Play in One Act*. 1923. NY. 1st ed. VG. C1. $5.00

CANIFF, Milton. *Male Call*. 1945. NY. VG. $17.50

CANNING, Victor. *Circle of the Gods*. 1979. London. 1st ed. dj. M. C1. $11.00

CANNING, Victor. *Circle of the Gods*. 1979. London. 2nd print. dj. M. C1. $9.50

CANNING, Victor. *Crimson Chalice*. pb. VG. C1. $3.50

CANNING, Victor. *Crimson Chalice*. 1978. 1st Am ed. dj. VG. scarce. C1. $14.50

CANNING, Victor. *Dragon Tree*. 1958. Sloane. 1st ed. dj. VG. $10.00

CANNING, Victor. *Python Project*. 1968. Morrow. 1st ed. dj. EX. $15.00

CANNING, Victor. *Raven's Wind*. 1983. 1st Am ed. dj. EX. C1. $10.00

CANNON, D.D. *Flags of Confederacy*. 1988. Ils. 91 p. M. J4. $8.50

CANNON, H.D. *Box Seat Over Hell*. 1985. San Antonio. Ils. 138 p. wraps. M. T5. $18.00

CANNON, H.G. *Evolution of Living Things*. 1958. Manchester U. 180 p. dj. EX. M2. $10.00

CANNON, R. *Sea of Cortez*. 1973. Sunset. dj. VG. $28.00

CANOT, Theodore. *Adventures of an African Slaver*. 1928. Boni. Ils Covarrubias. 376 p. dj. G. $25.00

CANTIN, Eugene. *Yukon Summer*. 1974. Chronicle. photos. map. 198 p. dj. VG. M2. $9.00

CANTOR, Eddie. *Caught Short*. 1929. NY. Ils 1st ed. dj. VG. $15.00

CANTOR & FREEDMAN. *Ziegfeld: A King*. 1934. photos. dj. VG. scarce. $100.00

CANTWELL, R. *Alexander Wilson: Naturalist & Pioneer*. 1961. Lippincott. Ils 1st ed. 4to. 319 p. EX. M2. $30.00

CANU & BASSLER. *Bryozoa of the Philippine Region*. 1929. US Nat Mus. 94 pl. 685 p. EX. M2. $45.00

CANU & BASSLER. *Bryozoan Fauna of the Galapagos Islands*. 1930. US Nat Mus. 14 pl. 78 p. EX. M2. $13.00

CANU & BASSLER. *Fossil & Recent Bryozoa From the Gulf of Mexico Region*. 1928. US Nat Mus. 33 pl. cloth bound. EX. M2. $25.00

CANU & BASSLER. *N American Later Tertiary & Quaternary Bryozoa*. 1923. US Nat Mus. 47 pls. 294 p. EX. M2. $35.00

CANU & BASSLER. *Synopsis of American Tertiary Bryozoa*. 1917. US Nat Mus. 6 pl. EX. M2. $13.00

CAPA, Cornell. *Margin of Life*. 1974. Grossman. dj. VG. $15.00

CAPA, Robert. *Battle of Waterloo Road.* 1941. Random House. dj. VG. $50.00

CAPA, Robert. *Death in the Making.* 1938. Covici Friede. 1st ed. 4to. VG. $50.00

CAPA, Robert. *Images of War.* 1964. Grossman. 1st ed. dj. VG. $30.00

CAPA, Robert. *Russian Journal.* 1948. Viking. dj. VG. $65.00

CAPA, Robert. *Slightly Out of Focus.* 1947. Holt. 1st ed. VG. $30.00

CAPA, Robert. *Slightly Out of Focus.* 1947. Holt. 1st ed. 8vo. dj. EX. $45.00

CAPART, J. *Documents Pour Servir a l'Etude de l'Art Egyptien. Vol. 1.* 1927. Paris. 1/612. $175.00

CAPE, C.B. *Stronghold of Hinduism.* 1910. London. 41 photos. G. rare. $40.00

CAPEN, O.B. *Country Homes of Famous Americans.* 1905. NY. Ils 1st ed. folio. 176 p. fair. $30.00

CAPON, Paul. *World at Bay.* 1954. Winston. 1st ed. G. P1. $6.00

CAPON, R.F. *Capon on Cooking.* 1983. Boston. 1st ed. dj. $8.00

CAPONIGRO, Paul. *Wise Silence.* 1983. NY. dj. EX. $50.00

CAPOTE, Truman. *Breakfast at Tiffany's.* 1958. Random House. 1st ed. dj. VG. $50.00

CAPOTE, Truman. *Christmas Memory.* 1966. NY. Ltd ed. 1/600. sgn. boxed. EX. $75.00

CAPOTE, Truman. *Christmas Memory.* 1966. Random House. 1st trade ed. slipcase. EX. $30.00

CAPOTE, Truman. *Dogs Bark.* 1973. NY. 1st ed. dj. EX. $30.00

CAPOTE, Truman. *Grass Harp.* 1951. NY. 1st ed. sgn. dj. EX. $125.00

CAPOTE, Truman. *Grass Harp.* 1951. Random House. 1st ed. 1st bdg. dj. EX. $100.00

CAPOTE, Truman. *Local Color.* 1950. Random House. 1st ed. 8vo. dj. EX. $75.00

CAPOTE, Truman. *Muses Are Heard.* 1956. Random House. 1st ed. sgn. dj. $100.00

CAPOTE, Truman. *Music for Chameleons.* 1980. Random House. 1st ed. 2nd print. dj. EX. $12.50

CAPOTE, Truman. *One Christmas.* 1983. NY. 1st ed. 1/500. sgn. boxed. EX. $200.00

CAPOTE, Truman. *Other Voices Other Rooms.* c 1948. NY. Random House. 3rd print. $20.00

CAPOTE, Truman. *Other Voices Other Rooms.* 1948. NY. 1st ed. dj. M. $85.00

CAPOTE, Truman. *Tree of Night & Other Stories.* 1949. NY. 1st ed. dj. EX. $75.00

CAPOTE, Truman. *Tree of Night & Other Stories.* 1949. NY. 1st ed. dj. G. $55.00

CAPRON, F.H. *Highway to Heaven & Byway to Nowhere.* 1937. London. $10.00

CAPUTO, Philip. *Del Corso's Gallery.* 1983. Harper Row. dj. VG. $12.00

CAPUTO, Philip. *Horn of Africa.* 1980. NY. 1st ed. 1/200. sgn/#d. slipcase. EX. $55.00

CAPUTO, Philip. *Indian Country.* 1987. NY. 1st ed. sgn. dj. EX. $22.00

CARAS, R. *Animals in Their Places: Tales From the Natural World.* 1987. Sierra Club. 1st ed. EX. M2. $16.00

CARAS, R. *Custer Wolf: Biography of an American Renegade.* 1966. Little Brown. Ils. 175 p. dj. VG. M2. $12.00

CARAS, R. *Dangerous to Man.* 1964. Chilton. Ils 1st ed. 433 p. dj. EX. M2. $15.00

CARAS, R. *Monarch of Deadman Bay: Life & Death of a Kodiak Bear.* 1969. Little Brown. Ils 1st ed. 195 p. dj. EX. M2. $13.00

CARAS, R. *Roger Caras Treasury.* 1966-1969. Outdoor Life. 551 p. dj. EX. M2. $12.00

CARAS, R. *Venomous Animals of the World.* 1974. Prentice Hall. Ils 1st ed. 4to. 362 p. dj. EX. M2. $17.00

CARCEAU, Jean. *Dear Mr. G.* 1961. Little Brown. 1st ed. dj. VG. J2. $20.00

CARD, Orson Scott. *Capitol.* 1979. Baronet. 1st ed. wraps. EX. $40.00

CARD, Orson Scott. *Planet Called Treason.* nd. Book Club. dj. VG. P1. $4.50

CARD, Orson Scott. *Planet Called Treason.* nd. Book Club. sgn. dj. VG. P1. $10.00

CARD, Orson Scott. *Songmaster.* nd. Book Club. dj. VG. P1. $4.50

CARD, Orson Scott. *Unaccompanied Sonata.* 1981. Dial. 1st ed. dj. G. $12.50

CARD, Orson Scott. *Wyrms.* 1987. Arbor House. 1st ed. dj. EX. P1. $16.95

CARDANO, Hieronymi. *De Rerum Varietate Libri XVIII.* 1580. Lugduni. 12mo. 881 p. $400.00

CARELL, Paul. *Foxes of the Desert.* 1960. London. 1st ed. 370 p. dj. VG. B2. $42.50

CARELL, Paul. *Scorched Earth.* 1970. Boston. 1st Am ed. dj. EX. $50.00

CAREY, A.M. *American Firearms Makers.* 1953. Crowell. Standard 1st ed. G. $32.00

CAREY, M. *Beads & Beadwork of E & S Africa.* 1986. Shire, England. Ils 1st ed. 64 p. M2. $14.00

CAREY, M.V. *Memoirs of a Murder Man.* 1930. Doubleday. 1st ed. VG. P1. $18.25

CAREY, M.V. *Mystery of the Singing Serpent.* nd. Random House. EX. P1. $7.50

CAREY, Mary. *Walt Disney's Sword in the Stone.* 1963. Whitman. 1st/only ed. scarce. VG. C1. $14.00

CAREY, Peter. *Fat Man in History & Other Stories.* 1908. Random House. 1st ed. dj. VG. $15.00

CAREY, R.N. *Herb of Grace.* 1901. Lippincott. 1st ed. $12.00

CARISELLA & RYAN. *Who Killed the Red Baron.* 1969. Wakefield. 1st ed. presentation. sgns. dj. B2. $40.00

CARLETON, George. *Life & Adventures of Private Miles O'Reilly.* 1864. Ils. K1. $21.00

CARLEY. *MN in the Civil War.* 1961. MN. 1st ed. dj. EX. $12.50

CARLISLE, CLEVELAND & WOOD. *Modern Wonder Book of the Air.* 1945. Phil. Ils 1st ed. 316 p. dj. VG. T5. $22.50

CARLON, Patricia. *See Nothing...Say Nothing.* 1968. Walker. 1st ed. dj. VG. P1. $7.00

CARLSON, E.W. *Recognition of Edgar A. Poe.* 1966. MI U. 1st ed. black cloth. VG. D1. $11.00

CARLTON & HARDY. *Tumble-Down Pictures.* c 1900. NY. Ils. VG. $55.00

CARLYLE, Thomas. *Complete Works.* 1897. NY. 1st ed. 16 vols. $150.00

CARLYLE, Thomas. *French Revolution.* 1851. Leipzig. Tauchnitz. 3 vols. VG. $45.00

CARMAN, Bliss. *Ballads & Lyrics.* 1923. Toronto. 1st ed. blue cloth. VG. $45.00

CARMAN, Bliss. *Kinship of Nature.* 1903. Boston. 1st ed. 8vo. VG. $30.00

CARMAN, W.Y. *British Military Uniforms From Contemporary Pictures.* 1957. London. 1st ed. photos. dj. VG. $35.00

CARMAN & MILLER. *Roentgen Diagnosis of Diseases of Alimentary Canal.* 1917. Phil. Ils. 8vo. 558 p. VG. P3. $45.00

CARMER, Carl. *Dark Trees to the Wind.* 1949. NY. Sloane. 1st ed. inscr. 8vo. VG. $27.00

CARMER, Carl. *French Town: Book of Poems.* 1968. NY. McKay. facsimile of 1929 ed. sgns. EX. $25.00

CARMER, Carl. *Susquehanna.* 1955. NY. 1st ed. dj. VG. B2. $25.00

CARMER & CARMEL. *Hurricane's Children.* 1937. NY. presentation. sgns. dj. G. B2. $17.50

CARMICHAEL, B. *Incredible Collectors' Weird Antiques & Odd Hobbies.* 1975. NJ. $15.00

CARMICHAEL, Henry. *Condemned.* 1967. Collins Crime Club. 1st ed. dj. P1. $5.00

CARMICHAEL, Hoagy. *Sometimes I Wonder.* 1965. Farrar Straus. 1st print. dj. M. $65.00

CARMICHAEL, Hoagy. *Stardust Road.* 1946. NY. 1st ed. dj. VG. B2. $17.50

CARMICHAEL, Jim. *Do-It-Yourself Gunsmithing.* 1977. Outdoor Life. Ils. sm 4to. 372 p. dj. EX. $8.50

CARNAC, Carol. *Long Shadows.* 1958. Collins Crime Club. 1st ed. VG. P1. $12.50

CARNAHAN, A.E. *Pyeatts & Carnahans of Old Cane Hill.* 1954. WA Co Hist Soc. 4to. 41 p. EX. M2. $10.00

CARNEAL, G. *Conqueror of Space.* 1930. NY. 1st ed. 296 p. $50.00

CARNEGIE, Andrew. *Problems of Today.* 1908. 1st ed. presentation. $75.00

CARNEGIE, Andrew. *Triumphant Democracy.* 1891. NY. sgn. VG. $80.00

CARNEGIE, Dale. *Five-Minute Biographies.* 1937. NY. 8vo. inscr. EX. $18.00

CARNEGIE, Dale. *Five-Minute Biographies.* 1949. Perma P35. VG. P1. $4.75

CARO, Robert. *Power Broker.* 1974. Knopf. 1st ed. dj. EX. $45.00

CARPENTER, Don. *Hard Rain Falling.* 1969. NY. 1st ed. dj. VG. $8.00

CARPENTER, F.B. *Six Months at White House With Lincoln.* 1961. Century. reprint of 1866 ed. EX. $16.00

CARPENTER, F.G. *AK: Our N Wonderland.* 1923. Ils 1st ed. 2 fld maps. EX. $18.00

CARPENTER, F.G. *Asia.* 1897. Am Book Co. Ils. 307 p. EX. $5.00

CARPENTER, Humphrey. *Letters of J.R.R. Tolkien.* 1981. 1st ed. dj. M. C1. $9.50

CARPENTER, K.E. *Life in Inland Waters With Especial Reference to Animals.* 1928. Macmillan. Ils. 267 p. EX. M2. $17.00

CARPENTER, Richard. *Robin of Sherwood.* 1985. Penguin. pb. M. C1. $4.00

CARPENTER & ARTHUR. *History of OH From Its Earliest Settlement to Present Time.* 1854. Phil. 1st ed. VG. T5. $125.00

CARPENTER. *History of American Schoolbooks.* 1963. PA. dj. VG. $20.00

CARPENTIER. *Kingdom of This World.* Ltd Ed Club. slipcase. M. B3. $400.00

CARPOZI, George. *Gary Cooper Story.* 1970. Arlington Heights. 1st ed. dj. J2. $10.00

CARR, A. *Everglades.* 1973. Time Life. photos. map. 194 p. EX. M2. $8.00

CARR, A. *Reptiles.* 1963. Time Life. photos. 4to. 192 p. EX. M2. $14.00

CARR, A. *So Excellent a Fish: Natural History of Sea Turtles.* 1967. Nat Hist Pr. 45 photos. map. 248 p. EX. M2. $15.00

CARR, A. *World & William Walker.* 1963. Harper. 1st ed. dj. M. $23.00

CARR, Charles. *Colonists of Space.* 1954. Ward Lock. dj. VG. P1. $18.25

CARR, Charles. *Salamander War.* 1955. Ward Lock. dj. EX. P1. $18.25

CARR, Clark. *Stephen A. Douglas: Life, Public Services, Patriotism...* 1909. McClurg. VG. $45.00

CARR, D.E. *Deadly Feast of Life.* 1971. Doubleday. 396 p. dj. EX. M2. $10.00

CARR, Emily. *Growing Pains: Autobiography of Emily Carr.* 1946. Oxford. 1st ed. VG. J2. $17.50

CARR, J. *Pioneer Days in CA Times.* 1891. 1st ed. G. $250.00

CARR, J.D. *Below Suspicion.* nd. Book Club. P1. $4.00

CARR, J.D. *Below Suspicion.* 1949. Harper. 1st ed. dj. VG. P1. $27.50

CARR, J.D. *Blind Barber.* 1934. Harper. 1st ed. VG. $20.00

CARR, J.D. *Bride of Newgate.* nd. BOMC. dj. VG. P1. $5.00

CARR, J.D. *Bride of Newgate.* 1950. Harper. 1st ed. VG. P1. $20.00

CARR, J.D. *Bride of Newgate.* 1955. Hamish Hamilton. 1st ed. VG. P1. $40.00

CARR, J.D. *Captain Cut-Throat.* 1955. Harper. 1st ed. dj. EX. P1. $80.00

CARR, J.D. *Captain Cut-Throat.* 1955. Harper. 1st ed. dj. VG. $25.00

CARR, J.D. *Dark of the Moon.* 1967. Harper. 1st ed. dj. xl. P1. $7.50

CARR, J.D. *Dead Man's Knock.* nd. Book Club. dj. xl. P1. $4.00

CARR, J.D. *Dead Man's Knock.* 1958. Harper. Book Club. inscr. dj. VG. $23.00

CARR, J.D. *Death Turns the Tables.* nd. Collier. VG. P1. $9.25

CARR, J.D. *Demoniacs.* 1962. NY. 1st ed. dj. EX. $22.50

CARR, J.D. *Devil in Velvet.* 1951. Harper. 1st ed. dj. $18.00

CARR, J.D. *Emperor's Snuffbox.* 1946. Books Inc. P1. $15.00

CARR, J.D. *He Who Whispers.* 1946. Harper. 1st ed. dj. $40.00

CARR, J.D. *He Who Whispers.* 1971. Hamish Hamilton. dj. xl. P1. $7.50

CARR, J.D. *In Spite of Thunder.* nd. Book Club. dj. G. P1. $4.00

CARR, J.D. *It Walks by Night.* 1930. Harper. 4th ed. VG. P1. $50.00

CARR, J.D. *It Walks by Night.* 1976. Hamish Hamilton. dj. VG. P1. $15.00

CARR, J.D. *Maiden Murders.* nd. Book Club. dj. VG. P1. $7.50

CARR, J.D. *Man Who Could Not Shudder.* nd. Collier. VG. P1. $9.25

CARR, J.D. *Most Secret.* 1964. Harper. 1st ed. dj. VG. $23.00

CARR, J.D. *Patrick Butler for Defense.* nd. Book Club. dj. VG. P1. $3.50

CARR, J.D. *Patrick Butler for Defense.* 1956. Hamish Hamilton. P1. $25.00

CARR, J.D. *Poison in Jest.* nd. Harper. VG. P1. $18.25

CARR, J.D. *Poison in Jest.* 1977. Hamish Hamilton. dj. EX. P1. $15.00

CARR, J.D. *Problem of the Green Capsule.* 1939. Harper. 1st ed. xl. G. P1. $18.25

CARR, J.D. *Problem of the Green Capsule.* 1944. Books Inc. G. P1. $7.50

CARR, J.D. *Problem of the Green Capsule.* 1945. Books Inc. 2nd ed. VG. P1. $10.00

CARR, J.D. *Problem of the Green Capsule.* 1946. Books Inc. 3rd ed. dj. G. P1. $15.00

CARR, J.D. *Problem of the Wire Cage.* 1939. Harper. 1st ed. $20.00

CARR, J.D. *Sleeping Sphinx.* nd. Collier. VG. P1. $9.25

CARR, J.D. *Sleeping Sphinx.* 1947. Harper. 1st ed. P1. $15.00

CARR, J.D. *To Wake the Dead.* 1945. Books Inc. 2nd ed. VG. P1. $12.00

CARR, Jayge. *Rabelaisian Reprise.* 1988. Doubleday. 1st ed. dj. EX. RS. P1. $17.50

CARR, Jayge. *Treasure in the Heart of the Maze.* 1985. Doubleday. 1st ed. dj. EX. RS. P1. $17.50

CARR, Robert Spencer. *Room Beyond.* 1948. Appleton. G. P1. $11.50

CARR, Terry. *Best SF Novellas No. 1.* 1979. Del Rey. xl. rebound. P1. $4.00

CARR, Terry. *Best SF of the Year No. 8.* nd. Book Club. dj. EX. P1. $4.00

CARR, Terry. *Cirque.* 1977. Bobbs Merrill. 1st ed. dj. xl. P1. $6.00

CARR, Terry. *Cirque.* 1977. Bobbs Merrill. 2nd ed. dj. EX. P1. $12.50

CARR, Terry. *Creatures From Beyond.* nd. Book Club. dj. VG. P1. $4.00

CARR, Terry. *Fantasy Annual 4.* nd. Book Club. dj. EX. P1. $10.00

CARR, Terry. *Fellowship of the Stars.* nd. Book Club. dj. G. P1. $4.00

CARR, Terry. *Universe 10.* 1980. Doubleday. 1st ed. dj. VG. P1. $15.00

CARR, Terry. *Universe 11.* 1981. Doubleday. 1st ed. dj. EX. P1. $12.50

CARR, Terry. *Universe 15.* 1985. Doubleday. 1st ed. dj. EX. RS. P1. $15.00

CARR, Terry. *Universe 16.* 1986. Doubleday. 1st ed. dj. EX. P1. $12.95

CARR, Terry. *Universe 17.* 1987. Doubleday. 1st ed. dj. EX. RS. P1. $17.50

CARR, Terry. *Universe 17.* 1987. Doubleday. 1st ed. dj. VG. P1. $12.95

CARR, Terry. *Universe 7.* 1977. Doubleday. 2nd ed. dj. EX. P1. $7.00

CARR, Terry. *Universe 8.* 1978. Doubleday. 1st ed. dj. EX. P1. $12.50

CARRAWAY, G.S. *Historic New Bern.* 1942. New Bern, NC. Ils. 64 p. printed wraps. $7.50

CARRE, Leon. *Livre des Milles Nuits et Une Nuit.* 1926-1932. Paris. 1/2200. 12 vols. slipcases. $1000.00

CARREL & LINDBERGH. *Culture of Organs.* 1938. NY. Ils 1st ed. 221 p. VG. B2. $90.00

CARRIGHAR, S. *Moonlight at Midday.* 1959. Knopf. photos. map. 392 p. VG. M2. $9.00

CARRIGHAR, S. *One Day on Beetle Rock.* 1946. Knopf. 196 p. dj. EX. M2. $12.00

CARRIGHAR, S. *Twilight Seas: A Blue Whale's Journey.* 1975. Weybright Talley. 179 p. dj. M2. $5.00

CARRINGTON, Grant. *Time's Fool.* 1981. Doubleday. 1st ed. dj. EX. P1. $9.25

CARRINGTON, H. *Atlantis: Lost Continent.* 1948. Haldeman Julius. 32 p. EX. M2. $5.00

CARRINGTON, Henry B. *Battle Maps & Charts of the American Revolution.* 1881. NY. 41 maps. 88 p. fair. T5. $65.00

CARRINGTON, Mrs. M.I. *Absaraka. Home of the Crows.* 1950. Donnelley. Lakeside Classic. A3. $45.00

CARRINGTON, W.T. *Mary Holloway Carrington, As Her Husband Knew Her.* c 1930s. np. 125 p. VG. T5. $8.50

CARROLL, D. *Notes on All-Too-Brief Visit to New Yamanaka Galleries.* 1918. NY. 11 pls. oblong 4to. J2. $200.00

CARROLL, Dixie. *Lake & Stream Game Fishing.* 1919. OH. 1st ed. 2nd print. blue cloth. VG. $25.00

CARROLL, Eugene A. *Rosso Fiorentino: Drawings, Prints & Decorative Arts.* 1988. WA, D.C. Nat Gallery of Art. 390 p. D2. $39.95

CARROLL, J.M. *Custer in TX.* 1975. Lewis. Ils. photos. 288 p. EX. M2. $27.00

CARROLL, J.M. *General Custer & Battle of the Washita: Federal View.* 1978. Bryan, TX. EX. $45.00

CARROLL, J.M. *Readings From Hunter-Trader-Trapper. Vol. 1.* nd. Bryan TX. 1/100. wraps. VG. A3. $35.00

CARROLL, James. *Fault Lines.* 1980. Little Brown. 1st ed. dj. EX. $12.00

CARROLL, Jim. *Basketball Diaries.* 1978. Bolinas. 1st ed. dj. VG. $40.00

CARROLL, Lewis. *Alice in Wonderland. Pop-Up Classic.* 1968. Random House. Graphics Internat. 1st ed. $25.00

CARROLL, Lewis. *Alice's Adventures in Wonderland & Through Looking Glass.* c 1950s. Phil. Jacobs. Ils Tenniel/Abbott. G. $17.00

CARROLL, Lewis. *Alice's Adventures in Wonderland & Through Looking Glass.* nd. Grosset. 1 vol ed. 298 p. VG. $12.50

CARROLL, Lewis. *Alice's Adventures in Wonderland & Through Looking Glass.* 1931. London. Ils. 2 vols. AEG. Riviere bdg. VG. $200.00

CARROLL, Lewis. *Alice's Adventures in Wonderland & Through Looking Glass.* 1946. Random House. Special ed. 2 vols. boxed. EX. $37.00

CARROLL, Lewis. *Alice's Adventures in Wonderland.* 1901. NY. Ils Newell. VG. $45.00

CARROLL, Lewis. *Alice's Adventures in Wonderland.* 1929. Black. P1. $5.50

CARROLL, Lewis. *Alice's Adventures in Wonderland.* 1948. Collins. Ils Watson. 4th ed. dj. VG. P1. $13.75

CARROLL, Lewis. *Alice's Adventures in Wonderland.* 1982. Berkeley. Ils Mosher. Ltd ed. sgn. slipcase. $120.00

CARROLL, Lewis. *Alice's Adventures in Wonderland.* 1982. CA U. Ils 1st ed. EX. $30.00

CARROLL, Lewis. *Alice's Adventures Underground.* 1932. NY. 1st Am ed. $65.00

CARROLL, Lewis. *Feeding the Mind.* 1907. London. 1st ed. VG. $40.00

CARROLL, Lewis. *Hunting of Snark & Other Poems & Verses.* 1903. NY. Ils Peter Newell. 1st ed. VG. $35.00

CARROLL, Lewis. *Rhyme? Reason?* 1884. Macmillan. Ils 1st ed. EX. $75.00

CARROLL, Lewis. *Sylvie & Bruno.* 1889. London. Ils Furniss. 1st ed. sgn. $100.00

CARROLL, Lewis. *Sylvie & Bruno.* 1889. London. 1st ed. VG. $65.00

CARROLL, Lewis. *Through the Looking Glass & What Alice Found There.* nd. NY. Stokes. Ils Kirk/Tenniel. VG. $60.00

CARROLL, Lewis. *Through the Looking Glass & What Alice Found There.* 1983. CA U. Ils Barry Moser. dj. EX. $25.00

CARROLL, Robert. *Disappearance.* 1975. Dial. dj. xl. P1. $4.75

CARROLL, W.L. *From Under Sun Mountain.* 1961. Vantage. Ils 1st ed. 76 p. dj. EX. M2. $9.00

CARRUTH, Hayden. *Mr. Milo Bush & Other Worthies.* 1899. NY. Ils Frost. 1st ed. 8vo. VG. $20.00

CARRUTH, William. *Each in His Own Tongue.* 1909. 2nd print. VG. C1. $5.00

CARSE, Robert. *Blockade: Civil War at Sea.* 1958. Ils 279 p. K1. $9.50

CARSE, Robert. *Blockade: Civil War at Sea.* 1958. Rinehart. 1st ed. dj. M. $27.50

CARSON, Hampton. *Supreme Court: History & Centennial Celebration.* 1891. Phil. 4to. 745 p. VG. $45.00

CARSON, J. *Recollections of CA Mines.* 1950. Bio Books. Ltd ed. 1/750. EX. $60.00

CARSON, Kit. *Kit Carson's Autobiography.* 1935. Donnelley. Lakeside Classic. A3. $45.00

CARSON, Rachel. *Sea Around Us.* Ltd Ed Club. slipcase. M. B3. $40.00

CARSON, Robert. *Outsiders.* nd. Book Club. dj. VG. P1. $17.50

CARSTAIRS, Carroll. *Generation Missing.* 1930. Doubleday. 259 p. dj. M1. $6.50

CARTE, V.B. *Winston S. Churchill: Intimate Portrait.* 1965. Book Club. 1st ed. black cloth. dj. EX. D1. $30.00

CARTE & LUCIUS. *Secession & Reunion.* 1935. Chapel Hill. 1st ed. VG. J2. $25.00

CARTER, A.C. *Kingdom of Siam.* 1904. Putnam. Ils 1st ed. 280 p. VG. $10.00

CARTER, Angela. *Black Venus.* 1985. Hogarth. dj. EX. P1. $17.50

CARTER, Angela. *Nights at the Circus.* 1984. Hogarth. dj. VG. P1. $20.00

CARTER, C.E. *Territory NW of the River OH, 1787-1803.* 1934. WA. 2 vols. cloth bdg. EX. $100.00

CARTER, D. *Butterflies & Moths in Britain & Europe.* 1982. Heinemann. Ils 1st ed. 4to. 192 p. dj. EX. M2. $32.00

CARTER, Hodding. *Floodcrest.* 1947. NY. 1st ed. dj. VG. B2. $17.50

CARTER, Jimmy. *Blood of Abraham.* 1985. Boston. 1st ed. inscr/sgn. dj. M. $65.00

CARTER, Jimmy. *Keeping Faith.* 1983. Bantam. 1st trade ed. sgn. pb. EX. $25.00

CARTER, John. *ABC for Book Collectors.* 1981. NY. Revised 5th ed. 211 p. dj. M. T5. $18.95

CARTER, John. *Taste & Technique in Book Collecting.* 1948. Bowker. 203 p. dj. VG. $40.00

CARTER, John. *Taste & Technique in Book Collecting.* 1970. London. dj. $25.00

CARTER, Lin. *Dreams From R'lyeh.* 1975. Arkham House. 1st ed. dj. EX. P1. $17.50

CARTER, Lin. *Flashing Swords! #5.* nd. Book Club. dj. EX. P1. $4.00

CARTER, Lin. *Horror Wears Blue.* 1987. Doubleday. 1st ed. dj. EX. P1. $12.95

CARTER, Lin. *Horror Wears Blue.* 1987. Doubleday. 1st ed. dj. EX. RS. P1. $17.50

CARTER, Lin. *Invisible Death.* 1975. Doubleday. 1st ed. dj. EX. P1. $15.00

CARTER, Lin. *Kellory the Warlock.* 1984. Doubleday. 1st ed. dj. EX. P1. $15.00

CARTER, Lin. *Look Behind the Lord of the Rings.* 1969. 1st ed in any form. pb. EX. C1. $5.00

CARTER, Lin. *Volcano Ogre.* 1976. Doubleday. 1st ed. dj. EX. P1. $9.25

CARTER, Morris. *Isabella Stewart Gardner & Fenway Court.* 1925. Houghton. 1st ed. VG. J2. $17.50

CARTER, Nick. *Nick Carter Detective.* 1963. Macmillan. 1st ed. dj. G. P1. $20.00

CARTER, R.S. *Those Devils in Baggy Pants.* 1951. NY. 1st ed. dj. VG. B2. $35.00

CARTER, R.S. *Those Devils in Baggy Pants.* 1951. NY. 299 p. dj. xl. VG. T5. $15.00

CARTER, Rosalyn. *1st Lady From Plains.* 1984. Boston. Ltd ed. 1/750. sgn. dj. EX. B2. $47.50

CARTER, S. *Siege of Atlanta.* 1973. Bonanza. reprint. 425 p. dj. EX. M2. $10.00

CARTER, T.D. *Mammals of the Pacific World.* 1945. Macmillan. 1st print. map. 227 p. dj. EX. M2. $16.00

CARTER, V.B. *Winston Churchill.* 1965. NY. Harcourt Brace. dj. EX. $8.00

CARTER, Vincent. *Bern Book.* 1970. NY. 1st ed. dj. EX. $22.50

CARTER, W.A. *McCurtain Co. & SE OK: History, Biography, Statistics.* 1923. Idabel, OK. 1st ed. brown bdg. EX. $150.00

CARTER, Youngman. *Mr. Campion's Farthing.* 1969. Heinemann. 1st ed. dj. xl. P1. $7.00

CARTER & CARTER. *Secret Knowledge Disclosed; or, A Plain Way to Wealth.* nd. Boston. Ils 210 p. fair. T5. $19.50

CARTER & CROSS. *Twinsburg, 1817-1917.* 1984. Twinsburg, OH. Ils 533 p. index. EX. T5. $45.00

CARTER & GANNETT. *Angry Scar: Story of Reconstruction.* 1959. Garden City. 1st ed. sgn. 425 p. dj. G. $20.00

CARTHY, J.D. *Animals & Their Ways: Science of Animal Behavior.* 1965. Mus Nat Hist. 1st Am ed. 156 p. dj. EX. M2. $15.00

CARTHY, J.D. *Behavior of Arthropods.* 1965. Edinburgh. Oliver Boyd. 1st ed. dj. EX. M2. $17.00

CARTIER-BRESSON, Henri. *Decisive Moment.* 1952. VG. S2. $210.00

CARTIER-BRESSON, Henri. *Europeans.* 1955. NY. EX. P3. $300.00

CARTIER-BRESSON, Henri. *From One China to the Other.* 1955. NY. 1st ed. G. $56.00

CARTIER-BRESSON, Henri. *From One China to the Other.* 1956. Universe. M. $150.00

CARTIER-BRESSON, Henri. *Les Europeans. Photographies.* 1955. Verve/Simon Schuster. VG. $275.00

CARTIER-BRESSON, Henri. *Man & Machine.* 1971. Viking. dj. VG. $37.50

CARTIER-BRESSON, Henri. *People of Moscow.* 1955. NY. 1st ed. 4to. dj. EX. $65.00

CARTIER-BRESSON, Henri. *Visage d'Asie...* 1972. Paris. Eds Chene. French text. 207 p. $150.00

CARTIER-BRESSON, Henri. *World of Henri Cartier-Bresson.* 1968. NY. 1st ed. oblong folio. 210 p. dj. T5. $85.00

CARTIER-BRESSON, Henri. *World of Henri Cartier-Bresson.* 1968. Viking. 1st ed. G. $65.00

CARTWRIGHT, Julia. *Jean Francois Millet.* 1902. NY. Ils 1st ed. VG. $40.00

CARUS, Paul. *Goethe With Special Consideration of His Philosophy.* 1915. Chicago. Open Court. Ils 1st ed. EX. $95.00

CARUTHERS, E.W. *Revolutionary Incidents: Sketches of Character...* 1854. Phil. 1st ed. VG. scarce. $150.00

CARUTHERS, William. *Loafing Along Death Valley Trails.* c 1951. Ontario, CA. 1st ed. dj. EX. $15.00

CARUTHERS, William. *Loafing Along Death Valley Trails.* 1951. Death Valley. later print. 191 p. dj. VG. M2. $12.00

CARVALHO, S.N. *Incidents of Travel & Adventure in Far W With Fremont.* 1857. NY. Derby Jackson. 380 p. A3. $120.00

CARVALHO, S.N. *Incidents of Travel & Adventure in Far W With Fremont.* 1973. NY. facsimile of 1857 ed. VG. $17.50

CARVER, J. *Three Years' Travels Through Interior Parts of N America.* 1792. Phil. rebound. VG. M2. $125.00

CARVER, Raymond. *At Night the Salmon Move.* 1976. Capra. Ltd ed. 1/1000. blue wraps. M. $35.00

CARVER, Raymond. *Collectors.* 1975. Chicago. VG. T6. $15.00

CARVER, Raymond. *My Father's Life.* nd. 1st ed. 1/200. sgn/#d. wraps. G. $50.00

CARVER, Raymond. *My Father's Life.* 1986. Derry, NH. Babcock. 1/200. sgn/#d. EX. T6. $75.00

CARVER, Raymond. *Night the Mill Boss Died.* 1963. Chapel Hill. wraps. VG. T6. $30.00

CARVER, Raymond. *Painter & the Fish.* 1988. NH. Ils Azarian. 1/26. sgns. M. $200.00

CARVER, Raymond. *This Water.* 1985. Ewert. 1st ed. 1/100. sgn. wraps. M. $60.00

CARVER, Raymond. *Ultramarine.* 1986. NY. Review 1st ed. dj. VG. $45.00

CARVER, Raymond. *What We Talk About When We Talk About Love.* 1981. NY. 1st ed. dj. VG. $50.00

CARVER, Raymond. *What We Talk About When We Talk About Love.* 1982. London. 1st ed. dj. EX. $35.00

CARVER, Raymond. *Where I'm Calling From.* 1988. NY. 1st trade ed. sgn. dj. M. $125.00

CARVER, Raymond. *Where I'm Calling From.* 1988. NY. 1st ed. 1/250. sgn. slipcase. M. $150.00

CARVER, Raymond. *Will You Be Quiet Please?* 1976. NY. 1st ed. dj. EX. $100.00

CARY, James. *Tanks & Armor in Modern Warfare.* 1966. NY. Ils 1st ed. dj. VG. T5. $15.00

CARY, Joyce. *Horse's Mouth.* 1944. NY. 1st ed. dj. VG. $40.00

CARY, M. *Life Zone Investigations in WY.* 1917. USDA. Ils. fld map. 95 p. M2. $6.00

CASANOVA, J.D.S. *Memoirs of Casanova.* nd. np. 1/750. 12 vols. TEG. VG. $125.00

CASANOVA, J.D.S. *Memoirs of Casanova.* 1972. Haarlem. Ils Sussan. dj. EX. $60.00

CASANOWICZ, I.M. *Collection of Ancient Oriental Seals in US National Museum.* 1926. WA. GPO. wraps. G. $17.00

CASE, David. *Cell: Three Tales of Horror.* 1969. Hill Wang. 1st ed. dj. VG. P1. $25.00

CASE, David. *Fengriffen.* nd. Hill Wang. 2nd ed. dj. xl. P1. $8.00

CASE, E.C. *Revision of the Cotylosauria of N America.* 1911. Carnegie Inst. 14 pls. 4to. 122 p. VG. P1. $135.00

CASE, Frank. *Tales of a Wayward Inn.* 1938. NY. 1st ed. with sgn letter. $45.00

CASE. *Stereoentgenography: Alimentary Tract.* 1915. Baltimore. 25 photos. slipcase. EX. P3. $45.00

CASERTA, P. *Going Down With Janis.* 1973. Stuart. VG. $35.00

CASEY, D. *Leaving Locke Horn.* 1986. Chapel Hill. 1st ed. inscr. dj. EX. $30.00

CASEY, R.J. *Easter Island, Home of the Scornful Gods.* 1931. Bobbs Merrill. Ils 1st ed. maps. 337 p. EX. M2. $45.00

CASEY, R.J. *Land of Haunted Castles.* 1921. Century. Ils. photos. G. $45.00

CASEY, Silas. *Infantry Tactics. Vol. 3.* 1862. NY. 1st ed. 29 pls. 24mo. 183 p. scarce. G2. $59.00

CASEY & DOUGLAS. *Lackawanna Story.* 1951. NY. Ils. 223 p. EX. $25.00

CASEY. *American Romance.* 1977. NY. 1st ed. dj. VG. $20.00

CASH, Johnny. *Man in Black.* 1975. Zondervan. dj. EX. $19.00

CASLER, J.O. *Four Years in the Stonewall Brigade.* 1951. reprint of 1906 ed. EX. J4. $20.00

CASPARY, Vera. *Bedelia.* nd. Book Club. dj. VG. P1. $2.75

CASPARY, Vera. *Bedelia.* 1947. Triangle. dj. G. P1. $7.00

CASPARY, Vera. *Music in the Street.* nd. Grosset Dunlap. VG. P1. $4.75

CASS, A.R.H. *Catching the Wily Sea Trout.* nd. Jenkins. Ils 1st ed. dj. VG. $10.00

CASSELL, C.A. *Liberia: History of 1st African Republic.* 1970. NY. Ils 1st ed. 457 p. dj. VG. T5. $25.00

CASSIDY, Bruce. *Floater.* 1960. Abelard Schuman. dj. VG. P1. $7.00

CASSIDY, Bruce. *Floater.* 1960. NY. Abelard Schuman. 1st ed. dj. EX. $10.00

CASSIDY, John. *Station in the Delta.* 1979. Scribner. 1st ed. dj. M. $10.00

CASSON, H.N. *History of the Telephone.* 1910. Chicago. Ils. fair. $22.00

CASSON, Herbert. *Romance of Reaper.* 1908. Doubleday Page. 1st ed. photos. green bdg. VG. $22.00

CASSON, Stanley. *Murder by Burial.* 1938. NY. 1st ed. dj. VG. $12.50

CASSOU & FEDIT. *Kupka.* 1964-1965. Abrams. dj. D2. $30.00

CASSUTT, Michael. *Star Country.* 1986. Doubleday. 1st ed. dj. EX. P1. $12.95

CASTANEDA, C. *Eagle's Gift.* 1981. NY. 1st ed. VG. B2. $17.50

CASTEL, Albert. *Quantrill: His Life & Times.* 1962. NY. Ils 1st ed. dj. VG. B2. $35.00

CASTELLI, Enrico. *Simboli e Immagini: Studi di Filosofia Dell'Arte Sacra.* 1966. Rome. Ils. 41 p. dj. D2. $35.00

CASTERET, Norbert. *Ten Years Under the Earth.* 1938. NY. Greystone. Stated 1st ed. VG. $35.00

CASTIGILIONE. *Book of the Courtier.* 1959. Anchor. Trans Singleton. pb. VG. C1. $4.50

CASTIGLIONI. *History of Medicine.* 1941. NY. 1st ed. $25.00

CASTLE, Jeffery Lloyd. *Satellite E One.* 1954. Eyre Spottiswoode. dj. VG. P1. $7.00

CASTRO, J.I. *Sharks of N American Waters.* 1983. TX A&M. Ils 1st ed. 180 p. dj. EX. P1. $18.00

CASWELL, J.E. *Arctic Frontiers: US Explorations in the Far N.* 1956. OK U. Ils 1st ed. dj. EX. P1. $18.00

CATCOTT, E.J. *Feline Medicine & Surgery: Text & Reference Work.* 1964. Wheaton. Am Veterinary Pub. 1st ed. VG. $20.00

CATER, Douglas. *Irrelevant Man.* 1970. McGraw Hill. 1st ed. dj. $7.00

CATHELL, D.W. *Book on the Physician Himself.* 1892. Phil. VG. $18.00

CATHER, Thomas. *Voyage to America.* c 1961. NY. Ils Taylor. dj. VG. $12.50

CATHER, Willa. *December Night.* 1933. NY. 1st ed. dj. EX. $50.00

CATHER, Willa. *Lost Lady.* Ltd Ed Club. slipcase. M. B3. $100.00

CATHER, Willa. *Lucy Gayheart.* 1935. NY. 1st ed. dj. B2. $25.00

CATHER, Willa. *Lucy Gayheart.* 1935. NY. 1st ed. 231 p. dj. T5. $17.50

CATHER, Willa. *My Mortal Enemy.* 1926. NY. 1st ed. 1/200. sgn. 4to. $75.00

CATHER, Willa. *My Mortal Enemy.* 1926. NY. 1st trade ed. 8vo. $30.00

CATHER, Willa. *Obscure Destinies.* 1932. Knopf. 1st ed. dj. EX. $30.00

CATHER, Willa. *Obscure Destinies.* 1932. NY. Knopf. Ltd ed. 1/260. sgn. dj. slipcase. $250.00

CATHER, Willa. *Old Beauty & Others.* 1948. NY. 1st ed. dj. B2. $25.00

CATHER, Willa. *Sapphira & the Slave Girl.* 1940. NY. ARC. 1st ed. dj. EX. $175.00

CATHER, Willa. *Sapphira & the Slave Girl.* 1940. NY. 1st ed. dj. EX. $50.00

CATHER, Willa. *Scene From Willa Cather's Novel Death Comes for Archbishop.* 1933. Knopf. Pynson Printers. VG. scarce. A3. $90.00

CATHER, Willa. *Shadows on the Rock.* 1931. Knopf. 1st ed. 1/619. sgn. VG. $125.00

CATHER, Willa. *Willa Cather on Writing.* 1949. NY. 1st ed. dj. VG. B2. $45.00

CATHER, Willa. *Woman & Her Works.* 1970. Scribner. dj. VG. $10.00

CATICH, Edward. *Origin of the Serif: Brush Writing & Roman Letters.* 1968. Catfish Pr. 1st ed. dj. EX. $55.00

CATLIN, George. *Catlin Book of American Indians.* 1977. NY. dj. EX. $30.00

CATLIN, George. *G. Catlin: Episodes From Life Among Indians & Last Rambles.* 1959. Norman. Ils. dj. EX. $45.00

CATLIN, George. *Indians of N American.* 1924. Berlin. 24 pls. 355 p. B2. $125.00

CATLIN, George. *N American Indians.* 1841. London. Ils 191 pls. 3 maps. 2 vols. EX. $950.00

CATLIN, George. *N American Indians.* 1926. Edinburgh. 8vo. 320 pls. 2 vols. red cloth. VG. A3. $700.00

CATON, J.D. *Last of the IL & a Sketch of the Potowatomies.* 1876. Chicago. Fergus Hist Series. wraps. VG. $50.00

CATTELL, Ann. *Mind Juggler & Other Ghost Stories.* 1966. Exposition. dj. EX. P1. $10.00

CATTELL. *American Men of Science: Biographical Dictionary. Vol. I.* 1959. Lancaster. 4to. 2180. VG. $45.00

CATTELLE, W.R. *Diamond.* 1911. John Lane. 1st ed. VG. J2. $35.00

CATTON, Bruce. *American Heritage Picture History of Civil War.* 1960. Ils. 630 p. dj. EX. J4. $20.00

CATTON, Bruce. *Battle of Gettysburg.* 1963. Ils 1st ed. 153 p. EX. J4. $15.00

CATTON, Bruce. *Civil War.* 1984. NY. 3 vols in 1. dj. VG. $18.00

CATTON, Bruce. *Gettysburg: Final Fury.* 1974. Ils. maps. 114 p. boxed. EX. J4. $12.50

CATTON, Bruce. *Gettysburg: Final Fury.* 1974. Doubleday. 1st ed. dj. M. $16.00

CATTON, Bruce. *Grant Moves S.* 1960. Boston. 1st ed. inscr. dj. EX. $55.00

CATTON, Bruce. *Grant Takes Command.* 1969. Little Brown. maps. 556 p. dj. M2. $8.00

CATTON, Bruce. *Mr. Lincoln's Army.* 1951. Doubleday. G. $7.50

CATTON, Bruce. *Never Call Retreat.* 1965. Doubleday. 555 p. dj. $21.00

CATTON, Bruce. *Reflections on the Civil War.* 1981. Doubleday. Ils 1st ed. 246 p. dj. EX. M2. $35.00

CAUDILL, Rebecca. *My Appalachia.* 1966. Holt Rinehart. Ils. 155 p. dj. VG. $12.50

CAULFIELD, M. *Tomorrow Never Came: Sinking of S.S. Athenia.* 1958. NY. 1st ed. 223 p. dj. VG. B2. $17.50

CAULFIELD, M.F. *Black City.* 1953. Dutton. 1st ed. dj. VG. $25.00

CAULFIELD, P. *Everglades.* 1970. San Francisco. Sierra Club. 1st ed. dj. VG. B2. $37.50

CAULFIELD, S.F.A. *House Mottoes & Inscriptions: Old & New.* 1908. London. Ils New Revised ed. EX. $35.00

CAVALIER, Julian. *N American Railroad Station.* 1979. photos. 215 p. $17.50

CAVALIERO, Glen. *Charles Williams: Poet of Theology.* 1983. dj. M. C1. $11.00

CAVE, Roderick. *Private Presses.* 1971. London. 1st ed. dj. EX. $65.00

CAVE, Roderick. *Private Presses.* 1971. Watson Guptill. Ils. 376 p. rust linen. dj. VG. $37.50

CAVENDISH, Richard. *Encyclopedia of the Unexplained.* 1974. McGraw Hill. 1st ed. dj. EX. $25.00

CAVENDISH. *History of WWII.* 1972. 2nd ed. wraps. VG. $80.00

CAWEIN, Madison. *Accolon of Gaul & Other Poems.* 1889. Louisville. Morton. 1st/only ed. EX. C1. $95.00

CAYCE, Hugh Lynn. *Venture Inward.* nd. Book Club. VG. P1. $1.75

CAZALET-KEIR, Thelma. *Homage to P.G. Wodehouse.* 1973. Barrie Jenkins. 1st ed. dj. VG. P1. $25.00

CAZENEUVE, J. *Sociologie de la Television.* 1963. Paris. 128 p. wraps. $10.00

CEASAR, Sid. *Where Have I Been?* 1982. NY. 1st ed. dj. VG. $11.00

CECIL, Henry. *Friends at Court.* 1956. NY. Harper. 1st ed. presentation. sgn. dj. $30.00

CECIL, Henry. *Woman Named Anne.* 1967. London. 1st ed. dj. EX. $27.00

CELAIRIE, Henrietta. *Behind Moroccan Walls.* 1931. NY. Trans/sgn Morris. 1st ed. dj. J2. $50.00

CELLIER, A. *L'Orgue Moderne.* 1925. Paris. Ils 4th ed. inscr. 4to. gilt bdg. $50.00

CELLINI, Benvenuto. *Autobiography of Benvenuto Cellini.* 1946. NY. Ltd ed. Trans Symonds. Ils/sgn Dali. boxed. $300.00

CELLINI, D.A.S. *Wobby Wennedy, Hero.* 1966. Zenger. 2nd print. paper wraps. VG. M1. $9.50

CENDRARS, Blaise. *Panama; or, Adventures of My Seven Uncles.* 1931. NY. Trans/Ils Dos Passos. dj. VG. P3. $50.00

CEPLAIR & ENGLUND. *Inquisition in Hollywood: Politics, 1938-1960.* 1980. NY. 1st ed. dj. EX. $23.00

CERAM. *Secret of the Hittites.* 1956. Knopf. 1st Am ed. 281 p. EX. $12.50

CERF, Bennett. *At Random.* 1977. NY. 1st ed. dj. M. $12.00

CERF, Bennett. *Famous Ghost Stories.* 1946. Modern Lib. dj. VG. P1. $2.75

CERF, Bennett. *Out on a Limerick.* 1960. NY. Harper. G. $3.00

CERF, Bennett. *Shake Well Before Using.* 1948. Simon Schuster. 1st ed. sgn. 306 p. M1. $10.50

CERF, Bennett. *Sound of Laughter.* 1970. Doubleday. 1st ed. sgn. dj. $12.50

CERF, Bennett. *3 Famous Spy Novels.* 1942. Random House. VG. P1. $4.75

CERNI, Vincente A. *Julio, Joan & Roberta Gonzalez: Itinerario de un Dinastia.* 1973. Barcelona. Poligrafa. Ils. dj. D2. $75.00

CERNY, W. *Field Guide in Color to Birds.* 1975. Cathay. Ils. maps. VG. P1. $15.00

CERVANTES, Saavedra. *Don Quixote de la Mancha.* c 1930. NY. Hogarth. Ils Dore. 4to. 855 p. VG. $60.00

CERVANTES, Saavedra. *Don Quixote de la Mancha.* 1655. Madrid. 2 parts in 1 vol. vellum bdg. B2. $1000.00

CERVANTES, Saavedra. *Don Quixote de la Mancha.* 1933. Barcelona. Ltd Ed Club. Ils Ricart. 2 vols. $100.00

CERVANTES, Saavedra. *Don Quixote de la Mancha.* 1950. Heritage. Ils Legrand. slipcase. VG. $17.50

CERVANTES, Saavedra. *Don Quixote de la Mancha.* 1979. Franklin Lib. Ils Jiminez y Aranda. M. C1. $19.50

CERVANTES, Saavedra. *History & Adventures of Renowned Don Quixote.* 1755. Ils Hayman. Trans Smollett. 2 vols. VG. J2. $575.00

CHABER, M.E. *Bonded Dead.* 1971. Holt Rinehart. 1st ed. dj. EX. P1. $13.75

CHABER, M.E. *Born To Be Hanged.* 1973. Holt Rinehart. 1st ed. dj. EX. P1. $13.75

CHABER, M.E. *Day It Rained Diamonds.* 1966. Holt Rinehart. 1st ed. dj. VG. P1. $13.75

CHABER, M.E. *Green Grow the Graves.* 1970. Holt Rinehart. 1st ed. dj. EX. P1. $13.75

CHABER, M.E. *Green Grow the Graves.* 1970. Holt Rinehart. 1st ed. dj. xl. P1. $5.00

CHABER, M.E. *Man in the Middle.* 1967. Holt Rinehart. 1st ed. dj. VG. P1. $12.50

CHABER, M.E. *Six Who Ran.* 1964. Holt Rinehart. 1st ed. dj. VG. P1. $8.50

CHABER, M.E. *So Dead the Rose.* 1960. Boardman. dj. VG. P1. $15.00

CHABER, M.E. *Softly in the Night.* 1963. Holt Rinehart. 1st ed. dj. EX. P1. $10.00

CHABER, M.E. *Wanted: Dead Men.* 1965. Holt Rinehart. 1st ed. dj. EX. P1. $12.50

CHABON, Michael. *Mysteries of Pittsburgh.* 1988. Morrow. 1st ed. dj. M. $10.00

CHADWICK, L. *Baseball Joe on the School Nine.* 1912. Cupples Leon. dj. VG. $26.00

CHAFETZ, Henry. *Play the Devil.* nd. Bonanza. VG. P1. $9.25

CHAFFEE, A.B. *Adventures of Twinkly Eyes, the Little Black Bear.* 1925. Springfield. Milton Bradley. Ils. 193 p. 12mo. $15.00

CHAFFEE, A.B. *Fuzzy Wuzz, Little Brown Bear of the Sierras.* 1922. Springfield. Milton Bradley. Ils. 142 p. VG. $15.00

CHAGALL, Marc. *Jerusalem Windows.* 1962. NY. 1st ed. dj. EX. B2. $395.00

CHAGALL, Marc. *Jerusalem Windows.* 1962. NY. dj. slipcase. with 2 lithographs. EX. $1000.00

CHAGALL, Marc. *Jerusalem Windows.* 1967. Braziller. Revised 1st ed. dj. VG. J2. $22.50

CHAGALL, Marc. *Jerusalem Windows.* 1988. NY. reprint of 1962 ed. EX. $18.00

CHAGALL, Marc. *Le Message Biblique.* 1972. Paris. Ils. 4to. dj. slipcase. EX. J2. $150.00

CHAGALL, Marc. *Les Vitraux de Jerusalem.* 1961. Paris. Musee Arts Decoratifs. sgn. wraps. $375.00

CHAGALL, Marc. *Musee National, Message Biblique.* 1973. Nice. Ils. 237 p. stiff wraps. EX. J2. $75.00

CHAGALL, Marc. *World of Marc Chagall.* 1968. NY. 1st ed. dj. EX. $35.00

CHAGALL & ELOUARD. *Le Dur Desir de Durer. Poemes de Paul Elouard.* 1946. Paris. Jacomet/Arnold-Bordas. sgns. wraps. $1000.00

CHALIAPIN, F. *Autobiography As Told to Maxim Gorky.* 1967. Stein Day. dj. VG. $40.00

CHALKER, Jack L. *Messiah Choice.* 1985. Bluejay. 1st ed. dj. EX. P1. $16.95

CHALLIS, George. *Monsieur.* 1926. Bobbs Merrill. VG. P1. $15.00

CHALMERS, G. *Historical View of Domestic Economy of Great Britain...* 1812. New ed. presentation. $250.00

CHALMERS, H. *Last Stand of Nez Perce.* 1962. NY. 1st ed. dj. VG. B2. $25.00

CHALON, Jean. *Portrait of a Seductress: World of Natalie Barney.* 1979. NY. Crown. Trans Barko. xl. D2. $35.00

CHAMBERLAIN, B.H. *Classical Poetry of the Japanese.* 1880. Boston. Osgood. 227 p. TEG. brown cloth. EX. $20.00

CHAMBERLAIN, E.B. *Rare & Endangered Birds of S National Forest.* 1974. USFS. EX. P1. $10.00

CHAMBERLAIN, E.C. *Shoes & Ships & Sealing Wax.* 1928. Akron. VG. $15.00

CHAMBERLAIN, Elinor. *Manila Hemp.* 1947. Dodd Mead. 1st ed. dj. VG. P1. $15.00

CHAMBERLAIN, Elinor. *Snare for Witches.* 1948. Dodd Mead. dj. VG. P1. $7.00

CHAMBERLAIN, F.E. *Revelations of Life.* 1931. LA. $5.00

CHAMBERLAIN, Frederick. *Lighted Pathway.* 1945. LA. $8.00

CHAMBERLAIN, G.E. *Summit Co. Historical Society, 1939-1940.* 1940. Akron. printed wraps. G. T5. $15.00

CHAMBERLAIN, S. *S Interiors of Charleston, SC.* 1956. 1st ed. dj. VG. $15.00

CHAMBERLAIN, S.E. *My Confession.* 1956. Ils. 302 p. dj. K1. $12.50

CHAMBERLAIN, Samuel. *Sketches of N Spanish Architecture.* 1926. NY. 51 pls. portfolio. J2. $25.00

CHAMBERLIN, A.B. *Hans Holbein the Younger.* 1913. London. 1st ed. 4to. 2 vols. VG. G2. $70.00

CHAMBERLIN, Everett. *Struggle of '72.* 1872. Chicago. Ils. 570 p. VG. T5. $35.00

CHAMBERLIN, H.D. *Training Hunters, Jumpers & Hacks.* 1952. dj. EX. B1. $30.00

CHAMBERLIN, W. *Thames & Hudson Manual of Wood Engraving.* 1978. dj. $5.00

CHAMBERLIN & IVIE. *N American Spiders of the Genera Cybaeus & Cybaeina.* 1932. UT U. 61 pls. 43 p. M2. $8.00

CHAMBERLIN & IVIE. *Spiders of the Raft River Mountains of UT.* 1933. UT U. 12 pls. 79 p. M2. $10.00

CHAMBERS, E.K. *Arthur of Britain.* 1967. 1st pb ed. VG. C1. $15.00

CHAMBERS, J. *MS River.* 1910. NY. Am Literature Series. 1st ed. B2. $65.00

CHAMBERS, J. *MS River.* 1910. NY. Ils 1st ed. 308 p. VG. B2. $55.00

CHAMBERS, Jack. *NV Whalen Avenger.* nd. Saalfield. Big Little Book. G. P1. $10.50

CHAMBERS, James. *This Must Be the Place.* 1936. London. 1st ed. dj. EX. $45.00

CHAMBERS, Peter. *Don't Bother To Knock.* 1966. Robert Hale. 1st ed. dj. xl. P1. $6.00

CHAMBERS, Peter. *Downbeat Kill.* 1964. Abelard Schuman. VG. P1. $9.25

CHAMBERS, Peter. *No Peace for the Wicked.* 1968. Robert Hale. 1st ed. dj. G. P1. $10.00

CHAMBERS, Peter. *Wreath for a Redhead.* 1962. Abelard Schuman. 1st ed. dj. G. P1. $10.00

CHAMBERS, R.W. *Ailsa Paige.* 1910. Appleton. 1st ed. $12.00

CHAMBERS, R.W. *Common Law.* 1911. McLeod Allen. G. P1. $4.75

CHAMBERS, R.W. *Flaming Jewel.* 1942. Triangle. dj. VG. P1. $10.00

CHAMBERS, R.W. *Hidden Children.* 1914. McLeod Allen. G. P1. $10.00

CHAMBERS, R.W. *In Search of Unknown.* 1904. NY. EX. $45.00

CHAMBERS, R.W. *Rogue's Moor.* 1929. NY. Ils Price. inscr. VG. $35.00

CHAMBERS, R.W. *Secret Service Operator 13.* 1942. Triangle. 2nd ed. G. P1. $7.50

CHAMBERS, R.W. *Slayer of Souls.* 1972. Tom Stacey. dj. EX. P1. $15.00

CHAMBERS, Whitman. *Coast of Intrigue.* nd. World. VG. P1. $6.50

CHAMBERS, William. *Atlas of Ancient & Modern Geography.* 1845. Edinburgh. 33 maps. quarto. A3. $210.00

CHAMLER, W.A. *Through Jungle & Desert: Travels in E Africa.* 1896. Macmillan. Ils. 2 pocket maps. VG. $125.00

CHAMOUIN. *Collection de Vues de Paris Prises au Daguerreotype.* c 1850. Paris. Ils. oblong 4to. G. $100.00

CHAMPFLEURY, M. *Cat: Past & Present.* 1885. London. Chiswick. Ils. 214 p. EX. $55.00

CHAMPION. *Jungle in Sunlight & Shadow.* 1934. NY. VG. $35.00

CHAMPLIN, J.D. *Chronicle of the Coach.* 1886. NY. Ils Chicester. poor. $15.00

CHAMSON, A. *Le Livre de Coeur d'Amour Epris du Roi Rene.* 1949. Paris. 16 pls. folio. VG. J2. $50.00

CHANCE, John Newton. *Death Under Desolate.* 1964. Robert Hale. 1st ed. dj. xl. P1. $6.00

CHANCE & JOLLY. *Social Groups of Monkeys.* 1970. NY. 1st Am ed. $20.00

CHANCELLOR, J. *Audubon: A Biography.* 1978. Viking. 16 pls. 224 p. dj. EX. M2. $14.00

CHANDLER, A.G. *Asa Griggs Chandler.* 1950. Emory U. 1st ed. 503 p. EX. scarce. B1. $65.00

CHANDLER, C. *How Our Army Grew Wings.* 1943. NY. Ils. 333 p. VG. $22.00

CHANDLER, D.G. *Atlas of Military Strategy.* 1980. Free Pr. Ils 1st ed. 200 maps. dj. EX. $15.00

CHANDLER, David. *Aphrodite.* 1977. Morrow. 1st ed. dj. xl. P1. $4.75

CHANDLER, M.C. *History of 7th US Cavalry Regiment.* 1960. Annadale. Ils 1st ed. maps. 4to. dj. EX. T1. $100.00

CHANDLER, Raymond. *Big Sleep.* 1946. Forum Books. Movie ed. dj. VG. P1. $30.00

CHANDLER, Raymond. *Farewell, My Lovely.* nd. Modern Lib. EX. P1. $18.25

CHANDLER, Raymond. *Farewell, My Lovely.* 1946. Tower. 3rd ed. dj. G. P1. $25.00

CHANDLER, Raymond. *Farewell, My Lovely.* 1946. World. Movie 3rd ed. dj. VG. P1. $25.00

CHANDLER, Raymond. *High Window.* 1942. NY. 1st ed. inscr. dj. EX. $25.00

CHANDLER, Raymond. *High Window.* 1946. Tower. 2nd ed. dj. VG. P1. $25.00

CHANDLER, Raymond. *Killer in Rain.* 1964. London. 1st ed. dj. VG. $15.00

CHANDLER, Raymond. *Lady in the Lake.* 1944. Hamish Hamilton. G. P1. $27.25

CHANDLER, Raymond. *Lady in the Lake.* 1947. Hamish Hamilton. 5th ed. VG. P1. $20.00

CHANDLER, Raymond. *Little Sister.* 1949. Hamish Hamilton. VG. P1. $45.00

CHANDLER, Raymond. *Little Sister.* 1949. Houghton Mifflin. 1st ed. xl. P1. $20.50

CHANDLER, Raymond. *Long Good-Bye.* 1953. Hamish Hamilton. 1st ed. dj. P1. $75.00

CHANDLER, Raymond. *Long Good-Bye.* 1953. Hamish Hamilton. 2nd ed. VG. P1. $22.75

CHANDLER, Raymond. *Long Good-Bye.* 1953. London. Penguin. 1st ed. dj. VG. $50.00

CHANDLER, Raymond. *Long Good-Bye.* 1954. Houghton. 1st ed. glassine dj. VG. $50.00

CHANDLER, Raymond. *Mystery Omnibus.* 1944. Forum. 1st ed. G. P1. $11.50

CHANDLER, Raymond. *Playback.* nd. Book Club. dj. VG. P1. $4.50

CHANDLER, Raymond. *Playback.* 1958. Hamish Hamilton. dj. VG. P1. $40.00

CHANDLER, Raymond. *Raymond Chandler Speaking.* 1962. Boston. 2nd print. dj. VG. B2. $25.00

CHANDLER, Raymond. *Raymond Chandler's Unknown Thriller: Screenplay of Playback.* 1985. Mysterious Pr. Intro/sgn Parker. 1st ed. dj. VG. $40.00

CHANDLER, Raymond. *Red Wind.* 1946. Tower. G. P1. $12.50

CHANDLER, Raymond. *Simple Art of Murder.* 1950. Hamish Hamilton. 2nd ed. dj. P1. $30.00

CHANDLER, Raymond. *Simple Art of Murder.* 1950. NY. 1st ed. dj. B2. $50.00

CHANDLER, Raymond. *Spanish Blood.* 1946. Tower. dj. EX. P1. $27.25

CHANDLER, Raymond. *Spanish Blood.* 1946. Tower. dj. VG. P1. $25.00

CHANG, Diana. *Woman of Thirty.* 1959. Random House. 1st ed. presentation. sgn. dj. EX. $10.00

CHANIN, A. & M. *This Land, These Voices: Different View of AZ History...* 1977. Northland. 1st ed. 266 p. dj. EX. M2. $22.00

CHANIN, P. *Natural History of Otters.* 1985. Facts on File. Ils 1st ed. 179 p. EX. M2. $27.00

CHANNING, Mark. *King Cobra.* 1934. Lippincott. 1st ed. VG. P1. $30.00

CHANNING, Mark. *Nine Lives.* 1937. Phil. 1st ed. dj. EX. $45.00

CHANNING, Mark. *White Python.* 1934. Phil. 1st ed. dj. EX. $40.00

CHANNING, W.E. *Reviews & Miscellanies.* 1830. Boston. 1st ed. 2 vols. EX. J2. $85.00

CHANNING, W.E. *Sermon Preached in Boston, July 23, 1912...* 1812. Boston. 1st ed. 20 p. VG. $55.00

CHANNING, W.E. *Works of William E. Channing.* 1848. Boston/NY. 8th ed. 6 vols. VG. $45.00

CHANT, Joy. *Gray Mane of Morning.* 1977. Allen Unwin. 1st ed. dj. EX. P1. $25.00

CHANT, Joy. *Gray Mane of Morning.* 1978. Allen Unwin. 2nd ed. P1. $11.50

CHANT, Joy. *High Kings.* 1985. 1st pb ed. EX. C1. $2.50

CHANT, Joy. *Red Moon & Black Mountain.* nd. Book Club. dj. VG. P1. $4.75

CHANT, Joy. *Red Moon & Black Mountain.* 1976. Dutton. 1st ed. dj. EX. P1. $25.00

CHAPATTI & ROSCI. *Octavianus Monfort.* 1985. Turin. Umberto Allemandi. Ils. 127 p. D2. $60.00

CHAPEL, C.E. *Art of Shooting.* 1960. Ils 2nd ed. dj. $18.00

CHAPEL, C.E. *Boys' Book of Rifles.* 1948. Crowell. dj. G. $30.00

CHAPEL, C.E. *Gun Collectors' Handbook of Values.* 1940. San Leandro. 1st ed. VG. B2. $50.00

CHAPEL, C.E. *Simplified Rifle Shooting.* 1950. NY. 1st ed. dj. VG. $20.00

CHAPELLE, Howard. *History of American Sailing Ships.* 1935. 2nd print. G. $25.00

CHAPELLE, Howard. *History of the American Sailing Navy.* 1949. Norton. 1st ed. dj. EX. $60.00

CHAPELLE, Howard. *Search for Speed Under Sail, 1700-1855.* 1967. NY. 1st ed. dj. EX. $75.00

CHAPIN, A.A. *Everyday Fairy Boat Book.* nd. London. Ils Smith. B4. $75.00

CHAPIN, Bela. *Poets of NH.* 1883. Claremont. 8vo. 784 p. gilt cloth. VG. T1. $30.00

CHAPIN, Carl M. *Three Died Beside the Marble Pool.* 1936. Crime Club. 1st ed. VG. P1. $18.25

CHAPIN, D. *Wizard of Westwood.* 1973. Boston. 1st ed. 322 p. dj. VG. B2. $17.50

CHAPIN, E.H. *Catalog of Library of Late E.H. Chapin.* 1881. NY. orig wraps. fair. $35.00

CHAPIN & PAGE. *Chapin & Page's Hudson Directory & Historical Record.* 1869. Tecumseh. 1st/only ed. VG. rare. $160.00

CHAPLIN, Charlie. *My Trip Abroad.* 1922. Harper. Ils 1st ed. dj. VG. $55.00

CHAPLIN, Gordon. *Joy Ride.* 1982. Coward. 1st ed. dj. M. $10.00

CHAPLIN, Jeremiah. *Chips From the White House.* 1881. Boston. 12mo. G. $17.50

CHAPLIN, Ralph. *Bars & Shadows.* 1922. NY. dj. EX. $50.00

CHAPLIN, Ralph. *Somewhat Barbaric.* 1944. Seattle. Dogwood. EX. $45.00

CHAPMAN, A. *Savage Sudan: Its Wild Tribes, Big Game & Bird Life.* 1921. London. Ils. photos. map. 452 p. VG. M2. $165.00

CHAPMAN, Allen. *Radio Boys With the Forest Rangers.* 1923. Grosset. dj. VG. P1. $10.00

CHAPMAN, Arthur. *Pony Express.* 1932. NY. Ils 1st ed. 319 p. B2. $40.00

CHAPMAN, Arthur. *Pony Express.* 1932. NY. 1st ed. dj. C4. $45.00

CHAPMAN, C.E. *Founding of Spanish CA.* 1916. NY. 1st ed. G. $22.50

CHAPMAN, E. *Latest Night: A. Lincoln Wartime Memories.* 1917. NY. 1st ed. 570 p. VG. B2. $35.00

CHAPMAN, F.M. *Autobiography of a Bird-Lover.* 1933. Appleton. Ils Fuertes. 420 p. dj. VG. P1. $25.00

CHAPMAN, F.M. *Color Key to N American Birds.* 1903. Doubleday. Ils 1st ed. 312 p. VG. P1. $20.00

CHAPMAN, F.M. *Color Key to N American Birds.* 1912. Appleton. Ils Revised 2nd ed. 356 p. G. M2. $16.00

CHAPMAN, F.M. *Nesting Habits of Wagler's Oropendola on Barro Island, CO.* 1930. Smithsonian. Ils Jaques. M2. $4.00

CHAPMAN, F.M. *Warblers of N America.* 1907. Appleton. Ils Fuertes/Horsfall. 1st ed. M2. $45.00

CHAPMAN, F.M. *Warblers of N America.* 1917. Appleton. Ils Fuertes/Horsfall. 3rd ed. M2. $40.00

CHAPMAN, F.S. *Jungle Is Neutral.* 1949. NY. 1st ed. dj. VG. B2. $17.50

CHAPMAN, Vera. *Green Knight.* 1978. Avon. 1st Am ed. EX. C1. $3.50

CHAPMAN, Vera. *Three Damsels.* 1978. Magnum. 1st Eng ed. VG. C1. $9.00

CHAPMAN, W. *Loneliest Continent: Story of Antarctic Discovery.* 1964. NY Graphic Soc. Ils 1st ed. 279 p. dj. EX. M2. $13.00

CHAPPELL, F. *Brighten the Corner Where You Are.* 1989. NY. UCP. EX. $45.00

CHAPPELL, F. *Inkling.* 1965. London. 1st ed. dj. EX. scarce. $40.00

CHAPPELL, F. *World Between the Eyes.* 1971. Baton Rouge. 1st ed. dj. EX. $25.00

CHAPPELL, G.S. *Logging Along the Denver & Rio Grande.* 1971. Co Railroad Mus. 190 p. dj. A3. $45.00

CHAPPELL, G.S. *Rollo in Society.* 1922. NY. VG. $20.00

CHAPPELL, Matthew N. *How To Control Worry.* 1949. Perma P46. VG. P1. $4.50

CHAPPELL, Warren. *Let's Make a B for Bennett.* 1953. Typophiles. wraps. EX. $20.00

CHAPPELL, Warren. *Short History of Printed Word.* 1970. Knopf. Stated 1st ed. dj. EX. $12.50

CHAPPELL, William. *Fonteyn: Impressions of a Ballerina.* 1951. London. 8vo. 136 p. dj. VG. P3. $29.00

CHAPPELL, William. *Old English Popular Music.* 1961. NY. Revised ed. $27.50

CHAPPELL & DUYCKINCK. *National Portrait Gallery.* 1862. NY. Ils. 2 vols in 1. dj. G. $125.00

CHAPUY & DE JOLIMONT. *Vues Pittoresques de la Cathédrale de Paris.* 1823. Paris. Ils Chapuy. G. J2. $200.00

CHARBONNEAU, Louis. *No Place on Earth.* nd. Book Club. dj. VG. P1. $3.50

CHARD, Thomas. *CA Sketches.* 1888. Chicago. 12mo. 26 p. green bdg. $10.00

CHARLES, C.J. *Elizabethan Interiors.* nd. NY. 3rd ed. 1/500. sgn/inscr/#d. J2. $65.00

CHARLIP & SUPREE. *Harlequin & the Gift of Many Colors.* 1973. NY. Parents Magazine. Ils. VG. $10.00

CHARLTON, T.U.P. *Life of Major General James Jackson.* 1898. Atlanta. 1st ed. 1/250. VG. $200.00

CHARTERIS, Evans. *John Sargent.* 1927. NY. Scribner. Ils. 4to. 308 p. cloth. $50.00

CHARTERIS, Leslie. *Call for the Saint.* 1948. Crime Club. 1st ed. dj. G. P1. $25.00

CHARTERIS, Leslie. *Call for the Saint.* 1948. Crime Club. 1st ed. xl. P1. $7.50

CHARTERIS, Leslie. *Featuring the Saint.* nd. Hodder Stoughton. G. P1. $7.50

CHARTERIS, Leslie. *Follow the Saint.* 1943. Triangle. 2nd ed. VG. P1. $10.00

CHARTERIS, Leslie. *Juan Belmonte: Killer of Bulls.* nd. Book League. VG. P1. $15.00

CHARTERIS, Leslie. *Saint & Mr. Teal.* 1943. Triangle. VG. P1. $10.00

CHARTERIS, Leslie. *Saint & the People Importers.* 1972. Crime Club. 1st ed. dj. xl. P1. $6.00

CHARTERIS, Leslie. *Saint at Large.* 1945. Triangle. VG. P1. $10.00

CHARTERIS, Leslie. *Saint at the Thieves' Picnic.* 1937. London. $25.00

CHARTERIS, Leslie. *Saint Bids Diamonds.* 1944. Triangle. 7th ed. dj. VG. P1. $10.00

CHARTERIS, Leslie. *Saint Goes On.* 1941. Sun Dial. dj. VG. P1. $16.00

CHARTERIS, Leslie. *Saint in Miami.* nd. Book Club. P1. $2.75

CHARTERIS, Leslie. *Saint in Miami.* 1945. Triangle. 4th ed. dj. VG. P1. $11.50

CHARTERIS, Leslie. *Saint in Pursuit.* 1970. Doubleday. 1st ed. dj. xl. P1. $10.00

CHARTERIS, Leslie. *Saint on Guard.* 1944. Doubleday. 1st ed. dj. EX. scarce. $45.00

CHARTERIS, Leslie. *Saint on Guard.* 1945. Musson. VG. P1. $20.00

CHARTERIS, Leslie. *Saint Overboard.* 1941. Triangle. 2nd ed. dj. VG. P1. $16.00

CHARTERIS, Leslie. *Saint Overboard.* 1942. Triangle. VG. P1. $9.25

CHARTERIS, Leslie. *Saint Plays With Fire.* 1942. Triangle. VG. P1. $10.00

CHARTERIS, Leslie. *Saint Sees It Through.* 1947. Musson. 1st Canadian ed. G. P1. $6.50

CHARTERIS, Leslie. *Saint Steps In.* 1944. Musson. dj. xl. P1. $6.50

CHARTERIS, Leslie. *Saint vs. Scotland Yard.* nd. Book Club. dj. VG. P1. $4.50

CHARTERIS, Leslie. *Saint: Good As Gold.* nd. Ellery Queen Mystery Club. dj. P1. $7.50

CHARTERIS, Leslie. *Saint's Getaway.* 1945. Triangle. VG. P1. $10.00

CHARTERIS, Leslie. *Send for the Saint.* 1978. Crime Club. 1st ed. dj. xl. P1. $7.50

CHARTERIS, Leslie. *Trust the Saint.* 1962. Crime Club. 1st ed. dj. xl. P1. $7.50

CHARTERIS, Leslie. *X Esquire.* nd. Ward Lock. VG. P1. $40.00

CHARTERS. *Bibliography of Works by Jack Kerouac.* 1975. NY. Revised ed. VG. $25.00

CHASE, A.W. *Dr. Chase's Recipes or Information for Everyone.* 1870. Ils. 384 p. K1. $18.50

CHASE, A.W. *Guide to Wealth: Over Seventy Valuable Receipts.* 1859. Hornellsville. Revised 4th ed. 14 p. wraps. T5. $22.50

CHASE, Allan. *Five Arrows.* nd. Book Club. dj. VG. P1. $4.50

CHASE, E. *Memorial Life of General Sherman.* 1891. Chicago. Ils. 8vo. 558 p. G2. $29.00

CHASE, Francis. *Gathered Sketches From NH & VT.* 1871. Claremont. pls. VG. $27.50

CHASE, James Hadley. *Cade.* 1967. Thriller Book Club. dj. VG. P1. $3.75

CHASE, James Hadley. *Double Shuffle.* nd. Thriller Book Club. dj. VG. P1. $6.00

CHASE, James Hadley. *Have This One on Me.* 1967. Thriller Book Club. dj. VG. P1. $4.50

CHASE, James Hadley. *I Would Rather Stay Poor.* 1962. Robert Hale. dj. VG. P1. $7.00

CHASE, James Hadley. *I'll Bury My Dead.* 1954. Dutton. xl. P1. $4.75

CHASE, James Hadley. *I'll Bury My Dead.* 1954. Dutton. 1st ed. dj. VG. P1. $10.00

CHASE, James Hadley. *Strictly for Cash.* nd. Thriller Book Club. dj. VG. P1. $5.50

CHASE, James Hadley. *Tiger by the Tail.* 1954. Robert Hale. VG. P1. $11.00

CHASE, James Hadley. *World in My Pocket.* 1958. Robert Hale. dj. VG. P1. $7.25

CHASE, James Hadley. *You've Got It Coming.* 1955. Robert Hale. dj. VG. P1. $8.25

CHASE, M.E. *Dawn in Lyonesse.* March, 1938. 1st reprint ed. VG. C1. $6.50

CHASE, M.E. *ME & Its Role in American Art.* 1963. NY. 1st ed. dj. VG. B2. $47.50

CHASE, M.E. *Windswept.* 1941. NY. 1st ed. sgn. G. $20.00

CHASE, N. *Locksley.* 1984. pb. EX. C1. $4.50

CHASE, Stuart. *Men & Machines.* 1929. NY. Ils 1st ed. dj. $10.00

CHASE, Stuart. *Road We Are Traveling 1914-1942.* 1942. NY. 20th-C Fund. sgn. 106 p. VG. M1. $25.00

CHASTAIN, Thomas. *911.* nd. Book Club. dj. VG. P1. $4.00

CHATFIELD, Judith. *Tour of Italian Gardens.* 1988. NY. Rizzoli. Ils. 224 p. dj. D2. $25.00

CHATHAM. *Anecdotes of William Pitt, 1st Earl of Chatham.* 1797. London. 6th ed. 3 vols. VG. $250.00

CHATTERJI, J.C. *India's Outlook on Life.* 1931. NY. $55.00

CHATTERTON, E.K. *In Great Waters.* 1932. Warne. VG. P1. $12.50

CHATTERTON, E.K. *Windjammers & Shellbacks.* nd. Phil. pls. G. $7.50

CHATWIN, Bruce. *On the Black Hill.* 1983. NY. Viking. 1st ed. EX. $12.00

CHATWIN, Bruce. *Utz.* 1978. London. 1st ed. dj. EX. $45.00

CHATWIN, Bruce. *Viceroy of Ouidah.* 1980. London. 1st ed. dj. EX. $20.00

CHAUCER, Geoffrey. *Canterbury Tales.* 1907. London. Ils Clark. blue calf. EX. $150.00

CHAUCER, Geoffrey. *Canterbury Tales.* 1934. NY. Ils Kent. not Deluxe ed. $30.00

CHAUVIN, R. *World of the Insect.* 1967. McGraw Hill. Ils. 254 p. dj. xl. M2. $4.00

CHAYEFSKY, P. *Middle of the Night.* 1957. NY. 1st ed. dj. VG. $25.00

CHAYEFSKY, P. *Television Plays.* 1955. NY. 1st print. dj. VG. $22.50

CHEEL, C. *Truth About VA City, 1850-1940.* wraps. VG. $80.00

CHEERS, G. *Carnivorous Plants.* 1983. Australia. Ils. 95 p. EX. M2. $11.00

CHEESMAN, E. *Six Legged Snakes in New Guinea: Collecting Expedition.* 1949. Harrap. Ils 1st ed. 281 p. dj. EX. M2. $14.00

CHEEVER, John. *Atlantic Crossing. Excerpts From a Journal.* 1986. Ex-Ophidia Pr. 1/90. 4to. full leather. fld case. $350.00

CHEEVER, John. *Brigadier & the Golf Widow.* 1964. NY. 1st ed. dj. EX. $35.00

CHEEVER, John. *Bullet Park.* 1969. NY. 1st ed. sgn. dj. VG. $32.50

CHEEVER, John. *Enormous Radio.* 1953. NY. 1st ed. dj. VG. $30.00

CHEEVER, John. *Falconer.* 1977. London. AP. proof dj. EX. $60.00

CHEEVER, John. *Falconer.* 1977. London. 1st ed. dj. EX. $40.00

CHEEVER, John. *Housebreaker of Shady Hill.* 1958. NY. 1st Am ed. dj. VG. $50.00

CHEEVER, John. *Leaves, Lion Fish & Bear.* 1980. LA. 1st ed. 1/330. sgn. EX. $75.00

CHEEVER, John. *National Pastime.* 1982. LA. 1st ed. 1/330. sgn. EX. $75.00

CHEEVER, John. *Oh What a Paradise It Seems.* 1982. Knopf. Stated 1st ed. dj. EX. $17.50

CHEEVER, John. *Stories of John Cheever.* 1978. NY. 1st ed. dj. EX. $35.00

CHEEVER, John. *Wapshot Chronicle.* 1964. London. 1st ed. dj. M. $36.00

CHEEVER, John. *Wapshot Scandal.* 1964. NY. 1st trade ed. dj. EX. $35.00

CHEEVER, John. *Way Some People Live.* 1943. NY. 1st ed. EX. $55.00

CHEEVER, John. *What a Paradise It Seems.* 1982. NY. 1st ed. dj. VG. $15.00

CHEEVER, John. *World of Apples.* 1973. Knopf. 1st ed. dj. EX. $25.00

CHEIRO. *Fate in the Making.* 1931. NY. $70.00

CHEN-CHI, Chang. *Practice of Zen.* 1959. NY. $24.00

CHENEY, E.D. *Louisa May Alcott: Her Life, Letters & Journals.* 1889. Boston. 1st ed. VG. $45.00

CHENEY, J.V. *Lyrics.* 1901. Boston. presentation. sgn. $10.00

CHENWETH, W.W. *How To Make Candy.* 1936. NY. Ils 1st ed. 8vo. 212 p. $20.00

CHERNOV, L.A. *Wave Propagation in Random Medium.* 1960. McGraw Hill. sgn. G. $12.00

CHERRIE, G.K. *Contribution to the Ornithology of San Domingo.* 1896. Field Mus. 26 p. M2. $3.00

CHERRINGTON, E.M. *Standard Encyclopedia of Alcohol Problem.* 1935-1930. Westerville, OH. 4to. 6 vols. $150.00

CHERRY, P.P. *Portage Path.* 1911. Akron. Ils 1st ed. fld map. 106 p. T5. $35.00

CHERRY, P.P. *W Reserve & Early OH.* 1921. Akron. Pub/inscr Fouse. 333 p. T5. $37.50

CHERRY-GARRARD, A. *Worst Journey in the World.* 1930. NY. 1st Am ed. 485 p. VG. B2. $67.50

CHERRYH, C.J. *Arafel's Saga.* nd. Book Club. dj. VG. P1. $4.50

CHERRYH, C.J. *Cuckoo's Egg.* 1985. Phantasia. 1/350. sgn. dj. slipcase. EX. P1. $40.00

CHERRYH, C.J. *Faded Sun Shon'Jir.* nd. Book Club. dj. EX. P1. $4.00

CHERRYH, C.J. *Forty Thousand in Gehenna.* nd. Book Club. dj. VG. P1. $4.50

CHERRYH, C.J. *Forty Thousand in Gehenna.* 1983. Phantasia. 1/350. sgn. dj. slipcase. EX. P1. $50.00

CHERRYH, C.J. *Kif Strike Back.* 1985. Phantasia. 1/2400. dj. VG. $20.00

CHERRYH, C.J. *Kif Strike Back.* 1985. Phantasia. 1/350. sgn. dj. slipcase. EX. P1. $40.00

CHERRYH, C.J. *Port Eternity.* pb. VG. C1. $3.00

CHERRYH, C.J. *Port Eternity.* Book Club. dj. VG. C1. $3.00

CHERRYH, C.J. *Pride of Chanur.* nd. Book Club. dj. EX. P1. $4.00

CHESELDEN, W. *Anatomy of Human Body.* 1756. London. Ils 7th ed. inscr. 8vo. 334 p. $350.00

CHESELDINE, R.M. *OH in the Rainbow: Official Story of 166th Infantry...* 1924. Columbus. 528 p. G. T5. $55.00

CHESNEY, A.M. *Johns Hopkins Hospital & School of Medicine Early Years...* 1943. Baltimore. Ils 1st ed. fld map. dj. VG. B2. $32.50

CHESNUT & WOODWARD. *Mary Chesnut's Civil War.* c 1981. New Haven. dj. VG. $15.00

CHESSICK, Richard. *Intensive Psychotherapy of the Borderline Patient.* 1977. NY. 2nd ed. dj. EX. $14.00

CHESSMAN, Caryl. *Face of Justice.* 1957. NY. Crime Club. 1st ed. dj. VG. B2. $22.50

CHESSMAN, Caryl. *Trial by Ordeal.* 1955. NY. 1st ed. dj. VG. $18.00

CHESTER, George Randolph. *Making of Bobby Burnit.* 1909. McLeod Allen. G. P1. $3.75

CHESTERFIELD & TRUSLER. *Principles of Politeness & of Knowing the World.* 1775. London. $55.00

CHESTERTON, G.K. *Autobiography.* 1936. NY. 1st ed. dj. G. B2. $20.00

CHESTERTON, G.K. *Colored Lands.* 1938. Sheed Ward. Ils Chesterton. dj. VG. B4. $55.00

CHESTERTON, G.K. *Crimes of England.* 1916. NY. 1st Am ed. xl. VG. $30.00

CHESTERTON, G.K. *Father Brown Book.* 1959. Cassell. 2nd ed. xl. P1. $7.25

CHESTERTON, G.K. *Innocence of Father Brown.* nd. Macaulay. VG. P1. $15.00

CHESTERTON, G.K. *Innocence of Father Brown.* 1913. Cassell. 4th ed. VG. P1. $18.25

CHESTERTON, G.K. *Magic.* 1914. NY. G. $18.00

CHESTERTON, G.K. *Man Who Knew Too Much.* nd. Burt. xl. rebound. P1. $6.00

CHESTERTON, G.K. *Man Who Was Thursday.* nd. Dodd Mead. dj. VG. P1. $20.00

CHESTERTON, G.K. *Man Who Was Thursday.* nd. Modern Lib. VG. P1. $20.00

CHESTERTON, G.K. *Man Who Was Thursday.* 1946. Arrowsmith. 3rd ed. VG. P1. $20.00

CHESTERTON, G.K. *Possessors.* 1964. Simon Schuster. dj. VG. $17.50

CHESTERTON, G.K. *Sword of Wood.* 1938. Woburn Books. Ltd ed. sgn. $50.00

CHESTERTON, G.K. *Tales of the Long Bow.* 1925. Tauchnitz. VG. P1. $60.00

CHESTERTON, G.K. *What's Wrong With the World.* 1913. Cassell. 8th print. G. P1. $20.00

CHESTNUT, M.B. *Diary From Dixie.* 1949. Boston. Houghton Mifflin. dj. $25.00

CHETWYND-HAYES, R. *Quiver of Ghosts.* 1984. William Kimber. 1st ed. sgn. dj. EX. P1. $30.00

CHETWYND-HAYES, R. *Tales From the Dark Lands.* 1984. William Kimber. 1st ed. P1. $20.00

CHEVALIER, Haakon. *For Us the Living.* 1949. Knopf. 1st ed. sgn. $15.00

CHEVALIER, Maurice. *I Remember It Well.* 1970. NY. 1st ed. dj. EX. $20.00

CHEVALIER, Maurice. *My Paris.* 1972. NY. Macmillan. 1st ed. dj. EX. $40.00

CHEVALLIER, Gabriel. *Clochemerle.* nd. Paris. Ils Dubout. Ltd ed. 4to. wraps. $125.00

CHEVREUL. *Principles of Harmony & Contrast of Colors.* 1967. NY. Ils. 256 p. dj. EX. C4. $59.00

CHEW, Samuel. *Pilgrimage of Life.* 1962. Yale. dj. VG. $18.00

CHEYNEY, Peter. *Can Ladies Kill?* 1938. Collins. 1st ed. xl. VG. P1. $15.00

CHEYNEY, Peter. *Dark Bahama.* 1950. Collins. dj. VG. P1. $13.75

CHEYNEY, Peter. *Dark Street.* 1944. Dodd Mead. dj. VG. P1. $10.00

CHEYNEY, Peter. *Dark Wanton.* 1948. Collins. dj. VG. P1. $9.25

CHEYNEY, Peter. *I'll Say She Does!* 1946. Dodd Mead. G. P1. $7.00

CHEYNEY, Peter. *Ladies Won't Wait.* 1972. Collins. dj. VG. P1. $12.50

CHEYNEY, Peter. *Lady, Behave!* 1950. Collins. dj. VG. P1. $15.00

CHEYNEY, Peter. *No Ordinary Cheyney.* 1949. Faber. 3rd ed. dj. VG. P1. $9.25

CHEYNEY, Peter. *One of Those Things.* 1949. Collins. VG. P1. $10.00

CHEYNEY, Peter. *One of Those Things.* 1950. Dodd Mead. VG. P1. $10.00

CHEYNEY, Peter. *Poison Ivy.* 1937. Collins. xl. VG. P1. $15.00

CHEYNEY, Peter. *Stars Are Dark.* nd. Book Club. VG. P1. $5.00

CHEYNEY, Peter. *This Man Is Dangerous.* 1938. Collins. 5th ed. xl. P1. $10.00

CHEYNEY, Peter. *Trying Anything Twice.* 1948. NY. 1st ed. dj. VG. T1. $22.00

CHEYNEY, Peter. *Uneasy Terms.* 1947. Dodd Mead. xl. VG. P1. $6.00

CHEYNEY, Peter. *Uneasy Terms.* 1958. Collins. VG. P1. $7.50

CHEYNEY, Peter. *You Can Call It a Day.* 1949. Collins. dj. xl. P1. $7.00

CHIARENZA & SISKIND. *Pleasures & Terrors.* 1982. Boston. Little Brown. sgn. M. $40.00

CHICHESTER, F.C. *Seaplane Solo.* 1934. NY. Ils 1st ed. fld map. 314 p. dj. T5. $37.50

CHICHESTER, John Jay. *Rogues of Fortune.* 1929. Chelsea House. xl. VG. P1. $13.75

CHICKERING, C.R. *Flowers of Guatamala.* 1973. OK U. Ils 1st ed. 131 p. dj. EX. $15.00

CHIDSEY, D.B. *CA Gold Rush.* 1968. NY. Crown. 1st ed. dj. EX. $10.00

CHIDSEY, D.B. *Panama Passage.* nd. Book Club. dj. VG. P1. $3.50

CHIERA, Ed. *Sumerian Epics & Myths.* 1934. Chicago. Chicago U. VG. $60.00

CHILD, Julia. *French Chef Cookbook.* 1968. NY. 1st ed. dj. EX. $20.00

CHILD, L.M. *American Frugal Housewife.* 1838. NY. 22nd ed. orig bdg. EX. T5. $95.00

CHILD, L.M. *Letters From NY.* 1843. London. 12mo. full leather. VG. $60.00

CHILD, L.M. *Letters From NY.* 1845. 3rd ed. 288 p. $30.00

CHILD, Steven. *Landscape Architecture: Series of Letters.* 1927. Stanford. 1st ed. 4to. 279 p. $60.00

CHILD, Theodore. *Spanish-American Republics.* 1891. Harpers. Ils. VG. $40.00

CHILD. *English & Scottish Popular Ballads.* 1925. Rome. 4to. xl. VG. $30.00

CHILDCRAFT. *Vol. 13: Art & Music.* 1947. Ils. VG. B4. $35.00

CHILDS, G.W. *Recollections of General Grant.* 1890. Phil. 1st ed. VG. $25.00

CHILDS, M.F. *De Namin' ob de Twins & Other Sketches From Cotton Land.* 1923. Macon, GA. Burke. 139 p. $45.00

CHILDS, Timothy. *Cold Turkey.* 1979. Harper Row. dj. EX. P1. $7.00

CHILERS. *Erskine Ramsay: His Life.* 1942. presentation. sgn. VG. B1. $25.00

CHILTON, John. *Who's Who of Jazz.* 1978. Time Life. black cloth. VG. $13.00

CHINDAHL, George. *History of the Circus in America.* 1959. Caxton. 1st ed. dj. VG. J2. $20.00

CHIPPENDALE, Thomas. *Cabinet Makers' & Gentlemen's Directory.* 1938. NY. Towse Pub. folio. dj. G. $125.00

CHIPPERFIELD. *Seokoo of the Black Wind.* 1963. NY. Ils. dj. EX. $8.00

CHISHLOLM, Louey. *Enchanted Land: Tales Told Again.* nd. NY. Ils Cameron. 1st ed. VG. J2. $40.00

CHITTENDEN, Hiram. *History of American Fur Trade in Far W.* 1954. Stanford, CA. 1st ed. 2 vols. djs. VG. J2. $40.00

CHITTENDEN, L.E. *Invisible Siege: Journal of Lucius E. Chittenden...* 1969. San Diego. 1/1500. 133 p. slipcase. EX. M2. $45.00

CHITTY, A.B. *Reconstruction at Sewanee...* 1954. Sewanee U. Ils 1st ed. 1/1000. sgn. 206 p. $35.00

CHRETIEN DE TROYES. *Erec et Enide.* 1924. Paris. Trans Lot-Borodine. 1/50. C1. $15.00

CHRISTENSEN, C.M. *Common Edible Mushrooms.* 1969. MN U. 3rd print. VG. $11.00

CHRISTENSEN, C.M. *Common Fleshy Fungi.* 1965. Burgess. Ils. 237 p. spiral bdg. EX. M2. $13.00

CHRISTENSEN, E.O. *Museum Directory of US & Canada.* 1961. WA. 1st ed. VG. $35.00

CHRISTIAN, Catherine. *Pendragon.* 1980. 1st ed. pb. VG. C1. $3.50

CHRISTIANSEN, Harry. *N OH's Interurbans & Rapid Transit Railways.* 1965. Cleveland. Ils 1st ed. 176 p. wraps. VG. T5. $35.00

CHRISTIE, Agatha. *After the Funeral.* 1953. Collins Crime Club. dj. VG. P1. $30.00

CHRISTIE, Agatha. *After the Funeral.* 1953. Collins Crime Club. VG. P1. $12.50

CHRISTIE, Agatha. *Appointment With Death.* 1938. Collins. 1st Eng ed. orange cloth. VG. D1. $75.00

CHRISTIE, Agatha. *Appointment With Death.* 1938. Dodd Mead. 1st Am ed. VG. D1. $48.00

CHRISTIE, Agatha. *At Bertram's Hotel.* 1965. Collins. 1st Eng ed. dj. VG. D1. $30.00

CHRISTIE, Agatha. *Big Four.* nd. Collins. dj. VG. P1. $20.00

CHRISTIE, Agatha. *Big Four.* 1927. Dodd Mead. 1st Am ed. blue cloth. VG. D1. $85.00

CHRISTIE, Agatha. *Body in the Library.* 1942. Dodd Mead. 1st Am ed. orange cloth. VG. D1. $40.00

CHRISTIE, Agatha. *Boomerang Clue.* 1935. Dodd Mead. 1st ed. G. P1. $30.00

CHRISTIE, Agatha. *By the Pricking of My Thumbs.* 1968. Collins. 1st Eng ed. green cloth. D1. $25.00

CHRISTIE, Agatha. *By the Pricking of My Thumbs.* 1968. Collins. 1st Eng ed. orange cloth. dj. D1. $30.00

CHRISTIE, Agatha. *By the Pricking of My Thumbs.* nd. Book Club. dj. VG. P1. $2.75

CHRISTIE, Agatha. *By the Pricking of My Thumbs.* 1968. Collins Crime Club. 1st ed. dj. P1. $20.00

CHRISTIE, Agatha. *By the Pricking of My Thumbs.* 1968. Dodd Mead. 1st Am ed. dj. VG. D1. $20.00

CHRISTIE, Agatha. *Cards on the Table.* 1936. Collins. 1st Eng ed. orange cloth. G. D1. $15.00

CHRISTIE, Agatha. *Cards on the Table.* 1937. Dodd Mead. 1st ed. VG. P1. $40.00

CHRISTIE, Agatha. *Caribbean Mystery.* 1964. Collins. 1st Eng ed. dj. VG. D1. $35.00

CHRISTIE, Agatha. *Caribbean Mystery.* 1965. Dodd Mead. 1st ed. dj. xl. P1. $6.00

CHRISTIE, Agatha. *Cat Among the Pigeons.* 1959. Collins Crime Club. P1. $10.00

CHRISTIE, Agatha. *Cat Among the Pigeons.* 1959. Collins. 1st Eng ed. red cloth. dj. D1. $35.00

CHRISTIE, Agatha. *Clocks.* 1963. Collins Crime Club. 1st ed. dj. P1. $30.00

CHRISTIE, Agatha. *Clocks*. 1963. Collins. 1st Eng ed. red cloth. dj. VG. D1. $30.00

CHRISTIE, Agatha. *Clocks*. 1963. Dodd Mead. 1st Am ed. gray/orange cloth. dj. $25.00

CHRISTIE, Agatha. *Crooked House*. 1949. Collins. 1st Eng ed. orange cloth. dj. G. $35.00

CHRISTIE, Agatha. *Crooked House*. 1949. Dodd Mead. 1st Am ed. gray cloth. VG. D1. $30.00

CHRISTIE, Agatha. *Crooked House*. 1950. Australia. Collins Crime Club. 1st ed. dj. P1. $25.00

CHRISTIE, Agatha. *Curtain*. 1975. Collins. 2nd Eng ed. black cloth. dj. D1. $18.00

CHRISTIE, Agatha. *Curtain*. 1975. Dodd Mead. dj. P1. $15.00

CHRISTIE, Agatha. *Curtain*. 1975. Dodd Mead. 1st ed. blue/tan cloth. dj. D1. $10.00

CHRISTIE, Agatha. *Dead Man's Folly*. 1956. Collins Crime Club. 1st ed. dj. P1. $30.00

CHRISTIE, Agatha. *Dead Man's Folly*. 1956. Collins. 1st ed. orange cloth. dj. VG. D1. $50.00

CHRISTIE, Agatha. *Dead Man's Folly*. 1956. Collins. 1st ed. orange cloth. VG. D1. $30.00

CHRISTIE, Agatha. *Dead Man's Folly*. 1956. Dodd Mead. 1st Am ed. red cloth. dj. VG. D1. $20.00

CHRISTIE, Agatha. *Dead Man's Folly*. 1957. Collins. 2nd ed. blue cloth. VG. D1. $15.00

CHRISTIE, Agatha. *Death in the Air*. 1935. Dodd Mead. 1st Am ed. gray cloth. VG. D1. $60.00

CHRISTIE, Agatha. *Destination Unknown*. 1954. Collins Crime Club. 1st ed. dj. P1. $30.00

CHRISTIE, Agatha. *Destination Unknown*. 1954. Collins. 1st ed. orange cloth. dj. VG. D1. $40.00

CHRISTIE, Agatha. *Elephants Can Remember*. 1972. Collins Crime Club. dj. VG. P1. $7.25

CHRISTIE, Agatha. *Elephants Can Remember*. 1972. Collins. 1st ed. orange cloth. dj. VG. D1. $22.00

CHRISTIE, Agatha. *Elephants Can Remember*. 1972. Dodd Mead. Book Club. beige cloth. dj. VG. D1. $15.00

CHRISTIE, Agatha. *Elephants Can Remember*. 1972. Dodd Mead. 1st ed. violet cloth. dj. VG. D1. $20.00

CHRISTIE, Agatha. *Endless Night*. 1967. Collins. 1st Eng ed. red cloth. dj. VG. D1. $35.00

CHRISTIE, Agatha. *Endless Night*. 1967. London. 1st ed. dj. EX. $42.00

CHRISTIE, Agatha. *Floating Admiral*. 1932. Crime Club. 1st Am ed. black cloth. VG. D1. $80.00

CHRISTIE, Agatha. *Halloween Party*. 1969. Collins. 1st Eng ed. orange cloth. dj. D1. $40.00

CHRISTIE, Agatha. *Halloween Party*. 1969. Dodd Mead. 1st ed. black/orange cloth. dj. D1. $30.00

CHRISTIE, Agatha. *Halloween Party*. 1969. UK Book Club. green cloth. dj. VG. D1. $15.00

CHRISTIE, Agatha. *Hickory Dickory Death*. 1955. Dodd Mead. 1st Am ed. green cloth. dj. EX. D1. $38.00

CHRISTIE, Agatha. *Hickory Dickory Dock*. 1955. Collins. 1st ed. red cloth. dj. VG. D1. $48.00

CHRISTIE, Agatha. *Hollow (A Play)*. 1952. French's Acting #8 ed. wraps. D1. $40.00

CHRISTIE, Agatha. *Hollow*. 1946. Collins. 1st ed. orange cloth. dj. VG. D1. $55.00

CHRISTIE, Agatha. *Hound of Death & Other Stories*. 1933. Odhams. 1st ed. maroon cloth. VG. D1. $35.00

CHRISTIE, Agatha. *Hound of Death & Other Stories*. 1939. Collins Crime Club. dj. VG. P1. $45.00

CHRISTIE, Agatha. *Labors of Hercules*. 1963. Collins Crime Club. dj. VG. P1. $10.00

CHRISTIE, Agatha. *Make Mine Murder!* nd. Book Club. dj. VG. P1. $4.75

CHRISTIE, Agatha. *Man in the Brown Suit*. 1924. Dodd Mead. 1st Am ed. brown cloth. VG. D1. $185.00

CHRISTIE, Agatha. *Mirror Cracked From Side to Side*. nd. Collins Crime Club. dj. VG. P1. $20.00

CHRISTIE, Agatha. *Mirror Cracked From Side to Side*. 1962. Collins. 1st ed. red cloth. dj. VG. D1. $32.00

CHRISTIE, Agatha. *Mirror Cracked From Side to Side*. 1962. Dodd Mead. 1st ed. yellow bdg. dj. VG. D1. $25.00

CHRISTIE, Agatha. *Miss Marple Meets Murder*. nd. Book Club. dj. EX. P1. $7.50

CHRISTIE, Agatha. *Miss Marple's 6 Final Cases*. 1979. Collins. dj. EX. P1. $15.00

CHRISTIE, Agatha. *Mousetrap*. 1954. London. 1st ed. wraps. $12.00

CHRISTIE, Agatha. *Mr. Parker Pyne, Detective*. 1933. Dodd Mead. 1st ed. orange cloth. VG. D1. $100.00

CHRISTIE, Agatha. *Mrs. McGinty's Dead*. 1952. Collins Crime Club. 1st ed. dj. P1. $30.00

CHRISTIE, Agatha. *Murder at the Vicarage*. 1930. Collins. 1st ed. orange cloth. VG. D1. $105.00

CHRISTIE, Agatha. *Murder in Mesopotamia*. 1936. Collins. 1st ed. orange cloth. G. D1. $45.00

CHRISTIE, Agatha. *Murder in the Calais Coach*. 1934. Dodd Mead. 1st ed. beige cloth. VG. D1. $60.00

CHRISTIE, Agatha. *Murder in the Calais Coach*. 1934. NY. 1st Am ed. yellow cloth. EX. $145.00

CHRISTIE, Agatha. *Murder Is Announced*. 1950. London. 1st Eng ed. orange cloth. $35.00

CHRISTIE, Agatha. *Murder of Roger Ackroyd*. nd. Grosset. G. P1. $4.75

CHRISTIE, Agatha. *Murder of Roger Ackroyd*. 1944. Collins. 13th ed. dj. VG. P1. $7.25

CHRISTIE, Agatha. *Murder of Roger Ackroyd*. 1950. Collins. 19th imp. orange cloth. dj. VG. D1. $35.00

CHRISTIE, Agatha. *Murder on Board*. nd. Book Club. dj. VG. P1. $3.75

CHRISTIE, Agatha. *Murder on the Orient Express*. nd. Book Club. VG. P1. $1.75

CHRISTIE, Agatha. *Mysterious Affair at Styles*. 1927. Grosset Dunlap. 1st ed. red cloth. dj. EX. $75.00

CHRISTIE, Agatha. *Mysterious Affair at Styles*. 1975. NY. Commemorative ed. dj. $15.00

CHRISTIE, Agatha. *Mysterious Mr. Quin*. June, 1935. Collins. 5th imp. black cloth. D1. $25.00

CHRISTIE, Agatha. *Nemesis*. 1971. Collins. 1st ed. red cloth. dj. VG. D1. $30.00

CHRISTIE, Agatha. *Nemesis*. 1971. Dodd Mead. 1st Am ed. dj. VG. D1. $25.00

CHRISTIE, Agatha. *Nemesis*. 1971. Dodd Mead. 3rd ed. green/white bdg. dj. D1. $8.00

CHRISTIE, Agatha. *Ordeal by Innocence*. 1958. Collins Crime Club. 1st ed. VG. P1. $25.00

CHRISTIE, Agatha. *Ordeal by Innocence*. 1958. Collins. 1st ed. red cloth. dj. VG. D1. $35.00

CHRISTIE, Agatha. *Pale Horse*. 1961. Collins. 1st ed. red cloth. dj. VG. D1. $46.00

CHRISTIE, Agatha. *Partners in Crime*. 1929. Dodd Mead. 1st Am ed. blue bdg. G. D1. $65.00

CHRISTIE, Agatha. *Passenger to Frankfurt*. nd. Dodd Mead. 3rd ed. dj. VG. P1. $10.00

CHRISTIE, Agatha. *Passenger to Frankfurt*. 1970. Collins. 1st ed. red cloth. dj. VG. D1. $35.00

CHRISTIE, Agatha. *Passenger to Frankfurt*. 1970. Dodd Mead. Book Club. red cloth. dj. D1. $20.00

CHRISTIE, Agatha. *Passenger to Frankfurt*. 1970. Dodd Mead. 1st Am ed. black cloth. G. D1. $8.00

CHRISTIE, Agatha. *Peril at End House*. 1932. Dodd Mead. 1st Am ed. beige cloth. VG. D1. $45.00

CHRISTIE, Agatha. *Pocket Full of Rye*. nd. Book Club. VG. P1. $1.75

CHRISTIE, Agatha. *Pocket Full of Rye*. 1953. Collins Book Club. 1st ed. dj. P1. $30.00

CHRISTIE, Agatha. *Poirot Loses a Client*. 1937. Dodd Mead. 1st Am ed. orange cloth. VG. D1. $50.00

CHRISTIE, Agatha. *Postern of Fate*. nd. Book Club. dj. VG. P1. $2.75

CHRISTIE, Agatha. *Postern of Fate*. nd. Dodd Mead. 3rd ed. dj. EX. P1. $9.25

CHRISTIE, Agatha. *Postern of Fate*. 1973. Collins. 1st ed. turquoise cloth. dj. D1. $25.00

CHRISTIE, Agatha. *Postern of Fate*. 1973. Dodd Mead. 1st ed. red cloth. dj. VG. D1. $15.00

CHRISTIE, Agatha. *Regatta Mystery*. 1939. NY. 1st ed. dj. $30.00

CHRISTIE, Agatha. *Remembered Death*. 1945. Dodd Mead. G. P1. $12.50

CHRISTIE, Agatha. *Secret Adversary*. 1922. Dodd Mead. 1st ed. brown cloth. G. D1. $100.00

CHRISTIE, Agatha. *Seven Dials Mystery*. 1929. Collins. 1st ed. D1. $125.00

CHRISTIE, Agatha. *Sleeping Murder*. nd. Book Club. VG. P1. $2.25

CHRISTIE, Agatha. *Sleeping Murder*. 1976. Collins Crime Club. dj. VG. P1. $9.25

CHRISTIE, Agatha. *Sleeping Murder*. 1976. Dodd Mead. 1st ed. yellow/brown bdg. dj. D1. $30.00

CHRISTIE, Agatha. *Sparkling Cyanide*. 1945. Collins. 1st ed. orange cloth. VG. D1. $30.00

CHRISTIE, Agatha. *Spies Among Us*. nd. Book Club. VG. P1. $4.00

CHRISTIE, Agatha. *Spies Among Us*. 1968. Dodd Mead. dj. xl. VG. P1. $7.00

CHRISTIE, Agatha. *Taken at the Flood*. 1948. Collins. 1st ed. orange cloth. VG. D1. $30.00

CHRISTIE, Agatha. *Ten Little Niggers (A Play)*. 1944. French's Acting ed. blue wraps. D1. $45.00

CHRISTIE, Agatha. *They Came to Baghdad*. nd. Book Club. VG. P1. $2.50

CHRISTIE, Agatha. *They Came to Baghdad*. 1951. Collins. 1st ed. orange cloth. dj. VG. D1. $40.00

CHRISTIE, Agatha. *They Came to Baghdad*. 1951. Collins. 1st ed. orange cloth. G. D1. $20.00

CHRISTIE, Agatha. *They Do It With Mirrors*. 1952. Collins Crime Club. 1st ed. VG. P1. $25.00

CHRISTIE, Agatha. *They Do It With Mirrors*. 1952. Collins. 1st ed. red cloth. dj. VG. D1. $35.00

CHRISTIE, Agatha. *Third Girl*. 1966. Collins. 1st ed. red cloth. dj. VG. D1. $32.00

CHRISTIE, Agatha. *Third Girl*. 1966. Collins. 1st ed. red cloth. VG. D1. $20.00

CHRISTIE, Agatha. *Third Girl*. 1966. Dodd Mead. 1st ed. blue cloth. VG. D1. $15.00

CHRISTIE, Agatha. *Third Girl*. 1967. Dodd Mead. dj. xl. P1. $7.00

CHRISTIE, Agatha. *Three Act Tragedy*. nd. (1935?) Collins. not 1st ed. dj. G. D1. $80.00

CHRISTIE, Agatha. *Towards Zero*. 1944. Collins. 1st Eng ed. G. D1. $45.00

CHRISTIE, Agatha. *Towards Zero*. 1944. Collins. 1st India ed. orange cloth. dj. D1. $50.00

CHRISTIE, Agatha. *Underdog*. nd. (1936?) Daily Express. not 1st ed. D1. $30.00

CHRISTIE, Agatha. *What Mrs. McGillicudy Saw!* 1957. Dodd Mead. 1st ed. brown cloth. dj. VG. D1. $25.00

CHRISTIE, Agatha. *4.50 From Paddington*. 1957. Collins Crime Club. 1st ed. dj. P1. $20.00

CHRISTIE, Agatha. *4.50 From Paddington*. 1957. Collins. 1st ed. orange cloth. dj. D1. $45.00

CHRISTIENNE & LISSARRAGUE. *History of French Military Aviation*. 1986. WA. 1st Am ed. photos. 531 p. dj. EX. T5. $37.50

CHRISTMAN, H.E. *Ladder of Rivers*. 1962. Denver. Sage. 1st ed. presentation. 426 p. A3. $45.00

CHRISTMAN, H.E. *Tin Horns & Calico*. 1945. NY. Ils. 377 p. dj. VG. B2. $17.50

CHRISTOPHER, John. *Little People*. nd. Book Club. dj. VG. P1. $4.00

CHRISTOPHER, John. *Little People*. 1966. Simon Schuster. 1st ed. dj. xl. P1. $5.50

CHRISTOPHER, John. *Pendulum*. nd. Book Club. dj. xl. P1. $3.00

CHRISTOPHER, John. *Pendulum*. 1968. Simon Schuster. 1st ed. dj. VG. P1. $15.00

CHRISTOPHER, John. *Pendulum*. 1969. Man's Book. dj. VG. P1. $13.75

CHRISTOPHER, John. *White Voyage*. nd. Book Club. dj. VG. P1. $2.75

CHRISTOPHER, Milbourne. *Illustrated History of Magic*. 1973. NY. Ils. 452 p. dj. $5.00

CHRISTY, H.C. *American Girl*. 1906. NY. 18 color pls. $55.00

CHRISTY, H.C. *Christy Girl*. 1906. Bobbs Merrill. G. $50.00

CHRISTY, H.C. *Christy Girl*. 1906. Bobbs Merrill. 1st ed. 4to. EX. $125.00

CHUBBUCK, Emily. *Alderbrook: Collection of Fanny Forester's Village Sketches*. 1847. Boston. 4th ed. 2 vols. VG. $27.50

CHUIKOV, Vasili I. *Battle for Stalingrad*. 1964. NY. Ils 1st Am ed. 364 p. dj. VG. T5. $22.50

CHUNTER, Roland. *Old Houses in England*. 1930. NY/London. photos. 4to. VG. $85.00

CHURCH, A.C. *Whale Ships & Whaling.* 1938. NY. 1st ed. VG. $27.00

CHURCH, K.E. *KS Quail Annual Report.* 1987. KS Wildlife/Parks. 31 p. M2. $4.00

CHURCH, T.D. *Gardens Are for People.* 1955. NY. 1st ed. sgn. VG. $75.00

CHURCH, W.C. *Life of John Erickson.* 1890. NY. 1st ed. xl. VG. $18.00

CHURCHILL, David. *It, Us & the Others.* 1979. Harper Row. dj. EX. P1. $7.00

CHURCHILL, J.W. *History of First Church in Dunstable-Nashua, NH...* 1918. Boston. Ils. 99 p. G. T5. $35.00

CHURCHILL, Robert. *Churchill's Shotgun Book.* 1955. NY. 1st ed. dj. VG. $35.00

CHURCHILL, Robert. *Gun Shooting: Revised by M. Hastings.* 1967. London. dj. VG. $20.00

CHURCHILL, W.S. *Blood, Sweat & Tears.* 1941. Putnam. Book Club. dj. VG. D1. $25.00

CHURCHILL, W.S. *Blood, Sweat & Tears.* 1941. Putnam. Book Club. VG. D1. $15.00

CHURCHILL, W.S. *Crisis.* 1905. NY. Grosset. Ils Christy. 522 p. $12.50

CHURCHILL, W.S. *Dawn of Liberation.* 1945. Little Brown. 1st Am ed. red cloth. VG. D1. $45.00

CHURCHILL, W.S. *End of the Beginning.* 1943. Little Brown. 1st Am ed. inscr by cousin. VG. D1. $95.00

CHURCHILL, W.S. *End of the Beginning.* 1943. Little Brown. 1st Am ed. red cloth. dj. EX. D1. $60.00

CHURCHILL, W.S. *End of the Beginning.* 1943. London. Cassell. 1st ed. dj. VG. D1. $55.00

CHURCHILL, W.S. *Great Contemporaries.* 1949. Odham. reprint of 1937 ed. red cloth. D1. $45.00

CHURCHILL, W.S. *History of English-Speaking Peoples: Age of Revolution.* 1956. Dodd Mead. Book Club. dj. VG. D1. $20.00

CHURCHILL, W.S. *History of English-Speaking Peoples: Great Democracies.* 1956. Dodd Mead. Book Club. dj. VG. D1. $20.00

CHURCHILL, W.S. *History of English-Speaking Peoples: New World.* 1956. Dodd Mead. Book Club. dj. EX. D1. $20.00

CHURCHILL, W.S. *If Lee Had Not Won the Battle of Gettysburg.* 1930. Scribner. SftCvr. VG. D1. $35.00

CHURCHILL, W.S. *If Lee Had Not Won the Battle of Gettysburg.* 1931. Longman. 1st HrdCvr ed. brown cloth. VG. D1. $50.00

CHURCHILL, W.S. *In the Balance: Speeches of 1949 & 1950.* 1951. Cassell. 1st Eng ed. blue cloth. dj. VG. D1. $50.00

CHURCHILL, W.S. *Island Race.* 1964. Cassell. 1st ed. 4to. green cloth. dj. D1. $40.00

CHURCHILL, W.S. *London to Ladysmith Via Pretoria.* 1900. Longman. 1st Am ed. 1/3000. maps. VG. D1. $550.00

CHURCHILL, W.S. *Marlborough: His Life & Times.* 1933. Scribner. 1st Am ed. 2 vols. djs. VG. D1. $325.00

CHURCHILL, W.S. *My African Journey.* 1908. London. Hodder. 1st ed. rebound. G. D1. $125.00

CHURCHILL, W.S. *My Early Life.* 1941. Macmillan. later print. blue cloth. G. D1. $45.00

CHURCHILL, W.S. *My Early Life: Roving Commission.* 1949. London. Odahm. later print. red cloth. dj. VG. D1. $35.00

CHURCHILL, W.S. *Onwards to Victory: War Speeches.* 1944. Little Brown. 1st Am ed. dj. VG. D1. $50.00

CHURCHILL, W.S. *Painting As a Pastime.* 1948. Odham. 1st ed. gray cloth. dj. VG. D1. $40.00

CHURCHILL, W.S. *Painting As a Pastime.* 1949. Odham. 3rd ed. gray cloth. VG. D1. $30.00

CHURCHILL, W.S. *Painting As a Pastime.* 1950. NY. Ils 1st ed. dj. VG. $12.00

CHURCHILL, W.S. *Painting As a Pastime.* 1965. Cornerstone. later Am print. VG. D1. $20.00

CHURCHILL, W.S. *Roving Commission.* 1930. NY. 1st Am ed. 377 p. T5. $65.00

CHURCHILL, W.S. *Roving Commission.* 1930. Scribner. 1st ed. red cloth. D1. $75.00

CHURCHILL, W.S. *Savrola: Tale of Revolution in Laurania.* 1900. London. 1st ed. 345 p. rebound. VG. T5. $300.00

CHURCHILL, W.S. *Second World War.* 1948-1953. Book Club. 6 vols. djs. VG. D1. $60.00

CHURCHILL, W.S. *Second World War.* 1948-1953. Boston. 1st ed. 6 vols. djs. D1. $95.00

CHURCHILL, W.S. *Second World War.* 1960. Time Life. 2nd issue. 4to. VG. D1. $45.00

CHURCHILL, W.S. *Secret Session Speeches.* 1946. Simon Schuster. 1st ed. gray cloth. dj. G. D1. $25.00

CHURCHILL, W.S. *Step by Step.* 1939. Putnam. 1st ed. blue cloth. VG. D1. $55.00

CHURCHILL, W.S. *Step by Step.* 1942. London. Macmillan. later issue. VG. D1. $35.00

CHURCHILL, W.S. *Step by Step.* 1949. Odham. later print. red cloth. dj. VG. D1. $35.00

CHURCHILL, W.S. *Ten Chapters.* 1945. Hutchinson. 1st ed. black cloth. VG. D1. $75.00

CHURCHILL, W.S. *Thoughts & Adventures.* 1933. Keystone. 1st ed. 1/2764. green cloth. G. D1. $45.00

CHURCHILL, W.S. *Thoughts & Adventures.* 1942. London. later issue. blue cloth. G. D1. $30.00

CHURCHILL, W.S. *Tree Trade.* 1977. NY. 1st Am ed. VG. $22.00

CHURCHILL, W.S. *Unrelenting Struggle.* 1942. Little Brown. 1st Am ed. dj. EX. D1. $65.00

CHURCHILL, W.S. *Victory.* 1946. Little Brown. 1st Am ed. dj. VG. D1. $55.00

CHURCHMAN, John. *Account of Gospel Labors...* 1779. Phil. 1st ed. 8vo. $125.00

CHURCHWARD, J. *Lost Continent of Mu.* 1947. Washburn. Ils. 335 p. VG. M2. $18.00

CHUTE, Carolyn. *Letourneau's Used Auto Parts.* 1988. NY. 1st Am ed. dj. VG. $30.00

CHUTE, L.A. *Story of Cheerio.* 1936. NY. Subscription ed. sgns. G. $4.00

CHUTE, Marchette. *Two Gentlemen: Lives of George Herbert & Robert Herrick.* 1959. Dutton. 1st ed. with letter. VG. $18.00

CHUTE, W.H. *Guide to the John G. Shedd Aquarium.* 1953. Ils. 236 p. EX. M2. $9.00

CIARDI, John. *As If.* 1955. Rutgers. 1st ed. inscr. dj. EX. $90.00

CIARDI, John. *Ciardi's Translation of Dante's Inferno.* 1954. Rutgers. 1st ed. presentation. sgn. EX. $75.00

CIARDI, John. *Lives of X.* 1971. Rutgers. 1st ed. dj. EX. $22.00

CIARDI & BASKIN. *Drawings for Dante's Inferno by Rico Lebrun.* 1963. Kathos. 1/2000. with 4 loose lithographs. EX. D2. $195.00

CIOFFI, Frank. *Formula Fiction?* 1982. Greenwood. 1st ed. no dj issued. EX. P1. $25.00

CIRKER. *Dictionary of American Portraits.* 1967. Dover. reprint. folio. EX. $60.00

CIST, Charles. *Cincinnati in 1841.* 1841. Cincinnati. 1st ed. 300 p. VG. T5. $165.00

CIST, Henry M. *Army of the Cumberland.* 1882. NY. 1st ed. maps. 289 p. G. T5. $30.00

CITY LIGHTS. *City Lights Journal. No. 1.* 1963. San Francisco. City Lights Books. G. $24.00

CLAFLIN, Burt. *American Waterfowl.* 1952. Knopf. 1st ed. dj. VG. $35.00

CLAIN-STEFANELLI, E. *Select Numismatics.* 1911. New Enlarged ed. dj. EX. $75.00

CLAIR, Colin. *Chronology of Printing.* 1969. NY. 1st ed. 4to. dj. EX. T1. $30.00

CLAIRE, Mabel. *O'Neil's Cookbook for the Busy Woman.* 1932. NY. Ils. 416 p. G. T5. $15.00

CLANCEY, P.A. *Birds of Natal & Zululand.* 1964. Edinburgh. Boyd. Ils. 511 p. dj. EX. M2. $165.00

CLANCEY, P.A. *Check List of S African Birds.* 1980. Pretoria. Ils. maps. EX. M2. $18.00

CLANCY, Tom. *Patriot Games.* 1987. Putnum. 1st ed. dj. EX. $15.00

CLANCY, Tom. *Red Storm Rising.* 1986. NY. 1st ed. dj. EX. B2. $37.50

CLANCY, Tom. *Red Storm Rising.* 1986. NY. 1st ed. VG. B3. $30.00

CLAP & WOODWARD. *New Records of Birds From HI Leeward Islands.* 1968. US Nat Mus. 39 p. M2. $4.00

CLAPHAM, R. *Book of the Fox.* 1931. Derrydale. 1/750. 8vo. red cloth. VG. $100.00

CLAPP, F.M. *Said Before Sunset.* 1938. NY. presentation. sgn. $10.00

CLAPP. *Life & Work of James Leon Williams.* 1925. NY. Ils. 8vo. 299 p. VG. $25.00

CLARESON, Thomas. *Voices for the Future. Vol. 3.* 1984. Bowling Green. dj. EX. P1. $15.00

CLARK, A. *Barbarossa.* 1956. NY. 1st ed. dj. EX. $27.50

CLARK, A. *Reefs of Taprobane.* 1957. Harper. Ils 1st ed. map. VG. M2. $10.00

CLARK, C.M. *History of Australia From Earliest Times...* 1822-1838. Melbourne. 1st ed. 2 vols. djs. J2. $35.00

CLARK, C.M. *Picturesque OH: Historical Monograph.* 1887. Cincinnati. 238 p. G. T5. $27.50

CLARK, D.L. *Fossils, Palentology & Evolution.* 1976. Brown. Ils. 121 p. EX. M2. $13.00

CLARK, Douglas. *Rhythmic Ramblings in Battle-Scarred Manassas.* 1905. Phil. 26 p. printed wraps. $45.00

CLARK, E.A. *Indian Legends of the Pacific NW.* 1953. CA U. Ils. 225 p. dj. EX. M2. $25.00

CLARK, E.H. *Carleton Case.* 1910. McLeod Allen. 1st Canadian ed. G. P1. $4.75

CLARK, E.L. *Daleth; or, Homestead of the Nations: Egypt Illustrated.* 1864. Boston. 14 pls. VG. $85.00

CLARK, Glenn. *Man Who Tapped the Secrets of the Universe.* nd. np. $20.00

CLARK, Glenn. *Windows of Heaven.* 1954. NY. $16.00

CLARK, H.W. *History of AK.* 1930. Macmillan. Ils 1st ed. maps. 208 p. VG. M2. $14.00

CLARK, I.G. *Then Came the Railroads: From Steam to Diesel in SW.* 1958. Norman. Ils 1st ed. 336 p. dj. G. T5. $27.50

CLARK, J. *Rivers Ran Fast.* 1953. Funk Wagnall. Ils 1st ed. dj. VG. M2. $14.00

CLARK, J.I. *WI Defies Fugitive Slave Law: Case of Sherman Booth.* 1955. Madison. 1st ed. 20 p. wraps. VG. $5.00

CLARK, Janet MacDonald. *Legends of King Arthur & His Knights.* c 1910. London/NY. Ils Margetson. VG. C1. $19.50

CLARK, Jason. *Civil War Recollections With Unpublished Material...* 1862. TX A&M. Ils 1st ed. dj. EX. $25.00

CLARK, Kenneth. *Florence Baptistery Doors.* 1980. Viking. 321 pls. 328 p. dj. D2. $75.00

CLARK, L. *Marching Wind.* 1955. London. Hutchinson. 347 p. dj. VG. $10.00

CLARK, L.H. *They Sang for Horses: Impact of Horses on Navajo & Apache...* 1966. Tucson. Ils De Grazia. 225 p. dj. VG. $25.00

CLARK, M.H. *Cry in the Night.* 1982. NY. 1st ed. sgn. dj. M. $25.00

CLARK, M.W. *Calculated Risk.* 1950. NY. Ils 1st ed. 400 p. dj. VG. T5. $22.50

CLARK, Mark. *From the Danube to the Yalu.* 1954. NY. Ils 1st ed. 369 p. dj. VG. T5. $22.50

CLARK, N. *E Birds of Prey.* 1983. Thorndike. Ils. 174 p. EX. M2. $17.00

CLARK, N.B. *Poems.* 1883. NY. Little. 1st ed. $47.50

CLARK, R.B. *Flowering Trees.* 1963. Van Nostrand. Ils. 241 p. dj. EX. M2. $12.00

CLARK, R.W. *Life of Bertrand Russell.* 1975. NY. 1st Am ed. dj. VG. $17.50

CLARK, Rene. *Faust.* 1932. Ltd Ed Club. 1/1500. sgn. boxed. VG. C1. $25.00

CLARK, Roland. *Gunner's Dawn.* 1927. Derrydale. 1/950. sgn. EX. $420.00

CLARK, Roland. *Pot Luck.* 1945. W Hartford. 1/460. sgn. boxed. VG. B2. $115.00

CLARK, Sydney. *All the Best in S America.* 1960. Dodd Mead. Ils. maps. VG. P1. $9.25

CLARK, Thomas. *Pills, Petticoats & Plows: S Country Store.* 1944. Bobbs Merrill. 1st ed. dj. VG. J2. $15.00

CLARK, Tom. *Air.* 1970. Harper. 1st ed. dj. EX. $15.00

CLARK, W.V.T. *City of Trembling Leaves.* 1945. NY. 1st ed. dj. VG. $35.00

CLARK, W.V.T. *Ox-Bow Incident.* 1940. NY. 1st ed. sgn/dtd. dj. M. $550.00

CLARK, W.V.T. *Track of the Cat.* 1949. NY. 1st ed. dj. EX. $55.00

CLARK, W.V.T. *Track of the Cat.* 1949. NY. 1st ed. dj. VG. P3. $50.00

CLARK, W.V.T. *Watchful Gods.* 1950. NY. 1st ed. dj. VG. B2. $40.00

CLARK, William Bell. *Lambert Wickes: Sea Raider & Diplomat.* 1932. Yale. 1st ed. presentation. inscr. J2. $15.00

CLARK & ETHINGTON. *Conodonts & Zonation of Upper Devonian in the Great Basin.* 1967. Geol Soc Am. Ils. EX. M2. $20.00

CLARK & STROMBERG. *Mammals in WY.* 1987. KS U. Ils 1st ed. 314 p. EX. M2. $30.00

CLARK & WHEELER. *Field Guide to Hawks of N America.* 1987. Houghton. Ils. 198 p. VG. M2. $20.00

CLARK. *I Remember.* private print. EX. S2. $25.00

CLARKE, A.C. *Expedition of the Moon.* 1954. London. Ils Smith. VG. $20.00

CLARKE, A.C. *From the Ocean, From the Stars.* nd. Book Club. dj. VG. P1. $6.00

CLARKE, A.C. *Going Into Space.* 1954. NY. Ils 1st Am ed. 117 p. dj. G. T5. $35.00

CLARKE, A.C. *Imperial Earth.* nd. Book Club. dj. VG. P1. $4.00

CLARKE, A.C. *Islands in the Sky.* 1954. Winston. 2nd ed. VG. P1. $15.00

CLARKE, A.C. *Islands in the Sky.* 1956. Signet. EX. $20.00

CLARKE, A.C. *Lion of Comarre & Against Fall Night.* nd. Book Club. dj. VG. P1. $4.00

CLARKE, A.C. *Prelude to Space.* 1970. Harcourt Brace. dj. VG. P1. $15.00

CLARKE, A.C. *Promise of Space.* 1968. Harper Row. Ils 1st ed. dj. EX. $15.00

CLARKE, A.C. *Report on Planet Three.* 1972. Harper Row. 1st ed. dj. VG. P1. $25.00

CLARKE, A.C. *Sands of Mars.* nd. Book Club. dj. VG. P1. $4.50

CLARKE, A.C. *Songs of Distant Earth.* 1986. NY. 1st ed. dj. VG. $12.00

CLARKE, A.C. *Tales From the White Hart.* 1970. Harcourt Brace. 1st ed. dj. VG. P1. $100.00

CLARKE, A.C. *Tales of Ten Worlds.* 1962. Harcourt Brace. 1st ed. dj. VG. P1. $50.00

CLARKE, A.C. *2010: Odyssey Two.* 1982. NY. 1st ed. dj. VG. $10.00

CLARKE, A.C. *2010: Odyssey Two.* 1982. NY. 1st trade ed. dj. EX. $25.00

CLARKE, Anna. *Cabin 3033.* 1986. Crime Club. 1st ed. dj. EX. P1. $12.95

CLARKE, Anna. *Soon She Must Die.* 1984. Doubleday Book Club. VG. P1. $7.50

CLARKE, D.H. *Alabam.* 1946. Tower. dj. VG. P1. $5.50

CLARKE, D.H. *Housekeeper's Daughter.* 1940. Triangle. Movie ed. dj. G. P1. $15.00

CLARKE, D.H. *Louis Beretti.* 1943. Triangle. 11th print. dj. EX. P1. $7.00

CLARKE, D.H. *Tawny.* 1936. Vanguard. 1st ed. $12.00

CLARKE, D.L. *William Tecumseh Sherman: Gold Rush Banker.* 1969. CA Hist Soc. Ils 446 p. dj. M2. $20.00

CLARKE, E.P. *Winnipesaukee: Potpourri.* 1935. Ils. photos. inscr. VG. $12.00

CLARKE, George. *History of Needham, MA.* 1912. Cambridge. private print. dj. EX. $30.00

CLARKE, Harry. *Faust.* nd. Three Sirens Pr. VG. $15.00

CLARKE, Harry. *Years at the Spring.* 1920. NY. 12 color pls. $45.00

CLARKE, Joseph I.C. *Manhattan & Henry Hudson.* 1910. Roycrofters. 62 p. TEG. VG. T5. $75.00

CLARKE, P.D. *Origin & Traditional History of Wyandots & Indian Tribes...* 1870. Toronto. 16mo. VG. $200.00

CLARKE, S.A. *Pioneer Days of OR History.* 1905. Portland. Gill. Ils. 2 vols. VG. A3. $120.00

CLARO, Joe. *Alex Gets the Business.* 1986. Weekly Reader. VG. P1. $5.00

CLASON, Clyde B. *Ark of Venus.* 1955. Knopf. 1st ed. Lib bdg. VG. P1. $20.00

CLAUDY, C.H. *Tell Me Why Stories.* 1912. NY. Ils Rockwell. 1st ed. G. B2. $60.00

CLAVELL, James. *King Rat.* 1962. Boston. 1st ed. dj. EX. $75.00

CLAVELL, James. *Whirlwind.* 1986. NY. Morrow. 1st ed. dj. EX. T6. $10.00

CLAVIERE & DE WARVILLE. *De la France et des Etats-Unis.* 1787. London. 344 p. VG. scarce. $175.00

CLAY, Beatrice. *King Arthur & His Round Table.* nd. c 1910. Ils Dora Curtis. VG. C1. $24.00

CLAY, Henry. *Life & Speeches.* 1843. NY. Bixby. 1st ed. 8vo. 2 vols. VG. G2. $45.00

CLAY, John. *My Recollections of Ontario.* 1918. Chicago. private print. 1st ed. VG. scarce. $75.00

CLAY & COURT. *History of the Microscope.* 1985. London. Holland. Ils. 266 p. dj. EX. M2. $23.00

CLAY & MEDWIN. *Acoustical Oceanography.* 1977. Wiley. dj. M. $25.00

CLAYBURN, B.B. *Prairie Stationmaster.* 1979. 128 p. $12.50

CLAYTON, P. *Aftermath of the Civil War in AR.* 1915. Neale. M2. $80.00

CLEATHER & CRUMP. *Parsifal Lohengrin & Legend of Holy Grail.* 1904. London. probably 1st ed. 16mo. VG. G1. $25.00

CLEATON & CLEATON. *Books & Battles: American Literature 1920-1930.* 1937. Boston. 1st ed. pls. dj. $20.00

CLEAVELAND, C.H. *Pronouncing Medical Lexicon.* 1865. pocket size. 302 p. K1. $13.50

CLEEVE, Brian. *Dark Blood, Dark Terror.* 1965. Random House. 1st ed. dj. xl. P1. $5.00

CLEEVE, Brian. *Tread Softly This Place.* 1973. John Day. VG. P1. $10.00

CLEGG & LAVALLEE. *Catenary Through the Counties.* nd. 64 p. $25.00

CLEIFE, Philip. *Tour de Force.* nd. Book Club. dj. EX. P1. $2.75

CLEMENCEAU, George. *American Reconstruction: 1865-1870.* 1928. NY. Trans MacVeagh. 300 p. VG. $20.00

CLEMENS, Clara. *My Father, Mark Twain.* 1931. NY. 1st ed. photos. VG. $30.00

CLEMENT, Charles. *Gericault.* 1974. NY. DaCapo. reprint of 1879 ed. D2. $80.00

CLEMENT, Hal. *Ice World.* 1953. Gnome. 1st ed. dj. EX. $15.00

CLEMENT, Hal. *Needle.* 1950. Doubleday. 1st ed. dj. VG. P1. $60.00

CLEMENT, Hal. *Small Changes.* 1969. Doubleday. 1st ed. dj. xl. P1. $10.00

CLEMENT, Hal. *Still River.* 1987. Del Rey. 1st ed. dj. EX. P1. $16.95

CLEMENT & FRENCH. *Trip of the Steamer Oceanus to Ft. Sumpter & Charleston.* 1865. Ils. 173 p. HrdCvr dj. VG. scarce. J4. $35.00

CLEMENTINA, Lady Hawarden. *Ovenden.* 1974. St. Martin. dj. VG. $12.50

CLEMENTS, E.S. *Flowers of Coast & Sierra.* 1928. 1st ed. 32 pls. VG. $35.00

CLEMENTS, E.S. *Flowers of Coast & Sierra.* 1959. Wilson. Ils. 226 p. EX. M2. $25.00

CLEMENTS, F.C. & E.S. *Rocky Mountain Flowers.* 1945. Wilson. Ils. 390 p. VG. M2. $20.00

CLENDENEN, C.C. *Blood on the Border.* 1969. London. 1st ed. EX. $17.00

CLENNELL, J.E. *Cyanide Handbook.* 1910. McGraw Hill. Ils. 520 p. EX. $7.50

CLEVELAND, Grover. *Fishing & Shooting Sketches.* 1906. Outing Pub. not 1st ed. VG. $27.50

CLEVELAND, Grover. *Government in Chicago Strike of 1894.* 1913. Princeton. 12mo. $15.00

CLEVELAND, M. *NH Fights the Civil War.* 1969. New London. EX. $100.00

CLEVELAND, R.M. *Air Transport at War.* 1946. NY. Ils 1st ed. 324 p. VG. T5. $35.00

CLEVELAND, R.M. *Air Transport at War.* 1946. NY. Ils 1st ed. 324 p. VG. T5. $35.00

CLEVER, Edlridge. *Soul On Fire.* 1978. Waco, TX. World. 240 p. dj. M1. $4.50

CLIFFORD, Francis. *All Men Are Lonely Now.* nd. Book Club. dj. VG. P1. $2.75

CLIFFORD, Francis. *Naked Runner.* nd. British Book Club. dj. EX. P1. $2.75

CLIFFORD, Martin. *Encyclopedia of Home Wiring & Electricity.* nd. Drake. dj. EX. P1. $10.00

CLIFFORD, W.G. *Books in Bottles: Curious in Literature.* 1926. London. Ils 1st ed. $20.00

CLIFTON, V. *Book of Talbot.* 1933. Harcourt Brace. 2nd ed. 439 p. M1. $35.00

CLIFTON-TAYLOR, Alec. *Pattern of English Building.* 1962. London. 1st ed. 1/50. presentation. sgn. djs. J2. $30.00

CLINTON, G.P. *Ustilagineae or Smuts of CT.* 1905. CT Nat Hist Survey. Ils. 45 p. M2. $10.00

CLINTON. *Printed Ephemera: Collection, Organization & Access.* 1981. London. 125 p. dj. EX. $35.00

CLIVE, William. *Dando & the Summer Palace.* 1972. Macmillan. dj. VG. P1. $7.00

CLODD, Edward. *Story of the Alphabet.* 1909. NY. McClure. Ils. 209 p. rebound. VG. $25.00

CLOQUET, M.J. *Recollections of Private Life of Lafayette.* 1936. Leavitt Lord. 1st ed. M1. $125.00

CLOSS, Hannah. *Silent Man.* 1955. London. 1st Eng ed. dj. VG. C1. $8.00

CLOSS, Hannah. *Tarn Trilogy.* 3 vols. pb. VG. C1. $7.00

CLOSSON, Ernest. *History of the Piano.* 1947. London. Ils Clossen. 1st ed. dj. G. T5. $25.00

CLOSTERMAN, Pierre. *Flames in the Sky.* 1954. London. reprint. 247 p. T5. $15.00

CLOUDSLEY-THOMPSON, J. *Wildlife of the Deserts.* 1979. Hamlyn. Ils. 4to. 96 p. dj. EX. P1. $13.00

CLOUZOT. *Painted & Printed Fabrics.* 1927. NY. MOMA. 92 pls. VG. $40.00

CLUNE, F. *Across the Snowy Mountains.* 1961. Robertson. Ils 1st ed. 262 p. dj. EX. M2. $11.00

CLUTE, John. *Interzone.* 1986. St. Martin. 1st ed. dj. EX. P1. $17.50

CLUTTON & DANIELS. *Watches.* 1965. Viking. Studio Book. 2nd ed. 159 p. D2. $75.00

CLUTTON-BROCK, T.H. *Red Deer: Behavior & Ecology of Two Sexes.* 1982. Chicago. 1st ed. M. M2. $14.00

CLYMER, W.B. *Robert Frost: a Bibliography.* 1937. Amherst. 1st ed. 1/650. EX. $100.00

COATES, Harold. *Stories of KY Feuds.* 1942. Holmes Darst Coal Co. Ils. EX. $30.00

COATES, Lydia. *American Dressmaking Step by Step.* 1917. Ils. 254 p. VG. $15.00

COATS, Peter. *Great Gardens of W World.* 1963. NY. dj. VG. $45.00

COATS, Peter. *Roses.* 1973. Octopus. Ils. dj. EX. M2. $5.00

COATSWORTH, Elizabeth. *Cat Who Went to Heaven.* 1930. Ils Lynd Ward. 1st ed. 4to. 57 p. $20.00

COATSWORTH, Elizabeth. *Especially ME.* 1970. Stephen Green. inscr/sgn. dj. $35.00

COATSWORTH, Elizabeth. *ME Ways.* 1947. NY. inscr/sgn. dj. VG. $30.00

COB, Ernest. *Mind's Eye.* 1941. Arlo. 1st ed. sgn. dj. VG. $15.00

COBB, B. *Hunting Dogs.* 1931. Crafton. Ils. VG. M2. $20.00

COBB, Frank. *Aviator's Luck.* nd. Saalfield. VG. P1. $7.50

COBB, Frank. *Dangerous Deeds.* 1927. Saalfield. VG. P1. $7.50

COBB, Humphrey. *Paths of Glory.* 1935. NY. Viking. 1st ed. xl. $7.50

COBB, I.S. *Exit Laughing.* 1941. Indianapolis. sgn. VG. $30.00

COBB, I.S. *Irvin Cobb, His Book...* 1915. NY. Ils. tall 8vo. 28 p. $45.00

COBB, I.S. *Old Judge Priest.* nd. Grosset. VG. P1. $7.50

COBB, I.S. *This Man's World.* 1929. London. Brentano. 1st ed. 288 p. $15.00

COBB, Lyman. *Cobb's Abridgement of J. Walker's Critical Dictionary.* 1829. Ithaca. 440 p. full leather. fair. T5. $45.00

COBBETT, William. *American Gardener: Treatise on Soil, Fencing...* 1842. Concord. 1st Am ed. 272 p. $195.00

COBIA, Daniel. *House of God in Ashes...* 1835. Charleston. Miller. 23 p. wraps. $65.00

COBIANCHI, Mario. *Pionieri Dell' Avianzione in Italia.* 1943. Roma. 1st ed. 470 p. wraps. slipcase. EX. T5. $225.00

COBLENTZ, Stanton A. *Crimson Capsule.* 1967. Abalon. 1st ed. dj. xl. P1. $5.50

COBLENTZ, Stanton A. *Crimson Capsule.* 1967. Avalon. 1st ed. dj. EX. P1. $10.00

COBURN, A.L. *More Men of Mark.* 1922. Knopf. 1st ed. photos. M. $250.00

COBURN, K. *Notebooks of Samuel T. Coleridge.* 1957. Bollingen. 2 vols. boxed. VG. $70.00

COBURN, Walt. *Pioneer Cattleman in MT: Story of Circle C Ranch.* 1968. Norman. Ils. dj. EX. $35.00

COBURN, Walt. *Walt Coburn: Autobiography.* 1973. Flagstaff. 1st ed. 255 p. dj. VG. $25.00

COCHRAN, Hamilton. *Blockade Runners of the Confederacy.* 1958. NY. Ils. 350 p. dj. VG. $20.00

COCHRAN, Jacqueline. *Stars at Noon.* 1954. Boston. 1st ed. dj. VG. $15.00

COCHRAN & GOIN. *New Field Book of Reptiles & Amphibians.* 1970. Putnam. Ils. 359 p. dj. EX. M2. $25.00

COCHRAN & STOBBS. *Search for the Perfect Swing.* 1968. Phil. 1st ed. 242 p. dj. VG. B2. $40.00

COCHRANE, J.D. *Pedestrian Journey Through Russia & Siberian Tartary.* 1829. Edinburgh. 2 vols. full leather. $100.00

COCKERELL, Douglas. *Bookbinding & Care of Books.* 1912. Appleton. Ils. 342 p. G. $20.00

COCKERELL, M.F. *Gunner With Stonewall. Reminiscences of Wm. T. Poague...* 1903. Special ed. sgn. 191 p. dj. M. J4. $20.00

COCTEAU, Jean. *Knight of Round Table.* Trans Auden. reprint. pb. VG. C1. $11.50

COCTEAU, Jean. *La Mort et les Statues.* 1946. Paris. Ils Jahan. 1/450. 4to. wraps. $125.00

COCTEAU, Jean. *La Rappel a L'Ordre.* 1926. Paris. 1st Collected ed. 1/550. $75.00

CODMAN, John. *Arnold's Expedition to Quebec.* 1902. NY. later ed. fld maps. 340 p. xl. G. T5. $17.50

CODMAN, John. *Round Trip.* 1879. NY. 331 p. K1. $17.50

CODY, L.F. *Memories of Buffalo Bill by His Wife.* 1919. NY. Appleton. 1st ed. VG. $40.00

CODY, M. *Favorite Restaurants of American in Paris.* 1966. Paris. Ils Man Ray. wraps. VG. $40.00

CODY, Morrill. *Hemingway's Paris.* 1965. Tower. VG. P1. $5.00

CODY, W.F. *Life & Adventures of Buffalo Bill, Colonel W.F. Cody.* 1917. Chicago. Ils. green cloth. G. $40.00

COE, A. *Shocking Truth.* 1969. NJ. $19.00

COE, G.W. *Frontier Fighter.* 1984. Lakeside Pr. Ils. VG. $10.00

COE, M.D. *Maya.* 1967. Ediciones Lars. 83 pls. maps. VG. M2. $9.00

COE, Tucker. *Don't Lie to Me.* nd. Book Club. dj. xl. P1. $3.00

COE, Tucker. *Kinds of Love, Kinds of Death.* nd. Random House. 2nd ed. dj. VG. P1. $10.00

COE, Tucker. *Kinds of Love, Kinds of Death.* nd. Book Club. dj. VG. P1. $4.00

COE, W.R. *Echinoderms of CT.* 1912. CT Geol Nat Hist Survey. VG. M2. $35.00

COE. *Sociology of Medicine.* 1970. 8vo. 388 p. VG. $20.00

COEN, Franklin. *Plunderers.* c 1980. Coward McCann. dj. G. $20.00

COETZEE, J.M. *From the Heart of the Country.* 1976. NY. 1st ed. dj. EX. $25.00

COFFIN, A.I. *Treatise on Midwifery & Diseases of Women & Children.* 1849. Manchester. fair. $50.00

COFFIN, C.C. *Four Years of Fighting.* 1866. Boston. Ils. 558 p. M2. $20.00

COFFIN, Charles. *Building the Nation.* 1883. Harper. Ils. maps. G. $22.00

COFFIN, Charles. *Freedom Triumphant.* 1891. Ils. 506 p. gilt bdg. K1. $14.50

COFFIN, Charles. *Life & Services of Major General John Thomas.* 1844. NY. 1st ed. presentation. 33 p. wraps. EX. $75.00

COFFIN, Charles. *Redeeming the Republic.* 1890. NY. Ils. index. K1. $12.50

COFFIN, Charles. *Story of Liberty.* 1878. Harper. Ils. VG. $24.00

COFFIN, Lewis. *Small French Buildings.* 1926. Scribner. Ils. 4to. VG. $45.00

COFFIN, R.P.T. *Ballads of Square-Toed Americans.* 1933. NY. 1st ed. sgn. dj. EX. $25.00

COFFIN, R.P.T. *Salt-Water Farm.* 1937. NY. dj. with sgn letter. VG. B2. $47.50

COFFMAN, Virginia. *From Satan With Love.* 1983. Piatkus. dj. EX. P1. $15.00

COGGINS, J. *Arms & Equipment of the Civil War.* 1983. Fairfax. Ils. 160 p. dj. EX. M2. $15.00

COGSWELL, F.H. *Regicides: Tale of Early Colonial Times.* 1896. Baker Taylor. 1st ed. $12.00

COHEN, A.A. *Admirable Woman.* 1983. Godine. 1st ed. dj. EX. $15.00

COHEN, Daniel. *Secrets From Ancient Graves.* 1968. NY. Ils. dj. VG. $15.00

COHEN, Leonard. *Favorite Game.* 1963. NY. 1st ed. dj. EX. $40.00

COHN, Art. *Around the World in 80 Days Almanac.* 1956. Random House. Movie 1st ed. P1. $9.25

COHN, Art. *Joker Is Wild: Story of Joe E. Lewis.* 1955. Random House. 1st ed. dj. VG. J2. $10.00

COIT, M. *Mr. Baruch.* 1957. Boston. Houghton Mifflin. BOMC. 784 p. $7.50

COKE, O. *Scrapbook of AR Literature.* 1939. Caxton. Ltd 1st ed. 1/100. EX. M2. $80.00

COKER, R.E. *Habits & Relations of Guano Birds of Peru.* 1919. US Nat Mus. 17 pls. map. M2. $9.00

COKER, R.E. *Natural History & Propagation of Fresh-Water Mussels.* 1921. Fish Bureau. Ils. VG. M2. $10.00

COKER, R.E. *Streams, Lakes & Ponds.* 1954. NC U. Ils. 327 p. dj. EX. M2. $18.00

COKER, W.C. *Saprolegniaceae With Notes on Other Water Molds.* 1923. Chapel Hill. 1st ed. 4to. VG. very scarce. $150.00

COLBERG, M.R. *Human Capital in S Development, 1939-1963.* 1965. Chapel Hill. 136 p. xl. $15.00

COLBERT, E.H. *Age of Reptiles.* 1965. Norton. Ils 1st ed. 228 p. dj. EX. M2. $18.00

COLBERT, E.H. *Great Dinosaur Hunters & Their Discoveries.* 1984. Dover. Ils. 283 p. wraps. EX. $12.00

COLBERT & CHAMBERLINE. *Chicago & the Great Conflagration.* 1871. Vent. 1st ed. photos. fld map. G. $45.00

COLBURN, W. *Introduction to Algebra.* 1838. Hilliard Gray. 12mo. leather. $15.00

COLBURN, Zerah. *Locomotive Engine.* 1881. 187 p. $27.50

COLBY, Benjamin. *Guide to Health Being Exposition of Thomsonian System...* 1846. Milford, NH. Ils Revised 3rd ed. 181 p. VG. $125.00

COLBY, C.B. *Wild Deer.* 1966. Duell Sloan. Ils 1st ed. 126 p. dj. EX. M2. $12.00

COLBY, Merle. *Big Secret.* 1949. Viking. 1st ed. VG. P1. $9.25

COLCORD. *Wings & Paws.* 1927. Phil. Ils 1st ed. EX. $15.00

COLE, A.H. *Charleston Goes to Harvard...* 1940. Harvard. 108 p. dj. $35.00

COLE, Burt. *Blue Climate.* 1977. Harper Row. 1st ed. dj. VG. P1. $12.50

COLE, Cornelius. *CA 350 Years Ago.* 1888. San Francisco. 1st ed. gilt brown cloth. $50.00

COLE, Cyrenus. *I Am a Man: Indian Blackhawk.* 1938. IA City. glassine dj. EX. $75.00

COLE, E.B. *Philosophical Corps.* 1961. Gnome. 1st ed. dj. EX. P1. $20.00

COLE, E.B. *Philosophical Corps.* 1961. Gnome. 1st ed. dj. VG. P1. $13.75

COLE, Ernest. *House of Bondage.* 1967. Random House. dj. VG. $25.00

COLE, H.E. *Baraboo Bear Tales.* 1915. Baraboo, WI. Ils. 110 p. G. T5. $22.50

COLE, H.E. *Baraboo Bear Trails.* 1915. Baraboo, WI. 1st ed. dj. VG. B2. $32.50

COLE, H.E. *Stagecoach & Tavern Tales of Old NW.* 1930. Cleveland. Clark. 1st ed. dj. EX. J3. $80.00

COLE, Herbert. *Heraldy & Floral Forms As Used in Decoration.* 1922. Dutton. 1st ed. dj. VG. J2. $30.00

COLE, Herbert. *Rubaiyat of Omar Khayyam.* 1928. Bodley Head. Ils Herbert Cole. dj. EX. $25.00

COLE & COLE. *End of an Ancient Mariner.* 1933. Crime Club. 2nd ed. VG. P1. $15.00

COLE & COLE. *End of an Ancient Mariner.* 1938. Crime Club. 8th print. dj. VG. P1. $20.00

COLE & COLE. *Last Will & Testament.* 1936. Crime Club. 1st ed. xl. P1. $11.00

COLEMAN, C. *Trail of the Stanley Cup. Vol. I.* 1964. Sherbrooke. 1st ed. 1/1000. boxed. B2. $40.00

COLEMAN, R.A. *Golden W in Story & Verse.* nd. Harper. G. $75.00

COLEMAN, Terry. *S Cross.* 1979. Viking. 1st ed. dj. VG. $12.50

COLEMAN, Wanda. *Mad Dog Black Lady.* 1979. Black Sparrow. 1/200. sgn/#d. EX. $25.00

COLERIDGE, S.T. *Kubla Khan.* 1933. NY. Ils Vassos. $45.00

COLERIDGE, S.T. *Rime of Ancient Mariner in Seven Parts.* nd. (1889) Ils Dore. folio. G. T5. $75.00

COLERIDGE, S.T. *Rime of the Ancient Mariner.* 1899. Roycroft. 1/910. 8vo. VG. D1. $75.00

COLERIDGE, S.T. *Rime of the Ancient Mariner.* 1945. Heritage. Ils Wilson. slipcase. EX. $15.00

COLERIDGE, S.T. *Selected Poems.* 1935. London. Nonesuch. 1/500. TEG. slipcase. EX. $170.00

COLES, C. *Game Birds.* Dodd Mead. 1st Am ed. slipcase. EX. M2. $65.00

COLES, C. *Game Birds.* 1981. London. Collins. Ils. slipcase. EX. M2. $65.00

COLES, Manning. *Basle Express.* nd. Book Club. dj. VG. P1. $5.00

COLES, Manning. *Basle Express.* 1956. Hodder Stoughton. 1st ed. dj. P1. $10.00

COLES, Manning. *Basle Express.* 1956. Crime Club. 1st ed. VG. P1. $15.00

COLES, Manning. *Drink to Yesterday.* 1946. Tower. dj. VG. P1. $15.00

COLES, Manning. *Fifth Man.* nd. Collier. VG. P1. $12.50

COLES, Manning. *No Entry.* nd. Book Club. VG. P1. $3.50

COLES, Manning. *They Tell No Tales.* 1942. Book League Am. VG. P1. $20.00

COLES, Manning. *Toast to Tomorrow.* 1943. Musson. dj. VG. P1. $13.75

COLES, Manning. *Without Lawful Authority.* nd. Book Club. dj. VG. P1. $5.00

COLES, Manning. *Without Lawful Authority.* nd. Book Club. VG. P1. $3.25

COLES, Manning. *Without Lawful Authority.* 1943. Crime Club. G. P1. $10.00

COLETTE. *Blue Lantern.* 1963. NY. Intro Flanner. 1st ed. dj. VG. $20.00

COLETTE. *Break of Day.* 1983. Ltd Ed Club. Ils/sgn Gilott. slipcase. B3. $110.00

COLETTE. *Cat.* 1936. NY. Ils Suba. 1st Am ed. dj. EX. $40.00

COLIN, Aubrey. *Hands of Death.* 1963. Hammond. 1st ed. dj. VG. P1. $7.50

COLIN, M.L. *Simon Perkins of W Reserve.* 1968. Cleveland. W Reserve Hist Soc. 215 p. dj. T5. $9.50

COLLIAS, N.E. & E.C. *Some Mechanisms of Family Integration in Ducks.* 1956. Auk. M2. $3.00

COLLIE, G.F. *Highland Dress.* 1948. London. 1st ed. pls. VG. $27.00

COLLIER, Basil. *Battle of the V-Weapons, 1944-1945.* 1965. NY. Ils 1st Am ed. 191 p. dj. VG. T5. $15.00

COLLIER, Eric. *Three Against the Wilderness.* 1960. Dutton. Ils. 349 p. dj. EX. $10.00

COLLIER, John. *Defy the Foul Fiend.* 1934. London. 1st ed. VG. $47.50

COLLIER, John. *His Monkey Wife.* 1930. London. 1st ed. EX. $100.00

COLLIER, John. *Presenting Moonshine.* 1941. London. 1st ed. fair. $45.00

COLLIER, John. *Scandal & Credulities of John Aubrey.* 1932. London. 2nd ed. G. $30.00

COLLIER, John. *Tom's A-Cold.* 1933. London. 1st ed. EX. $75.00

COLLIER & HOROZITZ. *Fords: American Epic.* 1987. Summit Books. Ils 1st ed. 496 p. dj. VG. $7.50

COLLIER MACMILLAN. *Encyclopedia of Philosophy.* 1972. 8 vols in 4. G. $50.00

COLLIER. *Awakening Valley.* 1949. dj. EX. S2. $30.00

COLLINGS, Michael. *Shorter Works of Stephen King.* 1985. Starmont. EX. P1. $9.95

COLLINGWOOD & WOOLAMS. *Le Cuisinier Anglais Universel.* 1810. Paris. 1st French ed. 2 vols in 1. scarce. $120.00

COLLINS, Francis A. *Boys' Book of Model Aeroplanes.* 1910. NY. Ils 1st ed. 308 p. $55.00

COLLINS, G.N. *New Type of Indian Corn From China.* 1909. USDA. 30 p. M2. $3.00

COLLINS, H.H. *Complete Field Guide to American Wildlife.* 1959. Harper. Ils. 683 p. VG. M2. $5.00

COLLINS, Henry. *Wildlife, Companion Field Guide...* 1959. Harper. 683 p. EX. $25.00

COLLINS, J.S. *My Experiences in the W.* 1970. Donnelley. Lakeside Classic. A3. $40.00

COLLINS, J.T. *Amphibians & Reptiles in KS.* 1982. KS U. Ils 2nd ed. 179 p. EX. M2. $18.00

COLLINS, J.T. *Tales From the New Mabinogion.* 1923. London. 1st/only ed. xl. VG. scarce. C1. $19.50

COLLINS, Joan. *King Arthur.* 1986. Ladybird Books. 1st ed. M. C1. $7.00

COLLINS, M.A. *Million Dollar Wound.* 1986. NY. 1st ed. dj. EX. $15.00

COLLINS, M.P. *Song of Love, Selections From Song of Songs...* 1970. NY. sm 4to. 60 p. dj. $25.00

COLLINS, Max. *Shroud for Aquarius.* 1985. Walker. 1st ed. P1. $14.95

COLLINS, Michael. *Blood-Red Dream.* 1976. Dodd Mead. 1st ed. dj. VG. P1. $12.00

COLLINS, Michael. *Blue Death.* nd. Book Club. dj. VG. P1. $2.75

COLLINS, Michael. *Carrying the Fire.* 1974. NY. Ils 1st ed. 478 p. dj. G. T5. $22.50

COLLINS, Michael. *Freak.* 1983. Dodd Mead. 1st ed. dj. EX. P1. $9.95

COLLINS, Michael. *Walk a Black Wind.* 1971. Dodd Mead. dj. VG. P1. $9.25

COLLINS, Robert. *Practical Treatise on Midwifery.* 1841. Boston. 320 p. G. B1. $75.00

COLLINS, Wilkie. *Moonstone.* 1868. NY. 1st Am ed. G. E2. $25.00

COLLINS, Wilkie. *Moonstone.* 1946. Literary Guild. dj. VG. P1. $5.50

COLLINS & BOYAJIAN. *Familiar Garden Birds of America.* 1965. Harper Row. Ils. 309 p. EX. M2. $8.00

COLLINS & LAPIERRE. *Is Paris Burning?* 1963. Hammond. 1st ed. dj. VG. P1. $7.50

COLLODI, Carlo. *Adventures of Pinocchio.* nd. NY. Ils Mussino. 3rd ed. J2. $75.00

COLLODI, Carlo. *Adventures of Pinocchio.* 1920. Phil. Ils Kirk. Deluxe ed. VG. $50.00

COLLODI, Carlo. *Adventures of Pinocchio.* 1946. Grosset Dunlap. Ils Kredel. VG. B4. $20.00

COLLODI, Carlo. *Pinocchio.* 1924. Saalfield. Ils Brundage. yellow cloth. VG. $35.00

COLLYER, J. *Messiah, From German of Mr. Klopstock.* 1788. Elizabeth, NJ. sm 8vo. leather. $65.00

COLMAN & TRIER. *Artisten.* 1928. Dresden. Ils. G. $25.00

COLMERY, R.C. *Memoir of Life & Character of Josiah Scott.* 1881. Columbus. 190 p. G. T5. $17.50

COLNAGI. *Rubens & His Engravers: An Exhibition.* 1977. Ils. 20 pls. price list insert. D2. $9.00

COLONNA, F. *Strife of Love in a Dream Being Elizabethan Version...* 1890. 1/500. VG. $100.00

COLTON, Walter. *Deck & Port; or Incidents of Cruise in US Frigate...* 1850. NY. Barnes. Ils. maps. A3. $90.00

COLUM, Padraic. *Ado of Odysseus.* 1920. London. Ils Pogany. 1st ed. 8vo. 254 p. VG. $57.50

COLUM, Padraic. *Arabian Nights.* 1923. Macmillan. Ils Pape. $35.00

COLUM, Padraic. *Creatures.* 1927. Macmillan. Ils Artzybasheff. 1/300. sgns. EX. $95.00

COLUM, Padraic. *Creatures.* 1927. NY. Ils Artzybasheff. 1st ed. dj. J2. $30.00

COLUM, Padraic. *Crossroads in Ireland.* 1931. NY. Ils. 375 p. xl. G. $6.00

COLUM, Padraic. *Half-Day's Ride.* 1932. NY. 1st ed. dj. EX. $30.00

COLUM, Padraic. *King of Ireland's Son.* 1921. NY. Ils Pogany. dj. $45.00

COLUM, Padraic. *Orpheus: Myths of the World.* 1930. NY. Ils Artzybasheff. 1st ed. J2. $30.00

COLUM, Padraic. *Road 'Round Ireland.* 1926. NY. 1st ed. inscr. VG. $40.00

COLUM, Padraic. *White Sparrow.* 1933. NY. Macmillan. Ils Ward. 8vo. $50.00

COLUM, Padraic. *Wild Earth & Other Poems.* 1927. NY. later print. inscr. VG. $30.00

COLVILLE, John. *Churchillians.* 1981. London. Nicolson. red cloth. dj. EX. D1. $40.00

COLVILLE, John. *Winston S. Churchill & His Inner Circle.* 1981. Wyndham. 1st Am ed. dj. EX. D1. $30.00

COLVIN, Fred H. *Aircraft Mechanics Handbook.* 1918. McGraw Hill. 5th ed. VG. P1. $9.25

COLYTON, Henry. *Sir Pagan.* 1947. 2nd imp. dj. VG. C1. $4.50

COMBE, Andrew. *Physiology of Digestion.* 1840. Boston. 4th ed. 12mo. VG. $15.00

COMBE, George. *System of Phrenology.* 1830. Edinburgh. 3rd ed. 8vo. 707 p. $35.00

COMBE, Jacques. *Hieronymus Bosch.* 1946. Paris. 142 pls. $45.00

COMBE, William. *Tour of Dr. Syntax in Search of the Picturesque.* 1813. London. Ils Rowlandson. 4th ed. 276 p. T5. $195.00

COMBS, B.B. *W to Promontory.* 1969. Ils. 79 p. $16.00

COMBS, G.H. *Himmler: Nazi Spider Man.* 1942. Phil. 64 p. dj. VG. C4. $22.00

COMBS & CAIDIN. *Kill Devil Hill: Discovering Secret of Wright Brothers.* 1979. Boston. Ils. sgn. 389 p. dj. VG. T5. $17.50

COMEAU, Napoleon. *Life & Sport on N Shore of Lower St. Lawrence.* 1923. Quebeck. Ils 2nd ed. 440 p. G. B2. $40.00

COMFORT, Will Levington. *Son of Power.* nd. Gundy. 1st Canadian ed. VG. P1. $10.00

COMMAGER, H.S. *Blue & the Gray.* 1950. Bobbs Merrill. Ils. 2 vols. slipcase. EX. $25.00

COMMONS, John. *History of Labor in the US.* 1918. NY. 2 vols. VG. $50.00

COMMONS, John. *Races & Immigrants in America.* 1907. Chautauqua. G. $12.50

COMMONS, M.A. *Log of Tanger Hill.* 1938. private print. Ils. 244 p. EX. M2. $5.00

COMPTON, D.G. *Windows.* 1979. Berkley Putnam. 1st ed. dj. VG. P1. $12.50

COMPTON-BURNETT, I. *Mighty & Their Fall.* 1962. Simon Schuster. 1st print. dj. EX. $60.00

COMSTOCK, C. *Comstock Genealogy.* 1907. NY. inscr. VG. $60.00

COMSTOCK, J.H. *Introduction to Entomology.* 1933. Comstock. Ils. 1044 p. VG. M2. $20.00

COMSTOCK, J.H. *Spider Book.* 1980. Cornell. Ils Revised ed. 729 p. EX. M2. $23.00

COMSTOCK, J.H. & A.B. *How To Know the Butterflies.* 1929. Comstock. 45 pls. 311 p. VG. M2. $35.00

COMSTOCK, W.P. *Butterflies of the American Tropics: Genus Anaea.* 1961. NY. Am Mus Nat Hist. 30 pls. 214 p. EX. $200.00

CONARD & HUS. *Water Lilies.* 1914. Garden City. G. $20.00

CONARD & REDFEARN. *How To Know the Mosses & Liverworts.* 1979. Brown. Ils 1st ed. 302 p. EX. M2. $22.00

CONDIE. *Lectures on Principles & Practice of Psysics.* 1958. Phil. Ils. 8vo. 1224 p. full calf. VG. P3. $59.00

CONDIT, Carl. *Rise of the Skyscraper.* 1952. Chicago. 1st ed. dj. VG. $20.00

CONDIT, D.M. *Case Study in Guerrilla War: Greece During WWII.* 1961. Am U. G. M1. $12.50

CONDON, Eddie. *Eddie Condon's Treasury of Jazz.* 1956. NY. 1st ed. 488 p. dj. VG. B2. $22.50

CONDON, Eddie. *We Called It Music.* 1947. NY. 1st ed. 328 p. dj. B2. $22.50

CONDON, Richard. *Mile High.* 1969. Dial. 1st ed. dj. EX. $15.00

CONES, Elliot. *Biogen: Speculation on Origin & Nature of Life.* 1884. Boston. Estes Lauriat. dj. EX. $100.00

CONEY, M.G. *Fang the Gnome.* 1988. 1st ed. dj. M. C1. $17.00

CONEY, M.G. *Fang the Gnome.* 1988. 1st pb ed. M. C1. $4.00

CONEY, M.G. *King of the Scepter'd Isle.* 1989. 1st ed. dj. M. C1. $19.50

CONEY, M.G. *Syzygy.* 1973. Elmfield Pr. dj. EX. P1. $18.25

CONEY, M.G. *Winter's Children.* 1975. Readers Union Book Club. dj. P1. $5.00

CONFUCIUS. *Analects of Confucius.* 1970. Heritage. sm quarto. slipcase. EX. $15.00

CONGDON, Don. *Combat: Civil War.* 1967. NY. 1st ed. 564 p. dj. VG. $15.00

CONGDON, H.W. *Covered Bridge.* 1941. Brattleboro. Ils 1st ed. EX. T1. $35.00

CONGDON, R.T. *Our Beautiful W Birds.* 1954. Exposition. Ils. 408 p. G. M2. $9.00

CONGER, S.P. *Old China & Young America.* 1913. Browne. Ils. photos. G. $20.00

CONKLIN, Groff. *SF Galaxy.* 1950. Perma P67. VG. P1. $50.00

CONKLING, M.C. *Memoirs of Mother & Wife of WA.* 1851. Auburn. Ils. 12mo. 248 p. xl. VG. G2. $17.00

CONN & WEBSTER. *Algae of the Fresh-Waters of CT.* 1908. CT Geol Nat Hist Survey. M2. $9.00

CONNELL, E.S. *Mrs. Bridge.* 1959. NY. 1st ed. dj. EX. $30.00

CONNELLEY. *Wild Bill & His Era.* 1933. NY. VG. C4. $75.00

CONNELLY, T.L. *Will Sucess Spoil Jeff Davis?* 1963. NY. Ils Grant. dj. EX. $10.00

CONNER, D.E. *Confederate in the CO Gold Fields.* 1970. OK U. Ils 1st ed. 186 p. dj. EX. M2. $10.00

CONNER, H.M. *Spearhead: WWII History of 5th Marine Division.* 1950. WA. Ils 1st ed. 325 p. dj. G. T5. $65.00

CONNER, Michael. *I Am Not the Other Houdini.* 1978. NY. Harper. 1st ed. dj. EX. $10.00

CONNER, Ralph. *Corporal Cameron.* 1912. Westminster. G. P1. $18.25

CONNER, Stanley J. *Sock It To Her.* 1970. Land's End. dj. VG. P1. $10.00

CONNETT, E.V. *Fishing a Trout Stream.* 1934. Derrydale. 1/95. 8vo. blue buckram. EX. $150.00

CONNETT, E.V. *Random Casts.* 1939. Derrydale. 1/1075. 8vo. acetate dj. EX. $160.00

CONNETT, E.V. *Upland Game Bird Shooting in America.* 1930. Derrydale. 1/850. EX. $450.00

CONNICK, Charles. *Adventures in Light & Color.* 1937. Random House. Ils. 428 p. dj. VG. $150.00

CONNINGTON, J.J. *Eye in the Museum.* nd. Grosset. VG. P1. $7.50

CONNOLLY, Cyril. *Condemned Playground. Essays 1927-1944.* 1945. London. Routledge. dj. EX. $50.00

CONNOLLY, Cyril. *Evening Colonnade.* 1975. NY. 1st Am ed. dj. EX. $12.00

CONNOLLY, J.B. *Port of Gloucester.* 1940. NY. Ils Kuehne. 1st ed. xl. G. R1. $17.50

CONNOLLY, Joseph. *P.G. Wodehouse.* 1979. London. Ils 1st ed. dj. EX. $35.00

CONNOR, H.G. *George Davis: A Biographical Sketch.* 1911. Daughters of CSA. 1st ed. R1. $35.00

CONNOR, Ralph. *Sky Pilot in No Man's Land.* 1919. Doran. VG. P1. $15.00

CONNOR, Ralph. *Sky Pilot.* nd. Revell. VG. P1. $7.50

CONOVER, Ted. *Rolling Nowhere.* 1984. 274 p. $15.00

CONRAD, Earl. *Governor & His Lady.* 1960. 433 p. dj. VG. J4. $8.50

CONRAD, H.L. *Uncle Dick Wootton: Pioneer Frontiersman of Rocky Mountains.* 1957. Donnelley. Lakeside Classic. 462 p. M. M2. $30.00

CONRAD, Joseph. *Almayer's Folly.* 1895. NY. 1st Am ed. VG. $295.00

CONRAD, Joseph. *Arrow of Gold.* 1919. London. 1st ed. $45.00

CONRAD, Joseph. *Arrow of Gold.* 1919. NY. 1st ed. 1st issue. EX. $30.00

CONRAD, Joseph. *Arrow of Gold.* 1919. NY. 1st ed. 2nd issue. VG. $15.00

CONRAD, Joseph. *Children of the Sea.* 1897. NY. 1st ed. 1st issue. EX. scarce. $225.00

CONRAD, Joseph. *Congo Diary.* 1978. NY. 1st ed. dj. M. $12.00

CONRAD, Joseph. *Conrad to a Friend.* 1928. NY. 1st ed. EX. $25.00

CONRAD, Joseph. *Da Vinci Machine.* 1968. Fleet Pr. dj. VG. P1. $7.25

CONRAD, Joseph. *Falk.* 1903. NY. 1st Am ed. EX. $115.00

CONRAD, Joseph. *Inheritors.* 1901. London. 1st Eng ed. 1st state. $75.00

CONRAD, Joseph. *Inheritors.* 1901. NY. 1st ed. 2nd issue. VG. $115.00

CONRAD, Joseph. *Last Essays.* 1926. London/Toronto. 1st ed. dj. EX. $50.00

CONRAD, Joseph. *Last Twelve Years of Joseph Conrad.* 1928. London. 1st ed. VG. $35.00

CONRAD, Joseph. *Laughing Anne & One Day More.* 1924. London. 1st ed. EX. $50.00

CONRAD, Joseph. *Letters to Cunninghame Graham.* 1969. Cambridge. 1st ed. dj. EX. $25.00

CONRAD, Joseph. *Letters to William Blackwood & David S. Meldrum.* 1958. Durham. 1st ed. dj. EX. $25.00

CONRAD, Joseph. *Lord Jim.* 1900. NY. 1st Am ed. 2nd state. VG. $35.00

CONRAD, Joseph. *Mirror of the Sea.* 1905. NY. 1st Am ed. VG. $50.00

CONRAD, Joseph. *Nature of a Crime.* 1924. London. 1st ed. dj. EX. $50.00

CONRAD, Joseph. *Nature of a Crime.* 1924. NY. 1st ed. VG. P3. $25.00

CONRAD, Joseph. *Nigger of Narcisus.* 1898. London. 1st ed. 1st issue. $225.00

CONRAD, Joseph. *Nigger of Narcisus.* 1965. Heritage. slipcase. VG. $20.00

CONRAD, Joseph. *Nostromo.* 1904. NY. 1st Am ed. dj. EX. $95.00

CONRAD, Joseph. *Nostromo.* 1961. Heritage. slipcase. EX. $30.00

CONRAD, Joseph. *One Day More: Play in One Act.* 1919. London. Beaumont Pr. 1/250. VG. $200.00

CONRAD, Joseph. *Outcast of the Islands.* 1896. NY. 1st Am ed. EX. scarce. $125.00

CONRAD, Joseph. *Outcast of the Islands.* 1975. Ltd Ed Club. 212 p. slipcase. EX. $50.00

CONRAD, Joseph. *Point of Honor.* 1908. NY. McClure. 1st ed. dark green cloth. EX. $75.00

CONRAD, Joseph. *Rescue.* 1920. London. Dent. 1st ed. VG. EX. $60.00

CONRAD, Joseph. *Romance.* 1904. NY. 1st Am ed. EX. $95.00

CONRAD, Joseph. *Rover.* 1923. Garden City. blue cloth. VG. $30.00

CONRAD, Joseph. *Rover.* 1923. London. 1st ed. P3. $40.00

CONRAD, Joseph. *Rover.* 1923. London. Unwin. 1st ed. J2. $25.00

CONRAD, Joseph. *Secret Agent.* 1907. London. Ltd ed. dj. VG. $90.00

CONRAD, Joseph. *Secret Agent.* 1907. NY. Harper. 1st Am ed. EX. $65.00

CONRAD, Joseph. *Secret Sharer.* Ltd Ed Club. slipcase. M. B3. $125.00

CONRAD, Joseph. *Shadowline.* 1917. Doubleday. 1st Am ed. dj. M. $38.00

CONRAD, Joseph. *Shadowline.* 1917. London. 1st ed. 1st issue. EX. $50.00

CONRAD, Joseph. *Suspense.* 1925. Doubleday. 1st Am ed. dj. VG. $40.00

CONRAD, Joseph. *Suspense.* 1925. London. 1st ed. EX. $60.00

CONRAD, Joseph. *Tales of Hearsay.* 1925. London. Unwin. Ltd 1st ed. dj. EX. $150.00

CONRAD, Joseph. *Tales of Hearsay.* 1925. NY. 1st Am ed. VG. $25.00

CONRAD, Joseph. *Tales of Unrest.* 1898. London. 1st ed. VG. $175.00

CONRAD, Joseph. *Twixt Land & Sea.* 1912. London. 1st ed. 3rd state bdg. VG. $65.00

CONRAD, Joseph. *Typhoon.* nd. Readers Lib. $18.25

CONRAD, Joseph. *Under W Eyes.* 1911. NY. 1st Am ed. VG. $40.00

CONRAD, Joseph. *Victory.* 1915. London. Methuen. red cloth. VG. $38.00

CONRAD, Joseph. *Youth (With Heart of Darkness).* 1903. NY. 1st Am ed. VG. $60.00

CONRAD, T.N. *Rebel Scout.* 1904. WA. 1st ed. VG. $75.00

CONRAD & FORD. *Nature of a Crime.* 1924. Garden City. 1st ed. EX. $45.00

CONRAN, Terrance. *House Book.* 1976. Crown. 1st Am ed. folio. dj. M. $65.00

CONROY, Jack. *Disinherited.* c 1933. Covici Friede. 1st ed. 2 djs. VG. $175.00

CONROY, Jack. *Midland Humor.* 1947. NY. Currents. 1st ed. 446 p. $25.00

CONROY, Pat. *Boo.* 1981. NY. Pinnacle. 1st ed. pb. wraps. VG. T6. $30.00

CONROY, Pat. *Great Santini.* 1976. Boston. Houghton. 1st ed. sgn. dj. EX. $60.00

CONROY, Pat. *Great Santini.* 1977. NY. Avon. 1st ed. pb. EX. T6. $15.00

CONROY, Pat. *Lords of Discipline.* 1980. Boston. Houghton. 1st ed. sgn. dj. EX. T6. $50.00

CONROY, Pat. *Lords of Discipline.* 1980. Boston. 1st ed. sgn. dj. VG. $45.00

CONROY, Pat. *Lords of Discipline.* 1981. Secker Warburg. 1st Eng ed. dj. M. T6. $60.00

CONROY, Pat. *Prince of Tides.* 1986. Boston. Houghton. 1st ed. dj. EX. $12.00

CONROY, Pat. *Prince of Tides.* 1986. Houghton. 1st ed. dj. M. T6. $15.00

CONROY, Pat. *Prince of Tides.* 1986. NY. Putnam. 1st ed. dj. EX. $15.00

CONSIDINE. *Remarkable Life of Dr. Armand Hammer.* 1975. NY. Ils 1st ed. 287 p. dj. VG. B2. $20.00

CONSTABLE, W.G. *Canaletto.* 1964-1965. Eng/French text. 176 p. D2. $45.00

CONTE, Pierre. *Ecriture de la Danse Theatrale et Dance en General.* 1931. Niort. private print. 1/200. folio. wraps. $110.00

CONTINI, Mila. *Fashion.* 1965. NY. dj. EX. $15.00

CONTOR, R. & J. *Bighorn, Elk & Deer of Rocky Mountain National Park.* 1970. Rocky Mt Nat Assn. EX. M2. $9.00

CONTROVICH, J.T. *US Army Unit Histories.* 1987. Manhattan, KS. 131 p. wraps. M. T5. $17.50

CONWAY, A. *Reconstruction of GA.* 1966. MN U. 248 p. xl. M2. $10.00

CONWAY, Hugh. *Called Back.* nd. Detective Club. dj. G. P1. $13.75

CONWAY, Jim. *Fishin' Holes.* 1969. 1st ed. sgn. VG. $10.00

CONWAY, M.D. *Life of Thomas Paine.* 1892. NY. 1st ed. 2 vols. VG. $80.00

CONWAY, M.D. *Travels in S Kensington: Art & Architecture in England.* 1882. Harper. 1st ed. VG. $35.00

CONWAY, M.D. *Wandering Jew.* 1881. NY. Holt. 292 p. G. $25.00

CONWELL, R.H. *History of Great Fire in Boston.* 1873. Boston. Ils. 12mo. 312 p. G. G2. $22.00

CONWELL, R.H. *Life of General James A. Garfield.* 1880. Boston. 12mo. 356 p. G. G2. $18.00

COOK, A.J. *Manual of the Apiary.* 1878. Chicago. 3rd ed. G. $25.00

COOK, Chris. *History of Great Trains.* 1977. NY. Ils. dj. EX. $12.50

COOK, F. *Walter Reuther: Building the House of Labor.* 1963. dj. VG. $20.00

COOK, F.A. *My Attainment of the Pole.* 1912. Kennerley. Ils. sgn. 604 p. G. M2. $30.00

COOK, F.A. *Return From the Pole.* 1953. London. Burke. Ils 1st ed. map. VG. M2. $20.00

COOK, F.F. *Bygone Days in Chicago.* 1910. McClurg. Ils. VG. $50.00

COOK, Helen. *Maverick With Paint Brush.* 1977. Ils Benton. 1st ed. dj. EX. $10.00

COOK, J. *Pursuing the Whale.* 1926. Boston. 1st ed. 344 p. dj. VG. B2. $55.00

COOK, J.F. *Governors of GA.* 1979. Huntsville. Strode. Ils. 320 p. $15.00

COOK, J.L. *Lane of Llano: Being Story of Lane As Told to T.M. Pearce.* 1936. Boston. 1st ed. dj. EX. $55.00

COOK, J.R. *Border & Buffalo: Untold Story of SW Plains.* 1938. Donnelley. reprint of 1907 ed. 480 p. EX. M2. $25.00

COOK, James. *Voyage to Pacific Ocean.* 1784. London. Stockdale. 4 vols. VG. $2500.00

COOK, Joel. *Pen Pictures of America.* 1903. 6 vols. M. K1. $21.00

COOK, Oscar. *Borneo: Stealer of Hearts.* 1924. Boston. 1st Am ed. photos. dj. G. T5. $25.00

COOK, T.A. *Twenty-Five Great Houses of France.* nd. London. dj. J2. $190.00

COOK, W.L. *Flood Tide of Empire: Spain & Pacific NW, 1543-1819.* 1973. New Haven. Ils 1st ed. pocket maps. dj. M. T1. $35.00

COOK, William. *Platto: Master Book of All Plots.* 1941. Writer's Digest. 29 p. J2. $20.00

COOK & STEVENSON. *Weapons of War.* 1980. Crescent. 1st ed. 4to. dj. $20.00

COOKE, A. *Six Men.* 1977. NY. 1st ed. 1/400. sgn. slipcase. EX. $60.00

COOKE, A.H. *Molluscs: Brachiopods (Recent) & Brachiopods (Fossil).* 1968. London. Macmillan. reprint. EX. M2. $18.00

COOKE, Alistair. *America.* 1973. NY. Ils 1st ed. sgn. 400 p. dj. VG. T5. $22.50

COOKE, Donald E. *Silver Horn of Robin Hood.* 1957. Ils 2nd print. VG. C1. $6.00

COOKE, J.E. *Life of Stonewall Jackson.* 1863. 305 p. gilt bdg. J4. $40.00

COOKE, J.E. *Outlines From the Outpost.* 1961. Donnelley. 410 p. EX. M2. $25.00

COOKE, J.E. *Stonewall Jackson: Military Biography.* 1866. NY. 1st ed. 8vo. 470 p. scarce. G2. $46.00

COOKE, J.E. *Wearing of the Gray.* 1867. pls. 601 p. J4. $50.00

COOKE, Jacob. *Alexander Hamilton.* 1982. NY. 1st ed. dj. EX. $15.00

COOKE, Morris. *Organized Labor & Production.* 1940. 3rd ed. inscr. dj. $20.00

COOKE. *Outlines From the Outpost.* 1961. Donnelley. Lakeside Classic. A3. $40.00

COOLIDGE, Dane. *Texican.* 1911. Chicago. Ils 1st ed. EX. $35.00

COOLIDGE, L.A. *Life of Ulysses S. Grant.* 1922. index. 596 p. K1. $13.50

COOLIDGE, Susan. *What Katy Did at School.* ND. Little Brown. VG. P1. $9.25

COOMBS, David. *Churchill: His Paintings.* 1967. London. Hamish Hamilton. 4to. VG. D1. $60.00

COOMBS, David. *Sport & Countryside in English Paintings.* 1973. Oxford. Ils. VG. $25.00

COOMER, B.G. *Genealogical History of Coomer Family, 1710-1892.* 1893. Flint, MI. Ils. 143 p. G. T5. $22.50

COON, C.S. *Hunting Peoples.* 1971. Little Brown. Ils 1st ed. 413 p. dj. EX. M2. $14.00

COONEY, Barbara. *Chaucer's Chanticleer & the Fox.* 1958. Crowell. Ils. VG. B4. $25.00

COONEY, Barbara. *Lear's the Owl & the Pussycat in French by Steegmuller.* 1961. Little Brown. 1st ed. dj. VG. B4. $30.00

COONEY, Ellen. *Silver Rose.* 1979. Duir Pr. 1st ed. sgn. wraps. EX. $25.00

COONS, J.W. *IN at Shiloh. Report of the Commission.* 1904. pocket map. 310 p. VG. scarce. J4. $29.50

COONTS, S. *Flight of the Intruder.* 1986. Annapolis. 1st ed. dj. M. $20.00

COOPER, A. *Complete Distiller.* 1797. London. Ils. fld plt. rebound. VG. $100.00

COOPER, A.R. *N American Pseudophyllidean Cestodes From Fishes.* 1919. IL U. 13 pls. 212 p. M2. $5.00

COOPER, Alonzo. *In & Out of Rebel Prisons.* 1888. Oswego. 1st ed. dj. VG. $45.00

COOPER, Astley. *Testis & Thymus Gland.* 1845. Phil. VG. $65.00

COOPER, Basil. *And Afterward, the Dark.* 1977. Arkham House. 1st ed. dj. VG. P1. $15.00

COOPER, C.R. *Lions 'n Tigers 'n Everything.* 1925. Boston. Ils. 260 p. M. $20.00

COOPER, Douglas. *Great Private Collections.* 1963. Macmillan. 400 photos. 303 p. dj. D2. $65.00

COOPER, Douglas. *Picasso Theatre.* 1968. London. 1st ed. dj. EX. $175.00

COOPER, Edmund. *Five to Twelve.* nd. Book Club. dj. VG. P1. $4.00

COOPER, Edmund. *Overman Culture.* nd. Book Club. dj. VG. P1. $3.75

COOPER, Edmund. *Sea Horse in the Sky.* 1970. Putnam. dj. EX. P1. $4.75

COOPER, Edmund. *Tenth Planet.* 1973. Putnam. dj. EX. P1. $9.25

COOPER, G.R. *Invention of Sewing Machine.* 1968. Smithsonian. 2nd ed. VG. $20.00

COOPER, J.F. *Deerslayer.* 1929. Scribner. Ils Wyeth. VG. $40.00

COOPER, J.F. *Historical Sketch of Indiantown Presbyterian Church...* 1957. np. 1st ed. wraps. EX. $25.00

COOPER, J.F. *History of the Navy of the USA.* 1839. Phil. 1st ed. 2 vols. G. $175.00

COOPER, J.F. *History of the Navy of the USA.* 1840. Phil. 2nd ed. 2 vols. T5. $150.00

COOPER, J.F. *Last of the Mohicans.* 1932. Ltd Ed Club. Ils Wilson. slipcase. EX. $55.00

COOPER, J.F. *Last of the Mohicans.* 1935. NY. Scribner. reprint. 4to. EX. $20.00

COOPER, J.F. *Lionel Lincoln.* 1825. NY. 1st ed. 1st state. 2 vols. $275.00

COOPER, J.F. *Notions of the Americans: Picked Up by Traveling Bachelor.* 1838. Phil. 12mo. 340 p. 1 vol only. G. G2. $28.00

COOPER, J.F. *Oak Openings; or, Bee Hunter.* 1848. NY. Burgess Stringer. 228 p. G. $100.00

COOPER, J.F. *Pioneers.* 1923. London. 1st Eng ed. 3 vols. VG. $250.00

COOPER, J.F. *Prairie.* 1940. Ltd Ed Club. Ils John Curry. G. $85.00

COOPER, J.F. *Red Rover: A Tale.* 1838. Phil. 1st ed. 2 vols. G. $95.00

COOPER, J.F. *Stories of the Sea: Narratives of Adventure.* 1863. Gregory. Ils Darley. VG. $50.00

COOPER, J.F. *Technique of Contraception.* 1928. NY. Day Nichols. 2nd ed. EX. $45.00

COOPER, J.F. *Wing & Wing: A Tale.* 1842. Phil. Lea Blanchard. 12mo. 2 vols. $125.00

COOPER, Louise. *Thorn Key.* 1988. 1st ed. dj. M. C1. $8.50

COOPER, M. *Munsters.* 1937. Avon. pb. G. $25.00

COOPER, Patricia. *Quilters, Women & Domestic Art.* 1977. Doubleday. Ils. 4to. 157 p. $15.00

COOPER, S. *Concise System of Instructions & Regulations for Militia...* 1836. Phil. Ils. 288 p. T5. $95.00

COOPER, S.F. *Pages & Pictures From Writings of James Fenimore Cooper.* 1861. NY. embossed leather. VG. $125.00

COOPER, Samuel. *Dictionary of Practical Surgery.* 1832. NY. reprint of 6th London ed. 2 vols. $140.00

COOPER, Susan. *Dark Is Rising.* nd. Atheneum. Ils Cober. pb. VG. C1. $5.50

COOPER, Treat. *Man O'War.* 1954. NY. Ils. 230 p. dj. G. B2. $27.50

COOPER, W.M. *Illustrated History of the Rod.* 1988. England. $30.00

COOVER, Robert. *Origin of Brunists.* 1967. London. 1st ed. dj. VG. $75.00

COOVER, Robert. *Theological Position.* 1972. Dutton. 1st ed. dj. RS. EX. $60.00

COOVER, Robert. *Universal Baseball Association.* 1968. Random House. 1st print. dj. EX. $75.00

COPE, E.D. *Batrachia of N America.* 1963. Lundberg. reprint of 1889 ed. M2. $45.00

COPE, E.D. *Crocodilians, Lizards & Snakes of N America.* 1898. Nat Mus. 36 pls. 1143 p. $75.00

COPE, E.D. *Vertebrate of Cretaceous Formations of the W.* 1875. WA. Ils. 4to. 303 p. EX. M2. $165.00

COPE. *15th OH Volunteers & Its Campaigns.* 1916. Columbus. VG. $110.00

COPELAND, Aaron. *Copeland on Music.* 1968. Doubleday. 1st ed. sgn. dj. $25.00

COPELAND, Aaron. *Music & Imagination.* 1952. Harvard. 1st ed. sgn. $20.00

COPELAND, Aaron. *New Music.* 1968. Norton. sgn. dj. $20.00

COPELAND, R.M. *Country Life: Handbook of Agriculture, Horticulture...* 1866. Boston. 5th ed. 8vo. 912 p. $50.00

COPELAND, R.M. *Picturesque Pocket Companion & Guide Through Mt. Auburn.* 1839. Boston. Ils. 16mo. 252 p. $50.00

COPELAND & PERLIS. *Copeland, 1800-1942.* 1984. NY. Ils 1st ed. sgn. dj. M. $30.00

COPPARD, A.E. *Adam & Eve & Pinch Me.* 1922. Knopf. 2nd ed. dj. G. P1. $30.00

COPPARD, A.E. *Fearful Pleasures.* 1946. Arkham House. 1st ed. dj. VG. P1. $35.00

COPPARD, A.E. *Fearful Pleasures.* 1946. Arkham House. 1st ed. EX. $40.00

COPPARD, A.E. *Hundredth Story.* 1931. Berkshire. Golden Cockerel. 1/1000. dj. VG. $75.00

COPPARD, A.E. *Man From Kilsheelan.* 1930. London. Chiswick. 1/550. sgn. EX. $50.00

COPPARD, A.E. *Pink Furniture.* 1930. London. Cape. Ils Gurney. 1st ed. dj. EX. $25.00

COPPEL, Alfred. *Gate of Hell.* 1967. Harcourt Brace. 1st ed. dj. VG. P1. $7.00

COPPER, Basil. *Curse of the Fleers.* 1976. Harwood Smart. 1st ed. dj. EX. P1. $25.00

COPPER, Basil. *From Evil's Pillow.* 1973. Arkham House. dj. EX. P1. $15.00

COPPER, Basil. *Great White Space.* 1975. St. Martin. 1st ed. dj. xl. VG. P1. $8.00

COPPER, Basil. *House of the Wolf.* 1983. Arkham House. 1st ed. dj. EX. P1. $15.00

COPPER, Basil. *Necropolis.* 1980. Arkham House. 1st ed. dj. EX. P1. $17.50

CORBEN, Richard. *Bloodstar.* 1976. Morning Star. 1st ed. dj. VG. P1. $30.00

CORBEN, Richard. *Flights Into Fantasy.* 1981. Thumb Tack Books. 1st ed. dj. P1. $30.00

CORBEN, Richard. *Neverwhere.* nd. Ariel. 2nd ed. pb. G. $3.50

CORBET, A.S. *Butterflies of the Malay Penninsula.* 1956. Edinburgh. Oliver Boyd. Ils 537 p. dj. M2. $85.00

CORBETT, Jim. *Jungle Lore.* 1953. NY. dj. EX. $20.00

CORBETT, Jim. *Man Eaters Kumaon.* 1944. NY. Stated 1st ed. dj. VG. B2. $15.00

CORBETT, Jim. *My India.* 1952. NY. 1st ed. dj. VG. B2. $37.50

CORBETT, Mrs. E.T. *Karl & the Queen of Queer-Land.* 1880. NY. G. $25.00

CORBETT & HAMLIN. *Peacemaker.* 1952. Salt Lake City. Desert Book. 538 p. dj. VG. A3. $65.00

CORBETT-SMITH, A. *Parsifal.* 1922. 2nd print. xl. VG. C1. $4.00

CORBIN & KERKA. *Steam Locomotives of Burlington Route.* 1960. Red Oak. Ils 1st ed. 4to. 304 p. C4. $65.00

CORCORAN, William. *Blow Desert Winds.* 1935. Appleton Century. 1st ed. $12.00

CORDASCO. *American Medical Imprints, 1820-1910.* Prentice Hall. folio. 2 vols. $110.00

CORDELL, Alexander. *If You Believe the Soldiers.* 1974. Doubleday. 1st ed. dj. VG. P1. $7.25

CORDUS, Valerius. *Il Dispensario di Valerio Cordo i Speciali Necessarie...* 1627. Venice. 12mo. 373 p. $385.00

COREY, J.W. *Soul: Its Organization & Development.* 1913. LA. $12.50

CORKILL, Louis. *Fish Lane.* 1951. Bobbs Merrill. 1st ed. dj. VG. P1. $7.25

CORLEY. *Fifth Son of the Shoemaker.* 1930. NY. 1st ed. dj. VG. $30.00

CORMACK, M.B. *Star-Crossed Woman.* 1962. Crown. dj. EX. P1. $9.25

CORMACK, Malcolm. *J.M.W. Turner, R.A.: 1775-1851 Catalog of Drawings...* 1975. Cambridge. 1st ed. dj. VG. J2. $17.50

CORN, Alfred. *Notes From a Child of Paradise.* 1984. Viking. 1st ed. dj. EX. $20.00

CORN, Wanda. *Art of Andrew Wyeth.* 1973. Greenwich. 1st print. VG. B1. $25.00

CORNE, M.E. *Death at the Manor.* 1938. Mill. 1st ed. xl. G. P1. $10.00

CORNELL, Katherine. *I Wanted To Be an Actress.* 1939. NY. 1st ed. dj. VG. B2. $27.50

CORNELL, W.W. *Brief Sketch of Family History of Walter W. Cornell...* 1943. Pawnee City, NE. G. $30.00

CORNELL, William. *Horace Greeley: Voice of the People.* 1950. 1st ed. dj. EX. B1. $15.00

CORNER, George. *Dr. Kane of the Arctic Seas.* 1972. Phil. 1st ed. dj. VG. $20.00

CORNWALL, A.B. *Francis the First.* 1936. England. $60.00

CORODIMAS, P. *In Trout Country.* 1971. Boston. 1st ed. dj. EX. $20.00

CORRELL, A. Boyd. *Murder Is an Art.* 1950. Phoenix. dj. VG. P1. $7.50

CORRINGTON, Julian. *Adventures With the Microscope.* 1934. Rochester. VG. $27.50

CORSO, Gregory. *American Express.* 1961. Olympia. 1st ed. wraps. EX. $40.00

CORSO, Gregory. *Ankh.* 1971. Pheonix. 1/100. sgn/#d. EX. $40.00

CORSO, Gregory. *Hitting the Big 50.* 1983. Catchword Papers. 1/126. sgn. $35.00

CORTADA, James. *Historical Dictionary of the Spanish Civil War, 1936-1939.* 1982. Greenwood Pr. 1st ed. VG. J2. $25.00

CORTAZAR, Julio. *Hopscotch.* 1966. NY. 1st ed. dj. EX. $45.00

CORTAZAR, Julio. *We Love Glenda So Much.* 1983. Knopf. $25.00

CORTAZAR, Julio. *Winners.* 1965. Pantheon. 1st ed. dj. EX. $35.00

CORTI, E.C. *Rise of the House of Rothschild.* 1928. NY. Ils 1st ed. 8vo. 427 p. VG. $35.00

CORTISSOZ, R. *John La Farge: Memoir & Study.* 1911. Boston. 15 pls. 8vo. TEG. VG. J2. $60.00

CORTISSOZ, R. *Works of Edwin Howland Blashfield.* 1937. NY. 75 pls. 4to. cloth bdg. VG. J2. $50.00

CORWIN, H.D. *Kiowa Indians: Their History & Life Stories.* 1958. Lawton, OH. Ils. sgn. EX. $50.00

CORWIN, Norman. *Overkill & Megalove.* 1963. Cleveland. 1st ed. inscr. dj. EX. $45.00

CORWIN, Norman. *They Fly Through the Air With the Greatest of Ease.* 1939. Vrest Orton. 1st ed. dj. EX. $75.00

CORWIN, W. *Plot to Overthrow Christmas.* 1952. NY. 1st ed. 32 p. VG. $37.50

CORWIN, W. *Thirteen Radio Dramas.* 1946. NY. 8th print. dj. VG. $27.50

CORWIN, W. *Untitled & Other Radio Dramas.* 1947. NY. 1st print. 553 p. dj. VG. $37.50

CORY, C.B. *Birds of IL & WI.* 1908. Field Mus. Ils. 764 p. EX. M2. $60.00

CORY, C.B. *Mammals of IL & WI.* 1912. Field Mus. pls. wraps. VG. $20.00

CORY, David. *Red Feather & Star Maiden.* 1935. Grosset Dunlap. 1st ed. VG. $15.00

CORY, Desmond. *Even If You Run.* 1972. Crime Club. 1st ed. dj. xl. P1. $5.00

CORY, Desmond. *Feramontov.* 1966. Muller. VG. P1. $5.50

CORY, Desmond. *Sunburst.* 1971. Hodder Stoughton. dj. xl. P1. $5.00

COSENTINO, Frank. *Edward Marshall Boehm, 1913-1969.* 1970. Lakeside Pr. 1st ed. boxed. VG. J2. $35.00

COSMAN, M.P. *Fabulous Feasts: Medieval Cookery & Ceremony.* 1976. 1st ed. VG. C1. $12.00

COSTAIN, T.B. *History of the Plantagenets.* 1952. NY. 1/400. boxed. EX. B2. $30.00

COSTAIN, T.B. *Last Platagents.* 1962. Garden City. 1st ed. sgn. 8vo. VG. $30.00

COSTAIN, T.B. *Silver Chalice.* 1952. Doubleday. Special ed. 1/750. sgn. slipcase. $70.00

COSTAIN, T.B. *Silver Chalice.* 1952. Garden City. 1st ed. presentation. slipcase. EX. $75.00

COSTELLO, D.F. *Desert World.* 1972. Crowell. Ils. 264 p. dj. EX. M2. $12.00

COSTELLO, D.F. *World of the Prairie Dog.* 1970. Lippincott. Ils 1st ed. 160 p. dj. EX. M2. $13.00

COSTIGAN, J. *Little Moon of Alban & Wind From the S: 2 Plays.* 1959. NY. Ils. 147 p. dj. VG. $25.00

COT, Pierre. *Triumph of Treason.* 1944. Chicago. 432 p. G. T5. $17.50

COTHRAN, S. *Charleston Murders.* 1947. NY. 1st ed. Regional Murders Series. dj. B2. $17.50

COTLER, Gordon. *Mission in Black.* nd. Book Club. dj. EX. P1. $2.75

COTLOW, Lewis. *In Search of the Primitive.* 1966. Little Brown. Ils. 454 p. dj. VG. M2. $10.00

COTON, A.V. *New Ballet: Kurt Joose & His Work.* 1946. London. Dobson. 4to. 156 p. dj. VG. $25.00

COTTER, C.H. *Physical Geography of the Oceans.* 1965. Am Elsevier. maps. 317 p. dj. EX. M2. $13.00

COTTERILL, R.S. *Old S.* 1939. Clark. Revised 2nd ed. VG. J2. $22.50

COTTERILL, R.S. *S Indians: Story of Civilized Tribes Before Removal.* 1954. Norman. Ils. dj. EX. $40.00

COTTRELL, Kent. *Sunburnt Sketches.* c 1950. S Africa. Ils. dj. VG. $22.50

COUES, Elliot. *Birds of NW: Handbook of Ornithology of Region...MS River...* 1874. GPO. 1st ed. 791 p. G. $45.00

COUES, Elliot. *Birds of the CO Valley: Passeres to Laniidae.* 1878. WA. Ils. 807 p. EX. M2. $155.00

COUES, Elliot. *Field Ornithology...* 1874. Salem. 1st ed. VG. $60.00

COUES, Elliot. *Key to N American Birds.* 1872. Ils 1st ed. pls. 4to. $100.00

COUES, Elliot. *Third Installment of American Ornithological Bibliography.* 1879. WA. VG. M2. $95.00

COUES, Elliott. *Field Notes on Birds Observed in Dakota & MT.* 1878. WA. 201 p. wraps. A3. $35.00

COUES, Elliott. *Monographs of N American Rodentia.* 1877. WA. Ils. 4to. 1091 p. EX. M2. $145.00

COUES, Elliott. *Monographs of N American Rodentia.* 1877. GPO. 1091 p. orig bdg. A3. $75.00

COUES, Elliott. *Third Installment of American Ornithological Bibliography.* 1879. WA. 551 p. disbound. A3. $45.00

COUFFER, Jack. *Song of Wild Laughter.* 1963. Simon Schuster. Ils. 190 p. dj. EX. M2. $5.00

COUGHLIN, W.J. *Her Honor.* 1987. NY. 1st ed. dj. EX. $7.00

COULTER, E.M. *College Life in the Old S.* 1928. NY. Ils 1st ed. 381 p. G. $30.00

COULTER, E.M. *Daniel Lee: Agriculturalist.* 1972. Athens. 165 p. dj. VG. $20.00

COULTER, E.M. *GA Waters: Tallulah Falls, Madison Spring, Scull Shoals...* 1965. Athens. Ltd ed. sgn. 208 p. VG. $55.00

COULTER, E.M. *History of the S. Vol. 8: S During Reconstruction...* 1947. 426 p. VG. J4. $9.50

COULTER, E.M. *Joseph Wallace Bevan: GA's First Historian.* 1964. Athens. Wormsloe. 1/750. 157 p. dj. VG. $35.00

COULTER, E.M. *Parson Brownlow.* 1937. Chapel Hill. Ils 1st ed. 432 p. VG. $30.00

COULTER, E.M. *Travel the Confederate States: A Bibliography.* 289 p. M. scarce. J4. $40.00

COULTER & SAYE. *List of Early Settlers of GA.* 1967. Athens. 2nd print. 111 p. VG. $15.00

COUNSELMAN, Mary Elizabeth. *Half in Shadow.* 1978. Arkham House. 1st ed. dj. EX. P1. $15.00

COUP, W.C. *Sawdust & Spangles.* 1901. Chicago. Ils. 262 p. VG. $30.00

COUPLAND, R. *Kirk of the Zambesi.* 1970. Negro U. reprint of 1928 ed. EX. M2. $18.00

COURBOIN, Francois. *L'Estampe Francais: Graveurs & Marchands.* 1914. Bruxelles/Paris. wraps. scarce. D2. $115.00

COURSEY, O.W. *Pioneering in Dakota.* 1937. Mitchell, SD. Ils. 12mo. 160 p. VG. $30.00

COURSEY, O.W. *Wild Bill.* 1942. Mitchell, SD. Educator Supply Co. 1st ed. VG. $60.00

COURSEY, O.W. *Woman With a Stone Heart: Romance of Philippine War.* 1914. Mitchell, SD. Ils. 12mo. 178 p. VG. $15.00

COURTHION, P. *Georges Rouault.* nd. NY. Ils. 4to. dj. EX. J2. $125.00

COURTIER, S.H. *Ligny's Lake.* 1971. Robert Hale. 1st ed. dj. G. P1. $15.00

COURTNEY, M.A. *Cornish Feasts & Folklore.* 1973. reprint of 1890 ed. dj. EX. C1. $14.50

COURTNEY & BURDSALL. *Field Guide to Mushrooms & Their Relatives.* 1982. Van Nostrand. Ils 1st ed. 144 p. dj. EX. M2. $18.00

COURVILLE, C.B. *Cerebral Anoxia.* 1953. Los Angeles. St. Lucas Pr. 1st ed. xl. $60.00

COUSINS, Norman. *Modern Man Is Obsolete.* 1945. NY. Viking. 1st ed. inscr. VG. $20.00

COUSINS, Norman. *Present Tense.* 1967. NY. 1st ed. dj. EX. $25.00

COUSTEAU, Jacques-Yves. *Living Sea.* 1963. Harper Row. Ils. dj. VG. M2. $8.00

COUSTEAU, Jacques-Yves. *Shark: Splendid Savage of the Sea.* 1970. Doubleday. Ils 1st Am ed. 277 p. dj. EX. M2. $14.00

COUTIERE, H. *American Species of Snapping Shrimps of Genus Synalpheus.* 1973. USFWS. 31 p. M2. $10.00

COVARRUBIAS, Miguel. *Eagle, Jaguar & Serpent.* 1954. Knopf. Ils 1st ed. dj. VG. $65.00

COVARRUBIAS, Miguel. *Island of Bali.* 1937. Knopf. 2nd ed. VG. $40.00

COVARRUBIAS, Miguel. *Mexico S.* 1946. NY. Ils 1st ed. dj. VG. B2. $32.50

COVARRUBIAS, Miguel. *Negro Drawings.* 1927. Knopf. Ils. 56 p. black cloth. $175.00

COVENTRY, F. *History of Pompey the Little.* 1751. London. 1st ed. rebound. $120.00

COWAN, T.J. *No One Is So Small.* 1963. private print. Ils. 102 p. EX. M2. $10.00

COWARD, Noel. *Bittersweet & Other Plays.* 1929. Doubleday. Ltd 1st ed. 1/1000. sgn. VG. $75.00

COWARD, Noel. *Cavalcade.* 1932. London. Heinemann. 138 p. VG. $20.00

COWARD, Noel. *Conversation Piece.* 1934. NY. 1st Am ed. dj. VG. $15.00

COWARD, Noel. *Design for Living: A Comedy.* 1933. Garden City. 1st ed. sgn. EX. $65.00

COWARD, Noel. *In War Services Fund: 70 Years of Song.* 1940. London. 1st ed. wraps. $15.00

COWARD, Noel. *Last Encore. Words by Noel Coward, Pictures From Life...* 1973. Little Brown. 1st Am ed. photos. dj. G. $7.50

COWARD, Noel. *Pomp & Circumstance.* 1960. NY. 1st Am ed. dj. EX. $25.00

COWARD, Noel. *Present Laughter.* 1943. London. Heinemann. VG. $15.00

COWARDIN, L.M. *Mallard Recruitment in Agricultural Environment of ND.* 1985. Wildlife Soc. Ils. 37 p. M2. $6.00

COWARDIN & JOHNSON. *Preliminary Classification of Wetland Plant Communities.* 1973. USFWS. 31 p. M2. $3.00

COWBURN, Benjamin. *No Cloak No Dagger.* nd. Adventurers Club. VG. P1. $3.75

COWDEN, J. *Cameleons: Little Lions of the Reptile World.* 1977. McKay. Ils 1st ed. 58 p. dj. EX. M2. $9.00

COWELL, A. *Heart of the Forest.* 1961. Knopf. Ils 1st ed. dj. VG. M2. $10.00

COWLES, Charles. *Leaves From a Lawyer's Life Alfoat & Ashore.* 1879. Lowell, MA. VG. $65.00

COWLES, R.B. *Distant Drums.* 1932. London. Methuen. 1st ed. sgn. EX. $17.50

COWLES, R.B. *Zulu Journal: Field Notes of a Naturalist in S Africa.* 1959. CA U. Ils. map. 267 p. dj. EX. M2. $12.00

COWLEY, Abraham. *Mistress.* 1923. London. 1/725. VG. $100.00

COWLEY, M. *Dry Season.* 1941. New Directions. ARC. wraps. VG. $20.00

COWLEY, M.F. *Talks on Doctrine.* nd. Chicago. Later Day Saints. dj. G. $40.00

COWLEY, Malcolm. *Blue Juniata: Collected Poems.* 1968. NY. 1st ed. dj. EX. $35.00

COWLEY, Malcolm. *Exile's Return.* Ltd Ed Club. slipcase. B3. $60.00

COWLEY, Malcolm. *Second Flowering.* 1973. NY. 1st ed. dj. VG. B2. $15.00

COWLEY, Malcolm. *Second Flowering.* 1973. NY. 2nd print. inscr. dj. EX. $20.00

COWLEY, Malcolm. *Writers at Work: Paris Review Interviews.* 1958. NY. Viking. dj. VG. $12.00

COWLEY, Stewart. *Spacecraft 2000 to 2100 A.D.* 1978. Chartwell. dj. EX. P1. $7.00

COWLEY, Stewart. *Spacewreck.* 1979. Hamlyn. dj. EX. P1. $10.00

COWLEY & HERRIDGE. *Great Space Battles.* 1979. Chartwell. dj. EX. P1. $5.50

COWPER, Richard. *Clone.* nd. Book Club. dj. VG. P1. $3.75

COWPER, Richard. *Clone.* 1973. Doubleday. 1st ed. dj. EX. P1. $10.00

COWPER, Richard. *Road to Corlay.* nd. Book Club. dj. EX. P1. $3.75

COWPER, Richard. *Twilight of Briareus.* 1974. John Day. 1st ed. dj. EX. P1. $20.00

COWTAN, Robert. *Memories of the British Museum.* 1872. London. 1st ed. $59.50

COX, B. *All Color Guide to Prehistoric Animals.* 1970. Grosset Dunlap. Ils. 159 p. dj. EX. M2. $8.00

COX, E.H.M. *Modern Shrubs.* 1968. Nelson. dj. VG. $10.00

COX, G.F. *Tropical Marine Aquaria.* 1974. Grosset Dunlap. Ils Revised ed. 160 p. EX. M2. $10.00

COX, Ian. *Scallop: Studies of a Shell.* 1957. London. Ils. 4to. VG. $11.00

COX, J.D. *Atlanta: Campaigns of the Civil War.* 1882. NY. 1st ed. 274 p. VG. T5. $30.00

COX, J.D. *Battle of Franklin, TN, November 30, 1864.* 1897. 1/1000. maps. 351 p. EX. scarce. J4. $85.00

COX, J.H. *Folk Songs of the S.* 1925. Cambridge. Ils 2nd print. sgn. TEG. $50.00

COX, James. *My Native Land.* 1895. St. Louis. Ils. 400 p. K1. $13.50

COX, Palmer. *Brownies: Their Book.* 1887. NY. $75.00

COX, Peter. *Dwarf Rhododendrons.* 1973. London. dj. VG. $18.00

COX, Samuel. *Buckeye Abroad.* 1852. NY. Ils 1st ed. 444 p. VG. $25.00

COX, Sidney. *Swinger of Birches: Robert Frost.* 1961. Collier. EX. P1. $10.00

COX, W.E. *Book of Pottery & Porcelain. Vol. I.* 1970. Crown. Ils Revised ed. 1158 p. M1. $110.00

COX, Wally. *Mr. Peepers.* 1955. NY. 1st ed. wraps. EX. $20.00

COX & FORD. *Parish Churches of England.* 1943-1944. London. dj. VG. J2. $15.00

COXE, Betty J. *New Sexuality.* 1969. Medical Pr. EX. P1. $7.50

COXE, George Harmon. *Camera Clue.* 1937. Knopf. 1st ed. G. P1. $11.50

COXE, George Harmon. *Dangerous Legacy.* 1946. Knopf. dj. VG. P1. $9.25

COXE, George Harmon. *Eye Witness.* nd. Book Club. VG. P1. $2.00

COXE, George Harmon. *Fenner.* 1971. Knopf. 1st ed. dj. VG. P1. $9.25

COXE, George Harmon. *Glass Triangle.* 1944. Triangle. dj. VG. P1. $7.00

COXE, George Harmon. *Groom Lay Dead.* 1947. Triangle. dj. VG. P1. $7.00

COXE, George Harmon. *Groom Lay Dead.* 1947. Triangle. VG. P1. $4.75

COXE, George Harmon. *Inland Passage.* nd. Book Club. dj. EX. P1. $2.75

COXE, George Harmon. *Murder for Two.* nd. Grosset. dj. VG. P1. $7.50

COXE, George Harmon. *Murder With Pictures.* nd. Grosset. G. P1. $5.50

COXE, George Harmon. *Never Bet Your Life.* nd. Book Club. dj. VG. P1. $7.00

COXE, George Harmon. *Ring of Truth.* nd. Book Club. dj. VG. P1. $2.75

COXE, George Harmon. *Top Assignment.* nd. Book Club. dj. VG. P1. $2.75

COXE, George Harmon. *With Intent To Kill.* nd. Book Club. dj. VG. P1. $2.75

COXE, William. *Memoirs of Duke of Marlborough.* 1848. London. Revised 1st ed. 12mo. 3 vols. $125.00

COYKENDALL, T. *Duck Decoys & How To Rig Them.* 1955. NY. Ils 1st ed. 125 p. dj. VG. B2. $40.00

COYLE, David Cushman. *Age Without Fear.* 1937. Nat Home Lib. VG. P1. $5.00

COYLE, E.R. *Ambulance on the French Front.* 1918. Britton. Ils. 243 p. $8.50

COYNE, John. *Piercing.* nd. Book Club. dj. VG. P1. $4.50

COYNE, John. *Searing.* nd. Book Club. dj. VG. P1. $4.50

COZZENS, J.G. *Just & the Unjust.* 1942. Harcourt Brace. 1st ed. $5.00

COZZENS, J.G. *Last Adam.* 1933. Harcourt Brace. 1st ed. xl. rebound. VG. P1. $10.00

COZZENS, S.W. *Ancient Cibola; or, Three Years in AZ & NM.* 1891. Boston. EX. $65.00

CRABB, A.L. *Nashville: Personality of a City.* 1960. Bobbs Merrill. 1st ed. sgn. 12mo. dj. VG. $25.00

CRABTREE, B.G. *NC Governors, 1585-1958.* 1958. Ils. 137 p. EX. J4. $10.00

CRABTREE, J.B. *Passing of Spain & Ascendency of America.* 1898. Springfield. Ils. 8vo. 460 p. G. G2. $13.00

CRADDOCK, C.E. *In the TN Mountains.* 1885. 322 p. G. J4. $6.50

CRADDOCK, Phyllis. *Gateway to Remembrance.* 1950. London. dj. VG. C1. $7.50

CRADY, K.M. *Free Steppin'.* 1944. Dallas. 5th print. 83 p. dj. M1. $25.00

CRAFTS. *Pioneers in Settlement of America.* 1876. Boston. 2 vols. VG. $95.00

CRAGE, E.G. *Scene.* 1923. London. Ltd ed. 1/100. sgn. 4to. xl. VG. $150.00

CRAIG, Alisa. *Murder Goes Mumming.* nd. Book Club. dj. G. P1. $4.00

CRAIG, David. *Contact Lost.* 1970. Stein Day. dj. VG. P1. $7.00

CRAIG, E.G. *On the Art of the Theatre.* 1911. Chicago. EX. P3. $39.00

CRAIG, J.D. *Danger Is My Business.* 1938. Simon Schuster. VG. $7.50

CRAIG, J.D. *Danger Is My Business.* 1939. Literary Guild. Ils. 309 p. dj. G. M2. $4.00

CRAIG, N.B. *History of Pittsburgh.* 1851. Pittsburgh. 1st ed. 2 fld maps. rebound. xl. $35.00

CRAIG, N.B. *Sketch of Life & Services of Isaac Craig.* 1854. Pittsburgh. 1st ed. 70 p. fair. T5. $95.00

CRAIG, Neville. *Recollections of Ill-Fated Expedition to Brazil.* 1907. Phil. 1st ed. VG. $85.00

CRAIG, Philip. *Gate of Ivory, Gate of Horn.* 1970. 1st Eng ed. dj. VG. C1. $6.00

CRAIG. *Coins of the World, 1750-1850.* 1971. 2nd ed. $20.00

CRAIGHEAD, F.C. *Track of the Grizzly.* 1979. Sierra Club. Ils. 261 p. dj. EX. M2. $15.00

CRAIGIE, David. *Voyage of the Luna-1.* 1965. Messner. 8th print. dj. xl. P1. $5.00

CRAIK. *Bow-Wow & Mew-Mew.* 1911. Flanagan. Ils. G. $10.00

CRAM, R.A. *Ruined Abbeys of Great Britain.* c 1905. NY. Pott. 1st imp. photos. TEG. $28.00

CRAMER, C.H. *Royal Bob.* 1952. Indianapolis. 1st ed. 314 p. dj. VG. B2. $17.50

CRAMER, Carl. *Dark Trees to the Wind.* 1949. NY. 1st ed. inscr. dj. EX. $45.00

CRAMER, Carl. *Listen for a Lonesome Drum.* 1950. NY. 1st ed. sgn. dj. EX. $40.00

CRAMER, Carl. *Windfall Fiddle.* 1950. NY. 1st ed. dj. VG. $20.00

CRAMER, Rie. *Het Land Van de Lotus Van de Zon.* nd. Utrecht. 1/200. Ils sgn. VG. P3. $75.00

CRAMER. *Miro: Catalogue Raisonne of Illustrated Works.* 1989. 4to. 600 p. boxed. VG. $250.00

CRAMOND, M. *Of Bears & Men.* 1986. OK U. Ils 1st ed. 433 p. dj. M. M2. $28.00

CRAMPTON, C.G. *Standing Up Country: Canyon Lands of UT & AZ.* 1964. Knopf. 1st ed. dj. VG. $30.00

CRAMPTON, H.E. *Doctrine of Evolution: Its Basis & Scope.* 1924. Columbia U. 320 p. EX. M2. $25.00

CRANE, Caroline. *Circus Day.* 1986. Dodd Mead. 1st ed. dj. EX. P1. $14.95

CRANE, Frances. *Black Cypress.* 1948. Random House. 1st ed. VG. P1. $15.00

CRANE, Frances. *Cinnamon Murder.* 1946. Random House. 1st ed. xl. P1. $10.00

CRANE, H. *Bridge.* Ltd Ed Club. slipcase. M. B3. $65.00

CRANE, Hart. *Voyages: Six Poems.* 1957. MOMA. Ils Baskin. oblong 4to. wraps. G. $40.00

CRANE, Robert. *Hero's Walk.* 1954. Ballantine. dj. EX. P1. $31.75

CRANE, Robert. *Hero's Walk.* 1954. Ballantine. dj. VG. P1. $22.75

CRANE, Stephen. *Battle in Greece.* 1936. Peter Pauper. Ils Angelo. 1/425. slipcase. EX. $30.00

CRANE, Stephen. *Complete Novels of Stephen Crane.* 1967. Doubleday. 1st ed. dj. EX. $20.00

CRANE, Stephen. *George's Mother.* 1896. NY. 1st ed. 8vo. VG. $125.00

CRANE, Stephen. *Great Battles of the World.* 1901. Phil. 1st ed. green cloth. VG. $50.00

CRANE, Stephen. *Little Regiment.* 1896. NY. 1st ed. 8vo. VG. $125.00

CRANE, Stephen. *Maggie: Girl of the Streets.* 1896. NY. 1st HrdCvr ed. EX. $100.00

CRANE, Stephen. *Maggie: Girl of the Streets.* 1974. Norwalk. Heritage. quarto. slipcase. EX. $15.00

CRANE, Stephen. *Red Badge of Courage.* 1896. Appleton. EX. J3. $50.00

CRANE, Stephen. *Third Violet.* 1897. NY. 1st ed. 203 p. tan bdg. G. T5. $65.00

CRANE, Stephen. *Third Violet.* 1897. NY. 1st ed. 8vo. tan cloth. EX. $125.00

CRANE, Stephen. *Works of Crane.* 1925. Knopf. Intro Hergesheimer. 12 vols. VG. $175.00

CRANE, Walter. *Artist's Reminiscences.* 1907. Macmillan. 1st ed. G. J2. $15.00

CRANE, Walter. *Artist's Reminiscences.* 1907. NY. Ils 1st ed. photos. 520 p. M. $75.00

CRANE, Walter. *Baby's Opera.* Warne. Ils. B4. $40.00

CRANE, Walter. *Bases for Design.* 1898. London. 1st ed. 8vo. gilt cloth. VG. G2. $125.00

CRANE, Walter. *Beauty & the Beast.* 1982. NY. Thames Hudson. 21 color pls. 4to. $7.00

CRANE, Walter. *Flora's Feast: Masque of Flowers.* 1892. London. pls. VG. $45.00

CRANE, Walter. *Line & Form.* 1900. London. VG. P3. $65.00

CRANE, Walter. *Line & Form.* 1900. London. Bell. Ils. TEG. gilt blue bdg. EX. $85.00

CRANE, Walter. *Mrs. Mundi at Home.* c 1885. London. 2nd ed. oblong 4to. dj. VG. $75.00

CRANE, Walter. *Queen Summer; or, Tourney of Lily & Rose.* 1981. London. pls. 4to. VG. $65.00

CRAPO, Thomas. *Strange But True.* 1893. New Bedford. G. $20.00

CRAPSEY, A.S. *Ways of the Gods.* 1921. NY. $40.00

CRASY, John. *Hang the Little Man.* 1963. NY. 1st ed. dj. VG. $20.00

CRAVEN, Avery. *Edmund Ruffin, Southerner: Study in Secession.* 1932. Appleton. photos. 283 p. EX. M2. $12.00

CRAVEN, Thomas. *Modern Art.* 1934. Simon Schuster. VG. P1. $18.25

CRAVEN, Thomas. *Treasury of American Prints.* 1939. slipcase. VG. $25.00

CRAVEN & MARAIS. *Namib Flora.* 1986. S Africa. Ils. 126 p. M. M2. $16.00

CRAWFORD, Dan. *Back to the Long Grass: My Link With Livingstone.* nd. NY. Ils. 373 p. G. T5. $25.00

CRAWFORD, Dan. *Thinking Black.* 1913. Doran. Ils. 484 p. G. M2. $12.00

CRAWFORD, Dan. *Thinking Black.* 1914. NY. Ils. 499 p. VG. T5. $22.50

CRAWFORD, F.M. *Adam Johnston's Son.* 1896. Macmillan. Ils Edwards. 1st ed. VG. $15.00

CRAWFORD, F.M. *Cigarette Maker's Romance.* 1890. London. 2nd ed. TEG. VG. $20.00

CRAWFORD, F.M. *Little City of Hope.* 1907. Macmillan. VG. P1. $5.50

CRAWFORD, F.M. *To Leeward.* 1911. Ward Lock. VG. P1. $12.50

CRAWFORD, F.M. *White Sister.* nd. Grosset. Photoplay ed. G. P1. $5.50

CRAWFORD, Isabel. *Kiowa: History of Blanket Indian Mission.* 1914. NY. Ils 1st ed. dj. EX. $40.00

CRAWFORD, Jack. *Broncho Book.* 1908. Roycroft. 16mo. brown suede. G. D1. $25.00

CRAWFORD, James. *Studies in SE Indian Languages.* 1975. Athens. 453 p. VG. $15.00

CRAWFORD, L.F. *Badlands & Broncho Trails.* 1922. Bismark. Capitol Book Co. Ils. scarce. A3. $80.00

CRAWFORD, M.C. *Romance of American Theatre.* 1925. Little Brown. VG. $12.00

CRAWFORD, Medorem. *Journal of Medorem Crawford.* 1897. Eugene. Star Job Office. 26 p. wraps. A3. $75.00

CRAWFORD, W.R. *Bibliography of Chaucer, 1954-1963.* 1967. Seattle. 1st ed. dj. VG. B2. $25.00

CRAWFORD, William Jr. *Gore & Glory.* 1944. Phil. Ils 192 p. T5. $12.50

CRAWFORD. *Social Life in Old New England.* 1914. NY. G. $30.00

CRAY, Ed. *Levi's.* 1978. Houghton Mifflin. dj. VG. $10.00

CRAYON, G. *Sketchbook (WA Irving).* 1891. NY. Crowell. G. $20.00

CREASE & MANN. *Second Creation.* 1986. NY. 1st ed. dj. EX. $12.50

CREASEY, John. *Baron & the Stolen Legacy.* 1967. Scribner. dj. EX. P1. $7.00

CREASEY, John. *Baron on Board.* 1968. Walker. 1st ed. dj. EX. P1. $7.00

CREASEY, John. *Blight.* 1968. Walker. 1st ed. dj. EX. P1. $9.25

CREASEY, John. *Bundle for the Toff.* 1968. Walker. 1st ed. dj. EX. P1. $7.00

CREASEY, John. *Croaker.* 1973. Holt Rinehart. 1st ed. dj. VG. P1. $7.50

CREASEY, John. *Depths.* 1967. Walker. dj. VG. P1. $7.00

CREASEY, John. *Dissemblers.* 1967. Scribner. dj. VG. P1. $7.00

CREASEY, John. *Famine.* 1968. Walker. 1st ed. dj. EX. P1. $7.00

CREASEY, John. *Fool to the Toff.* 1966. Walker. 1st ed. dj. EX. P1. $10.00

CREASEY, John. *Holiday for Inspector W.* nd. Stanley Paul. dj. VG. P1. $7.00

CREASEY, John. *House of the Bears.* 1975. Walker. VG. P1. $7.50

CREASEY, John. *Hunt the Toff.* 1969. Walker. dj. VG. P1. $7.50

CREASEY, John. *Insulators.* 1973. Walker. dj. VG. P1. $9.25

CREASEY, John. *Kill the Toff.* 1966. Walker. dj. EX. P1. $7.00

CREASEY, John. *League of Dark Men.* 1968. John Long. dj. xl. P1. $5.00

CREASEY, John. *Life for a Death.* 1973. Holt Rinehart. 1st ed. dj. VG. P1. $10.00

CREASEY, John. *Missing Monoplane.* nd. Sampson Low. G. P1. $20.00

CREASEY, John. *Plague of Silence.* 1968. Walker. dj. VG. P1. $9.25

CREASEY, John. *Six for the Toff.* 1969. Walker. 1st ed. dj. EX. P1. $7.00

CREASEY, John. *Stars for the Toff.* 1968. Walker. 1st ed. dj. VG. P1. $7.00

CREASEY, John. *Taste of Treasure.* 1966. John Long. 1st ed. dj. xl. P1. $5.00

CREASEY, John. *This Man Did I Kill?* 1974. Stein Day. dj. VG. P1. $7.00

CREASEY, John. *Thunder in Europe.* 1936. Andrew Melrose. xl. G. P1. $10.00

CREASEY, John. *Toff & the Deep Blue Sea.* 1967. Walker. dj. VG. P1. $10.00

CREASEY, John. *Toff & the Golden Boy.* 1969. Walker. 1st ed. dj. EX. P1. $7.00

CREASEY, John. *Toff & the Toughs.* 1968. Walker. 1st ed. dj. EX. P1. $7.00

CREASEY, John. *Toff Proceeds.* 1968. Walker. 1st ed. dj. EX. P1. $7.00

CREASEY, John. *Wait for Death.* 1972. Holt Rinehart. dj. xl. P1. $5.00

CREEKMORE, Hubert. *Long Reprieve.* 1946. New Directions. 1/1000. $30.00

CREELEY, Robert. *Away.* 1976. Black Sparrow. Ils Creeley. 1/200. sgn. EX. $35.00

CREELEY, Robert. *Day Book.* 1972. NY. 1st ed. dj. $25.00

CREELEY, Robert. *For Love: Poems, 1950-1960.* 1962. NY. 1st ed. wraps. EX. $40.00

CREELEY, Robert. *Island.* 1963. NY. 1st ed. wraps. EX. $40.00

CREELEY, Robert. *Later.* 1978. Toothpaste Pr. 1/800. inscr. wraps. $25.00

CREIGHTON, W.S. *Ants of N America.* 1950. Harvard. 57 pls. 585 p. EX. M2. $45.00

CREMER, R. *Lugosi, Man Behind the Cape.* 1976. Chicago. dj. EX. $50.00

CRESPELLE, J. *Fauves.* 1962. Greenwich. Ils. 4to. cloth. dj. EX. J2. $75.00

CREW, Henry. *Portraits of Famous Physicists With Biographical Accounts.* 1942. NY. Scripta Mathematica. photos. J2. $45.00

CREWS, Harry. *All We Need of Hell.* 1987. NY. Harper. 1st ed. dj. EX. T6. $15.00

CREWS, Harry. *Blood & Grits.* 1988. Perennial Lib. 1st ed. EX. $10.00

CREWS, Harry. *Childhood: Biography of a Place.* 1st ed. dj. VG. B7. $30.00

CREWS, Harry. *Feast of Snakes.* 1976. NY. Atheneum. 1st ed. dj. xl. $22.50

CREWS, Harry. *Hawk Is Dying.* 1973. 1st ed. dj. EX. $25.00

CREWS, Harry. *Hawk Is Dying.* 1973. Literary Guild. wraps. VG. T6. $15.00

CREWS, Harry. *Knockout Artist.* Harcourt Brace. 1st ed. dj. M. $10.00

CREWS, Harry. *Knockout Artist.* nd. NY. Harper. UCP. 1st ed. yellow printed wraps. $20.00

CREWS, Harry. *Naked in Garden Hills.* 1969. NY. 1st ed. dj. EX. $35.00

CREWS. *Pooh Perplex.* 1963. Dutton. 4th print. dj. VG. $5.00

CRICHTON, Michael. *Andromeda Strain.* 1969. Knopf. 1st ed. dj. VG. $20.00

CRICHTON, Michael. *Eaters of the Dead.* 1976. Knopf. 1st ed. dj. EX. P1. $15.00

CRICHTON, Michael. *Terminal Man.* nd. BOMC. dj. EX. P1. $5.00

CRICHTON, Robert. *Secret of Santa Vittoria.* 1960. Simon Schuster. sgn. dj. $8.50

CRILE, George. *Bipolar Theory of Living Processes.* 1926. NY. 1st ed. 8vo. 404 p. $50.00

CRISLER, Lois. *Arctic Wild.* 1958. Harper. sgn. 301 p. dj. M1. $17.50

CRISLER, Lois. *Captive Wild.* 1968. Harper. Ils 1st ed. 238 p. dj. EX. M2. $17.00

CRISP, N.J. *Gotland Deal.* 1976. Weidenfeld Nicolson. 2nd ed. P1. $10.00

CRISP, N.J. *Gotland Deal.* 1976. Viking. dj. EX. P1. $7.00

CRISP, Quentin. *Wit & Wisdom of Quentin Crisp.* 1984. NY. 1st ed. sgn. wraps. $25.00

CRISPIN, Edmund. *Beware of the Trains.* 1962. NY. 1st Am ed. dj. EX. $40.00

CRISPIN, Edmund. *Fen Country.* 1979. London. 1st ed. dj. VG. $27.00

CRISPIN, Edmund. *Glimpses of the Moon.* nd. Walker. 3rd ed. dj. VG. P1. $10.00

CRISPIN, Edmund. *Long Divorce.* 1951. Gollancz. 1st ed. VG. P1. $30.00

CRISPIN, Edmund. *Love Lies Bleeding.* 1948. Lippincott. 1st ed. G. P1. $12.50

CRISPIN, Edmund. *Love Lies Bleeding.* 1981. Walker. dj. VG. P1. $10.00

CRISWELL, Grover. *N American Currency.* 1969. Ils 2nd ed. 941 p. EX. J4. $20.00

CRITE, Allan. *Three Spirituals From Earth to Heaven.* 1948. dj. EX. $60.00

CROCE, B. *Grundriss der Asthetick.* 1913. Leipzig. fair. $25.00

CROCKER, Betty. *Betty Crocker's Cake & Frosting Cookbook.* 1966. 1st ed. spiral bdg. VG. $12.50

CROCKER, Betty. *Betty Crocker's New Good & Easy Cookbook.* 1962. sm 4to. 192 p. spiral bdg. EX. $2.50

CROCKER, Betty. *Betty Crocker's Picture Cookbook.* 1950. McGraw. 1st ed. later print. VG. J2. $20.00

CROCKER, Betty. *Dinner in a Dish.* 1965. 1st ed. $12.50

CROCKETT, G.L. *Two Centuries in E TX: History of San Augustine...* 1972. Dallas. SW Pr. facsimile of 1932 ed. dj. A3. $65.00

CROFT, Terrell. *Wiring for Light & Power.* 1920. NY. Ils. $12.50

CROFTS, F.W. *Box Office Murders.* 1929. London. 1st ed. VG. $55.00

CROFUTT, G.A. *Crofutt's Gripsack Guide to CO.* 1966. Cubar. reprint of 1885 ed. VG. A3. $40.00

CROFUTT, G.A. *Crofutt's Transcontinental Tourist.* 1945. reprint of 1874 ed. 162 p. G. A3. $30.00

CROGHAN, George. *Army Life on the W Frontier, 1826-1845.* 1958. Norman. 1st ed. dj. EX. $18.00

CROGHAN, George. *Colonial Army Life on the W Frontier.* 1958. Norman. Ils. dj. EX. $35.00

CROLL, P.C. *Ancient Historic Landmarks in Lebanon Valley.* 1895. Phil. 1st ed. presentation. sgn. G. B2. $37.50

CROMPTON, J. *Ways of the Ant.* 1954. Houghton. Ils. 242 p. EX. M2. $5.00

CROMPTON, Sidney. *English Glass.* 1986. Hawthorne. 1st Am ed. 8vo. 255 p. dj. EX. $15.00

CRONE, G.R. *Explorers.* 1962. Crowell. Ils. 261 p. dj. EX. M2. $6.00

CRONE, G.R. *Roaring Veldt.* 1930. Putnam. Ils 1st ed. 286 p. EX. M2. $80.00

CRONIN, A.J. *Adventures in Two World.* 1952. People Book Club. 1st ed. dj. VG. $5.00

CRONIN, A.J. *Adventures in Two Worlds.* 1952. London. 1st ed. dj. VG. $15.00

CRONIN, A.J. *Citadel.* 1937. Boston. 8th print. presentation. dj. VG. $15.00

CRONIN, A.J. *Citadel.* 1937. London. 1st ed. dj. EX. $30.00

CRONIN, A.J. *Green Years.* 1944. Boston. 1st ed. inscr. dj. EX. $20.00

CRONIN, A.J. *Hatter's Castle.* 1st Am ed. VG. $25.00

CRONIN, A.J. *Inkeeper's Wife.* 1958. NY. 1st ed. VG. $15.00

CRONIN, A.J. *Jupiter Laughs.* 1941. London. 1st ed. dj. EX. $30.00

CRONIN, A.J. *Keys of the Kingdom.* 1942. London. 1st ed. inscr. dj. EX. $30.00

CRONIN, A.J. *Pocketful of Rye.* 1969. Boston. 1st ed. dj. EX. $20.00

CRONIN, A.J. *Song of Sixpence.* 1964. Boston. 1st ed. dj. EX. $15.00

CRONIN, A.J. *Spanish Gardener.* 1950. Boston. 1st ed. inscr. dj. EX. $20.00

CRONIN, A.J. *Stars Look Down.* 1935. Grosset Dunlap. 1st ed. G. $5.00

CRONIN, Michael. *Night of the Party.* 1958. Ives Washburn. 1st ed. dj. VG. P1. $12.50

CRONKITE, Walter. *N by NE.* 1st ed. sgn. dj. with pl. EX. $35.00

CRONKITE & ELLIS. *S by SE.* 1983. AL. 1st ed. oblong folio. dj. EX. $40.00

CRONYN, George. *Fool of Venus.* 1934. 2nd print. VG. C1. $7.50

CROOK, George. *Autobiography.* 1946. Norman. 1st ed. pls. dj. VG. $22.50

CROOK, W.B. *Yeast Connection.* 1983. TN. $16.50

CROOK, W.H. *Through Five Administrations.* 1910. NY. Ils 1st ed. 280 p. $50.00

CROOKALL, Robert. *Study & Practice of Astral Projection.* 1966. New Hyde Park. $27.50

CROOKS, William. *Phenomena of Spiritualism.* 1874. London. fair. $65.00

CROSBY, A.L. *Steamboat Up the CO.* 1965. Little Brown. Ils 1st ed. 112 p. dj. VG. A3. $25.00

CROSBY, Frank. *Life of Abraham Lincoln.* c 1865. Phil. 12mo. 476 p. G. G2. $22.00

CROSBY, Frank. *Life of Abraham Lincoln.* 1865. 476 p. possible later bdg. K1. $18.50

CROSBY, Kathryn. *My Life With Bing.* 1983. Collage. Ils 1st ed. sgn. dj. EX. $25.00

CROSBY, Percy. *Skippy.* nd. Grosset Dunlap. Ils. VG. P1. $4.75

CROSBY, W.O. *Tables for Determination of Common Minerals.* 1891. Boston. 2nd ed. 86 p. EX. $50.00

CROSBY. *Black Sun.* 1976. Random House. 1st ed. dj. EX. $25.00

CROSS, Amanda. *James Joyce Murder.* 1967. Macmillan. 1st ed. dj. VG. P1. $20.00

CROSS, Amanda. *James Joyce Murder.* 1967. Macmillan. 2nd ed. dj. VG. P1. $10.00

CROSS, Amanda. *Question of Max.* 1976. Knopf. 1st ed. dj. xl. P1. $6.00

CROSS, G. *Little Heroes of Hartford.* 1947. NY. 1st ed. sgn. dj. VG. $15.00

CROSS, John Keir. *Best Black Magic Stories.* 1960. Faber. 1st ed. dj. EX. P1. $35.00

CROSS, John Keir. *Best Horror Stories 2.* 1965. Faber. dj. EX. P1. $35.00

CROSS, John Keir. *Other Passenger.* 1946. Phil. 1st Am ed. dj. VG. $65.00

CROSS, John Keir. *Red Journey Back.* 1954. Coward McCann. VG. P1. $15.00

CROSS, Mark. *Perilous Hazard.* 1961. Ward Lock. dj. VG. P1. $15.00

CROSS, W.L. *CT Yankee: Autobiography.* 1943. Yale. Ltd ed. sgn. boxed. EX. R1. $75.00

CROSS & COLLINS. *Fishes in KS.* 1975. KS U. Ils. maps. EX. M2. $8.00

CROSSEN, Kendell Foster. *Adventures in Tomorrow.* 1950. Greenberg. dj. VG. P1. $11.50

CROSSLEY, F. *English Abbey.* 1943. Batsford. Ils 2nd ed. dj. VG. C1. $27.00

CROTHERS, S.M. *Children of Dickens.* 1926. NY. Ils Smith. G. $27.50

CROTHERS, S.M. *Children of Dickens.* 1935. Scribner. Ils Smith. VG. B4. $40.00

CROTHERS, S.M. *Children of Dickens.* 1944. NY. Scribner. Ils Smith. VG. $35.00

CROTHERS, S.M. *Gentle Reader.* 1903. Houghton Mifflin. 1st ed. $12.00

CROUCH, T.D. *Eagle Aloft: Two Centuries of the Balloon in America.* 1983. WA. Ils. 770 p. dj. EX. T5. $27.50

CROW, Carl. *America & the Philippines.* 1914. Doubleday. Ils. G. $22.50

CROW, Carl. *City of Flint Grows Up.* 1945. Harper. 1st ed. dj. VG. J2. $12.50

CROWELL, Pers. *First Horseman.* 1948. Ils 1st ed. 95 p. fair. $18.00

CROWLEY, John. *Aegypt.* 1987. Bantam. 1st ed. dj. VG. P1. $17.95

CROWLEY, John. *Aegypt.* 1987. NY. Review 1st ed. sgn. dj. VG. $65.00

CROWLEY, John. *Engine Summer.* 1979. Doubleday. 1st ed. dj. EX. P1. $25.00

CROWLEY, John. *Little Big.* nd. London. 1st ed. sgn. wraps. $25.00

CROWNFIELD, Gertrude. *Little Tailor of the Winding Way.* 1921. Macmillan. Ils Pogany. G. $30.00

CROWNINSHIELD, F.B. *Story of George Crowninshield's Yacht on Voyage...* 1913. Boston. private print. 259 p. EX. T5. $175.00

CROWQUILL, Alfred. *Strange Surprising Adventures of Venerable Gooroo Simple...* 1861. London. Trubner. 1st ed. 8vo. gilt bdg. $125.00

CROXTON, Smith. *Hounds & Dogs.* nd. Phil. Londsdale. EX. $22.00

CROY, Homer. *He Hanged Them High.* 1952. Duell Sloan. photos. 278 p. dj. EX. M2. $25.00

CROY, Homer. *Headed for Hollywood.* 1932. Harper. 1st ed. VG. P1. $13.75

CROY, Homer. *Last of the Great Outlaws: Story of Cole Younger.* 1956. Duell Sloan. Ils 1st ed. 242 p. dj. EX. M2. $25.00

CRUIKSHANK, A.D. *Hunting With the Camera: Guide to Technique & Adventures...* 1957. Harper. 1st ed. photos. 215 p. dj. $20.00

CRUIKSHANK, A.D. *Wings in the Wilderness.* 1947. Oxford U. Ils. EX. M2. $15.00

CRUIKSHANK, George. *Comic Almanac 1840, 1841, 1842.* 1840-1842. London. Tilt. 3 parts in 1. VG. $55.00

CRUIKSHANK, George. *Comic Almanac.* 1835. 12mo. 2 vols. full calf. $450.00

CRUIKSHANK, George. *Comic Almanac. First & Second Series.* 1871. London. 2 vols. $210.00

CRUIKSHANK, George. *Eighty-Two Illustrations on Steel, Stone & Wood.* nd. London. Tegg. 1st ed. VG. J2. $75.00

CRUIKSHANK, George. *Illustrations to Mornings at Bow Street.* 1827. London. Ils. rebound leather. wraps. G. $100.00

CRUIKSHANK, George. *Omnibus.* 1869. London. Lanman Blanchard. 100 engravings. $95.00

CRUIKSHANK & CRUIKSHANK. *Flight Into Sunshine: Bird Experiences in FL.* 1948. Macmillan. 1st ed. sgn. 132 p. EX. M2. $37.00

CRUIKSHANK & CRUIKSHANK. *1,001 Questions Answered About Birds.* 1958. NY. 291 p. G. $10.00

CRUMB, R. *Snatcher Sampler.* 1977. San Francisco. wraps. EX. $30.00

CRUME, P. *TX at Bay.* 1961. McGraw Hill. 1st ed. sgn. 212 p. dj. EX. M2. $13.00

CRUMLEY, James. *Last Good Kiss.* 1978. NY. 1st ed. sgn. dj. VG. $45.00

CRUMLEY, James. *One to Count Cadence.* 1969. NY. 1st Am ed. dj. VG. $200.00

CRUMP, Irving. *Out of the Woods.* 1941. Dodd Mead. Ils Comstock. 269 p. dj. VG. $10.00

CUDAHY, B.J. *Destination: Loop.* 1982. 139 p. $13.50

CUDDON, J.A. *Acts of Darkness.* 1964. McKay. VG. P1. $3.75

CUDWORTH, W.H. *History of the First Regiment.* 1866. Boston. fair. $50.00

CULBERTSON, Ely. *Contract Bridge for Auction Players.* 1932. NY. Ils. G. $10.00

CULIN, S. *Chinese Games With Dice & Dominoes.* 1893. Nat Mus. 12 pls. 46 p. $12.00

CULLEN, Countee. *Copper Sun.* 1927. NY/London. 1st ed. sgn. dj. EX. scarce. $200.00

CULLEN, T.A. *When London Walked in Terror.* 1965. Boston. 1st ed. dj. VG. B2. $30.00

CULLEN, William. *First Lines in Practice of Physics.* 1806. NY. Nichols. 2 vols in 1. full calf. $125.00

CULLINGFORD, Guy. *Conjurer's Coffin.* 1954. Lippincott. 1st ed. dj. VG. P1. $20.00

CULLMAN, W. *Encyclopedia of Cacti.* 1986. Alphabooks. Ils. 4to. 340 p. dj. EX. M2. $45.00

CULLUM, Ridgwell. *Hound From the N.* nd. Burt. G. P1. $7.00

CULLUM, Ridgwell. *Men Who Wrought.* nd. Burt. G. P1. $4.75

CULLUM, Ridgwell. *Night Riders.* nd. Burt. VG. P1. $7.50

CULLUM, Ridgwell. *Triumph of John Kars.* 1917. Chapman Hill. G. P1. $10.00

CULPAN, Maurice. *Minister of Injustice.* 1966. Walker. 1st ed. dj. VG. P1. $10.00

CULVER, H.B. *Forty Famous Ships.* 1926. NY. Ils Grant. 1/501. sgn. slipcase. VG. $50.00

CUMING, E.D. *Idlings in Arcadia.* 1935. Dutton. Ils Shepherd. 1st ed. dj. EX. M2. $18.00

CUMMINGS, E.E. *Eimi.* 1933. NY. Ltd 1st ed. dj. VG. $155.00

CUMMINGS, E.E. *Him.* 1927. NY. 1st ed. VG. $55.00

CUMMINGS, E.E. *One Times One.* 1944. Harcourt. 1st ed. dj. EX. $50.00

CUMMINGS, E.E. *Poesis Scelte.* 1958. Milan. Trans Quasimodo. 1/1000. wraps. EX. $55.00

CUMMINGS, E.E. *Puella Mea.* 1923. Golden Eagle. Ils Ltd ed. $100.00

CUMMINGS, E.E. *Santa Claus: Morality.* 1946. NY. 1st ed. 1/250. sgn. slipcase. $295.00

CUMMINGS, E.E. *Tom.* 1935. Santa Fe. Arrow. 1st ed. 8vo. dj. EX. $75.00

CUMMINGS, E.E. *Tulips & Chimneys.* 1937. Golden Eagle. 1st ed. 1/481. sgn. EX. $200.00

CUMMINGS, E.E. *95 Poems.* 1958. Derrydale. 1st ed. 1/300. sgn. slipcase. EX. $240.00

CUMMINGS, Ray. *Shadow Girl.* 1946. Swan. VG. P1. $20.00

CUMMINGS, Ray. *Tarrano the Conqueror.* 1930. Chicago. EX. $30.00

CUMMINGS, Thomas S. *Historic Annals of National Academy of Design.* 1965. NY. DaCapo. reprint of 1865. 364 p. D2. $42.50

CUMMINGS & FIRMAGE. *E.E. Cummings: A Miscellany.* 1958. NY. 1st ed. glassine dj. EX. $55.00

CUMMINS, C.L. *My Days With the Diesel.* 1967. NY. 1st ed. 190 p. dj. VG. B2. $40.00

CUNDALL, H.M. *Birket Forster.* 1906. London. Ils. TEG. blue bdg. VG. $34.00

CUNEO, John. *Robert Rogers of the Rangers.* 1959. NY. 1st ed. dj. xl. G. $24.00

CUNLIFFE, Barry. *Celtic World.* 1979. Ils 1st ed. M. C1. $19.00

CUNNINGHAM, A.B. *One Man Must Die.* 1946. Dutton. 1st ed. xl. P1. $11.50

CUNNINGHAM, A.B. *Who Killed Pretty Becky Low?* 1951. Dutton. 1st ed. dj. VG. P1. $17.50

CUNNINGHAM, Allan. *Life of Robert Burns.* 1835. London. 2nd ed. 12mo. 380 p. VG. $45.00

CUNNINGHAM, E. *Triggernometry: Gallery of Gunfighters With Technical Notes.* 1956. Caxton. photos. 441 p. VG. M2. $35.00

CUNNINGHAM, E.V. *Assassin Who Gave Up His Gun.* 1969. Morrow. 1st ed. dj. VG. P1. $15.00

CUNNINGHAM, E.V. *Case of the Poisoned Eclairs.* nd. Book Club. dj. VG. P1. $4.00

CUNNINGHAM, E.V. *Case of the Russian Diplomat.* 1978. Holt Rinehart. dj. xl. P1. $6.00

CUNNINGHAM, E.V. *Case of the Sliding Pool.* nd. Book Club. dj. VG. P1. $4.00

CUNNINGHAM, E.V. *Penelope.* 1965. Doubleday. dj. VG. P1. $12.00

CUNNINGHAM, E.V. *Samatha.* 1967. Morrow. 1st ed. dj. EX. P1. $15.00

CUNNINGHAM, H.H. *Doctors in Gray.* Ils. statistics. 339 p. M. J4. $20.00

CUNNINGHAM, H.H. *Doctors in Gray.* LA U. 2nd ed. VG. J2. $17.50

CUNNINGHAM, I.S. *Frank N. Meyer: Plant Hunter in Asia.* 1984. IA U. Ils 1st ed. 317 p. dj. EX. M2. $29.00

CUNNINGHAM, Jere. *Abyss.* 1981. Wyndham. 1st ed. dj. VG. P1. $15.00

CUNNINGHAM, Peter. *Story of Nell Gwyn & Sayings of Charles II.* 1892. London. 1/750. VG. $40.00

CUNNINGHAM, Viscount. *Sailor's Odyssey: Autobiography of Admiral of the Fleet...* 1951. NY. Ils 1st Am ed. 715 p. dj. VG. T5. $12.50

CUPPY, Will. *How To Become Extinct.* 1941. NY. Ils Steig. 1st ed. dj. VG. $17.50

CURL & KNIGHT. *Wonderful World of Aunt Tuddy.* 1958. NY. 1st ed. dj. VG. B2. $17.50

CURLE, Richard. *Collecting American 1st Editions.* 1930. Bobbs Merrill. 1/1250. sgn. TEG. boxed. G. $50.00

CURLEY, J.M. *I'd Do It Again.* 1957. Prentice Hall. dj. VG. B2. $15.00

CURLEY, Thomas. *Nowhere Man.* 1967. NY. 1st ed. dj. VG. $8.00

CURRAN, C.H. *Families & Genera of N American Diptera.* 1965. Tripp. Ils. 515 p. EX. M2. $30.00

CURRER-BRIGGS, Noel. *Shroud & the Grail.* 1987. 1st Am ed. dj. EX. C1. $16.00

CURREY, J.S. *Story of Old Ft. Dearborn.* 1912. McClurg. Ils. G. $35.00

CURREY, Richard. *Fatal Light.* 1988. Dutton. 1st ed. dj. M. $10.00

CURRO, Evelyn. *American Print Book: Paddlewheel Steamboats.* 1955. NY. 1st ed. VG. J2. $20.00

CURRY, Jane. *Over the Sea's Edge.* 1971. 1st Am ed. dj. M. C1. $10.00

CURRY, Manfred. *Beauty of Flight.* nd. (1932) NY. 1st ed. 100 p. dj. G. T5. $40.00

CURRY, Manfred. *Travers les Nuages.* c 1930. Paris. Arts et Metiers Graphiques. 4to. $28.00

CURRY, W.L. *History of Jerome Township, Union Co., OH.* 1913. Columbus. 1st ed. inscr. with photo. VG. T5. $250.00

CURTICE, C. *Animal Parasites of Sheep.* 1890. USDA. 36 pls. 333 p. G. M2. $12.00

CURTIN, J. *Seneca Indian Myths.* 1923. NY. 1st ed. 416 p. VG. B2. $25.00

CURTIN, Jeremiah. *Mongols in Russia.* 1908. Little Brown. 1st ed. VG. J2. $25.00

CURTIS, C. *Velazquez & Murillo.* 1883. NY. 12 pls. folio. 424 p. green cloth. VG. J2. $100.00

CURTIS, C.C. *Guide to the Trees.* 1925. Garden City. Ils. 208 p. EX. M2. $16.00

CURTIS, Charles. *Orchids.* 1950. London. 1st print. dj. VG. $50.00

CURTIS, G.T. *American Conveyancer.* 1846. Boston. 12mo. 269 p. G2. $14.00

CURTIS, G.W. *Nile Notes of a Howadji.* 1856. Dix. Edwards. $17.50

CURTIS, G.W. *Orations & Addresses.* 1894. Harper. Ltd ed. 8vo. TEG. EX. G2. $135.00

CURTIS, Jack. *Banjo.* 1971. Macmillan. 1st ed. dj. xl. P1. $4.75

CURTIS, Matton. *Book of Snuff & Snuff Boxes.* 1935. Bramhall House. dj. $15.00

CURTIS, N. *From Bull Run to Chancellorville.* 1906. Putnam. 3rd ed. VG. $75.00

CURTIS, P.A. *Sportsmen All.* 1938. NY. Derrydale. Ltd ed. 1/950. EX. $100.00

CURTIS, Paul A. *Guns & Gunning.* 1941. NY. VG. G1. $15.00

CURTIS, Paul. *Guns & Gunning.* 1934. Pen Pub. G. $22.00

CURTIS, R.E. *Vision Takes Form: Record of Building Sydney Opera House.* 1967. Sydney. Ils. 4to. dj. EX. $50.00

CURTIS, Robert. *Man Who Changed His Name.* nd. Hutchinson. G. P1. $18.25

CURTIS, William. *Practical Observations on British Grasses.* 1805. London. 6 pls. EX. $125.00

CURTIS. *Jewelry & Gold Work.* 1925. Rome. pls. xl. VG. $30.00

CURTISS, H.A. *Realms of the Living Dead.* 1933. Curtiss Philosophic Book Co. G. $15.00

CURTISS, Ursula. *Deadly Climate.* nd. Book Club. dj. VG. P1. $3.00

CURTISS, Ursula. *Face of the Tiger.* nd. Book Club. dj. G. P1. $3.00

CURTISS, Ursula. *Letter of Intent.* 1971. Dodd Mead. dj. xl. P1. $5.00

CURTISS, Ursula. *Widow's Web.* nd. Book Club. dj. VG. P1. $4.00

CURTIUS, E. *History of Greece.* 1871-1874. 5 vols. VG. $125.00

CURWOOD, J.O. *Baree, Son of Kazan.* nd. Grosset. dj. VG. P1. $10.00

CURWOOD, J.O. *Country Beyond.* 1922. Cosmopolitan. Ils Louderback. VG. $25.00

CURWOOD, J.O. *Gentleman of Courage.* 1924. Cosmopolitan. Ils Stewart. red cloth. G. $20.00

CURWOOD, J.O. *Steele of the Royal Mounted.* nd. Burt. VG. P1. $10.00

CURWOOD, J.O. *Valley of Silent Men.* nd. Grosset. dj. VG. P1. $20.00

CUSHING, Frank. *My Adventures in Zuni, American W.* 1970. Palo Alto. 1/1950. 125 p. dj. A3. $50.00

CUSHING, Harvey. *Life of Sir William Osler.* 1925. Oxford. 3rd imp. 2 vols. $50.00

CUSHION, J.P. *Animals in Pottery & Porcelain.* 1974. Crown. Ils 1st Am ed. dj. EX. M2. $23.00

CUSHION & HONEY. *Handbook of Pottery & Porcelain Marks.* 1956. London. Faber. Ils. 8vo. dj. EX. $30.00

CUSHMAN, Dan. *Good-Bye, Old Dry.* 1959. Hodder Stoughton. 1st ed. dj. P1. $15.00

CUSHMAN, Dan. *Great N Trail.* 1966. McGraw Hill. 1st ed. 383 p. dj. EX. $20.00

CUSHMAN, Dan. *Silver Mountain.* 1957. 1st ed. dj. VG. B2. $25.00

CUSHMAN, J.A. *Monograph of Formainiferal Family Valvulinidae.* 1937. Cushman Lab. 24 pls. 210 p. EX. M2. $25.00

CUSHMAN, Rebecca. *Swing Your Mountain Girl.* 1934. Boston. Ils. 151 p. dj. VG. $15.00

CUSTER, E.B. *Boots & Saddles; or, Life in Dakota With General Custer.* 1885. NY. 1st ed. 312 p. K1. $23.50

CUSTER, E.B. *Following the Guidon.* 1890. NY. Ils 1st ed. 341 p. K1. $14.50

CUSTER, E.B. *Following the Guidon.* 1890. Harper. Ils 1st ed. 341 p. T5. $42.50

CUSTER, E.B. *Tenting on the Plains; or, General Custer in KS & TX.* 1887. NY. Webster. 702 p. K1. $65.00

CUSTER, G.A. *My Life on the Plains.* 1952. Chicago. Lakeside Classic. 626 p. T5. $25.00

CUSTER, G.A. *My Life on the Plains.* 1952. Donnelley. Lakeside Classic. A3. $40.00

CUSTER, G.A. *My Life on the Plains.* 1952. Donnelley. reprint. 626 p. dj. M2. $35.00

CUSTER, Milo. *Custer Genealogies.* nd. Bryan TX. reprint. 160 p. VG. scarce. A3. $45.00

CUSTER & OSBORN. *Wading Birds As Biological Indicators.* 1977. USFWS. 28 p. M2. $3.00

CUTCHINS & STEWART. *History of 29th Division, Blue & Gray, 1917-1919.* 1921. Phil. Ils. 493 p. VG. T5. $67.50

CUTHBERT. *Lincoln & Baltimore Plot of 1861 From Pinkerton Records...* 1949. San Merino. 1st ed. dj. EX. $18.00

CUTLER, John Henry. *Tom Stetson & the Blue Devil.* 1951. Whitman. VG. P1. $12.50

CUTLER, John Henry. *Tom Stetson & the Giant Jungle Ants.* nd. Whitman. G. P1. $5.00

CUTLER, John Henry. *Tom Stetson & the Giant Jungle Ants.* 1948. Whitman. dj. VG. P1. $12.50

CUTLER & CUTLER. *Life, Journals & Correspondence.* 1888 & 1890. Cincinnati. 1st ed. 2 vols. VG. $95.00

CUTLER & ZOLLINGER. *Atlas of Surgical Operations.* 1949. Macmillan. dj. VG. $55.00

CUTRIGHT, P.R. *Great Naturalists Explore S America.* 1940. Macmillan. Ils 1st ed. 340 p. EX. M2. $25.00

CUTRIGHT & BRODHEAD. *Elliott Coues: Naturalist & Frontier Historian.* 1981. IL U. Ils. 509 p. dj. M. M2. $32.00

CUTTEN & CUTTEN. *Silversmiths of Utica.* 1936. Hamilton. Ltd ed. 1/250. EX. C4. $75.00

CUTTER, Calvin. *Physiological Family Physician.* 1845. W Brookfield. Merriam Cooke. 1st ed. 218 p. G. $30.00

CUTTER, W.R. *New England Families. Genealogical & Memorial.* 1913. NY. 1st ed. 4to. 4 vols. VG. T1. $100.00

CUTTING, Elisabeth. *Jefferson Davis.* 1930. Dodd Mead. 1st ed. VG. $30.00

CYRIAX, Tony. *Among Italian Peasants.* nd. NY. Ils. VG. $12.00

D'ALESSANDRO, A. *Lo Scenarioln Televisivo*. 1958. Milano. 1st ed. 234 p. wraps. VG. $17.50

D'AMOUR, F.E. *Black Widow Spider*. 1939. Smithsonian. 5 pls. M2. $5.00

D'ANTONIO, Nino. *Germano*. 1976. Rome. Ars Mior ed. 167 p. dj. D2. $45.00

D'ARCY, Thompson. *On Growth & Form*. 1917. 1st ed. 1/500. $30.00

D'AULAIRE, Ingri. *Abraham Lincoln*. 1940. NY. sgn. dj. VG. $22.00

D'AULAIRE, Ingri. *George WA*. 1940. NY. dj. VG. $20.00

D'AULAIRE & D'AULAIRE. *Leif the Lucky*. 1941. Doubleday. 1st ed. dj. EX. $40.00

D'AULAIRE & D'AULAIRE. *Lord's Prayer*. 1934. Doubleday. Ils 1st print. VG. B4. $35.00

D'HUMY, F. *Women Who Influence the World*. 1955. NY. dj. G. $12.00

D'OOGE, B.L. *Cicero Select Orations*. 1901. 371 p. TB. VG. $4.00

D'ORS, E. *Pablo Picasso*. 1930. NY. 48 pls. sm 4to. stiff wraps. VG. J2. $125.00

DABNEY, V. *Last Review: Confederate Reunion*. 1932. Chapel Hill. Ils. dj. EX. $40.00

DABRINGHAUS, Erhard. *Klaus Barbie*. 1984. WA. 1st ed. dj. VG. $7.50

DACIER, A. *Life of Pythagoras With Symbols & Golden Verses*. 1707. 1st Eng ed. rare. $300.00

DACUS, J.A. *Life & Adventures of Frank & Jesse James, Noted W Outlaws*. 1880. St. Louis. 1st ed. gilt bdg. VG. $65.00

DAFFAN, Katie. *TX Heroes*. 1924. Ennis, TX. Ils 1st ed. VG. $20.00

DAGMAR, Peter. *Alien Skies*. 1967. Arcadia. dj. VG. P1. $7.00

DAHL, Borghild. *Karen*. 1947. NY. 1st print. sgn. dj. VG. $7.00

DAHL, Folke. *Bibliography of English Corantos & Periodical Newsbooks...* 1952. London. VG. $18.00

DAHL, Roald. *Charlie & the Great Glass Elevator*. nd. Knopf. 7th ed. dj. VG. P1. $10.00

DAHL, Roald. *Charlie & the Great Glass Elevator*. 1972. Knopf. 1st ed. dj. VG. P1. $30.00

DAHL, Roald. *James & the Giant Peach*. 1961. Knopf. Ils Burkert. dj. VG. B4. $40.00

DAHL, Roald. *Switch Bitch*. 1974. NY. 1st ed. dj. VG. $15.00

DAHL, Roald. *Two Fables*. 1987. Farrar Straus. 1st ed. dj. EX. P1. $12.95

DAHL-WOLFE, L. *Photographer's Scrap book*. 1984. St. Martin. Ils 1st ed. 145 p. dj. $35.00

DAHLBERG, Edward. *Bottom Dogs*. 1930. London. 1st ed. $50.00

DAHLBERG, Edward. *Bottom Dogs*. 1930. Simon Schuster. Intro Lawrence. 1st Am ed. VG. $30.00

DAHLBERG & GUETTINGER. *White-Tailed Deer in WI*. 1956. WI Conservation Dept. Ils. EX. M2. $25.00

DAIL, Hubert. *Singing Fool*. 1929. Readers Lib. P1. $13.75

DAILEY, A.H. *Mollie Fancher: Brooklyn Enigma*. 1894. NY. $27.50

DAINGERFIELD, N.G. *Our Mammy & Other Stories*. 1906. Lexington. 1st ed. presentation. sgn. 8vo. T1. $85.00

DAIX, P. *Picasso: Blue & Red Periods: Catalog Raisonne 1900-1906*. 1967. Greenwich. 4to. dj. EX. J2. $250.00

DAKE, FLEENER & WILSON. *Quartz Family Minerals*. 1938. Whittlesey. Ils. sgn. 304 p. EX. M2. $25.00

DAKIN, Albert. *Descendants of Thomas Dakin of Concord, MA*. 1948. Rutland. 1st ed. 716 p. VG. T1. $35.00

DAKIN, D.M. *Sherlock Holmes Commentary*. 1972. NY. 320 p. dj. M. $22.50

DAKIN & HAYS. *Synopsis of Orthoptera (Sensulato) of AL*. 1970. Auburn U. 118 p. M2. $5.00

DAL, B. *Butterflies of N Europe*. 1982. London. Croom Helm. Ils. 128 p. dj. EX. M2. $12.00

DALE, E.E. *Cow Custom*. 1961. KS City. 1/117. sgn. wraps. EX. $35.00

DALE, E.E. *Indians of the SW*. 1951. Norman. Ils 2nd print. dj. EX. $35.00

DALE, E.E. *Range Cattle Industry*. 1930. Norman. 1st ed. 216 p. EX. rare. $150.00

DALE, Estil. *Last Survivor*. 1952. NY. 1st ed. dj. EX. T1. $35.00

DALE, William. *Tschudi: Harpsichord Maker*. 1913. NY. 82 p. VG. $35.00

DALES, R.P. *Pelagic Polychaetes of the Pacific Ocean*. 1957. CA U. Ils. EX. M2. $12.00

DALEY, Brian. *Han Solo at Stars' End*. nd. Book Club. dj. EX. P1. $4.00

DALI, Salvador. *Dali by Dali*. 1970. NY. 1st ed. $20.00

DALI, Salvador. *Dali: Study of His Life & Work*. 1958. NY Graphic Soc. 1st Am ed. folio. $125.00

DALI, Salvador. *Dali: Wines of Gala*. 1977. Abrams. folio. gilt white cloth. dj. M. J2. $75.00

DALI, Salvador. *Don Quixote*. nd. Modern Lib. VG. $12.00

DALI, Salvadore. *Les Diners de Gala*. 1973. NY. 1st ed. dj. EX. $75.00

DALI, Salvadore. *Maze: Story of Maurice Sandoz*. 1945. NY. 1st ed. dj. G. $60.00

DALI, Salvadore. *50 Secrets of Magic Craftsmanship*. 1948. NY. 1st ed. dj. $125.00

DALI & ROMERO. *Dali*. 1975. Barcelona. 1st ed. dj. M. scarce. $125.00

DALLAS, Harriet. *Teaching of Platonius*. 1941. Boston. $18.50

DALLIN, David. *Forced Labor in Soviet Russia*. 1947. Yale. 1st ed. dj. VG. J2. $15.00

DALLIN, David. *Soviet Foreign Policy After Stalin*. 1961. Lippincott. 1st ed. dj. J2. $15.00

DALLIN, David. *Soviet Russia's Foreign Policy 1939-1942*. 1942. Yale. 1st ed. dj. VG. J2. $15.00

DALMAIS, A.M. *Adventures of Henry Rabbit*. 1967. Golden Pr. VG. P1. $2.75

DALRYMPLE, B.W. *Plan for Promoting Fur Trade*. 1975. reprint of 1789 ed. 1/75. VG. $40.00

DALRYMPLE, Byron. *Hunting Across N America*. 1970. Outdoor Life. VG. P1. $9.25

DALRYMPLE, Byron. *N American Game Birds*. 1978. Crown. Ils. 480 p. dj. EX. M2. $15.00

DALRYMPLE, Jean. *From the Last Row*. 1975. NJ. White. inscr/sgn. $16.00

DALTON, E. *When the Daltons Rode*. 1937. Sun Dial. photos. 313 p. VG. M2. $32.00

DALTON, Stephen. *Borne on the Wind*. 1975. Readers Digest. photos. 4to. 159 p. dj. $32.50

DALY, Augustin. *Woffington: Tribute to Actress & Woman.* 1891. Troy, NY. Ils. almost disbound. $25.00

DALY, Carroll John. *Man in the Shadows.* nd. Grosset. G. P1. $20.00

DALY, Carroll John. *Mr. Strang.* 1936. Stokes. 1st ed. G. P1. $50.00

DALY, Elizabeth. *Nothing Can Rescue Me.* 1943. Doubleday Book Club. VG. P1. $10.00

DALY, Elizabeth. *Wrong Way Down.* 1946. NY. 1st ed. dj. VG. $20.00

DALY, H.C. *42nd Rainbow Infantry Division.* 1946. Baton Rouge. Ils 1st ed. 4to. 105 p. G. T5. $65.00

DALY, James. *Guilty Sun.* 1926. Pittsburg. 1/150. inscr. VG. $20.00

DALY, Maria. *Diary of Union Lady.* 1962. Funk Wagnall. 1st ed. VG. $18.00

DAMERON, J.L. *Edgar A. Poe: Check List of Criticism.* 1966. Biblio Soc. 1st ed. wraps. VG. D1. $20.00

DANA, J.D. *Corals & Coral Islands.* 1875. London. 2nd ed. VG. scarce. $75.00

DANA, J.D. *Geological Story.* c 1875. np. Ils. 12mo. 263 p. G. G2. $7.00

DANA, J.D. *New TB of Geology.* 1883. Ils. HrdCvr. sm 8vo. 412 p. EX. $2.50

DANA, Julian. *Sutter of CA.* 1936. NY. Macmillan. xl. G. R1. $12.00

DANA, Mrs. W.S. *How To Know the Wild Flowers.* 1900. Scribner. Ils Satterlee/Shaw. VG. $12.00

DANA, R.H. *Journal.* 1968. Cambridge. pls. 3 vols. VG. $35.00

DANA, R.H. *To Cuba & Back.* 1859. Boston. 1st ed. xl. VG. $65.00

DANA, R.H. *Two Years Before the Mast.* 1941. Heritage. slipcase. VG. $10.00

DANA, R.H. *Two Years Before the Mast.* 1964. Ward Ritchie. Ils Weinstein. 1st ed. 2 vols. J2. $40.00

DANBURY PRESS. *Grand Diploma Cooking Course.* 1972. 20 vols. EX. $37.50

DANE, C. *Saviours.* 1942. London/Toronto. 1st ed. inscr. dj. VG. $37.50

DANE & SIMPSON. *Enter Sir John.* 1971. Tom Stacey. dj. VG. P1. $7.25

DANEON, Emile. *Tides of Time.* 1952. Ballantine. dj. VG. P1. $30.00

DANI, A.H. *Indian Palaeography.* 1963. Oxford Clarendon Pr. dj. M. $17.00

DANIEL, Dan. *Babe Ruth.* 1930. Racine. Whitman. Ils. 108 p. VG. J3. $35.00

DANIEL, Dan. *Real Babe Ruth.* 1948. NY. VG. $20.00

DANIEL, Dorothy. *Circle 'Round the Square.* 1959. NY. Fun. Ils. sgn. yellow cloth. dj. VG. $16.00

DANIEL, Dorothy. *Cut & Engraved Glass, 1771-1905.* 1950. NY. Barrows. 1st ed. 446 p. dj. VG. $20.00

DANIEL, H. *Judge Medina.* 1952. NY. Funk. 373 p. dj. G. $10.00

DANIEL, Howard. *Callot's Etchings: 338 Prints.* 1974. NY. Dover. Ils. dj. D2. $40.00

DANIEL, J.W. *Bottom Rail.* 1915. Boston. Roxburgh. presentation. 239 p. $42.50

DANIEL, J.W. *Cateechee of Keeowee: Descriptive Poem.* 1868. Nashville. Ils 1st ed. presentation. xl. $15.00

DANIEL & GUNTER. *Confederate Cannon Foundaries.* 1977. Pioneer. Ils. 4to. 112 p. dj. EX. M2. $20.00

DANIEL & MINOT. *Inexhaustible Sea.* 1954. Dodd Mead. G. M2. $5.00

DANIEL & SULLIVAN. *Sierra Club Naturalist's Guide to N Woods of MI, WI, & MN.* 1981. 1st ed. map. 407 p. dj. EX. M2. $19.00

DANIEL-ROPS, Henri. *This Is the Mass.* 1958. NY. Ils Yousuf Karsh. 1st ed. dj. VG. $25.00

DANIELS, A.C. *A.C. Daniels, Cat Doctor: Home Treatment for Cats & Kittens.* 1911. Boston. 12mo. wraps. VG. scarce. T1. $35.00

DANIELS, Jonathan. *Frontier on the Potomac.* 1946. Macmillan. sgn. $16.00

DANIELS, Jonathan. *Stonewall Jackson.* 1959. Ils Moyers. 1st ed. dj. EX. J4. $7.50

DANIELS, Les. *Citizen Vampire.* 1981. Scribner. 1st ed. dj. VG. P1. $20.00

DANIELS, Mary. *Morris: Intimate Biography.* 1974. Morrow. sgn. $6.00

DANIELS, W.H. *Temperance Reform & Its Great Reformers.* 1878. NY. Ils. 612 p. gilt bdg. $50.00

DANIELSON, B. *Raroia: Happy Island of S Seas.* 1953. Rand McNally. Ils 1st ed. dj. EX. $12.00

DANIELSON, Richard. *Martha Doyle.* Derrydale. as issued. B2. $70.00

DANISH, M.A. *William Green.* 1952. NY. Internat Allied. 186 p. dj. G. $12.00

DANKERS & SLUYTER. *Journal of Voyage to NY & Tour of Several American Colonies.* 1867. Brooklyn. Trans Murphy. fld pls. G. $75.00

DANN & DOZOIS. *Future Power.* 1976. Random House. dj. VG. P1. $10.00

DANNETT, Sylvia. *Noble Women of N.* 1959. NY. Yoseloff. 1st ed. dj. M. $28.00

DANNETT, Sylvia. *Noble Women of N.* 1959. Yoseloff. dj. VG. $18.00

DANNETT, Sylvia. *She Rode With Generals But Regiment Thought She Was a Man.* 1960. NY. Nelson. 1st ed. dj. VG. $18.00

DANNETT, Sylvia. *Treasury of Civil War Humor.* 1963. Yoseloff. Ils. dj. EX. $30.00

DANTE. *Divine Comedy.* 1969. Grossman. Ils Baskin. 3 vols. VG. $150.00

DANTE. *Divine Comedy.* 1969. Grossman. 1st print. 3 vols. slipcase. $165.00

DARBY, Catherine. *Dream of Fair Serpents.* 1979. Popular Lib. 1st ed. pb. scarce. C1. $7.00

DARBY, William. *Tour From City of NY to Detroit in 1818.* 1962. NY. reprint. fld map. dj. VG. $12.50

DARGAN, J.J. *School History of SC.* 1906. Columbia. State Co. 286 p. xl. $27.50

DARK, Sidney. *London. With Illustrations by Joseph Pennell.* 1924. London. Macmillan. 1st ed. 176 p. TEG. EX. $25.00

DARLEY, F.O.C. *Selection of War Lyrics.* 1864. Ils 1st ed. 8vo. K1. $18.50

DARLING, Bert. *City in the Forest: Story of Lansing.* 1950. NY. 1st ed. dj. VG. J2. $12.50

DARLING, F.F. *Naturalist on Rona: Essays of Biologist in Isolation.* 1939. Oxford U. Ils. fld map. 137 p. dj. EX. M2. $17.00

DARLING, F.F. *Story of Scotland.* 1942. Ils 2nd ed. EX. C1. $9.50

DARLING, W.Y. *Private Papers of a Bankrupt Bookseller.* 1932. NY. 1st Am ed. $20.00

DARLINGTON, D. *In Condor Country: Portrait of Landscape.* 1987. Houghton. 1st ed. map. 242 p. dj. EX. M2. $15.00

DARLINGTON, M.C. *History of Colonel Henry Bouquet & W Frontiers of PA.* 1920. Pittsburgh. private print. 1/600. 1st ed. VG. $125.00

DARRACOTT. *England's Constable: Life & Letters.* 1985. London. Folio Soc. 1st ed. slipcase. M. C1. $15.00

DARRAH, J. *Real Camelot: Paganism & the Arthurian Romances.* 1981. 1st ed. dj. EX. C1. $12.00

DARRAH, W.C. *History of Stereographs in America & Their Collection.* 1964. Gettysburg. 255 p. $27.50

DARRELL, Margery. *Once Upon a Time: Fairy Tale World of Arthur Rackham.* 1972. NY. Ils 1st ed. 296 p. dj. VG. T5. $22.50

DARROW, Clarence. *Debate on Capital Punishment Versus A.J. Talley.* 1924. NY. Intro Marshall. 1st ed. wraps. B2. $45.00

DARROW, Clarence. *Skeleton in the Closet.* 1924. Boston. 1st ed. G. B2. $60.00

DARROW, Clarence. *Story of My Life.* 1932. NY. 1st ed. sgn laid in. VG. B2. $90.00

DARROW, G.M. *Strawberry: History, Breeding, Physiology.* 1966. Holt Rinehart. Ils 1st ed. 447 p. dj. EX. M2. $30.00

DARTON, Frederick. *Stories of Romance From the Age of Chivalry.* 1984. Ils Walker. gilt black cloth. M. C1. $7.50

DARTON, N.H. *Geology & Water Resources of N Portion of Black Hills.* 1909. WA. Ils. 106 p. xl. scarce. A3. $90.00

DARTON, N.H. *Guidebook of W US, Part C., Santa Fe Route.* c 1930s. WA. Ils. maps. 200 p. A3. $35.00

DARTON, N.H. *Guidebook to W US, Part F., S Pacific Lines.* 1933. WA. Ils. maps. 304 p. original wraps. G. A3. $40.00

DARWIN, Charles. *Charles Darwin: His Life in an Autobiographical Chapter...* 1893. NY. 1st Am ed. $40.00

DARWIN, Charles. *Darwin's Forgotten World.* 1978. Reed. Ils 1st ed. 4to. 176 p. dj. EX. M2. $22.00

DARWIN, Charles. *Descent of Man & Selection in Relation to Sex.* 1873-1874. Paris. 8vo. 2 vols. EX. T1. $150.00

DARWIN, Charles. *Descent of Man & Selection in Relation to Sex.* 1871. Appleton. 1st Am ed. 2 vols. G. $125.00

DARWIN, Charles. *Descent of Man & Selection in Relation to Sex.* 1872. Appleton. Ils. 2 vols. VG. $65.00

DARWIN, Charles. *Descent of Man & Selection in Relation to Sex.* 1875. NY. Ils. 8vo. red cloth. VG. T1. $35.00

DARWIN, Charles. *Descent of Man & Selection in Relation to Sex.* 1906. NY. Revised 2nd ed. VG. $45.00

DARWIN, Charles. *Descent of Man & Selection in Relation to Sex.* 1979. Easton. Ils. 8vo. AEG. black leather. EX. $32.00

DARWIN, Charles. *Descent of Man.* 1871. London. 1st ed. 1st issue. 2 vols. EX. $600.00

DARWIN, Charles. *Expression of Emotions in Man & Animals.* 1873. London. Murray. 8vo. green cloth. EX. $125.00

DARWIN, Charles. *Expression of Emotions in Man & Animals.* 1873. NY. 8vo. red cloth. VG. T1. $35.00

DARWIN, Charles. *Insectivorous Plants.* 1876. Stuttgart. 1st German ed. 8vo. VG. T1. $100.00

DARWIN, Charles. *Insectivorous Plants.* 1878. NY. 8vo. red cloth. VG. T1. $35.00

DARWIN, Charles. *Origin of Species & Descent of Man.* nd. Modern Lib. 1000 p. EX. M2. $10.00

DARWIN, Charles. *Origin of Species by Means of Natural Selection.* 1897. Appleton. 2 vols. EX. M2. $55.00

DARWIN, Charles. *Origin of Species by Means of Natural Selection.* 1979. Avenel. reprint of 1st ed. EX. M2. $18.00

DARWIN, Charles. *Structure & Distribution of Coral Reefs.* 1984. AZ U. maps. 214 p. EX. M2. $9.00

DARWIN, Charles. *Variation of Animals & Plants Under Domestication.* 1897. Appleton. Ils. 2 vols. EX. M2. $55.00

DARWIN, Erasmus. *Zoonomia; or, Laws of Organic Life.* 1796. London. 1st ed. 4to. 2 vols. T1. $350.00

DARWIN, Erasmus. *Zoonomia; or, Laws of Organic Life.* 1803. Boston. 2nd Am ed. 8vo. 524 p. $125.00

DARWIN, Francis. *More Letters of Charles Darwin.* 1903. NY. 2 vols. TEG. tan linen. $60.00

DATIG. *Luger Pistol.* 1962. Los Angeles. Revised Enlarged ed. dj. EX. $35.00

DAU, F.W. *FL: Old & New.* 1934. Putnam. Ils. maps. 377 p. EX. M2. $15.00

DAUMIER, Honore. *Married Life.* c 1920. Pantheon. 24 pls. folio folder. EX. $100.00

DAVARENNE, M. *Butterflies: Color Field Guide.* 1983. David Charles. Ils. 180 p. EX. M2. $14.00

DAVENPORT, Basil. *SF Novel.* 1971. Advent. 2nd ed. dj. VG. P1. $15.00

DAVENPORT, Basil. *13 Ways To Dispose of a Body.* 1966. Dodd Mead. dj. VG. P1. $12.50

DAVENPORT, Basil. *13 Ways To Kill a Man.* 1966. Faber. 1st ed. dj. VG. P1. $17.50

DAVENPORT, C.B. *Heredity in Relation to Eugenics.* 1911. NY. Holt. 1st ed. VG. $65.00

DAVENPORT, Cyril. *English Regalia.* 1897. London. 12 pls. crimson morocco. EX. $125.00

DAVENPORT, G. *Jonathan Williams, Poet.* 1969. Cleveland. 1st ed. inscr. wraps. EX. $50.00

DAVENPORT & MURPHY. *Lives of Winston S. Churchill.* 1945. Scribner. 1st ed. gray cloth. dj. VG. D1. $40.00

DAVENTRY, Leonard. *Man of Double Deed.* nd. Book Club. dj. VG. P1. $3.75

DAVENTRY, Leonard. *Man of Double Deed.* 1965. Doubleday. dj. VG. P1. $9.25

DAVEY, K.G. *Reproduction in Insects.* 1965. Edinburgh. Oliver Boyd. 1st ed. 96 p. dj. M2. $20.00

DAVEY, R. *History of Mourning.* c 1889. London. Ils. 4to. G. $55.00

DAVEY, Ray. *Don't Fence Me In.* 1954. Belfast. Ils Revised ed. 126 p. G. T5. $19.50

DAVID, Peter. *Knight Life.* Ace. pb. VG. C1. $3.50

DAVIDSON, Avram. *Best of Avram Davidson.* 1979. Doubleday. 1st ed. dj. VG. P1. $15.00

DAVIDSON, Avram. *Peregrine: Primus.* 1971. Walker. 1st ed. dj. xl. P1. $10.00

DAVIDSON, Avram. *Phoenix & the Mirror.* 1969. Doubleday. 1st ed. dj. xl. P1. $5.00

DAVIDSON, Avram. *Redward Edward Papers.* 1978. Doubleday. 1st ed. dj. EX. P1. $20.00

DAVIDSON, Avram. *Rork!* 1968. Rapp Whiting. dj. xl. P1. $7.50

DAVIDSON, Avram. *Strange Seas & Shores.* 1971. Doubleday. 1st ed. dj. EX. P1. $12.50

DAVIDSON, Basil. *Ghana: African Portrait.* 1976. Millerton. Aperture. 1st ed. dj. EX. $35.00

DAVIDSON, Donald. *Outland Piper.* 1924. Boston. 1st ed. VG. $50.00

DAVIDSON, Donald. *S Writers in the Modern World.* 1958. Athens, GA. reprint. EX. T6. $10.00

DAVIDSON, E.H. *Edgar A. Poe: A Critical Study.* 1969. Belknap. 4th print. dj. EX. D1. $22.00

DAVIDSON, Eugene. *Trial of the Germans.* 1966. NY. Ils. 636 p. G. T5. $17.50

DAVIDSON, J. *Amelia Earhart Returns From Saipan.* 1969. Canton. 1st ed. sgn. dj. VG. B2. $27.50

DAVIDSON, John. *Ballad of Lancelot.* 1904. London/NY. 1st ed. VG. C1. $7.50

DAVIDSON, Lionel. *Long Way to Shiloh.* 1966. Gollancz. 2nd ed. dj. VG. P1. $15.00

DAVIDSON, Lionel. *Menorah Men.* 1966. Harper Row. dj. VG. P1. $10.00

DAVIDSON, N.F.M. *Culligs From the Confederacy, 1862-1866.* 163 p. EX. very scarce. J4. $25.00

DAVIDSON. *Ral Property.* 1980. Garden City. 1st ed. dj. VG. $7.50

DAVIES, B. *Savage Luxury: Slaughter of Baby Seals.* 1970. London. Souvenir. Ils 1st ed. dj. EX. M2. $6.00

DAVIES, C.C. *Pelagic Copepoda of the NE Pacific Ocean.* 1949. WA. Ils. 117 p. EX. M2. $10.00

DAVIES, Charles. *Elements of Surveying.* 1835. Cincinnati. Revised 1st ed. full leather. T5. $45.00

DAVIES, Hunter. *Beatles: The Authorized Biography.* 1968. McGraw Hill. VG. P1. $13.75

DAVIES, L.P. *Artificial Man.* nd. Book Club. dj. VG. P1. $3.75

DAVIES, L.P. *Give Me Back Myself.* 1971. Doubleday. dj. xl. P1. $4.75

DAVIES, L.P. *Land of Leys.* 1979. Doubleday. 1st ed. dj. VG. P1. $12.50

DAVIES, L.P. *Psychogeist.* nd. Book Club. dj. VG. P1. $3.75

DAVIES, L.P. *Shadow Before.* 1970. Crime Club. 1st ed. dj. xl. P1. $4.75

DAVIES, L.P. *Shadow Before.* 1971. Barrie Jenkins. dj. xl. P1. $4.75

DAVIES, L.P. *Twilight Journey.* nd. Book Club. dj. VG. P1. $3.75

DAVIES, L.P. *Twilight Journey.* 1967. Herbert Jenkins. dj. xl. P1. $4.75

DAVIES, Randall. *Thomas Girtin's Watercolors.* 1924. London. Studio. Ils. xl. D2. $115.00

DAVIES, Robertson. *Lyre of Orpheus.* 1988. London. 1st ed. 1/50. sgn. 8vo. dj. M. $125.00

DAVIES, Robertson. *Papers of Samuel Marchbanks.* 1986. NY. 1st ed. dj. EX. $10.00

DAVIES, Thomas. *How To Make Money & How To Keep It.* 1867. 1st ed. G. $15.00

DAVIES, Valentine. *Miracle on 34th Street.* 1947. Harcourt Brace. 1st ed. P1. $7.00

DAVIES & PECK. *Mathematical Dictionary/Cyclopedia of Mathematical Science.* 1865. NY. VG. $17.00

DAVIES. *Rock Tombs of El Amarna.* 1903-1908. 6 vols. xl. $350.00

DAVILA, E.C. *Histoire des Guerres Civiles de France.* 1657. Paris. Rocolet. Corrected 3rd ed. folio. 2 vols. $300.00

DAVIS, A.J. *Genesis & Ethics of Conjugal Love.* 1874. NY. $125.00

DAVIS, A.J. *Magic Staff: Autobiography of a Clarivoyant & Spiritualist.* 1857. NY. 552 p. $60.00

DAVIS, A.J. *Present Age & Inner Life.* 1853. NY. Partridge Brittan. 1st ed. G. $35.00

DAVIS, A.M. *Confiscation of John Chandler's Estate.* 1903. Boston. 1st Am ed. dj. VG. $25.00

DAVIS, Adelle. *Let's Get Well.* 1956. NY. $18.00

DAVIS, Angela. *Autobiography.* 1974. NY. 1st ed. dj. EX. $30.00

DAVIS, Angela. *Autobiography.* 1974. NY. 1st ed. inscr/dtd. dj. VG. $45.00

DAVIS, Britton. *George WA & the American Revolution.* 1975. Random House. Ils 1st ed. 497 p. dj. EX. M2. $14.00

DAVIS, Britton. *Jeb Stuart: Last Cavalier.* 1957. Bonanza. Ils. 462 p. dj. EX. M2. $11.00

DAVIS, Britton. *Truth About Geronimo.* 1951. Donnelley. Lakeside Classic. dj. EX. M2. $30.00

DAVIS, Burke. *Gray Fox.* 1956. NY. sgn. dj. G. R1. $60.00

DAVIS, Burke. *Our Incredible Civil War.* 1966. 249 p. EX. J4. $6.00

DAVIS, Burke. *S Railway.* 1985. photos. 309 p. $20.00

DAVIS, Burke. *To Appomattox, Nine April Days, 1865.* 1959. photos. maps. 433 p. dj. EX. J4. $6.00

DAVIS, Burke. *War Bird: Life & Times of Elliott White Springs.* 1987. Chapel Hill. Ils 1st ed. 267 p. dj. M. T5. $19.95

DAVIS, Charles. *Life of Charles Henry Davis.* 1899. NY. 349 p. xl. K1. $23.50

DAVIS, D.R. *Revision of the Moths of the Subfamily Prodoxinae.* 1967. US Nat Mus. Ils. xl. M2. $17.00

DAVIS, Dorothy Salisbury. *Crime Without Murder.* 1970. Scribner. 1st ed. dj. xl. P1. $7.50

DAVIS, Duke. *Flashlights From Mountain & Plain.* 1911. NJ. Ils Russell. 266 p. $75.00

DAVIS, Edwards. *Lovers of Life.* 1934. NY. $14.00

DAVIS, F.C. *Detour to Oblivion.* 1947. Crime Club. 1st ed. dj. EX. $15.00

DAVIS, F.C. *Lilies in Her Garden Grew.* 1951. Crime Club. 1st ed. VG. P1. $20.00

DAVIS, G. *Gray Fox: Robert E. Lee & the Civil War.* 1956. Rinehart. Ils 1st ed. 466 p. dj. EX. M2. $21.00

DAVIS, Grania. *Moonbird.* 1986. Doubleday. 1st ed. dj. EX. RS. P1. $15.00

DAVIS, H.E. *Elmira: Girl Who Loved Poe.* 1966. Houghton. 1st ed. gray cloth. VG. D1. $11.00

DAVIS, H.J. *Great Dismal Swamp: Its History, Folklore & Science.* 1962. private print. Ils. 182 p. VG. M2. $10.00

DAVIS, Hubert. *Symbolic Drawings of Hubert Davis for an American Tragedy.* 1930. Ltd ed. sgn. slipcase. EX. $150.00

DAVIS, J. *Breeding Biology of the W Flycatcher.* 1963. Condor. M2. $5.00

DAVIS, J.C. *CA Salt-Water Fishing.* 1949. NY. 1st ed. dj. VG. $20.00

DAVIS, J.J. *Parasitic Fungi of WI.* 1942. private print. Ils. 157 p. EX. M2. $15.00

DAVIS, Jefferson. *Rise & Fall of Confederate Government.* 1881. 2 vols. J4. $40.00

DAVIS, John. *Travels of Four Years & a Half in USA, 1798-1802.* 1909. NY. 1st Am ed. fair. $7.50

DAVIS, K.S. *General Eisenhower.* 1949. Doubleday. 8vo. 217 p. dj. EX. $6.50

DAVIS, L.I. *Field Guide to Birds of Mexico & Central America.* 1972. TX U. Ils. 282 p. dj. EX. M2. $40.00

DAVIS, Lavinia R. *Threat of Dragons.* 1948. Crime Club. G. P1. $5.50

DAVIS, M.G. *Randolph Caldecott.* 1946. Lippincott. Ils. 46 p. dj. VG. $35.00

DAVIS, M.L. *Memoirs of Aaron Burr.* 1836. NY. Harper. 1st ed. 2 vols. G. R1. $45.00

DAVIS, M.L. *Uncle Sam's Attic: Intimate Story of AK.* 1930. Boston. Ils. photos. VG. $12.00

DAVIS, Mildred. *They Buried a Man.* nd. Book Club. dj. VG. P1. $4.00

DAVIS, Norbert. *Sally's in the Alley.* 1944. Boardman. 1st ed. dj. VG. P1. $75.00

DAVIS, R.H. *Bar Sinister.* 1903. NY. Ils 1st ed. VG. B2. $22.50

DAVIS, R.H. *Cuba in Wartime.* 1899. NY. Ils Remington. $65.00

DAVIS, R.H. *Cuban & Porto Rican Campaigns.* 1898. NY. Ils 1st ed. fld maps. 360 p. T5. $22.50

DAVIS, R.H. *In the Fog.* 1901. NY. Ils Steele. 1st ed. 8vo. G. $29.00

DAVIS, R.H. *Lion & the Unicorn.* 1904. Scribner. VG. P1. $4.75

DAVIS, R.H. *Ranson's Folly.* 1904. Scribner. G. P1. $4.75

DAVIS, R.H. *Soldiers of Fortune.* 1906. Scribner. VG. P1. $4.75

DAVIS, R.H. *W From a Car Window.* 1892. Ils Remington. 242 p. K1. $21.00

DAVIS, R.H. *White Mice.* 1914. Scribner. VG. P1. $4.75

DAVIS, R.H. *With Both Armies in S Africa.* 1900. NY. 1st issue. EX. $65.00

DAVIS, R.L. *George Cukor.* 1977. SMU Oral Hist. $150.00

DAVIS, Robert. *Canada Cavalcade.* 1937. Appleton Century. 1st ed. VG. P1. $18.25

DAVIS, Sammy Jr. *Hollywood in a Suitcase.* 1980. NY. 1st ed. dj. VG. B2. $20.00

DAVIS, W. *Dojo: Magic & Exorcism in Modern Japan.* 1980. Stanford. Ils. 332 p. dj. EX. M2. $10.00

DAVIS, W.B. *Mammals of TX.* 1978. TX Park/Wildlife. 294 p. EX. M2. $7.00

DAVIS, W.C. *Battle of Bull Run: History of First Major Campaign...* 1977. Doubleday. Ils. 298 p. dj. EX. M2. $12.00

DAVIS, W.C. *Orphan Brigade: KY Confederates Who Couldn't Go Home.* 1980. Doubleday. Ils. maps. dj. EX. M2. $13.00

DAVIS, W.H. *History of 104th PA Regiment.* 1866. Phil. 1st ed. VG. $75.00

DAVIS, W.J. *Air Conquest.* 1930. Los Angeles. Ils. 233 p. fair. T5. $25.00

DAVIS & BALDWIN. *Denver Dwellings & Descendants.* 1963. Denver. Sage. Ils. 250 p. dj. scarce. VG. A3. $35.00

DAVIS & RUSSELL. *Birds in SE AZ.* 1980. Tucson. Audubon Soc. 2nd print. 126 p. M2. $7.00

DAVIS. *Marine!* 1962. Boston. 1st ed. dj. EX. C4. $22.00

DAVISE, Robertson. *What's Bred in the Bone.* 1st Am ed. EX. C1. $7.00

DAVISON, Basil. *Tir a Mhurain. Outer Hebrides.* 1962. London. MacGibbon. 1st ed. 4to. dj. EX. $170.00

DAVISON, V.E. *Attracting Birds: From Prairies to Atlantic.* 1967. Crowell. Ils. 252 p. dj. EX. M2. $5.00

DAVISON, V.E. *Bobwhites on the Rise.* 1949. Scribner. Ils 1st ed. 150 p. VG. M2. $17.00

DAVISON, V.E. *Upland Non-Game Birds in the SE: Needs & Management.* 1959. USFS. 57 p. G. M2. $4.00

DAVISSON, Bud. *World of Sport Aviation.* 1982. NY. Hearst. Ils. 242 p. dj. M1. $16.50

DAVY, John. *Angler in the Lake District.* 1857. London. gilt green calf. EX. $125.00

DAWE, Grosvenor. *Melvil Dewey: Seer, Inspirer, Doer, 1851-1931.* 1932. Ltd Ed Club. photos. fld map. 391 p. T5. $42.50

DAWES, R.R. *Service With the 6th WI Volunteers.* 1890. Marietta. 1st ed. EX. $95.00

DAWES, R.R. *Service With the 6th WI Volunteers.* 1962. Madison. reprint of 1890 ed. dj. EX. $26.00

DAWIDOWICZ, L.S. *From That Place & Time.* 1989. NY. 1st ed. dj. EX. $11.00

DAWIDOWICZ, Lucy. *War Against the Jews.* 1975. NY. 1st ed. dj. EX. $20.00

DAWKINS, Cecil. *Live Goat.* 1971. Harper Row. 1st ed. dj. $17.50

DAWKINS, R.M. *Modern Greek Folk Tales.* 1953. Oxford. 1st ed. VG. J2. $25.00

DAWSON, Basil. *Dan Dare on Mars.* 1956. Hulton Pr. 1st ed. xl. P1. $7.50

DAWSON, Christopher. *Medieval Essays.* 1959. pb. VG. C1. $4.50

DAWSON, E. *TX Wildlife.* 1955. Banks Upshaw. Ils 1st ed. 4to. 174 p. EX. M2. $15.00

DAWSON, Elmer A. *Garry Grayson Showing His Speed.* nd. Grosset. VG. P1. $7.00

DAWSON, James. *Hell Gate.* 1971. McKay. dj. VG. P1. $7.00

DAWSON, Lucy. *Dogs As I See Them.* 1937. NY. Ils. VG. $30.00

DAWSON, Marshall. *19th-C Evolution & After.* 1924. NY. $8.00

DAWSON, Philip. *Electric Railways & Tramways: Construction & Operation.* 1897. London. Ils. quarto. 671 p. $37.50

DAWSON, W.J. *Literary Leaders of Modern Engish.* 1902. Chautauqua Pr. VG. $20.00

DAWSON, W.L. *Birds of OH.* 1903. Columbus. pls. 761 p. brown morocco. xl. T5. $150.00

DAWSON & HUDSON. *IA History & Culture: Bibliography...* 1898. IA U. 356 p. VG. T5. $17.50

DAY, Albert. *N American Waterfowl.* 1949. Stackpole. 1st ed. VG. J2. $20.00

DAY, Clarence. *Life With Mother.* 1949. Perma. G. P1. $4.00

DAY, D. *Hunting & Exploring Adventures of Theodore Roosevelt...* 1955. Dial. 1st ed. dj. G. $25.00

DAY, David. *Tolkien Bestiary.* Crescent. 1st ed. dj. M. C1. $15.00

DAY, F.H. *Slave to Beauty: Eccentric Life & Controversial Career...* 1981. Godine. dj. VG. $22.50

DAY, Gene. *Future Day.* 1979. Flying Buttress. 1st ed. P1. $15.00

DAY, Gina. *Tell No Tales.* 1967. Hart Davis. 1st ed. dj. EX. P1. $10.00

DAY, Harvey. *Study & Practice of Yoga.* 1955. University Books. P1. $3.75

DAY, Lewis F. *Ornament & Its Application.* 1904. London. VG. P3. $60.00

DAYRELL, Eleanore. *History of the Dayrells of Lillingstone Dayrell...* 1885. Jersey. 68 p. gilt bdg. G. T5. $22.50

DAYTON, F.E. *Steamboat Days.* 1925. NY. Ils. G. $30.00

DAYTON, F.E. *Steamboat Days.* 1939. NY. Tudor. VG. $30.00

DE ANGELI, Marguerite. *Book of Nursery & Mother Goose Rhymes.* 1954. Doubleday. Ils. dj. VG. B4. $50.00

DE ANGELI, Marguerite. *Copper-Toed Boots.* 1938. Doubleday. Ils. VG. B4. $18.00

DE ANGELI, Marguerite. *Door in the Wall.* 1st ed. sgn. dj. VG. E2. $25.00

DE ANGELI, Marguerite. *Henner's Lydia.* 1936. Doubleday. VG. B4. $25.00

DE ANGELI, Marguerite. *Up the Hill.* 1942. Doubleday. 1st ed. dj. VG. B4. $40.00

DE ARMENT, R.K. *Bat Masterson: Man & the Legend.* 1979. OK U. Ils 1st ed. 441 p. dj. EX. M2. $35.00

DE BACA, Carlos. *Vincente Silva: Terror of Las Vegas.* 1968. Truchas, NM. wraps. $18.00

DE BACA, F.C. *We Fed Them Cactus.* 1954. Albuquerque. 1st ed. dj. VG. B2. $20.00

DE BALZAC, Honore. *Droll Stories From Abbeys of Touraine.* 1874. London. Hotten. Ils Dore. TEG. red cloth. VG. $95.00

DE BALZAC, Honore. *Droll Tales: Second Decade.* 1929. Covici Friede. 1/1550. VG. J2. $35.00

DE BALZAC, Honore. *Love in a Mask.* 1911. NY. 1st ed. 8vo. VG. $35.00

DE BEAUMONT, E. *Sword & Womankind.* 1930. Panurge Pr. 1st Am ed. 1/1000. VG. $25.00

DE BEER, G.R. *Atlas of Evolution.* 1964. Nelson. Ils. 32 maps. folio. dj. EX. M2. $25.00

DE BERNATH. *Cleopatra: Her Life & Reign.* 1908. London. Humphreys. 8vo. EX. $150.00

DE BIBIENA. *Fairy Doll.* 1925. Chapman Hall. 1/1000. dj. VG. $15.00

DE BOER, J.H. *Electron Emission & Absorption Phenomena.* 1935. Cambridge. fair. $25.00

DE BOOY & FARIS. *Virgin Islands: Our New Possessions & British Islands.* 1918. Phil. Ils 1st ed. 5 maps. EX. $60.00

DE BORCHGRAVE & MOSS. *Spike.* 1954. Phil. 1st ed. dj. VG. $20.00

DE BOSSCHERE, Jean. *Folk Tales of Flanders.* 1918. NY. 1st Am ed. 4to. $80.00

DE BOUCHERVILLE & FOSTER. *War on the Detroit.* 1940. Chicago. Lakeside Classic. 320 p. VG. T5. $45.00

DE BOUCHERVILLE & FOSTER. *War on the Detroit.* 1940. Donnelley. Lakeside Classic. A3. $45.00

DE BOW, J.D. *Industrial Resources of S & W States.* 1852. New Orleans. 2 vols. VG. $47.00

DE BREVANS, J. *Manufacture of Liquors & Preserves.* 1972. Noyes. reprint. EX. $18.00

DE BRUNHOFF, Jean. *Story of Babar, the Little Elephant.* 1933. Smith Haas. Ils 1st Am ed. $75.00

DE BRUTELLE. *Sertum Anglicum, 1788.* 1963. Hunt Bot Lib. facsimile. 1/2000. 34 pls. EX. $50.00

DE BURE, G.F. *Bibliographie Instructive; or, Traite de la Connoissance...* 1763. Paris. full leather. J2. $60.00

DE CAMBREY, Leonne. *Lapland Legends.* 1926. Yale. 1st ed. VG. J2. $25.00

DE CAMP, L. Sprague. *Continent Makers.* 1953. Twayne. dj. VG. P1. $25.00

DE CAMP, L. Sprague. *Golden Wind.* 1969. Doubleday. 1st ed. dj. xl. P1. $20.00

DE CAMP, L. Sprague. *Great Fetish.* 1978. Doubleday. 1st ed. dj. EX. P1. $17.50

DE CAMP, L. Sprague. *Great Fetish.* 1978. Doubleday. 1st ed. dj. xl. P1. $5.00

DE CAMP, L. Sprague. *Hand of Zeil.* 1981. Owlswick. sgn. no dj issued. P1. $25.00

DE CAMP, L. Sprague. *Hostage of Zir.* 1977. Berkley Putnam. 1st ed. sgn. dj. EX. P1. $30.00

DE CAMP, L. Sprague. *Literary Swordsmen & Sorcerers: Makers of Heroic Fantasy.* 1976. Arkham House. 1st ed. dj. EX. $45.00

DE CAMP, L. Sprague. *Phantoms & Fancies.* 1972. Baltimore. Mirage. Ils Kirk. 1/1000. dj. C1. $12.00

DE CAMP, L. Sprague. *Prisoner of Zhamanak.* 1983. Phantasia. 1/500. sgn. dj. slipcase. EX. P1. $35.00

DE CAMP, L. Sprague. *Tritonian Ring.* 1977. Owlswick Pr. 1st ed. sgn. dj. EX. P1. $30.00

DE CAMP, L. Sprague. *Unbeheaded King.* 1983. Del Rey. 1st ed. sgn. dj. EX. P1. $25.00

DE CAMP & DE CAMP. *Bones of Zora.* 1983. Phantasia. 1/300. sgn. dj. slipcase. EX. P1. $35.00

DE CAMP & DE CAMP. *Citadels of Mystery: Unsolved Puzzles.* 1972. England. pb. VG. C1. $4.00

DE CAMP & DE CAMP. *Footprints on Sand.* 1981. Advent. 1st ed. dj. EX. P1. $20.00

DE CAMP & DE CAMP. *Incorporated Knight.* 1987. Phantasia. 1st ed. dj. EX. P1. $17.00

DE CAMP & KIRK. *Heroes & Hobgoblins.* 1981. Ils Kirk. 1/1200. sgns. dj. M. scarce. C1. $27.00

DE CAMP & LEY. *W Lands Beyond.* 1952. NY. 1st ed. VG. $30.00

DE CAMP & PRATT. *Wall of Serpents.* 1978. Phantasia. sgn. dj. EX. P1. $30.00

DE CAMPOS, Deoclecio Redig. *Art Treasures of Vatican: Architecture, Painting, Sculpture.* 1974. Park Lane. Ils. 410 pls. 398 p. dj. D2. $65.00

DE CARAVA, Roy. *Sweet Flypaper of Life.* 1955. Simon Schuster. 1st print. VG. $40.00

DE CARLE, Don Celestino. *Nas Noches de Santa Maria Magdalena.* 1838. Mexico City. VG. $75.00

DE CHAIR, Somerset. *Silver Crescent.* 1943. London. Golden Cockerel. 1/500. 4to. VG. $115.00

DE CHAMBRUN, Clara Longworth. *Cincinnati: Story of the Queen City.* 1939. NY. Ils 1st ed. 342 p. dj. VG. B2. $37.50

DE CHAMBRUN, M.A. *Impressions of Lincoln & the Civil War.* 1952. Random House. 1st ed. dj. VG. $20.00

DE CHASTELLUX, Marquis. *Travels in N America in Years 1780, 1781 & 1782.* c 1963. Chapel Hill. reprint. 2 vols. VG. $27.50

DE CHAVANNE, Countess. *Ouirda; or, American Gold Regilding the Coronets of Europe.* 1900. Phil. Drexel Biddle. 1st ed. VG. $7.50

DE COURMELLES, F. *Hypnotism.* 1895. London. Ils 1st ed. 321 p. $50.00

DE CREBILLON. *Divan.* 1927. NY. 1/975. EX. $20.00

DE DIESBACH, Ghislain. *Toys of Princes.* 1962. Chapman Hall. dj. EX. P1. $7.00

DE DILLMONT, Therese. *Encyclopedia of Needlework.* c 1925. France. Mulhouse. Ils. 24mo. $50.00

DE FILIPPI, Filippo. *Karakoram & W Himalaya, 1909.* 1912. London. Ils 1st ed. photos. 4to. 469 p. T5. $295.00

DE FOREST, Eleanor. *Armegeddon: Tale of the Antichrist.* 1938. MI. $27.50

DE FOREST, Izette. *Leaven of Love.* 1953. NY. $8.00

DE FOREST, J.D. *History of Indians of CT.* 1851. Hartford. 1st ed. map. $75.00

DE FOREST, J.W. *Union Officer in Reconstruction.* 1948. Yale. 1st ed. dj. EX. $26.00

DE FOREST, J.W. *Volunteer's Adventures.* 1946. Yale. 1st ed. dj. VG. $28.00

DE GAULLE, Charles. *Call to Honor, 1940-1942: War Memoirs.* 1955. London. 1st ed. 2 vols. djs. G. T5. $45.00

DE GRAZIA, Ted. *Flute Player.* 1952. Tuscon. Ltd ed. sgn. with photo. EX. P3. $300.00

DE GUOY. *Derrydale Cookbook.* Derrydale. as issued. VG. B2. $150.00

DE HAAS. *Jazz Singer.* 1927. NY. Movie ed. dj. EX. $15.00

DE HALSALLE, Henry. *Romance of Modern 1st Editions.* 1931. Phil. 1st ed. dj. VG. $25.00

DE HALSALLE, Henry. *Treasure Trove in Bookland.* 1931. London. 1st ed. dj. $25.00

DE HAURANNE, E.D. *Frenchman in Lincoln's America.* 1974. Chicago. Lakeside Classic. 2 vols. G. T5. $35.00

DE HOYOS, Ladislas. *Klaus Barbie: Untold Story.* 1985. NY. 1st ed. dj. EX. T5. $10.00

DE JOHNSTONE, Chevalier. *Memoirs of the Rebellion of 1745 & 1746.* 1820. London. Longman Hurst. 1st ed. rebound. VG. $800.00

DE JOLIMONT, F.G.T. *Les Mausolees Francais.* 1921. Paris. Ils. 4to. dj. xl. G. $250.00

DE JONG, Dola. *Whirligig of Time.* 1964. Crime Club. 1st ed. dj. xl. P1. $4.75

DE KAY, J.E. *Zoology of NY. Part 2.* 1844. Albany. 141 color pls. 4to. VG. $375.00

DE KRUIF, Paul. *Male Hormone.* 1948. Perma P12. VG. P1. $4.75

DE KUBINYI, Victor. *As We Are.* 1929. NY. $47.50

DE L'ARDECHE & LAURENT. *Histoire de l'Empereur Napoleon.* 1840. Paris. Dubochet. 46 pls. 852 p. G. $250.00

DE LA BARCA, F.C. *Life in Mexico.* 1843. Boston. Ils 1st ed. 2 vols. rebound. $75.00

DE LA BRETONNE. *Sara.* 1927. London. Rodker. 1/1000. dj. EX. $20.00

DE LA CREBILLON. *Divan.* 1927. NY. 1/975. EX. $20.00

DE LA FONTAINE, Jean. *Fables.* Merrymount. Ils Ruzicka. 2 vols. dj. VG. $80.00

DE LA FONTAINE, Jean. *Fables.* 1931. NY. 1/525. Trans Marsh. Ils Gooden. sgns. J2. $325.00

DE LA FONTAINE, Jean. *Selected Fables.* 1948. NY. Ils Alexander Calder. folio. dj. $50.00

DE LA MARE, Walter. *Alone.* nd. Curwen. wraps. EX. $20.00

DE LA MARE, Walter. *Best Stories of Walter de la Mare.* 1945. Faber. 4th ed. VG. P1. $17.50

DE LA MARE, Walter. *Down-Adown-Derry.* 1922. NY. Holt. Ils Lathrop. 2nd print. $50.00

DE LA MARE, Walter. *Eight Tales.* 1971. Arkham House. dj. EX. P1. $15.00

DE LA MARE, Walter. *Listeners.* 1916. Holt. 1st Am ed. green cloth. dj. VG. G2. $30.00

DE LA MARE, Walter. *On the Edge.* 1932. Faber. not 1st ed. VG. P1. $22.50

DE LA MARE, Walter. *Peacock Pie.* Jan., 1927. NY. Ils Robinson. 8vo. VG. $15.00

DE LA MARE, Walter. *Stuff & Nonsense.* 1927. Constable. Ils. 8vo. green cloth. dj. VG. G2. $20.00

DE LA MARE, Walter. *Veil & Other Poems.* 1921. London. Ltd 1st ed. 1/250. sgn. $125.00

DE LA MARE, Walter. *Veil.* 1921. Constable. 1st ed. 8vo. dj. VG. G2. $25.00

DE LA MARE, Walter. *Winged Chariot.* 1951. Faber. 1st ed. dj. $25.00

DE LA MARTINE, Alphonse. *Histoire des Girondins.* 1851. Bruxelles. 4to. EX. $125.00

DE LA MARTINE, Alphonse. *Ouvres Completes.* 1834. Paris. 8vo. 4 vols. leather. EX. $150.00

DE LA MOTHE FENELON, Salignac. *Adventures of Telemachus, Son of Ulysses.* 1859. Paris. 12mo. 2 vols. TEG. EX. T1. $100.00

DE LA RAME, L. *Bimbi.* 1910. TEG. red cloth. VG. $30.00

DE LA REE, Gerry. *Art of the Fantastic.* 1978. De La Ree. 1st ed. dj. EX. P1. $20.00

DE LA REE, Gerry. *More Fantasy by Fabian.* 1979. De La Ree. 1st ed. 1/1300. dj. EX. P1. $20.00

DE LA REE, Gerry. *Sixth Book of Virgil Finlay.* 1980. De La Ree. 1/1300. dj. EX. P1. $20.00

DE LA RUE, S. *Land of the Pepper Bird: Liberia.* 1930. Putnam. 1st ed. 330 p. G. M2. $13.00

DE LA TORRE, Lillian. *Villany Detected.* 1947. NY. 1st ed. 243 p. dj. VG. $17.00

DE LA TOURETTE, F. Gilles. *Robert Delaunay.* 1959. Paris. Ils. pls. photos. scarce. D2. $185.00

DE LAFAYETTE. *Princess of Cleves.* 1970. Norwalk. Heritage. quarto. slipcase. EX. $15.00

DE LAND, Margaret. *FL Days.* 1889. Boston. Ils. 200 p. $50.00

DE LANO, Alonzo. *Across the Plains & Among the Diggings.* 1936. NY. Ils 1st ed. 192 p. dj. VG. B2. $50.00

DE LAURENCE, L.W. *Book of Magical Art, Hindu Magic & Indian Occultism.* 1908. Chicago. De Laurence. 6th ed. VG. $67.50

DE LILLO, D. *Americana.* 1971. Boston. 1st ed. dj. EX. $95.00

DE LINT, Charles. *Jack the Giant Killer.* 1987. Ace. 1st ed. dj. VG. P1. $16.95

DE LINT, Charles. *Riddle of the Wren.* 1984. Ace. pb. VG. scarce. C1. $4.00

DE LINT, Charles. *Westlin Wind.* 1989. Axolotl Pr. 1st ed. 1/900. sgn. M. C1. $12.00

DE LINT, Charles. *Wolf Moon.* 1988. pb. EX. C1. $4.00

DE LISSER, H.G. *White Witch of Rosehall.* 1950. Ernest Benn. 4th ed. VG. P1. $5.50

DE LOI, Raimon. *Trails of the Troubadours.* 1926. NY. Ils 1st ed. VG. C1. $25.00

DE LONG, D.M. *Revision of the American Species of Empoasca in Mexico.* 1931. USDA. Ils. 59 p. M2. $3.00

DE LONG, Lea Rosson. *Nature's Forms/Nature's Forces: Art of Alexandre Hogue.* 1984. OK U. Ils. 211 p. index. D2. $37.50

DE LUC, W.G. *Recollections of Civil War Quartermaster.* 1963. St. Paul. 1st ed. dj. VG. $22.00

DE MARE, Eric. *Photography & Architecture.* 1961. London. dj. EX. P3. $60.00

DE MARIA, Robert. *Stone of Destiny.* 1985. pb. VG. C1. $4.00

DE MASSEY, E. *Frenchman in Gold Rush.* 1927. CA Hist Soc. Ils. 4to. 183 p. VG. $45.00

DE MEYER, Adolf. *Baron Adolf De Meyer.* 1976. Knopf. dj. EX. $45.00

DE MILFORD, L.L. *Milford's Memoir.* 1956. Donnelley. Lakeside Classic. A3. $40.00

DE MILLE, Agnes. *Book of the Dance.* 1963. NY. dj. EX. $30.00

DE MILLE, James. *Young Dodge Club: Seven Hills.* 1873. Lee Shepard. G. $20.00

DE MONTAIGNE, Michel. *Essays.* 1923. London. Navarre Soc. Trans Cotton. 5 vols. $100.00

DE MONTOLIEU, Isbelle. *Les Chateaux Suisses.* 1816. Paris. Bertrand. 3 vols. G. $75.00

DE MONVEL, M.B. *Chanson de France Pour les Petits Francais.* c 1920s. Paris. Ils. fair. $50.00

DE MONVEL, M.B. *Jeanne d'Arc.* nd. Paris. Ils. 47 p. fair. T5. $45.00

DE MORANT, G.S. *Chinese Love Tales.* 1935. Three Sirens. 161 p. wraps. boxed. VG. $55.00

DE MORANT, G.S. *E Shame Girl.* 1929. NY. Ltd ed. 1/1000. EX. $15.00

DE MORGAN, William. *Likely Story.* 1911. Heinemann. G. P1. $9.25

DE MUSSET, Paul. *Puylaurens.* 1856. Paris. $15.00

DE NADAILLAC, Marquis. *Prehistoric America.* 1884. NY. Trans D'Anvers. poor. $12.00

DE NADAILLAC, Marquis. *Prehistoric America.* 1895. NY. Trans D'Anvers. G. $22.50

DE NEVI, Don. *W Train Robberies.* 1976. Ils. 201 p. $9.50

DE NOLHAC, Pierre. *Nattier: Peintre de la Cour de Louis XV.* 1910. Paris. Goupil. Ils. orig wraps. D2. $85.00

DE NOON, Christopher. *Posters of the WPA.* 1987. Seattle. WA U. presentation. sgn. 175 p. dj. D2. $39.95

DE PONCINS, Gontran. *Eskimos.* 1949. NY. Ils 1st ed. 104 p. dj. G. T5. $19.50

DE PRIMA, Diane. *Loba As Eve.* 1975. Phoenix. 1/100. sgn. wraps. EX. $35.00

DE PUY. *People's Cyclopedia of Universal Knowledge.* 1882. Ils. maps. 2 vols. gilt bdg. K1. $23.50

DE QUINCEY, Thomas. *Confession of an English Opium Eater.* 1930. NY. Ils Sonia Woolf. slipcase. J2. $22.50

DE RICCI, Seymour. *Book Collector's Guide.* 1921. Rosenbach. 1/1000. $75.00

DE ROSIER, A.H. *Through the S With a Union Soldier.* 1969. 177 p. M. J4. $15.00

DE ROTHSCHILD, Salomon. *Casual View of America: Letters 1859-1861.* 1962. London. dj. VG. $8.50

DE ROUGE, E.M. *Inscription du Tombeau D'Ahmes.* 1851. 3 pls. presentation. VG. $60.00

DE RUBEIS, Domici. *Romanae Magnitudinis Monumenta.* 1699. Rome. 138 pls. J2. $750.00

DE SAINT-EXUPERY, Antoine. *Flight to Arras.* 1942. NY. 1st ed. dj. VG. $17.50

DE SAINT-EXUPERY, Antoine. *Little Prince.* 1943. Harcourt Brace. Ils. dj. VG. B4. $35.00

DE SALVO, Marquis. *Travels in the Year 1806 From Italy to England...* 1808. NY. 1st Am ed. VG. $50.00

DE SANTILLANA & VON DECHEND. *Hamlet's Mill.* 1969. Boston. Gambit. 1st ed. dj. EX. $22.00

DE SAUROG. *Masked Lady.* 1936. London. 1/1000. dj. VG. $15.00

DE SCHAUENSEE, R.M. *Birds of China.* 1984. Smithsonian. Ils. 602 p. EX. M2. $30.00

DE SCHAUENSEE & PHELPS. *Guide to the Birds of Venezuela.* 1978. Princeton. Ils. 424 p. EX. M2. $30.00

DE SCHWEINITZ, G.E. *Diseases of the Eye.* 1893. Phil. Ils. 4to. 641 p. $65.00

DE SCHWEINTZ, Edmund. *Life & Times of David Zeisberger: W Pioneer & Apostle...* 1971. NY. reprint of 1870 ed. 747 p. VG. T5. $19.50

DE SEINGALT, J.C. *Memoirs.* nd. private print. 2 vols. VG. $50.00

DE SEINGALT, J.C. *Memoirs.* 1940. Edinburgh. Ltd Ed Club. sgn. 4to. slipcase. $90.00

DE SEINGALT, J.C. *Memoirs.* 1972. Harlem. Ils Sussan. 4to. slipcase. EX. $45.00

DE SEVERSKY, A.P. *Air Power: Key to Survival.* 1950. NY. Ils 1st ed. 4to. 126 p. T5. $12.50

DE SMEDT. *Visual Evoked Potentials in Man.* 1977. 631 p. $57.00

DE TABIERS. *Coachman's Story.* 1922. London. 1/1000. dj. EX. $15.00

DE TOLEDANO, Ralph. *Spies, Dupes & Diplomats.* 1952. NY. dj. G. $12.00

DE TOLNEY, Charles. *Hieronymus Bosch.* 1966. Reynal. sm folio. dj. EX. $40.00

DE TROBRIAND, P.R. *Army Life in Dakota.* 1941. Chicago. Lakeside Classic. 387 p. VG. T5. $30.00

DE TROBRIAND, P.R. *Army Life in Dakota.* 1941. Donnelley. Lakeside Classic. A3. $45.00

DE TROBRIAND, P.R. *Military Life in Dakota: Journal.* 1951. St. Paul. Trans Kane. dj. EX. $28.00

DE VALLIERE. *Honneur et Fidelite, Histoire des Suisses Service Etranger.* c 1912. Neuchatel. Ils Mangold. 4to. $75.00

DE VALOIS, Ninette. *Invitation to the Ballet.* 1937. London. 1st ed. dj. VG. $15.00

DE VATTEL, Emmerich. *Law of Nations.* 1805. Northampton. 3rd Am ed. EX. $95.00

DE VIOSON. *All the Better for Her.* 1927. London. dj. EX. $15.00

DE VOMECOURT, Philippe. *Army of Amateurs.* 1961. Doubleday. 1st ed. M1. $4.50

DE VORE, I. *Primate Behavior: Field Studies of Monkeys & Apes.* 1965. Holt Rinehart. Ils. 654 p. EX. M2. $18.00

DE VOTO, Bernard. *Across the Wide MO.* 1947. Boston. Ltd 1st ed. 1/265. sgn. boxed. B2. $135.00

DE VOTO, Bernard. *Easy Chair.* 1955. Boston. 1st ed. dj. VG. B2. $15.00

DE VOTO, Bernard. *Journals of Lewis & Clark.* 1953. Boston. 1st ed. dj. VG. B2. $22.50

DE VOTO, Bernard. *Mark Twain's America.* 1967. 1st ed. dj. $12.50

DE VRIES, Peter. *Cat's Pajamas & Witch's Milk.* 1968. Boston. 1st ed. dj. VG. $15.00

DE VRIES, Peter. *Sauce for the Goose.* c 1981. Little Brown. 1st ed. sgn. dj. EX. $35.00

DE VRIES, Peter. *Tunnel of Love.* nd. Little Brown. dj. VG. P1. $7.00

DE WAAL, R.B. *Wild Biography of Sherlock Holmes & Dr. Watson.* 1974. Bramhall House. 1st ed. dj. EX. $35.00

DE WATERS, Lillian. *Who Am I?* 1942. np. $20.00

DE WITT, S.A. *Sermon on the Mount.* 1948. NY. Strathmore. inscr. VG. $50.00

DE WITT, S.A. *Shoes for the Stars: A Play in Three Acts...* 1944. NY. Parnassus. inscr. G. $50.00

DE WOLF, Gordon. *Flora Exotic: Collection of Flowering Plants.* 1972. Boston. Godine. 1/3500. dj. D2. $40.00

DEAKIN, Irving. *To the Ballet!* 1935. NY. Dodge. 1st ed. sgn. 12mo. VG. $20.00

DEAKS, Gloria. *Picturing America, 1497-1899.* 1988. NJ. Ils. lg 4to. 2 vols. EX. $175.00

DEAN, Amber. *Be Home by Eleven.* 1973. Putnam. dj. xl. P1. $5.00

DEAN, Amber. *Bullet Proof.* 1960. Crime Club. 1st ed. dj. xl. P1. $5.00

DEAN, Amber. *Call Me Pandora.* 1944. Crime Club. VG. P1. $10.00

DEAN, Amber. *Dead Man's Float.* 1944. Crime Club. EX. P1. $9.25

DEAN, Amber. *Wrap It Up.* nd. Collier. VG. P1. $10.00

DEAN, Amber. *Wrap It Up.* 1946. Crime Club. 1st ed. dj. VG. P1. $15.00

DEAN, Harry. *Adventures of Black Sea Captain in Africa...* 1929. Boston. 262 p. $50.00

DEAN, Robert George. *Affair at Lover's Leap.* 1953. Crime Club. 1st ed. dj. G. P1. $17.50

DEAN, Roy. *Time in Eden.* 1969. Rho Delta. 1st ed. dj. boxed. EX. $25.00

DEAN, S.W. *Knight of the Revolution.* 1941. Phil. Ils 1st ed. 312 p. T5. $17.50

DEAN, W.F. *General Dean's Story As Told to William L. Worden.* 1954. NY. Ils 1st ed. 305 p. dj. VG. T5. $22.50

DEANE, Samuel. *History of Scituate, MA...* 1831. Boston. Loring. $70.00

DEANE & BALDERSTON. *Dracula: Vampire Play.* 1971. Book Club. dj. VG. C1. $3.00

DEARBORN, Henry. *Revolutionary War Journals of Henry Dearborn, 1775-1783.* 1939. Caxton. 1st ed. 1/350. slipcase. EX. $165.00

DEBO, Angie. *Road to Disappearance.* 1941. Norman. Ils. inscr. dj. EX. $90.00

DEBRETT, Hal. *Before I Wake.* 1949. Dodd Mead. 1st ed. dj. VG. P1. $11.50

DEBS, Eugene. *Debs: His Life, Writings & Speeches.* 1908. Chicago. Kerr. EX. $25.00

DEBS, Eugene. *Walls & Bars.* 1927. Chicago. VG. $30.00

DEBS, Eugene. *Writings & Speeches.* 1948. NY. dj. VG. $20.00

DECKER. *Angiography of Cerebral Circulation.* 1969. Stuttgart. sm folio. 76 p. dj. VG. $48.00

DECKER-SAMMIS. *Cheese Making.* 1924. Revised 7th ed. presentation. EX. $22.00

DEEPING, Warwick. *Man on the White Horse.* 1st Eng ed. G. C1. $12.50

DEEPING, Warwick. *Man on the White Horse.* 1934. 1st Am ed. VG. C1. $11.00

DEEPING, Warwick. *Man Who Went Back.* 1940. Toronto. 1st Canadian ed. dj. EX. rare. C1. $27.50

DEEPING, Warwick. *Roper's Row.* 1929. Ryerson. dj. EX. P1. $7.25

DEFOE, Daniel. *Fortunes & Misfortunes of Famous Moll Flanders.* 1929. London. Ils Austen. New ed. dj. EX. J2. $35.00

DEFOE, Daniel. *Journal of the Plague Year 1665.* 1896. London. 315 p. G. $20.00

DEFOE, Daniel. *Journal of the Plague Year 1665.* 1968. Heritage. Ils Gnoli. slipcase. VG. $17.50

DEFOE, Daniel. *Moll Flanders.* 1954. Ltd Ed Club. Ils/sgn Marsh. slipcase. EX. $85.00

DEFOE, Daniel. *Novels & Selected Writings.* 1928. Oxford. Shakespeare Head. 1/500. 14 vols. $225.00

DEFOE, Daniel. *Robinson Crusoe.* c 1930s. NY/London. 24 pls. 352 p. T5. $22.50

DEFOE, Daniel. *Robinson Crusoe.* nd. Book League. dj. VG. P1. $9.25

DEFOE, Daniel. *Robinson Crusoe.* 1930. Ltd Ed Club. Ils/sgn Wilson. 4to. slipcase. EX. $90.00

DEFOE, Daniel. *Robinson Crusoe.* 1946. Grosset Dunlap. Ils Ward. VG. B4. $25.00

DEFOE, Daniel. *Roxanna.* Ltd Ed Club. slipcase. M. B3. $35.00

DEGLER, C.N. *Other S: S Dissenters in 19th C.* 1974. NY. Harper. 1st ed. 392 p. dj. $22.50

DEIGHTON, Len. *Berlin Game.* 1983. Hutchinson. 1st ed. dj. EX. P1. $17.50

DEIGHTON, Len. *Billion-Dollar Brain.* 1966. Jonathan Cape. 1st ed. dj. VG. P1. $20.00

DEIGHTON, Len. *Blitzkrieg.* 1979. London. 1st ed. dj. EX. $30.00

DEIGHTON, Len. *Catch a Falling Spy.* 1976. Doubleday Book Club. VG. P1. $7.50

DEIGHTON, Len. *Funeral in Berlin.* 1965. NY. 4th print. dj. VG. $25.00

DEIGHTON, Len. *Good-Bye Mickey Mouse.* 1982. NY. 1st Am ed. dj. EX. $15.00

DEIGHTON, Len. *Good-Bye Mickey Mouse.* 1983. Knopf. 4to. dj. $7.50

DEIGHTON, Len. *Mexico Set.* nd. Book Club. dj. EX. P1. $7.50

DEIGHTON, Len. *Spy Story.* 1974. NY. 1st Am ed. dj. EX. $15.00

DEIGHTON, Len. *Yesterday's Spy.* 1975. NY. 1st ed. dj. VG. $22.00

DEKLE, G.W. *FL Armored-Scaled Insects.* 1965. FL Dept Agric. Ils. 4to. 265 p. EX. M2. $18.00

DEKNATEL, Frederick. *Edvard Munch.* 1950. Boston. Inst Contemporary Art. $20.00

DEKOCK, C.P. *Queer Legacy.* 1906. NY. Ils Stein. red morocco. VG. $125.00

DEL CASTILLO, B.D. *Discovery & Conquest of Mexico.* 1942. Ltd Ed Club. Ils Covarrubias. sgn. slipcase. $50.00

DEL FRENCH, Chauncey. *Railroadman.* 1938. 292 p. xl. $25.00

DEL REY, Judy-Lynn. *Stellar SF Stories #4.* nd. Book Club. dj. EX. P1. $3.75

DEL REY, Lester. *Attack From Atlantis.* 1961. Winston. 3rd ed. dj. VG. P1. $15.00

DEL REY, Lester. *Moon of Mutiny.* 1961. NY. 1st ed. dj. EX. $30.00

DEL REY, Lester. *Runaway Robot.* 1965. Westminster. dj. EX. P1. $25.00

DELACOUR, J. *Birds of Malaysia.* 1947. Macmillan. Ils 1st ed. 382 p. EX. M2. $48.00

DELAND, Fred. *Dumb No Longer, Romance of the Telephone.* 1908. WA. Volta Bureau. 8vo. AEG. EX. T1. $45.00

DELAND, Margaret. *Around Old Chester.* nd. Harper. 1st ed. $12.00

DELAND, Margaret. *Awakening of Helena Richie.* 1906. Harper. Ils Walter Clark. 1st ed. $20.00

DELAND, Margaret. *Dr. Lavendar's People.* 1903. Harper. Ils Hitchcock. 1st ed. VG. $75.00

DELAND, Margaret. *Encore.* 1907. NY. Ils Alice Stevens. 1st ed. VG. $25.00

DELAND, Margaret. *Golden Yesterdays.* 1941. 1st ed. sgn. 8vo. 351 p. VG. $50.00

DELAND, Margaret. *Iron Woman.* 1911. Harper. Ils Taylor. 1st ed. G. $12.00

DELAND, Margaret. *Iron Woman.* 1911. Harper. Ils Taylor. 1st ed. sgn. $50.00

DELAND, Margaret. *Kays.* 1926. Ltd ed. 1/250. sgn. $50.00

DELAND, Margaret. *Kays.* 1926. 1st ed. 8vo. 336 p. dj. VG. $35.00

DELAND, Margaret. *Partners.* 1913. Ils Gibson. 1st ed. 8vo. 115 p. VG. $35.00

DELAND, Margaret. *Promises of Alice.* 1919. Harper. Ils Brett. 1st ed. $12.00

DELAND, Margaret. *Vehement Flame.* 1922. 1st ed. 8vo. 378 p. dj. VG. $35.00

DELAND, Margaret. *Voice.* 1912. 1st ed. 8vo. 85 p. VG. $25.00

DELAND, Margaret. *Where the Laborers Are Few.* 1909. Ils Stephens. 1st ed. VG. $35.00

DELANEY, J. *88th Division: Blue Devils in Italy.* 1947. WA. 1st ed. 40 p. G. R1. $80.00

DELANEY, R.F. *Literature of Communism in America.* 1962. WA, D.C. 1st ed. dj. VG. $35.00

DELANY, Samuel R. *Stars in My Pocket Like Grains of Sand.* 1984. Bantam. 1st ed. dj. VG. P1. $17.50

DELCROIX, E.A. *Patios, Stairways & Iron-Lace Balconies of Old New Orleans.* 1941. New Orleans. Harmanson. 92 pls. sgn. wraps. $50.00

DELDERFIELD, R.F. *To Serve Them All My Days.* c 1972. Simon Schuster. G. $10.00

DELGADO, Jose. *Physical Control of the Mind.* 1969. Harper. 1st ed. dj. EX. $30.00

DELKE, J.A. *History of NC Chowan Baptist Association, 1806-1881.* 1882. Raleigh. 1st ed. VG. $85.00

DELL, A. *Llama-Land.* 1927. NY. VG. $35.00

DELL, E.M. *Charles Rex.* 1922. Putnam. 1st ed. $12.00

DELL'ISOLA, Frank. *Thomas Merton: Bibliography.* 1956. NY. 1st ed. dj. EX. $30.00

DELLA CHIESA, Angela Ottino. *Pittura Lombarda del Quattrocento.* 1959. Bergamo. 62 pls. 103 p. D2. $35.00

DELLA PERFOLA, Paola. *Giorgione.* 1957. Milan. Martello. Ils. dj. D2. $125.00

DELLENBAUGH, F.S. *Breaking the Wilderness.* 1905. Putnam. Ils. 360 p. scarce. A3. $90.00

DELLENBAUGH, F.S. *Canyon Voyage, Narrative of Second Powell Expedition...* 1926. New Haven. Ils. 277 p. A3. $70.00

DELLENBAUGH, F.S. *N Americans of Yesterday.* 1906. Putnam. Ils. 486 p. scarce. A3. $90.00

DELTEIL, Loys. *Goya.* 1969. Collector Eds. reprint of 1922 ed. 2 vols. D2. $155.00

DELVING, Michael. *Bored to Death.* nd. Book Club. dj. VG. P1. $4.00

DELVING, Michael. *Bored to Death.* 1975. Scribner. 1st ed. dj. xl. P1. $7.50

DELVING, Michael. *Die Like a Man.* 1970. 1st Am ed. pb. G. C1. $3.00

DEMBECK, H. *Animals & Men.* 1965. Nat Hist Pr. Ils 1st Am ed. 390 p. dj. EX. M2. $5.00

DEMIJOHN, Thomas. *Black Alice.* nd. Book Club. VG. P1. $4.00

DEMING, Henry. *Life of Ulysses S. Grant.* 1868. Ils. 533 p. orig green bdg. K1. $14.50

DEMING, Richard. *Famous Investigators.* 1963. Whitman. VG. P1. $6.00

DEMING, Richard. *Whistle Past the Graveyard.* 1954. Rinehart. 1st ed. dj. xl. P1. $7.50

DEMING & DEMING. *Red Folk & Wild Folk: Indian Folklore Stories for Children.* 1902. NY. Ils 1st ed. inscr/sgns. dj. EX. $75.00

DEMOS, J.P. *Entertaining Satan.* 1982. NY. dj. EX. $25.00

DEMPSEY, Jack. *Dempsey.* 1977. Harper Row. Stated 1st ed. dj. EX. $15.00

DENBY, Charles. *China & Her People.* 1906. Boston. 2 vols. VG. $35.00

DENHAM, Bertie. *Two Thyrdes.* 1983. St. Martin. dj. EX. P1. $15.95

DENHARDT, R. *Quarter-Running Horse.* 1979. OK U. dj. EX. $15.00

DENIS, A. *Cats of the World.* 1964. Houghton. Ils 1st print. 144 p. dj. EX. M2. $25.00

DENIS, A. *On Safari: Story of My Life.* 1963. Collins. Ils. map. 320 p. EX. M2. $30.00

DENLINGER, Milo G. *Complete Dachsund.* 1954. Denlinger. 3rd ed. VG. P1. $9.25

DENNETT, J.R. *S As It Is: 1865-1866.* 1965. Viking. dj. EX. $25.00

DENNIS, F. *Man-Eating Sharks.* 1976. Castle. Ils. 4to. 96 p. dj. EX. M2. $15.00

DENNIS & WHITTELSEY. *Qualitative Analysis.* 1903. sm 8vo. 142 p. TB. EX. $2.00

DENSMORE, F. *Pawnee Music.* 1929. Smithsonian. VG. $50.00

DENT, Lester. *Dead at the Takeoff.* 1948. Cassell. G. P1. $20.00

DENT, Lester. *Lady To Kill.* 1946. Doubleday Book Club. VG. P1. $15.00

DEPEW, C.M. *My Memories of 80 Years.* 1923. 417 p. with sgn photo. $50.00

DER NISTER. *Family Mashber.* 1987. NY. 1st ed. dj. EX. $9.50

DERBY, Harry. *Hand Cannons of Imperial Japan.* 1981. Charlotte. Ils. sgn. 4to. VG. $55.00

DERBY, J.C. *50 Years Among Authors, Books & Publishers.* 1884. London/NY. Carleton Low. xl. G. $22.50

DERBY, Mark. *Sunlit Ambush.* nd. Book Club. dj. VG. P1. $2.75

DERI, Max. *Naturalismus, Idealismus, Expressionismus.* 1920. Leipzig. Ils. 83 p. D2. $35.00

DERLETH, August *Chronicles of Solar Pons.* 1973. Mycroft Moran. 1st ed. dj. EX. P1. $25.00

DERLETH, August. *Adventures of Solar Pons.* 1945. Mycroft Moran. 1st ed. inscr. EX. $60.00

DERLETH, August. *Adventures of Solar Pons.* 1975. Robson. dj. VG. P1. $20.00

DERLETH, August. *Bill's Diary.* nd. Stanton Lee. 1st ed. dj. VG. $5.00

DERLETH, August. *Boys' Way.* nd. Stanton Lee. 1st ed. dj. $5.00

DERLETH, August. *Chronicles of Solar Pons.* 1975. Robson. dj. EX. P1. $20.00

DERLETH, August. *Countryman's Journal.* 1963. Duell Sloan. Ils 1st ed. 215 p. dj. VG. M2. $10.00

DERLETH, August. *Dark Mind, Dark Heart.* 1962. Arkham House. 1st ed. dj. VG. P1. $35.00

DERLETH, August. *Dark of the Moon.* 1947. Arkham House. 1st ed. xl. rebound. P1. $15.00

DERLETH, August. *Dwellers in Darkness.* 1976. Arkham House. 1st ed. dj. EX. P1. $15.00

DERLETH, August. *Empire of Fur.* 1953. Aladdin. 1st ed. dj. VG. P1. $25.00

DERLETH, August. *Exploits of Solar Pons.* 1975. Robson. dj. EX. P1. $30.00

DERLETH, August. *Father Marquette & the Great Rivers.* nd. Book Club. dj. VG. P1. $4.00

DERLETH, August. *Fire & Sleet & Candlelight.* 1961. Arkham House. 1st ed. sgn. dj. EX. P1. $75.00

DERLETH, August. *Harrigan's File.* 1975. Arkham House. 1st ed. dj. EX. P1. $15.00

DERLETH, August. *Hills Stand Watch.* 1960. NY. 1st ed. sgn. dj. EX. $45.00

DERLETH, August. *House of Moonlight.* 1953. Prairie Pr. Ltd ed. dj. VG. $25.00

DERLETH, August. *House of the Mound.* 1958. NY. 1st ed. inscr. dj. EX. $50.00

DERLETH, August. *House on the Mound.* 1958. Duell Sloan. 1st ed. G. P1. $20.00

DERLETH, August. *In Re: Sherlock Holmes.* 1945. Mycroft Moran. 1st ed. inscr. EX. $60.00

DERLETH, August. *Memoirs of Solar Pons.* 1951. Mycroft Moran. 1st ed. dj. VG. P1. $35.00

DERLETH, August. *Mr. Fairlie's Final Journey.* 1968. Mycroft Moran. 1st ed. dj. VG. P1. $25.00

DERLETH, August. *New Poetry Out of WI.* 1969. Stanton Lee. 1st ed. dj. EX. P1. $50.00

DERLETH, August. *Place of Hawks.* 1935. Loring Mussey. 1st ed. G. P1. $13.75

DERLETH, August. *Reminiscences of Solar Pons.* 1961. Mycroft Moran. 1st ed. xl. VG. P1. $20.00

DERLETH, August. *Return of Solar Pons.* 1958. Mycroft Moran. 1st ed. xl. G. P1. $20.00

DERLETH, August. *Return to Walden W.* 1970. Candlelight Pr. dj. VG. P1. $15.00

DERLETH, August. *Shadow in Glass.* 1964. Duell Sloan. 2nd print. dj. VG. $7.00

DERLETH, August. *Sherlock Holmes.* 1945. Sauk City. 1st ed. sgn. 8vo. dj. $125.00

DERLETH, August. *Sleep No More.* 1944. Farrar Rinehart. 1st ed. EX. $45.00

DERLETH, August. *Sleep No More.* 1944. NY. 1st ed. red cloth. VG. $15.00

DERLETH, August. *Solar Pons Omnibus.* 1982. Arkham House. 2 vols. boxed. EX. P1. $50.00

DERLETH, August. *Someone in the Dark.* 1941. Arkham House. 2nd ed. EX. $30.00

DERLETH, August. *Something Near.* 1945. Arkham House. 1st ed. EX. $120.00

DERLETH, August. *Three Problems for Solar Pons.* 1952. Mycroft Moran. xl. P1. $40.00

DERLETH, August. *Three Problems for Solar Pons.* 1952. Mycroft Moran. 1st ed. dj. EX. $125.00

DERLETH, August. *Three Straw Men.* 1970. Candlelight Pr. 1st ed. dj. VG. $6.00

DERLETH, August. *Three Who Died.* 1935. NY. 1st ed. sgn. green cloth. EX. $30.00

DERLETH, August. *Time To Come.* 1954. Farrar Straus. 1st ed. dj. P1. $20.00

DERLETH, August. *Walden W.* 1961. Duell Sloan. sgn. dj. EX. $30.00

DERLETH, August. *WI Country.* 1965. Candlelight. 1st ed. sgn. dj. EX. $30.00

DERLETH, August. *Wilbur, Whipporwill.* nd. Stanton Lee. 1st ed. dj. VG. $5.00

DERLETH, August. *Wind Leans W.* 1969. Candlelight. dj. VG. $7.00

DERLETH, August. *Writing Fiction.* 1946. Boston. 210 p. dj. VG. T5. $35.00

DERLETH & SCHORER. *Colonel Markesan & Less Pleasant People.* 1966. Arkham House. 1st ed. dj. VG. P1. $30.00

DERMEK, A. *Mushrooms & Other Fungi.* 1985. Arco. Ils. 223 p. dj. EX. M2. $5.00

DERRICK, S.M. *Centennial History of SC Railroad.* 1930. Columbia. 1st ed. dj. EX. $85.00

DES PRES, Terrence. *Survivor: Anatomy of Life in the Death Camps.* 1976. NY. 2nd ed. dj. $6.50

DESCHARNES & CHABRUN. *Rodin.* 1967. NY. 1st Am ed. EX. $40.00

DESCHIN, Jacob. *Tabletop Photography.* 1941. Chicago. Ziff Davis. 5th print. 96 p. $7.50

DESCHNER, Donald. *Films of W.C. Fields.* 1966. NY. 1st ed. 4to. VG. $25.00

DESCOURTILZ, J.T. *Tropical American Birds.* 1960. NY. lg folio. boxed. EX. $90.00

DESSART, Gina. *Cry for the Lost.* 1959. Harper. 1st ed. dj. VG. P1. $7.00

DETMOLD, E.J. *Book of Insects.* 1939. NY. Tudor. dj. G. $30.00

DETMOLD, E.J. *Maeterlinck: News of Spring.* 1917. NY. 20 color pls. VG. scarce. $120.00

DETZER, Karl. *Carl Sandburg: A Study.* 1941. NY. 1st ed. dj. EX. with card. $55.00

DETZER, Karl. *Mightiest Army.* 1945. Pleasantville. Ils Shenton. 168 p. G. T5. $15.00

DEUTSCH, Harold. *Hitler & His Generals: Hidden Crisis, Jan.-June 1938.* 1974. MN U. 1st ed. dj. VG. J2. $15.00

DEUX-PONTS, William. *My Campaigns in America 1780-1781.* 1868. Boston. VG. $45.00

DEVALL, B. *Simple in Means, Rich in Ends: Practicing Deep Ecology.* 1988. Smith. 1st ed. 224 p. M. M2. $10.00

DEVERE, W. *Jim Marshall's New Pianner.* 1897. NY. VG. $40.00

DEVEREUX, James P.S. *Story of Wake Island.* 1947. NY. Ils 1st ed. 252 p. G. T5. $35.00

DEVI & RAMA RAU. *Princess Remembers.* 1976. Lippincott. VG. $35.00

DEVILLE, J. *Faune des Coleoteres du Bassin de la Seine: Tome II.* 1907. France. Soc Entomology. French text. M2. $5.00

DEVINE, Eric. *Down the Hatch.* 1945. Sheridan House. G. P1. $9.25

DEVLIN & NAISMITH. *World of Roger Tory Peterson: Authorized Biography.* 1977. Times. Ils Peterson. 266 p. dj. EX. M2. $18.00

DEVOE, A. *Lives Around Us: Book of Creaturely Biographies.* 1942. Creative Age. Ils. 221 p. G. M2. $5.00

DEWAR, A.C. *Russian War: 1855 Black Sea Offical Corres.* 1945. Navy Records Soc. 1st ed. J2. $20.00

DEWAR, D. *Jungle Folk: Indian Natural History Sketches.* 1912. London. Lane. 271 p. VG. M2. $18.00

DEWAR, G.A. *Wildlife in Hampshire Highlands.* 1899. London. Ils Rackham. VG. G2. $75.00

DEWAR & FINN. *Making of Species.* 1909. London. Lane. Ils. 400 p. VG. M2. $18.00

DEWEESE & COULSON. *Now You See It/Him/Them.* 1975. Doubleday. 1st ed. dj. EX. P1. $15.00

DEWEY, George. *Autobiography.* 1913. NY. Ils 1st ed. 337 p. VG. B2. $45.00

DEWEY, John. *Psychology.* Harper. 3rd print. VG. J2. $45.00

DEWEY, John. *Psychology.* 1887. Harper. 1st ed. VG. J2. $125.00

DEWEY, John. *School & Society.* 1916. Chicago. Ils 2nd ed. sgn. 164 p. VG. T5. $12.50

DEWEY, T.B. *Case of Chased & Unchaste.* nd. Book Club. dj. G. P1. $4.00

DEWEY, T.B. *Case of Chased & Unchaste.* 1959. Random House. dj. VG. P1. $25.00

DEWEY, T.B. *Deadline.* 1967. London. 1st ed. dj. EX. $15.00

DEWEY, T.B. *Death & Taxes.* 1969. London. 1st ed. dj. EX. $10.00

DEWEY, T.B. *Death Turns Right.* 1969. London. 1st ed. dj. EX. $10.00

DEWEY, T.B. *Draw the Curtain Close.* 1951. Dakers. VG. P1. $20.00

DEWEY, T.B. *Hue & Cry.* nd. Grosset. dj. VG. P1. $20.00

DEWEY, T.B. *Mean Streets.* 1955. Boardman. VG. P1. $20.00

DEWEY, T.B. *Taurus Trip.* nd. Simon Schuster. 2nd ed. dj. xl. P1. $5.50

DEWEY, T.B. *Taurus Trip.* 1970. Simon Schuster. 1st ed. dj. xl. P1. $7.50

DEWEY, T.E. *Twenty Against the Underworld.* 1974. NY. Ils 1st ed. 504 p. dj. T5. $9.50

DEWEY. *Reception of Admiral Dewey at WA, Oct. 2 & 3, 1899.* 1901. WA. 1/700. 4to. 127 p. VG. $65.00

DEWPEW, C.M. *My Memories of 80 Years.* 1923. 417 p. $25.00

DEXLER, Arthur. *Architecture of Ecole des Beaux-Arts.* 1977. NY. dj. VG. J2. $60.00

DEXTER, Colin. *Last Seen Wearing.* 1976. NY. 1st Am ed. dj. VG. $24.00

DEXTER, Colin. *Silent World of Nicholas Quinn.* 1977. Macmillan. 1st ed. dj. xl. P1. $7.50

DEXTER, F. *Anatomy of the Peritoneum.* 1892. Ils 1st ed. diagrams. EX. $24.00

DEXTER, F. Theodore. *Forty-Two Years Scrapbook of Rare Ancient Firearms.* 1954. Los Angeles. 1/2000. 320 p. VG. T5. $75.00

DEXTER, O.P. *Dexter Genealogy, 1642-1904.* 1904. Astor Place. Ils. 297 p. fair. T5. $12.50

DEXTER, Pete. *Deadwood.* 1986. NY. 1st Am ed. dj. VG. $35.00

DEZSO, K. *Magyar Irodalom Kepeskonyve.* 1956. Budapest. Ils. 344 p. G. $24.00

DI LAMPEDUSZ, Giuseppe. *Leopard.* 1988. Ltd Ed Club. Ils Guiccione. 1/750. sgn. dj. EX. $110.00

DI LILLO, Don. *End Zone.* 1972. NY. 1st Am ed. dj. VG. $50.00

DI LSIO. *MD: A Geography.* 1983. Westview Pr. VG. $15.00

DI SAN LAZZARO, G. *Homage to Georges Rouault: Special of XXe Siecle Review.* 1971. NY. Ils. 4to. dj. EX. J2. $100.00

DIAMOND, G.W. *Account of Great Hanging at Gainesville.* 1963. Austin. 1st ed. G. $18.00

DIBBLE, C.E. *Codex Hall.* 1947. Santa Fe. $45.00

DIBBLE, S.E. *Elements of Plumbing.* 1918. NY/London. 1st ed. G. $15.00

DIBDIN, Michael. *Last Sherlock Holmes Story.* 1978. Pantheon. 1st ed. dj. EX. P1. $25.00

DIBDIN, Thomas. *Bibliomania; or, Book Madness.* 1903. Boston. Bibliophile Soc. 1/483. 4 vols. G. $200.00

DICE, L.R. *Birds of Walla Walla & Columbia Counties, WA.* 1918. Auk. M2. $3.00

DICE, L.R. *Manual of Recent Wild Mammals of MI.* 1927. MI U. M2. $3.00

DICE, L.R. *Survey of the Mammals of Charlevoix County, MI.* 1925. MI U. photos. 33 p. M2. $3.00

DICENTA, Joaquin. *Juan Jose.* 1895. Madrid. 12mo. Spanish text. full calf. VG. T1. $45.00

DICK, J.H. *Commercial Carnation Culture.* 1915. NY. 1st ed. EX. $22.00

DICK, P.K. *Dark-Haired Girl.* 1988. Ziesing. 1st ed. dj. EX. P1. $19.50

DICK, P.K. *Divine Invasion.* 1981. Timescape. 1st ed. dj. EX. P1. $25.00

DICK, P.K. *Martin Time-Slip.* 1964. Ball. 1st ed. EX. $15.00

DICK, P.K. *Mary & the Giant.* 1987. Arbor House. 1st ed. dj. EX. P1. $20.00

DICK, P.K. *Radio Free Albemuth.* 1985. Arbor House. 1st ed. dj. EX. P1. $20.00

DICK, P.K. *Scanner Darkly.* 1977. Doubleday. 2nd ed. dj. EX. P1. $15.00

DICK, P.K. *Simulacra.* 1964. Ace. 1st ed. EX. $15.00

DICK, P.K. *Wonderland.* 1962. Pb Lib. 1st ed. dj. EX. $10.00

DICK, Stewart. *Arts & Crafts of Old Japan.* 1905. McClurg. Ils. 29 pls. 152 p. VG. $25.00

DICK, W.G. *Dick's Art of Gymnastics.* 1885. NY. Ils. 12mo. 120 p. EX. $35.00

DICK & ZELAZNY. *Deus Irae.* 1978. British SF Book Club. dj. VG. P1. $7.50

DICKENS, Charles. *American Notes.* 1970. Westvaco. Ltd ed. slipcase. VG. $18.50

DICKENS, Charles. *Annotated Dickens.* 1986. NY. 1st ed. folio. boxed. EX. $45.00

DICKENS, Charles. *Battle of Life: A Love Story.* 1846. London. 1st ed. 4th issue. gilt red bdg. $95.00

DICKENS, Charles. *Boys of Charles Dickens.* nd. McLoughlin. Ils. G. $24.00

DICKENS, Charles. *Character Sketches From Dickens.* c 1924. London. Ils Harold Copping. 4to. $70.00

DICKENS, Charles. *Christmas Carol in Prose.* 1934. Merrymount. Ils/sgn Gordon Ross. $125.00

DICKENS, Charles. *Christmas Carol.* nd. RTS Office. VG. P1. $7.00

DICKENS, Charles. *Christmas Carol.* 1902. Roycroft. 1/100. sgn. 8vo. VG. D1. $125.00

DICKENS, Charles. *Christmas Carol.* 1967. Ils Rackham. dj. VG. E2. $8.00

DICKENS, Charles. *Christmas Stories.* nd. Books Inc. Ils. VG. P1. $7.00

DICKENS, Charles. *Complete Works of Charles Dickens.* nd. Phil. U Lib Assn. 1/1000. 30 vols. $325.00

DICKENS, Charles. *Cricket on the Hearth.* 1846. London. 1st ed. AEG. gilt red cloth. $225.00

DICKENS, Charles. *Cricket on the Hearth.* 1927. Harper. Ils Bedford. red bdg. G. $15.00

DICKENS, Charles. *Cricket on the Hearth.* 1933. Ltd Ed Club. $75.00

DICKENS, Charles. *David Copperfield in Copperplate.* 1947. Berkeley. 1st ed. dj. $20.00

DICKENS, Charles. *Dickens Digest.* 1943. NY. 1st ed. EX. $12.50

DICKENS, Charles. *Dickens in Europe.* 1975. Folio Soc. Ils 1st ed. slipcase. M. C1. $14.00

DICKENS, Charles. *Dickens' Birthday Book.* 1888. NY. Ils. 16mo. 397 p. AEG. gilt bdg. $60.00

DICKENS, Charles. *Dickens' Originals.* 1912. Edwin Pugh. Ils 1st ed. VG. $30.00

DICKENS, Charles. *Dombey & Son.* 1848. London. Ils Browne. 1st ed. G. $150.00

DICKENS, Charles. *Dombey & Son.* 1848. London. 1st ed. gilt red calf. EX. $250.00

DICKENS, Charles. *Holly Tree.* 1903. Roycroft. 8vo. brown suede. VG. D1. $35.00

DICKENS, Charles. *Life of Our Lord.* 1934. London. 1st ed. EX. $40.00

DICKENS, Charles. *Life of Our Lord.* 1934. NY. Ils Updike. Ltd ed. facsimile. EX. $45.00

DICKENS, Charles. *Life of Our Lord.* 1934. NY. 1st ed. VG. $30.00

DICKENS, Charles. *Minor Writings of Charles Dickens.* 1900. London. 1st ed. $55.00

DICKENS, Charles. *Mr. Pickwick: Pages From Pickwick Papers.* nd. London. Ils Reynolds. folio. gilt bdg. $195.00

DICKENS, Charles. *Mystery of Edwin Drood.* 1870. London. Chapman Hall. 1st ed. $100.00

DICKENS, Charles. *Nicholas Nickleby.* 1839. London. Ils Phiz. 1st ed in book form. $175.00

DICKENS, Charles. *Our Mutual Friend.* 1865. Chapman Hall. 2 vols in 1. green morocco. $285.00

DICKENS, Charles. *People From Dickens Arranged by Rachel Field.* 1935. Ils Fogarty. 1st ed. VG. B4. $40.00

DICKENS, Charles. *Personal History of David Copperfield.* nd. London. Ils Frank Reynolds. J2. $40.00

DICKENS, Charles. *Pickwick Club Papers.* 1886. London. Macmillan. 2 vols. fair. $45.00

DICKENS, Charles. *Pictures From Italy.* 1846. London. 1st ed. 8vo. green cloth. $175.00

DICKENS, Charles. *Posthumous Papers of Pickwick Club.* nd. London. Ils Frank Reynolds. J2. $30.00

DICKENS, Charles. *Posthumous Papers of Pickwick Club.* 1910. London. Chapman Hall. 2 vols. VG. $250.00

DICKENS, Charles. *Posthumous Papers of Pickwick Club.* 1910. London. Ils Aldin. 24 pls. 2 vols. EX. $295.00

DICKENS, Charles. *Posthumous Papers of Pickwick Club.* 1933. Ltd Ed Club. Ils/sgn Austen. 2 vols. slipcase. $110.00

DICKENS, Charles. *Somebody's Luggage.* 1957. Phil. 1/1000. M. $20.00

DICKENS, Charles. *Unpublished Letters of Charles Dickens to Mark Lemon.* 1927. London. 1/525. $95.00

DICKENS, Charles. *Works of Charles Dickens.* 1911. NY. 36 vols. VG. $350.00

DICKENS, Charles. *People From Dickens Arranged by Rachel Field.* 1935. 1st ed. VG. B4. $40.00

DICKENS, Homer. *Films of Katherine Hepburn.* 1971. NY. 1st ed. $20.00

DICKENSON, Fred. *Kill 'Em With Kindness.* 1950. Bell. dj. VG. P1. $9.25

DICKEY, F.V. *Familiar Birds of Pacific SW.* 1936. Stanford. Ils 1st ed. 2nd print. 241 p. M2. $20.00

DICKEY, James. *Deliverance.* 1970. Boston. 1st ed. dj. EX. $18.00

DICKEY, James. *Deliverance.* 1970. Boston. 1st ed. sgn. dj. EX. $45.00

DICKEY, James. *Enemy From Eden.* 1978. Lord John. Ils Sauter. 1st ed. 1/275. sgn. EX. $55.00

DICKHOFF, R.E. *Eternal Fountain.* 1947. Boston. $40.00

DICKINSON, Emily. *Bolts of Melody.* 1945. NY. 1st ed. dj. EX. $50.00

DICKINSON, Emily. *Unpublished Poems.* 1936. Little Brown. 1st ed. 8vo. green cloth. dj. $85.00

DICKINSON, G. Lowes. *Modern Symposium.* 1916. Dent. VG. P1. $13.75

DICKINSON, Peter. *Devil's Children.* 1st Am ed. dj. EX. C1. $6.00

DICKINSON, Peter. *Heartsease.* 1986. 1st Am ed. dj. M. C1. $9.50

DICKINSON, Peter. *King & Joker.* 1976. Pantheon. dj. xl. P1. $5.00

DICKINSON, Peter. *Weathermonger.* 1974. Daw. 1st Am ed. pb. VG. C1. $3.00

DICKINSON, Peter. *Weathermonger.* 1986. 1st HrdCvr Am ed. dj. EX. C1. $9.50

DICKINSON, William Croft. *Dark Encounters.* 1963. Harvill. 1st ed. dj. VG. P1. $25.00

DICKINSON & LUCAS. *Color Dictionary of Mushrooms.* 1979. Van Nostrand. Ils 1st ed. 4to. M2. $12.00

DICKINSON & LUCAS. *Encyclopedia of Mushrooms.* 1983. Crescent. Ils. 4to. dj. EX. M2. $28.00

DICKSON, Carter. *Cavalier's Cup.* 1953. Morrow. VG. P1. $15.00

DICKSON, Carter. *Graveyard To Let.* nd. Book Club. dj. G. P1. $5.00

DICKSON, Carter. *Night at the Mocking Widow.* nd. Book Club. dj. VG. P1. $4.50

DICKSON, Carter. *Peacock Feather Murders.* 1937. Morrow. 1st ed. VG. P1. $40.00

DICKSON, Carter. *Seeing Is Believing.* 1945. Tower. dj. VG. P1. $17.50

DICKSON, Carter. *Skeleton in the Clock.* nd. Book Club. dj. VG. P1. $7.50

DICKSON, Carter. *Unicorn Murders.* Grosset Dunlap. VG. P1. $20.00

DICKSON, Carter. *Unicorn Murders.* 1935. Morrow. 1st ed. $20.00

DICKSON, Carter. *Unicorn Murders.* 1945. Tower. dj. G. P1. $20.00

DICKSON, Carter. *White Priory Murders.* 1944. Books Inc. 2nd ed. VG. P1. $12.50

DICKSON, Gordon R. *Alien Art.* 1973. Dutton. 1st ed. dj. EX. P1. $25.00

DICKSON, Gordon R. *Ancient My Enemy.* 1974. Doubleday. 1st ed. dj. xl. P1. $7.00

DICKSON, Gordon R. *Dragon & the George.* nd. Book Club. 1st ed. dj. EX. P1. $5.50

DICKSON, Gordon R. *Far Call.* nd. Book Club. dj. VG. P1. $4.50

DICKSON, Gordon R. *Masters of Everon.* nd. Book Club. dj. EX. P1. $4.00

DICKSON, Gordon R. *Mutants.* 1970. Macmillan. 1st ed. sgn. dj. EX. P1. $30.00

DICKSON, Gordon R. *Necromancer.* nd. Book Club. dj. VG. P1. $4.00

DICKSON, Gordon R. *Outposter.* 1972. Lippincott. 1st ed. dj. xl. P1. $6.00

DICKSON, Gordon R. *Pritcher Mass.* 1972. Doubleday. 2nd ed. dj. EX. P1. $12.00

DICKSON, Gordon R. *R-Master.* 1973. Lippincott. 1st ed. dj. xl. P1. $6.00

DICKSON, Gordon R. *Space Winners.* 1965. Holt Rinehart. 1st ed. xl. P1. $7.50

DICKSON, Gordon R. *Star Road.* 1973. Doubleday. 1st ed. sgn. dj. EX. P1. $25.00

DICKSON, Gordon R. *Star Road.* 1975. Robert Hale. 1st ed. P1. $15.00

DICKSON, Gordon R. *Three to Dorsai!* nd. Book Club. dj. EX. P1. $7.50

DICKSON, Harris. *Gabrielle Transgressor.* 1906. Lippincott. Ils Walter Everett. 1st ed. $12.00

DICKSON, J.L. *Journal of Joseph Lawrence Dickson.* 1956. WA Hist Soc. 4to. 44 p. EX. M2. $10.00

DICKSON, Paul. *Think Tanks.* 1971. NY. 1st ed. dj. VG. B2. $15.00

DICKSON & MAUGHAN. *Managing S Forests for Wildlife & Fish.* 1987. USFS. 4to. 85 p. M2. $5.00

DIDAY, P. *Exposition Critique et Pratique des Nouvelles Doctrines...* 1858. Paris. 8vo. 560 p. $120.00

DIDAY, P. *La Pratique des Maladies Veneriennes.* 1890. Paris. 8vo. 631 p. $100.00

DIDEROT. *Rameau's Nephew.* 1926. London. dj. VG. $15.00

DIDION, Joan. *Book of Common Prayer.* 1977. NY. 1st ed. 8vo. dj. VG. $50.00

DIDION, Joan. *Democracy.* 1984. NY. 1st ed. tall 8vo. dj. xl. VG. $15.00

DIDION, Joan. *Play It As It Lays.* 1970. NY. 1st ed. dj. VG. $20.00

DIDION, Joan. *Run River.* 1963. NY. dj. EX. $80.00

DIEBOW & GOELTZER. *Mussolini: Eien Biographie in 110 Bildern.* 1931. Verlag. photos. orig wraps. rare. D2. $125.00

DIEHL, Charles. *Emperor Who Lost His Nose.* 1927. England. Curwen. 1/50. EX. $35.00

DIEHL, Edith. *Bookbinding: Its Background & Technique.* 1942. Rinehart. 2 vols. slipcase. VG. $125.00

DIES, E.J. *Titans of the Soil.* 1949. Chapel Hill. dj. VG. $11.00

DIETRICH, P.J. *Silent Men.* 1983. Akron. Goodyear Tire & Rubber. 50 p. T5. $4.50

DIETRICK & FRANZ-WALSH. *Merry Ballads of Robin Hood.* 1931. NY. Macmillan. 1st/only ed. scarce. C1. $14.50

DIETZ, A.A. *Mad Rush for Gold in Frozen N.* 1914. Los Angeles. 281 p. fair. $9.00

DIFFIN, C.W. *Gray Smoke: Coyote of El Coronel.* 1940. NY. Ils Alyn. inscr. 4to. VG. $20.00

DIKTY, T.E. *Work of Julian May.* 1985. Borgo Pr. RS. VG. P1. $7.50

DILL & GARNETT. *Ideal Book.* 1932. Ltd Ed Club. 2nd print. EX. $35.00

DILLARD, Anne. *Weasel.* 1974. Rara Avis. 1/190. sgn/#d. wraps. M. $45.00

DILLARD, J.M. *Lost Years.* 1989. Pocket. HrdCvr. dj. VG. P1. $17.95

DILLIARD, M.E. *Old Dutch Houses of Brooklyn.* 1945. NY. photos. VG. $25.00

DILLIN, J. *KY Rifle.* 1924. Nat Rifle Assn. photos. 4to. 130 p. $95.00

DILLING, Elizabeth. *Red Network: Who's Who/Handbook of Radicalism for Patriots.* 1936. Dilling. 345 p. VG. $35.00

DILLING. *Roosevelt-Red Record & Its Background.* 1936. Kenilworth. dj. G. $14.50

DILLION, E.S. & L.S. *Manual of Beetles of E N America.* 1972. Dover. reprint of 1961 ed. EX. M2. $15.00

DILLON, Myles. *Cycles of the Kings.* 1946. Oxford. VG. C1. $29.50

DILLON, R.H. *Builders of CA Communities.* 1966. San Francisco. Ils. 144 p. EX. $17.50

DILLON, R.H. *J.R. Browne: Confidential Agent in Old CA.* 1965. Norman. Ils. dj. EX. $35.00

DILLON, William. *Narrative of My Professional Adventures, 1790-1839.* 1953. Navy Records Soc. 2 vols. J2. $35.00

DIMAND, Maurice. *Persian Miniature Paintings.* nd. (1945) Milan. 10 pls. folio. wraps. G. $20.00

DIMENT, Adam. *Dolly Dolly Spy.* 1967. Dutton. dj. EX. P1. $15.00

DIMENT, Adam. *Great Spy Race.* 1968. Dutton. 1st ed. dj. EX. P1. $15.00

DIMOND, S.J. *Social Behavior of Animals.* 1970. Harper Row. 256 p. dj. EX. M2. $4.00

DINES, Michael. *Operation Kill or Be Killed.* 1969. Robert Hale. 1st ed. dj. xl. P1. $5.00

DINESEN, Isak. *Anecdotes of Destiny.* 1958. NY. 1st ed. dj. VG. B2. $20.00

DINESEN, Isak. *Ehrengard.* 1963. NY. 1st Am ed. dj. EX. $25.00

DINESEN, Isak. *Last Tales.* 1957. NY. 1st ed. dj. EX. $30.00

DINESEN, Isak. *Out of Africa.* 1938. NY. 1st ed. dj. B2. $32.50

DINESEN, Isak. *Out of Africa.* 1938. Random House. 1st ed. dj. T6. $80.00

DINESEN, Isak. *Seven Gothic Tales.* 1934. NY. 1st ed. 420 p. gilt bdg. dj. G. T5. $35.00

DINESEN, Isak. *Seven Gothic Tales.* 1939. Modern Lib. 1st ed. dj. VG. $20.00

DINESEN, Isak. *Shadows on the Grass.* 1961. NY. 1st Am ed. dj. EX. $20.00

DINESEN, Isak. *Shadows on the Grass.* 1961. Random House. BOMC. dj. EX. $5.00

DINESEN, Isak. *Winter's Tales.* 1942. Random House. dj. G. P1. $4.75

DINESEN, Isak. *Winter's Tales.* 1942. Random House. 1st ed. dj. M. $40.00

DINKINS, James. *1861-1865 by an Old Johnie.* 1975. Dayton. facsimile. 280 p. VG. T5. $27.50

DINNEEN, Joseph F. *Anatomy of a Crime.* 1954. Scribner. 1st ed. xl. P1. $4.75

DINNEEN, Patrick S. *Irish-English Dictionary.* 1927. Dublin. Revised ed. VG. T6. $75.00

DINSMORE, Charles. *Teachings of Dante.* 1901. Houghton Mifflin. G. $24.00

DIOLE, Philippe. *Okapi Fever.* nd. Book Club. dj. VG. P1. $2.75

DIRINGER, David. *Alphabet: Key to History of Mankind.* 1968. NY. Ils 3rd ed. 2 vols. xl. VG. T5. $22.50

DIRLAM-SIMMONS. *Sinners This Is E Aurora: History of Roycrofters.* 1964. NY. Ils 1st ed. 263 p. dj. VG. B2. $30.00

DISCH, Thomas M. *Bad Moon Rising.* 1973. Harper Row. 1st ed. dj. VG. P1. $17.50

DISCH, Thomas M. *On Wings of Song.* 1979. St. Martin. dj. EX. P1. $20.00

DISCH & NAYLOR. *New Constellations.* 1976. Harper Row. 1st ed. dj. EX. P1. $20.00

DISHER, M.W. *Music Hall Parade.* 1938. Scribner. 1st ed. dj. VG. J2. $15.00

DISKINSON, Peter. *Devil's Children.* 1986. 1st Am ed. dj. EX. C1. $9.50

DISNEY, Doris Miles. *Day Miss Bessie Lewis Disappeared.* 1972. Doubleday Book Club. VG. P1. $7.50

DISNEY, Doris Miles. *Last Straw.* 1954. Crime Club. 1st ed. dj. VG. P1. $17.50

DISNEY, Doris Miles. *Shadow of a Man.* 1965. Crime Club. 1st ed. dj. G. P1. $15.00

DISNEY, Doris Miles. *Should Auld Acquaintance.* 1962. Crime Club. 1st ed. dj. xl. P1. $7.50

DISNEY, Doris Miles. *Three's a Crowd.* 1971. Crime Club. 1st ed. dj. VG. P1. $10.00

DISNEY, Doris Miles. *Trick or Treat.* nd. Book Club. VG. P1. $3.00

DISNEY, Doris Miles. *Who Rides a Tiger.* nd. Collier. VG. P1. $10.00

DISNEY, Dorothy Cameron. *Hangman's Tree.* 1949. Random House. 1st ed. dj. VG. P1. $9.25

DISNEY, Walt. *ABC Book.* nd. Disney. VG. $50.00

DISNEY, Walt. *Ferdinand the Bull.* 1938. Whitman. Ils. 31 p. G. $22.50

DISNEY, Walt. *Mickey Mouse's Picnic.* Little Golden Book. 7th print. P1. $5.00

DISNEY, Walt. *Snow White & Seven Dwarfs.* 1937. NY. Ils 1st ed. sm folio. 79 p. B2. $85.00

DISNEY, Walt. *Snow White & Seven Dwarfs.* 1938. NY. VG. $20.00

DISTURNELL, J. *Great Lakes, Inland Seas of America.* 1863. NY. fld map. VG. $115.00

DITMARS, R.L. *Reptiles of N America.* 1936. Doubleday. Ils. 4to. dj. G. M2. $17.00

DITMARS, R.L. *Reptiles of the World.* 1926. Macmillan. Ils. 373 p. EX. M2. $20.00

DITMARS, R.L. *Strange Animals I Have Known.* 1931. NY. Ils 1st ed. sgn. VG. $20.00

DITMARS, R.L. *Thrills of a Naturalist's Quest.* 1947. Halcyon House. Ils. 268 p. EX. M2. $10.00

DITMARS & BRIDGES. *Snake Hunters' Holiday Tropical Adventures...* 1935. NY/London. Ils. fair. $25.00

DIVINE, David. *Atom at Spithead.* 1953. Macmillan. 1st ed. xl. P1. $7.00

DIX, J.R. *Handbook of Newport & RI.* 1852. map. G. $53.00

DIX, M. *History of Parish Trinity Church.* 1898. Putnam. 5 vols. TEG. xl. VG. $200.00

DIXON, C. *Rural Bird Life of England: Essays on Ornithology.* 1895. Werner. Ils. 374 p. rebound. EX. M2. $8.00

DIXON, Charles. *Conquerors of the Atlantic by Air.* 1931. Phil. Ils. 246 p. dj. G. T5. $25.00

DIXON, Franklin W. *Arctic Patrol Mystery.* nd. Grosset. VG. P1. $4.75

DIXON, Franklin W. *Clue in the Embers.* nd. Grosset. VG. P1. $4.00

DIXON, Franklin W. *Clue of the Broken Blade.* nd. Grosset. VG. P1. $4.75

DIXON, Franklin W. *Clue of the Hissing Serpent.* nd. Grosset. VG. P1. $4.75

DIXON, Franklin W. *Crisscross Shadow.* nd. Grosset. VG. P1. $5.00

DIXON, Franklin W. *Disappearing Floor.* nd. Grosset. VG. P1. $4.75

DIXON, Franklin W. *Firebird Rocket.* nd. Grosset. VG. P1. $4.75

DIXON, Franklin W. *Flying Against Time.* 1929. Grosset. VG. P1. $7.50

DIXON, Franklin W. *Footprints Under the Window.* nd. Grosset. G. P1. $3.25

DIXON, Franklin W. *Ghost at Skeleton Rock.* nd. Grosset. VG. P1. $4.75

DIXON, Franklin W. *Great Airport Mystery.* nd. Grosset. VG. P1. $4.75

DIXON, Franklin W. *Hidden Harbor Mystery.* nd. Grosset. VG. P1. $4.75

DIXON, Franklin W. *Hooded Hawk Mystery.* nd. Grosset. VG. P1. $4.75

DIXON, Franklin W. *House on the Cliff.* 1959. Book Club. 193 p. dj. EX. $3.00

DIXON, Franklin W. *Mark on the Door.* nd. Grosset. VG. P1. $3.75

DIXON, Franklin W. *Melted Coins.* nd. Grosset. VG. P1. $4.75

DIXON, Franklin W. *Mysterious Caravan.* nd. Grosset. VG. P1. $4.75

DIXON, Franklin W. *Mystery at Devil's Paw.* nd. Grosset. VG. P1. $5.00

DIXON, Franklin W. *Mystery of Cabin Island.* nd. Grosset. VG. P1. $4.75

DIXON, Franklin W. *Mystery of the Aztec Warrior.* nd. Grosset. VG. P1. $4.75

DIXON, Franklin W. *Mystery of the Desert Giant.* nd. Grosset. VG. P1. $4.75

DIXON, Franklin W. *Mystery of the Flying Express.* nd. Grosset. VG. P1. $4.75

DIXON, Franklin W. *Mystery of the Spiral Bridge.* nd. Grosset. VG. P1. $4.75

DIXON, Franklin W. *Over the Rockies With the Air Mail.* nd. Grosset. G. P1. $6.00

DIXON, Franklin W. *Rescued in the Clouds.* nd. Grosset. VG. P1. $7.00

DIXON, Franklin W. *S of the Rio Grande.* nd. Grosset. VG. P1. $7.50

DIXON, Franklin W. *Secret Agent on Flight 101.* nd. Grosset. VG. P1. $4.00

DIXON, Franklin W. *Secret of the Lost Tunnel.* nd. Grosset. VG. P1. $4.75

DIXON, Franklin W. *Secret of Wildcat Swamp.* nd. Grosset. VG. P1. $4.75

DIXON, Franklin W. *Secret Panel.* nd. Grosset. VG. P1. $4.75

DIXON, Franklin W. *Shattered Helmet.* nd. Grosset. VG. P1. $4.75

DIXON, Franklin W. *Shortwave Mystery.* nd. Grosset. VG. P1. $4.75

DIXON, Franklin W. *Sigh of the Crooked Arrow.* nd. Grosset. VG. P1. $4.75

DIXON, Franklin W. *Tower Treasure.* nd. Grosset. dj. VG. P1. $7.50

DIXON, Franklin W. *Twisted Claw.* nd. Grosset. VG. P1. $4.75

DIXON, Franklin W. *Viking Symbol Mystery.* nd. Grosset. VG. P1. $4.75

DIXON, Franklin W. *Wailing Siren Mystery.* nd. Grosset. VG. P1. $4.75

DIXON, Franklin W. *Yellow Feather Mystery.* 1953. Grosset. sm 8vo. 216 p. EX. $3.00

DIXON, H.N. *Student's Handbook of British Mosses.* 1904. Sumfield. Ils. 583 p. EX. M2. $55.00

DIXON, J.D. *Neotropical Colubrid Snake Genus Liopis: Generic Concept.* 1980. Milwaukee Mus. Ils. 40 p. EX. M2. $5.00

DIXON, J.K. *Vanishing Race: Last Great Indian Council.* 1913. Doubleday. Ils Wanamaker. 4to. EX. $130.00

DIXON, J.K. *Vanishing Race: Last Great Indian Council.* 1913. Garden City. Ils. photos. VG. $85.00

DIXON, J.K. *Vanishing Race: Last Great Indian Council.* 1914. Doubleday. Revised 2nd ed. $65.00

DIXON, J.R. *Amphibians & Reptiles of TX With Keys: Taxonomic Synopses.* 1987. TX A&M U. Ils 1st ed. 434 p. M. M2. $18.00

DIXON, James. *Tour of America.* 1850. Lane Scott. 3rd ed. VG. $30.00

DIXON, Jeane. *Call to Glory.* 1972. NY. $12.50

DIXON, Jeane. *Reincarnation & Prayers To Live By.* 1970. NY. $12.00

DIXON, Joseph. *Study of Life, History & Food Habits of Mule Deer in CA.* 1934. Sacto. 1st ed. 146 p. stiff wraps. VG. J2. $15.00

DIXON, Roger. *Noah II.* 1975. Harwood Smart. dj. EX. P1. $9.25

DIXON, Royal. *Half Dark Moon.* 1939. TX. VG. $12.00

DIXON, S.H. *Men Who Made TX Free.* 1924. Houston. Ils. sgn. VG. $100.00

DIXON, Thomas. *Clansman.* 1905. Ils. 374 p. J4. $8.50

DIXON, Thomas. *Leopard's Spots.* 1903. Doubleday Page. 1st ed. VG. $35.00

DIXON & EDDY. *Personality of Insects.* 1924. Clark. 32 photos. 247 p. VG. M2. $4.00

DMITRI, Ivan. *Kodachrome & How To Use It.* 1940. Simon Schuster. dj. VG. $30.00

DOAK, W. *Fishes of the New Zealand Region.* 1972. Hodder Stoughton. 1st ed. dj. M2. $25.00

DOANE, F.H. *Young Married Lady's Private Medical Guide.* 1954. 264 p. K1. $17.50

DOANE, Gilbert. *About Collecting Bookplates.* 1941. Madison, WI. Black Mack. 1/360. boxed. VG. J2. $50.00

DOBBIN, C.N. *Fresh-Water Ostracoda From WA & Other W Localities.* 1941. WA U. Ils. repaired. M2. $8.00

DOBBINS, Paul H. *Fatal Finale.* 1949. Phoenix. dj. VG. P1. $7.00

DOBBINS, Paul H. *Kingdom of Cibola.* 1947. Boston. 1st ed. dj. VG. $10.00

DOBIE, C.C. *San Francisco's Chinatown.* 1936. NY. Ils Suydam. sgns. dj. VG. $60.00

DOBIE, J.F. *Cattle Industry of TX & Adjacent Territories.* 1959. Antiquarian. facsimile of 1894 ed. 2 vols. T6. $300.00

DOBIE, J.F. *Cow People.* 1964. 1st ed. dj. EX. B1. $30.00

DOBIE, J.F. *Guide to Life & Literature of the SW.* 1952. 2nd ed. dj. VG. $22.00

DOBIE, J.F. *Longhorns.* 1941. Boston. Ils Tom Lea. 1st ed. dj. T5. $65.00

DOBIE, J.F. *Mustangs.* 1952. Bramhall House. Ils Wilson. orange cloth. dj. VG. $15.00

DOBIE, J.F. *Mustangs.* 1952. NY. reprint. 376 p. VG. $15.00

DOBIE, J.F. *Out of the Old Rock.* 1972. Boston. Book Club. 237 p. dj. VG. T5. $12.50

DOBIE, J.F. *Rattlesnakes.* 1965. Little Brown. Ils. later print. dj. EX. M2. $15.00

DOBIE, J.F. *Texan in England.* 1945. Little Brown. 1st ed. inscr. $20.00

DOBKIN, Alexander. *Travel Sketchbook.* 1965. NY. 1st ed. inscr. dj. $35.00

DOBREE. *Japanese Sword Blades.* 1971. NY. 1st ed. dj. EX. $45.00

DOBROSZYCKI, Lucjan. *Chronicle of Lodz Ghetto, 1941-1944.* 1984. New Haven. Ils 2nd ed. dj. VG. $12.00

DOBSON, Austin. *Bookman's Budget.* 1917. London. 1st ed. pls. $25.00

DOBSON, Austin. *Complete Poetical Works.* 1923. Oxford. 1st ed. VG. C1. $6.00

DOBSON, Austin. *18th-C Vignettes.* 1892 & 1894. London. sgn. 2 vols in 1. M. $300.00

DOBSON, Austin. *18th-C Vignettes.* 1892. London. Ils. TEG. red morocco bdg. EX. $200.00

DOCKSTADER, Frederick. *Indian Art of Americas.* 1973. Am Indian Mus. photos. red bdg. VG. $23.00

DOCTOR, J.E. *Shotguns on Sunday.* 1958. LA. dj. G. $40.00

DOCTOROW, E.L. *Book of Daniel.* 1971. NY. sgn. dj. EX. $40.00

DOCTOROW, E.L. *Loon Lake.* 2nd print. sgn. dj. VG. $25.00

DOCTOROW, E.L. *Loon Lake.* 1980. NY. 1st ed. sgn. dj. M. $40.00

DOCTOROW, E.L. *Ragtime.* 1975. London. sgn. dj. $50.00

DOCTOROW, E.L. *Ragtime.* 1975. NY. Special ed. presentation. sgn. dj. $100.00

DOCTOROW, E.L. *Ragtime.* 1975. Random House. 1st trade ed. G. $7.50

DODD, B.T. *Certainty of a Future Life in Mars.* 1903. NY. 1st ed. VG. $50.00

DODD, William. *Cotton Kingdom.* 1919. 161 p. K1. $9.50

DODD & DODD. *Tugs & Barges: Story Collaborations.* 1927. Frederica. 1st ed. photos. sgns. dj. EX. $35.00

DODDS, J.E. *Gentleman From Heaven.* 1962. CA. $9.00

DODGE, David. *Carambola.* 1961. Little Brown. dj. xl. P1. $6.00

DODGE, David. *Death & Taxes.* 1941. Macmillan. 1st ed. dj. VG. P1. $11.50

DODGE, David. *Lights of Skaro.* 1954. Random House. 1st ed. dj. xl. P1. $7.50

DODGE, David. *Plunder of the Sun.* nd. Book Club. VG. P1. $2.25

DODGE, David. *Plunder of the Sun.* 1950. Michael Joseph. dj. G. P1. $7.25

DODGE, Ernest. *NW by Sea.* 1961. Oxford. 1st ed. dj. VG. J2. $15.00

DODGE, G.M. *Battle of Atlanta & Other Campaigns, Addresses, Etc.* 1985?. Ils. photos. EX. J4. $8.50

DODGE, G.M. *How We Built the Union Pacific Railway & Other Papers...* 1910. WA. Ils. 136 p. VG. A3. $35.00

DODGE, M.M. *Hans Brinker; or, The Silver Skates.* 1926. NY. Ils Edwards. not 1st ed. J2. $25.00

DODGE, M.M. *Hans Brinker; or, The Silver Skates.* 1935. Scribner. Ils Edwards. VG. B4. $30.00

DODGE, M.M. *Theophilius & Others.* 1876. NY. VG. $25.00

DODGE, N.N. *Poisonous Dwellers of the Desert.* 1974. SW Parks & Monuments Assn. VG. M2. $8.00

DODGE, R.I. *Black Hills.* 1965. Minneapolis. Ross Haines. reprint. dj. VG. A3. $35.00

DODGE, R.I. *Plains of the Great W & Their Inhabitants.* 1877. NY. Putnam. Ils. 448 p. VG. A3. $110.00

DODGE, R.I. *Plains of the Great W & Their Inhabitants.* 1959. Archer House. reprint of 1877 ed. xl. VG. M2. $13.00

DODGSON, Cambell. *Woodcuts of 15th C in John Ryland's Library.* 1915. Manchester. folio. portfolio. $100.00

DODRILL, W.C. *Moccasin Tracks & Other Imprints.* 1974. Parson, WV. reprint of 1915 ed. 298 p. VG. T5. $15.00

DODSON, Kenneth. *Away All Boats.* 1954. Boston. 44 p. dj. VG. T5. $4.50

DODSON, M.M. *OK Migratory Game Bird Study: 1949-1953.* 1954. OK Game/Fish. Ils. EX. M2. $4.00

DOGBOLT, Barnaby. *Eve's Second Apple.* 1946. Dutton. 2nd ed. dj. VG. P1. $9.25

DOGGETT, Carita. *Dr. Andrew Turnbull & the New Smyrna Colony.* 1919. VG. $20.00

DOGIEL, V.A. *Parasitology of Fishes.* 1961. Edinburgh. Oliver Boyd. 1st ed. dj. M2. $30.00

DOHERTY, Edward J. *Broadway Murders.* nd. Collier. VG. P1. $10.00

DOHERTY, P.C. *Death of a King.* 1985. 1st Am ed. dj. VG. C1. $6.00

DOHERTY. *Anatomical Works of George Stubbs.* 1974. London. folio. 345 p. dj. EX. $65.00

DOIG, Ivan. *This House of Sky.* 1978. NY. 1st ed. dj. B2. $27.50

DOIG, J.M. *Metropolitan Transportation Politics & NY Region.* 1966. 327 p. $20.00

DOISNEAU, Robert. *Three Seconds From Eternity.* 1979. Boston. 1st Am ed. folio. dj. EX. $25.00

DOITCH, E. *Springbok Prisoner in Germany.* 1917. London. wraps. xl. G. $25.00

DOKE, C.M. *Lambas of N Rhodesia.* 1931. London. Ils 1st ed. 408 p. B2. $32.50

DOLBEER & STEHN. *Population Trends of Blackbirds & Starlings in N America.* 1979. USFWS. 4to. 99 p. M2. $5.00

DOLGOFF. *Bakunin on Anarchy.* 1972. NY. 1st ed. dj. VG. $15.00

DOLPH, E.A. *Sound Off: Soldier Songs From Yankee Doodle to Parley Voo.* 1929. NY. Ils Lawrence Skick. 4to. $50.00

DONAHUE, Phil. *Donahue: My Own Story.* 1981. Fawcett. 1st ed. 318 p. pb. wraps. VG. $10.00

DONALD, D.H. *Gone for a Soldier: Civil War Memoirs of Private A. Bellard.* 1975. Boston. Ils. EX. $15.00

DONALDSON, D. *AK Deer Herd.* 1951. AR Game/Fish. Ils. maps. 72 p. G. M2. $6.00

DONALDSON, Frances. *P.G. Wodehouse: A Biography.* 1982. Weidenfeld. 1st ed. dj. EX. P1. $25.00

DONALDSON, Stephen R. *Daughter of Regals.* 1984. Del Rey. 1st ed. dj. EX. P1. $15.00

DONALDSON, T.L. *Ancient Architecture on Greek & Roman Coins & Medals.* 1966. Chicago. 1st ed. dj. VG. J2. $15.00

DONATI, Lamberto. *Incisioni Fiorentine del Quattrocento.* 1944. Bergamo. Ils. D2. $80.00

DONDERS, F.C. *On Anomalies of Accomodation & Refraction of the Eye.* 1864. London. 1st ed. 8vo. 635 p. $275.00

DONEHOO, J. *Apocryphal & Legendary Life of Christ.* 1903. NY. dj. G. $25.00

DONLEAVY, J.P. *Fairy Tale of NY.* 1973. NY. 1st Am ed. sgn. dj. VG. $35.00

DONLEAVY, J.P. *Further Adventures in Destinies of Darcy Dancer, Gentleman.* 1983. Delacorte. UCP. M. $40.00

DONLEAVY, J.P. *Ginger Man.* 1965. NY. 1st ed. dj. VG. $50.00

DONLEAVY, J.P. *Ginger Man.* 1978. Franklin Lib. Ltd ed. sgn. 8vo. EX. $35.00

DONLEAVY, J.P. *Leila.* 1983. NY. 1st Am ed. dj. VG. $20.00

DONLEAVY, J.P. *Singular Man.* 1963. Boston. 1st ed. dj. VG. $25.00

DONN, Draeger. *Asian Fighting Arts.* 1974. Kodansha. 7th print. dj. VG. $20.00

DONN, Draeger. *Classical Budo.* 1973. NY/Tokyo. 1st ed. dj. VG. $15.00

DONN, Draeger. *Classical Bujutsu.* 1973. NY/Tokyo. 1st ed. dj. VG. $15.00

DONNE, Jack. *Defense of Women for Their Inconstancy & Their Paintings.* Franfrolico. Ils Lindsay. 1/370. EX. $35.00

DONNE, John. *Donne's Sermon of Valediction.* 1932. London. 1/750. VG. $65.00

DONNE, John. *Everyman, a Mortality.* 1909. London. Ils Dudley. 1st ed. VG. C1. $12.50

DONNE, John. *Love Poems.* 1946. Golden Eagle. 1/1960. slipcase. M. C1. $17.50

DONNE, John. *Poems.* nd. NY. Oxford. Standard ed. G. $18.00

DONNEGAN, J. *Donnegan's Greek & English Lexicon.* 1847. Phil. 1st Am ed. 8vo. 1413 p. VG. $45.00

DONNEL, C.P. *Murder-Go-Round.* 1945. McKay. VG. P1. $10.00

DONNELL, A.H. *Rebecca Mary.* Sept., 1905. NY. Ils Green. G. $18.00

DONNELLY, B.G. *Range of the Booted Eagle Aquila Pennata in S Africa.* 1966. Cape Mus. G. M2. $3.00

DONNELLY, Ignatius. *Atlantis.* nd. Gramercy. dj. EX. P1. $5.50

DONNELLY, Ivon A. *Chinese Junks & Other Native Craft.* 1930. Shanghai. Kelly Walsh. Ils. fair. $35.00

DONNELLY, R.B. *Just Like Flowers Dear.* 1932. NY. Coventry Guild. 1/950. dj. EX. $15.00

DONNER, Daniel. *Confederate in CO Gold Fields.* 1970. Norman. 1st ed. maps. dj. EX. $33.00

DONNER, F. *Shabona.* 1982. Delacorte. 305 p. dj. EX. M2. $12.00

DONOGHUE, F.L. *Blue Devils All.* 1936. McLoughlin. Ils. VG. $12.00

DONOVAN, Duncan. *City Work at Country Prices. Portrait Photographs of...* 1977. Danbury, NH. Addison House. 54 pls. 4to. wraps. $35.00

DONOVAN, J.B. *Strangers on a Bridge: Case of Colonel Abel.* 1964. Atheneum. Book Club ed. dj. VG. M1. $4.50

DONSON, Theodore B. *Prints & the Print Market.* 1977. NY. Crowell. Ils 1st ed. dj. D2. $23.50

DONZELLI, Tomaso. *Theatro Farmaceutico Dogmatico, Spagirico del D.G. Donzeli.* 1713. Venedig. 4to. $520.00

DOOLITTLE, Hilda. *Hedylus.* 1928. Houghton. 1st ed. 1/775. $30.00

DORE, Gustave. *Adventures du Baron Munchhausen.* nd. Paris. Trans Gautier. sm folio. VG. $80.00

DORE & BLANCHARD. *London: A Pilgrimage.* 1890. NY. not 1st ed. VG. J2. $50.00

DOREY, J. Milnor. *Good English Made Easy.* 1949. Perma P19. VG. P1. $5.00

DOREY, J. Milnor. *Short History of the World.* 1949. Perma P28. VG. P1. $5.00

DORLAND & NANNEY. *Dust Off: Army Aeromedical Evacuation in Vietnam.* 1982. WA. 1st ed. 134 p. wraps. VG. T5. $9.50

DORMAN, Sonya. *Planet Patrol.* 1978. Coward McCann. 1st ed. dj. VG. P1. $10.00

DORN, Edward. *Twenty-Four Love Songs.* 1969. Frontier Pr. wraps. $20.00

DORNBUSH, C.E. *Military Bibliography of Civil War.* 1967. EX. scarce. J4. $30.00

DORNBUSH, C.E. *Military Bibliography of Civil War. Vol. 3.* 1922. 224 p. M. scarce. J4. $45.00

DORNBUSH, C.E. *Regimental Publications & Personal Narratives of Civil War.* 1961. 1 vol only. M. scarce. J4. $50.00

DORNBUSH, C.E. *Regimental Publications & Personal Narratives of Civil War.* 1962. NY. 88 p. wraps. G. T5. $15.00

DORPALEN, Andrewas. *Henrich Von Treitschke.* 1957. Yale. 1st ed. dj. VG. J2. $15.00

DORR & COVINGTON. *Life Dance.* 1975. Allendale, NJ. Alleluia Pr. 1st ed. 1/250. dj. EX. $75.00

DORSET, P.F. *CO Gold & Silver Rushes.* 1970. Ils 1st ed. 434 p. dj. K1. $14.50

DORSEY, J.M. *Jefferson-Dunglison Letters.* 1976. Charlottesville U. 1st ed. VG. $10.00

DORSON, Richard. *Davy Crockett: American Comic Legend.* 1939. NY. Rockland. 1st ed. VG. J2. $25.00

DORSON, Richard. *Jonathan Draws the Long Bow.* 1946. Harvard. 2nd print. dj. EX. $16.00

DORT & JONES. *Pleistocene & Recent Environments of Central Great Plains.* 1970. KS U. dj. EX. $20.00

DOS PASSOS, John. *Adventures of a Young Man.* 1939. NY. 1st ed. dj. EX. $45.00

DOS PASSOS, John. *Ground We Stand On: Some Examples From History...* 1941. Harcourt Brace. inscr. 8vo. VG. $35.00

DOS PASSOS, John. *Nineteen Nineteen.* 1932. Harcourt. 1st ed. dj. $50.00

DOS PASSOS, John. *USA Trilogy.* 1946. Boston. 1st trade ed. 3 vols. slipcase. T5. $95.00

DOSENBACH, H.D. *Family Life of Birds.* 1971. McGraw Hill. Ils. 185 p. dj. EX. M2. $7.00

DOSTER, J.F. *Railroads in AL Politics, 1875-1914.* 1957. . 273 p. $20.00

DOSTOEVSKY, Feodor. *House of the Dead.* Ltd Ed Club. slipcase. M. B3. $60.00

DOSTOEVSKY, Feodor. *Notebooks, Crime & Punishment.* 1967. Chicago. dj. EX. $12.00

DOSTOEVSKY, Feodor. *Notebooks, Possessed.* 1968. Chicago. dj. EX. $10.00

DOSTOEVSKY, Feodor. *Notebooks, Raw Youth.* 1969. Chicago. dj. EX. $10.00

DOSTOEVSKY, Feodor. *Notebooks for Brothers Karamazov.* 1971. Chicago. dj. EX. $10.00

DOUBLEDAY, Abner. *Chancellorsville & Gettysburg.* 1886. NY. Ils. maps. 243 p. T5. $35.00

DOUBOUT. *Gargantue par Francois Rabelais.* nd. Paris. Lib D'Amateurs. Ltd ed. wraps. G. $125.00

DOUGHTY, C.M. *Cabinet of Natural History & American Rural Sports.* Imprint Soc. dj. slipcase. EX. $55.00

DOUGHTY, C.M. *Some Early American Hunters.* Derrydale. as issued. VG. B2. $95.00

DOUGHTY, C.M. *Travels in Arabia Deserta.* c 1921. NY. 2 vols in 1. VG. $40.00

DOUGHTY, C.M. *Travels in Arabia Deserta.* 1953. Heritage. Ils. 453 p. VG. M2. $15.00

DOUGHTY, Oswald. *Victorian Romantic: Dante Gabriel Rossetti.* 1949. London. 1st ed. VG. C1. $7.00

DOUGLAS, Byrd. *Steamboatin' on the Cumberland.* 1961. Nashville. sgn. 407 p. dj. G. $25.00

DOUGLAS, C.L. *Cattle Kings of TX.* 1939. Dallas. Ils 2nd print. G. $35.00

DOUGLAS, C.L. *Cattle Kings of TX.* 1939. Dallas. 1st ed. dj. EX. $55.00

DOUGLAS, G.M. *Lands Forlorn.* 1914. NY. fair. $85.00

DOUGLAS, H.K. *I Rode With Stonewall.* 1940. Chapel Hill. not 1st ed. dj. G. $12.00

DOUGLAS, Hudson. *Million a Minute.* 1908. Watt. Ils Will Grefe. 1st ed. $12.00

DOUGLAS, L.C. *Affair of the Heart.* 1922. Akron. wraps. VG. T5. $12.50

DOUGLAS, L.C. *Disputed Passage.* 1939. Grosset. dj. VG. P1. $9.25

DOUGLAS, L.C. *Robe.* nd. Peoples Book Club. dj. VG. P1. $4.75

DOUGLAS, Norman. *Birds & Beasts of Greek Anthology.* 1929. NY. 1st ed. dj. VG. $30.00

DOUGLAS, Norman. *D.H. Lawrence & Maurice Magnus: Plea for Better Manners.* 1924. private print. sgn. wraps. EX. $150.00

DOUGLAS, Norman. *S Wind.* 1928. NY. Ils Angelo. 1/250. sgn. EX. $125.00

DOUGLAS, Norman. *S Wind.* 1929. Chicago. 2 vols. djs. boxed. EX. $75.00

DOUGLAS, Norman. *S Wind.* 1929. Ils Austen. 1st ed. 2 vols. VG. E2. $30.00

DOUGLAS, Norman. *Some Limericks.* 1967. Grove. 1st ed. EX. P1. $7.00

DOUGLAS, Stephen. *Speech of Mr. Douglas of IL on Territorial Question.* 1850. WA. 31 p. wraps. VG. J2. $25.00

DOUGLAS, W.O. *Mr. Lincoln & the Negroes.* 1963. Atheneum. 1st ed. dj. EX. $15.00

DOUGLAS, W.O. *My Wilderness.* 1960. Doubleday. Ils Jaques. 1st ed. dj. M2. $12.00

DOUGLAS, W.O. *My Wilderness.* 1960. NY. 2 vols. djs. EX. $20.00

DOUGLAS, W.O. *Of Men & Mountains.* 1950. Harper. Ils 1st ed. 338 p. VG. M2. $9.00

DOUGLAS & HAMILTON. *Among the Elephants.* 1975. Viking. Ils. maps. dj. EX. M2. $13.00

DOUGLAS & HAMILTON. *Among the Elephants.* 1978. Penguin. Ils. 285 p. M2. $9.00

DOUGLAS & STROUD. *Symposium on the Biological Significance of Estuaries.* 1971. Sport Fishing Inst. 111 p. M2. $10.00

DOUKAN, G. *World Beneath the Waves.* 1957. De Graff. Ils 1st Am ed. 356 p. VG. M2. $11.00

DOURNOVO, L.A. *Miniatures Armeniennes.* 1960. Paris. Ed Cercle d'Art. 87 pls. 4to. J2. $75.00

DOUTT, J.K. *Mammals of PA.* 1967. PA Game Com. photos. 281 p. VG. M2. $15.00

DOW, C.M. *Anthology & Bibliography of Niagara Falls. Vol. 1.* 1921. Albany. Ils. maps. xl. $17.50

DOW, Lorenzo. *Eccentric Preacher; or, Life of Lorenzo Dow.* 1841. Lowell. 204 p. $70.00

DOW, Lorenzo. *History of Cosmopolite.* 1849. Cincinnati. rebound. VG. $50.00

DOW, Lorenzo. *Life & Travels of Lorenzo Dow...* 1804. Hartford. 1st ed. G. $75.00

DOWDEN, P.B. *Parasites & Predators of Forest Insects Liberated in the US.* 1962. USDA. 70 p. M2. $4.00

DOWDEY, Clifford. *Lee's Last Campaign.* 1960. Boston. 1st ed. maps. 415 p. VG. T5. $35.00

DOWDEY, Clifford. *Seven Days: Emergence of Lee.* 1964. Boston. 1st ed. maps. 380 p. T5. $30.00

DOWDEY & MANARIN. *Wartime Papers of R.E. Lee.* 1961. 994. dj. M. J4. $20.00

DOWER, K.G. *Spotted Lion.* 1937. Boston. Ltd ed. 1/481. wraps. G. $30.00

DOWNES, R.C. *History of Lake Shore, OH.* 1952. NY. Ils 1st ed. 3 vols. VG. T5. $95.00

DOWNEY, Fairfax. *Cats of Destiny.* 1950. NY. 1st ed. dj. G. $15.00

DOWNEY, Fairfax. *Clash of Calvary: Battle of Brandy Station, June 9, 1863.* 1959. McKay. Ils. maps. 238 p. dj. EX. M2. $30.00

DOWNEY, Fairfax. *Portrait of an Era As Drawn by C.D. Gibson.* 1936. NY. 1st ed. VG. $25.00

DOWNEY, Sheridan. *They Would Rule the Valley.* 1947. San Francisco. private print. EX. $40.00

DOWNHOWER, J.F. *Biogeography of the Island Region of W Lake Erie.* 1988. OH U. photos. maps. 4to. 280 p. dj. M2. $30.00

DOWNIE, W. *Hunting for Gold.* 1893. San Francisco. VG. $150.00

DOWNING, A.J. *Architecture of Country Houses.* 1852. NY. Ils. xl. VG. $75.00

DOWNING, A.J. *Fruits & Fruit Trees of America.* 1860. NY. Ils. 760 p. VG. B1. $30.00

DOWNING, David. *Jack Nicholson.* 1984. NY. 1st ed. dj. EX. $15.00

DOWNING, R.L. *E Cougar Recovery Plan.* 1981. USFWS. 17 p. M2. $3.00

DOWNING, Todd. *Cat Screams.* 1934. Doubleday Crime Club. VG. P1. $15.00

DOWNING, Todd. *Vultures in the Sky.* 1935. Crime Club. 1st ed. VG. P1. $25.00

DOWNING, Warwick. *Mountains W of Town.* nd. Book Club. dj. VG. P1. $4.00

DOWNS, Joseph. *American Furniture: Queen Anne & Chippendale.* 1955. NY. 1st ed. $40.00

DOWNS, Mrs. G.S. *Gertrude Elliot's Crucible.* 1908. Dillingham. 1st ed. $12.00

DOWNS, Mrs. G.S. *Step by Step.* 1906. Dillingham. 1st ed. $12.00

DOWS, Olin. *Franklin Roosevelt at Hyde Park.* 1949. Am Artists. Ils. 4to. dj. VG. G2. $30.00

DOWSON, E. *Stories.* 1947. Allen. 1st Eng ed. dj. $30.00

DOWSON, W.L. *Birds of OH.* 1903. Columbus. EX. $80.00

DOYLE, A.C. *A.C. Doyle's Best Books in 3 Vols.* nd. Collier. Sherlock Holmes ed. 3 vols. VG. $25.00

DOYLE, A.C. *Adventure of the Blue Carbuncle.* Baker St. Irregulars. dj. VG. P1. $150.00

DOYLE, A.C. *Adventures of Gerard.* nd. Collier. G. P1. $7.50

DOYLE, A.C. *Adventures of Gerard.* 1903. NY. 1st ed. G. $18.00

DOYLE, A.C. *Adventures of Sherlock Holmes.* 1892. Harper. Ils 1st ed. plastic dj. VG. $275.00

DOYLE, A.C. *Adventures of Sherlock Holmes.* 1892. London. Newnes. 1st ed. 1st issue. $900.00

DOYLE, A.C. *Adventures of Sherlock Holmes.* 1902. Grosset. G. P1. $20.00

DOYLE, A.C. *Boys' Sherlock Holmes.* 1936. Harper. VG. P1. $18.25

DOYLE, A.C. *Casebook of Sherlock Holmes.* 1927. Doran. $20.00

DOYLE, A.C. *Casebook of Sherlock Holmes.* 1952. John Murray. 16th print. dj. VG. P1. $25.00

DOYLE, A.C. *Complete Adventures & Memoirs of Sherlock Holmes.* 1975. Barnahall. 1st ed. dj. EX. $30.00

DOYLE, A.C. *Complete Napoleonic Stories.* 1956. John Murray. dj. VG. P1. $25.00

DOYLE, A.C. *Complete Sherlock Holmes. Vol. I.* nd. Doubleday. Intro Morley. dj. VG. $30.00

DOYLE, A.C. *Doyle Diary: Last Great Conan Doyle Mystery.* 1978. NY. Ils 1st ed. oblong 8vo. dj. EX. $22.00

DOYLE, A.C. *Exploits of Brigadier Gerard.* 1896. London. Ils 1st ed. VG. $75.00

DOYLE, A.C. *Great Keinplatz Experiment.* 1919. Doran. VG. $25.00

DOYLE, A.C. *Great Shadow.* c 1890s. Harper. VG. P1. $75.00

DOYLE, A.C. *Heaven Has Claws.* 1953. Random House. Ils 2nd print. 245 p. dj. VG. M2. $14.00

DOYLE, A.C. *Heaven Has Claws.* 1953. Random House. 1st ed. dj. VG. P1. $11.50

DOYLE, A.C. *His Last Bow.* nd. Burt. VG. P1. $7.50

DOYLE, A.C. *His Last Bow.* 1917. Doran. 1st Am ed. VG. $20.00

DOYLE, A.C. *His Last Bow.* 1917. John Murray. 2nd ed. G. P1. $18.25

DOYLE, A.C. *Hound of the Baskervilles.* 1902. McClure Phillips. 1st Am ed. P1. $100.00

DOYLE, A.C. *Hound of the Baskervilles.* 1902. 1st Am ed. 2nd state. G. $75.00

DOYLE, A.C. *Hound of the Baskervilles.* 1902. London. Newnes. 1st ed. gold bdg. $850.00

DOYLE, A.C. *Illustrated Sherlock Holmes Treasury.* nd. Avenel. EX. P1. $10.00

DOYLE, A.C. *Last Galley.* 1911. Garden City. 1st Am ed. VG. rare. C1. $29.50

DOYLE, A.C. *Last of the Legions & Other Tales of Long Ago.* 1922. NY. 1st Am ed. 224 p. G. T5. $22.50

DOYLE, A.C. *Lost World.* 1912. Hodder Stoughton/Doran. 1st Am ed. $50.00

DOYLE, A.C. *Lost World.* 1912. NY. 1st Am ed. variant bdg. M. $135.00

DOYLE, A.C. *Memoirs of Sherlock Holmes.* 1894. London. Newnes. 1st ed. boxed. $750.00

DOYLE, A.C. *Memoirs of Sherlock Holmes.* 1894. NY. 1st ed. 1st issue. $500.00

DOYLE, A.C. *Memories & Adventures.* 1924. London. 2nd ed. 408 p. orig bdg. EX. $45.00

DOYLE, A.C. *Micah Clarke.* nd. Mershon. VG. P1. $20.00

DOYLE, A.C. *Micah Clarke.* 1894. NY. 1st ed. 8vo. brown bdg. G. $36.00

DOYLE, A.C. *Original Illustrated Sherlock Holmes.* Sept., 1983. Castle Books. Ils Paget. EX. $30.00

DOYLE, A.C. *Pheneas Speaks: Direct Spirit Communications.* 1927. Doran. 1st Am ed. $30.00

DOYLE, A.C. *Poison Belt.* 1913. Hodder Stoughton. 3rd ed. G. P1. $30.00

DOYLE, A.C. *Return of Sherlock Holmes.* nd. Newnes Sixpenny. poor. P1. $3.75

DOYLE, A.C. *Return of Sherlock Holmes.* 1905. Chicago. McClure. 1st ed. VG. $200.00

DOYLE, A.C. *Rodney Stone.* nd. Nash Grayson. G. P1. $15.00

DOYLE, A.C. *Rodney Stone.* 1897. Appleton. 1st Am ed. $40.00

DOYLE, A.C. *Rodney Stone.* 1930. Garden City. inscr. 8vo. VG. $35.00

DOYLE, A.C. *Sign of the Four & Other Stories.* nd. Collier. VG. P1. $13.75

DOYLE, A.C. *Stark Munro Letters.* 1895. NY. 1st ed. VG. B2. $30.00

DOYLE, A.C. *Study in Scarlet & Other Stories.* nd. Collier. VG. P1. $13.75

DOYLE, A.C. *Study in Scarlet.* nd. Ward Lock. G. P1. $18.25

DOYLE, A.C. *Study in Scarlet.* 1918. Ward Lock. VG. P1. $25.00

DOYLE, A.C. *Tales of Love & Hate.* 1960. John Murray. 1st ed. P1. $9.25

DOYLE, A.C. *Tales of Sherlock Holmes.* nd. NY. Grosset Dunlap. Ils Gillett. VG. $20.00

DOYLE, A.C. *Tales of Terror & Mystery.* 1977. Doubleday. 1st ed. dj. xl. P1. $7.00

DOYLE, A.C. *Treasury of Sherlock Holmes.* nd. Hanover House. P1. $9.25

DOYLE, A.C. *Valley of Fear.* 1914. Doran. Ils Keller. 1st Am ed. M. $60.00

DOYLE, A.C. *Valley of Fear.* 1965. John Murray. 14th print. dj. EX. P1. $20.00

DOYLE, A.C. *White Company & Beyond the City.* nd. Collier. G. P1. $10.00

DOYLE, A.C. *White Company.* nd. Grosset. VG. P1. $10.00

DOYLE, A.C. *White Company.* 1939. John Murray. 65th print. VG. P1. $15.00

DOYLE, A.C. *White Company.* 1945. Musson. VG. P1. $10.00

DOYLE, Brian. *Who's Who of Children's Literature.* 1971. Schocken. Ils 3rd print. 380 p. G. $10.00

DOYLE, C.W. *Taming of the Jungle.* 1899. Lippincott. inscr. VG. $30.00

DOYLE, J.B. *Frederic William Von Steuben & American Revolution.* 1913. Steubenville. Ils 1st ed. 1/600. 399 p. VG. T5. $75.00

DOYLE, Richard. *Journal Kept by Richard Doyle in Year 1840.* 1885. London. Ils. 4to. VG. $45.00

DOYLE & STEWART. *Stand in the Door!* 1988. Williamstown. Ils 1st ed. 428 p. M. T5. $25.00

DOZOIS, Gardner. *Strangers.* 1978. Berkley Putnam. 1st ed. dj. xl. P1. $7.50

DRABBLE. *Genius of Thomas Hardy.* 1925. NY. 1/2000. EX. $15.00

DRACHE, H.M. *Day of the Bonanza.* 1969. ND Inst. photos. maps. 239 p. EX. M2. $8.00

DRACO, F. *Devil's Church.* 1951. Holt Rinehart. 1st ed. dj. EX. $12.00

DRAGO, H.S. *Great American Cattle Trails.* 1963. NY. Dodd Mead. 1st ed. dj. VG. $15.00

DRAGO, H.S. *Great Range Wars: Violence on the Grasslands.* 1970. Dodd Mead. photos. 397 p. EX. M2. $17.00

DRAGO, H.S. *Road Agents & Train Robbers: Half a Century of W Banditry.* 1973. Dodd Mead. photos. 239 p. dj. EX. M2. $19.00

DRAGO, H.S. *Steamboaters From Early Sidewheelers.* nd. Bramhall. 2nd ed. dj. EX. P1. $9.25

DRAGO, H.S. *Steamboaters From Early Sidewheelers.* 1967. Bramhall. photos. red bdg. dj. VG. $20.00

DRAKE, Daniel. *N Lakes: Summer Resort for Invalids of S.* 1954. Torch Pr. reprint. 1/400. $27.50

DRAKE, David. *Dragon Lord.* 1st ed. dj. EX. C1. $16.00

DRAKE, David. *Dragon Lord.* 1979. Berkley Putnam. 1st ed. dj. P1. $15.00

DRAKE, George. *Mail Goes Through; or, Drake's Civil War Letters.* 1964. San Gelo. Anchor. sgn editor. dj. EX. $28.00

DRAKE, J.R. *Culprit Fay & Other Poems.* 1835. NY. 1st ed. AEG. rebound. boxed. T5. $45.00

DRAKE, S.A. *Historic Fields & Mansions of Middlesex.* 1874. Boston. 1st ed. EX. $125.00

DRAKE, S.G. *Indian Biography: History of Indian Wars.* 1832. Boston. 348 p. $75.00

DRANNAN, W.F. *Thirty-One Years on the Plains & in the Mountains.* 1902. Chicago. Ils 586 p. fair. T5. $22.50

DRAPER, J.W. *TB on Chemistry.* 1856. NY. Harper. 300 engravings. 412 p. full calf. $30.00

DRAPER, J.W. *Thoughts on Future Civil Policy of America.* 1866. NY. 12mo. 325 p. G. G2. $19.00

DRAPER, J.W. *Thoughts on Future Civil Policy of America.* 1875. 325 p. EX. J4. $7.50

DRAPER, Theodore. *84th Infantry Division in Germany.* 1946. NY. Viking. G. R1. $85.00

DREISER, Theodore. *American Tragedy.* 1925. Ltd Ed Club. slipcase. EX. $130.00

DREISER, Theodore. *American Tragedy.* 1925. NY. 1st ed. 2 vols. djs. VG. $45.00

DREISER, Theodore. *Aspirant.* 1929. Random House. Ltd ed. wraps. VG. $35.00

DREISER, Theodore. *Bulwark.* 1946. NY. 1st ed. dj. EX. $30.00

DREISER, Theodore. *Chains.* 1927. NY. 1st ed. sgn. VG. $50.00

DREISER, Theodore. *Color of a Great City.* 1923. NY. 1st ed. dj. VG. $25.00

DREISER, Theodore. *Color of the City.* 1930. London. Review 1st ed. slipcase. RS. EX. $25.00

DREISER, Theodore. *Dawn.* 1931. NY. 1st ed. dj. EX. $50.00

DREISER, Theodore. *Dawn.* 1931. NY. 1st ed. dj. VG. $35.00

DREISER, Theodore. *Epitaph.* 1929. Heron. Ils/sgn Fawcett. 1/1100. $60.00

DREISER, Theodore. *Fine Furniture.* 1930. NY. Ltd ed. 1/875. wraps. EX. $30.00

DREISER, Theodore. *Free & Other Stories.* 1918. NY. 1st ed. dj. EX. $60.00

DREISER, Theodore. *Gallery of Women.* 1929. NY. 1st ed. 2 vols. djs. slipcase. EX. $40.00

DREISER, Theodore. *Genius.* 1915. NY. 1st ed. 1st issue. $40.00

DREISER, Theodore. *Gennie Gerhardt.* 1911. NY. 1st ed. dj. $35.00

DREISER, Theodore. *Hand of the Potter.* 1918. NY. 1st ed. dj. VG. $70.00

DREISER, Theodore. *Hey Rub-A-Dub-Dub.* 1920. NY. 1st ed. dj. VG. $45.00

DREISER, Theodore. *Hoosier Holiday.* 1916. Bodley Head. Ils Booth. 513 p. TEG. VG. $45.00

DREISER, Theodore. *Hoosier Holiday.* 1916. NY. 1st ed. B2. $75.00

DREISER, Theodore. *Hoosier Holiday.* 1916. NY/London. 1st ed. 2nd issue. dj. $75.00

DREISER, Theodore. *Moods.* 1926. NY. Ltd ed. sgn. VG. $80.00

DREISER, Theodore. *Moods.* 1928. NY. 1st trade ed. dj. EX. $40.00

DREISER, Theodore. *Sister Carrie.* nd. Modern Lib. VG. P1. $7.00

DREISER, Theodore. *Sister Carrie.* 1907. Heritage. Ils 1st ed. VG. $25.00

DREISER, Theodore. *Sister Carrie.* 1939. Ltd Ed Club. Ils/sgn Marsh. 1/1500. dj. M. $115.00

DREISER, Theodore. *Sister Carrie.* 1965. Harper. Perennial Classic. 1st ed. dj. EX. $8.50

DREISER, Theodore. *Titan.* 1914. Lane. 1st ed. VG. $30.00

DREISER, Theodore. *Traveler at Forty.* 1914. NY. not 1st ed. VG. $25.00

DREISER & DRESSER. *Songs of Paul Dresser.* 1927. NY. 1st ed. 4to. VG. G1. $20.00

DREPPERD, C.W. *American Drawing Books.* 1946. NY. 20 p. wraps. fair. $6.00

DREPPERD, C.W. *American Pioneer Arts & Artists.* 1942. Springfield. Ils 1st ed. 172 p. dj. G. T5. $65.00

DRESLOV, Aksel. *River, a Town, a Poet: Walk Together With H.C. Andersen.* nd. Bogforlag. 1st ed. pls. dj. VG. J2. $20.00

DREW, Bernard. *Hard-Boiled Dames.* 1986. NY. 1st ed. dj. EX. $15.00

DREW, John. *Autobiographical Sketch of Mrs. John Drew.* 1899. NY. VG. B1. $25.00

DREW, John. *My Years on the Stage.* 1922. Dutton. VG. $10.00

DREXLER, R. *Line of Least Existence & Other Plays.* 1967. Random House. 1st print. dj. M. $35.00

DREXLER & HITCHCOCK. *Built in USA: Post-War Architecture.* 1952. NY. dj. J2. $20.00

DRIER, Thomas. *Power of Print & Men.* 1936. Merganthaler. VG. $12.00

DRIGGS, H. *Old W Speaks.* 1956. Prentice Hall. dj. VG. $12.00

DRIGGS, H. *W America.* 1942. NY. Pioneer. Ils Jackson. sgns. M. $40.00

DRIMMER, F. *Animal Kingdom.* 1954. Greystone. Ils. 3 vols. VG. M2. $28.00

DRINKER, C.K. *Clinical Physiology of the Lungs.* 1954. Thomas. 1st ed. inscr/sgn. VG. $100.00

DRINKWATER, John. *Book for Bookmen.* 1927. NY. $18.00

DRINKWATER, John. *Eighteen-Sixties.* 1932. Cambridge. 1st ed. dj. EX. $25.00

DRINKWATER, John. *Robert E. Lee, a Play.* 1923. London. Sidgwick. 1st ed. 95 p. $15.00

DRINKWATER, John. *World & the Artist.* nd. London. 1st ed. 1/140. sgn $60.00

DROEGE, J.A. *Passenger Terminals & Trains.* 1969. Ils. photos. 410 p. $27.50

DRONAMRAJU, K.R. *Haldane & Modern Biology.* 1968. Johns Hopkins. 333 p. dj. EX. M2. $20.00

DROSS, Friedrich. *Ernst Barlach: Aus Seinen Briefen.* 1947. Munich. Piper. 74 p. D2. $18.50

DROUET, B.C. *Station Astral.* 1932. NY. $20.00

DRUCKER, M.J. *Rubber Industry in OH.* 1937. np. 1st ed. 76 p. wraps. G. T5. $35.00

DRUCKER, P. *Ceramic Sequences at Tres Zapotes, Veracruz, Mexico.* 1943. Bull. Ils. 155 p. EX. M2. $25.00

DRUITT, Herbert. *Manual of Costume As Illustrated by Monumental Brasses.* 1906. Moring. 1st ed. with sgn letter. J2. $45.00

DRUITT, Robert. *Principles & Practice of Modern Surgery.* 1859. Phil. leather. $60.00

DRUMMOND, Charles. *Odds on Death.* 1969. Gollancz. 1st ed. dj. xl. P1. $5.00

DRUMMOND, H. *Ascent of Man.* 1894. Pott. 346 p. G. M2. $15.00

DRUMMOND, H. *Tropical Africa.* 1908. Hodder Stoughton. 228 p. G. M2. $15.00

DRUMMOND, June. *I Saw Him Die.* 1979. Gollancz. dj. EX. P1. $15.00

DRUMMOND, W.H. *Habitant & Other French Canadian Poems.* 1897. NY. Ils 1st ed. 12mo. VG. T1. $25.00

DRUMMOND, W.H. *Large Game & Natural History of S & SE Africa.* 1875. Edinburgh. Douglas. Ils. 428 p. M2. $190.00

DRURY, Allen. *Shade of Difference.* 1962. Doubleday. 1st ed. VG. P1. $9.25

DRURY, C.M. *Henry Harmon Spalding Cald.* 1936. 2nd print. dj. EX. $35.00

DRURY, John. *CA: Intimate Guide.* 1935. NY. 1st ed. VG. $20.00

DRURY, John. *Heritage of Early American Houses.* 1969. Coward McCann. Ils. folio. 298 p. orange cloth. $42.00

DRURY, John. *Old IL Houses.* 1948. Springfield. 1st ed. VG. J2. $15.00

DRURY, W.P. *Peradventures of Private Pagett.* 1904. London. Ils Rackham. 1st ed. $75.00

DRY, Thomas. *Manual of Cardiology.* 1943. Phil. 2nd print. EX. $27.50

DRYDEN, John. *Poems on Various Occasions...* 1701. London. 1st 1 vol ed. $250.00

DU BOIS, Theodora. *Armed With a New Terror.* 1936. Houghton. 1st ed. dj. VG. P1. $25.00

DU BOIS, Theodora. *Fowl Play.* 1951. Doubleday Book Club. VG. P1. $7.50

DU BOIS, Theodora. *High King's Daughter.* 1965. Ariel. dj. xl. P1. $5.00

DU BOIS, Theodora. *Listener.* 1953. Crime Club. 1st ed. dj. VG. P1. $11.50

DU BOIS, W.E. *Negro.* 1915. NY. Holt. 254 p. $15.00

DU BOIS, W.E. *Souls of the Black Folk: Essays & Sketches.* 1903. Chicago. Ils music scores. EX. T1. $30.00

DU BOIS, W.P. *Twenty-One Balloons.* 1947. NY. Ils 1st ed. 179 p. dj. G. T5. $25.00

DU CANE, Ella. *Flowers & Gardens of Japan.* 1908. London. Black. Ils 1st ed. 8vo. dj. VG. T1. $55.00

DU CANE, Ella. *Italian Lakes.* 1905. London. Black. VG. $15.00

DU CHAILLU, Paul. *African Forest & Jungle.* 1903. NY. 1st ed. VG. $22.50

DU CHAILLU, Paul. *Country of the Dwarfs.* 1969. Negro U. reprint of 1872 ed. EX. M2. $16.00

DU CHAILLU, Paul. *Viking Age.* 1890. London. Ils. map. VG. $25.00

DU CHAILLU, Paul. *Wildlife Under the Equator. Narrated for Young People.* 1869. NY. 1st ed. 12mo. 231 p. scarce. $40.00

DU MAURIER, Daphne. *Classics of the Macbre.* 1987. Doubleday. 1st ed. dj. EX. P1. $18.95

DU MAURIER, Daphne. *Come Wind Come Weather.* 1940. London. 82 p. wraps. $30.00

DU MAURIER, Daphne. *Mary Anne: A Novel.* 1954. London. 1st ed. dj. EX. $45.00

DU MAURIER, Daphne. *Rule Britannia.* 1973. Doubleday. dj. xl. P1. $4.75

DU MAURIER, George. *Martian.* 1897. NY. Ltd ed. 1/500. VG. $50.00

DU MAURIER, George. *Trilby.* 1894. Harper. 1st ed. VG. $12.00

DU MAURIER, George. *Trilby.* 1894. NY. Ils 1st ed. EX. $25.00

DU MAURIER, George. *Trilby.* 1895. London. 1st 1 vol ed. VG. $35.00

DU MONT, P.A. *Birds of Polk County, IA.* 1931. Des Moines. Audubon Soc. 72 p. M2. $5.00

DU NOUY, Lecomte. *Human Destiny.* 1949. Signet. Lib pb bdg. VG. P1. $5.00

DU PONT, Pierre. *Chants et Chansons.* 1855. Paris. Ils. French text/music. 4 vols. $100.00

DU PRE LUMPKIN, Katherine. *Making of a Southerner.* 1947. Knopf. 1st ed. dj. EX. $8.00

DU PUY, Henry. *Ethan Allen & the Green Mountain Heroes of `76.* 1853. Boston. Ils 1st ed. gilt cloth. VG. T1. $30.00

DU SABLON, Leclerc. *Nos Fleurs, Plantes Utiles et Nuisibles.* 1890. Paris. 16 pls. 128 p. gilt red cloth. VG. A3. $250.00

DU VALL, L. *AR: Colony & State.* 1973. Rose Pub. 264 p. EX. M2. $3.00

DUANE, Diane. *So You Want To Be a Wizard.* 1983. Delacorte. 1st ed. dj. VG. P1. $15.00

DUBE, J.P. *Lets Save Our Salmon.* 1972. Canada. private print. 1/850. slipcase. M2. $80.00

DUBKIN, L. *White Lady.* 1952. Putnam. 165 p. dj. EX. M2. $10.00

DUBOIS, Gaylord. *George O'Brien & the Hooded Riders.* 1940. Whitman. Big Little Book. VG. P1. $13.75

DUBOIS, Gaylord. *Tim McCoy & Sandy Gulch Stampede.* 1939. Whitman. Big Little Book. P1. $9.25

DUBUS, Andre. *Blessings.* 1987. Elmwood. 1st ed. 1/60. sgn/#d. dj. VG. $150.00

DUBUS, Andre. *Lieutenant.* 1967. NY. 1st ed. dj. EX. $65.00

DUBUS, Andre. *Separate Flights.* 1975. Boston. 1st ed. dj. VG. $40.00

DUBY, Georges. *History of Private Life II: Revelation of Medieval World.* 1988. Harvard. Trans Goldhammer. 1st Eng ed. C1. $27.00

DUCHARTRE, P.L. *Italian Comedy.* 1929. NY. 1st ed. 331 p. VG. B2. $35.00

DUCKER, J.H. *Men of the Steel Rails.* 1983. 220 p. $17.50

DUCOS DU HAURON, Alcide. *La Triplice Photographique des Couleures et L'Imprimerie...* 1897. Paris. Gauthier Villars. 488 p. wraps. $175.00

DUDEN, G. *Report on Journey to W States of N America & a Stay in MO...* 1980. MO Hist Soc. map. 327 p. dj. EX. M2. $24.00

DUELLMAN, W.E. *S American Herpetofauna: Its Origin, Evolution & Dispersal.* 1979. KS U. Ils. maps. 485 p. EX. M2. $30.00

DUFF, E.G. *Printers, Stationers & Bookbinders of Westminster & London.* 1906. Cambridge. 1st ed. pls. $75.00

DUFF, Grant. *Notes From a Diary, 1889-1891.* 1901. London. Murray. 2 vols. VG. $60.00

DUFF, W.A. *History of N Central OH.* 1931. Topeka/Indianapolis. 3 vols. G. T5. $95.00

DUFFUS, R.L. *Santa Fe Trail.* 1934. NY. Ils. 283 p. dj. K1. $18.50

DUFFUS, R.L. *Santa Fe Trail.* 1936. Tudor. Ils. 283 p. VG. M2. $17.00

DUFFUS, R.L. *Williamstown Branch.* 1958. NY. Norton. 252 p. dj. G. $10.00

DUFFY, Maureen. *Erotic World of Faery.* 1972. 1st Eng ed. sgn. dj. VG. C1. $37.50

DUFFY, Maureen. *Erotic World of Faery.* 1980. 1st pb ed. VG. scarce. C1. $5.00

DUFFY, Warden. *88 Men & 2 Women (90 San Quentin Executions).* 1962. NY. 1st ed. dj. VG. B2. $15.00

DUFFY. *European Swords & Daggers in Tower of London.* 1974. London. dj. EX. $25.00

DUFFY. *Selections From By-the-Way.* 1936. Grabhorn. 1/250. VG. $40.00

DUFOUR, C.L. *Nine Men in Gray.* 1963. Doubleday. 1st ed. dj. EX. $30.00

DUFRESNE, F. *AK Animals & Fishes.* 1955. Binfords Mort. Ils Hines. 2nd ed. dj. EX. M2. $20.00

DUFRESNE, F. *No Room for Bears.* 1965. Holt Rinehart. Ils. 252 p. dj. EX. M2. $14.00

DUGAN, J. *Ploesti.* 1962. NY. 2nd ed. dj. VG. B2. $30.00

DUGAN, J. *World Beneath the Sea.* 1967. Nat Geog Soc. Ils. 204 p. dj. M2. $9.00

DUGANNE, A.J.H. *Fighting Quakers: True Story of War for Our Union.* 1866. NY. 1st ed. $35.00

DUGGAN, Alfred. *Cunning of a Dove.* 1st Am ed. xl. C1. $7.00

DUGGAN, Alfred. *Lady for Ransom.* 1969. NY. dj. VG. C1. $9.50

DUGMORE, A.R. *Romance of Beaver.* c 1920. Phil. Lippincott. Ils. 224 p. A3. $50.00

DUKE, Donald. *Night Train.* 1961. Ils. photos. 127 p. $30.00

DUKE. *Henry Duke, Counselor: His Descendants & Connections.* 1949. orig bdg. VG. B1. $25.00

DULAC, Edmund. *Dulac's Fairy Book.* nd. NY/London/Toronto. VG. $75.00

DULAC, Edmund. *Edmund Dulac's Picture Book for the Red Cross.* 1915. London. pls. 4to. VG. $55.00

DULAC, Edmund. *Fairy Garland Being Fairy Tales From the Old French.* 1929. NY. 1st Am ed. VG. J2. $85.00

DULAC, Edmund. *Novels of Anne, Charlotte & Emily Bronte.* 1922. London. 12mo. 6 vols. VG. $275.00

DULAC, Edmund. *Rubaiyat of Omar Khayyam.* nd. London/NY. Trans Fitzgerald. 4to. J2. $200.00

DULAC, Edmund. *Rubaiyat of Omar Khayyam.* 1934. NY. Ils. VG. $35.00

DULAC, Edmund. *Sindbad der Seefahrer. Die Geschichte der Prinzessin...* nd. Potsdam. 1st German ed. 4to. VG. scarce. $80.00

DULLES, Foster. *Lowered Boats: Chronicle of American Whaling.* 1933. Harcourt. 1st ed. G. J2. $15.00

DUMAS, Alexandre. *Celebrated Crimes Vol. 5.* 1910. Collier. VG. P1. $20.00

DUMAS, Alexandre. *Chicot the Jester.* nd. Collins. leather bdg. VG. P1. $20.00

DUMAS, Alexandre. *Man in the Iron Mask.* nd. Burt. P1. $4.75

DUMAS, Alexandre. *Man in the Iron Mask.* nd. Collins. leather bdg. VG. P1. $20.00

DUMAS, Alexandre. *Queen's Necklace.* nd. Collins. leather bdg. EX. P1. $20.00

DUMAS, Alexandre. *Taking the Bastille.* nd. Oxford Soc. leather bdg. VG. P1. $20.00

DUMESNIL, Rene. *Histoire Illustree de la Medecine.* 1935. Paris. Ils 1st ed. 4to. $90.00

DUMESNIL, Rene. *Histoire Illustree du Theatre Lyrique.* 1953. Paris. Ils. 240 p. wraps. VG. T5. $12.50

DUMKE, R.T. *Habitat Development for Quail on Private Lands in WI.* 1982. WI Fish/Game. 46 p. M2. $5.00

DUMOND, A.N. *Life of a Book Agent.* 1892. St. Louis. $60.00

DUMONT, Frank. *Burnt Cork; or, Amature Minstrel.* 1881. NY. Wehman. 16mo. 113 p. wraps. VG. $40.00

DUMONT & GNUDI. *Gothic Painting.* 1954. Geneva/NY. Skira. 110 pls. 216 p. dj. D2. $65.00

DUNBAR, G.S. *Historical Geography of the NC Outer Banks.* 1958. LA U. Ils. maps. 234 p. M2. $14.00

DUNBAR, Janet. *J.M. Barrie: Man Behind the Image.* 1970. Boston. 1st ed. 413 p. dj. EX. $17.00

DUNBAR, M.J. *Ecological Development in Polar Regions.* 1968. Prentice Hall. Ils 1st ed. 119 p. dj. EX. M2. $13.00

DUNBAR, P.L. *Li'l Gal.* 1904. NY. Ils Miner. 1st ed. VG. $55.00

DUNBAR, P.L. *Poems of Cabin & Field.* 1901. NY. Ils. 125 p. VG. B1. $75.00

DUNBAR, P.L. *Poems of Cabin & Field.* 1904. NY. Ils Hampton Camera Club. VG. $40.00

DUNBAR, P.L. *When Malindy Sings.* 1903. Dodd Mead. 1st ed. VG. $75.00

DUNBAR, P.L. *When Malindy Sings.* 1903. NY. Ils Hampton Camera Club. G. $35.00

DUNBAR, S. *History of Travel in America.* 1937. 2nd print. dj. VG. $25.00

DUNBAR, S. *History of Travel.* 1915. Indianapolis. 1st ed. 4 vols. VG. $65.00

DUNCAN, A. *Art Nouveau & Art Deco Lighting.* 1978. NY. 1st ed. dj. $45.00

DUNCAN, Andrew. *Practical Surveyor's Guide.* 1902. Phil. Ils. 12mo. 214 p. $15 00

DUNCAN, D.D. *Good-Bye Picasso.* 1974. NY. 1st ed. dj. VG. B2. $95.00

DUNCAN, D.D. *Picasso's Picassos.* 1961. NY. 1st ed. folio. dj. M. $85.00

DUNCAN, D.D. *Picasso's Picassos.* 1964. Harper. dj. EX. $45.00

DUNCAN, D.D. *This Is War!* 1951. NY. 1st ed. photos. 315 p. dj. T5. $145.00

DUNCAN, D.D. *War Without Heroes.* 1970. NY. 1st ed. photos. 252 p. dj. VG. T5. $115.00

DUNCAN, D.D. *Yankee Nomad.* 1966. Harper Row. 1st ed. VG. $28.00

DUNCAN, D.D. *Yankee Nomad.* 1966. NY. 1st ed. 500 photos. dj. EX. $35.00

DUNCAN, D.D. *Yankee Nomad.* 1967. Harper Row. 2nd ed. dj. EX. $25.00

DUNCAN, D.D. *Yankee Nomad.* 1967. Harper Row. 2nd ed. VG. E2. $15.00

DUNCAN, L.C. *Medical Men in American Revolution, 1775-1783.* 1931. Carlisle Barracks. wraps. EX. $140.00

DUNCAN, Marion. *Mountain of Silver Snow.* 1929. Powell White. dj. G. $30.00

DUNCAN, Robert. *As Testimony.* 1964. White Rabbit. inscr. wraps. EX. $45.00

DUNCAN, Robert. *As Testimony.* 1964. White Rabbit. wraps. EX. $30.00

DUNCAN, Robert. *Five Songs.* 1981. La Jolla. 1/100. sgn/#d. wraps. EX. $50.00

DUNCAN, Robert. *Ground Work Before the War.* 1984. New Directions. 1/150. sgn/#d. slipcase. EX. $85.00

DUNCAN, Robert. *Medea at Dolchis the Maiden Head.* 1965. Oyez. 1/500. inscr. EX. $50.00

DUNCAN, Robert. *Names of People.* 1968. Black Sparrow. Ils Jess. 1/250. sgns. $100.00

DUNCAN, Robert. *Selected Poems.* 1959. San Francsico. 1st ed. wraps. VG. $30.00

DUNCAN, Robert. *Truth & Life of Myth.* 1968. House of Books. 1/300. sgn/#d. EX. $50.00

DUNCAN, Robert. *Veil, Turbine, Cord & Bird.* 1979. Jordan Davies. 1/200. sgn/#d. wraps. EX. $50.00

DUNCAN, W.H. & M.B. *Trees of the SE US.* 1988. GA U. Ils. maps. dj. M. M2. $19.00

DUNCAN, Winifred. *Webs in the Wind.* 1949. Ronald. VG. $35.00

DUNCAN & SPICER. *Medieval Scenes 1950 & 1959.* 1978. Kent State. 1/624. inscr. EX. $45.00

DUNCAN. *Self-Portrait of USA.* EX. S2. $35.00

DUNCAN. *65 Drawings.* 1970. Black Sparrow. 1/300. sgn/#d. slipcase. EX. $125.00

DUNDAS, David. *Military Movements, Chiefly Applied to Infantry...* 1795. London. 2nd ed. EX. J4. $45.00

DUNGLISON, Robley. *Human Health.* 1844. Phil. New ed. leather. $75.00

DUNLAP, O.E. *Understanding Television: What It Is & How It Works.* 1948. NY. VG. $20.00

DUNLAP, R.F. *Gunsmithing.* 1950. Georgetown. Ils 1st ed. 714 p. VG. B2. $50.00

DUNLEAVY, S. *Elvis: What Happened?* 1977. NY. 1st ed. 392 p. wraps. $35.00

DUNLOP, J. *Anatomical Diagrams for Use of Art Students.* nd. NY. VG. $22.00

DUNLOP, W.S. *Lee's Sharpshooters.* 1899. 1st AR ed. orig red cloth. G. R1. $375.00

DUNN, Eliza. *Rugs in Their Native Land.* 1916. NY. 1st ed. EX. $36.00

DUNN, J.P. *Massacres of the Mountains: History of Indian Wars...* 1958. Archer House. reprint of 1886 ed. dj. VG. M2. $30.00

DUNN, J.T. *St. Croix: Midwest Border River.* 1965. NY. 1st ed. sgn. dj. VG. $30.00

DUNN, Samuel. *Government Ownership of Railways.* 1913. NY. Appleton. 12mo. $12.00

DUNNAHOO, Terry. *Nellie Bly, a Portrait.* nd. Chicago. Ils. 168 p. dj. VG. T5. $6.50

DUNNE, P. *Hawks in Flight.* 1988. Houghton. Ils 1st ed. 254 p. dj. EX. M2. $27.00

DUNNING, John. *Portraits of Tropical Birds.* 1970. Ils. dj. EX. E2. $18.00

DUNNING, W.A. *Essays on Civil War & Reconstruction.* 1904. NY. 397 p. VG. $20.00

DUNSANY, Lord. *Book of Wonder.* c 1930. Boston. Ils. $22.50

DUNSANY, Lord. *Book of Wonder.* 1972. Books for Lib Pr. P1. $7.50

DUNSANY, Lord. *Fourth Book of Jorkens.* 1948. Arkham House. 1st ed. dj. VG. P1. $40.00

DUNSANY, Lord. *King of Elfland's Daughter.* 1977. pb. EX. C1. $3.50

DUNSANY, Lord. *Last Book of Wonder.* 1916. Boston. Ils 1st ed. VG. B2. $37.50

DUNSANY, Lord. *Plays Near & Far.* 1922. Putnam. 1/500. VG. $45.00

DUNSANY, Lord. *Seven Modern Comedies.* 1929. NY. 1st ed. dj. VG. $20.00

DUNSANY, Lord. *Sword of Welleran.* 1908. London. Ils. $45.00

DUNSANY, Lord. *Sword of Welleran.* 1954. Devin Adair. 1st ed. dj. VG. P1. $35.00

DUNSANY, Lord. *Tales of Three Hemispheres.* 1976. Owlswick. dj. EX. P1. $20.00

DUNSANY, Lord. *Tales of War.* 1918. Talbot Pr. 1st ed. VG. P1. $75.00

DUNSCOMB, G.L. *Century of S Pacific Steam Locomotives, 1862-1962.* 1963. Ils. 18 maps. 496 p. $75.00

DUNSDORFS, Edgars. *Australian Wheat-Growing Industry: 1788-1848.* 1956. Melbourne. 1st ed. dj. VG. J2. $20.00

DUNSHEE, K.H. *As You Pass By.* 1952. Hastings. VG. $12.00

DUNSHEE, Kenneth. *Enjine! Enjine!* Sept., 1939. Ils. 4to wraps. EX. scarce. $20.00

DUNTHORNE, Gordon. *Flower & Fruit Prints of 18th & Early 19th Centuries.* 1938. GPO. VG. $335.00

DUNTHORNE, Gordon. *Flower & Fruit Prints of 18th & Early 19th Centuries.* 1970. Da Capo. reprint. folio. dj. EX. $125.00

DUPLESSIS, George. *Histoire de la Gravure en France.* 1861. Paris. 1st ed. wraps. M. $75.00

DUPUY, R.E. *St. Vith: Lion in the Way, 106th Infantry Division in WWII.* 1949. WA. 1st ed. photos. maps. 252 p. xl. G. T5. $37.50

DUPUY & DUPUY. *Compact History of Civil War.* 1960. NY. 40 maps. dj. EX. $25.00

DURAND, James. *Able Seaman of 1812.* 1926. New Haven. reprint of 1817 ed. dj. T5. $25.00

DURANT, Will. *Our Oriental Heritage.* 1935. NY. 1st ed. sgn. dj. VG. B2. $60.00

DURAS, Marguerite. *Hiroshima Mon Amour.* 1960. Paris. 1st ed. wraps. EX. P3. $25.00

DURAS, Marguerite. *War: A Memoir.* 1986. NY. 1st Am ed. dj. EX. $15.00

DURDEN, K. *Fine & Peaceful Kingdon.* 1975. Simon Schuster. Ils 1st ed. 159 p. dj. EX. M2. $8.00

DURDEN, K. *Gifts of an Eagle.* 1972. Simon Schuster. Ils. 160 p. VG. M2. $8.00

DURHAM, David. *Hounded Down.* nd. Detective Club. dj. VG. P1. $18.25

DURIE, Alistair. *Weird Tales.* 1979. Jupiter. dj. EX. P1. $20.00

DURKIN, J.T. *General Sherman's Son: Life of Thomas Ewing Sherman.* 1959. photos. 276 p. dj. EX. J4. $6.50

DURLING. *Catalog of 16th-C Books in National Library Medicine.* 1967. GPO. xl. VG. $40.00

DURRELL, G.M. *Bafut Beagles.* 1954. Viking. Ils 1st ed. 238 p. VG. M2. $14.00

DURRELL, G.M. *Fauna & Family: Account of Durrell Family of Corfu.* 1978. Simon Schuster. 219 p. dj. EX. M2. $5.00

DURRELL, G.M. *Golden Bats & Pink Pigeons.* 1977. Simon Schuster. Ils 1st ed. 190 p. dj. EX. M2. $15.00

DURRELL, G.M. *Rosy Is My Relative.* 1968. NY. 1st Am ed. 239 p. dj. VG. T5. $17.50

DURRELL, G.M. *Two in the Bush.* 1966. Viking. Ils. 256 p. dj. VG. M2. $9.00

DURRELL, G.M. *Whispering Land.* 1961. London. 1st ed. dj. EX. $30.00

DURRELL, G.M. *Whispering Land.* 1962. Viking. Ils 1st ed. dj. VG. M2. $12.00

DURRELL, Lawrence. *Black Book.* 1938. Paris. Obelisk. 1st ed. black morocco. wraps. T5. $750.00

DURRELL, Lawrence. *Clea.* 1st Am ed. dj. VG. B7. $20.00

DURRELL, Lawrence. *Esprit de Corps.* c 1957. Dutton. 1st ed. G. $20.00

DURRELL, Lawrence. *Tunc.* 1968. NY. 1st ed. sgn. dj. VG. $25.00

DUSENBERRY, W.H. *Mexican Mesta.* 1963. Urbana, IL. dj. EX. $35.00

DUTTON, C.E. *Report on Geology of High Plateaus of UT.* 1880. WA. GPO. Ils. 307 p. very scarce. A3. $180.00

DUTTON, Charles J. *Streaked With Crimson.* nd. Collier. VG. P1. $10.00

DUVEEN, J.H. *Rise of the House of Duveen.* 1957. Knopf. 1st Am ed. EX. $60.00

DUYCKINCK & DUYKIN. *Encyclopedia of American Literature.* 1965. Gale Research. xl. VG. P1. $20.00

DVORKIN, David. *Budspy.* 1987. Watts. 1st ed. dj. EX. P1. $17.95

DWIGGINS, Don. *They Flew the Bendix Race.* 1965. Ils 1st ed. 198 p. dj. EX. $20.00

DWIGGINS, W.A. *Check List of Exhibition of Work of W.A. Dwiggins.* 1949. Boston. Ltd ed. 1/350. wraps. EX. $27.00

DWIGGINS, W.A. *Layout in Advertising.* 1928. NY. Ils 1st ed. VG. $25.00

DWIGHT, Nathaniel. *Short But Comprehensive System of Geography of World...* 1795. Hartford. Hudson Goswin. 2nd ed. 218 p. G. $200.00

DWIGHT, T. *Travels in New England & NY. Vol. 1.* 1821. New Haven. 1st ed. 8vo. 524 p. xl. G2. $32.00

DWYER, K.R. *Shattered.* 1973. Random House. 2nd print. dj. EX. $25.00

DYE, J.S. *History of Plots & Crimes of Great Conspiracy...* 1866. NY. poor. $15.00

DYER, K.G. *Turkey Trott & the Black Santa.* 1942. Platt Munk. Ils Robson. 1st ed. dj. EX. $20.00

DYER & FRASER. *Rocking Chair: American Institution.* 1928. NY. 1st ed. 50 photos. G. B2. $32.50

DYKE & DAVIDOFF. *Roentgen Treatment of Diseases of Nervous System.* 1942. Phil. Lea Febiger. 1st ed. VG. $95.00

DYKES, J.C. *Billy the Kid: Bibliography of a Legend.* 1952. Albuquerque. 1st ed. 2nd print. with sgn card. $55.00

DYKSTRA, Robert. *Cattle Towns.* 1968. Knopf. 1st ed. dj. M. $28.00

DYLAN, Bob. *Tarantula.* 1971. NY. 1st ed. dj. VG. $15.00

DYOTT, D.M. *Man Hunting in the Jungle.* 1930. NY. G. $25.00

EADE, Charles. *Churchill by His Contempories.* 1953. Hutchinson. 1st ed. dark blue cloth. dj. D1. $35.00

EAGAN, P. *Life of an Actor.* 1892. London. Ils Lane. 257 p. G. $26.00

EAGER, Edward. *Half Magic.* 1954. NY. Voyager. pb. juvenile. VG. C1. $14.00

EAKINS, Thomas. *Family Album: Photographs by Thomas Eakins 1880-1890.* 1976. Phil. 35 photos. D2. $18.50

EARHART, Amelia. *Fun of It.* 1932. NY. later print. sgn. with record. T5. $395.00

EARHART, Amelia. *Last Flight.* 1937. NY. 229 p. $20.00

EARHART, Amelia. *20 Hours 40 Minutes.* nd. Grosset Dunlap. Ils. dj. VG. $25.00

EARL, L. *Crocodile Fever.* 1954. London. Collins. photos. 255 p. G. M2. $18.00

EARL, W.H. *Cacti of the SW.* 1973. AZ Desert Bot Garden. EX. M2. $7.00

EARLE, A.M. *Home Life in Colonial Days.* 1900. NY. 1st ed. G. $15.00

EARLE, A.M. *Home Life in Colonial Days.* 1910. NY. VG. $20.00

EARLE, A.M. *Sun Dials & Roses of Yesterday.* 1922. NY. VG. $20.00

EARLE, G.F. *History of 87th Mountain Infantry, Italy 1945.* 1945. np. photos. maps. 215 p. VG. T5. $75.00

EARLE, Helen L. *Biographical Sketches of American Artists.* 1912. Lansing. MI State Lib. very scarce. D2. $135.00

EARLE, Mrs. C.W. *More Potpourri From a Surrey Garden.* 1899. London. 1st ed. G. $20.00

EARLE & CASE. *Potpourri Mixed by Two.* 1914. London. 1st ed. green cloth. G. $22.00

EARNEST, A. *Art of the Decoy: American Bird Carving.* 1965. Bramhall. reprint. Ils. 4to. dj. EX. M2. $20.00

EAST, B. *Bears.* 1978. Crown. Ils. 269 p. dj. EX. M2. $15.00

EAST, B. *Danger! Explosive True Adventures of Great Outdoors.* 1970. Outdoor Life. 371 p. EX. M2. $7.00

EAST, B. *Narrow Escapes & Wilderness Adventures.* 1960. Outdoor Life. 321 p. G. M2. $6.00

EAST, Robert. *John Quincy Adams: Critical Years 1785-1794.* 1962. Bookman. 1st ed. dj. VG. J2. $12.50

EASTMAN, A.M. *Norton Anthology of Poetry.* 1970. NY. Stated 1st ed. blue bdg. VG. $12.50

EASTMAN, E.C. *Eastman's White Mountain Guide.* 1865. Boston. Lee Shepard. map. G. $20.00

EASTMAN, Edwin. *Seven & Nine Years Among Comanches & Apaches.* 1874. Jersey City. Ils. 309 p. A3. $70.00

EASTMAN, Elaine. *George Pratt: Red Man's Moses.* 1935. Norman. Ils. dj. EX. $65.00

EASTMAN, George. *George Eastman Centennial Issue, 1854-1954.* 1954. Rochester. 1st ed. wraps. VG. J2. $12.50

EASTMAN, M.H. *Index to Fairy Tales, Myths & Legends.* 1926. Boston. Faxton. 606 p. A3. $60.00

EASTMAN, Max. *Heroes I Have Known.* 1942. NY. 1st ed. dj. EX. $30.00

EASTMAN, Max. *Love & Revolution.* 1964. NY. 1st ed. dj. VG. B2. $25.00

EASTMAN KODAK COMPANY. *How To Make Good Movies.* 1940. NY. xl. VG. $35.00

EASTMAN KODAK COMPANY. *Kodak & Kodak Supplies.* 1907. VG. $35.00

EASTMAN. *Soul of the Indian.* 1911. Cambridge. red cloth. G. $10.00

EASTON, Carol. *Straight Ahead.* 1973. NY. 1st ed. 252 p. dj. VG. B2. $22.50

EASTON, Malcolm. *Artists & Writers in Paris.* 1964. London. Ils. dj. wraps. VG. $22.00

EASTON, Nat. *Bill for Damages.* 1958. Roy. xl. VG. P1. $4.75

EASTON, Nat. *Right for Trouble.* 1960. Boardman. 1st ed. dj. VG. P1. $7.00

EASTON & BROWN. *Lord of the Beasts: Saga of Buffalo Jones.* 1961. AZ U. Ils. 287 p. dj. EX. M2. $22.00

EATON, A.H. *Handicrafts of S Highlands.* 1937. NY. Ils. 370 p. G. T5. $22.50

EATON, Chester. *250th Anniversary of Ancient Town of Redding.* 1896. Redding. Loring Twombly. 4to. 398 p. fair. $35.00

EATON, Clement. *Civilization of Old S...* 1968. KY U. Intro Albert Kirwan. 307 p. $25.00

EATON, Clement. *History of S Confederacy.* 1954. NY. 1st ed. 351 p. dj. T5. $19.50

EATON, E.H. *Birds of NY.* 1910-1914. NY State Mus. 1st ed. 4to. VG. M2. $115.00

EATON, E.H. *Birds of NY.* 1914. Albany. 106 color pls. 2 vols. $40.00

EATON, Harold. *Poisoners of Women.* nd. Detective Club. dj. VG. P1. $18.25

EATON, W.P. *In Berkshire Fields.* 1926. Wilde. Ils Stone. 312 p. VG. M2. $18.00

EAYRS, J. *In Defense of Canada: From Great War to Great Depression.* c 1965. Toronto. dj. VG. $18.00

EBAN, Abba. *Civilizations & the Jews.* 1984. Heritage. 1st ed. dj. EX. $20.00

EBAN, Abba. *My Country: Story of Modern Israel.* 1972. NY. 1st ed. 1/300. sgn. boxed. M. $35.00

EBEREIN, H.D. *Practical Book of American Arts & Crafts.* 1916. Phil. 1st ed. EX. $29.00

EBERHART, Dikkon. *Paradise.* 1983. 1st ed. dj. M. C1. $7.50

EBERHART, Mignon G. *Bayou Road.* 1979. Random House. 1st ed. dj. VG. P1. $5.00

EBERHART, Mignon G. *Call After Midnight.* 1964. Random House. 1st ed. dj. VG. P1. $7.50

EBERHART, Mignon G. *Cases of Susan Dare.* 1935. Bodley Head. 1st ed. P1. $10.00

EBERHART, Mignon G. *Five Passengers From Lisbon.* 1946. Collins Crime. P1. $7.00

EBERHART, Mignon G. *Hangman's Whip.* nd. Book League Am. VG. P1. $10.00

EBERHART, Mignon G. *Hangman's Whip.* 1942. Triangle. VG. P1. $7.50

EBERHART, Mignon G. *House of Storm.* 1949. Random House. 1st ed. xl. P1. $5.50

EBERHART, Mignon G. *Man Next Door.* 1943. NY. 1st ed. dj. VG. B2. $15.00

EBERHART, Mignon G. *Man Next Door.* 1943. Random House. 1st ed. dj. xl. P1. $7.50

EBERHART, Mignon G. *While the Patient Slept.* 1933. Heinemann. 7th print. VG. P1. $9.25

EBERHART, Mignon G. *Wings of Fear.* nd. Collier. VG. P1. $7.50

EBERHART, Mignon G. *With This Ring.* nd. Grosset. dj. VG. P1. $8.00

EBERHART, Mignon G. *With This Ring.* 1941. Random House. 1st ed. P1. $12.50

EBERHART, Mignon G. *Witness at Large.* 1966. NY. 1st ed. 1st print. dj. T1. $20.00

EBERHART, Mignon G. *Witness at Large.* 1966. Random House. 1st ed. dj. P1. $10.00

EBERHART, Richard. *Poems to Poets.* 1974. Penamen Pr. 1st ed. presentation. sgn. dj. EX. $35.00

EBERHART, Richard. *Quarry.* 1964. NY. 1st ed. sgn. dj. VG. $25.00

EBERHART. *Ways of Light.* 1980. Oxford. sgn. dj. EX. $25.00

EBERLE, J. *Treatise of Materia Medica & Therapeutics. Vol. II.* 1825. Phil. 400 p. full calf. VG. $125.00

EBERLE, J. *Treatise on Practice of Medicine. Vol. II.* 1835. Phil. 479 p. full calf. VG. $100.00

EBERLEIN & RAMSDELL. *Small Manor Houses & Farmsteads in France.* 1926. Phil/London/NY. photos. 4to. G. $75.00

EBERT, Katherine. *Collecting American Pewter.* 1973. NY. Ils 1st ed. 163 p. dj. EX. $15.00

EBERT. *Ellgemeines Bibliographisches Lexikon.* 1821. Leipzig. 1st ed. 2 vols in 1. $200.00

ECCLESTON, James. *Introduction to English Antiquities.* 1847. London. gilt red calf. EX. $75.00

ECHAGUE, J.O. *Espana Mistica.* 1950. Bilbao. 2nd ed. dj. J2. $40.00

ECHARD, Margaret. *If This Be Treason.* 1944. Crime Club. 1st ed. dj. xl. P1. $7.00

ECKENRODE, H.J. *Jefferson Davis: President of the S.* 1923. 371 p. K1. $14.50

ECKENRODE, H.J. *Jefferson Davis: President of the S.* 1930. Macmillan. 371 p. dj. EX. M2. $15.00

ECKERT, A.W. *Conquerors.* 1970. Boston. 1st ed. dj. VG. B2. $22.50

ECKERT, A.W. *Great Ark.* 1963. 1st ed. dj. VG. B2. $27.50

ECKERT, A.W. *Owls of N America (N of Mexico).* 1987. Weathervane. Ils Karalus. 4to. dj. EX. M2. $35.00

ECKERT, A.W. *Owls of N America.* 1974. NY. 1st ed. 278 p. dj. VG. B2. $50.00

ECKERT, A.W. *Owls of N America.* 1974. NY. 1st trade ed. dj. M. $60.00

ECKERT, A.W. *Wading Birds of N America (N of Mexico).* 1987. Weathervane. Ils Karalus. 4to. dj. EX. M2. $35.00

ECKERT, A.W. *Wild Season.* 1967. Little Brown. Ils 1st ed. 244 p. dj. EX. M2. $9.00

ECKERT, A.W. *Wilderness Empire.* 1969. Boston. 1st ed. dj. EX. $15.00

ECKERT, A.W. *Wilderness War.* 1978. Boston. 1st ed. dj. VG. B2. $17.50

ECKHARDT. *Electronic Television.* 1936. Chicago. Ils 162 p. VG. C4. $65.00

ECKSTROM, F.H. *Old John Neptune & Other ME Indian Shamans.* 1945. Portland. Southworth Anthoensen. 1st ed. EX. $45.00

ECKSTROM, F.H. *Woodpeckers.* 1901. Houghton. Ils Fuertes. 131 p. VG. M2. $25.00

ECO, UMBERTO & ZORZOLI. *Pictorial History of Inventions.* 1962. Macmillan. dj. VG. $20.00

EDDISON, E.R. *Fish Dinner in Memison.* 1941. NY. Dutton. 1st Am ed. 1/998. dj. $90.00

EDDISON, E.R. *Mistress of Mistresses.* 1935. NY. Dutton. 1st Am ed. dj. $50.00

EDDY, A.J. *Ganton & Co.* 1908. McClurg. Ils Thomas Fogarty. 1st ed. $12.00

EDDY, J.W. *Hunting the AK Brown Bear.* 1930. Putnam. Standard 1st ed. 3 fld maps. $180.00

EDDY, M.B. *Poems.* 1910. Boston. 1st ed. 8vo. EX. $35.00

EDDY, M.B. *Science & Health With Key to Scriptures.* 1908. 32mo. 700 p. leather. EX. $30.00

EDE, H.S. *Savage Messiah.* 1931. NY. pls. xl. G. $20.00

EDEN, Guy. *Portrait of Churchill.* nd. (1946?) Hutchinson. 1st print. dj. VG. D1. $35.00

EDEN. *Dish of Apples.* 1921. London. Hodder. Ils Rackham. 1st ed. EX. $65.00

EDER, J.M. *Ausfuhrliches Handbuch der Photographie.* 1930. Knapp. Ils. diagrams. 595 p. wraps. $20.00

EDEY, M. *Cats of Africa.* 1970. Time Life. Ils Dominis. square 4to. 192 p. M2. $25.00

EDGAR, John. *History of Early Scottish Education.* 1893. James Thin. 1st ed. VG. J2. $20.00

EDGELL, G.H. *American Architecture of Today.* 1928. NY. Ils 1st ed. 8vo. 401 p. $35.00

EDGERLY, Beatrice. *From Hunter's Bow: History & Romance of Musical Instruments.* 1942. Putnam. 1st ed. dj. VG. J2. $15.00

EDGEWORTH, Maria. *Tales & Novels.* 1832. London. 1st Collected ed. 18 vols. VG. $250.00

EDGLEY, Leslie. *Judas Goat.* 1952. Crime Club. 1st ed. dj. VG. P1. $15.00

EDIDIN, Ben. *Rebuilding Palestine.* 1939. Behrman. Ils. maps. inscr. 264 p. VG. $28.00

EDLIN, H. *Atlas of Plant Life.* 1973. Day. Ils. 4to. dj. EX. M2. $8.00

EDMINSTER, F.C. *African Game Birds.* 1954. NY. Ils. 490 p. dj. VG. B2. $45.00

EDMINSTER, F.C. *American Game Birds of Field & Forest.* 1954. Castle. reprint. 4to. 490 p. dj. M2. $23.00

EDMINSTER, F.C. *Ruffed Grouse: Its Life Story, Ecology & Management.* 1947. Macmillan. 1st print. 385 p. EX. M2. $65.00

EDMONDS, George. *Facts & Falsehood Concerning the War on S, 1861-1865.* 1904. Memphis. 271 p. printed wraps. $125.00

EDMONDS, Harry. *Secret Voyage.* 1946. MacDonald. VG. P1. $7.00

EDMONDS, I.G. *Black Magic of Kings.* 1981. 197 p. dj. M. $18.00

EDMONDS, I.G. *Iron Monster Raid.* 1968. Whitman. VG. P1. $12.50

EDMONDS, I.G. *Wild Mountain Trail.* 1966. Whitman. P1. $4.50

EDMONDS, S.E. *Nurse & Spy.* 1865. Ils. 384 p. K1. $13.50

EDMONDS, Walter. *Musket & the Cross.* 1968. Boston. 1st ed. 514 p. dj. EX. $10.00

EDMONDS, Walter. *Young Ames.* 1942. Boston. 1st ed. dj. VG. B2. $25.00

EDMONDSON, W.T. *Fresh-Water Biology.* 1959. Wiley. Ils 2nd ed. dj. EX. M2. $35.00

EDNEY, E.B. *Water Relations of Terrestrial Arthropods.* 1957. Cambridge. Ils. 109 p. dj. EX. M2. $14.00

EDWARDS, A.B. *Pharoahs, Fellahs & Explorers.* 1891. VG. $45.00

EDWARDS, Agnes. *Cape Cod: New & Old.* 1918. Cambridge. Riverside. Ils Ruyl. fair. $12.00

EDWARDS, Agnes. *Old Coast Road From Boston & Plymouth.* 1920. Houghton. Ils Ruyl. G. $23.00

EDWARDS, Anne. *Road to Tara: Life of Margaret Mitchell.* 1983. NY. 1st ed. dj. EX. B2. $25.00

EDWARDS, Clinton. *Aboriginal Watercraft on Pacific Coast of S America.* 1965. CA U. 1st ed. 28 pls. 138 p. stiff wraps. J2. $15.00

EDWARDS, E.P. *Finding Birds in Mexico.* 1968. private print. Ils Revised ed. dj. EX. M2. $20.00

EDWARDS, Eleanor. *World Famous Great Mystery Stories.* 1960. Hart. VG. P1. $15.00

EDWARDS, G.C. *Legal Laughs, a Joke for Every Jury.* 1915. Clarkesville. Legal Pub. 2nd print. 416 p. $35.00

EDWARDS, G.W. *Alsace-Lorraine.* 1918. Phil. Ils 1st ed. 4to. VG. G1. $25.00

EDWARDS, G.W. *Book of Old English Ballads.* 1906. Ils. VG. C1. $14.00

EDWARDS, G.W. *Spain.* 1926. Phil. Ils 1st ed. 4to. VG. G1. $20.00

EDWARDS, G.W. *Vanished Halls & Cathedrals of France.* 1917. Phil. TEG. gilt blue cloth. VG. J2. $30.00

EDWARDS, G.W. *Vanished Towers & Chimes of Flanders.* 1916. Phil. Ils 1st ed. $25.00

EDWARDS, Harry. *Eneas Africanus.* 1930. TX Book Club. 1/300. 8vo. boxed. EX. J2. $40.00

EDWARDS, Harry. *Eneas Africanus.* 1940. Grosset Dunlap. 1st ed. map. dj. VG. $25.00

EDWARDS, Harry. *Guide to Spirit Healing.* 1950. London. $37.50

EDWARDS, Harry. *Mediumship of Jack Webber.* 1953. London. $35.00

EDWARDS, Jonathan. *History of Work of Redemption.* 1782. Boston. 296 p. leather. $125.00

EDWARDS, Jonathan. *Memoirs of Rev. David Brainerd.* 1822. New Haven. rebound. G. $75.00

EDWARDS, Jonathan. *Treatise Concerning Religious Affections in Three Parts.* 1794. Phil. 8vo. 351 p. M1. $47.50

EDWARDS, Jonathan. *Treatise on Religious Affections.* nd. NY. Am Tract Soc. 16mo. 276 p. M1. $22.50

EDWARDS, Leo. *Poppy Ott & the Galloping Snail.* nd. Grosset Dunlap. VG. P1. $5.00

EDWARDS, Lionel. *Beasts of the Chase.* 1950. London. 1/100. leather. EX. $165.00

EDWARDS, Ruth Dudley. *St. Valentine's Day Murders.* 1984. St. Martins. dj. VG. P1. $12.00

EDWARDS, Tyron. *World's Laconics: In Prose & Poetry.* 1860. NY. Dodd. $12.50

EDWARDS, W.B. *Story of Colt's Revolver.* 1953. Harrisburg. 4to. dj. VG. G1. $60.00

EDWARDS, W.S. *Into the Yukon.* 1909. Jennings Graham. 3rd ed. VG. $65.00

EDWARDS, William. *Civil War Guns.* 1962. Harrisburg. 1st ed. 438 p. dj. EX. $25.00

EDWARDS, William. *Through Scandanavia to Moscow.* 1906. Cincinnati. Clark. 1st ed. 237 p. EX. $22.50

EDWARDS & RATTRAY. *Whale Off: Story of American Shore Whaling.* 1956. NY. boxed. EX. $45.00

EDWARDS. *Football Days.* 1916. NY. Moffat Yard. 1st ed. VG. J3. $30.00

EFFINGER, George Alec. *Death in Florence.* 1978. Doubleday. 1st ed. xl. P1. $4.75

EFFINGER, George Alec. *Mixed Feelings.* 1974. Harper Row. 1st ed. dj. EX. P1. $15.00

EFFINGER, George Alec. *Nick of Time.* 1985. Doubleday. 1st ed. dj. EX. P1. $20.00

EFFINGER, George Alec. *Relatives.* 1973. Harper Row. 1st ed. dj. EX. P1. $15.00

EFFINGER, George Alec. *What Entropy Means to Me.* 1972. Doubleday. 1st ed. dj. EX. P1. $15.00

EFFINGER, George Alec. *When Gravity Fails.* 1987. Arbor House. 1st ed. dj. EX. P1. $16.95

EGAN, Lesley. *Blind Search.* nd. Book Club. dj. VG. P1. $4.00

EGAN, Lesley. *Dream Apart.* nd. Book Club. dj. VG. P1. $4.00

EGAN, Lesley. *Dream Apart.* 1978. Crime Club. 1st ed. dj. xl. P1. $5.00

EGAN, Lesley. *Hunters & the Hunted.* nd. Book Club. VG. P1. $3.00

EGAN, Lesley. *Hunters & the Hunted.* 1979. Doubleday. 1st ed. dj. xl. P1. $6.00

EGAN, Lesley. *Look Back on Death.* nd. Book Club. dj. VG. P1. $3.75

EGAN, Lesley. *Look Back on Death.* 1978. Doubleday. 1st ed. dj. xl. P1. $6.00

EGAN, Lesley. *Run to Evil.* 1963. Gollancz. 1st Eng ed. dj. EX. $12.00

EGAN, Lesley. *Serious Investigaton.* nd. Book Club. dj. VG. P1. $4.50

EGAN, Lesley. *Wine of Violence.* nd. Book Club. dj. VG. P1. $4.00

EGAN, M.F. *Everybody's St. Francis.* 1913. Century. Monvel. TEG. VG. $22.50

EGAN & KENNEDY. *Knights of Columbus in Peace & War.* 1920. New Haven. Ils. 2 vols. TEG. VG. $25.00

EGBERT, S. *Manual of Hygiene & Sanitation.* 1898. 1st ed. G. $5.00

EGER. *Danny & Fanny & Spot, the Fox-Terrier Hero.* 1939. Rand McNally. Ils. G. $15.00

EGERTON & SNELGROVE. *British Sporting & Animal Drawings, 1500-1850.* 1978. London. 21 pls. lg 4to. dj. EX. $50.00

EGERTON. *British Sporting & Animal Paintings, 1655-1867.* 1978. London. Ils. 4to. 382 p. dj. EX. $95.00

EGGERT, J.H. *Technischer Grundriss der Photographie...* 1931. Berlin. Ils. 53 p. printed wraps. $20.00

EGGLESTON, Edward. *Christ in Art.* 1875. NY. Ford. 100 pls. gilt leather. $55.00

EGGLESTON, Edward. *Circuit Rider.* 1874. NY. 1st ed. VG. B2. $22.50

EGGLESTON, Edward. *Hoosier Schoolboy.* c 1882-1886. Scribner. $12.00

EGGLESTON, Edward. *Hoosier Schoolmaster.* 1871. NY. 1st ed. G. $50.00

EGGLESTON, Edward. *Hoosier Schoolmaster.* 1871. NY. 1st ed. 2nd state. VG. $45.00

EGGLESTON, William. *William Eggleston's Guide.* 1976. NY. MOMA. 94 photos. oblong 4to. 110 p. $45.00

EGLETON, Clive. *Piece of Resistance.* 1970. Hodder Stoughton. VG. P1. $4.75

EGLINTON, J.Z. *Greek Love.* 1964. NY. 1st ed. dj. VG. J2. $15.00

EHLE, J. *Road.* 1967. NY. 1st ed. dj. VG. B2. $32.50

EHRLICH, Max. *Big Eye.* nd. Book Club. dj. VG. P1. $2.75

EHRLICH, Max. *Big Eye.* 1949. Doubleday. 1st ed. green cloth. dj. $40.00

EHRLICH, Max. *Reincarnation of Peter Proud.* nd. Book Club. dj. VG. P1. $3.75

EHWA, Carl. *Book of Pipes & Tobacco.* 1974. NY. 1st ed. dj. VG. $20.00

EICHELBERGER, R.L. *Our Jungle Road to Tokyo.* 1950. NY. 1st ed. 306 p. T5. $25.00

EICHENBERG, Fritz. *Art of the Print: Masterpieces, History, Techniques.* 1976. NY. Abrams. Ils. 611 p. dj. D2. $125.00

EICHHOFF, F. *Poesie Heroique des Indiens.* 1860. Paris. $75.00

EICHLER, Alfred. *Death of an Ad Man.* 1954. Abelard Schuman. dj. VG. P1. $9.25

EICHLER, Alfred. *Election by Murder.* 1947. Lantern Pr. xl. P1. $5.00

EICHLER, Lillian. *Customs of Mankind.* 1925. NY. 753 p. G. $12.00

EIMERL & DE VORE. *Primates.* 1977. Time Life. Ils Revised ed. 4to. 200 p. VG. M2. $7.00

EINARSEN, Arthur. *Pronghorn Antelope.* 1948. WA. VG. $25.00

EINSTEIN, Albert. *L'Ether et la Theorie de la Relativite.* 1921. Paris. Gauthier Villars. 1st ed. wraps. $125.00

EINSTEIN, Albert. *Out of My Later Years.* 1950. Philosophical Lib. 1st print. dj. $50.00

EINSTEIN, Albert. *Relativity.* 1921. Holt. 1st Am ed. VG. J2. $65.00

EISELEY, Loren. *Darwin & Mysterious Mr. X.* 1979. NY. 1st ed. dj. VG. B2. $17.50

EISEN, G. *Great Chalice of Antioch.* 1923. NY. 60 pls. folio. 2 vols. TEG. EX. J2. $300.00

EISEN, G. *Portraits of WA.* 1932. NY. 1/300. sgn. 3 vols. slipcase. EX. $300.00

EISENBERG, J.F. *Comparative Study in Rodent Ethology.* 1967. US Nat Mus. 49 p. M2. $3.00

EISENBERG, Larry. *Best-Laid Schemes.* 1971. Macmillan. 1st ed. dj. EX. P1. $9.25

EISENHOWER, D.D. *At Ease.* 1967. Doubleday. EX. $7.50

EISENHOWER, D.D. *Crusade in Europe.* 1941. Doubleday. photos. maps. G. $20.00

EISENHOWER, D.D. *Crusade in Europe.* 1948. Garden City. Ils 1st trade ed. 559 p. dj. G. T5. $25.00

EISENHOWER, D.D. *Crusade in Europe.* 1949. Ltd ed. 1/1401. sgn/#d. TEG. plastic dj. EX. $45.00

EISENHOWER, D.D. *Peace With Justice.* 1961. NY. 273 p. dj. $8.00

EISENHOWER & COOKE. *Military Churchill.* 1970. Norton. 1st ed. black cloth. dj. VG. D1. $25.00

EISENSCHIML, Otto. *Why the Civil War?* 1958. Bobbs Merril. 1st ed. 208 p. dj. VG. M2. $10.00

EISENSCHIML, Otto. *Why Was Lincoln Murdered?* 1937. Boston. 1st ed. dj. B2. $35.00

EISENSCHIML & LONG. *As Luck Would Have It.* 1948. Indianapolis. Ils 1st ed. 258 p. dj. G. T5. $37.50

EISENSCHIML & NEWMAN. *American Iliad: Epic Story of Civil War by Eyewitnesses.* 1947. Bobbs Merrill. Ils 1st ed. 720 p. VG. M2. $14.00

EISENSCHIML & NEWMAN. *American Iliad: Epic Story of Civil War by Eyewitnesses.* 1947. Bobbs Merrill. Ltd 1st ed. dj. EX. $65.00

EISENSCHIML & NEWMAN. *Civil War: American Iliad As Told by Those Who Lived It.* 1959. 43 maps. 719 p. VG. J4. $5.00

EISENSTADT, B.Z. *Otzer Hatemunot.* 1909. NY. photos. $400.00

EISENSTAEDT, Alfred. *Witness to Our Time.* 1966. NY. 1st ed. pub presentation. 343 p. dj. T5. $45.00

EISENSTAEDT. *Winbleton.* 1972. 1st ed. VG. S2. $30.00

EISERER, L. *American Robin: Backyard Institution.* 1976. Nelson Hall. photos. 175 p. dj. EX. M2. $11.00

EISLER, Colin. *Seeing Hand: Treasury of Great Master Drawings.* 1975. Harper Row. Ils 132 pls. D2. $110.00

EISLER, Steven. *Space Wars, Worlds & Weapons.* 1979. Crescent. dj. EX. P1. $6.00

EISNER & WILSON. *Animal Behavior.* 1975. Freeman. Ils 4to. 339 p. M2. $10.00

EKLUND, Gordon. *Beyond the Resurrection.* 1973. Doubleday. 1st ed. dj. EX. $20.00

EKLUND, Gordon. *Grayspace Beast.* 1976. Doubleday. 1st ed. dj. EX. P1. $9.25

ELAM, Richard M. *Teen-Age SF Stories.* nd. Grosset Dunlap. P1. $7.00

ELAM, Richard M. *Young Readers' SF Stories.* nd. Grosset Dunlap. dj. P1. $15.00

ELDER, Art. *Blue Streak & Dr. Medusa.* nd. Whitman. dj. VG. P1. $9.25

ELDER, Joseph. *Eros in Orbit.* 1973. Trident. 1st ed. dj. VG. P1. $10.00

ELDER, Michael. *Oil-Seeker.* 1977. Readers Union Book Club. P1. $5.00

ELDER, William. *Biography of Elisha Kent Kane.* 1858. Phil. G. $65.00

ELDREDGE, Z.S. *March of Portola & the Discovery of Bay of San Francisco.* 1909. San Francisco. Ils. 71 p. A3. $60.00

ELDRIDGE, Eleanor. *Memoirs of Eleanor Eldridge.* 1842. Providence. Albro. 128 p. orig bdg. scarce. $200.00

ELGIN, Suzatte Haden. *Star-Anchored, Star-Angered.* 1979. Doubleday. 1st ed. dj. EX. P1. $15.00

ELGIN, Suzette Haden. *And Then There'll Be Fireworks.* 1981. Doubleday. 1st ed. dj. xl. P1. $5.00

ELGIN, Suzette Haden. *Grand Jubilee.* 1981. Doubleday. 1st ed. dj. VG. P1. $11.50

ELGIN, Suzette Haden. *Grand Jubilee.* 1981. Doubleday. 1st ed. dj. xl. P1. $5.00

ELGIN, Suzette Haden. *Twelve Fair Kingdoms.* 1981. Doubleday. 1st ed. dj. EX. P1. $15.00

ELI LILLY COMPANY. *De Re Medicina.* 1938. Indianapolis. EX. $20.00

ELIADE, Mircea. *Myth of the Eternal Return.* 1954. NY. Bollingen. 1st ed. dj. EX. $35.00

ELIAS, R.H. *Letters of Theodore Dreiser.* 1969. Phil. 3 vols. slipcase. VG. $45.00

ELIGOULASHWILY, Nathan. *Flight of the Clan, Diary of 1865...* 1954. Atlanta. 14 p. printed wraps. $27.50

ELIOT, Charles. *Landscape Architect.* 1903. Boston. Ils. fld maps. 770 p. $75.00

ELIOT, George. *Scenes of Clerical Life.* 1859. Leipzig. Tauschnitz. 2 vols. VG. $45.00

ELIOT, George. *Works of George Eliot.* 1893. Estes Lauriat. Ltd ed. 1/1000. 24 vols. TEG. EX. $295.00

ELIOT, John. *Biographical Dictionary 1st Settlers...New England.* 1809. Salem/Boston. 8vo. 511 p. rebound. VG. $80.00

ELIOT, Marc. *Death of a Rebel, Starring Phil Ochs.* 1979. Garden City. Ils 1st ed. pb. VG. $30.00

ELIOT, T.S. *Anabasis.* 1st ed. dj. VG. B7. $25.00

ELIOT, T.S. *Burnt Norton.* 1941. London. Faber. 1st ed. tall 8vo. wraps. EX. $95.00

ELIOT, T.S. *Cocktail Party.* 1950. London. 1st ed. dj. M. $30.00

ELIOT, T.S. *Confidential Clerk: A Play.* 1954. London. 1st ed. dj. M. $40.00

ELIOT, T.S. *Cultivation of Christmas Trees.* nd. Faber. Ils David Jones. EX. $30.00

ELIOT, T.S. *For Lancelot Andrews.* 1928. London. Faber Gwyer. 1st ed. 143 p. $50.00

ELIOT, T.S. *Four Quartets.* 1944. Harcourt. 1st ed. 2nd imp. dj. G. $50.00

ELIOT, T.S. *Murder in the Cathedral.* 1935. NY. Harcourt. 2nd ed. $40.00

ELIOT, T.S. *Old Possum's Book of Practical Cats.* 1939. Faber. Ils Bentley. 5th imp. dj. VG. $50.00

ELIOT, T.S. *Sweeney Agonistes.* 1932. London. 1st ed. dj. EX. $125.00

ELIOT & GILLEY. *ME Farmer & Fisherman.* 1904. Am Unitarian Assn. presentation. $50.00

ELISOFON, Eliot. *Color Photography.* 1961. Viking. 1st ed. dj. VG. $30.00

ELISOFON, Eliot. *Nile.* 1964. Viking. VG. $30.00

ELKIN, Stanley. *Stanley Elkin's Greatest Hits.* 1980. NY. 1st ed. dj. VG. $20.00

ELKINGTON, E.W. *Savage S Seas.* 1907. Black. Ils. 211 p. VG. M2. $16.00

ELLENBERGER, H.E. *Discovery of the Unconscious.* 1970. NY. 2nd ed. dj. EX. $20.00

ELLET, E.F. *New Cyclopedia of Domestic Economy & Practical Housekeeper.* 1872. Norwich. Ils. 8 vols. $30.00

ELLIN, Stanley. *Bind.* 1970. Random House. 1st ed. VG. P1. $10.00

ELLIN, Stanley. *Eighth Circle.* nd. Book Club. dj. VG. P1. $4.00

ELLIN, Stanley. *House of Cards.* 1967. MacDonald. 1st ed. dj. VG. P1. $12.50

ELLIN, Stanley. *Stronghold.* 1974. Random House. 1st ed. dj. VG. P1. $20.00

ELLIN, Stanley. *Winter After This Summer.* 1960. Random House. 1st ed. dj. VG. P1. $35.00

ELLING, Christian. *Rome: Biography of Her Architecture...to Thorvalsen.* 1975. Boulder. dj. EX. J2. $65.00

ELLINGTON, Duke. *Music Is My Mistress.* 1973. Doubleday. 1st ed. dj. VG. $27.00

ELLIOT, E.C. *Kemlo & the Gravity Rays.* 1956. Nelson. VG. P1. $10.00

ELLIOT, E.C. *Kemlo & the Martian Ghosts.* 1954. Nelson. dj. VG. P1. $15.00

ELLIOT, E.C. *Kemlo & the Zombie Men.* 1958. Nelson. 1st ed. dj. VG. P1. $20.00

ELLIOT, J.M. *Pulp Voices.* 1983. Borgo Pr. 1st ed. P1. $17.50

ELLIOTT, D.G. *Catalog of Collection of Mammals in Field Columbian Museum.* 1907. Field Mus. Ils. 694 p. rebound. M2. $60.00

ELLIS, Chamberlain. *Fighting Vehicles.* 1973. Hamlyn. 1st ed. 2nd imp. 4to. dj. EX. $15.00

ELLIS, E.S. *Young Gold Seekers of the Klondyke.* 1899. Phil. Ils. 311 p. VG. A3. $25.00

ELLIS, Elizabeth. *Barbara Winslow Rebel.* 1906. Dodd Mead. Ils John Rae. 1st ed. $12.00

ELLIS, Frank. *Canada's Flying Heritage.* 1961. Toronto. Ils. 4to. 398 p. dj. EX. $30.00

ELLIS, H.C. *Pioneer Life of the Firelands.* 1939. Norwalk, OH. 35 p. mimeographed. VG. T5. $12.50

ELLIS, Havelock. *Kanga Creedk: Australian Idyll.* 1938. Oriole Pr. Ils Sleigh/Ellis. dj. VG. $50.00

ELLIS, Havelock. *Studies in Psychology of Sex.* 1942. NY. 2 vols. $35.00

ELLIS, Havelock. *Study of British Genius.* 1904. Hurst. 1st ed. VG. J2. $17.50

ELLIS, John. *Sights & Secrets of the National Capital.* 1869. NY. VG. $35.00

ELLIS, K. *American Civil War.* 1971. Putnam. Ils. 128 p. dj. EX. M2. $5.00

ELLIS, Leo R. *Octopus Caper.* 1971. Whitman. VG. P1. $7.50

ELLIS, M. *Peg-Leg Pete.* 1973. Holt Rinehart. 169 p. dj. EX. M2. $5.00

ELLIS, M. *Wild Goose, Brother Goose.* 1970. Holt Rinehart. 159 p. dj. EX. M2. $6.00

ELLIS, M.D. *Dangerous Plants, Snakes, Arthropods & Marine Life of TX.* 1975. GPO. Ils. maps. 277 p. EX. M2. $35.00

ELLIS, Mel. *No Man for Murder.* 1973. Holt Rinehart Winston. dj. EX. P1. $7.50

ELLIS, W.D. *Bounty Lands.* 1952. Cleveland. 1st ed. 492 p. dj. VG. T5. $17.50

ELLIS, W.D. *Brooks Legend.* 1st ed. sgn. 467 p. dj. VG. T5. $17.50

ELLIS, W.D. *Cuyahoga.* 1966. Holt Rinehart. Ils 1st ed. maps. dj. xl. M2. $6.00

ELLIS, W.D. *Jonathan Blair: Bounty Lands' Lawyer.* 1954. Cleveland. 1st ed. sgn. 462 p. dj. VG. T5. $17.50

ELLIS, W.E. *Art & Philosophy of Jules de Gaultier.* 1928. Seattle. Chapbook. 16mo. wraps. $25.00

ELLIS, W.T. *Memories: My Seventy-Two Years in Romantic Co. of Yuba, CA.* 1939. Eugene, OR. Ils. inscr. 4to. dj. EX. $80.00

ELLIS & CUNNINGHAM. *Clarke of St. Vith: Sergeants' General.* 1974. Cleveland. Ils 1st ed. inscr Clarke. dj. T5. $45.00

ELLIS. *Is Objectivism a Religion?* 1968. Lyle Stuart. dj. VG. $20.00

ELLIS. *Lost in the Rockies.* 1898. Burt. Ils. G. $8.00

ELLISON, Harlan. *Again, Dangerous Visions.* nd. Book Club. VG. P1. $4.50

ELLISON, Harlan. *Again, Dangerous Visions.* 1972. NY. 1st ed. sgn. dj. EX. $100.00

ELLISON, Harlan. *Alone Against Tomorrow.* 1971. NY. Macmillan. 1st ed. sgn. dj. $30.00

ELLISON, Harlan. *Angry Candy.* 1988. Boston. AP. sgn. EX. $65.00

ELLISON, Harlan. *Angry Candy.* 1988. Boston. 1st ed. sgn. dj. EX. $40.00

ELLISON, Harlan. *Approaching Oblivion.* nd. Book Club. dj. VG. P1. $5.00

ELLISON, Harlan. *Approaching Oblivion.* 1974. Walker. sgn. dj. EX. P1. $100.00

ELLISON, Harlan. *City on the Edge of Forever.* 1977. Bantam. photos. EX. P1. $17.50

ELLISON, Harlan. *Dangerous Visions.* 1967. Doubleday. 1st ed. dj. VG. P1. $200.00

ELLISON, Harlan. *Doomsman.* 1972. Belmont/Tower. pb. VG. $35.00

ELLISON, Harlan. *Edge in My Voice.* 1985. Donning. 1st ed. dj. EX. P1. $15.00

ELLISON, Harlan. *From the Land of Fear.* 1967. NY. Belmont. 1st pb ed. EX. $15.00

ELLISON, Harlan. *Illustrated Harlan Ellison.* nd. Baronet. sgn. no dj issued. EX. P1. $60.00

ELLISON, Harlan. *Paingod.* 1965. Pyramid. 1st ed. wraps. $15.00

ELLISON, Harlan. *Partners in Wonder.* 1971. NY. Walker. 1st ed. sgns. dj. EX. $50.00

ELLISON, Harlan. *Rockabilly.* 1961. Greenwich. Fawcett. 1st ed. pb. EX. $30.00

ELLISON, P. *Common Wild Flowers of NY State.* 1975. Cornell. 31 p. M2. $3.00

ELLS, B.F. *History of the Romish Inquisition.* 1835. Hanover, IN. 120 p. fair. T5. $45.00

ELLSON, Hal. *Tomboy.* 1950. Scribner. dj. xl. P1. $7.50

ELLSWORTH & RICHMOND. *History of Woodstock.* 1901. Cazenovia. Ils. G. $40.00

ELLUL, Jacques. *Histoire des Institutions.* 1958. Paris. 3 vols. wraps. VG. $15.00

ELLWANGER, George. *Story of My House.* 1891. NY. 12mo. 286 p. $20.00

ELMORE, W.T. *Dravinian Gods in Modern Hinduism.* 1925. India. $10.00

ELSEN, Albert. *Seymour Lipton.* 1971. NY. Abrams. Ils. 244 p. dj. D2. $85.00

ELSEN, Albert. *Seymour Lipton.* 1974. NY. Abrams. dj. EX. $75.00

ELSON, Louis. *Modern Music & Musicians.* 1918. NY. Ils. 4to. 10 vols. gilt cloth. EX. T1. $100.00

ELTON, C.S. *Ecology of Invasions by Animals & Plants.* 1958. London. Methuen. 1st ed. 51 pls. 191 p. EX. $55.00

ELTON & ELTON. *Great Book Collectors.* 1893. London. 1st ed. VG. $65.00

ELWIN, M. *Lord Byron's Wife.* 1962. Harcourt Brace. dj. VG. $23.00

ELWOOD, Roger. *And Walk Now Gently Through Fire.* 1972. Chilton. 1st ed. dj. EX. P1. $12.50

ELWOOD, Roger. *Continuum 4.* 1975. Putnam. dj. VG. P1. $9.25

ELWOOD, Roger. *Dystopian Visions.* 1975. Prentice Hall. 1st ed. dj. VG. P1. $15.00

ELWOOD, Roger. *Far Side of Time.* 1974. Dodd Mead. 1st ed. dj. VG. P1. $12.50

ELWOOD, Roger. *Future Kin.* 1974. Doubleday. 1st ed. dj. EX. P1. $9.25

ELWOOD, Roger. *In the Wake of Man.* 1975. Bobbs Merrill. 1st ed. dj. EX. P1. $15.00

ELWOOD, Roger. *Other Side of Tomorrow.* 1973. Random House. 1st ed. dj. VG. P1. $9.25

ELWOOD, Roger. *Showcase.* 1973. Harper. 1st ed. dj. VG. P1. $11.00

ELWOOD, Roger. *Way Out.* 1973. Whitman. P1. $3.00

ELY, David. *Seconds.* 1963. NY. 1st ed. dj. VG. $25.00

EMERSON, E.W. *Emerson in Concord.* 1889. London. 1st ed. 266 p. B2. $25.00

EMERSON, Ellen. *Indian Myths.* 1884. Boston. Ils 1st ed. 677 p. TEG. fair. T5. $47.50

EMERSON, Ellen. *Masks, Heads & Faces With Some Considerations...* 1891. Houghton. 1st ed. VG. J2. $65.00

EMERSON, N.B. *Unwritten Literature of HI: Sacred Songs of the Hula.* 1909. WA. Ils. 288 p. A3. $45.00

EMERSON, R.W. *Compensation.* 1904. Roycroft. 8vo. red suede. G. D1. $25.00

EMERSON, R.W. *Essay on Friendship.* 1899. Roycroft. 1/50. sgns. 53 p. VG. T5. $125.00

EMERSON, R.W. *Essay on Nature.* Roycroft. gray suede. G. D1. $25.00

EMERSON, R.W. *Essay on Nature.* 1905. Roycroft. red suede. VG. D1. $35.00

EMERSON, R.W. *Essay on Nature.* 1905. Roycroft. 8vo. green suede. VG. D1. $40.00

EMERSON, R.W. *Essay on Self-Reliance.* 1908. Roycroft. green linen. VG. D1. $30.00

EMERSON, R.W. *Essay on Self-Reliance.* 1908. Roycroft. 8vo. brown linen. G. D1. $35.00

EMERSON, R.W. *Essays of Ralph Waldo Emerson.* 1962. Norwalk. Heritage. quarto. slipcase. EX. $15.00

EMERSON, R.W. *Essays of Ralph Waldo Emerson.* 1979. Easton Pr. 4to. AEG. full red leather. EX. $32.00

EMERSON, R.W. *Friendship.* 1899. Roycroft. 1/50. 8vo. gray bdg. VG. D1. $100.00

EMERSON, R.W. *Poems of Ralph Waldo Emerson.* 1945. Norwalk. Heritage. quarto. slipcase. EX. $15.00

EMERSON, R.W. *Society & Solitude.* 1870. 1st ed. EX. $65.00

EMERSON, W.C. *Land of the Midnight Sun.* 1956. Phil. 1st ed. sgn. dj. VG. $10.00

EMERTON, J.H. *Common Spiders of the US.* 1902. Ginn. Ils 1st ed. 225 p. EX. M2. $23.00

EMERY, S.A. *My Generation.* 1893. Newburyport. Sargent. G. $25.00

EMET, R. *New World for Nellie.* 1952. Harcourt Brace. Ils. xl. $7.50

EMMANUEL, Maurice. *Antique Greek Dance.* 1916. Dodd Mead. 1st ed. VG. J2. $45.00

EMMETT, Chris. *TX Camel Tales...* 1932. San Antonio. Naylor. 1st ed. 1/300. sgn. 275 p. $425.00

EMMITT, Robert. *Last War Trail: Utes & Settlement of CO.* 1954. Norman. dj. VG. $40.00

EMMONS, S.B. *Vegetable Family Physician...* 1842. Boston. 12mo. 179 p. VG. B1. $75.00

EMORY, W.H. *Report on the Mexican Boundary Survey.* 1987. TX Hist Assn. 1/750. 2 vols. slipcase. M. M2. $175.00

EMOTT, James. *Speech of in House of Representatives January 12, 1813.* 1813. NY. Seymour. 1st NY ed. 40 p. $65.00

EMPEY, A.G. *First Call.* 1918. Putnam. Ils. VG. $20.00

EMPSON, R.H.W. *Cult of the Peacock Angel (Yezidi Tribes of Kurdistan).* 1928. London. Ils. photos. VG. $20.00

EMPSON, W. *Milton's God.* 1961. New Directions. dj. EX. $15.00

EMURIAN, Ernest. *Stories of Civil War Songs.* 1960. Wilde. 1st ed. dj. EX. $15.00

ENDE, Michael. *Momo.* 1984. Doubleday. 1st ed. dj. VG. P1. $13.75

ENDE, Michael. *Neverending Story.* 1983. Doubleday. 2nd print. dj. EX. T6. $15.00

ENDE, Michael. *Neverending Story.* 1983. NY. Doubleday. AP. 1st ed. wraps. VG. $25.00

ENDERS, J. *Fox Hunter's Scrapbook.* 1945. private print. Hartford. 1/500. $35.00

ENDORE, Guy. *King of Paris.* nd. Book Club. VG. P1. $2.25

ENDORE, Guy. *Methinks the Lady.* nd. Duell Sloan Pearce. 3rd ed. dj. P1. $15.00

ENDORE, Guy. *Werewolf of Paris.* 1933. Grosset Dunlap. $65.00

ENDORE, S.G. *Casanova: His Known & Unknown Life.* 1929. NY. 390 p. G. $12.00

ENEFER, Douglas. *Seven Nights at the Resort.* 1976. Robert Hale. dj. xl. P1. $5.00

ENGDAHL, Sylvia. *Anywhere, Anywhen.* 1976. Atheneum. dj. xl. P1. $17.50

ENGDAHL, Sylvia. *Far Side of Evil.* 1972. Ateneum. dj. xl. P1. $15.00

ENGDAHL, Sylvia. *Far Side of Evil.* 1975. Gollancz. dj. EX. P1. $15.00

ENGEL, David. *Japanese Gardens for Today.* 1959. Tuttle. rebound. $30.00

ENGEL, Howard. *Murder Sees the Light.* 1984. Viking. 1st ed. dj. VG. P1. $12.50

ENGEL, Howard. *Ransom Game.* 1981. Clarke Irwin. 1st ed. sgn. dj. EX. P1. $30.00

ENGEL, J.M. *IN Bat, Myotis Sodalis: A Bibliography.* 1976. USFWS. 9 p. M2. $3.00

ENGEL, L. *Sea.* 1969. Time Life. Ils. 190 p. EX. M2. $5.00

ENGEL, P.L. *Juris Canonici.* 1717. Salisburgi. thick quarto. 1300 p. VG. $95.00

ENGELDINGER, E.A. *Spouse Abuse: Annotated Bibliography of Violence...* Scarecrow Pr. 331 p. VG. T5. $9.50

ENGELHARDT, Conrad. *Demark in Early Iron Age.* 1866. London. Williams Norgate. 33 pls. $100.00

ENGELMAN & OBST. *Snakes: Biology, Behavior & Relationship to Man.* 1982. Exeter. Ils 1st Am ed. 4to. VG. M2. $20.00

ENGELMANN, Bernt. *Weapons Merchants.* 1986. NY. Crown. 1st Am ed. dj. EX. $10.00

ENGELMANN, C.F. *W Patriot & Canton Almanac for Year of Our Lord 1847.* 1946. Canton. Ils. wraps. G. T5. $45.00

ENGEMAN, Jack. *Airline Stewardess: A Picture Story.* 1960. np. Ils. 119 p. dj. VG. T5. $17.50

ENGEN, R.K. *Kate Greenaway.* 1976. London. Academy. Ils. 4to. 68 p. dj. VG. $20.00

ENGEN, Rodney. *Richard Doyle.* 1983. Catalpa Pr. Ils. 216 p. D2. $55.00

ENGLE, Paul. *World of Love.* 1951. NY. 1st ed. 8vo. dj. VG. $20.00

ENGLE & URGANG. *Prize Stories 1957: O. Henry Awards.* 1957. Garden City. 1st ed. dj. EX. $25.00

ENGLISH, W.A. *Geology & Oil Resources of Puente Hills Region, S CA.* 1926. WA. Ils. sgn. EX. $35.00

ENOCK, G.R. *Andes & the Amazon: Life & Travel in Peru.* 1910. Unwin. Ils. 379 p. G. M2. $20.00

ENRIQUES, R.D.Z. *Case of Mexico & Policy of President Wilson.* 1914. NY. 209 p. G. $8.00

ENSTROM, Robert. *Encounter Program.* 1977. Doubleday. dj. EX. P1. $9.25

EPHRON, Nora. *Heartburn.* 1983. NY. 1st Am ed. dj. EX. $12.00

EPICTETUS. *Discourses of Epictetus With Encheiridion & Fragments.* 1890. Bohn's Classical Lib. EX. $25.00

EPLER, Percy. *Life of Clara Barton.* 1915. NY. index. 438 p. K1. $21.00

EPPES, S.B. *Negro in Old S.* 1942. Macon, GA. Ils. 203 p. VG. $35.00

ERASMUS, Desiderius. *In Praise of Folly.* 1900. Gibbings. G. $25.00

ERASMUS, Desiderius. *Moriae Encomium.* 1954. NY. Ils Masereel. 1st ed. slipcase. $45.00

ERDMAN, Paul. *Paul Erdman's Money Book.* 1984. Random House. 1st ed. dj. EX. P1. $14.95

ERDRICH, Louise. *Tracks.* 1988. NY. Holt. ARC. wraps. M. $20.00

ERGANG, Robert. *Frederick William I: Father of Prussian Militarism.* 1941. Columbia. 1st ed. presentation. sgn. dj. J2. $15.00

ERICHSEN, Hugo. *Cremation of Dead Considered From Aesthetic, Religious...* 1887. Detroit. 1st ed. 12mo. 264 p. $100.00

ERICHSON-BROWN, C. *Use of Plants for the Past 500 Years.* 1980. Breezy Creek. Ils. 512 p. EX. M2. $15.00

ERLANGER, Philippe. *Age of Courts & Kings: Manners & Morals, 1558-1715.* 1967. London. Ils. photos. dj. VG. $38.00

ERMISCH, Richard. *Portrait Eines Baumeister. Querschnitt Einer Zeit.* 1971. Berlin. Ernst. Ils. 4to. dj. $27.50

ERNEST, Edward. *Animated Circus Book.* 1943. NY. Ils. 20 p. spiral bdg. dj. VG. T1. $55.00

ERNST & BARBOUR. *Turtles of the World.* 1989. Smithsonian. Ils 1st ed. 313 p. dj. M. M2. $45.00

ERNST & CHAR. *Dent Prompte.* Paris. 1/240. sgns. with 10 orig lithographs. $2500.00

ERRINGTON, P.L. *Muskrats & Marsh Management.* 1978. NE U. photos. 183 p. EX. M2. $6.00

ERSKINE, G.S. *Bronco Charlie: Saga of the Saddle.* 1934. NY. Crowell. Ils. 316 p. A3. $60.00

ERSKINE, John. *Adam & Eve.* 1927. Bobbs Merrill. 1st ed. VG. P1. $12.50

ERSKINE, John. *Adam & Eve.* 1927. Indianapolis. 1st ed. dj. M. $20.00

ERSKINE, John. *Adam & Eve.* 1927. McClelland. 1st Canadian ed. VG. P1. $7.00

ERSKINE, John. *Brief Hour of Francois Villon.* 1937. 1st ed. VG. C1. $6.00

ERSKINE, John. *Cinderella's Daughter.* 1930. 1st ed. VG. C1. $10.00

ERSKINE, John. *Galahad: Enough of His Life To Explain His Reputation.* 1926. 1st ed. VG. C1. $5.00

ERSKINE, John. *Helen Retires.* 1934. Bobbs Merrill. 1st ed. VG. scarce. C1. $12.00

ERSKINE, John. *Penelope's Man.* 1928. Odysseus. 1st ed. VG. C1. $5.00

ERSKINE, John. *Private Life of Helen of Troy.* 1925. Bobbs Merrill. P1. $17.50

ERSKINE, John. *Tristan & Isolde.* 1932. 1st ed. C1. $15.00

ERSKINE, John. *Venus: Lonely Goddess.* 1949. 1st ed. VG. C1. $10.00

ERSKINE, Margaret. *Brood of Folly.* 1971. Hodder Stoughton. 1st ed. xl. P1. $6.00

ERSKINE, Margaret. *Ewe Lamb.* 1968. Crime Club. 1st ed. dj. xl. P1. $6.00

ERSKINE. *Philharmonic-Symphony Society of NY: 1st 100 Years.* 1943. 1st ed. EX. $15.00

ERTE, Romain de Tirtoff. *Erte's Costumes & Sets for Der Rosenkavalier.* 1980. NY. Ltd 1st ed. 1/1750. sgn. 4to. EX. $175.00

ESAREY, Logan. *History of IN to 1850.* 1915. Indianapolis. VG. $37.50

ESAREY, Logan. *IN Home.* 1953. IN U. Ils. 4to. red cloth. slipcase. G2. $45.00

ESDAILE, Arundell. *British Museum Library: A History.* 1948. London. VG. $15.00

ESDAILE, Arundell. *Student's Manual of Bibliography.* 1931. NY. Scribner. 383 p. G. $25.00

ESHBACH, Lloyd Arthur. *Of Worlds Beyond.* 1965. Dobson. dj. VG. P1. $10.00

ESHBACH, Lloyd Arthur. *Over My Shoulder.* 1983. Oswald Train. 1st ed. dj. EX. P1. $20.00

ESHBACH, Lloyd Arthur. *Tyrant of Time.* 1955. Fantasy Pr. Donald Grand bdg. dj. M. P1. $12.50

ESHLEMAN, Clayton. *Hades in Manganese.* 1981. Black Sparrow. glassine dj. EX. $15.00

ESKEW, G. *Williard's of WA.* 1954. NY. 1st ed. dj. VG. $9.00

ESKEW, Harry. *Fair Prize: World's Fair Story.* 1904. Bloomfield, NJ. Ils. 64 p. cloth wraps. T5. $19.50

ESPOSITO, V.J. *Military History & Atlas of Napoleonic Wars.* 2nd ed. G. $50.00

ESPOSITO, V.J. *Military History & Atlas of Napoleonic Wars.* 1968. NY. 169 maps. cloth bdg. VG. T5. $150.00

ESPOSITO, V.J. *W Point Atlas of American Wars.* 1959. NY. 2 vols. slipcase. T5. $125.00

ESPOSITO, V.J. *W Point Atlas of American Wars.* 1960. 2nd print. 2 vols. VG. $55.00

ESQUEMELING, John. *Buccaneers of America.* nd. London. 3rd print. 480 p. G. $25.00

ESSES, Michael. *Michael, Michael, Why Do You Hate Me?* 1973. Logos. 1st ed. dj. EX. $9.50

ESTABROOK, E.F. *Ancient Lovers of Peace: Recollections of Unspoiled SW.* 1959. Boston. private print. xl. scarce. A3. $45.00

ESTABROOKE, Edward. *Ferrotype & How To Make It.* 1872. Cincinnatti/Louisville. 1st ed. G2. $47.00

ESTEP, E.R. *El Toro: Motor Car Story of Interior Cuba.* 1909. Detroit. Packard. photos. 107 p. EX. $22.50

ESTEP, W. *Eternal Wisdom & Health With Light on Scriptures.* 1932. MO. $22.00

ESTEROW, Milton. *Art Stealers.* 1966. Macmillan. Ils. photos. dj. D2. $25.00

ESTLEMAN, L.D. *Bloody Season.* 1988. Bantam. 1st ed. dj. EX. P1. $15.95

ESTLEMAN, L.D. *Downriver.* 1988. Boston. Houghton Mifflin. 1st ed. dj. M. $10.00

ESTLEMAN, L.D. *Dr. Jekyll & Mr. Holmes.* Garden City. Stated 1st ed. 214 p. dj. M. $22.50

ESTLEMAN, L.D. *Every Bright Eye.* 1986. Boston. Houghton Mifflin. 1st ed. dj. M. $12.00

ESTLEMAN, L.D. *Hider.* 1978. Doubleday. 1st ed. dj. xl. P1. $6.00

ESTLEMAN, L.D. *Lady Yesterday.* 1987. Boston. 1st ed. dj. EX. $15.00

ESTLEMAN, L.D. *Midnight Man.* 1982. Houghton. 1st ed. dj. EX. $15.00

ESTLEMAN, L.D. *Sugartown.* 1987. Boston. 1st ed. dj. EX. $15.00

ETHERIDGE, Y.W. *History of Ashley Co., AR.* 1959. Van Buren. EX. M2. $30.00

ETTINGER, Elzbieta. *Kindergarten.* 1986. Boston. 1st pb ed. VG. $4.00

ETTMULLER, M. *Opera Omnia in Compendium Redacta.* 1727. Venice. 8vo. 454 p. xl. $260.00

EUCLID. *Elements.* 1546. Latin text. scarce. $700.00

EUSLIN, Bernard. *Green Hero: Early Adventures of Finn McCool.* 1975. Ils 1st ed. dj. M. C1. $9.50

EVANS, A.J. *Devota.* 1907. Dillingham. dj. VG. $25.00

EVANS, A.J. *Macaria.* 1864. 1st ed. very scarce. J4. $35.00

EVANS, A.J. *St. Elmo.* nd. Grosset Dunlap. Movie ed. dj. G. $35.00

EVANS, C.A. *Confederate Military History. Vol. 3.* 1975. Dayton, OH. Ils. VG. T5. $32.50

EVANS, C.A. *Confederate Military History: GA.* nd. Blue/Gray Pr. 345 p. dj. EX. M2. $15.00

EVANS, C.A. *Confederate Military History: KY & MO.* nd. Blue/Gray Pr. 2 vols. dj. EX. M2. $20.00

EVANS, Christopher. *Lightship.* 1985. Paper Tiger. Ils Jim Burns. 1/250. sgns. dj. EX. $75.00

EVANS, Christopher. *Writing SF.* 1988. St. Martin. 1st ed. dj. RS. EX. P1. $15.00

EVANS, G.B. *Best of Nash Buckingham.* 1973. NY. dj. EX. $25.00

EVANS, H. *Falconry.* 1978. Arco. Ils 2nd print. 160 p. dj. EX. M2. $28.00

EVANS, H.E. *Pleasures of Entomology: Portraits of Insects & People.* 1988. Smithsonian. Ils. 238 p. M. M2. $14.00

EVANS, H.E. *Wasp Farm.* 1963. Nat Hist Pr. Ils. 178 p. dj. EX. M2. $14.00

EVANS, Jessie Benton. *Giulietta & Romeo.* 1934. Ils 1st/only ed. 1/1000. M. C1. $12.50

EVANS, Kenneth. *Oasis of Fear.* 1968. Roy. 1st ed. dj. EX. P1. $7.00

EVANS, Peter. *Peter Sellers.* 1968. Prentice Hall. 1st ed. VG. J2. $7.50

EVANS, Sebastian. *High History of the Holy Grail.* 1898. London. Dent. 1/200. sgn. 2 vols. VG. rare. C1. $95.00

EVANS, Walker. *American Photographs.* 1938. 1st ed. inscr/sgn. EX. $175.00

EVANS, Walker. *American Photographs.* 1938. NY. MOMA. 1st ed. square 8vo. VG. $95.00

EVANS, Walker. *Many Are Called.* 1966. Boston. Houghton. 1st ed. 8vo. wraps. VG. $110.00

EVANS, Walker. *Message From the Interior.* 1966. NY. EX. $185.00

EVANS, Walker. *Walker Evans at Work.* 1982. NY. Harper. 1st ed. 745 photos. 4to. 239 p. dj. $50.00

EVANS & ABRAHAMS. *Ancient Greek Dress.* 1964. Chicago. 1st Am ed. dj. G. $8.00

EVANS & KIRKMAN. *Guide to Bird Habitats of the Ozark Plateau.* 1981. USFS. Ils. 79 p. M2. $4.00

EVANS. *Our Sister Republic: Mexico.* 1880. CT. VG. with Columbian Expo clipping. $20.00

EVARTS. *Yellow Horde.* 1921. Boston. Ils 1st ed. dj. EX. $12.50

EVENS, W.M. *Ballots & Fence Rails: Reconstruction.* 1967. Chapel Hill. 1st ed. 293 p. dj. VG. $15.00

EVERARD, John. *Artist's Model.* 1952. Bodley Head. reprint of 1951 ed. D2. $35.00

EVERARD, John. *Oriental Model.* 1955. London. Ils. VG. $50.00

EVERETT, Edward. *Address Delivered at Lexington on 19th of April, 1835.* 1835. Charleston. 2nd ed. 36 p. EX. $55.00

EVERETT, Fred. *Fun With Trout.* 1952. PA. Stackpole. VG. $25.00

EVERETT, Marshall. *Complete Story of San Francisco Earthquake.* 1906. Bible House. G. $30.00

EVERETT, Michael. *Birds of Paradise.* 1978. Putnam. Ils Gould/Hart/ Keulmans/ Hayman. M2. $80.00

EVERETT, P.L. *Suder.* 1983. NY. 1st ed. dj. VG. $30.00

EVERHARED & MORLEY. *Wild Flowers of the World.* 1970. NY. Putnam. 1st ed. dj. EX. $25.00

EVERHART, W.H. *Principles of Fishery Science.* 1975. Cornell. Ils. 288 p. dj. EX. M2. $15.00

EVERITT, C. *Birds of the Edward Marshall Boehm Aviaries.* 1973. Boehm. Ils. 4to. 297 p. EX. M2. $16.00

EVERITT, C.P. *Adventures of a Treasure Hunter.* 1951. Boston. 1st ed. dj. M. $20.00

EVERSON, W.K. *Films of Laurel & Hardy.* 1967. NY. 4to. G. $20.00

EVERSON, William. *Birth of a Poet.* 1982. Black Sparrow. 1/250. sgn. $35.00

EVERSON, William. *Tendril in the Mesh.* 1973. San Francisco. Cayucos. 1/250. sgn. 4to. EX. $110.00

EVERSON & FENIN. *W.* 1962. Orion. 1st ed. dj. VG. J2. $15.00

EWALD, C.A. *Diseases of the Stomach.* 1894. NY. Ils. xl. VG. $75.00

EWER, James K. *3rd MA Cavalry.* 1903. Ils. 452 p. K1. $57.50

EWING, J.H. *Mary's Meadow.* c 1886. London. VG. $35.00

EXLEY, Frederick. *Fan's Notes.* 1968. Harper. 1st print. dj. M. $95.00

EXLEY, Frederick. *Last Notes From Home.* 1988. Random House. UCP. wraps. M. $40.00

EXLINE. *Valhalla in the Smokies.* 1938. Ltd ed. sgn. S2. $65.00

EYLES, Allen. *Sherlock Holmes: A Centenary Celebration.* 1986. NY. Harper. 1st Am ed. 4to. 144 p. dj. M. $20.00

EYRE, Frank. *20th-C Children's Books.* 1952. London. 1st ed. pls. 72 p. pictorial wraps. T5. $17.50

EYRE, S.R. *Vegetation & Soils: A World Picture.* 1963. Aldine. Ils 1st ed. dj. EX. M2. $20.00

FAANES, C.A. *Birds of the St. Croix River Valley, MN & WI.* 1981. USFWS. maps. 196 p. EX. M2. $13.00

FABER, E. *Evolution of Chemistry: History of Idea, Method, & Material.* 1952. Ronald. Ils. 349 p. EX. M2. $10.00

FABER, Elmer. *Behind the Law: True Story of PA State Police.* 1933. Greensbury. Henry. VG. $12.00

FABER, G.S. *Dissertation on Mysteries.* 1803. Oxford. 2 vols. xl. VG. B1. $45.00

FABER, J. *TX With Guns.* 1950. Naylor. Ils possible 1st ed. sgn. VG. M2. $25.00

FABER, R.S. *Bibliotheque de la Providence. Catalog of Library...* 1887. London. 1/50. $150.00

FABER. *Moments in News Photography.* 1950. EX. S2. $16.00

FABES, Gilbert. *Autobiography of a Book.* 1926. London. 1st ed. inscr. dj. $50.00

FABIAN, Robert. *Fabian of the Yard.* 1950. Naldrett. 2nd ed. dj. VG. P1. $10.00

FABIAN. *Fabian Essays & New Fabian Essays.* 1890 & 1952. 1st ed. 2 vols. dj. scarce. J2. $85.00

FABOR, John. *Great Moments in News Photography.* 1960. NY. Ils. 4to. 126 p. dj. VG. T5. $15.00

FABRE, J.H. *Book of Insects.* 1936. Tudor. Ils Detmold. 3rd print. VG. $40.00

FABRE, J.H. *Fabre's Book of Insects.* 1931. Dodd Mead. Ils Detmold. 4to. gilt bdg. VG. G2. $130.00

FAGAN, B. *Elusive Treasure: Story of Early Archaeologists in Americas.* 1977. Scribner. Ils 1st ed. 369 p. dj. EX. M2. $26.00

FAGAN, J.O. *Autobiography of an Individualist.* 1912. Houghton Mifflin. 1st ed. $12.00

FAHEY, J. *Inland Empire: D.C. Corbin & Spokane.* 1965. WA U. photos. maps. 270 p. dj. EX. M2. $13.00

FAIR, A.A. *Bats Fly at Dusk.* 1942. Triangle. dj. VG. P1. $10.00

FAIR, A.A. *Beware the Curves.* 1956. Morrow. 1st ed. dj. VG. $30.00

FAIR, A.A. *Kept Women Can't Quit.* 1960. Morrow. 1st ed. dj. xl. P1. $10.00

FAIR, A.A. *Owls Don't Blink.* 1947. Triangle. VG. P1. $10.00

FAIR, A.A. *Pass the Gravy.* 1959. Morrow. dj. VG. $25.00

FAIR, A.A. *Spill the Jackpot.* 1944. Triangle. VG. P1. $7.50

FAIRBANKS & BERKLEY. *Life & Letters of R.A.F. Penrose.* 1952. Geol Soc Am. 765 p. EX. M2. $35.00

FAIRBRIDGE, Dorothea. *Historic Houses of S Africa.* 1922. London. Ils 1st ed. 4to. gilt cloth. T1. $85.00

FAIRCHILD, David. *Garden Islands of the Great E.* 1943. NY. 1st ed. VG. $15.00

FAIRCHILD, David. *World Grows Round My Door.* 1947. NY. 1st ed. G. $30.00

FAIRCHILD, David. *World Was My Garden: Travels of a Plant Explorer.* 1938. Scribner. Ils 1st ed. sgn. 494 p. VG. M2. $30.00

FAIRCHILD, T.B. *History of Town of Cuyhoga Falls, Summit Co., OH.* 1876. Cleveland. 1st ed. stiff wraps. fair. T5. $85.00

FAIRFIELD, J.H. *Known Violin Makers.* 1942. NY. 1st ed. G. $65.00

FAIRHOLT, F.W. *Tobacco: Its History & Associations...* 1859. London. Chapman Hall. 1st ed. 332 p. $125.00

FAIRLEY, J. *Lion River: The Indus.* 1975. Day. Ils 1st Am ed. dj. EX. M2. $18.00

FAIRLEY, J.A. *Agnes Campbell, Lady Roseburn...* 1925. Aberdeen. 1st ed. 1/150. EX. $65.00

FAIRWEATHER, Sally. *Picasso's Concrete Sculptures.* 1982. NY. 1st ed. $50.00

FALCONER, B.L. *Flying Around the World.* 1937. Boston. Ils. sgn. 104 p. dj. VG. T5. $45.00

FALCONER, Sovereign. *To Make Death Love Us.* 1987. Doubleday. dj. EX. P1. $17.50

FALL, B.B. *Anatomy of a Crisis.* 1969. Doubleday. 1st ed. dj. EX. $10.00

FALLIS, E.H. *When Denver & I Were Young.* 1956. Mountain Pr. 198 p. dj. VG. A3. $35.00

FALLON, David. *Big Fight (Gallipoli to the Somme).* 1918. NY. EX. $10.00

FALLOPIO, Gabriel. *La Chirurgia die Gabriel Falloppio Modonese, Fisico...* 1603. Venedig. 4to. 290 p. $500.00

FALLS, Cyril. *Great Military Battles.* 1964. NY. Ils. photos. maps. 303 p. G. T5. $35.00

FAMILY HANDYMAN MAGAZINE. *America's Handyman's Book.* 1961. Scribner. Ils. photos. 513 p. dj. EX. $5.50

FANNIN, Cole. *Danger at the Ranch.* 1961. Whitman. VG. P1. $12.50

FANNIN, Cole. *Sea Hunt.* 1960. Whitman. EX. P1. $15.00

FANT & ASHLEY. *Faulkner at W Point.* 1964. Random House. 1st ed. dj. EX. $35.00

FANTE, John. *Dago Red.* 1940. NY. 1st ed. sgn. dj. EX. $100.00

FARABEE, W.C. *Indian Tribes of E Peru.* 1922. Peabody Mus. map. sgn. VG. $40.00

FARADAY. *European & American Carpets & Rugs.* 1929. Grant Rapids. 4to. gilt red cloth. EX. $95.00

FARAGO, Ladislas. *Game of the Foxes.* 1971. McKay. Book Club ed. dj. M1. $5.00

FARAGO, Ladislas. *German Psychological Warfare.* 1942. Putnam. 1st ed. dj. VG. J2. $15.00

FARAGO, Ladislas. *Patton: Ordeal & Triumph.* 1st ed. dj. $22.00

FARAH, Cynthia. *Literature & Landscape Writers of SW.* 1988. 1st ed. 1st state. sgn. dj. EX. $50.00

FARB, P. *Ecology.* 1970. Time Life. Ils. 192 p. EX. M2. $5.00

FARB, P. *Land & Wildlife of N America.* 1966. Time Life. Ils. maps. 200 p. EX. M2. $5.00

FARB, P. *Man's Rise to Civilization.* 1979. Revised 2nd ed. 413 p. dj. $35.00

FARBER, Norma. *As I Was Crossing Boston Common.* 1973. Dutton. Ils Lobel. 1st ed. VG. B4. $25.00

FARBMAN. *Masterpieces of Russian Painting.* 1930. London. Europa. 4to. VG. G2. $50.00

FARIS, J.T. *Seeing Canada.* 1924. Lippincott. Ils Holloway. 8vo. 265 p. VG. $25.00

FARIS, Lillie. *Old Testament Stories Retold for Children.* 1938. NY. Ils White. 4to. EX. $12.00

FARJASSE, D.D. *L'Italie...* 1836. Paris. pls. VG. $125.00

FARJEON, E. *Unlocked Book.* 1938. NY. 1st ed. 205 p. dj. VG. B2. $50.00

FARJEON, J.J. *Mystery Underground.* 1932. Collins. 5th ed. G. P1. $9.25

FARJEON, J.J. *Shadow of Thirteen.* 1949. Collins. 1st ed. dj. VG. P1. $15.00

FARJEON, J.J. *5:18 Mystery.* c 1936. NY. Mason. 1st ed. VG. $8.00

FARLEY, R.M. *Radio Man.* 1948. LA. 1st ed. 1st bdg. 1st issue dj. EX. $50.00

FARLEY, Walter. *Black Stallion Returns.* 1945. NY. 1st ed. dj. EX. $25.00

FARLEY, Walter. *Island Stallion.* 1948. Random House. 8vo. G. $7.50

FARMER, B.J. *Gentle Art of Book Collecting.* 1940. London. 1st ed. dj. $20.00

FARMER, Fannie. *Food & Cookery for Sick & Convalescent Centers.* 1907. Little Brown. VG. $16.50

FARMER, Hugh. *Inquiry Into the Nature & Design of Christ's Temptation.* 1765. London. 160 p. orig bdg. K1. $12.50

FARMER, Philip Jose. *Book of Philip Jose Farmer.* 1976. Elmfield Pr. 1st ed. dj. EX. P1. $20.00

FARMER, Philip Jose. *Classic Farmer 1964-1973.* 1984. Crown. 1st ed. dj. EX. P1. $8.95

FARMER, Philip Jose. *Dark Design.* 1977. Berkley Putnam. 1st ed. dj. VG. P1. $15.00

FARMER, Philip Jose. *Dayworld Rebel.* 1987. NY. 1st Am ed. dj. VG. $25.00

FARMER, Philip Jose. *Dayworld.* 1985. Putnam. 1st ed. dj. VG. P1. $16.95

FARMER, Philip Jose. *Doc Savage: His Apocalyptic Life.* 1973. Doubleday. 1st ed. dj. EX. P1. $50.00

FARMER, Philip Jose. *Gods of Riverworld.* 1983. Phantasia. 1/650. sgn. dj. slipcase. EX. P1. $35.00

FARMER, Philip Jose. *Lovers.* 1979. Del Rey. 1st ed. dj. EX. P1. $20.00

FARMER, Philip Jose. *Magic Labyrinth.* 1980. Berkley Putnam. 1st ed. dj. EX. P1. $15.00

FARMER, Philip Jose. *Unreasoning Mask.* 1981. Putnam. 1st ed. dj. EX. P1. $20.00

FARMILOE, Edith. *One Day.* 1904. NY. Dutton. 1st ed. J2. $40.00

FARNHAM, A.B. *Home Manufacture of Furs & Skins.* 1941. Columbus. Harding. Ils. 16mo. 283 p. wraps. $20.00

FARNHAM, C.H. *Life of Francis Parkman.* 1900. Boston. 1st ed. 394 p. G. T5. $9.50

FARNOL, Jeffery. *Beltane the Smith.* nd. Musson. VG. P1. $10.00

FARNOL, Jeffery. *Black Bartlemy's Treasure.* nd. Ryerson. VG. P1. $7.50

FARNOL, Jeffery. *Broad Highway.* nd. Sampson Low. VG. P1. $7.50

FARNOL, Jeffery. *Broad Highway.* nd. Burt. VG. P1. $7.50

FARNOL, Jeffery. *Broad Highway.* 1912. London. Ils Brock. gilt bdg. EX. $30.00

FARNOL, Jeffery. *Chronicles of the Imp.* nd. Sampson Low. VG. P1. $15.00

FARNOL, Jeffery. *Loring Mystery.* nd. Sampson Low. VG. P1. $12.50

FARNOL, Jeffery. *Money Moon.* nd. Burt. VG. P1. $12.50

FARNOL, Jeffery. *Sir John Dering.* nd. Ryerson. G. P1. $6.00

FARNOL, Jeffery. *Way Beyond.* 1933. Ryerson. VG. P1. $10.00

FARNOL, Jeffery. *Winds of Chance.* 1924. Ryerson. VG. P1. $12.50

FARR, P. *King Arthur Companion.* 2nd ed. lg stiff wraps. EX. C1. $18.00

FARR. *Black Champion.* 1964. London. Ils Johnson. 1st ed. 245 p. dj. C4. $37.00

FARRAR, Emmie. *Old VA Houses Along the James.* 1957. Bonanza. Ils. maps. 4to. 231 p. dj. VG. $12.00

FARRAR, Leonard. *Art of Collecting Coins.* 1955. NY. 1st ed. dj. VG. $10.00

FARRAR, Stewart. *Death in the Wrong Bed.* 1964. Walker. 1st ed. dj. xl. P1. $7.50

FARRAR & HINES. *Old VA Houses Along the Fall Line.* 1971. NY. Ils 1st ed. 236 p. dj. EX. $15.00

FARRAR. *With the Poets.* c 1890. London. Suttaby. Ils Jennings. AEG. VG. $30.00

FARRELL, J.T. *Bernard Clare.* 1946. NY. 1st ed. dj. VG. $20.00

FARRELL, J.T. *Dunne Family.* 1976. Doubleday. 1st ed. dj. VG. P1. $20.00

FARRELL, J.T. *Ellen Rogers.* 1941. NY. 1st ed. dj. EX. $30.00

FARRELL, J.T. *Judith.* 1969. Schneider. 1/300. sgn. Beckett wraps. EX. $40.00

FARRELL, J.T. *Note on Literary.* 1936. NY. 1st ed. 8vo. VG. $28.00

FARRINGTON, Margaret. *Tales of King Arthur.* c 1882. NY/London. Ils Fredericks. VG. C1. $15.00

FARRINGTON, S.K. *Ducks Came Back.* 1945. NY. 1st ed. dj. VG. B2. $35.00

FARRINGTON, S.K. *Railroads at War.* 1944. NY. Ils. 320 p. index. VG. T5. $12.50

FARRINGTON, S.K. *Railroads of Today.* 1949. NY. Ils 1st ed. inscr. 306 p. VG. T5. $35.00

FARRIS, John. *Son of the Endless Night.* nd. Book Club. dj. VG. P1. $5.00

FARRIS, John. *Son of the Endless Night.* 1985. St. Martin. 1st ed. dj. EX. $10.00

FARRIS, John. *Uninvited.* nd. Book Club. dj. G. P1. $4.50

FARRIS, John. *Wildwood.* 1986. NY. 1st Am ed. dj. VG. $20.00

FARSON, Negley. *Sailing Across Europe.* 1926. Century. inscr/sgn. $12.00

FARWELL, Byron. *Gurkhas.* 1984. NY. dj. EX. $17.50

FARWELL, Byron. *Gurkhas.* 1984. NY. Ils. 317 p. dj. VG. T5. $15.00

FAST, Jonathan. *Inner Circle.* nd. Book Club. dj. VG. P1. $3.25

FAST, Jonathan. *Mortal Gods.* 1978. Harper Row. 1st ed. dj. EX. P1. $10.00

FAULK, O.B. *AZ: Short History.* 1970. OK U. Ils Review of 1st ed. dj. EX. M2. $10.00

FAULKNER, J.P. *Eighteen Months on a Greenland Whaler.* 1878. NY. 317 p. VG. scarce. $150.00

FAULKNER, James. *My Brother Bill.* 1963. NY. 1st ed. dj. VG. B2. $15.00

FAULKNER, Ray. *Art Today.* 1969. NY. 1st ed. dj. $25.00

FAULKNER, William. *Big Woods.* 1955. NY. 1st ed. dj. EX. $145.00

FAULKNER, William. *Collected Stories.* 1951. NY. 1st ed. dj. VG. $60.00

FAULKNER, William. *Dr. Martino & Other Stories.* 1934. NY. 1st ed. dj. VG. $60.00

FAULKNER, William. *Fable.* nd. NY. Random House. 1st trade ed. $45.00

FAULKNER, William. *Fable.* 1954. NY. 1st ed. 2nd state. dj. EX. $55.00

FAULKNER, William. *Fable.* 1954. Random House. 2nd ed. dj. EX. $15.00

FAULKNER, William. *Faulkner at Nagano.* 1956. Tokyo. 1st ed. dj. VG. $185.00

FAULKNER, William. *Faulkner Reader*. nd. Modern Lib. dj. G. $5.00

FAULKNER, William. *Faulkner Reader*. 1959. Modern Lib. 1st Giant ed. dj. EX. $35.00

FAULKNER, William. *Flags in the Dust*. 1973. NY. 1st ed. dj. EX. $25.00

FAULKNER, William. *Go Down Moses*. 1942. NY. 1st ed. dj. VG. B2. $250.00

FAULKNER, William. *Green Bough*. 1933. NY. 1st ed. dj. EX. $100.00

FAULKNER, William. *Green Bough*. 1933. NY. 1st trade ed. 67 p. G. T5. $75.00

FAULKNER, William. *Helen: Courtship & MS Poems*. 1981. Oxford/New Orleans. 165 p. dj. T5. $12.50

FAULKNER, William. *Hunting Stories*. Ltd Ed Club. slipcase. M. B3. $325.00

FAULKNER, William. *Hunting Stories*. 1988. Ltd Ed Club. Ils Welliver. 1/850. slipcase. EX. $270.00

FAULKNER, William. *Intruder in the Dust*. 1948. Random House. 6th print. dj. $12.50

FAULKNER, William. *Intruder in the Dust*. 1949. London. Chatto Windus. 1st ed. $75.00

FAULKNER, William. *Intruder in the Dust*. 1949. Signet. 1st ed. printed wraps. VG. $50.00

FAULKNER, William. *Knight's Gambit*. 1st ed. dj. EX. B7. $120.00

FAULKNER, William. *Knight's Gambit*. 1951. London. 1st ed. dj. VG. $105.00

FAULKNER, William. *Light in August*. 1950. Random House. VG. P1. $13.75

FAULKNER, William. *Mansion*. 1959. NY. 1st trade ed. 436 p. VG. T5. $75.00

FAULKNER, William. *Mansion*. 1959. Random House. 1st ed. blue cloth. dj. EX. $80.00

FAULKNER, William. *Mansion*. 1959. Random House. 1st trade ed. 1st print. dj. M. $90.00

FAULKNER, William. *Mayday*. 1978. Notre Dame. 1st trade ed. M. C1. $19.00

FAULKNER, William. *Mosquitoes*. 1937. Dial. 1st ed. VG. $30.00

FAULKNER, William. *New Orleans Sketches*. 1958. NJ. 1st ed. dj. $55.00

FAULKNER, William. *Pylon*. 1935. Harrison Smith. 1st ed. dj. $175.00

FAULKNER, William. *Pylon*. 1935. NY. 2nd print. dj. VG. $95.00

FAULKNER, William. *Reivers*. 1962. Ltd 1st ed. 1/500. 8vo. wraps. $275.00

FAULKNER, William. *Reivers*. 1962. Chattow Windus. 1st ed. dj. EX. $45.00

FAULKNER, William. *Reivers*. 1962. Random House. 1st ed. dj. EX. $50.00

FAULKNER, William. *Reivers*. 1962. Random House. 1st trade ed. 1st print. dj. M. $37.50

FAULKNER, William. *Requiem for a Nun*. 1951. NY. Ltd ed. 1/750. sgn. wraps. $145.00

FAULKNER, William. *Requiem for a Nun*. 1951. NY. 1st ed. 1st print. gray bdg. $110.00

FAULKNER, William. *Requiem for a Nun*. 1953. London. 1st ed. dj. EX. $95.00

FAULKNER, William. *Sanctuary*. 1931. Cape. 1st ed. 2nd print. VG. $20.00

FAULKNER, William. *Sanctuary*. 1958. Random House. Book Club ed. $5.00

FAULKNER, William. *Town*. 1957. NY. 1st ed. 371 p. dj. T5. $75.00

FAULKNER & CHESHER. *Living Corals*. 1979. Potter. Ils 1st ed. square 4to. dj. EX. M2. $40.00

FAURE, Gabriel. *Gardens of Rome*. 1926. Medici. 14 pls. 4to. VG. G2. $75.00

FAURE, Gabriel. *Gardens of Rome*. 1960. Fair Lawn, NJ. 1st ed. gray cloth. dj. VG. $40.00

FAUST, E.C. *Life History Studies of MT Trematodes*. 1917. IL U. Ils. G. M2. $8.00

FAUVEL, P. *Faune de France: Polychetes Sedentaires*. 1927. Paris. Ils. 492 p. rebound. EX. M2. $25.00

FAUVEL, P. *L'Architecture et la Decoration aux Palais Versailles...* 1899. Paris. 120 pls. folio. TEG. J2. $250.00

FAVRE, H. *Dictionary of Fresh-Water Aquarium*. 1977. Barrons. Ils 1st Am ed. dj. EX. M2. $16.00

FAVRETTI, Rudy. *New England Colonial Gardens*. 1964. Stonington. CT Pequot Pr. wraps. VG. $10.00

FAWCETT, Edgar. *New King Arthur: Opera Without Music*. 1885. London/NY. 1st/only ed. G. C1. $95.00

FAY, Bernard. *Revolution & Freemasonary: 1680-1800*. 1935. Little Brown. 1st ed. dj. VG. $25.00

FAY, C.E. *Mary Celeste*. 1942. Ltd ed. 1/500. VG. $15.00

FAY, Frank. *How To Be Poor*. 1945. NY. Ils Flagg. 172 p. G. $7.00

FEAMSTER, C.N. *Calendar of Papers of John Jordan Crittenden*. 1913. Lib Congress. 335 p. xl. VG. A3. $60.00

FEARING, Kenneth. *Big Clock*. 1946. NY. 1st ed. dj. G. $12.00

FEARING, Kenneth. *Complete Poems*. 1940. NY. 1st ed. inscr. dj. VG. $35.00

FEARING, Kenneth. *Lonelist Girl in the World*. 1951. NY. 1st ed. dj. VG. $20.00

FEATHERSTON, S.R. *True Romantic Tales of the W*. 1978. private print. photos. map. 122 p. dj. EX. M2. $10.00

FEATHERSTONAUGH, G.W. *Excursions Through Slave States*. 1844. 1st Am ed. late wraps. $95.00

FEATHERSTONAUGH, G.W. *Geological Report of Examination Made in 1834...* 1835. Gales Seaton. extremely scarce. A3. $180.00

FEATHERSTONAUGH, G.W. *Report of Geological Reconnaissance Made in 1835...* 1836. pls. 160 p. orig calf. scarce. A3. $140.00

FECHET, J.E. *Flying*. 1933. Baltimore. Williams Wilkins. 138 p. M1. $7.50

FECHTER, Paul. *Der Expressionismus*. 1920. Munich. Piper. Ils 2nd ed. D2. $75.00

FEDER, N. *American Indian Art*. nd. NY. Ils. 4to. dj. EX. J2. $65.00

FEDERBUSH, Arnold. *Man Who Lived in Inner Space*. 1973. Houghton. 1st ed. dj. VG. P1. $15.00

FEDUCCIA, A. *Age of Birds*. 1980. Harvard. Ils. 4to. M2. $9.00

FEDUCCIA, A. *Catesby's Birds of Colonial America*. 1985. NC U. Ils Catesby. 176 p. dj. EX. M2. $35.00

FEHL, Fred. *Stars of Ballet & Dance in Performance Photographs*. 1984. NY. Dover. Ils. 4to. 234 p. wraps. $25.00

FEIBELMAN, W.A. *Rails to Pittsburgh*. 1979. 1st ed. photos. 192 p. $22.50

FEIN, Helen. *Accounting for Genocide.* 1984. Chicago. 1st pb ed. $9.50

FEININGER, Andreas. *Anatomy of Nature.* 1956. dj. EX. S2. $35.00

FEININGER, Andreas. *Face of NY.* 1954. VG. S2. $45.00

FEININGER, Andreas. *Face of NY.* 1954. NY. photos. sgn. EX. $65.00

FEININGER, Andreas. *New Paths in Photography.* 1939. 1st ed. 47 pls. 4to. G. $110.00

FEININGER, Andreas. *NY.* 1964. Darmstadt. Ils 1st ed. D2. $55.00

FEININGER, Andreas. *Principles of Compostition in Photography.* 1973. NY. Amphoto. photos. 176 p. dj. $20.00

FEININGER, Andreas. *Trees.* 1968. Viking. dj. VG. $40.00

FEININGER, Andreas. *World Through My Eyes.* 1963. Crown. dj. VG. $60.00

FEIST, Raymond E. *Darkness at Sethanon.* 1986. Doubleday. 1st ed. dj. EX. P1. $22.50

FEIST, Raymond E. *Silverthorn.* 1985. Doubleday. 1st ed. dj. EX. P1. $22.50

FELD, Charles. *Picasso: His Recent Drawings, 1966-1968.* 1969. NY. Abrams. 1st ed. dj. EX. $60.00

FELDMAIER, Carl. *Lilies.* 1970. London. 1st ed. dj. VG. $15.00

FELDMAN, Stephen. *Fabled Land, Timeless River: Life Along the MS.* 1970. Quadrangle. VG. $12.50

FELDMAN & FALK. *Jews in American Wars.* 1954. WA. Revised Enlarged ed. 276 p. dj. T5. $19.50

FELLOWES, P.F.M. *First Over Everest: Houston-Mt. Everest Expedition, 1933.* 1934. NY. 1st ed. photos. maps. 265 p. dj. G. T5. $45.00

FELLOWS. *This Way to the Big Show.* 1936. NY. Ils. 362 p. VG. C4. $45.00

FELSENTHAL, B. *Practical Grammar of Hebrew Language.* 1868. NY. Frank. 8vo. EX. $125.00

FENADY, Andrew J. *Man With Bogart's Face.* 1977. Regnery. 1st ed. dj. VG. P1. $9.25

FENELLOSA, Ernest. *Chinese Written Character As Medium for Poetry.* 1926. NY. Intro Ezra Pound. VG. $65.00

FENISONG, Ruth. *Desperate Cure.* 1946. Crime Club. 1st ed. dj. xl. P1. $4.75

FENISONG, Ruth. *Lost Caesar.* 1945. Crime Club. 1st ed. xl. P1. $5.00

FENISONG, Ruth. *Miscast for Murder.* nd. Book Club. dj. VG. P1. $2.75

FENISONG, Ruth. *Snare for Sinners.* 1949. Crime Club. 1st ed. dj. VG. P1. $3.00

FENISONG, Ruth. *Widows' Plight.* nd. Book Club. VG. P1. $3.00

FENNER, Phyllis R. *Ghosts Ghosts Ghosts.* 1955. Chatto Windus. 1st ed. dj. VG. P1. $17.50

FENTON, C. *Our Amazing Earth.* 1943. Garden City. maps. 346 p. VG. M2. $5.00

FERBER, Edna. *Giant.* 1952. NY. 1st ed. dj. VG. $20.00

FERENCZ, Benjamin. *Less Than Slaves.* 1980. Cambridge. 2nd ed. G. $3.00

FERENCZI, Sandor. *Thalassa: Theory of Genitality.* 1938. NY. 1st Eng text ed. VG. $50.00

FERGUSON, James. *Two Scottish Soldiers.* 1888. Aberdeen. 1st ed. $150.00

FERGUSON, John. *Man in the Dark.* 1928. Collier. 4th ed. G. P1. $5.50

FERGUSON, John. *Some Aspects of Bibliography.* 1900. Edinburgh. 1/300. $45.00

FERGUSON, Robert. *Indians of the SE: Then & Now.* 1973. NY. Ils. 304 p. dj. EX. $15.00

FERGUSON, W.J. *I Saw Booth Shoot Lincoln.* 1930. Boston. 1/1000. VG. $65.00

FERGUSSON, Bernard. *Black Watch & the King's Enemies.* 1950. London. 1st ed. dj. EX. T1. $45.00

FERGUSSON, Bruce. *Shadow of His Wings.* 1987. Arbor House. 1st ed. dj. EX. P1. $16.95

FERGUSSON, Erna. *Murder & Mystery in NM.* 1948. Albuquerque. Merle Armitage. sgn. G. $18.00

FERGUSSON, Erna. *NM: Pageant of Three Peoples.* 1955. Knopf. dj. VG. $10.00

FERGUSSON, J. *Illustrated Handbook of Architecture.* 1855. 2 vols. rebound. VG. $200.00

FERLINGHETTI, Lawrence. *Canticle for Jack Kerouac.* 1988. Lowell. 1st ed. 1/350. sgn. M. $40.00

FERLINGHETTI, Lawrence. *Canticle of Jack Kerouac.* 1987. Spotlight. 1st ed. 1/350. sgn. $25.00

FERLINGHETTI, Lawrence. *One Thousand Words for Fidel Castro.* 1961. City Lights. 1st ed. presentation. sgn. $45.00

FERLINGHETTI, Lawrence. *Starting From San Francisco.* New Directions. 1st ed. sgn. with record. EX. $45.00

FERLINGHETTI, Lawrence. *Trip to Italy & France.* 1981. New Directions. 1/250. sgn/#d. EX. $30.00

FERMAN, Edward L. *Best Fantasy Stories From Fantasy & SF.* 1985. Octopus. dj. EX. P1. $15.00

FERMAN, Edward L. *Best From Fantasy & SF: 15th Series.* 1966. Doubleday. dj. xl. P1. $5.00

FERNANDEZ, J.A. *Donana: Spain's Wildlife Wilderness.* 1975. Taplinger. Ils 1st ed. 253 p. dj. EX. M2. $25.00

FERRA, Bartomeu. *Chopin & George Sand in Majorca.* 1961. Palma De Mallorca. stiff wraps. J2. $12.50

FERRARI, L. *Onomasticon, Bibliographico, Italiani, 1501 al 1850.* 1947. Milan. Ltd ed. 1/1000. xl. G1. $50.00

FERRARS, Elizabeth X. *Count the Cost.* 1957. Crime Club. 1st ed. xl. P1. $5.00

FERRARS, Elizabeth X. *Death in Botanist's Bay.* 1941. Hodder Stoughton. VG. P1. $25.00

FERRARS, Elizabeth X. *Death of a Minor Character.* 1983. Doubleday. 1st ed. dj. VG. P1. $11.95

FERRARS, Elizabeth X. *I, Said the Fly.* 1945. Crime Club. VG. P1. $15.00

FERRARS, Elizabeth X. *Thinner Than Water.* 1982. Doubleday. 1st ed. dj. VG. P1. $10.00

FERRETTO, G. *Bibliographiche Archeologia Cristiana.* 1942. Vatican. xl. G1. $40.00

FERRI, Enrico. *Criminal Sociology.* 1897. NY. P3. $18.00

FERRIDAY, Peter. *Victorian Architecture.* 1964. NY/Phil. dj. VG. J2. $17.50

FERRIER, Neil. *Churchill: Man of the Century.* 1955. no pub given. 1st ed. red cloth. VG. D1. $25.00

FERRIS, A.B. *Magic Box.* 1922. NY. Council of Women for Home Missions. $35.00

FERRIS & BROWN. *Butterflies of Rocky Mountain States.* 1981. OK U. Ils 1st ed. 442 p. dj. EX. M2. $40.00

FERRISS, Hugh. *Metropolis of Tomorrow.* 1929. Ives Washburn. facsimile ed. dj. D2. $35.00

FERRY, Les Allen. *Make-Believe World of Sue Lewin: Photographs by M. Parrish.* 1978. Los Angeles. 1st print. photos. D2. $27.50

FERRY, W.H. *Buildings of Detroit: A History.* 1969. Wayne U. 2nd print. dj. VG. J2. $22.50

FESSENDEN. *Ladies Monitor.* 1818. Bellows Falls. 1st ed. poor. $38.00

FEST, Joachim. *Face of the Third Reich.* 1970. NY. dj. EX. $17.50

FEST, Joachim. *Hitler.* 1973. NY. 1st ed. dj. VG. $10.00

FETZER, Herman. *Bulls of Spring.* 1937. NY. 1st ed. 93 p. dj. T5. $27.50

FETZER, Herman. *Come Back to Wayne Co.* 1942. Boston. Ils Lynd Ward. 244 p. dj. VG. T5. $17.50

FETZER, Herman. *Jocoby's Corners.* 1949. Boston. Ils 1st ed. 242 p. dj. VG. T5. $17.50

FEYLING-HANSSEN, R.W. *Barnacle Balanus Balanoides in Spitzbergen.* 1953. Oslo. Ils. 64 p. M2. $8.00

FICHTER, G.S. *Birds of FL.* 1971. Seeman. Ils. 114 p. dj. EX. M2. $15.00

FIEDLER, Leslie. *Being Busted.* 1969. Stein Day. 1st ed. dj. VG. $20.00

FIELD, Eugene. *Child's Garland of Verses.* after 1901. Fenno. Ils Powers. VG. $25.00

FIELD, Eugene. *Clink of the Ice.* 1905. G. C1. $4.00

FIELD, Eugene. *Little Book of Tribune Verse.* 1901. Denver. 1st ed. 1/750. M. $45.00

FIELD, Eugene. *Little Book of W Verse.* 1889. Chicago. 1st ed. 1/250. VG. $50.00

FIELD, Eugene. *Little Book of W Verse.* 1915. not 1st ed. VG. C1. $4.50

FIELD, Eugene. *Works of Eugene Field.* 1903. NY. Ils. 12mo. 12 vols. TEG. gilt blue cloth. T1. $90.00

FIELD, Eugene. *Works of Eugene Field.* 1950. Scribner. gilt green cloth. VG. $35.00

FIELD, Evan. *What Nigel Knew.* 1981. Potter. 1st ed. dj. EX. P1. $12.50

FIELD, H.M. *Bright Skies & Dark Shadows.* 1890. NY. 1st ed. 316 p. VG. T5. $45.00

FIELD, H.M. *Old Spain & New Spain.* 1888. Scribner. 1st ed. TEG. VG. $15.00

FIELD, H.M. *Track of Man.* 1955. London. $40.00

FIELD, M. *City Architecture; or, Designs for Dwelling Houses...* 1854. NY. 8vo. 75 p. $45.00

FIELD, M.A. *Where Castilian Roses Bloom: Memoirs.* 1954. San Francisco. Grabhorn. 1/500. sgn. 4to. EX. $125.00

FIELD, S.B. *Darkling Plain.* 1936. Grabhorn. 1st ed. 8vo. VG. $28.00

FIELD, Thomas. *Catalog of Library of Thomas W Field...* 1875. NY. 376 p. poor. $125.00

FIELD & ROSWELL. *Echoes From Sabine Farm.* 1893. Chicago. 1/500. 8vo. VG. T1. $35.00

FIELDING, A. *Death of John Tait.* 1932. Kinsey. 1st ed. VG. P1. $15.00

FIELDING, A. *Eames Erskin Case.* nd. Burt. VG. P1. $4.75

FIELDING, Henry. *History of Adventures of Joseph Andrews.* 1929. NY. Ils Norman Tealby. J2. $22.50

FIELDING, Henry. *History of Tom Jones.* 1964. NY. Ils Lawrence Smith. slipcase. J2. $20.00

FIELDING, Henry. *Journey From This World to the Next.* 1930. Golden Cockerel. 1/500. 8vo. VG. $80.00

FIELDING, Henry. *Late Mr. Jonathan Wild the Great.* 1943. Ltd Ed Club. Ils Cleland. 4to. slipcase. EX. $30.00

FIELDING, Sean. *They Sought Out Rommel: Diary of Libyan Campaign...* 1942. London. Ministry of Information. 72 p. T5. $12.50

FIENNES, R. *Order of Wolves.* 1976. Bobbs Merrill. Ils 1st ed. dj. EX. M2. $25.00

FIFIELD, William. *Sign of Taurus.* 1960. Holt Rinehart Winston. 1st ed. P1. $7.00

FILLEY, William. *Indian Captive; or, Long-Lost Jackson Boy.* 1867. Chicago. Ils 2nd ed. 112 p. G. B2. $350.00

FILMUS, T. *Selected Drawings.* 1971. Ils. 4to. dj. EX. $19.00

FINBERG, A.J. *In Venice With Turner.* 1930. Cotswold Gallery. Ils Turner. J2. $45.00

FINCH, J.S. *Sir Thomas Browne: Doctor's Life of Science & Faith.* 1950. Schuman. Ils 1st ed. 319 p. VG. M2. $9.00

FINCH-DAVIS, C.G. *Game Birds & Waterfowl of S Africa.* 1986. Winchester. Ils. 4to. 190 p. slipcase. M. M2. $9.00

FINDLAY, Hugh. *Imperishable Earth.* 1934. NY. 1/2000. inscr. dj. $45.00

FINDLEY, R. *Great American Deserts.* 1972. Nat Geog Soc. Ils. map. 207 p. dj. EX. M2. $10.00

FINE, R.E. *Gemini G.E.L. Art & Collaboration National Gallery of Art.* 1984. NY/WA. dj. EX. $25.00

FINE, R.E. *Prints of Benton Murdoch Spurance: Catalog Raisonne.* 1986. Phil. PA U. Ils. 340 p. dj. D2. $57.95

FINE, Reuben. *Ideas Behind the Chess Opening.* 1943. Phil. Ils 1st ed. 240 p. dj. T5. $19.50

FINERTY, J.F. *War Path & Bivouac.* 1955. Donnelley. Lakeside Classic. A3. $40.00

FINGER, C.J. *Frontier Ballads Heard & Gathered.* 1927. NY. Ils Paul Honore. 1/201. sgns. fair. $50.00

FINGER, C.J. *Highwaymen: Book of Gallant Rogues.* 1925. NY. 3rd print. dj. G. $18.00

FINGLETON, D. *Kiri.* 1983. Atheneum. dj. M. $37.00

FINKEL, George. *Watch Fires to the N.* 1967. 1st Am ed. scarce. dj. EX. C1. $34.50

FINLEY, J.B. *Autobiography of Rev. James B. Finley...* nd. (1853) Cranston. 1st ed. 455 p. VG. A3. $70.00

FINLEY, J.B. *Life Among the Indians; or, Personal Reminiscences...* 1857. Cincinnati. Ils 1st ed. 548 p. rebound. T5. $62.50

FINLEY, J.B. *Selected Chapters From History of Wyandott Mission...* 1916. Cincinnati. 147 p. dj. VG. T5. $37.50

FINN, F. *Fancy Waterfowl.* 1985. Nimrod. Ils. 85 p. dj. EX. M2. $20.00

FINNEY, C.G. *Circus of Dr. Lao.* 1935. NY. Ils Artzybasheff. 1st ed. dj. VG. $65.00

FINNEY, C.G. *Circus of Dr. Lao.* 1948. London. Ils Fish. 1st ed. $50.00

FINNEY, C.G. *Circus of Dr. Lao.* 1982. Ltd Ed Club. sgn. slipcase. M. $300.00

FINNEY, C.G. *Past the End of the Pavement.* 1939. NY. 1st ed. dj. with sgn leaf. EX. $150.00

FINNEY, C.G. *Unholy City.* 1937. Vanguard Pr. 1st ed. dj. M. $40.00

FINNEY, Jack. *Assault on a Queen.* nd. Book Club. dj. VG. P1. $5.00

FINNEY, Jack. *Forgotten News.* 1983. NY. 1st ed. dj. EX. $20.00

FINNEY, Jack. *I Love Galesburg in the Springtime.* 1963. NY. 1st ed. dj. VG. $20.00

FINNEY, Jack. *Marion's Wall.* nd. Simon Schuster. 3rd ed. VG. P1. $12.50

FINNEY, Jack. *Marion's Wall.* 1973. NY. 1st ed. dj. VG. B2. $25.00

FINNEY, Jack. *Night People.* 1977. NY. 1st ed. dj. G. $15.00

FINNEY, Jack. *Third Level.* nd. Book Club. dj. G. P1. $6.00

FINNEY, Jack. *Time & Again.* nd. BOMC. dj. VG. P1. $7.00

FIOCCO, Giusepe. *Giorgione.* 1948. Bergamo. Ils 2nd ed. D2. $45.00

FIORE & STRAUSS. *Promotable Now.* 1972. NY. $5.00

FIREBAUGH, E.M. *Physician's Wife.* 1894. Phil. 49 pls. VG. $25.00

FIREBAUGH, W.C. *Inns of Greece & Rome.* 1923. Chicago. Ltd ed. 271 p. $70.00

FIREMAN, Judy. *Ultimate TV Book.* 1977. Workman. dj. EX. P1. $20.00

FIRSOFF, V.Z. *Moon Atlas.* 1962. Viking. 2 fld maps. folio. EX. $25.00

FIRTH, Henry. *King Arthur.* 1932. Ils Schoonover. 1st ed. VG. C1. $17.00

FISCH, G. *Nine Months in the US During the Crisis.* 1863. 1st ed. very scarce. K1. $35.00

FISCHEL, Oskar. *Raphael.* 1949. London. 302 pls. 8vo. 2 vols. djs. EX. J2. $75.00

FISCHEL, Oskar. *Raphael.* 1962. Berlin. Hartmann. Ils. 278 p. D2. $75.00

FISCHEL, Oskar. *Raphael.* 1964. London. Spring Books. Ils. 387 p. D2. $65.00

FISCHELLI. *Pompeii: Past & Present.* 1895. VG. S2. $200.00

FISCHER, Erwin. *Berlin Indictment.* 1971. World. 1st ed. dj. xl. P1. $4.75

FISCHER, Fritz. *Germany's Aims in WWI.* 1967. NY. 1st ed. dj. EX. $30.00

FISCHER, Louis. *Men & Politics.* 1941. Duell. 1st ed. sgn. $8.50

FISH, Robert L. *Trouble in Paradise.* 1975. Doubleday. dj. VG. P1. $10.00

FISH, Robert L. *Whirligig.* 1970. World. 1st ed. dj. xl. P1. $6.00

FISH, Robert L. *With Malice Toward All.* 1968. Putnam. 1st ed. dj. xl. P1. $7.50

FISH, Robert L. *Xavier Affair.* 1969. Putnam. 1st ed. dj. xl. P1. $5.00

FISH, T. *Sidney Lanier: America's Sweet Singer of Songs.* 1963. Darien, GA. 1st ed. dj. VG. B2. $22.50

FISHBEIN, Anna Mantel. *Modern Woman's Medical Encyclopedia.* nd. Book Club. dj. VG. P1. $7.50

FISHBERG, A.M. *Heart Failure.* 1937. Phil. Lea Febiger. 1st ed. VG. $75.00

FISHBERG, A.M. *Hypertension & Nephritis.* 1930. Phil. Lea Febiger. 1st ed. VG. $95.00

FISHER, Bud. *Mutt & Jeff, Book 8.* 1922. NY. 48 p. pictorial wraps. fair. T5. $8.50

FISHER, C.J.Z. *Posterity of John Adam Stager...* 1983. Baltimore. Ils. fld map. 1195 p. M. T5. $22.50

FISHER, Harrison. *American Beauties.* 1909. Indianapolis. 4to. EX. $85.00

FISHER, Harrison. *American Girls in Miniature.* 1912. Scribner. 32 color pls. boxed. VG. $50.00

FISHER, Harrison. *Dream of Fair Women.* 1907. NY. G. $75.00

FISHER, Harrison. *Hiawatha.* 1906. Indianapolis. Ils 1st ed. 8vo. EX. T1. $90.00

FISHER, J. *Birds of Britain.* 1947. London. Collins. Ils. 48 p. dj. G. M2. $11.00

FISHER, J. *Wildlife in Danger.* 1969. Viking. Ils Gould/Lear/Gilbert. dj. M2. $20.00

FISHER, J.D. *Description of Distinct, Confluent & Inoculated Small Pox...* 1834. Boston. 2nd ed. sm folio. VG. rare. $600.00

FISHER, John. *Papers of Admiral Sir John Fisher.* 1960. Navy Records Soc. 2 vols. J2. $25.00

FISHER, L.B. *18th-C Garland.* 1951. Williamsburg. Ils 1st ed. 91 p. dj. EX. $35.00

FISHER, M.F.K. *Among Friends.* 1971. NY. 1st ed. dj. VG. B2. $30.00

FISHER, M.F.K. *Physiology of Taste.* nd. Heritage. boxed. VG. $20.00

FISHER, M.F.K. *With Bold Knife & Folk.* 1969. Putnam. 4to. 318 p. dj. EX. $25.00

FISHER, R.M. *Appalachian Trail.* 1972. Nat Geog Soc. Ils. maps. 199 p. dj. EX. M2. $9.00

FISHER, Richard. *Gazetteer of the US.* 1859. Colton. 960 p. G. $55.00

FISHER, Steve. *Hell-Black Night.* 1970. Los Angeles. 1st ed. dj. EX. $15.00

FISHER, Steve. *Image of Hell.* 1961. NY. 1st ed. inscr. dj. EX. $35.00

FISHER, Steve. *Night Before Murder.* 1939. Hillman Curl. 1st ed. G. $18.25

FISHER, Vardis. *Children of God.* 1939. NY. 1st ed. dj. VG. B2. $27.50

FISHER, Vardis. *Gold Rushes & Mining Camps of the Early American W.* 1979. Caxton. 4to. dj. VG. $32.50

FISHER, Vardis. *Intimations of Eve.* 1946. Vanguard. VG. P1. $13.75

FISHER, Vardis. *Mothers.* 1943. NY. 1st ed. dj. VG. B2. $22.50

FISHER, Vardis. *Valley of Vision.* 1951. NY. 1st ed. dj. VG. B2. $22.50

FISHER & PETERSON. *World of Birds.* 1964. Crescent. New Revised ed. 4to. dj. EX. M2. $11.00

FISHMAN. *Sex in Prison.* 1934. Nat Lib Pr. 1st ed. dj. EX. $15.00

FISK, E.J. *Parrot's Wood.* 1985. Norton. 1st ed. 240 p. dj. EX. M2. $17.00

FISK & ELLENBERGER. *Ice Cream Laboratory Guide.* 1917. Orange Judd. 1st ed. sgn. cloth. VG. $15.00

FISKE, D.W. *Book of the First American Chess Congress.* 1859. NY. Ils 1st ed. 561 p. very scarce. T5. $195.00

FISKE, Dwight. *Without Music, That Man at the Taft!* 1933. Chatham. Intro Benchley. 4to. EX. $40.00

FISKE, John. *Critical Period of American History, 1783-1789.* 1879. Riverside Pr. 1/250. VG. $45.00

FISKE, John. *MS Valley in the Civil War.* 1900. Houghton. maps. 368 p. VG. $16.00

FISKE, John. *MS Valley in the Civil War.* 1901. maps. 368 p. EX. J4. $15.00

FISKE, John. *Myths & Myth-Makers.* 1886. not 1st ed. dark blue cloth. VG. C1. $17.00

FISKE, John. *Old VA & Her Neighbors.* 1902. 2 vols. EX. K1. $14.50

FITCH, E.M. *AK Railroad.* 1967. NY. Ils 1st ed. fld map. dj. EX. $45.00

FITCH, F.W. *Life History & Ecology of Scissor-Tailed Flycatcher.* 1950. Auk. no cover. M2. $3.00

FITCH, G.W. *Outlines of Physical Geography.* 1867. NY. Ils. maps. 12mo. 225. p. VG. G2. $15.00

FITCH, J. *Annals of Army of Cumberland Comprising Biographies...* 1863. Lippincott. portraits. maps. 671 p. M2. $50.00

FITCH, M.H. *Ranch Life & Other Sketches.* 1914. Franklin Pr. VG. $175.00

FITCH, S.S. *Six Lectures on Uses of Lungs.* 1847. NY. Ils. 325 p. VG. $45.00

FITELSON, H.W. *Theatre Guild on the Air.* 1947. NY/Toronto. 1st ed. VG. $35.00

FITT, Mary. *Banquet Ceases.* 1949. MacDonald. 1st ed. dj. VG. P1. $25.00

FITT, Mary. *Clues to Cristabel.* 1944. Crime Club. 1st ed. xl. P1. $7.00

FITZ, Grancel. *N American Head Hunting.* 1957. NY. dj. EX. $20.00

FITZGERALD, Edward. *Rubaiyat of Omar Khayyam.* nd. London. Hodder. Ils Dulac. 4to. VG. J2. $200.00

FITZGERALD, Edward. *Rubaiyat of Omar Khayyam.* nd. NY. Crowell. Ils Pogany. dj. J2. $45.00

FITZGERALD, Edward. *Rubaiyat of Omar Khayyam.* 1903. London/NY. Ils Herbert Cole. full leather. $150.00

FITZGERALD, Edward. *Rubaiyat of Omar Khayyam.* 1911. London. Ils. VG. $125.00

FITZGERALD, Edward. *Rubaiyat of Omar Khayyam.* 1946. NY. Heritage. Ils Szyk. slipcase. VG. T5. $25.00

FITZGERALD, F.S. *Beautiful & Damned.* 1922. NY. 1st ed. VG. $60.00

FITZGERALD, F.S. *Beautiful & Damned.* 1922. Scribner. G. $50.00

FITZGERALD, F.S. *Beautiful & Damned.* 1922. Scribner. 1st ed. 1st issue. M. $85.00

FITZGERALD, F.S. *Beautiful & Damned.* 1950. London. 2nd ed. dj. EX. $40.00

FITZGERALD, F.S. *Correspondence.* 1980. NY. 1st ed. dj. EX. $20.00

FITZGERALD, F.S. *Cruise of the Rolling Junk.* 1976. Bruccoli Clark. 1st ed. dj. EX. T6. $75.00

FITZGERALD, F.S. *Dear Scott/Dear Max.* 1971. NY. 1st ed. dj. EX. $20.00

FITZGERALD, F.S. *F. Scott Fitzgerald's St. Paul Plays, 1911-1914.* 1978. Princeton. 1st ed. dj. EX. T6. $25.00

FITZGERALD, F.S. *Great Gatsby.* Ltd Ed Club. slipcase. M. B3. $60.00

FITZGERALD, F.S. *Great Gatsby.* nd. Modern Lib. VG. $20.00

FITZGERALD, F.S. *Great Gatsby.* 1925. NY. Scribner. 1st ed. 2nd state. gilt bdg. T6. $80.00

FITZGERALD, F.S. *Great Gatsby.* 1980. Lunenburg, VG. Ils Fred Meyer. 1/2000. sgn. dj. $70.00

FITZGERALD, F.S. *Pat Hobby Stories.* 1962. NY. 1st ed. presentation. sgn editor. dj. B2. $22.50

FITZGERALD, F.S. *Porcelain & Pink.* 1927. NY. T6. $15.00

FITZGERALD, F.S. *Six Tales of Jazz Age & Other Stories.* 1960. NY. 1st ed. dj. VG. $55.00

FITZGERALD, F.S. *Tales of the Jazz Age.* 1922. NY. 1st ed. 1st print. VG. $120.00

FITZGERALD, F.S. *Taps at Reveille.* 1935. NY. Scribner. 1st ed. 1st state. boxed. $200.00

FITZGERALD, F.S. *Tender Is the Night.* Ltd Ed Club. slipcase. M. B3. $65.00

FITZGERALD, F.S. *Tender Is the Night.* 1934. Scribner. 1st ed. 2nd state. T6. $60.00

FITZGERALD, F.S. *Vegetable.* 1923. NY. 1st ed. 12mo. M. $100.00

FITZGERALD, Francis. *America Revised.* 1979. Boston. 1st ed. dj. VG. $25.00

FITZGERALD, Kevin. *Quiet Under the Sun.* 1954. Little Brown. 1st ed. dj. VG. P1. $10.00

FITZGERALD, Nigel. *Candles Are All Out.* 1961. Macmillan. 1st ed. dj. xl. P1. $6.00

FITZGERALD, Nigel. *Midsummer Malice.* 1959. Macmillan. VG. P1. $13.75

FITZGERALD, T.C. *Coturnix Quail: Anatomy & Histology.* 1969. IA U. Ils 1st ed. 306 p. EX. M2. $20.00

FITZGERALD, Zelda. *Couple of Nuts.* 1932. NY. Scribner. VG. T. $15.00

FITZGERALD, Zelda. *Save Me the Waltz.* 1953. Grey Walls Pr. 1st ed. dj. T6. $90.00

FITZGERALD, Zelda. *Save Me the Waltz.* 1985. Greece. 1st Greek ed. wraps. EX. T6. $25.00

FITZGERALD, Zelda. *Scandalabra.* 1980. Lancaster. Wickersham. 1/500. slipcase. T6. $150.00

FITZGIBBON, Constantine. *Life of Dylan Thomas.* 1965. NY. 1st Am ed. 4to. 370 p. dj. EX. $20.00

FITZGIBBON, R.H. *Agatha Christie Companion.* 1980. Bowling Green. dj. EX. P1. $15.00

FITZHUGH, George. *Antebellum: Three Classic Works on Slavery in Old S.* 1960. NY. 1st ed. dj. EX. $12.00

FITZHUGH, George. *Cannibals All! Or, Slaves Without Masters.* 1960. Cambridge. 1st ed. dj. EX. $18.00

FITZHUGH, P.K. *Pee-Wee Harris in Darkest Africa.* 1929. dj. EX. $12.00

FITZHUGH, P.K. *Westy Martin in the Yellowstone.* 1924. dj. EX. $12.00

FITZPATRICK, J.C. *Calendar of Correspondence of George WA, Commander in Chief.* 1915. Lib Congress. Ils. 4 vols. xl. VG. A3. $240.00

FITZPATRICK, J.C. *Diaries of George WA, 1748-1799.* 1925. Boston. 1st ed. 4 vols. VG. $55.00

FITZPATRICK, J.C. *Some Historic Houses: Their Builders & Places in History.* 1939. NY. VG. J2. $35.00

FITZPATRICK, P. *Jock of the Bushveld.* 1949. Longman Green. Ils. 475 p. rebound. EX. M2. $40.00

FITZSIMMONS, Cortland. *Sudden Silence.* 1938. Stokes. 1st ed. dj. VG. P1. $13.75

FITZSIMMONS, J.O. *Pheasants & Their Enemies.* 1979. Spur. Ils. 101 p. dj. EX. M2. $15.00

FLAGG, J.M. *Roses & Buckshot: Autobiography.* 1946. Putnam. 3rd ed. dj. VG. $15.00

FLAMING, Edmond. *Voyages & Discoveries in S Seas: 1792-1832.* 1924. Salem, MA. 330 p. VG. $50.00

FLAMINI, Roland. *Scarlett, Rhett & a Cast of Thousands.* 1975. Macmillan. 1st ed. dj. EX. $25.00

FLANNAGAN, Roy. *Story of Lucky Strike.* 1939. NY. World Fair ed. VG. $10.00

FLANNER, J. *American in Paris.* 1940. Simon Schuster. dj. EX. $45.00

FLATTE. S.M. *Sound Transmission Through a Fluctuating Ocean.* 1979. Cambridge. dj. M. $30.00

FLAUBERT, Gustave. *Salambo.* 1931. Golden Cockerel. 1/500. 4to. VG. $85.00

FLAUBERT, Gustave. *Salambo.* 1932. private print. Ils Gibbings. 4to. 318 p. VG. $22.00

FLAUBERT, Gustave. *Three Tales.* Ltd Ed Club. slipcase. M. B3. $40.00

FLAUBERT, Gustave. *Three Tales.* 1923. Chatto Windus. Trans McDowell. 1st ed. G. $40.00

FLAUBERT, Gustave. *Three Tales.* 1923. London. Ils Diaz de Soria. VG. C1. $12.00

FLAVEL, John. *Husbandry Spiritualized; or, Heavenly Use of Earthly Things.* 1795. Elizabethtown. Shepard Kellock. 8vo. calf. fair. $30.00

FLEAY, D. *Nightwatchmen of Bush & Plain: Australian Owls & Birds.* 1968. Jacaranda. Ils 1st ed. dj. EX. M2. $35.00

FLECKER, J.E. *Last Generation.* 1906. London. wraps. VG. $50.00

FLECKLES, E.V. *Willie Speaks Out.* 1974. MN. $12.00

FLECTER, E.L. *Practical Instructions in Quantitative Assaying...* 1894. Wiley. 1st ed. 140 p. EX. $6.00

FLEET, S. *Clocks.* 1961. NY. Ils. 128 p. slipcase. EX. $8.50

FLEETWOOD, Frances. *Concordia Errant.* 1973. London. 1st ed. dj. EX. $8.50

FLEETWOOD, John. *History of Medicine in Ireland.* 1951. Dublin. 1st ed. dj. VG. J2. $45.00

FLEISCHER, Nat. *Gene Tunney: Enigma of the Ring.* 1931. NY. 1st ed. 127 p. VG. B2. $40.00

FLEISHER, Edwin. *Edwin A. Fleisher Music Collection in Free Library of Phil.* 1933. Phil. 1st ed. 1/700. 2 vols. VG. J2. $45.00

FLEMING, A.L. *Archibald of the Arctic.* 1956. NY. Appleton Century. 1st ed. dj. M1. $16.50

FLEMING, Ian. *Diamond Smugglers.* 1957. Jonathan Cape. 1st ed. dj. VG. P1. $35.00

FLEMING, Ian. *Diamond Smugglers.* 1957. London. 1st ed. dj. EX. $55.00

FLEMING, Ian. *Dr. No.* 1958. Jonathan Cape. 1st ed. dj. P1. $75.00

FLEMING, Ian. *Dr. No.* 1958. London. 1st ed. silhouette on bdg. dj. EX. $90.00

FLEMING, Ian. *For Your Eyes Only.* 1960. Jonathan Cape. 1st ed. dj. EX. P1. $75.00

FLEMING, Ian. *From Russia With Love.* 1957. Jonathan Cape. 1st ed. VG. P1. $100.00

FLEMING, Ian. *Goldfinger.* 1959. Jonathan Cape. 1st ed. dj. EX. $125.00

FLEMING, Ian. *Jamaica.* 1965. London. 1st ed. dj. VG. $12.00

FLEMING, Ian. *Live & Let Die.* nd. Macmillan. dj. VG. P1. $20.00

FLEMING, Ian. *Man With the Golden Gun.* nd. Book Club. P1. $3.00

FLEMING, Ian. *Man With the Golden Gun.* 1965. Doubleday. 3rd ed. dj. VG. P1. $22.75

FLEMING, Ian. *Man With the Golden Gun.* 1965. Jonathan Cape. 1st ed. dj. EX. P1. $50.00

FLEMING, Ian. *Man With the Golden Gun.* 1965. Jonathan Cape. 1st ed. dj. VG. P1. $40.00

FLEMING, Ian. *Man With the Golden Gun.* 1965. Jonathan Cape. 1st ed. dj. xl. P1. $22.75

FLEMING, Ian. *Moonraker.* 1954. Macmillan. 1st ed. dj. VG. $60.00

FLEMING, Ian. *Octopussy & Living Daylights.* 1966. London. 1st ed. dj. EX. $35.00

FLEMING, Ian. *Octopussy & Living Daylights.* 1966. NY. 1st ed. dj. EX. $20.00

FLEMING, Ian. *On Her Majesty's Secret Service.* 1963. Jonathan Cape. 1st ed. dj. EX. P1. $65.00

FLEMING, Ian. *On Her Majesty's Secret Service.* 1963. New Am Lib. 1st Am ed. dj. EX. $40.00

FLEMING, Ian. *Spy Who Loved Me.* 1962. Jonathan Cape. 1st ed. dj. P1. $65.00

FLEMING, Ian. *Thrilling Cities.* 1964. New Am Lib. 1st ed. EX. $15.00

FLEMING, Ian. *Thunderball.* 1961. Jonathan Cape. 1st ed. VG. P1. $50.00

FLEMING, Ian. *You Only Live Twice.* nd. Book Club. G. P1. $4.00

FLEMING, Ian. *You Only Live Twice.* 1964. Jonathan Cape. 1st ed. dj. P1. $45.00

FLEMING, Ian. *You Only Live Twice.* 1964. Jonathan Cape. 2nd ed. dj. xl. P1. $13.75

FLEMING, Ian. *You Only Live Twice.* 1964. Jonathan Cape. 2nd ed. G. P1. $11.50

FLEMING, Ian. *You Only Live Twice.* 1964. London. 1st ed. dj. B1. $35.00

FLEMING, Joan. *Daisy Chain for Satan.* 1950. Crime Club. 1st ed. dj. xl. P1. $5.00

FLEMING, Joan. *Deeds of Dr. Deadcert.* 1957. Ives Washburn. dj. xl. P1. $5.00

FLEMING, Joan. *You Won't Let Me Finish.* 1974. Putnam. 1st ed. dj. xl. P1. $5.00

FLEMING, P. *Brazilian Adventure.* 1934. Scribner. Ils 1st ed. 412 p. M2. $10.00

FLEMING, T.J. *Now We Are Enemies: Story of Bunker Hill.* 1960. St. Martin. map. 366 p. VG. M2. $9.00

FLEMING, T.J. *Now We Are Enemies: Story of Bunker Hill.* 1969. 559 p. dj. EX. J4. $5.00

FLEMING, Walter. *Sequel of Appomattox.* 1921. Yale. index. 322 p. K1. $9.50

FLESHMAN, Bob. *Theatrical Movement: Bibliographical Anthology.* Scarecrow Pr. 756 p. VG. T5. $15.00

FLETCHER, Banister. *History of Architecture on the Comparative Method.* 1931. NY. 9th ed. VG. J2. $20.00

FLETCHER, Banister. *History of Architecture on the Comparative Method.* 1967. NY. 17th ed. dj. EX. J2. $22.50

FLETCHER, Benton. *Royal Homes Near London.* 1930. London. dj. VG. with presentation card. J2. $25.00

FLETCHER, Colin. *Complete Walker: Joys & Techniques of Hiking & Backpacking.* 1973. Knopf. Ils. 353 p. VG. M2. $10.00

FLETCHER, Colin. *Man Who Walked Through Time.* March, 1968. NY. photos. dj. VG. $9.50

FLETCHER, Colin. *Thousand-Mile Summer.* 1964. Howell N. Ils. 207 p. dj. EX. M2. $5.00

FLETCHER, Curley. *Songs of the Sage.* 1931. Los Angeles. Frontier Pub. sgn. VG. scarce. $30.00

FLETCHER, David. *Loveable Man.* 1975. Coward McCann. 1st ed. dj. xl. P1. $4.75

FLETCHER, George U. *Well of the Unicorn.* 1948. Sloane. 1st ed. dj. G. P1. $31.75

FLETCHER, Inglis. *Bennett's Welcome.* 1950. Bobbs Merrill. 1st ed. sgn. 8vo. EX. $30.00

FLETCHER, Inglis. *Coromant's Brood.* 1959. Lippincott. Stated 1st ed. sgn. dj. EX. $25.00

FLETCHER, Inglis. *Roanoke Hundred.* 1948. Bobbs Merrill. 1st ed. sgn. EX. $32.50

FLETCHER, J.S. *Amaranth Club.* nd. Grosset. VG. P1. $11.50

FLETCHER, J.S. *Diamond Murders.* c 1929. NY. Dodd Mead. 1st ed. VG. $8.00

FLETCHER, J.S. *Guarded Room.* nd. John Long. xl. P1. $10.00

FLETCHER, J.S. *Lost Mr. Linthwaite.* 1923. Knopf. 1st ed. VG. P1. $20.00

FLETCHER, J.S. *Makenmore Mystery.* nd. Grosset. dj. VG. P1. $15.00

FLETCHER,   J.S.   *Rayner-Slade Amalgamation.* 1922. Knopf. G. P1. $9.25

FLETCHER, Lucille. *And Presumed Dead.* 1963. Random House. 1st ed. VG. P1. $10.00

FLETCHER, P. *Purple Island; or, Isle of Man...* 1633. Cambridge. 1st ed. 4to. Larkins bdg. $350.00

FLETCHER, R.H. *Free Grass to Fences.* MT Hist Soc. Ils Russell. dj. EX. $50.00

FLETCHER, R.H. *Marjorie & Her Papa.* 1891. Century. Ils Birch. VG. B4. $85.00

FLETCHER, S.W. *Strawberry Growing.* 1917. Macmillan. Ils. 352 p. EX. $8.00

FLETCHER. *Account of Descendants of Robert Fletcher of Concord, MA.* 1871. Boston. private print. G. B1. $50.00

FLETCHER, J.S. *False Scent.* 1925. Macmillan. VG. P1. $15.00

FLEXNER, James. *American Painting: First Flowers of Our Wilderness.* 1947. Houghton. 1st ed. dj. VG. J2. $12.50

FLEXNER, James. *John Singleton Copley.* 1948. Houghton. VG. J2. $22.50

FLEXNER. *Quaker Childhood, 1781-1888.* 1940. New Haven. 1st ed. presentation. sgn. dj. EX. $22.00

FLINT, Abel. *System of Geometry & Trigonometry...* 1818. Hartford. 4th ed. 8vo. full calf. $25.00

FLINT, Timothy. *History & Geography of MS Valley.* 1833. Cincinnati. 3rd ed. 2 vols. rebound. EX. $75.00

FLINT, Timothy. *Recollections of the Last Ten Years.* 1932. NY. reprint of 1826 ed. dj. VG. T5. $27.50

FLINT, W.R. *Models of Propriety.* 1951. London. Joseph. 2nd print. 31 pls. dj. $30.00

FLOMEN, Michael. *Still Life, Draped Stone.* 1985. Paget Pr. dj. VG. $12.50

FLOOD, C.B. *Lee: The Last Years.* 1981. Houghton. Ils 1st ed. 308 p. dj. EX. M2. $12.00

FLORA, Fletcher. *Irrepressible Peccadillo.* 1962. Macmillan. 1st ed. dj. VG. P1. $20.00

FLORESCU & MC NALLY. *Dracula: Biography of Vlad the Impaler: 1431-1476.* 1973. 2nd print. dj. EX. $30.00

FLORIN, Lambert. *Boot Hill: History of Graves of Old W.* 1966. Seattle. dj. VG. $11.00

FLORIN, Lambert. *W Ghost Towns.* 1961. Seattle. 1st ed. 200 photos. dj. EX. $17.50

FLORINSKY, M.T. *Encyclopedia of Russia & the Soviet Union.* 1961. McGraw Hill. Ils 1st ed. 4to. 624 p. dj. M2. $22.00

FLOWER, Desmond. *Paper Book: Its Past, Present & Future.* 1959. London. private print. presentation. EX. $35.00

FLOWER, Pat. *Crisscross.* 1976. Crime Club. 1st ed. dj. EX. P1. $12.50

FLOWER, Pat. *Crisscross.* 1977. Stein Day. dj. VG. P1. $10.00

FLOWER, Pat. *Vanishing Point.* 1977. Stein Day. dj. VG. P1. $10.00

FLOWER & REEVES. *War: 1939-1945.* 1960. London. Cassell. 8vo. 1120 p. EX. $35.00

FLUCKIGER, F. *Chinchona Barks: Pharmacognostically Considered.* 1884. Phil. 8 pls. sm folio. 100 p. EX. $65.00

FLYNN, Errol. *Showdown.* 1946. NY. 1st ed. dj. VG. B2. $22.50

FOBES, H.K. *Mystic Gems.* 1924. Boston. $75.00

FODOR, Nandor. *Encyclopedia of Psychic Science.* 1933. London. $100.00

FODOR, Nandor. *Kalandok a Sing-Sing Fegyhazban.* nd. Budapest. $60.00

FOGAZZARO, Antonio. *Saint.* 1907. Copp Clarke. VG. P1. $9.25

FOGEL, R.W. *Railroads & American Economic Growth.* 1964. 296 p. $17.50

FOGEL, R.W. *Union Pacific Railroad: Case in Premature Enterprise.* 1960. 129 p. $15.00

FOGEL & ENGERMAN. *Time on the Cross: Economics of American Negro Slavery.* 1974. 1st ed. tables. charts. 286 p. dj. M. J4. $17.50

FOGG, G.E. *Algal Cultures & Phytoplankton Ecology.* 1971. WI U. Ils. 126 p. dj. EX. M2. $15.00

FOLEY, Daniel. *Complete Book of Garden Ornaments, Compliments...* 1972. NY. dj. VG. $20.00

FOLEY, Edwin. *Book of Decorative Furniture: Its's Form, Color & History.* c 1910. NY. Dodge. 100 pls. 2 vols. VG. A3. $350.00

FOLEY, Rae. *Girl Who Had Everything.* 1977. Dodd Mead. 1st ed. dj. VG. P1. $12.50

FOLEY, Rae. *Malice Domestic.* 1968. Dodd Mead. 1st ed. dj. G. P1. $10.00

FOLEY, Rae. *Reckless Lady.* 1973. Dodd Mead. 1st ed. dj. xl. P1. $7.50

FOLEY, Rae. *Shelton Conspiracy.* 1967. Dodd Mead. dj. G. P1. $15.00

FOLGER, FOLGER & LUPOLD. *W Reserve.* 1981. Garrettsville. 1st ed. fld map. 243 p. wraps. T5. $8.50

FOLIO SOCIETY. *First Colonists: Hakluyt's Voyages.* 1986. 4to. slipcase. EX. $22.00

FOLIO SOCIETY. *Life & Campaigns of Black Prince.* 1979. 8vo. slipcase. EX. $15.00

FOLLETT, Ken. *Gentlemen of 16 July.* 1978. Arbor House. 1st ed. dj. VG. P1. $12.00

FOLLETT, Ken. *Key to Rebecca.* 1980. Morrow. 3rd ed. dj. EX. $10.00

FOLLETT, Ken. *Lie Down With Lions.* 1986. Morrow. 3rd ed. dj. EX. $10.00

FOLLETT, Ken. *Man From St. Petersburg.* 1986. Morrow. 3rd ed. dj. EX. $10.00

FOLLETT, Ken. *On Wings of Eagles.* 1983. NY. 1st ed. dj. VG. M1. $10.00

FOLLETT, Ken. *Triple.* 1979. Arbor House. 5th print. dj. EX. $10.00

FOLSOM, Franklin. *Exploring American Caves: Their History, Geology, Lore...* 1956. Crown. 1st ed. dj. VG. J2. $20.00

FOLSOM, Franklin. *Life & Legend of George McJunkin, Black Cowboy.* 1973. Ils 2nd ed. dj. VG. $15.00

FONER, E. *Tom Paine & Revolutionary America.* 1976. Oxford U. Ils. 326 p. dj. EX. M2. $14.00

FONER & LEWIS. *Black Worker, Vol. IV.* 1979. 402 p. $25.00

FONT. *Font's Complete Diary.* 1931. CA U. 1st ed. xl. VG. J2. $45.00

FONTEYN, Margot. *Magic of Dance.* 1979. NY. 1st Am ed. 326 p. dj. EX. $25.00

FOOSE, S. *Scrap Savers' Stichery Book.* 1978. 1st ed. dj. EX. $15.00

FOOTE, H. *Casket of Reminiscences.* 1874. WA. 8vo. 498 p. VG. $52.00

FOOTE, H. *Harrison, TX: 8 Television Plays.* 1956. NY. 1st ed. 266 p. dj. VG. $27.50

FOOTE, J.T. *Hell Cat.* 1936. Appleton. 1st ed. dj. VG. B2. $30.00

FOOTE, J.T. *Jing.* 1936. Derrydale. 1/950. inscr/sgn. M. $120.00

FOOTE, Shelby. *Civil War: A Narrative.* 1958. NY. maps. 3 vols. G. T5. $35.00

FOOTE, Shelby. *Civil War: A Narrative. Vol. I: Ft. Sumter to Perryville.* 1958. 1st ed. maps. 840 p. EX. J4. $9.50

FOOTE, Shelby. *September September.* 1977. Random House. 1st ed. dj. $45.00

FOOTE & COOK. *Mosquitos of Medical Importance.* 1959. USDA. Ils. 4to. EX. M2. $18.00

FOOTNER, Hulbert. *Dark Ships.* 1937. Harper. 1st ed. G. P1. $10.00

FOOTNER, Hulbert. *Unneutral Murder.* 1944. Crime Club. 1st ed. VG. P1. $10.00

FORBES, Allan. *Towns of New England & Old England, Ireland & Scotland.* 1936. NY. Tudor. Ils. G. T5. $19.50

FORBES, M. *More Than I Dreamed. Lifetime of Collecting.* 1989. NY. 1st ed. dj. M. $25.00

FORBES, R. *From Red Sea to Blue Nile: An Abyssinian Adventure.* 1925. Macaulay. Ils. 367 p. VG. M2. $16.00

FORBES, R.H. *Crabb's Filibustering Expedition Into Sonora, 1857.* 1952. Tucson. 1/650. maps. 60 p. T5. $45.00

FORBES & FOSTER. *Automotive Giants of America.* 1926. Forbes. EX. $27.50

FORBES & RICHARDSON. *Fishes of IL.* 1920. IL Nat Hist Div. 2 vols. M2. $90.00

FORBIS, W. *Cowboys.* Time Life. Old W Series. 4to. padded leather. $8.50

FORBUSH, E.H. *Natural Enemies of Birds.* 1916. MS Agric. Ils. 58 p. M2. $4.00

FORBUSH, E.H. *Utility of Birds.* nd. MA Audubon Soc. Ils. 83 p. M2. $5.00

FORBUSH & MAY. *Natural History of Birds of E & Central N America.* 1955. Bramhall. reprint. 4to. dj. EX. M2. $22.00

FORCE, M.F. *Personal Recollections of Vicksburg Campaign.* 1885. Cincinnati. 15 p. wraps. xl. fair. T5. $15.00

FORD, Alexander. *Robin Hood: Earl of Huntington.* 1930. Chicago. 1st ed. dj. VG. C1. $11.00

FORD, Alice. *Bird Biographies of James John Audubon.* 1957. Macmillan. Ils 1st print. 282 p. dj. EX. M2. $14.00

FORD, Alice. *John James Audubon.* 1965. OK U. 488 p. dj. EX. M2. $15.00

FORD, Alice. *1826 Journal of John James Audubon.* 1967. OK U. Ils 1st ed. 409 p. dj. EX. M2. $21.00

FORD, Arthur. *Nothing So Strange.* 1958. NY. 1st ed. dj. EX. $10.00

FORD, Arthur. *Unknown But Known.* 1968. NY. $28.00

FORD, C. *Where the Sea Breaks Its Back.* 1966. Little Brown. Ils 1st ed. 206 p. dj. EX. M2. $45.00

FORD, C.H. *Flag Ecstasy.* 1972. Black Sparrow. 1/200. sgn. $40.00

FORD, Corey. *Minutes of the Lower Forty.* 1962. NY. 1st ed. dj. VG. $60.00

FORD, F.M. *Man Could Stand Up.* 1926. London. 1st ed. EX. $20.00

FORD, F.M. *NY Is Not America.* 1927. NY. 1st Am ed. sgn. VG. $75.00

FORD, G.L. *TX Cattle Brands.* 1936. Dallas. Ils. dj. EX. $25.00

FORD, G.R. *Portrait of the Assassin.* 1965. NY. 1st ed. dj. VG. B2. $30.00

FORD, G.R. *Time To Heal.* 1979. NY. 1st ed. presentation. dj. EX. $110.00

FORD, Hugh. *Nancy Cunard, Brave Poet.* 1960. NY/London. Stated 1st ed. dj. M. $25.00

FORD, J.H. *Conversion of Buster Drumwright.* 1964. Nashville. Vanderbilt U. dj. VG. $27.50

FORD, J.L. *Forty-Odd Years in the Literary Shop.* 1922. NY. pls. $30.00

FORD, James Allan. *Judge of Men.* 1968. Hodder Stoughton. dj. VG. P1. $7.00

FORD, John M. *Dragon Waiting.* nd. Book Club. dj. EX. C1. $4.50

FORD, John M. *Dragon Waiting.* 1983. Timescape. 1st ed. dj. VG. P1. $17.50

FORD, John M. *Dragon Waiting.* 1985. pb. VG. C1. $3.00

FORD, Julia. *Imagine.* 1923. NY. Ils Rackham. 4to. G. $25.00

FORD, Julia. *Snickerty Nick & the Giant.* 1935. LA. Sutton House. 3rd print. dj. VG. $65.00

FORD, Leslie. *By the Watchman's Clock.* nd. Grosset Dunlap. VG. P1. $7.50

FORD, Leslie. *False to Any Man.* 1939. Scribner. dj. VG. $25.00

FORD, Leslie. *Murder in MD.* 1942. NY. Triangle. 1st ed. dj. $12.50

FORD, Leslie. *Philadelphia Murder Story.* 1945. Scribner. dj. G. P1. $13.75

FORD, Leslie. *Road to Folly.* nd. Collier. VG. P1. $7.50

FORD, Leslie. *Simple Way of Poison.* nd. Grosset Dunlap. dj. xl. P1. $9.25

FORD, Leslie. *Washington Whisper's Murder.* 1953. Scribner. 1st ed. VG. P1. $10.00

FORD, P.L. *House Party.* 1901. Boston. 1st ed. 8vo. red cloth. EX. T1. $35.00

FORD, P.L. *Love Finds a Way.* 1904. Dodd Mead. Ils Fisher/Armstrong. 1st ed. B4. $115.00

FORD, P.L. *Wanted: A Chaperone.* 1902. NY. Ils Christy. G. $20.00

FORD, Richard. *Communist.* 1987. Babcock Koontz. 1/200. sgn/#d. wraps. $45.00

FORD, Richard. *Piece of My Heart.* 1976. Harper. ARC. wraps. $165.00

FORD, Richard. *Piece of My Heart.* 1976. Harper. 1st ed. dj. $100.00

FORD, Richard. *Piece of My Heart.* 1976. Random House. 1st ed. EX. $40.00

FORD, Richard. *Sportswriter.* 1986. NY. Vintage. 1st ed. wraps. M. $25.00

FORD, Thomas. *History of IL.* 1945 & 1946. Lakeside Classic. 2 vols. A3. $70.00

FORD, Tirey. *Dawn & Dons. Romance of Monterey.* 1926. San Francisco. Ils Jo Mora. VG. $30.00

FORD, W.C. *George WA.* 1900. NY. Memorial ed. VG. $85.00

FORD & STILES. *Portrait of the Assassin.* 1965. NY. 1st ed. presentation. sgns. dj. EX. B2. $130.00

FORD MOTOR COMPANY. *Instruction Book for Ford Model A.* 1928. 52 p. wraps. VG. $32.00

FORD. *Time To Heal.* 1979. NY. 1st ed. dj. EX. $10.00

FORDMAN, Henry James. *Rembrandt Murder.* 1931. Richard Smith. 1st ed. dj. xl. P1. $10.00

FOREMAN, C.T. *OK Imprints: 1835-1907.* 1936. Norman. Ils. dj. EX. $85.00

FOREMAN, Grant. *Advancing the Frontier, 1830-1860.* 1933. Norman. Ils. 10 maps/plans. EX. $40.00

FOREMAN, Grant. *Indians & Pioneers: Story of American SW Before 1830.* 1936. Norman. Ils Revised ed. sgn. dj. VG. $130.00

FOREMAN, Grant. *Last Trek of the Indians.* 1946. Chicago. fld maps. dj. EX. $85.00

FORES, Thomas. *Guide to Better Archery.* 1955. PA. 307 p. dj. G. $15.00

FORESTER, C.S. *Bedchamber Mystery.* 1944. Toronto. only ed. dj. $165.00

FORESTER, C.S. *Captain Horatio Hornblower.* 1940. Little Brown. 12th print. VG. P1. $15.00

FORESTER, C.S. *Commodore Hornblower.* nd. BOMC. dj. VG. P1. $7.50

FORESTER, C.S. *Commodore Hornblower.* 1945. Boston. 1st Am ed. 384 p. dj. G. T5. $35.00

FORESTER, C.S. *Flying Colors Including a Ship of the Line.* 1938. London. 1st ed. VG. $60.00

FORESTER, C.S. *Good Shepherd.* nd. BOMC. dj. G. P1. $7.50

FORESTER, C.S. *Gun.* 1933. Boston. 1st ed. dj. VG. B2. $27.50

FORESTER, C.S. *Hornblower Companion.* 1964. Bonzanza. EX. $45.00

FORESTER, C.S. *Hunting the Bismarck.* 1959. London. Joseph. 1st ed. dj. EX. $25.00

FORESTER, C.S. *Lord Hornblower.* nd. Grossett. G. P1. $5.00

FORESTER, C.S. *Lord Hornblower.* 1946. Boston. 1st ed. VG. $47.50

FORESTER, C.S. *Mr. Midshipman Hornblower.* 1951. Reprint Soc. dj. EX. P1. $20.00

FORESTER, C.S. *Ship.* 1943. Clipper Books. dj. VG. P1. $30.00

FORESTER, C.S. *Sky & the Forest.* nd. BOMC. dj. VG. P1. $7.50

FORESTER, C.S. *Sky & the Forest.* 1948. Michael Joseph. 1st Canadian ed. P1. $9.25

FORESTER, E.M. *Life To Come & Other Stories.* 1972. London. 1st ed. dj. EX. $25.00

FORESTER, Frank. *Deer Stalkers.* Derrydale. 1/750. EX. $100.00

FORESTER, Frank. *Field Sports in US & British Provinces of America.* 1848. London. Bentley. 1st ed. 2 vols. scarce. $140.00

FORESTER, Frank. *Sporting Scenes & Sundry Sketches.* 1842. NY. 1st ed. 2 vols. rebound. VG. B2. $70.00

FORESTER, Frank. *Trouting Along the Catasaqua.* 1927. NY. 1/423. 41 p. $80.00

FOREY & FITZSIMONS. *Instant Guide to Reptiles & Amphibians.* 1987. Bonanza. Ils. 124 p. EX. M2. $8.00

FORGE, Andrew. *Rauschenberg.* nd. NY. Abrams. Ils. stiff paper wraps. D2. $25.00

FORKERT, O.M. *From Gutenberg to the Cuneo Pr.* 1933. Chicago. Ils. $30.00

FORMAN, Alfred. *Nibelung's Rings.* 1877. London. 1st Trans. gilt cloth. VG. T1. $35.00

FORMAN, H.C. *Architecture of Old S.* 1948. Harvard. 1st ed. dj. M. $32.50

FORMAN, H.C. *Architecture of Old S.* 1948. Harvard. 1st ed. dj. VG. J2. $25.00

FORMAN, H.C. *Architecture of Old S: Medieval Style, 1585-1850.* 1949. Cambridge. xl. G. $20.00

FORMAN, W. & B. *Prehistoric Art.* nd. (c 1950) 22 color pls. B2. $40.00

FORNEY, J.W. *Life & Military Career of Winfield Scott Hancock.* 1880. 504 p. EX. $15.00

FORREST, Edwin. *Report of Forrest Divorce Case.* 1852. NY. wraps. $25.00

FORREST & ALBI. *Denver's Railroads: Story of Union Station & Railroads...* 1981. Golden. Ils. 244 p. dj. VG. A3. $45.00

FORREST & HILL. *Lone War Trail of the Apache Kid.* 1947. Trails End Pub. Deluxe Ltd ed. 1/250. sgns. dj. VG. $135.00

FORRESTEL, E.P. *Admiral Raymond A. Spruance, USN: Study in Command.* 1966. WA. 275 p. EX. T5. $22.50

FORRESTER, Francis. *Minnie Grown; or, The Gentle Girl.* 1856. Rand Avery. VG. B4. $35.00

FORRESTER, Larry. *Skymen: Heroes of Fifty Years of Flying.* 1961. NY. Ils. 256 p. dj. VG. T5. $12.50

FORSTER, E.M. *Passage to India.* 1924. London. 1st ed. VG. $185.00

FORSTER, E.M. *Two Cheers for Democracy.* 1951. London. 1st ed. G. $20.00

FORSTER, F.J. *Country Houses.* 1931. NY. 4to. maroon cloth. $90.00

FORSYTH, Frederick. *Day of the Jackal.* 1971. NY. Review 1st ed. VG. $45.00

FORSYTH, Frederick. *Day of the Jackal.* 1971. NY. 1st Am ed. dj. EX. $16.00

FORSYTH, Frederick. *Day of the Jackel.* 1971. NY. ARC. wraps. EX. T5. $150.00

FORSYTH, Frederick. *Devil's Alternative.* 1979. Hutchinson. 1st ed. dj. EX. P1. $18.25

FORSYTH, Frederick. *Fourth Protocol.* 1984. Stoddart. 1st ed. dj. EX. P1. $18.25

FORSYTH, Frederick. *No Comebacks & Other Stories.* 1982. Helsinki. 1st ed. 1/350. sgn. dj. wraps. EX. $65.00

FORT, I.S. *Flag Paintings of Childe Hassam.* 1988. NY. pls. 8vo. 128 p. EX. $15.00

FORTUIN, Leonard. *Sea Surface As Random Filter for Underwater Sound Waves.* 1973. Uitgeverij Waltman-Delft. pb. VG. $10.00

FORTUNE, Dion. *Glastonbury: Avalon of the Heart.* 1989. pb. M. C1. $12.00

FORTUNE, Dion. *Goat Foot God.* 1988. pb. M. C1. $11.00

FORTUNE, Dion. *Moon Magic.* 1985. pb. M. C1. $9.50

FORTUNE, Dion. *Winged Bull.* 1971. dj. EX. C1. $12.50

FORTUNE & BURTON. *Elisabeth Ney.* 1943. Knopf. 1st ed. VG. J2. $10.00

FORWARD, Robert L. *Dragon's Egg.* 1980. Del Rey. 1st ed. dj. EX. P1. $15.00

FORYS, Marsha. *Antonio Buero Vallejo & Alfonso Sastre.* Scarecrow Pr. 209 p. VG. T5. $9.50

FOSDICK, Charles. *Five Hundred Days in Rebel Prisons.* 1887. Bethany, MO. G. $35.00

FOSDICK, Charles. *Five Hundred Days in Rebel Prisons.* 1887. np. 118 p. EX. very scarce. J4. $60.00

FOSS, Michael. *Undreamed Shores: England's Wasted Empire in America.* c 1974. London. dj. VG. $7.50

FOSTER, Alan Dean. *Cachalot.* nd. Book Club. dj. EX. P1. $4.00

FOSTER, Alan Dean. *Day of the Dissonance.* 1984. Phantasia. 1/375. sgn. dj. slipcase. EX. P1. $40.00

FOSTER, Alan Dean. *Icerigger.* 1976. New Eng Lib. 1st ed. dj. P1. $40.00

FOSTER, Alan Dean. *Man Who Used the Universe.* nd. Book Club. dj. EX. P1. $4.50

FOSTER, Alan Dean. *Midworld.* nd. British SF Book Club. dj. VG. P1. $5.00

FOSTER, Alan Dean. *Midworld*. nd. Book Club. dj. VG. P1. $4.50

FOSTER, Alan Dean. *Mission to Moulokin*. nd. Book Club. dj. EX. P1. $4.50

FOSTER, Alan Dean. *Moment of the Magician*. 1984. Phantasia. 1/375. sgn. dj. slipcase. EX. P1. $40.00

FOSTER, Alan Dean. *Splinter of the Mind's Eye*. nd. Book Club. dj. VG. P1. $3.75

FOSTER, Alan Dean. *Splinter of the Mind's Eye*. 1978. Del Rey. 2nd ed. dj. EX. P1. $15.00

FOSTER, B. *Powdersmoke Fence*. 1940. Doubleday Doran. orange cloth. M. $12.00

FOSTER, David. *Adventures of Christian Rosy Cross*. 1986. Penguin. pb. EX. C1. $5.00

FOSTER, H.L. *Rock Gardening*. 1968. Boston. 1st ed. dj. VG. $20.00

FOSTER, Hal. *Prince Valiant Fights Attila the Hun*. 1952. Hastings House. 1st ed. dj. VG. C1. $12.50

FOSTER, Hal. *Young Knight: Tale of Medieval Times*. 1945. Kenosha, WI. Martin House. Ils 1st ed. dj. VG. $45.00

FOSTER, J. *Miniature Painters, British & Foreign*. 1903. London. folio. 2 vols. TEG. VG. J2. $150.00

FOSTER, Joseph. *Some Feudal Coats of Arms From Heraldic Rolls 1298-1418*. 1902. London. Ils. 268 p. xl. VG. T5. $25.00

FOSTER, R.F. *Mystery at Chillery*. c 1931. NY. Fiction League. 1st ed. VG. $8.00

FOSTER, T.S. *Travels & Settlements of Early Man*. 1929. Stokes. 1st ed. VG. J2. $15.00

FOSTER, W.D. *Cottages, Manors & Other Minor Buildings of Normandy...* Ils Rosenberg. photos. sgn. folio. fair. $75.00

FOSTER & HARRIES. *Look of the Old W.* 1955. NY. 1st ed. dj. EX. $35.00

FOSTER & WEIR. *Rhymes & Roundelayes in Praise of Country Life*. 1857. London. Ils. gilt morocco. EX. $90.00

FOSTER & WHITNEY. *Report on Geology Lake Superior Land District: Iron Region*. 1850. WA. orig leather. VG. $50.00

FOTHERGILL, J.M. *Practitioner's Handbook of Treatments*. 1887. Phil. full calf. $55.00

FOTHERGILL, John. *Fothergill Omnibus*. 1931. London. 1/250. 17 sgns. $300.00

FOUCHET, Max Pol. *Wildredo Lam*. 1976. NY. Rizzoli. pls. photos. 266 p. dj. D2. $125.00

FOULKES, Charles. *Armor & Weapons*. 1909. London. Ils 1st ed. EX. $65.00

FOURCADE, Francois. *Art Treasures of Peking Museum*. 1965. Abrams. Ils. folio. 177 p. dj. EX. $60.00

FOURNIER, A. *Les Affections Parasyphilitiques*. 1894. Paris. 1st ed. 8vo. 375 p. $180.00

FOWKE, Gerard. *Antiquities of Central & SE MO*. 1910. Smithsonian. VG. $50.00

FOWLER, D.D. *Photographed All the Best Scenery: Jack Hiller's Diary...* 1972. Salt Lake City. Ils. 225 p. dj. A3. $30.00

FOWLER, Gene. *Trumpet in the Dust*. 1930. Liveright. 1st ed. inscr. VG. $28.00

FOWLER, H.W. *Dictionary of Modern English Usage*. 1965. NY. 2nd ed. VG. $14.00

FOWLER, Horace. *Industrial Public*. 1921. LA. VG. $25.00

FOWLER, O.S. *Fowler's Practical Phrenology*. 1845. NY. 430 p. full calf. EX. $65.00

FOWLER, O.S. *Practical Phrenologist*. 1869. Boston. $16.00

FOWLER, Sydney. *Bell Street Murders*. 1932. Harrap. 3rd ed. dj. VG. P1. $20.00

FOWLER, W.W. *Ten Years in Wall Street*. 1870. Worthington Dustin. 1st ed. EX. $60.00

FOWLER, W.W. *Ten Years in Wall Street*. 1870. Hartford. Ils 1st ed. 8vo. VG. T1. $40.00

FOWLER & FOWLER. *Self-Instructor in Phrenology & Physiology*. 1859. NY. $37.50

FOWLES, John. *Cinderella*. 1974. London. Ils Beckett. 1st ed. sgns. dj. EX. $40.00

FOWLES, John. *Collector*. 1963. Boston. ARC. 1st Am ed. wraps. VG. $80.00

FOWLES, John. *Collector*. 1963. Boston. Little Brown. 1st Am ed. dj. EX. $75.00

FOWLES, John. *Daniel Martin*. 1977. Little Brown. 1st ed. dj. EX. $30.00

FOWLES, John. *Daniel Martin*. 1977. London. 1st ed. sgn. dj. EX. $37.00

FOWLES, John. *Ebony Tower*. 1974. Boston. Ltd 1st ed. dj. EX. $150.00

FOWLES, John. *Ebony Tower*. 1974. London. AP. proof dj. M. $350.00

FOWLES, John. *Ebony Tower*. 1974. London. 1st ed. dj. EX. $125.00

FOWLES, John. *French Lieutenant's Woman*. 1969. Boston. 1st ed. dj. P3. $65.00

FOWLES, John. *French Lieutenant's Woman*. 1969. London. 1st ed. sgn. dj. $225.00

FOWLES, John. *Islands*. 1978. London. 1st ed. sgn. dj. EX. $60.00

FOWLES, John. *Maggot*. 1985. Little Brown. 1st ed. dj. EX. T6. $15.00

FOWLES, John. *Mantissa*. 1982. Boston. 1st ed. dj. EX. $25.00

FOWLES, John. *Ourika*. 1977. TX. 1/500. sgn. M. $100.00

FOWLES, John. *Short History of Lyme Regis*. 1983. Boston. ARC. 1st Am ed. dj. RS. EX. $30.00

FOWLES, John. *Steep Holm: Case Study of Evolution*. 1978. Dorset. sgn. dj. EX. $45.00

FOWNEY, Fairfax. *Storming of the Gateway, Chattanooga 1863*. 1969. 303 p. stiff wraps. M. J4. $3.00

FOX, C.K. *This Wonderful World of Trout*. 1963. Carlisle. Ltd ed. sgn. dj. M. $75.00

FOX, Ebenezer. *Adventures of Ebenezer Fox in Revolutionary War*. c 1847. Boston. gilt bdg. VG. $40.00

FOX, Fontaine. *Toonerville Trolley*. 1972. NY. 4to. VG. $22.00

FOX, G.H. *Photographic Atlas of Diseases of Skin*. 1900-1905. NY. 96 pls. 4to. 4 vols. VG. $145.00

FOX, G.H. *Photographic Illustrations of Skin Disease*. 1886. NY. 85 pls. $50.00

FOX, H.M. *Gardening With Herbs*. 1933. NY. 1st ed. VG. $25.00

FOX, J.J. *Steps to Parnassus*. 1943. NY. 1st ed. dj. $18.00

FOX, James M. *Iron Virgin*. 1951. Little Brown. 1st ed. VG. P1. $7.00

FOX, James M. *Operation Dancing Dog*. 1974. Walker. 1st ed. dj. VG. P1. $12.50

FOX, James M. *Shroud for Mrs. Bundy*. 1952. Little Brown. 1st ed. VG. P1. $15.00

FOX, James. *My Native Land*. 1895. St. Louis. 400 p. EX. K1. $18.50

FOX, John. *Little Shepherd of Kingdom Come*. 1931. Scribner. Ils Weyth. 1st ed. 322 p. EX. $50.00

FOX, S. *John Muir & His Legacy*. 1981. Little Brown. Ils 1st ed. 436 p. dj. EX. M2. $16.00

FOX, W.P. *Dixiana Moon.* 1981. NY. Viking. AP. sgn. printed wraps. $65.00

FOX, W.P. *Dixiana Moon.* 1981. NY. Viking. 1st ed. 275 p. dj. RS. M. $22.50

FOX, W.P. *Dr. Golf.* 1963. Lippincott. 1st ed. 176 p. dj. EX. $55.00

FOX, W.P. *Dr. Golf.* 1963. Phil. 1st ed. dj. VG. B2. $25.00

FOX-DAVIES, Arthur Charles. *Complete Guide to Heraldry.* c 1900. London/ Edinburgh. Ils. VG. C1. $35.00

FOX-SMITH, Cicely. *Ocean Racers.* 1932. NY. McBride. 245 p. dj. VG. $25.00

FOX-SMITH, Cicely. *There Was a Ship: Chapters From History of Sail.* 1930. Hartford. Mitchell. 201 p. dj. VG. $15.00

FOXX, Jack. *Penguin Island.* 1925. Bodley Head. 12th print. VG. P1. $5.00

FRAIGNAU. *Cocteau.* 1961. London/NY. 1st ed. photos. VG. $20.00

FRALIN, Frances. *Indelible Image: Photographs of War 1846 to Present.* 1985. Abrams. 185 photos. oblong 4to. 254 p. dj. $45.00

FRANCE, Anatole. *At the Sign of the Reine Pedaque.* 1922. London. Ils Pape. VG. J2. $25.00

FRANCE, Anatole. *Girls & Boys.* 1923. NY. Ils De Monvel. xl. VG. $40.00

FRANCE, Anatole. *Gods Are A'Thirst.* 1927. NY/London. Ils Austen. 1st ed. VG. J2. $25.00

FRANCE, Anatole. *Gods Are A'Thirst.* 1941. London. Nonesuch. slipcase. VG. $25.00

FRANCE, Anatole. *Le Jardin d'Epicure.* 1895. Paris. Ltd ed. sgn. G. $85.00

FRANCE, Anatole. *Mother of Pearl.* 1929. NY. Ils Pape. dj. VG. J2. $25.00

FRANCE, Anatole. *Penguin Island.* 1925. NY. reprint of Ils 1st ed. dj. J2. $25.00

FRANCE, Anatole. *Red Lily.* 1930. London/NY. Ils Donia Nachshen. VG. J2. $25.00

FRANCE, Anatole. *Revolt of Angels.* 1930. Bodley Head. Ils Pape. gilt black bdg. VG. $25.00

FRANCE, Anatole. *Romance of Queen Pedaque.* 1932. Three Sirens. Ils King. 214 p. VG. $12.00

FRANCE, Anatole. *Selected Works.* 1930. NY. Wise. Book Lover's ed. 10 vols. G. $50.00

FRANCE, L.B. *Mountain Trails & Parks in CO.* 1888. Denver. 2nd ed. 224 p. VG. A3. $45.00

FRANCHERE, G. *Voyage to NW Coast of America.* 1954. Donnelley. reprint of 1854 ed. dj. M. M2. $30.00

FRANCIS, Devon. *Mr. Piper & His Cubs.* 1973. Ames, IA. Ils 1st ed. 256 p. G. T5. $35.00

FRANCIS, Dick. *Banker.* 1982. Book Club Assn. dj. EX. P1. $6.00

FRANCIS, Dick. *Banker.* 1982. London. 1st ed. dj. EX. $20.00

FRANCIS, Dick. *Bolt.* 1986. Michael Joseph. 1st ed. dj. VG. P1. $17.50

FRANCIS, Dick. *Bolt.* 1987. NY. 1st ed. dj. VG. $8.00

FRANCIS, Dick. *Bonecrack.* nd. Book Club. dj. VG. P1. $4.00

FRANCIS, Dick. *Danger.* 1983. Book Club Assn. dj. EX. P1. $6.00

FRANCIS, Dick. *High Stakes.* 1975. London. 1st ed. dj. EX. $30.00

FRANCIS, Dick. *In the Frame.* 1976. London. 1st ed. sgn. dj. M. $85.00

FRANCIS, Dick. *In the Frame.* 1977. NY. 1st ed. dj. EX. $30.00

FRANCIS, Dick. *Knockdown.* 1975. NY. 1st ed. dj. EX. $30.00

FRANCIS, Dick. *Proof.* 1985. Putnam. 1st ed. dj. VG. P1. $17.50

FRANCIS, Dick. *Proof.* 1985. Putnam. 1st ed. sgn. dj. M. $45.00

FRANCIS, Dick. *Rat Race.* 1971. Michael Joseph. 3rd ed. dj. xl. P1. $5.00

FRANCIS, Dick. *Reflex.* 1980. London. 1st ed. dj. EX. $35.00

FRANCIS, Dick. *Risk.* 1978. NY. 1st ed. dj. EX. $30.00

FRANCIS, Dick. *Slayride.* 1973. NY. 1st ed. dj. EX. $45.00

FRANCIS, Dick. *Trial Run.* nd. Book Club. dj. VG. P1. $5.00

FRANCIS, Dick. *Trial Run.* 1978. NY. 1st ed. dj. EX. $25.00

FRANCIS, Dick. *Twice Shy.* 1982. Putnam. 1st Am ed. dj. EX. $15.00

FRANCIS, Dick. *Whip Hand.* 1979. Harper. 1st Am ed. dj. EX. $20.00

FRANCIS, Rene. *Story of Tower of London.* nd. Winston. Ils Weister. xl. VG. $100.00

FRANCK, Harry. *Roving Through S China.* 1925. NY/London. Ils. fair. $45.00

FRANCO, Eloise. *Journey Into a Strange Land.* 1956. NH. $20.00

FRANCOIS, Yves Regis. *Ctz Paradigm.* 1975. Doubleday. 1st ed. dj. EX. P1. $7.50

FRANDSEN & MARKHAM. *Manufacture of Ice Cream & Ices.* 1919. Orange Judd. Ils. EX. $25.00

FRANK, Anne. *Diary of a Young Girl.* 1952. NY. 1st Am ed. dj. EX. $125.00

FRANK, Gerold. *American Death.* 1972. Doubleday. 467 p. dj. M1. $6.50

FRANK, Pat. *Mr. Adam.* nd. Lippincott. 10th print. VG. P1. $5.00

FRANK, Philip. *Einstein: His Life & Times.* 1947. NY. 1st ed. 298 p. dj. B2. $17.50

FRANK, S. *Pictorial Encyclopedia of Fishes.* 1971. Hamlyn. Ils. 552 p. dj. VG. M2. $17.00

FRANK, Waldo. *America & Alfred Steiglitz.* 1934. NY. Stated 1st ed. black cloth. VG. $35.00

FRANK, Waldo. *America & Alfred Steiglitz.* 1934. NY. S2. $45.00

FRANK, Waldo. *America & Alfred Stieglitz.* 1934. NY. Literary Guild. 339 p. $20.00

FRANK, Waldo. *City Block.* 1922. private print. Waldo. VG. $15.00

FRANKAU, Gilbert. *Seeds of Enchantment.* 1921. Doubleday Page. G. P1. $3.00

FRANKFURTER, Alfred. *Winston Churchill, the Painter.* 1958. Intro Eisenhower. SftCvr. VG. D1. $25.00

FRANKL, P.T. *New Dimensions: Decorative Arts of Today...* 1928. NY. VG. J2. $70.00

FRANKLIN, Allan. *Trail of the Tiger: Tammany 1789-1928, Facts From Records.* 1928. np. (NY?) Ils. 314 p. G. T5. $35.00

FRANKLIN, B. *Way to Wealth.* 1950. Czechoslovakia. Vojtech Preissig. slipcase. EX. $85.00

FRANKLIN, Benjamin. *Works of Benjamin Franklin.* 1800. Huntington. 2 vols in 1. G. $65.00

FRANKLIN, Colin. *Private Presses.* 1969. Dufour, PA. Ils. 240 p. dj. VG. $30.00

FRANKLIN, S.R. *Memories of Rear Admiral Franklin.* 1898. Harper. Ils. 398 p. G. M2. $15.00

FRANZIUS, Enno. *History of Order of Assassins.* 1969. Funk Wagnalls. 1st ed. dj. VG. $35.00

FRAPIE & JORDAN. *Photographic Hints & Gadgets.* 1937. Am Photographic. Ils. G. $30.00

FRARY, I.T. *Early Homes of OH.* 1936. Richmond, VA. Ils 1st ed. 336 p. $60.00

FRASER, C.L. *Nursery Rhymes.* c 1930. NY. EX. G1. $40.00

FRASER, David. *Wales in History. Book 1.* 1965. U of Wales Pr. Ils 2nd ed. VG. C1. $15.00

FRASER, G.L. *Textiles by Britain.* 1948. Allen Unwin. Ltd ed. G. $20.00

FRASER, G.M. *Flashman at the Charge.* 1973. NY. 1st ed. dj. VG. B2. $22.50

FRASER, G.M. *Flashman in Great Game.* 1975. NY. 1st ed. dj. B2. $27.50

FRASER, G.M. *McAuslan in the Rough.* 1974. NY. 1st ed. dj. VG. $30.00

FRASER, G.M. *Royal Flash.* 1970. NY. 1st ed. dj. VG. B2. $27.50

FRASER, Ronald. *City of the Sun.* 1961. Jonathan Cape. dj. xl. P1. $5.00

FRASER-BRUNNER, A. *Danger in the Sea.* 1973. Hamlyn. Ils. 4to. 128 p. dj. EX. M2. $14.00

FRASSANITO, W.A. *Antietam: Photographic Legacy of America's Bloodiest Day.* 1978. Scribner. photos. maps. 304 p. dj. EX. $17.00

FRAUCA, H. *Encounters With Australian Animals.* nd. Heinemann. Ils. 152 p. M2. $14.00

FRAZEE, Steve. *Apache Way.* 1969. Whitman. G. P1. $5.00

FRAZEE, Steve. *Apache Way.* 1969. Whitman. VG. P1. $7.50

FRAZEE, Steve. *Killer Lion.* 1966. Whitman. VG. P1. $7.50

FRAZEE, Steve. *Mystery of Bristlecone Pine.* 1967. Whitman. G. P1. $4.50

FRAZER, James. *Golden Bough.* 1894. London. Macmillan. 1st ed. 2 vols. VG. J2. $250.00

FRAZER, James. *Golden Bough.* 1926. NY. 1 vol ed. 752 p. G. $9.00

FRAZER, James. *Golden Bough.* 1951. Book Club. dj. VG. C1. $8.50

FRAZER, P.D. *Elementary Gunsmithing.* 1938. Sm Arms Tech. Ils. $20.00

FRAZIER, Robert. *Apaches of White Mountain Indian Reservation.* 1885. Phil. Indian Rights Assn. wraps. xl. A3. $90.00

FREAR, Mary. *Flowers of HI.* 1938. Ils McLean. 1st ed. VG. E2. $35.00

FREDBORG, Arvid. *Behind the Steel Wall.* 1944. Viking. G. M1. $7.50

FREDERICK, Harold. *March Hares.* 1896. Appleton. 292 p. blue cloth. G. $10.00

FREDERICKSON, O.A. *American Military Occupation of Germany, 1945-1953.* 1953. Darmstadt. Ils. quarto. 222 p. VG. $35.00

FREDERICKSON, O.A. *Silence of the N.* 1972. Crown. Ils. 209 p. dj. EX. M2. $8.00

FREDMAN, John. *Epitaph to a Bad Cop.* 1973. David McKay. dj. VG. P1. $7.50

FREDMAN, John. *False Joanna.* 1970. Bobbs Merrill. dj. EX. P1. $7.50

FREDMAN & FALK. *Jews in American Wars.* 1954. WA, DC. Ils Revised ed. 276 p. dj. VG. T5. $12.50

FREEBORN, Brian. *Good Luck, Mr. Cain.* 1976. St. Martin. 1st ed. dj. VG. P1. $12.00

FREEDMAN, Nancy. *Joshua, Son of None.* nd. Book Club. dj. VG. P1. $4.00

FREELING, Nicolas. *Dresden Green.* nd. Book Club. dj. EX. P1. $3.00

FREELING, Nicolas. *Night Lords.* 1978. Pantheon. 1st ed. dj. xl. P1. $5.00

FREELING, Nicolas. *Question of Loyalty.* nd. Book Club. dj. VG. P1. $3.00

FREELING, Nicolas. *Wolfnight.* 1982. Pantheon. 1st ed. dj. EX. P1. $12.50

FREEMAN, A.A. *Case for Dr. Cook.* 1961. Coward McCann. 315 p. dj. EX. M2. $15.00

FREEMAN, D.S. *Lee of VA.* 1958. Scribner. Ils. 243 p. dj. EX. M2. $15.00

FREEMAN, D.S. *Lee's Lieutenants.* 1942-1944. NY. 1st ed. not 1st print. 3 vols. $90.00

FREEMAN, D.S. *Robert E. Lee.* 1934. Scribner. 1st ed. 4 vols. VG. $75.00

FREEMAN, Dan. *Elephants: Vanishing Giants.* 1980. Gallery. Ils 1st ed. 4to. 192 p. dj. EX. M2. $15.00

FREEMAN, Devery. *Father Sky.* 1979. Morrow. 1st ed. dj. EX. $12.00

FREEMAN, H.C. *Butte, Above & Below Ground.* 1900. Chicago. G. $50.00

FREEMAN, Harley. *FL Obsolete Notes & Script.* 1967. 1st ed. 103 p. gilt bdg. EX. J4. $30.00

FREEMAN, J. *American Testament.* 1936. Farrar. 1st ed. VG. $32.00

FREEMAN, J.D. *Household of Fairth.* 1951. MO. $20.00

FREEMAN, John. *Portrait of George Moore in Study of His Work.* 1922. Appleton. VG. $25.00

FREEMAN, R. Austin. *Mystery of 31, New Inn.* 1913. Winston. VG. P1. $45.00

FREEMAN, R. Austin. *Red Thumb Mark.* 1967. Norton. 1st ed. dj. VG. P1. $10.00

FREEMAN, Samuel. *Valuable Assistant to Every Man...* 1800. Boston. Thomas Andrews. leather. VG. A3. $60.00

FREEMAN. *Earthquake Damage & E Insurance.* 1932. McGraw. Ils. 4to. 904 p. G. $100.00

FREEMAN. *Works of Charles Darwin: Annotated Bibliography.* Revised 2nd ed. EX. $35.00

FREEMANTLE, Brian. *Deaken's War.* 1982. Hutchinson. 1st ed. dj. xl. P1. $6.00

FREEMANTLE & HASKELL. *Two Views of Gettysburg.* 1964. Donnelley. Lakeside Classic. A3. $35.00

FREIDEL, Frank. *Over There.* 1964. NY. 300 photos. dj. VG. $25.00

FREIND, John. *History of Physick From the Time of Calen.* 1725. London. 1 vol only. modern bdg. VG. $125.00

FREMANTLE, J.A.L. *Fremantle Diary...on His Three Months in S States.* 1954. Little Brown. 1st ed. dj. $25.00

FREMANTLE & HASKELL. *Two Views of Gettysburg.* 1962. Donnelley. Lakeside Classic. A3. $35.00

FREMONT, J.B. *Souvenirs of My Time.* 1887. Ils. 393 p. K1. $6.50

FREMONT, J.B. *Story of the Guard: Chronicle of the War.* 1863. Boston. Ils 1st ed. 227 p. T5. $30.00

FREMONT, J.C. *Exploration of Country Lying Between MO River.* 1843. Ils 1st ed. fld map. VG. A3. $275.00

FREMONT, J.C. *Exploring Expedition to Rocky Mountains.* 1845. WA. 1st ed. fld maps. 583 p. B2. $295.00

FREMONT, J.C. *Exploring Expedition to Rocky Mountains.* 1845. WA. 1st ed. 5 fld maps. orig bdg. A3. $575.00

FREMONT, J.C. *Exploring Expedition to Rocky Mountains.* 1852. Buffalo. 456 p. G. $210.00

FRENCH, Allen. *Lost Baron.* 1940. Boston. Houghton. 1st ed. VG. C1. $15.00

FRENCH, J.L. *Book of the Rogue.* 1926. Boni Liveright. 398 p. G. $12.50

FRENCH, S.G. *Two Wars.* 1901. Nashville. 1st ed. 404 p. K1. $95.00

FRENCH, S.L. *Reminiscenes of Plymouth, Luzerne Co., PA.* 1914. Plymouth, PA. Ils 1st ed. 94 p. G. T5. $19.50

FRENCH, W. *Some Recollections of a W Ranchman.* 1927. London. 1st ed. 283 p. red cloth. EX. $125.00

FRENCH & EBERLEIN. *Smaller Houses & Gardens of Versailles.* 1926. NY. Pencil Points Lib. Ils. G. $85.00

FRERE-COOK, Gervis. *Decorative Arts of the Mariner.* 1966. Little Brown. 1st Am ed. dj. EX. $30.00

FRERE-COOK, Gervis. *Decorative Arts of the Mariner.* 1966. Little Brown. 1st ed. dj. VG. J2. $27.50

FREUCHEN, Peter. *Adventures in the Arctic.* 1960. Messner. photos. maps. 383 p. dj. EX. M2. $10.00

FREUCHEN, Peter. *Arctic Adventure: My Life in the Frozen N.* 1935. Farrar Rinehart. 467 p. VG. M2. $10.00

FREUCHEN, Peter. *Book of the Eskimos.* 1961. World. photos. maps. dj. VG. M2. $10.00

FREUCHEN, Peter. *Book of the Seven Seas.* 1957. Messner. Ils. maps. 512 p. dj. EX. M2. $10.00

FREUCHEN, Peter. *Ivalu.* 1935. NY. G. $10.00

FREUCHEN, Peter. *Vagrant Viking: My Life & Adventures.* 1953. Messner. Ils. 422 p. EX. M2. $10.00

FREUD, Anna. *Ego & Mechanisms of Defense.* Internat Pr. dj. G. $6.00

FREUD, Sigmund. *Collected Papers. Vols. 1-5.* 1950. London. Hogarth. 5 vols. G. $25.00

FREUD, Sigmund. *Collected Papers. Vols. 1-5.* 1959. NY. Riviere. 5 vols. $87.00

FREUD, Sigmund. *Interpretation of Dreams.* 1950. Modern Lib. 12mo. gray cloth. $7.50

FREUD, Sigmund. *Question of Lay Analysis.* London. 1st ed. dj. EX. $25.00

FREUD & BURLINGHAM. *War & Children.* 1943. 1st ed. VG. $15.00

FREUD. *Biblioteca: Interpretacion de Los Suenos. Tomo I-IV.* 1936. Chile. 662 p. rebound. G. $10.00

FREUDENTHAL, Elisabeth. *Flight Into History: Wright Brothers & Air Age.* 1949. OK U. 1st ed. J2. $17.50

FREUND, Gisele. *Gisele Feund, Photographer.* 1985. NY. Abrams. Ils. sm folio. 223 p. dj. $45.00

FREUND, Gisele. *World in My Camera.* 1974. NY. Dial. Trans Guicharnaud. 4to. 259 p. dj. $65.00

FREWIN, Leslie. *Immortal Jester.* 1973. Frewin Pub Ltd. reprint. white cloth. dj. VG. D1. $20.00

FREY, D.G. *Limnology in N America.* 1963. WI U. Ils. 734 p. dj. EX. M2. $30.00

FREYRE, G. *Sasa-Grande & Senzala.* 1946. Rio de Janiero. 2 vols. wraps. $9.00

FREYTAG, G.W. *Lexicon Arabico-Latium.* 1837. Halis Saxonum. 4to. xl. G. $150.00

FRIED, Frederick. *Artists in Wood.* 1970. NY. Bramhall. 1st ed. dj. EX. $65.00

FRIED, Frederick. *Artists in Wood: American Carvers of Cigar Store Indians...* 1970. Potter. 1st ed. dj. VG. J2. $35.00

FRIEDENWALD & RUHRAD. *Diet in Health & Disease.* 1906. Revised 2nd ed. VG. $18.00

FRIEDHEIM & TAYLOR. *Fighters Up.* 1945. Phil. Ils 1st ed. 275 p. dj. VG. T5. $45.00

FRIEDHEIM. *Seattle General Strike.* 1964. Seattle. dj. VG. $15.00

FRIEDLANDER, C.P. *Biology of Insects.* 1977. Pica. Ils. dj. EX. M2. $9.00

FRIEDLANDER, F.G. *Sound Pulses.* 1958. Cambridge. dj. EX. $12.00

FRIEDMAN, Bruce Jay. *Dick.* 1970. Knopf. 1st ed. dj. xl. P1. $6.00

FRIEDMAN, Bruce Jay. *Scuba Duba.* 1967. Simon Schuster. 1st ed. dj. EX. $20.00

FRIEDMAN, I.R. *Escape or Die: True Stories of Young People Who Survived...* 1982. NY. 1st ed. Lib bdg. dj. G. $9.50

FRIEDMAN, Joseph. *History of Color Photography.* 1944. Am Photographic Pub. 1st ed. J2. $20.00

FRIEDMAN, Kinky. *Greenwich Killing Time.* 1986. NY. 1st ed. dj. EX. $20.00

FRIEDMAN, M. *Buried Alive.* 1973. Morrow. dj. EX. $30.00

FRIEDMAN, R. *History of Dermatology in Phil.* 1955. Ft. Pierce Beach, FL. 4to. xl. $40.00

FRIEDMAN, Stuart. *Free Are the Dead.* 1954. Abelard Schuman. VG. P1. $12.00

FRIEDMAN & FRIEDMAN. *Shakespearean Ciphers Examined.* 1957. Cambridge. dj. EX. $60.00

FRIEL, A.O. *River of Seven Stars.* 1924. NY. 1st ed. VG. $40.00

FRIESNER, Esther. *Druid's Blood.* 1988. 1st ed. pb. VG. C1. $3.50

FRIESNER, Esther. *Elf Defense.* VG. C1. $3.50

FRINCKE & TERRY. *Birds of Point Lobos.* 1971. CA. Ils. 53 p. M2. $5.00

FRINK, Maurice. *Cow Country Cavalcade: 80 Years of WY Stock Growers Assn.* 1954. Denver. Old W. 1st ed. sgn. dj. scarce. J3. $65.00

FRINK, Maurice. *When Grass Was King...* 1956. Boulder. Ils. dj. EX. $40.00

FRISWELL, J.H. *Varia: Readings From Rare Books.* 1886. London. 1st ed. $50.00

FROEST, Frank. *Grell Mystery.* nd. Detective Club. dj. VG. P1. $15.00

FROEST & DILNOT. *Crime Club.* nd. Detective Club. dj. G. P1. $18.25

FROHMAN, C.F. *History of Sandusky & Erie Counties.* 1965. Columbus, OH. Ils. sgn. 61 p. G. T5. $15.00

FROMAGET. *Prophet's Cousin.* 1926. London. dj. EX. $15.00

FROME, David. *Homicide House.* 1950. Rinehart. 1st ed. Lib bdg. xl. P1. $5.00

FROME, David. *Mr. Pinkerton Goes to Scotland Yard.* nd. Grosset. G. P1. $7.50

FROME, David. *Scotland Yard Can Wait!* nd. Grosset. dj. G. P1. $20.00

FROME, Michael. *Strangers in High Places: Story of Great Smoky Mountains.* 1966. Garden City. 1st ed. map. 394 p. dj. EX. $25.00

FROMM, Erich. *Heart of Man.* 1964. NY. 1st ed. dj. EX. $12.00

FROST, A.B. *Book of Drawings.* 1904. NY. Collier. Intro Harris. Ils. folio. $50.00

FROST, Frances. *Woman of This Earth.* 1934. Boston. 1st ed. 8vo. dj. VG. $20.00

FROST, John. *Art of Swimming: Series of Practical Instructions...* 1818. NY. Gallaudet. 12 fld pls. 8vo. scarce. $400.00

FROST, John. *Great Cities of the World.* 1857. Beardsley. Ils. G. $40.00

FROST, John. *Panorama of Nations.* 1854. NY. Ils. 12mo. 512 p. G2. $16.00

FROST, John. *Pictorial History of the US.* 1851. Hartford. Ils. 8vo. 328 p. disbound. G2. $10.00

FROST, L.A. *Arrest General Custer.* 1987. Monroe, MI. photos. map. sgn. 21 p. dj. VG. T5. $6.50

FROST, L.A. *Custer Album Sea.* 1964. 1st ed. dj. EX. $40.00

FROST, L.A. *Custer Slept Here.* 1974. Monroe, MI. 1st ed. sgn. 22 p. wraps. EX. T5. $4.50

FROST, L.A. *U.S. Grant Album: Pictorial History of U.S. Grant.* 1966. Bonanza. reprint. 192 p. dj. EX. M2. $14.00

FROST, Lesley. *Digging Down to China.* 1968. NY. 1st ed. sgn. dj. M. $15.00

FROST, Lesley. *Going on Two.* 1973. Ils Hudnut. 1st ed. sgn. wraps. M. $10.00

FROST, Lesley. *Really Not Really.* 1962. NY. 1st ed. sgn. dj. M. $15.00

FROST, Robert. *Aforesaid.* 1954. NY. Ltd ed. 1/650. slipcase. M. $300.00

FROST, Robert. *Boy's Will.* nd. NY. Holt. sgn. blue cloth. VG. P3. $175.00

FROST, Robert. *Boy's Will.* 1913. London. 1st ed. 4th state. sgn. wraps. $450.00

FROST, Robert. *Collected Poems.* 1930. NY. 1/1000. sgn. EX. $150.00

FROST, Robert. *Further Range.* c 1936. Holt. dj. VG. $8.00

FROST, Robert. *Further Range.* 1936. Holt. Ltd 1st ed. sgn. dj. EX. $155.00

FROST, Robert. *Further Range.* 1936. NY. Ltd 1st ed. sgn. VG. $120.00

FROST, Robert. *Further Range. Book Six.* 1936. Holt. 1st ed. VG. $15.00

FROST, Robert. *Guardeen.* nd. Ritchie Pr. 1/96. orig mailing envelope. M. $250.00

FROST, Robert. *In the Clearing.* 1962. NY. 1st ed. dj. EX. $20.00

FROST, Robert. *Letters of Robert Frost to Louis Untermeyer.* 1963. NY. 1st ed. dj. EX. $17.50

FROST, Robert. *Letters of Robert Frost to Louis Untermeyer.* 1963. NY. 1st ed. 388 p. dj. VG. T5. $12.50

FROST, Robert. *Masque of Mercy.* 1947. NY. 1st ed. dj. EX. $35.00

FROST, Robert. *Masque of Mercy.* 1947. NY. Holt. Ltd ed. 1/751. sgn. slipcase. EX. $160.00

FROST, Robert. *Memoirs of Notorius Stephen Burroughs of NH.* 1924. NY. 1st ed. VG. $35.00

FROST, Robert. *Mountain Interval.* NY. 2nd ed. sgn. with sgn program. M1. $135.00

FROST, Robert. *Mountain Interval.* 1916. NY. 1st ed. 99 p. blue cloth. EX. $100.00

FROST, Robert. *N of Boston.* 1915. Boston. 2nd ed. 137 p. blue cloth. EX. $40.00

FROST, Robert. *NH: A Poem.* 1923. NY. 1st ed. EX. $55.00

FROST, Robert. *NH: A Poem.* 1928. NY. Ils Lankes. VG. $12.00

FROST, Robert. *Robert Frost at Agnes Scott College.* 1963. wraps. $65.00

FROST, Robert. *Robert Frost: Bibliography.* 1937. Amherst. 1st ed. 1/650. EX. $65.00

FROST, Robert. *Steeple Bush.* 1947. NY. Ltd ed. 1/751. sgn. boxed. EX. $130.00

FROST, Robert. *Steeple Bush.* 1947. NY. Holt. 1st ed. dj. EX. $25.00

FROST, Robert. *W Running Brook.* 1928. NY. 1st trade ed. VG. $40.00

FROST, Robert. *Way Out.* 1929. NY. Harbor Pr. 1st ed. 1/485. inscr/sgn twice. $125.00

FROST, Robert. *Wishing Well.* 1959. NY. 1st ed. Christmas Keepsake. wraps. $40.00

FROST, Stanley. *Labor & Revolt.* 1920. NY. dj. VG. $25.00

FROST, W.H. *Fairies & Folk of Ireland.* 1900. NY. $25.00

FROTHINGHAM, Richard. *History of Siege of Boston & Battles of Lexington...* 1849. Boston. 1st ed. pls. fld maps. G. $47.50

FROTHINGHAM, Richard. *Rise of Republic of the US.* 1872. Boston. 1st ed. presentation. 640 p. VG. T5. $65.00

FROTHINGHAM, Robert. *Songs of the Sea & Sailors' Chanteys.* 1924. Cambridge. Riverside. xl. poor. $12.00

FRY, Christopher. *Thor With Angels.* 1950. Oxford. 4th imp. red cloth. VG. C1. $4.50

FRY, Daniel. *White Sands Incident.* 1966. Louisville. 1st ed. dj. VG. with photo. $12.50

FRY, H.P. *Modern Ku Klux Klan.* 1922. Boston. 8vo. 259 p. VG. $40.00

FRY, J.R. *Life of General Zachary Taylor.* 1848. Phil. Ils 332 p. gilt bdg. K1. $21.00

FRY & WHITE. *Big Trees.* 1945. Stanford. photos. 126 p. VG. M2. $10.00

FRYER, Donald S. *Songs & Sonnets Atlantean.* 1971. Arkham House. 1st ed. dj. EX. P1. $15.00

FRYER, Jane. *Mary Frances' First Aid Book.* 1916. Ils 1st ed. VG. B2. $35.00

FUCHS, F. *Das Fernsehen Museum.* 1937. Munchen. Auflage. Ils. 47 p. xl. wraps. $10.00

FUCHS, F. *Grundriss der Funktechnick.* 1936. Berlin. Auflage. Ils. 215 p. wraps. $17.50

FUELL, Melissa. *Blind Boone: His Early Life & His Achievements.* 1915. KS City. 256 p. gilt bdg. VG. $35.00

FUERMAN, George. *Reluctant Empire: Mind of TX.* 1957. Doubleday. Ils Schwietz. 1st ed. $15.00

FUERST & D'ARCY. *Versailles.* 1950. Vienna. French/Eng text. wraps. D2. $50.00

FUGINA, Frank. *Lore & Lure of Upper MS River.* 1945. Winona, MN. 1st ed. dj. VG. J2. $30.00

FUHRER, B. *Field Companion to Australian Fungi.* 1985. Austin. Five Mile Pr. 1st ed. EX. M2. $18.00

FULDHEIM, Dorothy. *Where, Where the Arabs?* 1967. Cleveland. Ils 1st ed. sgn. 110 p. dj. T5. $15.00

FULLER, A.S. *Small Fruit Culturist.* 1867. NY. Ils. $17.00

FULLER, Anne. *Peak & Prairie From CO Sketchbook.* c 1894. NY. VG. $12.50

FULLER, Claude. *Confederate Currency & Stamps.* 1949. 1st ed. EX. rare. K1. $50.00

FULLER, Claude. *Rifled Musket.* 1958. reprint. 302 p. EX. J4. $25.00

FULLER, E. *Extinct Birds.* 1988. Facts on File. Ils 1st ed. 4to. dj. EX. M2. $32.00

FULLER, G. *History of Pacific NW With Emphasis on Inland Empire.* 1952. Knopf. Revised ed. maps. 383 p. M2. $10.00

FULLER, George. *Bibliography of Bookplate Literature.* 1926. Spokane. Public Lib. 1/500. sgn. VG. J2. $75.00

FULLER, Hector. *Abroad With Mayor Walker Shields.* nd. IL. VG. $20.00

FULLER, J. *Magical Dilemma of Victor Neuberg.* 1965. London. Allen. 1st ed. 295 p. dj. VG. B2. $22.50

FULLER, J.F.C. *Generalship of U.S. Grant.* 1958. Bloomington. 1st ed. dj. EX. $28.00

FULLER, J.F.C. *Grant & Lee: Study in Personality & Generalship.* 1957. Bloomington. 2nd ed. maps. 323 p. VG. T5. $27.50

FULLER, J.G. *Great Soul Trial.* 1969. Toronto. $16.00

FULLER, Joseph. *Bismarck's Diplomacy at Its Zenith.* 1922. Harvard. 1st ed. VG. J2. $15.00

FULLER & HOLMES. *Life of the Far N.* 1972. McGraw Hill. Ils 1st ed. 232 p. dj. EX. M2. $11.00

FULLERTON, Alexander. *Bury the Past.* 1954. Peter Davies. dj. VG. P1. $7.50

FULLERTON & WALDO. *Down the Mackenzie.* 1923. NY. 1st ed. EX. $38.00

FULMER, Genie. *Cabins & Campfires in SE MT.* 1973. 1st ed. sgn. stiff wraps. VG. J2. $10.00

FULTON, M.G. *S Life in S Literature.* 1917. Boston. Ginn. 53 p. xl. $12.50

FULTON, R.L. *Epic of the Overland.* 1954. Los Angeles. VG. $20.00

FULTON & THOMSON. *Benjamin Silliman: Pathfinder in American Science.* 1947. NY. dj. EX. $15.00

FUNK, E. *64 Years of Newspapering in AR 1896-1960.* 1960. WA Co Hist Soc. photos. 4to. 87 p. M2. $10.00

FUNK & WAGNALLS. *Jewish Encyclopedia.* 1901. 12 vols. blue Lib buckram. VG. J2. $350.00

FUNKHOUSER & WEBB. *Ancient Life in KY.* 1928. KY Geol Survey. Ils. maps. 349 p. M2. $16.00

FURBUSH, C.C. *Catalog of Library of Caroline C. Furbush.* 1903. NY. 1/206. with sgn letter. $75.00

FURGUSON, John. *Grouse Moor Murder.* 1934. Dodd Mead. VG. P1. $18.25

FURLANI, G. *La Televisione.* 1931. Trieste. Ils 1st ed. 201 p. $45.00

FURLONG, C.W. *Let 'Er Buck: Story of Passing of the Old W.* 1921. NY. 1st ed. 52 photos. 242 p. VG. $30.00

FURMAN, Laura. *Watch Time Fly.* 1985. NY. 1st ed. dj. $15.00

FURNAS, J.C. *Good-Bye to Uncle Tom.* 1956. 435 p. dj. VG. J4. $12.50

FURNEAUX, R. *Money Pit Mystery.* 1972. NY. 1st ed. dj. VG. B2. $22.50

FURNEAUX, W. *Butterflies & Moths (British).* 1919. Longman Green. 12 pls. 350 p. VG. M2. $18.00

FURNESS, Clifton. *Walt Whitman's Workshop.* 1928. Cambridge. 1/750. 4to. EX. $50.00

FURNILL, John. *Culmination.* 1933. Mathews Marrot. 2nd ed. xl. VG. P1. $6.00

FURNISS, Harry. *Some Victorian Women.* 1923. NY. 1st Am ed. J2. $20.00

FURST, Herbert. *Decorative Art of Frank Brangwyn.* 1924. Bodley Head. Ils. folio. 229 p. $85.00

FUTRELL. *US Air Force in Korea.* 1961. NY. 1st ed. 4to. 774 p. dj. VG. $35.00

FYE. *William Osler's Collected Papers on Cardiovascular System.* 1985. Birmingham. 8vo. AEG. red bdg. EX. $45.00

FYLEMAN, Rose. *Princess Dances.* 1933. London. Ils Leslie. dj. VG. J2. $15.00

FYSON, P.F. *Flora of the S Indian Hill Stations.* 1932. Madras. Ils. 2 vols. xl. G. $47.50

G

GABO, Naum. *Of Divers Arts.* 1962. Pantheon. Ils 205 p. dj. D2. $35.00

GABORIAU, Emile. *Blackmailer.* nd. Detective Club. dj. G. P1. $15.00

GABORIAU, Emile. *Honor of the Name.* 1902. Scribner. VG. P1. $20.00

GABORIAU, Emile. *Monsieur Lecoq.* 1902. Scribner. VG. P1. $20.00

GABORIAU, Emile. *Other People's Money.* 1902. Scribner. VG. P1. $20.00

GABORIAU, Emile. *Widow Lerouge.* 1902. Scribner. VG. P1. $20.00

GACHE PUBLISHING. *Encyclopedia of US Government Benefits.* 1968. Ils. 2 vols. EX. $7.50

GADD, L. *Deadly Beautiful: World's Most Poisonous Animals & Plants.* 1980. Macmillan. Ils 1st ed. 208 p. dj. EX. M2. $20.00

GADDIS & LONG. *Killer.* 1970. NY. Macmillan. 1st ed. dj. EX. $25.00

GADE, G. *Norwegian Ex-Libris.* 1917. Boston. Ltd 1st ed. 1/300. VG. J2. $50.00

GAGE, S.M. *Microscope.* 1935. Ithica. Dark Field ed. $21.50

GAILEY, H.A. *Historical Dictionary of the Gambia.* 1987. Metuchen. 2nd ed. VG. $12.50

GAILLARDET, F. *Sketches of Early TX & LA.* 1966. Austin. TX U. dj. EX. $65.00

GAINES, F.P. *Lee: Final Achievement (1865-1870).* 1933. Ltd ed. 31 p. J4. $20.00

GAINES, T.R. *Achieving Life.* 1926. NY. $18.00

GAINES, T.R. *Higher Mental Action.* 1936. LA. $12.50

GAINES, T.R. *Vitalic Breathing.* 1947. LA. $18.00

GAINHAM, Sarah. *Appointment in Vienna.* 1958. Dutton. 1st ed. dj. VG. P1. $7.50

GAINHAM, Sarah. *Cold Dark Night.* 1961. Walker. dj. VG. P1. $7.50

GAITHER, Frances. *Double Muscadine.* 1949. Macmillan. Book Club ed. 335 p. dj. $7.50

GALANOY, T. *Tonight.* 1972. Garden City. Ils 1st ed. photos. 229 p. dj. VG. $17.50

GALARDI, Albert. *New Italian Architecture.* 1967. NY/WA. dj. EX. $20.00

GALBRAITH. *Journey to Poland & Yugoslavia in 1958.* Cambridge. Harvard. 1st ed. dj. EX. $15.00

GALBREATH, C.B. *Mill Creek Park & Source of Mill Creek.* 1934. np. photos. maps. 74 p. wraps. T5. $8.50

GALE, H.W. *Holidays & Anniversaries of the World.* 1985. Detroit. xl. EX. $37.50

GALE, J.S. *Korea in Transition.* 1909. NY. Ils 1st ed. map. 8vo. VG. T1. $40.00

GALE, R.L. *Plots & Characters in Poe.* 1970. Archon Books. 1st ed. blue cloth. VG. D1. $15.00

GALE, Zona. *Loves of Pellaes & Etarre.* 1910. Macmillan. Ils Edwards. VG. $15.00

GALLAGHER, Tess. *Lover of Horses.* 1986. NY. 1st ed. dj. EX. $35.00

GALLAND, Adolf. *First & the Last.* 1955. London. Trans Savill. 368 p. fair. T5. $22.50

GALLAND, I. *Galland's IA Emigrant.* nd. IA City. facsimile of 1840 ed. dj. VG. $32.00

GALLATIN, A.E. *Art & the Great War.* 1919. NY. Ils 1st ed. VG. T5. $145.00

GALLATIN, Albert. *Synopsis of Indian Tribes Within US E of Rocky Mountains...* 1836. Cambridge. 1st ed. fld map. 574 p. xl. EX. A3. $1600.00

GALLICO, Paul. *Hand of Mary Constable.* 1964. Heinemann. 1st ed. xl. P1. $6.00

GALLICO, Paul. *Man Who Was Magic.* 1966. Garden City. 1st ed. dj. VG. $10.00

GALLUP. *Ezra Pound: Bibliography.* 1983. VA. 548 p. dj. EX. $45.00

GALSWORTHY, John. *Devoted to the Disabled Sailor & Soldier.* 1918. London. Ils Beerbohm. wraps. VG. $35.00

GALSWORTHY, John. *Loyalties.* 1930. London. 1/315. sgn. dj. EX. $150.00

GALSWORTHY, John. *Memories.* 1914. NY. Ils Maud Earl. $30.00

GALSWORTHY, John. *Roof.* 1931. NY. dj. EX. $4.00

GALSWORTHY, John. *Soames & the Flag.* 1930. London. Heinemann. 1/1025. sgn. boxed. VG. $25.00

GALSWORTHY, John. *Soames & the Flag.* 1930. NY. 1st ed. sgn. $75.00

GALSWORTHY, John. *Swan Song.* 1928. London. 1st ed. gilt bdg. EX. $20.00

GALVIN, John. *Etchings of Edward Borein: Catalog of His Work.* 1971. San Francisco. Howell. 1st ed. 318 pls. dj. EX. $70.00

GAMBLING, John. *Rambling With Gambling.* 1972. Prentice Hall. 2nd print. inscr. VG. $8.50

GAMBRELL, Herbert. *Anson Jones: Last President of TX.* 1948. Doubleday. 1st ed. dj. VG. J2. $17.50

GAMMON, Roland. *Faith Is a Star.* 1964. NY. $10.00

GAMSON, W.A. *Power & Discontent.* 1968. Homewood, IL. Dorsey. 1st ed. pb. $3.00

GANDOLFI, Simon. *France-Security.* 1981. Blond Briggs. 1st ed. dj. EX. P1. $15.00

GANN, Ernest K. *Getting Them Into the Blue.* 1942. NY. Ils 1st ed. 154 p. dj. G. T5. $25.00

GANN, W.D. *US Years in Wall Street.* 1949. Mami. 1st ed. VG. B2. $42.50

GANNETT PUBLISHING. *Homes of Ready-Made Farmers...* 1915. Augusta, ME. Ils. 4to. 80 p. $30.00

GANPAT. *Voice of Dashin.* 1927. Doran. 1st ed. dj. G. $15.00

GANSSER, E.B. *History of the 126th Infantry in War With Germany.* 1920. private print. xl. G. $20.00

GANTILLON, Simon. *Maya.* 1930. Golden Cockerel. Ils Stanton. G. $50.00

GANTZ, Kenneth F. *Not in Solitude.* nd. Book Club. dj. VG. P1. $4.00

GANZ, Jeffrey. *Mabinogion.* Penguin. pb. M. C1. $4.00

GANZ, P. *Paintings of Hans Holbein.* 1956. London. 1st ed. 220 pls. 4to. dj. EX. J2. $80.00

GANZ. *World of Coins & Coin Collecting.* 1985. Scribner. dj. EX. $20.00

GARD, R.M. *End of the Morgan Raid.* 1963. Lisbon, OH. Ils. 22 p. wraps. VG. T5. $22.50

GARD, Wayne. *Chisholm Trail.* 1954. Norman. Ils 1st ed. dj. EX. $40.00

GARD, Wayne. *Great Buffalo Hunt.* 1959. NY. Knopf. Ils Eggenhofer. 1st ed. dj. EX. $22.00

GARD, Wayne. *Great Buffalo Hunt.* 1960. Knopf. Ils. 324 p. VG. M2. $20.00

GARD, Wayne. *Great Buffalo Hunt.* 1960. NY. Ils Eggenhoffer. dj. G. $17.50

GARD, Wayne. *Rawhide TX.* 1965. Norman. Ils. dj. VG. $35.00

GARD & VODREY. *Sandy & Beaver Canal.* 1972. E Liverpool. reprint. inscr Gard. 210 p. VG. T5. $45.00

GARDINER, Dorothy. *Lion in Wait.* 1963. Crime Club. 1st ed. dj. VG. P1. $12.50

GARDINER, J.T. *Report of NY State Survey for 1878-1884. Vols. I-V.* 1879-1885. Albany. 8vo. wraps. xl. $100.00

GARDNER, A. *English Medieval Sculpture.* 1951. Cambridge. 8vo. blue buckram. dj. EX. J2. $100.00

GARDNER, Albert. *Winslow Homer.* 1961. NY. 1st ed. dj. EX. $40.00

GARDNER, Alexander. *Gardner's Photographic Sketchbook of Civil War.* 1959. Dover. Unabridged reprint of 1886 ed. dj. $35.00

GARDNER, E.J. *History of Biology.* 1968. Burgess. Ils 2nd ed. 376 p. EX. M2. $18.00

GARDNER, E.S. *Case of the Backward Mule.* 1946. Morrow. 1st ed. dj. VG. $37.00

GARDNER, E.S. *Case of the Beautiful Beggar.* nd. Book Club. dj. VG. P1. $4.00

GARDNER, E.S. *Case of the Buried Clock.* 1943. Morrow. 1st ed. dj. VG. $35.00

GARDNER, E.S. *Case of the Careless Cupid.* 1968. NY. 1st ed. dj. EX. $20.00

GARDNER, E.S. *Case of the Crimson Kiss.* 1970. Morrow. 1st ed. dj. EX. P1. $15.00

GARDNER, E.S. *Case of the Crooked Candle.* 1944. Morrow. 1st ed. dj. VG. $33.00

GARDNER, E.S. *Case of the Crying Swallow.* 1971. NY. 1st ed. dj. EX. $20.00

GARDNER, E.S. *Case of the Dubious Bridegroom.* 1949. Morrow. 1st ed. dj. VG. P1. $25.00

GARDNER, E.S. *Case of the Fabulous Fake.* 1969. Morrow. 1st ed. dj. EX. P1. $15.00

GARDNER, E.S. *Case of the Fan Dancer's Horse.* 1947. Morrow. VG. P1. $12.50

GARDNER, E.S. *Case of the Ice-Cold Hands.* 1962. Morrow. 1st ed. dj. VG. P1. $12.00

GARDNER, E.S. *Case of the Negligent Nymph.* nd. Black. dj. VG. P1. $7.50

GARDNER, E.S. *Case of the Reluctant Model.* 1968. Thiller Book Club. dj. xl. P1. $4.00

GARDNER, E.S. *Case of the Shoplifter's Shoe.* 1938. Morrow. 1st ed. dj. VG. $35.00

GARDNER, E.S. *Case of the Stepdaughter's Secret.* 1963. Morrow. Lib bdg. xl. P1. $5.00

GARDNER, E.S. *Case of the Stuttering Bishop.* 1936. Morrow. 1st ed. dj. VG. $40.00

GARDNER, E.S. *Case of the Sulky Girl.* 1944. Triangle. dj. VG. P1. $12.50

GARDNER, E.S. *Case of the Waylaid Wolf.* 1959. NY. Morrow. 1st ed. dj. EX. $30.00

GARDNER, E.S. *Case of the Worried Waitress.* 1966. Morrow. 1st ed. dj. VG. $15.00

GARDNER, E.S. *D.A. Breaks an Egg.* 1949. Morrow. 1st ed. dj. VG. $42.00

GARDNER, E.S. *D.A. Holds a Candle.* 1938. Morrow. 1st ed. dj. VG. $40.00

GARDNER, E.S. *D.A. Holds a Candle.* 1942. Triangle. 2nd ed. dj. VG. P1. $12.50

GARDNER, E.S. *Desert Is Yours.* 1963. NY. 1st ed. presentation. sgn. VG. G1. $25.00

GARDNER, E.S. *Hidden Heart of Baja.* 1962. NY. 1st ed. presentation. sgn. VG. G1. $25.00

GARDNER, E.S. *Host With the Big Hat.* 1969. NY. Ils 1st ed. 8vo. dj. VG. $27.50

GARDNER, E.S. *Hovering Over Baja.* 1961. NY. 1st ed. presentation. sgn. VG. G1. $25.00

GARDNER, E.S. *Hunting the Desert Whale: Travels in Baja.* 1960. NY. Ils. 8vo. dj. VG. $20.00

GARDNER, E.S. *Neighborhood Frontiers.* 1954. Morrow. 1st ed. inscr. dj. VG. $50.00

GARDNER, E.S. *Two Clues.* 1947. Morrow. 1st ed. dj. $35.00

GARDNER, J. *Construction of Christian Poetry in Old English.* 1975. S IL U. dj. EX. $100.00

GARDNER, J. *Construction of the Wakefield Cycle.* 1974. S IL U. dj. EX. $100.00

GARDNER, John. *Complete State of Death.* 1969. Jonathan Cape. dj. xl. P1. $7.50

GARDNER, John. *Every Night's a Bullfight.* 1971. London. 1st ed. dj. VG. $25.00

GARDNER, John. *For Special Services.* 1982. Coward McCann. 1st ed. dj. EX. P1. $17.50

GARDNER, John. *Grendel.* 1st Eng ed. sgn. dj. EX. $100.00

GARDNER, John. *Grendel.* NY. Ltd 1st ed. slipcase. $150.00

GARDNER, John. *Gudgekin the Thistle Girl & Other Tales.* 1978. Ils Spoorn. 1st ed. VG. C1. $6.00

GARDNER, John. *Icebreaker.* 1983. Putnam. 1st ed. dj. EX. P1. $17.50

GARDNER, John. *Invective Against Mere Fiction.* 1967. Baton Rouge. S Review. T6. $10.00

GARDNER, John. *King of the Hummingbirds & Other Tales.* 1977. 1st ed. dj. EX. C1. $7.50

GARDNER, John. *King's Indian.* 1974. NY. Knopf. 1st ed. dj. VG. T6. $20.00

GARDNER, John. *License Renewed.* 1981. Jonathan Cape. 1st ed. dj. EX. P1. $17.50

GARDNER, John. *Madrigal.* 1967. Frederick Muller. dj. xl. P1. $7.50

GARDNER, John. *Madrigal.* 1968. Viking. 1st ed. dj. VG. P1. $22.50

GARDNER, John. *MSS, Vol. I, No. 2.* 1962. Chico, CA. 2nd issue. T6. $25.00

GARDNER, John. *Notes on Malory's le Morte d'Arthur.* 1967. Cliff Notes. 1st ed. wraps. EX. T6. $15.00

GARDNER, John. *Notes on the Gawian Poet.* 1967. Cliff Notes. 1st ed. wraps. EX. T6. $15.00

GARDNER, John. *Resurrection.* 1974. Ballantine. 1st pb ed. wraps. VG. T6. $20.00

GARDNER, John. *Secret Generations.* 1985. Putnam. dj. EX. P1. $22.50

GARDNER, John. *Wreckage of Agathon.* 1970. NY. 1st ed. dj. EX. $90.00

GARDNER, Paul V. *Glass of Frederick Carder.* 1971. Crown. 1st print. dj. D2. $125.00

GARDNER, Percy. *Coins of the Greek & Scythic Kings of Bactria & India.* 1966. Chicago. Argonaut. dj. M. $20.00

GARDNER, R.D. *Horatio Alger; or, American Hero Era.* 1964. Mendota. 102 p. dj. EX. $40.00

GARDNER & DUNLAP. *Forms of Fiction.* 1962. NY. 1st ed. dj. VG. $85.00

GARFIELD, Brian. *Recoil.* nd. BOMC. dj. VG. P1. $3.00

GARFIELD, J.A. *Wild Life of Army.* 1964. Lansing. 1st ed. dj. G. $8.00

GARIEPY, L.J. *Saw-Ge-Mah.* 1950. St. Paul. $20.00

GARIS, H.R. *Rocket Riders Over the Desert; or, Seeking the Lost City.* 1933. NY. Burt. 12mo. 250 p. VG. $20.00

GARIS, Roger. *My Father Was Uncle Wiggly.* 1966. McGraw Hill. 217 p. dj. EX. $20.00

GARLAND, H. *Tyranny of the Dark.* 1905. London. 1st ed. G. $35.00

GARLAND, Hamlin. *Back Trailers From Middle Border.* 1928. NY. 1st ed. VG. $25.00

GARLAND, Hamlin. *Book of American Indian.* 1923. NY. Ils. 274 p. VG. B2. $75.00

GARLAND, Hamlin. *Daughter of Middle Border.* 1921. NY. 1st ed. presentation. sgn. VG. B2. $37.50

GARLAND, Hamlin. *Friendly Contemporaries.* 1932. 1st ed. dj. VG. B2. $20.00

GARLAND, Hamlin. *Son of the Middle Border.* 1917. NY. 1st ed. inscr/sgn. VG. $40.00

GARLAND, Hugh A. *Life of John Randolph of Roanoke.* 1851. Appleton. 2 vols. xl. $45.00

GARNER, Alan. *Weirdstone of Brisingamen.* 1978. Intro Norton. pb. VG. C1. $2.50

GARNER, Elvira. *Ezekiel.* 1937. NY. Black FL Juvenile. dj. B2. $32.50

GARNER, Philippe. *Emile Galle.* 1976. London. presentation. sgn. 167 p. dj. D2. $45.00

GARNER, R.L. *Apes & Monkeys: Their Life & Language.* 1900. Ginn. Ils 1st ed. 297 p. EX. M2. $23.00

GARNER, W. *Production of Tobacco.* 1946. Boston. Blakiston. Ils. 8vo. 516 p. $45.00

GARNER, William. *Strip Jack Naked.* 1977. Bobbs Merrill. dj. G. P1. $10.00

GARNER, William. *Us or Them War.* nd. Companion Book Club. dj. EX. P1. $3.50

GARNER, William. *Us or Them War.* nd. Book Club. dj. VG. P1. $3.00

GARNER, William. *Us or Them War.* 1969. Collins. xl. P1. $5.00

GARNETT, David. *Letters of T.E. Lawrence.* 1939. Doubleday. Stated 1st ed. VG. $16.50

GARNETT, David. *Man in the Zoo.* 1924. Macmillan. dj. VG. P1. $10.00

GARNETT, David. *Shot in the Dark.* 1958. Little Brown. 1st ed. dj. G. P1. $7.50

GARNETT, Richard. *Twilight of the Gods.* 1924. Bodley Head. Ils Lawrence. 1st ed. $75.00

GARNETT, Richard. *Twilight of the Gods.* 1924. NY. Ils Keen. 1st ed. VG. J2. $35.00

GARNETT & GOSS. *History of English Literature.* 1903. Macmillan. 1st ed. 4to. 4 vols. $60.00

GARNIER, F. *Traite'sur les Puits Artesiens.* 1926. Paris. 2nd ed. 25 fld pls. VG. $150.00

GARRETSON, Martin. *American Bison.* 1938. NY Zool Soc. 1st ed. dj. VG. J2. $45.00

GARRETT, G. *People's Pottage.* 1953. Caxton. 1st ed. M. $35.00

GARRETT, P.F. *Authentic Life of Billy the Kid.* 1954. Norman. Ils 5th ed. dj. EX. $25.00

GARRETT, P.F. *Authentic Life of Billy the Kid.* 1980. Time Life. reprint of 1882 ed. 137 p. M2. $15.00

GARRETT, Randall. *Lord Darcy.* nd. Book Club. dj. VG. P1. $6.00

GARRETT, Randall. *Unwise Child.* nd. Book Club. dj. VG. P1. $6.00

GARRETT, William. *From Dusk Till Dawn.* 1931. Bodley Head. VG. P1. $10.00

GARRIOTT, E.B. *Weather Folklore & Local Weather Signs.* 1903. GOP. fair. $20.00

GARRISON, J.B. *Piedmont Garden: How To Grow by the Calendar.* 1981. SC U. 1st ed. spiral bdg. $10.00

GARROTT. *Hal Squiffer.* 1924. NY. Ils Dugald Walker. $17.50

GARSIDE, A.H. *Cotton Goes to Market.* 1935. NY. Ils 1st ed. 411 p. G. $15.00

GARSON, Paul. *Great Quill.* 1973. Doubleday. 1st ed. dj. VG. P1. $7.50

GARST, S. *Kit Carson: Trailblazer & Scout.* 1946. Messner. 241 p. G. M2. $7.00

GARST, S. *Scotty Allan, King of the Dog Team Drivers.* 1947. NY. Ils 4th print. dj. VG. $10.00

GARTH, David. *Bermuda Calling.* 1944. Thomas Allen. 1st ed. dj. VG. P1. $15.00

GARTHOFF, Raymond. *Soviet Military Doctrine.* 1953. Free Pr. 1st ed. dj. VG. J2. $15.00

GARVE, Andrew. *Ascent of D.13.* 1969. Thriller Book Club. dj. VG. P1. $4.50

GARVE, Andrew. *Hero for Leanda.* nd. Book Club. dj. VG. P1. $3.00

GARVE, Andrew. *Hide & Go Seek.* nd. Book Club. dj. VG. P1. $3.00

GARVE, Andrew. *Long Short Cut.* 1968. Harper Row. 1st ed. dj. xl. P1. $5.00

GARVE, Andrew. *Megstone Plot.* nd. Book Club. dj. VG. P1. $3.00

GARWOOD, Darrell. *Artist in IA: Life of Grant Wood.* 1944. Norton. 1st ed. VG. J2. $45.00

GASCOIGNE, Bamber. *Great Moghuls.* 1971. NY. Harper Row. Ils. 264 p. dj. D2. $45.00

GASH, Jonathan. *Grail Tree.* nd. Book Club. dj. EX. P1. $4.50

GASH, Jonathan. *Moonspender.* 1986. London. 1st ed. dj. EX. $35.00

GASH, Jonathan. *Pearlhanger.* c 1985. NY. St. Martin. 1st ed. dj. EX. $10.00

GASKELL, Jane. *Atlan Saga. Vol. III.* 1965. St. Martin. 1st ed. dj. EX. $8.50

GASKELL, Jane. *City.* 1978. St. Martin. 1st ed. dj. EX. P1. $15.00

GASKELL, Jane. *City.* 1978. St. Martin. 1st ed. dj. VG. P1. $12.00

GASKELL, T. *Gulf Stream.* 1965. 1st ed. dj. EX. $5.00

GASKELL. *Life of Charlotte Bronte.* 1895. London. TEG. $25.00

GASPARINETTI, A. *L'Uniforme Italiana.* 1961. Rome. Ils. Italian text. dj. VG. $50.00

GASPER. *Complete Sportsman.* 1883. NY. 1st ed. G. $35.00

GASS, William. *In the Heart of the Heart of the Country & Other Stories.* 1968. NY. Harper. 1st ed. dj. $40.00

GASS, William. *Omensetter's Luck.* 1966. NY. 1st ed. dj. EX. $65.00

GASSER, M. *World of Werner Bishof.* 1959. Dutton. dj. EX. $25.00

GASSIER & WILSON. *Life & Complete Work of Francisco Goya.* 1971. NY. Morrow. Revised ed. 400 p. slipcase. D2. $120.00

GASTER, Theodore. *Dead Sea Scriptures in English.* 1956. Garden City. VG. $22.50

GASTON, Paul. *New S Creed: Study in S Mythmaking.* 1970. NY. 1st ed. 304 p. dj. VG. $20.00

GAT, Dimitri V. *Shepherd Is My Lord.* 1971. Doubleday. 1st ed. dj. xl. P1. $5.00

GATENBY, Rosemary. *Deadly Relations.* nd. Book Club. dj. VG. P1. $3.00

GATENBY, Rosemary. *Fugitive Affair.* nd. Book Club. dj. VG. P1. $3.00

GATES, Macburney. *Black Pirate.* 1926. Grosset Dunlap. Movie ed. dj. VG. P1. $20.00

GATES, S.Y. *Life Story of Brigham Young Written by Daughter.* 1930. NY. 1st ed. 388 p. dj. VG. B2. $47.50

GATEWOOD, R.L. *Faulkner Co., AR, 1778-1964: A History.* 1964. Conway. Ils. 4to. 188 p. EX. M2. $15.00

GAUGUIN, Paul. *Intimate Journals.* 1936. Crown. Trans Van Wyck Brooks. 1st ed. J2. $25.00

GAUGUIN, Paul. *Noa Noa.* 1919. NY. 1st ed. dj. $10.00

GAULT, William Campbell. *Convertible Hearse.* 1957. Random House. 1st ed. xl. P1. $8.00

GAULT, William Campbell. *Dead Hero.* 1963. Dutton. 1st ed. dj. xl. P1. $7.50

GAULT, William Campbell. *Death in Donegal Bay.* 1984. Walker. 1st ed. dj. EX. P1. $15.00

GAUTIER, E.F. *Sahara: Great Desert.* 1935. Columbia U. Revised ed. fld map. 264 p. EX. M2. $18.00

GAUTIER, Leon. *Chivalry: Everyday Life of the Medieval Knight.* 1989. reprint. 500 p. dj. M. C1. $15.00

GAUTIER, Theophile. *Madame de Maupin.* nd. np. Ils/sgn Clara Tice. dj. EX. $25.00

GAUTIER, Theophile. *Wife of King Candaules.* 1942. Wisdom House. Ils Roth. green bdg. dj. EX. $22.50

GAVARNI. *Oeuvres Choises de Gavarni.* 1846. Paris. 4to. green leather. $135.00

GAVIN, Antonio. *Frauds of Romish Monks & Priests Set Forth in 8 Letters.* 1725. London. 12mo. 360 p. leather. VG. G2. $56.00

GAVIN, James M. *Airborne Warfare.* 1947. WA. Ils 1st ed. 186 p. dj. VG. T5. $45.00

GAVIN, William. *Accoutrement Plates N & S, 1861-1865.* 1963. 1st ed. dj. M. J4. $50.00

GAVIN, William. *Accoutrement Plates N & S, 1861-1865.* 1975. 2nd ed. M. J4. $45.00

GAWRON, Jean Mark. *Apology for Rain.* 1974. Doubleday. 1st ed. dj. EX. P1. $7.50

GAY, J.A. *History of Oaxaca.* 1881. Mexico. 1st ed. 2 vols. VG. T1. $65.00

GAY, John. *Beggar's Opera.* 1937. NY. Ils. 4to. 113 p. slipcase. EX. $15.00

GAY, John. *Fables by the Late Mr. Gay.* 1746. London. 6th ed. 2 vols. VG. $240.00

GAY, M.A. *Transplanted: Story of Dixie Before the War.* 1907. Neale. VG. B1. $35.00

GAZDANOV, Gaito. *Buddha's Return.* 1951. Dutton. 1st ed. VG. P1. $5.00

GEARD, V. *Meisonnier: His Life & His Art.* 1897. NY. Ils. 4to. VG. J2. $70.00

GEDDES, N.B. *Magic Motorways.* 1940. NY. 1st ed. presentation. sgn. VG. B2. $67.50

GEDGE, Pauline. *Eagle & the Raven.* 1978. 1st ed. dj. VG. C1. $9.50

GEE, Nancie. *Reflections in Pike Place Markets.* 1968. Seattle. 1st ed. folio. 128 p. VG. B2. $27.50

GEER, A. *New Breed: US Marine in Korea.* 1952. NY. 1st ed. dj. VG. B2. $22.50

GEER, H.A. *Trooper's Scrapbook.* 1966. Ravenna, OH. 1st ed. 1/300. inscr. 107 p. G. T5. $45.00

GEER, J.J. *Beyond the Lines; or, Yankee Prisoner Loose in Dixie.* 1863. Phil. 1st ed. G. $25.00

GEFVERT, C.J. *Edward Taylor: Annotated Bibliography.* 1971. Kent State. green cloth. EX. $15.00

GEHLBACK, F.R. *Mountain Islands & Desert Seas.* 1981. TX A&M. Ils 1st ed. 298 p. dj. EX. M2. $25.00

GEHMAN, J.M. *Smoke Over America.* 1943. Roycroft. 8vo. tan cloth. VG. D1. $25.00

GEHRIG, Eleanor. *My Luke & I.* 1976. NY. 1st ed. dj. VG. B2. $15.00

GEHRING, W. *Charlie Chaplin: Bio-Bibliography.* 1983. Greenwood. 1st ed. VG. J2. $10.00

GEHRTS, A. *Der Fernsehdienst der Deutschen Reichspost.* 1938. Leipzig. 1st/only ed. 30 p. wraps. xl. G. $25.00

GEIGER, Maynard. *Martyrs of FL: 1513-1616.* 1936. Franciscan Studies. 1st ed. J2. $17.50

GEIKIE, Archibald. *Geology.* nd. Am Book Co. Ils. 137 p. EX. $3.00

GEIRINGER, Karl. *Johann Sebastian Bach: Culmination of an Era.* 1966. Oxford. 1st ed. VG. J2. $15.00

GEIRINGER, Karl. *Musical Instruments: History From Stone Age to Present Day.* 1945. Allen. 2nd ed. dj. VG. J2. $15.00

GEIST, Valerius. *Mountain Sheep: Study in Behavior & Evolution.* 1971. Chicago U. 1st ed. dj. VG. J2. $20.00

GELATT, R. *Fabulous Phonograph: From Tin Foil to High Fidelity.* 1955. NY. 1st ed. dj. VG. B2. $32.50

GELATT, R. *Hi-Fi Record Annual for 1955.* 1st ed. EX. $15.00

GELD, E.B. *Heritage: Daughter's Memories of Louis Bromfield.* 1962. NY. Ils 1st ed. 204 p. dj. T5. $19.50

GELD, E.B. *Heritage: Daughter's Memories of Louis Bromfield.* 1962. NY. 1st ed. dj. B2. $17.50

GELDERS & O'HARE. *Handbook for House Repairs.* 1949. Perma P27. G. P1. $2.75

GELLER, Eli. *Window Episode.* 1958. Mystery House. 1st ed. xl. P1. $5.00

GELLER, Michael. *Major League Murder.* 1988. St. Martin. 1st ed. dj. M. $10.00

GENAUER. *Chagall at Met.* 1971. NY. Tudor. dj. VG. $35.00

GENESTE, John. *Some Account of British Stage From Restoration, 1630-1830.* 1832. Bath. 1st ed. 10 vols. rebound. xl. $350.00

GENET, E.C. *Memorial on Upward Forces of Fluids.* 1969. Austin. reprint of 1825 ed. dj. T5. $22.50

GENET, Jean. *Miracle of the Rose.* 1966. Grove. 1st ed. dj. M. $25.00

GENET, Jean. *Thief's Journal.* 1954. Olympia Pr. sgn. wraps. $95.00

GENTHE, Arnold. *As I Remember.* 1936. NY. Ltd ed. 112 photos. sgn. VG. $140.00

GENTHE, Arnold. *As I Remember. With One Hundred & Twelve Photographs.* 1936. NY. 3rd print. 4to. 290 p. M. $45.00

GENTHE, Arnold. *Book of the Dance.* 1916. NY. 1st ed. $115.00

GENTHE, Arnold. *Book of the Dance.* 1920. Boston. 2nd ed. VG. $50.00

GENTHE, Arnold. *Highlights & Shadows.* 1937. NY. Greenberg. photos. 4to. spiral bdg. wraps. $37.50

GENTHE, Arnold. *Impressions of Old New Orleans.* 1926. Doran. EX. S2. $150.00

GENTHE, Arnold. *Impressions of Old New Orleans.* 1926. Doran. VG. $75.00

GENTHE, Arnold. *Pictures of Old Chinatown.* 1908. NY. Moffat. 1st ed. 4to. orange cloth. VG. $110.00

GENTHE, Arnold. *Yellow-Jacket, Chinese Play Done in Chinese Manner...* 1913. Bobbs Merrill. later ed. 190 p. $35.00

GENTRY. *Frame-Up.* 1967. 2nd print. dj. VG. $20.00

GENUNG, J.F. *Stevenson's Attitude to Life.* 1901. Crowell. 44 p. VG. $25.00

GEORGE, D. *Sweet Man.* 1981. NY. 1st ed. 272 p. dj. VG. B2. $22.50

GEORGE, J.B. *Shots Fired in Anger.* 1947. Plantersville. Ils 1st ed. 421 p. VG. B2. $60.00

GEORGE & LEONARD. *Roentgen Diagnosis of Surgical Lesions...* 1915. Boston. Ils. 4to. P3. $59.00

GEORGIOU, Constantine. *Children & Their Literature.* 1969. Prentice Hall. 401 p. VG. $13.50

GEPHART. *Revolutionary America: Bibliography.* 1894. GPO. 1600 p. EX. $65.00

GERALDY. *Toi et Moi.* 1946. Stockholm. Ils Hallman. wraps. EX. $15.00

GERARD, Francis. *Secret Sceptre.* 1971. Tom Stacey. dj. EX. P1. $15.00

GERARD, Francis. *Sinister Secret.* 1952. MacDonald. 1st Eng ed. dj. EX. $15.00

GERARD, Max. *Dali.* 1968. Abrams. 1st ed. dj. EX. B2. $95.00

GERARD, Max. *Dali.* 1968. Abrams. 1st ed. dj. VG. J2. $45.00

GERBER, Albert. *Howard Hughes: Bashful Billionaire.* 1967. Lyle Stuart. 384 p. EX. $16.00

GERDTS, William H. *Painters of the Humble Truth.* 1981. Tulsa. Philbrook Art Center. 293 p. D2. $37.50

GERHARDSTEIN, V.B. *Fourth Edition, Dickinson's American Historical Fiction.* Scarecrow Pr. 312 p. VG. T5. $6.50

GERLACH. *Atlas de Couronnes.* c 1890. 10 pls. VG. $75.00

GERNSBACK, Hugo. *Ralph 124C41: Romance of Year 2660.* 1925. Statford Co. 1st ed. B1. $50.00

GERNSHEIM, Helmut. *Creative Photography: Aesthetic Trends, 1839-1960.* 1962. Boston. Boston Book Art. 1st Am ed. dj. EX. $70.00

GERNSHEIM, Helmut. *Masterpieces of Victorian Photography.* 1951. London. Phaidon. 1st ed. 4to. VG. $35.00

GERNSHEIM & CHURCHILL. *Churchill: His Life in Photographs.* 1955. NY. Rinehart. 1st ed. dj. $30.00

GERNSHEIM & GERNSHEIM. *History of Photography, 1685-1914.* 1969. McGraw. 1st ed. 4to. dj. $225.00

GERONIMO. *Geronimo's Story of His Life.* 1907. NY. photos. 216 p. VG. T5. $45.00

GERRARD & BARTOLOTTI. *Bald Eagle: Haunts & Habits of a Wilderness Monarch.* 1988. Smithsonian. Ils. maps. 177 p. dj. EX. M2. $24.00

GERRISH, Theodore. *Life in the World's Wonderland.* 1887. Biddeford. Ils 1st ed. 8vo. VG. T1. $40.00

GERRISH, Theodore. *Reminiscences of the War.* 1882. 1st ed. 372 p. K1. $23.50

GERROLD, David. *Man Who Folded Himself.* 1973. Random House. 1st ed. dj. EX. P1. $35.00

GERSCHENKRON, Alexander. *Bread & Democracy in Germany.* 1943. CA U. 1st ed. VG. J2. $15.00

GERSON, Horst. *Rembrandt Paintings.* 1968. Reynal Morrow. Ils. 527 p. D2. $75.00

GERSTACKER, F. *Wild Sports in the Far W.* 1968. Duke U. Ils. 409 p. dj. EX. M2. $35.00

GERSTER, George. *Below From Above: Aerial Photography.* 1986. NY. Ils. dj. VG. T5. $19.50

GESNER, Conrad. *On the Admiration of Mountains.* 1937. Grabhorn. 1/325. tall 4to. EX. $85.00

GESSLER, C. *Tropic Landfall: Port of Honolulu.* 1942. Doubleday. Ils 1st ed. 331 p. G. M2. $11.00

GETLEIN, Frank. *Chaim Gross.* 1974. NY. Abrams. Ils. 235 p. dj. D2. $115.00

GEYL, P. *Beautiful Play of Lancelot of Denmark.* 1923. Hague. 1st ed. VG. C1. $7.00

GHENT, W.J. *Early Far W Narrative Outline, 1554-1850.* 1936. Ils. 411 p. G. $10.00

GHIRSHMAN, Roman. *Persian Art: Parthian & Sassanian Dynasties 249 BC-AD 651.* 1962. Golden Pr. Ils. dj. D2. $95.00

GHIRSHMAN, Roman. *Persian Art: Parthian & Sassanian Dynasties 249 BC-AD 651.* 1962. NY. Ils. 4to. dj. slipcase. EX. J2. $60.00

GIBBINGS, Robert. *Coming Down the Seine.* 1953. London. 1st ed. gilt bdg. EX. $20.00

GIBBINGS, Robert. *Coming Down the Seine.* 1953. London. Dent. Ltd ed. 1/75. sgn. EX. $175.00

GIBBON, Edward. *History of the Decline & Fall of Roman Empire.* 1946. Heritage. 3 vols. boxed. VG. J2. $30.00

GIBBON, Edward. *Memoirs of My Life.* 1966. Funk Wagnall. dj. M. $55.00

GIBBON, Edward. *Miscellaneous Works of Edward Gibbon.* 1796. London. Stratan Cadell Davies. 2 vols. $150.00

GIBBONS, Felton. *Dosso & Battista Dossi: Court Painters at Ferrara.* 1968. Princeton. pls. dj. D2. $165.00

GIBBONS, P.E. *PA Dutch & Other Essays.* 1882. Phil. VG. $40.00

GIBBONS, Walter. *Tragedy of the Heavens.* 1930. London. $125.00

GIBBS, H.J. *Miller's Daughter; or, Bound in Honor.* 1894. Clyde, OH. Ames. 30 p. wraps. G. T5. $12.50

GIBBS, Philip. *Darkened Rooms.* 1929. Doubleday Doran. VG. P1. $6.00

GIBBS, Philip. *England Speaks.* 1935. Ils Landers. 1st Am ed. 341 p. dj. VG. $12.00

GIBBS, Philip. *Now It Can Be Told.* 1920. Harper. G. $10.00

GIBBS, Sharon. *Greek & Roman Sundials.* 1976. Yale. 1st ed. dj. VG. J2. $17.50

GIBBS-SMITH, C.H. *Balloons.* 1956. London. Ariel Pr. 12 pls. wraps. T5. $45.00

GIBLIN, J.J. *Private Detective.* 1944. Providence. 1st ed. 98 p. EX. $35.00

GIBRAN, Kahlil. *Prophet.* 1966. Knopf. Ils. pls. 84 p. black cloth. boxed. $25.00

GIBRAN, Kahlil. *Self-Portrait.* 1969. NY. $7.00

GIBSON, A.M. *Chickasaws.* 1971. Norman. Ils. dj. EX. $35.00

GIBSON, C.D. *Drawings.* 1894. NY. 1st ed. $125.00

GIBSON, C.D. *Pictures of People.* 1896. NY. Russell. 1st ed. folio. rebound. $175.00

GIBSON, C.D. *Sketches & Cartoons.* 1/200. sgn. with sgn pl. $625.00

GIBSON, Charles. *Enchanted Trails.* 1949. London. Mus Pr. Ils 1st ed. VG. M2. $14.00

GIBSON, Charles. *Story of the Ship.* 1948. Schuman. 1st ed. dj. VG. J2. $15.00

GIBSON, R. *St. Thomas Moore: Preliminary Bibliography of Works...* 1961. Yale. dj. VG. $55.00

GIBSON, Strickland. *Some Oxford Libraries.* 1914. London. pls. $25.00

GIBSON, W.B. *Rod Serling's the Twilight Zone.* 1963. Grosset Dunlap. dj. VG. P1. $15.00

GIBSON, W.H. *Camp Life in the Woods & Tricks of Trapping & Trap Making.* 1881. NY. 300 p. G. $30.00

GIBSON, W.H. *Our Edible Toadstools & Mushrooms.* 1895. Ils 1st ed. 30 pls. TEG. $40.00

GIBSON, W.H. *Sharp Eyes.* 1892. NY. Ils. EX. $35.00

GIBSON, W.W. *Collected Poems.* 1917. VG. C1. $14.00

GIBSON, Walter. *Crime Over Casco & Mother Goose Murder.* 1979. Crime Club. 1st ed. dj. xl. P1. $15.00

GIBSON, Walter. *Magic Explained.* 1949. Perma P54. G. P1. $15.00

GIBSON, William. *Mona Lisa Overdrive.* 1988. NY. Bantam. ARC. wraps. EX. $20.00

GIDDINGS, J.L. *Ancient Men of the Arctic.* 1967. Knopf. Ils 1st ed. 381 p. dj. EX. M2. $20.00

GIDE, Andre. *Imaginary Interviews.* 1944. NY. Trans Cowley. dj. VG. C1. $7.50

GIDE, Andre. *Montaigne: Essay in Two Parts.* 1929. Liveright. 1/500. sgn. dj. VG. $55.00

GIDE, Andre. *Pages de Journal.* 1944. NY. 1st ed. G. $20.00

GIDEON, Henry L. *New Jewish Hymnal.* 1917. NY. Bloch. 173 p. VG. T6. $20.00

GIEDION-WELCKER, Carola. *Paul Klee.* 1952. NY. Viking. Ils. 156 p. dj. D2. $85.00

GIELGUD, John. *Camera Studies by Gordon Anthony.* 1938. London. sm 4to. $20.00

GIELGUD, John. *Gielgud: An Actor & His Time.* 1980. NY. 1st Am ed. dj. EX. $15.00

GIELGUD, Val. *Death at Broadcasting House.* 1935. Rich Cowan. 5th ed. dj. VG. P1. $16.00

GIELGUD, Val. *White Eagles.* 1929. np. G. $10.00

GIESBRECHT & SCHMEIL. *Copepoda I.: Gymoplea.* 1898. Berlin. Ils. German text. rebound. EX. M2. $30.00

GIESY, J.U. *Jason, Son of Jason.* 1966. Avalon. dj. VG. P1. $10.00

GIEURE, Maurice. *Georges Braque.* 1956. Paris. Tisne. Ils. 131 p. slipcase. D2. $110.00

GIFFORD, John. *History of Political Life of Right Honorable William Pitt.* 1809. London. 1st/only ed. 6 vols. $175.00

GILBERT, A.C. *Man Who Lives in Paradise.* 1954. NY. sgn. EX. $22.00

GILBERT, Anthony. *And Death Came Too.* 1956. Crime Club. 1st ed. xl. P1. $6.00

GILBERT, Anthony. *Death Knocks Three Times.* 1949. Crime Club. 1st ed. dj. G. P1. $20.00

GILBERT, Anthony. *Give Death a Name.* 1975. Hamish Hamilton. dj. EX. P1. $10.00

GILBERT, Anthony. *Mr. Crook Lifts the Mask.* 1970. Random House. 1st ed. dj. xl. P1. $6.00

GILBERT, Anthony. *Murder's a Waiting Game.* 1972. Random House. 1st ed. dj. xl. P1. $6.00

GILBERT, Anthony. *Mystery of the Open Window.* 1930. Dodd Mead. G. P1. $25.00

GILBERT, Anthony. *Nice Little Killing.* 1973. Random House. 1st ed. dj. xl. G. P1. $5.00

GILBERT, Davies. *Some Ancient Christmas Carols With Tunes...* 1822. London. Niclos. $175.00

GILBERT, G.K. *Report on Geology of Henry Mountains.* 1877. WA. GPO. 5 maps. 160 p. scarce. VG. A3. $125.00

GILBERT, G.M. *Nuremberg Diary.* 1947. NY. 1st ed. dj. VG. B2. $27.50

GILBERT, Henry. *King Arthur's Knights.* 1911. Edinburgh. Ils Crane. 1st ed. VG. C1. $49.50

GILBERT, Henry. *King Arthur's Knights.* 1986. Ils Crane. not 1st ed. dj. M. C1. $12.00

GILBERT, Henry. *Robin Hood.* c 1925. Ils Crane. VG. C1. $17.00

GILBERT, Henry. *Robin Hood.* nd. McKay. Ils Godwin. 12mo. 348 p. dj. $15.00

GILBERT, Martin. *Winston S. Churchill: Wilderness Years.* 1982. London. 1st ed. mauve cloth. dj. M. D1. $25.00

GILBERT, Michael. *Body of a Girl.* 1972. Harper Row. 1st ed. dj. VG. P1. $12.50

GILBERT, Michael. *Death Has Deep Roots.* nd. Book Club. dj. xl. P1. $3.00

GILBERT, Michael. *Night of the Twelfth.* nd. Harper Row. dj. EX. P1. $7.50

GILBERT, Michael. *Overdrive.* 1967. Harper Row. 1st ed. dj. VG. P1. $20.00

GILBERT, Michael. *Petrella at Q.* 1977. Harper Row. 1st ed. dj. VG. P1. $12.50

GILBERT, O.P. *Men in Women's Guise.* 1926. London. Ils. 284 p. gilt bdg. $30.00

GILBERT & SULLIVAN. *Treasury of Gilbert & Sullivan.* 1941. NY. 1st ed. folio. dj. boxed. EX. $22.00

GILBEY, Walter. *Thoroughbred & Other Ponies.* 1903. London. 2nd ed. VG. $20.00

GILCHRIST, Ellen. *Anna Papers.* 1988. Boston. 1st ed. sgn. dj. EX. $35.00

GILCHRIST, Ellen. *Victory Over Japan.* 1984. Boston. 1st ed. dj. EX. $45.00

GILCK, Allen. *Winter's Coming, Winter's Gone.* 1984. NY. Pinnacle. 1st print. dj. M. scarce. $25.00

GILDER, Rodman. *Battery.* 1936. Boston. 1st ed. dj. G. $22.00

GILES, F.W. *Thirty Years in Topeka: Historical Sketch.* 1886. Topeka. EX. $22.00

GILES, J.A. *Works of Gildas & Nennius.* 1841. London. orig ed. rebound. rare. C1. $49.50

GILES, J.H. *Around Our House.* 1971. Boston. Ils 1st ed. 358 p. dj. VG. B2. $27.50

GILES, J.H. *Kinta Years.* 1973. Boston. Houghton. 1st ed. dj. EX. $20.00

GILES, J.H. *Miss Willie.* nd. Book Club. dj. VG. P1. $5.00

GILES, Kenneth. *Death Among the Stars.* 1969. Walker. 1st ed. dj. EX. P1. $10.00

GILIPIN, Laura. *Rio Grande: River of Destiny.* 1949. Duell Sloan. Ils 1st ed. 243 p. dj. scarce. A3. $100.00

GILIPIN, Laura. *Temples in Yucatan.* 1948. Hastings House. sgn. 124 p. dj. VG. scarce. A3. $200.00

GILL, Bartholomew. *McGarr & Method of Descartes.* 1984. Viking. 1st ed. dj. EX. P1. $15.00

GILL, Brendan. *Tallulah.* nd. np. 1st ed. folio. 297 p. dj. EX. $22.00

GILL, Elizabeth. *Crime Coast.* 1931. Crime Club. 1st ed. VG. P1. $20.00

GILL, Eric. *Last Essays.* 1942. London. 1st ed. dj. VG. $35.00

GILL, R.C. *White Water & Black Magic.* 1940. Holt. Ils. 369 p. VG. M2. $17.00

GILLESPIE, Dizzy. *To Be or Not To Be.* 1979. NY. 1st ed. 522 p. dj. VG. B2. $35.00

GILLESPIE, Janet. *Joyful Noise.* 1971. NY. 1st ed. dj. VG. B2. $15.00

GILLESPIE, N.C. *Charles Darwin & the Problem of Creation.* 1980. Chicago U. 201 p. dj. EX. M2. $20.00

GILLESPIE, R.B. *Empress of Coney Island.* 1986. Dodd Mead. 1st ed. dj. M. $10.00

GILLESPY, F.B. *Derby Porcelain.* 1961. London. Spring. 168 pls. folio. dj. EX. $35.00

GILLETT, J.B. *Six Years With the TX Rangers: 1875-1881.* 1943. Chicago. Lakeside Classic. 364 p. VG. T5. $32.50

GILLETT, J.B. *Six Years With the TX Rangers: 1875-1881.* 1943. Donnelley. Lakeside Classic. A3. $50.00

GILLHAM, M.E. *Naturalist in New Zealand.* 1965. Reed. Ils 1st ed. dj. xl. M2. $15.00

GILLIARD, E.T. *Birds of Paradise & Bower Birds.* 1969. NY. 1st Am ed. dj. M. $65.00

GILLIE, M.H. *Forging the Thunderbolt.* 1947. Harrisburg. 1st ed. 330 p. VG. T5. $35.00

GILLIES, M.D. *All About Modern Decorating.* 1942. NY/London. Harper. G. $25.00

GILLINGHAM, John. *Richard the Lionhearted.* VG. C1. $7.50

GILLIS, W.R. *Gold Rush Days With Mark Twain.* 1930. Boni. Ils Glintenkamp. 264 p. VG. $45.00

GILLMORE, Parker. *Lone Life: Year in the Wilderness.* 1875. London. 2 vols. G. $70.00

GILLMORE, Parker. *Prairie & Forest.* 1874. Harper. G. $48.00

GILLMORE, Rufus. *Ebony Bed Murder.* 1932. Mystery League. VG. P1. $10.00

GILMAN, Dorothy. *Mrs. Pollifax & Hong Kong Buddha.* 1985. Doubleday. 1st ed. dj. EX. P1. $15.00

GILMAN, Harry. *Four Years in the Saddle.* 1886. NY. 1st ed. presentation. sgn. $85.00

GILMAN, Laselle. *Red Gate.* 1953. Ballantine. dj. VG. P1. $30.00

GILMAN, Lawrence. *Music & Cultivated Man.* 1929. NY. Rudge. Ltd ed. sgn. EX. $14.00

GILMOUR, D. *Metabolism of Insects.* 1965. Edinburg. Oliver Boyd. 195 p. EX. M2. $15.00

GILMOUR, Pat. *Artists at Curwen.* 1977. London. Ils. 167 p. dj. D2. $30.00

GILPATRICK, Guy. *Last Glencannon Omnibus.* 1957. NY. 1st ed. dj. VG. B2. $22.50

GILPATRICK, Guy. *Second Glencannon Omnibus.* 1952. NY. dj. VG. B2. $15.00

GILPIN, Laura. *Pueblos: Camera Chronicle.* 1941. Hastings. VG. $40.00

GILPIN, Laura. *Rio Grande, River of Destiny: Interpretation of River...* 1949. NY. 1st ed. 243 p. dj. T5. $35.00

GILPIN, Laura. *Temples in Yucatan.* 1948. Hastings. 1st ed. dj. VG. $60.00

GIMPEL, Rene. *Diary of an Art Dealer.* 1966. Farrar Straus. 2nd print. dj. D2. $35.00

GINGER, Ray. *Altgeld's America.* 1958. NY. 1st ed. dj. VG. $22.00

GINGER, Ray. *Bending Cross.* 1940. 460 p. $16.00

GINGRICH, Arnold. *Well-Tempered Angler.* 1965. NY. Ils Groth. 1st ed. 337 p. dj. T5. $12.50

GINSBERG, Allen. *Airplane Dreams.* 1968. Anansi. inscr/sgn. wraps. EX. $50.00

GINSBERG, Allen. *Airplane Dreams.* 1968. Toronto. 1st ed. sgn. dj. EX. $45.00

GINSBERG, Allen. *Allen Verbatim.* 1974. McGraw Hill. 1st ed. sgn. dj. EX. $35.00

GINSBERG, Allen. *Angkor Wat.* 1968. Folcrum. Ils Lawrence. 1/100. dj. EX. $125.00

GINSBERG, Allen. *Angkor Wat.* 1968. London. AP. wraps. scarce. $100.00

GINSBERG, Allen. *Bixby Canyon Ocean Path Word Breeze.* 1972. Gotham. 1/26. inscr/sgn. $200.00

GINSBERG, Allen. *Careless Love.* 1978. Red Ozier. 1/280. sgn/#d. wraps. EX. $40.00

GINSBERG, Allen. *Collected Poems, 1947-1980.* 1984. NY. Harper. 1st ed. sgn. 8vo. 837 p. dj. EX. $25.00

GINSBERG, Allen. *Fall of America.* 1972. City Lights. 1st ed. sgn. wraps. EX. $40.00

GINSBERG, Allen. *First Blues.* 1975. Full Court. 1/100. sgn/#d. EX. $45.00

GINSBERG, Allen. *Gates of Wrath.* 1972. Grey Fox. 1/100. EX. $47.50

GINSBERG, Allen. *Gay Sunshine.* 1973. Ginsberg. 1st ed. sgn. EX. $35.00

GINSBERG, Allen. *Howl.* 1986. City Lights. Ltd ed. 1/250. sgn/#d. slipcase. $100.00

GINSBERG, Allen. *Mind Breaths: Poems, 1972-1977.* 1977. City Lights. wraps. EX. $15.00

GINSBERG, Allen. *Mostly Sitting Haiku.* 1978. From Here. inscr. wraps. EX. $50.00

GINSBERG, Allen. *Planet News.* 1968. City Lights. 1/500. sgn/#d. slipcase. EX. $65.00

GINSBERG, Allen. *Planet News.* 1968. San Francisco. 1st Am ed. VG. $35.00

GINSBERG, Allen. *Scrap Leaves.* 1968. Sri Ram Ashram. 1/150. sgn/#d. wraps. EX. $65.00

GINSBERG, Allen. *To Eberhart From Ginsberg.* 1976. Penmen Pr. 1/300. sgns/#d. acetate bdg. $65.00

GINSBERG, Allen. *White Shroud: Poems 1980-1985.* 1986. NY. 1st ed. 1/200. sgn. boxed. M. $65.00

GINSBERG, Louis. *Everlasting Minute & Other Lyrics.* 1937. NY. 1st ed. inscr/sgn. EX. $40.00

GINSBERG & ORLOVSKY. *Straight Hearts' Delight.* 1980. Gay Sunshine. 1st ed. sgn. dj. $50.00

GINSBURG, Ralph. *Eros.* 1962. 4 vols. S2. $95.00

GINZBURG. *Legends of the Jews. Vol. 3.* 1913. Jewish Pub Soc. G. $6.50

GIRARD, J. *Adventures of a French Captain, at Present a Planter in TX.* 1878. NY. M1. $185.00

GIRARD, J. *La Chambre Noire et le Microscope.* 1870. Paris. Ils. 222 p. wraps. $110.00

GIRAUDOUX, Jean. *Mirage de Bessines.* 1931. Paris. Ltd ed. 1/900. inscr/sgn. G. $125.00

GIRL SCOUTS OF AMERICA. *Girl Scout Handbook.* 1947. NY. 12mo. green cloth. G. $5.00

GIRODIAS, Maurice. *Frog Prince: Autobiography.* 1980. NY. 411 p. dj. G. $12.00

GIROUARD, Mark. *Return to Camelot.* 1981. Yale. 1st ed. dj. EX. C1. $22.50

GIRSON, A.M. *Life & Death of Colonel Albert Jennings Fountain.* 1965. Norman. Ils. dj. VG. $40.00

GISH, Lillian. *Dorothy & Lillian Gish.* 1972. NY. 1st ed. 800 photos. sgn. $30.00

GISH, Lillian. *Movies, Mr. Griffith & Me.* 2nd print. inscr. 399 p. VG. $25.00

GIST, B.D. *High Sierra Adventure.* 1950. private print. Ils. 108 p. M2. $7.00

GISWOLD, F.G. *Sport on Land & Water.* 1931. Plimpton. VG. $40.00

GIVENS, Charles G. *Rose Petal Murders.* 1935. Bobbs Merrill. G. P1. $7.50

GJERSET, Knut. *Norwegian Sailors in American Waters.* 1933. Norwegian/Am Hist Assn. 1st ed. J2. $20.00

GLACKENS, Ira. *Pope Joan: Unorthodox Interlude.* 1965. NY. Ils. 4to. 110 p. T5. $12.50

GLADSTONE, T.H. *Englishman in KS; or, Squatter Life & Border Warfare.* 1857. NY. 1st Am ed. 328 p. VG. $75.00

GLASSER, Otto. *Dr. W.C. Roentgen.* 1945. Springfield. 1st ed. 169 p. dj. VG. B2. $27.50

GLASSPELL, Susan. *Road to the Temple: George Cram Cook & Provincetown Theatre.* 1927. NY. 1st ed. 404 p. dj. VG. B2. $47.50

GLATTHAAR, J.T. *March to the Sea & Beyond.* 1985. NY U. photos. 318 p. dj. EX. $15.00

GLAZE, Eleanor. *Fear & Tenderness.* 1st ed. dj. EX. B7. $35.00

GLAZIER, R. *Historical Textile Fabrics: Tradition & Development...* 1923. NY. Ils. 120 p. G. $30.00

GLAZIER, Willard. *Down the Great River.* 1892. Hubbard. Ils. fld map. $30.00

GLAZIER, Willard. *Headwaters of the MS.* 1893. Rand McNally. Ils. photos. maps. VG. $25.00

GLAZIER, Willard. *Heroes of Three Wars.* 1882. Ils. 450 p. EX. J4. $12.50

GLEASON, C.W. *Gate to Vergil.* 1898. Ginn. 162 p. EX. $5.00

GLEASON, D. *Islands & Ports of CA.* 1958. NY. Ils 1st ed. dj. VG. $25.00

GLEASON, H.W. *Through the Year With Thoreau With Photo Illustrations.* July, 1917. Boston. Ils 1st ed. 135 p. EX. $75.00

GLEASON, Madeline. *Collected Poems, 1944-1979.* 1983. San Francisco. 1/15. bdg for U Lib. 162 p. T5. $25.00

GLEASON. *W Wilderness of N America.* 1972. dj. EX. S2. $75.00

GLEN, Lois. *Charles W.S. Williams: A Check List.* 1975. Kent State. 1st ed. VG. C1. $12.50

GLENN, William. *Between N & S: MD Journalist Views of Civil War: 1861-1869.* 1976. Rutherford. 1st ed. dj. EX. $32.00

GLICK, Carl. *Treasury of Masonic Thought.* 1953. NY. $15.00

GLIMCHER, A. *Sketchbooks of Picasso.* Boston/NY. Ils. 349 p. EX. $32.00

GLINES, C.V. *Lighter-Than-Air Flight.* 1965. NY. Ils 1st ed. 276 p. dj. G. T5. $37.50

GLINES & MOSELEY. *Grand Old Lady: Story of DC-3.* 1959. Cleveland. Ils. 250 p. VG. T5. $17.50

GLISAN, R. *Journal of Army Life.* 1874. San Francisco. Ils. VG. $100.00

GLOAG, John. *Englishman's Chair.* 1964. London. Ils 1st ed. dj. VG. B2. $37.50

GLOAG & WALKER. *Home Life in History: Social Life & Manners of Britain.* 1927. NY. Ils Read. 1st ed. VG. C1. $17.50

GLOTZ, Gustave. *Ancient Greece at Work.* 1936. Knopf. 1st ed. VG. J2. $12.50

GLOVER. *Bobbed Wire II Bible.* 1971. Sunset. wraps. M. $14.00

GLUBB, John. *Story of Arab Legion.* 1948. London. Ils. maps. VG. $30.00

GLUCK, G. *Pieter Brueghel the Elder.* nd. Paris. 63 color pls. 4to. dj. EX. J2. $75.00

GLYCK. *Photographic Vision.* 1965. dj. EX. $28.00

GLYN, Elinor. *Elizabeth Visits America.* 1909. NY. 1st ed. dj. EX. $20.00

GOBER, K. *Children's Toys of Bygone Days.* 1928. NY. Ils. 4to. 63 p. orange cloth. $120.00

GODDARD, Anthea. *Vienna Pursuit.* 1976. Walker. dj. VG. P1. $7.50

GODDARD, Henry. *Feeble-Mindedness.* 1914. NY. Macmillan. 1st ed. VG. $60.00

GODDARD, Robert. *Papers of Robert H. Goddard.* 1970. McGraw. 1st ed. 3 vols. boxed. VG. J2. $100.00

GODDARD & KRITZLER. *Catalog of Frederick & Carrie Beineck Collection Americana.* 1965. Yale. Ils. 1 vol only. dj. VG. $22.00

GODDEN, Goeffrey. *Coalport & Coalbrookdale Porcelains.* 1970. NY. Praeger. 1st Am ed. dj. VG. $35.00

GODDEN, Rumer. *Episode of Sparrows.* 1955. Viking. 1st ed. dj. VG. $10.00

GODDEN, Rumer. *Fugue in Time.* 1945. London. 1st ed. dj. $25.00

GODDEN, Rumer. *Gone.* 1968. Viking. 1st Am ed. dj. EX. $20.00

GODDEN, Rumer. *Home Is the Sailor.* 1964. London. 1st ed. dj. EX. $18.00

GODDEN, Rumer. *Little Plum.* 1963. Viking. Ils 1st ed. $25.00

GODDEN, Rumer. *Peacock Spring.* 1976. Viking. 1st ed. dj. VG. $10.00

GODDEN, Rumer. *Raphael Bible.* 1970. NY. Viking. Studio Book. 248 p. dj. D2. $25.00

GODECKER, Mary. *Simon Brute De Remur: First Bishop of Vincennes.* 1931. St. Meinrad. 1st ed. xl. VG. J2. $20.00

GODEY, John. *Taking of Pelham: One, Two, Three.* c 1973. Putnam. dj. G. $20.00

GODFREY, A.A. *Government Operation of Railroads, 1918-1920.* 1974. 190 p. $14.50

GODFREY, W.E. *Birds of Canada.* 1979. Canada Nat Mus. Ils. dj. EX. M2. $48.00

GODIN, Alfred. *Wild Mammals of New England.* 1977. Johns Hopkins. 1st ed. dj. EX. $14.00

GODON, Julien. *Painted Tapestry.* 1879. London. EX. P3. $180.00

GODWIN, E. & S. *Warrior Bard: Life of William Morris.* 1947. London. 1st ed. dj. VG. B2. $20.00

GODWIN, Gail. *Finishing School.* 1985. Viking. 1st ed. sgn. dj. M. $20.00

GODWIN, Parke. *Beloved Exile.* 1984. Bantam. 1st ed. oversized pb. EX. C1. $6.50

GODWIN, Parke. *Beloved Exile.* 1984. 1st ed. oversized pb. VG. C1. $4.50

GODWIN, Parke. *Fire When It Comes.* 1st ed. dj. VG. C1. $10.00

GODWIN, Parke. *Firelord.* 1980. 1st ed. dj. VG. scarce. C1. $15.00

GODWIN, Parke. *Invitation to Camelot.* Ace. 1st ed. pb. VG. scarce. C1. $4.50

GODWIN, Parke. *Last Rainbow.* pb. VG. C1. $3.00

GODWIN, Tom. *Survivors.* 1958. NY. 1st ed. dj. VG. $25.00

GOEHRING. *TN Folk Culture: Annotated Bibliography.* 1982. 1st ed. VG. $12.50

GOERCH, Carl. *Carolina Chats.* 1944. Raleigh. Ils 1st ed. 405 p. dj. VG. $20.00

GOERCH, Carl. *Down Home.* 1943. Raleigh. 1st ed. sgn. dj. EX. $23.00

GOETHE. *Faust.* nd. London. Ils Pogany. VG. $75.00

GOETHE. *Faust.* 1925. London. Harrap. Trans Anster. Ils/sgn Clarke. T5. $550.00

GOETHE. *Faust.* 1930. NY. Ils Ward. Trans/sgn Raphael. 1/500. J2. $80.00

GOETHE. *Faust.* 1932. Ltd Ed Club. 1/1500. sgn. boxed. VG. C1. $25.00

GOETHE. *Reynard the Fox.* 1855. London. Ils Joseph Wolf. 320 p. VG. T5. $35.00

GOETSCH, W. *Ants.* 1957. MI U. Ils. 169 p. dj. EX. M2. $13.00

GOETZMANN, W.H. *Army Exploration in the American W: 1803-1863.* 1979. NE U. Ils 1st ed. 489 p. EX. M2. $30.00

GOETZMANN & SLOAN. *Looking Far N: Harriman Expedition to AK in 1899.* 1982. Viking. Ils 1st ed. 244 p. dj. EX. M2. $15.00

GOFF & GOFF. *Painter.* Florence. Black. color pls. $17.50

GOGOL. *Evenings on Farm Near Dikanka.* 1926. Knopf. VG. $6.00

GOGUEN, R.J. *329th Buckshot Infantry Regiment.* 1945. Wolfenbuttel. Ils. 186 p. VG. T5. $37.50

GOLD, H.L. *Bodyguard.* nd. Book Club. G. P1. $4.00

GOLD, H.L. *Fourth Galaxy Reader.* 1959. Doubleday. 1st ed. dj. VG. P1. $15.00

GOLD, H.L. *Mind Partner.* 1961. Doubleday. dj. G. P1. $10.00

GOLD, Herbert. *Optimist.* 1959. Boston. 1st ed. dj. EX. $20.00

GOLD, Ivan. *Nickel Miseries.* 1963. NY. 1st ed. inscr. dj. EX. $35.00

GOLDBERG, B.Z. *World of Sholom Aleichem.* 1953. np. Ils Shahn. wraps. scarce. $35.00

GOLDBERG, N. *John Crome the Elder.* 1978. NY. Ils. 4to. 2 vols. djs. EX. J2. $100.00

GOLDBERGER, E. *Unipolar Lead Electrocardiography.* 1947. Phil. Lea Febiger. 1st ed. VG. $45.00

GOLDBRUNNER, J. *Individuation: Depth Psychology of Carl Jung.* 1965. Pantheon. 1st ed. EX. $45.00

GOLDEN, Harry. *Little Girl Is Dead.* 1965. Cleveland. World. 1st ed. dj. EX. $35.00

GOLDEN, Harry. *Only in America.* 1958. Cleveland. World. inscr/sgn. $10.00

GOLDFARB, Israel. *Avodath Yisro-El. Sabbath Morning Service for Cantor...* 1946. NY. 1st ed. wraps. $17.50

GOLDHURST, R. *Many Are the Hearts: Agony & Triumph of U.S. Grant.* 1975. Readers Digest. Ils 1st ed. 297 p. dj. EX. M2. $10.00

GOLDIN, Stephen. *Assault on the Gods.* 1977. Doubleday. dj. EX. P1. $10.00

GOLDIN, Stephen. *Assault on the Gods.* 1977. Doubleday. sgn. dj. EX. P1. $17.50

GOLDIN, Stephen. *World Called Solitude.* 1981. Doubleday. 1st ed. dj. EX. P1. $9.25

GOLDING, Louis. *Vicar of Dunkerly Briggs.* 1946. Vallancy. 2nd ed. dj. VG. P1. $15.00

GOLDING, William. *Inheritors.* 1962. NY. 1st Am ed. wraps. G. $15.00

GOLDING, William. *Lord of the Flies.* 1955. Coward McCann. 1st Am ed. dj. EX. $95.00

GOLDING, William. *Pyramid.* 1967. London. 1st ed. dj. RS. M. $85.00

GOLDING, William. *Pyramid.* 1967. London. 1st ed. 8vo. dj. EX. $50.00

GOLDING, William. *Pyramid.* 1967. NY. 1st ed. dj. P3. $20.00

GOLDING, William. *Rites of Passage.* 1980. Farrar Straus Giroux. 1st ed. P1. $12.00

GOLDING, William. *Spire.* 1964. London. 1st ed. dj. EX. $55.00

GOLDMAN, Albert. *Elvis.* 1981. McGraw. 1st print. dj. EX. $35.00

GOLDMAN, Emma. *Living My Life.* 1931. Knopf. 1st ed. 2 vols. G. J2. $45.00

GOLDMAN, James. *Man From Greek & Roman.* 1975. pb. VG. C1. $4.00

GOLDMAN, James. *Myself As Witness.* 1979. 1st Am ed. dj. EX. C1. $11.00

GOLDMAN, Lawrence Louis. *Tiger by the Tail.* 1946. McKay. dj. G. P1. $7.50

GOLDMAN, William. *Boys & Girls Together.* 1964. NY. 1st ed. dj. VG. $35.00

GOLDMAN, William. *Color of Light.* 1984. Warner. ARC. wraps. EX. $15.00

GOLDMAN, William. *Magic.* nd. Book Club. dj. VG. P1. $7.50

GOLDMAN, William. *Temple of Gold.* 1957. NY. 1st ed. dj. VG. B2. $40.00

GOLDMAN, William. *Thing of It Is.* nd. Book Club. dj. VG. P1. $4.00

GOLDMAN & FULLER. *Charlie Company: What Vietnam Did to Us.* 1983. NY. photos. 358 p. G. T5. $12.50

GOLDSCHEIDER, Ludwig. *Michelangelo: Paintings, Sculpture, Architecture.* 1964. Garden City. Ils 1st ed. 228 p. dj. D2. $75.00

GOLDSCHMIDT & NAEF. *Truthful Lens.* 1980. Grolier. 1/1000. boxed. VG. $200.00

GOLDSCHMIDT & NAEF. *Truthful Lens.* 1980. Grolier. 1/1000. slipcase. EX. $300.00

GOLDSMITH, Arthur. *Nude in Photography.* 1975. Chicago. 1st ed. dj. EX. $24.00

GOLDSMITH, M.O. *Designs for Outdoor Living.* 1941. NY. photos. VG. $25.00

GOLDSMITH, Oliver. *She Stoops To Conquer.* nd. London. Hodder Stoughton. 1/350. sgn. G2. $180.00

GOLDSMITH, Oliver. *Vicar of Wakefield.* Ils Mulready. facsimile of 1843 ed. G. $22.00

GOLDSMITH, Oliver. *Vicar of Wakefield.* nd. Phil. Ils Rackham. 1st Am ed. $65.00

GOLDSMITH, Oliver. *Vicar of Wakefield.* 1842. NY. Appleton. 8vo. black cloth. $30.00

GOLDSMITH. *Deserted Village.* 1912. Boston. Bibliophile Soc. 1/469. fair. $50.00

GOLDSTEIN, Milton. *Magnificent W: Yosemite.* 1973. 1st ed. 60 color photos. dj. EX. $24.00

GOLDSTEIN, Ruby. *Third Man in the Ring.* 1959. Funk Wagnall. 1st ed. dj. EX. $20.00

GOLDTHWAITE, Eaton K. *Don't Mention My Name.* 1942. Duell Sloan. P1. $7.00

GOLDTHWAITE, Eaton K. *Scarecrow.* 1946. Books Inc. dj. VG. P1. $10.00

GOLDWATER, Barry. *Face of AZ.* 1964. Ltd ed. presentation. sgn. S2. $300.00

GOLL, Ivan. *Noemi.* 1929. Berlin. Ils Steinhardt. 1/150. 8vo. EX. $100.00

GOLLER, Karl Heinz. *Alliterative Morte Arthur: Reassessment of the Poem.* 1981. Brewer. 1st ed. dj. M. C1. $29.50

GOLOMBECK, H. *World Chess Championship.* 1954. London. 1st ed. dj. VG. $15.00

GOMME, G.L. *Literature of Local Institutions.* 1886. London. 1st ed. $35.00

GOMME, Laurence. *London.* 1914. Williams. 1st ed. VG. J2. $15.00

GOMPERS, Samuel. *70 Years of American Labor.* 1948. NY. VG. $25.00

GONG, E.Y. *Tong War: History of Tongs in America.* 1930. NY. Ils 1st ed. 287 p. VG. B2. $22.50

GONGAWARE, G.J. *History of German Friendly Society of Charleston, SC, 1766.* 1935. Richmond. 1st ed. EX. $38.00

GONZALES, A.E. *Black Border.* 1922. Columbia. State Co. 348 p. $75.00

GONZALES, Juan. *Breve Resena Historica de la Virgen de Guadalupe.* 1888. Queretaro. VG. $50.00

GONZALES, N.G. *In Darkest Cuba.* 1922. Columbia. State Co. 1st ed. $85.00

GONZALES, R.E. *Poems & Paragraphs.* 1918. Columbia. State Co. 224 p. $30.00

GONZALEZ, Juan. *Breve Resena Historica de la Virgen de Guadalupe.* 1888. Queretaro. VG. $50.00

GOOD, P.P. *Family Flora & Materia Medica Botanica.* 1854. 2 vols. VG. $130.00

GOOD, P.P. *Materia Medica Animal Ia.* 1853. 25 pls. 8vo. 262 p. VG. $325.00

GOODCHILD, George. *CO Jim.* nd. Collins Wild W Club. VG. P1. $10.00

GOODCHILD, George. *CO Jim.* nd. Burt. G. P1. $3.00

GOODCHILD, George. *Jack O'Lantern.* 1930. Mystery League. 1st ed. G. P1. $10.00

GOODCHILD, George. *Trooper O'Neill.* 1935. Collins Wild W Club. VG. P1. $7.50

GOODDEN, Robert. *Wonderful World of Butterflies & Moths.* 1977. Hamlyn. photos. dj. VG. $17.00

GOODE, James. *Story of the Misfits.* 1963. Indianapolis. 1st ed. 331 p. dj. VG. B2. $27.50

GOODEN & THOMAS. *Sherlock Holmes: Bridge Detective.* 1973. LA. Ils 1st trade pb ed. sgns. VG. $35.00

GOODENOUGH, Caroline Leonard. *Legends, Loves & Loyalties of Old New England.* nd. Rochester. 1/1000. 344 p. T5. $25.00

GOODERS, J. *Birds That Came Back.* 1983. Deutsch. Ils. dj. EX. M2. $13.00

GOODERS & TREVOR. *Ducks of N America & N Hemisphere.* 1986. Facts on File. Ils 1st Am ed. dj. EX. M2. $30.00

GOODHUE, B.G. *Architecture & Gardens of San Diego Exposition.* 1916. Elder. 68 pls. $25.00

GOODING & HALL. *Flowers of the Islands in the Sun.* 1966. NY. Barnes. 1st ed. dj. EX. $22.00

GOODIS, David. *Dark Passage.* 1946. Messner. 1st ed. dj. VG. $50.00

GOODIS, David. *Fire in the Flesh.* 1957. Greenwich. Fawcett. 1st ed. pb. VG. $10.00

GOODIS, David. *Street of the Lost.* 1952. NY. Fawcett. 1st ed. pb. VG. $10.00

GOODLAND. *Bibliography of Sex Rites & Customs.* 1931. London. folio. 752 p. $135.00

GOODMAN, DAWS & SHEEHAN. *Hawaiians.* Deluxe Presentation ed. dj. VG. E2. $40.00

GOODMAN, J.M. *M.D.P.O.W.* 1972. NY. 1st ed. sgn. 218 p. dj. VG. T5. $25.00

GOODMAN, Paul. *Five Years.* 1966. NY. 1st ed. dj. VG. T5. $30.00

GOODMAN, Paul. *Kafka's Prayer.* 1976. NY. 1st ed. dj. VG. $15.00

GOODMAN, Paul. *Making Do.* 1963. NY. 1st ed. dj. $25.00

GOODMAN, Paul. *N Percy.* 1968. Black Sparrow. 1/200. sgn/#d. EX. $30.00

GOODMAN & MEININGER. *Birds of Egypt.* 1989. Oxford U. Ils 1st ed. 551 p. dj. M. M2. $95.00

GOODMAN. *Movement Towards a New America.* 1970. Knopf. 1st ed. 752 p. wraps. VG. $20.00

GOODRICH, C.A. *Visit to Principal Cities of W Continent.* 1848. Hartford. Ils. G. $35.00

GOODRICH, Carter. *Government Promotion of American Canals & Railroads, 1800...* 1960. 382 p. $25.00

GOODRICH, Lloyd. *Edward Hopper.* 1976. Abrams. pb. VG. $5.00

GOODRICH, Lloyd. *Edward Hopper.* 1978. NY. Abrams. 18 color pls. oblong folio. dj. J2. $250.00

GOODRICH, Lloyd. *Edward Hopper.* 1989. Abrams. dj. EX. $50.00

GOODRICH, Lloyd. *Raphael Soyer.* 1972. Abrams. 41 pls. folio. tan cloth. dj. EX. J2. $150.00

GOODRICH, Norma. *King Arthur.* 1st ed. 3rd print. dj. EX. C1. $16.00

GOODRICH, Norma. *King Arthur.* 1st ed. 2nd print. dj. EX. C1. $15.00

GOODRICH, Norma. *Merlin.* 1st ed. dj. EX. C1. $16.00

GOODRICH, Norma. *Ways of Love.* orig slipcase. VG. C1. $12.00

GOODRICH, S.G. *Celebrated Indians.* c 1844. Boston. pls. orig bdg. xl. VG. $12.50

GOODRICH, S.G. *Johnson's Natural History.* 1869. 1st ed. 2nd print. AEG. full leather. EX. $55.00

GOODRICH, S.G. *Peter Parley's Almanac for Old & Young.* 1836. Phil. Desilver Thomas. 16mo. wraps. G. $55.00

GOODRICH, S.G. *Peter Parley's Method of Telling About Geography.* 1839. NY. VG. $65.00

GOODRICH, S.G. *Peter Parley's Own Story From Personal Narrative...* 1864. NY. Sheldon. Ils 1st ed. 320 p. green bdg. G. $20.00

GOODRICH, Warren. *Change at Jamaica.* 1957. 100 p. $10.50

GOODRIDGE & DIETZ. *Seal Called Andre.* 1976. Praeger. Ils. 181 p. dj. EX. M2. $5.00

GOODRUM, C.A. *I'll Trade You an Elk.* 1967. Funk Wagnall. 220 p. dj. EX. M2. $10.00

GOODSPEED, C.E. *Yankee Bookseller.* 1937. Boston. Houghton. 2nd ed. EX. $35.00

GOODSPEED, T.H. *Plant Hunters in Andes.* 1941. NY. 1st ed. 429 p. dj. VG. B2. $35.00

GOODSPEED. *History of Craighead Co., AR.* nd. facsimle of 1889 ed. EX. M2. $15.00

GOODSTONE, Tony. *Pulps.* nd. Bonanza. dj. VG. P1. $15.00

GOODSTONE, Tony. *Pulps.* 1970. Chelsea House. 1st ed. dj. VG. P1. $20.00

GOODWIN, D. *Birds of Man's World.* 1978. British Mus. Ils 1st ed. dj. EX. M2. $8.00

GOODWIN, D. *Crows of the World.* 1976. Cornell U. Ils 1st ed. 354 p. dj. EX. M2. $40.00

GOODWIN, D. *Estrildid Finches of the World.* 1982. Cornell U. Ils 1st ed. 328 p. dj. EX. M2. $45.00

GOODWIN, D. *Pigeons & Doves & the World.* 1983. Cornell U. Ils 3rd ed. 363 p. dj. EX. M2. $45.00

GOODWIN, D.R. *S Slavery in Its Present Aspects...* 1864. Lippincott. 343 p. G. $65.00

GOODWIN, G. *History of Ottoman Architecture.* 1971. Baltimore. Johns Hopkins. dj. $55.00

GOODWIN, Gordon. *Catalog of the Harsnett Library.* 1888. London. 1/250. $69.50

GOODWIN, M.W. *Colonial Cavalier; or, S Life Before the Revolution.* 1897. Little Brown. 316 p. xl. $5.00

GOODWIN, Nathaniel. *Genealogical Notes; or, Contribution to Family History...* 1856. Hartford. 1st ed. 8vo. black cloth. EX. T1. $60.00

GOODWIN, T.S. *Natural History of Secession; or, Despotism & Democracy...* 1864. NY. fair. $20.00

GOODWIN, W.B. *Lure of Gold.* 1940. Boston. Ils. fair. $12.00

GOODYEAR AERONAUTICS DEPT. *Free Ballooning.* 1919. Akron. photos. 62 p. wraps. T5. $125.00

GOODYEAR TIRE & RUBBER CO. *Goodyear's Aeronautical Activities.* nd. np. fld series of photos. wraps. T5. $37.50

GOODYEAR TIRE & RUBBER CO. *Manual of Tire Repairing.* 1918. Akron. Ils. 60 p. wraps. T5. $22.50

GOOSE, Edmund. *Gossip in a Library.* 1891. London. 1st ed. $59.50

GORDIMER, Nadine. *Burger's Daughter.* 1979. London. 1st ed. dj. EX. $35.00

GORDIMER, Nadine. *Burger's Daughter.* 1979. Viking. 1st ed. $25.00

GORDIMER, Nadine. *Guest of Honor.* 1971. London. 1st ed. dj. $25.00

GORDIMER, Nadine. *July's People.* 1981. London. 1st ed. dj. EX. $30.00

GORDIMER, Nadine. *Late Bourgeois World.* 1966. NY. 1st ed. dj. VG. $35.00

GORDIMER, Nadine. *Livingstone's Companions.* 1972. London. 1st ed. dj. EX. $35.00

GORDIMER, Nadine. *Not for Publication.* 1965. NY. 1st ed. dj. EX. $35.00

GORDIMER, Nadine. *Soldier's Embrace.* 1980. London. 1st ed. dj. EX. $35.00

GORDIMER, Nadine. *Something Out There.* 1984. London. 1st ed. dj. EX. $30.00

GORDIMER, Nadine. *Sport of Nature.* 1987. London. 1st ed. dj. EX. $30.00

GORDIMER, Nadine. *Sport of Nature.* 1987. NY. AP. 1st Am ed. wraps. EX. $35.00

GORDIMER, Nadine. *Sport of Nature.* 1987. NY. 1st Am ed. sgn. dj. EX. $50.00

GORDIMER, Nadine. *World of Strangers.* 1958. London. 1st ed. dj. EX. $40.00

GORDIMER, Nadine. *World of Strangers.* 1958. NY. 1st ed. dj. VG. $35.00

GORDON, Caroline. *Collected Stories.* 1981. NY. 1st ed. dj. EX. $25.00

GORDON, Caroline. *Glory of Hera.* 1972. Garden City. 1st ed. dj. EX. $45.00

GORDON, Caroline. *Green Centuries.* 1941. Scribner. 1st ed. dj. EX. $85.00

GORDON, Caroline. *How To Read a Novel.* 1957. NY. 1st ed. dj. EX. $60.00

GORDON, Caroline. *Strange Children.* 1951. Scribner. 1st ed. dj. EX. $65.00

GORDON, Caroline. *Women on the Porch.* 1944. NY. 1st ed. dj. EX. $60.00

GORDON, Elizabeth. *Bird Children.* 1939. Wise Parslow. Ils Ross. Revised ed. VG. B4. $50.00

GORDON, Elizabeth. *Flower Children.* 1910. Vollard. Ils Ross. VG. B4. $45.00

GORDON, Esme. *Royal Scottish Academy of Painting, Sculpture, Architecture.* 1977. Canada. Macmillan. 1st ed. dj. VG. J2. $15.00

GORDON, G.A. *Witness to Immortality.* 1900. Boston. $47.50

GORDON, H. *Pammure, Land of the Almighty Dollar.* nd. London. Ils Montagu. VG. $7.50

GORDON, J.B. *Reminiscences of the Civil War.* 1903. 1st ed. 474 p. dj. K1. $65.00

GORDON, J.B. *Reminiscences of the Civil War.* 1904. Atlanta/NY. Ils. 474 p. K1. $55.00

GORDON, J.B. *Reminiscences of the Civil War.* 1981. Special Memorial ed. 474 p. J4. $35.00

GORDON, Mary. *Company of Women.* 1980. NY. Knopf. 1st ed. dj. VG. $20.00

GORDON, Maurice B. *Aesculapius Comes to Colonies.* 1949. Ventnor. 1st ed. dj. $20.00

GORDON, Paul *New Archery.* 1939. NY. Ils 1st ed. 423 p. dj. VG. B2. $30.00

GORDON, Richard. *Captain's Table.* 1955. Book Club. VG. P1. $5.00

GORDON, Richard. *Captain's Table.* 1956. Michael Joseph. 11th print. dj. xl. P1. $7.50

GORDON, Richard. *Doctor & Son.* 1959. Michael Joseph. dj. xl. P1. $15.00

GORDON, Richard. *Doctor at Sea.* 1955. Michael Joseph. 21st print. dj. VG. P1. $15.00

GORDON, Richard. *Doctor in Clover.* 1960. Michael Joseph. 1st ed. dj. VG. P1. $15.00

GORDON, Richard. *Doctor in Love.* 1957. Michael Joseph. VG. P1. $12.50

GORDON, Richard. *Doctor in the Swim.* nd. Book Club. dj. VG. P1. $17.50

GORDON, Richards. *Doctor in the House & at Sea.* 1955. Reprint Soc. dj. VG. P1. $10.00

GORDON, Stuart. *Smile on the Void.* 1981. Berkley Putnam. 1st ed. dj. VG. P1. $10.00

GORDON, T.C. *David Allan of Alloa, 1744-1796.* 1951. Cunningham. 1st ed. dj. VG. J2. $35.00

GOREN, C.H. *Standard Book of Bidding.* 1944. NY. Intro Maugham. 1st ed. dj. VG. $6.00

GORES, Joe. *Come Morning.* 1986. Mysterious Pr. 1st ed. dj. EX. P1. $20.00

GORES, Joe. *Gone, No Forwarding.* nd. Book Club. dj. VG. P1. $25.00

GOREY, Edward. *Doubtful Guest.* 1957. 1st ed. VG. B2. $25.00

GOREY, Edward. *Listing Attic.* 1954. Boston/NY. 1st ed. dj. EX. $150.00

GOREY, Edward. *Unstrung Harp.* 1953. Duell Sloan. 1st ed. dj. EX. $155.00

GOREY, Edward. *Willowdale Handcar.* 1979. NY. Dodd Mead. 1st reissue. square 8vo. EX. $4.50

GORHAM, Bob. *Churchill Downs 100th KY Derby.* 1973. np. 1st ed. EX. $25.00

GORHAM, George C. *Edwin M. Stanton.* 1899. 1st ed. 2 vols. K1. $21.50

GORHAM, Hazel. *Japanese & Oriental Ceramics.* 1980. Ils. boxed. EX. E2. $20.00

GORKI, Maxim. *Bystander.* 1930. NY. Literary Guild. 8vo. G. $7.50

GOSNELL, H. *Before Mast in Clippers.* Derrydale. as issued. VG. B2. $70.00

GOSNELL, H. *Guns on the W Waters.* 1949. Baton Rouge. VG. $24.00

GOSS, W.L. *Soldier's Story of Captivity at Andersonville, Belle Isle.* 1872. Boston. 357 p. VG. $15.00

GOSSAGE, John. *Pond. With Essay by Denise Sines.* 1985. Aperture. photos. dj. VG. $20.00

GOSSE, Philip. *Evenings at the Microscope.* 1889. NY. Appleton. 480 p. EX. $45.00

GOSSE, Philip. *Evenings at the Microscope.* 1902. NY. Ils. TEG. G. T1. $25.00

GOSSE, Philip. *My Pirate Library.* 1926. London. Intro Edmund Gosse. 1/300. sgn. VG. $50.00

GOSSELIN, P.F.J. *Recherches sur la Geographie Systematique et Positive...* 1797-1798. Paris. pls. 4to. 2 vols in 1. J2. $350.00

GOTCH, J.A. *Growth of English House From Feudal Times to 18th C.* 1928. Scribner. Revised 2nd ed. J2. $20.00

GOTLIEB, Phyllis. *O Master Caliban!* 1976. Harper Row. 1st ed. dj. EX. P1. $9.00

GOTO, S. *Studies of the Extoparasitic Trematodes of Japan.* 1894. Tokyo. Ils. 273 p. G. M2. $30.00

GOTTSCHANG, J.L. *Guide to the Mammals of OH.* 1981. OH U. Ils. 4to. 176 p. dj. EX. M2. $30.00

GOUDE, J.P. *Jungle Fever.* 1981. Moreau. 1st ed. VG. $20.00

GOUDGE, Elizabeth. *Child From the Sea.* 1970. NY. 1st Am ed. 8vo. dj. VG. $20.00

GOUDY, F.W. *Typologia.* 1977. CA U. EX. $15.00

GOULART, Ron. *Cowboy Heaven.* 1979. Doubleday. 1st ed. dj. EX. P1. $15.00

GOULART, Ron. *Odd Job #101.* 1975. Scribner. 1st ed. dj. EX. P1. $20.00

GOULD, Charles. *N OK Place Names.* 1933. OK U. 1st ed. VG. T6. $20.00

GOULD, E.K. *Major General Hiram G. Berry.* 1899. 1st ed. 312 p. gilt red bdg. M. J4. $45.00

GOULD, John. *Birds of Europe.* 1966. London. 160 pls. 321 p. EX. M2. $65.00

GOULD, John. *Gould's Exotic Birds.* 1988. Abrams. 40 pls. EX. M2. $16.00

GOULD, John. *John Gould's Birds.* 1981. Chartwell. Ils. folio. 239 p. dj. EX. M2. $30.00

GOULD, John. *Only in ME.* 1969. Barre, MA. 1st ed. dj. VG. B2. $17.50

GOULD, Lois. *Final Analysis.* 1974. NY. 1st ed. dj. VG. $15.00

GOULD, Lois. *Sea Change.* 1976. Simon Schuster. 1st ed. dj. EX. $15.00

GOULD, S.J. *Ontogeny & Phylogeny.* 1980. Harvard. Ils. 501 p. dj. EX. M2. $25.00

GOULD. *Book of Riviera.* 1905. London. 1st ed. VG. $15.00

GOVERNMENT PRINTING OFFICE. *Hearings...Assassination of President Kennedy.* 1964. GPO. 26 vols. orig shipping boxes. M. $325.00

GOVERNMENT PRINTING OFFICE. *Laws of the US & Other Documents, April 1810-Jan. 1817.* 1817. WA. 377 p. index. $175.00

GOVERNMENT PRINTING OFFICE. *Trails of War Criminals Before Nuernberg Military Tribunals.* 1950. 15 vols. VG. $675.00

GOYA. *Goya.* 1963. Milan. Ils 1st ed. folio. boxed. $125.00

GOYEN, William. *Arthur Bond.* 1979. Palaemon. 1st ed. 1/230. sgn. wraps. EX. $45.00

GOYEN, William. *Ghost & Flesh.* 1952. NY. 1st ed. dj. VG. $12.00

GOYEN, William. *House of Breath.* ARC. 1st ed. inscr. wraps. M. $115.00

GOYEN, William. *House of Breath.* 1950. NY. 1st ed. sgn. dj. $60.00

GOYTISOLO, Juan. *Young Assassins.* 1959. NY. 1st ed. dj. VG. $25.00

GRABER, A. *Early Medieval Painting From the 4th to the 11th C.* 1957. Geneva. 98 pls. 4to. dj. slipcase. EX. J2. $50.00

GRABER, J.W. *IL Birds: Wood Warblers.* 1983. IL Nat Hist. photos. map. 4to. 144 p. EX. M2. $9.00

GRABER, R.R. *IL Birds: Turdidae.* 1971. IL Nat Hist. photos. maps. 4to. 44 p. EX. M2. $4.00

GRABER, R.R. *IL Birds: Tyrannidae.* 1971. IL Nat Hist. photos. maps. 4to. 56 p. EX. M2. $4.00

GRABHORN PRESS. *Traits of American Indian Life & Character by a Fur Trader.* 1933. San Francisco. 1st ed. 6 pls. 107 p. VG. B2. $125.00

GRACE, L.H. *War Romance of Salvation Army.* 1919. Phil. 1st ed. dj. VG. B2. $40.00

GRACIAN, Baltazar. *Las Meditaciones.* 1805. Mexico City. VG. $75.00

GRACIE, Archibald. *Truth About Chickamauga.* 1911. blue cloth. xl. G. B7. $50.00

GRACIE, Archibald. *Truth About Titanic.* 1913. NY. Kennerly. Ils. G. $50.00

GRADY, James. *Six Days of the Condor.* 1974. Norton. 1st ed. dj. xl. P1. $5.00

GRAEBNER, Norman. *Politics & Crisis of 1860.* 1961. Urbana. 1st ed. dj. VG. $15.00

GRAEME, Bruce. *Body Unknown.* nd. Hutchinson. xl. P1. $5.00

GRAEME, Bruce. *Murder of Some Importance.* nd. Hutchinson. 9th print. VG. P1. $10.00

GRAEME, Bruce. *Unsolved.* 1932. Lippincott. G. P1. $15.00

GRAEME, Robert. *Never Mix Business With Pleasure.* 1968. Hutchinson. dj. xl. P1. $5.00

GRAETZ, H. *History of Jews.* 1891-1898. 1st Am ed. 8vo. 6 vols. G. $125.00

GRAFTON, Sue. *C Is for Corpse.* nd. Book Club. dj. VG. P1. $4.00

GRAGAN, E. *Ringolevio.* 1972. Little Brown. 1st ed. dj. VG. $40.00

GRAHAM, A. *Eyelids of Morning.* 1973. NY. Ils Beard. 2nd print. dj. VG. $45.00

GRAHAM, A. & F. *Alligators.* 1979. Delacarte. Ils 1st ed. 130 p. dj. EX. M2. $12.00

GRAHAM, A. & F. *Falcon Flight.* 1978. Delacorte. Ils 1st print. 112 p. dj. EX. M2. $9.00

GRAHAM, A.J. *Handbook of Standard or American Phonography.* 1858. private print. VG. scarce. $50.00

GRAHAM, Bessie. *Bookman's Manual.* 1935. NY. Bowker. 8vo. blue cloth. VG. $10.00

GRAHAM, Edward. *Legumes for Erosion Control & Wildlife.* 1941. GPO. VG. $15.00

GRAHAM, F. *Gulls: A Social History.* 1975. Random House. Ils 1st ed. 179 p. dj. EX. M2. $9.00

GRAHAM, F. *Since Silent Spring.* 1970. Houghton. Ils. 332 p. dj. EX. M2. $10.00

GRAHAM, F.D. *Audel's New Automobile Guide.* 1942. Ils. 1586 p. EX. $17.50

GRAHAM, G.F. *Songs of Scotland.* nd. Edinburgh. 256 p. gilt black morocco. $95.00

GRAHAM, Harvey. *Eternal Eve.* 1950. London. 1st ed. dj. $35.00

GRAHAM, J.A. *Aldeburg Cezanne.* nd. Book Club. dj. EX. P1. $3.00

GRAHAM, J.A. *Involvement of Arnold Wechsler.* nd. Book Club. dj. VG. P1. $3.00

GRAHAM, J.M. *Only Way To Cross.* 1972. NY. Ils 1st ed. 434 p. dj. VG. B2. $25.00

GRAHAM, John. *Writer's Voice, Converations With Contemporary Writers.* 1973. NY. Morrow. presentation. sgn. 294 p. $35.00

GRAHAM, M. *9th Regiment of NY Volunteers (Zouaves).* 1900. NY. Veteran Assn. 1st ed. VG. R1. $150.00

GRAHAM, S. *With Poor Immigrants to America.* 1914. London. Macmillan. Ils. TEG. VG. $17.50

GRAHAM, Stephen. *Soul of John Brown.* 1920. NY. 1st ed. 331 p. G. T5. $15.00

GRAHAM & BEARD. *Eyelids of the Morning.* 1973. Greenwich. 1st print. dj. EX. $95.00

GRAHAM-JONES, O. *First Catch Your Tiger.* 1973. Taplinger. photos. 223 p. dj. xl. G. M2. $6.00

GRAHAME, J. *History of the US of N America.* 1836. London. 1st ed. 4 vols. G. $50.00

GRAHAME, Kenneth. *Golden Age.* nd. (1905) Dodd Mead. Ils Parrish. VG. $50.00

GRAHAME, Kenneth. *Golden Age.* 1900. London. Ils Parrish. 1st ed. TEG. red bdg. $150.00

GRAHAME, Kenneth. *Golden Age.* 1904. London. Ils Parrish. $30.00

GRAHAME, Kenneth. *Wind in the Willows.* Heritage. Ils Rackham. 1st ed. EX. C1. $15.00

GRAHAME, Kenneth. *Wind in the Willows.* Heritage. Ils Rackham. 1st ed. EX. E2. $15.00

GRAHAME, Kenneth. *Wind in the Willows.* 1921. Ils Bransom. presentation. gilt bdg. $65.00

GRAHAME & SHEPARD. *Day Dreams.* 1930. London. Lane. 1/275. sgns. 8vo. TEG. G2. $225.00

GRANATELLI, Andy. *They Call Me Mr. 500.* inscr/sgn. dj. EX. $15.00

GRAND, Gordon *Silver Horn.* 1932. Derrydale. 1/950. 8vo. gilt bdg. VG. $90.00

GRAND, Gordon. *Colonel Weatherford & His Friends.* Derrydale. as issued. VG. B2. $50.00

GRAND, Gordon. *Colonel Weatherford & His Friends.* Derrydale. 1/1450. M. $85.00

GRAND, Gordon. *Colonel Weatherford & His Friends.* 1934. Derrydale. 1/1450. 8vo. EX. $70.00

GRAND, Gordon. *Colonel Weatherford's Young Entry.* Derrydale. as issued. VG. B2. $50.00

GRAND, Gordon. *Colonel Weatherford's Young Entry.* Derrydale. 1/1350. M. $125.00

GRAND, Gordon. *Old Man & Other Colonel Weatherford Stories.* Derrydale. as issued. VG. B2. $50.00

GRAND, Gordon. *Old Man & Other Colonel Weatherford Stories.* 1934. Derrydale. 1/1150. inscr/sgn. 8vo. EX. $85.00

GRAND, Gordon. *Redmond L. Stewart: Fox Hunter & Gentleman of MD.* 1938. NY. 1st ed. VG. $25.00

GRAND, Gordon. *Southborough Fox & Other Colonel Weatherford Stories.* Derrydale. as issued. VG. B2. $50.00

GRAND, Gordon. *Southborough Fox & Other Colonel Weatherford Stories.* 1939. Derrydale. 1/1450. sgn. 8vo. gilt bdg. EX. $75.00

GRANT, Asahel. *Nestorians; or, Lost Tribes.* 1841. NY. 1st ed. fld map. rebound. EX. $90.00

GRANT, Blanche. *Taos Indians.* 1926. Taos, NM. Ils. 127 p. wraps. VG. scarce. A3. $60.00

GRANT, Bruce. *Isaac Hull: Captain of Old Ironsides.* 1947. Pellegrini. 1st ed. dj. VG. J2. $15.00

GRANT, C.R. *Illustrated Summit Co., OH.* 1891. Akron. Ils 1st ed. maps. 184 p. fair. T5. $175.00

GRANT, Charles L. *Dodd Mead Gallery of Horror.* 1983. Dodd Mead. 1st ed. dj. VG. P1. $30.00

GRANT, Charles L. *Shadows 10.* 1987. Doubleday. 1st ed. dj. EX. P1. $12.95

GRANT, Charles L. *Shadows 2.* 1979. Doubleday. 1st ed. dj. EX. P1. $17.50

GRANT, Charles L. *Shadows 6.* 1983. Doubleday. 1st ed. dj. EX. P1. $10.95

GRANT, Charles L. *Shadows 7.* 1984. Doubleday. 1st ed. dj. EX. P1. $10.95

GRANT, Charles L. *Shadows 8.* 1985. Doubleday. 1st ed. dj. EX. P1. $11.70

GRANT, Charles L. *Shadows 8.* 1985. Doubleday. 1st ed. dj. EX. RS. P1. $17.50

GRANT, Charles L. *Shadows 9.* 1986. Doubleday. 1st ed. dj. EX. RS. P1. $12.95

GRANT, Charles L. *Tales From the Nightside.* 1981. Arkham House. 1st ed. dj. EX. P1. $20.00

GRANT, E.M. *Guide to Fishes.* 1978. Brisbane. pls. 768 p. dj. EX. M2. $65.00

GRANT, F.J. *Manual of Heraldry.* 1952. Edinburgh. 1st ed. VG. C1. $14.00

GRANT, F.J. *Manual of Heraldry.* 1962. Edinburgh. Ils. 142 p. VG. T5. $6.50

GRANT, George. *Picturesque Canada.* 1882. Toronto. 500 engravings. 2 vols. B2. $225.00

GRANT, Gordon. *Greasy Luck, a Whaling Sketchbook.* 1932. NY. 1st ed. 4to. VG. $45.00

GRANT, Gordon. *Snow, Wilbert Before the Wind.* 1938. NY. Ltd ed. 4to. dj. EX. $30.00

GRANT, Gordon. *Story of the Ship.* c 1920. McLoughlin. $12.00

GRANT, J.D. *Personal Memoirs of Julia Dent Grant.* 1975. Intro Catton. 346 p. EX. J4. $12.50

GRANT, James. *Boys' Single-Shot Rifles.* 1967. Morrow. 1st ed. dj. VG. $60.00

GRANT, Madison. *Passing of Great Race.* 1919. Scribner. 296 p. M1. $17.50

GRANT, Maxwell. *Shadow Laughs.* 1931. Street Smith. VG. P1. $75.00

GRANT, Robert. *Unleavened Bread.* 1900. Scribner. Ils Armstrong. 1st ed. VG. $15.00

GRANT, Roderick. *Private Vendetta.* 1974. Scribner. 1st ed. dj. EX. P1. $7.00

GRANT, U.S. *Personal Memoirs of U.S. Grant.* 1885-1886. NY. Webster. 1st ed. 2 vols. T6. $150.00

GRANT, U.S. *Personal Memoirs of U.S. Grant.* 1885. NY. 1st ed. 2 vols. morocco. T5. $125.00

GRANT, U.S. *Personal Memoirs of U.S. Grant.* 1892. Webster. 2 vols. gilt green bdg. K1. $37.50

GRANT, U.S. *Ulysses S. Grant: Warrior & Statesman.* 1969. Morrow. photos. 480 p. dj. M2. $16.00

GRANT, U.S. *Ulysses S. Grant: Warrior & Statesman.* 1969. NY. Ils 1st ed. 480 p. dj. T5. $22.50

GRANT, Verne. *Origin of Adaptations.* 1963. Columbia U. 606 p. M2. $15.00

GRANTHAM, D.W. *Hoke Smith & Politics of New S.* 1958. Baton Rouge. Ils. 396 p. dj. $10.00

GRAPPE, Georges. *La Vie & L'Oeuvre de J.H. Fragonard.* 1929. Neuchatel. 60 pls. 238 p. orig wraps. D2. $125.00

GRASS, Gunter. *Tin Drum*. 1962. NY. 1st ed. dj. G. $45.00

GRATTON, John. *Journal of His Life*. 1805. Stanford. 12mo. full calf. VG. G2. $75.00

GRATZ, Simon. *Book About Autographs*. 1920. Phil. 1st ed. 1/500. pls. $45.00

GRAU, S.A. *Condor Passes*. 1971. Knopf. 1st ed. 421 p. dj. EX. $15.00

GRAU, S.A. *Evidence of Love*. 1977. Franklin Lib. 1st ed. AEG. full blue leather. EX. $30.00

GRAU, S.A. *Evidence of Love*. 1977. Knopf. 1st trade ed. dj. $20.00

GRAU, S.A. *Hard Blue Sky*. 1958. Knopf. 1st ed. 466 p. dj. $22.50

GRAU, S.A. *Nine Women*. 1985. NY. 1st ed. sgn. dj. EX. $25.00

GRAUBARD, M. *Tidings Out of Brazil*. 1957. MN U. 1/1000. 12mo. dj. EX. G1. $20.00

GRAUBARD, Stephen. *British Babor & the Russian Revolution*. 1956. Harvard. 1st ed. VG. J2. $12.50

GRAVES, C.L. *War's Surprises & Other Verses*. 1917. London. 1st ed. inscr. $40.00

GRAVES, Charles. *Leather Armchairs: Guide to Great Clubs of London*. 1963. Coward. 1st ed. dj. VG. J2. $15.00

GRAVES, J.T. *Fighting S*. 1943. Putnam. presentation. sgn. 282 p. dj. $37.50

GRAVES, Robert. *Ancient Castle*. 1980. London. 1st ed. dj. EX. $30.00

GRAVES, Robert. *Catacrok!* 1956. London. 1st ed. dj. EX. $50.00

GRAVES, Robert. *Collected Poems*. 1961. Garden City. 1st Am ed. presentation. dj. EX. $25.00

GRAVES, Robert. *Fairies & Fusiliers*. 1918. NY. 1st Am ed. G. $35.00

GRAVES, Robert. *Golden Ass*. 1951. NY. 1st ed. dj. $35.00

GRAVES, Robert. *I, Claudis*. 1934. London. Barker. 1st ed. full black linen. $150.00

GRAVES, Robert. *Island of Unwisdom*. 1949. Garden City. 1st Am ed. dj. EX. $30.00

GRAVES, Robert. *Occupation: Writer*. 1950. NY. 1st ed. dj. EX. $35.00

GRAVES, Robert. *Original Rubaiyat of Omar Khayaam*. 1958. NY. Graves/All-Shah. 1/500. sgns. EX. $85.00

GRAVES, Robert. *Poems, 1968-1970*. 1971. Doubleday. 1st Am ed. dj. EX. $40.00

GRAVES, Robert. *Poems of Robert Graves*. Ltd Ed Club. slipcase. M. B3. $65.00

GRAVES, Robert. *Shout*. 1929. London. Ltd ed. 1/530. sgn. dj. EX. $100.00

GRAVES, Robert. *They Hanged My Saintly Billy*. nd. London. 1st ed. dj. EX. $35.00

GRAVES, Robert. *They Hanged My Saintly Billy*. 1957. NY. 1st ed. dj. VG. $25.00

GRAVES, Robert. *Translation of Lucan's Pharsalia*. 1957. NY. Penguin. 1st ed. dj. VG. $25.00

GRAVES, Robert. *Winter in Marjorca*. Valldemosa. wraps. EX. $25.00

GRAY, Asa. *Field, Forest & Garden Botany*. 1985. Am Book Co. Revised ed. 519 p. VG. M2. $18.00

GRAY, Asa. *Gray's New Manual of N US*. 1880. Ivison Blakeman Taylor. G. $37.50

GRAY, Asa. *Gray's School & Field Book*. 1857. Ivison Blakeman Taylor. G. $25.00

GRAY, Asa. *Structural Botany*. 1879. Ils. 442 p. EX. $17.50

GRAY, Berkeley. *Conquest Goes W*. 1973. Collins. dj. EX. P1. $10.00

GRAY, Berkeley. *Conquest in the Underworld*. 1974. Collins. dj. VG. P1. $10.00

GRAY, Curme. *Murder in Millennium VI*. 1951. Shasta. 1st ed. dj. VG. P1. $40.00

GRAY, F.D.P. *October Blood*. 1985. Simon Schuster. 1st ed. dj. M. $10.00

GRAY, Harold. *Little Orphan Annie & Gila Monster*. nd. Whitman. VG. P1. $9.25

GRAY, Henry. *Anatomy: Descriptive & Surgical*. 1859. Blanchard Lea. 1st Am ed. rebound. $850.00

GRAY, Howard. *English Field Systems*. 1915. Harvard. 1st ed. VG. J2. $15.00

GRAY, J.S. *Up: True Story of Aviation*. 1931. Strasburg. Ils 1st ed. 384 p. VG. T5. $65.00

GRAY, Nicholas. *Seventh Swan*. pb. EX. C1. $3.00

GRAY, Phoebe. *Little Sir Galahad*. 1915. 6th print. VG. C1. $12.50

GRAY, S. *Otherwise Engaged & Other Plays*. 1975. London. 1st pb ed. 135 p. wraps. VG. $10.00

GRAY, Thomas. *Elegy Written in Country Churchyard*. 1869. London. pls. gilt black bdg. VG. $50.00

GRAY, Thomas. *Elegy Written in Country Churchyard*. 1885. Lippincott. Artist ed. J2. $30.00

GRAY, Thomas. *Elegy Written in Country Churchyard*. 1979. Heritage. Ils Miller. quarto. slipcase. EX. $15.00

GRAY, Thomas. *Gray's Elegy*. 1903. Roycroft. 8vo. green suede. VG. D1. $75.00

GRAY, Thomas. *Odes*. 1757. Strawberry Hill. 1st ed. disbound. $550.00

GRAY, W.R. *Pacific Crest Trail*. 1975. Nat Geog Soc. Ils 1st ed. 199 p. dj. EX. M2. $11.00

GRAY, Zane. *Day of the Beast*. 1922. Harper Staro. 1st ed. dj. VG. B2. $145.00

GRAY & GRAY. *Wilderness Christians: Moravian Mission to DE*. 1956. Ithaca. VG. $35.00

GRAY & HOOKER. *Flora of the Rocky Mountain Region*. 1881. WA. 202 p. wraps. A3. $35.00

GRAY & LAWSON. *Adam of the Road*. 1944. NY. dj. VG. $15.00

GRAYBIEL & WHITE. *Electrocardiography in Practice*. 1941. Phil. Saunders. 1st ed. VG. $65.00

GRAYSON, W.J. *James Louis Petigur, Biographical Sketch*. 1866. Harper. 1st ed. 178 p. $45.00

GREARD, Vallery C.O. *Meissonier: His Life & Work*. 1897. NY. Armstrong. Ils. gilt red cloth. D2. $185.00

GREBER, Johannes. *Derkehr mit der Geisterweit*. 1937. NY. $20.00

GRECO, Antonella. *La Cappella di Niccolo V del Beato Angelico*. 1980. Rome. Ils. dj. D2. $75.00

GREELEY, A.W. *Handbook to AK*. 1906. NY. 1st ed. inscr. $40.00

GREELEY, Adolphus. *Three Years of Arctic Service*. 1886. NY. 1st ed. maps. G. $85.00

GREELEY, Andrew. *God Game*. 1986. Warner. 1st ed. dj. EX. P1. $16.95

GREELEY, Andrew. *Magic Cup*. 1985. 1st pb ed. VG. C1. $3.00

GREELEY, Horace. *American Conflict*. 1865. Hartford. 2 vols. VG. $50.00

GREELEY, Horace. *Recollections of a Busy Life*. 1868. NY. 1st ed. VG. B1. $75.00

GREELEY, Horace. *Recollections of a Busy Life*. 1869. NY. 624 p. VG. B1. $45.00

GREEN, Alan. *What a Body!* nd. Book Club. dj. VG. P1. $4.00

GREEN, B.K. *Ben Green Tales 1 Through 4.* 1974. Flagstaff. 1/1250. sgn. boxed. EX. $100.00

GREEN, B.K. *Horse Tradin'.* 1967. Knopf. 1st ed. dj. EX. $80.00

GREEN, B.K. *Last Trail Drive Through Downtown Dallas.* 1971. Flagstaff. Ils. 1/1750. dj. EX. $30.00

GREEN, B.K. *Some More Horse Tradin'.* 1972. NY. 1/350. sgn. boxed. EX. $160.00

GREEN, Benny. *P.G. Wodehouse: Literary Biography.* 1981. Rutledge. dj. EX. P1. $25.00

GREEN, E.L. *Indians of SC.* 1920. Columbia, SC. 81 p. $32.50

GREEN, E.P. *Perfect Fools.* 1982. NY. 1st ed. dj. M. $10.00

GREEN, Gerald. *Artist of Terezin.* 1st ed. dj. VG. E2. $18.00

GREEN, Graham. *Burnt-Out Case.* nd. London. 1st ed. dj. VG. $20.00

GREEN, H.D. *Furniture of the GA Piedmont Before 1830.* 1976. Atlanta. High Mus of Art. 143 p. pb. EX. $15.00

GREEN, Henry. *Nothing: A Novel.* 1950. London. 1st ed. dj. EX. $50.00

GREEN, Horace. *General Grant's Last Stand: A Biography.* 1936. Scribner. Ils 1st ed. 334 p. EX. M2. $15.00

GREEN, J. *Biology of Crustacea.* 1961. Witherby. Ils 1st ed. 180 p. dj. EX. M2. $18.00

GREEN, J. *Biology of Estuarine Animals.* 1975. WA U. Ils. 401 p. dj. M. M2. $20.00

GREEN, J.A. *Visit in 1929.* 1930. Columbus. 28 p. wraps. VG. T5. $8.50

GREEN, Joseph. *Conscience Interplanetary.* 1973. Doubleday. 1st ed. dj. EX. P1. $10.00

GREEN, L.S. *Tales of Buckeye Hills.* 1963. Mt. Vernon. 1st ed. sgn. 184 p. dj. G. T5. $19.50

GREEN, Martin. *Earth Again Redeemed.* 1977. Basic Books. 1st ed. dj. EX. P1. $10.00

GREEN, P. *Dramatic Heritage.* 1953. NY. 1st ed. dj. EX. $25.00

GREEN, P. *Laughing Pioneer.* 1932. McBride. 1st ed. dj. VG. $40.00

GREEN, P. *Salvation on a String & Other Tales of the S.* 1946. NY/London. 1st ed. dj. EX. $30.00

GREEN, Roger. *King Arthur & His Knights.* 1980. Penguin. pb. VG. C1. $3.50

GREEN, Roger. *Train.* 1982. 112 p. $9.50

GREEN, S.E. *Contemporary SF Fantasy & Horror Poetry.* 1989. Greenwood. 1st ed. EX. P1. $35.00

GREEN, S.P.M. *Cape Cod Folks.* 1904. Boston. Ils Atwood. 337 p. G. T5. $15.00

GREEN & DICK. *Oz Scrapbook.* 1977. NY. Stated 1st ed. 182 p. dj. M. $35.00

GREEN & ROWLANDSON. *Poetical Sketches of Scarborough.* 1813. London. Ils. 8 vols. VG. $325.00

GREENAN, R.H. *Nightmare: Contemporary Tale of Horror.* 1970. NY. 1st ed. dj. VG. $18.00

GREENAWAY, Kate. *A Apple Pie.* c 1880s. London. Warne. oblong 4to. VG. $65.00

GREENAWAY, Kate. *Almanac for 1883.* nd. London. Routledge. 1st state. sgn. VG. $175.00

GREENAWAY, Kate. *Kate Greenaway Pictures.* 1921. London. 20 pls. dj. EX. $350.00

GREENAWAY, Kate. *Kate Greenaway's Birthday Book for Children.* nd. London/NY. EX. $135.00

GREENAWAY, Kate. *Kate Greenaway's Birthday Book for Children.* nd. London. Warne. 16mo. G. $60.00

GREENAWAY, Kate. *Language of Flowers.* c 1885. London. Routledge. 1st ed. 12mo. $85.00

GREENAWAY, Kate. *Marigold Garden.* c 1890. London. Warne Evans. 4to. $75.00

GREENAWAY, Kate. *Marigold Garden.* nd. (1888) London/NY. 4to. VG. T1. $60.00

GREENAWAY, Kate. *Pied Piper of Hamelin.* nd. London. Warne. VG. $50.00

GREENAWAY, Kate. *Quiver of Love: Collection of Valentines.* 1876. London. Ward. Ils Crane. 1st ed. EX. rare. $650.00

GREENAWAY, Kate. *Under the Window.* nd. (1878) NY. Routledge. 1st ed. G. $85.00

GREENBERG, D.B. *Raising Game Birds in Captivity.* 1949. Van Nostrand. photos. 224 p. G. M2. $26.00

GREENBIE, S. *Furs to Furrows.* 1939. Caxton. inscr. VG. $37.50

GREENBLATT. *Hirsute Female.* 1965. Ils 2nd print. photos. dj. VG. $20.00

GREENE, C.S. *Sparks From the Campfires.* 1889. Keystone. Ils 528 p. G. M2. $10.00

GREENE, D.L. *Oz Scrapbook.* 1977. Random House. 1st ed. 4to. dj. VG. $15.00

GREENE, Frances. *Legends of King Arthur & His Court.* 1902. Boston/London. Ginn. Ils Garrett. VG. scarce. C1. $12.00

GREENE, Francis. *MS.* 1882. NY. Ils 1st ed. fld maps. xl. VG. T5. $35.00

GREENE, G.W. *German Element in War of American Independence.* 1876. NY. fair. $20.00

GREENE, Graham. *Collected Essays.* 1969. NY. 1st ed. dj. EX. $35.00

GREENE, Graham. *Complaisant Lover.* 1959. London. 1st ed. dj. EX. P3. $50.00

GREENE, Graham. *Confidential Agent.* 1954. Vanguard Lib. dj. VG. P1. $15.00

GREENE, Graham. *Dr. Fischer of Geneva.* 1980. NY. 1st ed. dj. EX. $9.00

GREENE, Graham. *End of the Affair.* 1951. Viking. 1st ed. dj. $45.00

GREENE, Graham. *Graham Greene Country Visited by Paul Hogarth.* 1986. London. Ils 1st ed. oblong folio. dj. EX. $75.00

GREENE, Graham. *Heart of the Matter.* 1948. NY. 1st Am ed. dj. VG. $40.00

GREENE, Graham. *Heart of the Matter.* 1948. NY. 1st trade ed. dj. EX. $20.00

GREENE, Graham. *Honorary Consul.* 1973. London. 1st ed. dj. EX. $35.00

GREENE, Graham. *Honorary Counsul.* 1973. Simon Schuster. 1st ed. dj. EX. $20.00

GREENE, Graham. *Human Factor.* 1978. Franklin Lib. 1st Am ed. full green leather. EX. $30.00

GREENE, Graham. *Human Factor.* 1978. London. dj. EX. $30.00

GREENE, Graham. *In Search of a Character.* 1962. NY. 1st ed. dj. EX. $20.00

GREENE, Graham. *It's a Battlefield.* 1934. NY. 1st ed. dj. VG. $120.00

GREENE, Graham. *Lost Childhood.* 1951. London. 1st ed. dj. EX. P3. $60.00

GREENE, Graham. *May We Borrow Your Husband?* 1967. London. 1st ed. dj. EX. $40.00

GREENE, Graham. *May We Borrow Your Husband?* 1967. NY. 1st ed. dj. EX. $35.00

GREENE, Graham. *Ministry of Fear.* 1944. Sun Dial. Movie ed. dj. G. P1. $125.00

GREENE, Graham. *Monsignor Quixote.* 1982. NY. 1st ed. dj. EX. $15.00

GREENE, Graham. *Our Man in Havana.* 1958. Heinemann. 1st ed. dj. VG. P1. $27.25

GREENE, Graham. *Our Man in Havana.* 1958. London. 1st ed. dj. EX. P3. $65.00

GREENE, Graham. *Quiet American.* 1955. London. 1st ed. dj. EX. $45.00

GREENE, Graham. *Quiet American.* 1956. NY. 1st ed. dj. VG. P3. $40.00

GREENE, Graham. *Reflections on Travels With My Aunt.* 1989. Firsts Co. 1/250. sgn. tall 8vo. as issued. M. $125.00

GREENE, Graham. *Return of A.J. Raffles.* 1975. NY. 1st ed. dj. EX. $15.00

GREENE, Graham. *Sense of Reality.* 1963. London. 1st ed. dj. EX. $40.00

GREENE, Graham. *Sort of Life.* 1971. NY. 1st ed. dj. EX. $25.00

GREENE, Graham. *Stamboul Train.* 1932. London. 1st ed. scarce. P3. $130.00

GREENE, Graham. *Third Man & Fallen Idol.* 1950. Heinemann. VG. P1. $20.00

GREENE, Graham. *Travels With My Aunt.* 1969. Bodley Head. 1st ed. dj. $35.00

GREENE, Harlan. *Why We Never Danced the Charleston.* 1984. St. Martin. 1st ed. sgn. dj. EX. T6. $25.00

GREENE, Harris. *Thieves of Timbuktu.* 1968. Doubleday. 1st ed. dj. EX. P1. $5.00

GREENE, Homer. *Lincoln Conscript.* 1909. Ils. 282 p. K1. $9.50

GREENE, Howard. *Rev. Richard Fish Cadle: Missionary...* 1936. Waukesha, WI. Ils 1st ed. 165 p. T5. $35.00

GREENE, Joseph. *Journey to Jupiter.* 1961. Golden Pr. P1. $10.00

GREENE, M. *Maya Sculpture From Lowlands, Highlands & Pacific Piedmont.* 1972. Berkeley. 202 pls. 4to. 432 p. dj. EX. J2. $50.00

GREENE, M.H. *Program Your Own Life.* 1982. VA. $5.00

GREENE, S.P. *Some Other Folks.* 1884. Boston. 1st ed. VG. $45.00

GREENE. *Little Steamroller.* 1974. Doubleday. Ils Ardizzone. M. $30.00

GREENER, W.W. *Gun & Its Development.* 1986. facsimile of 1910 ed. dj. M. $28.00

GREENFIELD, John. *Compleat Treatise of Stone & Gravel.* 1710. London. Ils. rare. $250.00

GREENHOUSE, Herbert. *Premonitions: Leap Into the Future.* 1972. London. $8.50

GREENLEAF, Stephen. *Death Bed.* 1980. Dial Pr. 1st ed. dj. EX. P1. $12.00

GREENLEAF, Stephen. *Fatal Obsession.* 1933. NY. Dial. 1st ed. dj. EX. $30.00

GREENLEAF, Stephen. *Toll Call.* 1987. NY. 1st ed. dj. EX. $15.00

GREENSTEIN, George. *Frozen Star.* 1983. NY. Ils. dj. EX. $12.50

GREENWALT, C.H. *Hummingbirds.* 1960. Am Mus Nat Hist. 70 pls. 250 p. M2. $300.00

GREENWOOD, Alice. *Cawn Dodgahs.* 1910. Chicago. VG. $25.00

GREENWOOD, Edwin. *Deadly Dowager.* 1935. Doubleday Doran. G. P1. $5.00

GREENWOOD, Gordon. *Australia: Social & Political History.* 1955. Praeger. 1st ed. dj. VG. J2. $15.00

GREENWOOD, Grace. *New Life in New Lands.* c 1872. Brooklyn. sgn. VG. $32.50

GREENWOOD, W.E. *Villa Madama Rame.* 1928. London. dj. VG. J2. $100.00

GREER, B.F. *Greer Family Reminiscences.* 1956. WA Co Hist Soc. 4to. 33 p. EX. M2. $8.00

GREER, Michael. *Inside Design.* 1962. NY. Ils. G. $30.00

GREERY, Edward. *Golden Lotus & Other Legends of Japan.* 1883. Boston. $30.00

GREEVER, W.S. *Bonanza W: Story of W Mining Rushes, 1848-1900.* 1963. Norman. 1st ed. dj. EX. $22.00

GREGG, J. *Commerce of the Prairies.* 1968. Citadel. reprint of Lakeside Classic. dj. $10.00

GREGG, William. *Controversial Issues in Scottish History.* 1910. Putnam. 1st ed. G. J2. $20.00

GREGG, Wilson. *Alexander Gregg, First Bishop of TX.* 1912. Sewanee. 1st ed. EX. $35.00

GREGG. *Gregg Shorthand.* 1966. Gregg Pub. 12mo. black cloth. $5.00

GREGORIETTI, Guido. *Jewelry Through the Ages.* 1969. Heritage. Ils. quarto. 319 p. dj. EX. $25.00

GREGORY, Augusta. *My First Play.* 1930. London. Elkin Mathews. 1/530. sgn/#d. EX. $70.00

GREGORY, C. *Labor & the Law.* c 1949. NY. Revised Enlarged ed. dj. $30.00

GREGORY, Claudius. *Case for Mr. Paul Savoy.* 1933. Scribner. 1st ed. VG. P1. $20.00

GREGORY, Claudius. *Valerie Hathaway.* 1933. McClelland Stewart. 1st ed. dj. P1. $7.50

GREGORY, Dick. *Political Primer.* 1971. NY. dj. EX. $15.00

GREGORY, Jackson. *Everlasting Whisper.* nd. Grosset. 1st ed. G. P1. $4.50

GREGORY, Julia. *Catalog of Early Books on Music Before 1800.* 1913. Lib Congress. 312 p. xl. VG. A3. $45.00

GREGORY, Mason. *If Two of Them Are Dead.* 1953. Arcadia. 1st ed. xl. P1. $5.00

GREIG, Francis. *Heads You Lose.* 1982. Crown. dj. EX. RS. P1. $9.25

GREIG, Ian. *Silver King Mystery.* c 1930. NY. Holt. 1st ed. VG. $9.50

GREINER, J. *Red Snow.* 1980. Doubleday. Ils 1st ed. 227 p. dj. EX. M2. $14.00

GRELIER. *To the Source of the Orinoco.* 1957. Jenkins. Ils 1st ed. maps. 190 p. EX. M2. $20.00

GRENDON, Stephen. *Mr. George & Other Odd Persons.* 1963. Arkham House. 1st ed. dj. EX. P1. $25.00

GRENFELL, Joyce. *Darling Ma: Letters to Her Mother, 1932-1944.* 1988. England. dj. EX. $15.00

GRENFELL, W.T. *Adrift on an Icepan.* 1937. Boston. Riverside. sgn. VG. $6.00

GRENFELL, W.T. *Down N on the Labrador.* 1911. NY. photos. fair. $12.00

GRENFELL, W.T. *Down to the Sea.* 1910. NY. dj. EX. $20.00

GRENFELL, W.T. *Laborador: Country & the People.* 1909. Macmillan. Ils 1st ed. 497 p. VG. M2. $10.00

GRESHAM, Otto. *Greenbacks; or, The Money That Won Civil War & World War.* 1927. Chicago. inscr. EX. $90.00

GRESS, E.G. *Art & Practice of Typography.* 1917. NY. Oswald. Ils. 4to. 300 p. TEG. VG. $45.00

GRESSLEY, Gene. *Bankers & Cattlemen.* 1966. NY. Knopf. 1st ed. dj. EX. $20.00

GREW, J.C. *Sport & Travel in the Far E.* 1910. Boston. 1st ed. inscr/sgn. blue bdg. VG. $75.00

GREWAL, R.S. *Lives & Teachings of Yogis of India.* 1939. CA. Grewal. $8.00

GREY, C. *Early Years of H.R.H. the Prince Consort.* 1867. NY. Harper. green cloth. VG. $50.00

GREY, Zane. *Adventures in Fishing.* nd. Harper. Stated 1st ed. VG. $30.00

GREY, Zane. *AZ Ames.* nd. Grosset Dunlap. VG. P1. $7.50

GREY, Zane. *Call of the Canyon.* 1924. Harper. 1st ed. G. P1. $25.00

GREY, Zane. *Call of the Canyon.* 1924. Musson. VG. P1. $10.00

GREY, Zane. *Deer Stalker.* nd. Grosset Dunlap. P1. $12.50

GREY, Zane. *Forlorn River.* nd. Grosset Dunlap. G. P1. $4.00

GREY, Zane. *Forlorn River.* 1927. Harper. VG. P1. $20.00

GREY, Zane. *Hash Knife Outfit.* nd. Grosset Dunlap. dj. VG. P1. $15.00

GREY, Zane. *Heritage of the Desert.* nd. Grosset Dunlap. VG. P1. $7.50

GREY, Zane. *Heritage of the Desert.* nd. Grosset. Movie ed. G. P1. $7.50

GREY, Zane. *Last of the Plainsmen.* nd. Grosset Dunlap. VG. P1. $7.50

GREY, Zane. *Last of the Plainsmen.* nd. Hodder Stoughton. dj. VG. P1. $12.50

GREY, Zane. *Last Ranger.* 1983. Ian Henry. dj. EX. P1. $10.00

GREY, Zane. *Last Trail.* nd. Grosset Dunlap. G. P1. $5.00

GREY, Zane. *Last Trail.* nd. Triangle. dj. VG. P1. $12.50

GREY, Zane. *Last Trail.* nd. Whitman. VG. P1. $5.00

GREY, Zane. *Last Trail.* 1950. Houghton Stoughton. 25th print. P1. $12.50

GREY, Zane. *Lone Star Ranger.* 1914. Grosset Dunlap. 373 p. EX. $4.50

GREY, Zane. *Man of the Forest.* 1920. Harper. VG. P1. $7.50

GREY, Zane. *Mysterious Rider.* 1921. Harper. G. P1. $7.50

GREY, Zane. *NV, Romance of the W.* 1928. NY. Harper. 1st ed. G. $15.00

GREY, Zane. *Raiders of Spanish Peaks.* nd. Collier. VG. P1. $7.50

GREY, Zane. *Rainbow Trail.* 1915. Harper. VG. P1. $12.50

GREY, Zane. *Rainbow Trail.* 1981. Ian Henry. dj. EX. P1. $10.00

GREY, Zane. *Reef Girl.* 1977. NY. 1st ed. dj. VG. $30.00

GREY, Zane. *Rogue River Feud.* nd. Grosset Dunlap. dj. G. P1. $12.50

GREY, Zane. *Roping Lions in the Grand Canyon.* 1924. NY. Harper. photos. 12mo. 191 p. EX. $25.00

GREY, Zane. *Shepherd of Guadaloupe.* nd. Grosset Dunlap. dj. G. P1. $12.50

GREY, Zane. *Spirit of the Border.* nd. Whitman. G. P1. $4.00

GREY, Zane. *Spirit of the Border.* nd. World. VG. P1. $7.50

GREY, Zane. *Spirit of the Border.* 1943. Triangle. 18th print. dj. VG. P1. $12.50

GREY, Zane. *Spirit of the Border.* 1944. Triangle. VG. P1. $7.50

GREY, Zane. *Stairs of Sand.* nd. Collier. VG. P1. $7.50

GREY, Zane. *Stairs of Sand.* 1943. Harper. 1st ed. dj. $60.00

GREY, Zane. *Stairs of Sand.* 1945. Musson. VG. P1. $7.50

GREY, Zane. *Sunset Pass.* nd. Grosset Dunlap. VG. P1. $7.50

GREY, Zane. *Tales of Fishing Virgin Seas.* 1925. Harper. 1st ed. G. $70.00

GREY, Zane. *Tales of Fresh-Water Fishing.* 1928. NY/London. Harper. 1st trade ed. 4to. dj. EX. $95.00

GREY, Zane. *Tales of Lonely Trails.* 1922. Blue Ribbon. 394 p. dj. VG. T5. $17.50

GREY, Zane. *Tales of Swordfish & Tuna.* 1927. NY/London. Harper. 1st ed. 4to. blue bdg. EX. $85.00

GREY, Zane. *Tales of Tahitian Water.* 1931. NY. $65.00

GREY, Zane. *Tappan's Burro & Other Stories.* 1923. NY. Ils 1st ed. 253 p. T5. $75.00

GREY, Zane. *Tappan's Burro.* nd. Grosset Dunlap. G. P1. $5.00

GREY, Zane. *Tenderfoot.* 1982. Ian Henry. dj. EX. P1. $10.00

GREY, Zane. *Thieves' Canyon.* 1981. Ian Henry. dj. EX. P1. $10.00

GREY, Zane. *Thunder Mountain.* 1935. Harper. dj. G. P1. $30.00

GREY, Zane. *Thundering Herd.* nd. Grosset Dunlap. VG. P1. $7.50

GREY, Zane. *Thundering Herd.* nd. Black. VG. P1. $7.50

GREY, Zane. *Thundering Herd.* 1924. NY. Harper. Ils. 12mo. 400 p. VG. $20.00

GREY, Zane. *To the Last Man.* nd. Grosset. G. P1. $5.00

GREY, Zane. *Twin Sombreros.* nd. Grosset Dunlap. VG. P1. $7.50

GREY, Zane. *Twin Sombreros.* nd. Collier. VG. P1. $7.50

GREY, Zane. *Wanderer of the Wasteland.* 1923. Harper. 1st ed. dj. EX. $30.00

GREY, Zane. *Wild Horse Mesa.* nd. Grosset Dunlap. dj. VG. P1. $12.50

GREY, Zane. *Wild Horse Mesa.* nd. Black. VG. P1. $7.50

GREY, Zane. *Wild Horse Mesa.* 1928. Musson. G. P1. $7.50

GREY, Zane. *Wildfire.* nd. Grosset Dunlap. G. P1. $4.00

GREY, Zane. *Wildfire.* nd. Grosset Dunlap. VG. P1. $7.50

GREY, Zane. *Wildfire.* 1917. Harper. 1st ed. EX. $30.00

GREY, Zane. *Zane Grey's Book of Camps & Trails.* 1931. NY. Ils 1st ed. 211 p. VG. T5. $295.00

GRIBBIN, John. *Spacewarps, Black Holes, White Holes, Quasars...* 1983. Delacorte. 1st ed. 211 p. dj. EX. $25.00

GRIBBLE, Leonard. *Don't Argue With Death.* 1959. NY. 1st Am ed. dj. EX. $15.00

GRIBBLE, Leonard. *Midsummer Slay Ride.* 1976. Robert Hale. 1st ed. dj. xl. P1. $5.00

GRIBBLE & LAUSANNE. *Paintings by J. Hardwick Lewis.* 1909. London. G. $20.00

GRIDLAND, R. *Practical Landscape Gardening.* 1924. Ils. G. $15.00

GRIEHL, K. *Giant Snakes & Non-Venomous Snakes in the Terrarium.* 1984. Barron. Ils 1st Eng language ed. 80 p. M2. $10.00

GRIER, A.C. *Spirit of the Truth.* 1930. NY. $15.00

GRIER, Eldon. *Ring of Ice.* 1957. Montreal. Ils Sylvia Tait. 1st ed. wraps. $45.00

GRIER, William. *Mechanic's Calculator.* 1849. Hartford. 3 pls. full leather. VG. $50.00

GRIERSON, Francis. *Murder at Wedding.* nd. Literary Pr. G. P1. $7.00

GRIFFEN, L.E. *Anatomy of Nautilus Pompilius.* 1900. Nat Acad Sc. Ils. 4to. EX. M2. $45.00

GRIFFIN, A. *List of Books on Danish W Indies.* 1901. Lib Congress. 18 p. $15.00

GRIFFIN, A. *List of Books on Porto Rico.* 1901. Lib Congress. 55 p. xl. $20.00

GRIFFIN, A.T. *Ship To Remember.* 1943. NY. Ils 1st ed. 288 p. dj. $30.00

GRIFFIN, Edward. *Plea for Africa: Sermon Preached Oct. 16, 1817.* 1817. NY. map. diagram. 8vo. disbound. $125.00

GRIFFIN, H. *AK & the Canadian NW: Our New Frontier.* 1944. Norton. 1st ed. 221 p. dj. M1. $11.50

GRIFFIN, J. *Devil Rides Outside.* 1952. Ft. Worth. 1st ed. dj. EX. $45.00

GRIFFIN, J. *Nuni.* 1956. Boston/Dallas. Houghton/Smith. 1st ed. dj. EX. $45.00

GRIFFIN, J.B. *Fort Ancient Aspect.* 1943. Ann Arbor. 1st ed. EX. G1. $35.00

GRIFFIN, Jeff. *Hunting Dogs of America.* 1964. 1st ed. dj. EX. $15.00

GRIFFIS, W.E. *Dutch Fairy Tales for Young Folks.* 1918. NY. $20.00

GRIFFITH, Corinne. *Hollywood Stories.* 1962. Frederick Fell. dj. VG. P1. $20.00

GRIFFITH, N.S. *Edward Bellamy: A Bibliography.* Scarecrow Pr. 185 p. VG. T5. $9.50

GRIFFITH, R.E. *Medicinal Botany...* 1847. Phil. Ils 1st ed. 704 p. VG. scarce. $200.00

GRIFFITH & TALMADGE. *GA Journalism, 1763-1950.* 1951. Athens. Ils 1st ed. 413 p. dj. VG. $35.00

GRIFFITHS, Arthur. *History & Romance of Crime.* nd. London. 1/1000. 12 vols. VG. $65.00

GRIFFITHS, W.H. *Story of the American Bank Note Co.* 1959. NY. Ils 1st ed. 4to. dj. EX. T1. $150.00

GRIFFITHS, W.H. *Story of the American Bank Note Co.* 1959. NY. Ils. photos. pls. 92 p. VG. T5. $125.00

GRIGG, E.R.N. *Trail of Invisible Light.* 1965. Springfield. $75.00

GRIMBBLE, Leonard. *Death Pays the Piper.* 1956. Jenkins. VG. P1. $8.00

GRIMES, Martha *Deer Leap.* 1985. Little Brown. 1st ed. dj. EX. P1. $15.95

GRIMES, Martha. *Help the Poor Struggler.* 1985. Little Brown. 1st ed. dj. VG. P1. $15.00

GRIMES, Martha. *I Am the Only Running Footman.* 1986. Boston. 1st ed. dj. EX. $12.50

GRIMKE & DYMOND. *Inquiry Into Accordancy of War With Principles...* 1834. Phil. 2nd ed. VG. $85.00

GRIMLEY, G.P. *Baltimore & OH Railroad.* 1933. WA. wraps. $25.00

GRIMM, Brothers. *Bruder Grimm.* c 1900. Leipzig. Ils. 87 p. G. $25.00

GRIMM, Brothers. *Grimm's Fairy Tales.* 1945. Grosset Dunlap. Ils Fritz Kredel. VG. $20.00

GRIMM, Brothers. *Little Brother, Little Sister.* 1917. NY. Dood Mead. Ils Rackham. 1st Am ed. EX. $100.00

GRIMMELSHAUSEN. *Adventures of Simplicissimus.* Ltd Ed Club. slipcase. M. B3. $65.00

GRINKER & SIEGEL. *Men Under Stress.* 1945. Phil. 8vo. 484 p. $25.00

GRINNELL, G.B. *Blackfoot Lodge Trails: Story of a Prairie People.* 1907. Scribner. Ils. 310 p. A3. $45.00

GRINNELL, G.B. *By Cheyenne Campfires.* 1926. New Haven. 1st ed. VG. $110.00

GRINNELL, G.B. *Indians of Today.* 1911. NY. Duffield. Ils. 426 p. G. A3. $35.00

GRINNELL, G.B. *Story of the Indian.* 1924. NY. Appleton. Ils. 268 p. A3. $35.00

GRINNELL, G.B. *Trail & Campfire: Book of Boone & Crockett Club.* 1897. NY. 1st ed. pls. xl. VG. $17.50

GRISCOM, L. *Warblers of America.* 1957. Devin Adair. Ils Dick. 1st print. 356 p. dj. M2. $55.00

GRISCOM & FOLGER. *Birds of Nantucket.* 1948. Cambridge. 1st ed. dj. VG. B2. $35.00

GRISET, Ernest. *Book of Fables.* 1880. Am Book Co. Ils. G. $15.00

GRISEWOOD, R. Norman. *Zarlah the Martian.* 1909. Fenno. G. P1. $50.00

GRISWOLD, George. *Checkmate by the Colonel.* 1953. Dutton. 1st ed. dj. VG. P1. $20.00

GRISWOLD, George. *Red Pawns.* 1954. Dutton. 1st ed. dj. VG. P1. $12.00

GROBER, Karl. *Children's Toys of Bygone Days.* 1928. London. Trans Hereford. photos. EX. $200.00

GROBLER, H. *Predators of S Africa: Guide to Carnivores.* 1984. S Africa. Ils 1st ed. 134 p. M. M2. $15.00

GRODINSKY, Julius. *IA Pool: Study in Railroad Competition, 1870-1884.* 1950. 184 p. $25.00

GROHMANN, Will. *Paul Klee.* 1954. NY. Abrams. Ils. 448 p. dj. D2. $100.00

GROLIER SOCIETY. *Book of Popular Science.* 1955. Grolier. 10 vols. EX. $27.50

GROLIER SOCIETY. *Catalog of Engraved Work of Asher B. Durand.* 1895. 1/350. wraps. VG. $35.00

GRONOW, Captain. *Reminiscences & Recollections of Captain Gronow.* 1892. London. Ils. 2 vols. EX. $125.00

GRONOWICZ, Antoni. *Bela Schick & the World of Children.* 1954. Abelard Schuman. 1st ed. dj. J2. $15.00

GROOM, Arthur. *Flying Doctor Annual.* 1963. Dean & Son. VG. P1. $30.00

GROPPER, William. *Di Goldene Medinah.* 1927. NY. sm folio. gilt bdg. $300.00

GROPPER, William. *Old Man of Lompadini & Other Stories.* 1948. Wroclaw, Poland. 8vo. wraps. $225.00

GROSLIER, B.P. *Indo-China: Art in Melting Pot of Races.* 1962. London. Art of World Series. EX. $35.00

GROSS, Charles. *Sources & Literature of English History to 1845.* 1915. London. 2nd ed. xl. VG. G1. $20.00

GROSS, H.I. *Antique & Classic Cameras.* 1965. NY. Amphoto. Ils. 4to. 192 p. dj. $65.00

GROSS, L.S. *Redefining the American Gothic.* 1989. UMI Research. 1st ed. dj. EX. P1. $35.00

GROSS, Milt. *Dear Dollink.* 1945. NY. 1st ed. dj. VG. B2. $15.00

GROSS, Milt. *He Done Her Wrong.* 1930. NY. 1st ed. VG. B2. $45.00

GROSS, S.D. *History of American Medical Literature From 1776 to Present.* 1972. reprint of 1876 ed. 85 p. EX. $35.00

GROSS, W. *Recollections of a Private.* 1890. Crowell. 1st ed. G. $90.00

GROSSBACH, Robert. *Never Say Die.* 1979. Harper Row. 1st ed. dj. EX. P1. $10.00

GROSSE, Edmund. *Books on the Table.* 1921. London. 1st ed. $40.00

GROSSE, P.H. *History of the British Sea: Anemones & Corals.* 1860. London. 362 p. gilt bdg. EX. M2. $75.00

GROSSMAN, E.B. *Edwin Booth: Recollections by His Daughter...* 1894. Century. $15.00

GROSSMAN & HAMLET. *Birds of Prey of the World.* 1964. Potter. Ils. 4to. 496 p. dj. EX. M2. $60.00

GROSSMAN. *Echo of a Distant Drum: Winslow Homer & the War.* nd. (1974) Abrams. pls. 4to. dj. VG. C4. $65.00

GROSSWRITH, Marvin. *Heraldry Book.* 1981. 1st ed. dj. VG. C1. $12.50

GROSVENOR, D. *Blue Whales.* 1977. Nat Geog Soc. Ils. 4to. EX. M2. $5.00

GROSVENOR, Gilbert. *Scenes From Every Land.* 1918. Nat Geog Soc. 4th Series. G. $25.00

GROSVENOR & WETMORE. *Book of Birds.* 1937. Nat Geog Soc. Ils. 3 vols. VG. A3. $45.00

GROSZ, George. *Das Neue Gesicht der Herrschenden Klasse.* 1930. Berlin. Malik. Ils. VG. D2. $350.00

GROSZ, George. *30 Drawings & Watercolors.* 1944. NY. spiral bdg. EX. $60.00

GROTH, John. *Studio Asia.* 1952. Cleveland. 1st ed. 208 p. dj. VG. B2. $30.00

GROTH, John. *Studio Europe.* 1945. Viking. Intro Hemingway. folio. dj. VG. $25.00

GROUSSET, Rene. *La Chine et Son Art.* 1951. Paris. VG. $45.00

GROVER, R. *One Hundred Dollar Misunderstanding.* 1962. NY. 2 djs. EX. $30.00

GRUBB, Davis. *Shadow of My Brother.* 1966. Hutchinson. 1st ed. dj. VG. P1. $25.00

GRUBE, E.J. *Islamic Pottery of 8th to 15th C in Keir Collection.* 1976. London. Faber. 29 pls. 4to. dj. EX. J2. $125.00

GRUBER, Frank. *Beagle-Scented Murder.* 1946. Holt Rinehart. 1st ed. EX. $20.00

GRUBER, Frank. *Freaky Mystery.* 1942. Avon. 1st ed. VG. $15.00

GRUBER, Frank. *Laughing Fox.* 1943. Tower. VG. P1. $12.50

GRUBER, Frank. *Outlaw.* 1941. NY. dj. VG. $80.00

GRUELLE, Johnny. *Beloved Belindy.* 1926. Chicago. Volland. dj. VG. $45.00

GRUELLE, Johnny. *Raggedy Andy Stories.* 1920. Chicago. Donohue. 1st ed. VG. $20.00

GRUELLE, Johnny. *Raggedy Anne in the Deep Woods.* 1930. Volland. 1st ed. B2. $35.00

GRUELLE, Johnny. *Sunny Bunny.* 1918. Algonquin. Ils. VG. B4. $35.00

GRUERBER, H.A. *Myths of N Lands.* 1985. 1st ed. VG. C1. $19.50

GRUMBACH, Doris. *Ladies.* 1984. NY. 1st ed. dj. EX. $8.00

GRUNER, L. *Das Grune Gewolbe zu Dresden.* 1862. Dresden. gilt blue cloth. J2. $200.00

GRYTZKO, Mascioni. *Disegni Di Maestri Moderni.* 1961. Milano. Soc Ed d'Arte. 1/450. slipcase. $225.00

GRZIMEK, B. *Among Animals of Africa.* 1970. Stein Day. Ils 1st Am ed. 368 p. dj. EX. M2. $15.00

GRZIMEK, B. *Animal Life Encyclopedia. Vol. 5.* 1984. Van Nostrand. Ils. HrdCvr. 555 p. dj. M. M2. $40.00

GUARD, David. *Deirdre: Celtic Legend.* 1981. Ils Gretchen Guard. dj. M. C1. $12.50

GUARESCHI, Giovanni. *Duncan & Clotilda.* 1968. Farrar Straus. 1st ed. dj. VG. P1. $10.00

GUARESCHI, Giovanni. *Little World of Don Camillo.* 1953. Gollancz. 16th print. VG. P1. $10.00

GUDERIAN, Heinz. *Panzer Leader.* 1952. NY. Ils. maps. 528 p. dj. G. T5. $35.00

GUEDALLA, Philip. *Mr. Churchill.* 1941. Hodder. 1st Eng ed. green cloth. dj. D1. $40.00

GUEDALLA, Philip. *Mr. Churchill.* 1942. Reynal Hitchcock. 1st ed. VG. D1. $30.00

GUENON, M.F. *Treatise on Milch Cows.* 1854. McElrath. Ils. 88 p. VG. M2. $37.00

GUERIN, Eddie. *I Was a Bandit.* 1929. NY. 1st ed. dj. fair. $40.00

GUERIN, M. *L'Oeuvre Grave de Manet.* 1969. NY. 4to. dj. EX. J2. $150.00

GUERIN, Mrs. E.J. *Mountain Charley; or, Adventures of Mrs. E.J. Guerin...* 1968. OK U. New ed. 1st print. 112 p. dj. M2. $15.00

GUERINET, Armand. *L'Oeuvre de Delafosse.* nd. Paris. 405 pls. 5 vols. G. T5. $120.00

GUERRA. *Iconografia Medica Mexicana.* 1955. Mexico. 1/550. 4to. wraps. VG. $275.00

GUEST, Edgar. *All That Matters.* 1922. Reilly Lee. Ils. dj. G. $20.00

GUEST, Edgar. *Harbor Lights of Home.* 1928. Chicago. boxed. EX. $10.00

GUEST, Edgar. *Heap O'Livin'.* 1916. Reilly Lee. sgn. fair. $12.00

GUGGENHEIM, Peggy. *Out of This Century: Confessions of Art Addict.* 1979. NY. Ils 1st ed. 396 p. dj. VG. B2. $20.00

GUGGISBERG, C.A. *Crocodiles: Their Natural History, Folklore & Conservation.* 1972. Stackpole. Ils. 195 p. dj. EX. M2. $15.00

GUGGISBERG, C.A. *Wilderness Is Free.* 1963. London. 4to. VG. $30.00

GUIDO, Rey. *Matterhorn.* 1907. Scribner. 1st ed. EX. rare. $135.00

GULICK, Paul. *Strings of Steel.* nd. Grosset Dunlap. Movie ed. VG. P1. $20.00

GULL, M.E. *Nobody's Darling.* c 1926. Greenwood. 30 p. printed wraps. $7.50

GUMMERE. *Old English Ballads.* 1894. Boston. G. C1. $19.50

GUNDEL, Karoly. *Hungarian Cookery Book.* 1964. Budapest. Ils 5th ed. 103 p. dj. EX. $15.00

GUNDELFINGER, George. *Decay of Bulldogism. Secret Chapters on Yale Football...* 1930. Sewickley. VG. $50.00

GUNN, James E. *Alternate Worlds.* 1975. Prentice Hall. 1st ed. dj. EX. P1. $25.00

GUNN, James E. *Deadlier Than the Male.* 1942. Duell Sloan. 2nd ed. VG. P1. $15.00

GUNN, James E. *End of the Dreams.* 1975. Scribner. 1st ed. dj. EX. P1. $10.00

GUNN, James E. *Joy Makers.* 1984. Crown. 1st ed. sgn. dj. EX. P1. $25.00

GUNN, James E. *Nebula Award Ten.* 1975. Harper. 1st ed. dj. VG. P1. $10.00

GUNN, James E. *Some Dreams Are Nightmares.* 1974. Scribner. 1st ed. dj. EX. P1. $10.00

GUNN, James E. *Some Dreams Are Nightmares.* 1974. Scribner. 1st ed. dj. VG. P1. $7.50

GUNN, Thomas. *Menace.* 1982. Ils Manroot. 1/250. sgns/#d. wraps. EX. $30.00

GUNN, Thomas. *To the Air.* 1974. Godine. 1st ed. EX. $12.50

GUNNISON, J.W. *Mormons; or, Latter-Day Saints...* 1856. Phil. 3rd ed. VG. $60.00

GUNSTON, Bill. *Rockets & Missiles.* 1979. Crescent. 1st ed. 264 p. dj. $25.00

GUNSTON & PEACOCK. *Fighter Missions. Modern Air Combat View From Cockpit.* 1989. NY. Ils. photos. dj. EX. $35.00

GUNTERS, A.C. *Small Boys in Big Boots.* 1890. NY. Home Pub. Ils Beard/others. G. $20.00

GUPTILL, A.L. *Norman Rockwell, Illustrator.* 1946. Watson Guptill. 1st ed. presentation. dj. EX. $110.00

GUPTILL, A.L. *Norman Rockwell, Illustrator.* 1972. Watson Guptill. reprint of 1946 ed. slipcase. EX. $8.50

GUPTILL, A.L. *Oil Painting Step by Step.* 1963. Watson Guptill. 1st ed. sgn. D2. $35.00

GURDJIEFF, G.I. *Meetings With Remarkable Men.* 1963. NY. 1st ed. dj. VG. B2. $17.50

GURNEY, David. *F Certificate.* 1968. Bernard Gets. 1st ed. G. P1. $7.50

GURNEY, Gene. *Great Air Battles.* 1963. NY. Ils 1st ed. 291 p. dj. VG. T5. $12.50

GURNEY, Gene. *Pictorial History of US Army in War & Peace...* 1966. NY. Ils. 815 p. dj. G. T5. $35.00

GURNEY, J.J. *Familiar Letters to Henry Clay Describing a Winter...* 1840. NY. 203 p. $75.00

GURTEEN, Humphreys. *Arthurian Epic.* 1965. reprint of 1895 ed. scarce. M. C1. $22.00

GUSMANI, Roberto. *Lydisches Worterbuch.* 1964. Heidelberg. German text. M. $16.00

GUTHRIE, A.B. *Blue Hen's Chick.* 1965. NY. 1st ed. dj. VG. B2. $22.50

GUTHRIE, A.B. *These Thousand Hills.* 1956. Boston. 1st ed. dj. VG. B2. $20.00

GUTHRIE, Edward. *Book of Butter.* 1918. Macmillan. Ils 1st ed. sgn. EX. $30.00

GUTHRIE, K.S. *Angelic Mysteries of the Nine Heavens.* 1926. Yonkers. $75.00

GUTIERREZ & ROUKES. *Painting With Acrylics.* 1968. Watson Guptill. 3rd print. dj. D2. $30.00

GUTMAN, Richard. *John Wilkes Booth, Himself.* 1979. 87 p. sgn. EX. $25.00

GUTTERIDGE, Lindsay. *Cold War in Country Garden.* 1971. Putnam. dj. VG. P1. $10.00

GUTTERIDGE, Lindsay. *Killer Pine.* 1975. British SF Book Club. dj. VG. P1. $4.00

GUYS, C. *Painter of Victorian Life: Study of Constantin Guys...* 1930. London. Ils. 8vo. 172 p. dj. EX. J2. $55.00

HAANEL, C.F. *You.* 1927. St. Louis. $22.00

HAARD & HAARD. *Foraging for Edible Wild Mushrooms.* 1978. Cloudburst. Ils. 156 p. EX. M2. $6.00

HAAS, Albert. *Doctor & the Damned.* 1984. NY. 1st ed. dj. $6.00

HAAS, Dorothy. *Sir Lancelot.* 1958. Whitman. 1st ed. Big Little Book. VG. C1. $14.00

HAAS, E. *Pride's Progress: Story of a Family of Lions.* 1967. Harper Row. Ils. 116 p. dj. EX. M2. $5.00

HAAS, H. *Manta: Under the Red Sea With Spear & Camera.* 1953. Rand McNally. Ils. 278 p. dj. VG. M2. $11.00

HABE, Hans. *Das Netz.* 1969. Verlag. 1st ed. inscr. dj. EX. $25.00

HABER. *Our Friend the Atom.* 1956. Disney Studio. 1st ed. dj. EX. $15.00

HACHIYA, M.D. *Hiroshima Diary: Journal of Japanese Physician.* 1955. Chapel Hill. 1st ed. 238 p. dj. EX. $45.00

HACKENBROCH, Yvonne. *English & Other Silver in Irwin Untermyer Collection.* 1969. NY. Ils. pls. 4to. dj. EX. J2. $75.00

HADAR & OFER. *Heyl Ha'Avir. The Israel Air Force.* c 1971. Israel. Ils 1st ed. G. T5. $45.00

HADER & HADER. *Reindeer Trail.* 1959. Macmillan. dj. G. $20.00

HADFIELD, Alice Mary. *Charles Williams: Exploration of His Life & Work.* 1983. NY/Oxford. 1st ed. dj. M. C1. $17.50

HADFIELD, John. *Chamber of Horrors.* 1965. Studio Vista. 1st ed. dj. VG. P1. $20.00

HADFIELD, Miles. *Pioneers in Gardening.* 1955. London. 1st ed. dj. VG. $21.00

HADGSON, William Hope. *Carnacki, the Ghost Finder.* 1972. Tom Stacey. dj. VG. P1. $20.00

HADLEY, Harold. *Come See Them Die.* 1934. Messner. 1st ed. G. P1. $10.00

HAFEN, L.R. *Overland Mail.* 1926. Clark. 1st ed. fld map. 361 p. K1. $85.00

HAFEN, L.R. & A.W. *Rufus B. Sage: His Letters & Papers, 1836-1847.* 1956. Clark. 2 vols. EX. M2. $65.00

HAFFNER, Sebastian. *Meaning of Hitler.* 1979. NY. 1st ed. dj. $6.00

HAFTMANN, W. *Emil Nolde.* nd. NY. 55 pls. 4to. dj. EX. J2. $50.00

HAGBERG, K. *Carl Linnaeus.* 1952. Cope. Ils. map. 264 p. dj. EX. M2. $28.00

HAGEL, B. *Game Loading & Practical Ballistics for American Hunter.* 1978. NY. Knopf. 1st ed. G. $28.00

HAGEMANN, E.R. *Fighting Rebels & Redskins: Experiences in Army Life.* 1969. OK U. photos. maps. dj. EX. M2. $25.00

HAGEMANN, E.R. *Index to Black Mask, 1920-1951.* 1982. Bowling Green. dj. EX. P1. $20.00

HAGEMANN, Otto. *New Face of Berlin.* 1959. Berlin. 3rd ed. dj. VG. J2. $15.00

HAGER, I.P. *Blue & Gray Battlefields.* 1978. Parsons, WV. McClain. 45 p. $12.50

HAGERDORN, Hermann. *Rough Riders: A Romance.* 1927. NY. 1st ed. 508 p. T5. $12.50

HAGGARD, H.R. *Allan Quatermain.* 1927. Harrap. 3rd ed. VG. P1. $15.00

HAGGARD, H.R. *Allan Quatermain.* 1933. Harrap. 7th print. VG. P1. $15.00

HAGGARD, H.R. *Allan Quatermain.* 1969. MacDonald. 6th print. dj. VG. P1. $7.50

HAGGARD, H.R. *Allan the Hunter.* 1898. 1st ed. VG. B1. $25.00

HAGGARD, H.R. *Allan's Wife.* 1969. MacDonald. 4th ed. dj. EX. P1. $12.50

HAGGARD, H.R. *Ancient Allan.* 1920. 1st ed. VG. B1. $25.00

HAGGARD, H.R. *Ayesha, the Return of She.* nd. Ward Lock. dj. VG. P1. $25.00

HAGGARD, H.R. *Ayesha.* 1972. MacDonald. dj. VG. P1. $12.50

HAGGARD, H.R. *Benita.* 1965. MacDonald. P1. $10.00

HAGGARD, H.R. *Brethern.* 1904. NY. VG. $12.00

HAGGARD, H.R. *Child of Storm.* 1913. 1st ed. VG. B1. $25.00

HAGGARD, H.R. *Cleopatra.* 1926. Harrap. 2nd ed. VG. P1. $15.00

HAGGARD, H.R. *Dawn.* 1928. London. dj. EX. $20.00

HAGGARD, H.R. *Elissa.* 1900. NY. Longman. 1st ed. VG. $35.00

HAGGARD, H.R. *Eric Brighteyes.* nd. WB Conkey. VG. P1. $15.00

HAGGARD, H.R. *Eric Brighteyes.* 1925. Harrap. VG. P1. $17.50

HAGGARD, H.R. *Eric Brighteyes.* 1936. Harrap. 3rd ed. xl. rebound. G. P1. $4.50

HAGGARD, H.R. *King Solomon's Mines.* nd. Readers Lib. dj. G. P1. $20.00

HAGGARD, H.R. *Love Eternal.* 1918. 1st ed. VG. B1. $35.00

HAGGARD, H.R. *Lysbeth.* London. 1st ed. red leather. boxed. EX. $175.00

HAGGARD, H.R. *Maiwa's Revenge.* 1888. London. 1st ed. gray/red bdg. EX. T5. $150.00

HAGGARD, H.R. *Montezuma's Daughter.* 1926. Harrap. 2nd ed. VG. P1. $15.00

HAGGARD, H.R. *Moon of Israel.* 1918. London. Murray. reprint. VG. $7.00

HAGGARD, H.R. *Mr. Meeson's Will.* 1888. NY. Longman. 1st ed. VG. $50.00

HAGGARD, H.R. *People of the Mist.* 2nd print. VG. B1. $20.00

HAGGARD, H.R. *People of the Mist.* 1953. MacDonald. 2nd ed. VG. P1. $10.00

HAGGARD, H.R. *She & Allan.* 1921. NY. 1st Am ed. 392 p. dj. T5. $25.00

HAGGARD, H.R. *She & Allan.* 1960. MacDonald. dj. xl. P1. $6.00

HAGGARD, H.R. *She.* nd. Grosset. G. P1. $5.00

HAGGARD, H.R. *She.* 1926. Grosset Dunlap. Movie ed. G. P1. $20.00

HAGGARD, H.R. *She.* 1927. London. reprint. EX. $6.00

HAGGARD, H.R. *When the World Shook.* June, 1919. 2nd print. VG. B1. $10.00

HAGGARD, H.R. *Yellow God, Idol of Africa.* 1929. London. dj. EX. $20.00

HAGGARD, Howard. *Devils, Drugs & Doctors: Science of Healing...* 1929. NY. $12.00

HAGGARD & LANG. *World's Desire.* 1920. Hodder Stoughton. VG. P1. $20.00

HAGUE, Harlan. *Road to CA: Search for S Overland Route.* 1848. Glendale. Clark. Ils Russell. 325 p. VG. A3. $60.00

HAGWOOD, Johnson. *Memoirs of War of Secession...* 1910. Columbia. State Co. maps. 496 p. $225.00

HAHM, Konrad. *Deutsche Volkskunst.* 1928. Berlin. Ils. 128 p. gilt bdg. scarce. D2. $145.00

HAHN, E. *On the Side of the Apes.* 1971. Crowell. Ils 1st ed. 239 p. dj. EX. M2. $18.00

HAHNEMANN, Samuel. *Chronic Diseases.* 1845-1846. NY/London. 5 vol set. VG. $375.00

HAHNEMANN, Samuel. *Organon; or, Art of Healing.* 1900. Boericke Tafel. 6th ed. 244 p. VG. $28.00

HAIBLUM, Isidore. *Mutants Are Coming.* 1984. Doubleday. 1st ed. dj. EX. RS. P1. $17.50

HAIBLUM, Isidore. *Wilk Are Among Us.* 1975. Doubleday. 1st ed. dj. VG. P1. $12.50

HAIG, D. *Dispatches, Dec. 1915-April 1919.* 1920. Dent. Dutton. 10 maps. dj. VG. $50.00

HAIG-BROWN, R.L. *Measure of the Year.* 1950. NY. 1st ed. dj. VG. $40.00

HAIG-BROWN, R.L. *River Never Sleeps.* 1946. NY. Ils 1st ed. 352 p. dj. VG. $45.00

HAIG-BROWN, R.L. *River Never Sleeps.* 1946. Toronto. Collins. 1st ed. dj. RS. VG. $60.00

HAIG-BROWN, R.L. *W Angler: Account of Pacific Salmon & W Trout.* Derrydale. as issued. VG. B2. $450.00

HAIG-BROWN, R.L. *W Angler: Account of Pacific Salmon & W Trout.* 1939. Derrydale. 1/950. 2 vols. acetate djs. M. $650.00

HAIGHT, A.L. *Banned Books.* 1935. NY. 1st ed. 1/1000. $35.00

HAIGHT, A.L. *Biography of a Sportsman.* 1939. NY. 1st ed. boxed. VG. B2. $25.00

HAILEY, Arthur. *In High Places.* nd. Doubleday. VG. P1. $5.00

HAILEY, Arthur. *Overload.* 1979. Doubleday. sgn. 8vo. EX. $25.00

HAILEY, T.L. *Handbook for Pronghorn Antelope Management in TX.* 1979. TX Parks. Ils 59 p. EX. M2. $5.00

HAIN, H.H. *History of Perry Co., PA.* 1922. Harrisburg. Ils. 1086 p. G. T5. $45.00

HAINE, E.A. *Seven Railroads.* 1979. 291 p. $18.50

HAINES, D.J.H. *Luck in All Weathers.* 1941. NY. 1st ed. dj. VG. $15.00

HAINES, E.K. *Tried Temptations: Old & New Cooking.* 1931. NY. dj. $20.00

HAINING, Peter. *Doctor Who Time-Traveler's Guide.* nd. WH Allen. dj. EX. P1. $24.95

HAINING, Peter. *Edgar A. Poe Scrapbook.* 1977. New Eng Lib. 1st ed. inscr. 4to. dj. EX. D1. $75.00

HAINING, Peter. *Evil People.* 1968. Leslie Frewin. dj. G. P1. $15.00

HAINING, Peter. *Ghouls.* nd. Book Club. dj. VG. P1. $4.00

HAINING, Peter. *Ghouls.* 1971. Stein Day. dj. VG. P1. $15.00

HAINING, Peter. *Gothic Tales of Terror.* 1972. Taplinger. 1st ed. dj. VG. P1. $20.00

HAINING, Peter. *H.G. Wells Scrapbook.* 1978. Clarkson Potter. dj. VG. P1. $15.00

HAINING, Peter. *Hollywood Nightmare.* 1970. MacDonald. 1st ed. dj. VG. P1. $15.00

HAINING, Peter. *Nightmare Reader.* 1973. Doubleday. 1st ed. dj. xl. P1. $7.50

HAINING, Peter. *Satanists.* 1969. Spearman. 1st ed. dj. VG. P1. $20.00

HAINING, Peter. *Satanists.* 1970. Taplinger. 1st ed. dj. VG. P1. $17.50

HAINING, Peter. *Wild Night Company.* 1971. Taplinger. 1st ed. dj. EX. P1. $20.00

HAINING, Peter. *Wild Night Company.* 1971. Taplinger. 1st ed. dj. xl. P1. $7.50

HAINING, Peter. *Witchcraft Reader.* 1969. Dobson. 1st ed. dj. EX. P1. $20.00

HAISLET, J.E. *Famous Trees of TX.* 1984. TX A&M. Ils 1st ed. map. EX. M2. $9.00

HAJEK & FORMAN. *Miniatures From the E.* 1960. London. photos. G. $25.00

HAKE, A.E. *Chinese Gordon: Story of A.E. Hake.* 1884. London. Ils. VG. scarce. $45.00

HAKES, Harry. *Hakes Family.* 1889. Wilkes-Barre. Ils 2nd ed. 220 p. G. T5. $25.00

HALAAS, David. *Boom Town Newspapers.* 1981. NM U. Ils. dj. VG. $12.00

HALACY, D.S. *Ripcord.* 1962. Whitman. G. P1. $5.00

HALDANE, A.R.B. *Three Centuries of Scottish Poets.* 1971. Edinburgh. 1st ed. dj. VG. J2. $20.00

HALDEMAN, Jack C. *Vector Analysis.* 1978. Berkley Putnam. 1st ed. dj. VG. P1. $12.00

HALDEMAN, Joe. *Dealing in Futures.* 1985. Viking. 1st ed. dj. EX. P1. $16.95

HALDEMAN, Joe. *Forever War.* 1974. St. Martin. 1st ed. dj. VG. P1. $20.00

HALDEMAN, Joe. *Infinite Dreams.* 1978. St. Martin. 1st ed. dj. VG. P1. $20.00

HALDEMAN, Joe. *Mindbridge.* nd. Book Club. dj. VG. P1. $3.00

HALDEMAN, Joe. *Mindbridge.* 1976. St. Martin. 1st ed. dj. EX. $30.00

HALDEMAN, Joe. *Worlds.* 1981. Viking. 1st ed. dj. VG. P1. $15.00

HALDIMAN, Linda. *Last Born of Elvinwood.* 1980. Avon. 1st pb ed. VG. rare. C1. $12.00

HALE, Edward Everett. *Man Without a Country.* 1908. Altemus. VG. P1. $15.00

HALE, Hilary. *Winter's Crimes 16.* 1984. Macmillan. 1st ed. dj. EX. P1. $15.00

HALE, J.P. *History & Mystery of Kanawha Valley.* 1897. Charleston. 1st ed. 18 p. printed wraps. T5. $42.50

HALE, J.P. *Trans-Allegheny Pioneers.* 1886. Cincinnati. 1st ed. 330 p. T5. $195.00

HALE, John. *Paradise Man.* 1968. Bobbs Merrill. dj. VG. P1. $8.00

HALE, Katherine. *Historic Houses of Canada.* 1952. Toronto. Ryerson Pr. 152 p. M1. $9.50

HALE, S.J. *Flora's Interpreter; or, American Book of Flowers...* 1932. Boston. pls. VG. M1. $135.00

HALE, S.J. *Mrs. Hale's Receipts for the Million..* 1857. Phil. 1st ed. 721 p. orig gilt bdg. EX. $250.00

HALEVY, Daniel. *My Friend, Degas.* 1964. Middletown. Wesleyan U. Ils. 128 p. dj. D2. $25.00

HALEY, Alex. *Roots.* 1976. Doubleday. UCP. gray wraps. VG. $75.00

HALEY, Alex. *Roots.* 1976. Garden City. 1st ed. 578 p. dj. VG. T5. $32.50

HALEY, D. *Seabirds of the E N Pacific & Arctic Waters.* 1984. Pacific Search. Ils. 4to. 214 p. dj. EX. M2. $35.00

HALEY, J.E. *George W. Littlefield, Texan.* 1943. Norman. Ils. dj. EX. $95.00

HALEY, J.E. *Jeff Milton, Good Man With a Gun.* 1948. Norman. Ils 1st issue. dj. EX. $95.00

HALEY, J.E. *Then Came Christmas for Mildred Taitt.* 1962. Amarillo. Shamrock Oil. Ils Hertzog. wraps. $18.00

HALEY, J.E. *XIT Ranch of TX & Early Days of Llanco Estacado.* 1953. Norman. Ils. dj. EX. $50.00

HALEY, J.E. *XIT Ranch of TX.* 1953. OK U. photos. 258 p. G. $15.00

HALFPENNY, J. *Gothic Ornaments in Cathedral Church of York.* 1795. 2 pls. folio. full morocco. $250.00

HALL, A. *Stars Upstream: Life Among the Ozark River.* 1976. Chicago U. Ils. map. 252 p. EX. M2. $8.00

HALL, A. *Wild Food Trail Guide.* 1976. Holt Rinehart. Ils. 230 p. VG. M2. $9.00

HALL, A.O. *Old Whitey's Christmas Trot.* 1857. NY. 16 pls. VG. $65.00

HALL, A.S. *Glossary of Important Symbols.* 1912. Boston. 8vo. VG. $75.00

HALL, Adam. *Sinkiang Executive.* 1978. Doubleday. 1st ed. dj. VG. P1. $15.00

HALL, B.M. *Best Remaining Seats.* 1961. NY. 1st ed. 266 p. dj. VG. B2. $27.50

HALL, Basil. *Voyages.* 1827. Edinburgh. 1st ed. 3 vols. VG. $75.00

HALL, C.M. *Atlantic Bridge to Germany. Vol. I: Baden-Wuerttemberg.* 1974. Logan, UT. Ils. 128 p. G. T5. $8.50

HALL, C.W. *Drifting Around the World.* 1882. Lee Shepard. Ils. 8vo. 372 p. G. $9.00

HALL, D. *Let `Er Buck.* 1973. Dutton. photos. 230 p. G. M2. $5.00

HALL, Delight. *Catalog of Alice Pike Barney Memorial Lending Collection.* 1965. Smithsonian. Ils. 196 p. dj. D2. $45.00

HALL, J.A. *Great Strike on the Q, With History of Organization...* 1889. Elliott/Beezley. 12vo. 124 p. $28.50

HALL, J.C. *When You Care Enough (Hallmark Cards).* 1979. KS City. 1st ed. 271 p. dj. VG. B2. $27.50

HALL, J.N. *Beginning of Tulsa.* c 1933. Tulsa. Ils 1st ed. VG. $85.00

HALL, J.N. *When Denver & I Were Young.* 1937. Denver. private print. 148 p. wraps. G. A3. $50.00

HALL, Leslie. *Judith, Phoenix & Other Anglo-Saxon Poems.* 1902. VG. C1. $19.50

HALL, Louis B. *Knightly Tales of Sir Gawain.* 1st ed. pb. VG. scarce. C1. $12.50

HALL, M.P. *First Principles of Philosophy.* 1935. LA. $25.00

HALL, M.P. *Freemasonry of Ancient Egyptians.* 1937. LA. 1st ed. sgn. 130 p. dj. VG. $55.00

HALL, M.P. *Man: Grand Symbol of the Mysteries.* 1932. LA. 1/1000. 4to. dj. VG. $35.00

HALL, M.P. *Old Testament Wisdom.* 1957. LA. $30.00

HALL, M.P. *Questions & Answers.* 1937. LA. $27.50

HALL, Mary. *Initiates of the Flame.* 1934. Phoenix Pr. Ils Knapp. 3rd ed. VG. C1. $19.50

HALL, Michael. *Leonardo da Vinci on the Human Body.* 1982. NY. reprint of 1952 ed. 506 p. dj. D2. $60.00

HALL, Mrs. S.C. *Swan's Egg. Bound With Poems for Young People.* 1851. Edinburgh. $20.00

HALL, Roger. *19.* nd. Norton. 2nd ed. dj. VG. P1. $8.00

HALL, S.C. *Book of British Ballads.* 1842. London. Jeremiah How. 234 p. VG. C1. $59.00

HALL, W.T. *History of Dekalb Co., TN.* 1915. Nashville. 1st ed. VG. $75.00

HALL, W.W. *Consumption.* 1859. NY. 2nd ed. 290 p. EX. $40.00

HALL, W.W. *Guidebook to Health, Peace & Competence.* 1869. 1st ed. 752 p. gilt bdg. K1. $21.50

HALL & STEINMANN. *Permanence of W.B. Yeats: Selected Criticism.* 1950. NY. Macmillan. 1st ed. dj. VG. $15.00

HALL. *History of State of CO.* 1889-1896. Chicago. 4 vols. full leather. $180.00

HALLE, Armin. *Tanks.* 1971. Crescent. 1st ed. 4to. $20.00

HALLE, L. *Storm Petrel & the Owl of Athena.* 1970. Princeton U. Ils. 268 p. dj. EX. M2. $14.00

HALLET, J.P. *Animal Kitabu.* 1967. Random House. Ils 1st print. dj. EX. M2. $10.00

HALLET, J.P. *Pygmy Kitabu. Origin & Legends of African Pygmies.* 1973. NY. Stated 1st ed. dj. EX. $20.00

HALLIBURTON, David. *Edgar A. Poe: Phenomenological View.* 1973. Princeton. 1st ed. black cloth. dj. EX. D1. $20.00

HALLIBURTON, Richard. *Book of Marvels.* 1937. NY. 1st ed. sgn. dj. $15.00

HALLIDAY, Brett. *Dividend on Death.* 1939. Holt. 1st ed. dj. VG. P1. $30.00

HALLIDAY, Brett. *Killers From the Keys.* 1961. Torquil. 1st ed. dj. xl. P1. $7.50

HALLIDAY, Brett. *Murder & the Married Virgin.* 1948. Triangle. dj. VG. P1. $12.00

HALLIDAY, Brett. *She Woke to Darkness.* 1954. Torquil. 1st ed. dj. VG. P1. $20.00

HALLIDAY, Brett. *Taste for Violence.* nd. Book Club. dj. VG. P1. $3.50

HALLIDAY, Brett. *This Is It Michael Shayne.* nd. Book Club. VG. P1. $2.50

HALLION, R.P. *Naval Air War in Korea.* 1986. Baltimore. Ils 1st ed. 244 p. dj. EX. T5. $17.50

HALLION & CROUCH. *Apollo: Ten Years Since Tranquility Base.* 1979. WA. photos. dj. VG. T5. $15.00

HALLOCK, Charles. *Angler's Reminiscences.* 1913. Cincinnati. Ils/inscr Pond. VG. $125.00

HALLOCK, Charles. *Camp Life in FL: Handbook for Sportsmen & Settlers.* 1876. US Forest Stream. 12mo. 348 p. VG. $65.00

HALLOCK, Charles. *Fishing Tourist.* 1873. NY. VG. $35.00

HALLS, L.K. *White-Tailed Deer Ecology & Management.* 1984. Stackpole. Ils. 870 p. dj. EX. M2. $35.00

HALPER, Albert. *Good-Bye, Union Square.* 1970. Chicago. dj. VG. $15.00

HALPERN, Daniel. *Life Among Others.* 1978. NY. 1st ed. dj. EX. $9.00

HALPIN, W.T. *Hoof Beats.* 1938. Lippincott. 1/1500. 4to. plaid bdg. VG. $75.00

HALSEY, Ashley. *Illustrating for the Saturday Evening Post.* 1951. Boston. Arlington House/Writer. 160 p. D2. $50.00

HALSEY, Ashley. *Who Fired First Shot & Other Untold Stories of Civil War.* 1963. NY. 1st ed. dj. EX. $12.00

HALSEY, C. *Halsey's Homeopathic Guide.* 1885. Chicago. 262 p. $50.00

HALSEY, Margaret. *Color-Blind: White Woman Looks at the Negro.* 1946. Simon Schuster. 1st ed. 163 p. dj. M1. $6.00

HALSTEAD, B.W. *Dangerous Marine Animals.* 1959. Cornell. Ils. 146 p. dj. EX. M2. $9.00

HALSTEAD, Murat. *Illustrious Life of William McKinley.* 1901. inscr/sgn. G. $15.00

HALSTEAD, Murat. *War Between Russia & Japan.* 1904. np. VG. $20.00

HALSTEAD, Ward. *Brain & Intelligence.* 1947. Chicago. 1st ed. VG. $60.00

HAMBIDGE, Jay. *Dynamic Symmetry: Greek Vase.* 1920. New Haven. Yale. 161 p. G. $35.00

HAMBLIN, H.T. *Story of My Life.* 1947. England. $10.00

HAMER, Philip. *Guide to Archives & Manuscripts in the US.* 1961. Yale. VG. $22.00

HAMERSTROM F. *Eagle to the Sky.* 1970. IA U. Ils. 142 p. EX. M2. $14.00

HAMERTON, P.G. *Intellectual Life.* 1899. Roycroft. 1/960. 4to. VG. D1. $150.00

HAMERTON, P.G. *Landscape.* 1885. London. Seeley. 1st ed. 386 p. gilt bdg. D2. $385.00

HAMERTON, P.G. *Portfolio Papers.* 1889. Boston. Robert Bros. VG. $25.00

HAMILL, Dorothy. *On & Off the Ice.* 1983. NY. 1st ed. dj. VG. B2. $15.00

HAMILTON, A. *Memoirs of Count de Grammont.* 1928. NY. Ils. dj. EX. $14.00

HAMILTON, Bob. *Gene Autry & the Redwood Pirates.* nd. Whitman. G. P1. $5.00

HAMILTON, Bruce. *To Be Hanged.* nd. Crime Club. VG. P1. $17.50

HAMILTON, Edmond. *Star of Life.* nd. Book Club. dj. VG. P1. $6.00

HAMILTON, H.S. *Reminiscences of a Veteran.* 1897. Concord. 1st ed. VG. $35.00

HAMILTON, H.W. *Dr. Syntax.* 1969. Kent, OH. Ils 1st ed. 340 p. dj. VG. T5. $8.50

HAMILTON, L.D. *Hotel Chelsea & the Sound.* 1980. Orange. UCP. EX. $25.00

HAMILTON, M. *Freedom of Henry Meredyth.* 1897. Appleton. 1st ed. $12.00

HAMILTON, P.J. *Colonial Mobile.* 1897. Boston/NY. 1st ed. 446 p. EX. M2. $75.00

HAMILTON, Patrick. *Resources of AZ: Its Mineral, Farming, Grazing & Timber...* 1884. San Francisco. Bancroft. 3rd ed. EX. A3. $200.00

HAMILTON, Thomas. *Men & Manners in America.* 1833. 1st Am ed. 410 p. original bdg. EX. K1. $42.50

HAMILTON, W.D. *Recollections of a Cavalryman of Civil War After 50 Years.* 1915. Columbus. Ils 1st ed. 309 p. scarce. T5. $175.00

HAMILTON, W.J. *American Mammals: Their Lives, Habits & Economic Relations.* 1939. McGraw Hill. Ils. 434 p. EX. M2. $14.00

HAMILTON. *Kvinnan I. Brahmas, Buddhas Och Muhameds Lander.* 1902. Stockholm. Ils Froleen. VG. $75.00

HAMMACHER, A.M. *Jacques Lipchitz: His Sculpture.* nd. Abrams. Ils 176 p. dj. D2. $95.00

HAMMATT, Abraham. *Hammatt Papers: Early Inhabitants of Ipswich, MA...* 1890. Baltimore. 1st book ed. 8vo. cloth. M. T1. $40.00

HAMMERSTROM F. *Harrier: Hawk of the Marshes, Hawk Ruled by a Mouse.* 1986. Smithsonian. Ils 172 p. dj. EX. M2. $24.00

HAMMETT, Dashiell. *Big Knockover.* ND. BOMC. VG. P1. $7.50

HAMMETT, Dashiell. *Blood Money.* 1943. Tower. VG. P1. $25.00

HAMMETT, Dashiell. *Blood Money.* 1944. Tower. 2nd ed. VG. P1. $20.00

HAMMETT, Dashiell. *Creeps by Night.* 1931. John Day. 1st ed. P1. $250.00

HAMMETT, Dashiell. *Creeps by Night.* 1932. John Day. 2nd ed. G. P1. $25.00

HAMMETT, Dashiell. *Creeps by Night.* 1932. Tudor. 2nd ed. G. P1. $45.00

HAMMETT, Dashiell. *Creeps by Night.* 1944. Forum. 2nd ed. VG. P1. $20.00

HAMMETT, Dashiell. *Dain Curse.* 1929. Knopf. 1st ed. 8vo. VG. EX. $125.00

HAMMETT, Dashiell. *Dain Curse.* 1929. NY. 1st ed. 1st print. 272 p. G. T5. $95.00

HAMMETT, Dashiell. *Dashiell Hammett's Mystery Omnibus.* 1944. Forum. VG. P1. $25.00

HAMMETT, Dashiell. *Glass Key.* nd. Grosset Dunlap. VG. P1. $6.00

HAMMETT, Dashiell. *Maltese Falcon.* nd. Book Club. VG. P1. $4.00

HAMMETT, Dashiell. *Red Harvest.* 1929. NY. 1st ed. red cloth. $295.00

HAMMETT, Dashiell. *Woman in the Dark.* 1988. NY. 1st ed. dj. EX. $12.50

HAMMIL, Joel. *Limbo.* 1980. Arbor House. 1st ed. dj. VG. P1. $12.50

HAMMOND, N. *20th-C Wildlife Artists.* 1986. Overlook. Ils. folio. 224 p. dj. EX. M2. $60.00

HAMMOND, P. *French Undressing Naughty: Post Cards From 1900 to 1920.* 1988. London. Ils. quarto. $22.00

HAMMOND, Ralph. *Antebellum Mansions of AL.* 1951. Bonanza. dj. VG. $13.00

HAMMOND, Ralph. *Quaint & Historic Forts of N America.* 1915. Phil. VG. $50.00

HAMMOND, Richard. *San Joaquin Valley.* 1979. Visalia. dj. VG. $17.50

HAMMOND. *Sexual Impotence in the Male.* 1883. NY. 1st ed. EX. $35.00

HAMNER, L.V. *Short Grass & Longhorns.* 1943. Norman. Ils. dj. EX. $90.00

HAMPE, T. *Der Zinnsoldat.* 1924. Berlin. VG. $25.00

HAMPSON, G.F. *Fauna of British India: Moths.* 1976. India. Ils. 609 p. EX. M2. $45.00

HAMPTON, Taylor. *Nickel Plate Road.* 1947. 365 p. $25.00

HAMPTON, Taylor. *Nickel Plate Road.* 1947. World. Ils 1st ed. 365 p. xl. EX. $7.50

HAMPTON, Wade. *Family Letters of Three Wade Hamptons, 1782-1901.* nd. SC U Pr. Ils 1st ed. 181 p. dj. $55.00

HAMSUN, Knut. *Chapter the Last.* 1929. NY. 1st Am ed. dj. VG. $25.00

HAMZETT, Car. *Light of Asia.* 1926. Bodley Head. 1/3000. TEG. EX. $90.00

HANAUER, E. *Rocks & Minerals of the W US: Collector's Guide.* 1976. Barnes. Ils. 237 p. dj. EX. M2. $10.00

HANBURY, David. *Sport & Travel in N Canada.* 1904. London. 2 fld maps. VG. $110.00

HANCE, Robert A. *Destination Earth II.* 1977. Vantage. dj. VG. P1. $8.00

HANCER, Kevin. *Paperback Price Guide #1.* 1980. Overstreet. VG. P1. $15.00

HANCOCK, Mrs. W.S. *Reminiscences of Winfield Scott Hancock.* 1887. Webster. Ils 1st ed. 340 p. K1. $32.50

HANCOCK & ELLIOTT. *Herons of the World.* 1978. Harper Row. Ils 1st Am ed. 304 p. dj. EX. M2. $110.00

HANCOCK. *Jiu-Jitsu Combat Tricks.* 1904. Putnam. Ils. VG. $10.00

HANCOCKS, D. *Master Builders of the Animal World.* 1973. Harper Row. Ils 1st Am ed. 144 p. dj. EX. M2. $12.00

HAND, S. *Signed Miniatures.* nd. London. 6 pls. 4to. EX. J2. $75.00

HANDLER, Andrew. *Holocaust in Hungary.* 1982. AL. 1st ed. dj. VG. $10.00

HANFF, Helene. *Duchess of Bloomsbury Street.* 1973. Phil. 1st ed. dj. VG. B2. $20.00

HANIGHEN, F.C. *Santa Anna: Napoleon of the W.* 1934. NY. Ils 1st ed. 326 p. dj. VG. B2. $35.00

HANISH, Otomen. *Ainyahita in Pearls.* 1913. Chicago. $50.00

HANKINS, R.M. *Lonesome River Range.* 1951. Hodder Stoughton Yellowjacket. P1. $10.00

HANLEY, W. *Natural History in America From M. Catesby to R. Carson.* 1977. Quadrangle. Ils. 339 p. dj. EX. M2. $18.00

HANNA, A.J. *Bibliography of Writing of Irving Bacheller.* 1939. Rollins. 12mo. 48 p. wraps. G. $10.00

HANNA, A.J. & K.A. *Lake Okeechobee, Wellspring of the Everglades.* 1948. Bobbs Merrill. Ils 1st ed. 379 p. EX. M2. $18.00

HANNAH, Barry. *Boomerang.* 1989. Boston. 1st ed. sgn. dj. VG. $35.00

HANNAH, Barry. *Captain Maximus.* 1985. NY. Knopf. 1st ed. dj. EX. T6. $15.00

HANNAH, Barry. *Hey Jack!* 1987. NY. AP. sgn. $65.00

HANNAH, Barry. *Hey Jack!* 1987. NY. UCP. printed pink wraps. RS. $55.00

HANNAH, Barry. *Hey Jack!* 1987. NY. 1st ed. sgn. dj. EX. $22.00

HANNAH, Barry. *Power & Light: Novella for Screen From Idea by Altman.* 1983. Palaemon. 1st ed. 1/75. sgn. EX. $75.00

HANNAH, Barry. *Tennis Handsome.* 1983. NY. 1st ed. sgn. dj. VG. $40.00

HANNAH, D. *Isak Dinesen & Karen Blixen.* 1971. NY. 1st ed. dj. VG. B2. $15.00

HANNUM, Alberta. *Spin a Silver Dollar.* 1946. Viking. Ils Yazz. dj. VG. $8.00

HANNUM, Alberta. *Spin a Silver Dollar: Story of Desert Trading Post.* 1950. Viking. Ils Little No-Shirt. 173 p. VG. M2. $5.00

HANRATTY, Peter. *Book of Mordred.* 1988. 1st pb ed. VG. C1. $3.50

HANS, F.M. *Great Sioux Nation.* 1907. Chicago. Ils 1st ed. 575 p. B2. $95.00

HANS, T. *NW to Hudson Bay: Life & Times of Jens Munk.* 1970. London. Collins. Ils. 348 p. dj. EX. M2. $16.00

HANSARD, G.A. *Trout & Salmon Fishing in Wales.* 1834. London. 16mo. rebound. $60.00

HANSCOM, W.W. *Archaeology of the Cable Car.* 1970. Pasadena. Ils 1st ed. 121 p. dj. VG. T5. $22.50

HANSEN, Harry. *Civil War.* 1962. NY. 1st ed. dj. VG. $8.00

HANSEN, Joseph. *Gravedigger.* 1982. NY. 1st ed. dj. EX. $15.00

HANSEN, Joseph. *Man Everybody Was Afraid Of.* 1978. NY. 1st ed. dj. EX. $20.00

HANSEN, Joseph. *Nightwork.* 1984. NY. Holt. 1st ed. dj. EX. $10.00

HANSEN, Joseph. *Skinflick.* 1979. Hold Rinehart. 1st ed. dj. EX. P1. $10.00

HANSEN, K.K. *Heroes Behind Barbed Wire.* 1957. Princeton. Ils 1st ed. 345 p. dj. G. T5. $9.50

HANSEN, Oscar. *Chien-Mi-Lo: Satiric Prose Fantasy.* 1927. Ils Shoji Osato. 1/700. sgn. VG. $15.00

HANSEN, Robert P. *Back to the Wall.* 1957. Mill Morrow. 1st ed. dj. VG. P1. $10.00

HANSEN, Robert P. *Deadly Purpose.* 1958. Mill Morrow. 1st ed. dj. VG. P1. $20.00

HANSEN, Robert P. *There's Always a Payoff.* 1959. Mill Morrow. VG. P1. $10.00

HANSEN, Ron. *Desperadoes.* 1979. Knopf. 1st ed. dj. EX. $10.00

HANSEN, T. *Arabia Felix: Danish Expedition of 1761-1767.* 1964. Harper Row. Ils 1st ed. 381 p. EX. M2. $27.00

HANSFORD, S. Howard. *Chinese Jade Carving.* 1950. London. Ils. maps. 145 p. dj. D2. $85.00

HANSON, J.C.M. *American & English Genealogies in Library of Congress.* 1910. Lib Congress. 805 p. xl. A3. $40.00

HANSON, J.W. *NY's Awful Excursion Boat Horror.* 1904. CA. Ils Slocum. 326 p. $45.00

HANSON, J.W. *World's Congress of Religions at Columbian Exposition.* 1894. Ils. 1196 p. green bdg. G. $27.00

HANSON, Maurice. *Pierpont the Foxhound.* 1939. NY. Ils Carlisle. 1st ed. $20.00

HAPGOOD, C.H. *Earth's Shifting Crust.* 1958. NY. Ils 1st ed. 438 p. dj. VG. B2. $15.00

HAPGOOD, Hutchins. *Spirit of Ghetto.* 1909. NY. Ils Epstein. 2nd ed. $35.00

HARBOR. *Labor in a Changing America.* 1966. NY. 2nd print. dj. VG. $15.00

HARCOURT, H. *FL Fruits & How To Raise Them.* 1886. Morton. Revised Enlarged ed. 347 p. VG. M2. $35.00

HARD, Curtis V. *Banners in the Air.* 1988. Kent. Ils. 147 p. dj. M. T5. $25.00

HARD, W. *CT.* 1947. NY. 1st ed. River Series. dj. VG. B2. $20.00

HARDEN, William. *History of Savannah & S GA.* 1981. Atlanta. Ils. 2 vols. EX. $30.00

HARDIE, James. *Description of the City of NY.* 1827. 1st ed. fld map. G. $90.00

HARDIE, James. *Description of the City of NY.* 1827. NY. 1st ed. VG. $125.00

HARDIE, John L. *22 Strange Stories.* nd. Art & Educational. 2nd ed. VG. P1. $15.00

HARDIN, A.C. *American Rides the Liners.* 1956. NY. Ils Enslow. presentation. dj. G. $18.00

HARDING, A.R. *Ginseng & Other Medicinal Plants.* 1908. Columbus. Harding. Revised ed. photos. VG. $25.00

HARDING, Chester. *Sketch of Chester Harding, Artist, Drawn by His Own Hand.* 1970. NY. Unabridged reprint of 1929 ed. D2. $37.50

HARDING, J.W. *Gate of the Kiss.* 1902. Lathrop. Ils Varian. 1st ed. $12.00

HARDING, Jane. *Arthurian Legend: Check List of Books in Newberry Library.* 1938. Chicago. 1st ed. stiff wraps. VG. C1. $12.50

HARDING, Jane. *Silver Land.* pb. VG. C1. $3.50

HARDING, Lee. *Weeping Sky.* 1977. Cassell Australia. dj. EX. P1. $20.00

HARDING, Robert. *Boy's Own Annual Vol. 63, 1940-1941.* 1941. Lutterworth. VG. P1. $30.00

HARDING, Walter. *Days of Henry Thoreau: A Biography.* 1965. Knopf. 1st ed. dj. VG. J2. $20.00

HARDING, William. *War in S Africa & the Dark Continent.* 1899. Chicago. Ils. map. 4to. EX. $18.00

HARDING. *Magic Fire.* 1953. Bobbs Merrill. 1st ed. VG. $5.50

HARDT & AUDOVIN-DEBREVIL. *Across the Sahara by Motor Car.* 1924. NY. Appleton. Ils. VG. $10.00

HARDWICK, E. *Sleepless Nights.* 1979. NY. 1st ed. dj. EX. $15.00

HARDWICK, Michael & Mollie. *Sherlock Holmes Companion.* 1962. John Murray. 1st ed. dj. VG. P1. $40.00

HARDWICK, Michael. *Sherlock Holmes: My Life & Crimes.* 1984. Garden City. Stated 1st ed. 208 p. dj. M. $35.00

HARDWICK, Richard. *Mystery of Black Schooner.* 1966. Whitman. EX. P1. $10.00

HARDWICKE, R. *Petroleum & Gas Bibliography.* 1937. Austin. 1st ed. VG. $25.00

HARDY, F. *Early Life of Thomas Hardy.* 1928. NY. xl. VG. $25.00

HARDY, Lindsay. *Nightshade Ring.* 1954. Appleton Century Crofts. dj. P1. $7.50

HARDY, R.M. *High Adventure.* 1954. CA. $4.00

HARDY, Thomas. *Duke's Appearance.* 1927. NY. Ltd ed. 1/89. EX. $50.00

HARDY, Thomas. *Dynasts.* 1904. London. 1st ed. scarce. P3. $45.00

HARDY, Thomas. *Far From the Madding Crowd.* 1918. Harper. Modern Classic. VG. $8.00

HARDY, Thomas. *Group of Noble Dames.* 1891. London. 2nd issue. VG. $55.00

HARDY, Thomas. *Human Shows & Far Phantasies.* 1925. London. dj. VG. $95.00

HARDY, Thomas. *Jude the Obscure.* 1896. London. 1st ed. P3. $145.00

HARDY, Thomas. *Jude the Obscure.* 1896. NY. 1st Am ed. $60.00

HARDY, Thomas. *Jude the Obscure.* 1903. Harper. Ils. 12 pls. 488 p. VG. $16.00

HARDY, Thomas. *Late Lyrics & Earlier.* 1922. London. 1st ed. dj. EX. $65.00

HARDY, Thomas. *Late Lyrics & Earlier.* 1922. Macmillan. 1st ed. VG. J2. $25.00

HARDY, Thomas. *Life's Little Ironies.* 1894. NY. 1st ed. EX. $45.00

HARDY, Thomas. *Life's Little Ironies.* 1894. NY. Harper. 1st Am ed. VG. $20.00

HARDY, Thomas. *Old Clock.* 1946. Portland. Anthoensen. 12 p. green wraps. EX. $65.00

HARDY, Thomas. *Old Mrs. Chundle.* 1929. NY. 1st ed. 1/742. glassine dj. EX. $35.00

HARDY, Thomas. *Pair of Blue Eyes.* 1895. NY. 1st ed. VG. $35.00

HARDY, Thomas. *Return of the Native.* 1929. Harper. Ils Leighton. Deluxe ed. sgn. VG. $60.00

HARDY, Thomas. *Return of the Native.* 1937. Book League. 1st ed. VG. $10.00

HARDY, Thomas. *Satires of Circumstance.* 1914. London. 1st ed. presentation. VG. $50.00

HARDY, Thomas. *Short Stories.* 1928. London. dj. EX. $40.00

HARDY, Thomas. *Trumpet Major.* 1896. NY. not 1st ed. VG. $15.00

HARDY, Thomas. *Under the Greenwood Tree.* nd. NY. 1st ed. G. $15.00

HARDY, Thomas. *Winter Words.* 1928. London. 1st ed. dj. EX. $95.00

HARDY, Thomas. *Woodlanders.* 1909. NY. not 1st ed. G. $10.00

HARDY, W.J. *Bookplates.* 1893. Kegan Paul. 1st ed. VG. J2. $45.00

HARDY & DARRELL. *American Locomotives 1871-1881.* 1950. Oakland, CA. Ils. plans. dj. M. $65.00

HARE, C.E. *Language of Field Sports.* 1949. Scribner. Ils Revised ed. dj. $15.00

HAREL, Isser. *House on Garibaldi Street.* 1975. NY. Viking. dj. EX. $20.00

HAREL, Isser. *House on Garibaldi Street.* 1975. Viking. G. M1. $4.50

HARGRAVE, C.P. *History of Playing Cards & Bibliography of Cards & Gaming.* 1930. Boston. Ils. 367 p. red cloth. VG. $225.00

HARGRAVE, John. *Harbottle.* 1924. Lippincott. G. P1. $6.00

HARGREAVES, H.A. *N by 2000.* 1975. Martin Assn. 1st ed. dj. EX. RS. P1. $25.00

HARGREAVES, H.A. *N by 2000.* 1975. Martin Assn. 1st ed. dj. VG. P1. $15.00

HARING, C.H. *Los Bucaneros de las Indias Occidentales en El Siglo XVII.* 1939. Paris. 274 p. wraps. fair. $12.00

HARKNESS, Albert. *Select Oration of Marcus Tutius Cicero.* 1882. 398 p. TB. EX. $5.00

HARLAN, G.H. *San Francisco Bay Ferry Boats.* 1967. Berkeley. Ils. 195 p. dj. VG. T5. $25.00

HARLAN. *Salt-Water Fishing Tackle.* 1930. NY. Ils. inscr. EX. $55.00

HARLAND, Marion. *Common Sense in the Household.* 1871. NY. Scribner. 1st ed. VG. $35.00

HARLEY, G.W. *Native African Medicine.* 1941. Cambridge, MA. 1st ed. 294 p. dj. T5. $95.00

HARLEY, G.W. *Native African Medicine.* 1941. Harvard. 1st ed. presentation. sgn. J2. $50.00

HARLEY, L.R. *Life of Charles Thomson.* 1900. Jacobs. 1/500. VG. $37.50

HARLOW, A.F. *Brass-Pounders.* 159 p. $18.50

HARLOW, A.F. *Paper Chase.* 1940. NY. 1st ed. dj. VG. B2. $40.00

HARMAN, Fred. *Red Death on the Range.* 1940. Whitman. Big Little Book. VG. P1. $15.00

HARMON, Tom. *Pilots Also Pray.* 1944. NY. Ils 1st ed. 184 p. dj. G. T5. $25.00

HARNSBERGER, Caroline. *Mark Twain at Your Fingertips.* 1948. NY. 1st ed. 559 p. dj. EX. $40.00

HARPENDING, A. *Great Diamond Hoax.* c 1913. San Francisco. 1st ed. VG. $12.50

HARPER, D.A. *Good Company.* 1982. Ils. 17 p. SftCvr. $14.50

HARPER, F. *Birds of the Ungava Peninsula.* 1958. KS U. Ils. maps. 171 p. M2. $10.00

HARPER, Frank. *Night Climb: Story of the Skiing 10th.* 1946. NY. 1st ed. 216 p. dj. VG. T5. $25.00

HARPER, George W. *Gypsy Earth.* 1982. Doubleday. dj. EX. P1. $10.00

HARPER & HARPER. *Old Ranches.* 1936. Dallas. Ils. wraps. EX. $75.00

HARPER PUBLISHING. *Harper's Cookbook Encyclopedia.* 1902. 473 p. VG. $55.00

HARRER, Heinrich. *Seven Years in Tibet.* 1954. Dutton. Ils 1st ed. 314 p. dj. EX. M2. $14.00

HARRER, Heinrich. *White Spider (Mountain Climbing) Eiger's N Face.* 1960. Dutton. 1st Am ed. dj. M. $65.00

HARRIMAN, F.J. *Mission to N.* 1941. Lippincott. 1st ed. sgn. $8.50

HARRINGTON, Joseph. *Last Doorbell.* nd. Book Club. dj. G. P1. $3.00

HARRIS, A.C. *AK & the Klondike Gold Fields.* 1897. 528 p. VG. B1. $25.00

HARRIS, A.H. *Ecological Distrbution of Vertebrates in San Juan Basin.* 1963. NM Mus. photos. 63 p. M2. $5.00

HARRIS, Arthur. *Bomber Offensive.* 1947. NY. 1st Am ed. 288 p. G. T5. $19.50

HARRIS, Bruce & Seena. *Complete Etchings of Rembrandt.* 1970. Bounty/Crown. Ils. 251 p. D2. $40.00

HARRIS, C.O. *Slide Rule Simplified.* 1943. Chicago. VG. $8.00

HARRIS, C.V. *Political Power in Birmingham: 1871-1921.* 1977. Knoxville. Ils. 318 p. dj. EX. $15.00

HARRIS, Dean. *By Path & Trail.* 1908. Chicago. Ils 1st ed. VG. $35.00

HARRIS, E. *Spanish Painting.* 1937. Paris/NY. Hyperion. pls. dj. D2. $55.00

HARRIS, Frank. *Bernard Shaw.* 1931. Gollancz. 2nd ed. VG. P1. $17.50

HARRIS, Frank. *Bernard Shaw.* 1931. Simon Schuster. 1st ed. VG. $50.00

HARRIS, Frank. *Joan La Romee.* 1926. London. Ltd 1st ed. 1/350. sgn. VG. $90.00

HARRIS, Frank. *Look of the Old W.* 1955. Bonanza. Ils. 4to. 316 p. dj. EX. M2. $14.00

HARRIS, Frank. *My Life & Loves.* 1922. Frank Harris. G. P1. $25.00

HARRIS, Frank. *My Life & Loves.* 1963. Grove Pr. 1st print. VG. $25.00

HARRIS, Frank. *My Life Vol. 2.* 1925. Frank Harris. VG. P1. $25.00

HARRIS, H. *American Labor.* 1939. G. $15.00

HARRIS, Herbert. *John Creasey's Crime Collection 1984.* 1908. St. Martin. dj. EX. P1. $15.00

HARRIS, J.C. *Chronicles of Aunt Minervy Ann.* 1899. Scribner. 1st ed. VG. J2. $35.00

HARRIS, J.C. *Daddy Jake the Runaway & Short Stories Told After Dark.* 1889. NY. Century. Ils Kemble. 1st ed. 4to. $125.00

HARRIS, J.C. *Free Joe.* 1975. Savannah. 232 p. dj. EX. $25.00

HARRIS, J.C. *Joel Chandler Harris: Editor, Essayist.* 1951. Chapel Hill. 1st ed. dj. VG. B2. $12.50

HARRIS, J.C. *Little Union Scout.* 1904. NY. 1st ed. VG. $62.00

HARRIS, J.C. *Making of a Statesman.* 1902. McClure. 1st ed. VG. J2. $25.00

HARRIS, J.C. *Plantation Pageants.* 1899. Boston. 1st ed. $50.00

HARRIS, J.C. *Sister Jane.* 1896. Boston. 1st ed. $25.00

HARRIS, J.C. *Tar Baby & Other Rhymes of Uncle Remus.* 1904. Appleton. Ils Frost/Kemble. 1st ed. TEG. EX. $125.00

HARRIS, J.C. *Uncle Remus & Brer Rabbit.* 1907. Stokes. G. $200.00

HARRIS, J.C. *Uncle Remus: His Songs & Sayings.* 1895. Appleton. Ils Frost. New Revised ed. $87.50

HARRIS, J.C. *Uncle Remus: His Songs & Sayings.* 1930. Appleton. Ils Frost. VG. $30.00

HARRIS, J.T. *Beregrine Falcon in Greenland: Observing Endangered Species.* 1981. MO U. Ils. 254 p. EX. M2. $11.00

HARRIS, John. *Artist & the Country House: History of Country House...* 1979. London. Ils 1st ed. square 4to. dj. M. T1. $200.00

HARRIS, John. *Catalog of British Drawings for Architecture, Decoration...* 1971. Upper Saddle River. 355 p. VG. T5. $95.00

HARRIS, John. *Old Trade of Killing.* 1966. Hutchinson. 1st ed. dj. xl. P1. $6.00

HARRIS, L. *Butterflies of GA.* 1972. OK U. Ils 1st ed. 326 p. dj. EX. M2. $15.00

HARRIS, M. *Field Guide to Birds of the Galapagos.* 1982. London. Collins. Ils Revised ed. EX. M2. $25.00

HARRIS, MacDonald. *Little People.* 1986. Morrow. 1st Am ed. dj. M. T6. $25.00

HARRIS, Mark. *Saul Bellow, Durmlin Woodchuck.* 1980. GA. 1st ed. dj. EX. $12.50

HARRIS, Mark. *Something About a Soldier.* 1957. 1st ed. 175 p. $15.00

HARRIS, Mark. *Southpaw.* 1953. Indianapolis/NY. 1st ed. dj. EX. $30.00

HARRIS, R.B. *Grizzly Bear Population Monitoring.* 1986. MT U. 80 p. EX. M2. $7.00

HARRIS, Richard. *Illustrations in Advocacy.* 1885. St. Louis. 1st Am ed. G. $25.00

HARRIS, T.M. *Assassination of Lincoln.* 1892. Boston. Ils 1st ed. VG. B2. $70.00

HARRIS, T.M. *Minor Encyclopedia; or, Cabinet of General Knowledge.* 1803. Boston. 12mo. 307 p. 1 vol only. G. G2. $19.00

HARRIS, Thomas. *Red Dragon.* 1981. NY. Putnam. 1st ed. dj. M. $35.00

HARRIS, Thomas. *Red Dragon.* 1981. Putnam. 1st ed. dj. VG. P1. $15.00

HARRIS, Thomas. *Silence of the Lambs.* 1988. St. Martin. ARC. wraps. M. $20.00

HARRIS, W. *Age of the Rainmaker.* 1971. London. 1st ed. dj. RS. EX. $20.00

HARRIS, W. *Ascent to Omai.* 1970. London. 1st ed. dj. EX. $20.00

HARRIS, W.C. *Portraits of Game & Wild Animals of S Africa.* 1969. Cape Town. Balkema. Ils. 195 p. dj. EX. M2. $110.00

HARRIS, Walter. *Story of Medicine in WI.* 1958. El Paso. 1st ed. sgn. dj. VG. J2. $20.00

HARRIS & SCHAAR. *Die Handzeichnungen von Andrea Sacchi & Carlo Maratta.* 1967. Dusseldorf. Ils. 348 p. D2. $75.00

HARRIS. *Constitution of Free & Accepted Masons.* 1798. Grand Lodge of MA. G. $127.00

HARRIS. *Gold Coins of the Americas With Values.* 1971. Anco. $12.50

HARRIS. *Guidebook of Modern Latin American Coins.* 1966. Whitman. 12mo. EX. $7.50

HARRISON, Constance. *Woman's Handiwork in Modern Homes.* 1881. NY. Ils 242 p. G. $24.00

HARRISON, Frederick. *Book About Books.* 1946. London. Ils. pls. $20.00

HARRISON, G.L. *Remains of William Penn.* 1882. Phil. Ils 94 p. TEG. G. T5. $9.50

HARRISON, H. *Contemporary American Women Poets.* 1936. NY. presentation. 4to. 320 p. VG. $25.00

HARRISON, H. *Larry Rivers.* 1984. 1st ed. dj. EX. $10.00

HARRISON, H.H. *Wood Warblers' World.* 1984. Simon Schuster. Ils 1st ed. 335 p. dj. EX. M2. $25.00

HARRISON, H.S. *V.V.'s Eyes.* 1913. Houghton Mifflin. 1st ed. $12.00

HARRISON, Harry & Aldiss. *Best SF 1969.* 1970. Putnam. dj. VG. P1. $10.00

HARRISON, Harry. *Astounding.* 1973. Random House. 1st ed. dj. VG. P1. $10.00

HARRISON, Harry. *Bill the Galactic Hero.* 1965. Doubleday. 1st ed. poor. xl. P1. $4.00

HARRISON, Harry. *Nova 1.* 1970. Delacorte. 1st ed. G. P1. $10.00

HARRISON, Harry. *Nova 4.* 1974. Walker. 1st ed. dj. VG. P1. $10.00

HARRISON, Harry. *SF Author's Choice 4.* 1974. Putnam. dj. VG. P1. $10.00

HARRISON, Harry. *Year 2000.* nd. Book Club. dj. VG. $3.00

HARRISON, J.T. *Story of the Dining Fork.* 1927. Ltd ed. 370 p. VG. J4. $45.00

HARRISON, Jack. *Flight From Youth.* 1973. np. Ils. 85 p. wraps. VG. T5. $15.00

HARRISON, Jim. *Letters to Yesenin.* 1973. Fremont. 1/1000. wraps. VG. $150.00

HARRISON, Jim. *Sundog.* 1984. NY. Dutton. 1st ed. dj. EX. T6. $15.00

HARRISON, L.H. *Civil War in KY.* 1975. Ltd ed. 116 p. EX. J4. $27.50

HARRISON, M. John. *Storm of Wings.* 1980. Doubleday. 1st ed. dj. EX. P1. $20.00

HARRISON, M. John. *Storm of Wings.* 1980. Doubleday. 1st ed. dj. xl. P1. $5.00

HARRISON, Martin. *Pre-Raphaelite Paintings & Graphics.* 1973. London/NY. Ils Revised ed. D2. $18.50

HARRISON, Michael. *Higher Things.* nd. MacDonald. VG. P1. $20.00

HARRISON, Michael. *In the Footsteps of Sherlock Holmes.* 1960. NY. Stated 1st Am ed. 292 p. dj. VG. $15.00

HARRISON, Michael. *World of Sherlock Holmes.* 1975. NY. Stated 1st Am ed. 227 p. dj. M. $27.50

HARRISON, Michael. *World of Sherlock Holmes.* 1975. NY. 1st ed. dj. EX. $20.00

HARRISON, P. *Seabirds: Identification Guide.* 1985. Houghton. Ils Revised ed. 448 p. dj. EX. M2. $25.00

HARRISON, P.D. *Stars & Stripes & Other American Flags.* 1906. Boston. 1st ed. 8vo. 419 p. xl. VG. $15.00

HARRISON & STOVER. *Stonehenge: Where Atlantis Died.* 1983. pb. VG. C1. $3.50

HARRISSE. *Discovery of N America.* 1961. Amsterdam. maps. 802 p. VG. $50.00

HARRITY & MARTIN. *Eleanor Roosevelt: Her Life in Pictures.* 1958. NY. 1st ed. dj. G. $15.00

HARROP, D. *History of Gregynog Press.* 1890. Pinner. Ils. 4to. $45.00

HARROW. *Atlas of Modern Geography.* 1870. London. 30 maps. tall quarto. A3. $150.00

HARRSEN, Meta. *Central European Manuscripts in Pierpont Morgan Library.* 1958. NY. 1st ed. 1/850. slipcase. $100.00

HARRSEN, Meta. *Italian Manuscripts in Pierpont Morgan Library.* 1953. NY. 1st ed. 1/750. #d. slipcase. $100.00

HARSHAW, Ruth. *Council of Gods.* 1931. Chicago. Ils Kaissaroff. sgn. $25.00

HARSHMAN, J.L. *Centennial History of Friendship Lodge No. 84...* 1927. Hagerstown, MD. 90 p. $12.50

HART, B.H.L. *Real War, 1914-1918.* 1930. Boston. maps. 508 p. dj. VG. T5. $22.50

HART, F.R. *Personal Reminiscences of Caribbean Sea & Spanish Main.* 1914. Boston. De Vinne Pr. 1/125. fair. $35.00

HART, Horace. *Bibliotheca Typographica, List of Books About Books.* 1933. Rochester. 142 p. dj. VG. $30.00

HART, Hornell. *Autoconditioning.* 1956. NY. $16.50

HART, Hornell. *Enigma of Survival.* 1959. London. $18.50

HART, Ivor B. *World of Leonardo da Vinci: Man of Science, Engineer...* 1961. Viking. Orig ed. 374 p. D2. $40.00

HART, L. *Europe in Arms.* 1937. NY. 1st Am ed. VG. $12.50

HART, S. *Life With Daktari: Two Vets in E Africa.* 1969. London. Bles Collins. 224 p. dj. VG. M2. $13.00

HART, Scott. *Tranquillity.* Derrydale. 1/950. EX. $225.00

HART & CLARK. *Interdisciplinary Biography of Fresh-Water Crayfishes.* 1989. Smithsonian. 1st ed. 4to. 498 p. dj. M. M2. $35.00

HART. *Moon Is Warning.* Derrydale. as issued. VG. B2. $50.00

HARTCOLLIS, Peter. *Borderline Personality Disorders.* 1977. NY. dj. VG. $14.00

HARTE, Bret. *Defense of the W.* 1950. Morrow. 1st ed. VG. J2. $12.50

HARTE, Bret. *In Carquinez Woods.* 1884. Houghton. 1st Am ed. blue bdg. VG. $20.00

HARTE, Bret. *Letters of Bret Harte.* 1926. Boston. Ils 1st ed. 515 p. dj. VG. T5. $35.00

HARTE, Bret. *Luck of Roaring Camp.* nd. Houghton Mifflin. VG. P1. $17.50

HARTE, Bret. *Luck of Roaring Camp.* 1941. Camden. Haddon Craftsmen. Ils/sgn Honore. $60.00

HARTE, Bret. *Openings in the Old Trail.* 1902. 1st ed. gilt brown cloth. EX. $20.00

HARTE, Bret. *Poems.* 1871. Fields Osgood. 1st ed. VG. $20.00

HARTE, Bret. *Poetical Works of Bret Harte.* 1887. Houghton. Ils. 8vo. 326 p. AEG. VG. $175.00

HARTE, Bret. *Prose & Poetry.* 1872. Leipzig. Tauchnitz. 2 vols in 1. VG. $45.00

HARTE, Bret. *Tales of the Argonauts.* 1875. Boston. 1st ed. 12mo. green bdg. $65.00

HARTE, Bret. *Tales of the Gold Rush.* 1972. Norwalk. Heritage. quarto. slipcase. EX. $15.00

HARTE, Bret. *Twins of Table Mountain.* 1879. Houghton. 1st ed. $22.00

HARTE & TWAIN. *Sketches of the Sixties.* 1926. San Francisco. 1/2250. VG. $45.00

HARTHAN, John. *History of Illustrated Book: W Tradition.* 1981. Thames Hudson. 465 Ils. 4to. dj. VG. $30.00

HARTLEY, C.B. *Life of Major General Henry Lee...* 1859. Phil. Evans. Ils White. 352 p. $55.00

HARTLEY, Fred. *Our New National Labor Policy.* 1948. dj. VG. $30.00

HARTLEY, Norman. *Shadowplay.* 1982. Atheneum. 1st ed. dj. EX. P1. $12.95

HARTLEY, Norman. *Viking Process.* 1976. Simon Schuster. 1st ed. dj. VG. P1. $6.00

HARTMAN, O. *Atlas of Sedentariate Polychaetous Annelids From CA.* 1968. S CA U. Ils. 812 p. EX. M2. $45.00

HARTMAN. *Valiant Knights of Daguerre.* 1979. dj. M. S2. $45.00

HARTMANN, John. *Praxis Chymiatrica. Herausgegeben von J.M. Hartmann.* 1639. Genf. 8vo. new leather. $1050.00

HARTMANN, Sadakichi. *Landscape & Figure Composition.* 1910. NY. Baker. Ils 1st ed. gilt red cloth. VG. $150.00

HARTSHORNE, A.C. *Japan & Her People.* 1902. Phil. Ils 1st ed. 2 vols. TEG. VG. T1. $35.00

HARTWELL, BLAIR & CHILTON. *Present State of VA & the College.* 1940. Williamsburg. Ils 1st ed. 105 p. dj. EX. $20.00

HARVARD CLASSICS. *Harvard Classics Shelf of Fiction.* 1917. NY. 8vo. 20 vol. TEG. gilt black cloth. T1. $65.00

HARVESTER, Simon. *Bamboo Screen.* 1968. Walker. 1st ed. dj. VG. P1. $15.00

HARVESTER, Simon. *Tiger in the N.* 1963. Walker. 1st ed. dj. xl. P1. $6.00

HARVESTER, Simon. *Zion Road.* 1968. Jarrolds. dj. xl. P1. $7.50

HARVESTER, Simon. *Zion Road.* 1968. Walker. 1st ed. dj. VG. P1. $10.00

HARVEY, A.D. *William Pitt the Younger, 1759-1806.* 1989. Westport. Meckler. 80 p. VG. T5. $9.50

HARVEY, F.I. *History of WA Monument & WA National Monument Society.* 1903. GPO. Ils. 362 p. orig calf. VG. A3. $50.00

HARVEY, G.C. *Robin Hood.* 1925. Winston. Ils Prittie. VG. B4. $18.00

HARVEY, John. *Life of Robert Bruce of Scots.* 1729. Edinburgh. Catanach. full leather. $50.00

HARVEY, Peter. *Reminiscences & Anecdotes of Daniel Webster.* 1877. Boston. 1st ed. VG. $35.00

HARVEY, W.F. *Arm of Mrs. Eagan.* 1952. NY. 1st ed. dj. EX. $20.00

HARVEY, Y.K. *Six Korean Women.* 1979. St. Paul. $15.00

HARVEY-GIBSON, R.J. *Outlines of the History of Botany.* 1919. London. Black. 274 p. VG. M2. $12.00

HARWELL, R.B. *Confederate Music.* 1950. 184 p. dj. J4. $35.00

HARWELL, R.B. *Confederate Reader.* 1957. Longman Green. Ils 389 p. VG. M2. $15.00

HARWELL, R.B. *Union Reader.* 1958. NY. 1st ed. dj. EX. $15.00

HARWELL, R.B. *Union Reader.* 1958. 1st ed. 362 p. dj. VG. J4. $6.50

HARWELL, Richard. *Confederate Hundred: Bibliographic Selection...Books.* 1964. Ils. M. J4. $20.00

HARWELL, Richard. *Fiery Trail, Union Officer's Account of Sherman's Campaigns.* 1986. Knoxville, TN. Ils 1st ed. 238 p. dj. $27.50

HARWELL, Richard. *In Tall Cotton.* 1978. 82 p. M. J4. $25.00

HARZOG, D. *Big Water Canoeing.* 1978. Chicago. Contemporary Books. photos. dj. VG. $10.00

HASBROUCK, M.B. *Pursuit of Destiny.* 1941. NY. $35.00

HASELTON, S.E. *Cacti for the Amateur.* 1941. Abbey Garden. Ils 134 p. VG. M2. $10.00

HASKELL, A.L. *Baron at the Ballet.* 1951. London. large 4to. 222 p. EX. P3. $29.00

HASKELL, A.L. *Black on White: Arbitrary Anthology of Drawing.* 1933. London. 1st ed. 41 p. T5. $25.00

HASKELL, John. *Haskell Memoirs.* 1960. NY. 1st ed. 176 p. dj. EX. T5. $22.50

HASKELL & FOWLER. *City of the Future: Narrative History of KS City 1850-1950.* 1950. Glenn. Ils 143 p. EX. M2. $10.00

HASKELL. *Leader of the Garment Workers: Isadore Nagler.* 1950. dj. VG. $25.00

HASKIN, F.J. *Panama Canal.* 1913. Garden City. Ils 1st ed. VG. $12.00

HASLAM, Malcolm. *Real World of Surrealists.* 1978. NY. 1st ed. dj. EX. $27.50

HASLUND, H. *Tents in Mongolia (Yabonah).* 1934. Dutton. Ils 1st ed. 366 p. EX. M2. $45.00

HASS, H. *Men & Sharks.* 1954. Doubleday. Ils 1st ed. 318 p. dj. VG. M2. $10.00

HASSE. *Province of NY, Journal of House of Representatives.* 1903. NY. facsimile of 1695 ed. 1/500. VG. $25.00

HASSRICK, P. *Frederic Remington: Paintings, Drawings, Sculpture...* 1973. NY. 94 pls. 4to. dj. EX. J2. $50.00

HASTINGS, Brook. *Demon Within.* 1953. Crime Club. 1st ed. xl. P1. $5.00

HASTINGS, Hugh. *Military Minutes of Council of Appointment of NY, 1784-1821.* 1901-1902. Albany. 4 vols. VG. $40.00

HASTINGS, Macdonald. *Cork on the Water.* nd. Book Club. dj. VG. P1. $3.00

HASTINGS, Thomas. *Mother's Nursery Songs.* 1835. NY. 1st ed. black cloth. G. T1. $35.00

HASTINGS & HASTINGS. *S Garden Book.* 1948. Garden City. 1st ed. sgns. 276 p. dj. VG. $35.00

HASTY, John Eugene. *Man Without a Face.* 1958. Dodd Mead. dj. G. P1. $8.00

HATCH, A. *Byrds of VA.* c 1969. NY. 1st ed. pls. dj. VG. $15.00

HATCH, A. *Full Tilt.* Derrydale. as issued. VG. B2. $50.00

HATCH, L. *History of Bowdoin College.* 1927. Portland. Ils 1st ed. 500 p. VG. B2. $27.50

HATCH, M.H. *Chelifera & Isopoda of WA & Adjacent Regions.* 1947. WA U. 18 pls. M2. $10.00

HATCHER, H. *Great Lakes.* 1945. Oxford U. photos. map. 384 p. G. M2. $5.00

HATFIELD, Audrey. *Pleasures of Herbs.* 1965. NY. 1st ed. dj. VG. $17.00

HATFIELD, M. *Physiology & Hygiene of House in Which We Live.* 1887. NY. Ils. 275 p. VG. $15.00

HATFIELD. *American House Carpenter.* 1872. NY. Revised 7th ed. VG. C4. $95.00

HATHAWAY. *Our Firemen: Record of Detroit Fire Department.* 1894. Detroit. G. $70.00

HATLAUB, G.F. *Die Graphik des Expressionismus in Deutschland.* 1947. Stuttgart. 1/5000. dj. D2. $65.00

HATTON, E. *Merchant's Magazine; or, Tradesman's Treasury.* 1719. London. VG. $650.00

HATTON & CLEAVER. *Bibliography of Periodical Works of Charles Dickens.* 1973. NY. 1/750. EX. $85.00

HAUCK, Louise Platt. *At Midnight.* nd. Grosset Dunlap. dj. VG. P1. $7.50

HAUGEN, Einar. *Voyages to Vinland: First American Saga.* 1942. NY. Knopf. Ils Chapman. EX. $40.00

HAUPT, Herman. *General Theory of Bridge Construction.* 1856. NY. Appleton. 16 pls. VG. $140.00

HAUSER, B.G. *Food Science & Health.* 1930. NY. $30.00

HAUSER, M. *Dark Dominion.* 1947. NY. 1st ed. dj. EX. $30.00

HAUSER, Mrs. I.L. *Orient & Its People.* 1876. Milwaukee. Hauser. 335 p. VG. $16.00

HAUSER, Thomas. *Dear Hannah.* 1987. NY. 1st ed. dj. M. $10.00

HAUSMAN, L.A. *Birds of Prey of NE N America.* 1948. Rutgers. Ils Abbott. 164 p. dj. VG. M2. $35.00

HAUSMAN, L.A. *Illustrated Encyclopedia of American Birds.* 1944. Halcyon House. Ils Abbott. 541 p. dj. EX. M2. $13.00

HAUT, F.J.G. *Pictorial History of Electric Locomotives.* 1970. NY. Ils. 147 p. dj. G. T5. $25.00

HAVEN, C.T. *Complete Small Arms Manual.* 1943. Morrow. 1st ed. dj. VG. $35.00

HAVEN & BELDEN. *History of Colt Revolver.* 1940. NY. 1st ed. sgn. slipcase. $75.00

HAVEN & BELDEN. *History of Colt Revolver.* 1978. NY. photos. 711 p. dj. EX. $40.00

HAVER, Ronald. *David O. Selznick's Gone With the Wind.* 1986. Bonanza. folio. dj. M. $25.00

HAVERMEYER, L. *Ethnography.* 1929. Ginn. Ils. 522 p. VG. M2. $18.00

HAVERSTOCK, M.S. *American Beastiary.* 1979. NY. Abrams. Ils. 248 p. EX. $13.00

HAVIGHURST, Walter. *Land of Promise: Story of NW Territory.* 1946. NY. G. $12.00

HAVIGHURST, Walter. *Voices on the River: Story of MS Waterways.* 1964. NY. Ils 1st ed. 310 p. dj. EX. T5. $25.00

HAVIGHURST, Walter. *Voices on the River: Story of MS Waterways.* 1964. NY. 1st ed. sgn. 310 p. dj. VG. B2. $25.00

HAVILAND, Virginia. *Children & Literature*. 1974. Lothrop Lee. 468 p. dj. VG. $15.00

HAVILAND, Virginia. *Children's Literature Guide to Reference Sources*. 1966. Lib Congress. Ils. 341 p. G. $20.00

HAWES, H.B. *Daughter of the Blood*. 1925. Boston. sgn. dj. VG. $30.00

HAWGOOD, John. *America's W Frontiers, Exploration & Settlement...* 1967. Knopf. 1st ed. dj. VG. $30.00

HAWK, John. *House of Sudden Sleep*. 1930. Mystery League. 1st ed. VG. P1. $15.00

HAWKE, Simon. *Wizard of 4th Street.* 1st ed. pb. VG. C1. $3.50

HAWKER, P. *Instructions to Young Sportsmen*. 1922. Phil. green bdg. EX. $75.00

HAWKES, Clarence. *Little Foresters*. 1903. Crowell. Ils Copeland. dj. G. $20.00

HAWKES, Clarence. *Patches, a WY Cow Pony*. 1930. Springfield. Milton Bradley. Ils Tyng. 8vo. VG. $30.00

HAWKES, John. *Cannibal*. 1962. London. 1st ed. dj. VG. $40.00

HAWKES, S. *Ivanhoe Gambit.* 1st ed. pb. VG. C1. $3.00

HAWKINS, Dean. *Skull Mountain*. 1941. Crime Club. 1st ed. dj. G. P1. $10.00

HAWKINS, Gerald. *Stonehenge Decoded.* 1965. 1st ed. dj. VG. C1. $7.50

HAWKINS, Kenneth. *Beekeeping in the S, a Handbook*. 1920. Hamilton, IL. Am Bee Journal. Ils. 120 p. $25.00

HAWKINS, W.E. *Technique of Salable Fiction*. 1939. Author Journalist. P1. $10.00

HAWKS, Ellisin. *Stars Shown to the Children*. 1910. Ils. 12mo. 116 p. EX. $2.50

HAWTHORNE, H. *CA's Missions: Their Romance & Beauty*. 1942. NY. Appleton. 2nd ed. 314 p. green cloth. dj. VG. $30.00

HAWTHORNE, H. *Contemplations*. Roycroft. brown suede. VG. D1. $25.00

HAWTHORNE, H. *Contemplations*. Roycroft. green suede. VG. D1. $30.00

HAWTHORNE, H. *Contemplations*. Roycroft. vellum bdg. G. D1. $35.00

HAWTHORNE, H. *Contemplations*. 1902. Roycroft. 4to. gray suede/boards. EX. D1. $60.00

HAWTHORNE, H. *Lure of the Garden*. 1911. Century. Ils Parrish. 1st ed. TEG. VG. $45.00

HAWTHORNE, Julian. *Mystery & Detective Stories*. 1908. Review of Reviews. P1. $15.00

HAWTHORNE, Nathaniel. *Arabian Nights*. 1928. Ils Sterrett. 4to. boxed. EX. G2. $125.00

HAWTHORNE, Nathaniel. *Dr. Grimshawe's Secret*. 1883. Boston. Osgood. Ils 1st ed. gray bdg. VG. $75.00

HAWTHORNE, Nathaniel. *Golden Touch*. nd. Mt. Vernon. Ils Angelo. 1/385. slipcase. EX. $30.00

HAWTHORNE, Nathaniel. *House of Seven Gables*. 1899. Houghton. Ils Cowles. 2 vols. TEG. VG. $40.00

HAWTHORNE, Nathaniel. *Marble Faun*. 1860. 1st ed. 1st issue. 2 vols. VG. $225.00

HAWTHORNE, Nathaniel. *Our Old Home*. 1863. Tickner Fields. 1st ed. 1st state. TEG. EX. $125.00

HAWTHORNE, Nathaniel. *Scarlet Letter*. 1928. NY. Grabhorn. Ils Angelo. 1/980. tall 8vo. $150.00

HAWTHORNE, Nathaniel. *Septimius Felton*. 1872. Boston. 1st ed. VG. $50.00

HAWTHORNE, Nathaniel. *Wonder Book & Tanglewood Tales*. 1910. Duffield. Ils Parrish. 1st ed. J2. $125.00

HAWTHORNE, Nathaniel. *Wonder Book for Girls & Books*. 1893. Boston. Ils Crane. VG. $50.00

HAWTHORNE, Nathaniel. *Wonder Book for Girls & Boys*. 1852. Boston. 1st ed. EX. $380.00

HAWTHORNE, Nathaniel. *Wonder Book for Girls & Boys*. 1885. Riverside Pr. Ils Church. 4to. 150 p. VG. $32.00

HAWTHORNE, Nathaniel. *Wonder Book*. 1913. Chicago. Ils Milo Winter. VG. $25.00

HAWTHORNE, Sophia. *Notes in England & Italy*. 1869. Putnam. 1st ed. VG. J2. $30.00

HAY, D. & J. *Last of the Confederate Privateers*. 1977. Crescent. Ils. 178 p. EX. M2. $10.00

HAY, J. *Spirit of Survival: Natural & Personal History of Terns*. 1974. Dutton. Ils 1st ed. 175 p. dj. EX. M2. $9.00

HAY, John. *Castilian Days*. 1903. Houghton. Ils Pennell. 1st ed. TEG. VG. $20.00

HAY, John. *Life of William Roscoe Thayer*. 1915. Houghton. 2nd imp. 2 vols. dj. VG. $20.00

HAY, John. *Memorial Address on Life & Character of William McKinley*. 1903. WA. Revised ed. 70 p. G. T5. $15.00

HAY, T.R. *Hood's TN Campaign*. 1929. 4 maps. 272 p. EX. J4. $20.00

HAYAKAWA, S.I. *Language in Action*. 1941. NY. presentation. inscr. 345 p. dj. $15.00

HAYCOX, Ernest. *Alder Gulch*. nd. Grosset Dunlap. dj. VG. P1. $7.50

HAYCRAFT, Howard. *10 Great Mysteries*. nd. Book Club. VG. P1. $3.00

HAYCRAFT & BEECROFT. *3 X 3 Omnibus*. nd. Book Club. dj. VG. P1. $4.00

HAYCRAFT & BEECROFT. *3 X 3 Vol. 1*. nd. Book Club. VG. P1. $2.50

HAYCRAFT & BEECROFT. *3 X 3 Vol. 2*. nd. Book Club. dj. VG. P1. $3.00

HAYDEN, F.V. *Report of US Geological & Geographical Survey Territories...* 1878. GPO. Ils. maps. 8vo. 546 p. G. G2. $85.00

HAYDEN, F.V. *Report of US Geological Survey at WY...* 1871. WA. Ils. 8vo. 511 p. VG. G2. $70.00

HAYDEN, F.V. *11th Annual Report of US Geological Survey Territories*. 1879. GPO. Ils. fld maps. charts. 720 p. xl. $50.00

HAYDEN, F.V. *7th Annual Report of US Geological & Geographical Survey...* 1874. GPO. Ils. presentation. 718 p. A3. $95.00

HAYDON, F.S. *Aeronautics in Union & Confederate Armies With Survey...* 1941. Johns Hopkins. 45 pls. 421 p. dj. EX. M2. $85.00

HAYES, Albert. *Science of Life; or, Self-Preservation...* 1868. Boston. 12mo. 267 p. $25.00

HAYES, E. *Forty Years on the Labrador: Life Story of Sir W. Grenfell*. 1930. Revell. photos. 128 p. VG. M2. $5.00

HAYES, I. *Open Polar Sea*. 1867. NY. orig wraps. VG. $55.00

HAYES, J.G. *Sheriff Thompson's Day: Turbulence in AZ Territory*. 1968. AZ U. possible 1st ed. 190 p. dj. EX. M2. $25.00

HAYES, J.W. *Tales of the Sierras*. 1912. NY. Ils. 136 p. wraps. VG. A3. $40.00

HAYES, John. *Thomas Gainsborough*. 1981. London. Tate Gallery. Ils. 158 p. D2. $30.00

HAYES, Ralph. *Visiting Moon*. 1971. Lenox Hill. dj. xl. P1. $5.00

HAYES, Woody. *You Win With People*. 1973. Columbus. 1st ed. dj. VG. B2. $30.00

HAYES. *War Between the States Biographical.* Ltd ed. 1/1000. 1500 facsimile sgns. J4. $32.50

HAYFORD, Otis. *History of Hayford Family, 1100-1900...* 1901. Canton, ME. Ils 1st ed. 8vo. green cloth. T1. $50.00

HAYLER, William. *Life & Posthumous Writings of William Cowper.* 1803-1804. Ils Blake. 1st ed. sgn Beckford. $400.00

HAYMAKER, R.E. *From Pampas to Hedgerows & Downs: Study of W.H. Hudson.* 1954. Bookman. 398 p. EX. M2. $16.00

HAYMAKER, W. *Founders of Neurology.* 1953. Thomas. 1st ed. inscr/sgn/dtd. dj. EX. $120.00

HAYMAN, L.R. *O Captain! Death of Abraham Lincoln.* 1968. NY. Four Winds. 1st ed. dj. M. $20.00

HAYNE. *Second Speech of Mr. Hayne of SC...* 1830. Gales Seaton. 32 p. disbound pamphlet. $45.00

HAYNES, B.D. & E. *Grizzly Bear: Portraits From Life.* 1979. OK U. Ils. 386 p. EX. M2. $11.00

HAYNES, Dorothy K. *Thou Shalt Not Suffer a Witch.* 1949. Methuen. Ils Mervyn Peake. 1st ed. VG. P1. $30.00

HAYNES, E.M. *History of 10th VT Volunteers.* 1870. Leiston, ME. 1st ed. 1st issue. VG. T1. $125.00

HAYNES, G.W. *American Paint Horse.* 1976. OK U. Ils 1st ed. dj. EX. M2. $10.00

HAYNES, William. *Stone That Burns: Story of American Sulfur Industry.* 1942. Ils. VG. $10.00

HAYS, Tom. *Hunting the White-Tailed Deer.* 1960. NY. dj. EX. $20.00

HAYTER, S.W. *About Prints.* 1962. London. Oxford. 1st ed. dj. $30.00

HAYWARD, H.L. *Lives of the Most Remarkable Criminals.* 1927. NY. 1st ed. dj. VG. J2. $50.00

HAYWARD, Helena. *World of Furniture.* 1970. London. Hamlyn. 4th print. dj. EX. $60.00

HAYWARD, Mildred. *Christ Appears.* nd. NY. $16.00

HAYWARD, Mildred. *While Jesus Walked on Earth.* 1955. MA. $10.00

HAYWOOD, M.D. *Governor George Burrington.* 1896. Raleigh, NC. 34 p. wraps missing. G. T5. $12.50

HAYWORTH, P. *On the Headwaters of Peace River.* 1921. NY. VG. $70.00

HAZARD, Caroline. *Songs in the Sun.* 1927. Boston. 1st ed. G. $25.00

HAZARD, Thomas. *Jonny-Cake Papers of Shepherd Tom.* 1915. Boston. Ltd ed. 1/600. $30.00

HAZEL, Robert. *Lost Year.* 1953. Cleveland. 1st ed. dj. EX. $35.00

HAZELRIGG, J. *Astrosophia: Being Metaphysical Astrology.* 1915. NY. Hazelrigg. $50.00

HAZELRIGG, J. *Sun Book.* 1916. NY. $85.00

HAZELTON, E. *Sammy, the Crow Who Remembered.* 1969. Scribner. Ils Atwood. sgns. dj. VG. $35.00

HAZELTON, Elizabeth. *Treasure of Kilvarra.* nd. Book Club. VG. C1. $3.00

HAZELTON, John. *Declaration of Independence: Its History.* 1906. Dodd Mead. 1st ed. 629 p. VG. $45.00

HAZLITT, W.C. *Conversation of James Northcote.* 1830. London. 1st ed. $115.00

HAZLITT, W.C. *Gleanings in Old Garden Literature.* 1887. London. 1st ed. $50.00

HAZLITT, W.C. *Studies in Jocular Literature.* 1890. London. 1st ed. $40.00

HAZLITT, William. *Life of Napoleon.* nd. Grolier Deluxe ed. 1/1000. 5 vols. TEG. $100.00

HAZZARD, J.C. *Eutropius.* 1898. Am Book Co. 243 p. EX. $5.00

HAZZARD, Shirley. *Bay of Noon.* 1970. Boston. 1st ed. dj. VG. $20.00

HAZZARD, Shirley. *Evening of the Holiday.* 1965. Knopf. 1st ed. dj. VG. $20.00

HEAD, B. *Coins of the Ancients.* 1895. London. VG. $47.00

HEAD, Edith. *How To Dress for Success.* 1967. Random House. 1st ed. dj. VG. J2. $12.50

HEAD, Henry. *Studies in Neurology.* 1920. London. Frowde. 1st ed. VG. $225.00

HEAD, J.W. *History & Comprehensive Description of Loudon Co., VA.* 1908. WA. 1st ed. EX. scarce. $60.00

HEAD, Mathew. *Smell of Money.* 1944. Tower. dj. VG. P1. $12.50

HEAD, T.A. *Campaigns & Battles of 16th Regiment TN Volunteers.* 1961. reprint. 488 p. dj. very scarce. J4. $25.00

HEAD & KIRKMAN. *English Rogue.* 1928. NY. Ils Hayward. dj. J2. $50.00

HEADLAM, Cecil. *Oxford & Its History.* 1904. London. Dent. Ils Fanny Railton. 4to. TEG. $35.00

HEADLAND, I.T. *Chinese Mother Goose Rhymes in Chinese & English.* 1900. Revell. Trans/Ils Headland. VG. B4. $125.00

HEADLEY, J.T. *Adirondack.* 1849. NY. 1st ed. dj. VG. $60.00

HEADLEY, J.T. *Great Rebellion: History of Civil War in US. Vol. 1.* 1864. Hartford. Ils. 8vo. 506 p. G. G2. $19.00

HEADLEY, J.T. *Illustrated Life of WA.* 1859. NY. Ils. 8vo. 505 p. G. G2. $20.00

HEADLEY, J.T. *Letters From Italy With Alps & the Rhine.* 1848. NY. New Revised ed. VG. $20.00

HEADLEY, J.T. *Napoleon & His Marshals.* 1847. NY. 12 plts. 2 vols. $65.00

HEADLEY, J.T. *Tramps in Dark Mongolia.* 1910. NY/London. Ils. 371 p. TEG. VG. T5. $45.00

HEADLEY, P.C. *Island of Fire.* 1874. Boston. 357 p. EX. $40.00

HEADLEY, P.C. *Old Salamander: Life & Naval Career of Admiral Farracut.* 1883. Lee Shepard. 242 p. G. M2. $5.00

HEADSTROM, R. *Beetles of America.* 1977. Barnes. Ils. 488 p. EX. M2. $13.00

HEADSTROM, R. *Your Reptile Pet.* 1978. McKay. 40 photos. 120 p. EX. M2. $10.00

HEALD, Edward Thornton. *History of Stark Co.* 1963. Canton. Ils. 183 p. Ils wraps. VG. T5. $9.50

HEALD, Tim. *Unbecoming Habits.* 1973. Stein Day. 1st ed. dj. VG. P1. $10.00

HEALY, Jeremiah. *Staked Goat.* 1986. NY. 1st ed. dj. EX. $15.00

HEALY, Jeremiah. *Staked Goat.* 1986. NY. 1st ed. dj. VG. $6.00

HEALY, Raymond J. *9 Tales of Space & Time.* 1954. Holt. 1st ed. VG. P1. $12.50

HEANEY, Seamus. *Haw Lantern.* 1978. London. 1st ed. VG. $45.00

HEANEY, Seamus. *Poems & a Memoir.* 1982. Ltd Ed Club. slipcase. B3. $120.00

HEANEY, Seamus. *Poems & a Memoir.* 1982. Ltd Ed Club. 1st ed. sgn. slipcase. T6. $200.00

HEAPE, W. *Emigration, Migration & Nomadism.* 1931. England. Heffer. 369 p. VG. M2. $11.00

HEARD, H.F. *Lost Cavern.* 1948. Vanguard. 1st ed. dj. VG. P1. $35.00

HEARD, H.F. *Weird Tales, Terror & Detection.* 1946. Sun Dial. dj. VG. P1. $35.00

HEARD, I.V.D. *History of Sioux War & Massacres of 1862-1863.* 1865. NY. Harper. Ils. 354 p. VG. A3. $110.00

HEARN, C.V. *Foreign Assignment.* 1961. Adventurers Club. dj. VG. P1. $7.50

HEARN, Lafacido. *Kotto.* 1902. NY. 1st ed. EX. $120.00

HEARN, Lafacido. *Romance of Milky Way.* 1906. Houghton Mifflin. olive bdg. EX. $45.00

HEARN, Lafcadio. *Creole Sketches.* 1924. Boston. 1st ed. 201 p. G. T5. $15.00

HEARN, Lafcadio. *Gleanings in Buddha Fields.* 1897. Boston. 1st ed. EX. $125.00

HEARN, Lafcadio. *Japan: An Interpretation.* 1904. Macmillan. 1st ed. 541 p. VG. $85.00

HEARN, Lafcadio. *Japan: An Interpretation.* 1905. NY. 8vo. gilt cloth. VG. T1. $25.00

HEARN, Lafcadio. *Karma & Other Stories & Essays.* 1921. London. 1st ed. AEG. gilt morocco. VG. $65.00

HEARN, Lafcadio. *Kokoro.* 1896. Boston. 1st ed. VG. $55.00

HEARN, Lafcadio. *Life & Literature.* 1924. NY. 1st ed. VG. $25.00

HEARN, Lafcadio. *Out of E.* 1895. Boston. 1st ed. VG. $50.00

HEARN, Lafcadio. *Shadowings.* Boston. 1st ed. VG. $65.00

HEARN, Lafcadio. *Writings of Lafcadio Hearn.* Koizumi. 16 vols. EX. $450.00

HEARNE, John. *Eye of the Storm.* 1957. Boston. Little Brown. 1st Am ed. 328 p. $12.50

HEATH, M.H. *Elbert Hubbard I Knew.* 1929. Roycroft. 8vo. inscr/sgn. VG. D1. $50.00

HEATH, Sidney. *Cornish Riviera.* 1936. Ils 1st ed. dj. VG. C1. $7.50

HEAVEY, W.F. *Down Ramp! Story of Army Amphibian Engineers.* 1947. WA. 1st ed. maps. 272 p. dj. fair. T5. $45.00

HEBARD, M. *Blattidae From French Guiana.* 1927. Phil Acad Nat Sc. Ils. M2. $5.00

HEBER-PERCY, A. *Visit to Bashan & Argob.* 1895. Ils. VG. $50.00

HEBERDEN, M.V. *Murder of a Stuffed Shirt.* 1944. Crime Club. 1st ed. xl. P1. $10.00

HECHT, Anthony. *Venetian Vespers.* 1979. Atheneum. 1st ed. sgn. dj. VG. $25.00

HECHT, Ben. *Child of the Century.* 1954. NY. 1st ed. inscr. EX. $65.00

HECHT, Ben. *Fantazius Mallare.* 1922. Chicago. Ils Wallace Smith. 1/2025. dj. $60.00

HECHT, Ben. *Great Magoo.* 1933. Ils Rosse. 1st ed. 308 p. G. $30.00

HECHT, Ben. *Kingdom of Evil.* 1924. Chicago. Ils Angarola. 1/2000. dj. $55.00

HECHT, Ben. *Literature & the Bastinado.* 1922. NY. 1st ed. VG. $25.00

HECHT, Ben. *One Hell of an Actor.* 1977. 1st ed. dj. VG. $32.00

HECHT, Ben. *Sensualists.* 1959. NY. 1st ed. dj. VG. $20.00

HECHT, Ben. *1,001 Afternoons in Chicago.* 1927. Covici. Ils Herman Rosse. dj. VG. $25.00

HECHT, M.A. *Morte.* 1925. Chicago. Ils Riedel. 1st ed. 1/400. EX. $25.00

HECHT, M.A. *Morte.* 1925. Pascal Covici. 1/450. fair. $12.00

HECKELMANN, Charles. *Big Valley.* 1966. Whitman. VG. P1. $6.00

HECKENWELDER, J. *History, Manners & Customs of Indian Nations. Vol. XII.* 1876. PA Hist Soc. New Revised ed. VG. $78.00

HECKMAN, Hazel. *Island Year.* 1972. Seattle. 1st ed. dj. EX. $15.00

HEDGECOE, John. *Advanced Photography.* 1982. Simon Schuster. Ils. folio. 304 p. dj. $20.00

HEDGEPETH, W. *Hog Book.* 1978. Doubleday. Ils. 272 p. VG. M2. $11.00

HEDGEPETH & BELDEN. *Spurs Were Jinglin`: Brief Look at WY Range Country.* 1975. Northland. 1st ed. 104 p. dj. EX. M2. $29.00

HEDIN, Sven. *Central Asia & Tibet: Toward the Holy City of Lassa.* 1903. NY. Scribner. 2 vols. VG. $65.00

HEDIN, Sven. *My Life As an Explorer.* 1925. Garden City. Ils. 544 p. G. M2. $10.00

HEDIN, Sven. *Riddles of Gobi Desert.* 1933. NY. 1st Am ed. 382 p. dj. xl. G. $20.00

HEDIN & HOLTHAUS. *AK: Reflections on Land & Spirit.* 1989. AZ U. 1st ed. 322 p. dj. M. M2. $20.00

HEDLEY, F.Y. *Marching Through GA.* 1885. Chicago. Donnelley. Ils. $65.00

HEDRICK, U.P. *Cherries of NY.* 1915. NY. Ils. VG. $75.00

HEDRICK, U.P. *Cyclopedia of Hardy Fruits.* 1922. Macmillan. 1st ed. 4to. 370 p. EX. $50.00

HEDRICK, U.P. *Peaches of NY.* 1917. NY. ILs. 92 p. VG. $75.00

HEDRICK, U.P. *Small Fruit of NY.* 1925. Albany. 1st ed. color pls. 614 p. VG. B2. $135.00

HEEGAARD, P. *Parasitic Copepoda From Australian Waters.* 1962. Sydney. Ils. EX. M2. $14.00

HEEREN, A.H.L. *Ancient Greece & Three Historical Treatises.* 1847. London. 2nd ed. VG. $90.00

HEEREN, A.H.L. *Historical Researches Into Politics, Intercourse, Trade...* 1857. London. 2nd ed. VG. $90.00

HEERWAGEN, P.K. *Indian Scout, W Painter: Captain Charles L. VonBerg.* 1969. Pioneer Pr. photos. 119 p. dj. EX. M2. $10.00

HEG, H.C. *Letters.* 1936. Northfield. 1st ed. dj. EX. $30.00

HEGI, Ursula. *Intrusions.* 1981. NY. Viking. 1st ed. inscr/sgn. dj. EX. $15.00

HEGNER, Robert. *Parade of the Animal Kingdom.* 1951. Macmillan. 675 p. G. $10.00

HEIDEGGER, Martin. *Was Heisst Denken?* 1954. Tubingen. 8vo. 157 p. VG. $35.00

HEILMAIER, Hans. *Kososchka.* 1929. Paris. Cres. Ils. scarce. D2. $25.00

HEILNER, V.C. *Book on Duck Shooting.* 1939. Phil. Ils Hunt. 540 p. EX. $35.00

HEINE, Heinrich. *Book of Songs.* Roycroft. brown suede. VG. D1. $45.00

HEINE, Heinrich. *Book of Songs.* 1903. Roycroft. 8vo. green suede. VG. D1. $55.00

HEINE, Heinrich. *Works of Heinrich Heine.* 1891-1903. London. Trans Leland. 12 vols. T1. $75.00

HEINECKE, Samuel. *Genealogy From Adam to Christ, With Genealogy of Heinecke.* 1881. Lancaster. 2nd ed. sgn. 302 p. G. T5. $22.50

HEINEMANN, Larry. *Paco's Story.* 1986. NY. 1st ed. dj. M. $10.00

HEINEMANN, Larry. *Paco's Story.* 1987. London. 1st ed. dj. RS. EX. $45.00

HEININGER & HEININGER. *Great Book of Jewels.* 1974. Boston. NY Graphic Soc. 316 p. dj. D2. $135.00

HEINKEL, Ernst. *HE 1000.* 1957. London. photos. 287 p. T5. $25.00

HEINL, R.D. *Victory at High Tide.* 1968. Phil./NY. Ils 1st ed. maps. 315 p. dj. T5. $15.00

HEINLEIN, Robert. *Beyond This Horizon.* nd. Grosset. dj. VG. P1. $50.00

HEINLEIN, Robert. *Beyond This Horizon.* 1948. Fantasy. 1/500. inscr/sgn. dj. $190.00

HEINLEIN, Robert. *Cat Who Walks Through Walls.* 1985. Putnam. 1st ed. dj. VG. P1. $17.95

HEINLEIN, Robert. *Friday.* 1982. Holt Rinehart. 1st ed. dj. EX. P1. $20.00

HEINLEIN, Robert. *Glory Road.* 1963. Putnam. 1st ed. P1. $350.00

HEINLEIN, Robert. *Green Hills of Earth.* 1951. Chicago. Shasta. 1st ed. dj. VG. $98.00

HEINLEIN, Robert. *Heinlein Trio-Puppet Masters, Double Star, Door Into Summer.* nd. Book Club. dj. VG. P1. $5.00

HEINLEIN, Robert. *Heinlein Trio-Puppet Masters, Waldo, Magic Inc.* nd. Book Club. VG. P1. $7.50

HEINLEIN, Robert. *I Will Fear No Evil.* 1970. Putnam. 1st ed. dj. VG. P1. $60.00

HEINLEIN, Robert. *Jerry Is a Man: Complete Novelet.* 1947. NY. printed wraps. VG. $10.00

HEINLEIN, Robert. *Job: Comedy of Justice.* 1984. Del Rey. dj. EX. P1. $16.95

HEINLEIN, Robert. *Man Who Sold the Moon.* 1950. Shasta. 1st ed. dj. EX. $110.00

HEINLEIN, Robert. *Menace From Earth.* 1959. Hicksville. Gnome. 1st ed. EX. $260.00

HEINLEIN, Robert. *Menance From Earth.* 1966. London. 1st ed. dj. VG. $50.00

HEINLEIN, Robert. *Number of the Beast.* 1980. New English Lib. 1st ed. dj. P1. $35.00

HEINLEIN, Robert. *Revolt in 2100.* 1955. Tokyo. Tuttle. 1st ed. inscr. wraps. boxed. VG. $400.00

HEINLEIN, Robert. *Revolt in 2100.* 1957. Gengensha. 1st Japanese ed. sgn. wraps. $225.00

HEINLEIN, Robert. *Revolt in 21000.* 1965. Signet. EX. $10.00

HEINLEIN, Robert. *Rolling Stones.* 1952. NY. Longman. 1st ed. dj. VG. $95.00

HEINLEIN, Robert. *Space Cadet.* 1948. Scribner. 1st ed. dj. $300.00

HEINLEIN, Robert. *Space Cadet.* 1952. NY. presentation. sgn. dj. VG. $40.00

HEINLEIN, Robert. *Star Beast.* 1954. NY. Scribner. 1st ed. dj. G. $50.00

HEINLEIN, Robert. *Star Beast.* 1954. Scribner. 1st ed. xl. rebound. P1. $17.50

HEINLEIN, Robert. *Time for the Stars.* nd. Scribner. dj. VG. P1. $15.00

HEINLEIN, Robert. *Time for the Stars.* 1957. Scribner. 2nd ed. dj. VG. P1. $25.00

HEINLEIN, Robert. *To Sail Beyond the Sunset.* 1987. Ace Putnam. 1st ed. dj. EX. P1. $20.00

HEINRICH, B. *One Man's Owl.* 1987. Princeton. Ils 224 p. dj. EX. M2. $18.00

HEINRICH, Willi. *Crak of Doom.* 1958. NY. 1st ed. 313 p. dj. T5. $17.50

HEINRICH, Willi. *Mark of Shame.* 1959. NY. 1st Am ed. 316 p. dj. VG. T5. $15.00

HEINTZELMAN, D.S. *Manual for Bird Watching in the Americas.* 1979. Universe. Ils. maps. 254 p. dj. EX. M2. $10.00

HEINTZELMAN, D.S. *N American Ducks, Geese & Swans.* 1978. Winchester. Ils. maps. 236 p. EX. M2. $18.00

HEINTZELMAN, D.S. *World Guide to Whales, Dolphins & Porpoises.* 1981. Winchester. Ils 1st ed. maps. 156 p. EX. M2. $10.00

HEINZ. *Fireside Book of Boxing.* 1961. Simon Schuster. 1st ed. dj. EX. $20.00

HEISENFELT, Kathryn. *Ann Sheridan & Sign of the Sphinx.* 1943. Whitman. dj. VG. P1. $10.00

HEISENFELT, Kathryn. *Betty Grable & House of Iron Shutters.* 1943. Whitman. dj. VG. P1. $10.00

HEISENFELT, Kathryn. *Jane Withers & the Swamp Wizard.* 1944. Whitman. dj. VG. P1. $10.00

HEISTER, L. *Compendium Anatomicum.* 1755. Venice. tables. 8vo. 486 p. $380.00

HELD, John Jr. *Dog Stories.* 1930. NY. 1st ed. dj. VG. J2. $60.00

HELD, L. *Game of Checkers.* 1933. McKay. diagrams. VG. $14.00

HELDERMAN, L. *George WA: Patron of Learning.* 1932. NY. Century. 1st ed. photos. blue cloth. VG. $10.00

HELFER, T. *Gentle Jungle.* 1980. Bringham Young U. 245 p. dj. M2. $5.00

HELL'S ANGELS. *Debut of Harlow.* 1930. gold cloth. VG. $40.00

HELLER, Joseph. *Catch-22.* 1961. Simon Schuster. 1st Am ed. dj. EX. $375.00

HELLER, Joseph. *Catch-22.* 1966. Modern Lib. 1st ed. dj. EX. $10.00

HELLER, Joseph. *Catch-22.* 1978. Franklin Lib. Ltd ed. 4to. blue morocco. EX. $110.00

HELLER, Joseph. *God Knows.* 1984. Knopf. 1st trade ed. dj. EX. $20.00

HELLER, Joseph. *Good As Gold.* 1979. NY. 1/500. sgn. plastic wraps. M. $35.00

HELLER, Joseph. *No Laughing Matter.* 1986. Putnam. 1st ed. sgn. dj. $45.00

HELLER, Joseph. *Something Happened.* 1974. Knopf. 1/350. sgn. boxed. M. $165.00

HELLER, Joseph. *Something Happened.* 1974. NY. 1st ed. dj. EX. $35.00

HELLER, Joseph. *Something Happened.* 1974. NY. 1st ed. sgn. 8vo. dj. EX. $50.00

HELLER, Joseph. *We Bombed in New Haven.* 1968. Ltd ed. 8vo. dj. G. $275.00

HELLER & MAGEE. *Bibliography of Grabhorn Press, 1915-1940.* 1975. San Francisco. Wolfsy. 4to. gilt linen. EX. $185.00

HELLER. *Heller's Guide for Ice Cream Makers.* 1918. Ils. ads. recipes. cloth. EX. $30.00

HELLMAN, Lillian. *Maybe.* 1980. Boston. 1st ed. dj. EX. $15.00

HELLMAN, Lillian. *Unfinished Woman: Memoir.* 1969. Boston. 1st ed. inscr/sgn. dj. EX. $125.00

HELLWIG, S.C. *Our Ottawa Co.* nd. (1960s?) np. 48 p. wraps. VG. T5. $9.50

HELM, M. *Man of Fire.* 1953. 1st ed. EX. $10.00

HELM, T. *Dangerous Sea Creatures.* 1976. Funk Wagnall. Ils. 278 p. dj. EX. M2. $10.00

HELM, T. *Shark! Unpredictable Killer of the Sea.* 1961. Dodd Mead. Ils. 260 p. dj. EX. M2. $13.00

HELMER, W. *Gun That Made the '20s Roar.* 1969. Ils 1st ed. dj. $25.00

HELMER & HOWELL. *Railroads.* 1959. 2nd ed. dj. VG. $20.00

HELMUTH, William. *Surgery & Its Adaption to Homeopathic Practice.* 1855. Phil. Moss. pls. full leather. $110.00

HELPER, H.R. *Dreadful CA.* 1948. Bobbs Merrill. 1st ed. dj. EX. $12.00

HELPER, H.R. *Impending Crisis of the S: How To Meet It.* 1860. NY. 5th ed. G. $35.00

HELPER, H.R. *Nojoque: Question for a Continent.* 1867. NY. $20.00

HELPS, Arthur. *Conquerors of New World & Their Bondsmen...* 1848 & 1852. London. 1st ed. 2 vols. $150.00

HELPS, Arthur. *Leaves From Journal of Our Life in Highlands, 1848-1861.* 1868. Harper. $20.00

HEMANS, Felicia. *Poems.* c 1902. NY. VG. C1. $9.00

HEMERDINQUER, P. *La Television et ses Progres.* 1933. Paris. Ils 1st ed. 245 p. wraps. VG. $35.00

HEMINGWAY, Ernest. *Across the River & Into the Trees.* 1950. London. 1st ed. dj. EX. $125.00

HEMINGWAY, Ernest. *Across the River & Into the Trees.* 1950. NY. 1st ed. dj. EX. $65.00

HEMINGWAY, Ernest. *All the Brave Drawings.* 1939. NY. Ils. VG. $75.00

HEMINGWAY, Ernest. *Book of the XV Brigade.* 1938. Madrid, Spain. 1st ed. VG. scarce. $350.00

HEMINGWAY, Ernest. *Collected Poems of Ernest Hemingway.* 1960. San Francisco. Pirated ed. wraps. EX. $25.00

HEMINGWAY, Ernest. *Dangerous Summer.* 1985. Scribner. 1st ed. dj. EX. T6. $25.00

HEMINGWAY, Ernest. *Death in the Afternoon.* 1932. Halcoyn House. VG. $25.00

HEMINGWAY, Ernest. *Divine Gesture.* 1974. Aloe Eds. 1/250. wraps. $65.00

HEMINGWAY, Ernest. *Farewell to Arms.* 1929. London. 1st ed. EX. P3. $45.00

HEMINGWAY, Ernest. *Farewell to Arms.* 1929. London. 1st ed. VG. $30.00

HEMINGWAY, Ernest. *Farewell to Arms.* 1929. NY. Ltd 1st ed. VG. $120.00

HEMINGWAY, Ernest. *Farewell to Arms.* 1929. NY. Ltd 1st ed. 2nd state. sgn. dj. boxed. EX. $200.00

HEMINGWAY, Ernest. *For Whom the Bell Tolls.* 1940. 1st trade ed. VG. $15.00

HEMINGWAY, Ernest. *For Whom the Bell Tolls.* 1942. Princeton. Ltd Ed Club. sgn. slipcase. VG. $125.00

HEMINGWAY, Ernest. *For Whom the Bell Tolls.* 1954. Tel Aviv. 1st ed. dj. EX. $25.00

HEMINGWAY, Ernest. *Garden of Eden.* 1986. NY. 1st ed. dj. EX. $30.00

HEMINGWAY, Ernest. *In Our Time. Vol. 1.* 1930. Scribner. G. $30.00

HEMINGWAY, Ernest. *Islands in the Stream.* 1970. NY. 1st ed. dj. M. $35.00

HEMINGWAY, Ernest. *Men at War.* 1942. NY. 1st ed. 1072 p. G. T5. $25.00

HEMINGWAY, Ernest. *Men Without Women.* 1927. Scribner. 1st ed. 1st issue. VG. $50.00

HEMINGWAY, Ernest. *Moveable Feast.* 1964. London. 1st ed. dj. VG. $45.00

HEMINGWAY, Ernest. *Moveable Feast.* 1964. London. 1st ed. dj. M. P3. $75.00

HEMINGWAY, Ernest. *Nick Adams Stories.* 1972. NY. 1st ed. dj. VG. B2. $37.50

HEMINGWAY, Ernest. *Old Man & the Sea.* London. 1st ed. dj. VG. $50.00

HEMINGWAY, Ernest. *Old Man & the Sea.* 1952. NY. 1st ed. 1st print. 140 p. dj. VG. T5. $100.00

HEMINGWAY, Ernest. *Old Man & the Sea.* 1952. Scribner. 2nd ed. P1. $12.50

HEMINGWAY, Ernest. *Old Man & the Sea.* 1953. Reprint Soc. VG. $30.00

HEMINGWAY, Ernest. *Old Man & the Sea.* 1969. Tel Aviv. 1st ed. wraps. G. $12.50

HEMINGWAY, Ernest. *So Red the Nose.* 1935. NY. dj. EX. $60.00

HEMINGWAY, Ernest. *Spanish War.* 1935. NY. 1st ed. wraps. $85.00

HEMINGWAY, Ernest. *Sun Also Rises.* nd. Collier. VG. P1. $15.00

HEMINGWAY, Ernest. *Sun Also Rises.* 1926. NY. Modern Lib. Intro Canby. dj. EX. $20.00

HEMINGWAY, Ernest. *Sun Also Rises.* 1926. NY. 1st ed. 1st state. presentation. M. $125.00

HEMINGWAY, Ernest. *Sun Also Rises.* 1962. Tel Aviv. 1st ed. wraps. $12.50

HEMINGWAY, Ernest. *To Have & Have Not.* 1937. NY. 1st ed. 1st state. M. $75.00

HEMINGWAY, Ernest. *To Have & Have Not.* 1937. Scribner. 1st ed. dj. G. $35.00

HEMINGWAY, Ernest. *Wild Years.* 1962. Dell. VG. $10.00

HEMINGWAY, Ernest. *Winner Take Nothing.* 1933. NY. 1st A ed. VG. $85.00

HEMINGWAY, Ernest. *Winner Take Nothing.* 1933. NY. 1st ed. G. $30.00

HEMINGWAY, Ernest. *5th Column & the 1st 49th.* nd. Collier. VG. P1. $15.00

HEMINGWAY, Jack. *Misadventures of a Fly Fisherman.* 1986. Dallas. dj. EX. $12.50

HEMINGWAY, L. *My Brother, Ernest Hemingway.* 1962. Cleveland. 1st ed. dj. VG. B2. $17.50

HEMINGWAY, Taylor. *Sex Control: Curious Customs of Medieval Times.* 1953. Pioneer Pr. 1/2000. 8vo. $20.00

HEMPEL, Walter. *Methods of Gas Analysis.* 1902. Macmillan. Ils. 474 p. VG. $5.00

HENCK, J.B. *Field Book for Railroad Engineers.* 1854. . Ils. 243 p. gilt bdg. $27.50

HENDERSON, B. *Great War Between Athens & Sparta.* 1927. London. Ils. 517 p. VG. $22.00

HENDERSON, D. *From the Volga to the Yukon.* 1945. Hastings House. map. 255 p. dj. EX. M2. $12.00

HENDERSON, E.B. *Darky Ditties.* 1915. Columbus, OH. presentation. sgn. 54 p. $65.00

HENDERSON, E.F. *Germany's Fighting Machine...* 1914. Indianapolis. Ils. 97 p. VG. T5. $45.00

HENDERSON, G.F.R. *Stonewall Jackson & the American Civil War.* 1937. Longman Green. Ils. pocket map. 737 p. VG. M2. $22.00

HENDERSON, G.F.R. *Stonewall Jackson & the American Civil War.* 1968. Gloucester. maps. 576 p. VG. T5. $17.50

HENDERSON, George. *Survivals in Belief Among the Celts.* 1911. MacLehose. 1st ed. VG. J2. $50.00

HENDERSON, J.M. *Brief Stories of St. Charles.* nd. private print. 4to. 16 p. M2. $5.00

HENDERSON, John. *W Indies.* 1905. London. Black. color pls. G. $12.00

HENDERSON, Neville. *Failure of a Mission: Berlin, 1937-1939.* 1940. Putnam. 8vo. red buckram. VG. $20.00

HENDERSON, Peter. *Henderson's Handbook of Plants.* 1920. NY. 2nd ed. G. $21.00

HENDERSON, R. *Early American Sport. Check List of Books.* 1953. NY. Revised 2nd ed. $75.00

HENDERSON & CRAIG. *Economic Mammalogy.* 1932. Thomas. 397 p. dj. EX. M2. $19.00

HENDERSON & HARRINGTON. *Ethnozoology of the Tewa Indians.* 1914. WA. G. $12.00

HENDERSON & SCHWARTZ. *Guide to Amphibians & Reptiles of Hispaniola.* 1984. Milwaukee. Ils. maps. 76 p. M. M2. $8.00

HENDRICK, B.J. *Statesmen of Lost Cause: Jefferson Davis & His Cabinet.* 1939. Boston. Ils. dj. VG. $15.00

HENDRICK, C.T. *Hendrick Genealogy: Daniel Hendrick of Haverhill, MA...* 1923. Rutland. Ils. 699 p. G. T5. $42.50

HENDRICK, Ellwood. *Lewis Miller: Biographical Essay.* 1925. NY. Ils. 208 p. TEG. VG. T5. $45.00

HENDRICKS, G.D. *Bad Men of the W.* 1941. Naylor. 1st ed. photos. 310 p. G. M2. $24.00

HENDRICKS, G.D. *Photographs of Thomas Eakins.* 1972. NY. 1st ed. dj. VG. $110.00

HENDRY, L.C. *FL's Vanishing Wildlife.* 1982. FL U. Ils. 69 p. M2. $7.00

HENLE, Fritz. *American Virgin Islands.* 1971. Macmillan. 24 photos. boxed. $55.00

HENLE, Fritz. *Caribbean: Journey With Pictures.* 1957. NY. 1st ed. inscr. VG. $25.00

HENLE, Fritz. *HI.* 1948. Hastings House. dj. VG. $30.00

HENLE, Fritz. *Mexico.* dj. EX. S2. $50.00

HENLE, Fritz. *Mexico.* 1945. Ziff Davis. 64 photos. 4to. VG. $20.00

HENLE, Fritz. *New Guide to Rollei Photography.* 1965. Viking. $15.00

HENNACY, Ammon. *Autobiography of a Catholic Anarchist.* 1954. NY. Catholic Worker Books. sgn. dj. VG. $18.00

HENNEPIN, Father L. *New Discovery of Vast Country in America.* 1903. McClurg. Ils. maps. 2 vols. TEG. xl. VG. $42.50

HENNUS, M.F. *J.B. Jongkind.* nd. Amsterdam. Palet Series. Dutch text. D2. $35.00

HENREY, Mrs. Robert. *Madeleine's Journal.* 1953. London. 1st ed. dj. VG. B2. $17.50

HENRY, G.M. *Guide to Birds of Ceylon.* 1978. Sri Lanka. DeSilva. Ils. 498 p. dj. EX. M2. $45.00

HENRY, J.D. *Red Fox: Cat-Like Canine.* 1986. Smithsonian. Ils. 176 p. EX. M2. $22.00

HENRY, Marguerite. *Born To Trot.* color photos. 222 p. G. $12.00

HENRY, Marguerite. *Brightly of the Grand Canyon.* 1953. Rand McNally. Ils Dennis. 1st ed. dj. VG. $15.00

HENRY, Marguerite. *Hole Book.* 1908. Harper. 1st ed. dj. fair. $15.00

HENRY, Marguerite. *Mr. Munchausen, John Kendrick Gangs.* 1901. Noyes Platt. G. $20.00

HENRY, Matthew. *Exposition of Old & New Testament.* 1830. NY. Haven Pub. 6 vols. calf. G. $100.00

HENRY, O. *Postscripts.* 1923. NY/London. 1st ed. dj. EX. scarce. $85.00

HENRY, O. *Voice of the City & Other Stories.* 1935. NY. Ils/sgn Grosz. 4to. dj. EX. $275.00

HENRY, R.S. *As They Saw Forrest: Recollections...of Contemporaries.* 1956. reprint. photos. fld maps. EX. J4. $28.50

HENRY, R.S. *First With the Most, Forrest.* 1944. 1st ed. photos. maps. EX. dj. J4. $37.50

HENRY, R.S. *Story of the Confederacy.* 1931. Garden City. reprint. 514 p. G. M2. $10.00

HENRY, R.S. *Story of the Confederacy.* 1931. Indianapolis. Ils 1st ed. sgn. 514 p. G. $40.00

HENRY, R.S. *Story of the Confederacy.* 1936. Ils. 514 p. K1. $12.50

HENRY, S.J. *Foxhunting Is Different.* 1938. Derrydale. 1/950. VG. $85.00

HENRY, Sonja. *Let's Peel an Onion.* 1965. NY. $9.00

HENRY, W.C. *Memoirs of Life & Scientific Researches of John Dalton.* 1854. 1st ed. VG. $150.00

HENRY, Will. *TX Rangers.* 1957. 174 p. $9.00

HENRY. *Francis Gurney du Pont: Memoire.* 1951. Phil. 1st ed. 1/300. 2 vols. slipcase. EX. $48.00

HENSHAW. *Book of Birds.* 1918. Nat Geog Soc. Ils Fuertes. VG. $25.00

HENSON. *Father Henson's Story of His Own Life.* 1859. Boston. Intro Stowe. 1st ed. VG. $40.00

HENTOFF, Nat. *Jazz Is.* 1976. NY. dj. EX. $25.00

HENTZEN, Alfred. *Lyonel Feininger: Aquarelle.* 1961. Munich. Piper. Ils. D2. $15.00

HEPBURN, A.B. *Story of an Outing.* 1913. NY. Ils. VG. $22.00

HEPBURN, Katharine. *Making of the African Queen.* 1987. NY. 1st ed. dj. VG. $7.00

HEPBURN, Katharine. *Making of the African Queen.* 1987. NY. 1st ed. 131 p. dj. EX. $15.00

HEPPENHEIMER, T.A. *Colonies in Space.* 1977. Harrisburg. 1st ed. dj. EX. $17.50

HEPPLEWHITE. *Cabinet Maker & Upholsterer's Guide.* 1942. NY. Towse Pub. lg folio. dj. $150.00

HEPWORTH. *Victorian & Edwardian Norfolk From Old Photographs.* dj. EX. S2. $25.00

HERALD, E.S. *Living Fishes of the World.* 1961. Doubleday. Ils. 304 p. dj. EX. M2. $20.00

HERBERDEN, M.V. *Exit This Way.* 1960. Crime Club. dj. VG. P1. $12.50

HERBERDEN, William. *Introduction to the Study of Physic.* 1929. NY. Hoeber. 1/230. boxed. EX. $45.00

HERBERT, Frank *Worlds of Frank Herbert.* 1980. Gregg Pr. no dj issued. P1. $11.00

HERBERT, Frank. *Children of Dune.* Berkley Putnam. 10th print. dj. VG. P1. $5.00

HERBERT, Frank. *Children of Dune.* Berkley Putnam. 8th print. dj. VG. P1. $5.00

HERBERT, Frank. *Children of Dune.* Berkley Putnam. 9th print. dj. VG. P1. $5.00

HERBERT, Frank. *Dragon in the Sea.* 1956. Doubleday. 1st ed. dj. VG. P1. $175.00

HERBERT, Frank. *Eye.* 1986. Gollancz. 1st ed. dj. EX. P1. $17.50

HERBERT, Frank. *God Emperor of Dune.* 1981. Putnam. 1st ed. dj. VG. P1. $20.00

HERBERT, Frank. *Heretics of Dune.* 1984. Putnam. 1st ed. dj. VG. P1. $20.00

HERBERT, Frank. *Man of Two Worlds.* 1986. Putnam. 1st ed. dj. EX. P1. $18.95

HERBERT, Frank. *Santaroga Barrier.* 1970. Rapp Whiting. 1st ed. dj. VG. P1. $35.00

HERBERT, James. *Sepulchre.* 1987. Hodder Stoughton. 1st ed. dj. P1. $20.00

HERBERT, M. *Snow People.* 1973. Putnam. Ils. 277 p. dj. VG. M2. $10.00

HERBERT, W. *Fighting Joe Hooker.* 1944. Indianapolis. 1st ed. dj. VG. B2. $60.00

HERBERT, W.B. *Railway Ghosts.* 1985. 128 p. $10.50

HERBERT. *Houses for Town & Country.* 1907. NY. Ils. 249 p. VG. C4. $65.00

HERDON, G.M. *William Tatham & Culture of Tobacco.* c 1969. Miami. with facsimile booklet. dj. VG. $15.00

HERFORD, Oliver. *Laughing Willow.* 1918. NY. 1st ed. sgn. VG. $35.00

HERFORD, Oliver. *This Giddy Globe.* 1919. NY. Doran. 1st ed. VG. $10.00

HERKOMER, Hubert. *Autobiography of Hubert Herkomer.* 1890. private print. presentation. sgn. VG. $200.00

HERLAD, E.S. *Living Fishes of the World.* 1961. Doubleday. Ils. 4to. 304 p. VG. M2. $16.00

HERLIHY, J. *Midnight Cowboy.* 1965. NY. 1st ed. dj. EX. scarce. $50.00

HERLIHY, J. *Midnight Cowboy.* 1965. NY. 1st ed. dj. VG. $35.00

HERLIHY, J. *Sleep of Baby Filbertson.* 1959. NY. Dutton. 1st ed. dj. EX. $10.00

HERMAN, Gerhard. *Celts.* 1977. 1st Am ed. dj. EX. C1. $12.00

HERMAN, Gerhard. *Phoenicians.* 1975. 1st Eng ed. EX. C1. $7.50

HERMANNSSON, Halldor. *Cartography of Iceland.* 1931. Cornell. 1st ed. 81 p. stiff wraps. J2. $45.00

HERNDON, G.M. *William Tatham & the Culture of Tobacco...* 1969. Miami. 506 p. dj. $45.00

HERNDON, S.H. *Days on the Road, Crossing the Plains in 1865.* 1902. NY. 1st ed. 12mo. 270 p. VG. $25.00

HERNDON, W.L. *Exploration of Valley of Amazon Under Direction of Navy.* 1853. Ils. 414 p. xl. A3. $60.00

HERNDON & GIBBON. *Exploration of Valley of Amazon.* 1854. WA. Ils. pls. map. 3 vols. G. $125.00

HEROLD & PRESBYTER. *New Historical Atlas of Sandusky Co.* 1874. Chicago. maps. 90 p. G. T5. $150.00

HERON, Robert. *Dainty Work for Pleasure & Profit.* 1897. Chicago. Ils. 458 p. gilt bdg. VG. C4. $32.00

HERON, Robert. *Letters of Junius.* 1804. Phil. 2 vols. $75.00

HERRE, A.W. *Philippine Fish Tales.* 1935. Manila. 65 pls. 302 p. G. M2. $16.00

HERRICK, C.J. *Neurological Foundations of Animal Behavior.* 1924. Holt. Ils. 334 p. VG. M2. $17.00

HERRICK, M.F. *Engineer's & Fireman's Manual.* 1941. Omaha. Ils. 4to. 232 p. EX. $27.50

HERRICK, Robert. *Poems.* 1910. NY. Ils Abbey. VG. $22.00

HERRICK. *Genealogical Register of Name & Family of Herrick.* 1846. Bangor. 1st ed. 2 vols. G. J2. $40.00

HERRING, J.L. *Saturday Night Sketches.* 1918. Boston. Ils Nicholl. 1st ed. 303 p. G. $40.00

HERRING, Pendleton. *Politics of Democracy, American Parties in Action.* 1940. NY. 1st ed. $10.00

HERRLIGKOFFER, Karl. *Naga Parbat.* 1954. NY. 1st Am ed. EX. $30.00

HERRMANN, F. *Sotheby's Portrait of an Auction House.* 1981. NY. 1st Am ed. 468 p. dj. VG. B2. $27.50

HERRO, S. *Bear Attacks: Their Causes & Avoidance.* 1985. Winchester. Ils 1st ed. 297 p. dj. EX. M2. $15.00

HERRON, Don. *Dark Barbarian: Robert E. Howard.* 1984. Greenwood. 1st ed. no dj issued. EX. P1. $30.00

HERSEY, John. *Algiers Motel Incident.* 1968. Knopf. 1st ed. dj. xl. P1. $5.00

HERSEY, John. *Blues.* 1987. Phil. Franklin Mint. sgn. dj. VG. $35.00

HERSEY, John. *Child Buyer.* 1960. Knopf. 1st ed. dj. VG. P1. $10.00

HERSEY, John. *Hiroshima.* 1958. NY. 1st ed. dj. EX. $15.00

HERSEY, John. *Hiroshima.* Ltd Ed Club. slipcase. M. B3. $400.00

HERSEY, John. *Hiroshima.* nd. Modern Lib. dj. G. $5.00

HERSEY, John. *Single Pebble.* 1956. NY. 1st ed. dj. EX. $20.00

HERSEY, John. *Wall.* 1950. NY. 1st ed. dj. $15.00

HERSEY, John. *Walnut Door.* 1977. Phil. Franklin Mint. dj. VG. $30.00

HERTER, G.L. *Professional Guide's Manual.* 1960. 2nd ed. G. $45.00

HERTZ, L.H. *Collecting Model Trains.* 1956. NY. Ils 1st ed. 352 p. VG. B2. $42.50

HERTZLER, A.E. *Horse & Buggy Doctor.* 1938. Harper. photos. 322 p. dj. G. M2. $11.00

HERVEY, Harry. *King Cobra.* 1927. Cosmopolitan. Ils. map. 301 p. EX. M2. $23.00

HERVEY, Harry. *King Cobra.* 1927. NY. Ils 1st ed. fld map. VG. $12.50

HERVEY, John. *Messenger: Great Progenitor.* 1935. Derrydale. 1/500. 8vo. $150.00

HERVEY & HEMS. *Fresh-Water Tropical Aquarium Fishes.* 1952. Batchworth. Ils. 425 p. EX. M2. $16.00

HERZFELDE, Wieland. *Tragigrotesken der Nacht.* 1920. Berlin. Verlag. Ils. scarce. D2. $275.00

HERZOG, Arthur. *IQ 83.* 1978. Simon Schuster. 1st ed. dj. EX. P1. $10.00

HERZSTEIN, R.E. *Waldheim: Missing Years.* 1988. NY. 1st ed. dj. VG. $9.00

HESKY, Olga. *Sequin Syndicate.* 1969. Dodd Mead. 1st ed. dj. VG. P1. $8.00

HESKY, Olga. *Sequin Syndicate.* 1969. Dodd Mead. 1st ed. VG. P1. $6.00

HESKY, Olga. *Time for Treason.* 1967. Dodd Mead. 1st ed. dj. xl. P1. $5.00

HESLER, L.R. *Mushrooms of the Great Smokies.* 1975. TN U. Ils. 289 p. VG. M2. $14.00

HESLER & SMITH. *N American Species of Hygrophorus.* 1963. TN U. Ils. 416 p. EX. M2. $20.00

HESS, Hans. *George Grosz.* 1985. New Haven. Yale. Ils. D2. $18.95

HESS, Joan. *Mischief in Maggody: Ozarks Murder Mystery.* 1988. St. Martin. 1st ed. dj. M. $10.00

HESS, Joan. *Really Cute Corpse: Claire Malloy Mystery.* 1988. St. Martin. 1st ed. dj. M. $10.00

HESS, Stephen. *Ungentlemanly Art: History of American Political Cartoons.* 1968. NY. 1st print. dj. VG. T1. $35.00

HESSE, Herman. *Gertrude.* 1969. NY. 1st ed. dj. VG. $20.00

HESSELTINE, W.B. *Tragic Conflict.* 1962. Braziller. 1st ed. dj. EX. $15.00

HETHOM, R. *Strasberg at the Actor's Studio.* 1965. NY. Ils 1st ed. 428 p. VG. B2. $35.00

HEUSSER, Albert. *Homes & Haunts of the Indians.* 1923. Patterson. Ils. G. E2. $20.00

HEUVELMANS, B. *On Track of Unknown Animals.* 1959. Hill Wang. Ils. 558 p. VG. M2. $17.00

HEWES. *High Courts of Heaven.* 1943. NY. 1st Am ed. dj. VG. $15.00

HEWITT, E.L. *Ancient Life in American SW...* 1943. Tudor. 392 p. dj. A3. $45.00

HEWITT, E.L. *Pajarito Plateau & Its Ancient People.* 1938. NM U. VG. $17.50

HEWITT, E.R. *Handbook of Fly Fishing.* 1933. NY. Marchbanks. 1st ed. VG. scarce. J3. $40.00

HEWITT, R.H. *Across the Plains & Over the Divide, a Mule Journey...* 1906. Broadway Pub. Ils. 521 p. A3. $60.00

HEWLETT, Esther. *Temper; or, Story of Susan & Betsy.* nd. (1825) Salem. 1st ed. VG. rare. $75.00

HEYER, Georgette. *Charity Girl.* 1970. Bodley Head. 1st ed. dj. G. P1. $15.00

HEYER, Georgette. *Cotillion.* nd. Putnam. VG. P1. $7.50

HEYER, Georgette. *Lady of Quality.* nd. Book Club. dj. G. P1. $4.00

HEYER, Georgette. *Lady of Quality.* 1972. London. 1st ed. dj. EX. $27.00

HEYER, Georgette. *No Wind of Blame.* 1970. Dutton. dj. xl. P1. $7.50

HEYERDAHL, Thor. *Aku-Aku: Secrets of Easter Island.* 1958. Rand McNally. Ils. map. 384 p. VG. M2. $7.00

HEYERDAHL, Thor. *American Indians in the Pacific: Theory Behind Kon-Tiki...* 1953. Chicago. 1st Am ed. 821 p. dj. G. T5. $55.00

HEYERDAHL, Thor. *American Indians in the Pacific: Theory Behind Kon-Tiki...* 1953. Rand McNally. 1st ed. dj. VG. J2. $100.00

HEYERDAHL, Thor. *Kon-Tiki Expedition.* 1965. Rand McNally. 1st ed. 4to. 224 p. dj. M2. $12.00

HEYERDAHL, Thor. *Ra Expeditions.* 1971. NY. 1st Am ed. sgn. 4to. 341 p. VG. $20.00

HEYERDAHL & FERDON. *Archaeology of Easter Island.* 1961. NM Mus. Ils. 4to. 559 p. dj. EX. M2. $95.00

HEYLIGER, W. *Big Leaguer.* 1936. Chicago. dj. VG. $25.00

HEYMAN, Ken. *They Became What They Beheld.* 1970. Ballantyne. dj. EX. $120.00

HEYWARD, D.B. *Angel.* 1926. Doran. 1st trade ed. $27.50

HEYWARD, D.B. *Carolina Chansons, Legends of Low Country.* 1922. NY. 1st ed. dj. $37.50

HEYWARD, D.B. *Jasbo Brown & Selected Poems.* 1931. NY. Farrar Rinehart. 2nd print. dj. EX. $22.50

HEYWARD, D.B. *Peter Ashley.* nd. NY. Farrar Rinehart. $35.00

HEYWARD, D.B. *Porgy, Decorated by Theodore Nadejen.* nd. NY. Grosset Dunlap. presentation. sgn. $45.00

HEYWARD, D.B. *Porgy.* 1925. NY. Doran. not 1st ed. $25.00

HEYWARD, D.C. *Seed From Madagascar.* 1937. Chapel Hill. Ils Carl Julien. 256 p. $175.00

HEYWOOD, C.D. *Negro Combat Troops in World War: Story of 371st Infantry.* 1928. Worcester. 1st ed. EX. $145.00

HEYWOOD, Rosalind. *Beyond Reach of Sense.* 1961. Book Club ed. dj. EX. $5.00

HIASSEN, Carl. *Tourist Season.* 1986. NY. Putnam. 1st ed. dj. M. $15.00

HIBBARD, Addison. *Stories of the Old S.* 1931. Chapel Hill. 1st ed. 520 p. dj. VG. $30.00

HIBBARD, F. *Palestine: Its Geography & Bible History.* 1851. NY. 20 maps. 354 p. G. $150.00

HIBBEN, F.C. *Hunting American Bears.* 1950. Lippincott. 1st ed. dj. G. $35.00

HIBBEN, F.C. *Hunting in Africa.* 1950. Phil. 1st ed. $40.00

HIBBEN, Paxton. *Henry Ward Beecher, an American Portrait.* 1927. Doran. G. $25.00

HIBBERT, C.C. *Great Mutiny.* 1978. NY. dj. EX. $15.00

HICHENS, Robert. *Snakebite & Other Stories.* 1920. Cassell. 3rd ed. VG. P1. $25.00

HICKEY, Michael. *Out of the Sky.* 1979. NY. 1st ed. photos. maps. 286 p. dj. T5. $12.50

HICKMAN, Bill. *Brigham's Destroying Angel, Being Life, Confession...* 1872. NY. Crofutt. Ils 1st ed. 219 p. VG. scarce. A3. $75.00

HICKMAN & GUY. *Care of the Wild Feathered & Furred.* 1978. Kesend. Ils. 143 p. M. M2. $9.00

HIDDEN, Alexander. *Ottoman Dynasty.* 1912. NY. Ils Revised ed. photos. maps. G. $45.00

HIDY, R.W. *Timber & Men.* 1963. NY. Ils 1st ed. 704 p. dj. VG. B2. $30.00

HIELSCHER, Kurt. *Dutschland: Landschaft & Baukunst.* 1931. Leipzig. Brockhaus. photos. D2. $125.00

HIGBE, Kirby. *High Hard One.* 1967. Viking. 1st print. dj. VG. $45.00

HIGDON, Hal. *Crime of the Century.* 1975. NY. 1st ed. 380 p. dj. VG. B2. $22.50

HIGGINS, C.A. *New Guide to the Pacific Coast: Santa Fe Route, CA, NM...* 1894. Rand McNally. Ils. 292 p. G. A3. $30.00

HIGGINS, C.A. *To CA & Back: Book of Practical Information for Travelers...* 1904. Doubleday. Ils. 317 p. A3. $35.00

HIGGINS, D.S. *Rider Haggard, a Biography.* 1983. NY. 1st Am ed. dj. EX. $15.00

HIGGINS, George V. *Digger's Game.* 1973. Knopf. 1st ed. dj. EX. P1. $15.00

HIGGINS, George V. *Digger's Game.* 1973. Knopf. 4th ed. dj. VG. P1. $10.00

HIGGINS, George V. *Friends of Eddie Coyle.* 1972. Knopf. 1st ed. dj. G. P1. $10.00

HIGGINS, George V. *Friends of Eddie Coyle.* 1972. NY. 1st ed. dj. EX. $25.00

HIGGINS, George V. *Judgment of Deke Hunter.* 1976. Little Brown. 1st ed. dj. EX. P1. $15.00

HIGGINS, Jack. *Exocet.* 1983. Stein Day. 1st ed. dj. EX. $15.00

HIGGINS, Trumbull. *Winston Churchill & the Dardanelles.* 1963. NY. Ils 1st ed. dj. VG. T5. $22.50

HIGGINS, V.M. *Gingerbread Man: Old, Old Story Retold & Illustrated.* 1926. Chicago. Whitman. slipcase. EX. $40.00

HIGGINSON, A.H. *As Hounds Ran: Four Centuries of Fox Hunting.* 1930. NY. 1st ed. 1/990. EX. $65.00

HIGGINSON, A.H. *Foxhunting Theory & Practice.* 1948. Berryville. Blue Ridge. dj. $25.00

HIGGINSON, A.H. *Try Back.* 1931. NY. Huntington Pr. 1/401. EX. $55.00

HIGGINSON, Ella. *AK, the Greatest Country.* 1908. NY. 1st ed. $40.00

HIGGINSON, T.W. *Army Life in a Black Regiment.* 1870. 296 p. EX. very scarce. K1. $55.00

HIGGINSON, T.W. *Army Life in a Black Regiment.* 1960. reprint of 1870 ed. 235 p. dj. J4. $20.00

HIGH, Philip E. *These Savage Futurians.* 1969. Dobson. dj. EX. P1. $12.50

HIGHSMITH, Patricia. *Dog's Ransom.* 1972. Knopf. 1st ed. dj. VG. P1. $20.00

HIGHSMITH, Patricia. *Ripley Under Ground.* nd. Book Club. dj. xl. P1. $3.00

HIGHSMITH, Patricia. *Talented Mr. Ripley.* 1955. Harcourt. 1st ed. dj. VG. $75.00

HIGINBOTHAM. *Three Weeks in British Isles.* 1911. Reilly Britton. Ils Hazenplug. VG. $20.00

HIJUELOS, Oscar. *Mambo Kings Play Songs of Love.* 1989. ARC. wraps. $30.00

HILDEBRANDT, Greg. *Favorite Fairy Tales.* 1984. NY. Ils 1st ed. M. C1. $12.50

HILDEBRANDT, Greg. *Greg Hildebrandt's Fantasies Forever: Story & Coloring Book.* 1985. 1st ed. M. C1. $9.00

HILDICK, Wallace. *Bracknell's Law.* nd. Book Club. dj. VG. P1. $2.75

HILDRETH, A.G. *Lengthening Shadow.* 1942. Paw Paw, MI. 2nd ed. 475 p. VG. B2. $42.50

HILDRETH, Richard. *Despotism in America.* 1854. Jewett. 1st ed. $60.00

HILEY, M. *Frank Sutcliffe: Photographer of Whitby.* 1974. Godine. dj. EX. $25.00

HILGARTNER, Beth. *Necklace of Fallen Stars.* 1979. Little Brown. 1st ed. dj. EX. P1. $12.50

HILL, A.J. *History of Company E of 4th MN Regiment Volunteer Infantry.* 1899. Pioneer Pr. wraps. EX. $60.00

HILL, Douglas. *Illustrated Faerie Queene.* 1980. Ils 1st ed. M. C1. $12.50

HILL, Douglas. *Opening of the Canadian W: Where Strong Men Gathered.* 1967. NY. Day. dj. VG. $16.00

HILL, Douglas. *Young Legionary.* 1983. Atheneum. 1st ed. dj. EX. P1. $12.50

HILL, F.T. *On the Trail of Grant & Lee.* 1924. 305 p. VG. J4. $7.50

HILL, G.B. *Boswell's Life of Johnson.* 1887. Oxford. xl. G. B1. $75.00

HILL, Gene. *Tears & Laughter.* 1981. Los Angeles. 1st ed. 1/450. sgn. boxed. EX. $100.00

HILL, H.W. *Municipality of Buffalo.* 1923. NY/Chicago. $25.00

HILL, J.A. *Man Is a Spirit.* 1918. London. $15.00

HILL, J.E. *End of the Cattle Trail.* nd. Long Beach. Moyle. 120 p. wraps. G. A3. $65.00

HILL, N.P. *Birds of Cape Cod, MA.* 1965. Morrow. Ils. 364 p. xl. M2. $7.00

HILL, R. *Desert Conquest.* 1943. NY. 1st ed. dj. EX. $20.00

HILL, R.N. *Side-Wheeler Saga.* 1953. NY. 1st ed. dj. VG. $22.00

HILL, R.T. *Geography & Geology of Black & Grand Prairies, TX.* 1901. GPO. pls. maps. VG. $50.00

HILL, Reginald. *Deadheads.* 1983. Macmillan. dj. EX. P1. $12.95

HILL, Reginald. *Ruling Passion.* nd. Book Club. dj. VG. P1. $4.00

HILL, Reginald. *Ruling Passion.* 1973. Harper Row. dj. xl. P1. $6.00

HILL, S.J.F. *Mrs. Hill's Journal: Civil War Reminiscences.* 1980. Donnelley. Lakeside Classic. 343 p. EX. M2. $20.00

HILL, William. *History of Rise, Progress...American Presbyterianism.* 1839. WA. 1st ed. VG. scarce. $135.00

HILL & ADAMSON. *Early Victorian Album.* 1976. Knopf. 1st Am ed. dj. VG. $40.00

HILL & GRIFFITH COMPANY. *Manufacturers of Foundry Facings, Supplies & Equipment.* 1909. Cincinnati. $25.00

HILL & SMITH. *Bats: A Natural History.* 1984. TX U. Ils. maps. 243 p. dj. EX. M2. $30.00

HILLARD. *Hillard's Abridgment of American Law of Real Property.* 1838-1839. Little Brown. 2 vols. G. $90.00

HILLCOURT, William. *Baden-Powell: Two Lives of a Hero.* 1964. NY. 1st ed. presentation. dj. VG. B2. $32.50

HILLEARY, A.A. *Jew & the Klan.* c 1925. Harrisburg. 12mo. 139 p. VG. $45.00

HILLEARY, W.H. *Webfoot Volunteer Diary: 1864-1866.* 1965. Nelson Onstad. 1st ed. dj. EX. $35.00

HILLER, I. *Introducing Birds to Young Naturalists.* 1989. TX A&M. Ils 1st ed. 4to. 69 p. M. M2. $19.00

HILLERMAN, Tony. *Dark Wind.* 1982. NY. Harper. 1st ed. dj. EX. $30.00

HILLERMAN, Tony. *Words, Weather & Wolfmen. Conversations With Hillerman.* 1989. SW Books. 1st ed. 1/350. sgns. dj. M. $100.00

HILLES. *Memorials of the Hilles Family.* 1928. Cincinnati. Ils. 239 p. VG. C4. $55.00

HILLESUM, Etty. *Letters From Westerbork.* 1986. NY. 1st ed. dj. VG. $7.50

HILLIER, Bevis. *Victorian Studio Photographs.* 1976. Boston. Godine. 1st Am ed. quarto. dj. EX. $25.00

HILLS, N.E. *History of Kelley's Island, OH.* 1925. Toledo. Ils 1st ed. VG. T5. $95.00

HILLYER, V.M. *Child's Geography of the World.* 1951. Appleton Century. VG. $15.00

HILLYER, V.M. *Child's History of Art.* 1934. NY. VG. B2. $32.50

HILSCHER, H.H. *AK Now.* 1948. Little Brown. 1st ed. sgn. 8vo. tan bdg. dj. VG. $15.00

HILTON, G.W. *Great Lakes Car Ferries.* 1962. Ils. 292 p. $35.00

HILTON, G.W. *Ma & Pa.* 1963. 175 photos. 193 p. $16.50

HILTON, James. *Was It Murder?* 1935. Harper. VG. P1. $20.00

HILTON, John Buxton. *Corridors of Guilt.* 1984. St. Martin. 1st ed. dj. xl. P1. $7.50

HILTON, S. *Way It Was: 1876.* c 1975. Phil. Ils. 8vo. 216 p. red cloth. G2. $8.00

HILTY & BROWN. *Guide to Birds of Colombia.* 1986. Princeton U. Ils. 836 p. dj. M. M2. $90.00

HIMES, C.P. *Pinktoes.* 1965. NY. 1st A ed. dj. VG. $25.00

HIMES, Chester. *Case of Rape.* 1980. NY. Targ. 1st ed. 1/350. sgn. glassine dj. $40.00

HIND, Arthur M. *Catalog of Rembrandt's Etchings.* 1967. NY. Da Capo. reprint of 1923 ed. 2 vols. D2. $125.00

HIND, C.L. *Uncollected Works of Aubrey Beardsley.* 1925. London. Bodley Head. Ils. 4to. $75.00

HINDLE, Brooke. *Pursuit of Science in Revolutionary America, 1735-1789.* 1956. NC U. 1st ed. VG. J2. $15.00

HINDUS, Maurice. *Humanity Uprooted.* 1934. Blue Ribbon. 20th print. VG. $12.00

HINDWOOD, K. *Australian Birds in Color.* 1970. Reed. Ils. 112 p. dj. EX. M2. $12.00

HINE, L.W. *Lewis W. Hine & the American Social Conscience.* 1967. Walker. dj. VG. $17.50

HINE, L.W. *Portfolio.* 1970. S2. $125.00

HINEMEYER, Michael T. *4th Down Earth.* 1985. St. Martin. 1st ed. dj. EX. P1. $13.95

HINES, Gordon. *Alfalfa Bill.* 1932. OK City. EX. $75.00

HINES, Gustavus. *OR: Its History, Condition & Prospects.* 1851. Albany. Derby Miller. 438 p. G. A3. $75.00

HINES, Gustavus. *Wild Life in OR.* c 1881. NY. Ils. 12mo. 437 p. G. G2. $26.00

HINKLE. *Sierra NV Lakes.* 1949. Indianapolis. 1st ed. dj. EX. B2. $40.00

HINKLEY, Helen. *Rails From the W.* 1969. 207 p. $14.00

HINMAN, W.F. *Corporal Si Klegg & His Pard.* 1888. Cleveland. 1st ed. 706 p. rebound. fair. T5. $42.50

HINMAN, W.F. *Corporal Si Klegg & His Pard.* 1900. Cleveland. 12th ed. 706 p. T5. $25.00

HINSDALE, B.A. *Old NW.* 1888. NY. 11 color maps. TEG. VG. T5. $25.00

HINSIE, L.E. *Understandable Psychiatry.* 1948. NY. Hinsie. $20.00

HINTON, H.B. *Air Victory: Men & Machines.* 1948. NY. 1st ed. 428 p. G. T5. $19.50

HINTON, J.H. *History & Topography of the US of N America.* 1850. Ils 3rd ed. 2 vols in 1. EX. K1. $110.00

HINTON, R.J. *John Brown & His Men.* 1894. NY. 12mo. 752 p. maroon cloth. G2. $24.00

HINTZE, Naomi. *You'll Like My Mother.* nd. Putnam. 2nd ed. dj. VG. P1. $7.50

HIRSCH, A.H. *Huguenots of Colonial SC.* 1928. Durham. Duke U. 338 p. $45.00

HIRSCHFELD, Al. *American Theatre As Seen by Hirshfeld.* 1961. NY. 1st ed. dj. VG. B2. $25.00

HIRSCHFELD, Al. *Hirshfeld by Hirschfeld.* 1979. NY. 1st ed. dj. $30.00

HIRSCHFELD, Al. *World of Hirschfeld.* nd. Abrams. 189 pls. 233 p. dj. D2. $150.00

HIRSCHFELD, B. *Ewings of Dallas.* 1980. NY. 1st ed. 276 p. wraps. $12.50

HIRSCHMAN, Jack. *Black Alephs.* 1969. Phoenix. 1st ed. dj. $20.00

HISS & ZINSSER. *TB of Bacteriology.* 1910. NY. Ils 1st ed. VG. $45.00

HITCHCOCK, Alfred. *Daring Detectives.* 1969. Random House. VG. P1. $12.50

HITCHCOCK, Alfred. *Ghostly Gallery.* 1962. Random House. VG. P1. $15.00

HITCHCOCK, Alfred. *Haunted Houseful.* 1961. Random House. 1st ed. VG. P1. $15.00

HITCHCOCK, Alfred. *My Favorites in Suspense.* nd. Book Club. dj. VG. P1. $6.00

HITCHCOCK, Alfred. *Sinister Spies.* 1966. Random House. VG. P1. $15.00

HITCHCOCK, Alfred. *Stories Not for the Nervous.* nd. Book Club. dj. VG. P1. $5.00

HITCHCOCK, Alfred. *Suspense Stories.* 1945. Dell. pb. VG. $18.00

HITCHCOCK, C.H. *HI & Its Volcanoes.* 1911. Honolulu. Ils 2nd ed. G. $85.00

HITCHCOCK, Caroline. *Nancy Hanks.* 1899. NY. Doubleday McClure. 1st ed. EX. $20.00

HITCHCOCK, E. *Illustrations of Surface Geology.* 1956. Smithsonian. pls. fld maps. VG. $60.00

HITCHCOCK, E. *Outline of Geology of Globe & of US in Particular.* 1853. Boston. Phillips Samson. 1st ed. 136 p. M2. $165.00

HITCHCOCK, E.G. *Jonathan Goldsmith: Pioneer Master Builder of W Reserve.* 1980. Cleveland. Ils 1st ed. sgn. 131 p. dj. T5. $35.00

HITCHCOCK, H.R. *American Architectural Books Published Before 1895.* 1895. MN U. VG. $50.00

HITCHCOCK, H.R. *American Architectural Books Published Before 1895.* 1946. MN U. Latest Revised ed. 130 p. EX. $25.00

HITCHCOCK, J.R.W. *Etching in America.* 1886. NY. 12mo. $45.00

HITCHCOCK & CRONQUIST. *Flora of the Pacific NW: Illustrated Manual.* 1987. WA U. Ils. 730 p. M. M2. $40.00

HITCHENS, Dolores. *Bank With Bamboo Door.* 1965. Simon Schuster. 1st ed. dj. xl. P1. $5.00

HITCHENS, Dolores. *Collection of Strangers.* 1969. Putnam. 1st ed. dj. VG. P1. $12.50

HITLER, Adolf. *Bilder aus dem Leben des Fuhrers.* 1936. Hamburg. Ils. photos. 135 p. dj. VG. $100.00

HITLER, Adolf. *Deutschland Erwacht Werden, Kampf und Sieg der NSDAP.* 1933. Munchen. photos. folio. 151 p. $100.00

HITLER, Adolf. *Mein Kampf.* 1939. NY. 1st Unexpurgated ed. G. $18.50

HITSMAN, J.M. *Incredible War of 1812: Military History.* 1965. Toronto. Ils 1st ed. 265 p. dj. VG. T5. $22.50

HITTLE, J.D. *Military Staff: It's History & Development.* 1944. Harrisburg. 1st ed. 201 p. VG. T5. $25.00

HJORTSERG, William. *Gray Matters.* Simon Schuster. 2nd ed. dj. EX. P1. $10.00

HOARE, E.N. *Paths in Great Waters...* c 1889. London. Ils Gordon Browne. 320 p. $35.00

HOBAN, Russell. *Pilgermann.* 1983. NY. 1st ed. dj. EX. $16.00

HOBART, A.T. *Oil for Lamps of China.* 1933. Bobbs Merrill. 1st ed. dj. VG. $25.00

HOBBES, J.O. *Dream & Business.* 1906. London. Ils Beardsley. $35.00

HOBBS, H.H. *Crayfishes of FL.* 1942. FL U. 24 pls. map. 179 p. M. M2. $35.00

HOBBS, Robert. *Odilon Redon.* 1977. Boston. 1st ed. 4to. 192 p. EX. $13.00

HOBBS & ELLIOTT. *Gasoline Automobile.* 1915. NY. Ils 1st ed. 9th imp. 8vo. 259 p. $32.00

HOBSON, L.Z. *Laura Z.: A Life.* 1983. NY. 1st ed. dj. EX. $15.00

HOBSON, R.L. *Chinese Art.* 1927. NY. color pls. 4to. $60.00

HOBSON, R.P. *Grass Beyond the Mountains.* 1951. Lippincott. 256 p. dj. VG. M2. $10.00

HOCH, Edward D. *Best Detective Stories 1978.* 1978. Dutton. 1st ed. dj. EX. P1. $15.00

HOCHBAUM, H.A. *Canvasback on a Prairie Marsh.* 1944. Am Wildlife Inst. 1st ed. dj. J2. $22.50

HOCHBAUM, H.A. *Travels & Traditions of Waterfowl.* 1955. MN U. 1st ed. VG. J2. $22.50

HOCHBAUM, H.A. *Travels & Traditions of Waterfowl.* 1956. MN U. Ils 2nd print. 301 p. dj. VG. M2. $18.00

HOCHWALT. *Makers of Bird Dog History.* 1927. Dayton. 1st ed. VG. B2. $55.00

HOCKNEY & WESCHLER. *True to Life.* 1984. Knopf. 1st Am ed. square folio. dj. EX. $47.50

HODDER-WILLIAMS, Christopher. *Egg-Shaped Thing.* nd. Book Club. dj. VG. P1. $3.00

HODEL & WRIGHT. *Enter the Lion: Posthumous Memoir of Mycroft Holmes.* 1979. Hawthorne. 1st ed. dj. EX. P1. $20.00

HODEL & WRIGHT. *Enter the Lion: Posthumous Memoir of Mycroft Holmes.* 1979. NY. 237 p. dj. M. $25.00

HODGE, F.W. *Handbook of American Indians N of Mexico.* 1907 & 1910. WA. 2 vols. scarce. A3. $150.00

HODGE, L.T. *From a Sharecropper's Son to Independence.* 1977. NY. Vantage. 60 p. dj. $12.50

HODGES & HUGHES. *Select Naval Documents.* 1922. Cambridge. Ils 227 p. G. T5. $22.50

HODGSON, Fred. *ABC of Steel Square & Its Practical Uses.* 1908. 136 p. $4.00

HODGSON, Fred. *Modern Carpentry.* 1902. Chicago. Ils 1st ed. VG. T1. $30.00

HODGSON, Fred. *New Hardwood Finishing, Wood Manipulating, Staining...* 1904. Chicago. VG. C4. $32.00

HODGSON, Mrs. Willoughby. *Old English China.* 1913. London. 1st ed. pls. 201 p. VG. B2. $125.00

HODGSON, William Hope. *Carnacki, the Ghost Finder.* 1947. Mycroft Moran. 1st ed. EX. $35.00

HODGSON, William Hope. *Carnacki, the Ghost Finder.* 1979. Hawthorne. 1st ed. dj. EX. P1. $20.00

HODGSON, William Hope. *Deep Waters.* 1967. Arkham House. 1st ed. dj. EX. $75.00

HODGSON, William Hope. *Dream of X.* 1977. Donald Grant. 1st ed. dj. EX. P1. $20.00

HODGSON, William Hope. *House on the Borderland & Other Novels.* 1946. Sauk City. 1st Am ed. dj. $80.00

HODIN, Josef Paul. *Friedrich Karl Gotch: Olbilder, Oil Paintings, Huiles.* 1987. Hamburg. Verlag. Ils. D2. $150.00

HODSON, A.W. *Trekking the Great Thirst: Sport & Travel in Kalahari.* 1987. Zimbabwe. reprint of 1912 ed. dj. M. M2. $30.00

HOEHLING, A.A. *Last Train From Atlanta.* 1958. Yoseloff. Ils 1st print. sgn. dj. EX. M2. $25.00

HOESE & MOORE. *Fishes of the Gulf of Mexico, TX, LA & Adjacent Waters.* 1977. TX A&M U. Ils. 327 p. EX. M2. $19.00

HOFBAUER, Imre. *George Grosz.* 1948. London/Brussels. dj. D2. $45.00

HOFF, C.C. *Ostracods of IL: Their Biology & Taxonomy.* 1942. IL U. 9 pls. 196 p. M2. $12.00

HOFF, C.C. *Pseudoscorpions of IL.* 1949. IL Nat Hist Survey. Ils. VG. M2. $13.00

HOFF, Carol. *Johnny TX.* 1950. 150 p. G. $9.00

HOFF & FULTON. *Bibliography of Aviation Medicine.* 1942. Thomas. 1st ed. dj. VG. J2. $50.00

HOFF. *Dutch Firearms.* 1978. London. Ils. 252 p. dj. EX. $25.00

HOFFA, James. *Hoffa & the Teamsters.* 1965. sgn. dj. VG. $25.00

HOFFA, James. *Hoffa: The Real Story. As Told to Oscar Fraley.* 1975. 2nd print. dj. VG. $15.00

HOFFENBERG, Jack. *Thunder at Dawn.* 1965. Dutton. 1st ed. dj. VG. P1. $10.00

HOFFMAN, Abbie. *Soon To Be a Major Motion Picture.* 1980. Perigee. 1st print. EX. $15.00

HOFFMAN, Abbie. *Steal This Book.* 1971. NY. Black Cat. 1st ed. pb. wraps. G. $45.00

HOFFMAN, Abbie. *Steal This Book.* 1971. NY. Grove. 4th ed. VG. $20.00

HOFFMAN, Abbie. *Steal This Book.* 1971. NY. Zebra. later print. pb. wraps. EX. $35.00

HOFFMAN, Abbie. *Steal This Urine Test.* 1987. Penguin. 1st ed. sgn. wraps. M. $50.00

HOFFMAN, Abbie. *Woodstock Nation.* 1969. 3rd ed. pb. VG. $15.00

HOFFMAN, Abbie. *Woodstock Nation.* 1969. NY. 1st trade pb ed. wraps. VG. $45.00

HOFFMAN, Abbie. *Woodstock Nation.* 1969. Vintage. 1st print. SftCvr. EX. $65.00

HOFFMAN, E. *Kokoschka: Life & Work.* 1947. London. Ils. 8vo. gilt morocco. slipcase. J2. $90.00

HOFFMAN, Frederick. *Race Traits & Tendencies of American Negro.* 1896. Macmillan. 1st ed. 329 p. stiff wraps. VG. J2. $15.00

HOFFMAN, H.H. *Hoffman's Index to Poetry: European & Latin American...* Scarecrow Pr. 686 p. VG. T5. $15.00

HOFFMAN, J. *Alpen: Flora fur Touristen und Pflanzenfreunde.* 1904. Stuttgart. Ils. German text. VG. M2. $18.00

HOFFMAN, Lee. *Always the Black Night.* 1970. 1st ed. pb. EX. C1. $3.00

HOFFMAN, Lee. *Loco.* 1969. Doubleday. 1st ed. dj. xl. P1. $5.00

HOFFMAN, Malvina. *Yesterday Is Tomorrow.* 1965. NY. Crown. 1st ed. dj. VG. B2. $22.50

HOFFMAN, W.J. *Annotated List of Birds of NV.* 1881. WA. 195 p. wraps. A3. $35.00

HOFFMAN, Werner. *Das Irdische Paradies, Motive & Ideen des 19, Jahrhunderts.* 1974. Munich. Ils 2nd ed. 306 p. dj. D2. $45.00

HOFFMANN, Edith. *Kokoschka: Life & Work.* 1947. London. Faber. Ils. 367 p. VG. D2. $60.00

HOFFMANN, Heinrich. *Der Struwelpeter.* Ils Hoffmann. German text. juvenile. VG. $45.00

HOGAN, Ben. *Power Golf.* 1948. Barnes. dj. VG. $23.00

HOGAN, James P. *Endgame Enigma.* 1987. Bantam. 1st ed. dj. EX. P1. $16.95

HOGAN, W.R. *TX Republic: Social & Economic History.* 1946. OK U. Ils 1st ed. 338 p. EX. M2. $20.00

HOGARTH, Burne. *Dynamic Anatomy.* 1984. Watson Guptill. 11th print. dj. EX. P1. $20.00

HOGG, Ian. *Infantry Weapons.* 1977. Crowell. 1st ed. 4to. dj. $30.00

HOGNER, D.C. *Conservation in America.* 1958. Lippincott. Ils 1st ed. 240 p. dj. G. M2. $5.00

HOGUE, C.L. *Armies of the Ant.* 1972. World. Ils 1st ed. 234 p. dj. EX. M2. $12.00

HOHMAN, Elmo. *American Whaleman.* 1928. Longman. 1st ed. dj. VG. J2. $45.00

HOHN & PETERMAN. *Curiosities of the Plant Kingdom.* 1980. Universe. Ils. 212 p. dj. EX. M2. $12.00

HOIG, Stan. *Battle of the Washita: Sheridan-Custer Campaign, 1867-1869.* 1976. Doubleday. 1st ed. dj. M. $18.00

HOIG, Stan. *Sand Creek Massacre.* 1961. Norman. 1st ed. dj. EX. $22.00

HOIG, Stan. *W Odyssey of John Simpson Smith.* 1974. Clark. $15.00

HOKE, H. & J. *Music Boxes: Their Lore & Lure.* 1957. NY. Ils 1st ed. dj. with record. B2. $32.50

HOKE, Helen. *Mrs. Silk.* 1945. Veritas. Ils Thorne. dj. G. $20.00

HOKINSON, Helen. *So You're Going To Buy a Book!* 1931. NY. 1st ed. folio. VG. $15.00

HOLAND, Hjalmar. *American, 1355-1364.* 1946. Duell Sloan. 1st ed. dj. VG. J2. $10.00

HOLAND, Hjalmar. *Pre-Columbian Crusade to America.* 1962. Twayne. 1st ed. dj. VG. J2. $10.00

HOLAND, Hjalmar. *Westward From Vinland: Account of Norse Discoveries...* 1940. Duell Sloan. 1st ed. VG. J2. $17.50

HOLAND, Hjalmar. *Westward From Vinland: Account of Norse Discoveries...* 1942. Duell Sloan. 2nd print. VG. J2. $15.00

HOLBACH, M.M. *Bosnia & Herzegovia.* 1901. London. Ils. fld map. 242 p. TEG. G. T5. $22.50

HOLBROOK, J. *Ten Years Among Mailbags.* 1855. Phil. Ils. $60.00

HOLBROOK, S. *Age of the Moguls.* 1953. NY. 1st ed. EX. $15.00

HOLBROOK, S. *Age of the Monguls.* 1954. 373 p. M. $17.50

HOLBROOK, S. *Golden Age of Quackery.* 1959. NY. 1st ed. 302 p. index. dj. VG. B2. $17.50

HOLBROOK, S. *Holy Old Mackinaw.* 1940. 278 p. VG. $15.00

HOLBROOK, S. *Rocky Mountain Revolution.* 1956. 1st ed. dj. VG. $25.00

HOLBROOK, S. *Story of American Railroads.* 1947. NY. Bonanza. 3rd ed. dj. EX. $8.50

HOLDEN, E. *Country Diary of an Edwardian Lady.* facsimile of 1906 ed. dj. $12.00

HOLDEN, E. *Country Diary of an Edwardian Lady.* 1977. Holt Rinehart. Ils. 177 p. dj. M2. $17.00

HOLDEN, E.S. *Publications of Lick Observatory of U of CA. Vol. I.* 1887. Sacramento. $55.00

HOLDEN, G.P. *Idyl of the Split Bamboo.* 1920. Cincinnati. 1st ed. 278 p. VG. $75.00

HOLDEN, Richard Cort. *Snow Fury.* nd. Book Club. dj. G. P1. $3.00

HOLDREDGE, H. *Mammy Pleasant.* 1953. NY. 1st ed. dj. VG. B2. $17.50

HOLDRIDGE, D. *Pindorama; or, Jungle to You.* 1933. Minton Balch. Ils. map. 273 p. VG. M2. $11.00

HOLDSTOCK, Robert. *Mythago Wood.* 1984. Arbor House. 1st ed. dj. EX. P1. $14.95

HOLDSTOCK, Robert. *Mythago Wood.* 1984. Book Club. dj. VG. C1. $5.00

HOLESKI, C.J. & M.C. *In Search of Gold: AK Journals of Horace S. Conger...* 1983. AK Geog Soc. photos. maps. 313 p. EX. M2. $9.00

HOLLAENDER, A. *Radiation Biology.* 1954. NY. 3 vols in 4. $145.00

HOLLAND, Cecilia. *Lords of Vaumartin.* 1988. 1st ed. dj. M. C1. $12.00

HOLLAND, Jack. *Druid Time.* 1986. 1st ed. dj. EX. C1. $7.50

HOLLAND, Kenneth. *Youth in European Labor Camps.* 1939. WA. dj. VG. $20.00

HOLLAND, R.P. *Good Shot.* 1946. Knopf. 1st ed. 1/850. sgn. boxed. VG. B2. $60.00

HOLLAND, R.P. *My Gun Dogs.* 1929. Boston. 1st ed. VG. B2. $35.00

HOLLAND, R.P. *Nip & Tuck.* Derrydale. 1/74. pub bdg. slipcase. EX. $500.00

HOLLAND, R.P. *Now Listen Warden.* 1946. W Hartford. 1st ed. boxed. VG. B2. $70.00

HOLLAND, R.P. *Seven Grand Gun Dogs.* 1961. NY. 1st ed. dj. VG. B2. $35.00

HOLLAND, R.P. *Shotgunning in Uplands.* 1944. Barnes. 1st ed. VG. B2. $50.00

HOLLAND, R.S. *Historic Ships.* 1927. Phil. 3rd print. 390 p. G. $25.00

HOLLAND, W.J. *Butterfly Book.* 1899. Ils. color pls. G. $45.00

HOLLAND, W.J. *Moth Book.* 1903. Ils 1st ed. color pls. $100.00

HOLLANDER, Frederick. *Those Torn From the Earth.* 1941. NY. Intro Mann. 1st ed. inscr. EX. P3. $35.00

HOLLANDER, J.H. *Cincinnati S Railway.* 1894. 116 p. rebound. $32.50

HOLLANDS, D. *Eagles, Hawks & Falcons of Australia.* 1984. Melbourne. Nelson. Ils 1st ed. 212 p. dj. M2. $45.00

HOLLENBACK, F.R. *Argentine Central.* 1939. Ltd ed. 1/300. sgn. 80 p. $40.00

HOLLENBACK, F.R. *Laramie Plains Life.* 1960. Ltd ed. 1/300. sgn. 94 p. $40.00

HOLLIDAY, J.S. *World Rushed In.* 1981. Ils. 558 p. dj. K1. $14.50

HOLLING, H.C. *Book of Indians.* 1935. NY. 1st ed. dj. VG. B2. $25.00

HOLLING, H.C. *Minn of the MS.* 1951. Boston. 1st ed. dj. VG. B2. $22.50

HOLLINGS, E.F. *Case Against Hunger: Demand for National Policy...* 1970. NY. Cowles. 1st ed. presentation. sgn. 276 p. $22.50

HOLLINGSWORTH, B. *Her Garden Was Her Delight.* 1962. NY. 1st ed. 166 p. dj. VG. B2. $17.50

HOLLINGSWORTH, Brian. *Atlas of the World's Railways.* 1980. Ils. 350 p. $30.00

HOLLISTER, G.W. *History of CT.* 1855. New Haven. Ils 1st ed. 8vo. 2 vols. G. T1. $80.00

HOLLISTER, O.J. *CO Volunteers in NM.* 1962. Donnelley. Lakeside Classic. blue bdg. $35.00

HOLLISTER, U.S. *Navajo & His Blanket.* 1974. Glorieta. 2nd print. EX. $18.50

HOLLISTER. *History of Lackawanna Valley.* 1869. NY. Alvord. Revised 2nd ed. $45.00

HOLLOW, John. *Against the Night: The Stars.* nd. OH U. EX. P1. $9.95

HOLLOWAY, Emory. *Whitman: Interpretation in Narrative.* 1926. NY. Knopf. VG. $15.00

HOLLOWAY, G.N. *Beyond ESP.* 1969. NY. $10.00

HOLLOWAY, G.N. *Let the Heart Speak.* 1951. LA. $6.00

HOLLOWAY, J.N. *History of KS: From 1st Exploration of MS Valley.* 1868. Lafayette. Emmons. Ils 1st ed. VG. $40.00

HOLLOWAY, L.C. *Ladies of the White House.* 1881. Ils. 607 p. K1. $12.50

HOLMAN, Hugh. *World of Thomas Wolfe.* 1962. NY. Scribner. 197 p. printed wraps. $12.50

HOLME, C. *Art in Photography.* 1905. London. Studio. 1st ed. mounted photos. wraps. $95.00

HOLME, C. *Color Photography & Other Recent Developments...of Camera.* 1908. London. 1st ed. photos. 114 p. wraps. EX. $125.00

HOLME & HALTON. *Modern Book Illustrators & Their Work.* 1914. London. Studio. Special ed. pls. 4to. wraps. $75.00

HOLMER, M.R.N. *Indian Bird Life.* 1923. London/Bombay. Oxford U. 12mo. 100 p. VG. $27.50

HOLMES, F.L. *Badger Saints & Sinners.* 1939. Milwaukee. Ils 1st ed. 570 p. dj. G. T5. $22.50

HOLMES, F.S. *S Farmer & Market Gardner, Being Compilation of Articles...* 1852. Charleston. New Enlarged ed. fld chart. 249 p. $65.00

HOLMES, G.S. *Lenox China: Story of Walter Scott Lenox.* private print. Ils. 74 p. VG. $30.00

HOLMES, J.C. *Dire Coasts.* 1988. Limberlost. 1/500. hand-sewn wraps. M. $20.00

HOLMES, J.C. *Get Home Free.* 1964. NY. 1st ed. dj. EX. $30.00

HOLMES, J.C. *Go.* 1952. NY. 1st ed. sgn. dj. EX. $50.00

HOLMES, J.C. *Horn.* 1958. NY. 1st ed. dj. M. $95.00

HOLMES, J.C. *Nothing More To Declare.* 1967. Dutton. 1st ed. presentation. dj. RS. M. $140.00

HOLMES, James. *Dr. Bullie's Notes.* 1975. Atlanta. Cherokee Pub. Ils. 247 p. dj. EX. $15.00

HOLMES, John. *Mordred.* Ace. 1st ed. pb. VG. C1. $2.50

HOLMES, L. *Arctic Whale Men.* 1861. Boston. 1st ed. VG. $58.00

HOLMES, M.G. *From New Spain by Sea to CA, 1519-1668.* 1968. Glendale. Clark. Ils. maps. 308 p. VG. A3. $65.00

HOLMES, M.J. *Rose Mather.* 1874. np. $30.00

HOLMES, Maurice. *Some Bibliographical Notes on Novels of G.B. Shaw.* 1935. London. 1/500. wraps. VG. $35.00

HOLMES, O.W. *Currents & Counter Currents in Medicine.* 1861. Boston. 406 p. $100.00

HOLMES, O.W. *Over the Teacups.* 1891. Boston. Houghton Mifflin. 1st ed. VG. $25.00

HOLMES, O.W. *Poet at Breakfast Table.* 1872. Boston. 1st ed. 1st state. EX. $85.00

HOLMES, O.W. *Professor at Breakfast Table.* 1860. Large Paper ed. slipcase. $175.00

HOLMES, R.R. *Naval & Military Trophies & Relics of British Heroes.* 1896. London. Nimmo. Ils Gibb. folio. morocco. J2. $250.00

HOLMES, T.J. *Mather Literature.* 1927. Cleveland. 1/250. presentation. TEG. VG. $25.00

HOLMES & RUGGLES. *Roentgen Interpretation, a Manual.* 1919. Phil. 1st ed. 181 pls. red cloth. EX. $40.00

HOLMES. *Joan of Arc.* Ils Prittie. VG. E2. $20.00

HOLMES. *Report of Selby Smelter Commission.* 1915. GPO. 8vo. 528 p. VG. scarce. $60.00

HOLROYD, M. *Augustus John.* 1974-1975. London. 8vo. 2 vols. djs. EX. J2. $50.00

HOLROYD, Michael. *Dog's Life.* 1969. Holt Rinehart Winston. 1st ed. P1. $5.00

HOLSTEIN, H.L.V. *Memoirs of Gilbert M. Lafayette.* 1835. Geneva. 2nd ed. G. $45.00

HOLSTEIN, H.L.V. *Memoirs of Simon Bolivar.* 1829. Boston. 1st ed. G. $55.00

HOLT, Helen. *Exiled: Story of John Lathrop, 1584-1653.* 1987. Paramount. sgn. dj. EX. $25.00

HOLT, Henry. *Midnight Mail.* 1931. Crime Club. 1st ed. VG. P1. $15.00

HOLT, R. *George WA Carver.* 1943. sgn. dj. VG. $35.00

HOLT, Victoria. *King of the Castle.* nd. Book Club. dj. VG. P1. $2.75

HOLTON, I.F. *New Granda: Twenty Months in the Andes.* 1967. S IL U. reprint of 1857. 223 p. dj. EX. M2. $18.00

HOLTON, Leonard. *Corner of Paradise.* 1977. St. Martin. dj. EX. P1. $7.50

HOLTON, Leonard. *Out of the Depths.* nd. Book Club. VG. P1. $3.00

HOLTZHAUER, Helmet. *Goethe Museum.* 1969. Berlin. Ils 1st ed. 4to. 715 p. VG. T5. $45.00

HOLWAY, Hope. *Story of Water Supply.* 1929. Harper. Ils 1st ed. inscr. 12mo. dj. VG. $25.00

HOLWAY, John. *Voices From Great Black Baseball Leagues.* 1975. NY. 1st ed. 363 p. dj. VG. B2. $40.00

HOLZMEISTER, Clemens. *Worke fur das Theater. Vol. I.* 1953. Vienna. sgn. $65.00

HOLZWORTH, J. *Wild Grizzlies of AK.* 1930. NY. Ils 1st ed. 417 p. index. VG. B2. $50.00

HOLZWORTH, J. *Wild Grizzlies of AK.* 1930. Putnam. Ils 1st ed. 417 p. dj. EX. M2. $90.00

HOMANS, James. *Self-Propelled Vehicles.* 1907. NY. Ils. diagrams. EX. $50.00

HOME LIBRARY PUBLISHING. *Civil War: House Divided Cannot Stand.* 1976. 50 color pls. 96 p. M. J4. $8.50

HOMER. *Iliad. The First Twelve Staves.* 1938. London. Crescent. 1/725. tall 4to. TEG. $125.00

HOMER. *Odyssey of Homer.* c 1924. Ils Fling. TEG. dj. VG. $50.00

HOMER. *Odyssey.* Ltd Ed Club. slipcase. M. B3. $60.00

HOMER. *Odyssey. Translated by A. Pope.* 1806. London. 25 copper pls. 12mo. 6 vols. $100.00

HOMES, Geoffrey. *Man Who Didn't Exist.* 1937. Morrow. 1st ed. VG. P1. $20.00

HOMES, Geoffrey. *Then There Were Three.* 1944. Books Inc. VG. P1. $7.50

HOMMA, J. *Masterworks of Japanese Swords by Masamune & His School.* 1961. np. 96 pls. Japanese/Eng text. slipcase. J2. $200.00

HONE, Philip. *Diary.* 1889. NY. 1st ed. 2 vols. VG. $85.00

HONE, William. *Ancient Mysteries Described.* 1823. London. 2 vols. $45.00

HONEY, W.B. *Dresden China.* 1946. Troy, NY. 1st Am ed. VG. $22.00

HONIG, J.M. *Van Nostrand Chemist's Dictionary.* 1953. NY. 2nd print. EX. $20.00

HOOD, J.F. *When Monsters Roamed the Skies.* 1968. Grosset Dunlap. Ils. 143 p. dj. G. T5. $12.50

HOOKER, W.F. *Bullwacker.* 1988. NE U. Ils. 167 p. EX. M2. $6.00

HOOL & KINNIE. *Movable & Long-Spaned Steel Bridges.* 1923. NY. Ils. 496 p. $20.00

HOOPER, H. *Country House.* 1906. NY. Ils. 4to. 330 p. VG. C4. $55.00

HOOPER, R. *Hooper's Dictionary (Lexicon Medicum).* 1839. NY. 2 vols in 1. VG. $45.00

HOOVER, H.M. *Another Heaven, Another Earth.* 1981. Viking. 1st ed. dj. EX. P1. $12.50

HOOVER, H.M. *Bell Tree.* 1982. Viking. 1st ed. dj. EX. P1. $11.95

HOOVER, H.M. *Delikon.* 1977. Viking. 1st ed. dj. EX. P1. $15.00

HOOVER, Helen. *Gift of the Deer.* 1967. Knopf. Ils. 210 p. EX. M2. $8.00

HOOVER, Helen. *Years of the Forest.* 1973. Knopf. Ils. 318 p. dj. EX. M2. $8.00

HOOVER, Herbert. *Addresses Upon the American Road 1948-1950.* 1951. Stanford. 1st ed. sgn. dj. M1. $175.00

HOOVER, Herbert. *State Papers & Other Public Writings of Herbert Hoover.* 1934. Garden City. 1st ed. sgn. 2 vols. djs. EX. $220.00

HOPE, Bob. *They Got Me Covered.* 1941. Hollywood. 1st ed. EX. $20.00

HOPE, C.W. *Elphinstone: Star of the Fairies.* 1881. London. Ils Laurent. gilt bdg. J2. $100.00

HOPE, Laura Lee. *Bobbsey Twins of Lakeport.* nd. Grosset. dj. VG. P1. $4.00

HOPE, Laura Lee. *Bobbsey Twins on a Houseboat.* nd. Grosset. dj. VG. P1. $5.00

HOPE, Laura Lee. *Bobbsey Twins' Adventure in Country.* nd. Grosset. dj. VG. P1. $5.00

HOPE, Laura Lee. *Bobbsey Twins' Mystery at Meadowbrook.* nd. Grosset. VG. P1. $4.00

HOPE, Laura Lee. *Bobsey Twins & Mystery at Snow Lodge.* nd. Grosset. VG. P1. $4.00

HOPE, Laura Lee. *Outdoor Girls on a Hike.* nd. Grosset. VG. P1. $17.50

HOPE, W. *Royal House of Stuart.* 1890. London. 40 pls. folio. AEG. morocco. J2. $250.00

HOPE & MARTIN. *Have Tux Will Travel.* 1954. 308 p. EX. $4.00

HOPF, Albrecht. *Oriental Carpets & Rugs.* 1962. London. 62 pls. EX. $75.00

HOPKINS, Alphonsoa. *Life of Clinton Bowen Fisk.* 1888. NY. 1st ed. 295 p. G. T5. $25.00

HOPKINS, Arthur. *Glory Road.* 1935. NY. $5.00

HOPKINS, D.S. *Houses & Cottages: Book No. 5.* 1891. Grand Rapids. Ils. stiff wraps. VG. $40.00

HOPKINS, E.J. *Organ: Its History & Construction.* 1855. London. fld pl. 596 p. EX. $275.00

HOPKINS, G.M. *Poems.* 1974. Folio Soc. 8vo. slipcase. VG. $14.00

HOPKINS, J.H. *American Citizen: His Rights & Duties According to Spirit...* 1857. NY. 8vo. 459 p. brown cloth. G. G2. $22.00

HOPPE, E.O. *Bundestaatund Bundeskrieg...* 1885. Berlin. Ils. maps. 776 p. $75.00

HOPPE, E.O. *Fifth Continent.* 1931. London. Simpkin Marshall. 1st ed. EX. $35.00

HOPPE, E.O. *Hundred Thousand Exposures.* 1945. London. Focal Pr. 1st ed. $20.00

HOPPE, E.O. *Romantic American Westerman.* c 1927. VG. $50.00

HOPPENOT, H. *Extreme Orient.* 1951. Paris. French text. VG. $30.00

HOPPER, F. *Military Horse.* 1976. Barnes. Ils 1st ed. 4to. 105 p. EX. M2. $16.00

HOPPER, Hedda. *From Under My Hat.* 1952. NY. 1st ed. dj. VG. B2. $15.00

HORAN, J.D. *Across the Cimarron.* 1956. NY. 1st ed. dj. $25.00

HORAN, J.D. *Confederate Agent: Discovery in History.* 1954. Crown. Ils 1st ed. map. 326 p. EX. M2. $11.00

HORAN, J.D. *Desperate Men: Revelations From the Sealed Pinkerton Files.* 1949. Bonanza. reprint. 294 p. dj. EX. M2. $14.00

HORAN, J.D. *Desperate Women.* 1952. Putnam. possible 1st ed. 336 p. dj. EX. M2. $20.00

HORAN, J.D. *Great American W: Pictorial History.* 1959. Crown. Ils. 4to. 283 p. G. M2. $15.00

HORAN, J.D. *Great American W: Pictorial History.* 1959. NY. Crown. 1st ed. dj. EX. $22.00

HORAN, J.D. *Great River: Rio Grande in N American History.* 1954. BOMC. slipcase. VG. $20.00

HORAN, J.D. *Heroic Triad.* 1970. NY. 1st ed. dj. EX. $22.00

HORAN, J.D. *Life & Art of Charles Schreyvogel.* 1969. NY. folio. VG. $50.00

HORAN, J.D. *Mathew Brady: Historian With a Camera.* 1955. Crown. Ils. 4to. 244 p. dj. $25.00

HORAN, J.D. *Memories of the Future.* 1966. NY. 1st ed. dj. VG. $35.00

HORAN, J.D. *No Quarter Given.* 1935. NY. 1st ed. dj. VG. $28.00

HORAN, J.D. *Pinkerton Story.* 1951. Ils. 366 p. K1. $6.50

HORAN, J.D. *Pinkertons: Detective Dynasty That Made History.* 1967. np. brown cloth. dj. EX. $20.00

HORAN, J.D. *Timothy Sullivan: America's Forgotten Photographer.* 1966. NY. 1st ed. dj. $30.00

HORGAN, P. *Peach Stone.* 1967. NY. Farrar. 1st ed. dj. VG. $40.00

HORGAN, Paul. *Centuries of Santa Fe.* 1956. Dutton. Ils 1st ed. 363 p. M2. $14.00

HORGAN, Paul. *Centuries of Santa Fe.* 1956. NY. 1st ed. 363 p. dj. VG. $20.00

HORGAN, Paul. *Return of the Weed.* 1936. NY. Harper. Ils Hurd. 1/250. sgns. slipcase. $275.00

HORGAN, Paul. *Saintmaker's Christmas Eve.* 1955. NY. Ils 1st ed. dj. VG. $45.00

HORLER, Sydney. *Curse of Doone.* 1930. Mystery League. 1st ed. dj. VG. P1. $20.00

HORLER, Sydney. *Curse of Doone.* 1934. Hodder Stoughton. 9th print. G. P1. $10.00

HORLER, Sydney. *Evil Chateau.* nd. Grosset. dj. VG. P1. $25.00

HORLER, Sydney. *False Face.* 1926. Doran. 1st ed. dj. VG. P1. $30.00

HORLER, Sydney. *False Face.* 1926. Doran. 1st ed. VG. P1. $20.00

HORLER, Sydney. *False Purple.* 1932. Mystery League. 1st ed. dj. VG. P1. $30.00

HORLER, Sydney. *Harlequin of Death.* 1933. John Long. xl. P1. $10.00

HORLER, Sydney. *High Hazard.* 1950. Hodder Stoughton. 3rd ed. VG. P1. $12.00

HORLER, Sydney. *House of Secrets.* nd. Nelson. dj. G. P1. $17.50

HORLER, Sydney. *Man From Scotland Yard.* 1970. John Long. dj. VG. P1. $10.00

HORLER, Sydney. *Man Who Walked With Death.* nd. Grosset Dunlap. G. P1. $7.50

HORLER, Sydney. *Oh, Professor!* nd. London. 1st ed. VG. $15.00

HORLER, Sydney. *Peril.* 1930. Mystery League. 1st ed. G. P1. $12.50

HORLER, Sydney. *Peril.* 1930. Mystery League. 1st ed. VG. P1. $25.00

HORN, Edward Newman. *Faster, Faster.* 1946. Coward McCann. dj. xl. P1. $6.00

HORN, Maurice. *Women in the Comics.* 1977. Chelsea House. 1st ed. dj. VG. P1. $10.00

HORN, S.F. *Army of TN.* 1941. Ils 1st ed. 503 p. xl. scarce. J4. $15.00

HORN, S.F. *Army of TN.* 1953. OK U. Ils. map. 503 p. dj. EX. M2. $25.00

HORN, S.F. *Boy's Life of Robert E. Lee.* 1935. NY. presentation. dj. $35.00

HORN, S.F. *Invisible Empire.* 1939. 1st ed. 434 p. dj. VG. scarce. J4. $45.00

HORN, S.F. *Robert E. Lee Reader.* 1949. 1st ed. 542 p. dj. EX. J4. $18.50

HORNADAY, W.T. *Campfires in the Canadian Rockies.* 1906. Scribner. 1st ed. M. $85.00

HORNADAY, W.T. *Campfires in the Canadian Rockies.* 1909. NY. Ils. 353 p. VG. B2. $45.00

HORNADAY, W.T. *Campfires on Desert & Lava.* 1908. Scribner. VG. $85.00

HORNADAY, W.T. *Campfires on Desert & Lava.* 1983. AZ U. reprint of 1908 ed. 362 p. M. M2. $23.00

HORNADAY, W.T. *Extermination of American Bison.* 1889. US Nat Mus. fld map. wraps. VG. $35.00

HORNADAY, W.T. *Hornaday's American Natural History.* 1927. Scribner. Revised later print. 449 p. EX. M2. $16.00

HORNBLOW, Arthur. *History of Theatre in America.* 1965. Blom. reprint. 2 vols. xl. EX. $25.00

HORNE, Alistair. *Savage War of Peace.* 1975. NY. dj. G. $17.50

HORNE, C. *Great Events of Great War.* 1920. 7 vols. G. $30.00

HORNE, David. *Boards & Buckram, 1962-1969.* 1980. Hanover. EX. $9.00

HORNE, George. *Commentary of Book of Psalms.* 1792. Phil. 1st Am ed. 2 vols in 1. leather. $225.00

HORNE, T.H. *Revised Landscape Illustrations of the Bible.* 1836. London. 2 vols. full morocco. VG. $150.00

HORNER, Durbin Lee. *Murder by the Dozen.* 1935. Dingwall Rock. 1st ed. VG. P1. $25.00

HORNER, W.E. *US Dissector; or, Lessons in Practical Anatomy.* 1846. Phil. VG. $95.00

HORNUNG, E.W. *Amateur Cracksman.* 1908. Scribner. VG. P1. $25.00

HORNUNG, E.W. *Dead Men Tell No Tales.* 1909. Scribner. VG. P1. $15.00

HORNUNG, E.W. *Raffles.* 1090. Scribner. VG. P1. $15.00

HORNUNG, E.W. *Shadow of the Rope.* 1908. Scribner. VG. P1. $15.00

HORNUNG, E.W. *Stingaree.* 1909. Scribner. VG. P1. $15.00

HORNUNG, E.W. *Thief in the Night.* 1909. Scribner. VG. P1. $15.00

HORODISCH. *Picasso As a Book Artist.* 1962. London. Ils 136 p. dj. VG. $35.00

HORRY, P. *Life of General Francis Marion...* 1856. Lippincott. 5 pls. 252 p. xl. G. $22.50

HORSLEY, Terence. *Soaring Flight.* 1946. NY. Ils. 326 p. dj. VG. T5. $17.50

HORST. *Salute to the Thirties.* 1971. NY. 1st ed. 162 photos. 4to. 192 p. dj. $75.00

HORTON, C.W. *Signal Processing of Underwater Acoustic Waves.* 1969. Austin. M. $10.00

HORTON, H.L. *Ingenious Mechanism for Designers & Inventors.* 1956. NY. Ils. 3 vols. djs. VG. T5. $60.00

HORTON. *Frozen N.* 1904. Boston. Ils 1st ed. EX. $10.00

HORWICH & WERRENRATH. *Miss Frances' Ding-Dong School Book.* 1953. Rand McNally. dj. VG. $22.00

HORWITZ, James. *They Went Thataway.* 1976. Dutton. Review 1st ed. dj. RS. VG. $20.00

HORWOOD, William. *Dunction Wood.* 1980. McGraw Hill. 1st ed. dj. EX. P1. $15.00

HOSKING & KEAR. *Wildfowl.* 1985. Facts on File. Ils 1st Am ed. 153 p. dj. EX. M2. $22.00

HOSKING & LOCKLEY. *Sea Birds of the World.* 1983. Facts on File. Ils 1st Am ed. 159 p. dj. EX. M2. $18.00

HOSKING & SAGE. *Antarctic Wildlife.* 1982. Facts on File. Ils 1st Am ed. 4to. 160 p. dj. M2. $24.00

HOSKINS, Robert. *Shattered People.* 1975. Doubleday. 1st ed. dj. xl. P1. $5.00

HOSKINS, W.G. *Leicester Agrarian History.* 1949. Leicestershire. 1st ed. dj. VG. R1. $20.00

HOSMER, F.J. *Glimpse of Andersonville & Other Writings.* 1896. Greenfield. Ils. 90 p. wraps. $35.00

HOSMER, G.L. *Historical Sketch of Town of Deer Isle, ME...* 1886. Boston. Stanley Usher. $55.00

HOSOE, Eikoh. *Why, Mother, Why?* 1965. Kodansha. dj. xl. VG. $25.00

HOSS, Rudolf. *Kommandnt in Auschwitz.* 1958. Stuttgart. 1st ed. German text. dj. G. $14.00

HOSTETLER, Lester. *History: Amish-Mennonite Church, Walnut Creek, OH.* nd. np. Ils. 18 p. wraps. G. T5. $19.50

HOTCHKISS, Robert. *Fertility in Men.* 1944. Phil. Lippincott. dj. VG. $20.00

HOTCHNER, A.E. *Papa Hemingway.* 1966. Random House. 5th print. dj. $20.00

HOTSON, F. *De Havilland, Canada Story.* 1983. 1st ed. 244 p. dj. M. $23.00

HOTSON, J.L. *Death of Christopher Marlowe.* 1925. Nonesuch/Harvard. Ils 1st ed. G. $80.00

HOTTENROTH, Frederic. *Le Costome, les Armes, les Ustensiles Objeets Mobiliers...* nd. Paris. disbound color pls. xl. $75.00

HOTTON, N. *Ecology & Biology of Mammal-Like Reptiles.* 1986. Smithsonian. Ils. 4to. 326 p. dj. M. M2. $35.00

HOTTON, N. *Evidence of Evolution.* 1968. Am Heritage. Ils. 160 p. dj. EX. M2. $9.00

HOUDIN, Robert. *Life of Robert Houdin: King of Conjurers.* 1859. Phil. later issue. VG. $20.00

HOUGH, A.L. *Soldier in the W: Civil War Letters.* 1957. Phil. 1st ed. dj. VG. $15.00

HOUGH, E. *Firefly's Light.* 1916. NY. Trow. 1st ed. 8vo. EX. $85.00

HOUGH, Emerson. *Maw's Vacation.* 1924. St. Paul. 61 p. VG. A3. $30.00

HOUGH, F. *Island War: Marines in Pacific.* 1947. Phil. Ils 1st ed. dj. VG. B2. $32.50

HOUGH, G.W. *Description of Automatic Registering Printing Barometer.* 1856. Albany. 8 vo. $50.00

HOUGH, H.B. *Mostly on Martha's Vineyard.* 1975. NY. 1st ed. dj. VG. B2. $15.00

HOUGH, R.B. *Handbook of Trees of the N States & Canada.* 1907. Lowville. Ils. 8vo. scarce. $65.00

HOUGH, S.B. *Bronze Perseus.* 1962. Walker. dj. VG. P1. $10.00

HOUGH, S.B. *Dear Daughter Dead.* 1966. Walker. 1st ed. G. P1. $10.00

HOUGH, S.B. *Frontier Incident.* 1951. Crowell. dj. VG. P1. $10.00

HOUGHTON, Claude. *This Was Ivor Trent.* 1935. Heinemann. 1st ed. P1. $12.00

HOUGHTON, E.P. *Expedition of Donner Party & Its Tragic Fate.* 1911. McClure. G. $65.00

HOULDSWORTH, J. *Cheetham's Psalmody: Harmonized in Score for Organ...* 1853. Halifax. presentation. full leather. $25.00

HOURANI, A. *Arabic Thought in Liberal Age, 1798-1939.* 1967. London. $20.00

HOUSE, E.J. *Hunter's Campfires.* 1909. NY. Ils 1st ed. 402 p. EX. $60.00

HOUSE, H.D. *Wild Flowers.* 1937. Macmillan. 364 pls. 4to. 362 p. EX. M2. $35.00

HOUSE, J.T. *John G. Neilhardt: Man & Poet.* 1920. Wayne, NE. 1st ed. presentation. sgn. EX. $75.00

HOUSEHOLD, Geoffrey. *Arabesque.* 1948. Little Brown. 3rd ed. dj. VG. P1. $7.50

HOUSEHOLD, Geoffrey. *Summon the Bright Water.* 1981. 1st ed. dj. M. C1. $12.50

HOUSMAN, A.E. *Introductory Lecture: 1892.* 1937. Cambridge. 1st trade ed. dj. VG. $20.00

HOUSMAN, A.E. *Shropshire Lad.* 1914. London. Medici. 1/1000. $155.00

HOUSMAN, A.E. *Shropshire Lad.* 1922. London. polished crimson calf. EX. $75.00

HOUSMAN, A.E. *Shropshire Lad: Cameo Classic.* 1932. Grosset Dunlap. black/gold/cream bdg. EX. $20.00

HOUSMAN, Laurence. *Arabian Knights.* nd. NY. Ils Dulac. G. $25.00

HOUSMAN, Laurence. *Bethlehem.* 1927. London. Macmillan. 8vo. VG. $35.00

HOUSMAN, Laurence. *Princess Badoura. Tale From Arabian Nights.* nd. Hodder. Ils Dulac. $130.00

HOUSMAN, Laurence. *Stories From the Arabian Nights.* nd. Doran. Ils Dulac. not 1st ed. VG. J2. $35.00

HOUSMAN, Laurence. *Stories From the Arabian Nights.* 1907. NY. Scribner. Ils Dulac. J2. $75.00

HOUSMAN, Lawrence. *Stories From the Arabian Nights.* 1939. Hodder Stoughton. 1st print. B4. $90.00

HOUSTON, D. *Hell on Wheels.* 1977. San Rafael. 1st ed. dj. VG. B2. $30.00

HOUSTON, D.R. *Understanding the Game of Environment.* 1979. USDA. Ils 174 p. M2. $5.00

HOUSTON, E.J. *Death Valley Scotty Told Me.* 1954. Louisville. 106 p. wraps. G. $15.00

HOUSTON, E.J. *Elements of Physical Geography for Use of Schools.* 1879. Phil. $20.00

HOUSTOUN, R.A. *Light Color.* 1923. Longman. 1st ed. VG. J2. $20.00

HOUVET, Etienne. *Monographie de la Cathedrale de Chartres.* nd. np. J2. $20.00

HOW. *James B. Eads.* 1900. Boston. Houghton Mifflin. VG. $25.00

HOWARD, A.W. *Ching-Li & the Dragons.* 1931. NY. Ils Ward. 1st ed. dj. boxed. EX. J2. $125.00

HOWARD, Clark. *Brothers in Blood.* 1983. St. Martin. AP. printed wraps. $35.00

HOWARD, Elizabeth C. *Falconieri Palace in Rome: Role of Borromini...* 1981. NY. Garland. Ils 346 p. D2. $40.00

HOWARD, G.W. *Monumental City (Baltimore).* 1873. Baltimore. Ils fld maps. 1002 p. G. $80.00

HOWARD, Guy. *Give Me Thy Vineyard: Novel of the Ozarks.* 1949. Grand Rapids. Zondervan. 287 p. dj. $10.00

HOWARD, Hartley. *Key to the Morgue.* 1974. Collins. VG. P1. $10.00

HOWARD, Hartley. *Other Side of the Door.* 1953. Collins. 1st ed. dj. xl. P1. $10.00

HOWARD, L.O. *History of Applied Entomology.* 1930. WA. Ils. 4to. 564 p. xl. $80.00

HOWARD, L.R. *Quite Remarkable Father.* 1959. NY. Ils 1st ed. 307 p. dj. VG. B2. $17.50

HOWARD, Leland. *Insect Book.* 1905. Doubleday. Ils. 4to. 429 p. gilt green bdg. $30.00

HOWARD, R.W. *Dawnseekers: First History of American Paleontology.* 1975. Harcourt Brace. Ils 1st ed. 314 p. dj. EX. M2. $20.00

HOWARD, Robert E. *Black Colossus.* 1979. Donald Grant. 1st ed. dj. EX. P1. $35.00

HOWARD, Robert E. *Conan the Conqueror: Hyborean Age.* 1950. NY. Gnome. 1st ed. dj. EX. $65.00

HOWARD, Robert E. *Devil in Iron.* 1976. Donald Grant. dj. EX. P1. $35.00

HOWARD, Robert E. *Gent From Bear Creek.* 1975. Donald Grant. dj. EX. P1. $20.00

HOWARD, Robert E. *Jewels of Gwahlur.* 1979. Donald Grant. 1st ed. dj. EX. P1. $35.00

HOWARD, Robert E. *King Conan.* 1953. NY. 1st ed. dj. EX. $85.00

HOWARD, Robert E. *People of the Black Circle.* 1974. Donald Grant. dj. VG. P1. $40.00

HOWARD, Robert E. *People of the Black Circle.* 1978. Berkley Putnam. 1st ed. dj. VG. P1. $20.00

HOWARD, Robert E. *Pride of Bear Creek.* 1977. Donald Grant. 1st ed. dj. EX. P1. $15.00

HOWARD, Robert E. *Queen of the Black Coast.* 1978. Donald Grant. dj. VG. P1. $35.00

HOWARD, Robert E. *Red Nails.* 1975. Donald Grant. dj. EX. P1. $50.00

HOWARD, Robert E. *Red Shadows.* 1978. Donald Grant. 1st ed. artist sgn. dj. EX. P1. $75.00

HOWARD, Robert E. *Rogues in the House.* 1976. Donald Grant. dj. EX. P1. $35.00

HOWARD, Robert E. *Sowers of the Thunder.* 1973. Grant. 1st ed. dj. EX. $40.00

HOWARD, Robert E. *Sowers of the Thunder.* 1976. Donald Grant. 2nd ed. dj. VG. P1. $25.00

HOWARD, Robert E. *Sword of Conan.* 1952. Gnome. 1st ed. dj. EX. $60.00

HOWARD, Robert E. *Tower of the Elephant.* 1975. Donald Grant. dj. VG. P1. $35.00

HOWARD, Robert E. *Vultures.* 1975. Fictioneer. 2nd ed. dj. EX. P1. $10.00

HOWARD, Robert E. *Witch Shall Be Born.* 1975. Donald Grant. dj. EX. P1. $40.00

HOWARD, Thomas. *Novels of Charles Williams.* 1983. 1st ed. dj. M. C1. $10.00

HOWARTH, David. *We Die Alone.* 1955. Macmillan. 1st ed. dj. G. M1. $6.50

HOWATCH, Susan. *April's Grave.* 1974. Stein Day. dj. xl. P1. $5.00

HOWBERT, Irving. *Memories of a Lifetime in Pikes Peak Region.* 1925. Putnam. Ils. 298 p. VG. A3. $60.00

HOWE, George. *Heart Alone.* 1953. Putnam. 12mo. dj. M. $7.00

HOWE, Henry. *Historical Collections of OH.* 1889-1891. Columbus. 3 vols. rebound. VG. T5. $145.00

HOWE, Henry. *Historical Collections of OH.* 1852. Cincinnati. 180 engravings. 620 p. VG. M2. $42.00

HOWE, Henry. *Historical Collections of OH.* 1889. Columbus. 2 vols. $37.50

HOWE, Henry. *Historical Collections of OH.* 1902. Cincinnati. 2 vols. rebound. VG. T5. $65.00

HOWE, J.W. *Trip to Cuba.* 1860. Boston. 1st ed. VG. $30.00

HOWE, Octavius. *Argonauts of '49: History & Adventures of Emigrant Co.* 1923. Harvard. 2nd print. VG. J2. $20.00

HOWE, Percy. *American Annual of Photography, 1914.* 1913. NY. 350 p. G. $30.00

HOWE, R. *Children of the Wind.* 1980. Moonraker. Ils 1st ed. 68 p. dj. EX. M2. $10.00

HOWE, R.H. *Birds of MA.* 1901. Cambridge. Ltd 1st ed. 1/450. VG. $50.00

HOWE & LIBO. *How We Lived.* 1979. Phil. dj. VG. $20.00

HOWELL, A.H. *FL Bird Life.* 1932. FL Game/Fish. Ils Jaques. 579 p. EX. M2. $135.00

HOWELL, F.C. *Early Man.* 1970. Time Life. Ils. 200 p. EX. M2. $5.00

HOWELL, James. *Some Sober Inspections Made Into...Parliament...* 1646. London. 1st ed. 16mo. 184 p. VG. G2. $100.00

HOWELL. *US Army Headgear: 1855-1902.* 1975. Ils. 109 p. K1. $21.00

HOWELLS, J.M. *Architectural Heritage of Piscataqua.* 1965. NY. 1st ed. 217 p. dj. VG. B2. $40.00

HOWELLS, V. *Naturalist in Palestine.* 1956. London. Ils 1st ed. 180 p. dj. VG. B2. $22.50

HOWELLS, W.D. *Boy's Town.* 1890. NY. 1st ed. VG. $50.00

HOWELLS, W.D. *Lady of Aroostook.* 1879. Boston. G. $110.00

HOWELLS, W.D. *My Mark Twain.* 1910. NY. Ils 1st ed. 8vo. TEG. T1. $35.00

HOWELLS, W.D. *Shadow of a Dream.* 1890. NY. 1st ed. VG. $17.50

HOWELLS, W.D. *Undiscovered Country.* 1880. Boston. Houghton. 1st ed. VG. $20.00

HOWES, P.G. *Backyard Exploration.* 1927. NY. Ils 1st ed. 4to. 211 p. dj. $17.50

HOWES, P.G. *Giant Cactus Forest & Its World.* 1954. Duell. VG. $22.50

HOWES, Wright. *US-Iana (1650-1950).* 1962. NY. Bowker. Revised 1st ed. 652 p. VG. A3. $90.00

HOWLAND, E.A. *New England Economical Housekeeper & Family Receipt Book.* 1847. Worcester. Howland. 108 p. EX. $30.00

HOYLAND, John. *Historical Survey of Customs, Habits...of Gypsies.* 1816. York. 1st ed. recent bdg. $175.00

HOYLE, Fred. *Element 79.* nd. Book Club. dj. VG. P1. $3.00

HOYLE, Fred. *October the 1st Is Too Late.* nd. Book Club. dj. VG. P1. $3.00

HOYLE, John. *Roycroft Anthology.* 1917. Roycroft. 8vo. not Lib imp. VG. D1. $40.00

HOYLE. *In the Spotlight.* 1917. Roycroft. 8vo. purple suede. EX. D1. $45.00

HOYNINGEN-HUENE, George. *Baalbek-Palmyra.* 1946. dj. VG. $55.00

HOYT, E. *Antiquarian Researches: History of Indian Wars...* 1824. Greenfield, MA. 312 p. rebound. T5. $75.00

HSIEH, Tehyi. *Selected Pearls of Widsom & Buddhism.* 1943. Boston. $4.50

HUBBARD, Alice. *Garnett & the Brindled Cow.* 1913. Roycroft. 1/1003. sgn. 4to. VG. D1. $70.00

HUBBARD, Alice. *Life Lessons.* 1909. Roycroft. Ils Dard Hunter. VG. $45.00

HUBBARD, Alice. *Woman's Work.* 1908. Roycroft. 8vo. gray linen. VG. D1. $45.00

HUBBARD, B.S. *Mush You Malemutes!* 1932. NY. Ils 1st ed. sgn. $25.00

HUBBARD, Elbert. *Abe Lincoln & Nancy Hanks.* 1920. Roycroft. 16mo. tan wraps. VG. D1. $25.00

HUBBARD, Elbert. *Abe Lincoln & Nancy Hanks.* 1928. Roycroft. 16mo. coarse burlap. dj. VG. D1. $30.00

HUBBARD, Elbert. *American Bible.* 1912. Roycroft. 4to. brown leather. G. D1. $25.00

HUBBARD, Elbert. *Andrew Taylor Still.* 1912. Roycroft. 8vo. wraps. G. D1. $15.00

HUBBARD, Elbert. *As It Seems to Me.* 1898. Roycroft. 8vo. inscr/sgn. VG. D1. $75.00

HUBBARD, Elbert. *Beethoven.* 1901. Roycroft. 1/940. 8vo. VG. D1. $35.00

HUBBARD, Elbert. *Boy From MO Valley.* 1904. Roycroft. 8vo. wraps. G. D1. $10.00

HUBBARD, Elbert. *Boy From MO Valley.* 1916. Roycroft. 32mo. wraps. VG. D1. $15.00

HUBBARD, Elbert. *Catalog & Some Comments.* 1900. Roycroft. 8vo. green suede. VG. D1. $45.00

HUBBARD, Elbert. *Chicago Tongue.* 1900. Roycroft. 8vo. brown suede. VG. D1. $25.00

HUBBARD, Elbert. *Chicago Tongue.* 1913. Roycroft. beige wraps. VG. D1. $25.00

HUBBARD, Elbert. *Chopin.* 1901. Roycroft. 1/940. sgn. 8vo. VG. D1. $35.00

HUBBARD, Elbert. *City of Tagaste.* 1900. Roycroft. Ils Paine. 4to. VG. D1. $75.00

HUBBARD, Elbert. *Connersville.* 1914-1915. wraps. VG. D1. $25.00

HUBBARD, Elbert. *Consecrated Lives.* 1904. Roycroft. 8vo. gray suede. VG. D1. $45.00

HUBBARD, Elbert. *Divine in Man.* 1917. Roycroft. 24mo. wraps. VG. D1. $15.00

HUBBARD, Elbert. *Doctors: A Satire in Four Seizures.* 1909. Roycroft. green suede. VG. D1. $50.00

HUBBARD, Elbert. *Elbert Hubbard Speaks.* 1934. Roycroft. 2nd print. brown cloth. dj. VG. D1. $25.00

HUBBARD, Elbert. *Elbert Hubbard's Scrapbook.* 1923. Roycroft. 8vo. smooth leather. G. D1. $18.00

HUBBARD, Elbert. *Eminent Artists.* 1902. Roycroft. 8vo. 2 vols. suede. VG. D1. $35.00

HUBBARD, Elbert. *Eminent Orators.* 1903. Roycroft. 8vo. 2 vols. suede. VG. D1. $35.00

HUBBARD, Elbert. *English Authors.* 1900. Roycroft. 8vo. 2 vols. G. D1. $40.00

HUBBARD, Elbert. *Famous Women.* 1908. Roycroft. 4to. pink/white bdg. G. D1. $45.00

HUBBARD, Elbert. *Forbes of Harvard.* 1894. Arena. 1st print. white/gray bdg. VG. D1. $50.00

HUBBARD, Elbert. *Get Out or Get in Line.* nd. (1902?) Roycroft. beige wraps. VG. D1. $25.00

HUBBARD, Elbert. *Get Out or Get in Line.* nd. (1917?) Roycroft. 24mo. wraps. VG. D1. $15.00

HUBBARD, Elbert. *Great Americans.* nd. (1898) Putnam. 16mo. VG. D1. $35.00

HUBBARD, Elbert. *Great Businessmen.* 1909. Roycroft. 8vo. 2 vols. suede. VG. D1. $35.00

HUBBARD, Elbert. *Great Lovers.* 1906. Roycroft. 8vo. 2 vols. suede. VG. D1. $35.00

HUBBARD, Elbert. *Great Musicians.* 1901. Roycroft. 8vo. 2 vols. suede. VG. D1. $35.00

HUBBARD, Elbert. *Great Musicians. Vol. II.* Ils Granger. sgn. green suede. G. D1. $25.00

HUBBARD, Elbert. *Great Philosophers.* 1904. Roycroft. 8vo. 2 vols. suede. VG. D1. $30.00

HUBBARD, Elbert. *Great Reformers.* 1907. Roycroft. 8vo. 2 vols. suede. VG. D1. $35.00

HUBBARD, Elbert. *Great Scientists.* 1905. Roycroft. 8vo. 2 vols. suede. VG. D1. $30.00

HUBBARD, Elbert. *Great Teachers.* 1908. Roycroft. 8vo. 2 vols. suede. VG. D1. $40.00

HUBBARD, Elbert. *Help Yourself by Helping the House.* 1917. Roycroft. 24mo. wraps. VG. D1. $15.00

HUBBARD, Elbert. *Helpful Hints for Business Helpers.* 1916. Roycroft. 32mo. wraps. VG. D1. $15.00

HUBBARD, Elbert. *Homes of the Great.* 1928. Roycroft. Memorial ed. 8vo. 14 vols. djs. D1. $40.00

HUBBARD, Elbert. *Hundred Point Man.* 1915. Roycroft. 32mo. wraps. VG. D1. $20.00

HUBBARD, Elbert. *Impressions.* 1921. Roycroft. leather spine/gray boards. VG. D1. $40.00

HUBBARD, Elbert. *Joaquin Miller.* Roycroft. red suede. VG. D1. $35.00

HUBBARD, Elbert. *Joaquin Miller.* 1903. Roycroft. 8vo. brown suede. with letter. VG. D1. $45.00

HUBBARD, Elbert. *Journal of Koheleth.* 1896. Roycroft. 1/700. sgn. white bdg. G. D1. $250.00

HUBBARD, Elbert. *Justinian & Theodora.* 1906. Roycroft. brown suede. G. D1. $40.00

HUBBARD, Elbert. *Justinian & Theodora.* 1906. Roycroft. 8vo. gray suede. VG. D1. $55.00

HUBBARD, Elbert. *Legacy.* 1896. Roycroft. 16mo. 2 vols. brown suede. poor. D1. $50.00

HUBBARD, Elbert. *Little Journeys to Homes of English Authors.* 1900. Roycroft. 1/947. EX. $125.00

HUBBARD, Elbert. *Little Journeys to the Homes of Great Lovers.* 1913. Miriam ed. suede. VG. D1. $15.00

HUBBARD, Elbert. *Love, Life & Work.* 1906. Roycroft. brown suede. D1. $35.00

HUBBARD, Elbert. *Love, Life & Work.* 1906. Roycroft. 12mo. green suede. VG. D1. $45.00

HUBBARD, Elbert. *Loyalty in Business & One & Twenty Other Good Things.* 1922. Roycroft. VG. D1. $30.00

HUBBARD, Elbert. *Man of Sorrows.* 1904. Roycroft. 8vo. gray suede. orig box. EX. D1. $50.00

HUBBARD, Elbert. *Man of Sorrows.* 1905. Roycroft. 8vo. gray suede. VG. D1. $35.00

HUBBARD, Elbert. *Mendelssohn.* 1901. Roycroft. 1/940. 8vo. brown suede. VG. D1. $35.00

HUBBARD, Elbert. *Message to Garcia & 13 Other Things.* 1901. Roycroft. 8vo. suede. VG. D1. $45.00

HUBBARD, Elbert. *Message to Garcia.* 1899. Roycroft. wraps. D1. $35.00

HUBBARD, Elbert. *Message to Garcia.* 1899. Roycroft. 1/925. sgn. HrdCvr. D1. $75.00

HUBBARD, Elbert. *Message to Garcia.* 1899. Roycroft. 1/940. orig mailing envelope. $65.00

HUBBARD, Elbert. *Message to Garcia.* 1911. Roycroft. beige wraps. VG. D1. $20.00

HUBBARD, Elbert. *Message to Garcia.* 1913. Roycroft. beige wraps. VG. D1. $15.00

HUBBARD, Elbert. *Mintage: Being Ten Stories & One More.* 1910. Roycroft. 12mo. leather/cloth bdg. VG. D1. $40.00

HUBBARD, Elbert. *No Enemy But Himself.* 1894. Putnam. 1st ed. 8vo. rust/gray cloth. VG. D1. $50.00

HUBBARD, Elbert. *No Enemy But Himself.* 1907. Putnam. 4th imp. 8vo. gray cloth. VG. D1. $25.00

HUBBARD, Elbert. *Notebook of Elbert Hubbard.* 1927. Wise. 8vo. dj. boxed. EX. D1. $30.00

HUBBARD, Elbert. *Old John Burroughs.* 1901. Roycroft. white/gray bdg. VG. D1. $50.00

HUBBARD, Elbert. *Old John Burroughs.* 1901. Roycroft. 8vo. sgn. red suede. G. D1. $100.00

HUBBARD, Elbert. *Philistine.* 1899. Roycroft. 32mo. wraps. VG. D1. $50.00

HUBBARD, Elbert. *Philosophy of Elbert Hubbard.* 1916. Roycroft. sgn. 8vo. VG. D1. $45.00

HUBBARD, Elbert. *Philosophy of Elbert Hubbard.* 1930. Wise. 8vo. buckram bdg with ties. dj. VG. D1. $20.00

HUBBARD, Elbert. *Pig-Pen Pete.* 1914. Roycroft. full leather. VG. $30.00

HUBBARD, Elbert. *Pig-Pen Pete; or, Some Chums of Mine.* 1914. East Aurora. 1st ed. 12mo. full leather. EX. T1. $50.00

HUBBARD, Elbert. *Pitt.* 1903. Roycroft. 8vo. tan bdg. dj. VG. D1. $25.00

HUBBARD, Elbert. *Queen of the Porch & Other Droll Stories.* 1920. Roycroft. 8vo. green simulated leather. VG. D1. $25.00

HUBBARD, Elbert. *Reddy Ringlets.* 1915. Roycroft. 24mo. purple suede. VG. D1. $30.00

HUBBARD, Elbert. *Respectability: Its Rise & Remedy.* 1905. Roycroft. 8vo. rose suede. VG. D1. $45.00

HUBBARD, Elbert. *Romance of Business.* 1917. Roycroft. Lib imp. 8vo. VG. D1. $30.00

HUBBARD, Elbert. *Rubaiyat of Omar Khayyam.* 1900. Roycroft. 1/1000. sgn. 8vo. VG. D1. $85.00

HUBBARD, Elbert. *Rubaiyat of Omar Khayyam.* 1904. Roycroft. red suede. G. D1. $25.00

HUBBARD, Elbert. *Rubaiyat of Omar Khayyam.* 1906. Roycroft. 16mo. red suede. VG. D1. $50.00

HUBBARD, Elbert. *Selected Writings.* 1922. Roycroft. 8vo. 14 vols. embossed leather. VG. D1. $50.00

HUBBARD, Elbert. *Selected Writings.* 1928. NY. Wise. Memorial ed. 8vo. dj. G. $10.00

HUBBARD, Elbert. *Shoes & Character.* 1913. Roycroft. beige wraps. VG. D1. $20.00

HUBBARD, Elbert. *Song of Songs.* 1896. Roycroft. 1/600. sgn. white/gray bdg. EX. D1. $350.00

HUBBARD, Elbert. *Standard Oil Company.* 1910. Roycroft. 8vo. rust wraps. VG. D1. $50.00

HUBBARD, Elbert. *Three Great Women.* 1908. Roycroft. 8vo. inscr/sgn. calf. G. D1. $45.00

HUBBARD, Elbert. *Time & Chance.* 1899. NY. Ils 1st ed. 8vo. 2 vols. scarce. T1. $125.00

HUBBARD, Elbert. *Time & Chance.* 1899. Roycroft. 2 vols. D1. $60.00

HUBBARD, Elbert. *White Hyacinths.* 1907. Roycroft. 12mo. suede. VG. D1. $50.00

HUBBARD, Elbert. *Yellowstone Park.* 1915. Roycroft. 8vo. wraps. VG. D1. $35.00

HUBBARD, Elbert. *101 Epigrams.* 1973. Prentice Hall. 24mo. tan wraps. EX. D1. $25.00

HUBBARD, Elbert. *66 Etchings by Members of Print Society.* 1923. Hampshire. 73 pls. dj. EX. $30.00

HUBBARD, Freeman. *Encyclopedia of N American Railroading.* 1981. Ils. 377 p. $32.50

HUBBARD, Harlan. *Payne Hollow.* 1974. NY. 1st ed. dj. VG. B2. $17.50

HUBBARD, Kin. *Abe Martin's Broadcast.* 1930. Bobbs Merrill. 1st ed. EX. $35.00

HUBBARD, L. Ron. *Dianetics.* 1985. Bridge Pub. Commemorative ed. EX. T6. $25.00

HUBBARD, L. Ron. *Mission Earth.* nd. Bridge. 1st ed. 1/1000. 10 vols. djs. P1. $199.50

HUBBARD, Margaret Ann. *Murder Takes the Veil.* 1950. Bruce. 2nd ed. dj. VG. P1. $15.00

HUBBARD, Margaret Ann. *Sister Simon's Murder Case.* 1959. Bruce. dj. VG. P1. $15.00

HUBBARD, P.M. *Cold Waters.* 1969. Atheneum. 1st ed. dj. EX. P1. $5.00

HUBBARD, P.M. *Graveyard.* 1975. Atheneum. 1st ed. dj. EX. P1. $12.50

HUBBARD, P.M. *Graveyard.* 1975. Atheneum. 1st ed. dj. xl. P1. $5.00

HUBBARD, P.M. *Graveyard.* 1975. London. Macmillan. 1st ed. dj. xl. P1. $5.00

HUBBARD, R.H. *National Gallery of Canada Catalog of Painting & Sculpture.* 1960. Toronto. 1st ed. 1 vol only. dj. VG. J2. $27.50

HUBBARD, Ralph. *Queer Person.* 1930. NY. Ils Von Schmidt. 1st ed. dj. B2. $40.00

HUBBARD, W. *Narrative of Indian Wars in New England.* 1801. Worcester. 12mo. 410 p. $150.00

HUBBARD, W.O. *Ibamba.* 1962. Graphic Soc. Ils. map. 337 p. dj. VG. M2. $9.00

HUBBARD & CLARK. *Manhattan & Henry Hudson.* 1910. Roycroft. 12mo. green linen. VG. D1. $40.00

HUBBARD & HUBBARD. *Book of the Roycrofters: History & Some Comments.* 1921. Roycroft. Ils. brown wraps. VG. D1. $35.00

HUBBARD & HUBBARD. *Book of the Roycrofters: History & Some Comments.* 1923. Roycroft. 8vo. photos. tan wraps. VG. D1. $35.00

HUBBELL, Charles. *Record Breakers of the Air.* 1939. Akron. Ils. 4to. dj. VG. $85.00

HUBBELL, Raynor. *Confederate Stamps, Old Letters & History.* nd. Hubbell. gilt bdg. EX. J4. $30.00

HUBBS & LAGLER. *Fishes of Great Lakes Region.* 1958. Cranbrook. Revised ed. 213 p. EX. M2. $18.00

HUBERMAN. *Labor Spy Racket.* 1937. dj. VG. $25.00

HUBIN, Allen J. *Best Detective Stories 1971.* 1971. Dutton. 2nd ed. dj. xl. P1. $7.50

HUBIN, Allen J. *Best Detective Stories 1972.* 1972. Dutton. 1st ed. dj. xl. P1. $7.50

HUBIN, Allen J. *Bibliography of Crime Fiction, 1749-1975.* nd. Pub Inc. EX. P1. $75.00

HUBLER, R.G. *Brass God.* 1952. Coward McCann. $12.50

HUBLER, R.G. *Straight Up.* 1961. Duell Sloan. dj. M. $10.00

HUCKEL, Oliver. *Wagner's Parsifal.* 1903. Ils Stassen. 1st ed. xl. C1. $17.50

HUCKEL, Oliver. *Wagner's Siegfried.* 1910. 1st ed. VG. C1. $16.00

HUDDLESTON, F.J. *Gentleman Johnny Burgoyne: Misadventures of English General.* 1927. Bobbs Merrill. Ils. 367 p. dj. EX. M2. $10.00

HUDSON, Charles. *S Gardening.* 1953. Atlanta. sgn. 464 p. VG. $15.00

HUDSON, Derek. *Arthur Rackham: His Life & Work.* 1975. Scribner. dj. M. $60.00

HUDSON, G.H. *Amphibians & Reptiles of NE.* 1958. NE U. photos. maps. 146 p. EX. M2. $10.00

HUDSON, W.H. *Adventures Among Birds.* 1915. Kennerley. 316 p. VG. M2. $23.00

HUDSON, W.H. *British Birds.* 1898. Longman Green. 1st ed. TEG. J3. $450.00

HUDSON, W.H. *France: Nation & Development.* 1919. London. Harrap. VG. $15.00

HUDSON, W.H. *Green Mansions.* Three Sirens. Ils Henderson. 276 p. VG. $12.00

HUDSON, W.H. *Green Mansions.* 1944. Modern Lib. dj. G. P1. $10.00

HUDSON, W.H. *Green Mansions.* 1944. Random House. Ils. G. P1. $4.00

HUDSON, W.H. *Idle Days in Patagonia.* 1954. Dent. 248 p. dj. G. M2. $11.00

HUDSON, W.H. *Naturalist in La Plata.* 1892. Chapman Hall. Ils 1st ed. 388 p. VG. M2. $75.00

HUDSON, W.H. *Naturalist in La Plata.* 1922. Dutton. Ils. 394 p. G. M2. $25.00

HUEBINGER, Brothers. *Album of Davenport & Vicinity.* 1893. CA. $15.00

HUEI, W.B. *From Omaha to Okinawa: Story of the Seabees.* 1945. NY. Ils 1st ed. 257 p. VG. T5. $17.50

HUFF, Theodore. *Charlie Chaplin.* 1951. Schuman. 1st ed. dj. VG. J2. $20.00

HUGGINS, E.J. *Parasites of Fish in SD.* 1959. SD Fish/Game. Ils. 73 p. M2. $5.00

HUGGINS, William. *Atlas of Representative Stellar Spectra From 4870 to 3300...* 1899. London. Wesley. Ils. 12 pls. folio. 164 p. $225.00

HUGHES, Cledwyn. *He Dared Not Look Behind.* 1947. WYN. dj. VG. P1. $10.00

HUGHES, Dorothy B. *Blackbirder.* 1943. Duell Sloan. 1st ed. VG. P1. $10.00

HUGHES, Dorothy B. *Blackbirder.* 1944. Tower. dj. VG. P1. $15.00

HUGHES, Dorothy B. *Delicate Ape.* 1945. Tower. 1st ed. VG. P1. $7.50

HUGHES, Dorothy B. *Delicate Ape.* 1945. Tower. 2nd ed. VG. P1. $6.00

HUGHES, Dorothy B. *Dorothy B. Hughes Mystery Reader.* 1944. Forum. 2nd ed. G. P1. $5.00

HUGHES, Dorothy B. *Dread Journey.* nd. Duell Sloan. 3rd ed. dj. VG. P1. $15.00

HUGHES, Dorothy B. *Dread Journey.* 1946. Tower. dj. VG. P1. $15.00

HUGHES, Dorothy B. *Fallen Sparrow.* nd. Duell Sloan. 3rd ed. VG. P1. $10.00

HUGHES, Dorothy B. *Johnnie.* 1946. Tower. dj. VG. P1. $15.00

HUGHES, Dorothy B. *Ride the Pink Horse.* nd. Collier. VG. P1. $10.00

HUGHES, H.W. *TB in Coal Mining for Use of Colliery Managers & Others.* 1901. London. Griffin. 8vo. 527 p. G. $17.50

HUGHES, J.B. *Confederate Gunmakers, Armories & Arsenals.* 1961. 24 p. pb. VG. J4. $10.00

HUGHES, J.L. *How To Secure & Retain Attention.* 1889. 90 p. TB. VG. $3.00

HUGHES, Langston. *Big Sea.* 1940. NY. 1st ed. dj. VG. B2. $50.00

HUGHES, Langston. *Les Grandes Profondeurs.* 1947. Paris. Pierre Seghers. wraps. EX. $15.00

HUGHES, Langston. *Shakespeare in Harlem.* 1942. NY. 1st ed. dj. VG. B2. $125.00

HUGHES, Richard. *Fox in the Attic:* 1961. London. 1st ed. dj. EX. $30.00

HUGHES, Richard. *Gypsy Night & Other Poems.* 1922. Chicago. Will Ransom. Ltd 1st ed. 1/63. P3. $250.00

HUGHES, Richard. *Innocent Voyage.* 1944. Lit Ed Club. Ils Ward. sgn. printed folder. EX. $85.00

HUGHES, Richard. *Wooden Shepherdess.* 1973. NY. 1st Am ed. dj. EX. $25.00

HUGHES, Rupert. *She Goes To War.* nd. Grosset. Movie ed. VG. P1. $20.00

HUGHES, Ted. *Fangs the Vampire Bat & the Kiss of Truth.* 1986. London. 1st ed. dj. EX. $20.00

HUGHES, Ted. *Hawk in the Rain.* 1957. NY. 1st Am ed. dj. EX. $75.00

HUGHES, Thomas. *My Family Memoirs.* 1918. Baltimore. 51 p. fair. T5. $12.50

HUGHES, W.J. *Rebellious Ranger: Rip Ford & Old SW.* 1964. Norman. dj. EX. $35.00

HUGNINGEN-HUENE. *Baalbek Palmyra.* 1946. 1st ed. dj. EX. $60.00

HUGO, Victor. *Battle of Waterloo.* 1907. Roycroft. 1/194. glassine dj. EX. D1. $275.00

HUGO, Victor. *Hunchback of Notre Dame.* nd. Burt. Movie ed. VG. P1. $30.00

HUGO, Victor. *Works of Victor Hugo.* c 1900. Boston. Estes. Cabinet ed. 16 vols. VG. $65.00

HUGO, Victor. *Works of Victor Hugo.* 1894. Phil. Barrie. 1/250. 41 vols. slipcases. $495.00

HUHEEY, F.T. *Faces of the Land.* 1968. Fram Quarterly. 4to. 224 p. EX. $17.00

HUIE, W.B. *He Slew the Dreamer.* nd. Delacorte. 1st ed. presentation. sgn. dj. VG. $30.00

HUIE, W.B. *Klansman.* nd. Delacorte. 1st ed. dj. VG. $16.00

HUIE, W.B. *Klansman.* 1967. NY. ARC. wraps. EX. $25.00

HUISH, M.B. *Japan & Its Art.* 1912. London. Revised Enlarged ed. 373 p. VG. T5. $95.00

HUISMAN, P. *Lautrec by Lautrec.* 1964. NY. Trans Bellow. Ils. 4to. dj. EX. J2. $50.00

HUIZINGA, J. *Waning of the Middle Ages.* c 1985. Ils. M. C1. $7.50

HULBERT, A.B. *Forty-Niners.* 1931. Ils 1st ed. 340 p. K1. $21.00

HULBERT, A.B. *OH in the Time of the Confederation.* 1918. Marietta. VG. $40.00

HULL, A.L. *Campaigns of Confederate Army.* 1901. Atlanta. 1st ed. G. $75.00

HULL, F.M. *Robber Flies of the World.* 1962. Smithsonian. Ils. 2 vols. VG. $50.00

HULLEY. *Lullabies & Slumber Songs.* 1901. Lewisburg, PA. inscr. VG. $12.50

HULME, F.E. *Familiar Wild Flowers.* 1912. London/NY/Toronto/Melbourne. G. $10.00

HULME, K. *Look a Lion in the Eye: On Safari Through Africa.* 1974. Little Brown. Ils 1st ed. 223 p. dj. EX. M2. $9.00

HULT. *Steamboats in Timber.* 1952. Caxton. G. $17.00

HULTMAN, H.J. *Murder in French Room.* c 1931. NY. Mystery League. 1st ed. VG. $10.00

HUMBLE, Emil. *Gods in Plain Garb.* 1935. NY. $30.00

HUMBLE, Richard. *Hitler's Generals.* 1974. NY. Ils 1st ed. 167 p. VG. T5. $19.50

HUME, Abraham. *Learned Societies & Printing Clubs of United Kingdom.* 1847. London. 1st ed. $65.00

HUME, Cyril. *Myself & Young Bowman & Other Fantasies.* 1932. Doubleday. 1st ed. 1/1500. sgn. $15.00

HUME, David. *Dangerous Mr. Dell.* 1936. Collins. 3rd ed. VG. P1. $10.00

HUME, David. *Stand Up & Fight.* 1941. Collins. 1st ed. VG. P1. $22.50

HUME, H.H. *Gardening in the Lower S.* 1954. NY. 2nd ed. 377 p. VG. $20.00

HUMES. *Loyal Mountaineers of TN.* 1888. Knoxville. VG. $150.00

HUMFREVILLE, J.L. *Twenty Years Among Our Hostile Indians...* 1899. NY. Ils 2nd ed. 480 p. A3. $120.00

HUMPHREY, Seth. *Following the Prairie Frontier.* 1931. MN U. 1st ed. dj. VG. J2. $17.50

HUMPHREY, William. *Spawning Run.* 1970. NY. Ils 1st ed. dj. EX. $45.00

HUMPHREYS, Andrew A. *VA Campaign of '64 & '65.* 1883. NY. Ils 1st ed. 451 p. G. T5. $35.00

HUMPHREYS, F. *Manual of Veterinary Specific Homeopathy.* 1886. NY. fld chart. 416 p. $35.00

HUMPHREYS, J.R. *Lost Towns & Roads of America.* 1961. Garden City. Book Club. 1st ed. dj. EX. $5.00

HUMPHREYS, J.R. *Vandameer's Road.* nd. Book Club. xl. P1. $1.75

HUMPHREYS, Josephine. *Rich in Love.* 1987. NY. 1st ed. dj. EX. $25.00

HUMPHRIES, Rolfe. *Collected Poems.* 1966. 2nd print. VG. C1. $9.00

HUNCKE, Herbert. *Unspeakable Visions of the Individual.* 1973. 1st ed. with letter. EX. $25.00

HUNDLEY. *Social Relations in Our S States.* 1860. NY. 1st ed. scarce. $75.00

HUNEKER, James. *Chopin: Man & His Music.* 1911. NY. Scribner. inscr. 8vo. VG. $40.00

HUNG, L.F. *International Book of Orchids.* 1984. London. Cavendish. Ils. 4to. dj. EX. M2. $25.00

HUNGERFORD, Edward. *Daniel Willard Rides the Line.* 1938. NY. 1st ed. VG. $15.00

HUNGERFORD, Edward. *Transport for War.* 1943. 272 p. $17.50

HUNT, Aurora. *Kirby Benedict: Frontier Federal Judge.* 1961. Glendale. fld map. EX. P3. $25.00

HUNT, Elvid. *History of Ft. Leavenworth, 1827-1927.* 1827. Leavenworth. presentation. 298 p. VG. A3. $100.00

HUNT, Frazier. *Long Trail From TX: Story of Ad Spaugh, Cattleman.* 1940. NY. inscr. dj. EX. $40.00

HUNT, Frazier. *Tragic Days of Billy the Kid.* 1956. dj. EX. J4. $35.00

HUNT, Freeman. *Worth & Wealth: Maxims & Morals for Merchants.* 1856. Stringer/Townsent. 1st ed. G. $35.00

HUNT, Jonathan. *Illuminations.* 1989. 1st ed. dj. M. C1. $18.50

HUNT, L.B. *Artist's Game Bag.* Derrydale. 1/1225. dj. VG. $285.00

HUNT, L.B. *Artist's Game Bag.* 1936. Derrydale. 1/1225. EX. $300.00

HUNT, L.B. *Game Birds of America.* 1944. np. 12 pls. folio. wraps. $85.00

HUNT, Leigh. *Book for a Corner.* 1849. London. 2 vols. Zaehnsdorf bdg. VG. $65.00

HUNT, Mable. *Peddler's Clock.* 1943. Grosset Dunlap. Ils Jones. G. $15.00

HUNT, Percival. *If By Your Art: Testament to Percival Hunt.* 1948. Pittsburg U. 1st ed. VG. J2. $8.50

HUNT, R.S. *Law & Locomotives: Impact of Railroad on WI Law in 19th C.* 1958. Ils. 292 p. $22.50

HUNT, W.E. *Historical Collections of Coshocton Co., OH.* 1876. Cincinnati. Clarke. 1st ed. scarce. T5. $95.00

HUNT, W.H. *Pre-Raphaelitism & Pre-Raphaelite Brotherhood.* 1905. Macmillan. 2 vols. TEG. green bdg. VG. $25.00

HUNT, W.R. *Arctic Passage: Turbulent History of Land & People.* 1975. Scribner. Ils 1st ed. 395 p. dj. EX. M2. $20.00

HUNTER, Alan. *Gently Continental.* 1967. Cassell. 1st ed. dj. xl. P1. $6.00

HUNTER, Alan. *Landed Gently.* 1957. Cassell. 1st ed. dj. VG. P1. $12.50

HUNTER, Evan. *2nd Ending.* 1956. Simon Schuster. 1st ed. dj. VG. P1. $75.00

HUNTER, George. *Reminiscences of an Old Timer.* 1887. San Francisco. Crocker. Ils. 453 p. A3. $125.00

HUNTER, J.M. *Bloody Trail in TX: Sketches & Narratives of Indian Raids...* 1966. reprint of 1932 ed. 191 p. EX. M2. $20.00

HUNTER, J.M. *Trail Drivers of TX. Vol. 1.* 1924. San Antonio. 2nd ed. 1/500. G. $75.00

HUNTER, R. *Three Hundred Years of Psychiatry, 1535-1860.* 1982. Hartsdale. $45.00

HUNTER, R.C. *Old Houses in England.* 1930. London/NY. Ils. photos. folio. G. $75.00

HUNTER, Reginald. *Porlock.* 1940. Caxton. sgn. 8vo. dj. EX. $15.00

HUNTER, S.T. *Fear & Loathing in Las Vegas.* 1971. NY. 1st ed. dj. VG. $75.00

HUNTER, W.C. *Frozen Dog Tales.* 1905. Boston. Everett. Ils Border. 12mo. VG. $12.00

HUNTER & HAMMA. *Stagecoach Days.* 1963. Lane. Ils. 4to. 63 p. paper wraps. EX. M2. $4.00

HUNTING, Gardner. *Vicarion.* 1927. Unity Pr. dj. VG. P1. $7.50

HUNTINGTON, Dwight. *Our Big Game.* 1904. NY. 1st ed. dj. VG. $25.00

HUNTINGTON, H. *Defense of Nudism.* 1958. Sunshine. 1st ed. 234 p. VG. $13.00

HUNTINGTON, J. *On the Edge of Nowhere.* 1966. NY. 1st ed. dj. VG. B2. $32.50

HUNZIKER, Otto. *Condensed Milk & Milk Powder.* 1920. Hunziker. Revised Enlarged ed. EX. $25.00

HURD, D.H. *History of New London Co., CT.* 1882. Phil. Ils 1st ed. 4to. gilt leather. T1. $55.00

HURD, Peter. *Story of Roland.* 1930. Scribner. Ils. VG. $35.00

HURD. *History of Clinton & Franklin Counties.* 1978. NY. reprint of 1880 ed. 4to. EX. $30.00

HURLBURT, H.H. *Chicago Antiquities.* 1881. private print. $50.00

HURLEY, A.F. *Billy Mitchell, Crusader for Air Power.* 1975. Bloomington. 190 p. wraps. VG. T5. $8.50

HURLIMANN. *Germany.* 1961. dj. VG. S2. $35.00

HURN, Ethel. *WI Women in the War.* 1911. 1/5000. VG. $25.00

HURRELL, F.G. *John Lillibud.* 1935. Kendall Sharp. 1st ed. P1. $8.00

HURST, Fannie. *Anatomy of Me.* 1958. NY. 1st ed. dj. VG. $10.00

HURST, Fannie. *Appassionata.* 1926. NY. Ltd 1st ed. 1/220. sgn. VG. $25.00

HURST, Fannie. *Back Street.* 1931. Cosmopolitan. Ltd ed. 1/250. sgn. 8vo. VG. $60.00

HURST, Fannie. *Hands of Veronica.* 1947. Harper. G. P1. $6.00

HURSTON, Zora. *Moses: Man of the Mountain.* 1939. Phil. 1st ed. dj. VG. $95.00

HURTIG, G. *Masterpieces of Netsuke Art.* 1973. NY. Ils. 4to. silk bdg. slipcase. boxed. EX. J2. $125.00

HURWOOD, Bernhardt J. *Passport to the Supernatural.* 1972. Robert Hale. 1st ed. dj. VG. P1. $20.00

HUSBAND, Joseph. *Year in a Coal Mine.* 1911. Boston. Ils 1st ed. VG. $40.00

HUSE, Caleb. *Supplies of the Confederate Army.* 1904. Boston. 1st ed. xl. G. $150.00

HUSS, G.M. *Rational Building.* 1895. NY. Ils. 367 p. G. T5. $35.00

HUSSEIN, M.A. *Origins of the Book: From Papyrus to Codex.* 1972. NY Graphic Soc. 1st Am ed. 4to. dj. VG. $25.00

HUTCHENS, J.K. *Boots & Saddles at the Little Big Horn.* 1976. Old Army Pr. Ils. 81 p. paper wraps. EX. M2. $10.00

HUTCHENS, J.K. *One Mans's MT.* 1964. Phil. 1st ed. dj. VG. B2. $15.00

HUTCHINS, R.E. *Island of Adventure: Naturalist Explores a Gulf Coast.* 1968. Dodd Mead. Ils. 243 p. dj. EX. M2. $10.00

HUTCHINS & HUTCHINS. *VA: Old Dominion.* 1921. Boston. Ils. fld map. 299 p. $20.00

HUTCHINSON, B. *Fraser.* 1950. Rinehart. Ils. 368 p. dj. VG. M2. $10.00

HUTCHINSON, C. *Toward Daybreak.* nd. np. Ils Chagall. 1st ed. dj. VG. $25.00

HUTCHINSON, E. *Arts Revealed & Universal Guide.* 1853. NY. 136 p. K1. $27.50

HUTCHINSON, G.E. *Ecological Theater & the Evolutionary Play.* 1965. Yale U. Ils. 139 p. dj. EX. M2. $15.00

HUTCHINSON, Lucy. *Memoirs of Colonel Hutchinson & Siege of Lathom.* 1880. London. EX. $35.00

HUTCHINSON, Vernal. *ME Town in the Civil War.* 1967. Freeport. 1st ed. dj. VG. $22.00

HUTCHINSON, William. *Cyrus Hall McCormick.* 1930 & 1935. Century. Deluxe ed. VG. J2. $35.00

HUTCHINSON & HENRY. *Ancestry of Abraham Lincoln.* 1909. Boston. 1st ed. 4to. VG. $150.00

HUTCHISON, Harold. *Poster: An Illustrated History From 1860.* 1968. Viking. 1st ed. dj. VG. J2. $35.00

HUTT, Allen. *British Trade Unionism.* 1953. dj. EX. $15.00

HUTT, Allen. *Condition of Working Class in Britain.* 1933. NY. dj. VG. $25.00

HUTT, Allen. *Post-War History of British Working Class.* 1938. VG. $20.00

HUTTON, H. *Doc Middleton: Life & Legends of Notorious Plains Outlaw.* 1974. Sage. photos. maps. 290 p. dj. EX. M2. $25.00

HUTTON. *Sword & the Centuries; or, Old Sword Days & Ways.* 1901. London. EX. $90.00

HUXHAM, John. *Essay on Fevers, to Which Is Now Added Dissertation...* 1782. London. $175.00

HUXLEY, Aldous. *After Many a Summer.* 1939. London. 1st ed. dj. VG. $85.00

HUXLEY, Aldous. *After Many a Summer.* 1939. London. 1st ed. presentation. sgn. dj. $125.00

HUXLEY, Aldous. *After Many a Summer.* 1953. Vanguard. G. P1. $10.00

HUXLEY, Aldous. *Along the Road.* 1925. NY. Doran. 1st Am trade ed. $12.00

HUXLEY, Aldous. *Along the Road.* 1925. NY. Doran. 1/250. sgn. TEG. dj. EX. $175.00

HUXLEY, Aldous. *Ape & Essence.* 1948. Harper. 1st ed. dj. EX. $30.00

HUXLEY, Aldous. *Brave New World Revisited.* 1958. NY. 1st ed. dj. $20.00

HUXLEY, Aldous. *Brave New World.* 1932. Doubleday Doran. purple bdg. VG. $12.00

HUXLEY, Aldous. *Brave New World.* 1950. Harper. G. P1. $5.00

HUXLEY, Aldous. *Complete Etchings of Goya.* 1943. NY. Crown. Ils. dj. D2. $55.00

HUXLEY, Aldous. *Crome Yellow.* 1921. London. 1st ed. dj. $45.00

HUXLEY, Aldous. *Devils of Loudin.* 1st ed. dj. B7. $50.00

HUXLEY, Aldous. *Ends & Means.* Ltd 1st ed. sgn. EX. B7. $115.00

HUXLEY, Aldous. *Eyeless in Gaza.* 1936. Chatto Windus. 1st ed. dj. EX. $75.00

HUXLEY, Aldous. *Eyeless in Gaza.* 1936. Harper. 7th ed. VG. P1. $15.00

HUXLEY, Aldous. *Eyeless in Gaza.* 1936. London. 1st trade ed. dj. $35.00

HUXLEY, Aldous. *Genius & the Goddess.* 1955. Harper. 1st ed. dj. EX. T6. $20.00

HUXLEY, Aldous. *Heaven & Hell.* 1956. London. 1st ed. dj. EX. $75.00

HUXLEY, Aldous. *Jesting Pilate.* 1926. London. 1st trade ed. dj. EX. $30.00

HUXLEY, Aldous. *Leda.* 1929. Doubleday. Ltd ed. 1/361. sgn. VG. $95.00

HUXLEY, Aldous. *Limbo.* 1920. London. 1st trade ed. green bdg. G. $20.00

HUXLEY, Aldous. *Mortal Coils.* 1922. London. 1st ed. dj. M. $85.00

HUXLEY, Aldous. *Olive Tree & Other Essays.* 1936. London. Ltd 1st ed. dj. M. $85.00

HUXLEY, Aldous. *On the Margin: Notes & Essays.* 1923. Chatto Windus. 1st trade ed. dj. EX. $35.00

HUXLEY, Aldous. *Point Counter Point.* 1928. Doubleday. 432 p. $35.00

HUXLEY, Aldous. *Proper Studies.* Ltd 1st ed. sgn. EX. B7. $110.00

HUXLEY, Aldous. *Texts & Pretexts: An Anthology.* 1932. London. 1st trade ed. dj. EX. $30.00

HUXLEY, Aldous. *Those Barren Leaves.* 1925. Chatto Windus. 1st trade ed. dj. EX. $22.50

HUXLEY, Aldous. *Time Must Have a Stop.* 1944. NY. Stated 1st ed. dj. $25.00

HUXLEY, Aldous. *Time Must Have a Stop.* 1945. London. 1st ed. dj. $25.00

HUXLEY, Aldous. *Words & Their Meanings.* 1940. Ward Ritchie. 1st trade ed. dj. EX. $30.00

HUXLEY, E. *Flame Trees of Thika: Memories of an African Childhood.* 1959. Chatto Windus. later print. 280 p. dj. EX. M2. $12.00

HUXLEY, E. *Mottled Lizard.* 1982. Chatto Windus. 311 p. dj. EX. M2. $12.00

HUXLEY, J. *Evolution As a Process.* 1954. Unwin. 1st ed. 367 p. EX. M2. $25.00

HUXLEY, J. *Evolution in Action.* 1953. Harper. Ils 1st ed. 182 p. EX. M2. $15.00

HUXLEY, J. *Human Crisis.* 1963. WA U. 88 p. EX. M2. $10.00

HUXLEY, T.H. *Man's Place in Nature & Other Anthropological Essays.* 1896. Appleton. 328 p. VG. M2. $20.00

HUXLEY, T.H. *Manual of the Anatomy of Invertebrated Animals.* 1977. Churchill. Ils. 596 p. VG. M2. $27.00

HUXLEY, T.H. *Science & Christian Tradition: Essays.* 1904. Appleton. Authorized ed. TEG. EX. $30.00

HUXLEY & VAN LAWICK. *Last Days in Eden.* 1984. Amaryllis. Ils 1st ed. 192 p. dj. EX. M2. $17.00

HUYCKE, Harold. *To Santa Rosalia Further & Back.* 1970. Mariners Mus. 1st ed. inscr. VG. $20.00

HUYETTE. *MD Campaign & the Battle of Antietam.* 1915. Buffalo. G. $25.00

HUYGEN, W. *Gnomes.* 1977. NY. Ils. 4to. dj. EX. $12.00

HUYGHE, R. *Art Treasures of the Louvre.* 1960. Abrams. sm folio. dj. VG. $22.00

HUYSMANS. *Against the Grain.* 1931. Three Sirens. Ils Zaidenberg. 339 p. VG. $12.00

HVASS, E. & H. *Mushrooms & Toadstools.* 1973. Hippocrene. Ils 1st Am ed. 156 p. dj. EX. M2. $10.00

HYATT, A. *Pseudoceratites of the Cretaceous.* 1903. US Geol Survey. 47 pls. 4to. 351 p. VG. M2. $145.00

HYDE, D.O. *Yamsi.* 1971. Dial. Ils 1st ed. 318 p. dj. EX. M2. $13.00

HYLAND, Stanley. *Green Grow the Tresses-O.* 1965. Gollancz. 2nd ed. dj. xl. P1. $5.00

HYLANDER, C.J. *Cruisers of the Air.* 1931. NY. Ils 1st ed. 308 p. G. T5. $95.00

HYLL, Thomas. *Gardeners Labyrinth.* 1939. Milford. facsimile. VG. $40.00

HYMAN, Mac. *No Time for Sergeants.* 1954. NY. 1st ed. 214 p. dj. VG. T5. $12.50

HYMAN, S. *Edward Lear's Birds.* 1980. Morrow. Ils. folio. 96 p. dj. EX. M2. $85.00

HYNDS, E.C. *Antebellum Athens & Clarke Co., GA.* 1974. Athens. 200 p. dj. EX. $25.00

HYNE, C. *Lost Continent.* 1900. London. 1st ed. gilt bdg. G. $100.00

IAMBLICHUS. *De Vita Pythagorica.* 1707. Greek/Latin text. rebound. $200.00

IAMS, Jack. *Shot of Murder.* nd. Book Club. VG. P1. $3.00

IBANEZ, Blasco. *Mare Nostrum.* 1919. Prometeo. leather. G. $35.00

IBARRURI, Dolores. *They Shall Not Pass.* 1966. NY. 1st ed. dj. EX. $30.00

IDELSOHN, A.Z. *Gesaenge der Persischen, Bucharischen und Daghestanischen...* 1922. Jerusalem. Harz. folio. wraps. $50.00

ILES, George. *Flame, Electricity & the Camera.* 1900. NY. G. $35.00

ILES, George. *Flame, Electricity & the Camera.* 1901. Doubleday. sgn. VG. $50.00

ILF & PETROV. *Little Golden America.* 1937. Farrar Rinehart. 1st ed. fair. $7.00

ILIOWIZI, Henry. *In the Pale: Stories & Legends of Russian Jews.* 1897. Phil. 1st ed. 367 p. xl. $50.00

ILLINGWORTH, F. *Falcons & Falconry.* 1970. London House. Revised Enlarged ed. 126 p. dj. M2. $30.00

IMAIZUMI, Y. *Mammals of Japan.* 1960. Osaka. Ils Miyamoto. 196 p. slipcase. M2. $35.00

IND, Allison. *Sino-Variant.* 1969. McKay. dj. VG. P1. $7.50

INDERWOOD, T.R. *Thoroughbred Racing & Breeding.* 1945. NY. 1st ed. dj. VG. $20.00

INDIAN, Gray. *Horse Crazy.* 1989. NY. Grove. 1st ed. dj. M. $15.00

INFIELD, G.B. *Secrets of the SS.* 1988. NY. dj. EX. $10.00

INGALLS, A.G. *Amateur Telescope Making: Book One.* 1970. Sc Am. Ils. 510 p. VG. M2. $16.00

INGE, William. *Good Luck, Miss Wyckoff.* 1970. Boston. 1st ed. dj. VG. $15.00

INGERSOLL, Jared. *Diamond Fingers.* 1970. Robert Hale. 1st ed. dj. xl. P1. $5.00

INGERSOLL, R.G. *Crimes Against Criminals.* 1906. Roycroft. 8vo. brown suede. poor. D1. $20.00

INGERSOLL, R.G. *Mistakes of Ingersoll & His Answers Complete.* 1894. Rhodes McClure. G. $20.00

INGHAM, G. *Digging Gold.* 1882. 452 p. K1. $18.50

INGHAM, H. Lloyd. *Bury Me Deep.* 1963. Hammond Hammond. VG. P1. $7.50

INGLEHART, F.C.G. *Boy Captive of TX Mier Expedition.* 1910. San Antonio. Ils 1st ed. VG. $35.00

INGLIS, B.D. *Wild Flower Studies.* 1951. Studio/Crowell. 1st ed. pls. 144 p. dj. EX. $30.00

INGLIS, Grace. *Retrograde Planets.* 1976. New Delhi. $11.00

INGPEN & PECK. *Complete Works of P.B. Shelley.* 1926-1930. London/NY. 1/780. 10 vols. $150.00

INGRAHAM, Charles. *Elmer Ellsworth & Zouaves of '61.* 1925. Chicago. wraps. EX. $18.00

INGRAHAM, E.V. *Incarnation & Reincarnation.* 1930. LA. $11.00

INGRAHAM, J.H. *Prince of House of David.* London. Routledge. Ils. TEG. G. $10.00

INMAN & CODY. *Great Salt Lake Trail.* 1899. Topeka. Ils. 8vo. TEG. cloth. T1. $35.00

INNES, Hammond. *Angry Mountain.* 1950. Collins. 1st ed. VG. P1. $7.50

INNES, Hammond. *Campbell's Kingdom.* 1952. Collins. dj. VG. P1. $10.00

INNES, Hammond. *Doomed Oasis.* nd. Book Club. dj. VG. P1. $3.00

INNES, Michael. *Appleby & Honeybath.* 1983. Gollancz. 1st ed. dj. EX. P1. $17.50

INNES, Michael. *Appleby at Allington.* 1969. Gollancz. 2nd ed. dj. xl. P1. $5.00

INNES, Michael. *Appleby Talks Again.* 1957. NY. 1st ed. dj. VG. $20.00

INNES, Michael. *Appleby's Answer.* 1973. Gollancz. 1st ed. dj. EX. P1. $20.00

INNES, Michael. *Awkward Lie.* 1971. Dodd Mead. dj. xl. P1. $6.00

INNES, Michael. *Carson's Conspiracy.* 1984. Gollancz. 1st ed. dj. EX. P1. $17.50

INNES, Michael. *Death at the Chase.* 1970. Gollancz. 1st ed. dj. xl. P1. $6.00

INNES, Michael. *Honeybath's Haven.* 1977. Gollancz. 1st ed. dj. EX. P1. $20.00

INNES, Michael. *One-Man Show.* nd. Book Club. dj. VG. P1. $4.00

INNES, W.T. *Exotic Aquarium Fishes.* 1966. Metaframe. Ils. 593 p. EX. M2. $12.00

INNIS, P.B. *Gold in the Blue Ridge.* 1973. NY. 1st ed. 224 p. dj. B2. $17.50

INSH, George. *Company of Scotland: Trading to Africa & Indies.* 1932. Scribner. 1st ed. dj. VG. J2. $15.00

INSKIPP, C. & T. *Guide to the Birds of Nepal.* 1985. Tanager. Ils 1st ed. dj. EX. M2. $35.00

IONESCO, Eugene. *Story No. 1.* 1968. $15.00

IPCAR, Dahlov. *Dark Horn Blowing.* 1980. pb. VG. C1. $6.00

IRELAND, M.E. *Doctor's Family; or, Story of Erlaus American Tract Society.* 1896. 1st ed. $12.00

IRESON, Barbara. *April Witch & Other Strange Tales.* 1978. Scribner. 1st ed. dj. VG. P1. $20.00

IRISH, William. *Dancing Detective.* 1946. Lippincott. 1st ed. dj. $20.00

IRISH, William. *Marijuana.* 1961. NY. Dell. Separate 1st ed. wraps. VG. $65.00

IRISH, William. *Phantom Lady.* nd. Collier. VG. P1. $15.00

IRISH, William. *Phantom Lady.* 1944. Tower. dj. VG. P1. $15.00

IRISH, William. *Waltz Into Darkness.* Lippincott. 3rd ed. VG. P1. $7.50

IRISH, William. *Waltz Into Darkness.* 1947. Lippincott. 1st ed. G. P1. $20.00

IRON, Ralph. *Story of African Farm.* nd. Lupton. G. $20.00

IRVINE, W. *Apes, Angels & Victorians.* 1955. McGraw Hill. Ils. 399 p. EX. M2. $18.00

IRVING, David. *Rise & Fall of the Luftwaffe.* 1973. Boston. Ils 1st Am ed. 455 p. dj. VG. T5. $12.50

IRVING, Helen. *Ladies' Wreath & Parlor Annual.* c 1854. NY. 12 pls. 218 p. VG. T5. $45.00

IRVING, J.T. *Indian Sketches Taken During Expedition to Pawnee Tribes...* 1955. OK U. Ils. 275 p. VG. M2. $16.00

IRVING, Washington. *Alhambra.* 1894. Phil. Revised ed. TEG. $35.00

IRVING, Washington. *Alhambra.* 1942. Macmillan. Ils Goble. $35.00

IRVING, Washington. *Alhambra.* 1969. Norwalk. Heritage. quarto. slipcase. EX. $15.00

IRVING, Washington. *Astoria*. 1836. Paris. Eng text. G. scarce. $135.00

IRVING, Washington. *Beauties of WA Irving*. 1839. Phil. Lea Blanchard. 8vo. 349 p. $27.50

IRVING, Washington. *Bracebridge Hall*. 1896. NY. Putnam. Surrey ed. 2 vols. VG. $55.00

IRVING, Washington. *Complete Works*. NY. De Fau. 1/1000. 16 vols. VG. $90.00

IRVING, Washington. *History of Life & Voyages of Christopher Columbus*. 1828. London. 1st ed. maps. 4 vols. full leather. VG. C2. $350.00

IRVING, Washington. *Land of Sleepy Hollow & Home of WA Irving*. 1887. London/NY. Putman. Ltd Letterpress ed. VG. $150.00

IRVING, Washington. *Legend of Sleepy Hollow*. nd. Drexel Hill. Bell. dj. VG. $37.00

IRVING, Washington. *Legend of Sleepy Hollow*. 1906. Indianapolis. Ils Keller. EX. $40.00

IRVING, Washington. *Legend of Sleepy Hollow*. 1959. Braun. Ils Rackham. J2. $75.00

IRVING, Washington. *Life & Letters of WA Irving*. 1862. Putnam. Ils 1st ed. 8vo. 4 vols. VG. G2. $65.00

IRVING, Washington. *Life & Voyages of Christopher Columbus & Voyages...* 1892. NY. Putnam. Isabella ed. 3 vols. G. T5. $125.00

IRVING, Washington. *Old Christmas: From Sketchbook of WA Irving*. 1882. London. Macmillan. gilt cloth. AEG. EX. J2. $100.00

IRVING, Washington. *Rip Van Winkle & Legend of Sleepy Hollow*. 1893. London. Macmillan. Ils Boughton. 1/250. $180.00

IRVING, Washington. *Rip Van Winkle*. 1905. Roycroft. 8vo. red suede. VG. D1. $40.00

IRVING, Washington. *Rip Van Winkle*. 1916. Doubleday. Ils Rackham. J2. $75.00

IRVING, Washington. *Rural Life in England*. c 1910. London. Ils Stokes/Wright. EX. $30.00

IRVING, Washington. *Salmagundi*. 1859. Putnam. 1st ed. Railway Series. sgn. $125.00

IRVING, Washington. *Sketchbook*. 1895. Putnam. Van Tassell ed. 2 vols. VG. J3. $80.00

IRVING, Washington. *Tales of a Traveler*. 1824. London. 1st ed. 2 vols. $275.00

IRVING, Washington. *Tales of a Traveler*. 1895. NY/London. Ils Rackham. 2 vols. VG. $75.00

IRVING, Washington. *W Journals of WA Irving*. 1966. OK U. Ils. map. 201 p. dj. EX. M2. $15.00

IRVING, Washington. *Wolfert's Roost*. 1855. NY. 1st ed. 1st state. $75.00

IRWIN & JOHNSON. *What You Should Know About Spies & Saboteurs*. 1943. Norton. Ils 1st ed. xl. G. M1. $6.50

IRWIN & O'BRIEN. *Alone Across the Top of the World*. 1945. Phil. Ils 1st ed. VG. $35.00

ISAACS. *Close Relations*. 1980. NY. 1st ed. dj. EX. $12.00

ISAARSON, Dorris A. *ME: A Guide Down E*. 1970. Rockland, ME. Revised reprint of 1937 ed. T5. $19.50

ISAIAH. *Book of the Prophet Isaiah*. Ltd Ed Club. slipcase. M. B3. $65.00

ISBEN, Henrik. *Doll's House*. 1897. NY. Trans Lord. fair. $12.00

ISBEN, Henrik. *Peer Gynt*. 1929. NY. 1st ed. VG. $25.00

ISHAM, DAVIDSON & FURNESS. *Prisoners of War & Military Prisons*. 1890. 1st ed. 571 p. gilt bdg. very scarce. K1. $85.00

ISHERWOOD, Christopher. *Christopher & His Kind, 1929-1939*. 1976. NY. 1st ed. dj. EX. $20.00

ISHERWOOD, Christopher. *Memorial*. 1946. Norfolk. 1st ed. dj. VG. $35.00

ISHERWOOD, Christopher. *Single Man*. 1964. London. 1st ed. dj. EX. $55.00

ISHERWOOD, Christopher. *World in the Evening*. nd. NY. 1st ed. dj. EX. $45.00

ISHERWOOD, Christopher. *World in the Evening*. 1954. London. 1st Eng ed. dj. VG. $30.00

ISHIMOTO, Tatsuo. *Art of Driftwood & Dried Arrangements*. 1951. Ils 1st ed. 143 p. dj. VG. $18.00

ISHIMOTO, Tatsuo. *Japanese House*. 1963. NY. Crown. 1st ed. dj. EX. $20.00

ISLER, M.L. & P.H. *Tanagers: Natural History, Distribution & Identification*. 1987. Smithsonian. Ils. 464 p. dj. EX. M2. $70.00

ISMAN, Felix. *Weber & Fields: Their Tribulations, Triumphs & Associates*. 1924. NY. Ils 1st ed. 345 p. G. T5. $22.50

ISON, Walter. *Georgian Buildings of Bristol*. 1952. London. dj. VG. J2. $35.00

ITTEN, Johannes. *Art of Color: Subjective Experience & Objective Rationale*. 1961. NY. Reinhold. 1st Am ed. 155 p. dj. D2. $225.00

IVANOFF, Serge. *Tristan & Iseult*. 1960. Ltd Ed Club. 1/1500. sgn. slipcase. EX. C1. $59.00

IVES, Burl. *Sea Songs of Sailing, Whaling & Fishing*. 1956. NY. Ballantine. 134 p. pb. VG. $30.00

IVES, George. *Bibliography of Oliver Wendell Holmes*. 1907. Boston. Ltd ed. 1/530. $50.00

IZLAR, W.V. *Sketch of War Record of the Edisto Rifles, 1861-1865*. 1914. Columbia. Ils. 168 p. $150.00

IZZARD, R. *Abominable Snowman*. 1955. Doubleday. Ils. 250 p. dj. EX. M2. $13.00

IZZI, Eugene. *Bad Guys*. 1988. NY. St. Martin. 1st ed. dj. M. $20.00

IZZI, Eugene. *Take*. 1987. St. Martin. 1st ed. dj. M. $22.00

J

J.B. LIPPINCOTT CO. *Catalog of Rare & Choice English Books.* c 1890?. Phil. Lippincott. $30.00

JABLONSKI, Edward. *Flying Fortress.* 1965. 362 p. dj. EX. $10.00

JABOTINSKY & PERLMAN. *Atlas.* 1925. London. Hasepher. 48 maps. 4to. EX. $250.00

JACK, R. Ian. *Medieval Wales.* 1972. Cornell. 1st ed. dj. EX. C1. $12.50

JACKMAN, L. *History of 6th NH Regiment in the War for the Union.* 1981. Republican Pr. Ils. 630 p. M2. $75.00

JACKMAN & LONG. *OR Desert.* 1964. Caxton. Ils. 407 p. dj. EX. M2. $17.00

JACKS, L.P. *Last Legend of Smokeover.* 1939. Hodder Stoughton. dj. VG. P1. $30.00

JACKS, L.P. *Magic Formula.* 1927. Harper. 1st ed. dj. VG. P1. $25.00

JACKSON, Andrew. *Proclamation of Andrew Jackson...to People of NC, 1832.* 1862. Harrisburg. 1st ed. wraps. VG. very scarce. $60.00

JACKSON, Basil. *Epicenter.* 1971. Norton. 2nd ed. dj. VG. P1. $10.00

JACKSON, Clarence. *Picture Maker of the Old W: William Jackson.* 1947. Scribner. 1st ed. VG. J2. $45.00

JACKSON, D.D. *Sage of the '49ers.* 1980. NY. 1st ed. inscr. dj. VG. $12.50

JACKSON, F.G. *Lesson on Decorative Design.* 1894. London. VG. $55.00

JACKSON, G. *British Whaling Trade.* 1978. Archon. 1st Am ed. 310 p. dj. EX. M2. $10.00

JACKSON, G.E. *Dixie School Girl.* c 1935. NY. Donohue. dj. $12.50

JACKSON, H.H. *CA & Missions.* 1903. Little Brown. not 1st ed. 292 p. brown bdg. VG. $30.00

JACKSON, H.H. *Ramona.* 1912. Toronto. Ils Vroman. dj. EX. $20.00

JACKSON, H.L. *Some Descendants of John & Elizabeth Cummins Jackson...* 1976. Clarksville. 154 p. dj. VG. T5. $37.50

JACKSON, Hartley. *Taxonomic Review of American Long-Tailed Shrews.* 1928. USDA. pls. wraps. EX. $15.00

JACKSON, Holbrook. *Anatomy of Bibliomania.* 1930. London. 1/1048. sgn twice. 2 vols. VG. $240.00

JACKSON, Holbrook. *Anatomy of Bibliomania.* 1932. Scribner. 3rd ed. 854 p. dj. VG. $50.00

JACKSON, I.W. *Elementary Treatise on Optics.* 1867. Schenectady. xl. poor. $20.00

JACKSON, J.H. *Anybody's Gold: Story of CA Mining Towns.* 1941. NY. Ils Suydam. dj. EX. $50.00

JACKSON, J.H. *Gold Rush Album: To CA in '49.* 1949. NY. 1st trade ed. VG. $17.50

JACKSON, J.H. *Gold Rush Album: To CA in '49.* 1949. Scribner. Ils 1st ed. 4to. 239 p. dj. EX. M2. $19.00

JACKSON, J.S. & M.Y. *Miller, Quaker & the Square.* 1984. Akron. Ils 1st ed. 40 p. wraps. M. T5. $2.95

JACKSON, John A. *Diehard.* 1977. Random House. 2nd ed. dj. xl. P1. $5.00

JACKSON, Joseph. *American Colonial Architecture: Its Origin & Development.* 1924. Ils. 228 p. dj. EX. B1. $30.00

JACKSON, M.A. *Memoirs of Stonewall Jackson.* 1895. Prentice Pr. Ils Enlarged ed. 647 p. G. M2. $70.00

JACKSON, R.T. *Phylogeny of Echini: Revision of Paleozoic Species.* 1912. Boston. Soc Nat Hist. Ils. 4to. 2 vols. M2. $225.00

JACKSON, Radway. *Concise Dictionary of Artists' Signature.* 1981. NY. Alpine. dj. EX. $35.00

JACKSON, Shirley. *Haunting of Hill House.* 1965. Viking. 7th ed. dj. xl. P1. $5.00

JACKSON, Shirley. *Lottery.* 1949. Farrar Straus. ARC. 1st ed. dj. $225.00

JACKSON, Shirley. *Lottery.* 1949. Farrar Straus. dj. VG. P1. $50.00

JACKSON, Shirley. *Lottery.* 1949. NY. 1st ed. dj. EX. $125.00

JACKSON, W.H. *Descriptive Catalog of Photographs of N American Indians.* 1877. WA. 124 p. A3. $60.00

JACKSON, W.H. *Time Exposure: Autobiography of William Henry Jackson.* 1940. Putnam. Ils. sgn. 342 p. dj. rare. A3. $200.00

JACKSON, W.T. *Anatomy of Love: Tristan of Gottfried von Strassburg.* 1972. Columbia U. 1st ed. dj. EX. C1. $22.00

JACKSON, W.T. *Wells Fargo Staging Over the Sierra.* 1970. CA Hist Soc. Ils. paper wraps. EX. M2. $4.00

JACKSON, W.T. *Wells Fargo: Symbol of the Wild W?* 1972. W Hist Quarterly. paper wraps. M2. $4.00

JACKSON, W.T. *Wells Fargo's Pony Expresses.* 1972. W Journal. Ils. paper wraps. EX. M2. $4.00

JACKSON, William. *Bookkeeping in True Italian Form of Debtor & Creditor...* 1801. NY/London. pls. fld map. presentation. sgn. $25.00

JACKSON, William. *Westerner's Brand Book.* 1947. Ltd ed. EX. S2. $150.00

JACKSON & JACKSON. *At Home on the Hill: Perkins Family of Akron.* 1983. Akron. Ils. 95 p. wraps. M. T5. $5.95

JACKSON. *Alfred the Great.* 1901. London. Bowyer. inscr. VG. $20.00

JACKSON. *Romance of Flight.* 1926. London. Ils. 287 p. G. C4. $32.00

JACOB, Rabbi. *Ayn Jacob, 5712.* 1951. 4 vols. VG. $75.00

JACOBI, A. *Treatise on Diptheria.* 1880. NY. Wood. $35.00

JACOBI, Carl. *Disclosures in Scarlet.* 1972. Arkham House. dj. EX. P1. $17.50

JACOBI, Carl. *Revelations in Black.* Arkham House. 1st ed. dj. EX. $100.00

JACOBI, Carl. *Revelations in Black.* 1947. Random House. dj. EX. P1. $50.00

JACOBI, Carl. *Revelations in Black.* 1974. Neville Spearman. dj. EX. P1. $15.00

JACOBI, Charles. *Some Notes on Books & Printing.* 1902. London. Chiswick. New Enlarged ed. 1/500. $45.00

JACOBI, Lotte. *Theater & Dance Photographs.* 1982. Woodstock. Countryman Pr. 47 p. wraps. $17.50

JACOBOWITZ, Arlene. *James Hamilton: American Marine Painter.* 1966. Brooklyn Mus. Ils. D2. $25.00

JACOBS, David. *Chaplin: Movies & Charlie.* 1975. Harper. 1st ed. dj. VG. J2. $7.50

JACOBS, F. *Africa's Flamingo Lake.* 1979. Morrow. Ils 1st ed. 80 p. dj. EX. M2. $6.00

JACOBS, Frank. *Lt. Robin Crusoe USN.* nd. Golden Pr. Movie ed. VG. P1. $7.50

JACOBS, Fredric. *Greek Reader.* 1833. Collins Hanny. 73 p. M1. $12.50

JACOBS, Herbert. *Frank Lloyd Wright: America's Greatest Architect.* 1965. NY. Ils. 223 p. dj. EX. T5. $15.00

JACOBS, J. *Biographical Sketch of Life of Late Captain Michael Cresap.* 1971. NY. Arno. EX. $30.00

JACOBS, Michael. *Notes on Rebel Invasion of MD & PA & Battle of Gettysburg...* 1864. Lippincott. 47 p. G. A3. $75.00

JACOBS, T.C.H. *Aspects of Murder.* 1956. Stanley Paul Ltd. 1st ed. EX. $15.00

JACOBS, T.C.H. *Documents of Murder.* 1933. Macaulay. VG. P1. $17.50

JACOBSON & ANTONI. *Des Anticipations de Jules Verne aux Realisations...* c 1937. Paris. Ils. 197 p. VG. $27.50

JACOBY, H. *Architectural Drawings.* 1965. 1st ed. dj. G. $25.00

JACOBY & MOREHEAD. *Fireside Book of Cards.* 1957. Simon Schuster. Ils. dj. VG. $18.00

JACQUEMARD, Simonne. *Night Watchman.* 1964. Holt Rinehart. 1st ed. P1. $8.00

JACQUEMARD-SENECAL. *Body Vanishes.* 1980. Dodd Mead. 1st ed. dj. VG. P1. $7.50

JACQUES, Henry. *Modern Ballroom Dancing.* c 1930s. London. Ils. 4to. VG. T1. $50.00

JAEGER, E.C. *Desert Wild Flowers.* 1947. Stanford. Ils Revised ed. 322 p. G. M2. $13.00

JAEGER, E.C. *Desert Wildlife.* 1978. Stanford. Ils. 308 p. EX. M2. $15.00

JAEGER, E.C. *N American Deserts.* 1957. Stanford. Ils. maps. 308 p. dj. EX. M2. $18.00

JAEGER, E.C. *Tracks & Trailcraft.* 1948. Macmillan. Ils 1st ed. 381 p. VG. M2. $10.00

JAFFE, I.B. *Sculpture of Leonard Baskin.* 1980. NY. 1st ed. inscr. dj. EX. $35.00

JAFFE, Michael. *Jacob Jordaens: Selection & Catalog.* 1969. Ottawa. Nat Gallery Canada. 416 p. dj. D2. $75.00

JAFFE, Michael. *Van Dyck's Antwerp Sketchbook.* 1966. London. Macdonald. 2 vols. D2. $265.00

JAHN, M. *Switch.* 1976. NY. 1st ed. 138 p. wraps. VG. $7.50

JAHN, T.L. & F.F. *How To Know the Protozoa.* 1949. Brown. Ils. VG. M2. $17.00

JAHNS, P. *Frontier World of Doc Holliday.* 1957. Hastings House. xl. G. M2. $18.00

JAHNS, P. *Violent Years.* 1962. NY. 1st ed. 309 p. dj. EX. T5. $25.00

JAHODA, G. *Trail of Tears.* 1975. NY. 1st ed. 356 p. dj. VG. B2. $45.00

JAKEMAN, M. *Origins & History of Mayas. Part 1.* 1945. Los Angeles. 203 p. G. $12.00

JALLAND, G.H. *Sporting Adventures of Mr. Popple.* c 1895. London. pls. oblong 4to. VG. $50.00

JAMES, B. *Zodiac.* Ils 1/350. 4to. slipcase. EX. G2. $80.00

JAMES, Cary. *Imperial Hotel.* 1968. Rutland. dj. EX. P3. $95.00

JAMES, E. *Account of Expedition From Pittsburgh to Rocky Mountains.* 1966. Readex. reprint. 2 vols. EX. M2. $45.00

JAMES, G.W. *CA: Romantic & Beautiful.* 1921. 6th imp. map. EX. $25.00

JAMES, G.W. *Exposition Memories.* 1916. San Diego. 1st ed. EX. $45.00

JAMES, G.W. *In & Around the Grand Canyon.* 1913. Boston. presentation. sgn. 352 p. VG. B2. $70.00

JAMES, G.W. *In & Out of Old Missions of CA.* 1910. Boston. Ils. VG. $60.00

JAMES, G.W. *In & Out of Old Missions of CA.* 1910. Boston. xl. $18.00

JAMES, G.W. *Indian Basketry & How To Make Indian & Other Baskets.* 1903. Pasadina. Vroman. 3rd ed. xl. A3. $180.00

JAMES, G.W. *Indian Basketry.* 1902. NY. Maklin. 2nd ed. 274 p. A3. $120.00

JAMES, G.W. *Indian Blankets & Their Makers.* 1937. NY. pls. EX. $85.00

JAMES, G.W. *Indian Blankets & Their Makers.* 1937. Tudor. New ed. xl. VG. $55.00

JAMES, G.W. *NM.* 1920. Boston. 1st imp. map. TEG. EX. $35.00

JAMES, Henry. *Ambassadors.* 1903. NY. 1st ed. fabricoid dj. EX. P3. $175.00

JAMES, Henry. *American Scene & Portraits of Places.* 1946. Scribner. VG. $30.00

JAMES, Henry. *Better Sort.* 1903. London. 1st ed. G. $35.00

JAMES, Henry. *Better Sort.* 1903. NY. 1st ed. 428 p. T5. $65.00

JAMES, Henry. *English Hours.* 1905. Cambridge. Ltd 1st Am ed. 1/400. $150.00

JAMES, Henry. *English Hours.* 1905. Houghton. Ils Pennell. 1st ed. TEG. $65.00

JAMES, Henry. *Finer Grain.* 1910. NY. 1st ed. TEG. VG. $20.00

JAMES, Henry. *Hawthorne.* 1879. Macmillan. 1st ed. slim 8vo. VG. G2. $55.00

JAMES, Henry. *Notes of a Son & Brother.* 1914. NY. 1st ed. EX. P3. $55.00

JAMES, Henry. *Notes on Novelists.* 1914. NY. 1st ed. VG. $35.00

JAMES, Henry. *Other House.* 1896. NY. 1st Am ed. 388 p. TEG. T5. $80.00

JAMES, Henry. *Portraits of Places.* 1883. Boston/NY. 1st Am ed. brown cloth. $15.00

JAMES, Henry. *Small Boy & Others.* 1913. NY. 1st ed. VG. $30.00

JAMES, Henry. *Theatricals.* 1894. NY. 1st ed. as issued. $65.00

JAMES, Henry. *Turn of the Screw.* 1949. Ils. 4to. 145 p. slipcase. EX. $8.00

JAMES, Henry. *Turn of the Screw.* 1977. Norwalk. Heritage. quarto. slipcase. EX. $15.00

JAMES, Henry. *What Maisie Knew.* 1897. Chicago. 1st ed. VG. $40.00

JAMES, J.A. *Life of George Rogers Clark.* 1968. Greenwood. reprint. 534 p. EX. M2. $22.00

JAMES, Jesse Jr. *Jesse James, My Father.* 1906. Cleveland. 189 p. VG. $20.00

JAMES, M. *Alfred Durant: Family Rebel.* 1941. Indianapolis. Ltd ed. 1/250. boxed. VG. B2. $50.00

JAMES, M. *Andrew Jackson: Border Captain.* 1933. Literary Guild. Ils 1st ed. 461 p. EX. M2. $14.00

JAMES, M. *Life of Andrew Jackson.* 1938. Bobbs Merrill. Ils. 972 p. dj. EX. M2. $12.00

JAMES, M. *Life of Andrew Jackson.* 1938. Bobbs Merrill. VG. $6.00

JAMES, M. *Raven: Biography of Sam Houston.* 1929. Halcyon House. 489 p. VG. M2. $10.00

JAMES, P.D. *Innocent Blood.* nd. Scribner. 2nd ed. dj. VG. P1. $10.00

JAMES, P.D. *Innocent Blood.* nd. Scribner. 3rd ed. dj. VG. P1. $7.50

JAMES, P.D. *Innocent Blood.* 1980. Scribner. 1st ed. dj. G. P1. $10.00

JAMES, P.D. *Maul & Pear Tree.* 1971. London. 1st ed. $30.00

JAMES, P.D. *Mind to Murder.* 1963. London. 1st ed. dj. EX. $30.00

JAMES, P.D. *Unsuitable Job for a Woman.* nd. Book Club. dj. VG. P1. $4.00

JAMES, P.D. *Unsuitable Job for a Woman.* nd. London. 1st ed. dj. EX. $50.00

JAMES, P.S. *Stow, OH: Shadows of Its Past.* 1972. Ann Arbor. Ils. 307 p. EX. T5. $15.00

JAMES, Thomas. *Three Years Among the Indians & Mexicans.* 1953. Donnelley. Lakeside Classic. A3. $40.00

JAMES, Will. *American Cowboy.* 1942. Scribner. 1st ed. dj. VG. T6. $20.00

JAMES, Will. *Cowboy in the Making.* 1937. 1st ed. VG. $40.00

JAMES, Will. *Cowboy Life in TX.* 1895. Chicago. $25.00

JAMES, Will. *Cowboy Life in TX; or, 27 Years a Mavrick.* 1893. Chicago. Donohue. $45.00

JAMES, Will. *Cowboys: N & S.* 1924. NY. 1st ed. VG. B2. $75.00

JAMES, Will. *Dark Horse.* 1939. NY. 1st ed. VG. B2. $37.50

JAMES, Will. *Drifting Cowboy.* 1925. Grosset Dunlap. 241 p. VG. $15.00

JAMES, Will. *Drifting Cowboy.* 1925. Scribner. 241 p. $20.00

JAMES, Will. *Lone Cowboy: My Life Story.* 1930. NY. Ils 1st ed. 431 p. VG. T5. $25.00

JAMES, Will. *Sand.* 1929. Grosset Dunlap. 308 p. VG. $15.00

JAMES, William. *Memories & Studies.* 1911. NY. 1st Am ed. $45.00

JAMES. *Fifth Avenue.* 1972. dj. VG. S2. $25.00

JAMESON, E.W. *Hawking of Japan: History & Development of Falconry.* 1976. CA U. Ils 2nd print. 97 p. EX. M2. $110.00

JAMESON, H. *Heroes by the Dozen.* 1961. private print. photos. 203 p. dj. EX. M2. $9.00

JAMESON, J.F. *Privateering & Piracy in Colonial Period.* 1923. NY. VG. $20.00

JAMESON, Malcolm. *Bullard of the Space Patrol.* 1951. World. dj. VG. P1. $25.00

JAMESON, W. *Wandering Albatross.* 1959. Morrow. Ils 1st Am ed. 128 p. dj. EX. M2. $9.00

JAMISON. *Recollections of Pioneer & Army Life.* 1911. KS City. VG. C4. $65.00

JANIFER, Laurence M. *Knave & the Game.* 1987. Doubleday. dj. EX. P1. $12.95

JANIFER, Laurence M. *Reel.* 1983. Doubleday. 1st ed. dj. EX. RS. P1. $15.00

JANIN, Giovanni. *Memorie ed Osservazioni Anatomiche Fisiologiche...* 1784. Venice. 2 vols. $250.00

JANIS, Sidney. *They Taught Themselves: American Primitive Painters...* 1942. NY. Dial. Ils. photos. dj. D2. $75.00

JANNEY, Russell. *Miracle of the Bells.* 1946. McLeod. dj. G. P1. $7.50

JANOVY, J. *Yellowlegs.* 1980. St. Martin. 192 p. dj. EX. M2. $13.00

JANSKY, C.M. *Electrical Meters.* 1917. NY/London. 2nd ed. fair. $18.00

JANSON, C.W. *Stranger in America, 1793-1806.* 1935. NY. reprint of 1807 London ed. VG. $25.00

JANZARIK, Hilde. *Lively Adventures of Burly Woodcutter.* 1966. NY. Harper. Ils Flora. dj. VG. $12.00

JAPOUR, M.J. *Petroleum Refining & Manufacturing Processes.* 1939. Los Angeles. G. $25.00

JAPRISOT, Sebastien. *Lady in the Car.* nd. Book Club. dj. VG. P1. $3.00

JAPRISOT, Sebastien. *1030 From Marseille.* nd. Book Club. dj. G. P1. $3.00

JAQUES, Florence. *Francis Lee Jaques: Artist of the Wilderness World.* 1973. Doubleday. 1st ed. boxed. VG. J2. $125.00

JAQUES, Florence. *Snowshoe Country.* 1944. MN U. 1st ed. dj. J2. $20.00

JAQUES, Florence. *Snowshoe Country.* 1945. MN U. Ils Jaques. 110 p. dj. EX. M2. $14.00

JAQUES & JAQUES. *As Far As the Yukon.* 1951. Harper. 243 p. M1. $12.50

JAQUES & JAQUES. *As Far As the Yukon.* 1951. NY. 1st ed. sgns. dj. VG. B2. $25.00

JARDI, Enric. *Subira-Puig o el Latido de la Madera.* 1978. Barcelona. Spanish/Eng/French text. dj. D2. $35.00

JARDIN, Rex. *Devil's Mansion.* 1931. Fiction League. G. P1. $10.00

JARDINE, W. *Naturalist's Library of Animals.* c 1840s. London. 404 pls. 13 vols. EX. M2. $400.00

JARDINE, W. *Naturalist's Library of Entomology.* c 1840s. London. 202 pls. 7 vols. EX. M2. $250.00

JARDINE, W. *Naturalist's Library of Ichthyology.* c 1840s. London. 195 pls. 6 vols. EX. M2. $210.00

JARDINE, W. *Naturalist's Library of Ornithology.* 1944-1848. London. 452 pls. 15 vols. EX. M2. $450.00

JARDINE, W. *Naturalist's Library.* nd. Lizars. 437 of 438 pls. 14 vols. J2. $350.00

JARMAN, Rosemary. *We Speak No Treason.* 1971. 1st ed. VG. C1. $9.00

JARRELL, H.M. *Wade Hampton & the Negro: Road Not Taken.* 1950. SC U. 2nd print. 209 p. $35.00

JARRELL, H.M. *Wade Hampton & the Negro: Road Not Taken.* 1969. Columbia. 3rd print. dj. M. $10.00

JARRELL, Randall. *Pictures From an Institution.* 1954. NY. 1st ed. dj. VG. B2. $35.00

JARROTT, Charles. *Ten Years of Motors & Motor Racing.* 1906. NY. Ils 1st ed. 297 p. G. $75.00

JARVIS, Fred G. *Murder at the Met.* 1971. Coward McCann. dj. xl. P1. $5.00

JARVIS, G.H. *Hemrick & Allied Families (Germany to GA), 1727-1974.* 1975. 223 p. EX. $20.00

JARVIS, Stinson. *Ascent of Life...* 1894. Boston. $15.00

JASEN, David A. *P.G. Wodehouse: Portrait of Master.* nd. Continuum. Revised ed. dj. EX. P1. $25.00

JASEN, David A. *P.G. Wodehouse: Portrait of Master.* 1974. Mason Lipscomb. dj. VG. P1. $35.00

JASPERS, Karl. *Nietzche.* 1965. AZ U. Trans Wallraff/Schmitz. EX. $22.00

JAY, Charlotte. *Man Who Walked Away.* 1958. Crime Club. dj. VG. P1. $7.50

JAY, William. *Jay's Inquiry.* 1835. NY. xl. G. $20.00

JAY, William. *Review of the Mexican War.* 1849. Boston. 33 p. xl. K1. $18.50

JEAN, Marcel. *History of Surrealist Painting.* 1960. NY. Ils. 4to. 393 p. dj. EX. J2. $85.00

JEANCON, J.A. *Excavations in Chama Valley, NM.* 1923. Smithsonian. xl. VG. $45.00

JEFFERIES, R. *Pageant of Summer.* 1897. Portland, ME. 1/425. Art Nouveau bdg. EX. $150.00

JEFFERS, H. Paul. *Adventure of the Stalwart Companions.* 1978. Harper Row. dj. EX. P1. $25.00

JEFFERS, H. Paul. *Murder on Mike.* 1984. St. Martin. 1st ed. dj. EX. P1. $15.00

JEFFERS, H. Paul. *Rubout at the Onyx.* 1981. Ticknor Fields. 1st ed. dj. EX. P1. $12.50

JEFFERS, Robinson. *Continent's End: Anthology of Contemporary CA Poets.* 1935. Nash. Book Club of CA. 1/600. 4to. VG. $100.00

JEFFERS, Robinson. *Cowdor.* 1928. Liveright. 1/375. sgn. EX. $110.00

JEFFERS, Robinson. *Cowdor.* 1985. Covelo, CA. Yolla Bolley Pr. 1/225. M. $250.00

JEFFERS, Robinson. *Dear Judas & Other Poems.* 1929. NY. Ltd ed. 1/350. sgn. $85.00

JEFFERS, Robinson. *Dear Judas & Other Poems.* 1929. NY. 1st trade ed. dj. $40.00

JEFFERS, Robinson. *Deer Lay Down Their Bones.* 1954. Voices. EX. $20.00

JEFFERS, Robinson. *Descent to the Dead.* 1931. Random House. 1/500. sgn/#d. $275.00

JEFFERS, Robinson. *Give Your Heart to the Hawks.* 1933. Random House. 1st trade ed. EX. $25.00

JEFFERS, Robinson. *Meadea.* 1946. NY. 1st ed. 2nd state. inscr. EX. P3. $195.00

JEFFERS, Robinson. *Not Man Apart.* 1965. Sierra Club. 1st ed. $100.00

JEFFERS, Robinson. *Such Counsels You Gave to Me.* 1937. NY. 1st trade ed. dj. $38.00

JEFFERS, Robinson. *Such Counsels You Gave to Me.* 1937. Random House. 1/300. sgn. slipcase. EX. $225.00

JEFFERS, Robinson. *Tamar.* 1924. Boyle. 1st ed. VG. scarce. $200.00

JEFFERSON, Joseph. *Autobiography.* 1890. NY. 8vo. 501 p. EX. P3. $39.00

JEFFERSON, Thomas. *Jefferson Bible.* 1967. Potter. dj. $18.00

JEFFERSON & DUNBAR. *Documents Relating to Purchase & Exploration of LA.* 1904. NY. 1st ed. 1/550. M. $65.00

JEFFERY, L.H. *Local Scripts of Archaic Greece.* 1963. Oxford Clarendon Pr. dj. M. $35.00

JEFFRIES, Roderic. *Dead Against the Lawyers.* 1966. Dodd Mead. 1st ed. dj. VG. P1. $10.00

JEFFRIES, Roderic. *Just Deserts.* 1980. St. Martin. dj. VG. P1. $10.00

JEFFRIES, Roderic. *Three & One Make Five.* 1984. St. Martin. 1st ed. dj. EX. P1. $12.50

JEFFRIES. *History of Forsyth Family.* 1920. IN. Ils. 340 p. VG. C4. $42.00

JEHL, Francis. *Menlo Park Reminiscences.* 1935. Dearborn. Edison Inst. 1st ed. 430 p. $70.00

JEHOVAH WITNESSES. *Photo-Drama of Creation.* 1914. Brooklyn. maroon cloth. VG. B2. $42.50

JEKYLL & ELGOOD. *Some English Gardens.* 1904. London. Longman. 1st ed. VG. $150.00

JELLICOE, John. *Jellicoe Papers.* 1966. Navy Records Soc. 2 vols. J2. $25.00

JELLINEK-MERCEDES, Guy. *My Father, Mr. Mercedes.* 1961. Chilton. 1st ed. dj. VG. J2. $10.00

JENERETTE, Rita. *My Capitol Secrets.* 1981. Bantam. pb. $7.50

JENICKA, Jiriho. *Praha Deset Fotografii.* 1945. np. 10 photos. sgn. 4to. spiral bdg. $50.00

JENKINS, Alan C. *Thin Air.* 1972. Blackie. dj. EX. $15.00

JENKINS, Dan. *Dead Solid Perfect.* 1974. Atheneum. 1st ed. dj. EX. $20.00

JENKINS, Elizabeth. *Princes in the Tower.* 1978. 1st ed. dj. EX. C1. $12.50

JENKINS, Herbert. *Malcolm Sage Detective.* nd. Roy. dj. G. P1. $15.00

JENKINS, Herbert. *Return of Alfred.* nd. Jenkins. 6th ed. VG. P1. $10.00

JENKINS, J.S. *Daring Deeds of American Generals.* c 1857. NY. 12mo. 407 p. G. G2. $18.00

JENKINS, J.S. *James Knox Polk & History of His Administration.* 1851. Auburn. 395 p. fair. T5. $22.50

JENKINS, M.M. *Kangaroos, Opossums & Other Marsupials.* 1975. Holiday House. Ils. 160 p. dj. EX. M2. $14.00

JENKINS, P.B. *Battle of Westport.* 1906. 193 p. VG. very scarce. J4. $80.00

JENKINS, Peter. *Walk Across America.* nd. (1978?) NY. Morrow. UCP. VG. $15.00

JENKINS, W.F. *Murder of the USA.* 1947. Handi-Book. VG. P1. $25.00

JENKINS & FROST. *I'm Frank Hamer: Life of TX Peace Officer.* 1968. Austin. Pemberton. 1st ed. dj. M. $55.00

JENKINSON, R.C. *Collection of Books Chosen To Show Work of Best Printers.* 1929. Merrymount. 1/500. 8vo. TEG. VG. $47.00

JENNETT, Sean. *Making of Books.* c 1950. Pantheon. Ils. 474 p. dj. $25.00

JENNINGS, N.A. *TX Ranger.* 1959. Steck. facsimile of 1899 ed. slipcase. EX. $30.00

JENNINGS, O.E. *Wild Flowers of W PA & Upper OH Basin.* 1953. Pittsburgh. 1st ed. 2 vols. djs. EX. T5. $325.00

JENNINGS, W. *Founding of Belgrade.* 1808. NY. inscr. fair. $25.00

JENNISON, John W. *Thunderbirds Lost World.* 1966. World. VG. P1. $10.00

JENNY, Hans. *Kymatic/Cymatics. Structure & Dynamics of Waves...* 1974. Basel. dj. VG. $15.00

JENSEN, Bernard. *Science & Practice of Iridology.* 1974. Escondido. Jensen. Ils 5th ed. 372 p. VG. $20.00

JENSEN, Oliver. *Carrier War.* 1945. NY. Ils. 172 p. dj. VG. T5. $27.50

JENTSCH, Ralph. *Kaethe Kollwitz: Radierungen, Lithographien, Holzschnitte.* 1979. Esslingen. Kunstgalerie. Ils. wraps. D2. $27.50

JEPSON, Selwyn. *Man Dead.* 1951. Doubleday. VG. P1. $17.50

JERDON, T.C. *Birds of India: Natural History of Birds.* 1870. 1863-1870. Calcutta. 3 vols. rebound. EX. M2. $175.00

JERDON, T.C. *Mammals of India.* 1874. London. Wheldon. 335 p. rebound. EX. M2. $110.00

JERINGHAM & BETTANY. *Bargain Book.* 1911. London. pls. fld charts. $35.00

JERMAN. *Modern X-Ray Technique.* 1928. St. Paul. Ils. 4to. EX. P3. $45.00

JEROME, J.K. *Three Men in a Boat.* 1889. Bristol. Arrowsmith. 1st ed. later print. $55.00

JEROME, Owen Fox. *Corpse Awaits.* 1946. Mystery House. 1st ed. xl. P1. $5.00

JEROME, Owen Fox. *Corpse Awaits.* 1947. Handi-Book 58. G. P1. $7.50

JEROME, Owen Fox. *Five Assassins.* 1958. Mystery House. 1st ed. dj. xl. P1. $6.00

JEROME, V.J. *Negro in Hollywood Films.* 1952. NY. 64 p. pb. VG. $20.00

JEROME, V.J. *Treatment of Defeated Germany.* 1945. NY. Ils bdg Kent. 107 p. pb. VG. $25.00

JERROLD, Walter. *Big Book of Fables.* nd. NY. Ils Charles Robinson. J2. $35.00

JERROLD, Walter. *Big Book of Fables.* 1912. NY. Caldwell. 1st ed. J2. $100.00

JESSEE, Edward. *Summer's Day at Windsor & Visit to Eton.* 1841. London. 1st ed. 12mo. 151 p. VG. $25.00

JETER, K.W. *Death Arms.* 1987. Morrigan. 1st ed. dj. EX. P1. $22.50

JETER, K.W. *Infernal Devices.* 1987. St. Martin. dj. EX. P1. $16.95

JEUDY & TARAINE. *Jeep.* 1981. NY. Vilo. 1st ed. dj. EX. $35.00

JEWETT, Eleanore. *Hidden Treasure of Glaston.* 1966. 10th print. juvenile. dj. xl. VG. C1. $19.50

JEWETT, S.O. *Native of Winby & Other Tales.* 1893. Boston. 1st ed. $85.00

JEWISH BLACK BOOK COMMITTEE. *Black Book.* 1946. 560 p. black cloth. VG. $30.00

JILLSON, W.R. *Legrande Oil Pool.* 1930. Frankfort, KY. Ils 1st ed. 8vo. VG. T1. $45.00

JINGWEI, Z. *Alpine Plants of China.* 1982. Breach. 197 photos. 134 p. dj. EX. M2. $18.00

JINKS, R. *History of Smith & Wesson.* 1977. CA. 1st ed. 274 p. dj. EX. $20.00

JOACHIM & BOLLIGER. *Italian Drawings in Chicago Art Institute.* 1979. Chicago. Ils. 161 pls. map. 202 p. D2. $12.00

JOANNIDES, Paul. *Drawings of Raphael With Complete Catalog.* 1983. Berkeley. Ils. 271 p. dj. D2. $125.00

JOBSON, Hamilton. *Shadow That Caught Fire.* 1972. Scribner. 1st ed. dj. EX. P1. $10.00

JOCHERS, Ernest. *J. Otto Schweizer.* 1953. 1/200. photos. sgn. dj. VG. $40.00

JOCHIM, J.W. *MI & Its Resources.* 1893. Lansing. full brown leather. VG. $20.00

JOERG, W.L.G. *Work of Byrd Antarctic Expedition, 1928-1930.* 1930. NY. Ils 1st ed. maps. wraps. VG. T1. $45.00

JOHANNSEN, Albert. *House of Beadle & Adams.* 1962. Norman. OK U. 4to. VG. $37.50

JOHANNSEN, Robert. *To the Halls of Montezumas.* 1985. NY. dj. EX. $20.00

JOHN, Ivor B. *Maginogion.* 1911. London. 1st ed. VG. rare. C1. $19.50

JOHNES, E.R. *Johnes Family of Southampton, Long Island, 1629-1886.* 1886. NY. fld charts. 46 p. G. T5. $17.50

JOHNES, Merideth. *Boy's Book of Modern Travel & Adventure.* 1859. 8 pls. G. $25.00

JOHNS, Foster. *Victory Murders.* nd. Economy Book League. VG. P1. $12.50

JOHNS, V.P. *Servant's Problem.* 1963. Collier. VG. P1. $4.50

JOHNS, W.E. *Biggles Air Detective Omnibus.* 1959. Hodder Stoughton. VG. P1. $10.00

JOHNS, W.E. *Biggles Flies to Work.* nd. Dean & Son. VG. P1. $7.50

JOHNS, W.E. *Biggles in Africa.* 1946. Oxford. dj. VG. P1. $10.00

JOHNS, W.E. *Biggles in the Jungle.* 1944. Oxford. VG. P1. $10.00

JOHNS, W.E. *Not to the Stars.* 1956. Hodder Stoughton. 1st ed. VG. P1. $15.00

JOHNS, W.E. *Worrals Goes E.* 1946. Musson. VG. P1. $15.00

JOHNSGARD, P.A. *Bird Decoy: American Art Form.* 1976. NE U. Ils. sgn. 190 p. dj. EX. M2. $30.00

JOHNSGARD, P.A. *Diving Birds of N America.* 1987. NE U. Ils. 4to. 292 p. dj. EX. M2. $45.00

JOHNSGARD, P.A. *Ducks, Geese & Swans of the World.* 1978. NE U. Ils. 404 p. dj. EX. M2. $35.00

JOHNSGARD, P.A. *Grouse of the World.* 1983. NE U. Ils. 413 p. dj. EX. M2. $45.00

JOHNSGARD, P.A. *Hummingbirds of N America.* 1984. Smithsonian. Ils. 304 p. dj. EX. M2. $35.00

JOHNSGARD, P.A. *N American Game Birds of Upland & Shoreline.* 1975. NE U. Ils. 183 p. M. M2. $9.00

JOHNSGARD, P.A. *N American Owls: Biology & Natural History.* 1988. Smithsonian. Ils. 295 p. dj. M. M2. $45.00

JOHNSGARD, P.A. *Plovers, Sandpipers & Snipes of the World.* 1981. NE U. Ils. 493 p. dj. M. M2. $45.00

JOHNSGARD, P.A. *Song of the N Wind: Story of the Snow Goose.* 1974. Doubleday. 1st ed. dj. VG. J2. $10.00

JOHNSGARD, P.A. *Those of the Gray Wind: Sandhill Cranes.* 1981. St. Martin. Ils 1st ed. 116 p. dj. EX. M2. $17.00

JOHNSGARD, P.A. *Waterfowl of N America.* 1975. IN U. Ils 1st ed. 575 p. dj. EX. M2. $44.00

JOHNSGARD, P.A. *Waterfowl: Their Biology & Natural History.* 1968. NE U. Ils. 138 p. dj. EX. M2. $15.00

JOHNSON, A.W. *Birds of Chile & Adjacent Regions of Argentina, Bolivia...* 1965. Buenos Aires. Ils Goodall. 397 p. dj. EX. M2. $185.00

JOHNSON, Alexander. *Almshouse: Construction & Management.* 1911. NY. Ils 1st ed. 8vo. 263 p. dj. $35.00

JOHNSON, Allen. *Chronicles of America.* 1920. Yale. Extra-Ils ed. 50 vols. VG. $145.00

JOHNSON, Andrew. *Speeches...* 1866. Little Brown. 494 p. xl. $35.00

JOHNSON, B.W. *AR Frontier.* 1957. private print. Ils 1st ed. sgn. 162 p. EX. M2. $30.00

JOHNSON, C. *Among English Hedgerows.* 1899. Ils. 347 p. TEG. G. $10.00

JOHNSON, Charles A. *Wise County, VA.* 1938. HrdCvr. reprint. 416 p. index. J4. $28.00

JOHNSON, Charles. *General History of the Pirates.* 1926. Dodd Mead. reprint of 1726 ed. T6. $50.00

JOHNSON, Charles. *Lives & Actions of Highwaymen, Street Robbers, Pirates...* 1839. London. leather. VG. $100.00

JOHNSON, Clifton. *Isle of Shamrock.* 1901. EX. S2. $65.00

JOHNSON, Clifton. *Picturesque Hudson.* 1909. NY. 1st ed. 47 pls. 12mo. gilt blue cloth. T1. $22.00

JOHNSON, Clifton. *Picturesque St. Lawrence.* 1910. NY. photos. inscr. 16mo. $30.00

JOHNSON, D.F. *Uniform Buttons: American Armed Forces, 1784-1948.* 1948. 1st ed. 100 pls. 2 vols. VG. J4. $25.00

JOHNSON, D.W. *Biosystematics of American Crows.* 1961. WA U. 119 p. M. M2. $15.00

JOHNSON, Diane. *Dashiell Hammett: A Life.* 1983. Random House. 1st ed. dj. EX. P1. $15.00

JOHNSON, E. Richard. *Judas.* 1971. Harper. 1st ed. dj. xl. P1. $5.00

JOHNSON, F. *Nasty Nancy & Her Cat.* 1962. Mermaid Pr. Ltd ed. slipcase. EX. $65.00

JOHNSON, F. *Rockwell Kent: Anthology of His Works.* 1982. NY. Knopf. Ils 1st ed. 4to. 359 p. EX. $32.00

JOHNSON, G. *Sky Movies.* 1928. NY. Ils. dj. VG. $25.00

JOHNSON, H.A. *Sword of Honor: Story of Civil War.* 1906. Hallowell. 1st ed. presentation. VG. $55.00

JOHNSON, H.U. *From Dixie to Canada...* 1896. Orwell, OH. 2nd ed. 194 p. $55.00

JOHNSON, H.U. *W Reserve Centennial Souvenir.* 1896. Cleveland. 1st ed. 100 p. G. T5. $19.50

JOHNSON, I.M. *Botany of San Jose Island.* 1949. Harbard. 1st ed. 306 p. stiff wraps. VG. J2. $20.00

JOHNSON, Johanna. *King Arthur: His Knights & Their Ladies.* 1979. Scholastic Book. pb. VG. C1. $4.00

JOHNSON, L. *Manual of Medical Botany of N America.* 1884. NY. 9 pls. inscr. 8vo. 292 p. EX. $110.00

JOHNSON, L. *Manual of Medical Botany of N America.* 1884. NY. Wood. 9 pls. tall 8vo. G. $45.00

JOHNSON, L.B. *Vantage Point: Perspectives of Presidency, 1963-1969.* 1971. NY/Chicago. 1st ed. presentation. sgn. M. T5. $250.00

JOHNSON, L.F. *Famous KY Tragedies & Trials.* 1916. Louisville. VG. P3. $45.00

JOHNSON, M. *Over African Jungles.* 1935. Harcourt. 100 photos. 263 p. VG. M2. $18.00

JOHNSON, Malcolm. *Crime on the Labor Front.* 1950. dj. VG. $30.00

JOHNSON, Merle. *American First Editions.* 1932. Bowker. Ltd ed. 1/1000. $90.00

JOHNSON, Merle. *American First Editions: Bibliographic Check Lists.* 1936. NY. Bowker. 3rd ed. 507 p. G. $50.00

JOHNSON, Oliver. *Abolitionists Vindicated in Review of Eli Thayer's Paper...* 1887. Worcester. Rice. 29 p. wraps. VG. $40.00

JOHNSON, Osa. *Four Years in Paradise.* 1941. Garden City. 345 p. G. M2. $6.00

JOHNSON, Osa. *Four Years in Paradise.* 1941. London. 1st ed. sgn. VG. $37.50

JOHNSON, Osa. *I Married Adventure.* 1942. Halcyon House. photos. 376 p. M2. $8.00

JOHNSON, Osa. *Pantaloons. Adventures of Baby Elephant.* 1941. NY. Ils 1st ed. 4to. VG. T1. $40.00

JOHNSON, P.H. *Parker: America's Finest Shotgun.* 1963. Harrisburg. 2nd ed. 260 p. dj. VG. B2. $27.50

JOHNSON, R. *History of French War.* c 1882. NY. 12mo. 374 p. xl. G2. $10.00

JOHNSON, R. Brimley. *Book of British Ballads.* 1925. Everymans ed. dj. VG. C1. $7.50

JOHNSON, R.P. *Jacob Horner of the 7th Cavalry.* 1949. Bismark. Ils. 28 p. wraps. VG. A3. $35.00

JOHNSON, Samuel. *Letters of Samuel Johnson.* 1952. London. Chapman. 1st ed. 3 vols. $85.00

JOHNSON, Samuel. *Lives of Most Eminent English Poets.* 1783. London. 4to. 4 vols. full leather. $335.00

JOHNSON, Samuel. *Oriental Religions.* 1877. Boston. $75.00

JOHNSON, Samuel. *Prayers Composed by Dr. Samuel Johnson.* 1937. Golden Eagle. Ltd ed. 1/418. boxed. VG. J2. $35.00

JOHNSON, Stanley. *Doomsday Deposit.* 1980. Dutton. dj. EX. P1. $7.50

JOHNSON, T.L. *My Story.* 1911. NY. 326 p. G. T5. $22.50

JOHNSON, T.M. *Our Secret War.* c 1929. Bobbs Merrill. 1st ed. VG. $8.00

JOHNSON, T.R. *Amphibians of MO.* 1977. KS U. 67 photos. 42 maps. 142 p. EX. M2. $8.00

JOHNSON, Una E. *Milton Avery: Prints & Drawings 1930-1964.* 1966. Brooklyn Mus. Ils. D2. $42.50

JOHNSON, W.B. *From Pacific to Atlantic: Account of Journey Overland...* 1887. Webster, MA. Ils. 369 p. VG. A3. $90.00

JOHNSON, W.F. *History of Johnstown Flood.* 1889. Ils. 459 p. G. $12.50

JOHNSON, W.F. *Sitting Bull & the Indian Wars.* 1891. Ils. 544 p. K1. $18.50

JOHNSON, W.W. *Forty-Niners.* 1974. Time Life. photos. 4to. 240 p. EX. M2. $10.00

JOHNSON & MENCKEN. *Sunpapers of Baltimore.* 1937. Knopf. 1st ed. VG. J2. $20.00

JOHNSON & SNOOK. *Seashore Animals of the Pacific Coast.* 1935. Macmillan. Ils. 659 p. EX. M2. $23.00

JOHNSON & WARNER. *Johnson & Warner Almanac 1812.* 1812. Phil. Johnson/Warner. G. $15.00

JOHNSON. *About Mexico Past & Present.* 1887. Phil. Ils. maps. VG. $25.00

JOHNSON. *History of Franklin Co.* 1912. Frankford. 286 p. VG. C4. $57.00

JOHNSTON, A.F. *Mary Ware Doll Body* (paper dolls). 1914. Boston. 1st ed. 48 p. VG. B2. $125.00

JOHNSTON, A.F. *Ole Mammy's Torment.* 1897. Boston. Ils Johnson/Sacken. 1st ed. T5. $25.00

JOHNSTON, A.K. *Handy Royal Atlas of Modern Geography.* 1886. Edinburgh. 45 maps. folio. A3. $250.00

JOHNSTON, A.K. *Royal Atlas of Modern Geography.* 1895. Edinburgh. 56 maps. folio. A3. $400.00

JOHNSTON, Henry. *1,000 Islands of St. Lawrence.* 1937. 1st ed. photos. fld map. black silk bdg. EX. $18.00

JOHNSTON, J. *Eagle in Fact & Fiction.* 1966. Quist. Ils. 157 p. dj. EX. M2. $11.00

JOHNSTON, J.E. *Narrative of Military Operations.* 1874. Appleton. Ils. maps. VG. $70.00

JOHNSTON, Louise. *History & Homes of Liberty Hill.* nd. np. photos. sgn. 92 p. $25.00

JOHNSTON, Mary. *Audrey.* 1902. Houghton. Ils Yohn. 1st ed. $12.00

JOHNSTON, Mary. *Cease Firing.* 1912. Ils Wyeth. 1st ed. 457 p. K1. $14.50

JOHNSTON, Mary. *Long Roll.* 1911. Boston. Houghton. 1st ed. xl. $10.00

JOHNSTON, Mary. *Long Roll.* 1911. Ils Wyeth. 682 p. K1. $14.50

JOHNSTON, Mary. *Long Roll.* 1911. Toronto. Ils Wyeth. 683 p. xl. G. $15.00

JOHNSTON, Mary. *Pioneers of the Old S.* 1918. fld map. 260 p. K1. $9.50

JOHNSTON, Mary. *Sweet Rocket.* 1920. Harper. 1st ed. $12.00

JOHNSTON, Reginald. *Twilight in the Forbidden City.* 1934. NY. 1st Am ed. 486 p. dj. B2. $85.00

JOHNSTON, Reginald. *Twilight in the Forbidden City.* 1934. NY. 486 p. B1. $50.00

JOHNSTON, Richard. *Follow Me!* 1948. NY. Ils. 305 p. dj. VG. T5. $85.00

JOHNSTON, S.C. *Ordinances of the Town...* 1904. Columbia. Bryan. 57 p. wraps. $45.00

JOHNSTON, Stanley. *Grim Reapers.* 1943. Phil/NY. Ils 2nd print. 224 p. dj. VG. T5. $9.50

JOHNSTON, T.E. *Fauna of the Rockies.* 1977. Graphic Imp. Ils 1st ed. 101 p. EX. M2. $9.00

JOHNSTON, Velda. *Along a Dark Path.* 1967. Dodd Mead. 1st ed. dj. G. P1. $15.00

JOHNSTON, Velda. *I Came to a Castle.* 1969. Dodd Mead. 1st ed. dj. VG. P1. $10.00

JOHNSTON, Velda. *People on the Hill.* 1971. Dodd Mead. 2nd ed. dj. VG. P1. $7.50

JOHNSTON, Velda. *Room With Dark Mirrors.* nd. Book Club. dj. VG. P1. $3.50

JOHNSTON, Velda. *Voice in the Night.* nd. Book Club. dj. VG. P1. $4.00

JOHNSTON, W.P. *Life of General Albert Sidney Johnston.* 1879. 755 p. scarce. J4. $50.00

JOHNSTON, William. *Bewitched the Opposite Uncle.* 1970. Whitman. G. P1. $7.50

JOHNSTON, William. *Dr. Kildare: The Magic Key.* 1964. Whitman. VG. P1. $7.50

JOHNSTON, William. *Picture Frame Frame-Up.* 1969. Whitman. VG. P1. $7.50

JOHNSTON & OLIN. *Barberton & Kenmore, OH: The Golden Years.* 1976. Barberton. Ils. 128 p. VG. T5. $32.50

JOHNSTON. *Twenty Years of Hus'ling.* 1900. Chicago. fair. $20.00

JOHNSTONE, Christopher. *John Martin.* 1974. London/NY. Academy/St. Martin. 132 p. D2. $25.00

JOIRE, Paul. *Traite d'Hypnotisme: Experimental Psychotherapie.* 1914. Paris. 502 p. maroon cloth. VG. $75.00

JOLINE, A.H. *Book Collector & Other Papers.* 1904. Greenwich. private print. 1/150. $37.00

JOLLIVET, Gaston. *Goupil's Paris Salon 1893.* 1893. Paris/NY. Boussod. Trans Bacon. EX. D2. $350.00

JONES, A. *Wild Voyager: Story of a Canada Goose.* 1966. Little Brown. Ils 1st ed. 174 p. EX. M2. $6.00

JONES, Ben. *Sam Jones: Lawyer.* 1947. Norman. 1st ed. dj. EX. $30.00

JONES, Bobby. *Golf Is My Game.* 1960. NY. 1st ed. dj. B2. $45.00

JONES, Bobby. *How I Play Golf.* 1935. NY. Spalding Lib. 1st ed. wraps. B2. $75.00

JONES, C.A. *Memoirs of a Ozark Hill Boy As Pertaining to Childhood...* nd. private print. EX. M2. $3.00

JONES, C.H. *Africa: History of Exploration & Adventure.* 1875. VG. $75.00

JONES, D.A. *Taking of the Curtain Call: Life of Henry Arthur Jones.* 1930. Macmillan. VG. $20.00

JONES, D.F. *Fall of Colossus.* nd. Book Club. dj. VG. P1. $4.00

JONES, David. *Myth of Arthur.* 1942. London. 1st ed. dj. VG. scarce. C1. $17.50

JONES, Diana Wynne. *Archer's Goon.* 1984. Greenwillow. 1st ed. dj. VG. P1. $10.50

JONES, Diana Wynne. *Spellcoats.* 1979. Atheneum. 1st ed. dj. EX. P1. $25.00

JONES, Diana Wynne. *Witch Week.* 1982. Greenwillow. 1st ed. dj. VG. P1. $15.00

JONES, Electa. *Stockbridge: Past & Present.* 1854. Springfield. 1st ed. $55.00

JONES, Elwyn. *Barlow Comes To Judgement.* nd. Book Club. dj. VG. P1. $3.00

JONES, G. *Corregidora.* 1975. NY. 1st ed. dj. EX. $45.00

JONES, G. & T. *Mabinogion.* 1961. Everymans ed. VG. C1. $7.50

JONES, H.J. *History of Middle Sandy Presbyterian Church...* 1971. Alliance. Ils 200 p. VG. T5. $15.00

JONES, H.L. *Robert Lawson, Illustrator.* 1972. Little Brown. Ils. 121 p. dj. VG. $15.00

JONES, J.B. *Rebel War Clerk's Diary.* 1958. NY. Sagamore. reprint of 1866 ed. dj. VG. $25.00

JONES, J.B. *Wild W Scenes.* 1850. Phil. fair. B1. $25.00

JONES, James. *Friendship: Willie Morris.* 1978. Doubleday. 1st ed. dj. EX. $15.00

JONES, James. *From Here to Eternity.* 1951. NY. 1st ed. inscr/sgn. dj. M. $200.00

JONES, James. *From Here to Eternity.* 1951. Scribner. photo dj. fair. $65.00

JONES, James. *From Here to Eternity.* 1951. Scribner. 1st ed. dj. VG. $120.00

JONES, James. *Go to the Widow Maker.* nd. Delacorte. 1st print. dj. EX. $10.00

JONES, James. *Ice Cream Headache.* nd. Delacorte. 1st print. dj. EX. $22.00

JONES, James. *Ice Cream Headache.* 1968. Collins. 1st print. dj. EX. $20.00

JONES, James. *Into Eternity: Life of James Jones.* 1985. Houghton Mifflin. 1st ed. dj. VG. $14.00

JONES, James. *Merry Month of May.* nd. Delacorte. 1st print. dj. EX. $9.00

JONES, James. *Pistol.* 1958. NY. 1st ed. dj. $35.00

JONES, James. *Some Came Running.* 1957. Scribner. 1st ed. dj. VG. $25.00

JONES, James. *Thin Red Line.* 1962. NY. 1st ed. dj. EX. $45.00

JONES, James. *Thin Red Line.* 1962. NY. 1st ed. dj. G. $27.50

JONES, James. *Touch of Danger.* 1973. Doubleday. 1st ed. dj. M. $20.00

JONES, James. *Viet Journal.* 1974. Delacorte. 1st print. dj. EX. $20.00

JONES, James. *Whistle.* Delacorte. 1st trade ed. dj. $18.00

JONES, James. *Whistle.* 1978. Franklin Lib. 1st ed. full brown leather. EX. $30.00

JONES, James. *WWII: Chronicle of Soldiering.* nd. Grosset Dunlap. 1st print. dj. VG. $25.00

JONES, James. *WWII: Chronicle of Soldiering.* 1975. NY. 1st ed. dj. EX. $35.00

JONES, James. *Yankee Blitzkreig: Wilson's Raid Through AL & GA.* 1976. Athens. 256 p. dj. VG. $20.00

JONES, Jenkin L. *Artilleryman's Diary.* 1914. WI Hist Comm. 1/2500. $30.00

JONES, John. *Americanism: World War History of Troup Co., GA.* 1919. Atlanta. Webb Vary. 168 p. $37.50

JONES, John. *Stories of Great American Scouts.* 1924. Whitman. Ils. $5.00

JONES, John. *Stories of Great Explorers.* 1924. Whitman. Ils. 61 p. $5.00

JONES, K. *Ladies of Richmond.* 1962. Indianapolis. 1st ed. dj. VG. B2. $27.50

JONES, K. *Plantation S.* 1957. Bobbs Merrill. 1st ed. 412 p. VG. $45.00

JONES, L.C. *Copperstown.* 1949. NY. Otsego Co Hist Soc. 8vo. VG. $17.00

JONES, L.F. *Study of Thlingets of AK.* 1914. NY. Ils 1st ed. 261 p. G. T5. $57.50

JONES, L.R. *Dutchman & the Slave.* 1964. Morrow. 1st ed. wraps. EX. $15.00

JONES, L.R. *Moderns.* 1963. NY. dj. EX. $20.00

JONES, L.R. *Motion of History & Other Plays.* 1978. NY. dj. EX. $15.00

JONES, L.R. *Preface to a 20 Volume Suicide Note.* 1961. NY. 1st ed. VG. $20.00

JONES, L.R. *Raise: Essays Since 1965.* 1971. Random House. 1st ed. dj. EX. $20.00

JONES, L.R. *Reggae or Not.* 1981. Contact. 1st ed. sgn. wraps. EX. $25.00

JONES, L.R. *System of Dante's Hell.* 1965. Grove. 1st ed. dj. VG. $30.00

JONES, L.T. *Aboriginal American Oratory: Tradition of Eloquence...* 1965. SW Mus. Ils. 136 p. EX. M2. $17.00

JONES, Langdon. *Eye of the Lens.* 1972. Macmillan. 1st ed. dj. VG. P1. $15.00

JONES, Louise. *Human Side of Bookplates.* 1951. Ward Ritchie. 1st ed. VG. J2. $45.00

JONES, M.B. *VT in the Making: 1750-1777.* 1939. Harvard. 1st ed. xl. G. R1. $30.00

JONES, M.E. *Guide to Horoscope Interpretation.* 1941. Phil. $60.00

JONES, Madison. *Buried Land, a Novel.* 1963. Viking. 1st ed. dj. $35.00

JONES, Madison. *Exile.* 1967. Viking. 2nd print. xl. $4.50

JONES, Madison. *Forest of the Night.* 1960. NY. Harcourt Brace. 1st ed. dj. $35.00

JONES, Madison. *Innocent.* 1957. NY. 1st ed. dj. VG. $45.00

JONES, Madison. *Season of the Strangler.* 1982. Doubleday. 1st ed. 227 p. dj. $45.00

JONES, N. *Seattle.* 1973. Doubleday. photos. 371 p. VG. M2. $5.00

JONES, Nettie. *Fish Tales.* 1983. Random House. 1st ed. dj. M. $10.00

JONES, Owen. *Grammar of Ornament.* 1856. London. folio. disbound. lacks 1 pl. $90.00

JONES, Paul. *Irish Brigade.* 1969. WA. 1st ed. dj. M. $40.00

JONES, Peter. *History of Ojebway Indians...* 1861. London. 12 pls. xl. VG. $275.00

JONES, Raymond F. *Cybernetic Brains.* 1962. Avalon. dj. EX. P1. $15.00

JONES, Raymond F. *Renaissance.* 1951. NY. Gnome. 1st ed. dj. EX. $17.50

JONES, Raymond F. *Stories of Great Physicians.* 1963. Whitman. VG. P1. $7.50

JONES, Raymond F. *This Island Earth.* nd. Book Club. VG. P1. $5.00

JONES, Raymond F. *Voyage to the Bottom of the Sea.* 1965. Whitman. VG. P1. $7.50

JONES, Robert. *Civil War in the NW.* 1960. OK U. 1st ed. dj. $10.00

JONES, S. *English Village Homes & Country Buildings.* 1947. London. 2nd ed. dj. VG. J2. $15.00

JONES, S. *List of French Prose Fiction, 1700-1750.* 1939. NY. G1. $30.00

JONES, Sydney. *Art & Publicity: Fine Printing & Design.* 1925. London. Ils. 4to. VG. $17.00

JONES, T.C. *Ways of Game Fish.* 1972. Ferguson. Standard ed. dj. EX. M2. $60.00

JONES, T.C. *Ways of Game Fish.* 1972. Ferguson. 1/3000. folio. 326 p. slipcase. M2. $120.00

JONES, Terry. *Lee's Tigers: LA Infantry in Army of N VA.* 1987. Baton Rouge. 1st ed. dj. EX. $22.00

JONES, Thelma. *Piety Hill.* 1977. Turtinen. photos. sgn. 136 p. dj. M2. $6.00

JONES, Tristam. *Ice.* 1978. NY. 1st ed. VG. $15.00

JONES, Tristan. *Adrift.* 1980. Macmillan. 1st ed. VG. $15.00

JONES, U.J. *History & Settlement of Juiata Valley...* 1940. Harrisburg. pls. VG. $25.00

JONES, V.C. *Ranger Mosby.* 1944. Chapel Hill. 347 p. dj. VG. $25.00

JONES, W.D. *Principles of Powder Metallurgy.* 1939. London. Ils 2nd ed. 199 p. VG. $15.00

JONES, William. *Finger-Ring Lore: Historical, Legendary & Anecdotal.* 1898. Chatto Windus. Ils New ed. VG. J2. $25.00

JONES & JONES. *Mabinogion.* Ils Alan Lee. VG. C1. $14.50

JONES & REYNOLDS. *Coweta Co. Chronicles for One Hundred Years...* 1928. Atlanta. Ils 1st ed. 869 p. VG. $45.00

JONES & SCHLAEFFER. *SC in Short Story.* 1952. Columbia. 176 p. dj. EX. $45.00

JONES. *Prints of Rockwell Kent: Catalog Raisonne.* 1974. dj. VG. $65.00

JONG, Erica. *Fear of Flying.* 1973. NY. 1st ed. dj. EX. $25.00

JONG, Erica. *Fear of Flying.* 1975. Holt. dj. EX. $15.00

JONG, Erica. *Fruits & Vegetables.* 1971. NY. 1st ed. dj. EX. $20.00

JONG, Erica. *How To Save Your Life.* 1977. Holt. 1st ed. dj. EX. $15.00

JONG, Erica. *Loveroot.* 1975. NY. 1st ed. dj. EX. $15.00

JONG, Erica. *Ordinary Miracles.* 1983. NY. 1st ed. dj. VG. $40.00

JONG, Erica. *Parachutes & Kisses.* 1984. London. 1st ed. dj. M. $15.00

JONG, Erica. *Witches.* 1981. Abrams. VG. M1. $22.50

JONSON, Benjamin. *Volpone; or, The Fox.* 1898. NY. Ils Beardsley. 1/1000. VG. $125.00

JONSON, Benjamin. *Volpone; or, The Fox.* 1953. London. 4to. slipcase. EX. $45.00

JORDAN, David. *Nile Green.* 1973. John Day. 1st ed. dj. VG. P1. $7.50

JORDAN, G.E. *ID Reader.* 1963. Syms York. photos. 406 p. EX. M2. $17.00

JORDAN, J. *Give Me the Wind.* 1971. Prentice Hall. 253 p. dj. VG. M2. $10.00

JORDAN, J.A. *Elephants & Ivory.* 1956. Holt Rinehart. Ils. 250 p. dj. EX. $30.00

JORDAN, Millard L. *Good Years.* nd. Cleveland. Ils. 4to. sgn. 133 p. VG. T5. $8.50

JORDAN, Philip. *Frontier Law & Order: Ten Essays.* 1970. NE U. 1st ed. dj. VG. J2. $20.00

JORDAN, R.P. *Civil War.* 1969. Nat Geog Soc. Ils. maps. 215 p. dj. EX. M2. $10.00

JORDAN, S.R. *Modern Portraiture.* 1983. San Francisco. Camera Craft. 1st ed. 199 p. $25.00

JORDAN & EVERMANN. *American Food & Game Fishes.* 1904. Doubleday. Ils. 572 p. Lib bdg. EX. M2. $35.00

JORDAN & EVERMANN. *American Food & Game Fishes.* 1922. NY. Later ed. 4to. M. $50.00

JORDAN & SEALE. *Fishes of Samoa.* 1905. US Fisheries. 16 pls. 448 p. xl. VG. A3. $150.00

JORDON, June. *Things That I Do in the Dark.* 1977. Random House. dj. EX. $25.00

JORGENSEN, N. *Naturalist's Guide to S New England.* 1978. Sierra Club. Ils. maps. 417 p. EX. M2. $15.00

JORGENSEN, P. *Dressing Flies for Fresh-Water & Salt-Water.* 1973. NY. Ils. tall 8vo. 192 p. dj. EX. $15.00

JORGENSEN & SHARP. *Proceedings of Symposium on Rare & Endangered Mollusks.* 1971. USFWS. Ils. 79 p. M2. $5.00

JOSCELYN, Archie. *Golden Bowl.* 1931. Internat Fiction Lib. VG. P1. $7.50

JOSEPH, Robert. *Berlin at Midnight.* 1951. Harlequin 137. pb. G. P1. $4.50

JOSEPH. *Star Fleet Technical Manual.* 1975. Ballantine. 1st ed. EX. P1. $50.00

JOSEPHSON, E. *Your Life Is Their Toy.* 1940. NY. 1st ed. inscr/sgn. 449 p. VG. $20.00

JOSEPHSON, Matthew. *Edison: A Biography.* 1959. McGraw. 1st ed. dj. VG. J2. $12.50

JOSEPHSON, Matthew. *Union House, Union Bar.* 1956. NY. 1st ed. dj. VG. $18.00

JOSEPHY, A.M. *Indian Heritage of America.* 1969. Knopf. 2nd print. VG. $7.50

JOSEPHY, A.M. *Long & Short & Tall.* 1946. NY. 1st ed. dj. $22.00

JOSEPHY, A.M. *Nez Perce Indians & Opening of the NW.* 1965. 4to. 705 p. dj. EX. $35.00

JOSEPHY, A.M. *Patriot Chiefs.* 1961. NY. 1st ed. dj. EX. $18.00

JOSHI, S.T. *H.P. Lovecraft Annotated Bibliography.* Kent State. no dj issued. P1. $30.00

JOSLIN, E.P. *Homeopathic Epidemic Cholera.* 1854. NY. 3rd ed. VG. $35.00

JOWETT, George. *Drama of the Last Disciples.* 1967. London. 4th ed. dj. M. C1. $12.50

JOY, N.H. *How To Know British Birds.* 1943. London. Ils. 136 p. VG. M2. $7.00

JOY, William. *Aviators.* 1966. London. dj. VG. $20.00

JOYCE, James. *Anna Livia Plurabelle.* 1928. Crosby Gage. 1/800. sgn. 12mo. EX. $1200.00

JOYCE, James. *Anna Livia Plurabelle.* 1928. NY. Ltd ed. 1/800. sgn. VG. $850.00

JOYCE, James. *Anna Livia Plurabelle.* 1930. London. 1st ed. wraps. EX. $60.00

JOYCE, James. *Checkered Life.* 1883. Chicago. 1st ed. fair. $35.00

JOYCE, James. *Collected Poems of James Joyce.* 1936. Black Sun. Ltd 1st ed. 1/800. 12mo. VG. $300.00

JOYCE, James. *Critical Writings of James Joyce.* 1959. London. 1st ed. dj. VG. $30.00

JOYCE, James. *Dubliners.* Ltd Ed Club. slipcase. M. B3. $450.00

JOYCE, James. *Dubliners.* 1969. Modern Lib. dj. VG. P1. $12.50

JOYCE, James. *Exiles.* 1924. NY. Huebsch. 1st Am ed. 2nd issue. VG. $85.00

JOYCE, James. *Finnegan's Wake.* 1939. London. 1st ed. dj. EX. $275.00

JOYCE, James. *Finnegan's Wake.* 1949. London. Faber. reprint. dj. VG. $20.00

JOYCE, James. *Giacomo Joyce.* 1968. London. 1st ed. dj. EX. $45.00

JOYCE, James. *Giacomo Joyce.* 1968. Viking. 1st ed. 8vo. EX. $50.00

JOYCE, James. *Haveth Childers Everywhere.* 1931. London. 1st ed. wraps. VG. $50.00

JOYCE, James. *Jewels of Memory.* 1895. WA. 1st ed. G. $35.00

JOYCE, James. *Letters of James Joyce.* 1966. NY. 1st ed. 3 vols. EX. $35.00

JOYCE, James. *My Impossible Health.* 1977. London. Revised 2nd ed. wraps. $15.00

JOYCE, James. *Portrait of Artist As a Young Man.* 1916. NY. Heubsch. 1st ed. 8vo. blue cloth. VG. $295.00

JOYCE, James. *Portrait of Artist As a Young Man.* 1917. Huebsch. 2nd ed. VG. $75.00

JOYCE, James. *Portrait of Artist As a Young Man.* 1965. Folio Soc. VG. $15.00

JOYCE, James. *Portrait of Artist As a Young Man.* 1977. Garland. facsimile. 4to. 2 vols. EX. $85.00

JOYCE, James. *Stephen Hero.* 1944. New Directions. 1st ed. 234 p. VG. $25.00

JOYCE, James. *Two Tales of Shem & Shaun: Fragments From Work in Progress.* 1932. London. 1st ed. dj. EX. $75.00

JOYCE, James. *Two Tales of Shem & Shaun: Fragments From Work in Progress.* 1932. London. Faber. 1st ed. 8vo. VG. $60.00

JOYCE, James. *Ulysses.* 1924. Paris. Shakespeare. 4th print. $110.00

JOYCE, James. *Ulysses.* 1926. Paris. Shakespeare. 8th print. wraps. T6. $65.00

JOYCE, James. *Ulysses.* 1932. Hamsburg. Odyssey Pr. 1st ed. 1st print. $285.00

JOYCE, James. *Ulysses.* 1934. NY. 1st Authorized Am ed. dj. $110.00

JOYCE, James. *Ulysses.* 1934. Random House. 1st ed. 2nd print. VG. $50.00

JOYCE, James. *Ulysses.* 1936. London. John Lane. 1st ed. 1/100. EX. $400.00

JOYCE, Stanislaus. *My Brother's Keeper.* 1958. Viking. 1st ed. dj. EX. $37.00

JUBINAL, A. *Les Anciennes Tapisseries Historiees.* 1838. 1/330. 124 pls. xl. VG. $350.00

JUDD, Frances K. *Message in the Sand Dunes.* nd. Cupples Leon. G. P1. $7.50

JUDD, Harrison. *Shadow of a Doubt.* 1961. Gold Medal. pb. VG. P1. $6.00

JUDD, N.M. *Men Met Along the Trail.* 1968. OK U. Ils 1st ed. dj. EX. M2. $15.00

JUDSON, A.M. *History of 83rd Regiment, PA Volunteers.* 1865. Erie. 1st ed. VG. T5. $195.00

JUDSON, K.B. *Early Days of Old OR.* 1936. Metropolitan. Ils. maps. 275 p. dj. EX. M2. $28.00

JUDSON, K.B. *Myths & Legends of Great Plains.* 1913. McClurg. 1st ed. dj. VG. $40.00

JUDY, Will. *Dog Encyclopedia.* 1936. Chicago. Ils. VG. $20.00

JULIEN & MILLING. *Beneath So Kind a Sky.* 1948. Cola, SC. Ils. photos. dj. EX. $65.00

JULIEN & WATSON. *Ninety Six.* 1950. Columbia. 4to. dj. EX. $35.00

JUNG, C.G. *Man & His Symbols.* 1964. Doubleday. dj. EX. $15.00

JUNG, Leo. *Living Judaism.* 1927. NY. Night Day Pr. sgn. 360 p. EX. $55.00

JUNGGEFELLEN. *Wilhelm Bufch.* 1908. Munchen. Ils. G. $30.00

JUSDON, Clara. *Jerry & Jean Detectors.* 1923. Chicago. Ils. VG. $12.50

JUST, W.S. *To What End: Report of Vietnam.* 1968. Boston. 1st ed. 208 p. dj. T5. $17.50

K

KABOTIE, F. *Designs From Ancient Mimbrenos With Hopi Interpretation.* 1982. Northland. 1/100. sgn. folio. slipcase. M. M2. $90.00

KAFKA, Franz. *Amerika.* nd. Norfolk. 1st Am ed. dj. VG. $85.00

KAFKA, Franz. *Frank Kafka Miscellany Pre-Fascist Exile.* 1940. NY. 1st ed. dj. EX. $50.00

KAFKA, Franz. *Penal Colony.* 1948. Schocken. 1st ed. EX. $12.50

KAFKA, Franz. *Trial.* 1973. Knopf. 1st ed. dj. VG. $25.00

KAFKA, Franz. *Trial.* 1975. Ltd Ed Club. 1/2000. slipcase. EX. $50.00

KAGAN, S.R. *Modern Medical World's Portraits & Biographical Sketches...* 1945. Boston. 100 portraits. red cloth. EX. $95.00

KAHN, David. *Codebreakers.* 1967. London. 1st ed. dj. $25.00

KAHN, David. *Codebreakers.* 1967. NY. Ils 1st ed. dj. B2. $40.00

KAHN, David. *Codebreakers.* 1968. NY. 4th ed. dj. VG. B2. $22.50

KAHN, James. *Timefall.* 1987. St. Martin. 1st ed. dj. EX. P1. $16.95

KAHN, Joan. *Some Things Strange & Sinister.* Ellery Queen Mystery. VG. P1. $4.00

KAISER, Konrad. *Adolph Menzels Eisenwalzwerk.* 1953. Berlin. Ils. 132 p. D2. $65.00

KAKONIS, Tom. *MI Roll.* 1988. St. Martin. 1st ed. dj. M. $15.00

KALISHER, Simpson. *Railroad Men.* 1961. 84 p. $18.50

KALLEN, Lucille. *G.B. Greenfield: A Little Madness.* 1986. Random House. 1st ed. dj. EX. P1. $14.95

KALLEN, Lucille. *No Lady in the House.* nd. Book Club. dj. VG. P1. $3.50

KALLET, Arthur. *Counterfeit: Not Your Money But What It Buys.* 1935. NY. photos. dj. EX. $40.00

KALLIR, Otto. *Grandma Moses.* 1973. NY. Abrams. 1st ed. folio. dj. EX. $60.00

KALLIR, Otto. *Grandma Moses.* 1975. NY. Abrams. New Concise ed. dj. VG. $10.00

KALM, P. *Travels Into N America.* 1972. Imprint Soc. Ltd 1st ed. 1/1950. dj. EX. M2. $90.00

KALMBACH, A.C. *Railroad Panorama.* 1944. Kalmbach. Ils. 8vo. 228 p. $15.00

KALTENBORN. *I Broadcast the Crisis.* 1938. Random House. sgn. VG. $20.00

KAMARCK, Lawrence. *Dinosaur.* 1968. Random House. 2nd ed. dj. EX. P1. $7.50

KAMINSKY, S.M. *Bullet for a Star.* nd. Book Club. dj. EX. P1. $4.00

KAMINSKY, S.M. *Bullet for a Star.* 1981. London. 1st ed. dj. EX. $20.00

KAMINSKY, S.M. *Fine Red Rain.* 1987. Scribner. UCP. wraps. EX. $15.00

KAMINSKY, S.M. *Howard Hughes Affair.* nd. Book Club. dj. VG. P1. $4.50

KAMINSKY, S.M. *Never Cross a Vampire.* 1980. St. Martin. 1st ed. dj. VG. $25.00

KAMINSKY, S.M. *Smart Moves.* 1986. St. Martin. 1st ed. dj. M. $15.00

KANDAL, E.R. *Behavioral Biology of Aplysia.* 1979. Freeman. Ils. 463 p. EX. M2. $16.00

KANDER, S. *Settlement Cookbook.* 1943. Settlement Book. G. $15.00

KANDINSKY, Wassily. *Concerning the Spiritual in Art & Painting in Particular.* 1947. NY. Wittenborn Schultz. Ils. D2. $47.50

KANDINSKY, Wassily. *Concerning the Spiritual in Art & Painting in Particular.* 1964. reprint of 1947 ed. D2. $24.00

KANDINSKY, Wassily. *Kandinsky & Muchen: Begegnungen und Eandlungen, 1896-1914.* 1982. Munich. Prestel. Ils. D2. $50.00

KANDINSKY, Wassily. *Regards sur le Passe et Autres Textes: 1912-1922.* 1974. Paris. Hermann. Ils. D2. $40.00

KANDINSKY & MARC. *Blaue Reiter Almanac.* 1974. NY. Viking. 1st ed. 296 p. D2. $25.00

KANE, E.K. *Arctic Explorations.* 1857. Phil. 2 vols. VG. $85.00

KANE, E.K. *Arctic Explorations.* 1856. Phil. Childs Peterson. G. $85.00

KANE, E.K. *Arctic Explorations.* 1856. Phil. Childs Peterson. 2 vols. VG. $150.00

KANE, Frank. *Grave Danger.* 1954. Washburn. dj. VG. P1. $8.00

KANE, H.B. *Thoreau's Walden: Photographic Register.* 1946. NY. 1st ed. 169 p. dj. VG. T5. $27.50

KANE, H.T. *Bride of Fortune.* 1948. 301 p. dj. G. $7.50

KANE, H.T. *Gallant Mrs. Stonewall.* 1957. inscr/sgn. 320 p. dj. EX. J4. $20.00

KANE, H.T. *Gentlemen, Swords & Pistols.* 1951. Bonanza. reprint. 306 p. dj. EX. M2. $10.00

KANE, H.T. *Golden Coast.* 1959. NY. Ils 1st ed. 212 p. $6.00

KANE, H.T. *Gone Are the Days: Illustrated History of Old S.* 1960. Bramhall. reprint. 4to. 344 p. dj. M2. $10.00

KANE, H.T. *Natchez.* 1958. Morrow. dj. sgn. $7.50

KANE, H.T. *New Orleans Woman.* 1947. Doubleday. $5.50

KANE, H.T. *Plantation Parade.* 1946. NY. Morrow. Ils 3rd print. presentation. sgn. $30.00

KANE, H.T. *Spies for the Blue & Gray.* 1954. 311 p. dj. J4. $10.00

KANE, H.T. *Spies for the Blue & Gray.* 1954. Hanover House. 1st ed. sgn. 311 p. dj. M2. $20.00

KANE, Henry. *Conceal & Disguise.* 1966. Macmillan. 1st ed. dj. VG. P1. $12.50

KANE, Henry. *Hang by Your Neck.* nd. Book Club. dj. VG. P1. $3.50

KANE, Henry. *Hang by Your Neck.* 1949. Simon Schuster. 1st ed. dj. VG. P1. $12.50

KANE, Henry. *Narrowing Lust.* 1956. Boardman. 1st ed. VG. P1. $17.50

KANE, Henry. *Report for a Corpse.* 1948. Simon Schuster. 1st ed. dj. VG. P1. $8.00

KANE, Mary. *Bibliography of Works of Fiske Kimball.* 1959. Charlottesville. 12mo. dj. $20.00

KANE, Ruth. *Trolley Car Days.* 1984. np. 1st ed. photos. 214 p. T5. $19.50

KANE & JAKES. *Excalibur!* March, 1980. Dell. 1st ed. pb. VG. C1. $3.50

KANER, H. *Sun Queen.* 1946. Kaner. dj. VG. P1. $20.00

KANIN, Garson. *Hollywood.* 1974. Viking. ARC. inscr. with sgn letter. EX. $22.00

KANIUT, L. *AK Bear Tales.* 1985. AK NW. 318 p. EX. M2. $10.00

KANTNER, Rob. *Harder They Hit.* 1987. Bantam. UCP. wraps. M. $15.00

KANTOR, Alfred. *Book of Alfred Kantor.* 1971. NY. 1st ed. dj. EX. $25.00

KANTOR, MacKinlay. *Andersonville.* 1955. NY. World. 767 p. $10.00

KANTOR, MacKinlay. *Daughter of Bugle Ann.* 1953. Random House. 1st ed. 122 p. dj. EX. $12.00

KANTOR, MacKinlay. *Hamilton County.* 1970. NY. 1st ed. dj. VG. $20.00

KANTOR, MacKinlay. *Noise of Their Wings.* 1938. NY. Ils. VG. $7.50

KANTOR, MacKinlay. *Spirit Lake.* 1961. World. 1st ed. dj. VG. $17.50

KANTOR, MacKinlay. *Turkey in the Straw.* 1935. NY. Ils. VG. $7.50

KANTOR, MacKinley. *Romance of Rosy Ridge.* 1937. Coward McCann. Ils Crawford. 96 p. dj. VG. $6.50

KANTOR, MacKinley. *Sleepwalkers.* 1959. NY. 1st ed. dj. VG. $22.50

KANTOR, MacKinley. *Work of Saint Francis.* 1958. NY. 1st ed. inscr. dj. VG. $25.00

KANY, C.E. *Life & Manners in Madrid, 1750-1800.* 1932. Berkeley. Ils 1st ed. pls. $40.00

KAPLAN, BERGER & GROSS. *Rosso Case.* 1934. Central Book. 346 p. G. $7.50

KAPLAN, Justin. *Walt Whitman: A Life.* 1980. dj. EX. $17.50

KAPLAN, Stuart. *Tarot Classic.* 1972. NY. $30.00

KAPP, Colin. *Survival Game.* 1978. British SF Book Club. dj. VG. P1. $5.00

KAPP, Y. *Eleanor Marx.* 1972 & 1976. Pantheon. 1st Am ed. 2 vols. VG. $18.50

KAPPELL, Philip. *Jamaica Gallery.* 1961. London. Macmillan. Ils. 4to. dj. EX. $30.00

KAR, Chintamoni. *Classical Indian Sculpture 300 BC to AD 500.* 1950. London. Alec Tiranti Ltd. G. $20.00

KARFELD, E. *My Leica & I.* 1937. Berlin. VG. $20.00

KARIG, Walter. *Zotz!* 1947. Rinehart. dj. VG. P1. $5.00

KARIMS, Hadschic. *Traumbuch.* nd. Germany. 317 p. VG. $10.00

KARKLIS, Maruta. *Latvians in America, 1640-1973.* 1974. Dobbs Ferry. 151 p. xl. G. T5. $65.00

KARLIN, Nurit. *No Comment.* 1978. NY. 4to. dj. $17.00

KARLINS & ANDREWS. *Gomorrah.* 1974. Doubleday. 1st ed. VG. P1. $10.00

KARLOFF, Boris. *And the Darkness Falls.* 1946. World. G. P1. $17.50

KARLOFF, Boris. *Tales of Terror.* 1943. Tower. 2nd ed. VG. P1. $15.00

KARNES, T.L. *William Gilpin: W Nationalist.* 1970. TX U. Ils. map. 383 p. EX. M2. $18.00

KARNGA, Abayomi. *History of Liberia.* 1926. Liverpool. $25.00

KARR, Phyllis. *Idylls of the Queen.* 1985. pb. VG. C1. $3.50

KARR, Phyllis. *King Arthur Companion.* c 1986. 2nd ed. M. C1. $18.00

KARRAS, A.L. *N to Cree Lake.* 1970. NY. Ils Trident. 256 p. dj. G. $12.00

KARSH, Yousuf. *Faces of Our Time.* 1971. 1st ed. EX. S2. $60.00

KARSH, Yousuf. *Fifty Year Retrospective.* 1983. Little Brown. 1st ed. dj. EX. $25.00

KARSH, Yousuf. *In Search of Greatness.* 1962. Knopf. 1st ed. 8vo. black bdg. dj. EX. $20.00

KARSH & FISHER. *Karsh & Fisher See Canada.* 1960. Toronto. Allen. 1st ed. dj. VG. J2. $25.00

KARSHAN, Donald H. *Archipenko: Content & Continuity, 1908-1963.* 1968. Chicago. Kovler Gallery. Ils. 64 p. D2. $25.00

KARSKI, Jan. *Story of a Secret State.* 1944. Boston. Houghton. dj. G. M1. $6.50

KASSLER, Elizabeth. *Modern Gardens & the Landscape.* 1964. MOMA. SftCvr. VG. $15.00

KASTLE, Herbert. *Edward Berner Is Alive Again!* 1975. Prentice Hall. 1st ed. dj. EX. P1. $12.50

KASTNER, J. *Species of Eternity.* 1977. Knopf. Ils 1st ed. 350 p. dj. EX. M2. $20.00

KASTON, B.J. *Spiders of CT.* 1948. CT Nat Hist Survey. 874 p. M2. $65.00

KATACHI. *Japanese Pattern & Design in Wood, Paper & Clay.* 1963. Abrams. 1st ed. folio. 170 p. dj. VG. $90.00

KATAEV, Valentine. *Embezzlers.* 1929. Dial. 1st Am ed. $12.00

KATCHER. *Encyclopedia of British, Provincial & German Army Units...* 1973. Stackpole. dj. EX. $35.00

KATES, G.W. *Philosophy of Spirtualism.* 1916. Boston. 235 p. EX. $22.00

KATES, H.S. *Minute Glimpses of American Cities.* 1933. NY. Ltd ed. sgn. VG. $20.00

KATES. *Luggage & Leather Goods Manual.* 1948. EX. $35.00

KATSH, A.I. *Scroll of Agony: Warsaw Diary of Chaim Kaplan.* 1973. NY. 1st pb ed. VG. $2.50

KATZ, Welwyn. *Third Magic.* 1988. Vancouver/Toronto. dj. M. C1. $17.00

KATZ, William L. *Black W.* 1971. Doubleday. Ils 1st ed. dj. EX. $30.00

KATZENBACH, John. *In the Heat of the Summer.* nd. Book Club. dj. VG. P1. $4.00

KATZENBACH, John. *In the Heat of the Summer.* 1982. NY. 1st ed. inscr/sgn. dj. EX. $40.00

KATZENBACH, John. *In the Heat of the Summer.* 1982. NY. Atheneum. 1st ed. dj. VG. $25.00

KATZENBACH, John. *Traveler.* 1987. NY. 1st ed. sgn. dj. EX. $20.00

KAUFFELD, C. *Snakes & Snake Hunting.* 1957. Hanover House. Ils. 266 p. EX. M2. $35.00

KAUFFMAN, H.J. *PA Dutch American Folk Art.* 1946. NY. 1st ed. dj. VG. B2. $17.50

KAUFFMAN & FABRY COMPANY. *Official Pictures of a Century of Progress Exposition.* 1933. Chicago. photos. 4to. T5. $17.50

KAUFFMAN & FABRY COMPANY. *Souvenir Views of Chicago World's Fair.* 1934. Chicago. photos. wraps. T5. $12.50

KAUFMAN, Pamela. *Banners of Gold.* 1986. 1st ed. dj. M. C1. $12.00

KAUFMAN, Pamela. *Shield of Three Lions.* 1983. Crown. ARC. wraps. VG. $10.00

KAUFMAN, Wolfe. *I Hate Blondes.* 1946. Simon Schuster. 1st ed. dj. VG. P1. $10.00

KAUFMAN. *Moe Berg.* 1974. Little Brown. dj. EX. $42.00

KAUT, Herbert. *Alt-Wiener Spielzeu gschachtel.* 1961. Vienna. Hans Deutsch. Ils. dj. D2. $35.00

KAUTZ, A.V. *Company Clerk: Showing How & When To Make Out...Papers...* 1864. 142 p. gilt bdg. EX. J4. $50.00

KAVANAUGH, James. *There Are Men Too Gentle To Live Among Wolves.* 1970. Ils 1st ed. dj. VG. $15.00

KAVANAUGH, James. *Winter Has Lasted Too Long.* 1977. NY. 1st ed. dj. M. $12.00

KAVANAUGH, M. *Complete Guide to Monkeys, Apes & Other Primates.* 1984. Viking. Ils. maps. 224 p. dj. EX. M2. $19.00

KAWAI, Michi. *My Lantern.* 1939. Tokyo. boxed. VG. $23.00

KAWAI, Michi. *Sliding Doors.* 1950. Tokyo. sgn Eng/Japanese. boxed. VG. $30.00

KAWIN, B.F. *Faulkner & Film.* 1977. NY. Ungar. 1st ed. 194 p. dj. $15.00

KAY, Guy G. *Darkest Road.* 1st Am ed. M. scarce. C1. $18.00

KAY, Guy G. *Summer Tree.* Book Club. dj. EX. C1. $4.50

KAY, Guy G. *Summer Tree.* nd. London. 1st ed. sgn. EX. $35.00

KAY, Guy G. *Summer Tree.* 1985. Arbor House. 1st ed. dj. EX. P1. $15.95

KAY, Guy G. *Wandering Fire.* 1st Am ed. dj. M. C1. $9.50

KAY, Helen. *Picasso's World of Children.* 1965?. NY. Chanticleer. Ils. dj. G. $40.00

KAY & GODWIN. *Masters of Solitude.* 1978. Doubleday. 1st ed. dj. VG. P1. $12.50

KAYE, Barbara. *Company We Kept.* 1986. Blakeney. Ils 1st ed. sgn. EX. $30.00

KAYE, Marvin. *Devils & Demons.* 1987. Doubleday. dj. EX. P1. $15.95

KAYE, Marvin. *Masterpieces of Terror & Supernatural.* 1985. Doubleday. 2nd ed. dj. VG. P1. $15.95

KAYE, Marvin. *Possession of Immanuel Wolf.* 1981. Doubleday. 1st ed. dj. VG. P1. $12.50

KAYE & GODWIN. *Wintermind.* 1982. Doubleday. 1st ed. dj. EX. P1. $15.00

KAYE-SMITH, Sheila. *Ember Lane.* 1940. London. Cassell. 1st ed. G. $15.00

KAYE-SMITH, Sheila. *Superstition Corner.* 1934. Harper. 1st ed. VG. $10.00

KAYS, C.E. *Red Jungle Fowl Introductions in KY.* 1971. KY Fish/Game. 16 p. M2. $3.00

KAZAN, Elia. *Understudy.* 1975. NY. 1st ed. dj. VG. $5.00

KAZANTZAKIS, Nikos. *Freedom or Death.* 1956. London. 1st ed. dj. EX. $35.00

KAZANTZAKIS, Nikos. *Zorba the Greek.* 1953. NY. 1st ed. dj. VG. $65.00

KAZIN, Alfred. *Open Street.* 1948. NY. 1st ed. 1/1000. VG. $25.00

KAZIN, Alfred. *Walk in the City.* 1951. NY. 1st ed. dj. EX. $20.00

KEARTON, C. *In the Land of the Lion.* 1929. McBride. 298 p. VG. M2. $17.00

KEARTON, C. *Island of Penguins.* 1930. Longman. Ils. 223 p. G. M2. $12.00

KEARTON, R. *Wildlife at Home & How To Study & Photograph It.* 1899. London. Cassell. 193 p. $35.00

KEATING, B. *AK.* 1969. Nat Geog Soc. Ils. fld map. 207 p. dj. EX. M2. $10.00

KEATING, B. *Gulf of Mexico.* 1972. Viking. Review of 1st ed. 110 p. dj. M2. $14.00

KEATING, B. *Mighty MS.* 1971. Nat Geog Soc. dj. VG. $10.00

KEATING, B. *Mighty MS.* 1971. WA, D.C. photos. dj. EX. $15.00

KEATING, H.R.F. *Filmi Filmi Inspector Ghote.* 1977. Crime Club. 1st ed. dj. xl. P1. $5.00

KEATING, H.R.F. *Inspector Ghote Hunts the Peacock.* 1968. Dutton. 1st ed. dj. EX. P1. $15.00

KEATING, H.R.F. *Inspector Ghote Trusts Heart.* 1973. Crime Club. 1st ed. dj. xl. P1. $5.00

KEATING, H.R.F. *Is Skin-Deep Is Fatal.* nd. Collins Crime Club. dj. xl. P1. $5.00

KEATING, H.R.F. *Sherlock Holmes: Man & His World.* 1979. NY. Ils. 160 p. dj. M. $25.00

KEATING, H.R.F. *Whodunit? Guide to Crime, Suspense & Spy Fiction.* 1982. London. 1st ed. dj. EX. $25.00

KEATING, H.R.F. *Whodunit? Guide to Crime, Suspense & Spy Fiction.* 1982. NY. 1st ed. dj. VG. $20.00

KEATING, H.R.F. *Zen There Was Murder.* 1960. Gollancz. 1st ed. dj. xl. P1. $7.50

KEATING, Rex. *Nubian Twilight.* 1963. NY. 1st Am ed. 111 p. dj. VG. T5. $35.00

KEATON, Buster. *Wonderful World of Slapstick.* 1960. NY. 1st ed. dj. VG. $25.00

KEATS, John. *Letters of John Keats to Fanny Brawne.* 1878. NY. 128 p. EX. $95.00

KEATS, John. *Poems of John Keats.* 1966. Norwalk. Heritage. sm quarto. slipcase. $15.00

KEATS, John. *Unpublished Poem to His Sister Fanny.* 1909. Boston. Biblio Soc. 1/489. EX. $75.00

KEATS & SHELLEY. *Complete Poems.* nd. Modern Lib Giant. dj. EX. $8.00

KEBABIAN, P.B. *American Woodworking Tools.* 1978. NY Graphic Soc. 1st ed. 4to. dj. $35.00

KEBLE, Joseph. *Reports in Court of Kings Bench at Westminster.* 1685. London. sm folio. $60.00

KECKLEY, Elizabeth. *Behind Scenes: 30 Years a Slave & 4 Years in White House.* 1985. reprint of 1868 ed. M. J4. $18.50

KEEGAN, John. *Face of Battle.* 1976. NY. dj. VG. $15.00

KEEL, John A. *Jadoo.* 1957. Messner. 1st ed. dj. VG. P1. $15.00

KEELER, L.E. *Guide to Local History of Fremont, OH, Prior ot 1860.* 1905. Columbus. 28 p. wraps. T5. $8.50

KEELY, J. *Left-Leaning Antenna.* 1971. New Rochelle. 1st ed. 320 p. dj. VG. $22.50

KEELY & DAVIS. *In Arctic Seas: Voyage of the Kite With Peary Expedition.* 1893. Phil. Hartrand. Ils. maps. G. $30.00

KEEN, A.M. *Marine Molluscan Genera in W N America.* 1963. Stanford. 126 p. dj. EX. M2. $27.00

KEEN, A.M. *Seashells of Tropical W America: Marine Mollusks.* 1958. Stanford. Ils. 624 p. dj. EX. M2. $60.00

KEEN, W.W. *I Believe in God & Evolution.* 1923. Phil. VG. $10.00

KEENE, Carolyn. *Bungalow Mystery.* nd. Grosset Dunlap. VG. P1. $4.00

KEENE, Carolyn. *By the Light of Study Lamp.* 1934. Grosset Dunlap. violet bdg. VG. P1. $12.50

KEENE, Carolyn. *Clue in the Crossword Cipher.* nd. Grosset Dunlap. VG. P1. $4.00

KEENE, Carolyn. *Clue in the Crumbling Wall.* nd. Grosset Dunlap. EX. P1. $4.00

KEENE, Carolyn. *Clue in the Jewel Box.* nd. Grosset Dunlap. VG. P1. $4.00

KEENE, Carolyn. *Clue of the Dancing Puppet.* nd. Grosset Dunlap. EX. P1. $4.00

KEENE, Carolyn. *Clue of the Leaning Chimney.* nd. Grosset Dunlap. dj. EX. P1. $4.00

KEENE, Carolyn. *Clue of the Tapping Heels.* nd. Grosset Dunlap. VG. P1. $4.00

KEENE, Carolyn. *Clue of the Velvet Mask.* nd. Grosset Dunlap. EX. P1. $4.00

KEENE, Carolyn. *Ghost of Blackwood Hall.* nd. Grosset Dunlap. EX. P1. $4.00

KEENE, Carolyn. *Haunted Bridge.* nd. Grosset Dunlap. dj. VG. P1. $5.00

KEENE, Carolyn. *Haunted Lagoon.* nd. Grosset Dunlap. VG. P1. $6.00

KEENE, Carolyn. *Haunted Showboat.* nd. Grosset Dunlap. EX. P1. $4.00

KEENE, Carolyn. *Hidden Window Mystery.* 1956. Grosset Dunlap. VG. P1. $5.00

KEENE, Carolyn. *Invisible Intruder.* nd. Grosset Dunlap. VG. P1. $4.00

KEENE, Carolyn. *Moonstone Castle Mystery.* nd. Grosset Dunlap. EX. P1. $4.00

KEENE, Carolyn. *Mysterious Mannequin.* nd. Grosset Dunlap. EX. P1. $4.00

KEENE, Carolyn. *Mystery at Lilac Inn.* nd. Grosset Dunlap. VG. P1. $4.00

KEENE, Carolyn. *Mystery at the Ski Jump.* nd. Grosset Dunlap. EX. P1. $4.00

KEENE, Carolyn. *Mystery of the Fire Dragon.* nd. Grosset Dunlap. EX. P1. $4.00

KEENE, Carolyn. *Mystery of the Glowing Eye.* nd. Grosset Dunlap. VG. P1. $4.00

KEENE, Carolyn. *Mystery of the Moss-Covered Mansion.* nd. Grosset Dunlap. VG. P1. $4.00

KEENE, Carolyn. *Mystery of the Tolling Bell.* nd. Grosset Dunlap. VG. P1. $4.00

KEENE, Carolyn. *Mystery of 99 Steps.* nd. Grosset Dunlap. EX. P1. $4.00

KEENE, Carolyn. *Nancy's Mysterious Letter.* nd. Grosset Dunlap. VG. P1. $4.00

KEENE, Carolyn. *Password to Larkspur Lane.* nd. Grosset Dunlap. VG. P1. $4.00

KEENE, Carolyn. *Quest of the Missing Map.* nd. Grosset Dunlap. VG. P1. $4.00

KEENE, Carolyn. *Ringmaster's Secret.* nd. Grosset Dunlap. VG. P1. $4.00

KEENE, Carolyn. *Scarlet Slipper Mystery.* nd. Grosset Dunlap. VG. P1. $4.00

KEENE, Carolyn. *Secret at Lone Tree Cottage.* Grosset Dunlap. violet bdg. VG. P1. $12.50

KEENE, Carolyn. *Secret in the Old Attic.* nd. Grosset Dunlap. VG. P1. $4.00

KEENE, Carolyn. *Secret of Mirror Bay.* nd. Grosset Dunlap. VG. P1. $4.00

KEENE, Carolyn. *Secret of the Golden Pavilion.* nd. Grosset Dunlap. VG. P1. $4.00

KEENE, Carolyn. *Secret of the Old Clock.* nd. Grosset Dunlap. P1. $4.00

KEENE, Carolyn. *Secret of the Wooden Lady.* nd. Grosset Dunlap. EX. P1. $4.00

KEENE, Carolyn. *Sky Phantom.* nd. Grosset Dunlap. VG. P1. $4.00

KEENE, Carolyn. *Spider Sapphire Mystery.* nd. Grosset Dunlap. VG. P1. $4.00

KEES, Weldon. *Ceremony & Other Stories.* 1983. Abbatoir. Ltd ed. 1/295. $45.00

KEESY, W.A. *War, As Viewed From the Ranks.* 1898. Norwalk. Ils 1st ed. 240 p. fair. T5. $125.00

KEIGHTLEY, Thomas. *World Guide to Gnomes, Fairies & Elves.* 1978. Avenel. 560 p. dj. M. C1. $9.50

KEILEY, A.M. *In Vinculis; or, Prisoner of War.* 1866. Petersburg. 2nd ed. $45.00

KEILLOR, Garrison. *Happy To Be Here.* 1982. Atheneum. 1st ed. VG. $35.00

KEILLOR, Garrison. *Lake Wobegon Days.* 1985. Viking. 1st ed. dj. EX. $25.00

KEILLOR, Garrison. *Leaving Home.* 1987. NY. 1st ed. 1/1500. sgn. boxed. M. $75.00

KEILLOR, Garrison. *Leaving Home.* 1988. London. AP. EX. $75.00

KEILLOR, Garrison. *We Are Still Married.* nd. Franklin Lib. 1st ed. sgn. AEG. $45.00

KEIM, D.B.R. *Sheridan's Troopers on the Border.* 1870. Phil. Claxton. Ils. 308 p. VG. A3. $90.00

KEIM, D.B.R. *Sheridan's Troopers on the Border.* 1973. Corner House. reprint of 1889 ed. dj. EX. M2. $17.00

KEINZEL, William X. *Shadow of Death.* 1983. Andrews McMeel. 1st ed. dj. VG. P1. $15.00

KEITH, Brandon. *Affair of the Gentle Saboteur.* 1966. Whitman. VG. P1. $12.50

KEITH, Brandon. *Affair of the Gunrunners' Gold.* 1967. Whitman. G. P1. $7.50

KEITH, Brandon. *Case of the Disappearing Doctor.* 1966. Whitman. VG. P1. $10.00

KEITH, Brandon. *Message From Moscow.* 1966. Whitman. VG. P1. $7.50

KEITH, C.H. *Flying Years.* c 1937. London. Aviation Book Club. 315 p. VG. T5. $27.50

KEITH, Carlton. *Taste of Sangria.* 1968. Crime Club. 1st ed. VG. P1. $10.00

KEITH, E.C. *Countryman's Creed.* 1938. London. Country Life. 1st ed. dj. VG. B2. $30.00

KEITH, Elmer. *Big Game Rifles & Cartridges.* 1936. Sm Arms Tech. dj. $90.00

KEITH, Elmer. *Big Game Rifles & Cartridges.* 1936. Onslow Co., SC. 1st ed. VG. B2. $70.00

KEITH, Elmer. *Guns & Ammo for Big Game Hunting.* c 1965. Peterson. reprint. dj. G. $25.00

KEITH, Elmer. *Rifles for Big Game.* 1946. Huntington. 1st ed. VG. B2. $100.00

KEITH, Elmer. *Safari.* 1960. La Jolla. 1st ed. presentation. sgn. dj. EX. $150.00

KEITH, Elmer. *Shotguns.* 1950. Harrisburg. 1st ed. dj. VG. B2. $60.00

KEITH, Elmer. *Six-Guns.* 1961. Harrisburg. 2nd ed. VG. $50.00

KEITH, Lord. *Keith Papers.* 1950 & 1955. Navy Records Soc. 2 vols. J2. $20.00

KEITH, Thomas. *New Treatise on Use of Globes...* 1826. NY. 4th Am ed. 6 pls. 334 p. xl. T5. $65.00

KELEHER, William. *Turmoil in NM, 1846-1868.* 1952. Rydal Pr. 1st ed. sgn. VG. J2. $40.00

KELEMEN, P. *Medieval American Art.* 1943. NY. 4to. 2 vols. $35.00

KELEMEN, P. *Medieval American Art.* 1944. NY. 2nd ed. 4to. 2 vols. VG. $20.00

KELEMEN, P. *Medieval American Art.* 1956. Macmillan. 1 vol ed. 414 p. EX. M2. $45.00

KELLAND, C.B. *AZ.* 1948. Bantam 257. pb. EX. P1. $15.00

KELLAND, C.B. *Murder Makes an Entrance.* nd. NY. Abridged ed. 126 p. wraps. fair. $3.00

KELLER, Allan. *Morgan's Raid.* 1961. Indianapolis. Ils 1st ed. 272 p. dj. T5. $27.50

KELLER, C.E. *Check List & Finding Guide to IN Birds & Their Haunts.* 1986. IN U. map. 206 p. EX. M2. $10.00

KELLER, D.H. *Folson Flint.* 1969. Arkham House. 1st ed. dj. EX. P1. $25.00

KELLER, D.H. *Homunculus.* 1949. Phil. 1st trade ed. dj. VG. $30.00

KELLER, D.H. *Solitary Hunters & the Abyss.* 1948. New Era. 1st ed. dj. VG. P1. $35.00

KELLER, Ella Flatt. *Call of the Open Road.* 1930. Hudson, MI. inscr/sgn. VG. $10.00

KELLER, Frances Richardson. *American Crusade: Life of Charles Waddell Chesnutt.* 1978. Provo, UT. Ils. 304 p. VG. T5. $12.50

KELLER, Helen. *Song of the Stone Wall.* 1910. Century. photos. 8vo. G. $12.50

KELLER, Helen. *Story of My Life.* 1903. Doubleday Page. 1st print. VG. $45.00

KELLER, Mrs. S.A. *PA-German Cookbook.* nd. (c 1900?) np. 32 p. wraps. fair. T5. $35.00

KELLER, W.P. *Canada's Wild Glory.* 1961. Jarrold. Ils 1st ed. 336 p. dj. EX. M2. $14.00

KELLERHOVEN & DUTRON. *La Legende de Sainte Ursule.* 1860. 22 pls. xl. VG. $85.00

KELLERMAN, Jonathan. *Blood Test.* 1986. Atheneum. 1st ed. dj. RS. M. $15.00

KELLEY, A.P. *Anatomy of Antiques.* 1974. NY. Viking. Ils. dj. EX. $16.00

KELLEY, Francis Clement. *Mexico: Land of Blood-Drenched Alters.* 1935. Revised 2nd ed. sgn. dj. $25.00

KELLEY, Leo P. *Luke Sutton: Outrider.* 1984. Doubleday. 1st ed. dj. EX. RS. P1. $12.50

KELLEY, Leo P. *Time 110100.* 1972. Walker. 1st ed. dj. EX. P1. $10.00

KELLEY, W.M. *Dancers on the Shore.* 1965. London. Hutchinson. 1st ed. VG. $20.00

KELLEY, W.M. *Dunfords Travels Everywheres.* 1970. Doubleday. 1st ed. dj. $15.00

KELLOGG, J.H. *Rational Hydrotherapy.* 1903. Ils 2nd ed. EX. $35.00

KELLOGG, R. *Mexican Tailless Amphibians in the US National Museum.* 1932. US Nat Mus. Ils. 224 p. dj. VG. M2. $14.00

KELLOGG, R.H. *Life & Death in Rebel Prisons.* reprint of 1865 ed. 399 p. K1. $14.50

KELLOGG, R.H. *Life & Death in Rebel Prisons.* 1865. Hartford. 398 p. G. $45.00

KELLOGG, W.N. *Porpoises & Sonar.* 1961. Chicago U. Ils. 177 p. EX. M2. $13.00

KELLOGG. *Houdini.* 1928. NY. Ils 1st ed. fair. $10.00

KELLSEY, I. *Corrective Photography.* 1947. Deardorff. VG. $20.00

KELLY, Amy. *Eleanor of Aquitaine & the Four Kings.* 1981. dj. M. C1. $14.50

KELLY, Emmet. *Clown.* 1954. NY. 1st ed. VG. B2. $27.50

KELLY, F.C. *David Ross: Modern Pioneer.* 1946. NY. 1st ed. photos. 182 p. dj. T5. $25.00

KELLY, F.C. *One Thing Leads to Another.* 1936. Boston/NY. 1st ed. dj. VG. $35.00

KELLY, Fanny. *Narrative of My Captivity Among Sioux Indians.* 1871. Cincinnati. 1st ed. 8vo. gilt red cloth. T1. $60.00

KELLY, H.A. *Cyclopedia of American Medical Biography From 1610-1819.* 1912. Phil. 2 vols. xl. $95.00

KELLY, Mary. *Dead Corpse.* 1966. Michael Joseph. 1st ed. dj. xl. P1. $6.00

KELLY, Walt. *I Go Pogo.* 1952. NY. 1st ed. wraps. VG. $20.00

KELLY, Walt. *Pogo Peek-A-Book.* 1955. NY. 1st ed. wraps. VG. $20.00

KELLY, Walt. *Pogo Stepmother Goose.* c 1950s. NY. 1st ed. wraps. $20.00

KELLY, Walt. *Pogo's Bats & the Belles Free.* 1976. Fireside Books. 1st ed. wraps. T6. $10.00

KELLY, Walt. *Ten Ever-Loving, Blue-Eyed Years With Pogo, 1949-1959.* 1959. Simon Schuster. Fireside Book. SftCvr. VG. $25.00

KELLY & BASKERVILLE. *Story of Conservation in NC.* 1941. Charlotte. Ils 1st ed. 386 p. VG. $10.00

KELLY & CLEMENT. *Market Milk.* 1923. Ils Wiley. 1st ed. EX. $20.00

KELSEY, Albert. *Architectural Annual.* 1901. Phil. Ils. 4to. 303 p. G. $45.00

KELSEY, Vera. *Whisper Murder.* 1946. Crime Club. 1st ed. xl. VG. P1. $12.50

KELTIE, J.S. *Story of Emin's Rescue As Told in Stanley's Letters.* 1890. NY. $20.00

KELTON, Gerald. *Dolores.* 1934. Eldon. 1st ed. dj. VG. P1. $15.00

KEMBLE, F.A. *Journal of Residence on GA Plantation 1838-1839.* 1863. Harper. 1st ed. 337 p. purple cloth. $55.00

KEMBLE, F.A. *Record of a Girlhood.* 1978. London. 1st ed. 3 vols. C2. $80.00

KEMELMAN, Harry. *Someday the Rabbi Will Leave.* 1985. Morrow. 1st ed. dj. EX. P1. $16.00

KEMELMAN, Harry. *Thursday the Rabbi Walked Out.* nd. Book Club. dj. P1. $4.00

KEMELMAN, Harry. *Weekend With the Rabbi.* nd. Book Club. dj. EX. P1. $7.50

KEMP, D.C. *CO's Little Kingdom.* 1949. Denver. Sage. 1/1000. sgn/#d. 153 p. A3. $60.00

KEMP, Harry. *Don Juan's Notebook.* 1929. NY. private print. 1/1050. boxed. VG. $50.00

KEMP, J.F. *Handbook of Rocks for Use Without Petrographic Microscope.* 1950. Van Nostrand. Ils. 300 p. EX. M2. $8.00

KEMP, Sam. *Black Frontiers. Pioneer Adventures With Cecil Rhodes...* 1931. NY. 1st ed. VG. T1. $40.00

KENAMRE, Dallas. *Fire-Bird: Study of D.H. Lawrence.* 1952. NY. 1st ed. 8vo. dj. EX. T1. $25.00

KENDALL, E. *Phantom Prince: My Life With Ted Bundy.* 1981. Seattle. 1st ed. dj. VG. B2. $30.00

KENDALL, G.W. *Letters From TX Sheep Ranch.* 1959. Urbana. 1st ed. dj. EX. $28.00

KENDALL, G.W. *Narrative of TX Santa Fe Expedition.* 1844. NY. Harper. 1st ed. 2 vols. scarce. A3. $525.00

KENDALL, G.W. *Narrative of TX Santa Fe Expedition.* 1929. Donnelley. reprint of 1844 ed. EX. M2. $27.00

KENDALL, Henry. *Jerusalem: City Plan, Presevation & Development.* 1948. London. Ils. maps. plans. EX. $50.00

KENDALL, P.M. *Art of Biography.* 1965. London. 1st ed. dj. EX. $30.00

KENDRICK, Baynard. *Blind Man's Bluff.* 1946. Triangle. dj. VG. P1. $15.00

KENDRICK, Baynard. *Flames of Time.* nd. Book Club. dj. VG. P1. $3.00

KENDRICK, Baynard. *Flames of Time.* 1948. Scribner. VG. P1. $10.00

KENDRICK, Baynard. *Flight From a Firing Wall.* 1966. Simon Schuster. 1st ed. inscr. 8vo. dj. $25.00

KENDRICK, Baynard. *Out of Control.* 1945. Doubleday Book Club. VG. P1. $10.00

KENFIELD, S.D. *Akron & Summit Co., OH, 1825-1928.* 1928. Chicago/Akron. Ils. 3 vols. VG. T5. $75.00

KENK, R. *Index to the Genera & Species of Fresh-Water Tri-Clads.* 1974. Smithsonian. 90 p. M2. $8.00

KENNEALY, Patricia. *Throne of Scone.* 1986. 1st ed. dj. M. C1. $10.00

KENNEDY, C.E. *Fifty Years of Cleveland: By One Who Lived the Bulk of Them.* 1925. Cleveland. 352 p. fair. T5. $25.00

KENNEDY, Charles. *Poems of Cynewulf.* 1949. NY. VG. C1. $14.00

KENNEDY, J.F. *Why England Slept.* 1940. NY. Funk. 1st ed. dj. VG. G2. $300.00

KENNEDY, J.P. *Horseshoe Robinson: Tale of Tory Ascendency.* 1854. Putnam. Ils. 598 p. $35.00

KENNEDY, J.P. *I'm for Roosevelt.* 1936. NY. 2nd ed. 149 p. dj. VG. B2. $22.50

KENNEDY, J.S. *Insect Polymorphism.* 1961. London. EX. M2. $15.00

KENNEDY, J.W. *Holy Island.* 1958. NY. $8.50

KENNEDY, Leigh. *Journal of Nicholas the American.* 1986. Atlantic Monthly. dj. EX. P1. $16.95

KENNEDY, Ludovic. *Book of Railway Journeys.* 1980. NY. Rawson Wade. 1st ed. dj. EX. $5.00

KENNEDY, M. *Checkering & Carving of Gun Stocks.* 1952. Samworth. Ils. $35.00

KENNEDY, R.E. *Mellow: Negro Work Songs, Street Cries & Spirituals.* 1925. Boni. 1st ed. sgn. dj. $100.00

KENNEDY, S.B. *Joscelyn Cheshire: Story of Revolutionary Days in Carolinas.* 1901. Doubleday Page. Ils. 338 p. $22.50

KENNEDY, S.L. *H.S. Lehr & His School.* 1938. Ada, OH. Ada Herald. 1st ed. $10.00

KENNEDY, Stetson. *Passage to Violence.* 1954. Lion Lib. pb. VG. P1. $10.00

KENNEDY, William. *Billy Phelan's Greatest Game.* 1978. NY. 1st ed. dj. $65.00

KENNEDY, William. *Ink Truck.* 1969. Viking. 1st ed. dj. xl. VG. $25.00

KENNEDY, William. *Ironweed.* 1983. Viking. 1st ed. $40.00

KENNEDY, William. *Legs.* 1975. Coward McCann. 1st ed. dj. VG. $40.00

KENNEDY, William. *O Albany.* 1983. NY. 1st ed. dj. EX. $60.00

KENNEDY, William. *Quinn's Book.* 1987. NY. 1st ed. 1/500. sgn/#d. slipcase. $75.00

KENNELLEY, Brendan. *My Dark Fathers.* 1964. Dublin. inscr. $10.00

KENNETH, J.H. *Dictionary of Biological Terms.* 1963. Edinburgh. Oliver Boyd. 8th ed. 640 p. EX. M2. $15.00

KENT, Alexander. *Sloop of War.* 1972. London. 1st ed. dj. VG. $30.00

KENT, Alexander. *Sloop of War.* 1972. NY. 1st Am ed. dj. VG. $25.00

KENT, Alexander. *Tradition of Victory.* 1981. London. 1st ed. dj. VG. $20.00

KENT, L.A. *Summer Kitchen.* 1957. Boston. 1st ed. dj. VG. $15.00

KENT, Rockwell. *Beowulf.* 1932. Ltd ed. 1/950. EX. $150.00

KENT, Rockwell. *Birthday Book.* 1931. Ltd ed. 1/1850. sgn. VG. B4. $145.00

KENT, Rockwell. *Bookplates & Marks & Later Bookplates & Marks of Kent.* Random House. 1st ed. sgn. 2 vols. djs. J2. $275.00

KENT, Rockwell. *Canterbury Tales.* 1934. Covici Friede. dj. VG. $12.00

KENT, Rockwell. *Complete Works of Shakespeare.* 1936. NY. Ils. G. $30.00

KENT, Rockwell. *Decemeron of Giovanni Boccaccio.* Ltd ed. sgn. 2 vols. slipcase. EX. $125.00

KENT, Rockwell. *Dreams & Derisions.* 1927. NY. Ltd ed. sgn. poor. $120.00

KENT, Rockwell. *Greenland Journal.* 1962. Ltd ed. 1/1000. sgn. boxed. EX. $225.00

KENT, Rockwell. *Greenland Journal.* 1962. NY. 1st ed. dj. $35.00

KENT, Rockwell. *Isle of Long Ago.* 1933. Scribner. 1/1000. presentation. sgn. VG. B2. $50.00

KENT, Rockwell. *It's Me O Lord.* 1955. NY. 1st ed. dj. EX. $75.00

KENT, Rockwell. *Moby Dick.* 1930. NY. 1st trade ed. VG. B2. $30.00

KENT, Rockwell. *N by E.* Ltd ed. 1/900. 4to. boxed. EX. $150.00

KENT, Rockwell. *N by E.* 1930. Literary Guild. dj. $30.00

KENT, Rockwell. *N by E.* 1930. NY. 1st ed. dj. E2. $35.00

KENT, Rockwell. *N by E.* 1933. Blue Ribbon. 5th print. VG. $15.00

KENT, Rockwell. *Rockwellkentiana.* 1933. NY. 1st ed. blue/orange dj. VG. J2. $65.00

KENT, Rockwell. *Saga of Gisli.* 1936. NY. Trans Allen. VG. $45.00

KENT, Rockwell. *Salamina.* 1935. NY. 1st ed. dj. J2. $40.00

KENT, Rockwell. *Salamina.* 1935. NY. 1st ed. sgn. dj. J2. $60.00

KENT, Rockwell. *This I My Own.* 1940. NY. 1st ed. sgn. dj. VG. $75.00

KENT, Rockwell. *This Is My Own.* 1945. Duell Sloan. Ils 1st ed. 393 p. dj. $50.00

KENT, Rockwell. *To Thee! Toast in Celebration of Opportunity...* 1946. Manitowoc, WI. Rahr Malting Co. 4to. G. $75.00

KENT, Rockwell. *Treasury of Sea Stories.* 1948. NY. 1st ed. 644 p. dj. VG. B2. $27.50

KENT, Rockwell. *Voyaging S From Strait of Magellan.* 1924. Halcyon House. Ils 4th ed. M. $60.00

KENT, Rockwell. *Voyaging S From Strait of Magellan.* 1968. Revised 1st ed. dj. VG. B4. $40.00

KENT, Rockwell. *Wilderness: Journal of Quiet Adventures in AK.* 1920. Putnam. Ils 1st ed. 4to. beige linen. $100.00

KENT, Rockwell. *Wilderness: Journal of Quiet Adventures in AK.* 1937. Halcyon House. 5th print. 4to. dj. EX. $65.00

KENT, Samuel. *Grammar of Heraldry; or, Gentleman's Vade Mecum.* 1724. London. Ils 3rd ed. full leather. VG. $50.00

KENT, W.W. *Rare Hooked Rugs.* 1948. Springfield. Ils. 223 p. VG. T5. $37.50

KENTON, Edna. *Book of Earths.* 1928. NY. $35.00

KENWORTHY, J.D. *Fisherman's Philosophy.* 1933. Ils 1st ed. VG. $20.00

KENYON, Michael. *May You Die in Ireland.* 1965. Morrow. 2nd ed. dj. EX. P1. $12.00

KENYON, Michael. *Trouble With Series Three.* 1967. Morrow. 1st ed. dj. VG. P1. $10.00

KEPES, Gyorgy. *Nature & Art of Motion.* 1965. NY. Braziller. dj. VG. $40.00

KEPHART, Horace. *Our S Highlanders.* 1929. NY. 469 p. G. $30.00

KEPPLER, Herbert. *Nikon & Nikkormat Way.* 1977. Garden City. 1st ed. dj. EX. $22.00

KER, Henry. *Travels Through W Interior of US From 1808...* 1816. Elizabethtown. 1st ed. G. $375.00

KER, W.P. *Epic & Romance: Essays on Medieval Literature.* 1931. VG. C1. $12.50

KERENSKY, Alexander. *Russia & History's Turning Point.* 1965. Duell. 1st ed. dj. VG. J2. $15.00

KERKUT, G.A. *Implications of Evolution.* 1960. Pergamon. Ils. 174 p. EX. M2. $14.00

KERMODE, F. *Catalog of British Columbia Birds.* 1904. British Columbia Mus. 69 p. M2. $5.00

KERNER, Robert. *Urge to the Sea: Course of Russian History...* 1942. CA U. 1st ed. VG. J2. $20.00

KEROUAC, Jack. *American Haiku.* 1986. Caliban Pr. 1st ed. 1/125. wraps. EX. $45.00

KEROUAC, Jack. *Beat Road. Letters to Orlovsky & Ginsberg.* 1982. NY. M. $25.00

KEROUAC, Jack. *Big Sur.* 1962. NY. 1st ed. dj. VG. B2. $90.00

KEROUAC, Jack. *Book of Dreams.* 1961. San Francisco. City Lights. 184 p. pb. M. $45.00

KEROUAC, Jack. *Dharma Bums.* 1958. Viking. 1st ed. dj. VG. $50.00

KEROUAC, Jack. *Dr. Sax.* 1959. Grove. 1st ed. dj. rare. EX. $75.00

KEROUAC, Jack. *Dr. Sax.* 1959. Grove. 5th print. pb. VG. $10.00

KEROUAC, Jack. *Hugo Weber.* 1967. Ltd ed. 1/200. $125.00

KEROUAC, Jack. *Jazz of the Beat Generation.* 1955. New Am Lib. 1st ed. 12mo. wraps. VG. $20.00

KEROUAC, Jack. *Lonesome Traveler.* 1960. McGraw Hill. 1st ed. 183 p. dj. G. $40.00

KEROUAC, Jack. *Lonesome Traveler.* 1960. NY. 1st ed. dj. EX. $70.00

KEROUAC, Jack. *Lonesome Traveler.* 1962. Andre Deutsch. 1st ed. dj. VG. $75.00

KEROUAC, Jack. *Not Long Ago Christmas.* 1972. wraps. $60.00

KEROUAC, Jack. *On the Road.* 1957. NY. 1st ed. dj. B2. $195.00

KEROUAC, Jack. *On the Road.* 1958. Signet/New Am Lib. 1st ed. pb. M. $40.00

KEROUAC, Jack. *On the Road.* 1959. Signet. 1st print. pb. VG. $25.00

KEROUAC, Jack. *Pic & Subterraneans.* 1971. Andre Deutsch. 1st/only HrdCvr ed. dj. EX. $80.00

KEROUAC, Jack. *Pic.* 1973. Grove. 1st ed. 2nd print. pb. VG. $10.00

KEROUAC, Jack. *Satori in Paris.* 1966. Grove. 1st print. pb. G. $20.00

KEROUAC, Jack. *Satori in Paris.* 1967. Andre Deutsch. 1st ed. dj. EX. $85.00

KEROUAC, Jack. *Scattered Poems.* 1971. San Francisco. 1st ed. wraps. VG. $20.00

KEROUAC, Jack. *Scattered Poems.* 1973. City Lights. 4th print. pb. VG. $10.00

KEROUAC, Jack. *Take Care of My Ghost, Ghost.* 1977. Ghost Pr. 1/200. EX. $125.00

KEROUAC, Jack. *Town & City.* 1950. Harcourt Brace. ARC. orange wraps. slipcase. VG. $600.00

KEROUAC, Jack. *Trip Trap.* 1973. Bolinas. Grey Fox. 1st ed. wraps. EX. $60.00

KEROUAC, Jack. *Vanity of Duluoz.* 1968. NY. 1st ed. dj. VG. B2. $57.50

KEROUAC, Jack. *Visions of Cody.* 1972. McGraw Hill. 1st ed. inscr Ginsberg. EX. $100.00

KEROUAC, Jack. *Visions of Cody.* 1972. NY. 1st ed. tan dj. M. $55.00

KEROUAC, Jack. *Visions of Cody.* 1972. NY. 1st ed. white dj. VG. $35.00

KERR, E.M. *Yoknapatawpha.* 1969. NY. 1st ed. 284 p. dj. VG. T5. $25.00

KERR, J.G. *Naturalist in the Gran Chaco.* 1968. Greenwood. reprint. 235 p. EX. M2. $20.00

KERR, J.L. *Wilfred Grenfell: His Life & Works.* 1959. Dodd Mead. 270 p. dj. VG. M2. $7.00

KERR, Jean. *How I Got To Be Perfect.* 1978. Doubleday. 1st ed. dj. M. $12.00

KERR, John. *History of Curling.* 1890. Edinburgh. 440 p. $105.00

KERR, Katharine. *Daggerspell.* 1986. Doubleday. 1st ed. dj. EX. P1. $16.95

KERR, Katharine. *Daggerspell.* 1986. Doubleday. 1st ed. dj. EX. RS. P1. $20.00

KERR, Katharine. *Darkspell.* 1987. Doubleday. dj. EX. P1. $17.95

KERSH, Gerald. *Dead Look On.* 1943. London. 1st ed. dj. EX. $40.00

KERSH, Gerald. *Night & the City.* 1950. Harlequin. pb. G. P1. $15.00

KERSH, Gerald. *Prelude to a Certain Midnight.* 1947. Doubleday. 1st ed. VG. P1. $20.00

KERSH, Gerald. *Prelude to a Certain Midnight.* 1947. Heinemann. 1st ed. VG. P1. $30.00

KERSH, Gerald. *Sergeant Nelson of the Guards.* 1945. Winston. VG. P1. $15.00

KERSH, Gerald. *Weak & the Strong.* 1946. Simon Schuster. 1st ed. dj. G. P1. $17.50

KERSIS, S.C. *Plates & Buckles of American Military 1795-1874.* 448 pls. photos. 574 p. M. J4. $50.00

KERTESZ, Andre. *Day of Paris.* 1945. NY. Augustin. Ils 1st ed. 8vo. dj. VG. $110.00

KERTESZ, Andre. *Distortions.* 1976. NY. 1st ed. dj. VG. $65.00

KERTESZ, Andre. *From My Window.* 1981. Boston. 1st ed. dj. EX. $40.00

KERTESZ, Andre. *Hungarian Memories.* 1982. Boston. Little Brown. 1st ed. 187 p. dj. $65.00

KERTESZ, Andre. *Hungarian Memories.* 1982. NY. dj. EX. $40.00

KERTESZ, Andre. *Lifetime of Photography.* 1982. London. Thames Hudson. 1st ed. photos. dj. $50.00

KERTESZ, Andre. *On Reading.* 1971. Grossman. 63 photos. dj. VG. $50.00

KERTESZ, Andre. *Portraits; Landscapes; Birds; American.* 1979. NY. 1st pb ed. wraps. $17.50

KERTESZ, Andre. *Sixty Years of Photography, 1912-1972.* 1972. NY. Grossman. 1st ed. square 4to. dj. EX. $175.00

KESEY, Ken. *Sometimes a Great Notion.* 2nd ed. dj. EX. $25.00

KESEY, Ken. *Sometimes a Great Notion.* 1964. NY. 1st ed. dj. VG. B2. $40.00

KESSEL, Dmitri. *On Assignment: Dmitri Kessel, Life Photographer.* 1985. NY. Abrams. 150 photos. tall 4to. sgn. dj. EX. $85.00

KESSLER, Doyne. *AK Salt-Water Fishes & Other Sea Life.* 1985. AK NW. Ils. map. 358 p. EX. M2. $20.00

KESSLER, G.E. *City Plan for Dallas.* c 1911. np. photos. maps. 4to. stiff wraps. EX. $60.00

KESSLER, Lillian. *Inventory of Co. Archives of OH, No. 32: Hancock Co.* 1941. Columbus. 356 p. xl. T5. $32.50

KESTER, Vaughan. *Hand of the Mighty.* 1913. Bobbs Merrill. 1st ed. $12.00

KESTER, Vaughan. *Prodigal Judge.* 1911. Bobbs Merrill. Ils Bracker. 1st ed. $12.00

KESTLE, J.A. *This Is Lakeside, 1873-1973.* 1973. photos. sgn. 192 p. VG. T5. $17.50

KETCHUM, Philip. *Kill at Dusk.* 1946. Red Dagger 23. VG. P1. $12.50

KETRING, R.A. *Charles Obborn in Anti-Slavery Movement.* 1937. Columbus. OH Hist Soc. 1st ed. M. $33.00

KETTELL, T.P. *History of the Great Rebellion.* 1862. Worcester/NY. Ils. maps. G. G2. $46.00

KETTELL, T.P. *History of the Great Rebellion.* 1865. Ils. maps. 2 vols in 1. 778 p. EX. K1. $32.50

KETTERER, Bernadine. *Manderley Mystery.* 1937. Eldon. 1st ed. VG. P1. $20.00

KETTERER, David. *New Worlds for Old, Apocalyptic Imagination.* 1974. IN U. dj. EX. $12.00

KEY, J.S. *Field Guide to MO Ferns.* 1982. MO Conservation. Ils. EX. M2. $10.00

KEY, Ted. *If You Like Hazel.* 1952. NY. 1st ed. inscr Hazel/Key. EX. $17.50

KEYES, C.R. *Coal Deposits of IA.* 1894. IA Geol Survey. Ils. 18 pls. VG. M2. $5.00

KEYES, F.A. *Army Dentistry.* 1918. NY. Appleton. Ils 1st ed. VG. $12.00

KEYES, F.P. *Frances Parkinson Keyes' Cookbook.* 1955. NY. Ils 1st ed. 322 p. dj. B2. $30.00

KEYES, F.P. *Parts Unknown.* 1938. NY. 1st ed. presentation. sgn. dj. VG. B2. $32.50

KEYES, Roger S. *Male Journey in Japanese Prints.* 1989. Berkeley. Ils. dj. D2. $40.00

KEYHOE, D.E. *Flying Saucers: Top Secret.* 1960. NY. EX. $8.50

KEYNES, J.M. *General Theory of Employment, Interest & Money.* nd. (1936) Harcourt Brace. 1st Am ed. VG. $70.00

KEYNES, J.M. *Treatise on Money.* 1930. NY. 1st Am ed. 2 vols. djs. VG. $75.00

KEYON & INGOLD. *Trigonometry.* 1914. HrdCvr. 260 p. TB. EX. $2.00

KHAYYAM, Omar. *Rubaiyat of Omar Khayyam.* nd. np. Crowell. pls. 171 p. TEG. dj. T5. $75.00

KHAYYAM, Omar. *Rubaiyat of Omar Khayyam.* 1935. Ltd Ed Club. Ils Angelo. 12mo. wraps. slipcase. $85.00

KHOV, Voyette. *Last Days of Sevastopol.* 1943. NY. 1st ed. fld map. 224 p. dj. VG. B2. $25.00

KIBBY, G. *Mushrooms & Toadstools: A Field Guide.* 1979. Oxford U. Ils 1st ed. dj. EX. M2. $26.00

KIDD, J.H. *Personal Recollections of Cavalryman With Custer...* 1983. Time Life. facsimile of 1908 ed. M2. $45.00

KIDD, Virginia. *Millenial Women.* 1978. Delacorte. 1st ed. dj. EX. P1. $15.00

KIDDER, Glen M. *Railway to the Moon.* 1969. Littleton, NH. Ils. 184 p. dj. VG. T5. $19.50

KIDDER, J. *Japanese Temples: Sculpture, Paintings, Gardens...* 1964. Tokyo/ Amsterdam. slipcase. M. J2. $175.00

KIDDER, Tracy. *House.* 1985. Boston. Houghton. 1st ed. dj. EX. $18.00

KIDDER-SMITH, G.E. *New Church of Europe.* 1964. Holt Rinehart. Ils 1st ed. 291 p. dj. D2. $75.00

KIEBNAN, John. *Treasury of Great Nature Writings.* 1957. Hanover House. 1st ed. 640 p. EX. M2. $11.00

KIEFER, M. *American Children Through Their Books.* 1948. Phil. Ils 1st ed. dj. VG. B2. $40.00

KIEFER, P.W. *Practical Evaluation of Railroad Motive Power.* 1947. 65 p. $30.00

KIELAR, Wieslaw. *Annus Mundi: 1,500 Days in Auschwitz & Birkenau.* 1980. NY. 1st ed. dj. VG. $10.00

KIELL, Norman. *Psychological Studies of Famous Americans of Civil War Era.* 1964. NY. Twayne. 1st ed. dj. EX. $15.00

KIERAN, James. *Come Murder Me.* 1951. Gold Medal. EX. P1. $12.50

KIERNAN, John. *Footnotes on Nature.* 1950. Garden City. VG. $10.00

KIERNAN, Thomas. *White Hound of Mountain & Other Irish Folk Tales.* 1962. 1st ed. dj. EX. C1. $6.00

KIKKAWA & THORNE. *Behavior of Animals.* 1974. Plume. Ils. 223 p. M2. $3.00

KIKOSCHKA, Oskar. *Drawings, 1906-1965.* 1970. Miami U. Ils. dj. VG. $40.00

KIKUCHI, S. *Treasury of Japanese Wood Block Prints.* 1969. NY. 1st ed. dj. VG. B2. $70.00

KILBOURNE, William. *William Lyon Mackenzie & the Rebellion in Upper Canada.* 1956. Toronto. 1st ed. dj. J2. $15.00

KILBOURNE & GOODE. *Game Fishes of the US.* 1972. Winchester. 1/1000. orig wraps/carton. M2. $75.00

KILGOUR, Robert. *For Ancient Manuscripts in Bible House Library.* 1928. London. $30.00

KILHAM, L. *American Crow & the Common Raven.* 1989. TX A&M. Ils 1st ed. dj. M. $20.00

KILIAN, Crawford. *Icequake.* 1979. Douglas McIntyre. 1st ed. dj. P1. $10.00

KILIAN, Crawford. *Tsunami.* 1983. Douglas McIntyre. 1st ed. dj. P1. $20.00

KILLEFFER, D.H. *Banbury: Master Mixer.* 1962. NY. 1st ed. inscr. 165 p. dj. VG. T5. $75.00

KILMER, Aline. *Vigils.* 1921. VG. C1. $5.00

KIMBALL, Richard. *Life in Santa Domingo.* 1873. London. Carlfton. 12mo. G. $17.50

KIMBER. *Story of Old Press.* 1937. Cambridge. Stephen Daye. 1/1000. VG. $20.00

KIMBROUGH, E. *Thomas Kimbrough, 1805-1886, & His Descendants.* 1956. WA Co Hist Soc. 4to. 52 p. EX. M2. $10.00

KIMBROUGH, E. *Through Charlie's Door.* 1952. Harper. presentation. VG. $35.00

KIMBROUGH, Emily. *Better Than Oceans.* 1976. Harper Row. 1st ed. inscr/sgn. dj. VG. $15.00

KIMBROUGH, Emily. *Now & Then.* 1972. Harper Row. 1st ed. dj. VG. $10.00

KIMBROUGH, Emily. *Pleasure by the Busload.* 1961. Harper Row. 1st ed. dj. EX. $12.00

KIMBROUGH, Emily. *Time Enough.* 1974. Harper Row. 1st ed. inscr/sgn. dj. VG. $15.00

KIMIN, Maxine. *Long Approach.* 1985. NY. 1st ed. sgn. dj. EX. $45.00

KIMMEL, Stanley. *Mad Booths of MD.* 1940. Indianapolis. Ils 1st ed. 400 p. VG. B2. $37.50

KIMMEL, Stanley. *Mr. Davis's Richmond.* 1958. NY. Ils 1st ed. 4to. 214 p. dj. VG. T5. $27.50

KIMMEL, Stanley. *Mr. Lincoln's WA.* 1957. Coward McCann. Ils. 4to. dj. EX. M2. $10.00

KINDIG, Joe Jr. *Thoughts on the KY Rifle in Its Golden Age.* 1960. NY. 1st ed. 4to. dj. EX. $75.00

KINDSHER, K. *Edible Wild Plants of the Prairie.* 1987. KS U. Ils 1st ed. 276 p. M. M2. $10.00

KING, A.G. *Practical Steam: Hot Water & Vapor Heating & Ventilation.* 1925. NY. 5th ed. G. $12.00

KING, Alexander. *Is There a Life After Birth?* 1963. NY. 1st print. dj. EX. $18.50

KING, Arthur. *House of Warne.* 1965. Warne. Ils. 107 p. VG. $15.00

KING, B. *Ben King's Verse.* 1900. Forbes. Ils Denslow. Intro Rhead. $15.00

KING, C.S. *My Life With Martin Luther King Jr.* 1969. NY. Ils 1st ed. dj. EX. $30.00

KING, Charles. *Campaigning With Crook.* 1890. Ils. 295 p. K1. $23.50

KING, Charles. *Daughter of the Sioux.* 1903. Hobart. Ils Remington/Deming. 1st ed. VG. $20.00

KING, Charles. *Foes in Ambush.* 1893. 263 p. K1. $9.50

KING, Charles. *Laramie; or, Queen of Bedlam.* 1890. Lippincott. G. $23.00

KING, Charles. *Trooper Ross & Signal Butte.* 1896. Ils. 297 p. K1. $18.50

KING, Charles. *Under Fire.* 1895. Ils. 511 p. K1. $13.50

KING, Charles. *Wounded Name.* 1898. London. 1st ed. 1st issue. 353 p. VG. T5. $19.50

KING, Clarence. *Clarence King Memoirs: Helmet of Mambrino.* 1904. NY. Putnam. Memorial ed. 427 p. VG. A3. $50.00

KING, Clarence. *Mountaineering in Sierra, NV.* 1872. Boston. 1st Am ed. VG. $200.00

KING, Clarence. *Mountaineering in Sierra, NV.* 1872. Boston. 1st ed. G. $165.00

KING, Clarence. *Mountaineering in Sierra, NV.* 1875. Osgood. 5th ed. maps. $65.00

KING, F.H. *Farmers of 40 Centuries.* 1911. Madison, WI. Ils 1st ed. 441 p. VG. B2. $27.50

KING, Florence. *S Ladies & Gentlemen.* 1975. NY. 1st ed. dj. VG. B2. $22.50

KING, Grace. *Creole Families of New Orleans.* 1921. NY. Ils 1st ed. 464 p. EX. $30.00

KING, Grace. *De Soto & Men in the Land of FL.* 1898. NY. Macmillan. xl. G. R1. $12.00

KING, Grace. *Grace King of New Orleans: Selection of Her Writings.* 1973. LA U. 404 p. dj. M. $45.00

KING, Grace. *Monsieur Motte.* 1888. NY. 1st ed. VG. B1. $25.00

KING, Grace. *Pleasant Ways of St. Medard.* 1916. NY. ARC. 1st ed. B1. $25.00

KING, H.C. *History of the Telescope.* 1955. Cambridge. Ils 1st ed. 456 p. VG. B2. $35.00

KING, Harold. *Four Days.* 1976. NY. 1st ed. dj. VG. $6.00

KING, Jack. *Confessions of a Poker Player.* 1940. NY. 1st ed. 209 p. VG. B2. $22.50

KING, Kenneth. *Mission to Paradise.* 1956. Junipero Serra. 1st ed. sgn. 190 p. xl. G. $8.00

KING, M.L. *Strength To Love.* 1963. NY. 1st ed. dj. VG. $35.00

KING, M.L. *Stride Toward Freedom.* 1958. Harper. 1st ed. 230 p. dj. VG. $50.00

KING, Moses. *Photographic Views of NY.* 1895. Boston. Ils 1st ed. 720 p. $40.00

KING, O.A. *Gray Gold.* 1959. Denver. Big Mountain Pr. 2nd ed. dj. A3. $45.00

KING, O.B. *Five Million in Cash.* 1932. Doubleday Doran. VG. P1. $10.00

KING, Pauline. *American Mural Painting: Study of Important Decorations...* 1902. Noyes Platt. 264 p. D2. $95.00

KING, Pauline. *American Mural Painting: Study of Important Decorations...* 1902. Boston. 1st ed. J2. $20.00

KING, Rufus. *Constant God.* 1937. Crime Club. VG. P1. $10.00

KING, Rufus. *Dowager's Etchings.* 1944. Crime Club. 1st ed. VG. P1. $10.00

KING, Rufus. *Lesser Antilles Case.* 1934. Crime Club. 1st ed. dj. xl. P1. $10.00

KING, Rufus. *Lethal Lady.* 1948. Doubleday Book Club. VG. P1. $10.00

KING, Rufus. *Malice in Wonderland.* 1958. Crime Club. 1st ed. dj. G. P1. $15.00

KING, Rufus. *Murder by the Clock.* nd. Collier. VG. P1. $10.00

KING, Rufus. *Murder Masks Miami.* 1940. Sun Dial. VG. P1. $10.00

KING, Rufus. *Secret Beyond the Door.* 1947. Triangle. dj. VG. P1. $12.00

KING, Rufus. *Variety of Weapons.* 1943. Crime Club. dj. VG. P1. $12.00

KING, Stephen. *Bachman Books: Four Early Novels.* 1985. New Am Lib. 2nd ed. dj. P1. $20.00

KING, Stephen. *Carrie.* 1974. Doubleday. gold cloth. dj. EX. $20.00

KING, Stephen. *Carrie.* 1974. Doubleday. red cloth. dj. EX. $15.00

KING, Stephen. *Carrie.* 1974. Ltd 1st ed. inscr/sgn. 8vo. dj. EX. $300.00

KING, Stephen. *Christine.* 1983. NY. Review ed. dj. RS. M. $75.00

KING, Stephen. *Christine.* 1983. NY. Review ed. dj. VG. $50.00

KING, Stephen. *Christine.* 1983. NY. Grant. 1/1000. sgn. dj. boxed. M. $325.00

KING, Stephen. *Christine.* 1983. Viking. 1st trade ed. red/black bdg. dj. $30.00

KING, Stephen. *Cujo.* 1981. Mysterious Pr. Ltd ed. 1/750. sgn. slipcase. $350.00

KING, Stephen. *Cujo.* 1981. NY. Review ed. dj. RS. EX. $125.00

KING, Stephen. *Cujo.* 1981. NY. 1st trade ed. dj. EX. $30.00

KING, Stephen. *Cujo.* 1981. NY. Viking. 6th print. tan/black bdg. dj. EX. $15.00

KING, Stephen. *Cujo.* 1981. Viking. 1st ed. dj. EX. $40.00

KING, Stephen. *Cujo.* 1981. Viking. 1st ed. dj. VG. P1. $25.00

KING, Stephen. *Cujo.* 1982. London. MacDonald. 1st ed. dj. $30.00

KING, Stephen. *Cycle of the Werewolf.* 1985. Land of Enchantment. dj. P1. $150.00

KING, Stephen. *Cycle of the Werewolf.* 1985. Signet XE2111. EX. P1. $8.95

KING, Stephen. *Danse Macabre.* 1981. Everest House. Deluxe Ltd ed. 1/250. sgn/#d. M. $850.00

KING, Stephen. *Danse Macabre.* 1981. Everest House. 1/250. sgn. glassine dj. boxed. EX. $750.00

KING, Stephen. *Danse Macabre.* 1981. Everest House. 1st ed. red bdg. dj. EX. $25.00

KING, Stephen. *Danse Macabre.* 1981. Everest House. 2nd ed. red bdg. dj. EX. $15.00

KING, Stephen. *Dark Tower I: Gunslinger.* 1982. Grant. Ltd ed. 1/500. sgn/#d. EX. $500.00

KING, Stephen. *Dark Tower I: Gunslinger.* 1982. Grant. 2nd ed. dj. EX. $365.00

KING, Stephen. *Dark Tower I: Gunslinger.* 1982. W Kingston. Ils Whalen. 1st trade ed. dj. $180.00

KING, Stephen. *Dark Tower I: Gunslinger.* 1988. NY. Plume. 1st ed. 8vo. 224 p. wraps. EX. $20.00

KING, Stephen. *Dark Tower II: Drawing of the Three.* 1st trade ed. dj. M. $70.00

KING, Stephen. *Dark Tower II: Drawing of the Three.* 1987. Grant. Ltd ed. 1/850. sgn/#d. M. $450.00

KING, Stephen. *Dark Tower II: Drawing of the Three.* 1987. Grant. 1st ed. 1/3000. s/wrap. M. $85.00

KING, Stephen. *Dead Zone.* 1979. NY. 1st ed. dj. VG. $65.00

KING, Stephen. *Dead Zone.* 1979. NY. 1st ed. 426 p. VG. T5. $45.00

KING, Stephen. *Dead Zone.* 1979. Viking. 5th print. black bdg. dj. EX. $15.00

KING, Stephen. *Different Seasons.* 1982. Viking. 2nd print. blue bdg. dj. EX. $35.00

KING, Stephen. *Dolan's Cadillac.* 1989. AP. 1/100. blue wraps. EX. $100.00

KING, Stephen. *Dolan's Cadillac.* 1989. NY. Deluxe ed. presentation. sgn. slipcase. M. $600.00

KING, Stephen. *Dolan's Cadillac.* 1989. 1st ed. 1/1000. sgn. as issued. M. $175.00

KING, Stephen. *Eyes of the Dragon.* 1984. Philtrum. Ltd ed. 1/1000. sgn/#d. $550.00

KING, Stephen. *Eyes of the Dragon.* 1987. Viking. 1st ed. dj. EX. P1. $20.00

KING, Stephen. *Firestarter.* 1980. London. ARC. VG. $105.00

KING, Stephen. *Firestarter.* 1980. NY. 3rd print. black/red bdg. dj. EX. $20.00

KING, Stephen. *Firestarter.* 1980. Viking. 1st ed. black/red bdg. dj. VG. $25.00

KING, Stephen. *Firestarter.* 1980. Viking. 1st trade ed. dj. EX. $45.00

KING, Stephen. *It.* 1986. London. AP. EX. $105.00

KING, Stephen. *It.* 1986. NY. AP. $135.00

KING, Stephen. *It.* 1986. Viking. 1st ed. black bdg. dj. EX. $45.00

KING, Stephen. *It.* 1986. Viking. 1st ed. dj. G. P1. $20.00

KING, Stephen. *Letters From Hell.* 1988. Lord John Pr. 1/500. sgn. M. $150.00

KING, Stephen. *Misery.* 1987. Viking. 1st ed. dj. VG. P1. $20.00

KING, Stephen. *Misery.* 1987. Viking. 2nd ed. EX. P1. $10.00

KING, Stephen. *My Pretty Pony.* 1988. 1st trade ed. M. $60.00

KING, Stephen. *My Pretty Pony.* 1988. NY. 1st ed. slipcase. EX. $70.00

KING, Stephen. *Night Shift.* nd. Book Club. dj. G. P1. $7.50

KING, Stephen. *Night Shift.* 1978. Doubleday. red/black bdg. dj. EX. $15.00

KING, Stephen. *Night Shift.* 1979. Signet. VG. $45.00

KING, Stephen. *Pet Sematary.* 1983. Doubleday. 1st ed. dj. P1. $35.00

KING, Stephen. *Pet Sematary.* 1984. Hall. Large Print Ed. dj. EX. P1. $25.00

KING, Stephen. *Salem's Lot.* 1975. Doubleday. red/black bdg. dj. EX. $15.00

KING, Stephen. *Shining.* 1977. Doubleday. Book Club ed. dj. EX. $15.00

KING, Stephen. *Shining/Salem's Lot/Night Shift/Car.* 1984. Octopus. 4th ed. dj. EX. P1. $15.00

KING, Stephen. *Skeleton Crew.* 1985. NY. 1st trade ed. black bdg. dj. EX. $30.00

KING, Stephen. *Skeleton Crew.* 1985. Putnam. 1st ed. dj. EX. $40.00

KING, Stephen. *Skeleton Crew.* 1985. Putnam. 2nd ed. dj. VG. P1. $20.00

KING, Stephen. *Skeleton Crew.* 1985. Scream Pr. Ils/sgn Potter. Ltd ed. sgn. dj. $330.00

KING, Stephen. *Stand.* 1978. Doubleday. Stated 1st ed. gold/black bdg. dj. $50.00

KING, Stephen. *Stand.* 1978. Doubleday. 1st ed. dj. P1. $125.00

KING, Stephen. *Stand.* 1978. NY. Viking. 1st ed. dj. EX. $120.00

KING, Stephen. *Thinner.* 1984. New Am Lib. UCP. Special ABA ed. wraps. VG. $150.00

KING, Stephen. *Tommyknockers.* 1987. Putnam. 1st ed. dj. EX. T6. $15.00

KING, T.S. *White Hills.* 1862. Boston. Crosby Nichols. Ils. $40.00

KING, Tabitha. *Trap.* nd. Book Club. dj. EX. P1. $4.50

KING, Vincent. *Candy Man.* 1972. British SF Book Club. dj. EX. P1. $7.50

KING, W.B. *Endangered Birds of the World.* 1981. Red Data Books. VG. M2. $10.00

KING, W.J. *Search for the Masked Tawareks.* 1903. London. VG. $35.00

KING, Walter. *Battle Report of WWII.* 1944-1952. 6 vol set. VG. B2. $150.00

KING & DERBY. *Campfire Sketches & Battlefield Echoes.* 1890. Ils. 624 p. K1. $24.50

KING & STRAUB. *Talisman.* 1984. Kingston, RI. Grant. 11 pls. 2 vols. slipcase. $155.00

KING & STRAUB. *Talisman.* 1984. Viking. UCP. wraps. slipcase. $175.00

KING & STRAUB. *Talisman.* 1984. Viking. 1st ed. dj. VG. P1. $25.00

KING. *Ninny's Boat.* 1981. NY. Macmillan. 1st Am ed. dj. M. C1. $17.50

KING. *Wartime Wooing.* 1900. Ils. 195 p. K1. $9.50

KING-HALL, Magdalen. *Wicked Lady Skelton.* 1952. Dell. EX. P1. $20.00

KING-HELE, D. *Erasmus Darwin.* 1963. Scribner. Ils. 183 p. dj. EX. M2. $10.00

KINGERY, Don. *Death Must Wait.* 1956. Gold Medal. VG. P1. $7.50

KINGHORN, J.R. *Snakes of Australia.* 1956. MI U. Revised 2nd ed. 197 p. Lib bdg. M2. $25.00

KINGMAN, Lee. *Newberry & Caldecott Medal Books: 1956-1965.* 1966. Horn Book. 2nd print. VG. $12.00

KINGSBERRY, A. *Akron Negro Directory.* March, 1940. 128 p. Ils wraps. EX. T5. $95.00

KINGSLEY, Charles. *Heroes; or, Greek Fairy Tales for My Children.* 1855. Lovell. VG. $20.00

KINGSLEY, Charles. *Water Babies.* 1909. London. Macmillan. Ils Goble. J2. $250.00

KINGSLEY, Charles. *Water Babies.* 1916. NY. J2. $100.00

KINGSLEY, Charles. *Westward Ho!* 1920. Scribner. Ils Wyeth. 1st ed. J2. $75.00

KINGSLEY, J.S. *Standard Natural History.* 1885. Cassino. Ils. 6 vols. EX. M2. $65.00

KINGSLEY, M.H. *Travels in W Africa.* 1976. London. Folio Soc. Ils. map. slipcase. M2. $28.00

KINGSLEY, Michael. *Branches of Evil.* 1964. MacFadden. VG. P1. $4.50

KINGSLEY, Zaphania. *Treatis on Patriarchal or Cooperative System of Society...* Tallahassee. 2nd ed. 16 p. orig wraps. A3. $325.00

KINGSMILL, Hugh. *Behind Both Lines.* 1930. London. Kennerley. 255 p. dj. G. $9.50

KINGSTON, W.H.G. *Shipwrecks & Disasters at Sea.* 1873. London. Ils. 516 p. fair. T5. $35.00

KINIETZ, W.V. *Indians of W Great Lakes.* 1940. MI U. 1st ed. 427 p. stiff wraps. VG. J2. $22.50

KINIETZ, W.V. *John Mix Stanley & His Indian Paintings.* 1942. Ann Arbor. 1st ed. pls. glassine dj. EX. $45.00

KINLOCH, B. *Sauce for the Mongoose: Story of Real-Life Rikki-Tikki-Tavi.* 1965. Knopf. Ils 1st Am ed. 112 p. dj. EX. M2. $9.00

KINNAMAN, J.O. *Diggers for Facts.* 1940. Haverhill. 1st ed. $25.00

KINNELL, Galway. *Avenue Bearing Initial of Christ Into New World.* 1974. Boston. 1st pb ed. sgn. wraps. EX. $25.00

KINNELL, Galway. *Black Light.* 1966. Boston. 1st ed. dj. EX. $30.00

KINNELL, Galway. *Flower Herding on Mount Monadnock.* 1964. Boston. dj. EX. $60.00

KINNELL, Galway. *How the Alligator Missed Breakfast.* 1982. Boston. 1st ed. dj. EX. $35.00

KINNELL, Galway. *Mortal Acts, Mortal Words.* 1980. Boston. 1st ed. sgn. dj. M. $55.00

KINNELL, Galway. *Mortal Acts, Mortal Words.* 1980. Boston. 1st ed. sgn. dj. VG. $25.00

KINNELL, Galway. *Past.* 1985. Boston. Special ed. 1/200. sgn. slipcase. $75.00

KINNELL, Galway. *Poems of Francois Villon.* 1977. Boston. 1st bilingual pb ed. sgn. wraps. $20.00

KINNELL, Galway. *Poems of Night.* 1968. London. Rapp Carroll. 1st ed. dj. VG. $25.00

KINNELL, Galway. *Poems of Night.* 1968. London. 1st ed. sgn. dj. EX. $55.00

KINNELL, Galway. *Selected Poems.* 1982. Boston. Special ed. 1/200. sgn. slipcase. $65.00

KINNEY, Thomas. *Devil Take the Foremost.* 1947. Crime Club. 1st ed. VG. P1. $10.00

KINSELLA, W.P. *Dance Me Outside.* 1986. Boston. 1st ed. sgn. dj. EX. $45.00

KINSELLA, W.P. *Further Adventures of Slugger McBatt.* 1988. Toronto. 1st ed. sgn. dj. EX. $50.00

KINSELLA, W.P. *IA Baseball Confederacy.* 1986. Boston. proof 1st Am ed. brown wraps. $45.00

KINSELLA, W.P. *IA Baseball Confederacy.* 1986. Toronto. 1st ed. sgn. dj. EX. $60.00

KINSELLA, W.P. *Moccasin Telegraph & Other Indian Tales.* 1984. Boston. 1st Am ed. sgn. dj. EX. $40.00

KINSELLA, W.P. *Red Wolf, Red Wolf.* 1988. Toronto. 1st ed. sgn. dj. EX. $45.00

KINSELLA, W.P. *Thrill of Grass.* 1988. Vancouver. 1/200. sgn. dj. $75.00

KINSEY, POMEROY & MARTIN. *Sexual Behavior in the Human Female.* 1953. Phil. Japanese text. 2 vols. slipcase. $55.00

KINSEY, POMEROY & MARTIN. *Sexual Behavior in the Human Male.* 1948. Saunders. VG. $35.00

KINSTON, Rosemary. *Robin Hood & His Merry Men.* 1916. Whitman. Ils Chasey. VG. C1. $12.50

KINZIE, Mrs. J.H. *Wau-Bun: Early Day in the NW.* 1866. NY. 1st ed. 6 pls. 498 p. rebound. G. B2. $195.00

KINZIE, Mrs. J.H. *Wau-Bun: Early Day in the NW.* 1930. WI. 390 p. xl. fair. $8.00

KINZIE, Mrs. J.H. *Wau-Bun: Early Day in the NW.* 1932. Chicago. Lakeside Classic. 609 p. G. T5. $25.00

KIPLING, Rudyard. *Barrack Room Ballads.* 1909. Edinburgh Soc. Deluxe Ltd ed. VG. $20.00

KIPLING, Rudyard. *Benefactors.* 1930. NY. Ltd ed. 1/91. VG. $25.00

KIPLING, Rudyard. *Book of Words.* 1928. NY. dj. EX. $45.00

KIPLING, Rudyard. *Captains Courageous.* 1897. London. 1st ed. AEG. blue bdg. $90.00

KIPLING, Rudyard. *Collected Verse.* 1910. NY. Doubleday. Ils Robinson. 1st ed. J2. $125.00

KIPLING, Rudyard. *Day's Work.* 1898. NY. 1st Am ed. VG. $25.00

KIPLING, Rudyard. *Departmental Ditties.* c 1890. NY. US Book/Lovell. 1st Am ed. $250.00

KIPLING, Rudyard. *France at War.* 1915. Doubleday Page. VG. scarce. $40.00

KIPLING, Rudyard. *From Sea to Sea: Letters of Travel.* 1899. NY. 1st ed. 2 vols. VG. $45.00

KIPLING, Rudyard. *Indian Tales.* 1899. NY. Oriental ed. 8vo. TEG. G. T1. $25.00

KIPLING, Rudyard. *Jungle Book Vol. 1.* nd. BOMC. dj. VG. P1. $4.00

KIPLING, Rudyard. *Jungle Book Vol. 1.* nd. Doubleday. VG. P1. $5.00

KIPLING, Rudyard. *Kim.* 1901. London. 1st ed. VG. $75.00

KIPLING, Rudyard. *Life's Handicap.* 1891. London. 1st ed. olive cloth. VG. $45.00

KIPLING, Rudyard. *Limits & Renewals.* 1932. London. 1st ed. dj. VG. $35.00

KIPLING, Rudyard. *Many Inventions.* 1893. London. 1st ed. VG. $75.00

KIPLING, Rudyard. *Plain Tales From the Hills.* 1888. Calcutta. inscr. VG. $225.00

KIPLING, Rudyard. *Soldiers Three.* nd. NY. Cameo Classic. boxed. EX. $15.00

KIPLING, Rudyard. *Something of Myself.* 1937. Doubleday. VG. $24.00

KIPLING, Rudyard. *Song of the English.* 1909. Doubleday Page. Ils Robinson. VG. J2. $250.00

KIPLING, Rudyard. *Songs From Books.* 1912. NY. 1st Am ed. dj. VG. $30.00

KIPLING, Rudyard. *Songs of the Sea.* 1927. Doubleday. Ils Maxwell. 99 p. G. $37.50

KIPLING, Rudyard. *Stalky & Co.* 1899. NY. Ils 1st Am ed. 310 p. TEG. G. T5. $15.00

KIPLING, Rudyard. *Stalky & Co.* 1899. NY. 1st Am ed. dj. VG. $25.00

KIPLING, Rudyard. *With the Night Mail.* 1909. NY. 1st ed. EX. $100.00

KIPLING, Rudyard. *Works of Rudyard Kipling.* 1920-1923. NY. Scribner. 26 vols. $250.00

KIPLING, Rudyard. *Works of Rudyard Kipling.* 1899. Century Doubleday McClure. 15 vols. $100.00

KIPLING, Rudyard. *Years Between.* 1919. London. Ltd ed. 1/200. $75.00

KIPLING, Rudyard. *Years Between.* 1919. NY. 1st Am ed. $25.00

KIPLING & BALESTIR. *Naulahka: Story of W & E.* 1902. NY. 1st ed. VG. $25.00

KIRBY, R.L. *Confederate Invasion of NM & AZ, 1861-1862.* 1956. LA. Westernlore. 1/850. dj. M. $45.00

KIRBY, R.S. *Engineering in History.* 1956. McGraw Hill. 1st ed. VG. J2. $22.50

KIRBY, W.G. *Butterflies & Moths of the United Kingdom.* 1900. London. Rutledge. Ils. 463 p. EX. M2. $38.00

KIRBY & SPENCE. *Entomology.* 1818. London. 3rd ed. 4 vols. $125.00

KIRK, M.L. *Dog of Flanders.* 1909. Lippincott. Ils. VG. B4. $30.00

KIRK, M.L. *Little Lame Prince.* 1918. Lippincott. Ils. dj. B4. $15.00

KIRK, M.W. *Locust Hill.* 1976. AL U. Ils 2nd print. dj. $12.50

KIRK, Michael. *Cut in Diamonds.* 1986. Doubleday Crime Club. dj. VG. P1. $12.00

KIRK, Michael. *Mayday From Malaga.* 1983. Doubleday Book Club. VG. P1. $7.50

KIRK, Michael. *Mayday From Malaga.* 1983. Crime Club. 1st ed. dj. VG. P1. $12.50

KIRK, R. *Desert: American SW.* 1973. Houghton. Review of 1st print. 361 p. dj. M2. $23.00

KIRK, R. *Hunters of Whale: Adventure of NW Coast Archaeology.* 1974. Morrow. Ils. 160 p. dj. EX. M2. $12.00

KIRK, Russell. *Lord of the Hollow Dark.* 1979. St. Martin. 1st ed. dj. VG. P1. $15.00

KIRK, Russell. *Princess of All Lands.* 1979. Arkham House. 1st ed. dj. EX. P1. $15.00

KIRK & OTHMER. *Encyclopedia of Chemical Technology.* 1947. NY. 1st ed. 17 vols. EX. $495.00

KIRK. *Diseases of Cat.* 1925. 1st Am ed. EX. $24.00

KIRKBRIDGE, S.A. *Brief History of Kirkbride Family...1775-1830.* 1913. Alliance. Ils. 64 p. G. T5. $17.50

KIRKBRIDGE, T.S. *Kirkbride on Hospitals for the Insane.* 1880. Phil. sgn. TEG. xl. VG. $90.00

KIRKE, Edmund. *Among the Pines; or, S in Secession Time.* 1864. NY. VG. $22.50

KIRKE, Edmund. *Down in TN & Back by Way of Richmond.* 1864. NY. VG. $22.50

KIRKLAND & KENNEDY. *Historic Camden.* nd. Columbia. 2 vols. xl. G. $40.00

KIRKMAN, M.M. *Building & Repairing Railroads.* 1906. NY. World RR Pub. $35.00

KIRKPATRICK, E.S. *Tales of the St. John River.* 1904. Toronto. Briggs. 132 p. M1. $17.50

KIRKPATRICK, O.B. *Station Agent's Blue Book.* 1928. Order RR Telegraphers. 523 p. EX. $23.50

KIRKUP, James. *These Horned Islands: Journal of Japan.* 1962. NY. Ils. 48 p. VG. $15.00

KIRKUP. *History of Socialism.* 1892. London. 1st ed. EX. $18.00

KIRKWOOD, James. *Some Kind of Hero.* 1975. NY. Crowell. 1st ed. dj. M. $15.00

KIRMSE, Marguerite. *Dogs in the Field.* 1935. Derrydale. 1/685. with portfolio. boxed. EX. $500.00

KIRMSE, Marguerite. *Dogs.* 1930. Derrydale. 1/750. pls. with sgn etching. EX. $350.00

KIRSCH & MURPHY. *W of the W.* 1967. NY. dj. VG. $15.00

KIRSTEIN, Lincoln. *Pavel Tchelitchew Drawings.* 1947. Bittner. Ils. D2. $75.00

KIRTLAND, L.S. *Samurai Trails: Wandering on Japanese High Road.* 1918. Doran. Ils. 300 p. EX. M2. $14.00

KIRWAN, Richard. *Metaphysical Essays.* 1811. London. rebound. EX. $125.00

KISSINGER, Henry. *White House Years.* 1979. Boston. 1st ed. sgn. 1521 p. slipcase. EX. T5. $25.00

KITCHIN, George. *Prisoner of the OGPU (Siberian Gulag).* 1935. NY. AP. 1st ed. 8vo. 336 p. wraps. dj. T1. $100.00

KITCHIN, W.C. *Wonderland of the E.* 1920. Boston. 1st imp. maps. TEG. VG. $25.00

KITT, Eartha. *Thursday's Child.* 1958. London. Lansborough. 1st pb ed. 191 p. $10.00

KITTE, John. *Pictorial Sunday Book.* 1845. London. Ils. 12 maps. folio. $50.00

KITTON, F.G. *Dickens & His Illustrators.* 1972. Amsterdam. Emmering. reprint. 4to. VG. $25.00

KITTREDGE, Henry. *Cape Cod: Its People & Their History.* 1930. Houghton. Ils. G. $35.00

KITZIMMER, H.H. *One Hundred Years of W Reserve.* 1926. Hudson, OH. Ils Pogany. 52 p. wraps. fair. T5. $15.00

KIZER, C. *Ungrateful Garden.* 1961. Bloomington. 1st ed. inscr. wraps. $40.00

KLABER, Doretta. *Violets.* 1976. Barnes. Ils. 108 pls. folio. 208 p. dj. EX. $30.00

KLANE, Robert. *Where's Poppa?* 1970. 1st ed. dj. VG. B2. $22.50

KLANE, Robert. *Where's Poppa?* 1970. NY. 1st ed. dj. EX. B2. $35.00

KLARSFELD, Serge. *Children of Izieu.* NY. pb. (sealed) EX. $5.00

KLAUSNITZER, B. *Beetles.* 1983. Exeter. Ils 1st Am ed. square 4to. dj. M2. $24.00

KLEE, Paul. *On Modern Art.* 1948. London. Faber. 2nd print. D2. $28.50

KLEES, F. *PA Dutch.* 1950. NY. Review 1st ed. dj. VG. B2. $25.00

KLEIN, Ernst. *Blackmailer.* 1952. Avon 404. pb. VG. P1. $6.00

KLEIN, Gerard. *Overlords of War.* nd. Book Club. dj. VG. P1. $3.00

KLEIN, Herb. *Lucky Bwana.* 1953. Ltd ed. inscr. dj. EX. $80.00

KLEIN, Maury. *Great Richmond Terminal.* 1970. Charlottesville. 323 p. $20.00

KLEIN, Maury. *Life & Legend of Jay Gould.* 1986. Ils. 595 p. $21.50

KLEIN, T. *Loon Magic.* 1985. Paper Birch Pr. Ils. oblong 4to. 146 p. dj. EX. M2. $33.00

KLEIN, William. *Moscow.* 1964. NY. Crown. 1st ed. folio. VG. $125.00

KLEIN & KLEIN. *Kaethe Kollwitz: Life in Art.* 1972. Holt Rinehart. Ils 1st ed. 193 p. D2. $28.50

KLEIN & KLEIN. *OH River Handbook.* 1949. Cincinnati. Ils. 240 p. wraps. VG. T5. $9.50

KLEIN & KLEIN. *Peter Bruegel the Elder: Artist of Abundance.* 1968. NY. Macmillan. Ils. 188 p. dj. D2. $22.50

KLEIN. *NY Central System.* nd. Bonanza. dj. EX. $16.50

KLEMIN, Diana. *Art of Art for Children's Books.* 1966. Potter. 1st ed. 128 p. dj. VG. $15.00

KLEMIN, Diana. *Illustrated Books: Its Art & Craft.* 1970. Potter. 1st ed. 4to. 159 p. dj. VG. $30.00

KLETZLEY, R.C. *American Woodcock in WV.* 1976. WV Nat Resources. 46 p. M2. $6.00

KLIMO, Kate. *Labor Pains.* 1988. NY. 1st ed. dj. VG. $10.00

KLINE, Otis Adelbert. *Maza of Moon.* 1930. Chicago. dj. EX. $45.00

KLINE, Otis Adelbert. *Prince of Peril.* 1962. Avalon. dj. EX. P1. $25.00

KLINE, Otis Adelbert. *Prince of Peril.* 1962. Avalon. dj. xl. P1. $7.50

KLINGER, Max. *Malerei & Zeichnungen.* nd. Leipzig. Insel. D2. $18.50

KLIPPART, J.H. *Wheat Plant.* 1860. Cincinnati. Ils 1st ed. 706 p. T5. $25.00

KLOOT & MC CULLOUCH. *Birds of Australian Gardens.* 1980. Rigby. Ils Trusler. 1st ed. folio. dj. M2. $30.00

KLOSKY, B.A. *Pendleton Legacy.* 1971. Columbia. Sandlapper Pr. 1st ed. 4to. 110 p. $27.50

KLOTS, A.B. *Field Guide to Butterflies of N America E of Great Plains.* 1951. Houghton. Ils. 349 p. dj. EX. M2. $15.00

KLUGE, P.F. *Eddie & the Cruisers.* 1980. NY. 1st ed. dj. EX. $20.00

KLUMPKE, Anna. *Rosa Bonheur: Sa Vie, Son Oeuvre.* 1909. Paris. Flammarion. sgn. 445 p. D2. $450.00

KNAPF, J.L. *Travels & Missionary Labors: 18 Years in E Africa.* 1860. Boston. 1st Am ed. map. 464 p. $85.00

KNAPP, H.S. *History of Maumee Valley.* 1872. Toledo. Ils 1st ed. 667 p. rebound. xl. $45.00

KNAPP, S.L. *Lectures on American Literature.* 1829. NY. $100.00

KNATCHBULL-HUGESSEN, E.H. *Puss-Cat Mew & Other Stories for My Children.* 1871. NY. Ils. 317 p. G. $45.00

KNEALE, Nigel. *Year of the Sex Olympics.* 1976. Ferret Fantasy. 1st ed. dj. EX. P1. $12.50

KNEBEL. *Night of Camp David.* 1965. NY. 1st ed. dj. VG. $30.00

KNECHT, K. *Designing & Maintaining the CATV & Small TV Studio.* 1976. Blue Ridge Summit. 2nd ed. 297 p. $17.50

KNIGGE. *Brain-Endocrine Interaction: Median Eminese.* 1972. Basel. 368 p. $44.00

KNIGHT, Adam. *Girl Running.* 1956. Signet. EX. P1. $10.00

KNIGHT, Adam. *I'll Kill You Next.* 1954. Appleton. 1st ed. dj. VG. P1. $8.00

KNIGHT, Charles. *Shadows of the Old Booksellers.* 1865. London. 1st ed. $45.00

KNIGHT, Clifford. *Affair of the Limping Sailor.* 1942. Dodd Mead. VG. P1. $20.00

KNIGHT, Clifford. *Affair of the Splintered Heart.* 1942. Doubleday Book Club. VG. P1. $12.00

KNIGHT, Clifford. *Death of a Big Shot.* 1951. Dutton. 1st ed. dj. VG. P1. $12.50

KNIGHT, Damon. *Beyond Tomorrow.* 1965. Harper Row. 1st ed. dj. VG. P1. $20.00

KNIGHT, Damon. *Beyond Tomorrow.* 1965. Harper Row. 1st ed. dj. xl. P1. $5.00

KNIGHT, Damon. *Futurians.* nd. Book Club. dj. VG. P1. $5.00

KNIGHT, Damon. *Orbit 10.* 1972. Putnam. 1st ed. dj. VG. P1. $12.50

KNIGHT, Damon. *Orbit 12.* 1973. Putnam. 1st ed. dj. VG. P1. $9.25

KNIGHT, Damon. *Orbit 19.* 1977. Harper Row. 1st ed. dj. EX. P1. $10.00

KNIGHT, Damon. *Orbit 5.* 1969. Putnam. 1st ed. dj. xl. P1. $5.00

KNIGHT, Damon. *Orbit 7.* nd. Book Club. dj. VG. P1. $4.00

KNIGHT, Damon. *Three Novels.* nd. Book Club. dj. VG. P1. $2.75

KNIGHT, Damon. *Tomorrow & Tomorrow.* Simon Schuster. 2nd ed. VG. P1. $10.00

KNIGHT, Eric. *Flying Yorkshire.* 1938. Harper. 1st ed. dj. VG. P1. $10.00

KNIGHT, Eric. *Sam Small Flies Again.* 1942. Harper. 1st ed. P1. $15.00

KNIGHT, J.A. *Field Book of Fresh-Water Angling.* 1944. NY. 1st ed. 139 p. VG. T5. $15.00

KNIGHT, Kathleen Moore. *Intrigue for Empire.* 1944. Crime Club. 1st ed. dj. EX. P1. $12.50

KNIGHT, Kathleen Moore. *Port of Seven Strangers.* 1945. Doubleday Book Club. dj. VG. P1. $10.00

KNIGHT, Kathleen Moore. *Robineau Look.* 1955. Doubleday Book Club. VG. P1. $7.50

KNIGHT, Kathleen Moore. *Seven Were Veiled.* 1937. Crime Club. 1st ed. G. P1. $17.50

KNIGHT, Kathleen Moore. *Tainted Token.* 1939. Sun Dial. VG. P1. $17.50

KNIGHT, Kathleen Moore. *Trademark of a Traitor.* 1943. Crime Club. 1st ed. xl. P1. $6.00

KNIGHT, Ora. *Birds of ME.* 1908. Bangor. Ils. VG. $65.00

KNIGHT, R.P. *Discourse on Worship of Priapus.* 1875. London. TEG. VG. $95.00

KNIGHT, T.A. *Strange Disappearance of William Morgan.* 1932. NY. Ils 1st ed. sgn. 302 p. G. T5. $22.50

KNIGHT, W.C. *Birds of WY.* 1902. WY U. Ils Frank Bond. 172 p. VG. M2. $25.00

KNIGHT & KNIGHT. *Complete Book of Fly Casting.* 1963. NY. dj. VG. $20.00

KNIGHT PUBLISHING. *Yellow Spot.* 1936. NY. Ils. 287 p. G. $15.00

KNIGHT. *Ruffed Grouse.* 1947. Knopf. 1/210. dj. boxed. with sgn pls. B2. $295.00

KNIPE, H.R. *Nebula to Man.* 1905. London. pls. 4to. VG. $50.00

KNITTLE, R.M. *Early OH Taverns.* 1937. Ashland, OH. 46 p. VG. T5. $25.00

KNOBLOCH, Philip. *Good Practice in Construction. Part I.* 1923. NY. tall 4to. 52 p. VG. $45.00

KNOPF, Alfred. *Portrait of a Publisher, 1915-1965.* 1965. Typophiles. 1st ed. 2 vols. djs. boxed. VG. J2. $50.00

KNOPF, Richard. *Ancedotes of the Lake Erie Area, War of 1812.* 1957. Columbus. 4to. 63 p. T5. $19.50

KNOTT, William C. *Journey Across the Third Planet.* 1969. Chilton. 1st ed. dj. VG. P1. $12.50

KNOTTNERUS-MEYER, T. *Birds & Beasts of the Roman Zoo.* 1928. Century. photos. 378 p. G. M2. $5.00

KNOWLES, David. *English Mystical Tradition.* 1965. 1st pb ed. VG. C1. $6.50

KNOWLES, F.L. *Treasury of Humorous Poetry.* 1902. Dana Estes. Ils. G. $12.50

KNOWLES, J. *King Arthur & His Knights.* 1986. Ils Louis Rhead. M. C1. $10.00

KNOWLES, John. *Double Vision.* 1964. NY. 1st ed. dj. VG. $9.00

KNOWLES, John. *Morning in Antibes.* 1962. London. 1st ed. dj. EX. $45.00

KNOWLES, John. *Morning in Antibes.* 1962. London. 1st ed. dj. VG. $35.00

KNOWLES, John. *Private Life of Axie Reed.* 1986. NY. 1st ed. dj. EX. $9.00

KNOWLES, John. *Stolen Past.* 1983. NY. 1st ed. dj. M. $12.00

KNOWLES, Joseph. *Alone in the Wilderness.* 1913. Sm Maynard. photos. 295 p. VG. M2. $23.00

KNOX, Bill. *Bloodtide.* 1982. Hutchinson. dj. xl. P1. $5.00

KNOX, Bill. *Draw Batons!* 1973. Doubleday Crime Club. dj. VG. P1. $15.00

KNOX, Bill. *Sanctuary Isle.* 1962. John Long. 1st ed. dj. xl. P1. $6.00

KNOX, Bill. *Stormtide.* 1973. Crime Club. 1st ed. dj. VG. P1. $10.00

KNOX, Bill. *To Kill a Witch.* 1971. John Long. 1st ed. dj. xl. P1. $6.00

KNOX, Jennifer. *Lyle Official Arts Review.* 1983. 1st ed. dj. EX. $25.00

KNOX, Ronald A. *Footsteps at the Lock.* 1950. Methuen. 5th ed. dj. G. P1. $15.00

KNOX, T.W. *Siberian Exiles.* 1893. NY. Ils Victor Perard. EX. $10.00

KNOX & BOYD. *View From Daniel Pike.* 1974. St. Martin. 1st ed. dj. xl. P1. $7.50

KNYSTAUTAS, A. *Natural History of the USSR.* 1987. McGraw Hill. Ils 1st ed. 224 p. dj. EX. M2. $29.00

KNYVETON, John. *Diary of a Surgeon in Year 1751-1752.* 1937. Heinemann. 1st ed. dj. VG. $40.00

KNYVETON, John. *Diary of a Surgeon in Year 1751-1752.* 1937. NY. Appleton. 9 pls. dj. EX. $50.00

KOBAYSHI, K. *Birds of Japan in Natural Colors.* 1956. Osaka. Ils Miyamoto. dj. slipcase. EX. M2. $23.00

KOBBE, Gustav. *Famous Actors & Actresses & Their Homes.* 1903. Little Brown. TEG. VG. $25.00

KOBLER, J. *Capone.* 1971. Putnam. dj. VG. $24.00

KOCH, A.C. *Journey Through Part of US of N America in 1844-1846.* 1972. S IL U. Ils 1st ed. dj. EX. M2. $20.00

KOCH, Alexander. *Deutsche Kunst und Dekoration.* c 1896. Darmstadt. pls. $40.00

KOCH, Frederick. *Carolina Folk Plays.* 1922-1928. Holt. 1st ed. 3 vols. djs. VG. J2. $75.00

KOCH, K.P. *Folio of Cultural, Commercial & Industrial Symbols...* 1949. Bielefeld Studios. pls. portfolio. $40.00

KOCH, Robert. *Louis C. Tiffany: Rebel in Glass.* 1982. Crown. Revised 3rd ed. dj. M. $50.00

KOCH, T.W. *Les Livres a al Guerre.* 1920. Paris. presentation. sgn. morocco. wraps. $40.00

KOCH, T.W. *Notes on German Book Exhibit.* 1925. Chicago. Ils. xl. $35.00

KOEHLER, S.R. *American Art.* 1886. NY. 25 pls. 58 p. AEG. VG. T5. $395.00

KOESTER, Jane. *Writer's Market 75.* 1974. Writer's Digest. P1. $6.00

KOESTLER, Arthur. *Act of Creation.* 1964. NY. Macmillan. dj. EX. $25.00

KOESTLER, Arthur. *Age of Longing.* 1951. NY. 1st ed. dj. VG. B2. $15.00

KOESTLER, Arthur. *Age of Longing.* 1951. NY. 1st ed. inscr/sgn. dj. M. $60.00

KOESTLER, Arthur. *Darkness at Noon.* 1941. NY. 1st ed. dj. G. $30.00

KOESTLER, Arthur. *Darkness at Noon.* 1979. Franklin Lib. 1st ed. sgn. full leather. EX. $60.00

KOESTLER, Arthur. *Darkness at Noon.* 1984. London. Folio Soc. Ils Buday. slipcase. C1. $14.00

KOESTLER, Arthur. *Insight & Outlook.* 1949. NY. 1st ed. dj. VG. B2. $20.00

KOESTLER, Arthur. *Reflections on Hanging.* 1957. NY. 1st ed. dj. VG. $25.00

KOFOID, C.A. *On the Early Development of Limax.* 1895. Harvard. 8 pls. 118 p. M2. $8.00

KOGAN, Herman. *Traditions & Challenges: Story of Sidley & Austin.* 1983. Chicago. Ils 1st ed. 4to. TEG. slipcase. T1. $40.00

KOHL, J.G. *Travels in Canada.* 1861. London. 2 vols. EX. $225.00

KOHLER, Wolfgang. *Gestalt Psychology.* 1929. NY. Liveright. 1st Am ed. EX. $90.00

KOHLER, Wolfgang. *Mentality of Apes.* 1931. NY. Ils. VG. $12.00

KOHN, B.E. *Status & Management of Black Bears in WI.* 1982. WI Nat Resources. Ils. 31 p. M2. $3.00

KOHNER, F. *Gidget, Little Girl With Big Ideas.* 1957. Putnam. dj. VG. $6.00

KOHNER, Hanna & Walter. *Hanna & Walter: A Love Story.* 1984. NY. 1st ed. dj. EX. $6.50

KOKKINEN, Eils. *Lionel Feininger: Ruin by the Sea.* 1968. MOMA. 1st ed. stiff paper wraps. D2. $9.50

KOKOSCHKA, Oskar. *Die Traumenden Knaben.* 1968. Vienna/Munich. facsimile of 1908 ed. 1/2500. D2. $125.00

KOLBE, H. *Ornamental Waterfowl.* 1979. Gresham. Ils 1st Eng ed. dj. EX. M2. $25.00

KOLLER, Lawrence. *Shots at Whitetales.* 1970. Knopf. reprint. dj. G. $30.00

KOLLMAN, Franz. *Schonheit der Technik.* 1928. Munich. cloth bdg. J2. $37.50

KOLLWITZ, Hans. *Diary & Letters of Kaethe Kollwitz.* 1955. Chicago. Regnery. 1st Am ed. 223 p. D2. $85.00

KOLLWITZ, Hans. *Diary & Letters of Kaethe Kollwitz.* 1955. Regnery. 1st ed. dj. VG. J2. $85.00

KOMAN, Victor. *Jehovah Contract.* 1987. Watts. 1st ed. dj. VG. P1. $16.95

KONIGSBURG, E.L. *Proud Taste for Scarlet & Miniver.* 1973. NY. 1st ed. 6th print. dj. M. C1. $11.00

KONODY, P.G. *Art of Walter Crane.* 1902. London. Bell. 16 pls. folio. TEG. $300.00

KOO, T.S.Y. *Studies of Red Salmon.* 1962. WA U. photos. maps. 449 p. EX. M2. $14.00

KOONTZ, D.R. *Bad Place.* 1990. NY. AP. $65.00

KOONTZ, D.R. *Check List of First Editions.* 1989. Pandora. VG. P1. $2.00

KOONTZ, D.R. *Door to December.* London. 1st HrdCvr ed. $45.00

KOONTZ, D.R. *Dragonfly.* 1975. Random House. 1st ed. dj. EX. $50.00

KOONTZ, D.R. *Flesh in the Furnace.* 1979. Bantam. 1st ed. pb. EX. $15.00

KOONTZ, D.R. *House of Thunder.* 1988. Dark Harvest. 1st ed. 1/450. sgn. dj. slipcase. $110.00

KOONTZ, D.R. *Mask.* London. 1st HrdCvr ed. M. $50.00

KOONTZ, D.R. *Oddkins.* 1988. Warner. 1st ed. dj. EX. P1. $17.95

KOPPER, P. *Wild Edge: Life & Lore of the Great Atlantic Beaches.* 1979. Times. Ils. 280 p. dj. EX. M2. $14.00

KORCZAK, Janusz. *King Matt the First.* 1986. NY. 1st ed. dj. EX. $8.50

KORMAN, Gerd. *Hunter & the Hunted.* 1974. NY. 1st pb ed. G. $3.00

KORNBLUTH, C.M. *Best of C.M. Kornbluth.* 1977. Taplinger. 1st ed. dj. EX. P1. $15.00

KORNBLUTH, C.M. *Rebel Voices: WWI Anthology.* 1965. 4to. dj. VG. $30.00

KORNBLUTH, C.M. *Syndic.* nd. Book Club. VG. P1. $2.50

KORNBLUTH, C.M. *Syndic.* 1953. Doubleday. 1st ed. xl. VG. P1. $12.50

KORNBLUTH, C.M. *Syndic.* 1964. Faber. dj. EX. P1. $10.00

KORNBLUTH, C.M. *Takeoff.* 1952. Doubleday. 1st ed. dj. VG. P1. $30.00

KORNFELD, Eberhard W. *Paul Klee in Bern: Aquarelle & Zeichnungen 1897-1915.* 1962. Stampfli. Ils. D2. $30.00

KORSON, George. *Black Rock: Mining Folklore of PA Dutch.* 1960. Baltimore. 1st ed. 453 p. dj. VG. $20.00

KORTRIGHT, F.H. *Ducks, Geese & Swans of N America.* Am Wildlife Inst. 2nd ed. VG. M2. $16.00

KORTRIGHT, F.H. *Ducks, Geese & Swans of N America.* 1943. Am Wildlife Inst. Ils 1st ed. M2. $20.00

KOSCHATZKY, OBERHUBER & KNAB. *Italian Drawings in Albertina.* 1971. Greenwich. NY Graphic Soc. 100 pls. 322 p. D2. $100.00

KOSINSKI, Jerzy. *Blind Date.* 1977. Boston. 1st ed. dj. VG. $15.00

KOSINSKI, Jerzy. *Cockpit.* 1975. Boston. 1st ed. dj. VG. $15.00

KOSINSKI, Jerzy. *Der Bemalte Vogel.* 1965. Munchen. 1st German ed. inscr. dj. EX. $150.00

KOSINSKI, Jerzy. *Devil Tree.* 1973. NY. 1st ed. dj. EX. $15.00

KOSINSKI, Jerzy. *Future Is Ours Comrad.* 1960. London. Bodley Head. 1st ed. dj. VG. $50.00

KOSINSKI, Jerzy. *Painted Bird.* 1966. London. 1st ed. dj. VG. $45.00

KOSINSKI, Jerzy. *Passion Play.* 1979. NY. 1st ed. dj. EX. $15.00

KOSINSKI, Jerzy. *Passion Play.* 1979. NY. 1st ed. sgn. dj. EX. $40.00

KOSINSKI, Jerzy. *Steps.* 1968. Random House. 1st ed. dj. EX. $35.00

KOSINSKI, Jerzy. *Steps.* 1969. London. 1st ed. dj. VG. $40.00

KOSTER, W.J. *Guide to the Fishes of NM.* 1957. NM U. Ils 1st ed. 116 p. G. M2. $6.00

KOTZWINKLE, William. *Exile.* 1987. Dutton. AP. 1st ed. wraps. EX. $15.00

KOTZWINKLE, William. *Fata Morgana.* 1977. NY. 1st ed. dj. EX. $20.00

KOTZWINKLE, William. *Jack in the Box.* 1980. Putnam. 1st ed. dj. VG. P1. $12.50

KOUNTZ, W.J. *Billy Baxter's Letters.* c 1899. Duquesne Dist Co. Ils Hazenplug. $15.00

KOURY, M.J. *To Consecrate This Ground.* 1978. Ft. Collins. photos. 46 p. wraps. G. T5. $3.50

KOUWENHOVEN, John. *Adventures of America: 1857-1900.* 1938. NY. Ils. 4to. VG. $25.00

KOUWENHOVEN, John. *Columbia Historical Portrait of NY.* 1953. Doubleday. 1st ed. VG. J2. $40.00

KOVACS, Ernie. *Zooman.* 1957. NY. 1st ed. dj. VG. B2. $17.50

KOWALCZYK, Georg. *Decorative Sculpture.* 1927. London. 320 photos. J2. $50.00

KOWALCZYK & KOLL. *Fachkunde der Parfumerie und Kosmetik.* 1957. Leipzig. 358 p. dj. $25.00

KOWALIK, E.E. *Alone & Unarmed.* 1968. NY. 1st ed. sgn. 317 p. dj. T5. $32.50

KOZAKIEWICZ, S.B. *Bellotto.* 1972. London. 4to. 2vols. djs. slipcase. EX. J2. $250.00

KOZOL, Jonathan. *Death at an Early Age.* 1967. Boston. Mifflin. 1st ed. 240 p. dj. M1. $8.50

KRAEMER, R.S. *Drawings of Benjamin W.* 1975. NY. Morgan Lib. 1st ed. 4to. 231 p. EX. $13.00

KRAFT, J.L. *Adventure in Jade.* NY. 1/1500. gilt green cloth. EX. T1. $45.00

KRAKEL, D.F. *Saga of Tom Horn: Story of a Cattlemen's War.* 1988. NE U. 274 p. EX. M2. $18.00

KRAMER, E.L. *Pathway to Power.* 1952. MI. $16.00

KRAMER, F. *White House Gardens.* 1973. NY. 1st print. beige cloth. $15.00

KRAMER, Jack. *Cacti & Other Succulents.* 1977. Abrams. Ils Don Worth. sm folio. dj. $35.00

KRAMER, R.J. *HI Land Mammals.* 1971. Tuttle. Ils 1st ed. 347 p. dj. EX. M2. $13.00

KRANTZ, Judith. *Till We Meet Again.* 1988. Crown. UCP. wraps. EX. $20.00

KRASHES, Laurence. *Harry Winston: Ultimate Jeweler.* 1986. NY. Revised 2nd ed. dj. EX. $50.00

KRASNEY, S.A. *Death Cries in the Street.* 1956. Popular 749. pb. VG. P1. $5.00

KRATVILLE, W.W. *Steam, Steel & Limiteds.* 1962. Ils 1st ed. 413 p. $50.00

KRAUS, George. *High Road to Promontory.* 1969. Palo Alto. Ils 1st ed. 184 p. dj. VG. T5. $22.50

KRAUS, Rene. *Men Around Churchill.* 1941. Lippincott. 1st ed. red cloth. dj. VG. D1. $40.00

KRAUS & HUNT. *Tables for Determination of Minerals...* 1911. 254 p. G. $9.00

KRAUSE, Herbert. *Custer Prelude to Glory.* 1974. Brevet Pr. 1st ed. 279 p. dj. EX. $10.00

KRAUSE & THOMAS. *Tocharishches Elementarbuch.* 1960 & 1964. Heidelberg. German text. 2 vols. M. $35.00

KRAYBILL. *Mennonite Education.* 1978. Herald. pb. M. $4.50

KREADY, L.F. *Study of Fairy Tales.* 1916. Houghton. 313 p. G. $15.00

KREDEL, Fritz. *Anderson's Fairy Tales & Grimm's Fairy Tales.* 1945. Grosset Dunlap. 2 vols. slipcase. EX. $18.00

KREFTING, L.W. *Birds of Isle Royale in Lake Superior.* 1966. USFWS. Ils. map. 4to. 56 p. M2. $5.00

KREIG, Margaret. *Green Medicine.* 1964. Chicago. 4th print. dj. VG. $14.00

KREISLER, Fritz. *Four Weeks in the Trenches: War Story of a Violinist.* 1915. Boston. 1st ed. 86 p. VG. $35.00

KREPS, E. *Science of Trapping.* 1909. Columbus. Harding. Revised ed. VG. $17.00

KRESS, Nancy. *Alien Light.* 1987. Arbor House. UCP. inscr/sgn. dj. wraps. M. $40.00

KRESS, Nancy. *Golden Grove.* 1984. NY. Bluejay. 1st ed. inscr/sgn. dj. M. $30.00

KRICK, Robert. *Neale Books: Annotated Bibliography.* 1977. 234 p. gilt bdg. M. J4. $40.00

KRIEGER, L.C. *Mushroom Handbook.* 1936. Macmillan. Ils. 538 p. EX. M2. $15.00

KRISHNAI, B. *Shivaji the Great. Vol. 1.* 1932. Bombay. $65.00

KROEBER, Theodora. *Ishi in Two Worlds.* 1961. CA U. 1st ed. dj. scarce. J2. $40.00

KROEBER. *Almost Ancestors: First Californians.* 1968. dj. EX. S2. $35.00

KROLL, H.H. *I Was a Sharecropper.* 1937. Indianapolis. 1st ed. presentation. dj. VG. $45.00

KRON, Karl. *Ten Thousand Miles on a Bicycle.* 1887. NY. Autograph ed. sgn. T5. $95.00

KRONHAUSEN, Phyllis. *Erotic Art 2.* 1970. NY. Grove. Ils Grosz. 1st print. dj. D2. $50.00

KRONHAUSEN, Phyllis. *Erotic Art: Survey of Erotic Fact & Fancy in Fine Arts.* 1968. NY. Grove. 1st print. dj. D2. $55.00

KRONHAUSEN & KRONHAUSEN. *Complete Book of Erotic Art.* Ils. pls. 2 vols. VG. E2. $35.00

KRONSBERG, J.J. *Every Which Way But Loose.* 1979. Warner. Movie pb ed. VG. P1. $37.50

KROTT, P. *Demon of the N.* c 1958. Knopf. Standard 1st Am ed. dj. G. $20.00

KRUEGER. *I Was Hitler's Doctor.* 1953. NY. dj. VG. $12.00

KRUGER, Paul. *Bullet for a Blond.* 1958. Dell. 1st ed. pb. EX. P1. $15.00

KRUGER, Paul. *Finish Line.* 1968. Simon Schuster. 1st ed. dj. VG. P1. $7.00

KRUGER, Paul. *Message From Marise.* 1963. Gold Medal. pb. VG. P1. $4.50

KRUSEN. *Handbook of Physical Medicine & Rehabilitation.* 1971. 2nd ed. 4to. 920 p. VG. $35.00

KRUSI, Hermann. *Pestalozzi: His Life & Influence.* c 1875. Cincinnati/NY. 248 p. xl. $45.00

KRUTCH, J.W. *Baja, CA & the Geography of Hope.* 1967. Sierra Club. Ils. 160 p. M2. $7.00

KRUTCH, J.W. *Best Nature Writings of Joseph Wood Krutch.* 1970. Morrow. 384 p. dj. EX. M2. $10.00

KRUTCH, J.W. *Forgotten Peninsula: Naturalist in Baja, CA.* 1961. Sloane. Ils. map. 277 p. dj. EX. M2. $19.00

KRUTCH, J.W. *Gardener's World.* 1959. NY. 1st ed. dj. VG. $20.00

KRUTCH, J.W. *Henry David Thoreau.* 1948. Duell Sloan. 1st ed. dj. VG. J2. $17.50

KRUTCH & ERIKSSON. *Treasury of Bird Lore.* 1962. Doubleday. Ils 1st ed. 390 p. dj. EX. M2. $12.00

KUBLER, George. *History of Stereotyping.* 1941. NY. $30.00

KUCERA, C.L. *Grasses of MO.* 1961. MO U. Ils. 241 p. EX. M2. $18.00

KUCK, Loraine. *World of the Japanese Garden.* 1968. Tokyo. Walker Weatherhill. 1st ed. dj. EX. $40.00

KUCZYNSKI. *Labor Conditions in Great Britain: 1750-Present.* 1964. dj. VG. $15.00

KUDO, R.R. *Protozoology.* 1971. Thomas. Ils. 1174 p. EX. M2. $20.00

KUEBLER, Harold. *Treasury of SF Classics.* 1954. Hanover House. 1st ed. VG. P1. $12.50

KUES, Maurice. *Tolstoi Vivant.* 1940. Lausanne. VG. $55.00

KUHN, Charles L. *German & Netherlandish Sculpture 1200-1800.* 1965. Cambridge. Harvard. Ils. 146 p. D2. $55.00

KUHN, Fritz. *Kompositionen in Schwartz & Weiss.* 1959. Munich. dj. VG. $100.00

KUHN, Fritz. *Stufen.* 1964. Munich. Callwey. Ils. 155 p. D2. $45.00

KUHN, Herbert. *Die Kunst der Primitiven.* 1923. Munich. Delphin. Ils. D2. $120.00

KUHNE, Frederick. *Fingerprint Instructor.* 1916. NY. EX. P3. $45.00

KUHNS, William. *Memories of Old Canton.* 1937. np. 1st ed. inscr. 64 p. VG. T5. $27.50

KUHNS, William. *Movies in America.* 1975. London. Tantury. Ils. dj. EX. $25.00

KULYAR, S.P. *Swami Dayanand Saraswati.* 1914. India. $8.00

KUMIN, Maxine. *Designated Heir.* 1974. NY. 1st ed. dj. VG. $25.00

KUMIN, Maxine. *House, Bridge, Fountain, Gate.* 1975. NY. 1st ed. dj. RS. EX. $35.00

KUMIN, Maxine. *Nightmare Factory.* 1970. NY. 1st ed. sgn. dj. EX. $65.00

KUMIN, Maxine. *Why Can't We Live Together Like Civilized Human Beings?* 1982. NY. Review 1st ed. sgn. RS. EX. $55.00

KUMMER, F.A. *Clue of the Twisted Fact.* Detective Novel Classic. VG. P1. $12.50

KUMMER, F.A. *Design for Murder.* nd. Arrow Mystery. pb. P1. $12.50

KUMMER, F.A. *First Days of Knowledge.* 1923. Doran. 1st ed. VG. P1. $20.00

KUMMER, F.A. *Ladies in Hades.* nd. Grosset Dunlap. VG. P1. $7.50

KUMMER, F.A. *Song of Sixpence.* 1913. Watt. 1st ed. VG. P1. $10.00

KUNDERA, Milan. *Joke.* 1969. NY. 1st ed. dj. EX. $75.00

KUNZ, G.F. *Magic of Jewels & Charms.* 1915. Phil. pls. $80.00

KUNZ, G.F. *Shakespeare & Precious Stones.* 1916. Lippincott. 1st ed. sgn. VG. J2. $40.00

KUNZ, G.F. *Shakespeare & Precious Stones.* 1916. Lippincott. 1st ed. VG. J2. $35.00

KUNZ, T.H. *Ecological & Behavioral Methods for Study of Bats.* 1988. Smithsonian. photos. 533 p. dj. M. M2. $45.00

KUP, Karl. *Christmas Story.* 1956. NY. Typophiles. VG. $25.00

KUPPER & ROSHARDT. *Cacti.* 1960. London. Nelson. Ils. 4to. 127 p. EX. M2. $22.00

KUPRIN, Alexandre. *Yama.* 1922. NY. private print. 1/1335. G. $15.00

KURETSKY, Susan Donahue. *Paintings of Jacob Ochtervelt.* 1979. Oxford. Phaidon. Ils. 245 p. dj. D2. $65.00

KURSH, Harry. *Cobras in His Garden.* 1965. Harvey House. 192 p. dj. VG. $10.00

KURT, J.V. *Breakfast of Champions.* Delacorte. dj. EX. $50.00

KURT, J.V. *Happy Birthday Wanda June.* nd. Delacorte. 2nd ed. dj. EX. $70.00

KURT, J.V. *Player Piano.* 1952. Scribner. A ed. VG. $110.00

KURT, J.V. *Slaughterhouse Five.* 1978. Franklin Lib. Ltd ed. 5 sgns. $100.00

KURTZ, Katherine. *Bishop's Heir.* 1984. Del Rey. 1st ed. dj. EX. P1. $15.00

KURTZ, Katherine. *Camber of Culdi.* 1979. Del Rey. 1st ed. dj. EX. P1. $15.00

KURTZ, Katherine. *King's Justice.* 1985. Del Rey. 1st ed. dj. EX. P1. $17.50

KURTZ, Katherine. *Legacy of Lehr.* 1986. Walker. 1st ed. dj. EX. P1. $15.95

KURTZ, Katherine. *Saint Camber.* 1978. Del Rey. dj. EX. P1. $15.00

KURZ, Otto. *Fakes: Handbook for Collectors & Students.* 1948. Faber. 1st ed. dj. VG. J2. $20.00

KUSHNER, Sam. *Long Road to Delano.* 1975. NY. 1st ed. dj. VG. $15.00

KUTAK, Rosemary. *Darkness of Slumber.* 1946. Pocket 402. 2nd ed. EX. P1. $20.00

KUTSCHE, Paul. *Guide to Cherokee Documents in NE US.* Scarecrow Pr. 531 p. VG. T5. $25.00

KUTTNER, Henry. *Man Drowning.* 1952. Harper. 1st ed. dj. VG. P1. $25.00

KUTTNER, Henry. *Murder of Ann Avery.* 1956. Perma. VG. pb. P1. $15.00

KYLE, David. *Illustrated Book of SF Ideas & Dream.* 1977. Hamlyn. dj. EX. P1. $15.00

KYLE, David. *Pictorial History of SF.* 1977. Hamlyn. 2nd ed. EX. P1. $12.50

KYLE, Duncan. *Black Camelot.* 1978. 1st ed. dj. EX. C1. $9.00

KYLE, Duncan. *Stalking Point.* 1981. St. Martin. 1st ed. dj. EX. P1. $12.50

KYLE, Duncan. *Terror's Cradle.* 1975. Collins. 1st ed. dj. VG. P1. $10.00

KYLE, Robert. *Crooked City.* 1954. Dell. 1st ed. EX. P1. $10.00
KYLE, Robert. *Tiger in the Night.* 1955. Dell. 1st ed. EX. P1. $15.00

KYNE, Peter B. *Enchanted Hill.* 1924. Cosmopolitan. VG. P1. $25.00

KYNE, Peter B. *Never the Twain Shall Meet.* 1923. Grosset Dunlap. sgn. $15.00

KYNE, Peter B. *Valley of the Giants.* nd. Grosset Dunlap. G. P1. $6.00

KYNER, J.H. *End of the Track.* 1937. 117 p. $15.00

KYPER, Frank. *Railroad That Came Out at Night.* 1977. 160 p. $12.50

KYRIAZI, Gary. *Great American Amusement Parks.* 1976. Secaucus, NJ. Ils. 256 p. dj. VG. $30.00

KYTLE, Elizabeth. *Willie Mae.* 1958. Knopf. 1st ed. 243 p. dj. $20.00

L

L'ABBE, C. *Chevalier Promenades Pitoresques en Touraine.* 1869. Tours. 124 woodcuts. $125.00

L'AMOUR, Louis. *Daybreakers.* 1981. 197 p. $19.00

L'AMOUR, Louis. *Ferguson Rifle.* 1982. 165 p. $19.00

L'AMOUR, Louis. *Flint.* Bantam. 6th ed. imitation leather bdg. VG. P1. $15.00

L'AMOUR, Louis. *Haunted Mesa.* 1987. HrdCvr. dj. $19.00

L'AMOUR, Louis. *Jubal Sackett.* 1985. NY. 1st ed. dj. VG. $8.00

L'AMOUR, Louis. *Last of the Breed.* 1986. HrdCvr ed. 359 p. dj. $22.00

L'AMOUR, Louis. *Waking Drum.* 1984. NY. 1st ed. inscr. dj. EX. $30.00

L'ENGLE, Madeleine. *And Both Were Young.* 1983. Delacorte. 1st ed. dj. VG. P1. $13.95

L'ENGLE, Madeleine. *Many Waters.* 1986. NY. 1st ed. sgn. dj. EX. $45.00

L'ENGLE, Madeleine. *Summer of Great-Grandmother.* 1974. NY. 1st ed. dj. VG. $35.00

L'ERMITE, Pierre. *Mighty Friend.* 1913. NY. Benziger. 1st ed. dj. VG. $65.00

LA CROIX, Paul. *Arts in the Middle Ages & the Renaissance.* 1964. NY. dj. VG. $16.00

LA FARGE, Oliver. *As Long As the Grass Shall Grow.* 1940. NY/Toronto. Alliance. 1st ed. 4to. dj. VG. $60.00

LA FARGE, Oliver. *Laughing Boy.* 1929. Boston. 1st ed. dj. $85.00

LA FARGE, Oliver. *Pictorial History of American Indian.* 1956. NY. Ils. sgn. 4to. 272 p. dj. EX. $25.00

LA FARGE, Oliver. *Sparkes Fly Upward.* 1931. Boston. 1st ed. dj. VG. B2. $22.50

LA GUARDIA, F. *Making of an Insurgent: Autobiography.* 1948. Lippincott. 1st ed. dj. VG. $25.00

LA MONT. *Little Black Sambo.* 1959. Whitman. 28 p. EX. $5.00

LA MOTTA, Jake. *Raging Bull.* 1970. Prentice Hall. 1st ed. dj. M. $55.00

LA POINTE, J. *Legends of the Dakota.* 1976. Indian Hist Pr. Ils. 159 p. EX. M2. $10.00

LA SALE. *Fifteen Joys of Marriage.* 1933. NY. Trans Addington. Ils. $15.00

LA VIOLETTE, W. *Bhagavad Gita, Immortal Song.* 1945. LA. $22.50

LABISKY, W.R. *Waterfowl Shooting.* 1954. NY. 1st ed. dj. VG. $15.00

LACKEY, W.F. *History of Newton Co., AR.* 1950. private print. Ils 1st ed. 482 p. VG. M2. $45.00

LACKEY, W.F. *Newton Co. Homestead.* 1959. Newton Co Hist Soc. EX. M2. $5.00

LACKNER, Stephan. *Max Beckmann.* 1983. NY. Crown. Ils. 96 p. D2. $14.95

LACKNER, Stephan. *Max Beckmann: Memories of a Friendship.* 1969. Coral Gables. Ils. 126 p. D2. $25.00

LACY, Norris. *Arthurian Encyclopedia.* 1986. 649 p. VG. C1. $49.50

LACY, Norris. *Arthurian Encyclopedia.* 1987. 649 p. pb. M. C1. $16.00

LACY & ASHE. *Arthurian Handbook.* 1988. pb. M. C1. $22.00

LADER, Lawrence. *Bold Brahmins.* 1961. NY. 1st ed. dj. EX. $15.00

LAENNEC, R.T.H. *Treatise on Diseases of Chest & Mediate Auscultation.* 1835. Phil/London. xl. rebound. EX. $225.00

LAFFERTY, R.A. *Nine Hundred Grandmothers.* 1975. Dobson. 1st ed. dj. VG. P1. $35.00

LAFFERTY, R.A. *Not To Mention Camels.* 1976. Bobbs Merrill. 1st ed. dj. EX. P1. $12.50

LAFFERTY, R.A. *Serpent's Egg.* 1987. Morrigan. 1st ed. dj. EX. P1. $22.50

LAFUENTE, Ferrair. *El Greco: Expressionism of His Final Years.* nd. NY. 172 pls. folio. dj. slipcase. J2. $300.00

LAGERLOF, Selma. *Legend of the Christmas Rose.* 1942. Doubleday. 1st ed. VG. B4. $20.00

LAHEE, F.H. *Field Geology.* 1941. NY. Ils. 8vo. 853 p. VG. $15.00

LAHEE, H.C. *Famous Singers of Today & Yesterday.* 1898. Boston. Page. 1st ed. $15.00

LAIDLER, K. & L. *River Wolf.* 1983. London. Allen Unwin. Ils 1st ed. dj. M2. $20.00

LAIDLER, L. *Otters in Britain.* 1982. David Charles. Ils 1st ed. dj. EX. M2. $25.00

LAIDLER. *Boycotts & the Labor Struggle.* 1913. inscr. VG. $35.00

LAIGHTON, Oscar. *90 Years at Isles of Shoals.* 1929. Andover. inscr. dj. VG. $25.00

LAINEZ, Manuel M. *Wandering Unicorn.* Book Club. Trans Fitton. dj. VG. C1. $3.50

LAING, Alexander. *Cadaver of Gideon Wyck.* 1942. Triangle. VG. P1. $10.00

LAING, Alexander. *Cadaver of Gideon Wyck.* 1960. Macmillan. 1st ed. dj. xl. P1. $7.50

LAING, Alexander. *Clipper Ship Men.* 1944. Duell Sloan. 279 p. $20.00

LAING, Janet. *Honeycombers.* nd. Hodder Stoughton. VG. P1. $8.00

LAING, Patrick. *Murder From the Mind.* 1947. Red Dagger. VG. P1. $12.50

LAING & LAING. *Serving a Nation at the Time.* 1946. London. Ils. 124 p. G. $22.50

LAIRD, Dorothy. *How the Queen Reigns.* 1959. London. VG. $8.50

LAIRD & GRAEBNER. *Hitler's Reich & Churchill's Britain.* 1942. Batsford. 1st ed. gray cloth. dj. VG. D1. $45.00

LAIT, Jack. *Big House.* nd. Grosset. Movie ed. VG. P1. $25.00

LAKE, Simon. *Submarine: Autobiography As Told to Herbert Corey.* 1939. NY. Ils 1st ed. VG. $40.00

LAKE, Stuart W. *Wyatt Earp: Frontier Marshal.* 1955. Boston. Houghton Mifflin. Ils. dj. VG. $15.00

LAKE & DUTTON. *Parenteral Therapy.* 1936. Charles Thomas. 1st ed. presentation. J2. $20.00

LAKENBY, C.H. *Tread of Pioneers.* 1945. Pilot Pr. Ils. 206 p. VG. A3. $30.00

LAKIN, Richard. *Body Fell on Berlin.* nd. Detective Novel Classic. VG. P1. $12.50

LALANNE, M.L. *Bibliotheque de Poche, par un Societe de Gens de Lettres...* 1857. Paris. orig wraps. $50.00

LAMANTIA, Philip. *Narcotica.* 1959. Auerhahn. AP. wraps. $60.00

LAMANTIA, Philip. *Touch of the Marvelous.* Oyez. 1966. dj. VG. $45.00

LAMAR, E. *Notes on a Paper Napkin.* 1980. Caldwell. 1st ed. dj. EX. $7.50

LAMB, Charles. *Essays of Elia.* 1888. London. Ils Railton. 1/100. EX. $35.00

LAMB, Charles. *Life, Letters & Writings of Charles Lamb.* nd. London. Ils Enfield. VG. $90.00

LAMB, Charles. *Living Phantom.* 1934. Omaha. Ltd ed. 1/100. wraps. $50.00

LAMB, Charles. *Rosamund Gray.* 1835. London. Moxon. 356 p. VG. $175.00

LAMB, Charles. *Tale of Rosamund Gray & Old Blind Margaret.* 1928. Golden Cockerel. 1/500. VG. $50.00

LAMB, Charles. *Tale of Rosamund Gray & Old Blind Margaret.* 1928. London. Golden Cockerel. 1/500. 12mo. EX. $65.00

LAMB, Charles. *Tales of Shakespeare.* 1909. Dent Dutton. Ils Rackham. 1st ed. EX. $75.00

LAMB, D.S. *Where the Pools Are Bright & Deep.* 1973. NY. Ils 1st ed. dj. $12.50

LAMB, Harold. *Nur Mahal.* 1935. Doubleday Doran. VG. P1. $25.00

LAMB, Hugh. *Taste of Fear.* 1976. Taplinger. 1st ed. dj. EX. P1. $20.00

LAMB, Martha. *History of City of NY. Vol. II.* 1877. Barnes. Ils. G. $15.00

LAMB & HARRISON. *History of City of NY.* c 1896. NY. Ils. maps. 3 vols. VG. $75.00

LAMB & LAMB. *Pocket Encyclopedia of Cacti & Succulents in Color.* 1970. Macmillan. Ils 1st Am ed. 217 p. dj. EX. M2. $9.00

LAMB & LAMB. *Pocket Encyclopedia of Cacti in Color.* 1969. London. sgns. dj. VG. $13.00

LAMB & LAMB. *Tales From Shakespeare.* nd. NY. Ils Price. dj. J2. $20.00

LAMB & LAMB. *Tales From Shakespeare.* 1915. Ginn. School ed. VG. $22.50

LAMBERT, D. *Dinosaurs.* 1982. Bonanza. reprint. photos. map. 4to. dj. M2. $12.00

LAMBERT, D. *Field of Dinosaurs.* 1983. Avon. Ils 1st ed. 256 p. EX. M2. $14.00

LAMBERT, J.I. *One Hundred Years With the 2nd Cavalry.* 1939. Ft. Riley, KS. 1st ed. 9 maps. 441 p. VG. T5. $150.00

LAMBERT, Janet. *Miss Tippy.* 1949. NY. Dutton. 4th print. dj. VG. $10.00

LAMBERT, Jean Clarence. *Pierre Alchinsky: Central Park.* 1976. Yves Riviere. 1/600. with etching. D2. $245.00

LAMBOTTE, P. *Flemish Painting Before the 18th C.* 1927. London. Studio. Ils. 4to. VG. $15.00

LAMERS, William. *Edge of Glory.* 1961. Harcourt. 1st ed. maps. 499 p. dj. G. $18.00

LAMERS, William. *Edge of Glory.* 1961. NY. 1st ed. VG. $30.00

LAMMAN, Charles. *Farthest N.* 1885. NY. 1st ed. fld map. VG. $25.00

LAMMING, George. *Emigrants.* 1954. NY. 1st ed. dj. EX. $20.00

LAMMING, George. *In the Castle of My Skin.* 1954. McGraw Hill. 1st Am ed. 312 p. M. $22.50

LAMNECK, J.H. *Country Squire: Romance of Law-Abiding Citizen.* 1960. Boston. sgn. 289 p. dj. VG. T5. $19.50

LAMONT, James. *Seasons With the Sea Horse; or, Sporting Adventures...* 1861. NY. Harper. 7 pls. fld map. 8vo. J2. $75.00

LAMPE, David. *Tunnel.* 1963. London. Harrat. 1st ed. 219 p. dj. $17.00

LAMPLOUGH & FRANCIS. *Cairo & Environs.* 1909. London. 1st ed. VG. $25.00

LAMPMAN, B.H. *Leaf From French Eddy.* 1979. Harper. 1st ed. dj. EX. $10.00

LAMPORT, Felicia. *Cultural Slag.* 1966. Houghton. Ils Gorey. 1st ed. dj. VG. $18.00

LAMPSON, Robin. *Vulcan Among the Argonauts.* 1936. San Francisco. Ils/sgn Hans. 1/500. VG. $35.00

LAMPTON, Chris. *Gateway to Limbo.* 1979. Doubleday. 1st ed. dj. xl. P1. $5.00

LAMSA, G.M. *Secret of the Near E.* 1923. Phil. $35.00

LAMSA, George. *Shepherd of All Twenty-Third Psalm.* 1939. Phil. $15.00

LANCASTER, C. *Japanese Influence in America.* 1963. NY. Ils 1st ed. dj. VG. B2. $55.00

LANCASTER, Charles Maxwell. *Saints & Sinners in Old Romance.* 1972. reprint of 1942 ed. sgn. EX. C1. $19.00

LANCASTER, Osbert. *Progress at Pelvis Bay.* 1936. London. 1st ed. dj. VG. $50.00

LANCHNER, C. *Paul Klee.* 1987. NY. 283 pls. 4to. 344 p. dj. EX. J2. $55.00

LANCOUR, Gene. *Globes of Llarum.* 1980. Doubleday. 1st ed. dj. xl. P1. $5.00

LAND, H.C. *Birds of Guatemala.* 1970. Livingston Pub. Ils 1st ed. $30.00

LANDAIS, Hubert. *French Porcelain.* 1961. NY. Putnam. Ils. 128 p. slipcase. $25.00

LANDAU, Henry. *Enemy Within.* 1937. Putnam. 1st ed. M1. $30.00

LANDAY, J.M. *Silent Cities, Sacred Stones.* 1971. NY. Ils. 272 p. $15.00

LANDELL. *Landell's Boys' Own Toymaker: Practical Illustrated Guide.* 1860. NY. Ils. 12mo. 153 p. VG. scarce. B1. $75.00

LANDIS, Charles. *Rails Over the Horizon.* 1938. Harrisburg. Stackpole. Ils. $10.00

LANDON, Christopher. *Unseen Enemy.* nd. Book Club. dj. VG. P1. $3.00

LANDON, H.F. *N Country: History Embracing Jefferson, St. Lawrence...* 1932. Indianapolis. Ils 1st ed. 4to. 3 vols. VG. T1. $95.00

LANDOR, A.H.S. *In the Forbidden Land: Account of Journey Into Tibet.* 1909. Harper. 2 vols in 1. VG. M2. $38.00

LANDOUX, Armand. *Paris 1925.* 1959. Paris. Delpire. 2nd ed. D2. $45.00

LANDSBERGER, Franz. *Rembrandt: Jews & the Bible.* 1946. Phil. 66 pls. 189 p. D2. $35.00

LANE, Edward. *Modern Egyptians.* 1871. London. rebound. $20.00

LANE, Franklin. *American Spirit.* 1918. NY. inscr. VG. $20.00

LANE, Jeremy. *Kill Him Tonight.* nd. Black Knight. VG. P1. $12.50

LANE, John. *Elbert Hubbard & His Work.* trade ed. 8vo. G. D1. $30.00

LANE, John. *Elbert Hubbard & His Work.* 1901. Blanchard Pr. 1/200. 8vo. G. D1. $65.00

LANE, M. *Life With Ionides.* 1963. London. Hamilton. 1st ed. dj. VG. M2. $17.00

LANE, M. *Life With Ionides.* 1963. NY. Ils 1st ed. dj. VG. B2. $17.50

LANE, M. *Tale of Beatrix Potter: A Biography.* 1946. London. 1st ed. dj. VG. B2. $45.00

LANE, Margaret. *Edgar Wallace: Biography of Phenomenon.* 1939. NY. $12.50

LANE, Mark. *Citizen's Dissent.* 1968. Holt. 1st ed. dj. VG. $18.00

LANE, Mills. *General Oglethorpe's GA Letters, 1733-1743.* 1975. Savannah. 2 vols. boxed. VG. $75.00

LANE, R.D. *Images From the Floating World.* 1978. NY. Putnam. Ils. EX. $40.00

LANE, R.W. *Discovery of Freedom.* 1943. John Day. 1st ed. dj. VG. $22.50

LANE, W. *Commodore Vanderbilt: Epic of Steam Age.* 1942. NY. 1st ed. 357 p. dj. VG. B2. $27.50

LANE, W.P. *Adventures & Recollections of Walter P. Lane.* 1928. Marshall, TX. 2nd ed. VG. $45.00

LANE. *Emperor Norton.* 1939. Caxton. VG. $60.00

LANES, S.G. *Art of Maurice Sendak.* 1981. NY. Abrams. Ils. 4to. 278 p. EX. $40.00

LANG, Allen Kim. *Wild & Outside.* 1965. Chilton. dj. VG. P1. $12.50

LANG, Andrew. *Aucassin & Nicolette.* 1899. Roycroft. 8vo. green suede. VG. D1. $50.00

LANG, Andrew. *Blue Fairy Book.* 1930. Phil. Ils Richardson. dj. $15.00

LANG, Andrew. *Blue Poetry Book.* 1891. London. 1st ed. VG. $70.00

LANG, Andrew. *Chronicles of Pantouflia.* 1981. Godine. dj. EX. P1. $12.95

LANG, Andrew. *Green Fairy Book.* nd. Grosset Dunlap. Ils Ford. $8.00

LANG, Andrew. *Green Fairy Book.* 1964. Longman. 6th ed. dj. xl. P1. $5.00

LANG, Andrew. *Library.* 1881. London. Dobson. sm 8vo. VG. $25.00

LANG, Andrew. *Modern Mythology.* 1897. London. 1st ed. with errata slip. $60.00

LANG, Andrew. *Olive Fairy Book.* 1907. London. Ils Ford. 1st ed. VG. $72.50

LANG, Andrew. *Red True Storybook.* 1895. London. Longman Green. 1st ed. 12mo. EX. $60.00

LANG, H.J. *Whit & Wisdom of Abraham Lincoln.* 1942. Cleveland. 1st ed. dj. EX. $7.00

LANG, L.A. *Ranching With Teddy Roosevelt.* 1926. Phil. 1st ed. dj. EX. $40.00

LANG, V.R. *Poems & Plays.* 1975. Random House. 1st ed. dj. EX. C1. $10.00

LANG & LANG. *Highways & Byways in the Border.* 1913. London. Macmillan. dj. VG. $40.00

LANGDALE, C. *Monotypes by Maurice Pendergast.* 1984. Chicago. pls. 4to. 159 p. EX. $16.00

LANGDON, E.F. *Cripple Creek Strike.* 1905. Denver. Ils 1st ed. G. B2. $67.50

LANGE, Dorothea. *Looks at the American Country Woman.* 1967. Carter Mus. 2nd print. dj. VG. $32.50

LANGE, John. *Binary.* 1972. Knopf. 3rd ed. dj. VG. P1. $10.00

LANGE, Oliver. *Vandenburg.* 1971. Stein Day. dj. VG. P1. $10.00

LANGE & AMES. *St. Louis: Child of River, Parent of W.* 1939. Webster. Ils. G. $20.00

LANGE & MITCHELL. *To a Cabin.* 1973. Grossman. 1st ed. dj. EX. $50.00

LANGE & TAYLOR. *American Exodus: Record of Human Erosion.* 1939. NY. Reynal. 1st ed. 4to. VG. $75.00

LANGER, Joan. *Case of Missing Corpse.* nd. Bleak House. VG. P1. $12.50

LANGER, W.C. *Mind of Adolph Hitler.* 1872. Basic Books. dj. VG. $12.00

LANGERLOF, Slema. *Story of Gosta Berling.* 1899. Boston. 1st ed. VG. $20.00

LANGEWIESCHE, Wolfgang. *Light Plane Flying.* 1939. NY. Ils 1st ed. 213 p. dj. T5. $25.00

LANGFORD, Cameron. *Winter of the Fisher.* 1971. Norton. 222 p. dj. EX. $10.00

LANGFORD, N.P. *Vigilante Days & Ways.* 1912. Chicago. 2nd ed. VG. $30.00

LANGILLE & FOSTER. *Popular History of Life of Columbus.* 1893. WA. 1st ed. 581 p. VG. T5. $15.00

LANGLEY & MANLY. *Langly Memoir on Mechanical Flight...* 1911. Smithsonian. Ils. 307 p. wraps. A3. $200.00

LANGMAID, K. *Beat to Quarters!* 1968. London. Ils. VG. $15.00

LANGTON, M.B. *How To Know Oriental Rugs.* 1904. NY. Ils. 12mo. $25.00

LANHAM, Edwin. *Death of a Corinthian.* 1953. Harcourt Brace. 1st ed. dj. VG. P1. $8.00

LANHAM, U. *Insects.* 1964. Columbia. Ils. 292 p. dj. EX. M2. $10.00

LANIER, H.W. *A.B. Frost: American Sportsman's Artist.* 1933. Derrydale. 1/950. 4to. tan cloth. dj. $150.00

LANIER, R.S. *Photographic History of Civil War: Armies & Leaders.* 1983. 322 p. M. J4. $10.00

LANIER, Sidney. *Boy's King Arthur.* 1943. Scribner. Ils Wyeth. VG. $30.00

LANIER, Sidney. *Hymns of the Marshes.* 1907. Scribner. Ils 1st ed. $35.00

LANIER & DAMERON. *Curious Quests of Brigadier Fellowes.* 1986. 1st ed. 1/1200. sgns. dj. M. C1. $27.00

LANING, J.F. *Growth & History of OH.* 1897. Norwalk. 142 p. fair. T5. $9.50

LANKA & VIT. *Color Guide to Amphibians & Reptiles.* 1985. Hamlyn. Ils. 224 p. dj. EX. M2. $17.00

LANMAN, Charles. *Adventures in Wilds of the US. Vol. 2.* 1856. Phil. 12mo. 517 p. xl. G2. $18.00

LANMAN, Charles. *Japanese in America.* 1872. NY. 1st ed. 352 p. VG. $45.00

LANMAN, Charles. *Leading Men of Japan With Historical Summary of Empire.* 1883. Lathrop. G. $22.50

LANNER, R. *Trees of the Great Basin.* 1984. Reno. Ils. 215 p. VG. $8.00

LANSDALE, M.H. *Chateaux of Touraine.* 1906. NY. De Vinne. 1st ed. J2. $50.00

LANSDEN, J.M. *History of City of Cairo, IL.* 1910. Chicago. Ils. fld map. VG. $35.00

LANSDOWNE, J.F. *Birds of the W Coast. Vol. 2.* 1980. Toronto. Teheley. Ils. folio. dj. EX. M2. $75.00

LANSDOWNE & LIVINGSTON. *Birds of the E Forest. Vol. 1.* 1968. Houghton. Ils. 4to. dj. EX. M2. $65.00

LANSDOWNE & LIVINGSTON. *Birds of the E Forest. Vol. 2.* 1977. Toronto. McClelland Steward. dj. EX. M2. $65.00

LANTIS, M. *AK Indian Ceremonialism.* 1966. Am Ethnol Soc. map. 127 p. dj. EX. M2. $20.00

LANWORN, R.A. *Book of Reptiles.* 1972. Hamlyn. Ils. 4to. dj. EX. M2. $8.00

LANYON, W.E. *Biology of Birds.* 1963. Nat Hist Pr. Ils. 175 p. dj. EX. M2. $15.00

LAQUEUR, Walter. *Breaking the Silence.* 1986. NY. 1st ed. dj. $7.50

LAQUEUR, Walter. *Terrible Secret.* 1981. Boston. 1st ed. dj. RS. VG. $9.50

LARDNER, Dionysius. *History of Maritime & Inland Discovery.* 1833. Boston/London. 3 vols. cloth. T5. $75.00

LARDNER, Dionysius. *Popular Lectures on Science & Art.* 1846. NY. 1st ed. 2 vols. VG. $45.00

LARDNER, Dionysius. *Rudimentary Treatise on Steam Engine.* 1848. London. Ils. VG. $50.00

LARDNER, John. *Strong Cigars & Lively Women.* 1951. NY. Ils. dj. VG. $25.00

LARDNER, R.W. *Bib Ballads.* 1915. Volland. Ils Fox. 1st ed. TEG. cloth. $95.00

LARDNER, R.W. *Big Town.* 1921. NY. 1st ed. 244 p. EX. $35.00

LARDNER, R.W. *Ecstasy of Owen Muir.* 1954. London. 1st ed. dj. EX. $20.00

LARDNER, R.W. *Ecstasy of Owen Muir.* 1954. NY. 1st ed. dj. VG. $20.00

LARDNER, R.W. *How To Write Short Stories.* 1924. NY. 1st ed. EX. $30.00

LARDNER, R.W. *Round Up.* 1929. NY. 1st ed. EX. $40.00

LARDNER, R.W. *Story of a Wonder Man.* 1927. NY. 1st ed. VG. $45.00

LARDNER, R.W. *Symptoms of Being Thirty-Five.* 1921. Bobbs Merrill. 1st ed. EX. $25.00

LARDNER, R.W. *Treat 'Em Rough: Letters From Jack the Kaiser Killer.* 1918. Bobbs Merrill. 1st ed. 1st state. dj. VG. J2. $35.00

LARDNER, R.W. *What of It?* 1925. NY. 1st ed. VG. $30.00

LARGENT, D.L. *How To Identify Mushrooms to Genus III.* 1977. Mad River. Ils. 148 p. EX. M2. $9.00

LARIAR, Lawrence. *Girl With the Frightened Eyes.* 1949. Handi-Book. VG. P1. $10.00

LARIAR, Lawrence. *Man With the Lumpy Nose.* 1944. Dodd Mead. 1st ed. dj. G. P1. $15.00

LARIMORE, R.W. *Ecological Life History of Warmouth (Centrarchidae).* 1957. IL Nat Hist Survey. 83 p. EX. M2. $12.00

LARKIN, David. *Unknown Paintings of Kay Nielsen.* 1977. Toronto. Peacock. Ils 1st ed. $25.00

LARKIN, Margaret. *Six Days of Yad Mordechai.* 1970. Jerusalem. Mordechai Mus. EX. $25.00

LARKIN, Philip. *High Window.* 1974. NY. 1st ed. dj. M. $12.00

LARNED, J.N. *History of the World.* 1915. World. Revised ed. red cloth. VG. $40.00

LARNED, W.R. *American Indian Fairy Tales.* 1935. Wise. Ils Rae. 96 p. G. $18.00

LARNER. *Larner's Outlines of Universal History.* 1835. Phil. Hogan Thompson. 466 p. M1. $17.50

LARPENTEUR, Charles. *Forty Years a Fur Trader.* 1933. Donnelley. Lakeside Classic. A3. $50.00

LARRABEE, Eric. *American Panorama.* 1957. 1st ed. 376 p. dj. VG. $25.00

LARRABEE, William. *Railroad Question.* 1893. Chicago. Schulte. 4th ed. 12mo. $27.50

LARSELL. *Comparative Anatomy & Histology of Cerebellum.* 1970. MN. dj. VG. $38.00

LARSEN, Ernest. *Not a Through Street.* 1981. Random House. Review 1st ed. dj. EX. $17.50

LARSON, Henrietta. *Jay Cooke: Private Banker.* 1936. Harvard. 1st ed. J2. $30.00

LARSON, P. *Deserts of America.* 1970. Prentice Hall. 340 p. dj. $18.00

LARSON, P. & M.W. *All About Ants.* 1965. World. Ils. 220 p. VG. M2. $6.00

LARSON, William H. *7 Great Detective Stories.* 1968. Whitman. VG. P1. $4.75

LARSSON, Bernard. *Die Ganze Stadt Berlin.* 1964. Hamburg. wraps. VG. $55.00

LARSSON, Carl. *Ett Hem 25 Malninger.* nd. Stockholm. 25 pls. oblong folio. VG. $125.00

LARTIGUE, J.H. *Boyhood Photos.* 1966. Guichard. photos. EX. $200.00

LARTIGUE, J.H. *Les Femmes.* 1974. NY. 1st Am ed. EX. $45.00

LARWOOD, J. *History of Signboards.* 1908. London. Ils. 536 p. xl. G. $20.00

LASCELLES, G. *Art of Falconry.* 1985. London. Spearman. dj. EX. $12.50

LASH, J.P. *Dag Hammarskjold.* 1961. Garden City. 1st ed. dj. VG. $10.00

LASKER, R. *Marine Fish Larvae.* 1984. WA U. Ils. 131 p. M. M2. $9.00

LASKY, Muriel. *Proud Little Kitten.* 1944. NY. Universal. Ils. 4to. EX. $17.50

LASSAIGNE, Jacques. *Joan Ponc, Fondo del Ser: 1970-1977.* 1978. Barcelona. Ils. 215 p. dj. D2. $45.00

LASSAIGNE, Jacques. *Spanish Painting.* 1952. NY/Geneva. Skira. Orig ed. 2 vols. D2. $150.00

LASSON & SVENDSEN. *Life & Destiny of Isak Dinesen.* 1970. NY. 1st ed. dj. VG. B2. $17.50

LASSWELL, Mary. *I'll Take TX.* 1958. Boston. 1st ed. dj. VG. $12.50

LASSWELL, Mary. *Tio Pepe.* 1963. Boston. 1st ed. dj. M. $18.00

LASSWITZ, Kurd. *Two Planets.* 1971. IL U Pr. 1st ed. dj. VG. P1. $10.00

LATHAM, Charles. *In English Homes.* nd. London. J2. $50.00

LATHAM, Ian. *Joseph Maria Olbrich.* 1980. NY. Rizzoli. Ils. 156 p. dj. EX. D2. $65.00

LATHEN, Emma. *Ashes to Ashes.* nd. Book Club. dj. VG. P1. $3.00

LATHEN, Emma. *Ashes to Ashes.* Simon Schuster. 2nd ed. dj. VG. P1. $7.50

LATHEN, Emma. *Going for the Gold.* Simon Schuster. 2nd ed. dj. VG. P1. $7.50

LATHEN, Emma. *Longer the Thread.* nd. Book Club. dj. VG. P1. $3.00

LATHEN, Emma. *Murder To Go.* 1969. NY. 1st ed. dj. $25.00

LATHEN, Emma. *Murder Without Icing.* 1972. Simon Schuster. 1st ed. dj. $15.00

LATHEN, Emma. *Sweet & Low.* nd. Book Club. dj. VG. P1. $3.50

LATHROP, D.P. *Long Island.* 1929. Boston. Ils 1st ed. $12.00

LATHROP, D.P. *Skittle-Skattle Monkey.* 1945. Macmillan. Ils 1st ed. 8vo. $20.00

LATHROP, Elise. *Early American Inns & Taverns.* 1935. NY. photos. pls. $20.00

LATHROP, Elise. *Early American Inns & Taverns.* 1946. NY. 365 p. dj. $15.00

LATHROP, Elise. *Historic Houses of Early America.* 1927. NY. J2. $25.00

LATHROP, Elise. *Historic Houses of Early America.* 1927. NY. Tudor. 464 p. dj. slipcase. D2. $65.00

LATIMER, Jonathan. *Black Is the Fashion for Dying.* 1959. Random House. 1st ed. dj. G. P1. $12.50

LATIMER, Jonathan. *Headed for a Hearse.* nd. Jonathan Pr. VG. P1. $10.00

LATIMER, Jonathan. *Headed for a Hearse.* nd. Sun Dial. VG. P1. $10.00

LATIMER, Jonathan. *Headed for a Hearse.* 1980. Gregg Pr. 1st ed. dj. VG. P1. $20.00

LATIMER, Jonathan. *Lady in the Morgue.* nd. Book Club. dj. G. P1. $4.00

LATIMER, Jonathan. *Lady in the Morgue.* 1943. Sun Dial. P1. $7.50

LATIMER, Jonathan. *Red Gardenias.* 1939. Crime Club. dj. VG. P1. $35.00

LATROBE, F.C. *Iron Men & Their Dogs.* 1941. Baltimore. Ils. VG. $22.50

LATROBE, J.H.B. *Last Chapter in History of the Steamboat.* 1871. Baltimore. 44 p. wraps. VG. $47.00

LATTIMORE, Owen. *Desert Road to Turkestan.* 1929. Little Brown. Ils 1st ed. 373 p. EX. M2. $55.00

LATTIMORE, Owen. *Inner Asian Frontiers of China.* 1940. Am Geog Soc. Ils. 585 p. EX. $40.00

LATTIMORE, R.B. *Lee in Own Words & Those of Contemporaries.* 1964. WA. Colortone. Ils 1st ed. dj. M. $12.00

LAUBACH, F.C. *You Are My Friends.* 1942. NY. $7.50

LAUBENTHAL, Sanders Anne. *Excalibur.* 1977. Ballantine. 2nd print. pb. VG. C1. $12.50

LAUDER, Harry. *Minstrel in France.* 1918. Hearst. Ils. 338 p. EX. $8.00

LAUDER, Harry. *Wee Drappies.* 1932. NY. Laugh Club. Ils Cooper. 1st ed. VG. J2. $45.00

LAUDERDALE & DOAK. *Life of the Range & on the Trail.* 1936. San Antonio. Ils 1st ed. EX. $65.00

LAUFER, Berthold. *Chinese Clay Figures.* 1914. Field Mus Nat Hist. 1st ed. VG. J2. $65.00

LAUFFER, C.A. *Resuscitation From Electric Shock, Traumatic Shock...* 1913. NY. G. $18.00

LAUGHLIN, C.E. *Death of Lincoln: Story of Booth's Plot, Deed & Penalty.* 1909. Doubleday Page. 336 p. VG. $50.00

LAUGHLIN, C.J. *Ghosts Along the MS.* 1948. Scribner. 1st ed. VG. $55.00

LAUGHLIN, C.J. *Ghosts Along the MS.* 1961. NY. 4to. dj. EX. $35.00

LAUGHLIN, J.W. *Laughlin History, 1807-1912.* 1912. Barnesville. Ils. 121 p. wraps. G. T5. $19.50

LAUGHTON, R. *TV Graphics.* 1966. NY/London. Reinhold/Studio Vista. 1st ed. $17.50

LAUMER, Keith. *Dead Fall.* 1971. Doubleday. 1st ed. dj. xl. P1. $10.00

LAUMER, Keith. *Glory Game.* 1973. Doubleday. P1. $10.00

LAUMER, Keith. *Night of Delusions.* 1972. Putnam. 1st ed. dj. VG. P1. $17.50

LAUMER, Keith. *Once There Was a Giant.* 1971. Doubleday. dj. VG. P1. $10.00

LAUMER, Keith. *Other Side of Time.* 1971. Walker. 1st ed. dj. xl. P1. $7.50

LAUMER, Keith. *Retief's Ransom.* 1975. Dobson. 1st ed. dj. EX. P1. $20.00

LAUMER, Keith. *Star Treasure.* 1974. Sidgwick Jackson. 1st ed. dj. P1. $17.50

LAUMER, Keith. *Time Trap.* 1970. NY. 1st ed. dj. VG. $15.00

LAUMER, Keith. *Trace of Memory.* pb. VG. C1. $2.50

LAUMER, Keith. *Ultimax Man.* 1978. St. Martin. 1st ed. dj. xl. P1. $7.50

LAURD, N. *Last Wilderness: Journey Across Great Kalahari Desert.* 1981. Simon Schuster. Ils 1st ed. 222 p. dj. EX. M2. $13.00

LAURENTS, Arthur. *Clearing in the Woods.* 1957. NY. 1st ed. dj. VG. $10.00

LAURIE, Alex. *Flower Shop.* 1930. Chicago. Florists Pub. Ils. EX. $16.00

LAUT, A.C. *Enchanted Trails of Glacier Park.* 1926. NY. Ils 1st ed. 8vo. VG. T1. $35.00

LAUT, A.C. *Overland Trail: Epic Path of Pioneers to OR.* 1929. NY. Ils 1st ed. 358 p. $17.50

LAUTERBACH, Albert. *Economics in Uniform: Military Economy & Social Structure.* 1943. Princeton. 1st ed. dj. J2. $15.00

LAUTERBACH, R.E. *Danger From the E.* 1947. NY/London. VG. $15.00

LAUTERMILCH, I.P. *Book of Blue & Gold.* 1951. WA, D.C. $12.00

LAVALLEYE, Jacques. *Pieter Bruegel the Elder & Lucas van Leyden.* 1967. NY. Abrams. Ils. 491 pls. 231 p. D2. $125.00

LAVENDER, David. *Bret's Fort.* 1954. Doubleday. 1st ed. EX. $40.00

LAVENDER, David. *Fist in the Wilderness.* 1964. Doubleday. 1st ed. dj. EX. $40.00

LAVENDER, David. *Land of the Giants.* 1958. Garden City. dj. EX. $17.50

LAVER, James. *Costume of the W World.* 1951. NY. Ils 1st Am ed. EX. $25.00

LAVER, James. *Ladies' Mistakes.* 1943. Knopf. 1st ed. dj. EX. $20.00

LAVIN, Mary. *Memory & Other Stories.* 1973. Boston. 1st ed. dj. VG. $12.50

LAVINE, E.H. *Cops.* c 1936. NY. Vanguard. 1st ed. VG. $10.00

LAVINE, E.H. *3rd Degree: Detailed & Appalling Expose of Police Brutality.* 1930. NY. Vanguard. fair. $15.00

LAW, HARTLAND & HERBERT. *Viavi Hygiene: Viavi System of Treatment.* 1911. San Francisco. 8 pls. VG. $75.00

LAW, Janice. *Under Orion.* 1978. Houghton. 1st ed. dj. xl. P1. $6.00

LAWES, Lewis E. *Twenty Thousand Years in Sing Sing.* 1932. NY. Ils 1st ed. 412 p. dj. VG. T5. $22.50

LAWFORD, Valentine. *Horst: His Work & His World.* 1984. NY. Knopf. Ils 1st ed. 299 photos. 396 p. dj. $60.00

LAWHEAD, Stephen. *Pendragon Trilogy: Taliessin, Merlin, Arthur.* stiff wraps. slipcase. M. C1. $33.00

LAWRENCE, D.H. *Aaron's Rod.* 1922. London. 1st ed. G. $20.00

LAWRENCE, D.H. *Assorted Articles.* 1930. NY. 1st Am ed. dj. EX. $40.00

LAWRENCE, D.H. *Boy in the Bush.* 1924. NY. Seltzer. 1st ed. $25.00

LAWRENCE, D.H. *Etruscan Places.* 1932. London. Secker. 1st ed. dj. $110.00

LAWRENCE, D.H. *Etruscan Places.* 1972. Folio Soc. 8vo. slipcase. EX. $16.00

LAWRENCE, D.H. *Fantasia & the Unconscious.* 1922. NY. 1st ed. VG. $35.00

LAWRENCE, D.H. *Fire & Other Poems.* 1940. Grabhorn. Book Club of CA. 1/300. 4to. EX. $350.00

LAWRENCE, D.H. *Glad Ghosts.* 1926. London. Benn. 1/500. 12mo. 77 p. yellow wraps. M. $120.00

LAWRENCE, D.H. *Kangaroo.* 1923. London. Martin Seeker. 1st ed. $140.00

LAWRENCE, D.H. *Kangaroo.* 1925. NY. Seltzer. 1st ed. VG. $25.00

LAWRENCE, D.H. *Lady Chatterley's Lover.* 1928. Florence. 1/1000. sgn. dj. EX. $250.00

LAWRENCE, D.H. *Lady Chatterly.* c 1930s. Ils Edouard Chimot. Ltd ed. G. $135.00

LAWRENCE, D.H. *Lost Girl.* 1920. London. 1st ed. 2nd imp. $25.00

LAWRENCE, D.H. *Love Among the Haystacks.* 1930. London. Nonesuch. Ltd ed. dj. EX. $100.00

LAWRENCE, D.H. *Love Among the Haystacks.* 1952. Avon. pb. G. $10.00

LAWRENCE, D.H. *Mornings in Mexico.* 1927. NY. 1st ed. 1st print. dj. EX. $65.00

LAWRENCE, D.H. *My Skirmish With Jolly Roger.* 1929. Random House. Ltd 1st ed. 1/600. VG. $45.00

LAWRENCE, D.H. *Nettles.* 1930. London. 1st ed. dj. VG. $50.00

LAWRENCE, D.H. *New Poems.* 1918. London. 1st ed. VG. $25.00

LAWRENCE, D.H. *Pansies.* 1929. London. 1st ed. G. $65.00

LAWRENCE, D.H. *Rawdon's Roof.* 1928. London. Mathews Marrot. 1st ed. 1/530. $400.00

LAWRENCE, D.H. *Reflections on Death of a Porcupine.* 1925. Phil. 1/925. EX. $150.00

LAWRENCE, D.H. *St. Mawr.* 1925. Knopf. 1st Am ed. EX. $20.00

LAWRENCE, D.H. *Women in Love.* 1930. NY. 1/1250. VG. B2. $250.00

LAWRENCE, David. *True Story of Woodrow Wilson.* 1924. Doran. EX. $12.50

LAWRENCE, E.A. *Clover Passage.* 1954. Caxton. Ils. 260 p. dj. EX. M2. $12.00

LAWRENCE, Elizabeth. *S Garden: Handbook for the Middle S.* 1942. Chapel Hill. 241 p. dj. EX. $30.00

LAWRENCE, F.E. *About Old Tallmadge.* 1984. Akron. Tallmadge Hist Soc. wraps. VG. T5. $9.50

LAWRENCE, Freida. *Not I, But the Wind.* 1934. 1st trade ed. inscr/sgn. dj. $10.00

LAWRENCE, Frieda. *Not I, But the Wind.* 1934. Rydal Pr. Ltd ed. 1/100. sgn. VG. $85.00

LAWRENCE, Lars. *Old Father Antic.* 1961. NY. Internat Pub. 1st ed. dj. $35.00

LAWRENCE, Lars. *Out of the Dust.* 1956. NY. Putnam. 1st ed. dj. $20.00

LAWRENCE, Louise. *Cat Call.* 1980. 1st ed. dj. VG. C1. $6.00

LAWRENCE, Margery. *Number 7 Queer St.* 1969. Mycroft Moran. 1st ed. xl. P1. $10.00

LAWRENCE, R.D. *In Praise of Wolves.* 1986. Holt. Ils 1st ed. 245 p. dj. EX. M2. $18.00

LAWRENCE, R.D. *Paddy: Naturalist's Story of an Orphan Beaver.* 1977. Knopf. Ils 1st ed. 240 p. dj. EX. M2. $10.00

LAWRENCE, R.D. *Secret Go the Wolves.* 1980. Holt Rinehart. 1st ed. 277 p. dj. EX. M2. $18.00

LAWRENCE, R.F. *Centipedes & Millipedes of S Africa: A Guide.* 1984. Cape Town. Balakema. Ils. 148 p. EX. M2. $12.00

LAWRENCE, Robert. *Lohengrin: Adapted From Wagner's Opera.* 1938. NY. Metropolitan Opera. dj. M. C1. $12.50

LAWRENCE, T.E. *Home Letters of T.E. Lawrence & His Brothers.* 1954. Macmillan. 1st ed. $25.00

LAWRENCE, T.E. *Letters of T.E. Lawrence.* 1939. NY. 1st ed. EX. $30.00

LAWRENCE, T.E. *Lowell With Lawrence in Arabia.* nd. Century. VG. $50.00

LAWRENCE, T.E. *Men in Print.* 1940. Golden Cockerel. Ltd ed. EX. $375.00

LAWRENCE, T.E. *Men in Print.* 1940. London. Golden Cockerel. 1/500. 8vo. VG. $310.00

LAWRENCE, T.E. *Mint.* 1955. London. 1st trade ed. dj. VG. $65.00

LAWRENCE, T.E. *Odyssey.* 1932. 1st ed. 3rd print. VG. $20.00

LAWRENCE, T.E. *Seven Pillars of Wisdom.* 1934. NY. Doubleday Doran. 1st ed. dj. EX. $38.00

LAWRENCE, T.E. *Seven Pillars of Wisdom.* 1935. London. 1st ed. VG. $50.00

LAWRENCE, T.E. *Seven Pillars of Wisdom.* 1935. NY. 1st trade ed. dj. $15.00

LAWRENCE, T.E. *Seven Pillars of Wisdom.* 1937. Doubleday. not 1st ed. dj. VG. $25.00

LAWRENCE, W. *Pictures in Color: Lakes of Killarne.* nd. Jarrold. 48 photos. P1. $35.00

LAWRENCE, William. *Lectures on Physiology, Zoology & Natural History of Man...* 1828. Salem, MA. Foote Brown. 1st Am ed. 495 p. $75.00

LAWRENCE. *Botanico-Periodicum-Huntianum.* 1968. 1st ed. 1063 p. $50.00

LAWRIE, W.H. *English Trout Flies.* 1969. Barnes. Ils 1st Am ed. dj. VG. $8.00

LAWSON, M.A. *Sea Is Blue.* 1946. Viking. 1st ed. dj. EX. $15.00

LAWSON, Robert. *Country Colic.* 1944. Boston. Ils 1st ed. dj. EX. $25.00

LAWSON, Robert. *I Discover Columbus.* 1941. Boston. 1st ed. dj. VG. $30.00

LAWSON, Robert. *Mr. Revere & I.* 1953. Boston. 17th print. dj. EX. $10.00

LAWSON, Robert. *Mr. Twigg's Mistake.* 1947. Boston. Ils 1st ed. dj. EX. $25.00

LAWSON, Robert. *Rabbit Hill.* 1944. Viking. Ils. 8vo. EX. $12.50

LAWSON, Robert. *Robbut: Tale of Tails.* 1948. NY. Ils. dj. EX. $35.00

LAWSON, Robert. *Robbut: Tale of Tails.* 1948. NY. 1st ed. dj. VG. B2. $22.50

LAWSON, Robert. *They Were Strong & Good.* 1940. NY. 4th print. dj. EX. $10.00

LAWSON, Robert. *Tough Winter.* 1954. Viking. not Jr Lit Guild. dj. VG. $35.00

LAWSON, T.W. *Thirty Seconds Over Tokyo.* 1943. Random House. dj. EX. $7.00

LAWSON. *Aircraft Industry & Builder.* c 1930s. Detroit. Ils. 304 p. VG. C4. $75.00

LAWYER, J.P. *History of OH.* 1905. Collins. Ils 2nd ed. G. $12.50

LAYAL, Raja. *Princely India.* 1980. NY. photos. tall 8vo. dj. EX. $30.00

LAYCOCK, G. *Alien Animals: Story of Imported Wildlife.* 1966. Am Mus Nat Hist. 1st ed. dj. M2. $7.00

LAYCOCK, G. *Wild Hunters: N American Predators.* 1978. McKay. 1st ed. 121 p. dj. EX. M2. $7.00

LAYTHA, E. *N Again for Gold.* 1939. NY. 1st ed. dj. VG. B2. $22.50

LAZAREV, V.N. *Old Russian Murals & Mosaics.* 1966. London. Phaidon. Ils. 4to. dj. $60.00

LAZLO, Kate. *Forever After.* 1981. Dial. ARC. wraps. $12.50

LE CARRE, John. *Call for the Dead.* 1961. reprint of 1st Eng ed. dj. $15.00

LE CARRE, John. *Call for the Dead.* 1962. Walker. 1st Am ed. dj. VG. $20.00

LE CARRE, John. *Clandestine Muse.* 1986. Portland. Ltd ed. 1/250. sgn. wraps. EX. $60.00

LE CARRE, John. *Little Drummer Girl.* 1983. Hodder Stoughton. 1st ed. dj. P1. $25.00

LE CARRE, John. *Little Drummer Girl.* 1983. Knopf. 1st ed. dj. EX. $15.00

LE CARRE, John. *Looking Glass War.* nd. Book Club. dj. VG. P1. $3.00

LE CARRE, John. *Murder of Quality.* 1962. reprint of 1st ed. $15.00

LE CARRE, John. *Naive & Sentimental Lover.* 1972. Knopf. 1st Am ed. dj. EX. $20.00

LE CARRE, John. *Perfect Spy.* 1986. London. Hodder Stoughton. sgn. dj. $70.00

LE CARRE, John. *Perfect Spy.* 1986. London. Ltd ed. 1/250. sgn. wraps. M. $150.00

LE CARRE, John. *Perfect Spy.* 1986. NY. 1st Am ed. sgn. dj. EX. $95.00

LE CARRE, John. *Russia House.* 1989. London. 1st ed. dj. EX. $35.00

LE CARRE, John. *Small Town in Germany.* Coward McCann. 1st Am ed. dj. VG. $30.00

LE CARRE, John. *Small Town in Germany.* 1968. Heinemann. 1st ed. dj. VG. $55.00

LE CARRE, John. *Smiley's People.* 1980. Hodder Stoughton. 1st ed. dj. P1. $25.00

LE CARRE, John. *Smiley's People.* 1980. Knopf. 1st Am ed. dj. EX. $15.00

LE CARRE, John. *Spy Who Came in From Cold.* Coward McCann. 23rd print. xl. P1. $5.00

LE CARRE, John. *Spy Who Came in From Cold.* Coward McCann. 3rd ed. dj. xl. P1. $10.00

LE CARRE, John. *Spy Who Came in From Cold.* nd. Book Club. dj. VG. P1. $3.50

LE CARRE, John. *Spy Who Came in From Cold.* 1964. Gollancz. 16th print. VG. P1. $10.00

LE CARRE, John. *Spy Who Came in From Cold.* 1964. Gollancz. 17th print. dj. VG. P1. $10.00

LE CARRE, John. *Spy Who Came in From the Cold.* 1964. Coward McCann. 1st ed. dj. EX. $35.00

LE CARRE, John. *Tinker, Tailor, Soldier, Spy.* nd. BOMC. VG. P1. $4.00

LE CARRE, John. *Tinker, Tailor, Soldier, Spy.* 1974. Knopf. 1st Am ed. dj. VG. $15.00

LE CARRE, John. *Tinker, Tailor, Soldier, Spy.* 1974. London. 1st ed. dj. EX. $40.00

LE CORBUSIER. *Modulor.* 1958. Cambridge. 2nd ed. dj. EX. J2. $22.50

LE CORBUSIER. *Radiant City.* 1967. NY. 1st ed. EX. $40.00

LE CORBUSIER. *Towards a New Architecture.* 1946. London. 3rd ed. dj. VG. J2. $20.00

LE CORBUSIER. *When Cathedrals Were White.* 1947. NY. 1st Am ed. dj. VG. $25.00

LE DUC, W.G. *Recollections of Civil War Quartermaster.* 1963. St. Paul. 1st ed. dj. VG. $22.00

LE ENGLE, Madeleine. *Swiftly Tilting Planet.* 1st ed. dj. VG. C1. $7.50

LE FANU, J. Sheridan. *Hours After Midnight.* 1975. London. dj. G. $10.00

LE FANU, J. Sheridan. *In a Glass Darkly.* 1929. Peter Davies. VG. P1. $75.00

LE FANU, J. Sheridan. *Purcell Papers.* 1975. Arkham House. 1st ed. dj. EX. P1. $15.00

LE FEVRE, Edwin. *Wall Street Stories.* 1901. NY. VG. $40.00

LE FLEMING, H.M. *International Locomotives.* 1972. Ils. 192 p. $27.50

LE GALLIENNE, Richard. *Old Country House.* 1905. Harper. 4to. EX. $30.00

LE GALLIENNE, Richard. *Quest of the Golden Girl.* 1897. Bodley. 7th ed. 8vo. VG. G2. $45.00

LE GALLIENNE, Richard. *Romance of Perfume.* 1928. NY/Paris. Ils Barbier. 1st ed. dj. J2. $30.00

LE GALLIENNE, Richard. *Sleeping Beauty & Other Prose Fancies.* 1900. London. Lane. TEG. morocco. with sgn letter. M. $85.00

LE GROS CLARK, W.E. *Fossil Evidence for Human Evolution: Introduction.* 1960. Chicago U. Ils. 181 p. EX. M2. $10.00

LE GUIN, U.K. *Beginning Place.* 1980. Harper Row. 1st ed. sgn. dj. VG. $40.00

LE GUIN, U.K. *Catwings.* 1988. Orchard Books. Ils 1st ed. dj. M. $10.00

LE GUIN, U.K. *Compass Rose.* 1982. NY. 1st ed. sgn. dj. EX. $25.00

LE GUIN, U.K. *Dispossessed.* 1974. NY/London. 1st ed. dj. EX. $20.00

LE GUIN, U.K. *Eye of the Heron.* 1978. Harper Row. 1st ed. sgn. dj. VG. $45.00

LE GUIN, U.K. *Farthest Shore.* 1974. Atheneum. 3rd ed. dj. EX. P1. $15.00

LE GUIN, U.K. *From Elfland to Poughkeepsie.* 1973. Portland. Pendragon. Ltd ed. dj. $50.00

LE GUIN, U.K. *Language of the Night.* 1979. NY. 1st ed. dj. EX. $20.00

LE GUIN, U.K. *Malafrena.* Putnam. 2nd ed. dj. EX. P1. $15.00

LE GUIN, U.K. *Malafrena.* 1979. NY. 1st ed. dj. EX. $20.00

LE GUIN, U.K. *Orsinian Tales.* 1976. NY. 1st ed. dj. VG. $20.00

LE GUIN, U.K. *Planet of Exile.* 1978. NY. 1st ed. dj. EX. $22.50

LE GUIN, U.K. *Rocannon's World.* 1979. London. 1st ed. dj. EX. $20.00

LE GUIN, U.K. *Tombs of Atuan.* 1976. Atheneum. 5th print. dj. EX. P1. $15.00

LE GUIN, U.K. *Torrey Pines Reserve.* 1980. Lord John. Ltd ed. EX. $35.00

LE JEUNE. *German-English, English-German Dictionary for Physicians.* 1968. Stuttgart. 2 vols. VG. $45.00

LE MAITRE, Jules. *On the Margins of Old Books.* 1929. Coward McCann. 1/250. 322 p. VG. $25.00

LE MARCHAND, Elizabeth. *Death on Doomsday.* 1971. London. 1st ed. dj. VG. $20.00

LE MASTER, R. *Great Gallery of Ducks & Other Waterfowl.* 1985. Contemporary. Ils 1st ed. 4to. 340 p. EX. M2. $55.00

LE PLONGEON, A. *Queen Moo & Egyptian Sphinx.* 1900. private print. presentation. sgn. 277 p. $135.00

LE PLONGEON, A. *Queen Moo's Talisman.* 1902. NY. $27.50

LE PLONGEON, A. *Sacred Mysteries Among the Mayas & Quiches.* 1886. NY. 1st ed. 163 p. VG. $85.00

LE POINT. *Revue Artistique et Litteraire.* April, 1953. pls. 4to. 48 p. wraps. $65.00

LE PRADE, Ruth. *Debs & Their Poets.* 1920. Ltd ed. 1/500. sgn. VG. $75.00

LE PRAT. *Faces & Destinies.* 1963. Vaduz. Overseas Pub. 1st ed. VG. $25.00

LE QUEUX, William. *Crystal Claw.* 1924. Macaulay. 1st ed. VG. P1. $15.00

LE QUEUX, William. *Elusive Four.* 1930. Cassell. 3rd ed. VG. P1. $13.75

LE QUEUX, William. *Four Faces.* 1927. Shoe Lane. VG. P1. $10.00

LE QUEUX, William. *Golden Three.* 1931. Fiction League. VG. P1. $10.00

LE QUEUX, William. *Her Royal Highness.* 1914. London. Hodder. 1st ed. G. $8.00

LE QUEUX, William. *House of Evil.* 1930. Ward Lock. G. P1. $7.50

LE QUEUX, William. *House of the Wicked.* c 1906. London. Hurst Blackett. 1st ed. VG. $10.00

LE QUEUX, William. *Man From Downing Street.* nd. Hurst Blackett. VG. P1. $7.50

LE QUEUX, William. *Stretton Street Affair.* 1931. Cassell. Cheap ed. G. P1. $7.50

LE QUEUX, William. *Valrose Mystery.* 1928. Ward Lock. G. P1. $10.00

LE QUEUX, William. *Zoraida.* 1895. London. Tower. Ils 1st ed. $14.00

LE QUEX, William. *Secrets of Monte Carlo.* 1900. Dillingham. $6.50

LE VIEN & LORD. *Winston S. Churchill: Valiant Years.* 1962. Geis. 1st print. blue cloth. dj. VG. D1. $30.00

LEA, Homer. *Day of the Saxon.* 1912. Harper. 1st ed. $35.00

LEA, Homer. *Valor of Ignorance.* 1942. NY. Ils. 249 p. dj. VG. T5. $15.00

LEA, Tom. *Hand of Catu.* 1964. Ils 2nd ed. sgn. EX. $25.00

LEA, Tom. *King Ranch.* 1957. Boston. 1st ed. boxed. VG. B2. $75.00

LEA, Tom. *Picture Gallery.* 1968. Little Brown. 1st ed. slipcase. $85.00

LEA, Tom. *Tom Lea Gallery.* 1968. Little Brown. 1st ed. 2 vols. slipcase. EX. T6. $150.00

LEACH, Maria. *God Had a Dog: Folklore of the Dog.* 1961. Rutger. 1st ed. dj. VG. J2. $20.00

LEACH & WINTON. *Food Inspection & Analysis.* 1920. NY. Ils. 40 pls. 1090 p. $66.00

LEACOCK, Stephen. *Garden of Folly.* 1924. Dodd Mead. 2nd ed. dj. VG. P2. $35.00

LEACOCK, Stephen. *Hohenzollerns in America.* 1919. NY. Lane. 1st ed. VG. P2. $50.00

LEACOCK, Stephen. *Last Leaves.* 1946. NY. Dodd Mead. 2nd ed. dj. VG. P2. $20.00

LEACOCK, Stephen. *Moonbeams From the Larger Lunacy.* 1919. Bodley Head. 3rd ed. xl. P1. $7.50

LEACOCK, Stephen. *My Discovery of England.* 1923. NY. Dodd Mead. 6th ed. dj. VG. P2. $25.00

LEACOCK, Stephen. *My Discovery of the W.* 1937. Boston. Hale Cushman Flint. 1st ed. dj. P2. $35.00

LEACOCK, Stephen. *Short Circuits.* 1928. Dodd Mead. 1st ed. VG. P2. $25.00

LEACOCK, Stephen. *Wet Wit & Dry Humor.* 1931. NY. 2nd ed. dj. VG. P2. $30.00

LEACOCK, Stephen. *Winnowed Wisdom.* 1926. NY. 2nd ed. dj. VG. P2. $28.00

LEACOCK, Stephen. *Winsome Winnie.* 1926. NY. dj. VG. P2. $30.00

LEADER, Mary. *Triad.* 1973. Book Club. dj. VG. C1. $3.50

LEAF, Munro. *Fair Flay.* 1939. NY. VG. $20.00

LEAF, Munro. *Let's Do Better.* 1945. Lippincott. dj. G. $24.00

LEAF, Munro. *Manners Can Be Fun.* 1936. Stokes. VG. $15.00

LEAF, Munro. *Story of Ferdinand the Bull.* 1936. Viking. Ils Lawson. 3rd ed. $20.00

LEAF, Munro. *Story of Ferdinand the Bull.* 1938. NY. Ils Lawson. VG. $17.50

LEAF, Munro. *Wartime Handbook for Young Americans.* 1942. Stokes. 1st ed. EX. $25.00

LEAF, Munro. *Wee Gillis.* 1938. NY. 1st ed. VG. $55.00

LEAF & LAWSON. *Story of Simpson & Sampson.* 1941. NY. 1st ed. dj. VG. $25.00

LEAHY & CRAIN. *Land That Time Forgot.* 1937. NY. 1st ed. sgn. VG. B2. $30.00

LEAKEY, L.S.B. *Animals of E Africa.* 1969. Nat Geog Soc. Ils. map. 199 p. dj. EX. M2. $15.00

LEAR, Edward. *Book of Nonsense.* 1895. London. oblong 8vo. gilt black bdg. VG. $60.00

LEAR, Edward. *Collected Nonsense Songs.* 1947. London. Gray Walls. 1st ed. dj. $20.00

LEAR, Edward. *Nutcracker & the Sugar Tongs.* 1978. Boston. Ils Sewall. 1st ed. $10.00

LEAR, Peter. *Spider Girl.* 1980. Viking. 1st ed. dj. VG. P1. $15.00

LEARMONTH, David. *Checkmate & Stalemate.* 1939. Crime Book Soc. dj. VG. P1. $20.00

LEARY, Francis. *Golden Longing.* c 1960. dj. VG. C1. $7.00

LEARY, Timothy. *Confessions of a Dope Fiend.* 1973. Bantam. ARC. EX. $25.00

LEARY, Timothy. *Psychedelic Prayers.* 1964. NY. 1st issue. pink wraps. EX. $65.00

LEARY, Timothy. *Psychedelic Prayers.* 1964. NY. 2nd issue. $25.00

LEARY, Timothy. *Starseed.* 1973. Level Pr. wraps. EX. $30.00

LEASOR, James. *Millionth Chance.* nd. NY. Reynal. Ils. 244 p. dj. M1. $10.00

LEASOR, James. *Passport to Oblivion.* 1964. London. Heinemann. 1st ed. dj. VG. $25.00

LEASOR, James. *Spylight.* 1966. Lippincott. dj. VG. P1. $8.00

LEASOR, James. *They Don't Make Them Like That Any More.* 1969. Doubleday. 1st ed. dj. VG. P1. $17.50

LEASOR, James. *Who Killed Sir Harry Oaks?* 1983. Boston. Houghton Mifflin. 1st ed. dj. $10.00

LEASOR & BURT. *One That Got Away.* 1956. Collins. 1st ed. dj. VG. P1. $15.00

LEAVITT, David. *Equal Affections.* 1989. Weidenfeld. ARC. wraps. with promo sheet. M. $15.00

LEAVITT, David. *Family Dancing.* 1984. Knopf. 1st ed. dj. EX. $25.00

LEAVITT, David. *Lost Language of Cranes.* 1986. Knopf. 1st ed. dj. M. $10.00

LEAVITT. *Easy Lessons in Reading.* 1827. Ils. 156 p. full leather. K1. $10.00

LEBER, Annedore. *Conscience in Revolt.* 1957. Westport, CT. Ils. dj. G. M1. $20.00

LEBLANC, Maurice. *Confessions of Arsene Lupin.* 1967. Walker. xl. Lib bdg. VG. P1. $5.00

LEBLANC, Maurice. *Crystal Stopper.* 1922. Doubleday Page. VG. P1. $20.00

LEBLANC, Maurice. *Exploits of Arsene Lupin.* 1960. Bodley Head. dj. EX. P1. $20.00

LEBLANC, Maurice. *Fair-Haired Lady.* 1909. Grant Richards. G. P1. $25.00

LEBLANC, Maurice. *Hollow Needle.* 1960. Bodley Head. dj. EX. P1. $20.00

LEBLANC, Maurice. *Man of Miracles.* 1931. Macaulay. G. xl. P1. $15.00

LEBLANC, Maurice. *Three Eyes.* nd. Burt. VG. P1. $10.00

LEBRUN, Rico. *Drawings.* 1961. CA U. dj. G. $40.00

LECHFORD, Thomas. *Plain Dealing; or, News From New England.* 1868. Boston. 1/35. sgn Pub. VG. $50.00

LECKIE, W.H. *Military Conquest of S Plains.* 1963. Norman. Ils 1st ed. dj. EX. $35.00

LECKY. *History of European Morals From Augustus to Charlemagne.* 1929. Appleton. 3rd ed. 2 vols. G. $25.00

LECLER, B. *Sahara.* 1954. Hanover House. photos. 280 p. dj. EX. M2. $8.00

LECUYER, Raymond. *Histoire de la Photographie.* 1945. Paris. Ils. 4to. VG. $425.00

LEDERER & BURDICK. *Ugly American.* 1958. NY. 1st ed. 8vo. EX. $25.00

LEDWICH, E. *Antiquities of Ireland.* 1804. Dublin. Ils 1st ed. 525 p. G. $125.00

LEE, Alan. *Castles.* 1984. Ils 1st ed. dj. EX. C1. $22.00

LEE, Amy. *Hobby Horses.* 1940. Derrydale. 1/200. sgn. acetate dj. EX. $140.00

LEE, Asher. *German Air Force.* 1946. NY. Ils 1st Am ed. 310 p. dj. VG. T5. $35.00

LEE, Asher. *Goering: Air Leader.* 1972. NY. Ils 1st Am ed. 256 p. dj. VG. T5. $15.00

LEE, Austin. *Miss Hogg & the Bronte Murders.* 1956. Cape. 1st ed. dj. VG. P1. $20.00

LEE, Bourke. *Death Valley.* 1930. NY. Ils 1st ed. 210 p. EX. $35.00

LEE, C.F. *Merrie Olde Middlesex.* Ltd ed. 1/1719. dj. VG. E2. $20.00

LEE, C.H. *Judge Advocate's Vade Mecum.* 1863. Richmond. $150.00

LEE, D.L. *Physiology of Nematodes.* 1965. Edinburgh. Oliver Boyd. Ils 154 p. EX. M2. $8.00

LEE, Edward. *Needle's Eye.* 1944. Crime Club. 1st ed. VG. P1. $12.50

LEE, G.R. *G-String Murders.* c 1941. NY. World. 6th print. VG. $8.00

LEE, G.R. *G-String Murders.* 1942. Tower. 2nd ed. VG. P1. $10.00

LEE, G.R. *Gypsy.* 1957. NY. 1st ed. sgn. dj. VG. B2. $37.50

LEE, H. *Octopus: Devilfish of Fiction & Fact.* 1875. London. Chapman Hall. Ils. 114 p. VG. M2. $15.00

LEE, H. *Radio Joke Book.* 1935. Phil. 1st ed. dj. EX. $27.50

LEE, Harper. *To Kill a Mockingbird.* 1960. London. 1st ed. dj. EX. $70.00

LEE, J.D. *Mormonism Unveiled.* 1891. St. Louis. Ils 413 p. $40.00

LEE, J.H. *Powder River.* Boston. Christopher Pub. 2nd ed. sgn. dj. $50.00

LEE, J.H. *Stampede & Tales of the Far W.* c 1959. Greensburg, PA. Ils. VG. $40.00

LEE, James. *Introduction to Botany.* 1788. London. Rivington. 4th ed. VG. $50.00

LEE, John. *Fighter Facts & Fallacies.* 1942. NY. Ils. 63 p. dj. $15.00

LEE, Jonathan. *Fate of the Grosvenor.* 1938. NY. AP. 1st ed. 8vo. color wraps. VG. T1. $75.00

LEE, Laurie. *Cider With Rosie.* 1959. London. Ils Ward. 1st ed. dj. EX. $17.50

LEE, M.B. *Cripple Creek Days.* 1958. Ils 1st ed. sgn. dj. EX. $15.00

LEE, Nelson. *Three Years Among the Comanches: Narrative of Nelson Lee...* 1859. Albany. Taylor. 1st ed. 224 p. rare. A3. $900.00

LEE, R.E. *General Robert E. Lee After Appomattox.* 1922. Macmillan. 1st ed. J2. $20.00

LEE, R.E. *Recollections & Letters of Robert E. Lee.* 1904. NY. Ils. 461 p. VG. $35.00

LEE, R.E. *Recollections & Letters of Robert E. Lee.* 1909. 461 p. $18.50

LEE, S.E. *History of Far E Art.* 1964. NY. 1st ed. dj. EX. $50.00

LEE, S.E. *History of Far E Art.* 1965. Prentice Hall. dj. EX. $25.00

LEE, Stan. *Dunn's Conundrum.* 1984. Harper Row. 1st ed. dj. EX. P1. $15.00

LEE, Tanith. *E of Midnight.* 1978. St. Martin. 1st ed. dj. EX. P1. $30.00

LEE, Tanith. *Electric Forest.* nd. Book Club. dj. VG. P1. $5.00

LEE, Vernon. *Studies of 18th-C Italy.* 1880. London. later green leather. EX. $75.00

LEE, W.C. *Bat Masterson.* 1960. Whitman. G. P1. $7.50

LEE, W.S. *Great CA Deserts.* 1963. NY. Putnam. 1st ed. dj. EX. $15.00

LEE, W.S. *Yankees of CT.* 1957. NY. Holt. 1st ed. dj. $10.00

LEE, W.T. *Geologic Story of Rocky Mountain National Park.* 1917. WA. Nat Park Service. 89 p. wraps. A3. $40.00

LEE, Walt. *Reference Guide to Fantastic Films of SF, Fantasy & Horror.* 1972. 3 vols. wraps. EX. $20.00

LEE & MARTIN. *Koala: A Natural History.* 1988. New S Wales U. Ils. 102 p. M. M2. $13.00

LEE. *Big Game Hunting & Markmanship.* 1941. Plantersville. 1st ed. VG. B2. $45.00

LEE. *Bloodletting in Appalachia: Story of WV's 4 Major Mine Wars.* 1972. 3rd print photos. 216 p. dj. EX. $15.00

LEECH, John. *Little Tour of Ireland.* 1896. London. 3rd ed. EX. $100.00

LEECH, Margaret. *In the Days of McKinley.* 1959. NY. Ils 1st ed. 686 p. dj. VG. $12.50

LEECH, Margaret. *Reveille in WA: 1860-1865.* 1941. Harper. photos. map. M2. $10.00

LEECH, Samuel. *30 Years From Home; or, Voice From the Main Deck...* 1843. Boston. Ils. 305 p. orig bdg. VG. $115.00

LEECH, W.B. *Great Crystal Fraud; or, The Great P.J.* 1926. Chicago. $8.00

LEECH, W.L. *Calendar of Papers of Franklin Pierce.* 1917. Lib Congress. 102 p. xl. VG. A3. $40.00

LEEDS, L.W. *Lectures on Ventilation.* 1869. NY. 1st ed. 8vo. 60 p. $50.00

LEEKLEY, Thomas. *King Herla's Quest & Other Medieval Stories.* Britain in Pictures. xl. VG. C1. $6.50

LEEMANS, W.F. *Old Baylonian Merchant: His Business & Social Positions.* 1950. Brill. 1st ed. wraps. J2. $15.00

LEEPER, D.R. *Argonauts of '49: Recollections of Plains.* 1894. S Bend. Ils 1st ed. 146 p. VG. scarce. A3. $140.00

LEEPER, D.R. *Argonauts of '49: Recollections of Plains.* 1940. Columbus, OH. reprint of 1894 ed. dj. $35.00

LEES, A.D. *Physiology of Diapause in Arthropods.* 1955. Cambridge U. Ils. 151 p. dj. EX. M2. $15.00

LEES, Jim. *Ballads of Robin Hood.* Ltd Ed Club. slipcase. M. B3. $40.00

LEES, Jim. *Ballads of Robin Hood.* 1977. Cambridge. Ltd Ed Club. 1st ed. EX. C1. $39.50

LEESE, O. *Cacti.* 1973. London. Triume. Ils. 4to. 144 p. dj. M2. $20.00

LEFFINGWELL, W.B. *Shooting on Upland, Marsh & Stream.* 1890. Chicago/NY. Ils 1st ed. 473 p. G. $95.00

LEFLER, H.T. *NC History Told by Contemporaries.* 1948. Chapel Hill. 2nd ed. 502 p. VG. $20.00

LEGARET, Jean. *Tightrope.* 1968. Little Brown. dj. xl. P1. $5.00

LEGENDRE, S.L. *Okovango: Desert River.* 1971. Negro U. photos. map. 300 p. EX. M2. $18.00

LEGGET, R.F. *Canadian Railways in Pictures.* 1977. 96 p. $16.00

LEGLER, H.E. *Poe's Raven: Origin & Genesis.* 1907. Philosopher Pr. 1/164. presentation. slipcase. D1. $110.00

LEGMAN, Gershon. *Fake Revolt.* 1967. Breaking Point. 1st ed. 8vo. wraps. $30.00

LEGMAN, Gershon. *Love & Death: Study in Censorship.* 1949. NY. 1st ed. dj. $45.00

LEHMAN, J.O. *Sonnenberg: A Haven & a Heritage.* 1969. Kidron, OH. Ils. 384 p. dj. G. T5. $12.50

LEHMANN, Ernst. *Zeppelins.* 1927. NY. Ils 1st ed. VG. $80.00

LEHMANN, Rosamund. *Invitation to the Waltz.* 1932. NY. 1st ed. dj. EX. P3. $65.00

LEHMANN, Rosamund. *Echoing Grove.* 1953. London. 1st ed. dj. EX. $25.00

LEHMANN, V.W. *Bobwhites in the Rio Grande Plain of TX.* 1984. TX A&M. Ils 1st ed. 371 p. dj. EX. M2. $30.00

LEHMANN-HAUPT, H. *Gutenberg & the Master of Playing Cards.* 1966. Yale. 1st ed. dj. VG. J2. $35.00

LEHMER, D.J. *Introduction to Middle MO Archaeology.* 1971. Nat Park Service. 4to. 206 p. M2. $30.00

LEHNER, E. *Alphabets & Ornaments.* 1952. Cleveland. 1st ed. 4to. dj. EX. $70.00

LEHRS, Max. *Late Gothic Engravings of Germany & the Netherlands.* 1969. NY. Dover. 682 pls. D2. $65.00

LEIBER, Francis. *Letter to His Excellency Patrick Noble, Governor of SC...* c 1839. np. 1st ed. 27 p. wraps. VG. rare. $150.00

LEIBER, Fritz. *Best of Fritz Leiber.* nd. Book Club. dj. G. P1. $4.50

LEIBER, Fritz. *Best of Fritz Leiber.* 1974. NY. Ballantine. 1st ed. inscr/sgn. dj. $20.00

LEIBER, Fritz. *Big Time.* 1976. Severn House. 1st ed. dj. EX. P1. $25.00

LEIBER, Fritz. *Gather Darkness.* 1950. Pelligrini. 1st ed. dj. VG. P1. $40.00

LEIBER, Fritz. *Gather Darkness.* 1961. Grosset. 1st ed. sgn. dj. G. P1. $30.00

LEIBER, Fritz. *Green Millenium.* 1977. Severn House. 1st ed. dj. EX. P1. $25.00

LEIBER, Fritz. *Green Millenium.* 1977. Severn House. 1st ed. sgn. dj. VG. P1. $45.00

LEIBER, Fritz. *Night's Black Agents.* 1947. Arkham House. 1st ed. VG. P1. $60.00

LEIBER, Fritz. *Night's Black Agents.* 1980. Gregg Pr. 1st ed. P1. $25.00

LEIBER, Fritz. *Night's Black Agents.* 1980. Gregg Pr. 1st ed. sgn. no dj issued. P1. $45.00

LEIBER, Fritz. *Our Lady of Darkness.* 1977. Berkeley. 1st ed. inscr/sgn. dj. VG. $65.00

LEIBER, Fritz. *Rime Island.* 1977. Whispers Pr. dj. $25.00

LEIBER, Fritz. *Specter Is Haunting TX.* 1968. NY. 1st ed. dj. $20.00

LEIBER, Fritz. *Swords & Deviltry.* 1970. NY. 1st ed. 2nd print. inscr/sgn. $30.00

LEIBER, Fritz. *Swords Against Wizardry.* 1968. NY. Ace. 1st ed. sgn. pb. $15.00

LEIBER, Fritz. *Wanderer.* 1967. Dobson. 1st ed. dj. VG. P1. $35.00

LEIDET, F. *Coyote: Defiant Songdog of the SW.* 1977. Chronicle. Ils. 221 p. dj. EX. M2. $10.00

LEIDING, H.K. *Historic Houses of SC.* 1921. Lippincott. Ils. 4to. 318 p. $185.00

LEIDY, Joseph. *Contributions to Extinct Vertebrate Fauna of W Territories.* 1873. WA. Ils. 37 pls. 358 p. wraps. A3. $110.00

LEIDY, Joseph. *Flora & Fauna Within Living Animals.* 1853. Smithsonian. Ils. 4to. VG. M2. $40.00

LEIDY, Joseph. *Fresh-Water Rhizopods of N America.* 1879. WA. Ils. 48 pls. 324 p. VG. A3. $90.00

LEIGH, Oliver. *Edgar Allen Poe: Man, Master, Martyr.* 1906. Chicago. Dilettante I Series. VG. $65.00

LEIGH, Randolph. *American Enterprise in Europe.* 1945. Paris. Ils. photos. 233 p. T5. $45.00

LEIGH, W.R. *W Pony.* 1933. NY. 1st ed. 1/100. 6 pls. sgn. EX. $300.00

LEIGHTON, Ann. *Early American Gardens: For Meat or Medicine.* 1970. Boston. 1st print. dj. VG. $25.00

LEIGHTON, Clare. *Country Matters.* 1937. NY. Ils Leighton. 1st ed. $25.00

LEIGHTON, Clare. *Give Us This Day.* 1943. NY. 1st ed. sgn. 4to. dj. VG. $40.00

LEIGHTON, Clare. *Wood Engraving & Woodcuts.* 1932. London. Studio. 1st ed. sgn. EX. $130.00

LEIGHTON, Clare. *Wuthering Heights.* 1931. NY. Ltd ed. 1/450. sgn. EX. $125.00

LEIGHTON, F. *Cornhill Gallery, Containing One Hundred Engravings.* 1864. London. as issued unbound in folder. VG. $75.00

LEIGHTON, Lord. *Addresses Delivered to Students of Royal Academy.* 1896. Kegan Paul. 1st ed. VG. J2. $50.00

LEIGHTON, Margaret. *Singing Cave.* c 1945. Boston. dj. EX. $20.00

LEIMBACH, P.O. *All My Meadows.* 1977. Prentice Hall. Ils. 235 p. dj. EX. M2. $5.00

LEINSTER, Murray. *Forgotten Planet.* 1954. NY. Gnome. 1st ed. dj. $20.00

LEINSTER, Murray. *Four From Planet 5.* 1974. White Lion. 1st ed. dj. VG. P1. $25.00

LEINSTER, Murray. *Last Space Ship.* 1949. Frederick Fell. 1st ed. dj. VG. P1. $50.00

LEINSTER, Murray. *Sidewise in Time.* 1950. Chicago. Shasta. sgn. dj. EX. $80.00

LEINSTER, Murray. *Space Tug.* 1953. Shasta. 1st ed. sgn. dj. VG. P1. $60.00

LEISTER, M. *Seasons of Heron Pond.* 1981. Stemmer House. Ils 1st ed. 175 p. dj. EX. M2. $13.00

LEITFRED, Robert H. *Man Who Was Murdered Twice.* 1937. Green Circle. xl. P1. $12.50

LEITHAUSER, Brad. *Equal Distance.* 1985. Knopf. 1st ed. dj. EX. $20.00

LEITNER, Konradi. *Mystic World.* 1927. Boston. $7.00

LEKENA, A.T. *1919 God V'Sibiri (Year 1919 in Siberia).* 1962. Moscow. 1st ed. Russian text. 233 p. G. T5. $9.50

LELAND, C.G. *Gypsies.* 1882. Boston. Houghton Mifflin. VG. $35.00

LELAND, C.T. *Mean Time.* 1982. Random House. 1st ed. dj. EX. $15.00

LELLINGER, D.B. *Field Manual of Fern: Allies of the US & Canada.* 1985. Smithsonian. Ils. 446 p. EX. M2. $45.00

LEM, Stanislaw. *Fiasco.* 1987. Harcourt. 1st ed. dj. EX. P1. $17.95

LEM, Stanislaw. *His Master's Voice.* 1983. NY. Harcourt. 1st ed. dj. EX. $20.00

LEM, Stanislaw. *Imaginary Magnitude.* 1984. Harcourt. 1st ed. dj. EX. P1. $15.95

LEM, Stanislaw. *Memoirs From the Stars.* 1980. Harcourt. dj. EX. P1. $15.00

LEM, Stanislaw. *More Tales of Pirx the Pilot.* 1982. NY. 1st ed. dj. RS. $10.00

LEM, Stanislaw. *Return From the Stars.* 1980. NY. 1st ed. dj. M. $10.00

LEM, Stanislaw. *Tales of Pirx the Pilot.* 1979. Harcourt. dj. EX. P1. $15.00

LEMERY, Nicolas. *Mouveau Recueil des Plus Beaux Secrets de Medecine.* 1749. Paris. 8vo. 2 vols. leather. $375.00

LEMKE, W.J. *Early Colleges & Academies of WA Co., AR.* 1954. WA Co Hist Soc. 4to. 96 p. EX. M2. $10.00

LEMMING, Joseph. *Rayon: First Man-Made Fabric.* 1950. Brooklyn, NY. Ils 1st ed. 203 p. dj. G. T5. $15.00

LEMMON, Kenneth. *Covered Garden.* 1962. London. 1st ed. dj. VG. $21.00

LEMMON, R.S. *Our Amazing Birds: Little-Known Facts About Their Lives.* 1952. Doubleday. Ils 1st ed. 239 p. G. M2. $7.00

LEMMON & SHERMAN. *Flowers of the World.* 1964. Doubleday. Ils. 279 p. dj. EX. M2. $10.00

LENDY, A.F. *Elements of Fornification.* 1857. London. Ils 1st ed. 12mo. brown cloth. T1. $35.00

LENEHAN, J.C. *Tunnel Mystery.* c 1931. NY. Mystery League. 1st ed. VG. $10.00

LENGYEL, Emil. *Americans From Hungary.* 1948. Lippincott. 1st ed. dj. J2. $12.50

LENGYEL, Emil. *Siberia.* 1943. Random House. Ils 1st ed. 416 p. dj. EX. M2. $10.00

LENHOFF & LOOMIS. *Biology of Hydra & Some Other Coelenterates.* 1961. Miami U. Ils. 467 p. dj. EX. M2. $25.00

LENIN, Nikolai. *Imperialism: State & Revolution.* 1926. NY. 1st Am ed. VG. $30.00

LENNON, John. *Skywriting by Word of Mouth.* 1986. NY. Ltd 1st ed. sgn Yoko. boxed. M. $85.00

LENS. *Left, Right & Center: Conflicting Forces in American Labor.* 1949. dj. VG. $15.00

LENSKI, Lois. *Blueberry Corners.* 1940. NY. Stokes. 1st ed. dj. EX. $12.50

LENSKI, Lois. *Fireside Poems.* 1930. Minton Balch. Ils 1st ed. $30.00

LENSKI, Lois. *Judy's Journey.* 1947. Lippincott. 1st ed. VG. B4. $40.00

LENSKI, Lois. *Skipping Village.* 1927. Stokes. 1st ed. EX. $40.00

LENT, C.P. *Rocketry: Jets & Rockets.* 1947. NY. Ils 1st ed. 254 p. VG. T5. $35.00

LENT, H.B. *Aviation Cadet.* 1944. 5th print. dj. $10.00

LENT, Henry. *Straight Up.* 1944. Macmillan. 12mo. G. $7.50

LENTZ, T.L. *Cell Biology of Hydra.* 1966. N Holland. Ils. 199 p. dj. EX. M2. $11.00

LENZ, E.C. *Muzzle Flashes.* 1944. Huntington. 2nd ed. VG. B2. $60.00

LEODERER, R. *Voodo Fire in Haiti.* 1935. Literary Guild. Ils 1st ed. 274 p. VG. M2. $10.00

LEONARD, A.G. *Lead & Zinc Deposits in IA.* 1897. IA Geol Survey. Ils. 487 p. VG. M2. $5.00

LEONARD, Charles L. *Treachery in Trieste.* 1951. Crime Club. 1st ed. P1. $10.00

LEONARD, Elizabeth. *Call of the W Prairie.* 1952. Lib Pub. 1st ed. J2. $17.50

LEONARD, Elmore. *Bandits.* 1987. NY. 1st ed. sgn. dj. M. $30.00

LEONARD, Elmore. *Cat Chaser.* 1982. Arbor House. 1st ed. dj. $20.00

LEONARD, Elmore. *Cat Chaser.* 1982. NY. 1st ed. sgn. dj. EX. $35.00

LEONARD, Elmore. *City Primeval. High Noon in Detroit.* 1980. Arbor House. 1st ed. sgn. dj. VG. $45.00

LEONARD, Elmore. *Double-Dutch Treat.* 1980. Arbor House. AP. 1st ed. wraps. EX. $20.00

LEONARD, Elmore. *Dutch Treat.* Mysterious Pr. Ltd 1st ed. 1/350. sgn. dj. $50.00

LEONARD, Elmore. *Glitz.* 1985. Arbor House. AP. VG. P1. $10.00

LEONARD, Elmore. *Glitz.* 1985. NY. Ltd 1st ed. sgn. boxed. B2. $70.00

LEONARD, Elmore. *Glitz.* 1985. NY. 1st ed. sgn. dj. EX. $25.00

LEONARD, Elmore. *Gold Coast.* 1982. London. 1st Eng ed. dj. EX. $40.00

LEONARD, Elmore. *Moonshine War.* 1970. NY. Dell. 1st ed. pb. EX. $15.00

LEONARD, Elmore. *Split Images.* 1981. Arbor House. 1st ed. dj. EX. $25.00

LEONARD, Elmore. *Split Images.* 1981. London. 1st ed. dj. VG. $25.00

LEONARD, Elmore. *Touch.* 1987. Arbor House. 1st ed. dj. M. $10.00

LEONARD, Fred. *History of Physical Education.* 1923. Phil. 100 photos. 360 p. EX. $45.00

LEONARD, Zenas. *Narrative of Adventures of Zenas Leonard.* 1934. Chicago. Lakeside Classic. 278 p. G. T5. $25.00

LEONARD, Zenas. *Narrative of Adventures of Zenas Leonard.* 1934. Donnelley. Lakeside Classic. A3. $50.00

LEONARD & WARD. *Beowulf.* 1939. Heritage. Ils Lynd Ward. slipcase. EX. $15.00

LEONHARDT, Olive. *New Orleans Drawn & Quartered.* 1938. Richmond. Dale. Into/sgn Saxon. 4to. $125.00

LEONING, Grover. *Our Wings Grow Faster.* 1935. Doubleday. 1st ed. 4to. 203 p. dj. VG. $35.00

LEOPOLD, Aldo. *Round River: From the Journals of Aldo Leopold.* 1953. Oxford U. Ils. 173 p. dj. EX. M2. $12.00

LEOPOLD, Aldo. *Sand County Almanac & Sketches Here & There.* 1968. Oxford U. Ils. 226 p. M. M2. $7.00

LEOPOLD, E.F. *Lexicon Hebraicum et Chaldaicum in Libros.* 1891. Lipsiae. 12mo. G. $40.00

LERMAN, Rhoda. *Book of the Night.* 1984. 1st ed. dj. M. C1. $9.50

LEROI, A.G. *Treasures of Prehistoric Art.* 1967. NY. Abrams. 1st ed. dj. EX. $125.00

LEROUX, Gaston. *Nomads of the Night.* c 1925. NY. Macaulay. 1st ed. VG. $8.00

LEROUX, Gaston. *Phantom of the Opera.* 1911. Bobbs Merrill. 1st ed. dj. EX. T6. $100.00

LEROUX, Gaston. *Phantom of the Opera.* 1911. NY. Ils Movie ed. VG. B2. $22.50

LEROUX & GARNIER. *Acrobats & Mountebanks.* 1890. London. 1st ed. 336 p. $125.00

LESCROAT, J.T. *Son of Holmes.* 1986. NY. 1st ed. dj. EX. $20.00

LESESNE, T.P. *Landmarks of Charleston.* 1932. Richmond. Garrett Massie. photos. $6.50

LESKE, Gottfried. *I Was a Nazi Flier.* 1941. NY. 1st ed. 351 p. dj. VG. T5. $22.50

LESLIE, D. *Flying Saucers Have Landed.* 1953. 1st ed. dj. VG. $9.00

LESLIE, Frank. *Frank Leslie's Illustrated Famous Leaders & Battle Scenes...* 1896. NY. Ils. folio. 544 p. VG. $125.00

LESLIE, J.W. *Land of the Cypress & Pine.* 1976. Rose Pr. Ils. sgn/#d. 216 p. dj. EX. M2. $25.00

LESLIE, J.W. *Saracen's Country: Some SW AR History.* 1974. Rose Pr. Ils 1st ed. sgn. 216 p. dj. EX. M2. $20.00

LESLIE, R.F. *In the Shadow of a Rainbow.* 1974. Norton. 1st ed. 190 p. dj. EX. M2. $14.00

LESLIE, R.F. *Wild Pets.* 1970. Crown. photos. dj. EX. M2. $6.00

LESLIE, Shane. *Shane Leslie's Ghost Book.* 1955. London. 1st ed. dj. VG. $22.00

LESQUEREUX, Leo. *Contributions to Fossil Flora of W Territories, Part I.* 1874. WA. Ils. 133 p. A3. $75.00

LESQUEREUX, Leo. *Contributions to Fossil Flora of W Territories, Part II.* 1878. WA. 65 pls. 366 p. xl. A3. $75.00

LESQUEREUX, Leo. *Contributions to Fossil Flora of W Territories.* 1883. WA. GPO. Ils. 292 p. VG. scarce. A3. $90.00

LESSING, Doris. *Diary of Good Neighbor.* 1983. Knopf. 1st ed. dj. VG. $20.00

LESSING, Doris. *Golden Notebook.* 1962. London. Ltd 1st ed. dj. EX. $125.00

LESSING, Doris. *Good Terrorist.* 1985. Knopf. AP. wraps. $60.00

LESSING, Doris. *In Pursuit of the English.* 1961. NY. 1st Am ed. dj. EX. $15.00

LESSING, Doris. *Memoirs of a Survivor.* 1974. London. Octagon. sgn. dj. EX. $80.00

LESSING, Doris. *Memoirs of a Survivor.* 1975. NY. 1st ed. dj. VG. B2. $15.00

LESSING, Doris. *Shikasta.* 1979. NY. Knopf. 1st ed. dj. VG. $20.00

LESSING, Doris. *Sirian Experiments.* 1981. Knopf. 1st ed. dj. EX. $15.00

LESSING, Doris. *Summer Before the Dark.* 1973. London. Cape. 1st ed. dj. EX. $45.00

LESSING, Doris. *This Was the Old Chief's Country.* 1951. Joseph. 1st ed. dj. VG. $60.00

LESSING, Doris. *This Was the Old Chief's Country.* 1951. London. 1st ed. dj. M. $125.00

LESTER, C.E. *Life & Public Services of Charles Sumner.* c 1874. Muscatine, IA. Ils. 8vo. 693 p. G2. $19.00

LESTER, James. *History of GA Baptist Convention, 1822-1972.* 1972. Nashville. Ils 1st ed. 846 p. dj. VG. $15.00

LESTER, Julius. *Look Out Whitey Black Power's Gonna Get Your Mama!* 1971. wraps. EX. $15.00

LESTER, R.I. *Confederate Finance & Purchasing in Great Britain.* 1975. VA U. 1st ed. tall 8vo. 267 p. $22.50

LETHBRIDGE, T.C. *Gogmagog: Buried Gods.* 1957. London. Ils 1st ed. VG. C1. $19.00

LETTS. *British Imperial Atlas.* 1881. London. 76 maps. tall quarto. A3. $200.00

LETTY, C. *Trees of S Africa.* 1975. Cape Town. Ils 1st ed. dj. $10.00

LETULLE, C.J. *Nightmare Memoir.* 1987. LA U. 1st ed. dj. VG. $6.00

LEUBA, J.H. *Psychology of Religious Mysticism.* 1925. London. 1st ed. 8vo. TEG. VG. T1. $40.00

LEUTSCHER, A. *Keeping Reptiles & Amphibians As Pets.* 1976. Scribner. Ils. 164 p. $10.00

LEVANT, Oscar. *Importance of Being Oscar.* 1968. NY. 1st ed. sgn. dj. VG. B2. $22.50

LEVARIE, Norma. *Art & History of Books.* 1968. Heinemann. 1st ed. dj. VG. J2. $30.00

LEVER, Charles. *Fortunes of Glencore.* c 1860. London. 4 pls. $15.00

LEVER, Charles. *Jack Hinton.* Dublin. Curry. 1st ed. G. $45.00

LEVER, Charles. *Jack Hinton.* 1843. Phil. 1st ed. EX. $45.00

LEVER, Charles. *Martins of Cro' Martin.* 1856. London. Chapman Hall. 1st ed. VG. $55.00

LEVER, Charles. *Novels of Irish Life.* 1899. Boston. 16 vols. VG. $100.00

LEVER, Charles. *Roland Cashel.* 1850. NY. Ils 1st ed. VG. $35.00

LEVERETT, F.P. *New & Copious Lexicon of Latin Language.* 1840. Little Brown. 318 p. M1. $35.00

LEVERTOV, Denise. *Conversation in Moscow.* 1973. Hovey St Pr. 1/1000. dj. $20.00

LEVERTOV, Denise. *Life in the Forest.* 1978. New Directions. 1/150. slipcase. M. $60.00

LEVERTOV, Denise. *Tree Telling of Orpheus.* 1968. Black Sparrow. 1/250. sgn/#d. wraps. EX. $60.00

LEVERTOV, Denise. *Two Poems.* 1983. Ewert. Ltd ed. sgn. $85.00

LEVERTOV, Denise. *With Eyes at the Back of Our Heads.* 1959. New Directions. 1st ed. $45.00

LEVETT, Carl. *Crossings: Transpersonal Approach.* 1974. CT. $12.00

LEVETTO, G.C. *Return to Yesterday.* 1985. sgn. 193 p. dj. EX. J4. $5.00

LEVI, P. *Light Garden of the Angel Kings: Travels in Afghanistan.* 1972. Bobbs Merrill. dj. EX. $55.00

LEVI, Primo. *Drowned & Saved.* 1986. NY. 1st ed. dj. EX. $7.50

LEVI, W.M. *Pigeon.* 1957. Levi. Ils Revised ed. inscr/sgn. EX. M2. $55.00

LEVI, W.M. *Pigeon.* 1963. Sumter. Ils/inscr Levi. 4to. $65.00

LEVIN, Bob. *Best Ride to NY.* 1978. NY. 1st ed. dj. EX. $10.00

LEVIN, Gail. *Edward Hopper, Illustrator.* 1st ed. dj. EX. $10.00

LEVIN, Ira. *Rosemary's Baby.* 1967. Random House. dj. EX. $12.50

LEVIN, Meyer. *Obsession.* 1973. NY. 1st ed. dj. $10.00

LEVIN, Nora. *Holocaust: Destruction of European Jewry 1933-1945.* 1970. NY. 2nd ed. dj. VG. $10.00

LEVIN, Nora. *Holocaust: Destruction of European Jewry 1933-1945.* 1973. Schocken Books. SftCvr. VG. $17.50

LEVINE, David. *Arts of David Levine.* 1978. NY. 1st ed. dj. EX. $27.50

LEVINE, David. *No Known Survivors: David Levine's Political Plank.* 1970. Boston. 1st ed. 1/300. sgns. dj. EX. $60.00

LEVINE, I.D. *Stalin.* 1931. NY. Cosmopolitan. 421 p. G. $6.00

LEVINE, S.A. *Clinical Heart Disease.* 1936. Phil. Saunders. 1st ed. VG. $55.00

LEVINE & HARVEY. *Clinical Auscultation of the Heart.* 1949. Saunders. 1st ed. VG. $75.00

LEVINGER, L.J. *Anti-Semitism in US: Its History & Causes.* 1925. NY. Bloch. 1st ed. VG. J3. $15.00

LEVINREW, W. *Death Points a Finger.* c 1933. NY. Mystery League. 1st ed. VG. $8.50

LEVINSON & LINK. *Stay Tuned. Inside Look at Making of Prime-Time Television.* 1981. NY. 1st ed. 253 p. dj. $17.50

LEVINSON. *Labor on the March.* 1956. reprint of 1938 ed. dj. VG. $15.00

LEVISON, L.L. *Wall Street: Pictorial History.* 1961. NY. Ils 1st ed. boxed. $65.00

LEVITAN. *Blue Collar Workers: Symposium on Middle America.* 1971. dj. VG. $15.00

LEVITT, Saul. *Andersonville Trial.* 1960. Random House. 1st ed. dj. EX. $28.00

LEVY, G.R. *Gate of the Horn.* NY. Book Collectors Soc. 1/250. G. $25.00

LEVY, Leonard. *Legacy of Suppression: Freedom of Speech & Press...* 1960. Harvard. 1st ed. dj. VG. J2. $17.50

LEVY, Melvin. *Last Pioneers.* 1934. NY. sgn. EX. $17.50

LEWI, Grant. *Scorpio's Horoscope Book. Heaven Knows What.* 1947. NY. $60.00

LEWIN, M.Z. *Late Payments.* 1986. NY. 1st ed. dj. EX. $15.00

LEWIN, M.Z. *Out of Season.* 1984. Morrow. 1st ed. dj. RS. EX. $25.00

LEWINSOHN, R. *Animals, Men & Myths.* 1954. Harper. Ils 1st ed. 422 p. dj. EX. M2. $6.00

LEWIS, A. *Lament for the Molly Maguires.* 1964. NY. 1st ed. 308 p. dj. VG. B2. $17.50

LEWIS, C.B. *Classical Mythology & Arthurian Romance.* 1932. London. VG. C1. $29.50

LEWIS, C.D. *Gate.* 1962. London. dj. EX. $15.00

LEWIS, C.D. *Poems, 1943-1947.* 1948. NY. 1st Am ed. 8vo. dj. VG. $30.00

LEWIS, C.S. *Abolition of Man.* 1947. Macmillan. 1st Am ed. EX. $20.00

LEWIS, C.S. *Allegory of Love.* 1958. pb. VG. C1. $11.50

LEWIS, C.S. *Case for Christianity.* 1943. Macmillan. 1st Am ed. dj. VG. $45.00

LEWIS, C.S. *Patterns of Love & Courtesy: Essays in Memory of C.S. Lewis.* 1966. 1st ed. VG. C1. $14.50

LEWIS, C.S. *Perelandra.* 1944. Macmillan. 1st Am ed. dj. VG. $20.00

LEWIS, C.S. *Poems.* 1965. NY. 1st Am ed. dj. VG. $25.00

LEWIS, C.S. *Reflection on the Psalms.* 1958. London. 1st ed. dj. EX. $35.00

LEWIS, C.S. *Studies in Words.* 1960. Cambridge. 1st ed. dj. VG. B2. $17.50

LEWIS, C.S. *World's Last Night.* 1960. NY. 1st Am ed. dj. VG. $30.00

LEWIS, D.L. *Race to Fashoda.* 1987. Weidenfeld. Ils. 304 p. M. M2. $11.00

LEWIS, Dio. *New Gymnastics for Men, Women & Children.* 1862. Boston. Ils. $25.00

LEWIS, E. *Trader Horn.* 1927. Simon Schuster. Ils. VG. $12.50

LEWIS, E.F. *Young Fu of the Upper Yangtze.* 1932. Winston. sgn. VG. $18.00

LEWIS, E.W. *Motor Memories.* 1947. Detroit. sgn. $12.50

LEWIS, Frank. *Edward Ladell.* 1976. Lewis. Ltd ed. 1/500. D2. $85.00

LEWIS, Franklin. *Cleveland Indians.* 1949. Putnam. Ils. 276 p. EX. $8.00

LEWIS, G.G. *Mystery of the Oriental Rug.* 1914. Phil. Ils 1st ed. 103 p. VG. B2. $42.50

LEWIS, G.W. *Ape I Knew.* 1961. Caxton. 1st ed. dj. EX. $25.00

LEWIS, G.W. *Campaigns of the 124th Regiment, OH Volunteer Infantry...* 1894. Akron. Werner. Ils. 285 p. VG. T5. $225.00

LEWIS, H.H. *Gunner Aboard the Yankee.* 1898. NY. Ils. 312 p. G. T5. $19.50

LEWIS, H.L. *Butterflies of the World.* 1973. Follett. 208 pls. 4to. 312 p. dj. EX. M2. $40.00

LEWIS, J.C. *World of the Wild Turkey.* 1973. Lippincott. Ils 1st ed. 158 p. dj. EX. M2. $23.00

LEWIS, J.M. *Sing the S.* 1905. Houston. Dealy. Ils 2nd ed. green bdg. EX. $12.00

LEWIS, Lloyd. *Captain Sam Grant.* 1950. Little Brown. 1st ed. 512 p. dj. J4. $7.50

LEWIS, Lloyd. *Sherman, Fighting Prophet.* 1932. Harcourt Brace. Ils 1st ed. photos. maps. 690 p. $12.00

LEWIS, Marvin. *Mining Frontier.* 1967. Norman. not 1st ed. $12.00

LEWIS, Oscar. *Autobiography of the W.* 1958. NY. Holt. 1st ed. dj. M. $18.00

LEWIS, Oscar. *Sea Routes to the Gold Fields.* 1949. Knopf. Ils. 286 p. dj. VG. D1. $30.00

LEWIS, Oscar. *Silver Kings.* 1947. NY. 1st ed. 286 p. EX. $15.00

LEWIS, Oscar. *Sutter's Fort: Gateway to the Gold Field.* 1966. NY. 1st ed. dj. EX. $15.00

LEWIS, P. *British Racing & Record-Breaking Aircraft.* 1971. London. Putnam. 1st ed. dj. M. $35.00

LEWIS, P. *John Le Carre.* 1985. Ungar. AP. VG. P1. $20.00

LEWIS, P. *Man Who Lost America: Biography of Gentleman J. Burgoyne.* 1973. Dial. 1st ed. 282 p. dj. EX. M2. $13.00

LEWIS, R.H. *Fine Bookbinding in the 20th Century.* 1985. NY. Arco. Ils. 8vo. 151 p. $17.95

LEWIS, Richard. *Few Flowers for Shiner.* 1950. NY. 1st ed. dj. EX. $12.00

LEWIS, Robert. *Handbook of American Railroads.* 1951. 1st ed. photos. maps. $25.00

LEWIS, Robert. *Handbook of American Railroads.* 1956. NY. Simmons Boardman. 2nd ed. $12.50

LEWIS, Sinclair. *Ann Vicker.* 1933. Doubleday. $30.00

LEWIS, Sinclair. *Bethel Merriday.* 1940. NY. 1st ed. sgn. M. $85.00

LEWIS, Sinclair. *Bethel Merriday.* 1940. NY. 1st ed. sgn. VG. $45.00

LEWIS, Sinclair. *Cass Timberlane.* 1945. NY. 1st ed. dj. EX. P3. $45.00

LEWIS, Sinclair. *Elmer Gantry.* 1927. NY. 1st ed. 1st issue. VG. $75.00

LEWIS, Sinclair. *God Seeker.* 1949. Random House. 1st ed. dj. EX. $20.00

LEWIS, Sinclair. *Kingsblood Royal.* 1947. Random House. 1st ed. dj. T6. $25.00

LEWIS, Sinclair. *Main Street.* 1920. NY. 1st ed. 451 p. T5. $45.00

LEWIS, V.A. *History of WV.* 1889. Hubbard. Ils 1st ed. 744 p. VG. M2. $45.00

LEWIS, W.D. *Airway to Everywhere: History of All American Aviation.* 1988. Pittsburgh. Ils 1st ed. dj. RS. VG. T5. $15.00

LEWIS, W.S. *Horace Walpole.* 1961. NY. Bollingen. Ils. inscr/sgn. VG. $45.00

LEWIS, W.S. *Samothrace.* 1958. NY. Bolilingen. Ils. 4to. 3 vols. djs. EX. $75.00

LEWIS, W.S. *Yale Collections.* 1946. New Haven. presentation. sgn. $40.00

LEWIS, Wilmarth. *Collector's Progress.* 1952. London. Constable. 1st ed. dj. EX. $25.00

LEWIS, Wilmarth. *Horace Walpole's Library.* 1958. Cambridge. 1st ed. 1/750. 8vo. 74 p. dj. $40.00

LEWIS, Wilmarth. *One Man's Education.* 1967. NY. 1st ed. inscr. dj. $25.00

LEWIS, Wyndam. *Demon of Progress in the Arts.* 1954. London. 1st ed. dj. EX. $25.00

LEWIS, Wyndham. *Stuffed Owl.* 1930. London. Ils 1st ed. EX. $40.00

LEWIS, Wyndham. *Writer & the Absolute.* 1952. London. 1st ed. dj. EX. $30.00

LEWIS & CLARK. *Journals of Expedition Under Command of Lewis & Clark.* 1962. Ltd Ed Club. 1/1500. 2 vols. boxed. T5. $195.00

LEWIS & DIGNAM. *Marriage of Diamonds & Dolls.* 1947. NY. 1st ed. dj. VG. $22.50

LEWIS & EASSON. *Publishing & Printing at Home.* 1984. London. dj. M. $20.00

LEWIS & HALL. *Bonanza Inn.* 1939. NY. Ils 1st ed. EX. $25.00

LEWIS & KNEBERG. *Tribes That Slumber.* 1958. Knoxville. Ils 1st ed. 196 p. $15.00

LEWIS & MEWHA. *History of POW Utilization by US Army: 1776-1945.* 1955. WA. Army Dept. 1st ed. inscr. EX. $16.00

LEWISOHN, Florence. *St. Croix Under Seven Flags.* 1970. Hollywood, FL. Ils 1st ed. map. 8vo. dj. T1. $25.00

LEWISOHN, Ludwig. *Case of Mr. Crum.* 1926. Paris. Ltd ed. 1/500. dj. VG. $25.00

LEY, Willy. *Dawn of Zoology.* 1968. Prentice Hall. Ils. 280 p. G. M2. $5.00

LEY, Willy. *Lungfish, Dodo & Unicorn.* 1948. NY. Viking. VG. $5.00

LEY, Willy. *Salamanders & Other Wonders: Adventures of Naturalist.* 1955. Viking. Ils. 293 p. dj. VG. M2. $5.00

LEYDA, Jay. *Melville Log: Documentary Life of H. Melville, 1819-1891.* 1951. Harcourt Brace. 1st ed. 2 vols. boxed. VG. J2. $65.00

LEYDET, Francois. *Coyote: Defiant Songdog of the W.* 1988. OK U. Revised ed. 221 p. dj. EX. M2. $15.00

LEYLAND, J. *Adventures in Far Interior of Africa.* 1972. Cape Town. Struik. reprint of 1866 ed. M2. $38.00

LEYMARIE, Jean. *Picasso: Artist of the Century.* 1972. NY. 1st ed. folio. dj. EX. $85.00

LEYMARIE & MELOT. *Graphic Works of Impressionists: Manet, Pissarro, Renoir...* 1972. NY. Abrams. 391 pls. 353 p. D2. $285.00

LEYSON, Burr W. *Wings of Defense.* 1942. NY. Ils 1st ed. dj. T5. $12.50

LEZARD, Adele. *Great Gold Reef. Romantic History of Rand Gold Fields.* 1937. Indianpolis. Ils 1st ed. dj. VG. T1. $45.00

LIAUTARD. *Animal Castration.* 1892. Ils 5th ed. EX. $18.00

LIBBY, Bill. *Pro Hockey Heroes of Today.* 1974. Random House. Ils. EX. $12.50

LIBERACE. *Liberace Cooks.* 1970. NY. Ils 1st ed. 225 p. dj. VG. B2. $22.50

LIBERACE. *Wonderful Private World of Liberace.* 1986. Harper. 1st ed. dj. M. $14.00

LIBERMAN, Alexander. *Artist in His Studio.* 1960. Viking. dj. VG. $50.00

LIBRARY OF CONGRESS. *List of WA Manuscripts From the Year 1592 to 1775.* 1919. WA. 137 p. xl. VG. A3. $30.00

LICHTEN, Francis. *Folk Art of Rural PA.* 1946. NY. Ils 1st ed. 276 p. dj. B2. $27.50

LICHTENSTEIN, Roy. *Jerusalem: Portfolio.* 1941. 10 sgn pls. VG. $200.00

LIDDELL, Donald. *Chessmen.* 1937. Harcourt. 1st ed. G. J2. $30.00

LIDDELL, Hart. *War in Outline.* 1936. London. fld maps. dj. EX. $17.50

LIDDELL-HART, B.H. *Reputations Ten Years After.* 1928. Boston. Ils 1st Am ed. 316 p. T5. $37.50

LIDDY, G.G. *Out of Control.* 1979. NY. 1st ed. dj. VG. $15.00

LIDDY, G.G. *Will.* 1980. NY. 1st ed. dj. VG. B2. $15.00

LIDDY, G.G. *Will.* 1980. St. Martin. dj. M. $25.00

LIDELL, H.S. *Emotional Hazards in Animals & Man.* 1956. Thomas. 1st ed. simulated morocco. VG. $30.00

LIDMAN, Hans. *People of the Forest.* 1963. NY. 1st ed. dj. EX. $22.50

LIDO, Serge. *La Danse the Dance.* 1949. Paris. Masque. wraps. $65.00

LIEB, F.G. *Boston Red Sox.* 1947. Putnam. Ils. 257 p. $7.00

LIEBERMAN, W.S. *Manhattan Observed.* 1968. MOMA. Ils. 8vo. wraps. $20.00

LIEBLING, A.J. *Honest Rainmaker.* 1953. Doubleday. 1st ed. dj. EX. $35.00

LIEBLING, A.J. *Mollie & Other War Pieces.* 1964. Ballantine. 1st ed. wraps. EX. $17.50

LIEDERMAN, Earle. *Secrets of Strength.* 1925. NY. $37.50

LIEF, Alfred. *Firestone Story.* 1951. NY. Ils. 437 p. TEG. morocco. VG. T5. $22.50

LIEF, Alfred. *It Floats. Story of Proctor & Gamble.* 1958. NY. 1st ed. 338 p. dj. B2. $22.50

LIERS, E.E. *Otter's Story.* 1961. Viking. Ils. inscr/sgn. 191 p. dj. EX. M2. $13.00

LIFE, Page West. *Sir Thomas Malory & the Morte d'Arthur.* 1980. VA U. 1st ed. M. C1. $42.50

LIGHT, Mary. *More Signs & Wonders.* 1950. St. Paul. $3.50

LIGHT, Mose. *Light Genealogy in America.* 1896. private print. 12mo. wraps. 38 p. VG. B1. $30.00

LIGHT, Richard. *Focus on Africa.* 1938. Am Geog Soc. 323 photos. 4to. VG. $45.00

LIGHT & MARZANI. *Cuba Versus CIA.* 1961. NY. 72 p. pb. G. $25.00

LIGON, J.S. *History & Management of Merriam's Wild Turkey.* 1946. NM Fish/Game. Ils. map. 84 p. EX. M2. $17.00

LIGON, J.S. *NM Birds & Where To Find Them.* 1961. NM U. Ils Brooks. 1st ed. dj. EX. M2. $70.00

LILJENCRANTZ, O. *Thrall of Leif the Lucky.* 1902. Ils 1st ed. VG. C1. $9.50

LILJENCRANTZ, O. *Ward of King Canute.* 1903. Boston. 1st ed. VG. C1. $9.50

LILJESTRAND, G.R. *Land of the Wolf.* 1978. private print. Ils. 120 p. G. M2. $6.00

LILLARD, R.G. *Desert Challenge.* 1942. Knopf. 1st ed. fld map. dj. VG. $15.00

LILLIE, Leo. *Historic Grand Haven & Ottawa Co., MI.* 1931. Grand Haven. 1st ed. J2. $25.00

LIMITED EDITIONS CLUB. *Bibliography of Limited Editions Club, 1929-1985.* 1/800. $200.00

LIMITED EDITIONS CLUB. *Monthly Letters, 1929-1933.* 1/550. B3. $145.00

LIN, M.W. *Architectural Rendering Techniques: A Color Reference.* 1985. NY. dj. G. $20.00

LIN, Tsuifeng. *Secrets of Chinese Cooking.* nd. NY. Bonanza. EX. $7.50

LINCKE, J.R. *Jenny Was No Lady: Story of the JN-4D.* 1970. NY. Ils 1st ed. 288 p. dj. VG. T5. $35.00

LINCOLN, Abraham. *Famous Speeches of Abraham Lincoln.* 1935. Peter Pauper. 8vo. slipcase. EX. $20.00

LINCOLN, Abraham. *Old Abe's Jokes: Fresh From Abraham's Bosom.* 1864. NY. Dawley. 140 p. wraps. A3. $40.00

LINCOLN, Betty Woelk. *Festschriften in Art History, 1960-1975.* 1988. NY. Garland. D2. $35.00

LINCOLN, F.C. *Migration of Birds.* 1950. USFWS. maps. 102 p. M2. $8.00

LINCOLN, F.S. *Charleston, Photographic Studies.* 1946. NY. Corinthian Pub. 75 pls. 4to. $37.50

LINCOLN, F.S. *Photographic Studies of Charleston.* 1946. NY. Ils 1st ed. 76 p. VG. $15.00

LINCOLN, J.C. *Cape Cod Ballads & Other Verse.* 1902. Trenton, NJ. Ils Kemble. 1st ed. 198 p. G. T5. $45.00

LINCOLN, J.C. *Cape Cod Yesterdays.* 1935. Boston. Ils 1st ed. dj. VG. T1. $35.00

LINCOLN, J.C. *Keziah Coffin.* 1909. Grosset Dunlap. 387 p. $20.00

LINCOLN, J.C. *Old Home House.* 1907. NY. Barnes. 1st ed. 3rd print. $30.00

LINCOLN, J.C. *Rugged Water.* 1924. NY. 1st ed. $30.00

LINCOLN, Victoria. *Private Disgrace.* 1967. NY. 1st ed. dj. VG. B2. $17.50

LINCOLN & BRETT. *Christmas Days.* 1936. Coward McCann. Ltd ed. sgns/#d. VG. $48.00

LINCOLN & DOUGLAS. *Political Debates Between Lincoln & Douglas.* 1860. Columbus. 3rd ed. 5th state. very scarce. $175.00

LINCOLN & FREEMAN. *Blair's Attic.* 1929. NY. 1st ed. dj. $50.00

LIND, E. *Complete Book of Trick & Fancy Shooting.* 1972. Winchester Pr. Ils. dj. G. $16.00

LINDAUER, Gottfried. *Maoir Painting.* 1965. Honolulu. Ils. 117 p. dj. D2. $37.50

LINDAUER, Gottfried. *Prints & Drawings: Pictorial History.* 1970. Praeger. Trans Gerald Onn. 475 p. dj. D2. $65.00

LINDBERGH, A.M. *Bring Me a Unicorn.* 1972. NY. dj. G. $12.50

LINDBERGH, A.M. *Flower & the Nettle.* 1976. NY. 1st ed. dj. VG. $15.00

LINDBERGH, A.M. *Listen! The Wind.* 1938. NY. 1st ed. 275 p. dj. T5. $25.00

LINDBERGH, A.M. *N to the Orient.* 1935. NY. 1st ed. dj. EX. $30.00

LINDBERGH, C.A. *Of Flight & Life.* 1948. Scribner. 1st ed. inscr/sgn. EX. $275.00

LINDBERGH, C.A. *Wartime Journals of Charles A. Lindbergh.* 1970. NY. 1st ed. dj. VG. $25.00

LINDBERGH, C.A. *We.* 1927. 1st ed. B1. $25.00

LINDBERGH, C.A. *We.* 1927. NY. 1st ed. sgn. dj. VG. $95.00

LINDBERGH, C.A. *We.* 1927. NY. 1st ed. dj. boxed. B2. $37.50

LINDBURG, D.D. *Macaques: Studies in Ecology, Behavior & Evolution.* 1980. Van Nostrand. Ils 1st ed. maps. dj. EX. M2. $25.00

LINDER, Leslie. *History of Writings of Beatrix Potter...* 1971. Warne. 1st ed. dj. VG. J2. $45.00

LINDERMAN, F.B. *Indian Old Man Stories.* 1920. NY. Ils Russell. 1st ed. VG. B2. $95.00

LINDERMAN, F.B. *Indian Why Stories.* 1915. NY. Ils Russell. 1st ed. VG. B2. $125.00

LINDERMAN, F.B. *Indian Why Stories.* 1926. NY. Ils Russell. 236 p. VG. B2. $47.50

LINDERMAN, F.B. *Red Mother.* 1932. NY. 1st ed. VG. B2. $45.00

LINDGREN, E. *Art of the Film.* 1948. London. 1st ed. G. $20.00

LINDSAY, D.M. *Campfire Reminiscences.* 1912. Boston. 1st ed. VG. B2. $35.00

LINDSAY, John. *City.* 1969. NY. 1st ed. inscr. dj. VG. $25.00

LINDSAY, Merrill. *Miniature Arms.* 1970. Winchester. Ils. 8vo. VG. $10.00

LINDSAY, T.B. *Lives of Cornelius Nepos.* 1895. Ils. 362 p. EX. $6.00

LINDSAY, Vachel. *Candle in the Cabin.* 1926. Appleton. 1st ed. dj. VG. $65.00

LINDSAY, Vachel. *Collected Poems.* 1925. xl. VG. C1. $7.50

LINDSAY, Vachel. *Collected Poems.* 1925. NY. Macmillan. Special ed. 1/350. VG. $125.00

LINDSAY, Vachel. *Every Soul Is a Circus.* 1929. Macmillan. Ils. G. $30.00

LINDSAY, Vachel. *General William Booth.* 1921. NY. sgn. EX. $55.00

LINDSAY, Vachel. *Going to the Stars.* 1926. Appleton. 1st ed. VG. $25.00

LINDSAY, Vachel. *Johnny Appleseed & Other Poems.* 1928. NY. Ils Richards. 1st ed. VG. $35.00

LINDSAY, W.S. *Our Merchant Shipping: Its Present State Considered.* 1860. London. Longman. 2nd ed. 396 p. G. $25.00

LINDSEY, A. *Pullman Strike.* 1964. 385 p. VG. $10.00

LINDSEY, T.J. *OH at Shiloh.* 1903. Cincinnati. 1st ed. EX. $35.00

LINDSTROM E.G. *History of Lakewood.* nd. Lakewood. Ils. sgn. 156 p. wraps. G. T5. $45.00

LINE & RICCIUTI. *Audubon Society Book of Wild Cats.* 1985. Abrams. Ils. 4to. 256 p. dj. EX. M2. $45.00

LINEWEAVER & BACKUS. *Natural History of Sharks.* 1970. Lippincott. Ils 1st Am ed. 256 p. dj. VG. M2. $15.00

LINGREN, Waldemar. *Ore Deposits of NM.* 1910. WA. map. 361 p. xl. G. A3. $140.00

LINKLATER. *Juan in America.* 1931. London. 1st ed. dj. VG. $17.50

LINKS, J.C. *Canaletto.* 1982. Cornell/Ithaca. 239 pls. dj. D2. $50.00

LINN, Martha. *Come Into Life.* 1961. ME. $5.00

LINSDALE, Jean. *Herd of Mule Deer.* 1953. CA U. 1st ed. dj. $15.00

LINTON, W. *Masters of Wood Engraving.* 1889. New Haven. private print. pls. folio. $200.00

LIONEL, Edwards. *My Hunting Sketchbook.* 1928. London. Ltd ed. 1/250. $70.00

LIONNI, Leo. *Mouse Days.* 1981. NY. Ils 1st ed. dj. $15.00

LIPMAN, Jean. *Calder's Universe.* 1976. NY. Viking. dj. VG. $40.00

LIPMAN & WINCHESTER. *Primitive Painters in American, 1750-1950.* 1950. Dodd Mead. 1st ed. dj. VG. J2. $17.50

LIPPMANN, Walter. *Preface to Morals.* 1929. NY. 1st ed. inscr/sgn. $25.00

LIPPMANN, Walter. *US Foreign Policy: Shield of the Republic.* 1943. Little Brown. 1st ed. inscr. 12mo. VG. $25.00

LIPSKY, George. *John Quincy Adams: His Theory & Ideas.* 1950. Crowell. 1st ed. dj. VG. J2. $12.50

LIPSKY, Louis. *Tales of Yiddish Rialto.* 1962. NY. 234 p. EX. $45.00

LIPTON, Lawrence. *Holy Barbarians.* 1959. NY. Messner. 1st ed. dj. EX. $45.00

LIPTON, Lenny. *Foundations of Stereoscopic Cinema.* 1982. NY. 1st ed. dj. EX. $24.00

LISTER. *Earl Morris & SW Archaeology.* 1968. NM U. 1st ed. VG. $15.00

LISTER-KAYE, J. *White Island.* 1973. Dutton. Ils 178 p. dj. EX. M2. $9.00

LISZT, Franz. *Letters of Franz Liszt to Marie Zu Sayn-Wittgenstein.* 1953. Harvard. 1st ed. dj. VG. J2. $17.50

LITCHFIELD, Mary E. *Spenser's Britomart.* 1896. Boston/London. 1st ed. VG. C1. $9.50

LITCHFIELD, P.W. *Autumn Leaves: Reflections of an Industrial Lieutenant.* 1945. Cleveland. Ils Kent. 1st ed. 125 p. dj. T5. $12.50

LITCHFIELD, R.B. *Tom Wedgwood, the First Photographer...* 1903. London. Duckworth. Ils. 271 p. EX. $85.00

LITCHTEN, Frances. *Folk Art of Rural PA.* 1946. NY. Ils 1st ed. index. VG. T5. $45.00

LITTAUER & UPHOFF. *Air War in Indochina.* 1972. Boston. Revised ed. 289 p. G. T5. $27.50

LITTELL, Robert. *Debriefing.* 1979. Harper. 1st ed. VG. $12.50

LITTLE, Arthur. *From Harlem to the Rhine: Story of NY's Colored Volunteers.* 1936. NY. Ils 1st ed. 382 p. VG. T5. $95.00

LITTLE, J.P. *History of Richmond.* 1933. 1/682. VG. $85.00

LITTLE, Nina. *Abby Aldrich Rockefeller Folk Art Collection...* 1957. Little Brown. 1st ed. VG. J2. $65.00

LITTLE & HAMBLIN. *Narrative of His Personal Experience As Frontiersman...* 1909. Salt Lake City. Desert News. 151 p. A3. $65.00

LITTLE & HONKALA. *Trees & Shrubs of the US: Bibliography for Identification.* 1976. USFS. 56 p. M2. $5.00

LITTLE. *Abby Aldrich Rockefeller Folk Art Collection.* 1957. Boston. Houghton. 1st ed. boxed. EX. $50.00

LITTLE. *History of Lumsden's Battery, CSA.* nd. (1905) Tuskaloosa. 70 p. wraps. VG. C4. $125.00

LIU, F.F. *Military History of Modern China: 1924-1949.* 1956. Princeton. Ils 1st ed. map. 312 p. VG. T5. $17.50

LIVELY, Penelope. *Voyage of QV 66.* 1978. London. 1st ed. dj. EX. $55.00

LIVELY, Penelope. *Wild Hunt of the Ghost Hounds.* 1986. pb. VG. C1. $3.50

LIVERMORE, Mary. *My Story of the War.* 1896. Ils. 700 p. K1. $14.50

LIVERMORE, S.T. *History of Block Island From Its Discovery in 1514...* 1877. Hartford. 371 p. sgn. VG. $60.00

LIVERMORE, T.L. *Numbers & Losses in Civil War.* 1957. Bloomington. IN U. 1st ed. dj. EX. $25.00

LIVINGSTON, A.D. *Advanced Bass Tackle & Boats.* 1975. Lippincott. Ils 1st ed. 240 p. EX. $12.50

LIVINGSTON, A.D. *Fly Rodding for Bass.* 1976. Lippincott. Ils 1st ed. 203 p. VG. $10.00

LIVINGSTON, Don. *Film & the Director.* 1953. Ils 1st ed. VG. $10.00

LIVINGSTON, W. *Mystery of Villa Sineste.* c 1931. NY. Mystery League. 1st ed. VG. $8.00

LIVINGSTONE, David. *Missionary Travels & Researches in S Africa.* 1872. NY. fld map. 730 p. K1. $21.00

LIVINGSTONE, David. *Travels & Researches in S Africa.* 1858. Phil. 1st Am ed. 446 p. VG. $55.00

LIVINGSTONE, David. *Zambezi Expedition of D. Livingstone, 1858-1863.* Chatto Windus. 1st ed. 2 vols. djs. VG. J2. $85.00

LIVINGSTONE & LIVINGSTONE. *Narrative of Expedition to Zambesi & Its Tributaries 1858...* 1866. NY. Ils. map. orig red cloth. T1. $45.00

LIVIUS. *Romanae Historie.* 1589. London. 8vo. leather. G. $125.00

LIVSEY, C. *Manson Women.* 1890. NY. 1st ed. dj. VG. B2. $17.50

LLEWELLEN, Richard. *Night of Bright Stars.* 1979. Doubleday. 1st ed. dj. EX. $10.00

LLEWELLYN, Robert. *WA: Capital.* 1981. VA. 1st ed. presentation. 4to. dj. M. $30.00

LLOSA, M.V. *Conversation in Cathedral.* 1975. Harper. 1st Am ed. dj. $25.00

LLOSA, M.V. *War of End of World.* 1984. Farrar Straus. Trans Lane. 1st print. dj. EX. $15.00

LLOYD, Christopher. *Ships & Seamen: From Vikings to Present Day.* 1961. Cleveland. World. Ils 23 p. dj. VG. $20.00

LLOYD, G. & D. *All Color Guide: Birds of Prey.* 1970. Grosset Dunlap. Ils. 159 p. dj. EX. M2. $14.00

LLOYD, H.A. *Collector's Dictionary of Clocks.* 1964. NY. dj. VG. $40.00

LLOYD, J.U. *Our Willie.* 1934. Cincinnati. 1st ed. dj. EX. $40.00

LOBECK. *Airways of America.* 1933. WA. 1st ed. presentation. VG. $15.00

LOBLEY, J.L. *Mt. Vesuvius.* 1889. London. Ils. 400 p. EX. $45.00

LOCHER, A. *With Star & Crescent.* 1890. Aetna. Ils. VG. $20.00

LOCHTE, Dick. *Sleeping Dog.* 1985. NY. Arbor House. 1st ed. dj. $20.00

LOCKE, A. *New Negro.* 1925. NY. Ils 1st ed. 446 p. VG. B2. $42.50

LOCKE, C.G.W. *Tobacco: Growing, Curing & Manufacturing.* 1886. Span. Ils. 285 p. rebound. VG. M2. $47.00

LOCKE, E.W. *Three Years in Camp & Hospital.* 1870. 408 p. scarce. EX. $20.00

LOCKE, Frederick. *Quest for the Holy Grail.* 1960. Stanford. dj. VG. C1. $16.50

LOCKE, W.J. *Ancestor. Jorico.* 1929. Dodd Mead. 1st ed. $12.00

LOCKE, W.J. *Simon the Jester.* 1910. John Lane. Ils Flagg. 1st ed. $12.00

LOCKE, W.J. *Town of Tombarel.* 1930. Dodd Mead. 1st ed. $12.00

LOCKERT, Louis. *Petroleum Motor Cars.* 1899. Van Nostrand. Ils. 218 p. G. J3. $65.00

LOCKHART, John. *Memoir of Life of Sir Walter Scott.* 1901. Boston. 1/600. 10 vols. $250.00

LOCKHART, R.H. *British Agent.* 1933. Putnam. G. $30.00

LOCKLEY, R.M. *Islands Around Britain.* 1945. London. Ils. dj. VG. C1. $8.00

LOCKRIDGE, Norman. *Lese Majesty: Private Lives of Duke & Duchess of Windsor.* 1952. Boars Head. EX. $45.00

LOCKRIDGE, R.F. *George Rogers Clark: Pioneer Hero of Old NW.* 1927. NY. Yonkers-on-Hudson. 210 p. G. T5. $9.50

LOCKWOOD, C.A. *Tragedy at Honda.* 1960. Phil. 1st ed. dj. VG. B2. $22.50

LOCKWOOD, Charles. *Bricks & Brownstone: NY Row House, 1783-1929.* 1972. NY. dj. J2. $25.00

LOCKWOOD, F.C. *More AZ Characters.* 1943. Tucson. 1st ed. wraps. EX. $17.50

LOCKWOOD, F.C. *Pioneer Days in AZ.* 1932. NY. Ils 1st ed. maps. 387 p. VG. B2. $32.50

LOCKWOOD, F.C. *Pioneer Days in AZ.* 1932. NY. 1st ed. sgn. slipcase. EX. $75.00

LOCKWOOD, J.D. *Life & Adventures of a Drummer Boy...* 1893. Albany. 1st ed. square 8vo. 191 p. VG. J4. $20.00

LOCKWOOD, L.V. *Colonial Furniture in America.* 1957. NY. Scribner. 2 vols. $20.00

LODDIGE, Conrad. *Botanical Cabinet.* 1818-1823. London. 100 pls. 8vo. 3 vols. A3. $1200.00

LODGE, Oliver. *Past Years.* 1931. London. $75.00

LOEDERER, R. *Voodoo Fire in Haiti.* nd. NY. Ils. dj. VG. $15.00

LOEHR, Franklin. *Power of Prayer on Plants.* 1959. NY. $18.00

LOESSER, A. *Men, Women & Pianos.* 1954. NY. 1st ed. dj. VG. B2. $30.00

LOEWY, R. *Industrial Design.* 1979. Overlook. 1st ed. VG. $50.00

LOFGREN, L. *Ocean Birds.* 1984. Knopf. Ils 1st Am ed. 4to. dj. EX. M2. $25.00

LOFTIE, W.J. *English Lake Scenery.* 1875. NY. Ils Rowbotham. $45.00

LOFTING, Hugh. *Dr. Doolittle & the Green Canary.* 1950. Lippincott. Ils 1st ed. EX. $25.00

LOFTING, Hugh. *Dr. Doolittle in the Moon.* 1928. np. Stokes. 1st ed. M. $50.00

LOFTING, Hugh. *Dr. Doolittle's Return.* 1933. NY. Stokes. Ils 1st ed. VG. $40.00

LOFTING, Hugh. *Voyages of Dr. Doolittle.* 1922. NY. Stokes. Ils. 364 p. EX. $30.00

LOFTS, Norah. *Anne Boleyn.* 1979. NY. 1st Am ed. dj. M. C1. $15.00

LOFTS, Norah. *Knights Acre.* c 1975. Book Club. dj. VG. C1. $5.00

LOFTS, Norah. *Lute Player.* 1951. Book Club. dj. VG. C1. $7.50

LOGAN, Daniel. *Anatomy of Prophecy.* 1975. NY. $8.00

LOGAN, Daniel. *Your E Star.* 1972. NY. $10.00

LOGAN, J.A. *Great Conspiracy: Its Origin & History.* 1886. Hart. maps. 810 p. G. M2. $12.00

LOGAN, John. *Volunteer Soldier of America.* 1887. Ils 1st ed. 706 p. K1. $18.50

LOGAN, Olive. *Minic World & Public Exhibition.* 1871. New World. 591 p. scarce. $38.00

LOGAN, R.W. *What the Negro Wants.* 1944. Chapel Hill. 2nd print. 352 p. dj. VG. $30.00

LOGSDON, G. *Successful Berry Growing.* 1976. Rodale. 5th ed. EX. $6.00

LOHRMAN, H.P. *History of Tuscarawas Co., OH.* 1954. New Phil., OH. Ils. 61 p. wraps. T5. $12.50

LOKKE, Carl. *Birds in My Indian Garden.* 1961. Knopf. VG. $25.00

LOKKE, Carl. *Klondike Saga: Chronicle of MN Gold Mining Co.* 1965. MN U. 1st ed. VG. J2. $15.00

LOKVIG & MURPHY. *Star Trek (The Motion Picture): Pop-Up Book.* 1980. NY. 1st ed. EX. $20.00

LONDON, Charmain. *Book of Jack London.* 1921. Century. 1st ed. presentation. 2 vols. J2. $350.00

LONDON, Jack. *Assassination Bureau.* 1969. Berkley. 2nd ed. pb. VG. P1. $3.25

LONDON, Jack. *Before Adam.* 1908. London. Review 1st ed. VG. $105.00

LONDON, Jack. *Call of the Wild.* Grosset Dunlap. Anniversary ed. VG. $15.00

LONDON, Jack. *Call of the Wild.* 1903. NY. 1st ed. 1st bdg. VG. $110.00

LONDON, Jack. *Call of Wild, Scarlet Plague & Tales of Fish.* 1925. NY. Leslie-Judge. 12mo. VG. $10.00

LONDON, Jack. *Cruise of the Snark.* 1911. Macmillan. 1st ed. boxed. VG. $100.00

LONDON, Jack. *Daughter of the Snows.* 1902. 1st ed. VG. $100.00

LONDON, Jack. *Game.* 1905. Macmillan. Ils 1st ed. TEG. M. $85.00

LONDON, Jack. *Game.* 1905. Macmillan. 1st ed. 2nd state. EX. $50.00

LONDON, Jack. *John Barleycorn.* 1913. Century. 1st ed. VG. $50.00

LONDON, Jack. *John Barleycorn.* 1913. NY. 1st ed. later issue. VG. $25.00

LONDON, Jack. *Little Lady of the Big House.* 1916. NY. 1st ed. EX. $75.00

LONDON, Jack. *Lost Face.* 1910. Macmillan. 1st ed. VG. $50.00

LONDON, Jack. *Lost Face.* 1913. Regent Pr. VG. $15.00

LONDON, Jack. *Love of Life.* 1907. Macmillan. 1st ed. gilt blue cloth. EX. $90.00

LONDON, Jack. *Night Born.* 1913. Century. 1st ed. dj. EX. $100.00

LONDON, Jack. *Night Born.* 1913. NY. 1st ed. G. P3. $32.00

LONDON, Jack. *People of the Abyss.* nd. Macmillan. Standard ed. G. $20.00

LONDON, Jack. *Sea Wolf.* 1904. Macmillan. 1st ed. 2nd state. VG. $80.00

LONDON, Jack. *Sea Wolf.* 1961. Ltd Ed Club. Ils Martin. dj. EX. $65.00

LONDON, Jack. *Smoke Bellew.* 1912. NY. 1st ed. VG. B2. $65.00

LONDON, Jack. *Smoke Bellew.* 1912. NY. Century. 1st ed. EX. $85.00

LONDON, Jack. *Son of the Wolf.* nd. Grosset Dunlap. 251 p. EX. $6.50

LONDON, Jack. *Star Rover.* 1915. NY. 1st ed. $75.00

LONDON, Jack. *White Fang.* 1906. Macmillan. 1st ed. G. $35.00

LONDON, Jack. *White Fang.* 1906. NY. 1st ed. EX. $75.00

LONDON, Joan. *Jack London & His Times.* 1939. NY. Book League. 1st ed. VG. $10.00

LONG, A.L. *Memoirs of Robert E. Lee.* 1886. Ils. 707 p. EX. K1. $65.00

LONG, A.R. *Corpse Came Back.* 1950. Harlequin. pb. VG. P1. $20.00

LONG, C.C. *Central Africa: Naked Truths of Naked People.* 1877. NY. Ils 1st ed. 8vo. gilt bdg. VG. T1. $60.00

LONG, F.B. *Civil War Day by Day, Almanac 1861-1865...* 1971. Doubleday. Ils 1st ed. maps. 1133 p. dj. $47.50

LONG, F.B. *Horror From the Hills.* 1963. Arkham House. dj. $60.00

LONG, H.P. *Every Man a King.* 1933. New Orleans. Ils. rebound. T5. $25.00

LONG, H.P. *Every Man a King.* 1933. New Orleans. VG. $20.00

LONG, H.P. *My First Days in the White House.* 1935. Harrisburg. Telegraph Pr. 1st ed. dj. VG. M1. $60.00

LONG, Haniel. *Notes for a New Mythology.* 1926. Chicago. Torch Pr. 1st ed. 1/435. sgn. $75.00

LONG, M.F. *Growing Into Light.* 1955. CA. $65.00

LONG, M.F. *Secret Science Behind Miracles.* 1948. LA. $75.00

LONG, Manning. *Here's Blood in Your Eye.* 1949. Harlequin. pb. VG. P1. $20.00

LONG, Manning. *Modeled in Murder.* 1943. Margood. VG. P1. $10.00

LONG, Margaret. *Shadow of the Arrow.* 1941. Caldwell. 1st ed. sgn. dj. VG. B2. $35.00

LONG, Mason. *Life of a Converted Gambler.* 1878. Chicago. Ils 1st ed. $40.00

LONG, W.J. *Little Brother to Bear & Other Animal Studies.* 1904. Boston. Ginn. Ils Copeland. 178 p. 12mo. EX. $30.00

LONG & DENNIS. *Mail by Rail.* 1951. . 414 p. $31.50

LONGACRE, E.G. *From Union Stars to Top Hat.* 1972. Stackpole. photos. maps. dj. EX. M2. $10.00

LONGBAUGH, Harry. *No Way To Treat a Lady.* 1964. Gold Medal. EX. P1. $7.50

LONGFELLOW, H.W. *Aftermath.* 1873. Boston. VG. $35.00

LONGFELLOW, H.W. *Belfry of Bruges & Other Poems.* 1846. 1st ed. TEG. rebound Riviere bdg. $150.00

LONGFELLOW, H.W. *Courtship of Miles Standish & Other Poems.* 1858. Boston. 1st ed. 1st issue. rebound. $85.00

LONGFELLOW, H.W. *Courtship of Miles Standish.* nd. London/NY. Ils Dixon. 12mo. 159 p. AEG. $25.00

LONGFELLOW, H.W. *Courtship of Miles Standish.* 1903. Indianapolis. Ils Christy. boxed. EX. $45.00

LONGFELLOW, H.W. *Courtship of Miles Standish.* 1903. Indianapolis. Ils Christy. 4to. $20.00

LONGFELLOW, H.W. *Divine Tragedy.* 1871. Boston. 1st ed. VG. $40.00

LONGFELLOW, H.W. *Evangeline.* 1905. Indianapolis. Ils Christy. 132 p. G. T5. $22.50

LONGFELLOW, H.W. *Hanging of the Crane.* 1874. Boston. Houghton. gilt blue cloth. VG. $75.00

LONGFELLOW, H.W. *Kavanagh.* 1849. Boston. 1st ed. 1st bdg. EX. $75.00

LONGFELLOW, H.W. *Masque of Pandora.* 1875. Boston. 1st ed. VG. $75.00

LONGFELLOW, H.W. *Song of Hiawatha.* 1856. Boston. brown cloth. EX. G1. $60.00

LONGFELLOW, H.W. *Song of Hiawatha.* 1890. Boston/NY. Ils Remington. gilt bdg. T5. $50.00

LONGFELLOW, H.W. *Song of Hiawatha.* 1895. Boston. Ils Remington. VG. $40.00

LONGFELLOW, H.W. *Tales of a Wayside Inn.* 1863. Boston. 1st Am ed. 12mo. purple cloth. VG. $50.00

LONGFELLOW, H.W. *Tales of Wayside Inn.* 1863. Ticknor Fields. G. $37.00

LONGFELLOW, H.W. *Tales of Wayside Inn.* 1864. London. 1st ed. EX. $40.00

LONGFELLOW, H.W. *Three Books of Song.* 1872. Boston. 1st ed. dj. VG. $25.00

LONGHI, R. *Caravaggio.* 1952. Milan. Ils. 4to. dj. VG. J2. $50.00

LONGMAN NATURE LIBRARY. *Bats.* 1985. London. Ils 1st ed. 130 p. dj. EX. M2. $9.00

LONGSTREET, Charles. *GA Scenes: Characters, Incidents..in First Half-Century...* 1897. NY. Ils. 297 p. G. $40.00

LONGSTREET, James. *From Manassas to Appomattox.* 1896. Lippincott. 1st ed. 690 p. rebound. $225.00

LONGSTREET, James. *From Manassas to Appomattox.* 1960. Bobbs Merrill. 1st ed. $25.00

LONGSTREET, R.J. *Birds in FL.* 1965. Trend House. Ils Revised ed. dj. EX. M2. $20.00

LONGSTREET, Stephen. *War Cries on Horseback: Indian Wars on Great Plains.* 1970. Doubleday. 1st ed. dj. EX. $22.00

LONGSTREET, Stephen. *We All Went to Paris.* 1972. NY. 1st ed. $25.00

LONGSTRETH, Morris. *Rheumatism, Gout & Some Allied Disorders.* 1882. NY. 1st ed. 280 p. EX. $45.00

LONGUS. *Daphnis & Chloe.* 1977. Braziller. Trans Moore. 42 pls. dj. D2. $95.00

LONN, Ella. *Colonial Agents of S Colonies.* 1945. Chapel Hill. 1st ed. dj. EX. $60.00

LOOK MAGAZINE. *Santa Fe Trail.* 1946. Ils 271 p. $25.00

LOOMIS, A.F. *Great Blue-Water Yacht Races 1866-1935.* 1967. NY. reprint. dj. $20.00

LOOMIS, A.F. *Ranging the ME Coast.* 1939. NY. Loomis. Ils Wilson. 1st ed. inscr. dj. EX $60.00

LOOMIS, Andrew. *Creative Illustration.* 1947. NY. Ils 1st ed. VG. $45.00

LOOMIS, Andrew. *Creative Illustration.* 1948. NY. 2nd ed. dj. EX. B2. $50.00

LOOMIS, E.S. *Life & Appreciation of Dr. Aaron Schuyler.* 1936. np. 1/150. inscr. 190 p. VG. T5. $25.00

LOOMIS, Elias. *Tables of Logarithms of Numbers.* 1894. 204 p. TB. G. $8.00

LOOMIS, Elias. *Treatise on Meteorology With Collection of Tables.* 1868. NY. 1st ed. 305 p. VG. $45.00

LOOMIS, Frederick. *Consultation Room.* 1939. Knopf. 8vo. G. $10.00

LOOMIS, Leander. *Journal of Birmingham Emigrating Co.* 1928. UT. 1st ed. 1/1000. 17 pls. fld map. $85.00

LOOMIS, N.M. *TX-Santa Fe Pioneers.* 1958. Norman. Ils 1st ed. dj. EX. $40.00

LOOMIS, Roger S. *Arthurian Tradition & Chretien de Troyes.* 1949. Columbia. 1st ed. dj. VG. C1. $85.00

LOOMIS, Roger S. *Romance of Tristram & Ysolt.* 1923. NY. Ils 1st ed. VG. C1. $22.00

LOOMIS, Roger S. *Wales & the Arthurian Legend.* 1956. Cardiff. U of Wales Pr. 1st ed. dj. VG. C1. $95.00

LOOMIS & WEBSTER. *Van Zatzikhoven's Lanzelet (sic).* 1951. Columbia. 1st ed. VG. scarce. C1. $37.50

LOONEY, J.T. *Shakespeare Identified.* 1949. Duell Sloan. VG. $60.00

LOOS, Anita. *Gentlemen Prefer Blondes.* 1925. Boni Liveright. Ils Barton. 12mo. VG. $20.00

LOOS, Anita. *Gentlemen Prefer Blondes.* 1925. NY. Ils Barton. 9th print. $5.00

LOOS, Anita. *Mouse Is Born.* 1951. Doubleday. 1st ed. dj. $17.50

LOPEZ, B.H. *Arctic Dreams.* 1968. Scribner. Ils 1st ed. 464 p. dj. EX. M2. $20.00

LOPEZ, B.H. *Crossing Open Ground.* 1988. NY. 1st ed. sgn. dj. VG. $35.00

LOPEZ, B.H. *Of Wolves & Men.* 1978. Scribner. Ils 309 p. dj. EX. M2. $17.00

LOPEZ, Barry. *Desert Reservations.* 1980. Ltd ed. 1/300. sgn. dj. EX. $40.00

LOPEZ, Barry. *Winter Count.* 1981. Scribner. 1st ed. dj. EX. $8.00

LOPEZ, Vincent. *What's Ahead.* 1944. Phil. $14.00

LORAC, E.C.R. *Murder by Matchlight.* 1945. London. Collins. 1st ed. dj. EX. $25.00

LORANT, Stefan. *Abraham Lincoln: Life in Photographs.* 1941. NY. Ils 1st ed. dj. EX. $20.00

LORANT, Stefan. *New World: First Pictures of America.* 1946. NY. 1st ed. dj. EX. $45.00

LORD, A.B. *Handbook of Reinforced Concrete Building Design.* 1928. Am Concrete Inst. 262 p. EX. $5.00

LORD, E.L. *Gardener's Pick-Up Book.* 1943. Springfield. private print. sgn. VG. $15.00

LORD, Eleazar. *Lempriere's Universal Biography.* 1825. NY. 1st ed. 8vo. 2 vols. VG. T1. $100.00

LORD, F.A. *Civil War Collector's Encyclopedia.* 1965. Ils. 360 p. dj. J4. $30.00

LORD, F.A. *Civil War Collector's Encyclopedia.* 1965. Stackpole. Ils. 4to. 360 p. dj. M2. $22.00

LORD, F.A. *Civil War Sutlers & Their Wares.* 1969. 162 p. dj. J4. $22.50

LORD, F.A. *They Fought for the Union: Complete Reference Work...* 1960. Stackpole. Ils 1st ed. dj. EX. $40.00

LORD, M.B. *Mary Baker Eddy: Concise Story of Her Life & Works.* 1918. Boston. Ils 1st ed. 12mo. gilt cloth. T1. $30.00

LORD, Robert. *Origins of the War of 1870.* 1924. Harvard. 1st ed. dj. VG. J2. $15.00

LORD, Walter. *Incredible Victory.* 1967. Harper Row. 331 p. VG. $7.50

LORD, Walter. *Night To Remember.* 1955. NY. 1st ed. dj. VG. B2. $17.50

LORD & BROWN. *Illustrated Flora of N States & Canada.* 1898. 3 vols. EX. $128.00

LOREN, Eiseley. *Darwin & the Mysterious Mr. X.* 1979. NY. 1st ed. dj. VG. B2. $20.00

LORENZ, A.F. *Die Alte Burgerliche Baukunst in Rostock.* 1914. Rostock. Schen. Ils. German text. folio. wraps. $50.00

LORENZ, Frederick. *Savage Chase.* 1954. Lion Lib. pb. VG. P1. $10.00

LORENZ, K.Z. *King Solomon's Ring: New Light on Animal Ways.* 1952. Crowell. Ils. 202 p. dj. M2. $4.00

LORENZ, K.Z. *Year of the Greylag Goose.* 1978. Harcourt Brace. Ils 1st Am ed. 4to. 199 p. dj. M2. $18.00

LORIMER, G.H. *Master of Millions.* 1903. Revell. 1st ed. $12.00

LORIMER, G.H. *Old Gorgon Graham.* 1904. Doubleday Page. Ils Gruger. 1st ed. $12.00

LORING, Emilie. *Today Is Yours.* 1938. Little Brown. sgn. 314 p. VG. M1. $13.00

LORWIN, Lewis. *International Labor Movement.* 1953. 1st ed. dj. VG. $30.00

LORWIN, Lewis. *Labor & Internationalism.* 1929. 2nd print. dj. VG. $25.00

LOSSING, B.J. *Encyclopedia of US History.* 1902. Harper. 10 vols. VG. $85.00

LOSSING, B.J. *Harpers' Popular Encyclopedia of US History.* 1881. NY. Ils 1st ed. 2 vols. $25.00

LOSSING, B.J. *History of Civil War.* 1912. NY. War Memorial Assn. folio. 512 p. $60.00

LOSSING, B.J. *Mary & Martha WA.* 1886. Harper. Ils Rosa. AEG. gilt blue silk. VG. $25.00

LOSSING, B.J. *Our Country.* 1880. NY. Ils. 4to. 3 vols. VG. T5. $125.00

LOSSING, B.J. *Our Country.* 1888. Ils Darley. 3 vols. VG. $80.00

LOSSING, B.J. *Our Country.* 1892. Columubus. Anniversary ed. 3 vols. VG. $85.00

LOSSING, B.J. *Pictorial Field Book of the Revolution.* 1855. NY. 2nd ed. 2 vols. $110.00

LOSSING, B.J. *Pictorial Field Book of the Revolution.* 1976. NY. 2 vol set. $47.50

LOSSING, B.J. *WA & Mount Vernon.* 1859. NY. Ils 1st ed. VG. $50.00

LOTH, David. *Erotic in Literature.* 1961. London. Secker & Warburg. 1st ed. dj. $25.00

LOTH, David. *Gold Brick Cassie.* 1954. Gold Medal. pb. EX. P1. $10.00

LOTHROP, Elsie. *Historic Houses of Early America.* 1927. NY. McBridge. Ils. $47.50

LOTHROP, S. *Robert Woods Bliss Collection: Pre-Columbian Art.* 1959. NY. Ils. sm folio. gilt bdg. J2. $125.00

LOTI, Pierre. *Carmen Sylva.* 1912. NY. 1st ed. EX. $15.00

LOTI, Pierre. *Iceland Fisherman.* 1957. Alhambra. Ils Mugnaini. Trans Endore. T5. $45.00

LOTI, Pierre. *Iceland Fisherman.* 1957. Ltd Ed Club. black/yellow bdg. dj. $27.50

LOUDES, Mrs. Belloc. *Second Key.* nd. NY. Longman Green. inscr. $8.00

LOUDON, A. *Outrages Committed by Indians in Wars With White People.* 1971. Arno. reprint. 2 vols in 1. dj. VG. $25.00

LOUDON, J.C. *Encyclopedia of Agriculture.* 1839. London. 4th ed. rebound. $150.00

LOUDON, J.C. *Gardening for Ladies & Companion to the Flower Garden.* 1854. NY. VG. P3. $40.00

LOUGHEED. *Aeroplane Designing for Amateurs.* 1912. Chicago. VG. C4. $65.00

LOUGHEED. *Vehicles of the Air.* 1911. Chicago. 3rd ed. VG. C4. $105.00

LOUGHLIN, C.J. *Ghosts Along the MS.* 1948. Scribner. 1st ed. VG. $25.00

LOUGHRAN, J.X. *20th-C Health Science.* 1930. NY. $22.50

LOUIS, J.C. *Cola Wars.* 1980. NY. 1st ed. dj. VG. B2. $22.50

LOUYS, Pierre. *Ancient Manners.* nd. Paris. Ltd ed. 1/1000. EX. $65.00

LOUYS, Pierre. *Aphrodite.* 1925. np. Ltd ed. 1/1500. dj. EX. $45.00

LOUYS, Pierre. *Aphrodite.* 1932. Falstaff. Ltd ed. 1/500. VG. $30.00

LOUYS, Pierre. *Satyrs & Women.* 1930. Covici Friede. Ils/sgn Majeska. 1/1250. 4to. VG. $37.00

LOUYS, Pierre. *Songs of Bilitis.* 1904. Horace Brown. Aldus Soc. 1/971. $35.00

LOUYS, Pierre. *Songs of Bilitis.* 1926. NY. Ils/sgn Pogany. Ltd ed. sgn. M. $90.00

LOVE, E.M. *Rocking Island.* 1927. NY. 1st ed. 4to. VG. $30.00

LOVECRAFT, H.P. *Best Supernatural Stories.* 1945. Cleveland. World. 1st ed. $50.00

LOVECRAFT, H.P. *Collected Poems.* 1963. Arkham House. 1st ed. $55.00

LOVECRAFT, H.P. *Dagon.* 1965. Arkham House. 1st ed. dj. EX. $55.00

LOVECRAFT, H.P. *Dark Brotherhood & Other Pieces.* 1966. Arkham House. 1st ed. dj. EX. $37.50

LOVECRAFT, H.P. *Dunwich Horror.* 1963. Arkham House. dj. VG. $75.00

LOVECRAFT, H.P. *Marginalia.* 1944. Arkham House. 1st ed. dj. EX. $180.00

LOVECRAFT, H.P. *Marginalia.* 1944. Arkham House. 1st ed. EX. $150.00

LOVECRAFT, H.P. *Selected Letters.* 1965. Arkham House. 1st ed. dj. VG. $45.00

LOVECRAFT, H.P. *Shuttered Room.* 1959. Arkham House. 1st ed. dj. $100.00

LOVECRAFT, H.P. *Something About Cats & Other Pieces.* 1949. Arkham House. dj. $125.00

LOVECRAFT, H.P. *Supernatural Horror in Literature.* 1945. Ben Abramson. 1st ed. no dj issued. EX. $85.00

LOVECRAFT, H.P. *Watchers Out of Time & Others.* 1974. Sauk City. 1st ed. dj. M. $50.00

LOVECRAFT, H.P. *Weird Shadow Over Innsmouth.* 1944. NY. Bart House. wraps. EX. $95.00

LOVECRAFT & DERLETH. *Lurker at the Threshold.* 1945. Arkham House. 1st ed. sgn. dj. VG. $125.00

LOVEJOY, J.C. *Memoir of Charles Torrey Who Died in Penitentiary of MD.* 1847. Boston. 8vo. 346 p. VG. $75.00

LOVELACE, M.H. *Down Town.* 1943. NY. Ils Lenski. 1st ed. VG. $10.00

LOVELL, Caroline. *Golden Isles of GA.* 1932. Little Brown. 1st ed. J2. $15.00

LOVERIDGE, A. *Tomorrow's Holiday.* 1947. Harper. 1st ed. 278 p. EX. $20.00

LOVERING, T.S. *Geology & Ore Deposits of Breckenridge Mining District, CO.* 1934. WA. Ils. pocket maps. wraps. VG. A3. $100.00

LOVESEY, Peter. *Detective Wore Silk Drawers.* 1971. London. 1st ed. dj. VG. $55.00

LOVISI, Gary. *SF Detective Tales.* 1986. Gryphon. pb. EX. P1. $7.95

LOVISI, Gary. *Sherlock Holmes: Fifty Years of Great Detective Paperback.* 1984. Brooklyn. Fantasia. 1/200. 47 p. wraps. $7.50

LOW, Alfred. *Jews in the Eyes of the Germans.* 1979. Phil. 1st ed. dj. EX. $15.00

LOW, John. *Impartial & Correct History of War Bewteen US & Britain.* 1815. NY. 2nd ed. 312 p. rebound. T5. $125.00

LOW, L.H. *Sketch of Coinage of Mexican Revolutionary General Morelos.* 1886. NY. private print. xl. disbound. $45.00

LOW, R. *Complete Book of Parrots.* 1989. Barrons. Ils 1st Am ed. dj. EX. M2. $18.00

LOWDERER, R. *Voodoo Fire in Haiti.* 1935. Literary Guild. Ils 1st ed. 274 p. $15.00

LOWE, E.J. *Ferns: British & Exotic.* 1882. London. 479 pls. 8 vols. EX. $395.00

LOWE, Samuel E. *In the Court of King Arthur.* c 1921. VG. C1. $9.50

LOWE, Samuel E. *In the Court of King Arthur.* c 1922. Ils O'Keeffe. C1. $7.00

LOWELL, Amy. *Ballads for Sale.* 1927. Boston. 1st ed. VG. $25.00

LOWELL, Amy. *Pictures of the Floating World.* 1919. NY. 1st ed. sgn. VG. $40.00

LOWELL, Amy. *What's O'Clock.* 1925. Boston. Houghton. 1st ed. VG. $25.00

LOWELL, J.R. *Impressions of Spain.* 1899. Boston. 1st ed. EX. $30.00

LOWELL, J.R. *Political Essays.* 1888. Boston. 1st ed. EX. $17.50

LOWELL, J.R. *Vision of Sir Launfal.* 1904. London. Astolat Pr. gilt bdg. C1. $12.50

LOWELL, Robert. *Day by Day.* 1977. NY. 1st ed. sgn. dj. M. $40.00

LOWELL, Robert. *For Lizzie & Harriet.* 1973. NY. 1st ed. dj. EX. $20.00

LOWELL, Robert. *Lord Weary's Castle.* 1946. NY. 1st ed. dj. EX. $85.00

LOWELL, Robert. *Notebook, 1967-1968.* 1969. NY. 161 p. dj. EX. T5. $25.00

LOWELL, Robert. *Notebook.* 1970. NY. Revised Expanded ed. dj. EX. $12.50

LOWELL, Robert. *Old Glory.* 1965. Farrar. 1st ed. dj. EX. $40.00

LOWELL, Robert. *Selected Poems.* 1976. NY. 1st ed. 243 p. $15.00

LOWENFELS, Walter. *Sonnets of Love & Liberty.* 1955. Blue Heron. Ils Kent. dj. VG. $30.00

LOWERY, G.H. *LA Birds.* 1955. Ils Tucker. 1st ed. pls. photos. VG. $40.00

LOWERY, G.H. *LA Birds.* 1974. LA State U. Revised 3rd ed. dj. EX. M2. $30.00

LOWERY & DALQUEST. *Birds From the State of Veracruz, Mexico.* 1951. KS U. Ils. M2. $5.00

LOWIE, Robert. *Culture & Ethnology.* 1917. McMurtrie. 1st ed. $20.00

LOWNDES, M.B. *Duchess Laura.* c 1933. NY. Longman Green. 1st ed. VG. $12.50

LOWNDES, M.B. *Fortune of Bridget Malone.* c 1937. NY. Longman Green. 1st ed. VG. $12.50

LOWNDES, M.B. *Novels of Mystery.* c 1927. NY. Longman Green. VG. $20.00

LOWRIE, Walter. *Art in Early Church.* 1947. NY. 1st ed. dj. EX. $40.00

LOWRY, Beverly. *Daddy's Girl.* 1981. Viking. 1st Am ed. dj. VG. $15.00

LOWRY, Malcolm. *October Ferry to Gabriola.* 1970. World. 1st ed. dj. EX. $20.00

LOWRY, Malcolm. *Ultramarine.* 1962. NY. 1st Am ed. dj. EX. $75.00

LOWRY, Malcolm. *Under the Volcano.* 1984. NY. 1st ed. dj. EX. $20.00

LOWRY, Robert. *Wolf That Fed Us.* 1949. NY. 1st ed. 8vo. dj. EX. $20.00

LOWRY. *Table Atlas.* c 1850. London. 100 maps. quarto. A3. $200.00

LOWTHER, Minnie Kendall. *Blennerhassett Island in Romance & Tragedy.* 1974. Rutland. reprint of 1936 ed. 210 p. dj. T5. $7.50

LOXTON, H. *Beauty of Big Cats.* 1973. London. Triune. Ils. 144 p. dj. EX. M2. $11.00

LOYD, C. *Traveling Naturalists.* 1985. London. Croom Helm. Ils. 156 p. dj. EX. M2. $35.00

LOZOVSKY. *Marx & Trade Unions.* 1942. VG. $15.00

LUBBOCK, Basil. *Adventures by Sea From Art of Old Time.* 1925. Studio Ltd. 115 pls. gilt cloth. TEG. VG. J2. $250.00

LUBBOCK, Basil. *China Clippers.* 1914. Glasgow. 2nd ed. pls. G. $17.50

LUBBOCK, Basis. *China Clippers.* 1914. Boston. Lauriat. 433 p. dj. VG. $25.00

LUBBOCK, John. *Pleasures of Life.* nd. NY. 12mo. $6.00

LUCAS, E.V. *At the Shrine of St. Charles.* 1934. NY. 1st ed. dj. EX. $20.00

LUCAS, E.V. *Open Road.* 1914. Holt. Ils Stuart. later print. VG. $25.00

LUCAS, E.V. *Selected Essays.* 1954. London. 1st ed. dj. VG. $10.00

LUCAS, F.A. *Animals of the Past.* 1922. Am Mus Nat Hist. 207 p. EX. M2. $9.00

LUCAS, George. *Star Wars.* 1976. Ballantine. 1st ed. pb. $12.50

LUCAS, Jeremy. *Whale.* 1981. Summit. 1st ed. dj. $10.00

LUCAS, W.A. *From the Hills to the Hudson.* 1944. Ils. photos. maps. 320 p. $75.00

LUCIE-SMITH, Edward. *Dark Pagent.* 1986. 1st ed. pb. VG. C1. $6.00

LUCKHURST, Kenneth. *Story of Exhibitions.* 1951. Studio. 1st ed. dj. VG. J2. $20.00

LUCRETIUS. *De Renum Natura.* 1832. London. inscr. AEG. red leather. EX. $175.00

LUDLOW, F.H. *Heart of the Continent.* 1870. NY. Hurd Houghton. 8 pls. EX. $90.00

LUDLOW, William. *Report of Reconnaissance of Black Hills of Dakota in 1874.* 1875. WA. GPO. 121 maps. VG. A3. $175.00

LUDLUM, Robert. *Aquitaine Progression.* 1984. London. Granada. 1st ed. dj. VG. $35.00

LUDLUM, Robert. *Aquitaine Progression.* 1984. Random House. 1st ed. dj. VG. $25.00

LUDLUM, Robert. *Bourne Supremacy.* 1986. Random House. 1st ed. dj. EX. $20.00

LUDLUM, Robert. *Chancellor Manuscript.* 1977. NY. 1st ed. dj. VG. $20.00

LUDLUM, Robert. *Cry of the Halidon.* 1984. NY. 1st ed. dj. EX. $35.00

LUDLUM, Robert. *Gemini Contenders.* 1976. Dial. 1st ed. dj. EX. $20.00

LUDLUM, Robert. *Osterman Weekend.* 1972. World. 1st ed. dj. EX. $45.00

LUDLUM, Robert. *Rinemann Exchange.* 1974. NY. 1st ed. dj. $25.00

LUDLUM, Robert. *Scarlatti Inheritance.* 1971. NY. 1st ed. plastic dj. VG. $45.00

LUDWIG, E. *Clam Lake Papers: Winter in the N Woods.* 1977. Harper Row. 148 p. dj. EX. M2. $10.00

LUDWIG & MOLMENTI. *Vittore Carpaccio: La Vie & l'Oeuvre du Peintre.* 1910. Paris. Hachette. Ils. D2. $195.00

LUGT, Frits. *Les Marques de Collections de Dessins & d'Estampes...* 1975. San Francisco. reprint of 1921 ed. 596 p. D2. $85.00

LUHAN, M.D. *Winter in Taos.* 1935. NY. 1st ed. VG. $30.00

LUIGI, Belli. *Master-Mind Menace.* 1950. World Fantasy Classic. EX. P1. $20.00

LUKAS, J.A. *Don't Shoot-We Are Your Children!* 1971. NY. Ils. sgn. 461 p. dj. G. T5. $19.50

LUKEMAN, Tim. *Witchwood.* 1983. 1st ed. dj. EX. C1. $6.50

LULL, R.S. *Evolution of Man.* 1923. Yale U. 202 p. M2. $10.00

LUMBRERAS, L. *Peoples & Culture of Ancient Peru.* 1974. Smithsonian. Ils 248 p. VG. $20.00

LUMHOLTZ, C. *Among Cannibals: Four Years' Travels in Australia.* 1889. NY. VG. $90.00

LUMIANSKY, R.M. *Of Sondry Folk: Dramatic Principle in Cantebury Tales.* 1955. 1st Am ed. dj. VG. scarce. C1. $24.00

LUMMIS, Charles. *Some Strange Corners of Our Country.* 1892. Ils. 270 p. K1. $27.50

LUMPKIN, Grace. *Wedding.* 1939. NY. 1st ed. VG. $20.00

LUMPKIN, K.D.P. *Making of Southerner.* 1947. NY. Knopf. 1st ed. dj. VG. $5.00

LUNATCHARSKY. *Der Russiche Revolutions Film.* 1929. Leipzig/Zurich. 74 pls. $20.00

LUNDHOLM, Helge. *Schizophrenia.* 1932. Duke U. 1st ed. sgn. stiff wraps. J2. $25.00

LUNGE, G. *Techno-Chemical Analysis.* 1914. 1st ed. sm 8vo. 136 p. EX. $2.00

LUNN, Arnold. *Switzerland in English Prose & Poetry.* 1947. London. 1st ed. dj. EX. $20.00

LUNN, Harry H. Jr. *Milton Avery: Prints 1933-1955.* 1973. WA. Graphics Int Ltd. 66 pls. D2. $40.00

LUNT, D.C. *Taylor's Gut.* 1968. Knopf. Ils 1st ed. 303 p. dj. EX. M2. $11.00

LUPOFF, R.A. *Edgar Rice Burroughs: Master of Adventure.* 1965. NY. 1st trade ed. dj. VG. T5. $19.50

LUPOFF, Richard. *Sword of the Demon.* 1977. Harper. 1st ed. dj. EX. $15.00

LURIE, Alison. *Only Children.* 1979. NY. 1st ed. dj. EX. $25.00

LUSCOMB, S.C. *Collector's Encyclopedia of Buttons.* 1967. Bonanza. Ils. 242 p. dj. EX. $20.00

LUSK, William. *Science & Art of Midwifery.* 1893. Appleton. 4th ed. $15.00

LUTES, D.T. *Country Kitchen.* 1938. Boston. EX. $12.50

LUTZ, A. *Created Equal.* 1940. NY. 1st ed. 345 p. dj. VG. B2. $17.50

LUTZ, B. & G.A. *Brazilian Species of Hyla.* 1973. TX U. Ils. 4to. dj. EX. M2. $25.00

LUTZ, Cora. *Essays on Manuscripts & Rare Books.* 1975. Ils. 176 p. dj. M. K1. $12.50

LUTZ, E. *Animated Cartoons.* 1920. London. Chapman Hall. Ils. G. $30.00

LUTZ, F.E. *Field Book of Insects of US & Canada.* 1935. Putnam. 100 pls. 510 p. G. M2. $11.00

LUVAAS, Jay. *Battle of Gettysburg.* nd. np. trade pb ed. M. T5. $9.50

LUVAAS, Jay. *Battle of Gettysburg.* 1986. Carlisle, PA. Ils 1st ed. 232 p. VG. T5. $12.50

LUVAAS, Jay. *Battle of Gettysburg.* 1987. NY. Ils. 240 p. M. T5. $9.95

LUVAAS, Jay. *Military Legacy of the Civil War.* 1959. Chicago. 1st ed. dj. $10.00

LUZERNE, F. *Lost City: Chicago As It Is & Was.* 1872. NY. 1st ed. G. $35.00

LYALL. *Character of Russians & Detailed History of Moscow.* 1823. London. 1st ed. 23 pls. fld plan. VG. $600.00

LYASCHCHENKO, Peter. *History of National Economy of Russia to 1917 Revolution.* 1949. Macmillan. 1st ed. dj. J2. $17.50

LYDEKKER, R. *Handbook to British Mamalia.* 1896. Lloyd's Nat Hist. 31 pls. G. M2. $16.00

LYDEKKER, R. *Library of Natural History.* 1904. Saalfield. Ils. 6 vols. 3556 p. EX. M2. $130.00

LYDEKKER, R. *Reptiles, Amphibea, Fishes & Lower Chordata.* 1979. New Delhi. reprint. 510 p. rebound. VG. M2. $55.00

LYDENBERG, H.M. *Some Presses You Will Be Glad To Know About.* 1937. NY. $25.00

LYELL, Charles. *Manual of Elementary Geology.* 1852. Murray. Ils 4th ed. 8vo. 512 p. EX. $95.00

LYELL, Charles. *Travels in N America, Canada & Nova Scotia...* 1855. London. 2nd ed. pls. VG. $350.00

LYFORD, C.A. *Quill & Beadwork of the W Sioux.* 1940. WA. Bureau Indian Affairs. wraps. A3. $40.00

LYLE, D. *Art of Shorthand Improved.* 1762. London. 2 vols in 1. G. $100.00

LYMAN, H.M. *Insomnia: & Other Disorders of Sleep.* 1885. Chicago. Keener. 1st ed. VG. $70.00

LYMAN, P.A. *History of E Hampton.* 1866. Northampton. VG. $75.00

LYMAN, W.D. *Columbia River.* 1909. NY. Ils 1st ed. fld map. VG. $40.00

LYMINGTON, Lord. *Spring Song of Iscariot.* 1929. Black Sun. Ltd 1st ed. 1/125. slipcase. $110.00

LYNAM, Robert. *Beecher Island Annual.* 1930. Wray, CO. Ils. 124 p. wraps. scarce. A3. $75.00

LYNCH, Bohun. *History of Caricature.* 1927. Little Brown. 1st ed. J2. $22.50

LYNCH, Bohun. *Max Beerbohm in Perspective.* 1921. London. Ils 1st ed. $65.00

LYNCH, Bohun. *Prize Ring.* 1925. London. Country Life. 1st ed. 1/1000. VG. $125.00

LYNCH, Bohun. *Prize Ring.* 1925. London. 1/750. 40 pls. 4to. EX. B1. $175.00

LYNCH, E.C. *Furniture Antiques Found in VA.* 1954. WI. 1st ed. dj. VG. T1. $20.00

LYNCH, Jeremiah. *Three Years in the Klondyke.* 1967. Donnelley. Lakeside Classic. A3. $40.00

LYNCH, Stanislaus. *Echoes of the Hunting Horn.* nd. NY. 1st ed. dj. VG. $20.00

LYNCH & CLARK. *NY Volunteers in CA.* 1970. Gloriets, NM. 1st ed. VG. T5. $25.00

LYNDON, Lamar. *Storage Battery Engineering: Practical Treatise.* 1911. NY/London. 3rd ed. G. $20.00

LYON, G.F. *Journal of Residence & Tour in Republic of Mexico in 1826.* 1828. London. 2 vols in 1. rebound. VG. $95.00

LYON, Peter. *To Hell in a Day Coach.* 1968. Review 1st ed. 324 p. RS. $16.00

LYONS, Arthur. *Hard Trade.* 1981. Holt. 1st ed. dj. M. $15.00

LYONS, Nathan. *Notations in Passing.* 1974. MIT Pr. oblong 8vo. 121 p. dj. $42.50

LYONS, Nick. *Fisherman's Bounty.* 1970. NY. 1st ed. dj. EX. $45.00

LYONS, Nick. *Fishing Widows.* 1974. NY. dj. EX. $20.00

LYONS, Nick. *Seasonable Angler.* 1970. NY. dj. EX. $20.00

LYTLE, Andrew. *Alchemy.* 1979. Palaemon. Ltd ed. sgn. $35.00

LYTLE, Andrew. *Bedford Forrest & His Critter Company.* 1931. NY. 1st ed. 402 p. VG. B2. $80.00

LYTLE, Andrew. *Long Night.* 1936. Bobbs Merrill. 1st ed. dj. VG. $85.00

LYTLE, Andrew. *Wake for the Living.* 1975. NY. 1st ed. dj. VG. J2. $37.50

LYTTON, E.B. *Last Days of Pompeii.* 1926. NY. Ils Yohn. J2. $25.00

M

M'CONOCHIE, J.R. *Leisure Hours.* 1846. Louisville. 1st ed. 275 p. black morocco. T5. $75.00

MABBOTT & PLEADWELL. *Life & Works of Edward Koops Pinkney.* 1926. NY. 1st ed. inscr. $35.00

MABIE, H.W. *Fairy Tales Every Child Should Know.* 1923. Doubleday. Ils Frye. dj. $22.00

MABIE, H.W. *Great World.* 1911. Dodd Mead. 2nd ed. VG. $9.00

MABIE, H.W. *Nature & Culture.* 1904. Dodd Mead. Ils Eickenmeyer. TEG. VG. $35.00

MABIE, J. *Years Beyond.* 1960. E Northfield. 1st ed. 239 p. dj. VG. B2. $17.50

MAC LEISH, Archibald. *Fall of the City.* 1937. NY. 1st ed. EX. $37.50

MACADAMS, Cynthia. *Cynthia MacAdams: Rising Goddess.* 1983. Dobbs Ferry. 118 photos. D2. $25.00

MACARDLE, Dorothy. *Uninvited.* 1947. Bantam. EX. P1. $20.00

MACARTHUR, Arthur. *Annual Report of Major General Arthur MacArthur...* 1900. Manila. 1st ed. 2 vols. wraps. M. $70.00

MACARTNEY, C.E. *Grant & His Generals.* 1953. McBride. photos. maps. 352 p. VG. M2. $13.00

MACASKILL. *Out of Halifax.* 1937. 1/450. boxed. M. S2. $250.00

MACAULAY, T.B. *Critical & Historical Essays.* 1874. London. gilt crimson morocco. EX. $85.00

MACAULAY, T.B. *Critical & Miscellaneous Essays.* 1840-1844. Boston. 1st ed. 5 vols. $150.00

MACAULAY, T.B. *History of England.* 1906. NY/London/Bombay. 2 vols. M. $100.00

MACAULEY, Rose. *Pleasure of Ruins.* 1964. London. sm folio. dj. VG. $40.00

MACBETH, George. *Night of Stones.* 1969. Atheneum. 1st Am ed. dj. EX. $20.00

MACCLINTOCK, D. *Natural History of Raccoons.* 1981. Scribner. Ils 1st ed. 144 p. dj. EX. M2. $17.00

MACCLOSKEY, Monro. *American Intelligence Community.* 1967. Rosen Pr. 1st ed. dj. G. M1. $15.00

MACCLURE, Victor. *Mainly Fish.* 1959. London. 1st ed. VG. $10.00

MACCORD, C.W. *Kinematics: Treatise on Modification of Motion...* 1883. NY/London. Ils 4th ed. G. $20.00

MACDONALD, Alexander. *Design for Angling Dry Fly on W Trout Streams.* 1947. Boston. Ils. dj. EX. $20.00

MACDONALD, Betty. *Egg & I.* 1945. Lippincott. 1st ed. dj. VG. $37.00

MACDONALD, Betty. *Mrs. Piggle-Wiggle.* 1947. Phil. 1st ed. sgn. G. $35.00

MACDONALD, Bob. *Golf.* 1927. Chicago. Ils 1st ed. 212 p. VG. B2. $37.50

MACDONALD, D. *Encyclopedia of Mammals.* 1985. Facts on File. Ils. 4to. dj. EX. M2. $40.00

MACDONALD, D. *Expedition to Borneo: Search for Proboscis Monkey.* 1982. London. Dent. Ils 1st ed. 180 p. dj. EX. M2. $14.00

MACDONALD, Edwin. *Captain USN Polar Operations.* 1969. Naval Inst. Ils. 4to. dj. EX. $35.00

MACDONALD, F.W. *In a Nook With a Book.* c 1900s. Cincinnati. $25.00

MACDONALD, F.W. *Recreations of a Book Lover.* 1911. London. 1st ed. $30.00

MACDONALD, George. *At the Back of the N Wind.* 1919. Phil. McKay. Ils Smith. 1st ed. TEG. J3. $75.00

MACDONALD, George. *At the Back of the N Wind.* 1930. Macmillan. New ed of 1924 ed. dj. T6. $20.00

MACDONALD, George. *At the Back of the N Wind.* 1967. Dent Dutton. Ils Shepard. 8vo. dj. EX. $12.50

MACDONALD, George. *Light Princess & Other Fairy Tales.* nd. Putnam. Ils Humphrey. $30.00

MACDONALD, Gordon. *Volcanoes in Sea: Geology of HI.* 1970. Honolulu. 441 p. VG. $30.00

MACDONALD, Gregory. *Fletch Too.* 1986. Warner Bros. 1st ed. dj. VG. $10.00

MACDONALD, J. *Almost Human, the Baboon: Wild & Tame in Fact & Legend.* 1965. Chilton. Ils 1st ed. 161 p. dj. EX. M2. $14.00

MACDONALD, J.D. *April Eve.* 1956. NY. Dell. 1st ed. pb. $15.00

MACDONALD, J.D. *April Evil.* 1960. Dell. 1st Am ed. pb. VG. P1. $10.00

MACDONALD, J.D. *April Evil.* 1960. Dell. 1st Canadian ed. pb. VG. P1. $12.50

MACDONALD, J.D. *Area of Suspicion.* 1954. Dell. 1st ed. VG. P1. $10.00

MACDONALD, J.D. *Area of Suspicion.* 1961. Gold Medal. VG. P1. $7.50

MACDONALD, J.D. *Border Town Girl.* 1956. Popular. pb. VG. P1. $15.00

MACDONALD, J.D. *Bullet for Cinderella.* 1955. Dell. 1st ed. VG. P1. $17.50

MACDONALD, J.D. *Clemmie.* 1958. NY. Dell. 1st ed. pb. EX. $17.50

MACDONALD, J.D. *Empty Copper Sea.* 1978. NY. 1st ed. dj. EX. $20.00

MACDONALD, J.D. *Free Fall in Crimson.* 1981. Harper. 1st ed. dj. EX. $10.00

MACDONALD, J.D. *Green Ripper.* 1979. NY. 2nd ed. dj. EX. $7.50

MACDONALD, J.D. *Judge Me Not.* 1951. NY. Fawcett. 1st ed. pb. M. $10.00

MACDONALD, J.D. *Lonely Silver Rain.* 1985. Knopf. 1st ed. dj. M. $10.00

MACDONALD, J.D. *Murder for Money.* 1982. Harper Row. AP. EX. P1. $50.00

MACDONALD, J.D. *Purple Place for Dying.* 1964. Greenwich. Fawcett. 1st ed. pb. EX. $10.00

MACDONALD, J.D. *Turquoise Lament.* 1973. Phil. Lippincott. 1st ed. dj. EX. $15.00

MACDONALD, J.M. *Massilia-Carthago Sacrifice Tablets...* 1897. London. $20.00

MACDONALD, Malcolm. *Angkor.* 1958. London. Ils Loke Wan Tho. VG. $20.00

MACDONALD, Malcolm. *Borneo People.* 1958. Knopf. 1st Am ed. dj. EX. $12.50

MACDONALD, R.M.E. *Mrs. Robert E. Lee.* 1939. Boston. 1st ed. presentation. VG. $35.00

MACDONALD, Raymond. *Why the Chimes Rang.* 1909. Indianapolis. $17.50

MACDONALD, Ross. *Blue Hammer.* 1976. NY. 1st ed. dj. EX. $20.00

MACDONALD, Ross. *Blue Hammer.* 1976. NY. 1st ed. 4th imp. VG. $10.00

MACDONALD, Ross. *Chill.* 1964. NY. 1st ed. dj. EX. $95.00

MACDONALD, Ross. *Instant Enemy.* 1968. Knopf. 1st ed. dj. EX. $65.00

MACDONALD, Ross. *Sleeping Beauty.* 1973. NY. 1st ed. dj. EX. $12.50

MACDONELL, S. *W Trout.* 1948. NY. 1st ed. dj. VG. $25.00

MACDOUGALL, Arthur. *Trout Fisherman's Bedside Book*. 1963. Simon Schuster. 1st ed. VG. $17.50

MACDOUGALL, Arthur. *Under a Willow Tree*. 1946. Coward McCann. Ils 1st ed. 200 p. dj. VG. $22.50

MACDOWALL, Roddy. *Double Exposure*. 1966. VG. S2. $45.00

MACFADDEN, Bernarr. *Hair Culture*. 1925. NY. MacFadden. dj. VG. $12.00

MACFADDEN, Bernarr. *MacFadden's Encyclopedia of Physical Culture*. 1928. MacFadden. 5 vols. red cloth. VG. $45.00

MACFADDEN, Bernarr. *Physical Culture Cookbook*. 1924. NY. 1st ed. $12.00

MACFARREN, H.W. *TB of Cyanide Practice*. 1912. McGraw Hill. 291 p. EX. $6.50

MACGINITIE, G.E. *Natural History of Marine Animals*. 1949. McGraw Hill. Ils 473 p. VG. $17.50

MACGOWAN, Micheal. *Hard Road to Klondike*. 1962. London. Trans Iremonger. 1st ed. EX. $16.00

MACGREGOR, C. *Storybook Cookbook*. 1967. Doubleday. 1st ed. dj. EX. $22.50

MACGREGOR. *Inventor of the Thermionic Valve*. 1954. London. TV Soc. 1st ed. 22 photos. 141 p. $50.00

MACHEN, Arthur. *Anatomy of Tobacco*. 1926. NY. 1st Am ed. VG. C1. $12.00

MACHEN, Arthur. *Chronicle of Clemendy*. 1923. Cannonek. private print. 1/1050. VG. $45.00

MACHEN, Arthur. *Guinevere & Lancelot & Others*. 1986. Newport News. Purple Mouth Pr. Ils 1st ed. C1. $10.00

MACHEN, Arthur. *Ornaments of Jade*. 1924. NY. Ltd 1st ed. 1/1000. sgn. VG. $75.00

MACHEN, Arthur. *Shining Pyramid*. 1925. London. 2nd print. VG. scarce. C1. $14.50

MACINNES, Helen. *Agent in Place*. 1976. NY. 1st ed. dj. EX. $12.00

MACINNES, Helen. *Cloak of Darkness*. 1982. NY. 1st ed. dj. EX. $8.00

MACK, E.C. *Peter Cooper, Citizen of NY*. 1949. 432 p. $18.50

MACK, Gerstle. *Gustave Courbet*. 1951. NY. 1st ed. dj. VG. $30.00

MACKAL, R.P. *Monsters of Loch Ness*. 1976. Chicago. 1st ed. dj. VG. $12.50

MACKANESS, George. *Admiral Arthur Phillip: Founder of New S Wales*. 1937. Sydney. 1st ed. VG. $75.00

MACKANESS, George. *Life of Vice Admiral William Bligh*. 1931. Australia. 1st ed. sgn. 2 vols. VG. $100.00

MACKAY, Colin. *Song of the Forest*. 1987. 1st Am ed. lg pb. M. C1. $5.00

MACKAY, D. *Honorable Company*. 1936. Bobbs Merrill. 1st ed. dj. EX. $30.00

MACKAY, J.W. *Mark!* 1956. Coward McCann. Ils. 4to. 121 p. EX. $12.50

MACKAY, Neil. *Hole in the Card*. 1966. St. Paul. 1st ed. dj. EX. $12.50

MACKAY, Robert. *Letters of Robert MacKay to His Wife*. 1949. GA U. 1st ed. dj. J2. $15.00

MACKAYE, Percy. *Epoch: Life of Steele MacKaye*. 1927. NY. 8vo. 2 vols. VG. P3. $109.00

MACKENTY, J.G. *Duck Hunting*. 1953. Barnes. Ils. dj. EX. $15.00

MACKENZIE, Alexander. *Voyages From Montreal*. 1927. Toronto. reprint 1801 ed. $50.00

MACKENZIE, Compton. *My Life & Times*. 1971. London. inscr. dj. EX. $55.00

MACKENZIE, D.W. *Men Without Guns*. 1945. Phil. Ils 1st ed. dj. EX. $62.50

MACKENZIE & MACKENZIE. *Singers of Australia*. 1967. Melbourne. Ils 1st ed. dj. EX. $25.00

MACKEY, W. *American Bird Decoys With Chapter on Decoys As Folk Art*. 1979. Schiffer. Ils. 256 p. dj. EX. M2. $22.00

MACKEY, W. *American Bird Decoys*. 1965. Dutton. Ils 1st ed. 4to. 256 p. EX. $20.00

MACKEY & JERNEGAN. *Forward March*. 1934. folio. 2 vols. VG. $30.00

MACKEY & SINGLETON. *History of Freemasonry*. 1898. NY. Ils. 4to. 7 vols. gilt blue bdg. VG. $80.00

MACKINNON, Allan. *Red-Winged Angel*. 1958. London. Collins. 1st ed. dj. EX. $15.00

MACKINNON, J.R. *In Search of the Red Ape*. 1974. Holt Rinehart. Ils. 222 p. dj. EX. M2. $14.00

MACKINNON & HAWES. *Introduction to Study of Protozoa*. 1961. Oxford U. Ils. 506 p. dj. EX. M2. $32.00

MACKINSTRY, Elizabeth. *Puck in Pasture*. 1925. NY. Doubleday. 1st ed. VG. rare. C1. $19.50

MACLANACHAN, W. *Television & Radar Encyclopedia*. 1953. London. 1st ed. 216 p. dj. VG. $15.00

MACLAREN, Ian. *Beside the Bonnie Brier Bush*. 1895. Dodd Mead. 1st ed. $12.00

MACLAREN, Ian. *Days of Auld Lang Syne*. 1896. VG. S2. $65.00

MACLAREN, Ian. *Kate Carnegie*. 1896. Dodd Mead. 1st ed. $12.00

MACLEAN, Alistair. *Bear Island*. 1971. Doubleday. 1st ed. dj. EX. $12.00

MACLEAN, Alistair. *Breakheart Pass*. 1974. Doubleday. 1st Am ed. dj. EX. $9.00

MACLEAN, Alistair. *Captain Cook*. 1972. Doubleday. Ils. 192 p. dj. EX. M2. $18.00

MACLEAN, Alistair. *Force 10 From Navarone*. 1968. Doubleday. 1st ed. dj. EX. $20.00

MACLEAN, D.G. *Gene Stratton-Porter: Short Biography & Collector's Guide*. 1987. Decatur. Am Books. Ils. 28 p. wraps. T5. $3.95

MACLEAN, F. *To the Back of the Beyond*. 1974. Boston. Little Brown. 1st ed. dj. VG. $15.00

MACLEAN, Frank. *Henry Moore, R.A.* 1905. London/NY. Scott/Scribner. Ils. TEG. D2. $35.00

MACLEAN, G.L. *Birds of S Africa*. 1985. Cape Town. Ils. 848 p. dj. M. M2. $35.00

MACLEAN, Katherine. *Missing Man*. 1973. NY. Putnam. 1st ed. dj. EX. $15.00

MACLEAN, Norman. *River Runs Through It*. 1976. Chicago. 1st ed. dj. VG. B2. $35.00

MACLEAN, Norman. *River Runs Through It*. 1983. Chicago U. Ils Joel Snyder. 2nd print. dj. $35.00

MACLEISH, Archibald. *America Was Promises*. 1939. NY. 1st ed. sgn. dj. EX. $70.00

MACLEISH, Archibald. *Before March*. nd. Knopf. Ils Gorska. wraps. VG. $20.00

MACLEISH, Archibald. *Frescoes for Mr. Rockefeller's City*. 1933. NY. John Day. Day Pamphlet #29. pb. wraps. EX. $25.00

MACLEISH, Archibald. *New Found Land*. 1930. Boston. Houghton. Ltd ed. 1/500. $55.00

MACLEISH, Archibald. *Rides on the Earth.* 1978. Boston. 1st ed. dj. EX. $18.00

MACLEISH, Archibald. *Songs for Eve.* 1954. Boston. 1st ed. 58 p. red cloth. slipcase. $25.00

MACLEISH, R. *Prince Ombra.* 1st Eng ed. dj. EX. C1. $6.50

MACLEOD, Fiona. *Silence of Amor.* 1902. Portland. Mosher. 1st Am ed. 1/400. VG. C1. $19.00

MACLEOD, Mary. *King Arthur & His Knights.* c 1950. World. Ils Dobkin. VG. C1. $6.00

MACLEOD & BOULTON. *Songs of N Scotland.* c 1895. London. 2 vols. $75.00

MACMANUS, Seumas. *Well O' the World's End.* 1939. NY. Ils Bennett. 1st ed. VG. C1. $15.00

MACMIADHACHAN, Anna. *Spanish & Mexican Cooking.* 1979. London. dj. VG. $8.00

MACMILLAN, C. *Metaspermae of MN Valley.* 1892. MN Geol/Nat Hist Survey. 826 p. M2. $44.00

MACMILLAN, D. *How Peary Reached the Pole.* 1934. Boston. Ils 1st ed. 306 p. VG. B2. $40.00

MACMILLAN, Harold. *Blast of War: 1939-1945.* 1968. NY. VG. $10.00

MACMILLAN, M.T. *Story of Water Pictures.* 1936. Greenburg. VG. $40.00

MACMILLAN, Michael. *Globe Trotter in India.* 1895. London. VG. $12.50

MACMILLAN, Miriam. *Green Seas & White Ice.* 1948. Dodd Mead. photos. 287 p. G. M2. $9.00

MACNAIR, J. *Livingstone's Travels.* nd. Macmillan. photos. maps. VG. M2. $12.00

MACNAIR, J. *Livingstone's Travels.* 1954. Macmillan. Ils. maps. EX. $20.00

MACNAMARA, N.C. *Human Speech: Its Physical Basis.* 1909. Appleton. Ils. 267 p. $20.00

MACNEICE, Louis. *Holes in the Sky.* 1948. Random House. 1st ed. dj. EX. $15.00

MACOBOY, Stirling. *Tropical Flowers & Plants.* 1974. Sydney. 1st print. dj. VG. $18.00

MACOMB, J.N. *Report of Exploring Expedition From Santa Fe, NM...* 1876. WA. GPO. Ils Newberry. 152 p. VG. A3. $350.00

MACOUN, J. & J.M. *Catalog of Canadian Birds.* 1909. Canada Dept Mines. Ils. VG. M2. $38.00

MACQUIOD, Percy. *Dictionary of English Furniture From Middle Ages...* 1924-1927. London. 4to. 3 vols. TEG. $250.00

MACREADY, W.C. *Diaries 1833-1851.* 1912. Putnam. Ils. 2 vols. TEG. VG. $37.50

MACROBERT, T.M. *Printed Books. Short Introduction to Fine Typography.* 1957. Victoria Albert Mus. wraps. VG. $15.00

MACSWINEY, M. *Six Came Flying.* 1971. London. Joseph. Ils 1st ed. 190 p. EX. M2. $6.00

MADAN, Falconer. *What To Aim at in Local Bibliography.* 1887. np. orig printed wraps. $30.00

MADDEN, David. *Beautiful Greed.* 1961. Random House. 1st ed. EX. $20.00

MADDOCKS, R.F. *Recent Ostradodes of Family Pontocyprididae in Indian Ocean.* 1969. Smithsonian. 56 p. M2. $9.00

MADDOW, Ben. *Faces: Narrative History of the Portrait.* 1977. NY. sm folio. dj. EX. $30.00

MADDUX, Rachel. *Green Kingdom.* 1957. NY. 1st ed. dj. VG. B2. $15.00

MADER, Fredrich. *Distant Worlds.* 1932. NY. Ils 1st ed. 8vo. orange cloth. VG. T1. $200.00

MADIGAN, T.F. *Word Shadows of the Great: Lure of Autograph Collecting.* 1930. NY. Ils 1st ed. pls. inscr/sgn Ernest Dawson. $50.00

MADIS, George. *Winchester Book.* 1971. Brownsboro. 1st ed. sgn. EX. $30.00

MADISON, Lucy. *Joan of Arc: Warrior Maid.* nd. McKay. Ils Schoonover. dj. EX. $27.50

MADOX, Thomas. *History of Antiquities of Exchequer of Kings of England.* 1969. NY. reprint. 2nd ed. 4to. 2 vols. EX. $45.00

MAETERLINCK, Maurice. *Blue Bird.* 1925. Dodd Mead. Ils Robinson. $45.00

MAETERLINCK, Maurice. *Intelligence of Flowers.* 1907. Dodd Mead. Ils Coburn. 8vo. $85.00

MAETERLINCK, Maurice. *Intelligence of Flowers.* 1913. Dodd Mead. wraps. EX. $15.00

MAETERLINCK, Maurice. *Pelleas & Melisande.* 1908. NY. 1st ed. photos. TEG. gilt bdg. VG. $45.00

MAGEE, David. *Buccaneers: Grove Play.* 1964. Bohemian Club. 1st ed. dj. EX. $45.00

MAGEE, David. *Catalog of Examples of Printing of Grabhorn, 1917-1960.* 1960. San Francisco. 63 p. wraps. A3. $90.00

MAGGS BROS. *Catalog of Engraved Portraits & Decorative Prints.* 1929. $25.00

MAGINNIS, O.B. *How To Frame a House; or, House & Roof Framing...* 1901. NY. Ils. 8vo. 96 p. $20.00

MAGINNIS, O.B. *How To Measure Up Woodwork for Buildings.* 1909. NY. 12mo. 79 p. $15.00

MAGNUS, Albertus. *Egyptian Secrets.* c 1920s-1930s. Egyptian Pub. VG. $75.00

MAGOUN, H.I. *Osteopathy in Cranial Field.* 1976. Meridian, ID. 3rd ed. 367 p. gilt maroon leather. $60.00

MAGOUN, H.I. *Practical Osteopathic Procedures.* 1978. Kirksville. 128 p. gilt maroon leather. EX. $30.00

MAGRIEL, Paul. *Chronicles of American Dance.* 1948. Holt. 1st ed. dj. VG. J2. $22.50

MAGRIEL, Paul. *Isadore Duncan.* 1947. Holt. 1st ed. VG. J2. $10.00

MAGUIRE, Jack. *President's Country: Guide to Hill Country of TX.* 1964. Austin. Alcade. Ils 1st ed. dj. M. $18.00

MAHAFFY, J.P. *Greek Pictures Drawn With Pen & Pencil.* 1890. London. AEG. $16.00

MAHAN, A. *Critical History of Late American War...* 1877. Barnes. 1st ed. 461 p. poor. $55.00

MAHAN, A. *Fantastic Tales of Beroalde de Vervile.* 1923. Carbonneck. Ltd ed. 1/1050. sgn. G. B2. $85.00

MAHAN, A. *Interest of America in Sea Power: Present & Future.* 1897. Boston. 2 fld maps. TEG. cloth bdg. T5. $27.50

MAHER, Sigmund. *Die Wiener Juden, 1700-1900.* 1918. Berlin. 531 p. printed wraps. rare. $125.00

MAHON, Lord. *Life of Belisarius.* 1832. Phil. fld map. 306 p. G. T5. $25.00

MAHONY, Patrick. *Breath of Scandal.* 1957. CA. $15.00

MAHONY, Patrick. *Out of the Silence...* 1948. NY. $15.00

MAHRER, Alvin. *Experiencing. Humanistic Theory of Psychology & Psychiatry.* 1978. NY. dj. EX. $18.00

MAHRING, W. *No Road Back.* 1944. NY. Samuel Curl Inc. Ils Grosz. dj. $50.00

MAIER, P. *From Resistance to Revolution: Colonial Radicals...* 1972. Knopf. Review of 1st ed. 318 p. dj. M2. $15.00

MAILER, Norman. *Advertisements for Myself.* 1959. NY. 1st ed. dj. EX. $45.00

MAILER, Norman. *Armies of the Night.* 1968. New Am Lib. 1st ed. dj. VG. $22.50

MAILER, Norman. *Barbary Shore.* c 1951. Rinehart. 1st ed. VG. $85.00

MAILER, Norman. *Barbary Shore.* 1951. Rinehart. 1st ed. 312 p. green/black dj. EX. $125.00

MAILER, Norman. *Bullfight.* 1967. NY. Macmillan. CBS Legacy Collection Book. 4to. $37.50

MAILER, Norman. *Cannibals & Christians.* 1966. NY. 1st ed. dj. EX. $25.00

MAILER, Norman. *Idol & the Octopus.* 1968. NY. Dell. 1st pb ed. sgn. M. $50.00

MAILER, Norman. *Last Night.* 1984. NY. 1st ed. 1/250. sgn. dj. EX. $90.00

MAILER, Norman. *Marilyn: A Biography.* 1973. Grosset Dunlap. 1st ed. dj. VG. $25.00

MAILER, Norman. *Of Small & Modest Malignacy, Wicked & Bristling With Dots.* 1980. CA. 1st ed. 1/300. sgn. slipcase. M. $75.00

MAILER, Norman. *Of Women & Their Elegance.* 1980. NY. Ils Milton Greene. 1st ed. dj. EX. $45.00

MAILER, Norman. *Pieces & Pontifications.* 1983. London. 1st ed. dj. EX. $10.00

MAILER, Norman. *Presidential Papers.* 1963. Putnam. 1st ed. dj. EX. $45.00

MAILER, Norman. *Prisoner of Sex.* 1971. Boston. 1st ed. dj. VG. $15.00

MAILER, Norman. *Prisoner of Sex.* 1971. Little Brown. 1st ed. dj. EX. $20.00

MAILER, Norman. *Tough Guys Don't Dance.* 1984. NY. 1st Am ed. sgn. EX. $45.00

MAILER, Norman. *Tough Guys Don't Dance.* 1984. NY. 1st trade ed. dj. EX. $12.00

MAILER, Norman. *Why Are We in Vietnam?* 1967. NY. 1st ed. dj. EX. $25.00

MAILS, T. *Pueblo Children of Earth Mother.* 1983. 1st ed. 2 vols. djs. M. $75.00

MAIR, James. *Gardener's Calendar & Florist's Guide.* 1782. Birmingham. 326 p. brown polished calf. EX. $150.00

MAIRIANI. *Cocoa & Its Therapeutic Applications.* 1890. NY. Ils 2nd ed. AEG. VG. $65.00

MAITLAND, F.W. *Downing Professor of Laws of England.* 1910. Cambridge. Ils. G. $30.00

MAJDALANY, Fred. *Battle of Cassino.* 1957. Cambridge. Ils. 309 p. dj. VG. T5. $9.50

MAJOR, H. *Salt-Water Fishing Tackle.* 1939. Ils 1st ed. VG. $20.00

MAJORS, C.L. *WWI Jokes.* 1930. 112 p. stiff wraps. EX. J4. $7.50

MAKAROVA, Natalia. *Dance Autobiography.* 1979. Knopf. 1st ed. dj. M. $12.00

MALAMUD, Bernard. *Dubin's Lives.* 1979. Franklin Lib. 1st ed. green leather. EX. $30.00

MALAMUD, Bernard. *Fixer.* 1966. NY. 1st ed. dj. VG. $12.00

MALAMUD, Bernard. *New Life.* 1961. NY. 1st ed. dj. EX. $12.50

MALAMUD, Bernard. *Tenants.* 1971. NY. ARC. dj. RS. EX. $35.00

MALAMUD, Bernard. *Tenants.* 1971. NY. 1st ed. dj. EX. $25.00

MALAN, A.H. *Famous Homes of Great Britain & Their Stories.* 1913. NY. VG. J2. $32.50

MALANGA, Gerald. *This Will Kill That.* 1983. Black Sparrow. 1/200. sgn. acetate dj. EX. $20.00

MALCOLM, Ian. *Indian Pictures & Problems.* 1907. London. $37.50

MALCOLM, John. *Gwen John Sculpture.* 1986. NY. 1st Am ed. dj. EX. $10.00

MALINA, Fred. *Murder Over Broadway.* 1950. Harlequin. VG. P1. $15.00

MALINOWSKI, Bronislaw. *Magic, Science & Religion.* 1948. Boston. $27.50

MALITSKAYA, K.M. *Great Paintings From the Pushkin Museum, Moscow.* nd. Abrams. 100 color pls. dj. D2. $75.00

MALLARME, Stephane. *Five Letters From Mallarme to A.C. Swinburne.* 1922. private print. 1/30. wraps. slipcase. VG. J2. $45.00

MALLAY. *Essai sur les Eglises Romanes et Romano-Byzantines...* 1841. 51 pls. folio. xl. VG. $100.00

MALLET, J.W. *Chemistry Applied to the Arts.* 1868. Lynchburg. 38 p. lacks printed wraps. $35.00

MALLET, T. *Glimpses of Barren Lands.* 1930. Revillon Freres. 142 p. VG. M2. $18.00

MALLETTE, R.D. *Plan for CA Raptors.* 1978. CA Fish/Game. 42 p. M2. $6.00

MALLIS, A. *American Entomologists.* 1971. Rutgers. Ils. 549 p. VG. M2. $10.00

MALLORY, Garrick. *Calendar of the Dakota Nation.* 1877. WA. Ils. 182 p. disbound. A3. $35.00

MALLOY, Merrit. *Beware of Older Men.* 1980. London/NY. 1st ed. dj. EX. $12.00

MALO, David. *HI Antiquities.* 1951. Trans Bishop Museum. dj. $28.00

MALONE, H.L. *Brittlewings; or, Told by Fairy in Captivity.* 1926. London. Epworth. Ils Robinson. $30.00

MALONE, James H. *Chickasaw Nation.* 1919. 1st ed. presentation. G. B7. $110.00

MALONEY, T. *US Camera.* 1937. spiral bdg. VG. $25.00

MALOUIN, P.J. *Chimie Medicinale.* 1755. Paris. Nouvelle. 8vo. 2 vols. xl. $275.00

MALVERN, Gladys. *Curtain Going Up! Story of Katharine Cornell.* 1943. NY. Messner. 1st ed. dj. VG. $20.00

MANCHESTER, Herbert. *Diamond Match Co.: Century of Service, Progress & Growth...* 1935. NY. Ils. 108 p. stiff wraps. VG. T5. $37.50

MANCHESTER, William. *Last Lion: Winston S. Churchill.* 1983. Little Brown. Book Club. black cloth. dj. VG. D1. $15.00

MANDAHL-BARTH & ANTHON. *Cage Birds in Color.* 1959. Burrows. Ils. 149 p. dj. VG. M2. $5.00

MANDEL, P. *Great Battles of the Civil War.* 1963. Time. Ils. 4to. 48 p. EX. M2. $5.00

MANDUS. *Divine Awakening.* 1966. England. $9.00

MANGET, J.J. *Bibliotheca Pharmaceutica...* 1703. Geneve. 34 copper pls. folio. 2 vols. $2200.00

MANHOOD. *Photographer of the SW: Adam Clark Vroman, 1856-1916.* 1st ed. dj. EX. S2. $65.00

MANKER & TRYCKARE. *Peoples of Eight Seasons.* 1972. Crescent. dj. J2. $20.00

MANLEY, A. *Rushton & His Times in American Canoeing.* 1968. Syracuse U. Ils. 203 p. dj. xl. EX. M2. $12.00

MANLEY & LEWIS. *Ladies of Fantasy.* 1975. 1st ed. M. C1. $9.00

MANLY, W.L. *Death Valley in '49.* 1929. NY. 524 p. dj. VG. $45.00

MANN, A. *Regiment Historian: History of 45th Regiment, MA.* 1908. MA. Ils. 402 p. orig cloth. EX. R1. $160.00

MANN, E. *School for Barbarians.* 1938. NY. 3rd print. VG. C4. $22.00

MANN, E.P. *Buona Pasqua: Easter Greeting.* 1878. Boston. Marvin. wraps with silk ties. $15.00

MANN, F.S. *Bullet's Flight From Powder to Target.* 1909. 1st ed. 385 p. G. $85.00

MANN, Hans. *Strolling Through Rio.* 1958. Rio de Janeiro. Colibris. Eng/Portuguese text. dj. $37.50

MANN, Horace. *Lectures on Education.* 1845. Boston. 1st ed. EX. scarce. $300.00

MANN, Thomas. *Beloved Returns.* 1940. NY. Knopf. 1st Am ed. G. $22.00

MANN, Thomas. *Joseph & His Brothers.* 1934. NY. 1st Am ed. dj. VG. B2. $22.50

MANN, Thomas. *Joseph in Egypt.* 1938. Knopf. 6th print. 2 vols. slipcase. $25.00

MANN, Thomas. *Joseph the Provider.* 1944. NY. 1st ed. dj. VG. $20.00

MANN, Thomas. *Transposed Heads.* 1941. NY. 1st ed. dj. VG. P3. $35.00

MANN, Thomas. *Tristan.* 1960. German text. pb. VG. C1. $4.50

MANN, Thomas. *Young Joseph.* 1935. London. Secker. 1st ed. dj. VG. $75.00

MANNERS, D.X. *Great Tool Emporium.* 1979. Dutton. Ils. dj. VG. $15.00

MANNERS, D.X. *Memory of a Scream.* 1946. Hangman House. VG. P1. $15.00

MANNERS, Dorine. *Scarlet Patrol.* 1936. NY. Godwin. 1st ed. dj. VG. T6. $30.00

MANNING, A. *Miracle Spiritology.* 1975. Nyack. $19.00

MANNING, A. *Moon Lore & Moon Magic.* 1980. Nyack. $19.50

MANNING, A.G. *Helping Yourself With Psycho-Cosmic Power.* 1970. NY. $17.50

MANNING, A.I. *Eye of Newt in My Martini.* 1981. LA. $12.50

MANNING, H.P. *Fourth Dimension Simply Explained.* 1910. NY. 1st ed. small 8vo. 251 p. $75.00

MANNING, R.B. *Shrimps of Family Processidae From Atlantic Ocean.* 1971. Smithsonian. 39 p. EX. M2. $8.00

MANNING. *From Tee to Cup.* 1954. Phoenix. with golf cartoon. VG. C4. $32.00

MANNIX, D.P. *All Creatures Great & Small.* 1963. McGraw Hill. Ils 1st ed. 241 p. dj. EX. M2. $5.00

MANNIX, D.P. *More Backyard Zoo.* 1936. Coward McCann. Ils. 252 p. VG. M2. $4.00

MANNIX, J. *Adventure Happy.* 1954. Simon Schuster. Ils 1st print. 276 p. dj. EX. M2. $11.00

MANNIX, W.F. *Memoirs of Li Hung Chang.* 1913. Boston. Houghton Mifflin. 298 p. G. $25.00

MANSFIELD, E. *Life & Services of General Winfield.* 1852. NY. 1st ed. G. $22.50

MANSFIELD, E. *Lives of Ulysses S. Grant & Schuyler Colfax.* 1868. Cincinnati. 1st ed. 12mo. 425 p. G2. $34.00

MANSFIELD, I.F. *Historical Collections: Little Beaver River Valleys, PA-OH.* 1911. Beaver Falls. Ils. sgn. 224 p. G. T5. $37.50

MANSFIELD, Katherine. *Something Childish.* 1924. London. 1st ed. 2nd issue. VG. $65.00

MANSFORD, Wallis. *Bridging Two Worlds. Vol. 2.* 1939. London. $12.00

MANSUELLI. *Galleria Degli Uffizi: Le Sculture.* 1958 & 1961. Rome. 2 vols. D2. $120.00

MANTEGAZZA, P. *Sexual Relations of Mankind.* nd. Authropological Pr. Ltd ed. VG. $40.00

MANTER, H.W. *Some N American Fish Trematodes.* 1926. IL U. Ils. wraps. $11.00

MANTLE, Burns. *Best Plays of 1945-1946.* nd. NY. 515 p. xl. fair. $5.00

MANTLE, Mickey. *Quality of Courage.* 1964. Doubleday. 185 p. dj. $6.00

MAO, S.H. *Turtles of Taiwan.* 1971. Taiwan. Commerical Pr. Ils. 128 p. EX. M2. $25.00

MAPES, R.B. *Old Fort Smith: Cultural Center on SW Frontier.* 1965. private print. Ils. 160 p. dj. EX. M2. $25.00

MAPLET, John. *Greene Forest of a Natural History.* 1930. London. Hesperides Pr. Intro Davies. VG. $55.00

MAPP, A.J. *Frock Coats & Epaulets.* 1963. Yoseloff. Ils. 501 p. dj. M2. $14.00

MARA, Tim. *Thames & Hudson Manual of Screen Printing.* 1979. dj. EX. $5.00

MARACHE, N. *Manual of Chess.* 1866. NY. fair. $12.00

MARAINI, Antonio. *Goya Incisore.* 1927. Florence. 1/1000. D2. $40.00

MARAIS, E. *Soul of the Ape.* 1969. Atheneum. Ils 1st ed. 226 p. dj. EX. M2. $20.00

MARBEN, Rolf. *Zeppelin Adventures.* c 1930. London. Ils 1st ed. 220 p. dj. VG. T5. $95.00

MARBURY, M.O. *Favorite Flies & Their Histories.* 1896. Boston. 3rd ed. 8vo. VG. $175.00

MARCADE, J. *Roma Amor: Essay on Erotic Elements in Etruscan & Roman Art.* 1961. Geneva. Ils. quarto. dj. $60.00

MARCH, A.L. & K.G. *Mushroom Basket.* 1982. Meridian Hill. Ils. 160 p. EX. M2. $5.00

MARCH, J.M. *Wild Party.* 1928. Chicago. Ils Marsh. 1st ed. EX. $40.00

MARCH. *Night Scenes in Bible.* 1869. Phil. fair. $20.00

MARCHAM, F.G. *Louis Agassiz Fuertes & the Singular Beauty of Birds.* 1971. Harper Row. Ils 1st ed. folio. dj. EX. M2. $180.00

MARCHAND, L. *Byron: A Biography.* 1957. Knopf. 3 vols. boxed. M. $85.00

MARCHANT, James. *W.S. Churchill: Servant of Crown & Commonwealth, a Tribute.* 1954. London. 1st ed. T5. $25.00

MARCHINI, G. *Stained Glass Windows.* 1956. NY. 93 color pls. 36 pls. 4to. dj. J2. $100.00

MARCONI, D. *My Father, Marconi.* 1962. McGraw Hill. Ils 1st ed. 320 p. dj. EX. M2. $5.00

MARCOSSON, I.F. *Metal Magic: History of American Smelting & Refining Co.* 1949. NY. 1st ed. 313 p. dj. VG. B2. $22.50

MARCUS, Jacob. *Early American Jewry: Jews of PA & the S, 1655-1790.* 1955. Phil. 1 vol only. xl. EX. $20.00

MARCUS, Jacob. *Rise & Destiny of the German Jew.* 1934. Cincinnati. 1st ed. 417 p. dj. VG. B2. $37.50

MARCUS, M.F. *Period Flower Arrangement.* 1952. NY. 1st ed. 1st issue. VG. $22.50

MARCY, Mary. *Stories of Cave People.* 1917. Chicago. Kerr. inscr/sgn. VG. $100.00

MARCY, R.B. *Exploration of Red River of LA in Year 1852.* 1853. pls. fld maps. 320 p. orig leather. VG. A3. $275.00

MARDEN, O.S. *Cheerfulness As a Life Power.* 1899. Crowell. 1st ed. later print. $12.00

MARDEN, O.S. *Crime of Silence.* 1915. Physical Culture Pub. 1st ed. $12.00

MARGO, Elisabeth. *Taming the Forty-Niner.* 1955. NY. Rinehart. 1st ed. dj. EX. $10.00

MARGUIS, A.N. *Handy Business Directory of Cleveland, 1888-1889.* 1888. Cleveland. Ils. 443 p. VG. T5. $85.00

MARGULIES, Leo. *Flying Wildcats.* 1943. NY. 347 p. dj. T5. $12.50

MARIANI, Valerio. *Michelangelo, the Painter.* 1964. Abrams. 19 pls. photos. D2. $150.00

MARIANI, Valerio. *Michelangelo, the Painter.* 1964. Milano. folio. dj. slipcase. VG. $50.00

MARIANO, Nicky. *40 Years With Berenson.* 1967. Knopf. 3rd print. dj. VG. $8.50

MARIE, Alfred. *Les Chateaux des Rois de France.* 1964. Paris. Ils. French text. wraps. D2. $70.00

MARIE, Countess of Caithness. *Mystery of the Ages.* 1887. London. $95.00

MARITAIN, Raissa. *Chagall on L'Orage Enchante.* 1948. Paris. Ils. 8vo. 204 p. wraps. G. $100.00

MARK, Edward. *Walhous. Acuarelas de Mark. Un Testimento Pictario...* 1963. Bogata. 155 pls. folio. EX. $300.00

MARKALE, J. *King Arthur, King of Kings.* 1977. 1st ed. dj. VG. rare. C1. $59.00

MARKHAM, Beryl. *W With the Night.* 1942. Boston. 2nd ed. dj. VG. B2. $35.00

MARKHAM, Robert. *Colonel Sun.* 1968. Harper Row. 1st Am ed. dj. VG. $20.00

MARKHAM. *Life of Lazarillo Tormes.* 1908. Black. Ils. fld map. 8vo. VG. $25.00

MARKLAND. *Pterplegia.* Derrydale. as issued. VG. B2. $70.00

MARKS, A.A. *Manual of Artificial Limbs.* 1906. NY. Ils. 439 p. E2. $50.00

MARKS & SCHATZ. *Between N & S: MD Journalist Views the Civil War...* 1976. dj. M. J4. $15.00

MARLA, M.E. *Ward 81.* 1979. NY. 1st print. photos. dj. EX. $85.00

MARLOWE, Christopher. *Four Plays.* 1966. NY. Thistle. Ils Decaris. 4to. slipcase. $35.00

MARLOWE, Christopher. *Life & Death of Tamburlane the Great.* 1930. London. 1/400. J2. $35.00

MARQUAND, J.P. *Last Laugh, Mr. Moto.* 1942. Boston. Ltd 1st ed. sgn. dj. $85.00

MARQUAND, J.P. *Life at Happy Knoll.* 1957. Boston. 1st ed. dj. VG. B2. $17.50

MARQUAND, J.P. *Point of No Return.* 1949. Ltd ed. sgn. dj. EX. $75.00

MARQUIS, Don. *Archy's Life of Mehitabel.* 1933. NY. 1st ed. dj. VG. $22.50

MARQUIS, Don. *Carter & Other People.* 1921. NY. 1st ed. dj. EX. $27.50

MARQUIS, Don. *Dreams & Dust.* 1915. NY. 1st ed. G. C1. $7.00

MARQUIS, Don. *Old Soak & Hail & Farewell.* 1921. Doubleday. 141 p. $7.00

MARQUIS, Don. *Out of the Sea.* 1927. 1st ed. VG. C1. $15.00

MARRERO, Vicente. *Picasso & the Bull.* 1956. Chicago. 1st Am ed. dj. VG. $25.00

MARRIOTT, Alice. *Hell on Horses & Women.* 1953. Norman. 1st ed. dj. B1. $25.00

MARRIOTT, Alice. *Maria: Potter of San Ildefonso.* 1948. Norman. 3rd print. dj. EX. $30.00

MARRIOTT, Alice. *Maria: Potter of San Ildefonso.* 1963. Norman. EX. $25.00

MARRIOTT, Alice. *Maria: Potter of San Ildefonso.* 1976. Norman. Ils. 294 p. dj. EX. $10.00

MARRIOTT, Alice. *Ten Grandmothers.* 1945. Norman. 1st ed. dj. EX. $40.00

MARRYAT, Frederick. *Diary in America.* c 1960. IN U. reprint. dj. VG. $10.00

MARRYAT, Frederick. *Series of Diary in America.* 1840. Phil. 1st Am ed. VG. $125.00

MARRYAT, Frederick. *Twelve Novels.* 1895-1906. London. 12 vols. VG. $125.00

MARSH, Barton. *Uncompagre Valley & Gunnison Tunnel...* 1905. Montrose, CO. Ils. 149 p. VG. A3. $75.00

MARSH, G.D. *Copper Camp WPA, MT.* 1945. Hastings House. 308 p. $20.00

MARSH, George. *Sled Trails & White Waters.* 1929. Phil. Ils Schoonover. 1st ed. VG. $25.00

MARSH, George. *Toilers of the Trails.* 1921. Phil. Ils Schoonover. 1st ed. VG. $25.00

MARSH, Henry. *Dark Age Britain: Sources of History.* 1987. 3 maps. M. C1. $9.50

MARSH, Ngaio. *Black Beech & Honeydew.* 1965. Boston. 1st Am ed. 343 p. dj. G. T5. $12.50

MARSH, Ngaio. *Color Scheme.* 1943. London. Collins. 1st ed. dj. EX. $80.00

MARSH, Ngaio. *Death of a Peer.* 1940. NY. Book League Am. G. $5.00

MARSH, Ngaio. *Final Curtain.* 1947. London. Collins. 1st ed. dj. EX. $60.00

MARSH, Ngaio. *Hand in Glove.* 1962. Little Brown. 1st Am ed. dj. EX. $27.50

MARSH, Ngaio. *When in Rome.* 1971. Boston. 1st ed. dj. EX. $10.00

MARSH, W.L. *Wings, the ABC of Flying.* 1929. NY. 138 p. dj. VG. T5. $35.00

MARSHACK. *Roots of Civilization.* 1972. McGraw Hill. Ils. dj. VG. $10.00

MARSHAL, J.V. *Still Waters.* c 1983. Morrow. 1st ed. VG. $20.00

MARSHALL, Bruce. *White Rabbit.* 1952. Boston. Ils. xl. G. M1. $3.50

MARSHALL, D. *Ra'Ivavae: Expedition to Fascinating & Mysterious Polynesia.* 1961. Doubleday. Ils. 301 p. dj. VG. M2. $10.00

MARSHALL, D.W. *Campaigns of the American Revolution.* 1976. Ann Arbor. folio. 138 p. dj. T5. $22.50

MARSHALL, David. *Grand Central.* 1946. 280 p. $25.00

MARSHALL, E.F. *Spelling Book of English Language.* 1821. Saratoga. Davison. 12mo. 156 p. scarce. $85.00

MARSHALL, Edison. *Heart of the Hunter.* 1956. McGraw Hill. 1st ed. dj. VG. $20.00

MARSHALL, Edison. *Heart of the Hunter.* 1956. NY. 328 p. dj. G. $12.00

MARSHALL, Edison. *Pagan King.* Book Club. dj. VG. C1. $10.00

MARSHALL, Edison. *Shikar & Safari: Reminiscences of Jungle Hunting.* c 1947. 1st print. dj. G. $35.00

MARSHALL, J.T. *Miles Expedition of 1874-1875: Eyewitness Account...* 1971. Austin. Ils 1st ed. sgn editor. EX. $40.00

MARSHALL, John. *Guiness Book of Rail Facts & Feats.* 1975. 253 p. $17.50

MARSHALL, John. *Life of George WA.* 1926. Fredericksburg. Ils. 5 vols. VG. T5. $97.50

MARSHALL, Louis. *Selected Papers & Addresses.* 1957. Phil. 2 vols. boxed. EX. $15.00

MARSHALL, M. *King of Fowls.* 1981. England. Saiga. Ils 58 p. dj. EX. M2. $12.00

MARSHALL, N.B. *Life of Fishes.* 1965. Weidenfeld. Ils. 402 p. VG. M2. $17.00

MARSHALL, Nina. *Mushroom Book.* 1920. Doubleday. Ils. pls. dj. VG. B2. $27.50

MARSHALL, Paule. *Chosen Place, Timeless People.* 1970. London. Longman. 1st ed. EX. $40.00

MARSHALL, Raymond. *Mallory.* 1954. Harlequin. VG. P1. $10.00

MARSHALL, Raymond. *Paw in the Bottle.* 1954. Harlequin. VG. P1. $15.00

MARSHALL, S.L.A. *Battles in Monsoon.* 1967. NY. 1st ed. dj. EX. $22.50

MARSHALL, S.L.A. *Men Against Fire: Problem of Battle Command in Future War.* 1947. NY. 1st ed. inscr. 215 p. G. T5. $37.50

MARSHALL, S.L.A. *Pork Chop Hill.* 1956. Morrow. 1st ed. sgn. dj. EX. $25.00

MARSHALL, T.F. *Speeches & Writings of Honorable T.F. Marshall.* 1858. Cincinnati. 462 p. $15.00

MARSHALL, W.T. *AZ Cacti.* 1950. Desert Garden. Ils. sgn. 111 p. VG. M2. $7.00

MARSHALL, William. *Rural Economy of Midland (Ireland) Counties.* 1783. Dublin. 2 vols. full leather. $75.00

MARSHALL & ORR. *Biology of Marine Copepod Calanus Finmarchichus.* 1955. Edinburgh. Oliver Boyd. 1st ed. 188 p. EX. M2. $14.00

MARSTON, Edward. *Sketches of Booksellers of Other Days.* 1901. London. 1st ed. pls. $35.00

MARSTON, R.B. *Walton & Some Earlier Writers on Fish & Fishing.* 1894. London. 12mo. VG. $25.00

MARTEKA, V. *Mushrooms, Wild & Edible: Seasonal Guide.* 1980. Norton. Ils. 290 p. dj. EX. M2. $10.00

MARTI-IBANEZ, Felix. *All the Wonders We Seek.* 1963. Doubleday. Ils 1st ed. EX. $40.00

MARTIN, A.G. *Hand Taming Wild Birds at the Feeder.* 1963. Wheelwright. Ils. 144 p. dj. M2. $9.00

MARTIN, Albro. *Enterprise Denied: Origins of Decline of American Railroads.* 1917. 402 p. $16.50

MARTIN, Billy. *Billy Ball.* 1987. Doubleday. 1st ed. dj. RS. M. $15.00

MARTIN, Billy. *No. 1.* 1980. NY. 1st ed. dj. VG. B2. $15.00

MARTIN, Charles. *Room for Error.* 1978. Athens, GA. 67 p. $6.50

MARTIN, Chester. *Lord Selkirk's Work in Canada.* 1916. Oxford. 1st ed. J2. $20.00

MARTIN, D. *Tombstone's Epitaph.* 1951. NM U. Ils possible 1st ed. 272 p. dj. EX. $30.00

MARTIN, Edgar. *Boots & Her Buddies.* 1943. Whitman. Ils. dj. EX. $5.00

MARTIN, F. *Sea Bears: Story of Fur Seal.* 1960. Chilton. Ils 1st ed. 201 p. dj. EX. M2. $14.00

MARTIN, G.R.R. *Fevre Dream.* 1982. Poseidon. dj. EX. $15.00

MARTIN, Gregory. *Flemish School, Circa 1600 Through Circa 1900.* 1970. London. 304 p. D2. $24.50

MARTIN, H.H. *William Berry Hartsfield: Mayor of Atlanta.* 1978. Athens. 213 p. dj. EX. $15.00

MARTIN, Henry. *Comic Epitaphs.* 1957. Peter Pauper. 8vo. dj. $5.00

MARTIN, Hugh. *Battle: Life Story of Winston S. Churchill.* 1940. Gollancz. 2nd imp. blue cloth. VG. D1. $30.00

MARTIN, Hugh. *Battle: Life Story of Winston S. Churchill.* 1941. Gollancz. 8th imp. gray cloth. VG. D1. $20.00

MARTIN, Isaac. *Journal of Life, Travels, Labors & Religious Exercises...* 1834. Phil. 8vo. full calf. $125.00

MARTIN, John. *Ceiling Paintings for Jesuit Church in Antwerp.* 1968. Phaidon. Ils. 241 p. dj. D2. $85.00

MARTIN, John. *John Martin's Book of the Dance.* 1963. NY. dj. VG. $15.00

MARTIN, John. *World Book of Modern Ballet.* 1952. NY. dj. VG. $20.00

MARTIN, L.C. *Wild Flower Folklore.* 1984. E Woods Pr. Ils 1st print. 256 p. dj. EX. M2. $15.00

MARTIN, Les. *IN Jones & the Temple of Doom.* Random House. Movie ed. VG. P1. $4.00

MARTIN, M.E. *Friendly Stars.* 1907. Ils. small 8vo. 265 p. EX. $2.50

MARTIN, Malachai. *Hostage to Devil.* 1976. NY. Crowell. 1st ed. inscr/sgn. dj. EX. $20.00

MARTIN, R.G. *Jennie: Life of Lady Randolph Churchill. Vol. 2.* 1971. Prentice Hall. trade ed. blue cloth. dj. D1. $15.00

MARTIN, Russell. *Cowboy: Enduring Myth of Wild W.* 1983. NY. color pls. 4to. dj. VG. $22.50

MARTIN, T.C. *Inventions: Researches & Writings of Nikola Tesla.* 1952. Milwaukee. reprint of 1894 ed. 496 p. B2. $55.00

MARTIN, W.T. *Index: History of Franklin Co., OH.* nd. OH Geneal Soc. 29 p. wraps. T5. $9.50

MARTIN, W.W. *Manual of Ecclesiastical Architecture.* 1897. Cincinnati. 1st ed. 8vo. 429 p. $35.00

MARTIN & WRIGHT. *Pleistocene Extinctions.* 1967. Yale U. dj. EX. $25.00

MARTIN. *S America From a Surgeon's Point of View.* 1922. NY. Ils. 8vo. 325 p. EX. P3. $30.00

MARTINDALE, Thomas. *Hunting in the Upper Yukon.* 1913. Phil. Ils 1st ed. dj. EX. $75.00

MARTINE-BARNES, A. *Dragon Rises.* 1983. pb. EX. C1. $3.00

MARTINEAU, H. *Retrospect of W Travel.* 1938. NY. 12mo. 2 vols. $95.00

MARTINELL, Cesar. *Gaudi: His Life, His Theories, His Work.* 1975. Cambridge, MA. Trans Rohrer. VG. J2. $77.50

MARTINI, H. *My Zoo Family.* 1955. NY. photos. G. M2. $5.00

MARVEL, I. *Battle of Summer.* 1853. NY. 12mo. 289 p. G. G2. $16.00

MARVEL, I. *Reveries of a Bachelor.* 1906. Fenno. Ils Starkweather. $20.00

MARVIN, Arthur. *Olive.* 1888. San Francisco. VG. $60.00

MARVIN, E. *5th Regiment, CT Volunteers: A History.* 1889. 1st ed. xl. G. R1. $85.00

MARVIN, F.R. *Excursions of a Book Lover, Being Papers on Literary Themes.* 1910. Boston. 1st ed. $35.00

MARX, Groucho. *Beds.* 1930. NY. 2nd ed. dj. VG. B2. $40.00

MARX, Groucho. *Groucho & Me.* 1959. Holt. 1st ed. dj. VG. J2. $15.00

MARX, Groucho. *Many Happy Returns: Unofficial Guide to Income Tax Problems.* 1942. NY. Ils Soglow. 1st ed. dj. VG. $55.00

MARX, Groucho. *Memoirs of Mangy Lover.* 1963. NY. 1st ed. dj. B2. $37.50

MARX, Harpo. *Harpo Speaks.* 1961. Geis. 1st ed. dj. VG. $40.00

MARX, R.F. *Battle of the Spanish Armada 1588.* 1965. Cleveland/NY. Ils 1st ed. 137 p. dj. T5. $15.00

MARX & ENGELS. *Civil War in the US.* 1940. NY. 8vo. 325 p. red cloth. G2. $33.00

MARZIALS, T. *Pan Pipes: Book of Old Songs.* 1883. London. Ils Crane. oblong 4to. G. $50.00

MASARIK, Al. *Invitation to a Dying.* 1972. Redwood City. Vagabond. 68 p. pb. VG. $30.00

MASEFIELD, John. *Martin Hyde: Duke's Messenger.* 1925. Little Brown. Ils Dugdale. dj. VG. B4. $25.00

MASEFIELD, John. *Melloney Holtspur.* 1922. London. Ltd ed. sgn. $40.00

MASEFIELD, John. *Midnight Fox.* 1932. NY. Ils Rowland Hilder. 1st ed. $40.00

MASEFIELD, John. *Midsummer Night.* 1928. 1st Am ed. VG. scarce. C1. $14.00

MASEFIELD, John. *Nine Days' Wonder.* 1941. Macmillan. 1st ed. $75.00

MASEFIELD, John. *Poems.* 1929. dj. VG. C1. $12.50

MASEFIELD, John. *Reynard the Fox.* 1919. NY. 1st ed. 8vo. dj. VG. $20.00

MASEFIELD, John. *Right Royal.* 1920. London. Heinemann. 1/500. sgn. 8vo. EX. $95.00

MASEFIELD, John. *Right Royal.* 1922. London. Ils. EX. $37.50

MASEFIELD, John. *Rosas.* 1918. NY. 1st ed. 1/950. sgn. EX. $20.00

MASEFIELD, John. *Salt-Water Poems & Ballads.* 1936. NY. Ils. 163 p. G. $20.00

MASEFIELD, John. *So Long To Learn.* 1965. NY. 1st ed. dj. VG. $25.00

MASEFIELD, John. *Sonnets.* 1916. NY. 1st ed. sgn. EX. $40.00

MASEFIELD, John. *Tristan & Isolt.* 1927. NY. 1st ed. xl. G. C1. $7.50

MASEFIELD, John. *Wanderer of Liverpool.* 1930. NY. Macmillan. Ils. VG. $12.50

MASERELL, Frans. *Die Passion Eines Mechen.* 1927. Munich. 2nd ed. VG. J2. $60.00

MASLOW, J.E. *Owl Papers.* 1983. Dutton. Ils Baskin. 1st ed. 184 p. EX. M2. $16.00

MASON, A.E.W. *Musk & Amber.* 1946. Zephyr. dj. VG. P1. $20.00

MASON, A.E.W. *Prisoner in the Opal.* nd. Hodder Stoughton Yellowjacket. P1. $7.50

MASON, Arthur. *Wee Men of Ballywooden.* 1931. London. Ils Lawson. 1st ed. $20.00

MASON, B.A. *In Country.* 1985. NY. ARC. wraps. EX. $30.00

MASON, B.A. *In Country.* 1985. NY. 1st ed. 245 p. dj. VG. T5. $15.00

MASON, B.A. *Shiloh & Other Stories.* 1982. NY. 1st ed. sgn. dj. M. $65.00

MASON, B.A. *Shiloh & Other Stories.* 1983. London. Hogarth. 1st ed. dj. EX. $47.50

MASON, Bernard. *Drums, Tom-Toms & Rattles.* 1938. NY. Ils 1st ed. dj. EX. $25.00

MASON, C.M. *Anthology & Bibliography of Niagara Falls. Vol. I.* 1921. Albany. xl. G. $15.00

MASON, F.K. *Hawker Hurricane.* 1962. London. Macdonald. 1st ed. VG. $15.00

MASON, F.N. *John Norton & Sons.* 1937. Dietz Pr. EX. $17.50

MASON, F.V.W. *Harpoon in Eden.* 1969. Doubleday. 1st ed. dj. VG. $5.00

MASON, F.V.W. *Silver Leopard.* 1955. Doubleday. 1st ed. dj. EX. $6.00

MASLOW, F.V.W. *Spider House.* 1932. Mystery League. 1st ed. $15.00

MASON, John. *Self-Knowledge: A Treatise.* 1793. Ils. 210 p. full leather. K1. $17.50

MASON, K. *Abode of Snow.* 1955. NY. Ils. 372 p. dj. VG. B2. $32.50

MASON, Stuart. *Bibliography of Oscar Wilde.* 1914. London. wraps. $75.00

MASON, Stuart. *Bibliography of Oscar Wilde.* 1972. NY. reprint of 1914 ed. 2 vols. M. $45.00

MASON, W. *Poems of Thomas Gray To Which Are Prefixed Memoirs.* 1775. York. 1st ed. $150.00

MASON & SKINNER. *Mason's Farrier & Stud Book: Gentlemen's Pocket Farrier.* 1861. Lippincott. 415 p. gilt leather. VG. $55.00

MASON-MANHEIM, Madeline. *Hill Fragments.* 1925. London. $10.00

MASSENA, Victor. *Prince of Essling: Le Premier Livre Xylographique Italien.* 1903. Paris. Ils 1st ed. $60.00

MASSENGILL. *Sketch of Medicine & Pharmacy.* 1942. Bristol. Ils 2nd ed. presentation. sgn. P3. $35.00

MASSEY, A.B. *Ferns & Fern Allies of VA.* 1944. Blacksburg, VA. 110 p. printed wraps. $22.50

MASSEY, Gerald. *Ancient Egypt: Light of the World.* 1907. London. 1/500. 2 vols. VG. $175.00

MASSEY, Gerald. *Book of the Beginnings.* 1881. London. 2 vols. VG. $150.00

MASSEY, Gerald. *Natural Genesis.* 1883. London. 2 vols. VG. $175.00

MASSEY, Mrs. G.B. *Billingsley & the Garvins.* 1955. WA Co Hist Soc. 4to. 38 p. EX. M2. $8.00

MASSIE, Susanne. *Homes & Gardens in Old VA.* 1930. Richmond. Fergusson. 1st ed. 211 p. dj. $35.00

MASSIN. *Letter & Image.* 1970. NY. 1st ed. dj. EX. $45.00

MASSON, D. *Drummond of Hawthornden.* 1969. Greenwood. M. $28.00

MASSON, Georgina. *Italian Gardens.* nd. Abrams. Ils. 6 maps. 300 p. dj. D2. $150.00

MASSON, Oliver. *Les Inscriptions Chypriotes Syllabiques.* 1961. Paris. De Boccard ed. French Text. M. $30.00

MASSON. *Corner in Women.* 1905. NY. 2nd print. VG. C4. $22.00

MASTAI & MASTAI. *Stars & Stripes: American Flag As Art & History.* 1973. Knopf. 1st ed. 238 p. dj. M. $35.00

MASTER, A.M. *Electrocardiogram & X-Ray Configuration of the Heart.* 1939. Phil. 1st ed. VG. $100.00

MASTERMAN, J.C. *Double-Cross System in the War of 1939 to 1945.* 1972. Yale U. dj. VG. M1. $6.50

MASTERS, E.L. *Doomesday Book.* 1920. NY. 1st ed. 8vo. TEG. dj. VG. $20.00

MASTERS, E.L. *Great Valley.* 1916. NY. Macmillan. presentation. sgn. VG. $45.00

MASTERS, E.L. *Invisible Landscapes.* 1953. NY. 1st ed. dj. EX. $30.00

MASTERS, E.L. *Kit O'Brien.* 1927. NY. 1st ed. dj. EX. $45.00

MASTERS, E.L. *Lincoln, the Man.* 1931. Dodd Mead. 1st ed. G. $35.00

MASTERS, E.L. *Selected Poems.* 1925. NY. Macmillan. sgn. dj. $55.00

MASTERS, E.L. *Serpent in the Wilderness.* 1933. NY. 1/400. inscr/sgn. 4to. dj. boxed. EX. $60.00

MASTERS, E.L. *Songs & Satires.* 1916. reprint. VG. C1. $8.50

MASTERS, E.L. *Spoon River Anthology.* 1916. NY. later ed. sgn. 12mo. EX. $60.00

MASTERS, E.L. *Spoon River Anthology.* 1942. Ltd Ed Club. Ils Robinson. 1/1500. sgns. EX. $80.00

MASTERS, E.L. *Starved Rock.* 1919. NY. Macmillan. Stated 1st ed. presentation. VG. $110.00

MASTERS, John. *Bhowani Junction.* 1954. NY. Viking. 394 p. dj. $5.00

MASTERS & JOHNSON. *Human Sexual Response.* 1966. Boston. 1st ed. 2nd print. $50.00

MASTERS & LEA. *Sex Crimes in History.* 1966. NY. dj. EX. $10.00

MASTERSON, Bat. *Famous Gunfighters of W Frontier.* 1957. Frontier Pr. EX. $27.50

MASTERSON, Elsie. *Blueberry Hill Kitchen Notebook.* 1964. NY. 1st ed. dj. VG. B2. $17.50

MASTERSON, Elsie. *Blueberry Hill Menu Cookbook.* 1963. NY. 1st ed. dj. VG. B2. $17.50

MASUR, H.Q. *Mourning After.* 1984. NY. UCP. VG. $25.00

MATA. *Children of Santa Maria Cauque.* 1978. 8vo. 395 p. dj. VG. $30.00

MATBY, Isaac. *Elements of War.* 1915. Hartford. Revised 3rd ed. 12mo. $40.00

MATHER, A.S. *Extracts From Letter & Notebooks of Vol. II.* nd. Cleveland. private print. 8vo. G. $30.00

MATHER, Cotton. *Magnalia Christi Americana; or, Ecclesiastical History...* 1820. Hartford. 1st Am ed. 2 vols. $125.00

MATHER, Increase. *Testimony Against Profane Customs.* 1953. London. reprint of 1687 ed. EX. $20.00

MATHER, K.F. *Sons of Earth: Geologist's View of History.* 1930. Norton. Ils 1st ed. 272 p. dj. EX. M2. $12.00

MATHERS, E.P. *Red Wise.* 1926. Golden Cockerel. 1/500. 8vo. dj. $140.00

MATHERS, Michael. *Riding the Rails.* 1973. Gamit. 1st ed. $18.00

MATHES, C. Hodge. *Tall Tales From Old Smokey.* 1952. Kingport, TN. 1st ed. 241 p. dj. VG. T5. $9.50

MATHESON, Richard. *Scars.* 1987. Scream Pr. 1/250. sgn. boxed. M. $75.00

MATHESON, Richard. *Shrinking Man.* 1956. NY. 1st ed. pb. VG. $40.00

MATHESON, Richard. *What Dreams May Come.* 1978. Putnam. 1st ed. dj. xl. VG. $20.00

MATHEWS, F.A. *My Lady Peggy Goes to Town.* 1901. Bowen Merrill. Ils Fisher. VG. $20.00

MATHEWS, J.J. *Wah' Kon-Tah: Osage & the White Man's Road.* 1932. OK U. Ils. 359 p. dj. G. M2. $10.00

MATHEWS, Norris. *Bristol Public Libraries: Stucky Lean Collection.* 1903. Britsol. $69.50

MATHEWS, Washington. *Ethnology & Philology of Hidatsa Indians.* 1877. WA. 176 p. wraps. A3. $40.00

MATHEWS. *Long & Short Whist.* 1847. Cambridge. 1st Am ed. 12mo. wraps. VG. B1. $25.00

MATHIASSEN, T. *Sermermiut Excavations 1955.* 1958. Kobenhavn. Ils. 52 p. M2. $16.00

MATHIEWS, F.K. *Boy Scouts Yearbook.* 1931. NY. 1st ed. 223 p. VG. T5. $22.50

MATHISEN, J.E. *Bald Eagle & Osprey Populations.* 1987. Chippewa Nat Forest. 12 p. M2. $3.00

MATSCHAT, C.H. *Murder in Okefenokee.* 1941. NY. 1st ed. dj. VG. $17.50

MATSON, Norman. *Dr. Fogg.* 1929. NY. dj. EX. $30.00

MATTENKLODT, W. *Fugitive in the Jungle.* 1931. Little Brown. Ils. 292 p. VG. M2. $15.00

MATTESON, Porter. *Whose Feather Bed.* nd. c 1960s. 80 p. $14.00

MATTHEWS, Branden. *Last Meeting.* 1885. Scribner. 1st ed. $12.00

MATTHEWS, Frederick. *American Merchants' Ships, 1850-1900.* 1930. Salem, MA. 1st ed. 4to. VG. $50.00

MATTHEWS, Jack. *Dubious Persuasions.* 1981. John Hopkins. 155 p. $8.00

MATTHEWS, Joanna. *Bell's Pink Boots.* 1889. Dutton. Ils Waugh. 1st ed. VG. B4. $95.00

MATTHEWS, John. *Boadicea Warrior Queen.* Ils. sgn. stiff wraps. M. C1. $11.00

MATTHEWS, John. *Fionn Maccumhail: Champion of Ireland.* 1st ed. sgn. M. C1. $11.00

MATTHEWS, John. *Grail: Quest for the Eternal.* 1981. 1st Am ed. stiff wraps. M. C1. $14.00

MATTHEWS, John. *Thomas & the Book.* 1986. 1st ed. sgn. M. C1. $11.00

MATTHEWS, L.H. *Penguins, Whalers & Sealers.* 1977. Universe. 165 p. dj. EX. M2. $8.00

MATTHEWS, L.H. *Whale.* 1968. Simon Schuster. Ils 1st print. dj. EX. M2. $10.00

MATTHEWS, Richard. *Worlds Beyond the World: Fantastic Vision of Wm. Morris.* 1978. 1st ed. VG. C1. $6.00

MATTHEWS, S.K. *Photography in Archaeology & Art.* 1968. NY. dj. EX. $15.00

MATTHEWS, W.K. *Russian Historical Grammar.* 1960. London. Athlone Pr. dj. M. $12.00

MATTHEWS, William. *Medieval Secular Literature: Four Essays.* 1967. CA U. 2nd print. dj. VG. C1. $17.00

MATTHIES-MASUREN, F. *Die Kunstlerische Photographie...* 1922. Leipzig. Ils. photos. $67.50

MATTHIESSEN, F.O. *Achievements of T.S. Eliot.* 1935. NY. 1st ed. dj. VG. $20.00

MATTHIESSEN, F.O. *Henry James: Major Phase.* 1944. Oxford. dj. VG. $20.00

MATTHIESSEN, Peter. *Far Tortuga.* 1975. Random House. 1st ed. EX. $30.00

MATTHIESSEN, Peter. *In the Spirit of Crazy Horse.* 1983. NY. 1st ed. dj. EX. $95.00

MATTHIESSEN, Peter. *Oomingmak: Expedition to Musk Ox Island in Bering Sea.* 1967. NY. 1st ed. dj. EX. $55.00

MATTHIESSEN, Peter. *Race Rock.* 1954. NY. 1st ed. sgn. dj. VG. $100.00

MATTHIESSEN, Peter. *Raditzer.* 1961. NY. 1st ed. dj. EX. $55.00

MATTHIESSEN, Peter. *Sand Rivers.* 1981. Viking. Ils 1st ed. 213 p. dj. EX. M2. $13.00

MATTHIESSEN, Peter. *Snow Leopard.* 1978. Viking. maps. 298 p. dj. EX. M2. $18.00

MATTHIESSEN, Peter. *Tree Where Man Was Born.* 1972. Dutton. Ils 1st ed. 247 p. dj. EX. M2. $17.00

MATTHIESSEN, Peter. *Tree Where Man Was Born.* 1972. Dutton. 1st ed. dj. M. $25.00

MATTHIESSEN, Peter. *Under the Mountain Wall.* 1962. Viking. 1st ed. dj. VG. $30.00

MATTHIESSEN, Peter. *Wildlife in America.* 1959. NY. 1st ed. dj. VG. B2. $27.50

MATTHIESSEN, Peter. *Wildlife in America.* 1977. Penguin. Ils. 304 p. M2. $5.00

MATTISON, C. *Snakes of the World.* 1986. Facts on File. Ils. maps. 190 p. dj. EX. M2. $22.00

MATY, M. *Miscellaneous Works of Late Philip D. Stanhope.* 1779. London. 2nd ed. 4 vols. $300.00

MATZ, B.W. *Character Sketches From Dickens.* 1924. London. Ils Copping. 8vo. VG. $70.00

MAUCLAIR, Camille. *Art & Skies of Venice.* 1925. Brentanos. fair. $40.00

MAUERER, D.W. *Big Con.* 1940. Indianapolis. 1st ed. dj. VG. B2. $32.50

MAUGHAM, Robin. *Conversations With Willie.* 1978. London. 1st ed. dj. EX. $30.00

MAUGHAM, W.S. *Books & You.* 1940. London. 1st ed. $25.00

MAUGHAM, W.S. *Caesar's Wife: Comedy in Three Acts.* 1922. London. fair. $25.00

MAUGHAM, W.S. *Cakes & Ale.* 1953. Heinemann. Ils Sutherland. sgns. slipcase. M. $275.00

MAUGHAM, W.S. *Catalina.* 1948. NY. Stated 1st ed. EX. $25.00

MAUGHAM, W.S. *Great Novelists & Their Novels.* 1948. Phil. 1st ed. dj. VG. $15.00

MAUGHAM, W.S. *My S Sea Island.* 1936. 1st ed. 2nd issue. 1/50. wraps. EX. $100.00

MAUGHAM, W.S. *Of Human Bondage With Digression on Art of Fiction.* 1946. WA. Ltd ed. 1/500. sgn. EX. $100.00

MAUGHAM, W.S. *Of Human Bondage.* 1936. Doubleday. Ltd 1st ed. $135.00

MAUGHAM, W.S. *Summing Up.* 1938. London. 1st ed. dj. EX. $40.00

MAUGHAM, W.S. *Traveler in Romance.* 1984. NY. 1st ed. dj. EX. $20.00

MAUGHAM, W.S. *Up at the Villa.* 1941. London. 1st ed. dj. EX. $42.50

MAUGHAM, W.S. *Vagrant Mood: Six Essays.* 1952. London. Ltd ed. 1/500. sgn. EX. $125.00

MAUGHAM, W.S. *Writer's Notebook.* 1949. NY. 1st trade ed. dj. VG. $20.00

MAUITY, N.B. *Other Bullet.* c 1930. NY. Crime Club. VG. $10.00

MAULDIN, Bill. *Mud Mules & Mountains.* 1944. wraps. VG. M1. $20.00

MAUNDER, S. *History of World. Vol. 2.* 1849. NY. Ils. 8vo. 689 p. xl. VG. G2. $13.00

MAUNDER, S. *Treasury of History: Being History of World.* 1850. NY. Ils. 8vo. G2. $12.00

MAURICE, Frederick. *Robert E. Lee the Soldier.* 1925. Boston. ARC. dj. EX. $50.00

MAURICE, Frederick. *Robert E. Lee the Soldier.* 1925. Boston. maps. plans. 313 p. K1. $13.50

MAURICHEAU-BEAUPRE, Charles. *Versailles.* 1949. Monaco. Eng ed. pls. dj. J2. $50.00

MAUROIS, Andre. *From My Journal.* 1948. Harper. Stated 1st ed. sgn. dj. EX. $45.00

MAUROIS, Andre. *Life of Shelley.* 1924. Appleton. 1st ed. presentation. sgn. $40.00

MAUROIS, Andre. *Prophets & Poets.* 1935. Harper. 3rd ed. presentation. sgn. EX. $60.00

MAUROIS, Andre. *Tragedy in France.* 1940. NY/London. Harper. sgn. 8vo. VG. $30.00

MAURY, Dabney H. *Recollections of a Virginian.* 1894. 1st ed. K1. $45.00

MAURY, M.F. *Physical Geography of the Sea.* 1855. NY. 1st ed. $165.00

MAURY, M.F. *Physical Geography of the Sea.* 1856. Harper. 6th ed. maps. charts. VG. $50.00

MAXEY, R. *Airports of Columbia: History of Photographs & Headlines.* 1987. Columbia. 365 p. $30.00

MAXEY, R. *Columbia High School Story.* 1984. Columbia. Ils. $30.00

MAXEY, R. *Columbia's Bicentennial: 1786-1986.* 1986. Columbia. 180 photos. 100 p. $15.50

MAXIM, Hiram. *Dynate Stories & Some Interesting Facts About Explosives.* 1916. NY. presentation. sgn. $45.00

MAXIM & HAMMER. *Chronology of Aviation.* nd. (1912) np. 23 p. wraps. T5. $45.00

MAXWELL, G. *Otter's Tale.* 1962. Dutton. Ils 1st ed. 124 p. EX. M2. $15.00

MAXWELL, G. *Raven Seek Thy Brother.* 1969. Dutton. Ils 1st ed. 210 p. dj. VG. M2. $8.00

MAXWELL, G. *Ring of Bright Water.* 1961. Dutton. Ils 1st ed. 211 p. dj. VG. M2. $7.00

MAXWELL, G. *Rocks Remain.* 1963. Dutton. Ils 1st ed. 209 p. dj. EX. M2. $10.00

MAXWELL, H. *British Fresh-Water Fishes.* nd. London. Hutchinson. 25 pls. 320 p. EX. M2. $37.00

MAXWELL, H. *History of Tucker Co., WV.* 1884. Kingwood. Preston Pub. G. $45.00

MAXWELL, William. *Ancestors.* 1971. NY. 1st ed. dj. VG. $25.00

MAXWELL, William. *Chateau.* 1961. NY. 1st ed. dj. VG. $30.00

MAXWELL & HUTCHINSON. *Scottish Costume, 1550-1850.* 1958. Black. 1st ed. dj. J2. $20.00

MAY, E.C. *Century of Silver.* 1947. NY. Ils 1st ed. 388 p. dj. VG. B2. $25.00

MAY, J.B. *Hawks of N America.* 1935. NY. Nat Audubon Soc. 1st ed. B2. $42.50

MAY, Phil. *Gutter-Snipes.* 1896. London. Leadenhall Pr. 1/1050. 4to. VG. $20.00

MAY, Robin. *Story of the Wild W.* 1978. Hamlyn. Ils. 4to. 155 p. dj. EX. $18.00

MAY, Sophie. *Little Prudy.* 1904. Lee Shepard. VG. $10.50

MAY, Sophie. *Little Prudy's Captain Horace.* 1892. Lee Shepard. VG. $10.50

MAY, W.W. *Marine Painting.* nd. London. Cassell. 16 pls. VG. $150.00

MAY & GAUNT. *SC Secedes...* 1960. SC U. 1st ed. presentation. sgns. 231 p. $35.00

MAYA-NANDA, Jyotir. *Concentration & Meditation.* 1971. Miami. $12.00

MAYA-NANDA, Jyotir. *Death & Reincarnation.* 1970. Miami. $12.00

MAYA-NANDA, Jyotir. *Raja Yoga: Study of the Mind.* 1970. Miami. $12.00

MAYER, A.E. *Seashore Life.* 1905. NY Zool Soc. Ils. G. $6.00

MAYER, Arthur. *Merely Colossal: Story of the Movies.* 1953. Simon Schuster. 1st ed. dj. VG. J2. $10.00

MAYER, C. *Trapping Wild Animals in Malay Jungle.* 1921. Garden City. 207 p. dj. EX. M2. $13.00

MAYER, E. *International Auction Records.* 1980. France. 1st ed. EX. $45.00

MAYER, Grace M. *Once Upon a City: NY From 1890-1910.* 1958. Macmillan. Ils. 511 p. dj. D2. $85.00

MAYER, J.A. *Power Plant Testing.* 1934. NY. Ils 4th ed. 614 p. VG. $15.00

MAYER & VAN GELDER. *Physiological Mammalogy.* 1963. Academic. Ils. 2 vols. djs. EX. M2. $25.00

MAYERS, H. *Alger Biography Without a Hero.* 1928. NY. Ils 1st ed. 241 p. VG. B2. $30.00

MAYHALL, M.P. *Kiowas.* 1962. Norman. Ils 1st ed. dj. G. $25.00

MAYLAND, H.J. *Complete Home Aquarium.* 1976. Grosset Dunlap. Ils 1st Am ed. dj. EX. M2. $15.00

MAYNARD, C.J. *Manual of Taxidermy. Complete Guide...* 1883. Boston. Ils 1st ed. 12mo. 111 p. $35.00

MAYNARD, S.T. *Small Country Place.* 1908. Lippincott. 1st ed. dj. G. $12.00

MAYNE, A. *British Profile Miniaturists.* 1970. Boston. 1st Am ed. dj. VG. $22.00

MAYNE, William. *Earthfasts.* 1968. 4th print. xl. VG. scarce. C1. $14.00

MAYO, C.A. *Lloyd Library & Its Makers.* 1928. Cincinnati. Ils. pls. $40.00

MAYO, Charles. *Story of My Family & My Career.* 1968. NY. 1st ed. dj. VG. B2. $15.00

MAYOR, A. Hyatt. *Giovanni Battista Piranesi.* 1952. NY. Bittner. Orig ed. dj. D2. $85.00

MAYOR, A. Hyatt. *Prints & People: Social History of Printed Pictures.* 1972. NY. 2nd print. dj. D2. $65.00

MAYR, E. *Systematics & Origin of Species From Viewpoint of Zoologist.* 1949. Columbia U. Ils. 334 p. EX. M2. $25.00

MAZLISH, Bruce. *Railroad & the Space Program.* 1965. 223 p. $12.50

MCATEE, W.L. *Folk Names of Canadian Birds.* 1957. Nat Mus Canada. 1st ed. wraps. J2. $20.00

MCBRIDE, Bill. *Pocket Guide to Identification of First Editions.* 1985. McBride. Revised 3rd ed. EX. $6.00

MCBRIDE, H.W. *Rifleman Went To War.* 1935. Plantersville. 1st ed. dj. VG. B2. $60.00

MCCABE, J.D. *Life & Campaigns of General Robert E. Lee.* 1870. pls. maps. 732 p. VG. J4. $40.00

MCCABE, J.O. *San Juan Water Boundary Question.* 1964. Toronto U. dj. EX. $15.00

MCCAHILL, W.P. *First To Fight.* 1942. Phil. Ils Wittmack. 73 p. G. T5. $25.00

MCCALL, G.A. *NM in 1850: Military View.* 1968. OK U. Ils 1st ed. 222 p. dj. EX. M2. $13.00

MCCALLUM, J.D. *Ecerest Diary.* 1966. NY. dj. VG. $15.00

MCCALLUM & MCCALLUM. *Wire That Fenced the W.* 1965. Norman. Ils 1st ed. dj. EX. $35.00

MCCAMMON, Robert. *Bethany Sin.* London. 1st HrdCvr ed. M. $50.00

MCCAMMON, Robert. *They Thirst.* London. 1st HrdCvr ed. M. $35.00

MCCAMMON, Robert. *Usher's Passing.* 1984. 1st ed. dj. M. $35.00

MCCAMMON, Robert. *Wolf's Hour.* London. 1st HrdCvr ed. M. $50.00

MCCANLEY, L.M. *Joy of Gardens.* 1911. Chicago. VG. EX. P3. $30.00

MCCARRAN, Margaret. *Fabianism in Political Life of Britain, 1550-1850.* 1958. Black. 1st ed. 612 p. wraps. J2. $15.00

MCCARTER, M.H. *Winning the Wilderness.* 1917. Chicago. Ils Marchand. 1st ed. EX. $20.00

MCCARTHY, C. *Detailed Minutia of Soldier Life in Army of N VA: 1861-1865.* 1982. Time Life. reprint of 1882 ed. 224 p. AEG. M. $40.00

MCCARTHY, E.J. *Limits of Power: America's Role in the World.* 1967. Holt Rinehart. 1st ed. dj. $5.00

MCCARTHY, Eugene. *Familiar Fish: Their Habits & Capture.* 1900. Appleton. Ils 1st ed. 216 p. EX. $18.00

MCCARTHY, Mary. *Group.* 1963. NY. 1st ed. dj. VG. $22.00

MCCARTHY, Mary. *Memories of a Catholic Girlhood.* 1957. NY. 1st ed. dj. EX. $25.00

MCCARTHY, Mary. *Stones of Florence.* nd. NY. Harcourt Brace. Ils. dj. D2. $65.00

MCCARTHY, Mary. *17th Degree.* 1974. Harcourt Brace. 1st ed. dj. VG. $22.50

MCCARTHY. *Diagnosis & Treatment of Diseases of Hair.* 1940. St. Louis. 671 p. EX. $35.00

MCCARTY, J.L. *Maverick Town: Story of Old Tascosa.* 1946. Norman. 2nd ed. dj. VG. $35.00

MCCARTY, J.L. *Maverick Town: Story of Old Tascosa.* 1968. OK U. Enlarged ed. sgn. 297 p. dj. M2. $25.00

MCCAULEY, Kirby. *Dark Forces.* nd. Book Club. dj. VG. P1. $7.50

MCCAULEY, Kirby. *Frights.* 1976. St. Martin. 1st ed. sgns. dj. EX. $25.00

MCCAUSLAND, Elizabeth. *Work for Artists: What? Where? How?* 1947. Am Artist Group. 1st ed. dj. J2. $15.00

MCCLAIN, Emlin. *McClain's Annotated Statutes of State of IA.* 1882. sm 4to. 2 vols. leather. EX. $15.00

MCCLANAHAN, Ed. *Famous People I Have Known.* 1985. NY. Farrar. 1st ed. dj. $10.00

MCCLANE, A.J. *Practical Fly-Fisherman.* 1953. NY. dj. VG. $35.00

MCCLANE, A.J. *Spinning for Fresh-Water & Salt-Water Fish.* 1952. NY. dj. VG. $5.00

MCCLELLAN, Elisabeth. *History of American Costume 1607-1870.* 1937. NY. Tudor. 661 p. dj. slipcase. $35.00

MCCLELLAN, G.B. *Conduct of the War. Vol. III.* 1863. WA. index. 656 p. K1. $18.50

MCCLELLAN, G.B. *Life & Campaigns of Major General J.E.B. Stuart.* 1987. Little Rock. reprint of 1885 ed. 468 p. VG. T5. $35.00

MCCLELLAN, G.B. *McClellan's Own Story: War for the Union.* 1887. Webster. Ils. 678 p. VG. M2. $50.00

MCCLELLAN, G.B. *Report on Organization & Campaigns of Army of Potomac.* 1864. NY. 480 p. orig bdg. K1. $27.50

MCCLINTOCK, Alexander. *Best O'Luck.* 1917. Doran. sgn. $7.50

MCCLINTOCK, John. *Pioneer Days in Black Hills.* 1939. Deadwood, SD. 1st ed. VG. J2. $175.00

MCCLINTOCK, L. *Voyage of the Fox in the Arctic Seas.* 1859. London. VG. $85.00

MCCLINTON. *Chromolithography of Louis Prang.* 1973. 1st ed. 4to. dj. EX. B1. $30.00

MCCLUNG, J.W. *MN As It Is in 1870.* 1870. St. Paul. 1st ed. J2. $60.00

MCCLUNG, R.M. *Lost Wild Worlds.* 1976. Morrow. Ils 1st ed. maps. 288 p. dj. M2. $16.00

MCCLURE, A.K. *Col. Alexander K. McClure's Recollections of Half Century.* 1902. Salem. Ils. 502 p. TEG. T5. $35.00

MCCLURE, A.K. *Lincoln & Men of War Times.* 1962. Phil. reprint of 1892 ed. dj. EX. $15.00

MCCLURE, A.K. *Lincoln's Own Yarns & Stories.* nd. Winston. $12.00

MCCLURE, J.B. *Lincoln's Stories.* 1880. Rhodes McClure. G. $22.50

MCCLURE, James. *Steam Pig.* 1971. NY. Harper. 1st ed. dj. VG. $22.50

MCCLURE, Michael. *Beard.* 1967. Coyote. 1st print. pb. EX. $33.00

MCCLURE, Michael. *Dark Brown.* 1961. Auerhahn. 1/750. sgn. wraps. EX. $50.00

MCCLURE, Michael. *Grabbing of the Fairy.* 1978. Turck Pr. 1/100. sgn. $40.00

MCCLURE, Michael. *Hymns to St. Geryon & Dark Brown.* 1979. Gray Fox. wraps. EX. $15.00

MCCLURE, Michael. *Hymns to St. Geryon & Other Poems.* 1959. Auerhahn Pr. 1st ed. sgn. wraps. $85.00

MCCLURE, Michael. *Little Odes & the Raptors.* 1969. Black Sparrow. 1/200. sgn/#d. EX. $30.00

MCCLURE, Michael. *Scratching the Beat Surface.* 1980. San Francisco. N Point. 1st ed. dj. VG. $57.50

MCCLYMONT & FULLYLORE. *Greece.* 1906. London. Black. 1st ed. VG. $35.00

MCCOLVIN, Lionel. *Personal Library: Guide for the Bookbuyer.* 1953. London. dj. $25.00

MCCOMAS, E.S. *Journal of Travel.* 1954. Portland. Ltd ed. VG. $30.00

MCCOMMAS, B. *History of Sevier Co. & Her People.* 1980. Sevier Co Hist Soc. 352 p. M2. $30.00

MCCORD, David. *Star in the Pail.* 1975. Boston. Ils Simont. 1st ed. VG. $15.00

MCCORD, J.B. *My Patients Were Zulus.* 1951. Rinehart. 308 p. VG. M2. $5.00

MCCORMACK, L. *I Hear You Calling Me.* 1949. WI. $10.00

MCCORMICK, A.O. *Story of St. Agnes Parish, Cleveland, OH, 1893-1937.* 1937. Cleveland. Ils. 64 p. G. T5. $35.00

MCCORMICK, H.W. *Shadows in the Sea: Sharks, Skates & Rays.* 1963. Weathervane. reprint. 415 p. dj. EX. M2. $13.00

MCCORMICK, R.R. *Ulysses S. Grant: Great Soldier of America.* 1934. Appleton Century. Ils. 343 p. M2. $20.00

MCCORMICK, R.R. *War Without Grant.* 1950. 25 maps. 245 p. dj. EX. J4. $10.00

MCCOURT, E. *Yukon & NW Territories.* 1969. St. Martin. Ils. 236 p. dj. EX. M2. $10.00

MCCOWAN, D. *Animals of the Canadian Rockies.* 1941. Macmillan. Ils. sgn, 302 p. VG. M2. $11.00

MCCOWAN, D. *Naturalist in the Rockies.* 1946. Macmillan. Ils. 294 p. VG. M2. $6.00

MCCOY, H.J. *McCoy Company Catalog of Supplies & Equipment...* nd. Ils. 599 p. $45.00

MCCOY, J.J. *Hunt for the Whooping Crane.* 1966. Lothrop Lee. Ils. 223 p. dj. EX. M2. $11.00

MCCOY, J.J. *Saving Our Wildlife.* 1970. Crowell Collier. 232 p. dj. EX. M2. $4.00

MCCRACKEN, Harold. *American Cowboy.* 1973. NY. 1st ed after Ltd ed. dj. VG. $16.00

MCCRACKEN, Harold. *Beast That Walks Like a Man.* 1955. Garden City. Ils 1st ed. 319 p. dj. VG. B2. $35.00

MCCRACKEN, Harold. *Beast That Walks Like a Man.* 1955. Hanover House. 1st ed. $48.00

MCCRACKEN, Harold. *Charles M. Russell Book.* 1957. Doubleday. G. $25.00

MCCRACKEN, Harold. *Charles M. Russell Book.* 1957. NY. Deluxe 1st trade ed. dj. EX. $38.00

MCCRACKEN, Harold. *Frank Tenney Johnson Book.* 1974. Doubleday. 1st ed. dj. J2. $35.00

MCCRACKEN, Harold. *Frederic Remington Book: Pictorial History of W.* 1966. NY. 1st ed. pls. sm folio. EX. $75.00

MCCRACKEN, Harold. *Frederic Remington: Artist of Old W.* c 1947. Phil. 1st trade ed. 48 pls. dj. VG. $27.50

MCCRACKEN, Harold. *Frederic Remington: Artist of Old W.* 1947. Phil. 1st ed. VG. B2. $57.50

MCCRACKEN, Harold. *Frederic Remington's Won W.* 1960. Dial. dj. VG. $15.00

MCCRACKEN, Harold. *George Catlin & the Old Frontier.* 1959. NY. Ils 1st trade ed. 4to. 216 p. EX. $30.00

MCCRACKEN, Harold. *George Catlin & the Old Frontier.* 1959. NY. 1st ed after Ltd ed. dj. EX. $50.00

MCCRACKEN, Harold. *Portrait of Old W.* 1952. NY. 1st ed. $30.00

MCCULLERS, Carson. *Ballad of the Sad Cafe.* 1951. Boston. Houghton. dj. VG. $40.00

MCCULLERS, Carson. *Clock Without Hands.* 1961. Boston. Houghton Mifflin. 1st print. dj. M. $45.00

MCCULLERS, Carson. *Clock Without Hands.* 1961. Boston. 1st ed. dj. EX. $40.00

MCCULLERS, Carson. *Clock Without Hands.* 1961. London. 1st ed. dj. $25.00

MCCULLERS, Carson. *Member of the Wedding.* 1946. Boston. 1st ed. dj. B2. $85.00

MCCULLERS, Carson. *Mortgaged Heart.* 1971. Boston. 1st ed. dj. M. $30.00

MCCULLERS, Carson. *Reflections in a Golden Eye.* 1941. Boston. 1st ed. dj. EX. $47.50

MCCULLERS, Carson. *Square Root of Wonderful.* 1958. Boston. 1st ed. dj. B2. $40.00

MCCULLIN, Don. *Hearts of Darkness.* 1981. NY. Intro John Le Carre. 1st Am pb ed. $35.00

MCCULLO. *Pioneer With Wings.* 1951. Elgin, IL. Brethren. Ils. VG. $7.00

MCCULLOUGH, David. *Building of the Brooklyn Bridge.* 1972. NY. 1st ed. presentation. sgn. EX. $55.00

MCCULLOUGH, David. *Path Between the Seas.* 1977. NY. 1st ed. dj. EX. $20.00

MCCULLY, Anderson. *American Alpines in the Garden.* 1931. NY. 1st ed. dj. VG. $20.00

MCCUTCHEON, G.B. *Day of the Dog: A Love Story.* 1905. Dodd Mead. Ils Fisher/Armstrong. $7.50

MCCUTCHEON, G.B. *Flyers.* 1907. Dodd Mead. Ils Fisher. 1st ed. VG. $17.50

MCCUTCHEON, G.B. *Hollow of Her Hand.* 1912. Dodd Mead. Ils Keller. 1st ed. $12.00

MCCUTCHEON, G.B. *Mr. Bingle.* 1915. Dodd Mead. Ils Flagg. 1st ed. $12.00

MCCUTCHEON, G.B. *Purple Parasol.* 1905. NY. Ils Fisher. VG. $15.00

MCCUTCHEON, G.B. *Sherrods.* 1903. Dodd Mead. Ils Williams. 1st ed. $12.00

MCCUTCHEON, J.T. *Drawn From Memory.* 1950. Bobbs Merrill. Ils ed. VG. $15.00

MCDADE, M.T. *Annals of Murder.* 1961. Norman. 1st ed. dj. EX. $15.00

MCDADE, M.T. *Gulf.* 1986. NY. Harcourt. 1st ed. proof wraps. EX. $15.00

MCDANIEL, Ruel. *Vinegarroon: Saga of Judge Roy Bean, Law W of Pecos.* 1936. S Pub. 143 p. G. M2. $5.00

MCDANIEL, Ruel. *Vinegarroon: Saga of Judge Roy Bean, Law W of Pecos.* 1936. Kingsport. 1st ed. EX. $40.00

MCDANIEL, W.H. *History of Beech.* 1971. Wichita. Ils 1st ed. 336 p. VG. T5. $45.00

MCDERMAND, Charles. *Waters of Golden Trout Country.* 1946. Ils. 162 p. VG. $20.00

MCDERMAND, Charles. *Yosemite & Kings Canyon Trout.* 1947. Putnam. Ils. sgn. 178 p. EX. $28.00

MCDERMOTT, J.F. *Private Libraries of Creole St. Louis.* 1938. Baltimore. $45.00

MCDERMOTT, J.F. *Up the MO With Audubon: Journal of Edward Harris.* 1951. OK U. Ils 1st ed. dj. EX. M2. $37.00

MCDERMOTT, John. *Before Mark Twain.* 1968. 298 p. dj. M. K1. $17.50

MCDONALD, E.D. *Bibliography of D.H. Lawrence.* 1969. NY. EX. $25.00

MCDONALD, J.D. *No Deadly Drug.* 1968. NY. Doubleday. 1st ed. dj. EX. $15.00

MCDONALD, J.D. *One More Sunday.* 1984. Knopf. AP. 1st ed. wraps. EX. $20.00

MCDONALD, John. *Strategy in Poker, Business & War.* 1950. NY. Ils Osborn. 1st ed. dj. EX. $35.00

MCDONALD, Lucile. *Jewels & Gems.* 1940. Crowell. 1st ed. dj. VG. J2. $15.00

MCDOUGAL, H.C. *Recollections.* 1910. KS City. index. 466 p. K1. $27.50

MCDOWELL, Ian. *Albion.* Aries Fantasy Series. M. C1. $16.00

MCDOWELL, Ian. *Isaac Asimov's Fantasy?* 1985. 1st ed. dj. M. C1. $11.50

MCELROY, John. *Andersonville: Story of Rebel Military Prisons.* 1879. Toledo. Ils 1st ed. rebound. 654 p. T5. $45.00

MCELROY, John. *This Was Andersonville.* 1957. NY. 1st ed. dj. EX. $25.00

MCELROY, R. *Jefferson Davis: Real & Unreal.* 1937. Harper. 1st ed. sgn. 2 vols. EX. M2. $45.00

MCELROY, T.P. *Habitat Guide to Birding.* 1974. Knopf. Ils dj. VG. $8.00

MCEWEN, I.P. *So This Is Ranching.* 1948. Caldwell. Ils. 270 p. dj. VG. B2. $25.00

MCFALL, P.S. *So Lives Dream, History & Story of Old Pendleton District...* 1953. NY. Comet. presentation. sgn. 149 p. dj. $25.00

MCFARLAND, D. *Oxford Companion to Animal Behavior.* nd. Oxford U. Ils 1st ed. 653 p. dj. EX. M2. $25.00

MCFARLAND, Marvin. *Papers of Wilbur & Orville Wright.* 1953. NY. Ils 1st ed. 2 vols. djs. EX. $55.00

MCFARLANE, I.K. *Modern Culture: Some Sources of Oriental Influence.* 1919. np. $7.50

MCFEE, William. *Harbor Master.* 1931. Garden City. 1/377. sgn/#d. slipcase. EX. $65.00

MCFEE, William. *Harbor Master.* 1932. Garden City. Doubleday Doran. G. $5.00

MCFEE, William. *Life of Sir Martin Frobisher.* 1928. Harper. Ils 1st ed. 276 p. VG. M2. $25.00

MCFEE, William. *Race.* 1924. NY. 1st ed. sgn. 398 p. T5. $25.00

MCFEE, William. *Reflections of Marsyas.* 1933. Slide Mountain. 1st ed. 1/300. sgn. VG. $45.00

MCFEE, William. *Watch Below.* 1940. NY. Stated 1st ed. lg 8vo. VG. $20.00

MCFEELY, W.S. *U.S. Grant: Biography.* 1981. Norton. Ils 1st ed. 592 p. dj. EX. M2. $14.00

MCGAMMON, P. *Our Amazing World of Nature: Its Marvels & Mysteries.* 1969. Readers Digest. Ils. 4to. 320 p. EX. M2. $5.00

MCGARRY, Mary. *Great Fairy Tales of Ireland.* 1973. Avenel Books. 1st Am ed. 2nd issue. dj. VG. $5.50

MCGAW, W.C. *Savage Scene: Life & Times of James Kirker, Frontier King.* 1972. Hastings House. photos. 242 p. dj. EX. M2. $14.00

MCGILL, Ralph. *Fleas Come With the Dog.* 1954. Nashville. 1st ed. 128 p. dj. EX. $15.00

MCGILL, Ralph. *S & Southerner.* 1963. Little Brown. 3rd ed. inscr. dj. EX. $15.00

MCGILL, Ralph. *Selections From McGill's Column in Atlantic Constitution.* 1970. Atlanta. 80 p. $20.00

MCGINLEY, Patrick. *Foggage.* 1983. St. Martin. 1st ed. dj. EX. $25.00

MCGINNISS, Joe. *Going to Extremes.* 1980. NY. 1st ed. dj. VG. B2. $15.00

MCGLASHAN, C.F. *History of the Donner Party.* 1947. Stanford, CA. Ils. 261 p. G. T5. $17.50

MCGLOIN, John. *Eloquent Indian: Life of James Bouchard, CA Jesuit.* 1949. Stanford. 1st ed. presentation. dj. J2. $22.50

MCGOODWIN, Henry. *Architectural Shades & Shadows.* 1926. Boston. Ils. photos. G. $40.00

MCGOVERN, Ann. *Robin Hood of Sherwood Forest.* Ils Sugarman. reprint of 1968. pb. VG. C1. $3.00

MCGOVERN, G.S. *Great Coalfield War.* 1982. 1st ed. dj. VG. $30.00

MCGOVERN, W. *Jungle Paths & Inca Ruins.* 1927. NY. Ils. VG. $14.00

MCGRANE, Reginald. *William Allen: Study in W Democracy.* 1925. OH Hist Soc. 1st ed. VG. J2. $15.00

MCGRATH, Thomas. *To Walk a Crooked Mile.* 1974. Swallow. 1st ed. dj. EX. $22.50

MCGRAW & MCGRAW. *Forbidden Fountain of Oz.* 1980. Internat Wizard of Oz Club. wraps. $27.50

MCGRAW HILL. *Encyclopedia of World Drama.* 1972. 4 vols. xl. VG. $50.00

MCGUANE, Thomas. *Bushwacked Piano.* 1971. Simon Schuster. 1st ed. VG. $30.00

MCGUANE, Thomas. *Keep the Change.* 1989. Boston/NY. 1st ed. 1/150. sgn. boxed. EX. $100.00

MCGUANE, Thomas. *Keep the Change.* 1989. Houghton. ARC. wraps. M. $20.00

MCGUANE, Thomas. *Ninety-Two in the Shade.* 1973. Farrar. 1st ed. sgn. dj. EX. $60.00

MCGUANE, Thomas. *Ninety-Two in the Shade.* 1973. NY. 1st ed. dj. EX. $30.00

MCGUANE, Thomas. *Nobody's Angel.* 1982. Random House. 1st ed. sgn. dj. VG. $27.50

MCGUANE, Thomas. *Outside Chance.* 1980. Farrar. 1st ed. sgn. dj. VG. $32.50

MCGUANE, Thomas. *Something To Be Desired.* 1984. NY. 1st ed. dj. EX. $20.00

MCGUFFEY, W.H. *Fifth Eclectic Reader.* 1920. Revised ed. sm 8vo. 352 p. EX. $4.50

MCGUFFEY, W.H. *First Eclectic Reader.* 1920. Revised ed. sm 8vo. 96 p. EX. $2.50

MCGUFFEY, W.H. *Fourth Eclectic Reader.* 1920. Revised ed. sm 8vo. 256 p. EX. $4.00

MCGUFFEY, W.H. *McGuffey's Readers.* 1920. Revised ed. sm 8vo. 6 vols. VG. $18.00

MCGUFFEY, W.H. *Second Eclectic Reader.* 1920. Revised ed. sm 8vo. 160 p. EX. $3.00

MCGUFFEY, W.H. *Sixth Eclectic Reader.* 1921. Revised ed. sm 8vo. 464 p. EX. $5.00

MCGUFFEY, W.H. *Third Eclectic Reader.* 1920. Revised ed. sm 8vo. 208 p. EX. $3.50

MCGUFFIE, T.H. *Rank & File.* 1966. NY. Ils 1st Am ed. 424 p. dj. VG. T5. $12.50

MCGUIRE, C.E. *Catholic Builders of the Nation.* 1923. Boston. Ils. 5 vols. $60.00

MCHARGUE, G. *Elidor & the Golden Ball.* 1973. Book Club. Ils Schongut. VG. C1. $5.00

MCHATTON, T.H. *Armchair Gardening.* 1947. Athens. 130 p. VG. $20.00

MCHENRY & MYERS. *Home Is the Sailor.* 1948. NY. 1st ed. wraps. EX. $17.50

MCHUGH, Tom. *Time of the Buffalo.* 1972. Knopf. Ils 1st ed. 339 p. dj. EX. M2. $20.00

MCILROY, T. *Rose Is a Rose.* 1984. Doubleday. Ils MacPherson. wraps. VG. M1. $6.50

MCILWAINE, Shields. *Memphis: Down in Dixie.* 1948. Dutton. 1st ed. dj. J2. $12.50

MCINERNEY, Jay. *Bright Lights, Big City.* 1985. London. Cape. 1st HrdCvr ed. EX. $27.50

MCINERNY, Ralph. *Her Death of Cold.* 1977. Vanguard. dj. VG. $12.00

MCINERNY, Ralph. *Her Death of Cold.* 1977. Vanguard. 1st ed. dj. EX. $20.00

MCINERNY, Ralph. *Leave of Absence.* 1986. Atheneum. 1st ed. inscr/sgn. dj. EX. $20.00

MCINTOSH, James. *Origin of American Indians.* c 1850. New ed. 345 p. $50.00

MCINTOSH, William. *Sermons From a Philistine Pulpit.* 1898. Roycroft. 24mo. sgn. EX. D1. $70.00

MCINTYRE, J.T. *Ashton-Kirk: Criminologist.* c 1918. Phil. Ils. VG. $10.00

MCKAY, Claude. *Banjo.* 1929. NY. 1st ed. dj. VG. $50.00

MCKAY, Claude. *Selected Poems of Claude McKay.* 1953. NY. Bookman Assn. 1st ed. 112 p. $20.00

MCKAY, Donald. *Some Famous Sailing Ships & Their Builders.* 1928. NY. 1st Am ed. VG. $65.00

MCKAY, Richard. *S Street: Maritime History of NY.* 1934. Putnam. 1st ed. VG. J2. $15.00

MCKEARIN & MCKEARIN. *Two Hundred Years of American Blown Glass.* 1950. Bonanza. 382 p. dj. VG. M1. $35.00

MCKEE, Alexander. *How We Found the Mary Rose.* 1982. NY. Ils. sm 4to. dj. $30.00

MCKEE, Alexander. *Strike From the Sky.* 1960. Little Brown. 1st Am ed. 228 p. $20.00

MCKELVIE, Martha. *Quien Sabe? Montezuma, Emperor of the Aztecs.* 1965. Phil. presentation. sgn. 160 p. dj. VG. $15.00

MCKENDRY, J.J. *Aesop: 5 Centuries of Illustrated Fables.* 1965. Met Mus. 3rd print. 95 p. dj. VG. $15.00

MCKENNEY, Ruth. *Industrial Valley.* 1939. NY. 1st ed. dj. EX. $27.50

MCKENNEY & HALL. *History of Indian Tribes of N America.* 1934. Edinburgh. 3 vols. $400.00

MCKENNEY & HALL. *History of Indian Tribes of N America.* 1978. Volair. Ltd 1st ed. 2 vols. boxed. M. $225.00

MCKENNY, M. *Wildlife of Pacific NW.* 1954. Binfords Mort. Ils. 299 p. dj. EX. M2. $8.00

MCKENZIE, Lucia. *Astrographology.* 1971. AZ. $18.50

MCKEOWN, S. *HI Reptiles & Amphibians.* 1978. Oriental. Ils 1st print. 80 p. EX. M2. $12.00

MCKERROW. R.B. *Introduction to Bibliography.* 1927. Oxford. Clarendon. Ils. 358 p. dj. VG. $40.00

MCKIE, Ronald. *Company of Animals.* 1966. NY. 1st Am ed. 45 photos. dj. xl. VG. $8.50

MCKILLIP, Norman. *Ace Enginemen.* 1963. 117 p. $9.00

MCKILLIP, P.A. *Chronicles of Morgon.* 1979. London. Sidgwick. 1st ed. EX. $25.00

MCKILLIP, P.A. *Moon-Flash.* 1984. NY. Atheneum. 1st ed. dj. M. $10.00

MCKILLOP, Susan Regan. *Franciabigio.* 1974. Berkeley. Ils. 322 p. dj. D2. $95.00

MCKINLAY, W.L. *Karluk: Great Untold Story of Arctic Exploration.* 1977. St. Martin. Ils. 170 p. dj. EX. M2. $19.00

MCKINLEY, Robin. *Imaginary Lands.* 1986. 1st ed. dj. M. C1. $24.00

MCKINLEY & BENT. *Old Rough & Ready.* 1946. NY. 1st ed. 329 p. dj. VG. B2. $17.50

MCKUEN, Rod. *Moment to Moment.* 1974. NY. 1st ed. dj. VG. $7.00

MCLANE, B.J. *McClellans of AL & AR.* 1962. WA Co Hist Soc. 4to. 66 p. M2. $10.00

MCLAREN, Jack. *Stories of Fear.* 1947. Pendulum. dj. VG. P1. $45.00

MCLAUGHLIN, Jack. *Gettysburg: Long Encampment, Battle, Men, Memories.* 1962. NY. Ils 1st ed. dj. VG. $25.00

MCLAUGHLIN, Jack. *Gettysburg: Long Encampment, Battle, Men, Memories.* 1963. Bonanza. Ils. J4. $10.00

MCLAUGHLIN, M. *Dragonflies.* 1989. Walker. Ils 1st ed. dj. M. M2. $8.00

MCLAUGHLIN, P.A. *Comparative Morphology of Recent Crustacea.* 1980. Freeman. Ils 1st ed. 177 p. EX. M2. $28.00

MCLAURIN, Hamish. *What About N Africa?* 1927. NY. $35.00

MCLEAN, E.W. *Father Struck It Rich.* 1936. Boston. 1st ed. dj. VG. $17.50

MCLEARY, A.C. *Humorous Incidents of the War.* c 1903. 1st ed. wraps. VG. R1. $250.00

MCLEISH, Roderick. *Prince Ombra.* 1983. London. 1st Eng ed. dj. M. C1. $7.50

MCLIVER, Tom. *Anti-Evolution: Annotated Bibliography.* 1988. McFarland. 385 p. VG. T5. $12.50

MCLOUGHLIN, John. *White-Headed Eagle.* 1934. NY. 1st ed. sgn. VG. B1. $15.00

MCLUHAN, Marshall. *War & Peace in Global Village.* 1968. NY. Review 1st ed. dj. RS. EX. $25.00

MCMANUS, G.H. *Thomas Pierson McManus, His Ancestors & His Family.* 1949. np. Ils. sgn. 31 p. G. T5. $15.00

MCMARTHY, Mary. *Group.* 1963. NY. 1st ed. dj. VG. $10.00

MCMASTER, J.B. *Daniel Webster.* 1902. NY. Ils 1st ed. 333 p. TEG. VG. T5. $25.00

MCMECHEN, E.C. *Moffat Tunnel of CO, Epic of Empire.* 1927. photos. maps. charts. 280 p. $80.00

MCMILLAN, George. *Old Breed.* 1949. 1st ed. G. R1. $95.00

MCMILLAN, M. *AL Confederate Reader.* 1963. AL U. Ils 1st ed. VG. $35.00

MCMILLAN, P.J. *Marina & Lee (Harvey Oswald).* 1977. NY/London. 1st ed. 4to. 527 p. EX. $17.00

MCMINN & MAINO. *Illustrated Manual of Pacific Coast Trees.* 1981. CA U. Ils. 409 p. EX. M2. $10.00

MCMORRIES, E.Y. *History of 1st Regiment AL Volunteer Infantry, CSA.* 1904. Montgomery, AL. 1st ed. wraps. VG. $85.00

MCMURTRIE, D.C. *Book: Story of Printing & Bookmaking.* 1943. NY. Revised 3rd ed. dj. EX. $42.00

MCMURTRIE, D.C. *Book: Story of Printing & Bookmaking.* 1965. Oxford. 8th print. VG. M1. $30.00

MCMURTRIE, D.C. *Early Printing in TN.* 1933. TN Pr. 1/900. VG. $50.00

MCMURTRIE, D.C. *OR Imprints, 1847-1870.* 1950. Eugene. Ils. wraps. $40.00

MCMURTRIE, D.C. *Suggested Program for Augmenting Materials for Research...* 1939. Chicago. $15.00

MCMURTRIE, D.C. *Wings for Words.* 1940. NY. sgn. dj. EX. $27.50

MCMURTRIE, F.E. *Jane's Fighting Ships, 1940.* 1941. London. Ils. 527 p. fair. T5. $65.00

MCMURTRY, Larry. *Anything for Billy.* 1988. Simon Schuster. 1st ed. dj. EX. T6. $15.00

MCMURTRY, Larry. *Cadillac Jack.* 1982. NY. Ltd ed. sgn. slipcase. EX. $27.50

MCMURTRY, Larry. *Cadillac Jack.* 1982. Simon Schuster. 1st ed. dj. M. $15.00

MCMURTRY, Larry. *Daughter of Texas.* 1965. CT. Ray. 1st Am ed. dj. VG. $75.00

MCMURTRY, Larry. *Desert Rose.* 1983. Allen. 1st Eng ed. dj. EX. $45.00

MCMURTRY, Larry. *Desert Rose.* 1983. NY. 1st ed. dj. VG. B2. $30.00

MCMURTRY, Larry. *Film Flam.* 1987. NY. 1st ed. dj. EX. $20.00

MCMURTRY, Larry. *Film Flam.* 1987. Simon Schuster. 1st ed. sgn. dj. EX. $35.00

MCMURTRY, Larry. *In a Narrow Grave.* 1968. NY. 1st ed. 2nd issue. dj. EX. $55.00

MCMURTRY, Larry. *Lonesome Dove.* ARC. dj. EX. $150.00

MCMURTRY, Larry. *Lonesome Dove.* 1985. NY. 1st ed. dj. M. P3. $85.00

MCMURTRY, Larry. *Moving On.* 1970. Simon Schuster. 1st ed. dj. EX. $25.00

MCMURTRY, Larry. *Some Can Whistle.* 1989. NY. sgn. dj. EX. $15.00

MCMURTRY, Larry. *Somebody's Darling.* 1978. NY. 1st ed. dj. with sgn card. $85.00

MCMURTRY, Larry. *Terms of Endearment.* 1975. NY. 1st ed. dj. VG. $20.00

MCMURTRY, Larry. *Terms of Endearment.* 1975. Simon Schuster. 1st ed. dj. EX. $25.00

MCMURTRY, Larry. *Terms of Endearment.* 1977. London. 1st ed. dj. $40.00

MCMURTRY, Larry. *Terms of Endearment.* 1977. London. 1st ed. sgn. EX. $80.00

MCMURTRY, Larry. *Texasville.* 1987. NY. 1st ed. dj. EX. $25.00

MCMURTRY, Larry. *Texasville.* 1987. NY. 1st ed. sgn. dj. M. $75.00

MCNALLY, Dennis. *Desolate Angel: Jack Kerouac.* 1979. NY. 1st ed. dj. VG. $25.00

MCNALLY, R. *So Remorseless a Havoc of Dolphins, Whales & Men.* 1981. Little Brown. Ils 1st ed. 268 p. dj. EX. M2. $5.00

MCNAUGHTON, Arnold. *Book of Kings: Royal Genealogy.* 1973. Arcadia. 1/55. sgn Mountbatten. 3 vols. EX. $750.00

MCNEELY & WACHTEL. *Soul of the Tiger.* 1988. Doubleday. Ils 1st ed. 390 p. dj. EX. M2. $19.00

MCNEER, Mary. *Gold Rush.* 1944. NY. Ils Lynd Ward. 31 p. VG. T5. $22.50

MCNEER, May. *Golden Flash.* 1947. NY. 1st ed. dj. VG. $30.00

MCNEIL, Morris. *Hokum.* 1978. Sans Souci Pr. 1/26. sgn pub. $100.00

MCNEIL, Morris. *Hokum.* 1978. Sans Souci Pr. 1/73. #d. $50.00

MCNEILL, J.C. *Lyrics From Cotton Land.* 1922. Charlotte. Ils 1st ed. gingham bdg. B2. $47.50

MCNULTY, F. *Great Whales.* 1974. Doubleday. Ils 1st ed. dj. EX. M2. $5.00

MCNULTY, F. *Whooping Crane: Bird That Defies Extinction.* 1966. Dutton. Ils 1st ed. 190 p. dj. EX. M2. $10.00

MCPHAUL, Jack. *Johnny Torrio: First of Gang Lords.* 1971. NY. Ils. 489 p. dj. VG. B2. $20.00

MCPHEE, John. *Basin & Range.* 1981. Farrar. 216 p. dj. M2. $10.00

MCPHEE, John. *Coming Into the Country.* 1977. NY. 1st ed. dj. B2. $25.00

MCPHEE, John. *Deltoid Pumpkin Game.* 1969. NY. 1st ed. dj. EX. $35.00

MCPHEE, John. *Giving Good Weight.* 1979. Farrar Straus. 1st ed. dj. VG. T6. $15.00

MCPHEE, John. *Giving Good Weight.* 1979. NY. 1st ed. dj. EX. $25.00

MCPHEE, John. *Giving Good Weight.* 1979. NY. 1st ed. sgn. dj. VG. $35.00

MCPHEE, John. *Headmaster.* 1966. NY. 1st ed. presentation. dj. EX. $75.00

MCPHEE, John. *Levels of the Game.* 1969. NY. 1st ed. dj. B2. $32.50

MCPHEE, John. *Oranges.* 1967. NY. 1st ed. dj. EX. $40.00

MCPHEE, John. *Oranges.* 1967. NY. 1st ed. inscr/sgn. dj. M. $65.00

MCPHEE, John. *Survival of Bark Canoe.* 1975. Farrar Straus. 1st print. dj. xl. M2. $25.00

MCPHERSON, A.S. *Story of My Life.* 1927. Boni Liveright. Ils 1st ed. 316 p. dj. VG. B2. $35.00

MCPHERSON, A.S. *This Is That: Personal Experiences, Sermons & Writings.* nd. Los Angeles. sgn. 685 p. VG. M1. $32.50

MCPHERSON, J.A. *Railroads, Trains & Train People in American Culture.* 1976. 1st ed. 186 p. $18.00

MCPHERSON, J.L. *Good-Bye Rosie.* 1965. Knopf. 1st ed. dj. VG. $45.00

MCPHERSON, J.M. *Ordeal by Fire: Civil War & Reconstruction.* 1982. Knopf. Ils 1st ed. 694 p. dj. EX. M2. $15.00

MCQUEEN, A.S. *History of Charlton Co., GA.* 1932. Atlanta. $30.00

MCREYNOLDS, E.C. *MO: History of Crossroads State.* 1962. Norman. Ils 1st ed. EX. $20.00

MCREYNOLDS, E.C. *Seminoles.* 1957. Norman. Ils 1st ed. dj. EX. $22.50

MCSHERRY, Frank D. *Treasury of American Horror Stories.* 1985. Bonanza. 1st ed. dj. EX. P1. $12.50

MCSPADDEN, J.W. *Famous Ghost Stories.* nd. Cadmus Books. VG. P1. $15.00

MCSPADDEN, J.W. *Stories From Wagner.* 1914. NY. 16 pls. TEG. green cloth. VG. T1. $35.00

MCTAGGART. *Stable & Saddle.* 1930. NY. 4to. blue cloth. VG. $25.00

MCWILLIAMS, Carey. *Louis Adamic & Shadow-America.* 1935. Los Angeles. 1st ed. sgn. VG. J2. $10.00

MEAD, G.R.S. *Fragments of a Faith Forgotten.* 1960. U Books. dj. G. $35.00

MEAD, M.N. *Asheville in Land of the Sky.* 1942. Richmond. 1st ed. 188 p. dj. VG. $20.00

MEAD, Margaret. *Growth & Culture: Photographic Study of Balinese Childhood.* 1951. Putnam. brown cloth. $25.00

MEAD, P.B. *Elementary Treatise on American Grape Culture & Wine Making.* 1867. NY. 483 p. gilt lavender bdg. VG. $50.00

MEADE, Bishop. *Old Churches & Families of VA.* 1910. Richmond. 2 vols. VG. B1. $50.00

MEADE, Mary. *Mary Meade's Magic Recipes for the Osterizer Blender.* 1952. 500 recipes. 256 p. plastic dj. EX. $3.50

MEADE, Robert. *Judah P. Benjamin: Confederate Statesman.* 1943. NY. 2nd print. sgn. 432 p. EX. $25.00

MEADER, Stephen. *Shadow in the Pines.* 1944. NY. presentation. sgn. dj. VG. B2. $20.00

MEADOWCROFT, E.L. *Story of Crazy Horse.* 1954. Ils Reusswig. 1st ed. 191 p. $12.00

MEANLEY, B. *Waterfowl of Chesapeake Bay Country.* 1982. Tidewater. Ils 1st ed. dj. EX. M2. $30.00

MEANS, G.B. *Strange Death of President Harding.* NY. Guild Pub. 1st ed. 342 p. dj. G. $10.00

MEANY, Dee Morrison. *Iseult.* 1985. Ace. 1st ed. pb. M. C1. $4.00

MEARS, Eliot. *Maritime Trade of W US.* 1935. Stanford. 1st ed. J2. $15.00

MEARS, J.H. *Racing the Moon (& Winning).* 1928. NY. Henkle. 1st ed. 820 p. M1. $30.00

MEARS, P.H. *Fourteen Sermons.* nd. Augusta. presentation. sgn. 167 p. $25.00

MEDELEEFF, D. *Principles of Chemistry.* 1902. Collier. 4 vols. G. M2. $5.00

MEDER & DOGSON. *Drawings by Flemish & Dutch Masters.* 1930. 1/125. 41 pls. folio. portfolio. VG. $250.00

MEDER & DOGSON. *Drawings by Italian Masters.* 1930. 1/125. 40 pls. lg folio. portfolio. $250.00

MEDLIN, F. *Centuries of Owls in Art & the Written Word.* 1967. Silvermine. Ils 1st Am ed. 84 p. dj. EX. M2. $11.00

MEEGAN, G. *Longest Walk.* 1988. Dodd Mead. Ils 1st ed. dj. EX. M2. $10.00

MEEK, F.B. *Report of Invertebrate Cretaceous & Tertiary Fossils...* 1876. WA. Ils. 628 p. orig bdg. VG. A3. $120.00

MEEK, S.E. *Fresh-Water Fishes of Mexico N of Isthmus of Tehuantepec.* 1904. Field Mus. Ils. 252 p. EX. M2. $35.00

MEEROPOL & MEEROPOL. *We Are Your Sons: Legacy of Ethel & Julius Rosenberg.* 1975. Boston. Houghton. inscr. $18.00

MEIER-GRAEFE, Julius. *Degas.* 1923. London. Trans Holroyd-Reece. 1/1000. G. $75.00

MEIGS, Cornelia. *Critical History of Children's Literature.* 1959. NY. dj. EX. $30.00

MEIGS, Cornelia. *Critical History of Children's Literature.* 1964. Macmillan. 624 p. dj. G. $10.00

MEIGS, Cornelia. *Trade Wind.* 1942. Beacon Hill. Ils Pitz. VG. E2. $15.00

MEIGS, J.F. *Story of Seamen.* 1924. Phil. pls. 2 vols. xl. VG. $37.50

MEIKLE, James. *Traveler.* 1813. NY. sm 8vo. 232 p. G. $35.00

MEINHOLD, W. *Sidonia the Sorceress, Supposed Destroyer...* 1894. London. 2 vols. gilt bdg. VG. $225.00

MEISS & KIRSCH. *Visconti Hours.* 1972. NY. 1st ed. slipcase. EX. $40.00

MEIXNER, M.E. *Das Neu, Grosse, Gepruste und Bemahrte Linger Kochbuch...* 1822. Linz. G. extremely rare. $225.00

MELCHER, M.F. *Shaker Adventure.* 1941. Princeton. 1st ed. 319 p. dj. VG. B2. $40.00

MELHAM, Tom. *John Muir's Wild America...* 1976. Nat Geog Soc. photos. tall 8vo. dj. $22.50

MELINE, J.F. *Two Thousand Miles on Horseback: Summer Tour Through KS...* 1966. Horn Wallace. fld map. 317 p. dj. EX. M2. $35.00

MELLEN, Grenville. *Book of the US.* 1841. NY. Ils. 8vo. 804 p. leather. G. G2. $34.00

MELLEN, Grenville. *US History.* 1842. Ils. 847 p. full leather. K1. $12.50

MELLING, O.R. *Druid's Tune.* 1983. 1st ed. dj. M. C1. $9.00

MELLING, O.R. *Singing Stone.* 1986. 1st ed. EX. C1. $10.00

MELLINI, Gian Lorenzo. *Altichiero e Jacopo Avanzi.* 1965. Milan. Ils. dj. D2. $125.00

MELLNIK, Steve. *Philippine Diary, 1939-1945.* 1969. NY. Ils. 316 p. dj. VG. T5. $19.50

MELLON, P. *Alchemy & the Occult.* 1968. New Haven. pls. 4to. 2 vols. $200.00

MELONEY, William. *Chanty Man Sings.* 1926. NY. Ltd ed. 1/200. G. $75.00

MELTZER, David. *Agent.* 1968. Essex House. VG. P1. $40.00

MELTZER, David. *Ragas.* 1959. San Francisco. 1st ed. wraps. EX. $30.00

MELTZER, Milton. *Dorthea Lange: Photographer's Life.* 1975. NY. Review ed. 2 djs. with 2 photos. $75.00

MELTZER, Milton. *In Their Own Words: History of American Negro 1916-1966.* 1967. Crowell. 213 p. dj. M1. $14.50

MELVIL, James. *Memoirs.* 1683. London. 1st ed. folio. disbound. $37.50

MELVILLE, A.M. *Rue the Reservoir.* 1956. Milwaukee. 1st ed. dj. EX. $15.00

MELVILLE, Herman. *Benito Cereno.* 1926. Nonesuch. 1/1650. VG. $65.00

MELVILLE, Herman. *Moby Dick.* 1923. NY. Ils Mead/Schaeffer. J2. $17.50

MELVILLE, Herman. *Moby Dick.* 1931. Ils Anton Fischer. 1st ed. VG. C1. $12.50

MELVILLE, Herman. *Moby Dick.* 1977. Easton Pr. Collector ed. leather. M. $28.00

MELVILLE, Herman. *Omoo.* 1924. Dodd Mead. Ils Schaeffer. 1st ed. EX. $45.00

MELVILLE, Herman. *Omoo.* 1961. Oxford. Ltd Ed Club. Ils Stone. slipcase. $60.00

MELVILLE, Herman. *Typee.* 1847. Wiley Putnam. Revised ed. $175.00

MELVILLE, Herman. *Typee.* 1962. WV Pulp Paper. Ltd ed. boxed. EX. $50.00

MELVILLE, R.C. *God the Creator.* 1968. Chicago. $8.00

MENCKEN, August. *Railroad Passenger Car.* 1957. Johns Hopkins. 1st ed. dj. VG. J2. $17.50

MENCKEN, H.L. *Bathtub Hoax.* 1958. Knopf. 1st ed. dj. VG. $40.00

MENCKEN, H.L. *Boy of Calumny.* 1918. NY. 2nd ed. VG. B2. $40.00

MENCKEN, H.L. *Christmas Story.* 1946. Knopf. 1st ed. dj. EX. $35.00

MENCKEN, H.L. *Christmas Story.* 1946. NY. 1st ed. dj. VG. B2. $27.50

MENCKEN, H.L. *George Bernard Shaw: His Plays.* 1905. Boston. 1st ed. 107 p. black cloth. VG. $75.00

MENCKEN, H.L. *Happy Days.* 1940. NY. 2nd ed. dj. $10.00

MENCKEN, H.L. *Heathen Days, 1890-1936.* 1943. NY. 1st Am ed. sgn. VG. $90.00

MENCKEN, H.L. *James Branch Cabell.* 1927. NY. Ils 1st ed. wraps. $50.00

MENCKEN, H.L. *Letters...Selected & Annotated by Guy J. Forgue...* 1961. Knopf. 1st ed. 506 p. $45.00

MENCKEN, H.L. *Minority Report.* 1956. NY. 1st ed. dj. VG. B2. $25.00

MENCKEN, H.L. *Newspaper Days.* 1941. NY. 1st ed. dj. VG. B2. $35.00

MENCKEN, H.L. *Treatise on the Gods.* 1930. Knopf. 3rd ed. G. $20.00

MENDELSSOHN, Moses. *Abhundlung von der Unkorperlichkeit der Menschlichen Geele.* 1785. Bein. 16mo. G. $225.00

MENDELSSOHN, Moses. *Jerusalem Oder Uber Religiose Mact und Judentum.* 1783 & 1784. Berlin. 2 vols in 1. 8vo. VG. $375.00

MENDOZA, George. *Good-Bye, River, Good-Bye.* 1971. Doubleday. Ils/sgn Tice. 1st ed. 8vo. dj. EX. $35.00

MENEN, Aubrey. *Rome for Ourselves.* 1960. NY. dj. VG. J2. $15.00

MENKE, F.G. *Down the Stretch: Story of Col. Matt J. Winn.* 1944. NY. 1st ed. 1/1000. sgn Winn. EX. $75.00

MENKE, F.G. *Down the Stretch: Story of Col. Matt J. Winn.* 1945. NY. $20.00

MENNE, Bernhard. *Blood & Steel: Rise of the House of Krupp.* 1938. NY. Ils 1st Am ed. 424 p. dj. T5. $19.50

MENNINGER & MURO. *You & Psychiatry.* 1950. NY. $8.00

MENOCAL, A.G. *Report of the US Nicaragua Surveying Party, 1885.* 1886. GPO. Ils. sm folio. $225.00

MENPES & MENPES. *Venice.* 1927. London. 1/500. sgn. VG. J2. $100.00

MENTZER. *Descendants of John G. Gleim.* c 1930s. Harrisburg. Ils. 115 p. G. C4. $35.00

MENUHIN, Yehudi. *Unfinished Journey.* 1977. Knopf. 394 p. dj. VG. $12.00

MENZEL. *Das Graphische Werk.* 1976. Munich. Ils. 2 vols. djs. EX. $40.00

MENZIES & FRANKENBERG. *Handbook of Common Marine Isopod Crustacea of GA.* 1966. GA U. Ils. 93 p. M2. $8.00

MERCER, A.S. *Banditti of Plains of Cattleman's Invasion of WY in 1892.* 1954. OK U. Ils later print. 195 p. dj. EX. M2. $14.00

MERCER, D. *Parachute.* 1967. London. 1st ed. dj. VG. $22.50

MERCER, L.P. *New Birth.* 1887. Chicago. $4.50

MERCEY & GROVE. *Sea, Surf & Hell: US Coast Guard in WWII.* 1945. NY. photos. sgns. 352 p. G. T5. $9.50

MEREDITH, George. *Amazing Marriage.* 1895. London. 1st ed. 2 vols. EX. $85.00

MEREDITH, George. *Egoist.* 1988. Boston. Roberts. 12mo. $10.00

MEREDITH, George. *Modern Love.* 1989. Mosher. 1st ed. 1/925. EX. $45.00

MEREDITH, George. *Tale of Chloe.* nd. Ward Lock Bowder. 8vo. G. $10.00

MEREDITH, George. *Tale of Chloe.* 1894. London. 1st ed. VG. $35.00

MEREDITH, Roy. *Face of Robert E. Lee in Life & Legend.* 1947. Scribner. Ils 1st ed. 143 p. EX. M2. $15.00

MEREDITH, Roy. *Mathew Brady's Portrait of an Era.* 1982. 1st ed. photos. dj. K1. $14.50

MEREDITH, Roy. *Mr. Lincoln's Camera Man: Mathew B. Brady.* 1945. 1st ed. VG. S2. $30.00

MEREDITH, Roy. *Mr. Lincoln's Camera Man: Mathew B. Brady.* 1946. Scribner. 284 photos. 4to. 368 p. VG. M2. $20.00

MEREDITH, Roy. *Mr. Lincoln's General: U.S. Grant.* 1959. NY. Ils 1st ed. 252 p. dj. VG. T5. $22.50

MEREDITH, Roy. *Mr. Lincoln's General: U.S. Grant.* 1981. Bonanza. reprint. 252 p. dj. EX. M2. $10.00

MEREDITH, Roy. *This Was Andersonville.* 1957. NY. 1st ed. VG. $20.00

MERINGTON, M. *Custer Story.* 1950. NY. dj. VG. $15.00

MERLI, Frank. *Great Britain & the Confederate Navy, 1861-1865.* 1970. IN U. 1st ed. dj. VG. J2. $15.00

MERRIAM, C.H. *Dawn of the World.* 1910. Clark. 1st ed. VG. $75.00

MERRIAM, H.G. *Way Out W: Recollections & Tales.* 1970. OK U. 296 p. dj. EX. M2. $6.00

MERRICK, Elliott. *True N.* 1933. Scribner. 1st ed. 353 p. M1. $12.50

MERRICK, George. *Old Times on Upper MS: Recollections of Steamboat Pilot...* 1909. Clark. 1st ed. VG. J2. $125.00

MERRICK, Leonard. *House of Lynch.* 1919. NY. Ltd ed. 1/1500. VG. $20.00

MERRICK, Leonard. *Quaint Companions.* 1904. Leipzig. VG. $25.00

MERRILL, George. *Handbook & Descriptive Catalog of Collection Gems...* 1922. US Nat Mus. GPO. 1st ed. 225 p. wraps. J2. $15.00

MERRILL, J.M. *Dupont: Making of an Admiral.* 1986. NY. 1st ed. dj. EX. $16.00

MERRILL, James. *Braving the Elements.* 1972. Atheneum. 1st ed. dj. EX. $40.00

MERRILL, James. *From the Cutting-Room Floor.* 1983. Abattoir. wraps. EX. $25.00

MERRILL, James. *Metamorphosis of 741.* 1977. Banyan Pr. 1/440. wraps. EX. $35.00

MERRILL, James. *Santorini: Stopping the Leak.* 1982. Metacom. 1/300. sgn/#d. wraps. EX. $40.00

MERRILL, James. *Souvenirs.* 1984. Nadja. 1/200. sgn. wraps. EX. $50.00

MERRILL, James. *Spurts to Glory.* 1966. Rand McNally. 1st ed. dj. VG. $10.00

MERRILL, James. *Yannina.* 1973. Phoenix. 1/100. sgn/#d. EX. $40.00

MERRILL, Judith. *Best of the Best.* 1967. NY. Delacorte. 1st ed. dj. EX. $15.00

MERRILL, V. *Atlas of Roentgenographic Positions.* 1967. sm folio. VG. $75.00

MERRILL & GALBRAITH. *Republican Command, 1897-1912.* 1971. Lexington. 360 p. dj. $17.50

MERRIMAN, H.S. *Roden's Corner.* 1898. Harper. Ils Thulstrup. 1st ed. $12.00

MERRIMAN, H.S. *Young Mistley.* 1889. Leipzig. Tauchnitz. sgn. black bdg. VG. $45.00

MERRINS. *Swing the Handle Not the Club Head.* 1974. 2nd ed. inscr/sgn. dj. VG. $20.00

MERRITT, A. *Athenian Tribute.* 1939-1950. Harvard. 3 vols. VG. $125.00

MERRITT, A. *Dwellers in the Mirage.* 1932. NY. Liveright. VG. $12.00

MERRITT, A. *Moon Pool.* 1919. NY. 1st ed. presentation. wraps. $325.00

MERRITT, A. *Ship of Ishtar.* 1926. NY. 1st ed. Curry C bdg. $125.00

MERSHON, W.B. *Recollections of 50 Years' Hunting & Fishing.* 1923. Boston. 1st ed. VG. B2. $75.00

MERSKY & POLMAR. *Navy Air War in Vietnam.* 1986. Baltimore. Ils 2nd ed. 226 p. dj. VG. T5. $12.50

MERTENS. *Tactics & Technique of River Crossings.* 1918. Van Nostrand. Ils. maps. 253 p. $10.00

MERTON, Thomas. *Disputed Questions.* 1960. NY. 1st Am ed. dj. $20.00

MERTON, Thomas. *Last of Fathers.* 1954. NY. Harcourt. 1st ed. dj. EX. $35.00

MERTON, Thomas. *Living Bread.* 1956. NY. Farrar Straus. 1st ed. dj. EX. $40.00

MERTON, Thomas. *Prison Meditations of Father Delp.* 1963. NY. Herder. 1st Am ed. dj. EX. $25.00

MERTON, Thomas. *Seeds of Destruction.* 1964. NY. 1st ed. EX. $35.00

MERTON, Thomas. *Sign of Jonas.* 1953. NY. 1st ed. dj. VG. $20.00

MERTON, Thomas. *Silent Life.* 1957. Farrar Straus. 1st ed. dj. EX. $35.00

MERTON, Thomas. *Waters of Siloe.* 1949. NY. 1st ed. dj. EX. $45.00

MERWIN, W.S. *Three Poems.* 1968. Phoenix. 1/100. sgn/#d. wraps. EX. $30.00

MERYMAN, Richard. *Andrew Wyeth.* 1968. Boston. 1st ed. dj. boxed. EX. $125.00

MERYMAN, Richard. *Wyeth at Kuerners.* 1976. Boston. 1st ed. boxed. M. $90.00

MESERVE & SANDBURG. *Photographs of Abraham Lincoln.* nd. NY. Stated 1st ed. dj. EX. $45.00

MESNY, E. *Television et Transmission des Images.* 1933. Paris. Ils 1st ed. 216 p. G. $7.50

MESSEL, Rudolph. *This Film Business.* 1928. London. fair. $15.00

MESSICK, Hank. *Silent Syndicate.* 1967. NY. 1st ed. 303 p. dj. G. T5. $12.50

MESSICK, M.A. *History of Baxter Co., 1873-1973.* 1973. Centennial ed. dj. EX. M2. $35.00

METCALFE, John. *Feasting Dead.* 1954. Arkham House. 1st ed. dj. EX. P1. $85.00

METCALFE, S.L. *Caloric: Its Mechanical, Chemical & Vital Agencies...* 1843. London. Pickering. 1st ed. 2 vols. rebound. $80.00

METCHNIKOFF, Elie. *Prolongation of Life.* 1912. NY. 1st Am ed. EX. $150.00

METFESSELL, Milton. *Phonography in Folk Music.* 1928. Chapel Hill. 191 p. $50.00

METHVIN, J.J. *In Limelight; or, History of Anadarko & Vicinity...* 1925. OK City. Ils 1st ed. EX. $125.00

METKEN, Gunter. *Agam.* 1977. NY. Ils. 4to. dj. $20.00

METRAUX, Alfred. *Voodoo.* 1959. Oxford. 1st ed. dj. VG. J2. $20.00

METTHIESSEN, Peter. *Nine-Headed Dragon River.* 1986. Boston. dj. EX. $22.00

MEYER, A.E. *Chinese Painting As Reflected in Art of Li Lung-Mien.* 1923. Merrymount. 1st ed. VG. $45.00

MEYER, Dickey. *Girls at Work in Aviation.* 1943. NY. Ils 1st ed. 209 p. T5. $35.00

MEYER, Franz. *Marc Chagall: Das Graphisches Werk.* 1957. Zurich. Gutenberg. 152 pls. D2. $125.00

MEYER, Franz. *Marc Chagall: Life & Work.* 1963. Abrams. 1st ed. dj. xl. G. $75.00

MEYER, H.D. *Last Illusion: America's Plan for World Domination.* 1954. Anvil Atlas. inscr. $50.00

MEYER, H.N. *Colonel of Black Regiment: Life of Thomas Wentworth.* 1967. Norton. Ils 1st ed. dj. $27.50

MEYER, J.J. *Immortal Tales of Joe Shaun.* 1944. NY. 2nd ed. dj. VG. $35.00

MEYER, Nicholas. *Seven-Per-Cent Solution.* 1974. NY. 1st ed. dj. EX. $27.50

MEYER, S.E. *James Montgomery Flagg.* 1974. NY. dj. EX. $35.00

MEYER. *Great Children's Book Illustrators.* 1983. Abrams. M. $35.00

MEYER-OAKES, William J. *Prehistory of Upper OH Valley.* 1955. Pittsburgh. Ils. maps. dj. VG. T5. $12.50

MEYERS, J.B. *Tracking the Marvelous: Life in NY Art World.* 1983. Random House. Red Grooms Ils dj. M. $23.00

MEYERS, R.C.V. *Theodore Roosevelt: Patriot & Statesman.* c 1901. np. Ils. 8vo. 526 p. G. G2. $12.00

MEYERS. *Naval Sketches in CA.* 1939. NY. Ltd 1st ed. 1/1000. G. $45.00

MEZZROW & WOLFE. *Really the Blues.* 1946. NY. 1st Am ed. M. $30.00

MICHAELS, Leonard. *I Would Have Saved Them If I Could.* 1975. Farrar Straus. 1st ed. dj. EX. $10.00

MICHALS, Duane. *Photographic Illusion.* 1975. Dobbs Ferry. Morgan. 4to. 96 p. wraps. $25.00

MICHAUX, Henri. *Light Through Darkness.* 1963. Orion. 1st ed. dj. EX. $17.50

MICHAUX, Henri. *Miserable Miracle.* 1963. City Lights. Trans Varese. wraps. $18.00

MICHEAUX, Oscar. *Case of Mrs. Wingate.* 1945. NY. sgn. VG. $45.00

MICHEAUX, Oscar. *Story of Dorothy Stanfield.* 1946. NY. Book Supply. 1st ed. dj. EX. $50.00

MICHEL, Emile. *Rembrandt: His Life, His Work, His Time.* 1903. London/NY. 3rd ed. TEG. full leather. D2. $120.00

MICHELANGELO. *Complete Work of Michelangelo.* nd. NY. folio. dj. EX. $50.00

MICHELI, S. *Mongolia: In Search of Marco Polo & Other Adventures.* 1967. Harcourt Brace. Ils 1st Am ed. 366 p. dj. EX. M2. $23.00

MICHELL, David. *Monstrous Regiment: Story of Women in WWI.* 1965. NY. Ils 1st ed. 400 p. dj. VG. T5. $15.00

MICHELL, E.B. *Art & Practice of Hawking.* 1975. Branford. Ils. 219 p. dj. EX. M2. $30.00

MICHELSON, T. *Contributions to Fox Ethnology.* 1927. Bull. Ils. 168 p. EX. M2. $18.00

MICHENER, C.B. *Special Report on Diseases of the Horse.* 1890. USDA. Ills. 556 p. G. M2. $15.00

MICHENER, C.D. *Social Behavior of Bees: Comparative Study.* 1974. Harvard. Ils. 404 p. dj. EX. M2. $22.00

MICHENER, J. *Presidential Lottery.* 1969. NY. 1st ed. dj. VG. B2. $30.00

MICHENER, J.A. *AK.* Random House. Stated 1st ed. 868 p. dj. M. $18.00

MICHENER, J.A. *Caravans.* 1963. NY. 1st ed. dj. EX. $35.00

MICHENER, J.A. *Caribbean.* 1989. NY. Ltd ed. 1/1000. sgn. slipcase. s/wrap. EX. $95.00

MICHENER, J.A. *Chesapeake.* 1978. NY. 1st ed. 1/500. sgn. 865 p. slipcase. T5. $125.00

MICHENER, J.A. *Drifters.* 1971. NY. 1st ed. dj. EX. $30.00

MICHENER, J.A. *First Fruits: Harvest of 25 Years of Israeli Writing.* 1973. Phil. 1st ed. dj. EX. $55.00

MICHENER, J.A. *Floating World.* 1954. NY. 1st ed. 403 p. dj. VG. B2. $95.00

MICHENER, J.A. *HI.* 1959. Random House. 1st ed. dj. slipcase. VG. $45.00

MICHENER, J.A. *HI.* 1960. London. Secker Warburg. 1st ed. dj. M. $80.00

MICHENER, J.A. *Hokusai Sketchbooks.* 1969. Rutland. 9th print. dj. boxed. VG. B2. $90.00

MICHENER, J.A. *Hokusai Sketchbooks.* 1975. slipcase. M. $35.00

MICHENER, J.A. *Iberia: Spanish Travels & Reflections.* 1968. NY. Ils Vavra. 1st ed. dj. EX. $35.00

MICHENER, J.A. *Iberia: Spanish Travels & Reflections.* 1968. NY. 1st ed. photos. 818 p. dj. VG. T5. $25.00

MICHENER, J.A. *James Michener's USA: People & the Land.* 1981. NY. 1st ed. dj. EX. $30.00

MICHENER, J.A. *Japanese Prints From Early Masters to Modern.* 1959. Rutland. Tuttle. 1st ed. folio. dj. M. $120.00

MICHENER, J.A. *Quality of Life.* 1970. Girard. Ils Wyeth. slipcase. EX. $40.00

MICHENER, J.A. *Rascals in Paradise.* 1957. Random House. 1st ed. dj. VG. J2. $20.00

MICHENER, J.A. *Source.* 1965. NY. 1st ed. dj. EX. $35.00

MICHENER, J.A. *Space.* 1982. NY. 1st ed. 1/500. 622 p. slipcase. EX. T5. $75.00

MICHENER, J.A. *Sports in America.* 1976. Random House. 1st ed. dj. EX. $17.50

MICHENER, J.A. *Tales of S Pacific.* 1947. NY. 1st ed. dj. VG. B2. $195.00

MICHENER, J.A. *Voice of Asia.* 1951. NY. 1st ed. 338 p. dj. G. T5. $22.50

MICHIE, A.A. *Keep the Peace Through Air Power.* 1944. NY. 1st ed. 196 p. VG. T5. $22.50

MICHKLISH, Rita. *Sugar Bee.* 1972. Delacorte. 1st ed. 195 p. dj. $27.50

MICKEL, J.T. *How To Know the Ferns & Fern Allies.* 1979. Brown. Ils. 229 p. EX. M2. $18.00

MIDDLEBROOK, Martin. *Nuremberg Raid.* 1974. NY. Ils 1st ed. 369 p. dj. VG. T5. $15.00

MIDDLEMAS, Keith. *Double Market: Art Theft & Art Thieves.* 1975. Hampshire. Saxon. dj. VG. $7.50

MIDDLETON, D. *Baker of the Nile.* 1949. Falcon. Ils 1st ed. dj. EX. $22.50

MIDDLETON, Harry J. *Compact History of the Korean War.* 1965. NY. Ils 1st ed. 255 p. dj. VG. T5. $19.50

MIDDLETON, William D. *When the Steam Railroads Electrified.* 1974. Milwaukee. Kalmbach. Ils 1st ed. dj. VG. T5. $45.00

MIERS, E.S. *American Civil War: Popular History of Years 1861-1865...* 1961. Golden Pr. Ils. 324 p. dj. EX. M2. $20.00

MIERS, E.S. *Fundamental Creed of Robert E. Lee.* 1958. Newark. Curtis. Ltd ed. wraps. $8.00

MIERS, E.S. *Last Campaign: Grant Saves the Union.* 1972. Lippincott. Ils 1st ed. 213 p. VG. M2. $10.00

MIERS, E.S. *Web of Victory: Grant at Vicksburg.* 1955. Knopf. Ils 1st ed. maps. 320 p. M2. $17.00

MIERS, F.B. *History of Whites' Battalion VA Calvary.* 1956. reprint. xl. EX. scarce. J4. $28.50

MIETHE, A. *Spitzbergen. Das Alpenland im Eismeer.* 1925. Berlin. Ils. 4to. 261 p. $65.00

MIGDALSKI, E.C. *How To Make Fish Mounts & Other Fish Trophies.* 1960. Ronald. Ils. 218 p. VG. M2. $14.00

MIGEON, G. *Arts Musulmans.* 1926. 64 pls. wraps. VG. $60.00

MIKAN, George. *Mr. Basketball.* 1951. Greenberg. 1st ed. inscr. VG. $12.00

MIKELL, R.M. *Selma.* 1965. Charlotte, NC. Citadel. 276 p. wraps. M1. $8.50

MILAN, Victor. *Dragons of Darkness.* 1st ed. lg pb. VG. C1. $5.50

MILBANK, Jeremiah Jr. *First Century of Flight in America.* 1943. Princeton. Ils 1st ed. 248 p. VG. T5. $17.50

MILBANK, Kitty. *Flighty Prince.* 1963. NY. private print. G. $40.00

MILBANK & PERRY. *Turkey Hill Plantation.* 1966. np. Crown. 8vo. green leather. $35.00

MILBURN, George. *Hobo's Hornbook.* 1930. NY. Ils 1st ed. 295 p. G. B2. $27.50

MILBURN, L.H. *Progressed Horoscope Simplified.* nd. Berkeley. $19.50

MILBURN, W.H. *Rifle, Axe, Saddlebags, & Other Lectures.* 1857. NY. 1st ed. 209 p. G. T5. $37.50

MILES, A.H. *Universal Natural History.* 1895. Dodd Mead. 20 pls. 12mo. green cloth. G. $40.00

MILES, N.A. *Personal Recollections.* 1896. NY. Ils 1st ed. 1st issue. VG. T1. $125.00

MILES & WHITE. *Water Over the Dam: Miscellany About Warsaw, Benton Co., MO.* 1966. Democrat Pub. photos. 79 p. EX. M2. $5.00

MILES. *Gas War.* 1931. London. dj. EX. $35.00

MILFORD, Nancy. *Biography of Zelda Fitzgerald.* 1970. NY. Harper Row. 1st ed. dj. EX. $15.00

MILHOFFER, Stefan. *Color Treasury of Oriental Rugs.* dj. VG. E2. $15.00

MILHOUSE, Katherine. *Egg Tree.* 1950. Scribner. Ils 1st ed. VG. B4. $25.00

MILHOUSE, Katherine. *With Bells On.* 1955. Scribner. Ils 1st ed. VG. B4. $25.00

MILL, J.S. *System of Logic.* 1881. 659 p. TB. VG. $7.00

MILLAIS, J.G. *Breath From the Veldt.* 1986. S Africa. Ils reprint of 1895 ed. dj. EX. M2. $24.00

MILLAIS, J.G. *Newfoundland & Its Untrodden Ways.* 1907. Longman Green. Ils. gilt bdg. 340 p. EX. M2. $175.00

MILLAIS, J.G. *Newfoundland & Its Untrodden Ways.* 1967. Abercrombie. reprint of 1907 ed. dj. EX. M2. $25.00

MILLAR, Margaret. *Fiend.* 1964. NY. 1st ed. dj. VG. $12.50

MILLAR, Margaret. *How Like an Angel.* 1962. Random House. 1st ed. inscr/sgn. dj. VG. $60.00

MILLAR, Margaret. *It's All in the Family.* 1948. Random House. ARC. inscr. dj. $75.00

MILLARD, Christopher. *Printed Work of Claud Lovat Fraser.* 1923. Danielson. Ltd ed. sgn. 4to. RS. VG. $50.00

MILLARD, F.S. *Cowpuncher on the Pecos.* nd. np. 47 p. wraps. VG. scarce. A3. $45.00

MILLAY, E.S.V. *Ballad of the Harp Weaver.* 1922. NY. Ils 1st ed. wraps. slipcase. EX. $115.00

MILLAY, E.S.V. *Buck in the Snow.* 1928. Harper. 1st ed. 8vo. dj. VG. G2. $50.00

MILLAY, E.S.V. *Conversation at Midnight.* 1937. NY/London. Harper. 1st ed. 8vo. EX. $60.00

MILLAY, E.S.V. *Fatal Interview.* 1931. NY. Harper. Stated 1st ed. VG. $12.00

MILLAY, E.S.V. *Flowers of Evil. From French of Charles Baudelaire.* 1936. Harper. dj. EX. $50.00

MILLAY, E.S.V. *Huntsman, What Quarry?* 1st ed. dj. VG. B2. $27.50

MILLAY, E.S.V. *Huntsman, What Quarry?* 1939. NY. 1st ed. dj. EX. $35.00

MILLAY, E.S.V. *Renaissance & Other Poems.* 1917. NY. Harper. 1st ed. 1st print. $65.00

MILLAY, E.S.V. *Two Slaterns & a King.* 1921. Cincinnati. Stewart Kidd. 1st ed. wraps. EX. $75.00

MILLAY, E.S.V. *Wine From These Grapes.* 1934. Harper. 1st ed. 8vo. TEG. slipcase. EX. G2. $45.00

MILLER, A. *MS: Life & Legends of America's Greatest River.* 1975. Crescent. Ils. 4to. 127 p. dj. M2. $10.00

MILLER, A.H. *Field Experiences With Mountain-Dwelling Birds of S UT.* 1934. Wilson. M2. $3.00

MILLER, A.J. *Pioneer Doctor in the Ozarks' White River Country.* 1949. Burton. Ils. sgn. 161 p. dj. VG. M2. $12.00

MILLER, Arthur. *American Clock.* nd. NY. Studio. 1/200. sgn. wraps. T6. $80.00

MILLER, Arthur. *Chinese Encounters.* 1979. Farrar. 1st ed. dj. EX. $20.00

MILLER, Arthur. *Death of a Salesman.* Ltd Ed Club. slipcase. M. B3. $225.00

MILLER, Arthur. *Death of a Salesman.* 1949. Viking. 1st ed. 2nd print. dj. VG. $25.00

MILLER, Arthur. *Theater Essays.* 1978. NY. 1st ed. sgn. dj. EX. $25.00

MILLER, Arthur. *View From the Bridge.* 1955. NY. Viking. 1st ed. dj. VG. $40.00

MILLER, B.M. *Caldecott Medal Books, 1938-1957. Vol. II.* 1966. Boston. Horn Book. Ils. 329 p. VG. $12.00

MILLER, C.T. *Settlement of RI.* 1974. Providence. Ils Walter Brown. fair. T5. $37.50

MILLER, Caroline. *Lebanon.* 1945. Phil. Blakiston. reprint. $4.50

MILLER, D. *Story of Walt Disney.* 1959. Dell. 1st ed. pb. EX. $7.50

MILLER, Ernest. *Oil Mania: Sketches From Early PA Oil Fields.* 1941. Phil. presentation. EX. $35.00

MILLER, F.T. *Armies & the Leaders.* 1957. reprint. 352 p. dj. J4. $7.50

MILLER, F.T. *Photographic History of Civil War.* 1911. NY. 1st ed. 10 vols. K1. $265.00

MILLER, F.T. *Photographic History of Civil War.* 1957. NY. reprint of 1st ed. 10 vols. M. $100.00

MILLER, F.T. *World in the Air: Story of Flying in Pictures.* 1930. Putnam. Ils. 2 vols. EX. $55.00

MILLER, Floyd. *Bill Tilghman: Marshal of the Last Frontier.* 1968. Doubleday. Ils 1st ed. 252 p. dj. EX. M2. $30.00

MILLER, H.M. *Comparative Studies of Furcocercous Sercariae.* 1926. IL U. 8 pls. 112 p. EX. M2. $10.00

MILLER, H.R. *Gone a Hundred Miles.* 1968. Harcourt Brace. 1st ed. 240 p. dj. $12.50

MILLER, Henry. *Air-Conditioned Nightmare.* 1945. New Directions. 1st ed. sgn. $50.00

MILLER, Henry. *Letters to Anais Nin.* 1965. Putnam. 1st ed. dj. VG. J2. $15.00

MILLER, Henry. *Love Between the Sexes.* 1978. Greenwich. Ltd ed. sgn. $45.00

MILLER, Henry. *Max et les Phagocytes.* 1947. Eds Du Chene. 1st French ed. 1/300. wraps. VG. $175.00

MILLER, Henry. *Mother China & the World Beyond.* 1977. Santa Barbara. D2. $12.50

MILLER, Henry. *My Bike & Other Friends.* 1978. Capra. Ltd ed. sgn. dj. EX. $50.00

MILLER, Henry. *My Bike & Other Friends.* 1978. Santa Barbara. blueline proof. 1st ed. rare. $65.00

MILLER, Henry. *Of, By & About Henry Miller.* 1947. Yonkers, NY. Ltd ed. wraps. EX. $22.50

MILLER, Henry. *Order & Chaos: Chez Hans Reichel.* 1966. Tucson. Loujon Pr. 1st ed. sgn. 4to. dj. $65.00

MILLER, Henry. *Tropic of Capricorn.* 1961. Grove. 1st ed. dj. $25.00

MILLER, Hunter. *Treaties & Other International Acts of the USA. Vol. 2.* 1931. GPO. EX. $40.00

MILLER, J.C. *Alexander Hamilton: Portrait in Paradox.* 1959. Harper. 1st ed. 659 p. dj. EX. M2. $10.00

MILLER, J.C. *Origins of the American Revolution.* 1943. Little Brown. 1st ed. map. 519 p. dj. EX. M2. $10.00

MILLER, J.H. *Threadgills, Book II.* 1983. Baltimore. Review ed. 325 p. VG. T5. $7.50

MILLER, J.K.P. *Road to VA City.* 1960. Norman. dj. VG. $18.00

MILLER, James M. *Genesis of W Culture: Upper OH Valley, 1800-1825.* 1938. Columbus. 194 p. VG. T5. $22.50

MILLER, James. *Alcohol: Its Place & Power.* 1859. Phil. SftCvr. G. $25.00

MILLER, Joaquin. *Danties in the Sierras.* 1881. Chicago. 1st ed. VG. B2. $25.00

MILLER, Joaquin. *First Families of the Sierras.* 1876. Chicago. 1st Am ed. rebound. VG. $22.50

MILLER, Joaquin. *Shadows of Shasta.* 1881. Chicago. 184 p. xl. K1. $14.50

MILLER, Joaquin. *True Bear Stories.* 1900. Chicago. 1st ed. 1st print. M. $55.00

MILLER, Joaquin. *True Bear Stories.* 1926. Rand McNally. Ils. G. $25.00

MILLER, John. *San Adams: Pioneer in Propaganda.* 1936. Little Brown. 1st ed. VG. J2. $15.00

MILLER, KREH & HUBLEY. *Directory of State of MD by Post Office Address.* 1877. 189 p. VG. C4. $32.00

MILLER, M. *Saguaro: Desert Flower Book.* 1982. Johnson. Ils. 34 p. M2. $5.00

MILLER, M.H. *History & Genealogy of the Miller Family, 1725-1933.* 1933. Pittsburgh. 146 p. wraps. T5. $17.50

MILLER, Margaret. *Wall of Eyes.* 1943. Random House. 1st ed. dj. VG. $15.00

MILLER, Margery. *Joe Louis: American.* 1945. NY. 1st ed. presentation. sgn. 12mo. dj. T1. $75.00

MILLER, Marvin. *Breaking of a President.* 1976. Covina, CA. 3rd ed. 4to. 660 p. dj. VG. $22.50

MILLER, Max. *Skinny on Your Own Side.* 1958. NY. 1st ed. dj. EX. $10.00

MILLER, Merle. *Lyndon.* 1980. NY. 1/500. sgn. 645 p. slipcase. EX. T5. $35.00

MILLER, Merle. *Reunion.* 1954. Viking. 1st ed. dj. VG. $15.00

MILLER, O.B. *Book House for Children.* 1950. Chicago. Rainbow ed. 35th print. 12 vols. $80.00

MILLER, O.B. *Engines & Brass Bands.* 1933. NY. Ils 1st ed. dj. EX. $15.00

MILLER, O.B. *Little Pictures of Japan.* 1925. Book House. Ils Sturges. VG. $22.50

MILLER, O.B. *My Bookhouse.* 1925. Chicago. Bookhouse for Children. 6 vols. EX. $180.00

MILLER, O.B. *Nursery Friends From France.* nd. Chicago. Ils Petersham. 24th ed. VG. $15.50

MILLER, Perry. *Raven & Whale.* 1956. Harcourt Brace. 1st ed. 8vo. blue cloth. dj. D1. $30.00

MILLER, R.A. *For Science & National Glory.* 1968. OK U. Ils 1st ed. dj. EX. M2. $15.00

MILLER, Thomas. *Common Wayside Flowers.* 1860. London. 185 pls. $70.00

MILLER, W. *Prince & Mrs. Charming.* 1970. NY. 4to. dj. $20.00

MILLER, W.H. *Treatise on Crystallography.* 1839. Cambridge. 1st ed. 10 pls. inscr. 139 p. VG. $200.00

MILLER, W.J. *Introduction to Historical Geology.* 1941. 5th ed. 499 p. tan cloth. $25.00

MILLER, William. *Scottish Nursery Songs & Other Poems.* 1863. Glasgow. 1st ed. 4to. VG. rare. $200.00

MILLER, Zell. *Mountains Within Me.* 1976. Toccoa. 1st ed. sgn. 170 p. dj. EX. $15.00

MILLER & KELLOG. *List of N American Recent Mammals.* 1955. US Nat Mus. Ils 954 p. EX. M2. $22.00

MILLER. *Fifty Years of Sport.* c 1925. NY. Dutton. $15.00

MILLET, J.A.P. *Insomnia: Its Causes & Treatment.* 1938. NY. $10.00

MILLHAUSER, Steven. *Edwin Mullhouse.* 1972. Knopf. 1st ed. M. $25.00

MILLIN, S.G. *General Smuts.* 1936. London. Ils 1st ed. 393 p. T5. $35.00

MILLING, C.J. *Red Carolinians.* 1940. Chapel Hill. 1st ed. dj. EX. $65.00

MILLING, C.J. *Singing Arrows.* 1938. Columbia. Bostick. 1st ed. 84 p. dj. $15.00

MILLING, Chapman. *Buckshot & Hounds.* 1967. NY. photos. dj. EX. $20.00

MILLNER, Simon. *Face of Benedicutus Spinoza.* 1946. NY. 1st ed. inscr. $17.50

MILLNER, Simon. *Henry James & R.L. Stevenson: Record of Friendship...* 1948. London. dj. EX. $12.50

MILLON, H. *Key Moments in History of Architecture.* c 1965. NY. dj. $45.00

MILLS, Anson. *My Story.* 1918. WA. 1st ed. photos. 412 p. AEG. VG. scarce. T5. $225.00

MILLS, E.A. *Rocky Mountain Wonderland.* 1915. Houghton. Ils. 361 p. A3. $35.00

MILLS, E.A. *Spell of the Rockies.* 1911. Boston. Ils. dj. EX. T1. $25.00

MILLS, E.A. *Wildlife on the Rockies.* 1909. Boston. Houghton. Ils 1st ed. $22.00

MILLS, E.A. *Wildlife on the Rockies.* 1988. NE U. Ils. 271 p. M. M2. $9.00

MILLS, E.A. *Your National Parks.* 1917. Boston. Houghton. VG. $7.50

MILLS, W.C. *Maps & Guide to Ft. Ancient, Warren Co., OH.* 1920. Columbus. photos. fld map. 28 p. wraps. T5. $25.00

MILLS, W.S. *Story of W Reserve of CT.* 1900. NY. 1st ed. VG. T5. $37.50

MILNE, A.A. *Ascent of Man.* 1928. London. 1st ed. wraps. EX. scarce. $30.00

MILNE, A.A. *By Way of Introduction.* 1929. London. 1st ed. dj. VG. $35.00

MILNE, A.A. *Gallery of Children.* 1925. London. Ltd ed. 1/500. sgn. EX. $260.00

MILNE, A.A. *Gallery of Children.* 1925. McKay. Ils LeMair. VG. $85.00

MILNE, A.A. *House at Pooh Corner.* 1928. London. 1st ed. VG. $225.00

MILNE, A.A. *House at Pooh Corner.* 1928. NY. Dutton. Ils Shepard. 1st ed. EX. $60.00

MILNE, A.A. *Now We Are Six.* 1927. London. 1st ed. G. $125.00

MILNE, A.A. *Now We Are Six.* 1927. London. 1st print. scarce. EX. T5. $200.00

MILNE, A.A. *Now We Are Six.* 1950. Dutton. Ils Shepard. reprint. VG. B4. $35.00

MILNE, A.A. *Winnie the Pooh.* 1926. London. Ltd ed. sgn. dj. EX. $400.00

MILNE, A.A. *Winnie the Pooh.* 1926. London. 1st ed. G. $150.00

MILNE, A.A. *Year In, Year Out.* 1953. NY. Dutton. dj. EX. $50.00

MILNE, James. *Memoirs of a Bookman.* 1936. London. pls. $25.00

MILNE, L.J. *Cougar Doesn't Live Here Anymore.* 1971. Prentice Hall. Ils. 258 p. dj. EX. M2. $18.00

MILNE, L.J. *Mountains.* 1962. Time Life. Ils. 192 p. EX. M2. $5.00

MILNE, Leslie. *Shans at Home.* 1910. London. Murray. 1st ed. VG. $35.00

MILNE, W.J. *Standard Arithmetic.* 1895. Am Book Co. 459 p. VG. $5.00

MILOSZ, Czlaw. *Captive Mind.* Ltd Ed Club. slipcase. M. B3. $85.00

MILOSZ, Czlaw. *Native Realm.* 1965. NY. Stated 1st ed. presentation. dj. $35.00

MILTON, G.F. *Eve of Conflict: Stephen A. Douglas & the Needless War.* 1934. Houghton. photos. 608 p. G. M2. $10.00

MILTON, John. *Comus.* 1921. NY/London. Ils/sgn Rackham. 1st ed. 1/550. $225.00

MILTON, John. *L'Allegro & Il Penseroso.* 1954. Ltd Ed Club. Ils William Blake. slipcase. T5. $65.00

MILTON, John. *Mask of Comus.* 1937. Bloomsbury. 1/950. folio. EX. $95.00

MILTON, John. *Paradise Lost.* 1844. NY. Kearny. leather. $30.00

MILTON, John. *Paradise Lost; Paradise Regained.* 1760. Baskerville. 8vo. 2 vols. calf. J2. $300.00

MILTON, John. *Paradise Perdue.* 1805. Paris. French text. 3 vols. $125.00

MILTON, John. *Paradise Regained.* 1730. London. 7th ed. 12mo. calf. $125.00

MILTON, John. *Poems in English.* 1926. London. 1/1450. 2 vols. VG. $175.00

MILTON, John. *Poetical Works of John Milton.* 1966. Boston. Ltd ed. 1/100. 3 vols. $100.00

MILTOUN, Frances. *In Land of Mosques & Minarets.* 1908. Boston. Ils 1st ed. 8vo. TEG. EX. T1. $35.00

MILTS, M.H. *Only a Gringo Would Die for an Anteater.* 1979. Norton. Ils 1st ed. dj. EX. M2. $9.00

MIMS, Edwin. *Advancing S.* 1926. Garden City. 1st ed. 317 p. VG. $15.00

MINAHAN, John. *Arthur Tress: Dream Collector.* 1972. NY. Avon. photos. D2. $40.00

MINDLIN, H.E. *Modern Architecture in Brazil.* 1956. Rio. dj. xl. fair. $20.00

MINEHAN, Thomas. *Boy & Girl Tramps of America.* 1934. NY. Ils 2nd print. 267 p. dj. VG. T5. $15.00

MINER, Charles. *History of WY.* 1845. Phil. 1st ed. map. G. $75.00

MINER, E.H. *Cattle of the World.* 1926. Nat Geog Soc. Ils 1st ed. 142 p. VG. M2. $18.00

MINER. *Bibliography of Daniel Boone.* 1970. NY. reprint of 1901 ed. VG. $15.00

MINGOS, Howard. *American Heroes of the War in the Air. Vol. 1.* 1943. NY. Ils 557 p. G. T5. $95.00

MINIERO, G.A. *Roberto. Fotografia Aerea.* 1942. Rome. Societa Anonima Poligrafica. $35.00

MINIRIK. *Little Bear.* 1957. NY. Ils Maurice Sendak. VG. $15.00

MINK, O.J. *Meet the Parachute Chic.* 1944. Reliance Mfg. 98 p. EX. $7.50

MINNICH, L.W. *Gettysburg: What They Did There.* c late 1920s. Ils. fld map. 168 p. EX. J4. $12.50

MINTER, D. *William Faulkner.* 1980. Baltimore/London. ARC. dj. RS. EX. $25.00

MINTER, J.E. *Chagres: River of W Passage.* 1948. Rinehart. Ils 1st ed. 418 p. dj. EX. M2. $18.00

MINTON, S.A. & M.R. *Giant Reptiles.* 1973. Scribner. Ils. 345 p. EX. M2. $20.00

MIRO, Joan. *Catalan Notebooks.* 1977. NY. 1st ed. dj. M. $50.00

MIRO, Joan. *Farbide Lithographien.* 1959. Wiesbaden. German text. EX. $40.00

MIRSKY, Jeannette. *Elisha Kent Kane & the Seafaring Frontier.* 1954. Westport, CT. map. 201 p. VG. T5. $9.50

MIRSKY, Jeannette. *To the N: Story of Arctic Exploration.* 1934. NY. fld map. VG. $17.50

MIRSKY, Jeannette. *Westward Crossing.* 1946. NY. Knopf. 1st ed. 365 p. dj. G. $18.00

MISHIMA, Yukio. *After the Banquet.* 1963. Knopf. 1st ed. dj. $35.00

MISHIMA, Yukio. *Confessions of a Mask.* 1958. ND. 1st ed. dj. $40.00

MISHIMA, Yukio. *Decay of the Angel.* 1974. Knopf. 1st ed. dj. $30.00

MISHIMA, Yukio. *Forbidden Colors.* 1968. Knopf. 1st ed. dj. $35.00

MISHIMA, Yukio. *Runaway Horses.* 1973. Knopf. 1st ed. dj. $30.00

MISHIMA, Yukio. *Sound of Waves.* 1956. Knopf. 1st Am ed. dj. $50.00

MISHIMA, Yukio. *Spring Snow.* 1972. Knopf. 1st ed. dj. $30.00

MISHIMA, Yukio. *Temple of Dawn.* 1973. Knopf. 1st ed. dj. $30.00

MISHIMA, Yukio. *Temple of the Golden Pavilion.* 1959. Knopf. 1st ed. dj. $35.00

MISHIMA, Yukio. *Thirst for Love.* 1969. Knopf. 1st ed. dj. $35.00

MITCHELL, Donald. *Benjamin Britten: Commentary on His Works From Group...* 1952. Rockliff. 1st ed. VG. J2. $15.00

MITCHELL, E.V. *Morocco Bound: Adrift Among Books.* 1929. NY. Ils 1st ed. pls. $30.00

MITCHELL, Ella. *History of WA Co.* 1924. Atlanta. Ils 171 p. G. $45.00

MITCHELL, J. *Bottom of the Harbor.* 1959. Boston. 1st ed. dj. VG. B2. $30.00

MITCHELL, J.A. *Last American.* 1893. VG. $8.00

MITCHELL, J.L. *Earth Conquerors: Lives & Achievements of Great Explorers.* 1934. Simon Schuster. Ils. 370 p. G. M2. $5.00

MITCHELL, J.L. *Out-of-Body Experience: Handbook.* 1981. NC. $20.00

MITCHELL, Jack. *American Dance Portfolio.* 1964. NY. dj. VG. $30.00

MITCHELL, James. *Dead Ernest.* 1986. NY. 1st Am ed. dj. EX. $10.00

MITCHELL, Joseph. *McSorley's Wonderful Saloon.* 1943. Duell Sloan. dj. M. $50.00

MITCHELL, Julian. *Circle of Friends.* 1966. NY. 1st ed. dj. VG. $15.00

MITCHELL, M.K. *Recollections: Ten Women of Photography.* 1979. Viking. dj. VG. $17.50

MITCHELL, Margaret. *Gone With the Wind.* June, 1936. NY. Macmillan. 2nd ed. dj. G. R1. $125.00

MITCHELL, Margaret. *Gone With the Wind.* May, 1936. NY. 1st ed. 2nd issue dj. $400.00

MITCHELL, Margaret. *Gone With the Wind.* 1936. Macmillan. 7th imp. G. $25.00

MITCHELL, Margaret. *Gone With the Wind.* 1939. NY. Movie ed. 391 p. wraps. with record. G. T5. $37.50

MITCHELL, Margaret. *Gone With the Wind.* 1968. NY. Heritage. 2 vols. boxed. VG. B2. $60.00

MITCHELL, Margaret. *Von Winde Verweht.* 1937. Hamburg. 1st German ed. VG. B1. $75.00

MITCHELL, Paige. *Wilderness of Monkeys.* 1965. Dutton. 1st ed. dj. EX. $20.00

MITCHELL, S.A. *School Atlas.* 1839. Phil. maps. T1. $85.00

MITCHELL, S.W. *Fat & Blood.* 1878. Phil. 2nd ed. 109 p. $30.00

MITCHELL, S.W. *Hill of Stone & Other Poems.* 1883. 1st ed. $35.00

MITCHELL, William. *Winged Defense.* 1925. NY. Putnam. Ils 1st ed. EX. $45.00

MITCHELL & ZIM. *Butterflies & Moths.* 1964. Golden Pr. Ils. 160 p. M2. $4.00

MITCHELL. *Mean Things Happening in This Land.* 1979. inscr/sgn. dj. VG. $15.00

MITCHELL-HEDGES, F.A. *Danger Is My Ally.* 1954. Eleck. Ils. map. 255 p. VG. M2. $17.00

MITFORD, Jessica. *Fine Old Conflict.* 1977. London. 1st ed. dj. EX. $25.00

MITFORD, Mary. *Our Village.* 1880. Ils. EX. $175.00

MITFORD, N. *Water Beetle.* 1962. London. 1st ed. inscr. dj. EX. $40.00

MITHELL, R.A. *Today's Armies of the Air.* 1940. Paris. French text. 170 p. G. T5. $17.50

MITTELMAN, Joseph B. *Eight Stars to Victory.* 1948. WA. Ils. maps. 406 p. poor. T5. $45.00

MIYAMORI, Asataro. *Masterpieces of Chikamatsu.* 1936. London. Ils. 359 p. VG. scarce. $125.00

MIZALDO, Antonio. *Asterismi: Siue Stellatarum Octani Coeli Imaginum Officina.* 1553. Paris. vellum bdg. G. $425.00

MIZENER, Arthur. *Far Side of Paradise.* 1951. Boston. dj. VG. $15.00

MIZWA, S.P. *Nicholas Copernicus, 1543-1943.* 1943. NY. Kosciuszko. 2nd print. 8vo. VG. $20.00

MOCHI & MAC CLINTOCK. *African Images.* 1984. Scribner. Ils 1st ed. 158 p. dj. EX. M2. $30.00

MOCHULSKY, K. *Aleksandr Blok.* 1983. Wayne. dj. M. $28.00

MOCK, E.B. *Architecture of Bridges.* 1949. NY. Ils 1st ed. 4to. 127 p. P3. $35.00

MOCK, E.B. *If You Want To Build a House.* 1946. MOMA. EX. $22.50

MOCK, H. *Pemberton & Coulter.* 1933. Prior Co. 3 vols. $145.00

MOCK & COULTER. *Principles & Practice of Physical Therapy.* 1933. Prior Co. $145.00

MODAFFERI, R.D. *Lower Susitna Valley Moose Population Identity & Study.* 1988. AK Fish/Game. 60 p. M2. $10.00

MODE, Heinz. *Woman in Indian Art.* 1970. McGraw Hill. Ils. dj. D2. $45.00

MODERSOHN-BECKER, Paula. *Briefe & Tagebuchblatter.* 1920. Munich. Wolff. Ils. 248 p. D2. $39.50

MOEDEBECK & BARLEY. *Pocket Book of Aeronautics.* 1907. London. G. C4. $95.00

MOFFATT, A.T. *Queen's Gift.* 1923. Boston. 1st ed. EX. $30.00

MOGHISSI, Kamran. *Placenta: Biological & Clinical Aspects.* 1974. Thomas. 1st ed. dj. VG. J2. $20.00

MOHOLY & FERGUSSON. *Portrait of Eton.* 1949. London. Muller. 1st ed. 8vo. dj. $70.00

MOHOLY-NAGY, Laszlo. *Malerei, Fotografie. Film.* 1967. Berlin. Mainz. reprint of 1927 ed. 152 p. $45.00

MOHOLY-NAGY, Laszlo. *Painting Photography Film.* 1969. MA. 1st Am ed. dj. EX. $40.00

MOHOLY-NAGY, Laszlo. *Vision in Motion.* 1947. Chicago. 2nd ed. 371 p. dj. EX. $45.00

MOHOLY-NAGY, Sibyl. *Experiment in Totality.* 1950. NY. Harper. 1st ed. 253 p. D2. $55.00

MOHOLY-NAGY, Sibyl. *Pedagogical Sketchbook.* nd. London. Faber. Ils. D2. $40.00

MOHR, C.O. *Comparison of N American Small Mammal Censuses.* 1943. Am Mus Nat Hist. M2. $5.00

MOHR, Nicholas. *Excursions Through America.* 1973. Donnelley. Lakeside Classic. A3. $35.00

MOHR & POULSON. *Life of the Cave.* 1966. McGraw Hill. Ils. 232 p. dj. EX. M2. $10.00

MOIZUK, R.D. *Put-in-Bay Story.* c 1968. Put-in-Bay, OH. 1st ed. wraps. T5. $9.50

MOJUNNER & TROY. *Technical Control of Dairy Products.* 1922. Ils 1st ed. sgns. VG. $28.00

MOLDEA. *Hoffa Wars.* 1978. dj. EX. $15.00

MOLDENHAUER, J. *Descriptive Catalog of Poe.* 1973. TX U. 1st ed. 4to. black cloth. VG. D1. $35.00

MOLESWORTH. *Carrots: Just a Little Boy.* 1934. Macmillan. reprint. VG. B4. $25.00

MOLESWORTH. *Two Little Waifs.* 1920. London. Ils Crane. EX. $15.00

MOLEY, Raymond. *Hays Office.* 1945. Bobbs Merrill. 1st ed. dj. VG. J2. $12.50

MOLIERE. *Ouevres Complete.* nd. Paris. Ils Geffroy/Allouard. EX. $95.00

MOLINARD, Patrice. *Paris I Love.* nd. NY. Tudor. photos. G. $12.00

MOLLENHOFF. *Tentacles of Power.* 1965. Cleveland. dj. VG. $15.00

MOLLETT, John W. *Meissonier.* 1882. London/NY. Ils. D2. $20.00

MOLMENTI, P. *Life & Works of Vittorio Carpaccio.* 1907. London. Ils. pls. 4to. TEG. VG. J2. $100.00

MOLNAR, George. *Statues.* 1955. np. Dutton. 1st ed. dj. VG. M1. $6.50

MOLYNEAUX, P. *Romantic Story of TX.* 1936. Cordova Pr. 463 p. VG. M2. $19.00

MOMADAY, N.S. *House Made of Dawn.* 1968. NY. 1st ed. dj. EX. $65.00

MONACHESI, Mrs. N.D.R. *Manual for China Painters.* 1897. Boston. fair. $30.00

MONACO, Richard. *Final Quest.* 1983. pb. VG. C1. $3.00

MONACO, Richard. *Grail War.* 1979. Wallaby. 1st ed. pb. VG. C1. $4.00

MONACO, Richard. *Parsival: Knight's Tale.* 1977. 1st HrdCvr ed. VG. C1. $4.50

MONAGHAN, J. *Book of American W.* 1963. NY. Messner. Ils 1st ed. dj. M. $30.00

MONAGHAN, J. *Great Rascal: Life & Adventures of Ned Buntline.* 1951. Bonanza. reprint. 353 p. VG. M2. $15.00

MONAHAN, Michael. *Palms of Papyrus.* 1909. Papyrus Pub. 2nd ed. presentation. $45.00

MONCRIEFF, A.R. *Book About Authors: Reflections & Recollections...* 1914. London. 1st ed. $45.00

MONCRIF. *Les Chats.* Golden Cockerel. 1/300. sgn. M. $60.00

MONELL, S.H. *Practical Chapters on Static Electricity.* 1900. NY. 8vo. 46 p. wraps. $50.00

MONGAN, A. *Drawings in the Fogg Museum of Art.* 1940. Cambridge, MA. Ils. 4to. cloth. EX. J2. $400.00

MONGE & LANDSVERK. *Norse Medieval Cryptography in Runic Carvings.* 1967. Glendale. Ils. gilt bdg. EX. $35.00

MONKHOUSE, Cosmo. *British Contemporary Artists.* 1899. NY. Scribner. Ils. fair. $30.00

MONKHOUSE, Cosmo. *Life & Work of Sir John Tenniel.* 1901. London. Ils. 4to. VG. $40.00

MONNIER, P. *Le Quattrocento. Essai sur l'Historie...* 1904. Lausanne. 2 vols. $75.00

MONOT, G.R. *History of Insurrections in MA.* 1810. Boston. 2nd ed. orig leather. $95.00

MONRO, Alida. *Recent Poetry, 1923-1933.* 1933. London. Poetry Bookshop. 1st ed. VG. J2. $25.00

MONROE, Harriet. *Poets & Their Art.* 1926. Macmillan. 1st ed. presentation. VG. J2. $40.00

MONROE, Marilyn. *My Story.* 1974. NY. 1st ed. dj. VG. B2. $20.00

MONSARRAT, Nicholas. *Cruel Sea.* 1951. NY. Knopf. 1st ed. dj. $10.00

MONSELL, J. *Balderdash Ballads.* 1934. London. Heinemann. Ils. VG. $35.00

MONSON & SUMNER. *Desert Bighorn: Its Life History, Ecology & Management.* 1980. AZ U. Ils. map. 370 p. EX. M2. $15.00

MONTAGU, Ashley. *Touching.* 1971. NY. $25.00

MONTAGU, Ewen. *Man Who Never Was.* 1954. Lippincott. dj. M1. $4.50

MONTAGU, M.W. *Letters From the Levant.* 1838. London. VG. $95.00

MONTAGUE, C.E. *Right Off the Map.* 1927. London. Ltd 1st ed. 1/260. sgn. blue bdg. $30.00

MONTAGUE, S.R. *N to Adventure.* 1942. McBride. Ils. sgn. 284 p. G. M2. $13.00

MONTAGUE, S.R. *N to Adventure.* 1950. NY. 10th ed. sgn. 284 p. EX. $20.00

MONTAGUE, Summers. *Supernatural Omnibus.* 1932. NY. $15.00

MONTAIGNE. *Essays.* 1947. Doubleday. Ils/sgn Dali. 1/100. boxed. J2. $200.00

MONTGOMERY, D.H. *Leading Facts of English History.* 1901. Ils. 420 p. TB. VG. $6.00

MONTGOMERY, F.T. *Billy Whiskers in Mischief.* 1926. Saalfield. Ils Brundge. 158 p. M. $17.50

MONTGOMERY, F.T. *Billy Whiskers.* 1930. Saalfield. Ils. 156 p. VG. $12.50

MONTGOMERY, F.T. *Billy Whiskers' Grandchildren.* 1909. Chicago. VG. $18.00

MONTGOMERY, F.T. *Billy Whiskers' Kids.* 1931. Saalfield. Ils Fry. 134 p. VG. $12.50

MONTGOMERY, G.G. *Evolution & Ecology of Armadillos, Sloths & Vermilinguas.* 1986. Smithsonian. Ils. 462 p. M2. $45.00

MONTGOMERY, J.W. *Myth, Allegory & Gospel.* 1974. 1st ed. pb. VG. C1. $9.00

MONTGOMERY, L.M. *Jane of Lantern Hill.* 1937. Grosset. dj. VG. B2. $35.00

MONTGOMERY, R.G. *High Country.* 1938. Derrydale. 1/950. sgn. EX. $130.00

MONTGOMERY, Viscount. *Forward to Victory.* 1946. London. 1st ed. EX. $20.00

MONTGOMERY, Viscount. *Path to Leadership.* 1961. NY. 1st Am ed. 255 p. dj. VG. T5. $17.50

MONTGOMERY, Walter. *American Art & American Art Collections.* 1889. Boston. Walker. 2 vols. full leather. rare. D2. $395.00

MONTPELIER. *Recollections of Marion Du Pont Scott...* 1976. NY. oblong folio. dj. EX. $35.00

MONTROSS, Lynn. *US Marines: Pictorial History.* 1959. NY. Ils. 4to. 242 p. dj. T5. $9.50

MONTROSS, Lynn. *US Marines: Pictorial History.* 1959. NY. 1st ed. 4to. dj. T1. $35.00

MOODY, C.N. *Battle of Pea Ridge of Elkhorn Tavern, March 7-8, 1862.* 1956. AR Valley Print Co. Ils. 39 p. EX. $3.00

MOODY, D.W. *Life of a Rover.* 1926. Chicago. 116 p. $22.50

MOODY, E.W. *Journey Step by Step to Truth.* 1926. NY. $8.00

MOODY, John. *Railroad Builders.* 1920. 257 p. xl. $32.50

MOODY, Lonwood. *ME Two-Footers.* 1959. Berkeley. 2 fld maps. dj. VG. $25.00

MOODY, P.A. *Introduction to Evolution.* 1953. Harper. Ils 1st ed. 475 p. EX. M2. $12.00

MOODY, Ralph. *Horse of a Different Color.* 1968. NY. 1st ed. dj. VG. $27.00

MOODY, Ralph. *Old Trails W.* 1963. NY. 2nd ed. dj. VG. $15.00

MOODY, Ralph. *Old Trails W.* 1963. NY. Crowell. 1st ed. maps. dj. $22.00

MOODY, W.V. *Masque of Judgement.* 1900. Boston. Ltd 1st ed. 1/150. EX. $75.00

MOODY. *Fields of Home.* 1953. Peoples. EX. $6.80

MOORCOCK, Michael. *Chinese Agent.* 1970. NY. 1st ed. dj. EX. $15.00

MOORCOCK, Michael. *Cure for Cancer.* 1971. Holt Rinehart. Review 1st ed. $75.00

MOORCOCK, Michael. *End of All Songs.* 1976. NY. 1st ed. dj. EX. $20.00

MOORCOCK, Michael. *English Assassin.* 1972. NY. 1st ed. dj. VG. $20.00

MOORCOCK, Michael. *War Hound & the World's Pain.* 1982. 1st ed. pb. VG. C1. $3.00

MOORE, A.C. *My Roads.* 1939. NY. 1st ed. 399 p. dj. VG. B2. $22.50

MOORE, A.W. *Story of the Isle of Man.* 1902. London. 1st ed. VG. C1. $15.00

MOORE, Arthur. *Frontier Mind: Cultural Analysis of KY Frontiersman.* 1957. KY U. 1st ed. dj. VG. J2. $20.00

MOORE, Brian. *Feast of Lupercal.* 1957. Little Brown. 1st ed. dj. EX. $37.50

MOORE, C.B. *Aboriginal Sites on TN River.* 1915. Phil. Ils. folio. rebound. EX. M2. $90.00

MOORE, C.B. *Book of Wild Pets.* 1954. Branford. photos. 553 p. xl. M2. $5.00

MOORE, C.B. *Certain Aboriginal Mounds of GA Coast.* 1897. Phil. Ils. folio. 138 p. M2. $80.00

MOORE, C.B. *Certain Aboriginal Remains of AL River.* 1899. Phil. Ils. folio. M2. $60.00

MOORE, C.B. *Certain Antiquities of FL W Coast.* 1900. Phil. Ils. M2. $50.00

MOORE, C.B. *Some Aboriginal Sites on MS River.* 1911. Phil. Ils. folio. rebound. EX. M2. $100.00

MOORE, C.B. *Some Aboriginal Sites on the Red River.* 1912. Phil. Ils. folio. rebound. EX. M2. $100.00

MOORE, C.B. *Ways of Mammals in Fact & Fancy.* 1953. Ronald. 273 p. xl. VG. M2. $4.00

MOORE, C.L. *Shambleau & Others.* 1953. Gnome. 1st ed. dj. EX. $120.00

MOORE, Colleen. *Enchanted Castle.* 1936. Garden City. Ils Lawson. VG. B4. $55.00

MOORE, Colleen. *Silent Star.* 1968. NY. 1st ed. sgn. dj. VG. B2. $17.50

MOORE, F.G. *Judaism in First Centuries of Christian Era...* 1927. Cambridge, MA. 2nd ed. 2 vols. G. $25.00

MOORE, Frank. *Rebellion Record. Vol. IV.* 1862. $17.50

MOORE, Frank. *Songs & Ballads of the American Revolution.* 1856. NY. 1st ed. 12mo. EX. T1. $35.00

MOORE, Frank. *Women of the War.* 1866. steel engravings. 596 p. K1. $14.50

MOORE, G. *Strike at Arlingford.* 1893. London. 1st ed. VG. $35.00

MOORE, G.W. *Case of Mrs. Surratt: Her Controversial Trial...* 1954. OK U. Ils 1st ed. 142 p. dj. EX. M2. $10.00

MOORE, George. *Sister Theresa.* 1901. Lippincott. 1st ed. $12.00

MOORE, George. *Ulick & Soracha.* 1926. Boni Liveright. 1/1250. sgn. VG. $65.00

MOORE, H.E. *African Violets, Gloxinias & Their Relatives.* 1957. Macmillan. Ils 1st print. 323 p. dj. EX. M2. $17.00

MOORE, H.N. *Life & Services of Anthony Wayne.* 1845. Phil. Leary Getz. 16vo. 232 p. M1. $30.00

MOORE, H.T. *Intelligent Heart.* 1962. Grove. pb. EX. P1. $2.50

MOORE, J.P. *Leeches From China With Descriptions of New Species.* 1930. Phil. Ils. later paper cover. M2. $10.00

MOORE, J.T. *Bishop of Cottontown.* 1906. Phil. Ils Kinney. 1st ed. 644 p. dj. T5. $19.50

MOORE, J.T. *Summer Hymnal, Romance of TN.* 1901. Phil. Coates. Ils Dwiggins. xl. $5.00

MOORE, J.W. *Historical Notes on Printers & Printing 1420-1886.* 1886. Concord. 1st ed. VG. $50.00

MOORE, J.W. *Picturesque WA.* 1884. Providence. Ils. gilt bdg. VG. $55.00

MOORE, James. *History of the Civil War in the US.* 1881. Ils. 552 p. K1. $14.50

MOORE, James. *Kilpatrick & Our Cavalry.* 1865. NY. Ils Waud. 243 p. K1. $24.50

MOORE, John. *Journal During Residence in France.* 1797. Chambersburg. sm 8vo. VG. $95.00

MOORE, L.T. *Stories Old & New of Cape Fear Region.* 1956. Wilmington. Ils 1st ed. 261 p. dj. VG. $30.00

MOORE, LALICKER & FISHER. *Invertebrate Fossils.* 1952. McGraw hill. Ils 1st ed. 766 p. EX. M2. $35.00

MOORE, M.S. *Things I Can't Explain.* nd. London. $5.00

MOORE, Marianne. *Predilections.* 1955. NY. 1st ed. dj. EX. $37.50

MOORE, Marianne. *Tell Me, Tell Me.* 1966. Viking. 1st ed. sgn. dj. VG. $30.00

MOORE, Marianne. *Tipoo's Tiger.* 1967. Phoenix. 1/100. sgn. wraps. EX. $250.00

MOORE, Opha. *History of Franklin Co., OH.* 1930. Topeka, KS. 2 of 3 vols. G. T5. $45.00

MOORE, R. *Evolution.* 1970. Time Life. Ils. 192 p. EX. M2. $5.00

MOORE, R. *Man, Time & Fossils: Story of Evolution.* 1967. Knopf. Ils 2nd ed. 436 p. dj. EX. M2. $17.00

MOORE, R. *Universal Assistant & Complete Mechanic.* c 1879. NY. Ils. 12mo. 1016 p. G2. $29.00

MOORE, Thomas. *Loves of Angels: A Poem.* 1823. London. Littell. VG. $20.00

MOORE, Virginia. *VA Is a State of Mind.* 1942. NY. 1st ed. EX. T1. $19.00

MOORE & NICHOLS. *Overhead; or, What Harry & Nelly Discovered in the Heavens.* c 1878. Boston. Ils. 247 p. $25.00

MOORE. *Developing Human: Clinically Oriented Embryology.* 1973. 4to. 374 p. VG. $25.00

MOORE-LANDECKER, E. *Fundamentals of the Fungi.* 1982. Prentice Hall. Ils 2nd ed. 578 p. EX. M2. $33.00

MOOREHEAD, A. *Blue Nile.* 1962. Harper. Ils 1st ed. map. 308 p. VG. M2. $10.00

MOOREHEAD, A. *Darwin & the Beagle.* 1969. NY. Ils. 280 p. dj. VG. $20.00

MOOREHEAD, A. *Darwin & the Beagle.* 1970. Harper. Ils John Gould. 280 p. dj. EX. M2. $18.00

MOOREHEAD, A. *No Room in the Ark.* 1959. Harper. photos. map. 227 p. VG. M2. $5.00

MOOREHEAD, A. *White Nile.* 1960. Harper. Ils. 385 p. EX. M2. $14.00

MOOREHEAD, W.K. *Stone Ornaments Used by Indians in US & Canada.* 1917. Andover Pr. Ils. 448 p. scarce. A3. $325.00

MOOREHOUSE, G. *Fearful Void.* nd. Lippincott. Ils. map. dj. EX. M2. $8.00

MOOREPARK, C. *Book of Birds.* 1900. London. Ils. sm folio. dj. VG. $45.00

MORAN, Charles. *Sea of Memories: Story of Mediterranean Strife...* 1942. Scribner. 1st ed. dj. VG. J2. $15.00

MORAN, J.J. *Defense of Edgar A. Poe.* 1885. WA. Boogher. 1st ed. wraps. EX. scarce. D1. $125.00

MORAN. *Churchill: Taken From the Diaries of Lord Moran.* 1966. Houghton. 1st Am ed. blue cloth. dj. VG. D1. $30.00

MORAND, Paul. *Black Magic.* 1929. NY. Viking. Ils Douglas. Trans Miles. 218 p. $27.50

MORAND, Paul. *Open All Night.* 1923. London. 1/275. sgn. $50.00

MORATH, Inge. *From Persia to Iran: Historical Journey.* 1960. NY. Viking. 1st ed. D2. $55.00

MORATH & MILLER. *In the Country.* 1977. NY. 1st ed. dj. VG. $20.00

MORDAUNT & VERNEY. *Annals of Warwickshire Hunt, 1795-1895.* 1896. London. Ils. 2 vols. VG. scarce. $175.00

MORE, Colleen. *Silent Star.* 1968. NY. 1st ed. dj. VG. B2. $20.00

MORE, Hannah. *Structure on Modern System of Female Education.* 1802. Boston. rebound leather. VG. $125.00

MORE, Henry. *Epistola H. Mori ad V.C.* 1664. rebound. $225.00

MORE, Thomas. *Utopia.* 1750. Glascow. Latin text. full calf. EX. $125.00

MORE, Thomas. *Utopia.* 1963. Norwalk. Heritage. sm quarto. slipcase. $15.00

MORELAND, N.A. *Rope for the Hanging.* c 1939. NY. Farrar Rinehart. 1st ed. VG. $8.50

MORELY. *Life of Gladstone.* 1903. NY. 1st Am ed. VG. $25.00

MORETON, H.V. *This Is Rome.* 1960. NY. Hawthorne. Ils 1st ed. photos. dj. VG. $19.00

MORGAGNI. *De Sedibus et Causis Morbundum.* 2nd ed. VG. $450.00

MORGAN, A. *Study in Warwickshire Dilect...* 1900. Shakespeare Pr. 4th ed. xl. VG. $15.00

MORGAN, A.P. *Wireless Telegraphy & Telephone Simply Explained.* 1915. Henley. Ils 1st ed. EX. $20.00

MORGAN, Angela. *God Prays, Answer World.* 1917. NY. $12.00

MORGAN, B.E. *AR Angels.* 1967. College Bookstore. 176 p. M2. $20.00

MORGAN, Charles. *George Bellows: Painter of America.* 1965. NY. Reynal. Orig ed. 381 p. D2. $65.00

MORGAN, Charles. *Sparkenbroke.* 1936. NY. 1st Am ed. VG. C1. $7.50

MORGAN, D.P. *Locomotive 4501.* 1968. 127 p. $25.00

MORGAN, Dale. *Great Salt Lake.* 1947. Indianapolis. 1st ed. sgn. dj. EX. B2. $40.00

MORGAN, H.J. *Relations of Industry of Canada With Country & the US.* 1864. Montreal. fair. $60.00

MORGAN, J.A. *English Version of Legal Maxims.* 1878. Cincinnati. Clarke. 1st ed. 368 p. G. T5. $22.50

MORGAN, Keith N. *Charles A. Platt: Artist As Architect.* 1985. MIT Pr. Ils. 137 photos. dj. D2. $35.00

MORGAN, L.H. *Houses & House Life of American Aborigines.* 1881. GPO. 280 p. A3. $75.00

MORGAN, L.H. *Indian Journals, 1859-1862.* 1959. MI U. Ils Walton/Clyde. dj. VG. $16.00

MORGAN, L.H. *League of the Iroquois.* 1851. Rochester. Ils 1st ed. fld map. 477 p. B2. $225.00

MORGAN, M. *Last Wilderness.* 1956. Viking. Ils. 275 p. dj. EX. M2. $13.00

MORGAN, M.E. *Historical Souvenir of Clear Creek Country Co.* 1948. Georgetown Co. Ils. 25 p. wraps. VG. A3. $30.00

MORGAN, Morien O. *Royal Winged Son of Sonehenge & Avebury.* nd. c 1890. Ils 1st ed. VG. rare. C1. $85.00

MORGAN, S.O. *Moose.* 1988. AK Fish/Games. maps. 193 p. EX. M2. $20.00

MORGAN, Shepard. *History of Parliamentary Taxation in England.* 1911. Moffat. 1st ed. VG. J2. $15.00

MORGAN, Ted. *Churchill: Young Man in a Hurry 1874-1915.* 1982. Simon Schuster. 1st ed. white/red bdg. dj. VG. D1. $15.00

MORGAN & LESTER. *Graphic Graflex Photography.* 1940. NY. 1st ed. VG. $45.00

MORGAN & LESTER. *Stereo Realist Manual.* 1954. NY. Morgan. 1st ed. 400 p. dj. $37.50

MORGAN & MORGAN. *Keepers of Light: History...Photo Processes.* 1979. EX. $25.00

MORGAN. *History of Wichita Falls.* 1931. OK City. Ils. 221 p. VG. C4. $55.00

MORGAN. *Recollections of a Rebel Reefer.* 1917. Boston. Ils 1st trade ed. 491 p. VG. C4. $85.00

MORGENSTERN, George. *Pearl Harbor: Story of the Secret War.* 1947. NY. 1st ed. maps. 425 p. VG. T5. $12.50

MORI, F. *Ricordi di Alcuni Rimarchevoli Oggetti di Curiosita...* c 1849. Naples. 47 pls. 4to. J2. $75.00

MORICE, A.G. *History of N Interior of British Columbia.* 1971. Fairfield, WA. Ye Galleon Pr. Ltd ed. 368 p. M1. $40.00

MORIER, J.J. *Adventures of Hajji Baba of Ispahan.* 1947. Ils Guilbeau. 4to. 2 vols. djs. VG. $40.00

MORISON, S.E. *Battle of the Atlantic, Sept. 1939-May 1943. Vol. I.* 1950. Boston. Ils. 432 p. G. T5. $15.00

MORISON, S.E. *Breaking the Bismarks Barrier, 22 July 1942-1 May 1944.* 1950. Boston. Ils 1st ed. fld map. 463 p. T5. $15.00

MORISON, S.E. *Coral Sea, Midway & Submarine Actions, May 1942-August 1942.* 1950. Boston. Ils. fld maps. 307 p. T5. $15.00

MORISON, S.E. *European Discovery of America.* 1972. NY. dj. EX. $20.00

MORISON, S.E. *Maritime History of MA, 1783-1860.* 1921. Cambridge. Riverside. Ils. G. $40.00

MORISON, S.E. *Maritime History of MA, 1783-1860.* 1923. London. Heinemann. 401 p. gilt blue bdg. $30.00

MORISON, S.E. *Operations in N African Waters, October 1942-June 1943.* 1950. Boston. Ils. fld maps. 297 p. dj. G. T5. $15.00

MORISON, S.E. *Oxford History of American People.* 1965. NY. 1st ed. dj. VG. B2. $25.00

MORISON, S.E. *Puritan Pronaos: Studies in Intellectual Life...* 1936. NY U. 1st ed. VG. J2. $20.00

MORISON, S.E. *Rising Sun in the Pacific, 1931-April 1942.* 1948. Boston. Ils 1st ed. 411 p. T5. $15.00

MORISON, S.E. *Story of Mt. Desert Island.* 1960. Boston. Little Brown. 1st ed. dj. VG. $10.00

MORISON, S.E. *Struggle for Guadalcanal, August 1942-Feb. 1943.* 1950. Boston. Ils. fld map. 389 p. G. T5. $15.00

MORISON, S.E. *Victory in the Pacific, 1945.* 1975. Boston. Ils. fld map. 407 p. dj. G. T5. $15.00

MORISON, Stanley. *First Principles of Typography.* 1936. Merrymount. 12mo. 29 p. dj. EX. $42.00

MORLEY, Christopher. *Haunted Bookshop.* 1919. Grosset Dunlap. sgn. 8vo. VG. $30.00

MORLEY, Christopher. *Haunted Bookshop.* 1920. Doubleday. with sgn card. G. $28.00

MORLEY, Christopher. *Poems.* 1931. Doubleday. sgn. VG. $22.00

MORLEY, Christopher. *Really My Dear.* 1928. NY. 1st ed. 1/300. dj. EX. $65.00

MORLEY, Christopher. *Songs for a Little House.* 1917. NY. 1st ed. G. $10.00

MORLEY, Christopher. *Translations From the Chinese.* 1932. NY. 1st ed. VG. P3. $30.00

MORLEY, Christopher. *Trojan Horse.* 1957. Phil. 1st ed. inscr. EX. P3. $40.00

MORLEY, Christopher. *Where the Blue Begins.* 1922. NY/London. Ils Rackham. 4to. 227 p. VG. $55.00

MORLEY, Christopher. *Where the Blue Begins.* 1922. Phil. Ils Rackham. 1st ed. sgn. VG. $75.00

MORLEY, H.T. *Old & Curious Playing Cards.* 1989. Wellfleet Pr. Ils. 8vo. 235 p. $14.95

MORLEY, Iris. *Soviet Ballet.* 1945. London. dj. VG. $15.00

MORLEY, S.G. *Ancient Maya.* 1946. Stanford. dj. EX. $40.00

MORLEY, S.G. *Ancient Maya.* 1946. Stanford. Ils 1st ed. dj. VG. $26.00

MORPHET, Richard. *Richard Hamilton.* 1970. London. Tate Gallery. 100 p. D2. $28.50

MORRELL, C. *Tales of Genii.* 1805. London. 2 vols. $200.00

MORRELL, David. *League of Night & Fog.* 1987. Dutton. 1st ed. dj. M. $12.00

MORRELL, Ed. *25th Man: Strange Story of Ed Morrell...* 1924. Montclair. New Era. inscr. VG. $55.00

MORRELL. *Flowers & Fruits; or, 40 Years in TX.* 1886. Dallas. Ils. 426 p. VG. B1. $175.00

MORRIS, Desmond. *Animal Days.* 1980. Morrow. photos. 304 p. dj. EX. M2. $5.00

MORRIS, Desmond. *Naked Ape: Zoologist's Study of Human Animal.* 1967. McGraw Hill. 1st Am ed. 252 p. dj. VG. M2. $6.00

MORRIS, Donald. *Washing of the Spears.* 1965. NY. 1st ed. dj. VG. B2. $35.00

MORRIS, F.O. *History of British Birds.* 1895-1897. Nimmo. 4to. 6 vols. VG. J2. $750.00

MORRIS, F.O. *History of British Butterflies.* 1870. London. 72 pls. full calf. EX. $400.00

MORRIS, F.O. *History of British Butterflies.* 1895. London. Nimmo. 8th ed. VG. $175.00

MORRIS, F.O. *Natural History of Nests & Eggs of British Birds.* 1896. London. Nimmo. Ils 3 vols. EX. M2. $270.00

MORRIS, F.O. *Series of Picturesque Views of Seats of Noblemen...* c 1880. London. 234 pls. 6 vols. EX. C2. $600.00

MORRIS, Ivan. *Pageant of Japanese Art: Sculpture.* 1958. Tokyo. 1st Popular ed. 16mo. 169 p. VG. $15.00

MORRIS, Ivan. *World of Shining Prince: Court Life in Ancient Japan.* 1964. NY. 1st Am ed. 337 p. dj. EX. $25.00

MORRIS, John. *Age of Arthur.* 1973. 1st ed. VG. C1. $26.00

MORRIS, Kenneth. *Fates of the Princes of Dyfed.* 1978. Newcastle. reprint of 1914. M. C1. $12.50

MORRIS, R. & D. *Men & Snakes.* 1965. McGraw Hill. photos. 224 p. dj. EX. M2. $30.00

MORRIS, R.B. *Alexander Hamilton & the Founding of the Nation.* 1957. Dial. 617 p. dj. EX. M2. $15.00

MORRIS, R.L. *Opie Read: American Humorist.* 1965. Helios. 1st ed. sgn. 247 p. dj. EX. M2. $10.00

MORRIS, Richard. *Nature of Reality.* 1987. NY. 1st ed. dj. EX. $12.50

MORRIS, Robert. *Freemasonry in Holy Land; or, Handmarks of Hiram's Builders.* 1877. Chicago. Ils. 608 p. G. $35.00

MORRIS, Robert. *Freemasonry in Holy Land: A Narrative Made in 1868.* 1879. La Grange, KY. Ils. gilt bdg. G. $35.00

MORRIS, William. *Earthly Paradise.* 1868. Boston. 1st ed. VG. $50.00

MORRIS, William. *Hand & Brain.* 1898. Roycroft. 1/720. 8vo. VG. D1. $125.00

MORRIS, William. *Life & Death of Jason.* 1867. Boston. 1st ed. EX. $60.00

MORRIS, William. *Stories in Prose, Stories in Verse, Shorter Poems...* 1934. Nonesuch. EX. C1. $25.00

MORRIS, William. *Story of the Glittering Plain.* Kelmscott. facsimile of 1891 ed. slipcase. T6. $75.00

MORRIS, William. *Unpublished Lectures.* 1969. Detroit. Wayne. 1st ed. dj. VG. $15.00

MORRIS, William. *Well at the World's End.* 1977. Ballantine. VG. C1. $3.00

MORRIS, Willie. *Homecomings.* 1989. Jackson/London. Ils Dunlap. 1/174. sgns. slipcase. $65.00

MORRIS, Willie. *James Jones: A Friendship.* 1978. Garden City. 1st ed. dj. EX. $20.00

MORRIS, Willie. *N Toward Home.* 1967. Boston. 1st ed. dj. M. $40.00

MORRIS, Willie. *N Toward Home.* 1967. Boston. 1st ed. dj. VG. B2. $17.50

MORRIS, Willie. *Yazoo.* 1971. Harper. 1st ed. dj. EX. $35.00

MORRIS, Wright. *Cat's Meow.* 1975. Black Sparrow. 1/125. sgn. with photo. EX. $150.00

MORRIS, Wright. *Field of Vision.* 1956. NY. 1st ed. dj. EX. $50.00

MORRIS, Wright. *Fire Sermon.* 1971. Harper. 1st ed. dj. VG. $17.50

MORRIS, Wright. *God's Country & My People.* 1968. Harper. 1st ed. 2nd state dj. EX. $45.00

MORRIS, Wright. *Here Is Einbaum.* 1973. LA. 1st ed. 1/226. sgn. acetate dj. EX. $45.00

MORRIS, Wright. *Home Place.* 1948. NY/London. Scribner. 1st ed. 1st issue. xl. $45.00

MORRIS, Wright. *Home Place.* 1948. NY/London. 1st ed. dj. EX. $75.00

MORRIS, Wright. *Huge Season.* 1954. NY. 1st ed. dj. EX. $60.00

MORRIS, Wright. *Inhabitants.* 1946. NY. 1st ed. dj. VG. B2. $75.00

MORRIS, Wright. *Love Affair: A Venetian Journal.* 1972. NY. Harper. 1st ed. 8vo. dj. EX. S2. $40.00

MORRIS, Wright. *Man & Boy.* 1951. NY. 1st ed. dj. EX. $45.00

MORRIS, Wright. *Plains Song.* 1980. Harper. 1st ed. dj. EX. $15.00

MORRIS, Wright. *Works of Love.* 1951. Knopf. 1st ed. dj. EX. $55.00

MORRIS, Wright. *World in the Attic.* 1949. NY. 1st ed. dj. EX. $65.00

MORRISON, A.S. *Memoirs of Adele Sarpy Morrison.* 1911. St. Louis. presentation. sgn. 8vo. G. $150.00

MORRISON, H. *Louis Sullivan: Prophet of Modern Architecture.* 1952. NY. 2nd ed. 391 p. xl. B2. $45.00

MORRISON, H.A. *Preliminary Check List of American Almanacs 1639-1800.* 1907. Lib Congress. 160 p. xl. VG. A3. $50.00

MORRISON, L.P. *Introduction to World of Books.* 1934. Claremont. pls. $30.00

MORRISON, Toni. *Beloved.* 1987. NY. Knopf. 1st ed. 275 p. M. $40.00

MORRISON, Toni. *Bluest Eye.* 1979. London. 1st ed. sgn. dj. M. $100.00

MORRISON, Toni. *Tar Baby.* 1981. NY. 1st ed. dj. VG. B2. $35.00

MORRISON & LEE. *America's Atlantic Isles.* 1981. Nat Geog Soc. Ils. maps. dj. EX. M2. $8.00

MORRISON & MENZEL. *Adaptation of Free-Ranging Rhesus Monkey Group.* 1972. Wildlife Soc. Ils. 78 p. EX. M2. $5.00

MORRISON & MORRISON. *Stranger's Guide to WA City.* 1876. WA. Ils. fld map. 16mo. wraps. EX. $25.00

MORROW, J.E. *Fresh-Water Fishes in AK.* 1980. AK NW. Ils. 248 p. EX. M2. $24.00

MORROW & COONEY. *Bibliography of Black Sparrow Press.* 1981. sgn Morrow/Cooney/Kelly. dj. EX. $85.00

MORROW & LAFOURCADE. *Bibliography of Wyndham Lewis.* 1978. Santa Barbara. dj. EX. $50.00

MORSE, A.R. *Dali: A Collection.* 1973. Cleveland. Ltd 1st ed. 1/500. dj. M. $175.00

MORSE, E.S. *Japanese Homes & Their Surroundings.* 1886. Boston. Ticknor. Ils. plans. VG. J3. $100.00

MORSE, E.S. *Observations on Living Brachiopoda.* 1902. Appalachian Mt Club. New ed. M. M2. $9.00

MORSE, F.C. *Furniture of the Olden Time.* 1937. Macmillan. Ils. VG. $45.00

MORSE, J. *New Gazetteer of E Continent.* 1808. Boston. 8vo. 600 p. leather. G2. $48.00

MORSE, J.T. *Abraham Lincoln.* 1893. fld map. 2 vols. gilt blue bdg. K1. $12.50

MORSE, J.T. *Life of Hamilton.* 1876. Boston. 1st ed. 2 vols. with sgn letter. $55.00

MORSE, J.T. *Salmon P. Chase.* 1899. 1st ed. index. 465 p. K1. $10.00

MORSE, Noel. *Ancient Culture of Fremont River in UT.* 1931. Cambridge. Peabody Mus. 81 p. wraps. VG. A3. $45.00

MORTENSEN, M. *Management of Dairy Plants.* 1921. NY. Ils 1st ed. EX. $16.00

MORTENSEN, T. *On Some W Indian Echinoids.* 1910. US Nat Mus. 17 pls. 4to. M2. $27.00

MORTENSEN, W. *Flash in Modern Photography.* 1950. San Francisco. G. $27.50

MORTENSEN, W. *Model.* 1904. VG. S2. $35.00

MORTENSEN, W. *Mortensen on the Negative.* 1940. Simon Schuster. 3rd print. VG. $25.00

MORTENSEN, W. *New Projection Control.* 1942. San Francisco. G. $37.50

MORTENSEN, W. *Outdoor Portraiture.* 1940. San Francisco. Camera Craft. 1st ed. 4to. dj. EX. $35.00

MORTENSEN, W. *Print Finishing.* 1938. San Francisco. G. rare. $37.50

MORTENSEN, W. *Projection Control.* 1934. San Francisco. G. $35.00

MORTIER & AUBOUX. *Teilhard de Chardin Album.* 1966. NY. 4to. dj. VG. $25.00

MORTIMER, F.J. *Wall's Dictionary of Photography & Reference Book...* c 1930. Boston. Am Photo Pub. 701 p. dj. $22.50

MORTIMER, W.G. *Peru: History of Coca.* 1901. NY. Ils 1st ed. 576 p. scarce. T5. $225.00

MORTON, Anthony. *Branch for the Baron.* 1961. London. Hodder. 1st ed. dj. EX. $12.00

MORTON, E.P. *Lake Erie & the Story of Commodore Perry.* 1913. Chicago. Ainsworth. Ils. 104 p. T5. $22.50

MORTON, Eleanor. *Josiah White, Prince of Pioneers.* 1946. NY. 300 p. dj. VG. T5. $12.50

MORTON, F.S. *Foraminifera of the Marine Clays of ME.* 1897. Portland. Nat Hist Soc. M2. $5.00

MORTON, H.V. *Atlantic Meeting.* 1943. Methuen. 1st ed. green cloth. dj. VG. D1. $45.00

MORTON, H.V. *Atlantic Meeting.* 1943. Methuen. 2nd print. green cloth. VG. D1. $25.00

MORTON, H.V. *Atlantic Meeting.* 1943. Methuen. 4th print. green cloth. dj. VG. D1. $25.00

MORTON, J.F. *500 Plants of S FL.* 1974. Seeman. Ils. 163 p. dj. EX. M2. $18.00

MORTON, L. *Medical Bibliography.* 1976. London. 3rd ed. $50.00

MORTON, O.F. *History of Rockbridge Co., VA.* 1930. Stauton. 1st ed. EX. $95.00

MORTON, R.S. *Woman Surgeon.* 1937. NY. inscr. 399 p. $25.00

MORTON, William. *Mystery of Human Bookcase.* 1931. NY. dj. EX. $12.50

MORTON. *This Is Rome.* 1960. 1st ed. EX. S2. $15.00

MORTON. *This Is the Holy Land.* 1961. Ils Karsh. 1st ed. dj. EX. $20.00

MORWOOD, W. *Traveler in a Vanished Landscape: Life of David Douglas.* 1973. Potter. Ils 1st ed. 244 p. dj. EX. M2. $19.00

MOSAK. *Bibliography for Adlerian Psych.* 1975. WA. EX. $15.00

MOSBY, J.S. *Mosby's War Reminiscences.* 1887. NY. 1st ed. 264 p. G. B2. $75.00

MOSBY, J.S. *Stuart's Cavalry in Gettysburg Campaign.* 1908. NY. Revised 1st ed. VG. $90.00

MOSBY, J.S. *Stuart's Cavalry in Gettysburg Campaign.* 1908. NY. 1st ed. xl. G. $25.00

MOSCHCOWITZ, E. *Biology of Disease.* 1948. Grune Stratton. 1st ed. VG. $45.00

MOSCOW, A. *Collision Course Andrea Doria.* 1959. NY. 1st ed. 316 p. dj. VG. B2. $17.50

MOSELEY, W.M. *Essay on Archery.* 1792. Worcester. 4 pls. 8vo. 348 p. red morocco. $500.00

MOSER, G.P. *Johannes Schwalm: Hessian.* 1976. Millville. 1/750. 296 p. dj. VG. T5. $35.00

MOSER, Robert. *US Navy: Vietnam.* 1969. Annapolis. 4to. 243 p. dj. VG. $30.00

MOSKOVITER. *Cartoons of Albert Engstrom.* 1924. Stockholm. Swedish text. VG. $30.00

MOSKOWITZ, S. *Man Who Called Himself Poe.* 1976. 1st Am ed. dj. EX. $25.00

MOSKOWITZ, S. *Under the Moon of Mars.* 1970. NY. 1st ed. dj. VG. $20.00

MOSLEY, L.O. *No More Remains.* c 1937. NY. Doubleday Doran. VG. $8.00

MOSLEY, Leonard. *Marshall, Hero of Our Times.* 1982. NY. Ils 1st ed. 570 p. dj. G. T5. $8.50

MOSLOW. *Collision Course.* 1959. NY. 1st ed. dj. VG. B2. $15.00

MOSORIAK. *Curious History of Music Boxes.* 1943. Chicago. Ils 1st ed. 4to. 242 p. VG. C4. $85.00

MOSS, Frank. *American Metropolis.* 1897. Collier. 1st ed. 3 vols. VG. R1. $22.00

MOSS, Howard. *Buried City.* 1975. Atheneum. 1st ed. sgn. dj. VG. $18.00

MOSS, Howard. *Instant Lives.* 1974. Dutton. Ils Gorey. 1st ed. dj. EX. $60.00

MOSS, Howard. *Poet's Story.* 1973. NY. 1st ed. dj. EX. $45.00

MOSS, J.A. *Manual of Military Training.* c 1917. Menasha. 12mo. 666 p. G2. $12.00

MOSS, J.A. *Manual of Military Training.* 1917. Menasha, WI. Banta. Revised 2nd ed. 666 p. M1. $8.50

MOSS, J.A. *Memories of Campaign of Santiago.* 1899. Ils fld maps. 4to. VG. $60.00

MOSTEL, Zero. *Photographs by Max Waldman...* 1965. NY. Horizon. 1/250. sgn/#d. with sgn lithograph. $750.00

MOTLEY, J.L. *History of United Netherlands.* c 1867. 8vo. 4 vols. VG. $175.00

MOTLEY, Willard. *Knock on Any Door.* 1947. NY. 1st ed. 504 p. dj. VG. T5. $27.50

MOTLEY, Willard. *We Fished All Night.* 1951. NY. Appleton Century. 1st ed. 560 p. $12.50

MOTT, Abigail. *Biographical Sketches...of Persons of Color.* 1837. NY. Mahlon Day. 2nd ed. 255 p. orig bdg. G. $350.00

MOTT, S.B. *Campaigns of 52nd Regiment PA Volunteer Infantry.* 1911. 266 p. EX. very scarce. J4. $75.00

MOTTELAY, P.F. *Soldier in Our Civil War: Pictorial History of Conflict...* 1884 & 1885. Ils. 2 vols. VG. scarce. J4. $75.00

MOTTRAM, R.H. *Spanish Farm Trilogy, 1914-1918.* 1927. Chatto Windus. 1st ed. 6th print. 800 p. $13.00

MOUCHA, J. *Beautiful Moths.* 1966. Spring. 56 color pls. 139 p. dj. EX. M2. $18.00

MOUILLARD, L.P. *Empire of the Air: Ornithological Essay on Flight of Birds.* 1892. Smithsonian. no cover. M2. $3.00

MOULTON. *Portland by the Sea.* 1926. Augusta. VG. $15.00

MOUNT, Charles. *John Singer Sargent.* 1957. Cresset. 1st ed. dj. G. J2. $17.50

MOUNTEVANS. *Happy Adventurer.* 1951. NY. Ils 1st ed. dj. EX. $20.00

MOUNTFIELD, David. *History of Polar Exploration.* 1974. Dial. Ils. 4to. dj. EX. M2. $25.00

MOUNTFIELD, David. *Railway Barons.* 1979. Ils. 224 p. $16.00

MOUNTFORT, G. *Saving the Tiger.* 1981. Viking. Ils 1st ed. dj. EX. M2. $19.00

MOUNTFORT, G. *So Small a World.* 1974. Scribner. Ils 1st ed. dj. EX. M2. $15.00

MOUNTFORT, G. *Tigers.* 1973. Crescent. Ils. 96 p. dj. EX. M2. $10.00

MOURLOT, Fernand. *Picasso Lithographs.* 1970. Boston. Book & Art Pub. 4to. dj. slipcase. $150.00

MOUTBATTEN. *Biography of Philip Ziegler.* 1985. Knopf. Ils. 784 p. $10.00

MOWAT, F. *Never Cry Wolf.* 1963. Little Brown. 1st Am ed. dj. EX. M2. $20.00

MOWAT, F. *Whale for the Killing.* 1972. Boston. 1st ed. dj. VG. B2. $27.50

MOWREY, W.B. *Swift in the Night & Other Tales of Field & Wood.* 1956. NY. 1st ed. 254 p. dj. EX. $15.00

MOYER, J.W. *Practical Taxidermy.* 1979. Wiley. Ils Revised 2nd ed. dj. EX. M2. $12.00

MOYNAHAN, Jim. *Ace Powell Book.* 1974. Kalispell, MT. private print. 1st ed. dj. VG. $60.00

MOYNIHAN, Berkeley. *Abdominal Operations.* 1926. Saunders. 2 vols. EX. $15.00

MOZLEY, Charles. *State Funeral of Sir Winston S. Churchill.* 1965. London. Rainbird. Ils. 4to. dj. EX. D1. $40.00

MUCHA, Jiri. *Alphonse Maria Mucha: His Life & Work.* 1989. NY. Rizzoli. Ils. 300 p. dj. M. D2. $65.00

MUDD, N. *Life of Dr. Samuel A. Mudd.* reprint of 1906 ed. 383 p. EX. M2. $14.00

MUELLER, John. *American Symphony Orchestra: Social History Musical Taste.* 1951. IN U. 1st ed. presentation. dj. VG. J2. $17.50

MUELLER, Philipp. *Miracula & Mysteria Chimico Medica.* 1916. Frieburg im Breisgau. 12mo. 493 p. $800.00

MUHAMMAD, Elijah. *Message to Blackman.* 1965. Chicago. 1st ed. dj. EX. B1. $30.00

MUIR, Edwin. *Collected Poems.* 1953. 1st ed. VG. C1. $7.50

MUIR, John. *American Wilderness in Words of John Muir.* 1973. Country Beautiful. 4to. dj. M2. $17.00

MUIR, John. *Cruise of the Corwin.* Boston. 1/550. Lg Paper ed. G. $120.00

MUIR, John. *Cruise of the Corwin.* 1917. Boston. 1/550. VG. B2. $145.00

MUIR, John. *Mountains & Meadows.* 1969. S NV U. Ltd ed. 1/2100. gilt bdg. VG. $25.00

MUIR, John. *Mountains of CA.* 1894. NY. 1st ed. 1st issue. VG. T5. $150.00

MUIR, John. *Mountains of CA.* 1988. Golden, CO. reprint. dj. EX. $15.00

MUIR, John. *Muir Among the Animals: Wildlife Writing of John Muir.* 1986. Sierra Club. Ils 1st ed. 196 p. dj. EX. M2. $15.00

MUIR, John. *My First Summer in the Sierra.* 1911. Boston/NY. Ils 1st ed. $65.00

MUIR, John. *Picturesque CA.* 1888. India Proof ed. 1st issue. 109 of 120 pls. T1. $330.00

MUIR, John. *Story of My Boyhood & Youth.* 1913. Boston. 1st ed. dj. VG. B2. $75.00

MUIR, John. *Travels in AK.* 1915. Boston. 1st ed. inscr. VG. $75.00

MUIR, John. *Travels in AK.* 1920. Houghton. Ils. 327 p. xl. G. M2. $11.00

MUIR, John. *Travels in AK.* 1988. Sierra Club. 274 p. EX. M2. $10.00

MUIR, John. *Yosemite.* 1912. Century. fld map. VG. $150.00

MUIR, John. *1,000 Mile Walk to Gulf.* 1916. Boston. 1st ed. B2. $60.00

MUIR, P.H. *Book Collecting As a Hobby.* 1947. NY. 1st ed. dj. EX. $20.00

MUIR, P.H. *Children's Books of Yesterday. Catalog of Exhibit, 1946.* 1946. Cambridge. Nat Book League. 12mo. xl. G. $15.00

MUIR, P.H. *English Children's Books.* 1985. London. Batsford. 256 p. EX. $19.00

MUIR, P.H. *Minding My Own Business.* 1956. London. 1st ed. dj. VG. $55.00

MUIR, Percy. *Victorian Illustrated Books.* 1971. London. Ils 1st ed. dj. EX. $60.00

MUIR, Richard. *National Trust Guide to Dark Age & Medieval Britain.* 1985. London. 256 photos. map. dj. D2. $34.95

MUKERJI, D.G. *Bunny, Hound & Clown.* 1931. NY. $50.00

MUKERJI, D.G. *Rama, the Hero of India.* 1930. NY. $45.00

MULFORD, C.E. *Hopalong Cassidy Sees Red.* 1921. 1st ed. 353 p. $12.00

MULFORD, C.E. *Mesquite Jenkins.* 1928. Doubleday. 1st ed. VG. $7.50

MULFORD, I.S. *Civil & Political History of NJ.* 1848. Camden. Keen Chandler. 8vo. rebound. J2. $150.00

MULHOLLAND, Mary. *Early Guild Records of Toulhouse.* 1941. Columbia. 1st ed. 193 p. stiff wraps. J2. $15.00

MULLAN, John. *Report of Lieutenant John Mullan...* 1861. WA. 171 p. wraps. disbound. $200.00

MULLAN, John. *Report on Construction of Military Road From Ft. Walla...* 1863. WA. Ils. fld maps. VG. A3. $250.00

MULLER, C.G. *How They Carried the Goods.* 1932. NY. Dodd Mead. Ils 1st ed. dj. VG. $18.00

MULLER, Dan. *My Life With Buffalo Bill.* 1948. Reilly Lee. 1st ed. dj. EX. $15.00

MULLER, F.M. *My Autobiography.* 1901. Scribner. 1st ed. TEG. EX. $80.00

MULLER, Filip. *Eyewitness Auschwitz.* 1979. NY. 1st ed. dj. xl. $9.50

MULLER, Franz. *Pharmakologie: Theoretshe & Klinische.* 1921. Leipzig. 150 p. VG. $20.00

MULLER, Werner Y. *Ferdinand Hodler.* 1943. Zurich. Rascher. folio. wraps. D2. $40.00

MULLER & FRIEDMAN. *Recent Developments in Carbonate Sedimentology in Europe.* 1968. Verlag. 255 p. dj. EX. M2. $20.00

MULLER. *Manual of Military Aviation.* 1918. Manasha. Ils. TB. 486 p. VG. C4. $72.00

MULLER-HILL, Benno. *Murderous Science.* 1988. NY. 1st ed. dj. VG. $15.00

MULLINS & REED. *Union Bookshelf, Civil War Bibliography.* 1982. 80 p. scarce. J4. $32.50

MULOCK, D.T. *Adventures of a Brownie & Other Stories.* 1922. Ils Maris Kirk. Gift ed. VG. E2. $18.00

MULOCK, D.T. *Little Lame Prince.* 1918. Lippincott. Ils Kirk. dj. B4. $15.00

MUMBY & NORRIE. *Publishing & Bookselling.* 1974. London. Cape. Revised 5th ed. dj. xl. VG. $17.00

MUMFORD, J.K. *Oriental Rugs.* 1901. Scribner. 24 pls. fair. $35.00

MUMFORD, Lewis. *City in History.* 1961. Harcourt. 1st ed. dj. VG. J2. $25.00

MUMFORD, Lewis. *Story of Utopias.* 1922. Boni. 1st ed. G. J2. $45.00

MUMFORD, Lewis. *Technics & Civilization.* 1934. Harcourt Brace. 1st ed. $10.00

MUNCH, P.A. *Norse Mythology.* 1926. NY. Am-Scandinavian Foundation. G. $30.00

MUNDELL, E.H. *Erle Stanley Gardner: Check List.* nd. Kent State. EX. P1. $12.50

MUNDY, Talbot. *Her Reputation.* 1923. NY. Ils Ince. Movie ed. $17.50

MUNDY, Talbot. *Hira Singh.* 1918. NY. $15.00

MUNDY, Talbot. *Ivory Trail.* 1919. NY. $15.00

MUNDY, Talbot. *Jimgrim & Allah's Peace.* 1936. NY. 1st ed. dj. EX. $135.00

MUNDY, Talbot. *Jimgrim.* 1931. NY. 1st print. EX. T1. $45.00

MUNDY, Talbot. *Nine Unknown.* 1924. NY. $15.00

MUNDY, Talbot. *Om: Secret of Ahbor Valley.* 1924. NY. $15.00

MUNDY, Talbot. *Queen Cleopatra.* 1929. Indianapolis. 1/265. sgn. $100.00

MUNDY, Talbot. *Tros of Samothrace.* 1934. London. leather. $100.00

MUNDY, Talbot. *Winds of World.* 1917. NY. $15.00

MUNKACSI. *Style in Motion.* 1979. NY. Potter. 1st ed. dj. VG. $25.00

MUNN, Charles. *Uncle Terry.* 1900. Lee Shepard. Ils Higgenbotham. VG. $25.00

MUNN, Glen. *Encyclopedia of Banking & Finance.* 1973. Bankers Pub. 7th ed. EX. $15.00

MUNN, H. Warner. *Banner of Joan.* 1975. Ltd 1st ed. 1/975. dj. M. C1. $14.00

MUNN, H. Warner. *King of the World's Edge.* Ace. 1st ed. scarce. VG. C1. $4.00

MUNN, H. Warner. *Merlin's Godson & Merlin's Ring.* 2 vols. pb. VG. C1. $4.50

MUNRO, I.S.R. *Marine & Fresh-Water Fishes of Ceylon.* 1982. Delhi. reprint. 349 p. dj. EX. M2. $85.00

MUNRO & KIMBALL. *Population Ecology of the Mallard.* 1982. USFWS. 4to. 127 p. EX. M2. $10.00

MUNROE, J.P. *Life of Francis Amasas Walker.* 1923. Ils. index. 449 p. K1. $18.50

MUNSELL, A.H. *Color Notation.* 1926. Baltimore. Ils. VG. $30.00

MUNSON. *History of Lithographers Union.* 1963. Cambridge. dj. VG. $25.00

MUNSTERBERG, Hugo. *Art of Chinese Sculptor.* 1960. Tuttle. Stated 1st ed. dj. EX. $20.00

MUNSTERBERG, Hugo. *Japanese Print.* 1982. Weatherhill. Ils. dj. M. $35.00

MUNSTERBERG, Hugo. *Psychology & Social Sanity.* 1914. Garden City. 1st ed. VG. $20.00

MUNTZ, Hope. *Golden Warrior.* 1949. 1st Am ed. dj. M. C1. $11.50

MUNTZ, Hope. *Golden Warrior.* 1949. 1st Am ed. dj. xl. C1. $7.00

MURASKI, Lady. *Tale of Genji.* 1935. Boston. Houghton. 2 vols. slipcase. $25.00

MURATOFF, P. *35 Russian Primitives: Jacques Zolotnitsky's Collection.* 1931. Paris. Ils. 4to. 112 p. glassine dj. J2. $50.00

MURAY, Nickolas. *Revealing Eye.* dj. EX. S2. $30.00

MURAY, Nickolas. *Revealing Eye.* 1967. NY. Atheneum. Ils 1st ed. folio. 307 p. dj. $50.00

MURBARGER, N. *Ghost of the Adobe Walls: Human Interest & Highlights...* 1969. Westernlore. photos. maps. 398 p. dj. EX. M2. $16.00

MURCHISON, C. *Clinical Lectures on Diseases of the Liver.* 1877. NY. 644 p. EX. $45.00

MURDOCH, Iris. *Accidental Man.* London. 1st ed. dj. VG. $25.00

MURDOCH, Iris. *Accidental Man.* 1972. Viking. 1st ed. dj. EX. $20.00

MURDOCH, Iris. *Black Prince.* London. 1st ed. dj. M. $25.00

MURDOCH, Iris. *Bruno's Dream.* London. 1st ed. VG. $15.00

MURDOCH, Iris. *Flight From the Enchanter.* London. 1st ed. dj. VG. $40.00

MURDOCH, Iris. *Good Apprentice.* London. 1st ed. 1/250. sgn/#d. glassine dj. $80.00

MURDOCH, Iris. *Henry & Cato.* London. 1st ed. dj. VG. $23.00

MURDOCH, Iris. *Italian Girl.* London. 1st ed. dj. VG. $30.00

MURDOCH, Iris. *Italian Girl.* 1964. NY. 1st ed. dj. VG. $20.00

MURDOCH, Iris. *Philosopher's Pupil.* London. 1st ed. dj. VG. $23.00

MURDOCH, Iris. *Sacred & Profane Love Machine.* 1974. Viking. 1st Am ed. dj. EX. $15.00

MURDOCH, Iris. *Time of the Angels.* London. 1st ed. dj. EX. $25.00

MURDOCH, Iris. *Unicorn.* London. 1st ed. dj. M. $40.00

MURDOCH, Iris. *Unofficial Rose.* London. 1st ed. dj. M. $40.00

MURDOCK, E.C. *Patriotism Limited, 1862-1865.* 1967. 270 p. EX. J4. $12.50

MURDOCK, G.P. *Ethnographic Bibliography of N America.* 1960. Human Relations. 3rd ed. EX. M2. $45.00

MURIE, A. *Birds of Mount McKinley National Park, AK.* 1963. Mt. McKinley Hist Assn. EX. M2. $16.00

MURIE, A. *Grizzlies of Mt. McKinley, AK.* 1987. WA U. photos. 250 p. M. M2. $10.00

MURIE, A. *Naturalist in AK.* 1961. Devin Adair. Ils. 302 p. dj. EX. M2. $12.00

MURIE, A. *Wolves of Mt. McKinley.* 1971. Nat Park Service. Ils. 238 p. M2. $20.00

MURIE, A. *Wolves of Mt. McKinley.* 1987. WA U. photos. 238 p. M. M2. $10.00

MURIE, M.E. *AK Bird Sketches of Olaus Murie.* 1979. AK NW. Ils. oblong 4to. EX. M2. $12.00

MURIE, M.E. *Two in the Far N.* 1983. AK NW. Ils New ed. 385 p. EX. M2. $9.00

MURIE, M.E. *Wapiti Wilderness.* 1969. Knopf. Ils. 302 p. dj. EX. M2. $30.00

MURIE, Olaus. *AK-Yukon Caribou.* 1935. USDA. 1st ed. stiff wraps. VG. J2. $25.00

MURPHY, Brendan. *Butcher of Lyon.* 1983. NY. 1st ed. VG. $6.50

MURPHY, E.A. *30th Division in WWI.* 1936. HrdCvr. 342 p. VG. J4. $35.00

MURPHY, Joseph. *How To Use Your Healing Power.* 1957. CA. $14.00

MURPHY, Joseph. *Meaning of Reincarnation.* 1959. CA. $12.00

MURPHY, Joseph. *Miracles of Your Mind.* 1955. CA. $12.00

MURPHY, Joseph. *You Can Change Your Whole Life.* 1961. CA. $7.00

MURPHY, R. *Peregrine Falcon.* 1963. Houghton. Ils 1st print. 157 p. dj. EX. M2. $20.00

MURPHY, R.C. *Oceanic Birds of S America.* 1936. NY. Ils Jaques. 1st ed. 2 vols. EX. $200.00

MURPHY, Robert. *Logbook for Grace.* 1947. Macmillan. 2nd print. dj. VG. J2. $12.50

MURPHY, T.D. *OR the Picturesque.* 1917. Boston. Ils 1st ed. 8vo. VG. T1. $35.00

MURPHY, T.R. *SE States' Bald Eagle Recovery Plan.* 1984. USFWS. 147 p. M2. $10.00

MURPHY & AMADON. *Land Birds of America.* 1953. McGraw Hill. Ils 1st ed. VG. $12.50

MURPHY & AMADON. *Land Birds of America.* 1953. McGraw Hill. photos. 240 p. dj. EX. M2. $17.00

MURRAY, C.A. *Prairie Bird.* 1844. NY. 1st Am ed. rebound. VG. $110.00

MURRAY, Charles. *Hamewith.* 1920. London. Ils. G. $12.00

MURRAY, Hilda. *Echoes of Sport.* 1911. London. Foulis. 2nd ed. wraps. VG. $55.00

MURRAY, J.A. *Apparatus Medicaminum Tan Simplicium Quam Praeparatorum...* 1776-1792. Goettingen. 6 vols in 3. $580.00

MURRAY, J.J. *Wild Wings.* 1947. Knox. Ils. 123 p. VG. M2. $5.00

MURRAY, K.A. *Modocs & Their War.* 1959. Norman. Ils 1st ed. dj. VG. $45.00

MURRAY, K.M. *Wings Over Poland: Story of 7th Kosciuszko Squardron, WWI.* 1932. NY. 1st ed. 363 p. dj. VG. B2. $40.00

MURRAY, Lindley. *English Reader; or, Pieces in Prose & Poetry.* 1834. Phil. McDowell. 8vo. 263 p. M1. $26.50

MURRAY, Lindley. *Power of Religion on the Mind.* 1795. Trenton, NJ. Collins. Enlarged 7th ed. 220 p. $85.00

MURRAY, N. *Legacy of an Assassination.* 1964. NY. 1st ed. dj. EX. $35.00

MURRAY, Peter. *Architecture of the Renaissance.* 1971. NY. Abrams. Ils. 401 p. dj. D2. $50.00

MURRAY, William H. *Uncle Sam Needs a Doctor.* 1940. Boston. Meador. 1st ed. sgn. EX. T6. $25.00

MURRAY. *Mathematical Machines.* 1961. NY. 1st ed. 2 vols. EX. $20.00

MURRAY. *Practice of Osteopathy.* 1912. Elgin. Ils 3rd ed. 422 p. VG. C4. $45.00

MURSELL, W.A. *Byways in Bookland, Confessions & Digressions.* 1914. Boston. 1st Am ed. $25.00

MUSCHAMP, E.A. *Audacious Audubon: Story of Pioneer, Artist, Naturalist...* 1929. Brentanos. photos. 312 p. EX. M2. $15.00

MUSCIANO, W.A. *Eagles of the Black Cross.* 1965. NY. Ils 1st ed. 310 p. dj. T5. $22.50

MUSE, C. & S. *Birds & Birdlore of Samoa.* 1982. Pioneer. Ils 1st print. 156 p. EX. M2. $15.00

MUSEUM SCIENCE & INDUSTRY. *Treasures of Tiffany.* 1982. Chicago. 72 p. 4to. $17.00

MUSGRAVE, J.W. & M.R. *Waterfowl in IA.* 1953. IA Conservation. Ils Reece. M2. $20.00

MUSIL, Alois. *In the Arabian Desert.* 1930. NY. Liveright. Ils. VG. $35.00

MUSMANNO, Michael. *Eichmann Commandos.* 1961. Phil. 1st ed. 268 p. dj. VG. B2. $27.50

MUUS & DAHLSTROM. *Fresh-Water Fishes of Britain & Europe.* 1978. London. Collins. Ils. 222 p. EX. M2. $14.00

MUYBRIDGE, E. *Animals in Motion.* 1957. NY. Dover. reprint. dj. $27.50

MUZZEY, D.S. *James G. Glaine.* 1934. Dodd Mead. 1st ed. EX. $45.00

MYER, Geoffrey. *Final Exam.* 1981. Pinnacle. Movie ed. VG. P1. $3.75

MYERS, Bernard S. *German Expressionists: Generation in Revolt.* 1957. NY. Praeger. Ils. 401 p. dj. D2. $150.00

MYERS, Henry. *Utmost Island.* 1951. 1st ed. VG. C1. $5.50

MYERS, J.M. *Death of the Bravos.* 1962. Little Brown. 1st ed. 467 p. dj. M2. $15.00

MYERS, J.M. *Doc Holliday.* 1955. Little Brown. 1st ed. 387 p. dj. VG. M2. $20.00

MYERS, J.M. *Harp & the Blade.* 1985. pb. EX. C1. $3.00

MYERS, J.M. *Last Chance: Tombstone's Early Years.* 1950. NY. 1st ed. dj. EX. $37.50

MYERS, J.M. *Moon's Fire-Eating Daughter.* Ace. pb. VG. C1. $3.00

MYERS, J.M. *Silverlock.* pb. VG. C1. $3.00

MYERS, John. *San Francisco's Reign of Terror.* 1966. Doubleday. 1st ed. dj. EX. $15.00

MYERS, L.G. *Some Notes on American Pewterers.* 1926. Country Life. Ltd ed. 1/1000. xl. $50.00

MYERS, R.J. *Cross of Frankenstein.* 1975. Lippincott. 1st ed. dj. xl. P1. $5.00

MYERS, R.J. *Slave of Frankenstein.* 1976. Lippincott. 1st ed. dj. VG. P1. $9.25

MYERS, R.M. *Children of Pride.* 1972. New Haven. 1st ed. dj. VG. B2. $40.00

MYERS, R.M. *From Beowulf to Virginia Woolfe.* 1952. 1st ed. dj. EX. C1. $15.00

MYERS, S.A. *Martin's Natural History.* 1862. np. Ils 1st ed. 8vo. VG. $25.00

MYERS. *Memoirs of a Hunter: Story of 58 Years' Hunting & Fishing.* 1948. Davenport. dj. EX. $20.00

MYHAL, M.J. *Corps Badges of the Union Army.* 1973. 1/500. 80 p. EX. J4. $20.00

MYRER, Anton. *Evil Under the Sun.* 1951. Random House. 1st ed. dj. EX. $35.00

MYRICK, D.F. *NM Railroads.* 1970. Ils. photos. 206 p. $20.00

MYRICK, H. *Turkeys & How To Grow Them.* 1909. NY. Ils. 8vo. 159 p. $40.00

MYRICK, Susan. *White Columns in Hollywood.* 1982. Mercer U. Ils 1st ed. photos. dj. $25.00

MYTINGER, Caroline. *Headhunting in the Solomon Islands.* 1942. Macmillan. Ils 1st ed. EX. $10.00

NABHAN, G.P. *Gathering the Desert.* 1986. AZ U. Ils. 209 p. EX. M2. $14.00

NABOKOV, Vladimir. *Bend Sinister.* 1947. NY. 1st ed. dj. EX. $225.00

NABOKOV, Vladimir. *Glory.* 1971. NY. 1st Am ed. dj. EX. $30.00

NABOKOV, Vladimir. *King, Queen, Knave.* 1968. McGraw Hill. 1st ed. dj. EX. $35.00

NABOKOV, Vladimir. *Laughter in the Dark.* 1938. Indianapolis. 1st Am ed. 292 p. G. T5. $50.00

NABOKOV, Vladimir. *Laughter in the Dark.* 1960. NY. New ed. dj. EX. $10.00

NABOKOV, Vladimir. *Lolita.* Olympia. 2nd issue. 2 vols. wraps. EX. $350.00

NABOKOV, Vladimir. *Lolita.* 1955. NY. 1st Am ed. 319 p. dj. T5. $25.00

NABOKOV, Vladimir. *Lolita.* 1955. Paris. Olympia. 1st ed. 1st issue. 2 vols. wraps. $400.00

NABOKOV, Vladimir. *Look at the Harlequins!* 1974. McGraw Hill. 1st ed. dj. EX. $25.00

NABOKOV, Vladimir. *Mary.* 1970. NY. 1st Am ed. dj. VG. $25.00

NABOKOV, Vladimir. *Nabokov's Dozen.* 1958. NY. 1st ed. dj. EX. $50.00

NABOKOV, Vladimir. *Nabokov's Quartet.* 1966. NY. 1st ed. dj. EX. $35.00

NABOKOV, Vladimir. *Nikolai Gogol.* nd. London. 1st ed. $65.00

NABOKOV, Vladimir. *Pale Fire.* 1962. NY. 1st ed. dj. VG. B2. $57.50

NABOKOV, Vladimir. *Pnin.* 1957. Doubleday. 1st ed. dj. EX. $32.50

NABOKOV, Vladimir. *Poems.* 1959. Garden City. 1st ed. 1st issue. dj. EX. $150.00

NABOKOV, Vladimir. *Transparent Things.* 1972. NY. 1st ed. dj. EX. $25.00

NABOKOV, Vladimir. *Waltz Invention.* 1966. NY. 1st ed. dj. VG. B2. $30.00

NAEF, W. *Collection of Alfred Stieglitz.* 1978. NY. VG. $35.00

NAGLE. *Behind the Masque.* 1951. McMullen. 1st ed. EX. $6.00

NAIMY, Mikhail. *Kahlil Gibran: Biography.* 1950. NY. $30.00

NAIPAUL, V.S. *Congo Diary.* 1980. LA. 1st ed. 1/330. sgn. EX. $75.00

NAIPAUL, V.S. *Miguel Street.* 1959. NY. 1st ed. dj. VG. $15.00

NAIPAUL, V.S. *Mystic Masseur.* 1959. Vanguard. 1st ed. dj. EX. $75.00

NAIPAUL, V.S. *Return of Eva Peron.* 1980. NY. 1st ed. dj. EX. $20.00

NAKAYA, U. *Snow Crystals: Natural & Artificial.* 1954. Harvard. Ils. 410 p. dj. EX. M2. $55.00

NAMAIS, Rodolfo. *Il Processo Bromolio Ovvero la Bromoleotipia.* 1916. Milan. Ils. stiff wraps. $65.00

NANCE, J. *Gentle Tasaday: Stone Age People in Philippine Rain Forest.* 1976. London. Book Club. photos. 465 p. G. M2. $9.00

NANCE, J.J. *Splash of Colors: Self-Destruction of Braniff International.* 1984. Morrow. 426 p. dj. M1. $8.50

NANSEN, Fridtjof. *First Crossing of Greenland.* 1890. London. 2 vols. G. scarce. $100.00

NANSEN, Fridtjof. *In N Mists. Vol. I.* 1911. NY. Ils 1st ed. 384 p. B2. $47.50

NAPHEYS, G.H. *Physical Life of Woman.* 1890. index. 436 p. K1. $12.50

NAPIER, P. & J. *Monkeys & Apes.* 1976. Time Life. photos. 128 p. M2. $5.00

NAPOLEAO, Aluizio. *Santos-Dumont & the Conquest of the Air.* 1945. Rio de Janeiro. 1st ed. 2 vols. rebound. T5. $195.00

NAQUET, A. *Principes de Chimie, Fondee sur Les Theories Modernes.* 1867. Paris. Revised Enlarged 2nd ed. 2 vols. $40.00

NARAZAKI, Muneshige. *Kiyonaga.* 1969. Tokyo. Kodansha. 3rd print. 88 p. D2. $20.00

NARKISS. *Hebrew Illuninated Manuscripts.* 1974. NY. Amiel. 2nd ed. dj. EX. $25.00

NARRIEN, J. *Historical Account of Origin & Progress of Astronomy.* 1833. 5 pls. rebound. VG. $115.00

NASH, E. *History of 44th Regiment, NY Volunteers.* 1911. Chicago. Ils. R1. $225.00

NASH, J.N. *Poisonous Plants: Deadly, Dangerous & Suspect.* 1927. London. Curwen. 1/350. folio. orig bdg. EX. $200.00

NASH, Ogden. *Good Intentions.* 1942. Boston. 1st ed. dj. EX. $20.00

NASH, Ogden. *Happy Days.* 1933. NY. 1st ed. sgn. dj. EX. scarce. $90.00

NASH, Ogden. *Hard Lines.* 1931. NY. 1st ed. EX. $37.50

NASH, Ogden. *Many Long Years Ago.* 1945. Boston. 1st ed. VG. $20.00

NASH, Ogden. *Works of Ogden Nash.* 1945. Little Brown. 6 vols. djs. $25.00

NASIBOVA, Aida. *Faceted Chamber in the Moscow Kermlin.* 1978. Leningrad. dj. EX. J2. $40.00

NASON, E. *Gazetteer of State of MA.* 1890. Boston. Ils. 8vo. 724 p. G. G2. $27.00

NASON, E. *Life & Times of Charles Sumner.* 1874. Boston. 12mo. 356 p. G2. $18.00

NASSAU, R.H. *In Elephant Corral & Other Tales of W African Experiences.* 1969. Negro U. reprint of 1912 ed. EX. M2. $15.00

NAST, Thomas. *Flight of Dame Europa's School.* 1871. NY. Ils Nast. 34 p. $75.00

NAST, Thomas. *President's Message, 1887.* 1888. NY. Ils 1st ed. 38 p. wraps. EX. $100.00

NATHAN, Robert. *Bishop's Wife.* 1928. Grosset Dunlap. 1st ed. dj. G. $15.00

NATHAN, Robert. *Elixir.* 1971. 1st Am ed. cloth bdg. VG. C1. $10.00

NATHAN, Robert. *Elixir.* 1971. 1st Am ed. dj. EX. C1. $14.00

NATHAN, Robert. *Fair.* 1964. 1st ed. dj. EX. C1. $12.50

NATHAN, Robert. *Sir Henry.* 1979. Borgo. pb. VG. C1. $6.00

NATIONAL ACADEMY SCIENCE. *Effects of Atomic Radiation on Oceanography & Fisheries.* 1957. 137 p. EX. M2. $22.00

NATIONAL ARCHIVES. *Civil War Maps in the National Archives.* 1964. Ils. 453 maps. charts. plans. paper wraps. VG. $15.00

NATIONAL GEOGRAPHIC SOCIETY. *America's Majestic Mountains.* 1979. photos. maps. 207 p. dj. EX. M2. $10.00

NATIONAL GEOGRAPHIC SOCIETY. *America's Seashore Wonderlands.* 1985. color photos. maps. 199 p. dj. EX. M2. $10.00

NATIONAL GEOGRAPHIC SOCIETY. *Book of Birds.* 1939. 2 vols. VG. $28.00

NATIONAL GEOGRAPHIC SOCIETY. *Book of Dogs.* 1919. VG. B1. $40.00

NATIONAL GEOGRAPHIC SOCIETY.
Book of Dogs. 1958. Ils 1st ed. EX. M2. $16.00

NATIONAL GEOGRAPHIC SOCIETY.
Desert Realm: Lands of Mystery & Majesty.
1982. color photos. maps. 304 p. dj. EX. M2.
$10.00

NATIONAL GEOGRAPHIC SOCIETY.
Indians of the Americas. 1955. HrdCvr ed.
4to. EX. $27.50

NATIONAL GEOGRAPHIC SOCIETY.
Lake, Peaks & Prairies: Discovering the US-Canada Border. 1984. color photos. maps.
199 p. dj. EX. M2. $10.00

NATIONAL GEOGRAPHIC SOCIETY.
Majestic Island Worlds. 1987. color photos.
199 p. dj. EX. M2. $13.00

NATIONAL GEOGRAPHIC SOCIETY.
Marvels of Animal Behavior. 1972. Ils 1st
print. 421 p. dj. EX. M2. $10.00

NATIONAL GEOGRAPHIC SOCIETY.
Mysteries of the Ancient World. 1979. Ils.
maps. 223 p. dj. EX. M2. $8.00

NATIONAL GEOGRAPHIC SOCIETY.
Ocean Realm. 1978. Ils. 199 p. dj. EX. M2.
$10.00

NATIONAL GEOGRAPHIC SOCIETY.
Scenes From Every Land. 1909. EX. red cloth.
EX. J3. $30.00

NATIONAL GEOGRAPHIC SOCIETY.
Secret Corners of the World. 1982. color
photos. 199 p. dj. EX. M2. $10.00

NATIONAL GEOGRAPHIC SOCIETY.
Wild Animals of N America. 1960. Ils 1st
print. 399 p. dj. EX. M2. $15.00

NATIONAL GEOGRAPHIC SOCIETY.
*Wild Lands for Wildlife: America's National
Refuges.* 1984. color photos. maps. 207 p. dj.
EX. M2. $10.00

NATIONAL GEOGRAPHIC SOCIETY.
*Window on America: Discovering Her Natural
Beauty.* 1987. color photos. maps. dj. EX.
M2. $10.00

NATIONAL GEOGRAPHIC SOCIETY.
Wondrous World of Fishes. 1965. Ils 1st print.
367 p. EX. M2. $13.00

NATIONAL PARK SERVICE. *Lewis &
Clark.* 1975. GPO. 429 p. $36.00

NATIONAL PARK SERVICE. *Soldier &
Brave.* 1963. NY. 1st ed. photos. maps. dj.
VG. $20.00

NATIONAL WILDLIFE FEDERATION.
Wildlife Country: How To Enjoy It. 1977.
color photos. 4to. 208 p. dj. EX. M2. $9.00

NATIONAL WILDLIFE FEDERATION.
Wildlife Family Album. 1981. 190 photos. 4to.
208 p. dj. EX. M2. $8.00

NAUDE, Gabriel. *Advice on Establishing a
Library.* 1950. Berkeley. dj. $35.00

NAULT, A. *Staying Alive in AK's Wild.* 1980.
Loftion. photos. 210 p. EX. M2. $9.00

NAUMOV, N.P. *Ecology of Animals.* 1972.
IL U. maps. 650 p. dj. EX. M2. $20.00

NAVASKY, Victor. *Naming Names.* 1980.
Viking. 1st ed. dj. EX. $10.00

NAYLOR, B. *Technique of Dress Design.*
1967. London. Ils. 154 p. dj. VG. $20.00

NAYLOR, C.T. *Civil War Days in a (NY)
Country Village.* 1961. Peekskill. Ils. maps.
sgn. dj. EX. $35.00

NAYLOR, Gillian. *Arts & Crafts Movement.*
1971. Cambridge. MIT Pr. dj. VG. $35.00

NAYLOR, James Ball. *Cabin in the Big
Woods.* 1904. Akron. Ils 1st ed. 239 p. VG.
T5. $22.50

NAYLOR, James Ball. *Current Coins.* 1893.
Columbus. Ils 1st ed. inscr. 192 p. G. T5.
$42.50

NAYLOR, James Ball. *Ralph Marlowe.* 1901.
Akron. 1st ed. 412 p. VG. T5. $27.50

NAYLOR, James Ball. *Sign of the Prophet:
Tale of Tecumseh & Tippecanoe.* 1901.
Saalfield. 1st ed. 416 p. cloth. VG. T5. $22.50

NAYLOR, James Ball. *Songs From the Heart
of Things.* 1907. Columbus. Subscription ed.
1/750. 202 p. T5. $50.00

NEAL, E. *Natural History of Badgers.* 1986.
Facts on File. Ils 1st Am ed. dj. EX. M2.
$23.00

NEAL, R.M. *High Green & the Bark Peelers.*
1950. 275 p. $25.00

NEARING, Scott. *American Empire.* 1921.
Rand School Soc Science. 8vo. VG. $55.00

NEARING, Scott. *Next Step: Plan for
Economic World Federation...* 1922.
Ridgewood, NJ. 1st ed. 1/500. sgn. 8vo. VG.
$45.00

NEARING, Scott. *Poverty & Riches.* 1916.
Phil. 1st ed. 261 p. G. B2. $25.00

NECKER. *Four Centuries of Cat Books:
Bibliography, 1570-1970.* 1972. NY. VG.
$25.00

NEEDHAM & BETTEN. *Aquatic Insects in
Adirondacks.* 1901. NY State Mus. pls.
wraps. VG. $30.00

NEIDER, Charles. *Great W.* 1958. NY. Ils
1st ed. dj. VG. $22.00

NEIL, M.H. *Candies & Bonbons & How To
Make Them.* 1913. Phil. dj. VG. $30.00

NEILL, E.D. *Dakota Land & Dakota Life With
History of Fur Traders...* 1859. Lippincott. 98
p. wraps. scarce. A3. $120.00

NEILL, J.R. *Children's Stories That Never
Grow Old.* 1908. Reilly Britton. 1st ed. $35.00

NELL, William C. *Colored Patriots of the
American Revolution.* 1855. Boston. 396 p.
very scarce. K1. $27.50

NELLI, H.S. *Italians in Chicago, 1880-1930.*
1970. NY. 1st ed. dj. VG. B2. $17.50

NELSON, Bruce. *Brothers.* 1975. NY. 1st ed.
dj. VG. $8.00

NELSON, J.Y. *Fifty Years on the Trail: True
Story of W Life...* 1969. OK U. 291 p. dj. EX.
M2. $14.00

NELSON, James. *General Eisenhower on
Military Churchill.* 1970. NY. Ils 1st ed. 95 p.
dj. VG. T5. $17.50

NELSON, John. *Extract From the Journal of
John Nelson...* 1849. Lane Scott. leather. G.
$25.00

NELSON, M. *Home on the Range.* 1947.
Boston. Ils 1st ed. 285 p. dj. VG. B2. $22.50

NELSON, Ozzie. *Ozzie.* 1973. NY. 1st ed.
sgn. dj. VG. B2. $20.00

NELSON, R.K. *Shadow of the Hunter: Stories
of Eskimo Life.* 1980. Toronto U. $10.00

NELSON, Steve. *13th Juror: Inside Story of
My Trial.* 1955. NY. Masses Mainstream. pb.
sgn. G. $25.00

NELSON & BASS. *Orangeburg Massacre.*
1970. NY. World. Ils 1st print. 272 p. dj.
$45.00

NEMEROV, Howard. *Journal of the Fictive
Life.* 1965. NY. 1st Am ed. dj. VG. $35.00

NEPRUD, R.E. *Flying Minute Men: Story of
Civil Air Patrol.* 1948. NY. Ils 1st ed. 243 p.
dj. VG. T5. $22.50

NERO, R.W. *Great Gray Owl: Phantom of N
Forest.* 1980. Smithsonian. Ils. 168 p. M. M2.
$13.00

NERO, R.W. *Redwings.* 1984. Smithsonian.
Ils. 160 p. EX. M2. $12.00

NERUDA, Pablo. *Odas Elementales.* 1954.
Buenos Aires. wraps. $50.00

NESBIT, E. *Wouldbegoods.* 1901. Harper. Ils Reginald Birch. 1st ed. $12.00

NESBIT, R.C. *Torpedo Airmen.* 1983. London. Ils. dj. EX. $25.00

NESBITT, William. *How To Hunt With a Camera: Complete Guide...* 1926. Dutton. Ils 1st ed. 4to. 327 p. $65.00

NESS, Elliot. *Untouchables.* 1957. NY. 1st ed. dj. VG. $22.50

NETBOY, A. *Atlantic Salmon: Vanishing Species?* 1968. Houghton. Ils 1st ed. 457 p. EX. M2. $17.00

NETBOY, A. *Columbia River Salmon & Steelhead Trout.* 1980. WA U. photos. 180 p. dj. M. M2. $17.00

NETBOY, A. *Salmon: World's Most Harassed Fish.* 1980. Winchester. photos. 304 p. dj. EX. M2. $13.00

NETZER, Remigius. *Oskar Kokoschka: Lithographien.* 1960. Munich. Piper. Ils. sgn Kirk. D2. $24.50

NEU, John. *Chemical, Medical & Pharmaceutical Books Printed at WI U.* 1965. dj. VG. $9.00

NEUBAUER, W.G. *Acoustic Reflection From Surfaces & Shapes.* c 1986. WA. Naval Reasearch Lab. M. $20.00

NEUMANN, Erich. *Archetypal World of Henry Moore.* 1959. Pantheon. Ils. 138 p. dj. $20.00

NEUMANN, George. *History of Weapons of American Revolution.* 1967. NY. 1st ed. photos. 364 p. dj. EX. $40.00

NEUMANN-HODITZ, Reinhold. *Portrait of Ho Chi Minh.* 1972. np. Ils 1st Am ed. 187 p. dj. EX. T5. $12.50

NEUTRA, Richard. *Life & Shape.* 1962. Appleton. 1st ed. dj. VG. J2. $20.00

NEVILLE, A.W. *Red River Valley Then & Now.* 1948. Paris, TX. 1st ed. dj. EX. $75.00

NEVINS, Allan. *American Social History As Recorded by British Travelers.* 1931. NY. VG. $12.50

NEVINS, Allan. *Diary of George Templeton Strong.* 1952. Macmillan. 1st ed. 4 vols. boxed. scarce. M. $180.00

NEVINS, Allan. *Emergence of Lincoln.* 1950-1951. Ils. 2 vols. slipcase. EX. M2. $20.00

NEVINS, Allan. *Hamilton Fish.* 1936. NY. 2nd print. 932 p. dj. VG. B2. $22.50

NEVINS, Allan. *Letters of Grover Cleveland, 1850-1908.* 1933. Boston. 1st ed. 640 p. VG. T5. $25.00

NEVINS, Frank. *Yankee Dared. Romance of Our Railroads.* 1933. Chicago. O'Sullivan Pub. $10.00

NEVINS, R.T.W. *Civil War Books: Critical Bibliography Vol. I-II.* 1970. 2nd print. 2 vols. djs. EX. J4. $50.00

NEVINS, W.S. *Witchcraft in Salem Village in 1692.* 1892. Salem. Ils 1st ed. 12mo. VG. T1. $45.00

NEW YORK CITY. *Greater NY Guide.* 1895. Rand McNally. 1st ed. VG. $15.00

NEW YORK GRAPHIC SOCIETY. *Salvador Dali: Study of His Art...* 1959. boxed. with 3 pls. EX. $60.00

NEW YORK MUSEUM OF MODERN ART. *Vincent van Gogh.* 1936. Spiral Pr. Ils 3rd ed. 193 p. D2. $35.00

NEW YORK TIMES. *Churchill in Memoriam: Life, Death, Wit & Wisdom.* 1965. Bantam. pb. EX. D1. $10.00

NEW YORK TIMES. *Report of National Advisory Commission on Civil Disorders.* 1968. Dutton. 609 p. dj. $6.50

NEWBERRY, J.S. *Later Extinct Floras of N America.* 1898. US Geol Survey. Ils. 4to. 295 p. EX. M2. $65.00

NEWBOLT, Frank. *Etchings of Van Dyck.* 1906. London/NY. Newnes/Scribner. Ils D2. $30.00

NEWCOMB, F.J. *Hosteen Klah: Navaho Medicine Man & Sand Painter.* 1964. OK U. Ils. VG. $12.00

NEWCOMB, Rexford. *Architectural Monographs on Tiles & Tilework.* 1924. Beaver Falls. 4to. 3 vols. wraps. $35.00

NEWCOMB, Rexford. *Old KY Architecture.* 1940. NY. Ils. photos. VG. $65.00

NEWCOMB, Rexford. *Old Mission Churches & Historic Houses of CA.* 1925. 1st ed. rebound. VG. $70.00

NEWCOMB, Richard F. *Savo (Guadalcanal Naval Battle).* 1961. NY. 1st ed. dj. EX. B2. $17.50

NEWCOMB, Simon. *Astronomy for Everybody.* 1943. sm 8vo. 334 p. EX. $2.50

NEWELL, F.S. *Cesarean Section.* 1923. NY. Ils. 219 p. EX. $45.00

NEWHALL, Beaumont & Nancy. *Masters of Photography.* 1958. NY. 1st ed. photos. folio. 192 p. dj. VG. T5. $95.00

NEWHALL, Beaumont. *Airborne Camera: World From Air & Outer Space.* 1969. Hastings House. Ils. 4to. 143 p. dj. $30.00

NEWHALL, Beaumont. *Daguerreotype in America.* 1968. Boston. Revised ed. yellow cloth. dj. EX. $25.00

NEWHALL, Beaumont. *History of Photography From 1839 to Present Day.* 1949. NY. dj. EX. $55.00

NEWHALL, Beaumont. *In Plain Sight: Photographs of Beaumont Newhall.* 1983. Salt Lake City. 59 pls. 4to. dj. $75.00

NEWHALL, Beaumont. *Photography, 1839-1937.* 1937. MOMA. VG. $50.00

NEWHALL, Beaumont. *Photography, 1839-1937.* 1937. NY. dj. EX. $85.00

NEWHALL, C.S. *Trees of NE America.* 1901. Putnam. Ils. 250 p. EX. M2. $18.00

NEWHALL, Nancy. *Edward Weston: Flame of Recognition.* 1971. Grossman. photos. D2. $55.00

NEWHALL, Nancy. *Photographs of Edward Weston.* 1946. NY. 1st ed. wraps. VG. $40.00

NEWHOUSE, F.A. *Disciplines of the Holy Quest.* 1959. Escondido. $9.00

NEWHOUSE. *Trapper's Guide.* 1867. Oneida. 2nd ed. G. $85.00

NEWLANDS, J. *Carpenter's & Joiner's Assistant.* c 1880. London. Blackie. folio. xl. $125.00

NEWMAN, Arnold. *Great British.* 1979. Boston. 1st ed. inscr. dj. EX. $45.00

NEWMAN, H.H. *Nature of the World & of Man.* 1933. Garden City. photos. 562 p. dj. EX. M2. $5.00

NEWMAN, Harold. *Illustrated Dictionary of Glass.* 1977. London. Ils. green linen. dj. EX. $35.00

NEWMAN, Harold. *Veilleuses.* 1967. NY. Barnes. 1st ed. dj. VG. $25.00

NEWMAN, K. *Birds of S Africa.* 1988. S Africa. Ils. maps. 471 p. M. M2. $20.00

NEWMAN, Sharan. *Chessboard Queen.* 1st pb ed. VG. C1. $7.50

NEWMAN, Sharan. *Guinevere Evermore.* 1st pb ed. M. C1. $6.50

NEWMAN, Sharan. *Guinevere Evermore.* 1st ed. 2nd print. dj. VG. C1. $5.00

NEWMAN, Sharan. *Guinevere Evermore.* 1985. 1st ed. dj. M. C1. $11.00

NEWMAN, W.S. *Pianist's Problems.* 1956. Harper. Revised ed. dj. EX. $17.50

NEWMAN & LONG. *Civil War Digest.* 1960. New Enlarged ed. photos. 274 p. J4. $6.00

NEWNHAM, Maurice. *Prelude to Glory.* c 1947. London. Ils. 350 p. dj. T5. $29.50

NEWSWANGER, K. & C. *Amishland.* 1954. NY. Ils 1st ed. 128 p. dj. G. T5. $25.00

NEWTON, A.E. *Amenities of Book Collecting & Kindred Affections.* 1918. Boston. Ils 1st ed. 355 p. TEG. T5. $47.50

NEWTON, A.E. *Bibliography & Pseudo-Bibliography.* 1936. London. 124 p. VG. $35.00

NEWTON, A.E. *Bibliography & Pseudo-Bibliography.* 1936. Phil. Ils 1st ed. dj. $30.00

NEWTON, A.E. *Books & Business.* 1930. Appelicon/Rudge. 1/325. sgn. EX. $50.00

NEWTON, A.E. *Derby Day & Other Adventures.* 1934. Boston. Little Brown. 1st ed. dj. VG. $35.00

NEWTON, A.E. *Derby Day & Other Adventures.* 1934. Boston. Ltd 1st ed. sgn. VG. $55.00

NEWTON, A.E. *Dr. Johnson: A Play.* 1923. Boston. 1st ed. dj. EX. $25.00

NEWTON, A.E. *Greatest Book in the World & Other Papers.* 1925. Boston. 1st ed. 2nd state. 451 p. VG. T5. $95.00

NEWTON, A.E. *I Want! I Want!* 1932. Daylesford, PA. private print. 1st ed. wraps. $12.00

NEWTON, A.E. *Magnificent Farce.* 1921. Boston. Ils. VG. $15.00

NEWTON, A.E. *Nelson.* 1928. Daylesford, PA. private print. 1st ed. wraps. $12.00

NEWTON, A.E. *Newton on Blackstone.* 1937. Phil. Ltd ed. inscr. dj. EX. $55.00

NEWTON, A.E. *Reprimand & What Came of It.* 1927. Daylesford, PA. private print. 1st ed. wraps. EX. $12.00

NEWTON, A.E. *Staffordshire.* 1935. Daylesford, PA. private print. 1st ed. wraps. $30.00

NEWTON, A.E. *This Book-Collecting Game.* 1928. Boston. Ltd ed. sgn. EX. $50.00

NEWTON, A.E. *This Book-Collecting Game.* 1928. Boston. 1st ed. VG. B2. $22.50

NEWTON, A.E. *Thomas Hardy, Novelist or Poet.* 1929. private print. 1/950. 4to. EX. $55.00

NEWTON, A.E. *Tourist in Spite of Himself.* 1920. Boston. Little Brown. 1st ed. 3rd imp. dj. $22.50

NEWTON, A.E. *Trollope Society.* 1934. Phil. private print. 1st ed. wraps. $12.00

NEWTON, H.J. *Yellow Gold of Cripple Creek, Romances & Anecdotes...* 1928. Denver. Ils. 128 p. wraps. VG. A3. $60.00

NEWTON, Helmut. *Women.* 1976. NY. 1st ed. 1st print. dj. EX. $70.00

NEWTON, Isaac. *Principia.* 1871. Glasgow. reprint of 1726 ed. Latin text. EX. $150.00

NEWTON, R.E. *Kittens & Puppies.* 1934. Racine. Whitman. Ils. 4to. EX. $17.50

NIBLICK. *Hints to Golfers.* 1903. Boston. Ltd ed. 1/489. 147 p. VG. $65.00

NICHERSON, R. *Sea Otters: Natural History & Guide.* 1984. Chronicle. photos. 110 p. EX. M2. $15.00

NICHOLAS, F.C. *Across Panama & Around the Caribbean.* 1909. Boston. Ils. photos. VG. $12.00

NICHOLAS, S.H. *Coshocton Co. Centennial History, 1811-1911.* 1911. Coshocton Co. 75 p. wraps. T5. $47.50

NICHOLL, L.T. *Collected Poems.* 1953. Dutton. Ltd ed. 1/746. sgn. dj. VG. $18.00

NICHOLS, Beverly. *Cats' ABC.* 1960. Ils Sayer. 1st Am ed. dj. EX. $25.00

NICHOLS, Beverly. *Crazy Pavements.* 1927. London. Cape. 1st ed. 4th print. VG. $20.00

NICHOLS, D. *Echinoderms.* 1966. London. Hutchinson. Revised 2nd ed. EX. M2. $18.00

NICHOLS, E.J. *Zach Taylor's Little Army.* 1963. Garden City. Ils 1st ed. 280 p. dj. VG. T5. $17.50

NICHOLS, G.W. *Story of Great March From Diary of Staff Officer.* 1865. NY. fld map. B1. $60.00

NICHOLS, J.D. *Demography of the Everglade Kite.* 1980. Elsevier. no cover. M2. $3.00

NICHOLS, John. *American Blood.* 1987. NY. Holt. 1st ed. dj. M. $10.00

NICHOLS, John. *Ghost in Music.* 1979. NY. UCP. mustard wraps. EX. $45.00

NICHOLS, John. *Ghost in Music.* 1979. NY. 1st ed. dj. EX. $25.00

NICHOLS, John. *Magic Journey.* 1978. NY. 1st ed. dj. EX. $55.00

NICHOLS, John. *Milagro Beanfield War.* 1974. NY. 1st ed. dj. VG. B2. $125.00

NICHOLS, John. *Sterile Cuckoo.* 1965. NY. 1st ed. sgn. dj. EX. $95.00

NICHOLS, John. *Wizard of Loneliness.* 1966. NY. 1st ed. dj. EX. $42.50

NICHOLS, R.L. *General Henry Atkinson: W Military Career.* 1965. Norman. Ils 1st ed. dj. EX. $35.00

NICHOLS & PRESLEY. *Please, Doctor, Do Something!* 1972. TX. sgn. $22.50

NICHOLSON, Arnold. *American Houses in History.* 1965. NY. dj. VG. J2. $15.00

NICHOLSON, George. *Illustrated Dictionary of Gardening.* c 1897. London/NY. 35 pls. 4to. 6 vols. A3. $275.00

NICHOLSON, I. *Mexican & Central American Mythology.* 1968. Hamlyn. Ils. 141 p. dj. EX. M2. $15.00

NICHOLSON, J.U. *Before Dawn.* 1926. not 1st ed. VG. C1. $7.50

NICHOLSON, J.U. *King of the Black Isles.* 1924. Chicago. 1st ed. VG. scarce. C1. $8.00

NICHOLSON, Meredith. *Siege of the Seven Suitors.* 1910. Boston. Ils Phillips. 1st ed. VG. $30.00

NICHOLSON, William. *Almanac of Twelve Sports With Words by R. Kipling.* 1898. NY. Ils bdg Russell. VG. $22.50

NICKLAUS, Jack. *My 55 Ways To Lower Scores.* 1964. NY. 1st ed. dj. VG. $15.00

NICOL, C.W. *Moving Zen.* 1975. NY. 1st ed. dj. VG. $10.00

NICOLAY, J.G. *Abraham Lincoln.* 1890. NY. 10 vols. M. $225.00

NICOLAY, J.G. *Lincoln's Secretary Goes W, Two Reports on Frontier...* 1965. La Crosse. Sumac. 1/500. dj. EX. $20.00

NICOLAY, J.G. *Outbreak of Rebellion.* 1881. NY. Ils 1st ed. 220 p. G. T5. $35.00

NICOLSON, Harold. *Byron: Last Journey.* 1924. Houghton. 1st Am ed. M. $50.00

NICOLSON, Nigel. *Great Houses of Britain.* 1965. NY. VG. J2. $15.00

NICOLSON, Nigel. *Great Houses of W World.* 1968. NY. dj. J2. $15.00

NIEBAUM, Gustave. *Discoveries of Norsemen on NE Coast of America.* 1910. London. 1st ed. EX. $30.00

NIEBUHR, Carsten. *Voyage en Arabie & en d'Autres Pays Circonvoisins.* 1776-1780. Amsterdam. Baalde. 2 vols. J2. $400.00

NIELSEN, Kay. *Twelve Dancing Princesses.* 1923. NY. 1st ed. 16 mounted pls. $125.00

NIELSEN, P. *Zoology of Iceland: Diptera.* 1954. Copenhagen. Ils. 189 p. M2. $5.00

NIEMOELLER, Adolph. *American Encyclopedia of Sex.* 1935. NY. Panurge. 277 p. EX. $20.00

NIERENDORF, Karl. *Paul Klee: Paintings & Watercolors of 1913-1939.* 1941. NY. Oxford U. Ils. spiral bdg. D2. $125.00

NIETZKI, D.A. *Elementa Pathologiae Universae.* 1766. Halae ad Salem. 8vo. new leather. $320.00

NIGHTINGALE, Florence. *Notes on Nursing.* 1860. NY. very scarce. K1. $55.00

NIKHILANDANDA, Swami. *Upanishads.* Vol. 1. 1949. NY. $17.50

NILES, H. *Nile's Weekly Register From September 1820 to March 1824.* 1824. Baltimore. Franklin Pr. orig bdg. A3. $50.00

NILES, John. *View of S America & Mexico.* 1826. NY. 2 vols in 1. VG. $85.00

NIMMO & UNGS. *American Political Patterns.* 1967. Boston. Little Brown. 1st ed. dj. $5.00

NIN, Anais. *Children of the Albatross.* 1947. NY. 1st ed. dj. VG. $20.00

NIN, Anais. *Children of the Albatross.* 1959. Swallow Pr. 8vo. wraps. M. $15.00

NIN, Anais. *D.H. Lawrence: Unprofessional Study.* 1932. Paris. Ltd ed. 1/500. $95.00

NIN, Anais. *D.H. Lawrence: Unprofessional Study.* 1964. Chicago. wraps. EX. $25.00

NIN, Anais. *Diary of Anais Nin.* 1966. Swallow. EX. $55.00

NIN, Anais. *House of Incest. Photomontages by Val Telberg.* 1961. Denver. Swallow. 72 p. wraps. $25.00

NIN, Anais. *Photographic Supplement to Diary of Anais Nin.* 1974. Harcourt. 1st Harvest ed. wraps. $45.00

NIN, Anais. *Spy in House of Love.* 1954. Franklin Lib. 1st ed. dj. VG. $37.50

NIN, Anais. *Under a Glass Bell.* 1944. NY. Gemor Pr. 1/300. thin 8vo. EX. $85.00

NIN, Anais. *Under a Glass Bell.* 1948. Ann Arbor. Stated 1st ed. 8vo. wraps. VG. $15.00

NISBETT, A. *Konrad Lorenz.* 1976. Harcourt. Review of 1st Am ed. 240 p. VG. M2. $13.00

NISSENSON, S.G. *Patroon's Domain.* 1937. Columbia. 1st ed. J2. $15.00

NIVEN, John. *Gideon Welles: Lincoln's Secretary of Navy.* 1973. Oxford. 1st ed. dj. J2. $20.00

NIVEN, Larry. *World Out of Time.* 1976. Holt. 1st ed. sgn. dj. EX. $25.00

NIX, E.D. *Oklahombres: Particularly the Wilder Ones.* 1929. np. 1st ed. photos. 280 p. VG. M2. $47.00

NIXDORFF, Henry M. *Life of Whittier's Heroine: Barbara Fritchie.* 1902. 3rd ed. 80 p. VG. very scarce. J4. $25.00

NIXON, J.L. *Seance.* 1982. Dell. 3rd ed. pb. VG. P1. $3.00

NIXON, P.H. *Lesotho Kimberlites.* 1973. Lesotho Nat Development Corp. dj. $35.00

NIXON, Pat. *Century of Medicine in San Antonio.* 1936. San Antonio. 1st ed. EX. $100.00

NIXON, R.M. *Challenges We Face.* 1st ed of 1st book. dj. VG. E2. $40.00

NIXON, R.M. *Memoirs of Richard Nixon.* Book Club. 1st ed. dj. EX. $37.00

NIXON, R.M. *Memoirs of Richard Nixon.* 1978. Grosset Dunlap. 1st ed. 1st print. dj. EX. $45.00

NIXON, R.M. *Real War.* 1980. NY. 1st ed. dj. EX. $15.00

NIXON, R.M. *Real War.* 1980. Warner. presentation. dj. M. $55.00

NIXON, R.M. *Six Crises.* 1962. NY. 1st ed. sgn. dj. M. $70.00

NIXON. *Five Centuries of English Bookbinding.* 1978. London. Ils 241 p. dj. VG. $55.00

NOAKES, Aubrey. *Ben Marshall.* 1978. Lewis/Tithe House. 1/500. D2. $65.00

NOAKES, Aubrey. *William Frith: Extraordinary Victorian Painter.* 1978. London. Jupiter. Ils. dj. D2. $30.00

NOBILE, Umberto *My Five Years With Soviet Airships.* 1987. Akron. Trans Fleetwood. 153 p. M. T5. $14.95

NOBLE, R.C. *Nature of the Beast.* 1945. Doubleday. photos. 224 p. G. M2. $5.00

NOBLE. *Forces of Production.* 1984. NY. dj. VG. $20.00

NOCK, O.S. *Encyclopedia of Railroads.* 1977. Ils. 480 p. $30.00

NOCK, O.S. *World Atlas of Railways.* 1983. Ils. maps. 225 p. $20.00

NODIER, Charles. *Woodcutter's Dog.* 1921. London. Ils Fraser. 18 p. G. $25.00

NOEL, B. *Sinbad the Sailor.* 1972. Doubleday. Ils 1st Am ed. VG. $14.00

NOEL, J. *Footloose in Arcadia.* 1940. San Francisco. 1st ed. 330 p. dj. VG. B2. $27.50

NOEL, Ruth. *Mythology of Middle Earth: Study of Tolkien's Mythology.* 1977. 1st ed. dj. VG. C1. $12.50

NOETZLI, E. *Practical Drapery Cutting.* 1906. London. 4to. VG. $35.00

NOLAN, A.T. *Iron Brigade.* 1961. NY. 1st ed. dj. $25.00

NOLAN, E.H. *Illustrated History of Empire in India & the E...* c 1860. London. Ils. maps. 8 vols. G. T5. $250.00

NOLAN, J.B. *SW PA.* 1943. Phil. 3 vols. EX. $80.00

NOLAND, C.F.M. *Pete Whetstone of Devils Fork.* 1957. Argus. 131 p. EX. M2. $10.00

NOLL, M. *Angling Success.* 1935. Macmillan. Ils. dj. EX. $12.50

NOMEROV, Howard. *Salt Garden.* 1955. NY. 1st ed. inscr. dj. VG. $50.00

NONESUCH PRESS. *Nonesuch Dickensiana.* 1937. Bloomsbury. Ils. 128 p. blue bdg. VG. $25.00

NONIS, U. *Mushrooms & Toadstools: Color Field Guide.* 1982. Hippocrene. 168 photos. 229 p. EX. M2. $11.00

NOORBERGEN, Rene. *Jean Dixon: My Life & Prophecies.* 1969. NY. $15.00

NORAN, D.K. *Ring.* 1988. Doubleday. UCP. VG. $12.00

NORDAY, Michael. *Dark Magic.* 1956. Modern Pr. dj. VG. P1. $11.50

NORDENSKIOLD, E. *History of Biology.* 1928. Tudor. 629 p. EX. M2. $30.00

NORDHOFF, Charles. *Peninsular CA.* 1888. NY. $20.00

NORDHOFF & HALL. *Dark River.* 1938. Boston. AP. 1st ed. 336 p. white wraps. G. T1. $75.00

NORDHOFF & HALL. *Falcons of France.* 1930. Boston. 8th print. sgns. 332 p. VG. B2. $25.00

NORDHOFF & JAMES. *Mutiny on the Bounty.* NY. Large type ed. 4to. dj. T1. $45.00

NORDHOLL, Charles. *Communistic Societies of the US.* 1962. NY. Ils. 8vo. dj. EX. T1. $35.00

NORMAN, B. *Footsteps.* 1988. Salem House. 1st Am ed. 279 p. dj. M. M2. $28.00

NORMAN, Charles. *Magic Maker: E.E. Cummings.* 1958. NY. 1st ed. EX. $27.50

NORMAN, Philip. *London Signs & Inscriptions.* 1893. Elliot Stock. 1st ed. J2. $20.00

NORMAN, Vesey. *Arms & Armor.* 1972. London. Ils. dj. M. C1. $15.00

NORMAN, W.M. *Portion of My Life.* 1959. 242 p. dj. EX. J4. $7.50

NORMAN & FRASER. *Giant Fishes, Whales & Dolphins.* 1938. Norton. Ils 1st ed. 361 p. dj. EX. M2. $15.00

NORMAND, Charles. *J.B. Greuze.* 1892. Paris. Ils. 116 p. D2. $55.00

NORRIS, C. *Last of the Scottsboro Boys.* 1979. NY. Ils 1st ed. 281 p. dj. VG. B2. $17.50

NORRIS, Charles. *Easter Upland Shooting.* 1946. Phil. 1st ed. dj. VG. $65.00

NORRIS, Frank. *Deal in Wheat.* 1903. Doubleday Page. Ils Remington/others. VG. $45.00

NORRIS, Frank. *Moran of the Lady Letty.* 1898. Doubleday McClure. 1st ed. $35.00

NORRIS, Frank. *Octopus: Story of CA.* 1901. NY. 1st ed. VG. P3. $35.00

NORRIS, Frank. *Pit.* 1903. NY. EX. $45.00

NORRIS, Kathleen. *Foolish Virgin.* 1938. Doubleday Doran. 1st ed. $12.00

NORRIS, Kathleen. *Red Silence.* 1929. Doubleday Doran. 1st ed. $12.00

NORRIS, Kathleen. *Rose of the World.* 1924. Doubleday Page. Ils Gilbert. 1st ed. $12.00

NORRIS, Kathleen. *Venables.* 1941. Doubleday Doran. 1st ed. $12.00

NORROENA SOCIETY. *Flatey Book.* 1906. Copenhagen. $35.00

NORSE, Harold. *Hotel Nirvana.* 1974. City Lights. 1st ed. sgns. wraps. EX. $40.00

NORSE, Harold. *Roman Sonnets of G.G. Belli.* 1960. William. 1st ed. wraps. EX. $25.00

NORTH, John. *Alexander Memoirs, 1940-1945.* 1962. London. 1st ed. photos. maps. 208 p. dj. T5. $19.50

NORTH, Marianne. *Vision of Eden: Life & Work of Marianne N.* 1980. Holt. 1st ed. dj. VG. J2. $20.00

NORTH, Sterling. *Little Rascal.* 1965. Dutton. xl. G. $10.00

NORTH, Sterling. *So Dear to My Heart.* 1947. NY. 1st ed. sgn Walt Disney. dj. EX. scarce. $75.00

NORTH, Sterling. *Speak of the Devil.* nd. Book Club. VG. P1. $6.00

NORTHCOTE, H.S. *Churchill: Man of Destiny.* nd. (1963?) London. Newnes. wraps. VG. D1. $15.00

NORTHCOTT, Clarence. *Australian Social Development.* 1918. Columbia. 1st ed. 302 p. wraps. VG. J2. $15.00

NORTHCROFT, G.J.H. *Sketches of Summerland...* 1906. Nassau. Ils. pb. $12.00

NORTHEN, R.T. *Orchids As House Plants.* 1955. Van Nostrand. Ils. 122 p. VG. M2. $5.00

NORTHEND, Charles. *Book of Epitaphs: Amusing, Quaint.* 1873. NY. 1st ed. 171 p. EX. $55.00

NORTHROP, H.D. *Flowery Kingdom & Land of the Mikado, China, Japan & Korea.* 1894. Phil. Ils. 4to. gilt cloth. T1. $65.00

NORTHRUP, Solomon. *Twelve Years a Slave.* 1968. Baton Rouge. Ils. 273 p. dj. $15.00

NORTON, Andre. *Dragon Magic.* 1973. not 1st ed. pb. VG. C1. $2.50

NORTON, Andre. *Exiles of the Stars.* 1971. Viking. 1st ed. dj. EX. $40.00

NORTON, Andre. *Fur Magic.* 1968. Cleveland. World. 1st ed. dj. EX. $40.00

NORTON, Andre. *Iron Cage.* 1974. NY. 1st ed. dj. VG. $35.00

NORTON, Andre. *Merlin's Mirror.* pb. VG. C1. $2.50

NORTON, Andre. *Plague Ship.* 1956. NY. Gnome. 1st ed. dj. EX. $17.50

NORTON, Andre. *Small Shadows Creep.* 1974. Dutton. 1st ed. dj. EX. P1. $11.50

NORTON, Andre. *Steel Magic.* 1965. World. Ils Jaques. 1st ed. dj. EX. C1. $12.50

NORTON, Andre. *Tales of Witch World.* 1987. NY. 1st ed. sgn. dj. M. $25.00

NORTON, Andre. *Victory on Janus.* 1967. Gollanz. 1st ed. dj. EX. $25.00

NORTON, B. *Snake River Wilderness.* 1972. Sierra Club. photos. map. 159 p. EX. M2. $9.00

NORTON, F. *Illustrated Historical Register of Centennial Exhibition...* 1879. NY. 25 color pls. folio. $110.00

NORTON, S.V. *Motor Truck As an Aid to Business.* 1918. Chicago. Ils 1st ed. 4to. 509 p. dj. VG. T1. $75.00

NORTON, T.E. *Fur Trade in Colonial NY.* 1974. Madison. 1st ed. EX. $15.00

NORTON, Wesley. *Religious Newspapers in the Old NW of 1861.* 1977. Athens, OH. 196 p. dj. VG. T5. $7.50

NORWOOD. *Sketches of Brooks (ME) History.* 1935. Ils. presentation. G. $50.00

NOTT, C.C. *Sketches in Prison Camps.* 1865. NY. 204 p. EX. K1. $35.00

NOVAK, V.I.A. *Insect Hormones.* 1966. London. Methuen. 478 p. dj. EX. M2. $17.00

NOWARRA, H.J. *Von Richtofen & the Flying Circus.* 1959. Letchworth. Revised 2nd ed. 4to. 208 p. dj. T5. $45.00

NOWELL, Elizabeth. *Letters of Thomas Wolfe.* 1st ed. dj. EX. B7. $35.00

NOWELL-SMITH, Simon. *Edwardian England, 1901-1914.* 1964. Oxford. 1st ed. dj. VG. J2. $20.00

NOWLIN, William. *Bark-Covered House; or, Back in Woods Again.* 1937. Chicago. Lakeside Classic. 342 p. T5. $30.00

NOYES, P.B. *My Father's House.* 1933. Farrar Rinehart. Ils. photos. sgn. $22.00

NOYES, P.B. *My Father's House.* 1937. NY. Ils. photos. sgn. 312 p. dj. B2. $17.50

NOZIERE, Fernand. *Three Gallant Plays.* 1929. NY. Rudge. Trans Stratton. $6.00

NUTT, Alfred. *Fairy Mythology of Shakespeare.* 1900. London. 1st ed. VG. rare. C1. $19.50

NUTT, Alfred. *Ossian & the Ossianic Literature.* 1910. London. 2nd ed. VG. rare. C1. $19.50

NUTT, Alfred. *Studies on Legend of Holy Grail With Reference to Origin.* 1888. London. Nutt. 1st ed. VG. rare. C1. $145.00

NUTTALL, T. *Journal of Travels Into AK During the Year 1819.* 1980. OK U. Ils 1st ed. 361 p. dj. EX. M2. $25.00

NUTTING, Wallace. *Autobiography.* 1936. Framingham. Ils 1st ed. 295 p. dj. VG. B2. $27.50

NUTTING, Wallace. *Final Edition Furniture Catalog.* 1937. Framingham. Ils. 8vo. 136 p. wraps. VG. B1. $60.00

NUTTING, Wallace. *Furniture Treasury.* 1954. Macmillan. Ils. 2 vols in 1. dj. EX. $25.00

NUTTING, Wallace. *Ireland Beautiful.* 1925. Garden City. Ils 1st ed. T6. $25.00

NUTTING, Wallace. *Ireland Beautiful.* 1925. Garden City. Ils 1st ed. 4to. 294 p. xl. $12.00

NUTTING, Wallace. *MA Beautiful.* VG. S2. $35.00

NUTTING, Wallace. *PA Beautiful.* VG. S2. $35.00

NUTTING, Wallace. *VT Beautiful.* VG. S2. $35.00

NYE, Bill. *Bill Nye's Comic History of US.* 1906. Chicago. Ils Opper. G. $12.00

NYE, Bill. *Remarks.* 1896. NY. VG. $25.00

NYE, N.C. *Complete Guide of Quarter Horse.* 1967. Barnes. Ils 3rd print. dj. VG. $17.00

NYE, Robert. *Beowulf.* 1968. NY. Hill Wang. Ils Cober. 1st Am ed. dj. VG. C1. $14.50

NYE, Robert. *Taliesin.* 1967. NY. Hill Wang. Ils Maas. 1st Am ed. dj. VG. C1. $24.00

NYE, W.S. *Bad Medicine & Good.* 1962. OK U. Ils 1st ed. dj. VG. $15.00

NYE, W.S. *Carbine & Lance: Story of Old Ft. Sill.* 1942. Norman. Ils. maps. 345 p. dj. T5. $17.50

NYGARRD, Norman. *Walter Knott: 20th-C Pioneer.* 1965. Ils. 118 p. $10.50

NYSTROM, Daniel. *Ministry of Printing.* 1962. Rock Island. Augustana. photos. dj. EX. $20.00

O

O'BRIEN, C.C. *To Katanga & Back.* 1962. London. 1st ed. dj. VG. $20.00

O'BRIEN, Edna. *Casualties of Peace.* 1966. London. 1st ed. dj. EX. $30.00

O'BRIEN, Edna. *Tales for the Telling: Irish Folk & Fairy Stories.* 1986. NY. Ils Foreman. EX. $7.50

O'BRIEN, Jack. *Return of Silver Chief.* 1943. Phil. Ils Wiese. dj. EX. $7.50

O'BRIEN, Jack. *Silver Chief to the Rescue.* 1937. Phil. Ils Wiese. 1st ed. dj. EX. $7.50

O'BRIEN, Jack. *Silver Chief: Dog of the N.* 1933. Phil. Ils Wiese. 1st ed. dj. VG. $7.50

O'BRIEN, T. *If I Die in a Combat Zone.* 1972. London. dj. EX. $35.00

O'BRIEN, T.M. *Guardians of the Eighth Sea: History of US Coast Guard...* nd. (1976) np. (WA) Ils. 97 p. VG. T5. $9.50

O'CASEY, Sean. *Irish Fallen, Fare Thee Well.* 1949. NY. 1st ed. 396 p. dj. VG. $8.00

O'CONNOR, Flannery. *Everything That Rises Must Converge.* 1965. Farrar Straus. 2nd print. dj. $32.50

O'CONNOR, Flannery. *Memoir of Mary Ann.* 1961. NY. 1st ed. dj. EX. $20.00

O'CONNOR, Flannery. *Mystery & Manners.* 1st ed. dj. VG. B7. $30.00

O'CONNOR, Frank. *Set of Variations.* 1969. NY. 1st ed. dj. EX. $22.50

O'CONNOR, G.W. *Railroads of NY.* 1949. 1st ed. VG. $25.00

O'CONNOR, Harvey. *Empire of Oil.* 1955. NY. inscr. dj. VG. $25.00

O'CONNOR, Harvey. *Revolution in Seattle.* 1964. NY. 1st ed. sgn. dj. VG. $35.00

O'CONNOR, Harvey. *Steel Dictator.* 1935. dj. VG. $20.00

O'CONNOR, Jack. *Game in the Desert.* 1939. Derrydale. 1/950. snakeskin bdg. boxed. $375.00

O'CONNOR, Jack. *Hunting in the Rockies.* 1947. NY. 1st ed. VG. B2. $115.00

O'CONNOR, Jack. *Hunting Rifle.* 1970. NY. 1st ed. dj. VG. $20.00

O'CONNOR, Jack. *Shotgun Book.* 1965. NY. 1st ed. dj. VG. $18.00

O'CONNOR, Jean. *Horse & Buggy W.* 1st ed. dj. VG. B2. $60.00

O'CONNOR, Mary. *Vanishing Swede.* 1905. NY. 1st ed. G. $5.00

O'CONNOR, P.F. *Shark!* 1954. Norton. 1st Am ed. 255 p. VG. M2. $10.00

O'CONNOR, Richard. *Johnstown: Day the Dam Broke.* 1957. 1st ed. 55 p. $14.50

O'CONNOR, Richard. *Thomas Rock of Chickamauga.* 1948. NY. 1st ed. dj. VG. B2. $35.00

O'CROULEY, Pedro Alonso. *Description of the Kingdom of New Spain, 1774.* 1972. San Francisco. Howell Books. Ils. maps. D2. $175.00

O'DONNELL, Elliott. *Casebook of Ghosts.* 1969. Taplinger. dj. xl. P1. $7.00

O'DONNELL, Elliott. *Werewolves.* 1912. London. Methuen. 1st ed. 292 p. $55.00

O'FAOLAIN, Eileen. *Irish Sagas & Folk Tales.* c 1982. reprint of 1954 ed. dj. EX. C1. $10.00

O'FAOLAIN, S. *Come Back to Erin.* 1940. London. 1st ed. dj. VG. $35.00

O'FARRELL, Eddy. *Ghost Came Twice.* 1970. Bee-Line. VG. P1. $7.50

O'FLAHERTY, Liam. *Fairy Goose.* 1927. NY. Ltd 1st ed. sgn. 12mo. $55.00

O'FLAHERTY, Liam. *Hollywood Cemetery.* 1935. London. Gollancz. dj. VG. $135.00

O'FLAHERTY, Liam. *Red Barbara & Other Stories.* 1928. Gaige/Faber. 1st ed. 1/600. sgn. VG. $80.00

O'HARA, C.C. *Mineral Wealth of the Black Hills.* 1902. Rapid City. SD School Mines. wraps. fair. $17.50

O'HARA, Frank. *Jackson Pollock.* 1959. NY. Braziller. Ils. 125 p. $30.00

O'HARA, Frank. *Lovey Childs.* 1969. NY. Ltd 1st ed. 1/200. sgn. slipcase. EX. $75.00

O'HARA, John. *Appointment in Samarra.* 1934. NY. Harcourt. 1st trade ed. 8vo. dj. EX. $40.00

O'HARA, John. *Big Laugh.* 1962. NY. dj. VG. $9.00

O'HARA, John. *Family Party.* 1956. Random House. 1st ed. dj. EX. $30.00

O'HARA, John. *From the Terrace.* 1958. Random House. 1st ed. dj. EX. $25.00

O'HARA, John. *Sermons & Soda Water.* 1960. NY. 1st Am ed. 3 vols. boxed. VG. $30.00

O'HARA, John. *Sermons & Soda Water.* 1960. NY. 1st ed. sgn. 3 vols. slipcase. EX. $45.00

O'HARA, John. *Waiting for Winter.* 1966. Random House. 1st ed. dj. EX. $20.00

O'KANE, Walter. *Injurious Insects.* 1912. NY. VG. $20.00

O'KANE, Walter. *Intimate Desert.* 1969. AZ U. Ils. dj. EX. $10.00

O'MALLEY, Charles. *Leonardo Da Vinci on the Human Body.* 1952. Schuman. 1st ed. VG. J2. $25.00

O'MERA, Walter. *Duke of War.* 1966. 1st Am ed. dj. VG. scarce. C1. $29.50

O'NEAL, Hank. *Berenice Abbott: American Photographer.* 1982. NY. dj. VG. $45.00

O'NEAL, James. *Workers in American History.* 1921. NY. 4th ed. G. $18.00

O'NEALL, J.B. *Annals of Newberry in Two Parts.* 1949. Newberry. reprint of 1892 ed. rebound. $85.00

O'NEALL, J.B. *Biographical Sketches of Bench & Bar of SC.* 1859. Charleston. Ils 1st ed. 614 p. $250.00

O'NEILL, Eugene. *Ah, Wilderness.* 1933. NY. Ltd 1st ed. 1/325. sgn. $175.00

O'NEILL, Eugene. *Ah, Wilderness.* 1933. Random House. 1st ed. dj. EX. $45.00

O'NEILL, Eugene. *Ah, Wilderness.* 1972. Ltd Ed Club. Ils/sgn Sterneveis. slipcase. $60.00

O'NEILL, Eugene. *Anna Christie.* 1930. Liveright. Ils King. sgn. dj. EX. $225.00

O'NEILL, Eugene. *Dynamo.* 1929. Liveright. Ltd ed. 1/775. sgn. slipcase. EX. $245.00

O'NEILL, Eugene. *Emperor Jones, Diff'rent, Straw.* 1921. NY. 1st ed. 1st issue. VG. $75.00

O'NEILL, Eugene. *Emperor Jones.* 1928. Liveright. Ils King. 1/775. sgn. 4to. EX. $150.00

O'NEILL, Eugene. *Hughie.* 1962. London. 1st ed. dj. M. P3. $35.00

O'NEILL, Eugene. *Hughie: New One-Act Play.* 1959. New Haven. 1st ed. dj. VG. $18.00

O'NEILL, Eugene. *Iceman Cometh.* Ltd Ed Club. slipcase. M. B3. $60.00

O'NEILL, Eugene. *Lazarus Laughed.* 1927. Boni Liveright. 1st Am ed. 1/775. sgn. dj. VG. $135.00

O'NEILL, Eugene. *Lost Plays.* 1964. NY. 1st ed. dj. VG. $15.00

O'NEILL, Eugene. *Moon for the Misbegotten: Play.* 1952. NY. 1st ed. dj. EX. $75.00

O'NEILL, Eugene. *Plays of Eugene O'Neill (in 12 Vols.).* 1934-1935. NY. Wilderness ed. 1/775. sgn. djs. M. $800.00

O'NEILL, Eugene. *Strange Interlude.* 1928. NY. Ltd 1st ed. 1/775. wraps. boxed. $175.00

O'NEILL, Eugene. *Touch of the Poet.* 1957. New Haven. 1st ed. dj. EX. $400.00

O'NEILL, H. *Complete Poems & Stories of Poe.* 1946. Borzoi. 2 vols. blue cloth. boxed. VG. D1. $40.00

O'NEILL, Rose. *Loves of Edwy.* 1904. Boston. Ils 1st ed. EX. $45.00

O'REILLY, Maurice. *Goodyear Story.* 1983. Elmsford, NY. Ils 1st ed. photos. VG. T5. $15.00

O'REILLY, R.A. *Field List of Birds of Detroit-Windsor Region.* 1960. Cranbrook Inst. M2. $5.00

O'ROURKE, Frank. *E Company.* 1945. NY. Ils Glen Rounds. 166 p. G. T5. $12.50

O'SHERIDAN, Mary. *Gaelic Folk Tales.* c 1910. Chicago. Revised ed. VG. C1. $10.00

O'SULLIVAN, Maurice. *Twenty Years A-Growing.* 1933. Chatto Windus. 1st ed. 1st print. dj. EX. $85.00

OAKDEAN, J.P. *Alliterative Poetry in Middle English.* 1935. Manchester U. VG. scarce. C1. $49.50

OAKENFULL, J.C. *Brazil in 1911.* 1912. London. 3rd ed. fld map. VG. $60.00

OAKLEY, Amy. *Behold the W Indies.* 1951. NY. Ils Thornton Oakley. dj. VG. $12.00

OAKLEY, Violet. *Samuel F.B. Morse.* 1939. Cogslea. Ils/sgn Oakley. 8vo. VG. G2. $30.00

OAKLEY, Violet. *Samuel F.B. Morse.* 1939. Phil. Cogslea. 1/500. sgn. 97 p. T5. $75.00

OATES, J.C. *Angel Fire.* 1973. Baton Rouge. 1st ed. sgn. dj. VG. $45.00

OATES, J.C. *Cupid & Psyche.* 1970. Albadacondi Pr. 1/200. sgn/#d. EX. $50.00

OATES, J.C. *Invisible Woman: New & Selected Poems, 1970-1982.* 1982. Princeton. 1st ed. 1/300. sgn. slipcase. EX. $75.00

OATES, J.C. *Love & Its Derangements. Poems by Joyce Carol Oates.* nd. 1st ed. inscr. dj. EX. $40.00

OATES, S.B. *To Purge This Land With Blood.* 1970. 434 p. dj. EX. J4. $20.00

OBERDORFER, D. *Tet.* 1971. NY. 1st ed. dj. VG. $35.00

OERTER, M.F. *Centennial History of Sharon Moravian Church, 1815-1915.* nd. Canal Dover, OH. 36 p. wraps. T5. $8.50

OESTERLEY, W.O.E. *Hebrew Religion: Its Origin & Development.* 1930. NY. 1st ed. G. $7.50

OFFICER, H.R. *Australian Honey Eaters.* 1965. Bird Observers. Ils. map. 83 p. dj. EX. M2. $35.00

OGBURN, C. *Adventure of the Birds.* 1976. dj. EX. $5.00

OGDEN & NELSON. *Uniforms of the US Army.* 1959. NY. Oasis. 1/60. folio. boxed. EX. $250.00

OGILVIE, M. *Wildfowl of Britain & Europe.* 1982. Oxford U. Ils Cusa/Scott. map. 84 p. dj. M2. $25.00

OGILVIE, M. & C. *Flamingos.* 1986. Sutton. Ils 1st ed. 121 p. dj. M. M2. $15.00

OGILVY, J.S. *Relics & Memorials of London City.* 1910. London. 64 color pls. blue cloth. VG. J2. $35.00

OGILVY, J.S. *Relics & Memorials of London Town.* 1911. London. TEG. green cloth. VG. J2. $35.00

OH LIBRARY FOUNDATION. *Federal Population Census, 1830.* 1976. Columbus. reprint of 1964 ed. 2 vols. xl. T5. $47.50

OHWI, J. *Flora of Japan.* 1965. Smithsonian. Ils. 1067 p. EX. M2. $95.00

OKEY, T. *Venice & Its Story.* 1903. London. Ils Ward/others. 1/250. 4to. EX. $95.00

OLCOTT, Anthony. *May Day in Magadan.* 1983. NY. 1st ed. dj. EX. $15.00

OLDENBURG, C.W. *Leaps of Faith.* 1985. Pepper Pike. Ils. 4to. 183 p. dj. T5. $6.50

OLDENBURG, Claes. *Drawings & Prints.* 1969. Chelsea House. 1st ed. dj. EX. $75.00

OLDENBURG, Claes. *Store Days.* 1967. Something Else. dj. EX. $50.00

OLDER, Mrs. Fremont. *CA Missions & Their Romances.* 1939. Coward McCann. New ed. dj. EX. $25.00

OLDROYD, I.S. *Marine Shells of W Coast of N America.* 1924-1927. 164 pls. 4 vols. rebound. EX. M2. $265.00

OLDS, Sharon. *Dead & the Living.* 1983. NY. 1st Am ed. dj. VG. $25.00

OLENDORFF, R.R. *Golden Eagle Country.* 1975. Knopf. Ils 1st ed. 4to. 202 p. dj. EX. M2. $18.00

OLIN, Oscar Eugene. *Akron & Environs.* 1917. Chicago. 1st ed. full leather. scarce. T5. $95.00

OLIPHANT, Laurence. *Makers of Florence: Dante, Giotto & Savonrola & Their City.* 1889. London/NY. Ils Jeens/Delamotte. vellum bdg. $200.00

OLIPHANT, Laurence. *MN: Far W.* 1855. Edinburgh. 1st ed. 7 pls. fld map. $62.50

OLIVA, Leo. *Soldiers on the Santa Fe Trail.* 1967. Norman. 1st ed. dj. EX. $22.00

OLIVER, Andrew. *Portraits of John & Abigail Adams.* 1967. Harvard U. Ils. 284 p. dj. K1. $12.50

OLIVER, Basil. *Renaissance of English Public House.* 1947. Faber. 1st ed. dj. VG. J2. $20.00

OLIVER, E.R. *Journal of an Aleutian Year.* 1988. WA U. photos. maps. 248 p. EX. M2. $10.00

OLIVER, Laurence. *Confessions of an Actor.* 1st ed. sgn. dj. VG. B2. $35.00

OLIVER, Laurence. *Confessions of an Actor.* 1982. NY. 1st ed. dj. VG. B2. $20.00

OLIVER, Leon. *Great Sensation.* 1873. Chicago. Ils 1st ed. 360 p. G. T5. $35.00

OLIVER, Paul. *Shelter, Sign & Symbol.* 1977. NY. Woodstock. black cloth. dj. EX. J2. $25.00

OLIVER, R. *Sir Harry Johnston & Scramble for Africa.* 1957. Chatto Windus. Ils. 368 p. VG. M2. $19.00

OLMSTED, F.L. *Journey in the Back Country: Cotton Kingdom Through TX.* 1860. NY. 492 p. $60.00

OLMSTED, F.L. *Journey in the Seaboard States.* 1856. NY. 1st ed. 723 p. xl. K1. $35.00

OLMSTED, J.M.D. *Claude Bernard, Physiologist.* 1938. NY. sgn. 272 p. xl. $25.00

OLSHAN, Joseph. *Clara's Heart.* 1985. Arbor House. 1st ed. dj. EX. T6. $15.00

OLSON, H.W. *Earthworms of OH.* 1928. OH Biol Survey. maps. M2. $5.00

OLSON, John E. *Andersonville of the Pacific.* 1985. Lake Quivira. Ils. 249 p. dj. T5. $12.50

OLSON, Sigurd. *Listening Point.* 1958. NY. 1st ed. dj. VG. B2. $20.00

OLSON, Sigurd. *Lonely Land.* 1961. Knopf. 1st ed. dj. VG. J2. $20.00

OLSON, Sigurd. *Singing Wilderness.* 1956. Knopf. 1st ed. dj. VG. J2. $25.00

OLSON, Sigurd. *Wilderness Days.* 1972. Knopf. Ils 1st ed. maps. dj. EX. M2. $18.00

OLSON, Tilly. *Tell Me a Riddle.* 1978. New ed. 1/100. sgn. boxed. M. $60.00

OMEROD, H.A. *Piracy in the Ancient World: Essay on Mediterranean History.* 1967. Argonaut. 1st ed. dj. J2. $15.00

OMMANNEY, F.D. *Fishes.* 1977. Time Life. color photos. 4to. 192 p. VG. M2. $7.00

ONDAATJE, Michael. *Collected Works of Billy the Kid.* 1974. NY. 1st Am ed. EX. $20.00

ONDAATJE, Michael. *There's a Trick With a Knife I'm Learning To Do.* 1979. NY. 1st ed. inscr. dj. VG. $65.00

ONDERDONK, Elmer. *Genealogy of Onderdonk Family in America.* 1910. NY. VG. $35.00

ONIONS, Oliver. *Das Bemalte Geisicht.* 1982. Bastei Luebbe. German text. EX. P1. $4.00

ONO, Yoko. *Grapefruit.* 1970. NY. 1st ed. dj. VG. $15.00

OPARIN, A.I. *Genesis & Evolutionary Development of Life.* 1968. Academic Pr. 203 p. EX. M2. $22.00

OPARIN, A.I. *Origin of Life.* 1953. Dover. 270 p. VG. M2. $15.00

OPPE, A. *Sandro Botticelli.* 1913. Paris. 25 color pls. 4to. VG. J2. $60.00

OPPENHEIM, E.P. *Battle of Basinghall.* c 1935. Boston. Little Brown. 1st ed. VG. $8.00

OPPENHEIM, E.P. *Golden Beast.* c 1926. Boston. Little Brown. 1st ed. VG. $8.00

OPPENHEIM, E.P. *Great Prince Shan.* c 1922. Boston. Little Brown. 1st ed. VG. $10.00

OPPENHEIM, E.P. *Havoc.* 1911. Little Brown. Ils Christy. VG. $20.00

OPPENHEIM, E.P. *Milan Grill Room.* 1941. Boston. 1st ed. dj. VG. $20.00

OPPENHEIM, E.P. *Quest for Winter Sunshine.* 1927. Boston. 161 p. $15.00

OPPENHEIM, E.P. *Shy Plutocrat.* 1941. NY/Boston. 1st ed. dj. VG. $20.00

OPPENHEIM, E.P. *Up the Ladder of Gold.* c 1931. Boston. Little Brown. 1st ed. VG. $8.00

OPPENHEIMER, H.L. *March to the Sound of the Drums.* 1966. Danville, IL. 2nd print. sgn. 333 p. dj. VG. T5. $19.50

OPUSCULO. *El Catolicismo y las Corridas de Toros.* 1887. Mexico City. VG. $50.00

ORCHARD, Harry. *Confessions & Autobiography of Harry Orchard.* 1907. NY. McClure. VG. scarce. $75.00

ORCUTT, Samuel. *History of Town of Wolcott, CT, From 1731-1874.* 1874. Waterbury, CT. 608 p. rebound. G. T5. $45.00

ORCUTT, W.D. *Flower of Destiny.* 1905. McClurg. Ils Weber. G. $32.50

ORCUTT, W.D. *Flower of Destiny.* 1905. McClurg. Ils Weber. 1st ed. M. $125.00

ORCUTT, W.D. *From My Library Walls: Kaleidoscope of Memories.* 1946. London. 1st ed. dj. $40.00

ORCUTT, W.D. *Wallace Clement Sabine.* 1933. Plimpton Pr. presentation. sgn. 376 p. EX. $85.00

ORCZY, Baroness. *Beau Brocade.* nd. London. reprint. dj. VG. $12.50

ORCZY, Baroness. *Castles in the Air.* nd. London. Cheap ed. dj. VG. $12.50

ORCZY, Baroness. *Castles in the Air.* 1921. London. 1st ed. VG. $25.00

ORCZY, Baroness. *Celestial City.* nd. London. 1st ed. VG. $25.00

ORCZY, Baroness. *Divine Folly.* 1937. London. 1st ed. dj. VG. $45.00

ORCZY, Baroness. *Eldorado.* nd. London. reprint. dj. VG. $15.00

ORCZY, Baroness. *Elusive Pimpernel.* 1908. London. 1st ed. G. $40.00

ORCZY, Baroness. *Emperor's Candlesticks.* nd. London. reprint. dj. VG. $12.50

ORCZY, Baroness. *Fire in Stubble.* 1912. London. 1st ed. VG. $25.00

ORCZY, Baroness. *His Majesty's Well Beloved.* nd. London. reprint. dj. VG. $12.50

ORCZY, Baroness. *His Majesty's Well Beloved.* nd. London. 1st ed. VG. $25.00

ORCZY, Baroness. *Honorable Jim.* nd. London. 1st ed. dj. EX. $75.00

ORCZY, Baroness. *I Will Repay.* nd. London. reprint. dj. VG. $12.50

ORCZY, Baroness. *Laughing Cavalier.* 1914. London. 1st ed. VG. $25.00

ORCZY, Baroness. *Leatherface.* 1916. London. 1st ed. VG. $25.00

ORCZY, Baroness. *Leatherface.* 1916. NY. dj. VG. $20.00

ORCZY, Baroness. *Meadowsweet.* nd. London. reprint. dj. VG. $12.50

ORCZY, Baroness. *Meadowsweet.* 1912. London. 1st ed. VG. $25.00

ORCZY, Baroness. *Nest of the Sparrow Hawk.* 1909. London. 1st ed. VG. $35.00

ORCZY, Baroness. *Nicolette.* nd. London. dj. VG. $12.50

ORCZY, Baroness. *No Greater Love.* 1938. London. 1st ed. dj. VG. $45.00

ORCZY, Baroness. *Petticoat Government.* 1910. London. 1st ed. VG. $25.00

ORCZY, Baroness. *Pride of Race.* 1942. London. 1st ed. G. $17.50

ORCZY, Baroness. *Scarlet Pimpernel.* nd. London. reprint. dj. VG. $12.50

ORCZY, Baroness. *Scarlet Pimpernel.* nd. London. 1st ed. VG. $40.00

ORCZY, Baroness. *Sheaf of Bluebells.* 1917. London. 1st ed. EX. $30.00

ORCZY, Baroness. *Sir Percy Hits Back.* nd. London. reprint. dj. VG. $12.50

ORCZY, Baroness. *Sir Percy Hits Back.* nd. London. 1st ed. VG. $35.00

ORCZY, Baroness. *Sir Percy Leads the Band.* 1939. London. 1st ed. VG. $35.00

ORCZY, Baroness. *Spy of Napoleon.* nd. London. reprint. dj. VG. $12.50

ORCZY, Baroness. *Spy of Napoleon.* 1934. London. 1st ed. VG. $25.00

ORCZY, Baroness. *Triumph of the Scarlet Pimpernel.* nd. London. reprint. dj. VG. $12.50

ORCZY, Baroness. *True Woman.* nd. London. reprint. dj. VG. $12.50

ORCZY, Baroness. *True Woman.* 1911. London. 1st ed. VG. $25.00

ORCZY, Baroness. *Uncrowned King.* 1935. London. 1st ed. dj. EX. $45.00

ORCZY, Baroness. *Uncrowned King.* 1935. London. 1st ed. VG. $20.00

ORCZY, Baroness. *Unto Ceasar.* nd. London. 1st ed. G. $20.00

ORCZY, Baroness. *Way of the Scarlet Pimpernel.* nd. London. reprint. dj. VG. $12.50

ORCZY, Baroness. *Will O' the Wisp.* nd. London. 1st ed. dj. VG. $35.00

ORGEL, Irene. *Old Tales of Irene Orgel.* 1966. NY. 1st ed. inscr. dj. EX. $12.00

ORIANS, G. *Blackbirds of the Americas.* 1985. WA U. Ils Tony Angell. 4to. dj. M. M2. $25.00

ORLIAC, Antoine. *Veronese.* 1940. London/Paris. Trans Chamot. dj. VG. $35.00

ORLOVSKY, Peter. *Lepers Cry.* 1972. Phoenix. 1/26. sgn/lettered. wraps. EX. $35.00

ORMOND, Clyde. *Bear!* 1961. Stackpole. dj. VG. $20.00

ORMOND, Clyde. *Hunting Our Biggest Game.* 1956. Harrisburg. Ils 1st ed. 197 p. dj. VG. B2. $40.00

ORMOND, Clyde. *Hunting Our Medium-Sized Game.* 1958. Harrisburg. dj. VG. $12.50

ORMONDROYD. *David & the Phoenix.* 1957. Follett. dj. VG. $17.50

ORMSBY. *History of the Whig Party.* 1859. Boston. Crosby Nichols. 8vo. G. $15.00

ORNITZ, Samuel. *Allrightniks Row: Haunch, Paunch & Jowl; Making of a Jew.* 1985. reprint of 1923 ed. dj. M. $10.00

ORR, A. *World in Amber.* 1986. not 1st ed. VG. C1. $4.00

ORR, Dorothy. *History of Education of GA.* 1950. Chapel Hill. Ils 1st ed. 463 p. dj. EX. $30.00

ORR, R.T. *Animals in Migration.* 1970. Macmillan. Review 1st ed. 303 p. dj. M2. $11.00

ORR. *Handbook to Browning's Works.* 1930. London. Bell. G. $15.00

ORTON, J. *Andes & the Amazon: Across the Continent of S America.* 1870. Harper. Ils 356 p. fld map. dj. VG. M2. $70.00

ORTON, J.R. *Campfires of the Redmen; or, A Hundred Years Ago.* 1855. NY. Derby. Ils 1st ed. 401 p. A3. $60.00

ORVIS & CHENEY. *Fishing With the Fly.* 1898. Boston. Later ed. 12mo. VG. $55.00

ORWELL, George. *Animal Farm.* 1st Am ed. dj. B7. $110.00

ORWELL, George. *Animal Farm.* 1946. Harcourt. 1st ed. dj. VG. $65.00

ORWELL, George. *Down & Out in Paris & London.* 1986. London. 1st ed. dj. EX. $40.00

ORWELL, George. *English People.* 1947. London. 1st ed. dj. EX. $65.00

ORWELL, George. *Orwell Reader.* 1956. NY. 1st ed. dj. VG. B2. $12.50

ORWELL, George. *1984.* 1949. Harcourt. Stated 1st Am ed. VG. $45.00

ORWELL, George. *1984.* 1949. NY. 1st ed. 1st issue. red bdg. dj. M. $100.00

OSBORN, Campbell. *Let Freedom Ring.* 1954. Tokyo. unknown ed. dj. EX. T6. $15.00

OSBORN, H.F. *Man Rises to Parnassus.* 1927. NJ. $25.00

OSBORN, H.F. *Titanotheres of Ancient WY, Dakota & NE. Vol. 1.* 1929. US Geol Survey. Ils. 4to. rebound. M2. $185.00

OSBORN, H.S. *New Description of Geography of Palestine.* 1877. Oxford. 1st ed. VG. G1. $15.00

OSBORN, T.W. *Fiery Trail: Union Officer's Account of Sherman's Campaigns.* 1986. Knoxville. Ils 1st ed. dj. M. $25.00

OSBORNE, J. *Entertainer.* 1957. London. 1st ed. dj. M. $35.00

OSBORNE, Linda B. *Song of the Harp: Old Welsh Folk Tales.* 1976. Ils Taylor. 1st ed. dj. M. C1. $8.00

OSBORNE, O. *S American Mythology.* 1968. London. Hamlyn. Ils. 141 p. dj. EX. M2. $15.00

OSBOURNE, Alan. *Modern Marine Engineer's Manual.* 1941. NY. Cornell Maritime Pr. 2 vols. VG. $50.00

OSBOURNE, Lloyd. *Peril.* 1929. Garden City. $12.50

OSBURN, Burl. *Pewter.* 1947. Internat TB Co. 1st ed. 3rd print. 151 p. xl. M1. $18.50

OSGOOD, H.A. *Teeth & Jaws Roetgenologically Considered.* 1925. NY. Hoeber. Ils. 4to. 172 p. EX. $95.00

OSLER, William. *AL Student & Other Biographical Essays.* 1926. London. Oxford. 334 p. $45.00

OSLER, William. *Evolution of Modern Medicine.* 1921. Yale. 1st ed. EX. $125.00

OSLER, William. *Evolution of Modern Medicine.* 1923. New Haven. Ils 3rd print. VG. B2. $80.00

OSSA, H. *They Saved Our Birds.* 1973. Hippocrene. Ils. 287 p. dj. EX. M2. $9.00

OSSENDOWSKI, F. *From President to Prison.* 1925. NY. $25.00

OSTRANDER, A.B. *After 60 Years: Sequel to Story of the Plains.* 1925. Seattle. Gateway. Ils. 120 p. wraps. A3. $40.00

OSTROM & MC INTOSH. *Marsh's Dinosaurs: Collections From Como Bluff.* 1966. Yale U. Ils 1st ed. dj. EX. M2. $90.00

OSWALT, W. *This Land Was Theirs: Study of N American Indian.* 1966. Wiley. maps. 560 p. EX. M2. $15.00

OTERO, M.A. *My Life on the Frontier, 1864-1882.* 1935. NY. 1/750. sgn. VG. $95.00

OTERO, M.A. *My Nine Years As Governor of Territory of NM, 1897-1906.* 1940. Albuquerque. 1/400. 404 p. dj. scarce. A3. $120.00

OTERO, Miquel. *Real Billy the Kid With New Light on Lincoln Co. War.* 1936. NY. Ils. 200 p. VG. very scarce. A3. $90.00

OTIS, James. *Wan Lun & Dancy.* 1902. Burt. Ils Davis. G. $17.50

OTIS & BURNS. *MI Trees: Handbook of Native & Introduced Species.* 1931. MI U. Ils. 362 p. VG. M2. $10.00

OTIS. *Under the Liberty Tree.* 1896. Boston. Ils. VG. $12.00

OTT, John. *My Ivory Cellar.* 1958. Chicago. 3rd ed. sgn. dj. VG. $15.00

OTTENSOSER & SIGALL. *American Political Reality.* 1972. Random House. 1st ed. pb. $3.00

OUDARD, G. *Amazing Life of John Law.* 1928. NY. G. $10.00

OUIDA. *Dog of Flanders.* 1906. Roycroft. 8vo. brown cloth. VG. D1. $40.00

OUSBY, W.J. *Self-Hypnosis & Scientific Self-Suggestion.* 1966. London. $24.00

OUSPENSKY, P.D. *Tertium Organum: Key to Enigmas of the World.* 1922. NY. 336 p. G. $25.00

OUTDOOR LIFE. *Story of American Hunting & Firearms.* 1957. Coward McCann. dj. VG. $8.00

OUTDOOR LIFE. *Story of American Hunting & Firearms.* 1976. NY. Dutton. 168 p. dj. M. $8.50

OVENDEN, Graham. *Illustrators of Alice & Through Looking Glass.* 1972. London. Academy. 4to. 101 p. dj. VG. $25.00

OVENDEN, HILL & ADAMSON. *Photographs. With Introduction by Mariana Henderson.* 1973. NY/London. Ils 1st Am ed. dj. $35.00

OVER & THOMAS. *Birds of SD.* 1921. SD Geol/Nat Hist Survey. M2. $25.00

OVERSTREET, Harry. *War Called Peace.* 1961. NY. Norton. 1st ed. dj. $5.00

OVERTON, Grant. *Portrait of a Publisher & First Hundred Years of Appleton.* 1925. NY. 1st ed. 95 p. with presentation card. T5. $35.00

OVERTON, R.C. *Burlington Route.* 1965. Ils. maps. charts. 673 p. $35.00

OVID. *Art of Love.* 1971. Heritage. Ils Fraser. 8vo. slipcase. EX. $15.00

OVID. *Metamorphoses.* 1961. Heritage. boxed. EX. $15.00

OVITT, S.W. *Balloon Section of American Expeditionary Forces.* 1919. New Haven. 1st ed. photos. 286 p. T5. $275.00

OVSYANNIKOV, Yuri. *Lubok.* 1968. Moscow. 1st ed. Russian/English text. $35.00

OWEN, Bessie. *Aerial Vagabond.* 1941. NY. 1st ed. presentation. sgn. VG. B2. $75.00

OWEN, D.D. *Ilustrations to Geological Report of WI, IA & MN.* 1852. Phil. Lippincott. pls. maps. VG. $35.00

OWEN, D.D. *Report of Geological Exploration of Part of IA, WI & IL.* 1844. Ils. maps. 191 p. VG. A3. $70.00

OWEN, D.D. *Report of Geological Survey of WI, IA & MN...* 1852. Phil. Lippincott Grambo. 638 p. VG. A3. $90.00

OWEN, D.D. *Survey of Mineral Lands of IA, WI & N IL.* 1840. WA. fld pls. maps. rebound. VG. $95.00

OWEN, David. *Fantastic Planets.* 1979. Reed Books. dj. VG. P1. $15.00

OWEN, E.T. *Ft. Frye on the Muskingum.* nd. (c 1932) Beverly, OH. 16 p. wraps. G. T5. $12.50

OWEN, M. *Wild Geese of the World: Life History & Ecology.* 1980. London. Batsford. Ils 1st ed. dj. EX. M2. $45.00

OWEN, M.A. *Ole Rabbit's Plantation Stories As Told by Negroes of SW.* 1898. Phil. Jacobs. Ils Owen/Wain. 310 p. EX. $45.00

OWEN, R.B. *Leaves From a Greenland Diary.* 1935. Dodd Mead. 166 p. M1. $12.50

OWEN, Wilfred. *Cities in the Motor Age.* 1959. NY. Ils. dj. VG. $20.00

OWEN & OWEN. *Wind-Blown Stories.* 1930. Abingdon. Ils Tobins. VG. $30.00

OWENS, H.B. *GA Planting Prelate...* 1945. GA U. 1/1000. square 8vo. green bdg. $27.50

OWENS, M. & D. *Cry of the Kalahari.* 1984. Houghton. Ils. 341 p. dj. EX. M2. $15.00

OWENS & NEIMARK. *I Have Changed.* 1972. Morrow. 160 p. dj. M1. $10.00

OWENS. *Apostle of El Paso, 1892-1919.* 1951. sgn. orig bdg. VG. B1. $25.00

OXFORD UNIVERSITY. *Compact Edition of Oxford English Dictionary.* 1971-1978. sm folio. 2 vols. boxed. VG. $95.00

OZ, Amos. *Touch the Water, Touch the Wind.* 1973. Harcourt. 1st Am ed. dj. EX. $15.00

OZ, T. *Turkish Ceramics.* nd. np. 75 pls. VG. $100.00

OZENFANT, Amedee. *Journey Through Life.* 1939. Macmillan. dj. EX. $80.00

P

PA RAILROAD COMPANY. *History of the Floods.* 1937. Ils. maps. charts. 150 p. $65.00

PABEL. *Enemies Are Human.* 1955. Phil. 1st ed. dj. VG. $17.50

PACCAGNINI, G. *Andre Mantegna.* 1961. Milan. Ils. folio. slipcase. EX. J2. $300.00

PACE, N.G. *Acoustics & the Sea Bed: Conference Proceedings.* 1983. Bath, UK. EX. $25.00

PACH, Walter. *Art Museum in America: Its History & Achievement.* 1948. Pantheon. 1st ed. dj. VG. J2. $22.50

PACHTER, H.M. *Magic Into Science: Story of Paracelsus.* 1951. Schuman. Ils. 360 p. dj. VG. M2. $5.00

PACIONI, G. *Guide to Mushrooms.* 1981. Simon Schuster. Ils 1st Am ed. 511 p. dj. EX. M2. $18.00

PACKARD, A.S. *Monograph on Geometrid Moths or Phalaenide of US.* 1876. GPO. Ils. 607 p. A3. $75.00

PACKARD, E.L. *Molluscan Fauna From San Francisco Bay.* 1918. CA U. fld map. EX. M2. $60.00

PACKARD, Francis. *History of Medicine in the US.* 1901. Lippincott. 1st ed. G. J2. $30.00

PACKARD, Winthrop. *Young Ice Whalers.* 1903. Boston. 1st ed. VG. $14.00

PADEN, Irene. *Wake of the Prairie Schooner.* 1943. Macmillan. VG. $20.00

PADOA, Alless. *La Logique Deductive.* 1912. Paris. 1st ed. $110.00

PAGE, Curtis. *British Poets of the 19th C.* 1928. Revised ed. VG. C1. $6.50

PAGE, Jesse. *Land of the Peaks & Pampas.* 1913. London. Ils. fld map. G. $16.00

PAGE, Kirby. *National Defense.* 1931. NY. dj. G. $20.00

PAGE, Myra. *Soviet Main Street.* 1933. Moscow/Leningrad. 108 p. pb. $35.00

PAGE, T.N. *Burial of the Guns.* 1894. Scribner. 1st ed. 258 p. xl. $10.00

PAGE, T.N. *Old Gentleman of the Black Stock.* 1901. Scribner. Ils Christy. 169 p. $12.50

PAGE, T.N. *On Newfound River.* 1891. NY. 1st ed. 12mo. 240 p. scarce. T1. $20.00

PAGE, T.N. *Robert E. Lee, the Southerner.* 1908. 1st ed. 312 p. K1. $18.50

PAGE, T.N. *Social Life in Old VA Before the War.* 1897. NY. Ils. VG. $15.00

PAGE, T.N. *Under the Crust.* 1907. NY. 1st ed. EX. $22.50

PAGE, V.W. *Aviation Engines: Design, Construction, Operation, Repair.* 1917. NY. $20.00

PAIGE, L.S. *Maybe I'll Pitch Forever.* 1962. NY. 1st ed. dj. VG. B2. $27.50

PAIGE, L.S. *Maybe I'll Pitch Forever.* 1962. NY. 1st ed. 285 p. dj. xl. G. B2. $17.50

PAINE, A.B. *Captain Bell McDonald: TX Ranger.* 1986. State House. facsimile of 1909 ed. 454 p. M2. $20.00

PAINE, A.B. *Captain Bill McDonald: TX Ranger.* 1909. NY. Little Ives. 448 p. blue cloth. A3. $160.00

PAINE, A.B. *Mark Twain: Biography.* 1912. NY. 1st ed. 3 vols. TEG. VG. T5. $95.00

PAINE, A.B. *Mark Twain's Speeches.* 1923. London/NY. 1st ed. 396 p. VG. T5. $19.50

PAINE, R.D. *Book of Buried Treasure.* 1922. NY. Ils. G. $12.00

PAINE, R.D. *Ships & Sailors of Old Salem.* 1923. Boston. Lauriat. dj. VG. $25.00

PAINE, Thomas. *Common Sense.* 1928. NY. Rimington Hooper. 1/376. boxed. EX. $65.00

PAINE, Thomas. *Life & Writings of Thomas Paine.* 1908. NY. Independence ed. 1/500. 10 vols. $200.00

PAINTER, Muriel. *Yaqui Easter Sermon.* 1955. AZ U. 1st ed. stiff wraps. VG. J2. $15.00

PALEOLOGUE, Maurice. *Ambassador's Memoirs: 1914-1917.* 1973. London. Unabridged ed. dj. EX. $40.00

PALEY, Grace. *Later the Same Day.* 1985. NY. 1st ed. inscr. dj. RS. EX. $45.00

PALFREY, Francis Winthrop. *Antietam & Fredericksburg.* 1882. NY. Ils 1st ed. 228 p. G. T5. $35.00

PALGRAVE, Francis. *Five Days Entertainment at Wentworth Grange.* 1868. London. Ils. E2. $40.00

PALLIERE, Leon. *Leon Palliere: Diaro de Viaje Por la America del Sud.* 1945. Buenos Aires. dj. VG. P3. $75.00

PALLISTER, D.M. *Annual Bibliography of British & Irish History.* 1986. St. Martin. 165 p. VG. T5. $9.50

PALLUCCHINI, Rodolfo. *Carpaccio: Le Storie di Sant'Orsola.* nd. Milan. Martello. 31 pls. dj. D2. $28.50

PALLUCCHINI, Rodolfo. *Die Venezianische Malerei des 18: Jahrhunderts.* 1961. Munich. Bruckmann. Ils 303 p. dj. D2. $195.00

PALME, Arthur. *Berkshires. Through the Camera of Arthur Palme.* 1951. Pittsfield. 1st print. 8vo. dj. EX. T1. $35.00

PALMER, A.H. *Life of Joseph Wolf: Animal Painter.* 1895. Longman Green. Ils. 328 p. D2. $145.00

PALMER, Brooks. *Treasury of American Clocks.* 1971. Macmillan. Ils. 371 p. dj. EX. $17.50

PALMER, D.D. *Three Generations: Brief History of Chiropractic.* 1967. Davenport, IA. inscr. wraps. VG. $20.00

PALMER, E. *Plains of Camdeboo.* 1967. Viking. Ils. maps. 320 p. dj. EX. M2. $11.00

PALMER, Frederick. *Newton D. Baker: America at War.* 1931. Dodd Mead. 2 vols. xl. M1. $20.00

PALMER, G.T. *Conscientious Turncoat: Story of John M. Palmer.* 1941. New Haven. 1st ed. 297 p. dj. G. T5. $35.00

PALMER, Henrietta. *In Dixie Land: Stories of Reconstruction Era.* 1926. NY. Ils. 220 p. VG. $15.00

PALMER, Henry. *This Was Air Travel.* 1962. Bonanza. 208 p. dj. EX. $20.00

PALMER, Hugh. *Private Gardens of England.* 1986. Crown. folio. 223 p. dj. EX. $35.00

PALMER, John. *Studies in Contemporary Theatre.* 1927. Boston. 1st Am ed. dj. VG. $17.00

PALMER, Kingsley. *Folklore of Somerset.* 1976. 1st Am ed. dj. EX. C1. $18.00

PALMER, Marian. *White Boar.* pb. VG. C1. $3.00

PALMER, R.S. *Handbook of N American Birds: Loons Through Flamingos.* 1976. Yale U. Ils 2nd print. 567 p. dj. EX. M2. $40.00

PALMER, T.S. *Index Generum Mammalim.* 1904. USDA. 984 p. wraps. VG. $25.00

PALMER. *General Von Steuben.* 1937. Yale. VG. $22.00

PALMQUIST, P.E. *Carlton E. Watkins, Photographer of the American W.* 1983. NM U. dj. VG. $35.00

PALUDAN, P.S. *Covenant With Death.* 1975. Urbana U. Ils. 309 p. dj. $22.50

PANASSIE, H. *Hot Jazz.* 1936. Witmark. 1st ed. 1st print. EX. $60.00

PANCAKE, Breece. *Stories.* 1983. Boston. 1st ed. dj. EX. $45.00

PANCOAST, C.L. *Modern Templar.* 1932. NY. $45.00

PANGBORN, J.G. *Picturesque B&O Railroad.* 1882. Chicago. Knight Leonard. 8vo. 152 p. wraps. $37.50

PANKHURST, E.S. *Suffragette: History of Women's Militant Suffrage Movement.* 1911. Boston. Women's Journal. 1st ed. VG. $100.00

PANNETIRE. *Notes Cambodgiennes: Au Coeur du Pays Khmer.* 1921. Paris. 1st ed. VG. $35.00

PANOFSKY, Erwin. *Early Netherlandish Painting.* 1953. Harvard. 1st ed. 2 vols. djs. $200.00

PANSHIN, Alexei & Cory. *World Beyond the Hill: SF & Quest for Transcendence.* 1989. Tarcher. UCP. wraps. EX. $10.00

PANSU, Evelyne. *Ingres Dessins.* 1977. Paris. Ils. wraps. D2. $40.00

PAOLOZZI, Eduardo. *Kex, Kex, Kex, Kex, Kex.* nd. Chicago. Copley. Ils. D2. $40.00

PAPASHVILY, G. & H. *Thanks to Noah.* 1951. Harper. Ils 1st ed. 167 p. dj. EX. M2. $4.00

PAPE, F.C. *Works of Rabelais. Vol. 2.* 1937. London. Bodley Head. dj. EX. $50.00

PAQUIN, C. *Napoleon's Victories.* 1893. Chicago. Ils. folio. VG. $50.00

PARAMANANDA, Swami. *Srimed-Bhagavad-Gita.* 1913. Boston. $35.00

PARAMANANDA, Swami. *Way of Peace & Blessedness.* 1913. Boston. $60.00

PARAMORE, E.E. *Ballad of Yukon Jake.* 1928. NY. dj. $50.00

PARDEE, H.E.B. *Clinical Aspects of the Electrocardiogram.* 1924. NY. 1st ed. VG. scarce. $95.00

PARE, Richard. *Photography & Architecture, 1839-1939.* 1982. Callaway Eds. 147 pls. oblong folio. 282 p. dj. $65.00

PARE. *Catholic Church in Detroit.* 1951. Detroit. 1st ed. VG. $25.00

PAREKH, M.C. *Brahma Samaj.* 1929. India. $20.00

PARENT, Gail. *Sheila Levine Is Dead & Living in NY.* 1972. NY. 1st ed. dj. VG. B2. $25.00

PARET, J.P. *Lawn Tennis: Its Past, Present & Future.* 1904. NY. Ils. photos. 419 p. TEG. G. T5. $35.00

PARK, DAVIS & COMPANY. *Complete Catalog.* 1916. HrdCvr. 308 p. EX. $35.00

PARK, Orlando. *Sherlock Holmes, Esq. & John H. Watson, M.D.* 1962. NW U. 205 p. dj. M. $50.00

PARK & ERICKSON. *Atlanta Street Scenes: Best 10,000.* 1954. Atlanta. Ils. sgn. 100 p. dj. VG. $15.00

PARKER, Dorothy. *Death & Taxes.* 1931. NY. 1st ed. dj. T5. $35.00

PARKER, Dorothy. *Enough Rope.* 1926. Boni Liveright. 12mo. 110 p. VG. $12.00

PARKER, Dorothy. *Enough Rope.* 1940. Sun Dial. VG. $12.50

PARKER, Dorothy. *Not So Deep As a Well.* 1936. NY. 1st ed. 8vo. dj. VG. B2. $15.00

PARKER, Dorothy. *Not So Deep As a Well.* 1936. NY. Viking. 1/485. sgn. slipcase. EX. T5. $300.00

PARKER, Dorothy. *Portable Dorothy Parker.* 1972. NY. 1st ed. dj. EX. $10.00

PARKER, Dorothy. *Sunset Gun.* 1928. NY. 1st ed. 8vo. $35.00

PARKER, Dorothy. *You Might As Well Live.* 1970. Simon Schuster. Ils. VG. $10.00

PARKER, G.H. *World Expands: Recollections of a Zoologist.* 1946. Harvard U. 252 p. VG. M2. $10.00

PARKER, Gilbert. *Ladder of Swords.* 1904. Harper. Ils Kinneys. 1st ed. $12.00

PARKER, J. & P. *Ornamental Waterfowl.* 1970. Barnes. Ils 1st Am ed. dj. EX. M2. $14.00

PARKER, J.H. *Concise Glossary of Terms Used in...Architecture.* 1875. Oxford/London. Revised 4th ed. J2. $25.00

PARKER, K.T. *Drawings of Antoine Watteau.* 1932. NY. Ils. 100 pls. 4to. J2. $60.00

PARKER, K.T. *Drawings of Hans Holbein at Windsor Castle.* 1983. NY. 4to. dj. M. $50.00

PARKER, K.T. *Drawings of Hans Holbein in Collection of His Majesty King.* 1945. London. $40.00

PARKER, Nathan H. *IA Handbook for 1856.* 1956. Boston. 188 p. lacks map. gilt cloth. G. T1. $22.00

PARKER, Olivia. *Signs of Life.* 1978. Boston. Godine. 1st ed. sgn. dj. EX. $30.00

PARKER, R. *Yankee Saint.* 1935. NY. 1st ed. 322 p. dj. VG. $30.00

PARKER, R.B. *Catskill Eagle.* 1985. NY. 1st ed. dj. EX. $15.00

PARKER, R.B. *Catskill Eagle.* 1985. NY. 1st ed. sgn. dj. EX. $30.00

PARKER, R.B. *Ceremony.* 1982. NY. 1st ed. sgn. dj. EX. $40.00

PARKER, R.B. *Early Autumn.* 1981. NY. 1st ed. sgn. dj. EX. $35.00

PARKER, R.B. *God Save the Child.* 1974. Boston. Houghton. 1st ed. dj. EX. $50.00

PARKER, R.B. *Godwulf Manuscript.* 1974. Boston. 1st ed. inscr/sgn. dj. M. $175.00

PARKER, R.B. *Judas Goat.* nd. Boston. 1st ed. inscr/sgn. dj. M. $65.00

PARKER, R.B. *Judas Goat.* 1982. London. 1st ed. dj. EX. $35.00

PARKER, R.B. *Savage Place.* 1981. NY. 1st ed. sgn. dj. EX. $50.00

PARKER, R.B. *Taming a Sea Horse.* c 1986. Delacorte. 1st ed. sgn. dj. M. $40.00

PARKER, R.B. *Taming a Sea Horse.* 1986. Delacorte. 1st ed. 250 p. EX. $20.00

PARKER, R.B. *Valediction.* 1984. NY. 1st ed. sgn. dj. EX. $25.00

PARKER, R.B. *Widening Gyre.* 1983. NY. 1st ed. dj. EX. $30.00

PARKER, R.B. *Widening Gyre.* 1983. NY. 1st ed. sgn. dj. EX. $40.00

PARKER, R.B. *Wilderness.* 1979. NY. Review ed. sgn. dj. EX. $65.00

PARKER, R.B. *Wilderness.* 1979. NY. 1st ed. sgn. dj. RS. with photo. $85.00

PARKER, Samuel. *Exploring Tour Beyond the Rocky Mountains.* c 1967. Minneapolis. reprint. dj. VG. $15.00

PARKER, Samuel. *Journal of Exploring Tour Beyond Rocky Mountains.* 1846. Auburn. Derby. fld map. 422 p. VG. A3. $160.00

PARKER, Watson. *Gold in Black Hills.* 1966. Norman. 1st ed. dj. EX. $20.00

PARKER, William Belmont. *Edward Rowland Sill: His Life & Work.* 1915. Boston. Ils 1st ed. 307 p. VG. T5. $25.00

PARKER & BROWN. *Comparative Ecology of Two Colubrid Snakes.* 1980. Milwaukee Mus. 4to. 104 p. EX. M2. $10.00

PARKER & JENKINS. *Mushrooms: Separate Kingdom.* 1979. Oxmoor. Ils 1st ed. 101 p. dj. EX. M2. $12.00

PARKES, J.W. *Jew & His Neighbor: Study of Causes of Anti-Semitism.* 1931. NY. 1st ed. G. $8.50

PARKHILL, F. *Wildest of the W.* 1951. Holt. Ils 1st ed. 310 p. dj. EX. M2. $23.00

PARKINSON, C. *E & W.* 1963. NY. 1st ed. dj. VG. $15.00

PARKMAN, Francis. *Journals.* 1947. NY. Harper. 1st ed. 2 vols. djs. EX. $50.00

PARKMAN, Francis. *OR Trail.* 1925. Boston. 1/950. slipcase. EX. P3. $300.00

PARKMAN, Francis. *Works of Francis Parkman & Life of Francis Parkman.* 1910. Little Brown. 13 vols. VG. $75.00

PARKS, E.W. *Segments of S Thought.* 1938. Athens. 1st ed. 392 p. VG. $25.00

PARKS, Gordon. *Moments Without Proper Names.* 1975. Viking. dj. EX. $50.00

PARKS, Gordon. *Poet & His Camera.* 1968. Viking. dj. VG. $12.50

PARKS, Gordon. *Whispers of Intimate Things.* 1st ed. dj. EX. S2. $30.00

PARKS, Gordon. *Whispers of Intimate Things.* 1971. NY. Viking. 1st ed. dj. VG. $15.00

PARLEY, Peter. *Voyages, Travels & Adventures of Gilbert Go Ahead.* 1856. NY. 12mo. $50.00

PARMALA, M. *Nudism in Modern Life.* 1952. Sunshine. Ils 320 p. VG. $15.00

PARMALEE, R.D. *Pioneer Sonoma.* 1972. Sonoma, CA. sgn. EX. $25.00

PARMELIN, Helene. *Picasso: Women, Cannes & Mougins, 1854-1963.* nd. Paris/Amsterdam. dj. EX. $110.00

PARR, C.M. *Ferdinand Magellan: Circumnavigator.* 1964. Crowell. Ils. 423 p. dj. EX. M2. $11.00

PARRAMORE, D.D. *Scenes & Stories of Early W TX.* 1975. TW Pr. 1st ed. M. $25.00

PARRIS, John. *Roaming the Mountains.* 1955. Asheville. 1st ed. sgn. dj. VG. B2. $30.00

PARRISH, J.M. *Mammoth Book of Thrillers.* 1936. Odhams. G. P1. $20.00

PARRISH, Randall. *Maid of the Forest.* 1913. Chicago. Ils Schoonover. EX. $15.00

PARROTT, A. *Big Game Fishes & Sharks of New Zealand.* 1958. London. Hodder Stoughton. VG. M2. $24.00

PARRY, J.H. *Discovery of S America.* 1979. NY. Ils 1st ed. dj. EX. $20.00

PARRY, W.E. *Journal of a Voyage for Discovery of NW Passage, 1819-1820.* 1968. NY. reprint of 1821 ed. 4to. EX. $100.00

PARRY, W.E. *Journal of 2nd Voyage for Discovery of NW Passage.* 1824. London. Murray. 1st ed. 571 p. $350.00

PARRY, W.E. *Journal of 2nd Voyage for Discovery of NW Passage.* 1969. NY. reprint of 1824 ed. 8vo. EX. $100.00

PARRY & PUTNAM. *Birds of Prey.* 1979. London. Country Life. Ils. dj. EX. M2. $45.00

PARSON, E.C. *Christus Liberator, Outline Study of Africa.* 1905. Macmillan. Intro Johnston. fld map. 309 p. $22.50

PARSON, M. *Wild Flowers.* 1914. San Francisco. Ils. VG. $10.00

PARSONS, Albert. *Parsifal: Finding of Christ Through Art.* 1890. London/NY. 1st ed. VG. C1. $10.00

PARSONS, E.C. *Folklore of the Sea Islands, SC.* 1923. Cambridge. 219 p. $150.00

PARSONS, E.C. *I Flew With the Lafayette Escadrille.* 1963. Indianapolis. Ils. 335 p. dj. VG. T5. $12.50

PARSONS, F.A. *Interior Decoration: Its Principles & Practice.* 1922. Garden City. J2. $20.00

PARSONS, F.G. *Earlier Inhabitants of London.* 1927. Cecil Palmer. 1st ed. J2. $15.00

PARSONS, Kitty. *Ancestral Timber Ballads Without Music.* 1957. Francestown. Golden Quill. dj. VG. $12.00

PARSONS, Marion. *Old CA Houses, Portraits & Stories.* 1952. CA U. 1st ed. dj. VG. J2. $12.50

PARTINGTON, Wilfred. *Forging Ahead.* 1939. NY. 1st ed. sgn. dj. EX. $45.00

PARTINGTON, Wilfred. *Forging Ahead.* 1939. Putnam. 1st ed. VG. J2. $20.00

PARTNER, Peter. *Murdered Magicians: Templars & Their Myth.* pb. EX. C1. $9.00

PARTON, J. *General Butler in New Orleans.* 1864. NY. Ils. 8vo. 649 p. black cloth. VG. G2. $40.00

PARTON, J. *General Butler in New Orleans.* 1882. Boston. Ils. 661 p. VG. B2. $40.00

PARTON, J. *History & Administration of Department of the S.* 1864. NY. 661 p. K1. $21.50

PARTON, J. *Life of Horace Greeley, Editor of NY Tribune.* 1855. NY. $15.00

PARTRIDGE, Bellamy. *Sir Billy Howe.* 1932. NY. 1st ed. dj. VG. B2. $17.50

PASLEY, F.D. *Al Capone.* 1930. Garden City. 355 p. G. $5.00

PASSAVANT, J.D. *Le Peintre-Graveur.* 1966. NY. Burt Franklin. 6 vols in 3. D2. $100.00

PASSERON, Roger. *French Prints of the 20th C.* 1970. Prager. 1st ed. dj. VG. J2. $25.00

PASTERNAK, Boris. *Dr. Zhivago.* Aug., 1958. 2nd print. dj. VG. $25.00

PATAI. *Encounters: Life of Jacques Lipchitz.* 1961. NY. 1st ed. sgn. dj. EX. $20.00

PATCHEN, Kenneth. *Aflame & Afun of Walking.* 1970. New Directions. 1st ed. dj. EX. $15.00

PATCHEN, Kenneth. *Of the Lion the Teeth.* 1942. New Directions. 1st ed. dj. EX. $50.00

PATCHEN, Kenneth. *Patchen's Lost Plays.* 1977. Capra. 1/100. EX. $55.00

PATENT & SCHROEDER. *Beetles & How They Live.* 1978. Holiday House. photos. 159 p. dj. EX. M2. $7.00

PATER, Walter. *Marius the Epicurean.* 1929. London. Macmillan. Ltd ed. 1/300. sgn. $225.00

PATER, Walter. *Plato & Platonism.* 1893. London. 1st ed. $30.00

PATER, Walter. *Renaissance: Studies in Art & Poetry.* 1976. Verona. Ltd Ed Club. 1/2000. sgn. dj. EX. $110.00

PATOCKOVA-KOKOSCHKA, Berta. *Mein Leid.* 1952. Vienna. Gurlitt. Ils. D2. $25.00

PATON, W.A. *Down the Islands: Voyage to the Caribbees.* 1887. NY. Ils. 301 p. VG. $65.00

PATRICK, J.N. *Elements of Pedagogics.* 1894. 224 p. TB. EX. $4.00

PATRICK, Marsena. *Inside Lincoln's Army: Diary of Provost Marshal General...* 1964. Yoseloff. Ils 1st ed. dj. VG. $30.00

PATTEE, F.L. *Pasquaney: A Study.* 1893. Bristol, NH. Ils 1st ed. 83 p. VG. B2. $17.50

PATTEN, William. *Pioneering the Telephone in Canada.* 1926. Montreal. private print. 1/2000. EX. B1. $30.00

PATTERSON, C.B. *Seeking the Kingdom.* 1888. CT. $12.00

PATTERSON, F.B. *African Adventures.* 1928. 1st ed. VG. $10.00

PATTERSON, Harry. *Dillinger.* 1983. Stein Day. 1st ed. dj. VG. $15.00

PATTERSON, Harry. *Valhalla Exhange.* 1976. Stein Day. 1st ed. dj. VG. $15.00

PATTERSON, J.H. *In the Grip of the Nyika.* 1909. NY. Ils. 9 maps. $60.00

PATTERSON, James. *Virgin.* 1980. McGraw Hill. 1st ed. dj. VG. P1. $15.00

PATTERSON, James. *Virgin.* 1984. Golden Apple. VG. P1. $3.00

PATTERSON, Katherine. *Jacob Have I Loved.* 1980. NY. Crowell. 1st ed. dj. EX. $20.00

PATTERSON, M.C. *Author Newsletters & Journals.* 1979. Gale Research. M. P1. $23.75

PATTERSON, R.L. *Sage Grouse in WY.* 1952. WY Fish/Game. Ils. map. 341 p. dj. EX. M2. $7.00

PATTERSON, R.M. *Buffalo Head.* 1961. Sloane. Ils. map 273 p. dj. EX. M2. $10.00

PATTERSON, Robert. *In the Valley of the Shenandoah in 1861.* 1865. inscr/sgn. 542 p. scarce. K1. $32.50

PATTERSON & CONRAD. *Scottsboro Boy.* 1950. NY. dj. VG. $35.00

PATTERSSON, Hans. *Westward Ho With the Albatross.* 1953. NY. dj. VG. $9.00

PATTIE, J.O. *Personal Narrative of James O. Pattie of KY.* 1930. Donnelley. reprint of 1831 ed. EX. M2. $25.00

PATTISON, Barrie. *Seal of Dracula.* nd. Bounty. dj. VG. P1. $12.50

PATTON, G.S. *Was As I Knew It.* 1947. Boston. 425 p. G. T5. $19.50

PATTON, W. *Cottage Bible.* 1834. Hartford. Robinson Sumner. 2nd Am print. G. $55.00

PAUL, B. *This Was Cattle Ranching.* 1973. 1st ed. dj. EX. $25.00

PAUL, H.H. *Oxford Companion to English Literature.* 1969. NY. 4th ed. dj. EX. $20.00

PAUL, John. *Refutation of Arianism.* 1828. Lowry. 8vo. 319 p. full leather. M1. $25.00

PAUL & GEBBIE. *Stage & Its Stars: Past & Present.* nd. Phil. Gebbie. 128 pls. 2 vols. AEG. J2. $350.00

PAUL & QUINTANILLA. *With a Hay Nonny Nonny.* 1942. NY. 1st ed. 8vo. dj. $20.00

PAULLIN, C. *Atlas of Historical Geography of the US.* 1932. WA. VG. $75.00

PAULSSON, Thomas. *Scandinavian Architecture.* 1958. Leonard Hill. 1st ed. dj. VG. J2. $25.00

PAUSANIAS. *Description of Greece.* 1794. London. 3 vols. rebound gilt cloth. EX. T1. $195.00

PAUTZ & CRAMER. *Architecture of Fear.* 1987. NY. dj. G. $7.00

PAVIERE, Sydney H. *Dictionary of British Sporting Painters.* 1980. Lewis. reprint of 1965 ed. dj. D2. $55.00

PAVLOV, I.P. *Lectures on Conditioned Reflexes.* 1928. NY. 1st Am ed. G. $50.00

PAVLOVSKII, B.E. *Key to Parasites of Fresh-Water Fishes of the USSR.* 1964. Israel Sc Trans. Ils. 919 p. M2. $40.00

PAXON, Diana. *Silverhair the Wanderer.* 1986. 1st ed. pb. VG. C1. $3.00

PAXON, Diana. *White Raven.* 1st ed. pb. M. C1. $5.00

PAXON, Diana. *White Raven.* 1988. 1st ed. dj. M. C1. $18.00

PAYETTE, B.C. *OR Country Under the Union Jack.* 1962. Montreal. 1st ed. EX. $25.00

PAYNE, F.O. *One Hundred Lessons in Nature Study Around My School.* 1895. Ils. 201 p. TB. EX. $12.50

PAYNE, L.G.S. *Air Dates.* 1957. Heinemann. 565 p. dj. M1. $8.50

PAYNE, Robert. *Gold of Troy.* 1959. London. $11.00

PAYNE, Roger. *Extracts From the Diary of Roger Payne.* 1928. NY. 1/175. $45.00

PAYNE, Stephen. *Where the Rockies Ride Herd.* 1965. Denver. Sage. Ils. 359 p. scarce. A3. $30.00

PAYNE. *Payne's Royal Dresden Gallery.* Dresden. 136 pls. 4to. 2 vols. VG. B1. $175.00

PAYNTER & NUSSEY. *Kruger: Portrait of a National Park.* 1986. S Africa. Macmillan. Ils 1st ed. 4to. EX. M2. $28.00

PAZ, Ireneo. *Life & Adventure of Celebrated Bandit J. Murrietta...* 1937. Chicago. Trans Belle. 174 p. dj. VG. A3. $35.00

PAZ, Octavio. *On Poets & Others.* 1986. NY. 1st Am ed. dj. VG. $20.00

PAZAUREK, Gustav E. *Glaser der Empire & Biedermeierzeit.* 1923. Leipzig. Ils 412 p. D2. $125.00

PAZOS, D.V. *Letters on United Provinces of S America...* 1819. NY. 1st ed. map. G. $200.00

PE, Win. *Shwe Dagon.* 1972. Rangoon. Ils 1st ed. dj. EX. $14.00

PEABODY, F.C. *Education for Life.* 1919. NY. Ils. 393 p. VG. B2. $32.50

PEABODY, H.G. *Glimpses of the Grand Canyon of AZ.* 1902. KS City. Harvey. photos. 8vo. VG. $15.00

PEACHAM, H. *Compleat Gentleman.* 1627. London. fair. $150.00

PEACOCK, T.B. *Poems of Plains.* 1889. NY. Revised 3rd ed. inscr. with letter. $75.00

PEACOCK, Thomas Love. *Complete Novels of Thomas Love Peacock.* 1948. London. 1st ed. dj. VG. C1. $29.50

PEACOCK, Thomas Love. *Misfortunes of Elphin, Nightmare Alley & Crotchet Castle.* Rinehart. pb. VG. C1. $11.50

PEACOCK, V.T. *Famous American Belles of 19th C.* 1901. Lippincott. 297 p. $35.00

PEAKE & FLEURE. *Way of the Sea.* 1929. Yale U. Ils. 168 p. VG. M2. $5.00

PEALE. *Peale's Popular Educator & Cyclopedia of Reference...* 1884. Chicago. Ils. maps. diagrams. Art Deco bdg. $35.00

PEARCE, Cyril. *Toys & Models.* c 1947-1948. London. Ils 1st ed. dj. VG. T5. $25.00

PEARCE, D. *Cool Hand Luke.* 1965. NY. 1st ed. dj. EX. $35.00

PEARCE, E.H. *Sion College & Library.* 1913. Cambridge. 1st ed. pls. $40.00

PEARCE, J. *Effect of Deer Browsing on Certain Adirondack Forest Types.* 1937. Roosevelt Wildlife. 61 p. M2. $5.00

PEARCE, W.B. *Practical Bookbinding.* nd. London. Ils. 12mo. VG. $25.00

PEARCE, W.M. *Matador Land & Cattle Co.* 1964. Norman. Ils 1st ed. dj. EX. $40.00

PEARL, R.M. *CO Gem Trails.* 1951. Sage. photos. maps. 125 p. VG. M2. $10.00

PEARL, Raymond. *To Begin With: Being Prophylaxis Against Pedantry.* 1927. NY. 1st ed. dj. $40.00

PEARS, Charles. *From the Thames to the Seine.* nd. Phil. Jacobs. VG. $22.50

PEARSE, A.S. *Emigrations of Animals From Sea to Land.* 1936. Duke U. 176 p. EX. M2. $13.00

PEARSON, Edmund. *Dime Novels.* 1929. Boston. Ils. 280 p. VG. $35.00

PEARSON, Edmund. *Queer Books.* 1929. London. $20.00

PEARSON, Edmund. *Queer Books.* 1970. Kennikat Pr. reprint. EX. $8.00

PEARSON, Edmund. *Trial of Lizzie Borden.* 1937. Garden City. Ils 1st ed. dj. VG. B2. $60.00

PEARSON, G.W. *Records of MA Volunteer Militia.* 1913. 448 p. gilt bdg. EX. J4. $30.00

PEARSON, Grant. *My Life of High Adventure.* 1962. Prentice Hall. 1st ed. 234 p. dj. VG. $25.00

PEARSON, Hesketh. *A. Conan Doyle: His Life & Art.* 1943. Methuen. 1st ed. dj. VG. $20.00

PEARSON, Hesketh. *Dickens: His Character, Comedy & Career.* 1949. NY. 1st ed. dj. EX. $17.50

PEARSON, John. *Begin Sweet World.* 1976. NY. Doubleday. 1st ed. 112 p. wraps $20.00

PEARSON, T.G. *Birds of NC.* 1942. NC Mus. Ils Horsfall/Peterson. 416 p. M2. $85.00

PEARSON, T.G. *Birds of NC.* 1959. Raleigh. color pls. 434 p. dj. VG. $65.00

PEARY, Josephine. *Snow Baby.* 1901. Stokes. 1st ed. G. $22.00

PEARY, R.E. *N Pole.* 1910. NY. Stokes. Ils. map. VG. $80.00

PEASLEY, W.J. *Last of the Nomads.* 1983. Fremantle. photos. map. 119 p. EX. M2. $10.00

PEATTIE, D.C. *Audubon's America.* 1940. Houghton. Deluxe Lg ed. sgn. boxed. J2. $75.00

PEATTIE, D.C. *Bright Lexicon.* 1934. Putnam. presentation. sgn. dj. VG. $25.00

PEATTIE, D.C. *Natural History of Trees of E & Central N America.* 1966. Bonanza. reprint. Ils. 606 p. dj. EX. M2. $17.00

PEATTIE, Elia. *Annie Laurie & Azalea.* 1913. Reilly Britton. G. $12.00

PEATTIE, R. *Friendly Mountains: Green, White & Adirondacks.* 1942. Vanguard. Ils. map. 341 p. dj. EX. M2. $16.00

PEATTIE, R. *Great Smokies & the Blue Ridge.* 1943. Vanguard. photos. map. 372 p. dj. EX. M2. $16.00

PECK, A. *Rene & Patou.* 1938. Chicago. Whitman. dj. VG. $22.00

PECK, G.W. *Sunbeams.* 1900. Higgins. Ils Morgan. G. $25.00

PECK, G.W. *WY, PA: History, Stirring Incidents & Romantic Adventures.* 1858. NY. Ils 1st ed. 12mo. VG. T1. $45.00

PECK, R.M. *Celebration of Birds: Life & Art of Louis Agassiz Fuertes.* 1982. Walker. Ils. 4to. 178 p. dj. EX. M2. $15.00

PECKHAM, James. *General Nathaniel Lyon & MO in 1861.* 1866. NY. 447 p. K1. $32.50

PEDRICK. *Jungle Gold.* 1930. Bobbs Merrill. Ils 1st ed. VG. $37.50

PEEK, S.W. *Nursery & the Orchard: Practical Treatise on Fruit Culture.* 1885. Harrison. Ils. 208 p. gilt cloth. G. M2. $65.00

PEEKE, Marg. *Zenia the Vestal.* 1893. Arena. 2nd ed. $40.00

PEERY, R.B. *Lutherans in Japan.* 1900. Newberry, SC. Ils. maps. 192 p. $25.00

PEET, S.D. *Ashtabula Disaster.* 1877. Chicago. Ils 1st ed. 208 p. scarce. T5. $150.00

PEGGE, Samuel. *Anonymiana; or, Ten Centuries of Observations...Authors...* 1818. London. morocco. $35.00

PEGGOTT. *Innocent Diversion: Study of Music in Life of Jane Austen.* 1979. London. 1st ed. dj. EX. $30.00

PEGLER, D.N. *Pocket Guide to Mushrooms & Toadstools.* 1982. London. Beazley. Ils. 168 p. dj. EX. M2. $12.00

PEIRCE, Josephine. *Fire on the Hearth.* 9151. Pond Ekberg. 1st ed. dj. VG. J2. $20.00

PEISSEL, M. *Lost World of Quintana Roo.* 1963. Dutton. Ils 1st ed. 306 p. dj. EX. M2. $23.00

PEIXOTTO, Ernest. *American Front.* 1919. NY. Scribner. 8vo. TEG. morocco. boxed. M. J2. $90.00

PELLEY, W.D. *As Thou Lovest.* 1955. IN. $22.50

PELLEY, W.D. *Thinking Alive.* 1938. private print. Pelley. $60.00

PELLICER, A. Cirici. *1900 en Barcelona: Modernism, Modern Style, Art Nouveau...* 1972. Barcelona. Poligrafa. Ils 2nd ed. D2. $45.00

PELLOWE, William. *MI Methodist Poets.* 1927. VG. $12.50

PELS, Gertrude. *Easy Puppets.* 1951. NY. Crowell. Ils 1st ed. $10.00

PEMBER, P.Y. *S Woman's Story: Life in Confederate Richmond...* 1974. Ballantine. 1st pb ed. 12mo. 147 p. $5.00

PEMBERTON, Ebenezer. *Sermons & Discourses...* 1727. London. 1st ed. VG. $155.00

PENDEN, R. *Speak to the Earth: Pages From a Farm Wife's Journal.* 1974. Knopf. Ils 1st ed. 239 p. dj. EX. M2. $7.00

PENDER, Harold. *Electrical Engineers' Handbook.* 1950. Wiley. 4th ed. $20.00

PENFIELD & KRISTIANSEN. *Epileptic Seizure Patterns.* 1951. Thomas. 1st ed. VG. $40.00

PENFIELD & ROBERTS. *Speech & Brain Mechanisms.* 1959. Princeton. dj. EX. $45.00

PENHALLOW, D.P. *N American Gymnosperms.* 1907. Boston. 1st ed. VG. $28.00

PENHALLOW, S. *History of Wars of New England With E Indians.* 1924. Boston. facsimile of 1726 ed. 1/250. VG. $37.50

PENN, Irving. *Flowers.* 1980. Harmony. 1st ed. dj. VG. $35.00

PENN, Irving. *Issey Miyake.* 1988. Boston. 1st ed. square 4to. 62 p. EX. $22.00

PENN, Irving. *Moments Preserved.* 1960. Simon Schuster. 1st ed. EX. $195.00

PENN, Irving. *Worlds in a Small Room.* 1974. Viking. dj. EX. $25.00

PENNELL, E.R. *Life & Letters of Joseph Pennell.* 1929. Boston. Ils. 2 vols. djs. boxed. VG. B2. $35.00

PENNELL, Joseph. *Adventures of Illustrator Mostly in Following His Authors.* 1925. Boston. VG. $25.00

PENNELL, Joseph. *Etchers & Etching.* 1920. London. 1st ed. EX. $50.00

PENNELL, Joseph. *Etchers & Etching.* 1926. NY. 4th ed. 4to. 343 p. VG. $35.00

PENNIMAN. *Tanner Boy & How He Became Lieutenant General.* 1864. Boston. Ils. 12mo. 316 p. G. G2. $18.00

PENNINGTON, Myles. *Railways & Other Ways.* 1894. Toronto. 1st ed. presentation. rebound. $47.50

PENNY, M. *Birds of Seychelles & the Outlying Islands.* 1974. Taplinger. Ils 1st Am ed. 160 p. dj. EX. M2. $35.00

PENROSE, Boies. *Travel & Discovery in Renaissance.* 1955. Harvard. 2nd print. inscr. VG. J2. $35.00

PENROSE, R.A.F. *Last Stand of the Old Siberia.* 1922. Phil. Fell Co. Ils. VG. $50.00

PENROSE, Roland. *Sculpture of Picasso.* 1967. NY. 1st ed. dj. EX. $45.00

PENROSE, Roland. *Sculpture of Picasso.* 1967. NY. 1st ed. dj. VG. $17.50

PENZLER, Otto. *Great Detectives.* 1978. Little Brown. 1st ed. dj. VG. P1. $20.00

PEPPER, C.M. *Life & Times of Henry Gassaway Davis, 1823-1916.* 1920. NY. Ils. 318 p. G. T5. $15.00

PEPYS, Samuel. *Diary of Samuel Pepys.* 1893-1899. London. Bell. 1/250. 10 vols. $500.00

PEPYS, Samuel. *Diary of Samuel Pepys.* 1942. NY. Ltd Ed Club. Ils. VG. $95.00

PERCIVAL, Emily. *Golden Gift.* 1853. Boston. Ils 288 p. gilt bdg. K1. $13.50

PERCIVAL, Robert. *Account of Island of Ceylon.* 1805. London. 2nd ed. pls. fld map. $75.00

PERCY, Thomas. *Relics of Ancient English Poetry.* 1767. London. 3 vols. rebound. $450.00

PERCY, Thomas. *Relics of Ancient English Poetry.* 1887. London/NY. VG. C1. $12.50

PERCY, W.A. *Enzio's Kingdom.* 1924. Yale. 1st ed. inscr. $75.00

PERCY, W.A. *Lanterns on the Levee.* 1941. Knopf. 1st ed. dj. $50.00

PERCY, W.A. *Lanterns on the Levee.* 1941. Knopf. 1st ed. 9th print. 347 p. $6.50

PERCY, Walker. *Bourbon.* 1981. New ed. 1/50. sgn/#d. as issued. M. $75.00

PERCY, Walker. *Lancelot.* Book Club. dj. VG. C1. $3.50

PERCY, Walker. *Lancelot.* 1977. Farrar Straus. 1st ed. inscr/sgn. 12mo. VG. $20.00

PERCY, Walker. *Last Gentleman.* 1966. Farrar Straus. 1st ed. sgn. dj. EX. $65.00

PERCY, Walker. *Last Gentleman.* 1966. NY. 1st ed. dj. VG. $50.00

PERCY, Walker. *Lost in the Cosmos.* 1983. Farrar Straus. Ltd 1st ed. sgn. dj. EX. $60.00

PERCY, Walker. *Lost in the Cosmos.* 1983. Farrar Straus. 1st ed. dj. T6. $15.00

PERCY, Walker. *Lost in the Cosmos.* 1983. NY. 1st ed. sgn. dj. EX. $40.00

PERCY, Walker. *Love in the Ruins.* 1971. Farrar Straus. 1st ed. dj. M. $65.00

PERCY, Walker. *Love in the Ruins.* 1971. NY. 1st ed. 403 p. dj. VG. $35.00

PERCY, Walker. *Moviegoer.* 1976. Knopf. 5th print. dj. $15.00

PERCY, Walker. *Novel Writing in an Apocalyptic Time.* 1986. New Orleans. Deluxe ed. 1/100. sgns. EX. $125.00

PERCY, Walker. *Second Coming.* 1980. Franklin Lib. 1st ed. inscr/sgn. EX. $90.00

PERCY, Walker. *Second Coming.* 1981. Pocket Books. 1st ed. sgn. pb. EX. $15.00

PERCY, Walker. *Thanatos Syndrome.* 1987. NY. 1st trade ed. dj. M. $10.00

PEREIRA, H.B. *Aircraft Badges & Markings.* 1955. London. Ils 1st ed. 48 p. dj. VG. T5. $15.00

PERELAER, M.T.H. *Ran Away From the Dutch; or, Borneo From S to N.* 1887. Dodd Mead. 8vo. 376 p. EX. $45.00

PERELMAN, S.J. *Crazy Like a Fox.* 1944. Random House. 1st print. glassine dj. VG. $35.00

PERELMAN, S.J. *Look Who's Talking.* 1940. NY. 1st ed. dj. VG. B2. $75.00

PERELMAN, S.J. *Road to Miltown.* 1957. NY. 1st ed. dj. VG. $9.00

PERENYI, Eleanor. *Green Thoughts: Writer in the Garden.* 1981. NY. 1st ed. sgn. dj. EX. $35.00

PERHINS, D.C. *Homeopathic Therapeutics of Rheumatism & Kindred Diseases.* 1888. Phil. 1st ed. 180 p. VG. B1. $25.00

PERKINS, COMMINS & CHAMBERLIN. *Facts & Arguments.* 1861. Columbus. fld map. 15 p. self wraps. VG. T5. $45.00

PERKINS, J.H. *Annals of the W.* 1847. Cincinnati. 1st ed. 2nd issue. rebound. $80.00

PERKINS, J.H. *Annals of the W.* 1850. St. Louis. 2nd ed. rebound. VG. $45.00

PERKINS, J.N. *History of Parish of Incarnation of NY.* 1912. Howard Pr. VG. $27.50

PERKINS, J.R. *Trails, Rails & War.* 1929. Bobbs Merrill. G. $15.00

PERKINS, L.F. *French Twins.* 1918. Boston. Houghton. 203 p. VG. $30.00

PERKINS, Marlin. *My Wild Kingdom: An Autobiography.* 1982. Dutton. Ils. 263 p. dj. EX. M2. $17.00

PERKINS, Maxwell. *Editor to Author.* 1950. NY. 1st ed. dj. VG. $15.00

PERKINS, Michael. *Estelle.* 1969. Essex House. EX. P1. $40.00

PERLEMAN, S.J. *Old Gang O'Mine. Early & Essential Perleman.* 1984. Morrow. dj. EX. $15.00

PERLS, K. *Jean Fouquet.* 1940. London. Ils. 16 pls. 269 p. stiff wraps. J2. $85.00

PERRAULT, G. *L'Orchestre Rouge.* 1967. Paris. Fayard. 1st ed. 1st print. dj. M. $200.00

PERRIER, R. *La Faune de la France.* 1954. Paris. Ils. French text. 172 p. VG. M2. $10.00

PERRIN, W.H. *History of Summit Co.* 1881. Chicago. 1st ed. 1050 p. AEG. rebound. T5. $125.00

PERRINS, C.M. *Birds: Their Life, Their Ways, Their World.* 1976. Abrams. Ils Ad Cameron. 4to. 160 p. dj. M2. $14.00

PERRINS & MIDDLETON. *Encyclopedia of Birds.* 1986. Facts on File. Ils. 4to. 477 p. dj. EX. M2. $25.00

PERRY, Bliss. *Life & Letters of Henry Lee Higginson.* 1921. Boston. Ils. 557 p. VG. T5. $12.50

PERRY, Bliss. *Walt Whitman.* 1906. Riverside. Houghton Mifflin. VG. $15.00

PERRY, C.B. *Perrys of RI & Tales of Silver Creek...* 1913. NY. Ils Revised ed. 115 p. TEG. G. T5. $17.50

PERRY, Charles. *Portrait of a Young Man Drowning.* 1962. NY. 1st ed. dj. VG. $30.00

PERRY, Clay. *Underground Empire.* 1948. NY. Ils 1st ed. dj. T1. $30.00

PERRY, Clay. *Underground Empire.* 1948. NY. 1st ed. Am Cave Series. B2. $17.50

PERRY, Dick. *Reflections of Jesse Stuart on Land of Many Moods.* 1971. McGraw Hill. 1st ed. 229 p. dj. $15.00

PERRY, F.F. *Their Heart's Desire.* 1906. Dodd Mead. Ils Fisher. G. $60.00

PERRY, Frances. *Woman Gardener.* 1955. Farrar. 384 p. VG. $17.50

PERRY, J.H. *Chemical Engineers' Handbook: Chemical Engineering Series.* 1950. McGraw Hill. 3rd ed. 2nd imp. VG. $20.00

PERRY, Josephine. *Paper Industry.* 1946. Longman. 1st ed. dj. EX. $25.00

PERRY, M. *Patton & His Pistols.* 1957. Harrisburg. 1st ed. dj. VG. B2. $60.00

PERRY, R. *At the Turn of the Tide: Book of Wild Birds.* 1972. Taplinger. Ils 1st Am ed. 256 p. dj. EX. M2. $12.00

PERRY, R. *Life in Desert & Plain.* 1977. Taplinger. Ils 1st ed. 253 p. dj. EX. M2. $14.00

PERRY, R. *Mountain Wildlife.* 1981. Stackpole. Ils 1st ed. 179 p. dj. EX. M2. $12.00

PERRY, T.D. *Modern Plywood.* 1942. Chicago. Ils. dj. VG. $15.00

PERRY, Thomas. *Butcher's Boy.* 1982. Scribner. 1st ed. dj. with photo. $50.00

PERRY & SCHLEGEL. *Life of the Lava Beds.* 1975. Nat Park Service. Ils. 32 p. M2. $5.00

PERSHING, H. *Johnny Appleseed & His Time.* 1930. 1st ed. 379 p. VG. $20.00

PERSHING, J.J. *My Experiences in the World War.* Author Autograph ed. 2 vols. T5. $150.00

PETER, John. *Masters of Modern Architecture.* 1958. Braziller. Ils. 230 p. VG. $30.00

PETER, Lily. *Green Linen of Summer.* sgn. EX. B7. $12.00

PETERKIN, Julia. *Black April.* 1927. Bobbs Merrill. 1st ed. 315 p. $35.00

PETERKIN, Julia. *Bright Skin.* 1932. Bobbs Merrill. 1st trade ed. inscr. with photo. M. $80.00

PETERS, C. *Eldorado of the Ancients.* 1892. NY. Ils. 2 maps. VG. $55.00

PETERS, Charles. *Autobiography of LaGrave Co.* 1915. Sacramento. Ils. 231 p. orig wraps. A3. $45.00

PETERS, DeWitt. *Life & Adventures of Kit Carson.* 1859. Ils. 534 p. red embossed bdg. K1. $55.00

PETERS, E. *Camelot Caper.* pb. EX. C1. $4.00

PETERS, Elizabeth. *Die for Love.* 1984. NY. 1st ed. dj. EX. $22.00

PETERS, Elizabeth. *Mummy Case.* 1984. NY. 1st ed. dj. EX. $20.00

PETERS, Elizabeth. *Murders of Richard III.* VG. C1. $3.50

PETERS, Ellis. *Dead Man's Ransom.* 1984. London. 1st ed. sgn. dj. EX. $30.00

PETERS, Ellis. *Horn of Roland.* 1974. NY. dj. EX. C1. $9.00

PETERS, Ellis. *Morbid Taste for Bones.* 1987. Brother Cadfael Series. pb. EX. C1. $3.00

PETERS, Ellis. *Rainbow's End.* 1979. Morrow. 1st Am ed. dj. EX. $30.00

PETERS, Ellis. *Rare Benedictine.* 1988. London. 1st ed. sgn. dj. EX. $35.00

PETERS, Ellis. *Raven in the Foregate.* Book Club. Brother Cadfael Series. dj. EX. C1. $4.00

PETERS, Ellis. *Rose Rent.* Book Club. Brother Cadfael Series. dj. M. C1. $3.50

PETERS, Ellis. *Sanctuary Sparrow.* 1983. 1st ed. dj. VG. C1. $5.00

PETERS, Ellis. *Virgin in the Ice.* 1st ed. 2nd print. dj. EX. C1. $6.50

PETERS, H. *Der Arzt und die Heilkunst in der Deutschen Berganhenheit.* 1900. Leipzig. Ils. 138 p. xl. $120.00

PETERS, Harry. *Currier & Ives.* 1976. Arno. 2 vols. EX. $200.00

PETERS, J.A. *Dictionary of Herpetology.* 1964. Hafner. Ils. 392 p. dj. EX. M2. $25.00

PETERS, Jean. *Book Collecting: Modern Guide.* 1977. NY. dj. M. $15.00

PETERS, Joan. *From Time Immemorial: Origins of Arab-Jewish Conflict...* 1984. NY. 1st ed. dj. M. $15.00

PETERS, R. *Dance of the Wolves.* 1985. McGraw Hill. Ils 1st ed. 222 p. dj. EX. M2. $17.00

PETERS. *America on Stone.* 1976. NY. facsimile. $95.00

PETERS. *CA on Stone.* 1976. NY. facsimile. $50.00

PETERS. *Pictorial History of Ancient Pharmacy.* 1889. Chicago. Ils. 8vo. 184 p. G. P3. $49.00

PETERSON, B. *River of Light.* 1978. NY. 1st ed. dj. VG. $8.00

PETERSON, C.J. *Military Heroes of War of 1812.* 1849. Phil. 3rd ed. VG. $48.00

PETERSON, F.W. *Desert Pioneer Doctor & Experiences in Obstetrics.* 1947. Calexico. Ils. 8vo. 85 p. VG. P3. $45.00

PETERSON, H.L. *American Sword, 1775-1945.* 1965. Ils. 300 p. EX. scarce. J4. $42.50

PETERSON, H.L. *Arms & Armor in Colonial America.* 1956. PA. Ltd ed. sgn. leather. $65.00

PETERSON, H.L. *Notes on Ordnance of American Civil War: 1861-1865.* 1959. Am Ordnance Assn. 20 p. M2. $10.00

PETERSON, H.L. *Notes on Ordnance of American Civil War: 1861-1865.* 1959. WA. Ils. wraps. T5. $17.50

PETERSON, H.L. *Treasury of the Gun.* 1962. Deluxe ed. dj. EX. $16.00

PETERSON, R.T. *Field Guide to Birds.* 1947. Houghton. Ils Revised 2nd ed. 290 p. G. M2. $5.00

PETERSON, R.T. *Field Guide to the Birds of TX.* 1960. Houghton. Ils 1st ed. 304 p. dj. EX. M2. $14.00

PETERSON, R.T. *Field Guide to W Birds.* 1941. Houghton. Ils. 240 p. G. M2. $9.00

PETERSON, W.J. *Wolves in IA.* 1960. IA Hist Soc. Ils. EX. M2. $8.00

PETERSON, William. *Steamboating on Upper MS.* 1968. IA City. reprint of 1937 ed. dj. EX. $40.00

PETERSON & CHALIF. *Field Guide to Mexican Birds.* 1973. Houghton. 48 pls. dj. EX. M2. $20.00

PETERSON & FISHER. *Wild America.* 1955. Houghton. Ils. 434 p. VG. M2. $14.00

PETHERAM, John. *Bibliographical Miscellany.* 1859. London. rebound. $59.50

PETHICK, Derek. *First Approaches to NW Coast.* 1976. Vancouver. Ils. dj. M. $16.00

PETIEVICH, Gerald. *Money Men & One-Shot Deal.* 1981. Harcourt Brace. Review 1st ed. dj. RS. M. $75.00

PETIEVICH, Gerald. *To Die in Beverly Hills.* 1983. Arbor House. 1st ed. dj. EX. $25.00

PETRIE, George. *Ecclesiastical Architecture of Ireland...* 1845. Dublin. 2nd ed. J2. $150.00

PETRONE. *Le Satiricon. Traduit par Laurent Tailhade.* 1949. Paris. Ils Friesz. portfolio. slipcase. $185.00

PETRONIUS. *Satyricon.* nd. London. Ils Bosschere. 1/1000. VG. J2. $40.00

PETTERS, Ellis. *Never Pick Up Hitchhikers!* 1976. Morrow. 1st ed. dj. EX. $25.00

PETTIGREW, R.L. *Story of Ft. Liberty & Dauphin Plantation.* 1958. Richmond. 1st ed. presentation. sgn. 266 p. $37.50

PETTINGILL, O.S. *Guide to Bird Finding W of the MS.* 1953. Oxford U. Ils Sutton. 709 p. dj. EX. M2. $20.00

PEVSNER, Nikolaus. *History of Building Types.* 1976. Princeton. dj. J2. $30.00

PEW, W.A. *Colonel Ephraim Williams: An Appreciation.* 1919. Williamstown. map. 29 p. T5. $19.50

PEYRE, M.J. *Oeuvres d'Architecture.* 1796. Paris. 2nd ed. 21 pls. folio. VG. $550.00

PFANNER, H.F. *Exile in NY.* 1983. Detroit. 1st ed. dj. EX. $12.00

PFEIFFER, J. *Search for Early Man.* 1963. AM Heritage. Ils 1st ed. 151 p. EX. M2. $6.00

PFIEGER, W. *Distributional Study of MO Fishes.* 1971. KS U. 192 maps. 243 p. EX. M2. $14.00

PHAFF, H.J. *Life of Yeasts: Their Nature, Activity, Ecology...* 1966. Harvard. Ils. 186 p. dj. EX. M2. $17.00

PHAIR, Charles. *Atlantic Salmon Fishing.* Derrydale. as issued. VG. B2. $300.00

PHARES, Ross. *TX Traditions.* 1954. Holt. Ils 1st ed. 239 p. dj. EX. $20.00

PHARMACOPE-LEMERY, Nicolas. *Universelle Contenant.* 1754. Paris. $240.00

PHELAN, Richard. *TX Wild: Photographs by Jim Bones.* 1976. Excalibur. dj. EX. $15.00

PHELPS, Ethel. *Maid of the N: Feminist Folk Tales.* Ils Lloyd Bloom. pb. VG. C1. $7.50

PHILANDROS. *Astonishing Affair!* 1830. Concord. 1st/only ed. 16mo. VG. rare. T1. $275.00

PHILLIPS, A. *Birds of AZ.* 1983. AZ U. Ils Sutton. maps. 4to. dj. EX. M2. $40.00

PHILLIPS, C.C. *Coulterville Chronicle.* 1942. Grabhorn. EX. $160.00

PHILLIPS, Cabell. *From the Crash to the Blitz, 1929-1939.* 1969. Macmillan. 1st print. 596 p. dj. EX. $35.00

PHILLIPS, D.G. *Plum Tree.* 1905. Bobbs Merrill. Ils Richardson. VG. $12.00

PHILLIPS, David. *W: An American Experience.* 1973. Chicago. Regnery. Ils 1st ed. dj. EX. $45.00

PHILLIPS, Elizabeth. *American Imagination.* 1979. Kennikat Pr. Review ed. blue cloth. VG. D1. $20.00

PHILLIPS, Franklin. *Beekeeping.* 1939. Macmillan. Ils. photos. 490 p. EX. $18.00

PHILLIPS, J.A. *How Mickey Made It.* 1981. Minneapolis. 1st ed. 1/150. sgn. EX. $85.00

PHILLIPS, J.A. *Machine Dreams.* 1984. NY. 1st ed. sgn. dj. EX. $25.00

PHILLIPS, J.C. *Natural History of Ducks.* 1923-1926. London. 4to. 4 vols. VG. $22.50

PHILLIPS, J.C. *Natural History of Ducks.* 1986. Dover. 4 vols bound as 2. djs. EX. M2. $135.00

PHILLIPS, John. *Sportsman's Second Scrapbook.* 1933. Boston. 1st ed. VG. $20.00

PHILLIPS, M.E. *Edgar A. Poe: The Man.* 1926. Winston. 1st ed. blue cloth. 2 vols. VG. D1. $50.00

PHILLIPS, M.G. *Popular Manual of English Literature.* 1895. Harper. 2 vols. VG. $15.00

PHILLIPS, P.L. *List of Geographical Atlases in Library of Congress...* 1909-1914. GPO. 4 vols. xl. VG. A3. $320.00

PHILLIPS, P.L. *List of Maps of America in Library of Congress...* 1901. GPO. 1137 p. orig leather. EX. scarce. A3. $120.00

PHILLIPS, Paul. *Fur Trade.* 1961. Norman. Ils 1st ed. 2 vols. VG. B2. $135.00

PHILLIPS, S.N. *Famous Cases of Circumstantial Evidence.* 1873. Boston. 1st ed. 8vo. gilt brown cloth. G. T1. $40.00

PHILLIPS, S.S. *Excavated Artifacts From Battlefields & Campsites Civil War.* Ils. dj. M. J4. $32.50

PHILLIPS, Shine. *Big Spring.* 1942. Prentice Hall. inscr. VG. $10.00

PHILLIPS, Stephen. *Marpessa.* 1926. Windsor Pr. 1/750. EX. P3. $25.00

PHILLIPS, Stephen. *Ulysses.* 1902. Macmillan. 1st Am ed. 1/100. M. C1. $19.50

PHILLIPS, W.B. *Iron Making in AL.* 1896. Montgomery. rebound. $15.00

PHILLIPS, W.B. *Life & Labor in the Old S.* 1929. Grosset Dunlap. Ils. maps. 375 p. $22.50

PHILLIPS, W.S. *El Comancho: Indian Tales for Little Folks.* 1928. NY. Ils. VG. B2. $27.50

PHILLIPS, Wendell. *Agitator.* 1890. Funk Wagnall. 8vo. G. $17.50

PHILLIPS & LINCOLN. *American Waterfowl.* 1930. Houghton. Ils Brooks. 312 p. EX. M2. $65.00

PHILLIPS. *Black Tickets.* 1979. NY. dj. EX. $60.00

PHILLIPS. *Iron Making in AL.* 1912. AL U. Ils 3rd ed. 254 p. C4. $65.00

PHILLPOTTS, Eden. *Dish of Apples.* nd. (1921) London. Hodder Stoughton. $48.00

PHILLPOTTS, Eden. *Forest on Hill.* 1912. NY. 1st ed. VG. $18.00

PHILLPOTTS, Eden. *Green Alleys: A Comedy.* 1916. Macmillan. 1st Am ed. 396 p. RS. VG. $75.00

PHILO. *Opera.* 1613. Paris. Greek/Latin text. rebound. $300.00

PHIN, John. *Practical Hints on Selection & Use of Microscope.* 1892. NY. Ils 2nd ed. inscr. 12mo. 125 p. $25.00

PHINNEY, M.A. *Jirah Isham Allen, MT Pioneer, Government Scout Guide...* 1929. Rutland. 1/200. 8vo. black cloth. EX. T1. $75.00

PHISTERER, Frederick. *Statistical Record of the Armies of the US.* 1883. NY. 1st ed. 343 p. T5. $35.00

PHISTERER, Frederick. *Statistical Record of the Armies of the US.* 1883. NY. 343 p. K1. $14.50

PIANKA, E. *Evolutionary Ecology.* 1974. Harper Row. 356 p. EX. M2. $15.00

PIATT, D. *Memories of the Men Who Saved the Union.* 1887. 302 p. K1. $23.50

PIATT, J. *Adventures in Birding.* 1973. Knopf. 1st ed. dj. EX. M2. $8.00

PICASSO, Pablo. *Picasso Women, 1954-1963.* Abrams. 1st ed. dj. $100.00

PICASSO, Pablo. *Picasso.* 1957. Abrams. 1st ed. folio. dj. EX. $150.00

PICASSO, Pablo. *Variations on Velazquez Painting of Maids of Honor.* 1959. NY. Abrams. 1st ed. dj. EX. $175.00

PICHON, E. *Dan Sickles, Hero of Gettysburg & Yankee King of Spain.* 1945. 280 p. Lib bdg. J4. $10.00

PICHON, E. *Dan Sickles: Hero of Gettysburg & Yankee King of Spain.* 1945. Doubleday. Ils. 280 p. M2. $10.00

PICKARD & BULEY. *Midwest Pioneer: His Ills, Cures & Doctors.* 1946. NY. Ils 1st trade ed. dj. G. T5. $37.50

PICKERING, Ernest. *Homes of America.* 1951. NY. Crowell. Ils. 4to. 284 p. $15.00

PICKETT, W.P. *Negro Problem: Abraham Lincoln's Solution.* 1909. NY. inscr. 580 p. VG. T5. $22.50

PICQUET & BEST. *Post-Traumatic Stress Disorder, Rape Trauma, Delayed Stress.* Scarecrow Pr. VG. T5. $12.50

PIEKALKIEWICZ. *Moscow 1941.* 1981. Presidio Pr. 1st ed. dj. VG. $16.00

PIEPER. *Ft. Laurens, 1778-1779: Revolutionary War in OH.* 1976. Kent, OH. sgn. maps. 97 p. dj. VG. T5. $27.50

PIERCY, C.B. *Preyer-Andreae Family History.* 1937. Cleveland. sgn. 194 p. VG. T5. $25.00

PIERCY, M. *Small Changes.* 1973. NY. 1st ed. dj. EX. $30.00

PIERCY, Marge. *Breaking Camp.* 1968. CT. M. $35.00

PIERHAL, Jean. *Albert Schweitzer.* 1956. London. 1st ed. G. $18.00

PIETERS. *Dutch Settlement in MI.* 1923. Grand Rapids. Ils. 207 p. VG. C4. $37.00

PIGACHE, D.N. *Cafe Royal Days.* London. 2nd imp. fair. $12.00

PIGAFETTA, Antonio. *Voyage of Magellan.* 1969. NY. facsimile of 1525 Paris ed. M. $35.00

PIGGOTT, Stuart. *Ancient Europe: Survey.* 1965. Edinburgh U. 1st ed. dj. J2. $17.50

PIGNATTI, Terisio. *Golden Century of Venetian Paintings.* 1980. Braziller. 56 pls. 173 p. D2. $20.00

PIKE, G.D. *Jubilee Singers of Fisk U & Their Campaign To Raise $20,000.* 1873. Boston. Ils Black. 8vo. 219 p. EX. rare. $100.00

PIKE, J.A. *Beyond Anxiety.* 1955. NY. $8.00

PIKE, John. *Watercolor.* 1979. dj. $10.00

PIKE, W. *Barren Ground of N Canada.* 1892. London. Macmillan. 1st ed. 300 p. M2. $95.00

PIKE, Z.M. *SW Expedition of Zebulon M. Pike.* 1925. Chicago. Lakeside Classic. 239 p. VG. T5. $42.50

PILLSBURY COMPANY. *Pillsbury Grand National Baking Contest #1.* 1950. NY. VG. B2. $62.50

PILSBURY, H.A. *Land Mollusca of N America (N of Mexico).* 1939-1948. Phil Acad Sc. 4 vols. EX. M2. $225.00

PIMENTEL, D.F. *Situacion Actual de Raza Indigena de Mexico y Medios...* 1864. Mexico City. VG. $150.00

PINCHER, C. *Study of Fish.* 1948. Duell Sloan. 1st Am ed. 343 p. EX. M2. $15.00

PINCHERLE, Salvatore. *Operzioni Distributive E Le Lor Applicazioni All `Analisi.* 1901. Bologna. 1st ed. blue Lib buckram. VG. J2. $25.00

PINCHOT, G. *To the S Sea: Cruise of Schooner M. Pinchot.* 1930. Blue Ribbon. Ils. 370 p. VG. M2. $28.00

PINCKNEY, Josephine. *Hilton Head.* 1941. NY. 1st ed. dj. EX. $25.00

PINHEY, E.C.G. *Butterflies of Rhodesia.* 1949. Rhodesia Sc Assn. Ils. 208 p. M2. $80.00

PINKERTON, Allan. *Bank Robbers & the Detectives.* 1883. NY. Carlton. green cloth. xl. $60.00

PINKERTON, Allan. *Spy of the Rebellion.* 1886. NY. Ils. 658 p. $45.00

PINKERTON, Allan. *Spy of the Rebellion.* 1888. Chicago. Waverly. salesman sample. VG. $30.00

PINKERTON, R.E. *Canoe: Its Selection, Care & Use.* 1944. Macmillan. Ils. 162 p. dj. EX. $17.50

PINNEY, R. *Complete Book of Cave Exploration.* 1962. NY. 1st ed. dj. VG. B2. $17.50

PINTER & FOWLES. *French Lieutenant's Woman. A Screenplay.* 1981. Little Brown. 1/360. sgns. slipcase. M. $100.00

PIPER, R.F. *Hungry Eye.* 1956. LA. $10.00

PIPER, Watty. *Animal Storybook.* 1954. Platt Munk. Ils Dennis. dj. VG. $23.00

PIPER, Watty. *Bumper Book.* 1959. NY. Ils Eulailie. Revised ed. $20.00

PIPER, Watty. *Little Engine That Could.* 1930. NY. Ils Lois Lenski. dj. EX. $35.00

PIPER, Watty. *Little Engine That Could.* 1961. Platt Munk. Ils Haumans. EX. $8.00

PIRNIE, M.D. *MI Waterfowl Management.* 1935. MI Conservation. Ils. 328 p. M2. $19.00

PIRSIG, R.M. *Zen & the Art of Motorcycle Maintenance.* 1974. NY. dj. VG. $35.00

PIRTLE, Cable. *American Cowboy.* 1975. Oxmoor. sgn. 4to. dj. VG. $60.00

PISANO, R.G. *Long Island Landscape Painting, 1820-1920.* 1988. Boston. Ils. oblong 8vo. 167 p. EX. $23.00

PISANUS, Fraxis. *Bibliography of Prohibited Books.* 1962. Brussel Pub. 3 vols. M. $175.00

PITMAN, Benn. *Assassination of President Lincoln.* 1865. Cincinnati. 421 p. rebound. VG. T5. $95.00

PITMAN, Benn. *Manual of Phonography.* 1860. Cincinnati. 144 p. fair. T5. $27.50

PITMAN, N.H. *Chinese Wonder Book.* 1919. Dutton. Ils. blue cloth. VG. $40.00

PITOIS, E. *Le Secret du Temps de Pose, Secret de la Reussite...* 1923. Paris. Lib Delagrave. 102 p. wraps. $25.00

PITON, Camille. *Le Costume Civil en France.* c 1926. Paris. Ils. G. $60.00

PITTENGER, William. *Daring & Suffering: History of Great Railroad Adventure...* 1863. Phil. Daughaday. 1st ed. 288 p. EX. $57.50

PITTENGER, William. *Great Locomotive Chase.* 1929. 9th ed. 490 p. $17.50

PITZ, H.C. *Brandywine Tradition.* 1968. NY. 1st ed. dj. EX. $35.00

PLACE, C.A. *Charles Bulfinch: Architect & Citizen.* 1968. NY. reprint of 1925 ed. dj. VG. J2. $30.00

PLACZEK, Siegfried. *Geschlechtsleben der Hysterischen.* 1919. Bonn. Marcus Weber. 1st ed. EX. $30.00

PLAGENS, Peter. *Sunshine Muse: Comtemporary Art on W Coast.* 1974. NY. Praeger. Ils. 200 p. xl. D2. $25.00

PLAIDY, Jean. *Beyond the Blue Mountains.* 1947. NY. 1st ed. dj. EX. $12.50

PLANCHE, J.R. *Pursuivant of Arms.* c 1851. London. VG. $50.00

PLANCY, J.A.S. *Dictionaire Infernal ou Recherches et Anecdotes sur Demons.* 1818. Paris. Mongie. 1st ed. 8vo. 2 vols. $150.00

PLANTE, David. *Catholic.* 1985. London. 1st ed. sgn. dj. VG. $45.00

PLANTE, David. *Difficult Women.* 1983. London. 1st ed. dj. EX. $40.00

PLANTE, David. *Foreigner.* 1984. London. 1st ed. dj. EX. $30.00

PLANTE, David. *Ghost of Henry James.* 1970. Boston. Gambit. 1st ed. dj. VG. $30.00

PLANTE, David. *My Mother's Pearl Necklace.* 1987. NY. 1st ed. 1/150. sgn. wraps. M. $75.00

PLAT, Rutherford. *Our Flowering World.* 1947. NY. fair. $18.00

PLATH, I. *Decorative Arts of Sweden.* 1948. Scribner. Ils. dj. VG. $45.00

PLATH, Sylvia. *Bell Jar.* 1963. London. 1st ed. dj. VG. scarce. $50.00

PLATH, Sylvia. *Bell Jar.* 1971. Harper. 1st Am ed. dj. VG. $12.00

PLATH, Sylvia. *Letters Home: Correspondence.* 1975. NY. 1st ed. dj. EX. $20.00

PLATH, Sylvia. *Winter Trees.* 1971. London. 1st ed. dj. VG. $18.00

PLATT, Colin. *Abbeys & Priories of Medieval England.* 1984. Fordham U. 1st ed. 270 p. dj. M. C1. $24.00

PLATT, Frank C. *Great Battles of WWI: In the Air.* 1966. Weathervane. 206 p. dj. VG. T5. $19.50

PLATT, Rutherford. *This Green World.* 1949. NY. photos. VG. $18.00

PLATT, Rutherford. *Wilderness.* 1961. Dodd Mead. Ils. 310 p. dj. EX. M2. $5.00

PLATT, Ward. *Frontier, Eaton & Mains.* 1908. NY. Ils. fld map. 292 p. wraps. A3. $22.00

PLAUT, Frederick. *Unguarded Moment: Photographic Interpretation.* 1964. Englewood Cliffs. slipcase. T5. $35.00

PLAUTO, Tito Maccio. *I Tre Nummi & La Commedia del Fantasma.* 1951. Milan. Ils Chirico. 1/400. wraps. D2. $250.00

PLEASANTS, M.M. *Which One? And Other Antebellum Days.* 1910. Boston. Ils 1st ed. inscr. 90 p. VG. $30.00

PLEASANTS, W.S. *Stingaree Murders.* c 1932. NY. Mystery League. 1st ed. VG. $10.00

PLICKA, Karel. *Prague in Photographs.* 1961. Prague. Artia. 224 photos. folio. dj. slipcase. $75.00

PLIMPTON. *Bogey Man.* nd. NY. 1st ed. dj. VG. $10.00

PLOSSU, Bernard. *Surleanalisme.* 1972. Paris. Cheve. Ils. 4to. wraps. $32.50

PLOWDEN, David. *Bridges: Spans of N America.* 1974. photos. 328 p. $35.00

PLOWDEN, David. *Commonplace.* 1974. Dutton. 1st ed. VG. $22.50

PLOWDEN, David. *Time of Trains.* 1987. Ils. photos. 160 p. $35.00

PLOWDEN, Gene. *Those Amazing Ringlings & Their Circuses.* 1968. Caldwell. Ils. 312 p. dj. VG. $20.00

PLUM, M. *Killing of Judge MacFarlane.* c 1930. NY. Harper. 1st ed. VG. $8.00

PLUMLEY, Ladd. *With the Trout Fly.* 1929. 1st ed. VG. $20.00

PLUMMER, W. *Holy Goof.* 1981. Prentice Hall. 1st print. dj. M. $38.00

PLUMPELLY, Raphael. *Preliminary Report of Iron Ores & Coal Fields...of 1872.* 1873. NY. Bien. Ils. 442 p. VG. A3. $50.00

PLUTARCH & NORTH. *Lives of Noble Grecians & Romans.* 1928. Shakespeare Head Pr. 1/500. EX. $300.00

PLUTARCH & NORTH. *Lives of Noble Grecians & Romans.* 1929. Nonesuch. 1/1500. 4to. 5 vols. EX. $200.00

POCHIN, E. *More About British Wild Birds.* nd. Brockhampton. Ils. 56 p. G. M2. $4.00

PODESCHI. *Books on Horse & Horsemanship, 1400-1941.* 1981. London. Ils. 427 p. dj. EX. $65.00

POE, E.A. *Bells & Other Poems by Poe.* 1912. NY. Hodder. Ils Dulac. VG. $125.00

POE, E.A. *Bells.* nd. (1890?) London. Nister. Ils. wraps. G. D1. $8.00

POE, E.A. *Bells.* 1881. Phil. Porter Coates. green cloth. VG. D1. $30.00

POE, E.A. *Bells.* 1881. Porter Coates. beige/purple bdg. VG. D1. $22.00

POE, E.A. *Bells.* 1881. Porter Coates. Christmas/green bdg. G. D1. $10.00

POE, E.A. *Black Cat.* 1971. Weather Bird. 4to. VG. D1. $8.00

POE, E.A. *Centenary Poe.* 1909. Duffield. 8vo. TEG. gilt red cloth. G. D1. $35.00

POE, E.A. *Centenary Poe.* 1949. Bodley Head. 1st ed. blue cloth. VG. D1. $25.00

POE, E.A. *Chapter on Autography.* 1952. Graphoanaly Soc. 1/1239. VG. D1. $32.00

POE, E.A. *Complete Works.* 1908. NY. Centennial ed. 1/1000. 10 vols. G. $100.00

POE, E.A. *Edgar A. Poe Stories.* 1961. Platt Munk. blue bdg. dj. EX. D1. $8.00

POE, E.A. *Edgar A. Poe's Poetical Works.* 1866. Sampson Low. New Ils ed. gilt blue cloth. G. D1. $20.00

POE, E.A. *Fall of House of Usher.* Ltd Ed Club. slipcase. M. B3. $450.00

POE, E.A. *Fall of House of Usher.* 1928. Narcisse. 1/300. Ils Alastair. VG. D1. $180.00

POE, E.A. *Gold Bug & Other Tales.* nd. London. Downey. Ils McCormick. VG. D1. $35.00

POE, E.A. *Gold Bug.* nd. Little Leather Lib. 48mo. G. D1. $8.00

POE, E.A. *Gold Bug.* 1928. Lakeside Pr. 1/377. gilt cloth. slipcase. D1. $90.00

POE, E.A. *Gold Bug.* 1945. Comet Pr. Ils Morris. 1/1200. VG. D1. $25.00

POE, E.A. *Illustrated Edgar A. Poe.* 1976. Potter. Ils Satty. black cloth. dj. EX. D1. $35.00

POE, E.A. *Imp of the Perverse.* July, 1845. 1st print. lacks wraps. VG. D1. $65.00

POE, E.A. *Journal of Julius Rodman.* 1947. San Francisco. Colt Grabhorn. 4to. VG. D1. $75.00

POE, E.A. *Masque of Red Death.* 1946. England. Ils Wilks. 4to. gray bdg. EX. D1. $25.00

POE, E.A. *Memorial Edition of Muse.* 1938. NY. Special Ltd ed. 866 p. dj. VG. $25.00

POE, E.A. *Narrative of Arthur Gordon Pym.* 1898. London. Downey. Ils McCormick. red cloth. G. D1. $25.00

POE, E.A. *Narrative of Arthur Gordon Pym.* 1930. Heritage. Ils Clark. white bdg. slipcase. D1. $22.00

POE, E.A. *Narrative of Arthur Gordon Pym.* 1957. Norwalk. Heritage. quarto. slipcase. EX. $15.00

POE, E.A. *Oval Portrait.* 1980. 1st Class Pr. 1/30. gray wraps. EX. D1. $25.00

POE, E.A. *Poe's Masterpieces.* 1909. Caxton. 1/1000. VG. D1. $65.00

POE, E.A. *Poems of Edgar A. Poe With Memoir.* 1902. Crowell. Intro Kent. red cloth. G. D1. $10.00

POE, E.A. *Poems of Edgar A. Poe.* 1900. NY. Bell. Ils Robinson. green cloth. G. D1. $75.00

POE, E.A. *Poems of Edgar A. Poe.* 1901. Mosher. 1/925. 12mo. 87 p. vellum wraps. D1. $50.00

POE, E.A. *Poems.* 1901. Roycroft. 8vo. brown suede. VG. D1. $50.00

POE, E.A. *Poetical Works of Edgar A. Poe.* nd. (1880?) London. Griffin. Ils Weir. D1. $15.00

POE, E.A. *Poetical Works of Edgar A. Poe.* 1872. Edinburgh. Nimmo. gilt blue cloth. VG. D1. $21.00

POE, E.A. *Portable Poe.* 1977. Penguin. pb. VG. D1. $8.00

POE, E.A. *Prose Tales.* nd. (1920?) Crowell. Intro Lowell. VG. D1. $10.00

POE, E.A. *Raven & Other Poems.* 1936. Detroit. Fine Book Circle. 1/950. dj. D1. $45.00

POE, E.A. *Raven.* 1883. Sampson Low. folio. olive cloth. VG. D1. $130.00

POE, E.A. *Raven. With Comment by Edmund Stedman.* 1884. Harper. 26 pls. folio. AEG. J2. $300.00

POE, E.A. *Sallsamma Historier...* 1931. Malmo. Trans Nilsson. 185 p. $5.00

POE, E.A. *Selected Tales of Mystery.* 1909. Lippincott. 4to. black cloth. VG. D1. $50.00

POE, E.A. *Selected Writings.* 1976. Penguin. pb. VG. D1. $6.00

POE, E.A. *SF of Edgar A. Poe.* 1977. Penguin. pb. VG. D1. $7.00

POE, E.A. *Tales of Edgar A. Poe From 1809-1849.* 1964. VA Pulp Paper. Ils Thompson. slipcase. EX. D1. $34.00

POE, E.A. *Tales of Edgar A. Poe.* 1902. Knickerbocker. Ils Coburn. gilt blue cloth. D1. $22.00

POE, E.A. *Tales of Edgar A. Poe.* 1944. Random House. Ils Eichenberg. green cloth. D1. $15.00

POE, E.A. *Tales of Mystery, Imagination & Humor.* 1852. London. Vizetelly. 16mo. red cloth. VG. D1. $175.00

POE, E.A. *Tales of Mystery & Imagination.* nd. (1977?) reprint of 1935 ed. 8vo. dj. D1. $25.00

POE, E.A. *Tales of Mystery & Imagination.* nd. London/NY. Harrap/Brentanos. Ils Clarke. J2. $125.00

POE, E.A. *Tales of Mystery & Imagination.* 1933. NY. Tudor. Ils Clarke. TEG. EX. $75.00

POE, E.A. *Tales of Mystery & Imagination.* 1933. Tudor. Ils Clarke. black cloth. G. D1. $55.00

POE, E.A. *Tales of Mystery & Imagination.* 1941. Heritage. Ils Sharp. slipcase. VG. D1. $25.00

POE, E.A. *Tales.* 1964. WV Pulp Paper. Ltd ed. boxed. EX. $50.00

POE, E.A. *Tell-Tale Heart.* 1978. Harper Row. 1st ed. 8vo. dj. VG. D1. $25.00

POE, E.A. *Works of Edgar A. Poe.* nd. Plymouth. Midnight ed. 16mo. VG. D1. $12.00

POE, E.A. *Works of Edgar A. Poe.* 1904. Funk Wagnall. 10 vols. russet cloth. VG. D1. $30.00

POE, E.A. *Works of Edgar A. Poe.* 1905. NY. Nelson. 16mo. VG. D1. $27.00

POE, E.A. *Works of Edgar A. Poe.* 1927. Black Reader. Intro Hervey Allen. red cloth. D1. $10.00

POE, E.A. *Works of Edgar A. Poe. Vol. VII.* 1895. Stone Kimball. 1 of 10 vol set. VG. D1. $15.00

POETRY SOCIETY OF GEORGIA. *Anthology of Verse.* 1929. Savannah. G. $20.00

POGANY, Willie. *Witch's Kitchen.* nd. NY. possible 1st ed. green cloth. $50.00

POGANY, Willy. *Bobolink Books No. 1.* 4 color pls. oblong 4to. with record. EX. T1. $85.00

POGANY, Willy. *Rubaiyat of Omar Khayyam.* nd. NY. Crowell. sgn/inscr. 8vo. dj. J2. $45.00

POGANY, Willy. *Rubaiyat of Omar Khayyam.* nd. NY. Crowell. 4to. J2. $40.00

POGANY, Willy. *Rubaiyat of Omar Khayyam.* 1942. Phil. sgn. slipcase. J2. $100.00

POGANY, Willy. *Willy Pogany's Drawing Lessons.* 1942. Phil. Revised ed. with paper pad. J2. $35.00

POHL, Frederick. *Cool War.* 1981. Del Ray. 1st ed. dj. VG. $12.50

POHL, Frederick. *Starburst.* 1982. Del Ray. 1st ed. dj. VG. $12.50

POHL, Frederik. *Way the Future Was.* nd. Book Club. dj. VG. P1. $5.00

POHL, Frederik. *Way the Future Was.* 1978. Del Rey. dj. EX. P1. $10.00

POHL, John. *Kenny Concept of Infantile Paralysis & Its Treatment.* 1943. Bruce Pub. 1st ed. J2. $20.00

POIGNANT, A. *Animals of Australia.* 1967. Dodd Mead. Ils. 4to. 201 p. dj. EX. M2. $10.00

POINTER, Larry. *In Search of Butch Cassidy.* 1978. OK U. photos. 294 p. dj. EX. M2. $12.00

POINTER, Michael. *Sherlock Holmes File: Many Personae of Sherlock Holmes...* 1976. NY. Stated 1st Am ed. 168 p. dj. EX. $35.00

POIRE, Emmanuel. *Les Courses dans l'Antiquite par Caran d'Ache.* c 1900. Paris. oblong 4to. VG. $60.00

POLHAMUS, W.H. *Cedar Creek: A Poem.* 1901. Cleveland. Ils. 50 p. cloth bdg. G. T5. $35.00

POLI, F. *Sharks Are Caught at Night.* 1959. Regnery. Ils 1st Am ed. 158 p. dj. EX. M2. $14.00

POLLACK, Channing. *Enemy.* 1925. NY. 1/250. sgn. $10.00

POLLARD, A.W. *English Miracle Plays: Moralities & Interludes.* 1950. Oxford. dj. VG. C1. $16.00

POLLARD, A.W. *Le Morte d'Arthur.* 1961. 1 vol ed. dj. VG. C1. $16.00

POLLARD, A.W. *Romance of King Arthur.* 1979. Ils Rackham. reprint of 1917 ed. dj. M. C1. $11.50

POLLARD, E.A. *First Year of the War.* 1863. NY. 360 p. gilt bdg. K1. $28.50

POLLARD, E.A. *Lost Cause Regained.* 1868. NY. 1st ed. 214 p. K1. $27.50

POLLARD, E.A. *Lost Cause.* 1866. NY. 1st ed. 752 p. rebound brown cloth. K1. $45.00

POLLARD, E.A. *Lost Cause.* 1867. NY. Enlarged ed. 752 p. scarce. K1. $32.50

POLLARD, E.A. *S History of the War.* 1977. Fairfax. reprint. 2 vols. dj. EX. M2. $20.00

POLLARD & BARCLAY-SMITH. *British & American Game Birds.* 1939. Derrydale. 1/125. sgn. folio. slipcase. EX. $185.00

POLLARD & REDGRAVE. *Short Title Catalog of English Books, 1475-1640.* 1948. London. VG. $60.00

POLLEN, Arthur. *Great Delusion: Study of Aircraft in Peace & War by Neon.* 1927. MacVeagh. 1st ed. VG. J2. $20.00

POLLER, Walter. *Medical Block Buchenwald.* nd. NY. pb. VG. $7.00

POLLOCK, Edward. *Sketchbook of Suffolk, VA: Its People & Its Trade.* 1886. Portsmouth. wraps. $17.00

POLLOCK, Thomas. *Theatre in the 18th C.* 1933. PA U. 1st ed. J2. $20.00

POLSKY, Thomas. *Curtains for the Editor.* 1939. NY. 238 p. wraps. G. T5. $8.50

POMERLEAU, Rene. *Champignons de l'Est du Canada et des Etast-Unis.* 1951. Montreal. Ils. 5 color pls. 302 p. fair. T5. $19.50

POMERLEAU, Rene. *Mushrooms of E Canada & the US.* 1951. Montreal. Ils. 5 color pls. 302 p. fair. T5. $19.50

POMEROY, W.B. *Dr. Kinsey & Institute for Sex Research.* 1975. NY. $15.00

POND, B. *Sampler of Wayside Herbs: Rediscovering New Uses for Plants.* 1974. Chatham. Ils 1st ed. 4to. dj. EX. M2. $22.00

POND, F.E. *Sportsman's Directory & Yearbook.* 1892. Milwaukee. Pond & Goldey. 205 p. VG. A3. $145.00

POND, Grace. *Observer's Book of Cats.* 1961. Warne. Ils. 12mo. dj. EX. $14.00

POND, J.B. *Eccentricities of Genius: Memoirs of Men & Women...Stage.* 1900. NY. VG. $40.00

PONICSAN, Darryl. *Accomplice.* 1975. NY. 1st ed. dj. VG. $12.50

PONICSAN, Darryl. *Andoshen, PA.* 1973. NY. Dial. 1st ed. dj. EX. $10.00

PONICSAN, Darryl. *Last Detail.* 1970. NY. 1st ed. dj. M. $25.00

PONICSAN, Darryl. *Unmarried Man.* 1980. NY. 1st ed. dj. EX. $8.00

PONSOR, Y.R. *Gawain & the Green Knight.* Ils Darrell Sweet. dj. EX. C1. $6.50

PONSOR, Y.R. *Gawain & the Green Knight.* 1979. 1st ed. VG. C1. $6.00

PONTING, T.C. *Life of Tom Candy Ponting: Autobiography.* 1952. Evanston. Ils 2nd ed. 1/500. EX. $45.00

POOL, D.D.S. *Siddur: Traditional Prayer Book.* 1960. NY. 1st ed. boxed. M. scarce. $25.00

POOL, R.J. *Flowers & Flowering Plants.* 1941. McGraw Hill. Ils 2nd ed. 428 p. EX. M2. $17.00

POOL & PAVA. *Acoustic Nerve Tumors.* 1957. Thomas. 1st ed. dj. EX. $35.00

POOLE, AUGUSTUS & BUCKITT. *Walter J. Speculation: Wall Street Game Book.* 1929. NY. Farrar. dj. EX. $45.00

POOLMAN, K. *Zeppelins Against London.* 1961. NY. 1st ed. 246 p. dj. VG. B2. $22.50

POOR, C.L. *Men Against the Rule: Century of Progress in Yacht Design.* 1937. Derrydale. 1/950. 8vo. acetate dj. EX. $150.00

POPE, Alexander. *Essay on Man.* 1748. London. rebound. $65.00

POPE, Alexander. *Rape of the Lock.* 1896. Chiswick. Ils Beardsley. blue bdg. EX. $200.00

POPE, Arthur. *Persian Architecture.* 1965. Braziller. 1st ed. dj. VG. J2. $35.00

POPE, Charles. *Haverhill Emerson Part Second.* 1916. Cambridge. Ils. 248 p. VG. B1. $30.00

POPE, D. *Graf Spee: Life & Death of a Raider.* 1957. NY. 1st Am ed. dj. VG. B2. $20.00

POPE, Dudley. *Henry Morgan's Way.* 1977. London. 1st ed. dj. VG. $27.00

POPE-HENNESSY, John. *Catalog of Italian Sculpture in Victoria & Albert Museum.* 1964. London. 736 pls. 3 vols. djs. EX. J2. $150.00

POPE-HENNESSY, John. *Raphael.* 1970. NY U. 246 pls. 304 p. dj. D2. $65.00

POPE-HENNESSY, John. *Sienese Quattrocento Painting.* 1947. Oxford/London. Phaidon. Ils. dj. D2. $60.00

POPITZ, Klaus. *Plakate der Zwanziger Jahre aus der Kunstbibliothek Berlin.* 1977. Berlin. Ils. 119 p. D2. $55.00

POPULAR MECHANICS. *Boy Mechanic, Book 2.* 1915. Ils. 473 p. VG. $40.00

PORNY, M.A. *Elements of Heraldry...Dictionary of Technical Terms...* 1765. London. Newbery. leather. EX. $120.00

PORTALIS & BERALDI. *Les Graveurs du Dix-Huitieme Siecle.* 1970. NY. Burt Franklin. 3 vols. D2. $108.50

PORTER, Burton P. *Old Canal Days.* 1942. Columbus, OH. Premiere 1st ed. sgn. 469 p. T5. $42.50

PORTER, C. & M.R. *Matt Field on the Santa Fe Trail.* 1960. OK U. Ils. map. dj. VG. M2. $20.00

PORTER, D.D. *Naval History of the Civil War.* 1984. Castle. reprint. 843 p. dj. EX. M2. $20.00

PORTER, E.H. *Pollyanna Grows Up.* 1915. Page. 4th Glad Book. green bdg. G. $15.00

PORTER, Eliot. *All Under Heaven: Chinese World.* 1983. NY. Pantheon. dj. EX. $40.00

PORTER, Eliot. *Birds of N America: A Personal Selection.* 1972. Dutton. pls. dj. EX. $20.00

PORTER, Eliot. *Eliot Porter.* 1987. Boston. 1st ed. dj. EX. $75.00

PORTER, Eliot. *In Wildness Is the Preservation of the World.* 1962. San Francisco. 72 photos. folio. dj. T5. $45.00

PORTER, Eliot. *Moments of Discovery: Adventures With American Birds.* 1977. NY. 1st ed. dj. EX. $23.00

PORTER, G.S. *Birds of the Bible.* 1909. Cincinnati. 1st ed. VG. $195.00

PORTER, G.S. *Birds of the Bible.* 1916. London. Hodder Stoughton. dj. EX. $150.00

PORTER, G.S. *Daughter of the Land.* nd. Grosset Dunlap. VG. $12.00

PORTER, G.S. *Freckles.* nd. Grosset Dunlap. VG. $12.00

PORTER, G.S. *Harvester.* 1911. Garden City. 564 p. G. T5. $19.50

PORTER, G.S. *Her Father's Daughter.* nd. Grosset Dunlap. VG. $12.00

PORTER, G.S. *Her Father's Daughter.* 1923. Doubleday. dj. EX. $50.00

PORTER, G.S. *Keeper of the Bees.* 1925. Doubleday Page. 1st ed. VG. $25.00

PORTER, G.S. *Laddie.* 1913. Garden City. Ils 1st ed. 602 p. G. T5. $19.50

PORTER, G.S. *Little Story of Gene Stratton Porter.* 1926. Ils. 12mo. 51 p. G. B1. $55.00

PORTER, G.S. *Music of the Wild.* 1910. Cincinnati/NY. 1st ed. TEG. EX. $125.00

PORTER, G.S. *Song of the Cardinal.* 1st ed. G. $85.00

PORTER, G.S. *Tales You Won't Believe.* 1926. Doubleday. xl. G. $40.00

PORTER, G.S. *White Flag.* 1923. Garden City. 1st ed. 483 p. VG. T5. $22.50

PORTER, H. *Campaigning With Grant.* 1981. Time Life. reprint of 1897 ed. AEG. M2. $20.00

PORTER, Joyce. *Dover & the Unkindest Cut of All.* 1967. NY. 1st Am ed. dj. EX. $20.00

PORTER, Joyce. *Dover Goes to Pott.* 1968. NY. 1st Am ed. dj. EX. $20.00

PORTER, Joyce. *Package Included Murder.* 1976. NY. 1st Am ed. dj. EX. $15.00

PORTER, K.A. *Christmas Story.* 1967. NY. Ils Ben Shahn. dj. VG. J2. $10.00

PORTER, K.A. *Collected Essays & Occasional Writings.* 1970. NY. Deluxe ed. 1/250. sgn. boxed. M. $125.00

PORTER, K.A. *Defense of Circe.* 1954. NY. Ltd ed. 1/1700. VG. $35.00

PORTER, K.A. *Flowering Judas & Other Stories.* 1935. NY. 1st trade ed. 1st issue. dj. M. $50.00

PORTER, K.A. *French Songbook.* c 1933. Paris. Harrison. 1/595. sgn. 4to. dj. $175.00

PORTER, K.A. *Hacienda.* 1934. NY. 1st ed. 1/895. slipcase. EX. $85.00

PORTER, K.A. *Never-Ending Wrong.* 1977. Boston. 1st ed. dj. VG. $8.00

PORTER, K.A. *Ship of Fools.* 1962. Boston. 1st ed. dj. EX. $25.00

PORTER, Quincey. *Three Elizabethan Songs.* 1961. Yale. 1/500. dj. VG. $20.00

PORTER, R. *Mushroom Hunt.* 1983. Dutton. Ils 1st ed. 4to. 98 p. EX. M2. $10.00

PORTER & AUERBACH. *Mexican Churches.* 1987. NM U. Ils. dj. D2. $24.95

PORTER & COULTER. *Synopsis of Flora of CO.* 1874. WA. 176 p. wraps. A3. $30.00

PORTER & HUBLER. *Cole Porter Story.* 1965. World. 1st ed. 1st print. dj. EX. $55.00

PORTIS, Charles. *True Grit.* 1968. NY. 1st ed. dj. EX. $12.00

PORTOGHESI, Paolo. *Roma Barocca.* nd. Rome. dj. VG. J2. $50.00

PORTON, C. & M.R. *Ruxton on the Rockies.* 1979. OK U. Ils. 325 p. dj. EX. M2. $20.00

POSIN, D.Q. *Out of This World.* 1959. Chicago. $18.00

POSNER & TA-SHEMA. *Hebrew Book: An Historical Survey.* Ils. dj. VG. E2. $18.00

POSPAHALA, R.S. *Population Ecology of the Mallard.* 1974. USFWS. 73 p. M2. $5.00

POST, C.A. *Cuyahoga: Crooked River That Made a City Great.* nd. np. photos. maps. 44 p. wraps. VG. T5. $35.00

POST, C.A. *Doans Corners & City Four Miles W With Glance at Cuyahoga...* 1930. Cleveland. Ils 1st ed. 210 p. dj. G. T5. $47.50

POST, E.L. *Introduction to General Theory of Elementary Proposition.* 1921. 1st ed. VG. $140.00

POST, Emily. *How To Behave.* 1928. NY. Doubleday. EX. $15.00

POST, R.C. *History of European & American Sculpture.* 1921. Harvard. 1st ed. 2 vols. $125.00

POST, W.K. *Harvard Stories.* 1894. Putnam. 1st ed. $12.00

POTERII, Petri. *Pharmacopoe Spagyrica.* 1622. Bologna. 8vo. $200.00

POTOK, Chaim. *Book of Lights.* 1981. NY. 1st ed. dj. EX. $25.00

POTOK, Chaim. *Chosen.* 1967. NY. 1st ed. dj. EX. $40.00

POTOK, Chaim. *My Name Is Asher Lev.* 1972. Knopf. 1st ed. dj. EX. $20.00

POTOK, Chaim. *Promise.* 1969. NY. 1st ed. dj. VG. $25.00

POTTER, Beatrix. *House of Warne: 100 Years of Publishing.* 1965. London. EX. $40.00

POTTER, Beatrix. *Letters to Children.* 1966. NY. Harvard Lib/Walker. Ils. wraps. VG. $20.00

POTTER, Beatrix. *Letters to Children.* 1966. NY. 1st ed. clear acetate dj. EX. $30.00

POTTER, Beatrix. *Sister Anne.* 1932. Phil. 1st ed. 154 p. VG. B2. $25.00

POTTER, C.F. *Preacher & I.* 1951. NY. $22.50

POTTER, C.F. *Your Days Are Numbered.* 1973. PA. $15.00

POTTER, E.B. *US & World Sea Power.* 1955. Prentice Hall. 963 p. dj. VG. $35.00

POTTER, E.F. *Birds of the Carolinas.* 1986. NC U. Ils. 408 p. EX. M2. $24.00

POTTER, Jean. *AK Under Arms.* 1942. Macmillan. 4th ed. 8vo. blue cloth. VG. $15.00

POTTER, Stephan. *Art of Winning Games Without Actually Cheating.* nd. NY. Holt. green cloth. dj. $15.00

POTTER, Stephen. *Lifemanship.* 1951. NY. 1st ed. dj. VG. $10.00

POTTS, A.F. *Elegiac Mode.* 1967. Cornell. 1st ed. 8vo. dj. EX. $25.00

POULET. *Foreign Bodies in Surgery.* 1880. NY. Ils. 2 vols. green cloth. VG. $40.00

POULTON, E.B. *Colors of Animals: Their Meaning & Use.* 1890. London. Trench Trubner. 360 p. G. M2. $10.00

POUNCEY & GERE. *Italian Drawings in Department of Prints & Drawings...* 1962. London. Ils. 2 vols. djs. D2. $150.00

POUND, Arthur. *Detroit: Dynamic City.* 1940. Appleton. 1st ed. presentation. dj. VG. J2. $15.00

POUND, Arthur. *Lake Ontario.* 1945. Bobbs Merrill. Ils. maps. 384 p. dj. EX. $15.00

POUND, Arthur. *Twelve Years of the Telephone Pioneers.* 1923. Atlantic City. 86 p. VG. B1. $20.00

POUND, Ezra. *Ezra Pound Letters of 1907-1941.* 1950. NY. 1st ed. dj. VG. $40.00

POUND, Ezra. *Literary Essays of Ezra Pound.* 1954. London. 1st ed. 464 p. dj. VG. T5. $27.50

POUND, Ezra. *Lume Spente & Other Early Poems.* 1966. New Directions. 1st Am ed. acetate dj. EX. $25.00

POUND, Ezra. *Pisan Cantos.* 1949. London. Faber. 1st ed. VG. $45.00

POUND, J.B. *Memoirs of Jerome B. Pound With Histories...* 1949. np. $15.00

POURADE, R. *Time of the Bells. Vol. 2.* 1961. San Diego. Ils. 4to. 262 p. dj. VG. $16.00

POWELEIT, A.C. *KY Fighting 192nd Light G.H.Q. Tank Battalion.* 1981. Newport, KY. Ils. inscr. 228 p. VG. T5. $22.50

POWELL, A.G. *I Can Go Home Again.* 1943. Chapel Hill. 1st ed. 310 p. EX. $27.50

POWELL, A.M. *Trailing & Camping in AK.* 1909. Wessells. G. $20.00

POWELL, Anthony. *At Lady Molly's.* 1957. London. 1st ed. dj. EX. $27.00

POWELL, Anthony. *Faces in My Time.* 1980. NY. Holt. 1st Am ed. dj. EX. $15.00

POWELL, Anthony. *Military Philosphers.* 1968. London. 1st Eng ed. dj. EX. $60.00

POWELL, Anthony. *Question of Upbringing; Buyer's Market; Acceptance World.* 1962. London. 1st ed. 3 vols in 1. dj. VG. $95.00

POWELL, Anthony. *Temporary Kings.* 1973. London. 1st ed. dj. EX. $25.00

POWELL, David. *Autobiography of Rev. David Powell.* 1856. Phil. 8vo. black cloth. G. scarce. $25.00

POWELL, E.A. *End of the Trail.* 1914. NY. 1st ed. fld map. 402 p. G. T5. $22.50

POWELL, E.A. *End of the Trail.* 1915. Ils. fld map. 462 p. VG. K1. $22.50

POWELL, J.W. *Exploration of CO River of W & Its Tributaries 1869-1872.* 1875. WA. GPO. Ils. pocket map. 291 p. A3. $225.00

POWELL, J.W. *First Annual Report of Bureau of Ethnology.* 1881. WA. Ils. 4to. 603 p. K1. $75.00

POWELL, J.W. *Twentieth Annual Report of Bureau of American Ethnology.* 1903. WA. Ils. G. T5. $95.00

POWELL, L.C. *Bookman's Progress.* 1968. Ward Ritchie. 1st ed. dj. $40.00

POWELL, L.C. *Books in My Baggage.* 1960. World. 1st ed. inscr. dj. $50.00

POWELL, L.C. *Books W SW.* 1957. Ward Ritchie. 1st ed. inscr. $60.00

POWELL, L.C. *Check List of Published Writings of Lawrence C. Powell.* 1966. LA. wraps. $25.00

POWELL, L.C. *Fortune & Friendship.* 1968. NY. 1st ed. $30.00

POWELL, L.C. *Fountains in the Sand. From AZ & the W.* 1960. inscr. wraps. $40.00

POWELL, L.C. *Island of Books.* 1951. Los Angeles. 1st ed. presentation. sgn. EX. $55.00

POWELL, L.C. *Little Package.* 1964. World. 1st ed. dj. $35.00

POWELL, L.C. *Passion for Books.* 1958. World. 1st ed. inscr. dj. $60.00

POWELL, L.C. *Passion for Books.* 1959. London. 1st ed. dj. EX. $35.00

POWELL, L.C. *Robinson Jeffers.* 1934. San Pasqual. 1/650. $40.00

POWELL, L.C. *Robinson Jeffers.* 1940. San Pasqual. Revised ed. inscr. dj. $50.00

POWELL, L.C. *Roots of Regional Literature.* 1959. Hertzog. wraps. $50.00

POWELL, L.C. *SW Book Trails.* 1963. Albuquerque. 1st ed. dj. $50.00

POWELL, L.C. *Vroman's of Pasadena.* 1953. private print. wraps. $40.00

POWELL, Nicolas. *From Baroque to Rococo.* 1959. London. Ils. photos. dj. VG. $20.00

POWELL, Padgett. *Edisto.* 1984. Farrar Straus. 1st ed. dj. EX. T6. $25.00

POWELL, Padgett. *Woman Named Drown.* 1987. Farrar Straus. 1st ed. dj. EX. T6. $20.00

POWELL, T.G.E. *Celts.* 1966. 4th print. dj. VG. C1. $14.00

POWELL, T.S. *Five Years in S MS.* 1889. Cincinnati. 1st/only ed. VG. rare. $60.00

POWELL. *Mary Baker Eddy.* 1930. 4to. 364 p. with photo. S2. $75.00

POWER, E. *Small Birds of New Zealand Bush.* 1981. Collins. Ils. 45 p. EX. M2. $8.00

POWER, E.B. *General Issues of US Stamps: Their Shades & Varieties.* 1909. NY. Stanley Gibbons. VG. $15.00

POWERS, A. *Animals of the Arctic.* 1965. McKay. Ils. 272 p. dj. EX. M2. $13.00

POWERS, Stephen. *CA Indian Characteristics & Centennial Mission to Indians...* 1975. CA U. Friends Bancroft Lib. wraps. EX. $10.00

POWERS, Tim. *Drawing of the Dark.* 1979. Ace. 1st ed. pb. VG. C1. $5.00

POWERS, Tim. *On Stranger Tides.* 1987. NY. Ace. 1st ed. dj. EX. T6. $20.00

POWNAL, David. *White Cutter.* 1989. 1st ed. dj. M. C1. $14.00

POWYS, J.C. *Atlantis.* 1954. MacDonald. 1st ed. dj. EX. $37.50

POWYS, J.C. *Gastonbury Romance.* 1932. NY. 2nd print. VG. scarce. C1. $12.50

POWYS, J.C. *Pleasures of Literature.* 1938. London. 1st ed. $30.00

POWYS & POWYS. *Confessions of Two Brothers.* 1916. Mans. VG. $95.00

POWYS. *Psychoanalysis & Morality.* 1923. Grabhorn. 1/500. 8vo. EX. $60.00

POZNER, Vladimir. *First Harvest.* 1943. Viking. 1st ed. dj. VG. $20.00

PRAGNELL, F. *Green Man of Gray-Pec.* 1935. NY. 1st Am ed. dj. EX. $30.00

PRANGE, Gordon. *At Dawn We Slept.* 1981. NY. 1st ed. dj. EX. $25.00

PRANGE, Gordon. *Miracle at Midway.* 1982. NY. 1st ed. dj. EX. $22.00

PRATLEY, Gerald. *Cinema of Otto Preminger.* 1971. Castle. 1st ed. dj. VG. J2. $8.50

PRATT, A. *Lore of the Lyre Bird.* 1933. Endeavor Pr. Ils 1st ed. 71 p. VG. M2. $18.00

PRATT, Anne. *Ferns of Great Britain & Their Allies.* c 1880. London. Ils Dickes. $40.00

PRATT, Anne. *Wild Flowers.* 1853. London. 96 pls. 4to. 96 p. embossed blue cloth. A3. $450.00

PRATT, Fletcher. *Civil War in Pictures.* 1955. NY. Holt. Ils. 256 p. EX. J4. $5.00

PRATT, Fletcher. *Empire & the Sea.* 1946. NY. 1st ed. dj. VG. $10.00

PRATT, Fletcher. *Fleet Against Japan.* 1946. Harper. Ils 1st ed. photos. dj. EX. $15.00

PRATT, Fletcher. *Heroic Years: Fourteen Years of Republic 1801-1815.* 1934. Smith Haas. Ils. 352 p. dj. EX. M2. $10.00

PRATT, Fletcher. *Ordeal by Fire: Informal History of Civil War.* 1948. 426 p. VG. J4. $8.50

PRATT, Fletcher. *Secret & Urgent Codes & Ciphers.* 1939. NY. 1st ed. EX. $22.50

PRATT, Fletcher. *Stanton: Lincoln's Secretary of War.* 1953. Norton. 1st ed. 520 p. dj. EX. M2. $10.00

PRATT, Fletcher. *World of Wonder.* 1951. Twayne. 1st ed. dj. EX. $25.00

PRATT, H.D. *Field Guide to Birds of HI & Tropical Pacific.* 1987. Princeton U. 45 pls. maps. 409 p. dj. M. M2. $50.00

PRATT & OWEN. *Valley of Lower Fox (WI).* 1887. np. lg 4to. black cloth. $65.00

PRATT & WHITNEY AIRCRAFT CO. *Handbook for Series C Wasp.* 1929. Hartford. Ils. fld diagrams. 263 p. EX. T5. $35.00

PRATT. *Double in Space.* 1951. Garden City. 1st ed. dj. VG. $12.50

PRATT. *Gardens in Color.* 1944. Ils Steichen. VG. S2. $35.00

PRAZ, Mario. *House of Life.* 1964. Oxford. 1st ed. dj. VG. J2. $20.00

PREBLE, G.H. *Origin & History of American Flag.* 1917. Phil. 2 vols. VG. $45.00

PREECE, Harold. *Living Pioneers.* 1952. Cleveland. World. 1st ed. dj. EX. $16.00

PREECE, Harold. *Lone Star Man: Ira Aten, Last of Old TX Rangers.* 1960. NY. Ils 1st ed. dj. VG. $45.00

PRENDERGAST, M. *Watercolor Sketchbook: 1899.* 1960. Boston. 12mo. gray/black cloth. slipcase. VG. J2. $125.00

PRENDEVILLE, J. *Photographic Facsimiles of Antique Gems...* 1859. 471 photos. 2 vols. $135.00

PRENTICE, T.M. *Weeds & Wild Flowers.* 1973. Salem. dj. EX. $40.00

PRESCOTT, G.B. *Electricity & the Electric Telegraph.* 1877. NY. Appleton. Ils. 987 p. xl. $50.00

PRESCOTT, G.B. *History, Theory & Practice of Electric Telegraph.* 1863. Boston. Ils. 468 p. orig bdg. VG. $125.00

PRESCOTT, W.H. *Conquest of Mexico.* 1873. Lippincott. New Popular ed. gilt green cloth. $40.00

PRESCOTT, W.H. *Ferdinand & Isabella.* 1887. NY. Ils. 2 vols. TEG. G. $50.00

PRESCOTT, W.H. *History of Conquest of Peru.* 1847. 1st ed. 1st issue. G. $100.00

PRESCOTT, W.H. *History of Conquest of Peru.* 1847. NY. 1st ed. 2 vols. VG. $135.00

PRESCOTT, W.H. *History of Conquest of Peru.* 1890. Lippincott. Revised Lib ed. VG. $18.00

PRESLAND, John. *Satni.* 1929. London. 1/550. sgn. dj. EX. $25.00

PRESTON. *Surgical Management of Rheumatoid Arthritis.* 1968. 4to. 579 p. VG. $25.00

PREVETT & MAC INNES. *Family & Other Social Groups in Snow Geese.* 1980. Wildlife Soc. Ils. 46 p. M2. $5.00

PREVOST, Abbe. *Monon Lescaut.* 1931. private print. Ils Alastair. 197 p. dj. EX. $20.00

PRICE, A. *Final Letter.* 1980. Sylvester Orphanos. 1/330. sgn. $60.00

PRICE, Eugenia. *Beloved Invader.* 1965. Phil. 1st ed. sgn. dj. EX. $32.50

PRICE, Eugenia. *Diary of a Novel.* 1980. NY. 1st ed. dj. EX. $18.00

PRICE, F.J. *Troy H. Middleton: A Biography.* 1974. Baton Rouge. Ils 1st ed. 416 p. dj. T5. $17.50

PRICE, Frederic Newlin. *Etchings & Lithographs of Arthur B. Davies.* 1929. London/NY. Kennerley. 1/200. slipcase. D2. $825.00

PRICE, L.W. *Mountains & Man: Study of Process & Environment.* 1981. CA U. Ils 1st ed. 506 p. dj. EX. M2. $20.00

PRICE, M.E. *Real Storybook.* 1928. Rand McNally. Ils. VG. $45.00

PRICE, Reynolds. *Annual Heron.* 1980. Albondocani. 1/300. sgn. wraps. M. $65.00

PRICE, Reynolds. *Generous Man.* 1966. Atheneum. ARC. dj. EX. $50.00

PRICE, Reynolds. *Long & Happy Life*. 1962. Atheneum. 1st ed. dj. VG. $70.00

PRICE, Reynolds. *Names & Faces of Heroes*. 1963. NY. 1st Am ed. dj. VG. $50.00

PRICE, Reynolds. *Permanent Errors*. 1970. NY. Atheneum. 1st ed. dj. EX. $60.00

PRICE, Reynolds. *Things Themselves*. 1972. NY. 1st Am ed. dj. VG. $25.00

PRICE, Richard. *Ladies' Man*. 1978. Boston. Houghton. 1st ed. dj. EX. $20.00

PRICE, Richard. *Sermons on the Security & Happiness of a Virtuous Course*. 1794. Boston. 270 p. full leather. K1. $12.00

PRICE, Thomas. *Memoir of Wilberforce*. 1836. Boston. 2nd ed. 12mo. 163 p. VG. $50.00

PRICE & PRICE. *Treasury of Great Recipes*. 1965. Ampersand. 1st ed. glassine dj. EX. $35.00

PRICE & PRICE. *Treasury of Great Recipes*. 1965. NY. Ils Kredel. 5th ed. 4to. 488 p. EX. $30.00

PRICHETT, V.S. *On Edge of the Cliff*. 1979. NY. 1st ed. dj. EX. $10.00

PRIDE. *History of Ft. Riley*. 1926. np. Ils. 2 fld maps. 339 p. C4. $47.00

PRIEST, Christopher. *Anticipations*. nd. London. 1st ed. EX. $15.00

PRIEST, Christopher. *Perfect Lover*. 1977. NY. Scribner. 1st ed. dj. EX. $15.00

PRIEST, W.J. *American Antiquities & Discoveries in W.* Revised 2nd ed. EX. $150.00

PRIEST, W.J. *American Antiquities & Discoveries in W.* 1838. Albany. 4th ed. 1 pl. no map. rebound. $28.00

PRIESTLEY, J.B. *Adam in Moonshine*. 1927. NY. Harper. 1st ed. G. $10.00

PRIESTLEY, J.B. *Angel Pavement*. 1930. London. 1/1025. sgn. EX. P3. $85.00

PRIESTLEY, J.B. *Britain Speaks*. 1940. NY. Harper. 1st ed. VG. $10.00

PRIESTLEY, J.B. *Edwardians*. 1970. NY. 1st ed. dj. EX. $20.00

PRIESTLEY, J.B. *Found, Lost, Found*. 1977. Stein Day. 2nd ed. dj. xl. $5.00

PRIESTLEY, J.B. *Salt Is Leaving*. 1975. Harper Row. dj. EX. $12.50

PRIESTLEY, J.B. *Shapes of Sleep*. 1962. Heinemann. 1st ed. dj. EX. $27.50

PRIESTLEY, J.B. *Thirty-First of June*. 1962. 1st Am ed. dj. M. C1. $34.00

PRIESTLEY, J.B. *Wonder Hero*. 1933. NY. Harper. 1st ed. xl. G. $10.00

PRINCE, H.C. *Trans-Atlantic Chatelaine*. 1897. Houghton. 1st ed. $12.00

PRINCE, L.B. *Old Ft. Marcy, Santa Fe, NM*. Ils. 16 p. wraps. scarce. A3. $35.00

PRINGLE, E.W.A. *Chronicles of Chicora Wood*. 1922. Scribner. 1st ed. 366 p. dj. $65.00

PRINGLE, H.F. *Life & Times of William Howard Taft*. 1939. NY. 1st ed. 2 vols. G. T5. $37.50

PRINZ, Joachim. *Popes From the Ghetto*. 1966. NY. 1st ed. sgn. dj. EX. $20.00

PRITCHETT, V.S. *Dead Men Leading*. 1937. NY. 1st Am ed. dj. VG. $40.00

PRITCHETT, V.S. *NY Proclaimed*. 1965. Harcourt Brace. 1st Am ed. dj. D2. $50.00

PRITCHETT & HOFER. *London Perceived*. 1962. Harcourt Brace. 1st Am ed. dj. D2. $50.00

PRITCHETT & THEROUX. *Turn of Years*. 1982. London. 1/150. sgns. 8vo. glassine dj. M. $65.00

PRITTIE, E.J. *Robin Hood*. 1925. Winston. Ils. VG. B4. $18.00

PROBEST, Thomas. *Lost Mines & Buried Treasure of the W: Bibliography*. 1977. Berkeley. 1st ed. dj. VG. $22.50

PROCHASKA, E. *Coal Washing*. 1921. NY. Ils. fair. $20.00

PROCHAZKA. *Chopin & Bohemia*. 1969. Artia. dj. VG. $17.50

PROCTOR, A.P. *Sculptor in Buckskin*. 1971. OK U. 1st ed. pls. boxed. M. $70.00

PROCTOR, B.H. *Not Without Honor: Life of John H. Reagan*. 1962. TX U. Ils 1st ed. 361 p. dj. EX. M2. $15.00

PROFFITT, Nicholas. *Embassy House*. 1986. Bantam. ARC. wraps. EX. $10.00

PROKHUDIN-GORSKII, S.M. *Photographs for the Tsar*. 1980. Dial. 1st ed. dj. VG. $40.00

PRONZINI, Bill. *Arbor House Treasury of Horror*. 1981. Arbor House. dj. EX. P1. $30.00

PRONZINI, Bill. *Great Tales of Horror & Supernatural*. 1985. Castle. VG. P1. $10.00

PRONZINI, Bill. *Snatch*. 1971. Random House. 1st ed. dj. xl. $5.00

PRONZINI & MULLER. *Lighthouse*. 1987. NY. 1st ed. dj. EX. $15.00

PROTTENGEIER, A. *From Lisbon to Calicut*. 1956. MN U. 1/1000. 12mo. dj. EX. G1. $20.00

PROU, M. *Manuel Paleographie Latine et Francaise, VI Au XVII Siecle*. 1892. Paris. 2nd ed. xl. VG. G1. $20.00

PROUST, Marcel. *Letters of Marcel Proust*. 1949. NY. Trans Curtiss. 1st Am ed. G. T5. $35.00

PROUST, Marcel. *Past Recaptured*. 1959. Modern Lib. dj. VG. $15.00

PROUST, Marcel. *Pleasures & Regrets*. 1948. NY. Trans Varese. 1st Am ed. 221 p. T5. $35.00

PROWSE, A.L. *Churchills: From Death of Marlborough to Present*. 1958. Harper. 1st ed. red/black bdg. VG. D1. $30.00

PROZESKY, O.P.M. *Field Guide to the Birds of S Africa*. 1970. Collins. Ils. 350 p. dj. EX. M2. $25.00

PRUDDEN, Bonnie. *Fitness Book*. 1959. Ronald Pr. 90 p. dj. EX. $2.50

PRYCE-JONES, David. *Paris in the Third Reich*. 1981. NY. 1st ed. dj. EX. $20.00

PRYDE, D. *Nunga: Ten Years of Eskimo Life*. 1971. Walker. Ils 1st ed. 285 p. dj. EX. M2. $14.00

PRYOR, K. *Lads Before the Wind: Adventures in Porpoise Training*. 1975. Harper Row. Ils 1st ed. 278 p. dj. EX. M2. $9.00

PRYOR, Mrs. R.A. *Reminiscences of Peace & War...* 1904. Macmillan. 1st ed. 402 p. xl. $10.00

PUBLOW, Charles. *Fancy Cheese in America*. 1910. Ils 1st ed. EX. $18.00

PUCKETTE, C.C. *Old Mitt Laughs Last*. 1944. Bobbs Merrill. Ils James. Sea Islands ed. sgn. dj. $25.00

PUCKLE. *Funeral Customs*. 1968. facsimile of 1926 London ed. VG. $16.00

PUGIN & HEATH. *Paris & Its Environs...* 1829. London. 100 pls. 4to. 2 vols. $220.00

PULESTON, W.D. *Influence of Sea Power in WWII*. 1947. Yale. 1st ed. J2. $15.00

PULICH, W.M. *Birds of N Central TX*. 1988. TX A&M U. Ils 1st ed. 439 p. dj. M2. $17.00

PULLEN. *Twentieth ME*. 1957. NY. 1st ed. dj. $24.00

PURCELL, Mary. *Halo on the Sword: St. Joan of Arc*. 1952. 1st ed. dj. VG. C1. $7.50

PURCELL, Theodore. *Blue Collar Man.* 1960. dj. VG. $15.00

PURCELL, Theodore. *Worker Speaks His Mind on Co. & Union.* 1954. 2nd print. dj. VG. $25.00

PURDY, James. *Eustace Chisholm & Works.* 1967. Farrar. 1st ed. dj. EX. $25.00

PURDY, James. *In a Shallow Grave.* 1975. Arbor House. 1st ed. dj. VG. $18.00

PURDY, James. *Jeremy's Version.* 1970. NY. 1st ed. 308 p. dj. T5. $15.00

PURKIS, John. *Icelandic Jaunt.* 1962. London. Morris Soc. 1/750. wraps. EX. $20.00

PURNELL, Idella. *Wishing Owl.* 1931. NY. Macmillan. Ils Dehlsen. 1st ed. EX. $20.00

PURTELL, Joseph. *Tiffany Touch.* 1971. Random House. 1st ed. dj. $25.00

PURVER, M. *Royal Society: Concept & Creation.* 1967. MA Inst Technol. 1st ed. dj. M2. $16.00

PUSEY, M. *Charles Evans Hughes.* 1951. Macmillan. 1st print. 2 vols. boxed. VG. $50.00

PUSHKIN, Alexander. *Golden Cockerel.* nd. Heritage. Ils Dulac. J2. $25.00

PUSHKIN, Alexander. *Golden Cockerel.* nd. NY. Ils Dulac. slipcase. VG. T5. $22.50

PUTNAM, D.B. *David Goes to Greenland.* 1926. NY. Ils. photos. G. $12.00

PUTNAM, D.F. *Canadian Regions: Geography of Canada.* 1952. Toronto. Dent. 601 p. M1. $8.50

PUTNAM, G.H. *Memories of My Youth, 1844-1865.* 1914. NY. 1st ed. VG. $22.50

PUTNAM, N.W. *Sunny Bunny.* 1918. Algonquin. Ils Gruelle. VG. B4. $35.00

PUTNAM PUBLISHING. *Books & Their Makers in the Middle Ages.* 1962. NY. 2 vols. boxed. VG. E2. $35.00

PUZO, Mario. *Dark Arena.* 1955. NY. 1st ed. dj. VG. B2. $37.50

PUZO, Mario. *Fools Die.* 1979. 1st pb ed. VG. C1. $3.50

PYCRAFT, W.P. *Birds in Flight.* 1922. London. Ils Roland Green. green bdg. $75.00

PYE, J. *Patronage of British Art.* 1845. London. 442 p. orig green cloth. VG. J2. $80.00

PYLE, Howard. *Book of King Arthur.* 1970. Ils Ron King. reprint. VG. C1. $4.50

PYLE, Howard. *Book of Pirates.* 1921. London/NY. VG. J2. $50.00

PYLE, Howard. *Garden Behind the Moon.* 1916. NY. Ils. 192 p. green/gold/orange bdg. VG. B2. $30.00

PYLE, Howard. *Howard Pyle's Book of American Spirit.* 1923. Harper. 1st ed. VG. $85.00

PYLE, Howard. *Howard Pyle's Book of Pirates.* 1921. Harper. Ils. VG. $85.00

PYLE, Howard. *Men of Iron.* c 1891. NY/London. Ils Pyle. red cloth. $45.00

PYLE, Howard. *Merry Adventures of Robin Hood.* 1883. NY. 1st ed. AEG. rebound full leather. VG. $175.00

PYLE, Howard. *Merry Adventures of Robin Hood.* 1933. Brandywine ed. Lib bdg. xl. C1. $22.00

PYLE, Howard. *Merry Adventures of Robin Hood.* 1933. NY. Brandywine ed. EX. $150.00

PYLE, Howard. *Merry Adventures of Robin Hood.* 1946. Scribner. New ed. dj. M. $15.00

PYLE, Howard. *Otto of the Silver Hand.* 1926. Scribner. Ils. EX. $45.00

PYLE, Howard. *Ruby of Kishmoor.* 1908. London/NY. VG. J2. $65.00

PYLE, Howard. *Story of Champions of the Round Table.* 1905. NY. 1st ed. J2. $20.00

PYLE, Howard. *Story of Champions of the Round Table.* 1922. not 1st ed. VG. C1. $17.00

PYLE, Howard. *Story of King Arthur & His Knights.* 1931. NY. VG. J2. $10.00

PYLE, Howard. *Story of King Arthur & His Knights.* 1986. Ils Pyle. pb. M. C1. $2.50

PYLE, Howard. *Story of Sir Launcelot & His Companions.* 1907. 1st ed. VG. C1. $44.50

PYLE, Howard. *Story of the Grail & the Passing of Arthur.* c 1940s. Ils as (but not) 1st ed. VG. C1. $16.50

PYLE, Howard. *Story of the Grail & the Passing of Arthur.* 1910. London. Bickers. 1st Eng ed. VG. C1. $39.00

PYLE, Howard. *Story of the Grail & the Passing of Arthur.* 1910. NY. Ils 1st ed. tan cloth. VG. $80.00

PYLE, Howard. *Within the Capes.* 1885. Scribner. G. $45.00

PYLE, Howard. *Yankee Doodle: An Old Song.* 1881. NY. Dodd Mead. 1st ed. G. B2. $95.00

PYLE, Katherine. *Where the Wind Blows.* 1930. dj. VG. C1. $7.50

PYNCHON, Thomas. *Gravity's Rainbow.* 1973. NY. 1st ed. orange cloth. dj. EX. $125.00

PYNCHON, Thomas. *Gravity's Rainbow.* 1973. NY. 1st ed. wraps. EX. $40.00

PYNCHON, Thomas. *Low Lands.* 1978. London. Aloes Books. Ltd 1st ed. wraps. M. $60.00

PYNE, S.J. *Grove Karl Gilbert: Great Engine of Research.* 1980. TX U. Ils 1st ed. 306 p. dj. EX. M2. $20.00

PYRNELLE, L.C. *Diddie, Dumps & Tot; or, Plantation Child Life.* c 1882. VG. $27.50

PYRNELLE, L.C. *Diddie, Dumps & Tot; or, Plantation Child Life.* 1910. NY. Harper. 240 p. $10.00

QUAIFE, M.M. *Absalon Grimes: Confederate Mail Runner.* 1926. New Haven. Ils. 216 p. VG. C4. $49.00

QUAIFE, M.M. *Checagou, 1673-1835.* 1933. Chicago. 12mo. $35.00

QUAIFE, M.M. *Chicago's Highways Old & New: Indian Trail to Motor Road.* 1923. Chicago. Ils 1st ed. maps. black cloth. T1. $35.00

QUAIFE, M.M. *John Long's Voyages & Travels in Years 1768-1788.* 1922. Chicago. map. VG. $50.00

QUAIFE, M.M. *Yellowstone Kelly.* 1926. Yale. 1st ed. dj. EX. $70.00

QUAKENBOS, J.D. *Hypnotic Therapeutics.* 1908. NY. Harper. 1st ed. EX. $100.00

QUAKER OATS COMPANY. *Dick Daring's New Bag of Tricks.* 1934. sm 8vo. 64 p. wraps. VG. $3.00

QUARLES, B. *Lincoln & the Negro.* 1962. Oxford. 1st ed. dj. EX. $52.00

QUARLES, E.A. *American Pheasant Breeding & Shooting.* 1916. Wilmington. Ils. 132 p. wraps. fair. $15.00

QUARRINGTON, Paul. *Home Game.* 1983. NY. 1st Am ed. dj. VG. $20.00

QUAYLE, Eric. *Collector's Book of Books.* 1917. NY. Potter. 4to. 144 p. dj. VG. $22.50

QUAYLE, Eric. *Collector's Book of Children's Books.* nd. NY. 1st ed. VG. $40.00

QUAYLE, W.A. *God's Calendar.* 1907. OH. photos. TEG. VG. $17.50

QUEEN, Ellery. *Female of the Species.* 1943. Boston. 1st ed. $12.00

QUEEN, Ellery. *Perfect Crime.* 1942. Grosset Dunlap. EX. $10.00

QUEEN, Ellery. *Queen's Awards, 1946.* 1946. Little Brown. Stated 1st ed. dj. VG. $35.00

QUEEN, Ellery. *Siamese Twin Mystery.* 1942. Triangle. dj. EX. $8.00

QUEEN, Ellery. *There Was an Old Woman.* 1943. Boston. 1st ed. dj. VG. $30.00

QUEENY, E.M. *Cheechako.* 1941. Scribner. 1st ed. 1/1200. EX. $85.00

QUEENY, E.M. *Prairie Wings: Pen & Camera Flight Studies.* VG. S2. $100.00

QUEENY, E.M. *Prairie Wings: Pen & Camera Flight Studies.* 1946. Ducks Unltd. 1st ed. VG. J2. $150.00

QUEENY, E.M. *Prairie Wings: Pen & Camera Flight Studies.* 1947. Lippincott. Ils 2nd print. 256 p. EX. M2. $150.00

QUEENY, E.M. *Prairie Wings: Pen & Camera Flight Studies.* 1947. Phil. 1st trade ed. $115.00

QUEENY, E.M. *Prairie Wings: Pen & Camera Flight Studies.* 1979. Schiffer. Ils. 4to. 256 p. $40.00

QUENNELL, Nancy. *Epicure's Anthology.* 1936. Golden Cockerel. Ils Lancaster. VG. $70.00

QUENTIN, Patrick. *Ordeal of Mrs. Snow & Other Stories.* 1962. NY. 1st ed. dj. EX. $12.00

QUEZON, Manuel. *Good Fight.* 1946. NY. 1st ed. 336 p. dj. VG. B2. $37.50

QUICK, H. *American Inland Waterways.* 1909. NY. Ils 1st ed. 241 p. VG. B2. $65.00

QUICK, Jim. *Trout Fishing & Trout Flies.* 1957. Countryman Pr. Ils. 252 p. dj. VG. $10.00

QUILLER-COUCH, Arthur. *Brother Copas.* 1911. NY. 1st ed. EX. $12.00

QUILLER-COUCH, Arthur. *In Powder & Crinoline.* nd. np. Ils Kay Nielsen. VG. J2. $250.00

QUILLER-COUCH, Arthur. *On the Art of Reading.* 1920. Cambridge. 1st ed. G. $40.00

QUILLER-COUCH & DU MAURIER. *Castle Dor.* 1962. 1st ed. VG. C1. $5.00

QUIMBY, G.I. *Indian Life in the Upper Great Lakes.* 1961. Chicago. VG. $12.50

QUINEY, Anthony. *John Loughborough Pearson: Studies in British Art.* 1979. Yale. Ils 1st ed. 8vo. dj. EX. T1. $45.00

QUINN, A.H. *Edgar A. Poe: Letters & Documents in E. Pratt Free Library.* 1941. NY. Scolars Facsimiles. 1/500. EX. $40.00

QUINN, A.H. *French Face of Edgar A. Poe.* 1957. S IL U. 1st ed. black/red bdg. dj. VG. D1. $15.00

QUINN, Bernetta. *Ezra Pound.* 1972. Columbia. 1st ed. dj. VG. $18.00

QUINN, J.R. *Winter Woods.* 1976. Chatham. Ils. 124 p. jd. EX. M2. $7.00

QUINTANILLA, Luis. *All the Brave.* 1939. NY. Modern Age Books. Deluxe 1st ed. $150.00

QUINTANILLA, Luis. *Franco's Black Spain Drawings.* 1946. NY. Ils. VG. $60.00

R

RAABE, Paul. *Era of German Expressionism.* 1975. Woodstock. Overlook Pr. 423 p. dj. D2. $25.00

RABB, K.M. *Tour Through IN in 1840: Diary of John Parsons...* 1920. NY. Ils 1st ed. 391 p. G. T5. $35.00

RABBITT, M.C. *CO River Region & John Wesley Powell.* 1969. WA. Ils. 145 p. VG. A3. $40.00

RABINOWICZ, Harry. *Treasures of Judaica.* 1971. S Brunswick. Ils. tall 4to. dj. EX. $45.00

RABINOWITZ, A. *Jaguar: Struggle & Triumph in Jungles of Belize.* 1986. Arbor House. Ils 1st ed. 368 p. dj. EX. M2. $18.00

RACHILDE. *Monsieur Venus.* 1929. NY. Ils Majeska. Ltd ed. 1/1200. EX. $35.00

RACKHAM, Arthur. *Alice's Adventures in Wonderland.* 1978. Weathervane. dj. VG. E2. $9.00

RACKHAM, Arthur. *Allie's Fairy Book.* 1916. London/NY. 1st ed. 1/525. 4to. blue buckram. $500.00

RACKHAM, Arthur. *Comus.* 1921. London/NY. 1/550. sgn. VG. B2. $550.00

RACKHAM, Arthur. *Mother Goose: Old Nursery Rhymes.* 1913. NY. J2. $40.00

RACKHAM, Arthur. *Peter Pan in Kensington Gardens.* 1906. NY. 1st Am ed. VG. B2. $175.00

RACKHAM, Arthur. *Some British Ballads.* 1919. London. 16 color pls. VG. $85.00

RACKHAM, Arthur. *Wagner Siegfried & Twilight of the Gods.* 1911. London/NY. $100.00

RACKHAM, Arthur. *Wind in the Willows.* 1940. NY. Ltd Ed. 1/2020. sgn Bruce Rogers. VG. B2. $500.00

RACSTER, Olga. *Chats on Violins.* 1905. Lippincott. green cloth. $35.00

RACZ, I. *Treasures of Finnish Folk Art.* 1967. NY. 1st ed. dj. VG. B2. $27.50

RADAM, William. *Microbes & Microbe Killer.* 1890. NY. Ils. 8vo. 369 p. $50.00

RADDIN. *Hocquet Caritat & Early NY Literary Scene.* Ltd ed. 1/150. EX. $25.00

RADER, Dotson. *TN: Cry of the Heart.* 1985. NY. dj. EX. $8.00

RADFORD, R.L. *Mystery of Myrtle Grove.* c 1933. Phil. 1st ed. VG. $8.00

RADFORD, William. *House-Barn-Roof Framing.* 1909. Chicago. Ils 1st ed. EX. T1. $35.00

RADIN, Paul. *El Folklore de Oaxaca.* 1917. NY. 1st ed. Spanish text. 294 p. VG. T1. $50.00

RADOSH, Ronald. *American Labor & US Foreign Policy.* 1969. NY. dj. VG. $20.00

RAE, John. *Lucy Locket: Doll With the Pocket.* 1928. Saalfield. 1st ed. $50.00

RAFFALD, Elizabeth. *Experienced English Housekeeper for Use of Cooks...* 1807. Chester. Leadbeater. 260 p. VG. scarce. $200.00

RAFFLES, T.S. *Memoir of Sir Thomas Stamford Raffles.* 1830. London. Murray. 4to. VG. $125.00

RAGNAI, Miklos. *John Sell Cotman.* 1982. Ithaca. Ils. dj. D2. $35.00

RAGOSTA, Mille J. *Druid's Enchantment.* 1985. 1st ed. dj. EX. C1. $7.50

RAINE, D.F. *Canadian Tragedy.* 1980. Edmonton. Hurtig. VG. $10.00

RAINES. *Marcellus Laroon.* 1966. NY. quarto. $45.00

RAINIS, Jana. *Latviesu Tautas Dzejnieks.* 1960. Latvian Pub. Ils. photos. pls. VG. $45.00

RAIT, R.S. *Royal Palaces of England.* 1911. NY. Ils. 377 p. $25.00

RAMAGE, C.J. *Personal Historical Sketch of Peyton Randolph.* nd. Saluda, SC. 52 p. printed wraps. $20.00

RAMALEY, F. *CO Plant Life.* 1927. CO U. Ils 1st ed. 299 p. EX. M2. $35.00

RAMIE, G. *Ceramics of Picasso.* 1985. Ils. dj. EX. $10.00

RAMIE, G. *Picasso's Ceramics.* 1976. NY. 1st ed. dj. EX. $50.00

RAMSAY, David. *Life of George WA...* 1815. Baltimore. Ils. 16mo. 266 p. rebound. scarce. G2. $30.00

RAMSAY, David. *Life of George WA...* 1832. Baltimore. Jewett. Revised Enlarged ed. 252 p. $37.50

RAMSAY, David. *Memoirs of Life of Martha Laurens Ramsay...* 1811. Phil. Maxwell. 1st ed. 16mo. 308 p. $150.00

RAMSAY, J.A. *Physiological Approach to Lower Animals.* 1952. Cambridge U. Ils. 148 p. EX. M2. $12.00

RAMSBOTTOM, J. *Mushrooms & Toadstools.* 1959. London. Collins. Ils. 306 p. G. M2. $8.00

RAMSEY, A.H. *Veil, Duster & Tire Iron.* 1961. Covina, CA. private print. presentation. VG. $45.00

RAMSEY, J.G.M. *Annals of TN to End of 18th C.* 1860. 744 p. EX. J4. $35.00

RAMSEY, Thomas. *Battle of Kingsport.* 1864. 1st ed. 1/350. photos. map. M. J4. $20.00

RAMTHA & MAHR. *Voyage to the New World.* 1985. WA. $12.00

RANALD, Josef. *Hands of Destiny.* 1931. NY. $15.00

RAND, A.L. *American Water & Game Birds.* 1956. Dutton. Ils Mochi. 1st ed. 239 p. dj. M2. $37.00

RAND, A.L. *Stray Feathers From a Bird Man's Desk.* 1955. Doubleday. 1st ed. 224 p. EX. M2. $11.00

RAND, Ayn. *Atlas Shrugged.* 1957. NY. 1st ed. dj. $75.00

RAND, Ayn. *Night of January 16th.* 1968. World. 1st ed. dj. EX. $25.00

RAND, Ayn. *Philosophy? Who Needs It.* 1982. Bobbs Merrill. 1st print. dj. EX. $16.00

RAND, Ayn. *Virtue of Selfishness.* 1964. NY. 1st ed. dj. VG. B2. $27.50

RAND, C. *Nostalgia for Camels.* 1957. Little Brown. 1st ed. 279 p. dj. EX. M2. $11.00

RAND, F.P. *Village of Amherst MA Landmark of Light.* 1958. Amherst. 1st ed. dj. VG. B2. $27.50

RAND, J.S. *Run for the Trees.* 1967. NY. 1st ed. dj. VG. B2. $15.00

RAND, Paul. *Thoughts on Design.* 1947. Wittenborn. 1st ed. dj. scarce. D2. $70.00

RANDALL, Carl. *Life, Loves & Meat Loaf.* 1964. Random House. EX. P1. $7.50

RANDALL, D.A. *Dukedom Large Enough.* 1969. NY. Ils 1st print. EX. $30.00

RANDALL, E.O. *OH in the American Revolution.* 1903. Columbus. reprint. 146 p. wraps. VG. T5. $7.50

RANDALL, H.S. *Life of Thomas Jefferson.* 1871. Phil. Ils. 8vo. 3 vols. VG. T1. $65.00

RANDALL, J.G. *Civil War & Reconstruction.* 1966. Boston. Heath. 2nd ed. 820 p. VG. $25.00

RANDLE, E.H. *Safi Adventure, First Operation of Famous Regimental Team...* 1965. Clearwater. Eldnar. 1/750. presentation. dj. $35.00

RANDOLPH, E. *Hell Among the Yearlings.* 1955. Norton. Ils 1st ed. 308 p. dj. EX. M2. $20.00

RANDOLPH, Vance. *Devil's Pretty Daughter.* 1955. NY. 1st ed. dj. VG. B2. $20.00

RANDOLPH, Vance. *Down in the Holler: Gallery of Ozark Folk Speech.* 1953. OK U. 1st ed. dj. VG. J2. $25.00

RANDOLPH, Vance. *From an Ozark Holler.* 1933. NY. 1st ed. dj. EX. $30.00

RANDOLPH, Vance. *Ozark Folk Songs.* 1946. 1st ed. 4 vols. M. $75.00

RANDOLPH, Vance. *Ozark Superstitions.* 1951. Columbia. dj. EX. $15.00

RANDOW, H. *Zoo Hunt in Ceylon.* 1958. Doubleday. Ils 1st Am ed. 234 p. EX. M2. $15.00

RANHOFFER, C. *Epicurean.* 1920. Chicago. 1st ed. 1183 p. VG. B2. $47.50

RANKIN, H.F. *Narrative of the American Revolution As Told by Sailor...* 1976. Donnelley. Lakeside Classic. EX. M2. $17.00

RANKIN, R.H. *Uniforms of the Sea Services: Pictorial History.* 1962. Annapolis. US Naval Inst. 324 p. dj. VG. $35.00

RANSOME, Arthur. *Swallow Dale.* 1935. Lippincott. 2nd imp. dj. EX. $10.00

RANSOME, Stephen. *Shroud Off Her Back.* 1953. Doubleday. Crime Club. 1st ed. dj. VG. B2. $15.00

RANSOME-WALLIS, P. *Concise Encyclopedia of World Railway Locomotives.* 1959. 512 p. $25.00

RAO, Raja. *Kanthapura.* 1963. NY. 1st Am ed. inscr. dj. EX. $30.00

RAO, Raja. *Serpent & the Rope.* 1960. London. Murray. 1st ed. EX. $37.50

RAO, Raja. *Serpent & the Rope.* 1963. NY. 1st Am ed. inscr. dj. EX. $25.00

RAPHAEL, A. *Key to Astrology.* 1890. Raphael. 2nd ed. rust cloth. VG. $18.00

RAPIN, Henri. *La Sculpture Decorative.* nd. (1929?) 32 pls. portfolio. VG. J2. $150.00

RAPPOLE & BLACKLOCK. *Birds of TX Coastal Bend: Abundance & Distribution.* 1985. TX A&M U. Ils 1st ed. maps. dj. M. M2. $19.00

RASKY, Frank. *Polar Voyages.* 1976. McGraw Hill. EX. $12.50

RASMUSSEN, Knud. *Greenland by the Polar Sea.* c 1919. NY. 1st Eng Trans. xl. VG. $75.00

RASPAIL, F.V. *Nouveau Systeme de Physiologie Vegetale et de Botanique.* 1837. Burssels. Ils. pls. French text. G. $50.00

RATCHFORD, J.W. *Some Reminiscences of Persons & Incidents of Civil War.* 1971. Shoal Creek. reprint of 1909 ed. 69 p. EX. M2. $25.00

RATH, I.E. *Rath Trail: Non-Fiction Biography of Charles Rath.* 1961. Wichita, KS. Ils 1st ed. sgn. dj. EX. $40.00

RATH, I.E. *Year of Charles.* 1955. Antonio. Naylor. 1st ed. VG. $17.50

RATHBUN, M.J. *Crapsoid Crabs of America.* 1918. US Nat Mus. Ils. 461 p. rebound. EX. M2. $60.00

RATHBUN, M.J. *Oxystomatous & Allied Crabs of America.* 1937. Smithsonian. 86 pls. 278 p. VG. M2. $30.00

RATHBUN, M.J. *Spider Crabs of America.* 1925. US Nat Mus. 283 pls. cloth bdg. M2. $60.00

RATTRAY, J.E. *E Hampton History: Including Genealogies of Early Families.* 1953. E Hampton, NY. Ils 1st ed. 8vo. EX. T1. $45.00

RAUB, A.N. *Studies in English & American Literature.* 1882. 467 p. TB. G. $3.00

RAUSCHENBERG, Robert. *Robert Rauschenberg Photographs.* 1981. NY. presentation. dj. VG. $25.00

RAVEN, C.P. *Outline of Developmental Physiology.* 1954. McGraw Hill. Ils. 216 p. EX. M2. $10.00

RAVEN, Simon. *Close of Play.* 1962. London. 1st ed. dj. VG. $35.00

RAVENEL, B.S.J. *Architects of Charleston.* 1945. Charleston. Ils Julien. Intro Ball. 1st ed. $175.00

RAVENSDALE, T. *Coral Fishes: Their Care & Maintenance.* 1971. Great Outdoors. Ils. 137 p. dj. EX. M2. $9.00

RAVITCH, Diane. *Troubled Crusade.* 1983. NY. 1st ed. dj. EX. $17.50

RAVITCH, M. *Romance of Russian Medicine.* 1937. NY. 342 p. $75.00

RAWE, Donald. *Geraint, Last of the Arthurians.* 1972. Padstow. Lodenek Pr. 1st ed. VG. scarce. C1. $8.50

RAWLINGS, M.K. *Cross Creek Cookery.* 1942. NY. Ils 1st ed. dj. VG. T1. $40.00

RAWLINGS, M.K. *Cross Creek.* 1942. NY. 1st ed. dj. VG. B2. $22.50

RAWLINGS, M.K. *S Moon Under.* 1933. Scribner. 1st ed. dj. VG. B2. $95.00

RAWLINGS, M.K. *Yearling.* 1938. NY. 1st ed. dj. VG. B2. $25.00

RAWLINGS, M.K. *Yearling.* 1940. NY. Ils Wyeth. dj. EX. $12.00

RAWLINS, Dennis. *Peary at the N Pole, Fact or Fiction?* 1973. WA. $30.00

RAWLS, Walton. *Civil War Heroes & Their Battles.* 1985. photos. 303 p. M. J4. $10.00

RAWSON, Marion. *Candleday Art.* 1938. Dutton. 1st ed. dj. VG. J2. $12.50

RAY, D.J. *Artists of the Tundra & Sea.* 1961. WA U. Ils 1st ed. 170 p. dj. EX. M2. $11.00

RAY, D.L. *Marine Boring & Fouling Organisms.* 1959. WA U. 536 photos. dj. VG. M2. $10.00

RAY, Ginger. *Bending Cross.* 1949. Rutgers. VG. $10.00

RAY, James. *Complete History of Rebellion, From Its First Rifle in 1745.* 1749. York. 402 p. leather. G. $150.00

RAY, M.S. *Farallones: Painted World & Other Poems of CA.* 1934. Nash. 1/2000. 2 vols. VG. $55.00

RAY, M.S. *Poet & the Messenger Dune-Glade & Other Poems.* 1946. Pacific Book. dj. VG. $30.00

RAY, Man. *Self-Portrait.* 1963. London. 1st ed. dj. VG. scarce. $75.00

RAY, Marcia. *Collectible Ceramics.* 1974. NY. Crown. 1st ed. dj. VG. $20.00

RAY, R.J. *Hit Man Cometh.* 1988. St. Martin. 1st ed. dj. M. $10.00

RAY, R.J. *Murdock for Hire.* 1987. St. Martin. 1st ed. dj. EX. $10.00

RAY & CIAMPI. *Underwater Guide to Marine Life.* 1956. Barnes. 10 color pls. photos. 338 p. M2. $10.00

RAY & MCCORMICK-RAY. *Wildlife of the Polar Regions.* 1981. Abrams. Ils. 232 p. dj. EX. M2. $18.00

RAYBURN, O.E. *Forty Years in the Ozarks.* 1957. Eureka Spring. 1st ed. #d. 101 p. EX. M2. $20.00

RAYFIELD, Stanley. *Life Photographers: Their Careers & Favorite Pictures.* 1957. Doubleday. 89 p. dj. G. T5. $22.50

RAYMOND, A. *Vielles Faieces Turques.* 1923. 40 color pls. VG. $400.00

RAYMOND, Eleanor. *Early Domestic Architecture of PA.* 1931. NY. Ils. photos. folio. $60.00

RAYMOND, G.L. *Mountains About Williamstown, MA.* 1913. NY. Ils 1st ed. 100 p. VG. B2. $20.00

RAYMOND, H.J. *Life of Abraham Lincoln With State Papers, Letters...* 1865. NY. tall 8vo. 808 p. VG. $25.00

RAYMOND, Harold. *Publishing & Bookselling.* 1939. London. with sgn letter. $40.00

RAYMOND, Louise. *Child's Story of Nativity.* 1943. Random House. Ils Masha. 4to. dj. VG. $12.50

RAYMOND, Rossiter. *Mineral Resources of States & Territories W of Rockies.* 1869. GPO. VG. scarce. $165.00

RAYMOND, Thomas. *Stephen Crane.* 1923. NY. Carteret Book Club. 1/250. $70.00

RAYMONT, J.E.G. *Plankton & Productivity in the Oceans.* 1963. Pergamon. Ils. 660 p. EX. M2. $25.00

RAYTER, Joe. *Stab in the Dark.* 1955. Morrow. 1st ed. dj. VG. $17.50

RAYZER, G. *Flowering Cacti.* 1984. Hippercrene. Ils. 181 p. EX. M2. $12.00

READ, C. *Bibliography of British History: Tudor Period, 1485-1603.* 1933. Oxford. VG. $25.00

READ, K. *High Valley.* 1965. Scribner. Ils. 266 p. dj. EX. $12.00

READ, Louis. *Arabian Nights' Entertainments.* 1916. NY. Harper. 1st ed. J2. $35.00

READ, Opie. *AK Planter.* 1896. Chicago. Ils Denslow/Morgan. 1st ed. T5. $35.00

READ, Opie. *Bolanyo.* 1897. Chicago. Ils Parrish. EX. $75.00

READ. *History of CA Academy of Medicine, 1870-1930.* 1930. Grabhorn Pr. 1/951. 183 p. B1. $50.00

READE, Brian. *Aubrey Beardsley.* 1967. NY. Ils. 4to. VG. $30.00

READE, Charles. *Cloister & the Hearth.* 1932. Ltd Ed Club. Ils/sgn Ward. 2 vols. boxed. $40.00

READERS DIGEST. *Animals Can Be Almost Human.* 1980. Ils. 416 p. EX. M2. $10.00

READERS DIGEST. *Animals You Will Never Forget.* 1969. Ils. 413 p. G. M2. $6.00

READERS DIGEST. *Secrets & Spies Behind the Scenes: Stories of WWII.* 1964. Pleasantville. VG. M1. $6.50

REAGAN, Ronald. *Where's the Rest of Me?* 1965. NY. 1st ed. with sgn card. G. $65.00

REARDEN, M. & M. *Zulu Land: Wildlife Heritage.* 1984. Cape Town. Ils 1st ed. 159 p. dj. EX. M2. $15.00

REARICK, W.R. *Art of Paolo Veronese...* 1988. Cambridge. Ils. 212 p. D2. $30.00

REAVES, J.S. *Air Pilots Register, 1935.* 1935. NY. Ils. xl. G. T5. $45.00

REBAY, Hilla. *In Memory of Wassily Kandinsky.* 1945. Guggenheim. Ils. 119 p. D2. $135.00

RECHY, John. *City of Night.* 1964. Grove Pr. VG. P1. $6.00

RECHY, John. *Sexual Outlaw.* 1977. NY. Grove. 1st ed. dj. EX. $17.50

RECK, F.M. *On Time.* 1948. 1st HrdCvr ed. 184 p. $30.00

RECTOR, William. *Log Transportation in Lakes Lumber Industry, 1840-1918.* 1953. Ils. VG. $30.00

REDDING, Saunders. *Lonesome Road.* 1958. Doubleday. 1st ed. dj. M1. $9.50

REDDING, William. *Rom's Town.* 1947. Phil. 1st ed. 394 p. dj. VG. B2. $20.00

REDER, Gustav. *World of Steam Locomotives.* 1974. NY. Ils. 338 p. dj. G. T5. $42.50

REDFIELD, Holland. *Chief Training Captain, Pan-American...* 1981. presentation. printed wraps. VG. $20.00

REDFIELD, Robert. *Tepoztlan: Mexican Village.* 1941. Chicago. Ils. 8vo. gilt brown cloth. VG. T1. $40.00

REDIVIVUS, Quevedo. *Vision of Judgment.* 1867. NY. 12mo. VG. $30.00

REDLICH & FREEDMAN. *Theory & Practice of Psychiatry.* 1966. NY. 10th print. dj. EX. $18.00

REDNER, Morton. *Getting Out.* 1971. NY. Walker. 1st ed. dj. EX. $13.00

REDOUTE, P. *Redoute Treasury: 468 Watercolors From Les Liliacees.* 1986. Vendome. 1st Am ed. 4to. dj. EX. M2. $25.00

REDPATH, James. *Echoes of Harper's Ferry.* 1860. Boston. xl. EX. $22.00

REDPATH, James. *Guide to Hayti.* 1861. Boston. 1st ed. fld map. VG. $65.00

REDPATH, James. *Public Life of Captain John Brown.* 1860. 406 p. K1. $14.50

REDPATH, James. *Public Life of Captain John Brown.* 1860. Boston. 1st ed. 407 p. VG. T5. $25.00

REDSLOB, Edwin. *Richard Scheibe.* 1955. Berlin. Rembrandt. Ils. dj. D2. $55.00

REECE, Maynard. *Waterfowl Art of Maynard Reece.* 1985. Abrams. 94 pls. square 4to. 179 p. dj. M2. $45.00

REED, A. *Jose Clemente Orozco.* 1932. NY. sgn Orozco. black cloth. J2. $150.00

REED, Brian. *Locomotives in Profile. Vol. 1.* 1971. Garden City. Ils 1st ed. 292 p. dj. VG. T5. $22.50

REED, Brian. *Locomotives in Profile. Vol. 2.* 1972. Garden City. Ils. 288 p. dj. VG. T5. $22.50

REED, C.A. *American Game Birds.* 1912. Reed. Ils 1st ed. 64 p. VG. M2. $14.00

REED, C.A. *Birds of Rockies & W to Pacific.* 1920. Doubleday Page. Ils. 252 p. VG. M2. $13.00

REED, C.A. *Canadian Bird Book.* nd. Musson. Ils 1st Canadian ed. VG. M2. $65.00

REED, C.A. *Land Birds E of Rockies, Parrots to Bluebirds.* 1940. Doubleday Page. Ils. 229 p. VG. M2. $10.00

REED, Earl H. *Voices of Dunes & Other Etchings.* 1912. Chicago. Alderbrink. 1/125. sgn. VG. $75.00

REED, Edwin. *Francis Bacon, Our Shakespeare.* 1902. Boston. $60.00

REED, Eugene. *Masterpieces of German Art.* nd. Phil. 1st ed. folio. 2 vols. G. $100.00

REED, H.H. *NY Public Library: Architecture & Decoration.* 1986. NY. Norton. Ils 1st ed. 4to. pb. $30.00

REED, J. *War in E Europe.* 1919. NY. Ils Robinson. VG. $45.00

REED, John R. *Perception & Design in Tennyson's Idylly of the King.* 1969. OH U. 1st ed. dj. VG. C1. $16.00

REED, Myrtle. *Flowers of the Dusk.* 1910. Putnam. 341 p. $27.00

REED, Myrtle. *Love Affairs of Literary Men.* 1907. Knickerbocker. Ils. VG. $25.00

REED, Myrtle. *Master of the Vineyard.* 1910. Putnam. 1st ed. TEG. EX. $22.00

REED & KELLOGG. *Higher Lessons in English.* 1889. 16mo. 316 p. TB. VG. $2.00

REEP, Diana. *Rescue & Romance.* 1982. Popular Pr. VG. P1. $15.00

REES, David. *Son of Prophecy: Henry Tudor's Road to Bosworth.* 1985. 1st ed. dj. M. C1. $12.00

REESE, D.M. *Phrenology.* 1836. NY. 1st ed. 195 p. VG. $45.00

REESE, Trevor. *Colonial GA.* 1963. Athens. 172 p. dj. VG. $15.00

REESE, W.D. *Mosses of Gulf S From Rio Grande to Appalachicola.* 1984. LA U. Ils. 252 p. dj. EX. M2. $17.00

REEVES, Frank. *Century of TX Cattle Brands.* 1936. Ft. Worth. Ils. 80 p. wraps. VG. A3. $40.00

REEVES, J. *Arcadian Ballads.* 1977. Whittington Pr. 1/200. sgns. slipcase. EX. $40.00

REGARDIE, Israel. *Middle Pillar.* 1938. Aries Pr. M. $35.00

REGARDIE, Israel. *Philosopher's Stone.* 1970. 2nd ed. dj. VG. $35.00

REICHARD, Gladys. *Dezba: Woman of the Desert.* 1939. Augustin. 1st ed. sgn. VG. J2. $25.00

REID, D. *Mushrooms & Toadstools.* 1980. London. Kingfisher. 1st ed. 124 p. EX. M2. $8.00

REID, H.L. *Dixie of Desert: Brigham Young's Exploration & Settlement.* 1964. Zion, UT. Ils 1st ed. 8vo. dj. VG. T1. $35.00

REID, J.H. *Mountains, Men & Rivers.* 1954. Toronto. Ryerson Pr. 299 p. dj. M1. $15.00

REID, Mayne. *Scalp Hunters.* nd. London. Lea. Ils. $70.00

REID, S.C. *Scouting Expeditions of McCulloch's TX Rangers.* 1860. Phil. Ils. 251 p. G. $85.00

REID, W.M. *Lake George & Champlain & Mohawk War Trail.* 1910. NY. Ils 1st ed. dj. VG. B2. $85.00

REID, W.M. *Lake George & Lake Champlain.* 1910. NY. 1st ed. 381 p. EX. B2. $95.00

REID, Whitelaw. *OH in War: Her Statesmen, Her Generals & Soldiers.* 1868. Cincinnati. Ils 1st ed. 2 vols. T5. $225.00

REID, Whitelaw. *OH in War: Her Statesmen, Her Generals & Soldiers. Vol. II.* 1868. Cincinnati. Ils. 949 p. later cloth bdg. M2. $50.00

REID. *Cliff Climbers.* nd. London. 1st ed. G. $25.00

REILLY, C.W. *English Poetry of WWI.* 1978. London. 402 p. $17.50

REILLY, R. *British at the Gates: New Orleans Campaign...* 1974. Putnam. Ils. 376 p. EX. M2. $6.00

REIMER, John. *Diary of a Spiritualist.* 1930. NY. $16.50

REINFELDER, Al. *Bait Tail Fishing.* 1969. Barnes. Ils. photos. dj. VG. $9.00

REINHARD, E.G. *Witchery of Wasps.* 1929. Century. Ils 1st ed. 291 p. VG. M2. $14.00

REINHARDT, C.W. *Lettering for Draftsmen.* 1917. NY. oblong 4to. G. $20.00

REINHEMER, Sophie. *Bunte Blemen.* 1924. Germany. Ils. G. $25.00

REINO, Joseph. *Stephen King: The First Decade.* 1988. Twayne. dj. EX. P1. $17.95

REISER, O.L. *Philosophy & Concepts of Modern Science.* 1935. Macmillan. 1st ed. 323 p. dj. EX. M2. $12.00

REITSCH, Hanna. *Flying Is My Life.* 1954. NY. Ils 1st ed. 246 p. VG. $37.50

REMANE & SCHLIEPER. *Die Biologie des Brackwassers.* 1958. Stuttgart. Ils. map. German text. EX. M2. $15.00

REMARQUE, E.M. *All Quiet on the W Front.* 1929. Boston. 1st Am ed. dj. EX. $35.00

REMARQUE, E.M. *Flotsam.* 1941. Boston. 1st Am ed. inscr. EX. $40.00

REMARQUE, E.M. *Three Comrades.* 1946. Boston. 5th Am print. inscr. $30.00

REMARQUE, E.M. *Time To Love & Time To Die.* 1954. NY. 1st Am ed. sgn. dj. EX. $30.00

REMINGTON, Frederic. *Done in the Open.* 1902. NY. Russell. Ltd 1st ed. 1/250. slipcase. $650.00

REMINGTON, Frederic. *Done in the Open.* 1903. NY. Collier. folio. B2. $145.00

REMINGTON, Frederic. *Frontier Sketches.* nd. Franklin Lib. EX. $15.00

REMINGTON, Frederic. *Frontier Sketches.* 1898. Akron. 1st ed. VG. B2. $250.00

REMINGTON, Frederic. *Frontier Sketches.* 1898. Chicago. Werner. 1st ed. slipcase. $600.00

REMINGTON, Frederic. *Men With the Bark On.* 1900. Harper. 1st ed. 1st issue. M. $150.00

REMINGTON, Frederic. *Men With the Bark On.* 1900. NY. Harper. 1st ed. VG. B2. $80.00

REMINGTON, Frederic. *Pony Tracks.* 1895. NY. Ils. VG. $200.00

REMY, Nicolas. *Demonalatry.* 1930. London. Rodker. VG. $65.00

RENARD, Jules. *Natural Histories.* 1966. Horizon. Ils Lautrec. slipcase. VG. $16.00

RENAULT, Mary. *Mask of Apollo.* 1966. NY. Pantheon. 1st ed. dj. EX. $40.00

RENDELL, Ruth. *Best Man To Die.* 1970. Doubleday. 1st ed. dj. VG. $15.00

RENDELL, Ruth. *Killing Doll.* 1984. Pantheon. 1st Am ed. dj. EX. $15.00

RENDELL, Ruth. *Talking to Strange Men.* 1987. NY. Pantheon. 1st Am ed. dj. M. $10.00

RENDELL, Ruth. *Tree of Hands.* 1984. Pantheon. 1st Am ed. dj. M. $12.00

RENETZKY, A. *NASA Fact Book.* 1971. Orange. VG. $18.00

RENNELL, James. *Geographical System of Herodotus, Examined.* 1800. London. 1st ed. 11 maps. 4to. $350.00

RENNERT, Jack. *Poster Art of Tomi Ungerer.* 1971. Darien House. 1st ed. dj. VG. J2. $25.00

RENOUARD, P. *La Danse.* 1892. Paris. 20 color pls. cloth ties. VG. J2. $500.00

RENSE, Paige. *American Interiors: Architectural Digest Presents...* 1978. Los Angeles. Knapp. 287 p. dj. D2. $85.00

RENWICK, H.G. *Heaven's Own Mosaic & Other Poems.* 1929. Los Angeles. inscr. 95 p. VG. T5. $32.50

REPPLIER, Agnes. *Junipero Serra.* 1942. Doublday Doran. 312 p. dj. A3. $35.00

RESNICK, Louis. *Eye Hazards in Industry.* 1941. NY. 8vo. 321 p. dj. $20.00

RESNICK, Mike. *Official Guide to the Fantastics.* House of Collectibles. VG. P1. $12.50

RETI, Richard. *Masters of Chessboard.* 1932. NY. 5th ed. VG. $30.00

RETZLAFF, Erich. *Das Antlitz des Alters...* 1930. Dusseldorf. Ils. German text. sm folio. $125.00

REUBEN, W.A. *Atom Spy Hoax.* 1955. Action Books. VG. M1. $6.50

REULEAUX, F. *Constructor: Handbook of Machine Design.* 1895. Phil. 4to. 312 p. VG. $25.00

REUTHER, Victor. *Brothers Reuther & Story of UAW.* 1976. dj. VG. $25.00

REUTHER, Walter. *Selected Papers.* 1961. 1st ed. dj. VG. $20.00

REVEL, J.F. *On Proust.* 1972. London. 1st ed. dj. EX. $12.00

REVERE, J.W. *Tour of Duty in CA.* 1849. NY. pls. map. 305 p. rebound. EX. B1. $125.00

REVERE, J.W. *Tour of Duty in CA.* 1849. NY. 6 pls. fld map. 305 p. VG. $175.00

REWALD, John. *Les Fauves.* 1953. MOMA. Ils. 4to. wraps. $30.00

REWALD, John. *Renoir Drawings.* 1946. NY. Ils. 4to. cloth/buckram. VG. J2. $65.00

REWALD, John. *Woodcuts of Aristide Maillol.* 1943. 1st ed. 1/550. dj. slipcase. M. $125.00

REXROTH, Kenneth. *Autobiographical Novel.* 1966. NY. 1st ed. dj. EX. $25.00

REXROTH, Kenneth. *Pierre Reverdy: Selected Poems.* 1969. New Directions. 1st ed. 1/150. sgn/#d. slipcase. $75.00

REXROTH, Kenneth. *Saucy Limericks & Christmas Cheer.* 1880. Morrow. 1/299. sgn/#d. wraps. mailing envelope. $35.00

REXROTH, Kenneth. *Spark in the Tinder of Knowing.* 1968. Pym Randall. 1/200. sgn/#d. wraps. EX. $45.00

REY, H.A. *Find the Constellations.* 1954. Boston. Houghton. Ils. $22.50

REYDEN, H. *Bobcat Year.* 1981. Viking. Ils 1st ed. 211 p. dj. EX. M2. $13.00

REYHER, R. *Fon & His Hundred Wives.* 1952. Doubleday. Ils 1st ed. map. 314 p. EX. M2. $10.00

REYMONT, L. *Peasants.* 1924-1925. Knopf. 4 vols. VG. $25.00

REYNOLDS, C.B. *Old St. Augustine: Story of Three Centuries.* 1886. St. Augustine. Reynolds. Ils. VG. $35.00

REYNOLDS, E.G. *Myth of Manuscript Found: Absurdities of Spaulding Story.* 1883. Salt Lake City. 104 p. xl. G. T5. $35.00

REYNOLDS, Graham. *Introduction to English Watercolor Painting.* 1950. London/NY. Country Life/Scribner. Ils. D2. $35.00

REYNOLDS, James. *Andrea Palladio & the Winged Device.* 1948. NY. dj. J2. $15.00

REYNOLDS, James. *Gallery of Ghosts.* 1949. NY. $27.50

REYNOLDS, James. *Ghosts in Irish Houses.* 1947. Bonanza. Ils. 4to. 293 p. dj. VG. $22.00

REYNOLDS, Mack. *Mission to Horatius.* 1968. Whitman. VG. P1. $15.00

REYNOLDS, Quentin. *Fiction Factory.* 1955. NY. Ils 1st ed. 283 p. T5. $35.00

REYNOLDS, Quentin. *Fiction Factory.* 1965. NY. Ils. 283 p. VG. $28.00

REYNOLDS, Quentin. *Officially Dead.* 1945. NY. 1st ed. dj. VG. $15.00

REYNOLDS, Quentin. *They Fought for the Sky.* 1957. NY/Toronto. Ils 1st ed. RS. dj. VG. T5. $15.00

REYNOLDS, Tim. *Tlatelolco: Squence From Que.* 1970. Phoenix. 1/100. sgn/#d. EX. $25.00

REYNOLDS, Tim. *Women Poem.* 1972. Phoenix. 1/100. EX. $25.00

REYNOLDS, W.J. *Moving Targets.* 1986. St. Martin. 1st ed. dj. EX. $15.00

REZNIKOFF, Charles. *Family Chronicles.* 1971. NY. 1st ed. dj. EX. $25.00

RHEAD, Louis. *Bold Robin Hood & His Outlaw Band.* c 1922. Ils Rhead. VG. C1. $24.00

RHEADE, Brian. *Aubrey Beardsley.* 1967. NY. 1st ed. dj. EX. $20.00

RHEIMS. *Flowering of Art Nouveau.* nd. Abrams. plastic dj. VG. $85.00

RHINE, J.B. *New Frontiers of the Mind.* 1937. Duke. 1st ed. G. $10.00

RHINE, J.B. *New Frontiers of the Mind.* 1937. NY. 1st ed. VG. $15.00

RHODE, John. *Death at the Dance.* 1952. London. 1st ed. dj. EX. $37.50

RHODE, John. *Peril at Cranbury Hill.* 1930. London. 1st ed. dj. $35.00

RHODE, John. *Shadow of an Alibi.* nd. NY. Dodd Mead. EX. $15.00

RHODES, J.F. *Confederate Literature.* 1917. 213 p. EX. J4. $50.00

RHODES, J.F. *History of the Civil War, 1861-1865.* 1923. maps. 454 p. gilt bdg. VG. J4. $20.00

RHODES & JAUCHIUS. *Trial of Mary Todd Lincoln.* 1959. Indianapolis. 1st ed. sgns. 200 p. dj. VG. T5. $19.50

RHODES & VOSE. *Makin' Tracks: Story of Transcontinental Railroad.* 1975. NY. Ils. 216 p. dj. VG. T5. $25.00

RHYINER & MANNIX. *Wildest Game.* 1958. Lippincott. Ils. 320 p. VG. M2. $10.00

RHYS, Ernest. *English Fairy Book.* nd. NY. Stokes. VG. $30.00

RHYS, Jean. *Sleep It Off Lady.* 1976. London. 1st ed. dj. EX. $30.00

RHYS, Jean. *Smile Please.* 1979. London. 1st ed. dj. $25.00

RHYS, Jean. *Tigers Are Better Looking.* 1947. NY. 1st ed. dj. EX. $15.00

RHYS, John. *Studies in the Arthurian Legend.* 1891. Oxford. Clarendon. 1st ed. G. C1. $120.00

RICCI, Corrado. *Correggio.* 1930. London/NY. Ils. 200 p. TEG. dj. D2. $95.00

RICCIARDI, Mirella. *Vanishing Africa.* 1971. Morrow. 1st ed. dj. VG. $50.00

RICCIARDI, Mirella. *Vanishing Africa.* 1971. Reynal. dj. EX. $75.00

RICCIUTI, E.R. *Killers of the Sea.* 1973. Walker. Ils 1st ed. 308 p. EX. M2. $11.00

RICCIUTI, E.R. *Wild Cats.* 1979. Ridge Pr. Ils. 238 p. dj. EX. M2. $20.00

RICCIUTI, E.R. *Wildlife of the Mountains.* 1979. Abrams. Ils. 232 p. EX. M2. $16.00

RICE, A.H. *Lovey Mary.* 1903. NY. 1st ed. green cloth. EX. $20.00

RICE, A.H. *Sandy.* 1905. NY. 1st ed. EX. $16.00

RICE, A.T. *Reminiscences of Abraham Lincoln by Distinguished Men.* 1888. NY. VG. $65.00

RICE, Anne. *Belinda.* 1986. Arbor House. 1st ed. dj. EX. T6. $35.00

RICE, Anne. *Cry to Heaven.* 1982. Knopf. 1st ed. dj. EX. T6. $40.00

RICE, Anne. *Exit to Eden.* 1985. Arbor House. 1st ed. dj. EX. T6. $35.00

RICE, Anne. *Feast of All Saints.* 1979. NY. 1st ed. sgn. dj. VG. B2. $65.00

RICE, Anne. *Feast of All Saints.* 1979. Simon Schuster. 1st ed. dj. EX. T6. $75.00

RICE, Anne. *Interview With the Vampire.* 1976. Knopf. Book Club ed. dj. VG. $50.00

RICE, Anne. *Mummy.* 1989. Chatto. 1st Eng HrdCvr ed. dj. EX. T6. $60.00

RICE, Anne. *Queen of the Dammed.* 1988. 4th print. dj. M. C1. $14.00

RICE, Anne. *Queen of the Dammed.* 1988. Knopf. UCP. sgn. wraps. T6. $150.00

RICE, Anne. *Queen of the Dammed.* 1988. Ultramarine. 1/124. sgn. M. $350.00

RICE, Anne. *Vampire Lestat.* 1985. NY. 1st ed. dj. EX. T6. $75.00

RICE, B. *Tardiveau: French Trader in W.* 1938. Baltimore. M. $35.00

RICE, D.G. *Rockingham Pottery & Porcelain.* 1971. Barrie Jenkins. 1st ed. dj. VG. $30.00

RICE, Harvey. *Sketches of W Life.* 1887. Boston. 1st ed. 253 p. G. T5. $15.00

RICE, Robert. *Business of Crime.* 1956. 1st ed. 262 p. $10.00

RICE, W.G. *Carillons of Belgium & Holland.* 1914. John Lane. gilt green bdg. VG. $40.00

RICE & HARGER. *Effects of Alchol.* 1952. Chicago. TB. G. $10.00

RICH, Jeremiah. *Penns Dexterity.* 1674. London. full leather. G. $275.00

RICH, L.D. *Natural World of Louise Dickinson Rich.* 1962. Dodd Mead. Ils. 195 p. dj. EX. M2. $12.00

RICH, L.D. *Peninsula.* 1958. Phil. 1st ed. dj. VG. B2. $15.00

RICH, L.D. *We Took to the Woods.* 1942. Lippincott. Ils. 322 p. G. M2. $5.00

RICHARDS, E.A. *Arctic Mood.* 1949. Caxton. Ils 1st ed. EX. $15.00

RICHARDS, E.A. *Arctic Mood.* 1949. Caxton. photos. map. 282 p. G. M2. $7.00

RICHARDS, I.D. *Story of a River Town: Little Rock in the 19th C.* 1969. private print. Ils. 144 p. dj. EX. M2. $10.00

RICHARDS, Lee. *Punks.* 1964. Beacon. juvenile. VG. P1. $4.50

RICHARDS, R.K. *Arithmetic Operations in Digital Computers.* 1956. NY. 5th print. VG. $15.00

RICHARDS, R.K. *Digital Computer Components & Circuits.* 1959. NY. 2nd print. VG. $20.00

RICHARDS, T.A. *American Scenery.* 1854. NY. Ils. 4to. $75.00

RICHARDS, W.G. *Last Billionaire.* 1948. NY. sgn. dj. VG. B2. $15.00

RICHARDS & SAUNDERS. *Royal Air Force, 1939-1945.* 1953-1954. London. 3 vols. djs. T5. $115.00

RICHARDSON, Albert. *Beyond the MS.* 1867. Hartford. Ils Nast/Waud. 8vo. 572 p. G. G2. $23.00

RICHARDSON, Albert. *Beyond the MS.* 1867. Hartford. 1st ed. gilt bdg. VG. $50.00

RICHARDSON, Albert. *Secret Service, Field, Dungeon & Escape.* 1865. Hartford. Ils 1st ed. 8vo. 512 p. G2. $29.00

RICHARDSON, Charles. *New Dictionary of English Language.* 1839. London. Pickering. 2 vols. VG. $52.00

RICHARDSON, Dorothy. *John Austen & the Inseparables.* 1930. London. Ils Austen. 1st ed. VG. J2. $30.00

RICHARDSON, Edgar P. *WA Allston: Study of Romantic Artist in America.* 1948. Chicago. 1st ed. 4to. dj. $70.00

RICHARDSON, F.M. *Mars Without Venus: Study of Some Homosexual Generals.* 1981. Edinburg. photos. 188 p. dj. VG. T5. $12.50

RICHARDSON, James. *Wonders of the Yellowstone.* 1874. NY. Scribner. Ils. fld maps. 256 p. EX. $55.00

RICHARDSON, John. *Account of Life of John Richardson.* 1783. Phil. 8vo. leather. G. $125.00

RICHARDSON, M. *Fascination of Reptiles.* 1972. Hill Wang. Ils. 240 p. dj. EX. M2. $18.00

RICHARDSON, R.C. *Study of History: Bibliographical Guide.* 1988. Manchester U. 98 p. VG. T5. $12.50

RICHARDSON, R.N. *Frontier of NW TX, 1846-1876.* 1963. Glendale. Clark. 1st ed. EX. $35.00

RICHARDSON & BLOUT. *Along the Iron Trail.* 1938. Rutland. VG. $25.00

RICHLER, Mordecai. *Acrobats.* 1954. NY. Putnam. 1st ed. dj. VG. $20.00

RICHMOND, Ian. *Roman Britain.* 1947. Britain in Pictures. 1st ed. C1. $9.00

RICHMOND, W.D. *Grammar of Lithography.* 1880. London. VG. $35.00

RICHMOND. *Red Pepper Burns.* 1910. Burt. Ils. VG. $4.50

RICHTER, Conrad. *Brothers of No Kin & Other Stories.* 1924. Hinds Hayden. 1st ed. sgn. 340 p. VG. M1. $60.00

RICHTER, Gisela. *Sculpture & Sculptors of Greeks.* 1929. New Haven. Ils. pls. maps. folio. G. J2. $125.00

RICKENBACKER, Eddie. *Fighting the Flying Circus.* 1919. Stokes. presentation. VG. $95.00

RICKENBACKER, Eddie. *From Father to Son.* 1970. NY. Ils 1st ed. 204 p. dj. VG. T5. $12.50

RICKER. *Deppala: AK Dog Driver.* 1930. Boston. Ils 1st ed. EX. $25.00

RICKETT, H.W. *American Wild Flowers.* 1964. NY. Ils Grehan. photos. dj. G. $25.00

RICKETT, H.W. *Wild Flowers of America.* 1969. Crown. Ils. gilt green bdg. VG. $40.00

RICKETT, H.W. *Wild Flowers of the US: Central Mountains & Plains.* 1973. NY Bot Garden. Ils 1st ed. 3 vols. slipcase. M2. $145.00

RICKETT, H.W. *Wild Flowers of the US: SE States.* 1970. NY Bot Garden. Ils 1st ed. 3 vols. slipcase. M2. $145.00

RICKETT, H.W. *Wild Flowers of the US: SE States.* 1976. NY Bot Garden. 1st ed. 4to. 2 vols. slipcase. M2. $110.00

RICKETT, H.W. *Wild Flowers of US: TX.* 1969. NY. Stated 1st ed. 2 vols. boxed. G. $175.00

RICKETTS, Charles. *Passionate Pilgrim & Songs From Shakespeare's Plays.* 1896. London. Hacon/Ricketts. 1/310. very scarce. $200.00

RICKS, Beatrice. *Ezra Pound: Bibliography of Secondary Works.* Scarecrow Pr. 281 p. VG. T5. $15.00

RIDDLE, Kenyon. *Records & Maps of Santa Fe Trail.* 1948. Raton, NM. Raton Daily Range. maps. VG. A3. $40.00

RIDDLE, Maxwell. *Springer Spaniel.* 1939. Chicago. Ils 1st ed. 158 p. dj. VG. T5. $45.00

RIDEAL, S. *Glue & Glue Testing.* 1915. London. Ils 2nd ed. G. $22.00

RIDER, Sarah. *Misplaced Corpse.* 1940. Boston. 1st ed. sgn. $12.50

RIDGE, J.R. *Life & Adventures of Joaquin Murieta, Celebrated Bantit.* 1955. OK U. Ils. 1st print. 159 p. dj. M2. $14.00

RIDGE, L. *Ghetto & Other Poems.* 1918. NY. 1st ed. dj. EX. $50.00

RIDGE, W.P. *London Types.* 1926. London. Methuen. 1st ed. EX. $40.00

RIDGWAY & FRIEDMANN. *Birds of N & Middle America.* 1946. US Nat Mus. Ils. 484 p. EX. M2. $25.00

RIDGWAY & FRIEDMANN. *Birds of N Middle America. Part IX.* 1941. US Nat Mus. Ils. EX. M2. $20.00

RIDGWAY & MARTIN. *Soldier.* 1956. NY. Ils 1st ed. sgns. 371 p. dj. G. T5. $65.00

RIDGWAY & MARTIN. *Soldier.* 1956. NY. Ils 1st ed. 371 p. dj. EX. T5. $32.50

RIDING, Laura. *Description of Life.* 1980. NY. Targ. 1/350. sgn. glassine dj. EX. $50.00

RIDLEY, M.R. *Story of Gawian & the Green Knight in Modern English.* 1944. England. presumed 1st ed. dj. EX. C1. $8.00

RIDPATH, J.C. *History of the World.* 1885. Jones Pub. G. $40.00

RIDPATH, J.C. *Story of S Africa.* 1899. NY. Eaton Maims. Ils. 641 p. VG. $10.00

RIEFENSTAHL, Leni. *Coral Gardens.* 1978. London. dj. EX. $50.00

RIEFENSTAHL, Leni. *Coral Gardens.* 1978. NY. Harper. Ils 1st Am ed. 4to. 223 p. dj. M2. $25.00

RIEFENSTAHL, Leni. *People of Kau.* 1976. Harper. 1st ed. dj. EX. $65.00

RIEFENSTAHL, Leni. *Schonheit im Olympischen Kampf.* 1937. Berlin. EX. $450.00

RIEGEL, Robert. *Story of the W Railroads.* 1926. Macmillan. 1st ed. VG. J2. $20.00

RIEMER, J. *Shaft Sinking Under Difficult Conditions.* 1907. NY. 19 fld pls. VG. $35.00

RIES, Charles. *Sehende Maschinen.* 1916. Diessen. Ils. 120 p. wraps. G. $175.00

RIESS, Linel. *My Models Were Jews: Painter's Pilgrimage to Many Lands.* 1938. NY. Gordon. 1/1200. folio. VG. $145.00

RIGBY & RIGBY. *Lock, Stock & Barrell: Story of Collecting.* 1944. Phil. Ils. pls. dj. $35.00

RIGG, A.G. *Glastonbury Miscellany of the 15th C.* 1968. Oxford U. Ils. EX. C1. $15.00

RIGGS, A.F. *Birds of Grotan, MA.* 1947. MA Audubon Soc. 49 p. M2. $5.00

RIGGS, Stephen. *Forty Years With the Sioux.* 1880. Chicago. Holmes. Ils. 388 p. VG. scarce. A3. $75.00

RIHA & SUBIK. *Cacti & Other Succulents.* 1981. Octopus. Ils 1st Eng ed. 352 p. dj. EX. M2. $19.00

RIIS, J.A. *Making of an American.* 1902. NY. gilt blue cloth. VG. $45.00

RILEY, Alice. *Wishbone Boat.* 1906. Caldwell. Ils. G. $15.00

RILEY, J.W. *Boys of the Old Glee Club.* 1907. Nov., 1907. Indianapolis. Ils Vawter. G. $25.00

RILEY, J.W. *Old Sweetheart of Mine.* 1902. Bobbs Merrill. Ils Christy. VG. B4. $65.00

RILEY, J.W. *Out to Old Aunt Mary's.* 1904. Grosset Dunlap. Ils Christy. EX. $9.50

RILEY, J.W. *Riley Love-Lyrics. With Life Pictures by William B. Dyer.* 1899. Indianapolis. 1st ed. 2nd state. 192 p. EX. $65.00

RILEY, Judith M. *Vision of Light.* 1989. NY. 1st ed. dj. M. C1. $15.00

RILEY & MONETT. *Notes on the Aphidae of the US.* 1879. WA. Ils. 152 p. disbound. A3. $30.00

RILKE, R.M. *Die Weise Von Liebe und Tod des Cornetts Otto Rilke.* 1927. Leipzig. 1/150. German text. T5. $35.00

RILKE, R.M. *Duino Elegies.* 1969. NY. 1st ed. dj. EX. $45.00

RILKE, R.M. *Lay of Love & Death of Cornet Christopher Rilke.* 1948. London. 1/500. EX. P3. $225.00

RILKE, R.M. *Migration of Powers: French Poems.* 1984. Gray Wolf Pr. 1st print. dj. EX. $30.00

RILKE, R.M. *Notebooks of Malte Laurids Brigge.* 1987. Ltd Ed Club. 1/800. gilt full vellum. dj. EX. $140.00

RILKE, R.M. *Selected Poems.* Ltd Ed Club. slipcase. M. B3. $60.00

RIMMER, R.H. *Zolotov Affair.* 1967. Los Angeles. 1st ed. dj. EX. $10.00

RINARD, J. *Creatures of the Night.* 1977. Nat Geog Soc. color photos. EX. M2. $5.00

RINEHARD & HOPWOOD. *Bat.* 1926. Doran. $20.00

RINEHART, F.A. *Rinehart's Indians.* 1899. Omaha. Rinehart. Ils. VG. scarce. A3. $80.00

RINEHART, M.R. *Door.* c 1930. NY. Grosset Dunlap. reprint. VG. $5.00

RINEHART, M.R. *This Strange Adventure.* c 1929. NY. Doubleday Doran. 1st ed. VG. $10.00

RINGELBLUM, Emmanuel. *Notes From the Warsaw Ghetto.* 1958. NY. G. $7.00

RINGOLD, M.S. *Rose of the State Legislatures in the Confederacy.* 1966. Athens. 1st ed. 141 p. EX. $15.00

RINHART & RINHART. *American Daguerreian Art.* 1967. NY. Potter. 1st ed. dj. with errata slip. $100.00

RINTO, Oreste. *Spy-Catcher.* 1952. Harper. 1st ed. xl. M1. $5.00

RINTOUL, A.N. *Guide To Painting Photographic Portraits...* c 1870. London. Barnard. 5th ed. wraps. $125.00

RIPLEY, C.P. *Slaves & Freedmen in Civil War.* 1976. Baton Rouge. 237 p. dj. $25.00

RIPLEY, Edward. *Capture of Richmond.* 1907. Ils. 31 p. scarce. K1. $35.00

RIPLEY, Lassell. *Field & Stream Portfolio: Gunning in America.* 1947. np. 6 pls. wraps. $50.00

RIPLEY, S.D. *Paddling of Ducks.* 1957. Harcourt Brace. Ils Jaques. 1st ed. 256 p. dj. M2. $14.00

RIPLEY & LANDSDOWNE. *Rails of the World: Monograph of Family Rallidae.* 1977. Toronto. Feheley. 1st ed. folio. dj. M. M2. $200.00

RISER & MORSE. *Biology of the Trubellaria.* 1974. McGraw Hill. Ils 1st ed. 530 p. dj. EX. M2. $25.00

RISLEY, Mary. *House of Healing.* 1962. London. 1st ed. dj. VG. $35.00

RISSELL, R. *Bird Lives.* 1973. Charterhouse. dj. EX. $55.00

RISTER, C.C. *Ft. Griffin on the TX Frontier.* 1956. Norman. Ils 1st ed. dj. EX. $35.00

RISTER, C.C. *Robert E. Lee in TX.* 1946. Norman. Ils 1st ed. sgn. EX. $40.00

RITCH, W.G. *Illustrated NM: Historical & Industrial.* 1885. Santa Fe. Ils. fld map/pls. 234 p. Lib bdg. A3. $80.00

RITCHIE, A.C. *Abstract Painting & Sculpture in America.* 1951. NY. MOMA. 1st ed. 159 p. dj. VG. $20.00

RITCHIE, Jean. *Singing Family of Cumberlands.* 1955. Oxford. Ils Sendak. dj. VG. $18.00

RITTER, Mary Bennett. *More Than Gold in CA, 1849-1933.* 1933. Berkeley. presentation. sgn. 8vo. 451 p. P3. $59.00

RITZ, C. *Fly Fisher's Life.* 1972. NY. dj. EX. $45.00

RIUS, D.L. *Bibliografia de las Obras de M. de Cervantes Saavedra.* 1970. Burt Franklin. reprint. 3 vols. $65.00

RIVERA & WOLFE. *Portrait of Mexico.* 1937. Covici. 1st ed. VG. J2. $20.00

RIVERAIN, J. *Concise Encyclopedia of Explorations.* 1969. Collins Follett. 279 p. dj. M2. $10.00

RIVERE, Alec. *Wantons of Betrayal.* 1964. Scorpion. VG. P1. $8.00

RIVES, H.E. *Hearts Courageous.* 1902. Bowen Merrill. Ils Wenzell. 1st ed. $12.00

RIVIERE, Yves. *Messagier: Les Estampes & les Sculptures 1945-1974.* 1975. Paris. 25 color pls. 210 p. D2. $85.00

RIX, G.S. *History & Genealogy of Eastman Family of America, Part II.* 1901. Concord, NY. wraps. fair. T5. $7.50

RIX, H.H. *Christian Mind Healing.* 1914. LA. $7.50

RIX, Martyn. *Art of the Plant World.* 1981. Overlook. Ils 1st Am ed. 224 p. dj. EX. M2. $65.00

RIX, Martyn. *Art of the Plant World.* 1981. Overlook. Ils 64 pls. 224 p. dj. M. $85.00

ROBACK & KEIRNAN. *Pictorial History of Psychology & Psychiatry.* 1969. NY. 294 p. dj. VG. $34.00

ROBB, Stewart. *Prophecies on World Events by Nostradamus.* 1961. NY. $10.00

ROBBE-GRILLET, A. *La Maison de Rendezvous.* 1966. Grove Pr. 1st ed. $25.00

ROBBINS, Harold. *Inheritors.* 1969. NY. inscr. dj. G. $25.00

ROBBINS, Harold. *Stone for Danny Fisher.* 1951. Boston. 1st ed. dj. VG. B2. $17.50

ROBBINS, Harold. *Stone for Danny Fisher.* 1952. NY. Knopf. 1st issue. sgn. tall wraps. VG. $15.00

ROBBINS, R.A. *91st Infantry Division in WWII.* 1947. Journal Pr. 1st ed. VG. $45.00

ROBBINS, R.H. *Encyclopedia of Witchcraft & Demonology.* 1959. NY. Book Club. Ils 571 p. dj. EX. $9.50

ROBBINS, Tom. *Jitterbug Perfume.* 1984. Bantam. Review 1st ed. dj. EX. $17.50

ROBBINS, Tom. *Jitterbug Perfume.* 1984. NY. 1st ed. sgn. dj. EX. $35.00

ROBBINS, Tom. *Still Life With Woodpecker.* 1980. NY. 1st Am ed. dj. VG. $55.00

ROBERS, H.C.B. *Pageant Heraldry: Explanation of Its Principles & Uses...* 1955. London. Ils dj. VG. T5. $12.50

ROBERSON & LINDZEY. *Proceedings of the Second Mountain Lion Workshop.* 1984. UT Wildlife. 18 p. M2. $3.00

ROBERT & WORDE. *Code for Collector of Beautiful Books.* 1936. NY. Ltd Ed Club. $30.00

ROBERTS, Cecil. *Man Arose.* 1941. Macmillan. blue cloth. dj. G. D1. $10.00

ROBERTS, Charles. *Foulsham's Card & Conjuring Tricks.* nd. Phil. Ils. 12mo. dj. EX. T1. $35.00

ROBERTS, Dorothy James. *Enchanted Cup.* Book Club. 1st ed. dj. EX. C1. $9.00

ROBERTS, Dorothy James. *Enchanted Cup.* c 1953. Book Club. VG. C1. $4.00

ROBERTS, E. *Shoshone & Other W Wonders.* 1888. NY. Ils 1st ed. 275 p. G. $45.00

ROBERTS, E.M. *Buried Treasure.* 1931. NY. 1st ed. dj. EX. $25.00

ROBERTS, E.M. *Great Meadow.* 1930. NY. 1st ed. 1/295. sgn. 8vo. TEG. dj. boxed. $50.00

ROBERTS, F.H.H. *River Basin Surveys.* 1960. Smithsonian. 65 photos. 337 p. EX. M2. $20.00

ROBERTS, John Maddox. *King of the Wood.* 1st Am ed. dj. RS. EX. C1. $11.00

ROBERTS, Keith. *Corot.* 1965. London. Spring Art Books. Ils. dj. D2. $25.00

ROBERTS, Kenneth. *Oliver Wiswell.* 1940. Doubleday. Ltd ed. sgn. dj. VG. $125.00

ROBERTS, Kenneth. *Battle of Cowpens.* 1948. Garden City. 1st ed. dj. EX. B2. $40.00

ROBERTS, Kenneth. *Black Magic.* 1924. Indianapolis. 1st ed. VG. B2. $45.00

ROBERTS, Kenneth. *Boon Island.* 1956. Garden City. presentation. sgn. VG. $45.00

ROBERTS, Kenneth. *Boon Island.* 1956. NY. 1st ed. 275 p. dj. T5. $17.50

ROBERTS, Kenneth. *Henry Gross & His Dowsing Rod.* 1951. NY. 1st ed. dj. EX. B1. $30.00

ROBERTS, Kenneth. *Lively Lady.* 1935. NY. inscr. blue cloth. EX. $55.00

ROBERTS, Kenneth. *Moreau de St. Mery's American Journey (1793-1798).* 1947. Garden City. 1st ed. dj. VG. $20.00

ROBERTS, Kenneth. *NW Passage.* 1937. Doubleday. 1st ed. VG. $35.00

ROBERTS, Kenneth. *NW Passage.* 1937. NY. Ltd ed. sgn. dj. boxed. EX. $130.00

ROBERTS, Kenneth. *Oliver Wiswell.* 1940. Doubleday. 1st trade ed. $25.00

ROBERTS, Kenneth. *Oliver Wiswell.* 1940. NY. Ltd ed. 1/1050. sgn. 2 vols. boxed. EX. $150.00

ROBERTS, Kenneth. *Oliver Wiswell.* 1940. NY. 1st ed. 3rd print. inscr. VG. $75.00

ROBERTS, Kenneth. *Sun Hunting.* 1922. orig bdg. B1. $35.00

ROBERTS, Kenneth. *Trending Into ME.* 1938. Boston. Ils Wyeth. 1st ed. EX. M2. $65.00

ROBERTS, Kenneth. *Trending Into ME.* 1944. NY. Ils Wyeth. Revised 1st ed. dj. VG. B2. $30.00

ROBERTS, Kenneth. *Trending Into ME.* 1985. reprint of Arundel ed. dj. EX. $35.00

ROBERTS, Kenneth. *Water Unlimited.* 1957. Garden City. 1st ed. dj. EX. $45.00

ROBERTS, Leslie. *There Shall Be Wings: History of Royal Canadian Air Force.* 1960. London. Ils 1st ed. 290 p. dj. G. T5. $27.50

ROBERTS, Nancy. *Ghosts of the Carolinas. With Photographs by Bruce Roberts.* 1967. Charlotte, NC. Intro Legette Blyte. 2nd ed. 62 p. $27.50

ROBERTS, Nancy. *Goodliest Land: NC.* 1973. Doubleday. Ils Roberts. 2nd ed. 175 p. $10.00

ROBERTS, Octavia. *Lincoln in IL.* 1918. Houghton. Ltd ed. 1/1000. G. $35.00

ROBERTS, Octavia. *My Lady Valentine.* 1916. MA. Ils. VG. $30.00

ROBERTS, R.S. *True Likeness: Black S of Richard S. Roberts, 1920-1936.* 1986. Bruccoli. 1/100. sgn editor. folio. dj. EX. $150.00

ROBERTS, S.C. *Holmes & Watson: A Miscellany.* 1953. Oxford U. dj. VG. $35.00

ROBERTS, T.S. *Bird Portraits in Color.* 1960. MN U. Abridged ed. dj. EX. M2. $40.00

ROBERTS, T.S. *Birds of MN.* nd. 1/300. sgn. 2 vols. Kittredge bdg. EX. $200.00

ROBERTS, W.A. *Lake Pontchartrain.* 1946. Bobbs Merrill. Ils 376 p. dj. VG. M2. $8.00

ROBERTSON, Bruce. *Air Aces of the 1914-1918 War.* 1959. Letchworth. Revised 2nd ed. 4to. 211 p. dj. T5. $42.50

ROBERTSON, C.N. *Oneida Community, 1851-1876.* 1970. Syracuse. 1st ed. 364 p. dj. VG. $15.00

ROBERTSON, G. *Vita di Christofano Colombo.* 1794. Venezia. 140 p. VG. $75.00

ROBERTSON, J.I. *Concise Illustrated History of the Civil War.* 1971. Stackpole. Ils. 128 p. dj. EX. M2. $5.00

ROBERTSON, J.M. *Short History of Free Thought.* 1899. London. VG. $40.00

ROBERTSON, J.W. *Francis Drake Along Pacific Coast.* 1927. Grabhorn. Ltd ed. sgn. boxed. EX. $200.00

ROBERTSON, T. *Night Raider of the Atlantic.* 1956. NY. 1st ed. 256 p. dj. VG. $20.00

ROBERTSON, William. *History of America.* 1777. Dublin. 2 vols. full leather. $140.00

ROBESON, Dave. *A.G. Barnes: Master Showman.* 1935. Caxton. 1st ed. VG. J2. $25.00

ROBINSON, A. *Old New England Doorways.* 1920. NY. pls. VG. $25.00

ROBINSON, A.L. *Ten Commandments: Short Novels of Hitler's War...* 1943. NY. 1st ed. 488 p. dj. G. T5. $12.50

ROBINSON, Bert. *Basket Weavers of AZ.* 1954. Albuquerque. Review 1st ed. 8vo. dj. $90.00

ROBINSON, C.E. *Shakers & Their Homes.* 1893. Canterbury. Ils. 134 p. VG. $225.00

ROBINSON, D.H. *Giants in the Sky: History of Rigid Airship.* 1979. Seattle. Ils. 376 p. dj. M. T5. $19.50

ROBINSON, Doane. *History of SD.* 1904. Bowen. 1st ed. 4to. 2 vols. EX. $80.00

ROBINSON, E.A. *Cavender's House.* 1929. NY. 1st ed. 1/500. sgn. 8vo. TEG. boxed. EX. $50.00

ROBINSON, E.A. *Collected Poems.* 1929. NY. VG. C1. $15.00

ROBINSON, E.A. *Dionysus in Doubt.* 1925. NY. 1st ed. dj. VG. B2. $20.00

ROBINSON, E.A. *Merlin, Lancelot & Tristram.* 1927. 1 vol ed. leather. C1. $12.50

ROBINSON, E.A. *Roman Bartholow.* 1923. NY. 1st ed. 1/750. sgn. 191 p. TEG. G. T5. $65.00

ROBINSON, E.A. *Talifer.* 1933. NY. 1st ed. 8vo. gilt cloth. EX. T1. $25.00

ROBINSON, Fayette. *CA & Its Gold Regions.* 1849. NY. fld map. $90.00

ROBINSON, H.M. *Enchanted Grindstone.* 1952. NY. 1st ed. dj. VG. $9.00

ROBINSON, H.M. *Water of Life.* 1960. NY. 1st ed. sgn. 621 p. dj. G. T5. $25.00

ROBINSON, J.H. *Petrarch.* 1969. Greenwood. Revised Expanded 2nd ed. M. $35.00

ROBINSON, J.S. *Hilda Doolittle.* 1982. Houghton. 1st ed. 4to. 490 p. dj. EX. $25.00

ROBINSON, P.F. *Rural Architecture Being a Series of Designs for Cottages.* 1828. London. 3rd ed. 95 of 96 pls. J2. $150.00

ROBINSON, R.E. *Hunting Without a Gun.* 1905. NY. Ils 1st ed. 381 p. VG. $20.00

ROBINSON, Sara T. *KS: Its Interior & Exterior Life.* 1856. Boston/Cincinnati/London. 1st ed. $60.00

ROBINSON, Selma. *City Child.* 1931. NY. Colphon. Ils Kent. sgn Robinson. slipcase. $140.00

ROBINSON, Solon. *Facts for Farmers.* 1872. NY. 2 vols in 1. EX. $35.00

ROBINSON, Solon. *Hot Corn: Life Scenes in NY.* 1854. NY. Ils. $20.00

ROBINSON, Victor. *Victory Over Pain: History of Anesthesia.* 1946. Schuman. 1st ed. dj. VG. J2. $15.00

ROBINSON, W.H. *Under Turquoise Skies.* 1928. Macmillan. Ils 1st ed. 538 p. dj. VG. A3. $45.00

ROBINSON, W.M. *Confederate Privateers.* 1928. New Haven. 372 p. dj. VG. $45.00

ROBINSON. *Japanese Arms & Armor.* 1969. Crown. dj. VG. $30.00

ROBINSON. *Oriental Armor.* 1967. NY. 1st ed. dj. EX. $27.00

ROBINSON. *Robinson's Atlas of Norfolk City.* 1888. MA. 40 of 46 pls. VG. $160.00

ROBINSON. *Spotlight on Union: United Hatters, Cap & Millinery Workers.* 1948. dj. VG. $27.00

ROBRA, Gunther. *Mittelalterliche Holzplastic in Ostfriesland.* 1959. Osfriesland. tall 8vo. 140 p. dj. $37.50

ROCHE, E.L. *Historic Sketches of S.* 1914. NY. Ils. 8vo. 148 p. VG. $40.00

ROCHETTE, R. *Lectures on Ancient Art.* 1854. London. Hall Virtu. 184 p. VG. $45.00

ROCHLIN & ROCHLIN. *Pioneer Jews: New Life in the Old W.* 1984. Boston. Houghton. 180 photos. dj. M. $18.00

ROCKEY, Howard. *Honeymoon's End.* 1926. Macaulay. 1st ed. $12.00

ROCKWELL, John. *Sinatra: American Classic.* 1984. Rolling Stone. 1st ed. dj. M. $10.00

ROCKWELL, Norman. *My Adventures As an Illustrator.* 1960. Doubleday. 1st ed. dj. VG. J2. $15.00

ROCKWELL, Wilson. *Uncompahgre Country.* 1965. Denver. Sage. Ils 1st ed. 310 p. dj. VG. A3. $30.00

RODALE PRESS. *Feasting on Raw Foods.* 1980. 324 p. dj. EX. $20.00

RODALE PRESS. *Rodale Cookbook.* 1973. Ils. photos. 486 p. dj. EX. $20.00

RODMAN, Selden. *Mexican Journal.* 1958. NY. 1st ed. dj. EX. $17.50

RODMAN, Selden. *Renaissance in Haiti.* 1948. NY. Ils 1st ed. 4to. dj. VG. $35.00

ROE, A.S. *24th Regiment, VA Volunteers, 1861-1866.* 1907. Ils. rosters. 573 p. xl. EX. J4. $60.00

ROE, F.G. *Indian & Horses.* 1955. Norman. Ils 1st ed. dj. EX. $30.00

ROE, J.W. *English & American Tool Builders.* 1916. New Haven. 8vo. 315 p. VG. $100.00

ROE & SIMPSON. *Behavior & Evolution.* 1958. Yale. 557 p. EX. M2. $20.00

ROEDER, K.D. *Nerve Cells & Insect Behavior.* 1967. Harvard. Ils. 238 p. EX. M2. $15.00

ROEN, P.R. *Atlas of Genito-Urinary Surgery.* 1951. NY. Ils Stern. Intro Bandler. 325 p. EX. $40.00

ROESE, Wilhelm. *Meine Amerikafahrt zur Ausstellung, 1893.* nd. np. tall 4vo. gilt full leather. $40.00

ROETHEL & BENJAMIN. *Kandinsky: Catalog Raisonne of the Oil Paintings.* 1982-1984. Ithaca. 2 vols. dj. D2. $550.00

ROETHKE, Theodore. *Open House.* 1941. NY. Ltd 1st ed. dj. $275.00

ROETHKE, Theodore. *Straw for the Fire.* 1972. NY. Doubleday. 1st trade ed. dj. EX. $20.00

ROETHKE, Theodore. *Worlds for the Wind.* 1957. London. 1st ed. dj. EX. $75.00

ROFHEART, Martha. *Glendower Country.* 1978. pb. VG. C1. $4.00

ROGAN, R.K. *Benedict Arnold: Our First Marine.* 1931. Cincinnati. 1st ed. slipcase. very scarce. $85.00

ROGERS, A. *Women Are Here To Stay.* 1949. NY. G. $20.00

ROGERS, A.D. *Story of American Plant Sciences.* 1949. Princeton. Ils 1st ed. 506 p. dj. VG. B2. $40.00

ROGERS, Charles. *Book of Wallace.* 1889. Edinburgh. pls. 2 vols. with letter. $65.00

ROGERS, F.B. *Soldiers of Overland: Being Account of General P.E. Connor.* 1938. San Francisco. 1/1000. VG. $75.00

ROGERS, George C. *Charleston in the Age of the Pinckneys.* 1969. OK U. 1st ed. dj. EX. T6. $15.00

ROGERS, H.M. *Memories of Ninety Years.* 1928. 404 p. inscr/sgn. EX. J4. $15.00

ROGERS, J.A. *From Superman to Man.* 1978. NY. Rogers. reprint. 130 p. dj. $7.50

ROGERS, Meyric. *Carl Milles: Intrepretation of His Work.* 1948. Yale. 2nd print. VG. J2. $50.00

ROGERS, Richard. *Richard Rogers' Fact Book.* 1965. NY. 1st ed. 582 p. dj. EX. $25.00

ROGERS, Samuel. *Italy, a Poem.* 1830. London. 1st Complete ed. AEG. leather. $75.00

ROGERS, Samuel. *Italy, a Poem.* 1923. London. 2nd ed. AEG. gilt full leather. $30.00

ROGERS, Stanley. *Book of the Sailing Ship.* 1931. NY. Crowell. 282 p. dj. VG. $20.00

ROGERS, Stanley. *Ships & Sailors.* 1928. Boston. Ils. fair. $12.00

ROGERS, T.S. *Reference Manual of American Architect.* 1935. NY. G. $40.00

ROGERS, W.W. *Antebellum Thomas Co.: 1825-1861.* 1963. Tallahassee. 136 p. dj. VG. $30.00

ROGERS, William. *Pumps & Hydraulics. Part 2.* 1905. Audel. 8vo. 424 p. EX. $37.50

ROGERS & HAMMERSTEIN. *Pipe Dream: Musical Play Based on Sweet Thursday.* 1956. NY. 1st ed. dj. EX. $50.00

ROGERS & HAMMERSTEIN. *Rogers' & Hammerstein's Fact Book.* 1955. NY. 1st ed. EX. $25.00

ROGERS. *Wise Men Fish Here.* 1965. NY. 1st ed. dj. EX. $20.00

ROH, Franz. *German Painting in the 20th Century.* 1968. Greenwich. Ils. 259 p. D2. $20.00

ROHAN, M.S. *Anvil of Ice.* 1986. Morrow. 1st Am UCP. wraps. M. $15.00

ROHDE, Eleanor. *Old English Herbals.* 1922. Longman. 1st ed. G. J2. $55.00

ROHMER, Sax. *Gray Face.* 1924. Doubleday. 1st ed. VG. $10.00

ROLFE, Frederick. *Desire & Pursuit of the Whole.* 1934. London. Cassell. 1st ed. dj. EX. $90.00

ROLFE, Frederick. *Letters to James Walsh.* 1972. London. Bertram Rota. 1/500. dj. EX. $35.00

ROLFE, R.T. & F.W. *Romance of the Fungus World.* 1974. Dover. reprint of 1925 ed. EX. M2. $5.00

ROLFE, W.J. *Shakespeare's Comedy of Merchant of Venice.* 1899. Ils. 173 p. TB. VG. $10.00

ROLLIN, Charles. *Ancient History of Egyptians, Carthaginians...* 1847. Cincinnati. 2 vols. full leather. VG. $60.00

ROLLIN, Charles. *Ancient History.* 1834. NY. 1st Am ed. maps. 2 vols. EX. K1. $28.50

ROLLINS, A.W. *Three Tetons: Story of Yellowstone.* 1887. Cassell. presentation. 219 p. wraps. A3. $55.00

ROLLINS, P.A. *Cowboy: His Characteristics, Equipment, & Part Developing W.* 1922. NY. Ils 1st ed. VG. $55.00

ROLLINS, P.A. *Cowboy: His Characteristics, Equipment, & Part Developing W.* 1924. NY. G. $12.50

ROLPH, C.H. *Books in the Dock.* 1969. London. 1st ed. dj. EX. $25.00

ROLT, L.T.C. *Thames From Mouth to Source.* 1951. London. dj. J2. $20.00

ROLT-WHEELER, Francis. *Wonder of War in the Air.* 1917. NY. Ils 1st ed. 347 p. G. T5. $17.50

ROLVAAG, O.E. *Giants in the Earth.* 1927. NY. 1st ed. dj. EX. $45.00

ROLVAAG, O.E. *Their Father's God.* 1931. NY. 1st ed. dj. EX. $22.50

ROMANCES, Ethel. *Story of Port Royal.* 1907. London. pls. VG. $8.50

ROME, C. *Owl Who Came To Stay.* 1980. Crown. Ils. 144 p. EX. M2. $11.00

ROMMEL, Erwin. *Rommel Papers.* 1953. London. Ils 1st ed. 545 p. dj. VG. T5. $65.00

RONIS & MAC ORLON. *Belleville & Menilmontant.* c 1954. Ils. photos. dj. stiff wraps. VG. $18.00

ROOD, R. *Elephant Bones & Lonely Hearts.* 1977. Greene. 163 p. dj. EX. M2. $5.00

ROOKE, L. *Last One Home Sleeps in the Yellow Bed.* 1968. Baton Rouge. 1st ed. inscr. dj. EX. $40.00

ROONEY & HUTTON. *Story of Stars & Stripes.* 1946. NY. dj. G. $12.00

ROOP, P. & C. *Seasons of the Cranes.* 1989. Walker. Ils 1st ed. 28 p. dj. M. M2. $8.00

ROOSEVELT, Eleanor. *Christmas: A Story.* 1940. NY. Ils Kredel. 1st ed. 24mo. 42 p. T5. $17.50

ROOSEVELT, F.D. *Whither Bound?* 1926. Boston. 1st ed. dj. $45.00

ROOSEVELT, Theodore. *African Game Trails.* salesman's sample. G. B1. $30.00

ROOSEVELT, Theodore. *African Game Trails.* 1910. NY. Ils 1st ed. 529 p.$40.00

ROOSEVELT, Theodore. *African Game Trails.* 1924. Scribner. photos. 2 vols. M2. $25.00

ROOSEVELT, Theodore. *American Bears: Selections From Writings of T. Roosevelt.* 1983. CO U. photos. 193 p. dj. EX. M2. $10.00

ROOSEVELT, Theodore. *Autobiography.* 1913. NY. Ltd 1st ed. dj. boxed. M. $95.00

ROOSEVELT, Theodore. *Hunting Trips of a Ranchman.* 1886. Putnam. G. B2. $75.00

ROOSEVELT, Theodore. *Life Story of Theodore Roosevelt.* 1919. Rudge. VG. $12.50

ROOSEVELT, Theodore. *Through Brazilian Wilderness.* 1914. NY. 1st ed. VG. $50.00

ROOSEVELT, Theodore. *Through Brazilian Wilderness.* 1925. Scribner. EX. $17.50

ROOSEVELT, Theodore. *Winning of the W.* Presidential ed. 4 vols. K1. $23.50

ROOSEVELT, Theodore. *Winning of the W.* 1889. NY. 1st ed. 2 vols. EX. K1. $27.50

ROOSEVELT, Theodore. *Works of Theodore Roosevelt.* 1909. Scribner. 6 vols. gilt green bdg. VG. $60.00

ROOSEVELT & ROOSEVELT. *Trailing the Great Panda.* 1929. NY. Ils 1st ed. 278 p. dj. VG. T5. $19.50

ROOT, A.I. & E.R. *ABC & XYZ of Bee Culture.* 1929. Root. Ils. 815 p. VG. M2. $10.00

ROOT, C.P. *Automobile Troubles & How To Remedy Them.* 1909. Chicago. lG. $20.00

ROOT, G.F. *Story of Musical Life: Autobiography.* 1891. Cincinnati. 1st ed. 256 p. TEG. VG. T5. $35.00

ROOT, H.K. *People's Medical Lighthouse, Consumption, Marriage Guide.* 1856. NY. Ils. disbound. poor. $18.00

ROOT, L.C. *Quinby's New Beekeeping: Complete Guide...* 1879. Orange Judd. G. $20.00

ROPER, Stephen. *Handbook of Land & Marine Engines.* 1897. 9th ed. 598 p. AEG. $30.00

ROSA, J.G. *Devil To Pay in the Backlands.* 1953. NY. 1st Am ed. dj. VG. B2. $37.50

ROSA, J.G. *Gunfighter: Man or Myth?* 1969. Norman. sgn. dj. EX. $35.00

ROSA, J.G. *Gunfighter: Man or Myth?* 1969. OK U. Ils 1st ed. 229 p. dj. EX. M2. $15.00

ROSAMOND, Royal. *Bad Medicine.* 1948. OK City. 1st ed. sgn. dj. EX. $35.00

ROSCOE, Theodore. *US Destroyer Operations in WWII.* 1953. Annapolis. Ils. maps. dj. G. T5. $22.50

ROSCOE, Thomas. *Tourist in Spain.* 1836. London. leather. $65.00

ROSCOE & HARDEN. *New View of Origin of Dalton's Atomic Theory.* 1896. 1st ed. $90.00

ROSE, Andrea. *Pre-Raphaelites.* 1981. 48 pls. stiff wraps. M. C1. $14.00

ROSE, Barbara. *Alexander Liberman.* 1981. NY. 1st ed. dj. EX. $45.00

ROSE, H.J. *New General Biographical Dictionary.* 1853. London. 12 vols. VG. $320.00

ROSE, Lois. *Shattered Ring.* 1970. John Knox. VG. P1. $7.50

ROSE, R.R. *Advocates & Adversaries: Early Life & Times of R.R. Rose.* 1977. Donnelley. Ils. map. 322 p. EX. M2. $20.00

ROSE, W.G. *Cleveland: Making of a City.* 1950. Cleveland. Ils 1st ed. sgn. dj. VG. B2. $47.50

ROSE, W.L. *Rehearsal for Reconstruction.* 1964. Ils 1st ed. 442 p. EX. scarce. J4. $25.00

ROSE, W.R. *Stories.* 1927. Cleveland. 1st ed. 252 p. T5. $19.50

ROSEN, Richard. *Fadeaway.* 1986. NY. 1st ed. dj. EX. $12.50

ROSEN, S.R. *Judge Judges Mushrooms.* 1982. Highlander. Ils. 92 p. EX. M2. $3.00

ROSENBACH, A.S.W. *Book Hunter's Holiday.* 1936. Boston. Ils. 259 p. dj. B2. $25.00

ROSENBACH, A.S.W. *Book Hunter's Holiday.* 1936. Boston. 1/760. Ils. sgn. glassine dj. boxed. EX. $110.00

ROSENBACH, A.S.W. *Books & Bidders.* 1927. Boston. 1st ed. sgn. TEG. dj. EX. $65.00

ROSENBACH, A.S.W. *Books & Bidders.* 1927. Boston. 1st trade ed. VG. $45.00

ROSENBACH, A.S.W. *Early American Children's Books.* 1928. Phil. 16mo. wraps. VG. B1. $25.00

ROSENBACH, A.S.W. *Early American Children's Books.* 1971. Dover. Ils 1st ed. 354 p. G. $15.00

ROSENBACH, A.S.W. *Unpublishable Memoirs.* 1917. NY. 1st ed. $40.00

ROSENBAUM, Jeanette. *Myer Myers Goldsmith, 1723-1795.* 1954. Phil. sm 4to. cloth. $25.00

ROSENBERG, Adolf. *P.P. Rubens: Des Meisters Gemalde.* 1906. Stuttgart. 2nd ed. 519 p. TEG. gilt cloth. D2. $75.00

ROSENBERG, J. *Rembrandt.* 1948. Harvard. 1st ed. 2 vols. VG. J2. $45.00

ROSENBERG, J.N. *Self-Portrait.* 1958. NY. Ils. dj. VG. $50.00

ROSENBERG, M.M. *IA on the Eve of the Civil War: Decade of Frontier Politics.* 1972. OK U. 1st ed. map. 262 p. dj. EX. M2. $25.00

ROSENBERG, Pierre. *Chardin: 1699-1779.* 1979. Grand Palais. French text. 428 p. D2. $85.00

ROSENFELD, M.J. *Nuestes Augsburgishes Kochbuch.* 1838. Nordlingen. G. $200.00

ROSENFELD, Morris. *Lieder des Ghetto.* nd. Berlin. 3rd ed. EX. $200.00

ROSENGARREN, Theodore. *Tombee, Portrait of a Cotton Planter...* 1986. 1st ed. 750 p. dj. M. J4. $18.50

ROSENZWEIG, Franz. *Das Aelteste Systemprogramm des Deutschen Idealismus...* 1917. Heidelberg. wraps. $125.00

ROSKILL, S.W. *White Ensign: British Navy at War, 1939-1945.* 1960. Annapolis. Ils 1st ed. 480 p. dj. VG. T5. $15.00

ROSMANITH, Olga. *Unholy Flame.* 1952. Gold Medal. EX. P1. $15.00

ROSNY, J.H. *Printemps Parfume.* 1892. Paris. Ils Mittis. TEG. EX. $45.00

ROSS, Alexander. *Adventures of First Settlers on OR or Columbia River.* 1923. Chicago. Lakeside Classic. 388 p. G. T5. $42.50

ROSS, Alexander. *Adventures of First Settlers on OR or Columbia Rivers.* 1923. Donnelley. Lakeside Classic. A3. $60.00

ROSS, C.P. *E Front of the Bitterroot Range, MT.* 1950. US Geol Survey. Ils. fld map. M2. $6.00

ROSS, Charles. *Richard III.* 1981. CA U. Ils 1st ed. M. C1. $22.00

ROSS, Charles. *Richard III.* 1981. CA U. 1st ed. EX. C1. $19.50

ROSS, Frederick. *Ruined Abbeys of Britain.* 1882. London. MacKenzie. AEG. J2. $150.00

ROSS, Isabel. *Rebel Rose: Rose O'Neal Greenhow, Confederate Spy.* 1954. Harper. Ils 1st ed. 294 p. dj. EX. $16.00

ROSS, Isabel. *Rebel Rose: Rose O'Neal Greenhow, Confederate Spy.* 1954. NY. Harper. later print. dj. VG. $12.00

ROSS & EMERSON. *Wonders of Barnacles.* 1974. Dodd Mead. 78 p. dj. EX. M2. $5.00

ROSS & KENNEDY. *Bibliography of Negro Migration.* 1934. NY. 1st ed. dj. VG. $35.00

ROSSEN. *Columbian World's Fair Collectibles.* 1976. 1st ed. 148 p. K1. $14.50

ROSSETTI, D.G. *House of Life.* 1898. London. Zaehnsdorf bdg. G. $50.00

ROSSETTI, D.G. *House of Life.* 1904. Edinburgh. VG. $40.00

ROSSITER. *Mineral Resources of States & Territories W Rocky Mountains.* 1869. 1st ed. VG. $30.00

ROSSKAM, E. & L. *Towboat River.* 1948. NY. 1st ed. dj. VG. B2. $37.50

ROSTAN. *Cyrano de Bergerac.* 1931. Three Sirens. Ils Carbe. 184 p. VG. $12.00

ROSTOCK. *Germany: Portfolio of Photographs.* 1967. Berlin. loose as issued. $37.50

ROTCH. *Conquest of the Air.* 1910. NY. VG. C4. $37.00

ROTENSTREICH, Nathan. *Jews & German Philosophy.* 1984. NY. 1st ed. dj. VG. $10.00

ROTERS, Eberhard. *Realism & Expressionism in Berlin Art.* 1981. UCLA. Ils. D2. $17.50

ROTH, Philip. *Breast.* 1972. NY. 1st ed. dj. VG. $15.00

ROTH, Philip. *Breast.* 1973. London. 1st ed. dj. EX. $12.00

ROTH, Philip. *Farvel, Columbus.* 1965. Copenhagen. Trans/sgn Wright. 1st ed. wraps. $45.00

ROTH, Philip. *Good-Bye, Columbus.* 1959. Boston. 1st Am ed. dj. VG. $75.00

ROTH, Philip. *Good-Bye Columbus & Five Short Stories.* 1966. Modern Lib. 1st ed. dj. VG. $25.00

ROTH, Philip. *Good-Bye Columbus & Other Stories.* 1959. Boston. UCP. spiral bdg. salmon wraps. rare. T5. $550.00

ROTH, Philip. *Great American Novel.* 1973. NY. Holt. 1st ed. dj. VG. $30.00

ROTH, Philip. *Letting Go.* 1962. Random House. 1st ed. dj. VG. $55.00

ROTH, Philip. *My Life As a Man.* 1974. Holt Rinehart. 1st ed. dj. VG. $15.00

ROTH, Philip. *Our Gang.* 1971. NY. 1st ed. dj. VG. $12.00

ROTH, Philip. *Portnoy's Complaint.* 1969. London. 1st ed. dj. EX. $20.00

ROTH, Philip. *Portnoy's Complaint.* 1969. NY. 1st ed. dj. VG. $20.00

ROTH, Philip. *Professor of Desire.* 1977. NY. 1st ed. dj. VG. $10.00

ROTH, Philip. *When She Was Good.* 1967. Random House. 1st ed. dj. EX. $35.00

ROTH, S. *Europe: Book for America.* 1919. NY. 1st ed. VG. $35.00

ROTHCHILD, Sylvia. *Voices From the Holocaust.* 1981. NY. VG. $7.50

ROTHENBERG. *Creative Stained Glass. Techniques for Unfired Projects.* 1973. Crown. photos. tall folio. xl. EX. $20.00

ROTHENSTEIN, J. *16 Letters From Oscar Wilde.* 1930. London. 1/550. slipcase. EX. G1. $35.00

ROTHSCHILD, Alonzo. *Lincoln: Master of Men.* 1906. Boston. Houghton Mifflin. 1st ed. VG. $8.00

ROTHWELL, R.P. *Mineral Industry: Its Statistics, Technology & Trade...* 1892. Scientific Pub. Ils. 628 p. VG. A3. $120.00

ROTTENSTEINER, Franz. *SF Book.* 1975. Seabury. dj. EX. P1. $15.00

ROTTENSTEINER, Franz. *View From Another Shore.* 1973. Seabury. VG. P1. $7.50

ROUAULT, Georges. *Divertissement.* 1943. 1/1240. 12 color pls. VG. $200.00

ROULE, L. *Fishes: Their Journeys & Migrations.* 1933. Norton. Ils 1st Am ed. 270 p. EX. M2. $12.00

ROUMANIA, Queen Marie of. *Story of My Life.* 1935. Scribner. 1st ed. EX. $30.00

ROUNDS, Glen. *Swamp Life: An Almanac.* 1957. Prentice Hall. presentation. inscr. dj. VG. $35.00

ROURKE, C. *Audubon.* 1936. Harcourt Brace. 12 pls. 342 p. VG. M2. $10.00

ROWAN, M.K. *Doves, Parrots, Louries & Cuckoos of S Africa.* 1983. S Africa. Phillip. Ils. 429 p. dj. EX. M2. $48.00

ROWAN, Roy. *Four Days of Mayaguez.* 1975. NY. Ils 1st ed. 224 p. dj. T5. $12.50

ROWAN, Thomas. *Stormy Road.* 1934. NY. AP. 1st ed. 395 p. brown wraps. EX. T1. $75.00

ROWE, A.D. *Everyday Life in India.* 1881. Am Tract Soc. Ils. G. $18.50

ROWE, C.W. *Lawyers' Proof of the Hereafter.* 1938. Phil. $14.00

ROWE, J.P. Jr. *Letters From a WWI Aviator.* 1987. Boston. photos. 151 p. dj. M. T5. $15.95

ROWE, W.H. *Maritime History of ME.* 1948. Norton. 1st ed. dj. J2. $20.00

ROWE, W.H. *Shipbuilding Days.* 1924. Portland. Marks Print House. 1st ed. VG. $50.00

ROWELL, J.W. *Yankee Artilleryman: Through Civil War...* 1975. TN U. Ils 1st ed. 320 p. EX. M2. $20.00

ROWELL, Margit. *Miro.* 1970. NY. Abrams. Ils. dj. D2. $115.00

ROWES, Barbara. *Grace Slick: Biography.* 1980. Doubleday. 1st ed. dj. VG. T6. $15.00

ROWLAND, Mrs. Dunbar. *Andrew Jackson's Campaign Against the British...* 1948. NY. Ils 1st ed. 295 p. dj. VG. B2. $50.00

ROWLANDS, John. *Rubens: Drawings & Sketches.* 1977. 12 color pls. 176 p. dj. D2. $40.00

ROWLANDS, Walter. *Recent English Art: Selections...* 1889. Boston. Estes Lauriat. gilt cloth. D2. $65.00

ROWLANDS & KANE. *Cache Lake Country.* 1947. NY. 1st ed. dj. VG. B2. $17.50

ROWLANDSON, Thomas. *Tour of Dr. Syntax in Search of the Picturesque.* 1819. Ackermann. 9th ed. 30 pls. 8vo. slipcase. EX. $95.00

ROWLANDSON, Thomas. *Vicar of Wakefield.* 1903. London. Methuen. Ils. red cloth. VG. $35.00

ROWLANDSON, Thomas. *Watercolor Drawings of Thomas Rowlandson.* 1947. NY. 1st ed. dj. EX. $35.00

ROWLANDSON & PUGIN. *Microcosm of London.* 1943. King Penguin #9. 1st ed. $15.00

ROY, Jennet. *History of Canada for Use of Schools & Families.* 1847. Montreal. 1st ed. G. J2. $75.00

ROYCROFT. *Book of the Roycrofters.* nd. (1901) photos. green suede. VG. D1. $30.00

ROYCROFT. *Roycroft Catalog.* 1909. Roycroft. 8vo. wraps. G. D1. $40.00

ROYCROFT. *Roycroft Shop: A History.* 1909. Roycroft. 8vo. beige wraps. VG. D1. $45.00

ROYDEN, A.M. *Life's Little Pitfalls.* 1925. Putnam. 1st ed. $12.00

ROZE, L.A. *Josette et Jehan de Reims.* c 1930 Paris. Ils Damart. $25.00

RUARK, Robert. *Honey Badger.* 1965. McGraw Hill. 1st ed. dj. $45.00

RUARK, Robert. *Horn of the Hunter.* 1953. Doubleday. 1st ed. dj. EX. $50.00

RUARK, Robert. *Old Man & the Boy.* 1957. NY. 1st ed. dj. VG. B2. $60.00

RUARK, Robert. *Old Man & the Boy.* 1957. NY. 1st ed. dj. xl. VG. $30.00

RUARK, Robert. *Old Man & the Boy.* 1958. NY. 2nd ed. dj. EX. $37.50

RUARK, Robert. *Old Man's Boy Grows Older.* 1961. NY. 1st ed. dj. VG. B2. $60.00

RUARK, Robert. *Old Man's Boy Grows Up.* 1961. NY. 1st ed. dj. EX. $40.00

RUARK, Robert. *One for the Road.* 1949. NY. 1st ed. dj. VG. B2. $25.00

RUARK, Robert. *Poor No More.* 1959. NY. 1st ed. dj. M. $40.00

RUARK, Robert. *Something of Value.* 1955. NY. 1st ed. dj. VG. B2. $22.50

RUARK, Robert. *Uhuru.* 1962. NY. UCP. wraps. EX. scarce. $85.00

RUARK, Robert. *Use Enough Gun.* 1966. NY. 1st ed. dj. EX. $40.00

RUARK, Robert. *Women.* 1967. NY. New Am Lib. 1st ed. 233 p. dj. $47.50

RUBENS, Alfred. *History of Jewish Costume.* 1973. London. dj. EX. $125.00

RUBIN, William S. *Frank Stella.* 1970. MOMA. Ils. 176 p. xl. D2. $25.00

RUBIN, William S. *Pablo Picasso: Retrospective.* 1980. NY. 1st ed. dj. M. $70.00

RUBIN & KILPATRICK. *Lasting S: 14 Southerners Look at Their Home.* 1957. Chicago. Regnery. 1st ed. dj. VG. $12.00

RUBINSTEIN, Arthur. *My Many Years.* 1980. NY. Ils 1st ed. 626 p. dj. VG. B2. $22.50

RUBINSTEIN, C.S. *American Women Artists.* 1982. Boston. Hall. 4to. 560 p. EX. $15.00

RUBY & BROWN. *Half Sun on the Columbia: Biography of Chief Moses.* 1966. OK U. Ils. 377 p. dj. EX. M2. $18.00

RUCKERL, Adalbert. *Investigation of Nazi Crimes 1945-1978.* 1980. CT. 1st ed. dj. VG. $9.50

RUDHYAR, Dane. *Modern Man's Conflicts.* 1948. NY. $50.00

RUDHYAR, Dane. *Pulse of Life.* 1943. Phil. $45.00

RUDOLPH, Joseph. *Early Life & Civil War Reminiscences.* 1941. Hiram, OH. 36 p. wraps. VG. T5. $25.00

RUE, L.L. *Furbearing Animals of N America.* 1981. Crown. Ils 1st ed. 343 p. dj. EX. M2. $17.00

RUE, L.L. *Game Birds of N America.* 1976. Outdoor Life. Ils. 490 p. dj. EX. M2. $9.00

RUE, L.L. *Sportsman's Guide to Game Animals.* 1971. Outdoor Life. photos. 655 p. G. M2. $5.00

RUE, L.L. *World of White-Tailed Deer.* 1962. Lippincott. Ils. 134 p. dj. EX. M2. $10.00

RUFFIN, Edmund. *Diary of...Edited With Introduction by Wm. K. Scarborough.* 1972 & 1976. Baton Rouge. 2 vols. $85.00

RUGGLES, C.L. *Great American Scout & Spy, General Bunker.* 1870. 400 p. very scarce. J4. $40.00

RUGGLES, R.G. *One Rose: Biography of Rose O'Neill.* 1964. Oakland. 1st ed. sgn. VG. B2. $95.00

RUHMER, Eberhard. *Tura: Paintings & Drawings, Complete Edition.* 1958. London. Ils. 184 p. dj. D2. $85.00

RUIZ, Juan. *Book of Good Love.* 1970. NY. dj. VG. $25.00

RUMPEL, H. *Wood Engraving.* 1974. NY. Ils. pls. dj. EX. $22.00

RUNYAN. *Bloodhounds of Broadway & Other Stories.* 1981. NY. 1st ed. dj. VG. $18.00

RUPORT, A. *Art of Cockfighting: Handbook for Beginning & Old Timers.* 1949. NY. dj. EX. $50.00

RUPP, I.D. *History of Lancaster Co.* 1984. Spartanburg. reprint of 1844 ed. 566 p. VG. T5. $25.00

RUSAKOVA, Alla. *Borisov-Musatov.* 1975. Leningrad. Aurora. Revised 2nd ed. 222 p. D2. $35.00

RUSH, Allison. *Last of Danu's Children.* 1984. pb. VG. C1. $3.50

RUSH, P.S. *Merchandise of American Indian.* c 1920. np. reprint. wraps. VG. A3. $60.00

RUSH, W.M. *Red Fox of the Kinapoo.* 1950. Ils Wilson. 279 p. $12.00

RUSHA, Edward. *Few Palm Trees.* 1971. Hollywood. 1/3900. presentation. D2. $75.00

RUSHDIE, Salman. *Midnight's Children.* 1981. London. 1st ed. dj. EX. $250.00

RUSHDIE, Salman. *Satanic Verses.* 1st Am ed. 6th print. M. $60.00

RUSHDIE, Salman. *Satanic Verses.* 1989. NY. AP of 1st Am ed. wraps. EX. $200.00

RUSHDIE, Salman. *Shame.* 1983. NY. AP of 1st Am ed. wraps. EX. $75.00

RUSHMORE, G.M. *World With a Fence Around It: Tuxedo Park.* 1957. Pageant. dj. EX. $35.00

RUSKIN, John. *Aratra Pentelici.* 1870. Oxford. 1st Am ed. 21 pls. 181 p. xl. fair. $45.00

RUSKIN, John. *Elements for Drawing.* 1858. NY. 1st Am ed. EX. $75.00

RUSKIN, John. *Friendship's Offering of Sentiment & Mirth.* 1844. London. Ils. G. $50.00

RUSKIN, John. *King of Golden River.* 1900. Roycroft. 8vo. green suede. G. D1. $40.00

RUSKIN, John. *Modern Painters.* 1843. London. 1st ed. VG. $450.00

RUSKIN, John. *Modern Painters.* 1892. London. 5 vols. $175.00

RUSKIN, John. *Queen of the Air.* 1904. London. Art Nouveau bdg. $30.00

RUSKIN, John. *Stones of Venice.* c 1907. NY/London. Dent Dutton. 3 vols. VG. $55.00

RUSKIN, John. *Stones of Venice.* nd. Boston. Ils. 3 vols. EX. $45.00

RUSKIN, John. *Stones of Venice.* 1886. London. 4th ed. 3 vols. $135.00

RUSSELL, Bertrand. *German Social Democracy: Six Lectures by Bertram Russell.* 1896. Longman Green. 1st ed. J2. $600.00

RUSSELL, C.E. *A-Rafting on the MS.* 1928. NY. 1st ed. VG. $25.00

RUSSELL, C.E. *Julia Marlowe: Her Life & Art.* 1926. Appleton. 1st ed. VG. $12.00

RUSSELL, C.M. *Good Medicine.* 1930. Garden City. VG. $50.00

RUSSELL, C.P. *Firearms, Traps & Tools of Mountain Men: A Guide...* 1967. NY. Knopf. Ils. maps. dj. EX. $33.00

RUSSELL, C.T. *Pastor Russell's Sermons.* 1917. Brooklyn. Ils 1st ed. 803 p. VG. B2. $60.00

RUSSELL, Charlie. *Paper Talk: Charlie Russell's American W.* 1979. NY. dj. EX. $45.00

RUSSELL, Don. *Check List of Pictures Relating to Little Big Horn...* 1969. Ft. Worth. 88 p. wraps. VG. A3. $35.00

RUSSELL, E.F. *Three To Conquer.* 1957. Dobson. 1st Eng ed. dj. EX. scarce. $65.00

RUSSELL, Frank. *Okefenokee Swamp.* 1973. Time Life. Ils. map. 184 p. EX. M2. $9.00

RUSSELL, Frank. *Queen of Song: Life of Henrietta Sontag.* 1964. Exposition Pr. 1st ed. dj. VG. $24.00

RUSSELL, Franklin. *Season on the Plain.* 1974. NY. 1st ed. dj. EX. $8.50

RUSSELL, George. *Midsummer Eve.* 1928. NY. 1st ed. 1/450. sgn. VG. $75.00

RUSSELL, Irwin. *Christmas Night in the Quarters.* 1917. NY. Ils Kemble. 1st ed. VG. B1. $50.00

RUSSELL, Irwin. *Poems.* 1888. NY. Century. Intro Harris. 12mo. 109 p. VG. $12.00

RUSSELL, J. & R. *On the Loose.* 1967. Sierra Club. 118 photos. 121 p. EX. M2. $9.00

RUSSELL, Jim. *Bob Fudge: TX Trail Driver, Mountain WY Cowboy, 1862-1933.* 1962. Denver. dj. EX. $45.00

RUSSELL, John. *Tour in Germany & Austria in 1820-1822.* 1825. Boston. 469 p. $80.00

RUSSELL, L. *Love.* 1966. VA. $70.00

RUSSELL, Osborne. *Journal of a Trapper: 9 Years in Rockies, 1834-1843.* 1921. Boise. 2nd ed. 149 p. xl. $100.00

RUSSELL, Osborne. *Journal of a Trapper: 9 Years in Rockies, 1834-1843.* 1984. NE U. Ils. 191 p. EX. $25.00

RUSSELL, Phillips. *Woman Who Rang the Bell.* 1949. Chapel Hill. 1st ed. 293 p. dj. VG. $15.00

RUSSELL, R. *Bird Lives: High Life & Hard Times of Charlie Y. Parker.* 1973. NY. 1st ed. dj. xl. VG. B2. $30.00

RUSSELL, R.H. *Eden Versus Whistler: Paronet & Butterfly.* 1899. Ltd ed. 1/250. G. $150.00

RUSSELL, V.Y. *Indian Artifacts.* 1974. private print. Ils. 170 p. dj. EX. M2. $23.00

RUSSELL, W.L. *Invisible Forces.* 1959. TX. $18.50

RUSSELL, Walter. *Message of the Divine Iliad.* 1948. NY. $50.00

RUSSELL, Walter. *One-World Purpose.* 1960. VA. $50.00

RUSSELL, William Howard. *My Diary N & S.* 1863. Boston. 602 p. fair. T5. $35.00

RUSSELL & RUSSELL. *World Crisis.* 1958. Swannanoa. $25.00

RUSSO & SULLIVAN. *Bibliography of Booth Tarkington.* 1949. Indianapolis. VG. $30.00

RUSSO & SULLIVAN. *Seven Authors of Crawfordsville, IN.* 1952. Indianapolis. xl. VG. $25.00

RUTHERFORD, Edward. *Sarum: Novel of England.* 1987. 1st Am ed. dj. M. C1. $16.00

RUTLEDGE, Archibald. *From the Hill to the Sea...* 1958. Bobbs Merrill. 1st ed. sm 4to. 201 p. dj. $65.00

RUTLEDGE, Archibald. *Heart of the S.* 1924. State Co. 1st ed. sgn. 391 p. $87.50

RUTLEDGE, Archibald. *Heart's Citadel & Other Poems.* 1953. Dietz Pr. 1st ed. sgn. dj. $25.00

RUTLEDGE, Archibald. *It Will Be Daylight Soon.* 1938. NY. Revell. 4th print. 129 p. $10.00

RUTLEDGE, Archibald. *Peace in the Heart.* 1942. Doubleday. sgn. 316 p. M. $35.00

RUTLEDGE, Archibald. *Plantation Boyhood.* 1932. The Atlantic. 2 parts in printed wraps. $17.50

RUTLEDGE, Archibald. *World Around Hampton.* 1960. Indianapolis. Ils 1st ed. dj. VG. B2. $30.00

RYAN, Alan. *Quadripophia.* 1986. Doubleday. 1st ed. dj. RS. EX. $17.50

RYAN, Cornelius. *Last Battle.* 1966. NY. dj. G. $15.00

RYAN, D.J. *Civil War Literature of OH.* 1911. Cleveland. 517 p. G. M2. $75.00

RYAN, G.L. *Dances of Our Pioneers.* 1939. NY. Ils. 8vo. pictorial cloth. VG. T1. $25.00

RYAN, M.E. *Druid Path.* 1917. 1st Am ed. VG. C1. $10.00

RYAN, M.E. *Flute of the Gods.* 1909. Grosset Dunlap. VG. $15.00

RYAN, M.E. *Flute of the Gods.* 1909. NY. Stokes. Ils Curtis. EX. $35.00

RYAN, M.E. *Squaw Elouise.* 1892. Rand McNally. G. $24.00

RYDEN, H. *America's Last Wild Horses.* 1970. Dutton. Review of 1st ed. 311 p. dj. M2. $10.00

RYDER, J. *Trevayne.* 1973. NY. 1st ed. dj. EX. $50.00

RYE, R.A. *Libraries of London: Guide for Students.* 1910. London. 2nd ed. pls. $40.00

RYLAND, C.S. *1956 Brand Book of Denver W.* 1957. Denver. 1/500. 383 p. G. T5. $45.00

RYUS, W.H. *Second William Penn: True Account of Incidents...* 1913. KS City. Ils 1st ed. wraps. EX. $35.00

SAARINEN, A.B. *Proud Possessors.* 1958. NY. 1st ed. 2nd print. VG. $25.00

SABERHAGEN, F. *Dominion.* 1982. 1st ed. pb. VG. C1. $4.00

SABIN, E.L. *Kit Carson Days: 1809-1868.* 1935. Pioneer Pr. 1/1000. 2 vols. xl. scarce. A3. $90.00

SABIN, Joseph. *Dictionary of Books Relating to America. Vols. I-XXIX.* Readex Microprint. boxed. J2. $85.00

SABINE, Lorenzo. *Biographical Sketches of Loyalists of American Revolution.* 1864. Boston. $125.00

SACHS, Wulf. *Black Anger.* 1947. Boston. 1st ed. green cloth. VG. $27.00

SACKEN, R.O. *W Diptera.* 1877. WA. 164 p. disbound. A3. $30.00

SACKVILLE-WEST & NICHOLSON. *Another World Than This.* 1945. London. 247 p. dj. EX. $20.00

SAFARI CLUB. *Safari Club International Record Book of Trophy Animals.* 1980. EX. $120.00

SAFDIE, Moshe. *For Everyone a Garden.* 1974. London. Ils. 4to. 331 p. dj. VG. $22.00

SAFFORD, Ruth. *Cornelius of Beaufort.* 1969. Columbia. Bryan. 1st ed. dj. $27.50

SAGAN, Carl. *Contact.* 1985. NY. 1st ed. dj. EX. $15.00

SAGAN, Carl. *Cosmos.* 1980. NY. 1st ed. dj. EX. $20.00

SAGGS, H. *Greatness That Was Babylon.* 1962. NY. 1st ed. 562 p. dj. VG. B2. $25.00

SAINT-GAUDENS, Homer. *American Artist & His Times.* 1941. NY. Ils 1st ed. 332 p. dj. VG. T5. $45.00

SAKHAROV, Andrei. *Progress, Coexistence & Intellectual Freedom.* 1968. NY Times. 1st ed. dj. VG. J2. $20.00

SAKLATVALA, Beram. *Arthur: Roman Britain's Last Champion.* 1971. 3rd imp. dj. M. C1. $49.50

SAKURAI, Tadayoshi. *Human Bullets: Soldier's Story of Port Arthur.* 1907. Boston. 1st Am ed. 269 p. xl. G. T5. $22.50

SALAMAN, M.C. *London: Past & Present.* 1916. London. Studio. Ils. maps. 4to. $60.00

SALAMON, Ferdinando. *History of Prints & Printmaking From Durer to Picasso.* 1972. McGraw Hill. Ils. 303 p. D2. $40.00

SALE, R.T. *Blackstone Rangers.* 1972. NY. 1st ed. dj. EX. $25.00

SALESKI, Gdal. *Famous Musicians of Jewish Origin.* 1949. NY. Ils Saul Raskin. sgn. $100.00

SALINGER, J.D. *Catcher in the Rye.* 1951. Boston. 1st ed. dj. VG. $150.00

SALINGER, J.D. *Catcher in the Rye.* 1953. Signet. 1st ed. wraps. $95.00

SALINGER, J.D. *Franny & Zooey.* 1961. Little Brown. 1st ed. dj. EX. $30.00

SALINGER, J.D. *Franny & Zooey.* 1962. London. 1st ed. dj. $40.00

SALINGER, J.D. *Raise High the Roof Beam.* London. 1st ed. dj. $45.00

SALINGER, J.D. *Raise High the Roof Beam.* 1959. Boston. 1st ed. 3rd state. dj. $45.00

SALINGER, Margaretta. *Flowers: Flower Piece in European Painting.* 1949. Harper. VG. $25.00

SALLEY, A.S. *Lords & Proprietors of Carolina.* 1944. np. SC General Assembly. sgn. wraps. $27.50

SALLEY, J.S. *Seminole's Swan Song.* 1936. Boston. Ils. 90 p. $12.50

SALMI, M. *Complete Works of Michaelangelo.* 1965. NY. Reynal. Ils. folio. 600 p. dj. EX. J2. $125.00

SALMON, D.E. *Special Report on History & Present Condition of Sheep...* 1892. WA. USDA. Ils. 1000 p. VG. A3. $60.00

SALMON, Lucy. *Newspaper & Authority.* 1923. Oxford. 1st ed. J2. $22.50

SALMONSON, Jessica. *Heroic Visions.* 1983. 1st ed. pb. M. C1. $4.00

SALOMON, J. *Vuillard: Douze Pastels Presentes et Commentes.* 1966. 1/350. portfolio. VG. $175.00

SALT, H.B. *Animals Rights.* 1894. NY. 1st ed. 12mo. 176 p. $15.00

SALTER, Stefan. *Joys of Hunting Antiques.* 1971. NY. Ils. 4to. dj. EX. $35.00

SALTUS, Edgar. *Monster.* 1912. Pulitzer Pub. 1st ed. $12.00

SALTUS, Edgar. *Poppies & Mandragora.* 1926. NY. Murtrie. 1/500. 8 vols. black cloth. VG. $65.00

SALTUS, Edgar. *Purple & Fine Women.* 1925. Chicago. Covici. VG. $15.00

SALVADORI, M. *Italian People.* 1972. NY. 1st ed. photos. 396 p. dj. VG. B2. $27.50

SAMPSON, C. *Physiotherapy Technic.* 1923. St. Louis. Ils. 443 p. $35.00

SAMPSON, E.S. *Mammy's White Folks.* 1902. Grosset Dunlap. 4th print. 336 p. $15.00

SAMPSON, Faye. *White Nun's Telling.* 1st ed. pb. M. C1. $8.00

SAMPSON, H.E. *Progressive Redemption.* 1909. London. $85.00

SAMSON, J. *Modern Falconry.* 1984. Stackpole. Ils. 160 p. EX. M2. $14.00

SAMUELS, E.A. *Ornithology & Oology of New England.* 1867. Nichols Noyes. Ils. 583 p. rebound. M2. $120.00

SAMUELS, E.A. *With Fly Rod & Camera.* 1890. NY. 4to. VG. $60.00

SAMUELS, Lee. *Hemingway Check List.* 1951. NY. $5.00

SANBORN, E.D. *History of NH From Its Discovery to Year 1830-1874.* 1875. Manchester. 1st ed. presentation. sgn. 8vo. T1. $50.00

SANBORN, F.B. *Life & Letters of John Brown.* 1910. 3rd ed. 645 p. EX. J4. $25.00

SANBORN, Kate. *Old-Time Wallpapers.* 1905. Greenwich. Literary Collector Pr. Ils. VG. $120.00

SANBORN, Margaret. *Robert E. Lee, a Portrait (1807-1861).* 1966. Lippincott. Ils 1st ed. 353 p. $35.00

SANCHEZ, Thomas. *Mile Zero.* 1989. NY. 1st ed. sgn. dj. EX. $25.00

SAND, G.X. *Iron-Tail.* 1971. Scribner. Ils. 142 p. M2. $8.00

SANDBURG, Carl. *Abraham Lincoln: Prairie Years & War Years.* 1954. 1 vol ed. 762 p. K1. $12.50

SANDBURG, Carl. *Abraham Lincoln: Prairie Years.* Jan, 1926. NY. 2nd print. inscr. 2 vols. VG. $30.00

SANDBURG, Carl. *Abraham Lincoln: Prairie Years.* 1926. NY. sgn. dj. EX. $45.00

SANDBURG, Carl. *Abraham Lincoln: War Years.* 1939. Ils. 4 vols. J4. $30.00

SANDBURG, Carl. *Always the Young Strangers.* 1953. NY. 1st trade ed. dj. $25.00

SANDBURG, Carl. *Always the Young Strangers.* 1953. NY. Ltd ed. sgn. dj. VG. $80.00

SANDBURG, Carl. *American Songbag.* 1927. Harcourt Brace. presentation. sgn. EX. $150.00

SANDBURG, Carl. *Cornhuskers.* 1918. NY. 1st ed. later issue. dj. EX. scarce. $225.00

SANDBURG, Carl. *Good Morning, America.* 1928. NY. 1st trade ed. dj. EX. scarce. $55.00

SANDBURG, Carl. *Good Morning, America.* 1928. Rudge. Ltd ed. 1/811. sgn. $150.00

SANDBURG, Carl. *Home Front Memo.* 1943. Harcourt Brace. Stated 1st ed. presentation. dj. $125.00

SANDBURG, Carl. *Lincoln Collector.* 1949. Ils. 344 p. dj. K1. $17.50

SANDBURG, Carl. *Lincoln Collector.* 1950. NY. inscr/sgn. dj. B2. $50.00

SANDBURG, Carl. *Remembrance Rock.* 1948. Harcourt Brace. 1st trade ed. sgn. dj. VG. $50.00

SANDBURG, Carl. *Selected Poems of Carl Sandburg. Edited by Rebecca W.* 1926. Harcourt Brace. sgn. VG. $75.00

SANDBURG, Carl. *Slabs of Sunburnt W.* 1922. Harcourt Brace. presentation. sgn. VG. $90.00

SANDBURG, Carl. *Smoke & Steel.* 1920. Harcourt Brace. inscr/sgn. VG. $85.00

SANDBURG, Carl. *Smoke & Steel.* 1921. NY. 1st ed. 2nd print. EX. $75.00

SANDBURG, Carl. *Storm Over the Land.* 1939. Harcourt Brace. sgn. VG. $50.00

SANDER, August. *Citizens of the 20th C, 1892-1952.* 1980. MIT Pr. 431 pls. sm folio. dj. $125.00

SANDERLIN, W.S. *Great National Project.* 1946. 331 p. rebound. $32.50

SANDERS, A.H. *At the Sign of the Stockyard Inn.* nd. Chicago. Breeders Gazette. 322 p. A3. $60.00

SANDERS, D. *History of Indian Wars With First Settlers of US...* 1812. Montpelier, VT. 1st ed. $125.00

SANDERS, Ed. *Family.* 1971. NY. 1st ed. dj. EX. $15.00

SANDERS, F.K. *History of the Hebrews.* 1914. NY. Ils 1st ed. maps. G. $4.50

SANDERS, J. *Night Before Christmas.* 1963. NY. 1st ed. dj. VG. B2. $32.50

SANDERS & DINSMORE. *History of Percheron Horse.* 1917. Breeders Gazette. Ils. 602 p. M2. $40.00

SANDERS & SCHOTT. *Just Yesterday.* 1948. Clemens, MI. Ils. 44 p. wraps. T5. $12.50

SANDERSON, I.T. *Animal Tales: Anthology of Animal Literature.* 1946. Knopf. Ils 1st ed. 511 p. VG. M2. $10.00

SANDERSON, I.T. *Animal Treasure.* 1937. Viking. Ils. 325 p. VG. M2. $9.00

SANDERSON, I.T. *Dynasty of Abu: History & Natural History of Elephants.* 1962. Knopf. 1st ed. 376 p. dj. EX. M2. $15.00

SANDERSON, I.T. *Follow the Whale.* 1956. Little Brown. Ils 1st ed. 423 p. VG. M2. $14.00

SANDERSON, I.T. *Living Treasures.* 1937. Viking. dj. VG. $10.00

SANDERSON & LOTH. *Book of the Great Jungles.* 1965. Messner. Ils. 480 p. VG. M2. $11.00

SANDERSON & NALBANDOV. *Reproductive Cycle of the Raccoon in IL.* 1973. IL Nat Hist Survey. M2. $5.00

SANDERSON & SCHULTZ. *Wild Turkey Management: Current Problems & Programs.* 1973. MO Wildlife Soc. 355 p. dj. M2. $30.00

SANDHURST & STOTHERT. *Masterpieces of European Art.* nd. (c 1885?) Phil. Gebbie Barrie. AEG. D2. $375.00

SANDOZ, Mari. *Beaver Men.* 1964. NY. Ltd ed. 1/185. sgn. sgn map. boxed. EX. $225.00

SANDOZ, Mari. *Buffalo Hunters.* 1954. NY. 1st ed. dj. VG. $25.00

SANDOZ, Mari. *House Without Windows.* 1950. London. VG. $27.50

SANDOZ, Mari. *These Were the Sioux.* 1961. NY. 1st ed. dj. VG. B2. $22.50

SANDOZ, Maurice. *Maze.* 1946. NY. Ils/sgn Dali. Ltd ed. dj. $300.00

SANDOZ, Maurice. *On the Verge.* 1950. Garden City. Ils Dali. 1st ed. dj. VG. J2. $35.00

SANDS, Donald. *Middle-English Verse Romances.* 1966. stiff wraps. VG. C1. $9.50

SANGER, M.B. *Checkerback's Journey: Migration of the Ruddy Turnstone.* 1969. World. Ils. 159 p. dj. EX. M2. $12.00

SANGSTER, C. *St. Lawrence & the Saguenay & Other Poems.* 1856. Miller Orton. 1st ed. EX. rare. $30.00

SANKHALA, K. *Tiger! Story of the Indian Tiger.* 1977. Simon Schuster. Ils 1st ed. 220 p. dj. M2. $17.00

SANKHALA, K. *Tiger! Story of the Indian Tiger.* 1978. London. Collins. Ils 1st ed. 220 p. dj. M2. $25.00

SANSOM, William. *Fireman Flower.* 1944. London. 1st ed. dj. EX. $100.00

SANTAYANA, George. *Persons & Places.* 1944. Scribner. $12.00

SANTILLI, Marcos. *Madeira-Mamore: Image & Memory.* 1987. Sao Paulo. Ils. Eng/Portuguese text. 4to. EX. $40.00

SANTOS. *Religious Folk Art of NM.* 1943. CO Springs. Ils. 4to. red cloth. $85.00

SANTOS-TORREOLLA, Rafael. *Jorge Castillo: Seis Constantes de su Pintura.* 1978. Barcelona. Poligrafa. Ils. 65 p. dj. D2. $35.00

SAPHIRE, Lawrence. *Fernand Leger: Complete Graphic Works.* 1978. NY. Blue Moon. 1/1750. Eng text. 319 p. dj. D2. $250.00

SAPPENFIELD. *Sweet Instruction: Franklin's Journalism...* 1973. IL. dj. EX. $10.00

SARGENT, E. *Life & Public Services of Henry Clay.* 1852. Auburn, NY. gilt brown cloth. G. G2. $15.00

SARGENT, E. *Scientific Basis of Spiritualism.* 1882. 396 p. G. $15.00

SARGENT, Herbert. *Napoleon Bonaparte's First Campaign.* 1895. Chicago. 1st ed. maps. 12mo. EX. T1. $25.00

SARGENT, J.S. *Memorial Exhibition Museum of Fine Arts, Boston, 1925.* 1926. Boston. $25.00

SARGENT, L.M. *Dealings With the Dead.* 1856. Boston. 12mo. 2 vols. $15.00

SARGENT, Pamela. *Alien Upstairs.* 1983. Garden City. 1st ed. sgn. dj. EX. $25.00

SARGENT, Pamela. *Eye of the Comet.* 1984. NY. Harper. 1st ed. dj. M. $10.00

SARGENT, W. *Life & Career of Major John Andre.* 1861. Boston. 1st ed. G. $25.00

SARMIENTO, D.F. *Travels in US in 1847.* 1970. Princeton. Trans Rockland. pls. dj. VG. $12.50

SARMIENTO, F.L. *Life of Pauline Cushman: Celebrated Union Spy & Scout...* 1865. Phil. Potter. 1st ed. 374 p. $75.00

SAROYAN, William. *Daring Young Man on Flying Trapeze.* 1934. NY. 2nd ed. $11.00

SAROYAN, William. *Here Goes There Goes You Know Who.* 1961. NY. 1st ed. dj. EX. $20.00

SAROYAN, William. *Look at Us, Let's See, Here We Are...* 1967. NY. Cowles. Ils Rothstein. 2nd print. 4to. dj. $15.00

SAROYAN, William. *Sons Come & Go But Mothers Hang in Forever.* 1976. Franklin Lib. 1st ed. full leather. EX. $28.00

SARPI, Paolo. *Histoire du Concile de Trente Traduite en Francois...* 1736. Amsterdam. French text. 8 vols in 2. folio. $120.00

SARRANTINO, Al. *Campbell Wood.* 1986. Doubleday. 1st ed. dj. RS. EX. P1. $17.50

SARSON, Mary. *History of the People of Israel.* 1912. NY. Ils 1st ed. maps. G. $5.00

SARTON, George. *History of Ancient Science Though Golden Age Greece.* 1958. Harvard. 2nd ed. 646 p. VG. $20.00

SARTON, George. *History of Science.* 1952 & 1959. Harvard. 1st ed. 2 vols. J2. $45.00

SARTON, George. *Introduction to History of Science. Vol. I.* 1927. Carnegie Inst. 1st ed. VG. J2. $60.00

SARTON, May. *Anger.* 1982. Norton. 1st ed. dj. EX. $10.00

SARTON, May. *Anger.* 1982. NY. 1st ed. sgn. dj. M. $30.00

SARTON, May. *Blizzard.* 1987. Evert. Ltd ed. sgn/#d. $50.00

SARTON, May. *December Moon.* 1982. Ewert. Ltd ed. 1/36. sgn. $45.00

SARTON, May. *Selected Poems.* 1978. NY. 1st ed. dj. EX. $25.00

SARTRE, J.P. *Five Plays.* 1978. Franklin Mint. sgn. AEG. gilt red leather. EX. $75.00

SARTRE, J.P. *In French Writing on English Soil, 1940-1944.* 1945. London. 1st ed. G. $12.00

SARTWELL, Bruce. *USS Joseph Strauss War Cruise.* 1973. La Jolla. photos. 4to. 79 p. T5. $25.00

SASAKI, Hiroshi. *Modern Japanese House.* 1970. Tokyo. Ils 1st ed. 4to. dj. M. T1. $35.00

SASS, H.H. *Outspoken: 150 Years of the News & Courier.* 1953. Columbia. Ils. 120 p. dj. VG. $15.00

SASS, H.R. *Adventures in Green Places.* 1926. NY. Minton. 1st ed. 293 p. $35.00

SASS, H.R. *Adventures in Green Places.* 1935. Putnam. 297 p. xl. $65.00

SASS, H.R. *Charleston Grows: Economic, Social & Cultural Portrait...* 1949. Charleston. Carolina Art Assn. Ils. 353 p. $25.00

SASS, H.R. *Look Back to Glory.* 1933. Bobbs Merrill. 1st ed. 1/500. sgn. 360 p. $75.00

SASS, H.R. *War Drums.* 1928. Doubleday. 1st ed. 293 p. $27.50

SASSOON, Siegfried. *Centenary Celebration in Kent.* 1986. 1st ed. wraps. EX. $22.00

SASSOON, Siegfried. *Flower-Show Match & Other Pieces.* 1941. London. 1st ed. dj. EX. $40.00

SASSOON, Siegfried. *Memoirs of an Infantry Officer.* Ltd Ed Club. slipcase. M. B3. $60.00

SASSOON, Siegfried. *Old Century & Seven More Years.* 1838. London. 1st ed. 8vo. EX. T1. $35.00

SASSOON, Siegfried. *Vigils.* 1936. NY. 1st Am ed. dj. EX. $35.00

SATO, S. *Art of Arranging Flowers.* nd. Abrams. plastic dj. VG. $85.00

SATURDAY EVENING POST. *Post Scripts.* 1975. Hallmark. sm 8vo. dj. EX. $3.50

SAUCIER, Ted. *Bottoms Up!* October, 1952. Greystone. 4to. dj. RS. EX. $20.00

SAUL, George Brandon. *Wedding of Sir Gawain & Dame Ragnell.* 1934. Prentice Hall. 1st/only ed. sgn Ackerman. VG. C1. $39.00

SAUL, George Brandon. *Wild Queen.* 1967. Winston-Salem. Blair. 1st ed. dj. M. C1. $22.50

SAUL, John. *Nathaniel.* nd. Book Club. dj. VG. P1. $4.50

SAUNDERMAN, J.F. *WWII in the Air: Europe.* 1963. NY. Ils 1st ed. 345 p. dj. VG. T5. $32.50

SAUNDERS, Charles Francis. *Capistrano Nights.* 1930. Ils. K1. $9.50

SAUNDERS, Frederick. *Story of Some Famous Books.* 1877. London. 1st ed. $25.00

SAUNDERS, John Monk. *Wings.* 1927. NY. Ils. 249 p. dj. VG. T5. $22.50

SAUNDERS, M.G. *Soviet Navy.* 1958. Praeger. 1st ed. J2. $12.50

SAUNDERS, Marshall. *Beautiful Joe's Paradise; or, Island of Brotherly Love.* 1902. Boston. Ils Bull. 1st ed. 365 p. EX. $45.00

SAUNDERS, Richard. *Carolina Quest.* 1951. Columbia. 119 p. dj. VG. $35.00

SAUNDERS, Ruth. *Book of Artists` Own Bookplates.* 1933. Saunders. Ltd 1st ed. 1/360. sgn/#d. J2. $85.00

SAUNDERS & PARRISH. *Knave of Hearts.* c 1930. Ils Parrish. boxed. VG. T5. $350.00

SAUNDERS & PARRISH. *Knave of Hearts.* 1925. NY. Ils Parrish. 1st ed. wraps. G. B2. $300.00

SAUNDERS & PARRISH. *Knave of Hearts.* 1925. NY. 1st ed. folio. orig wraps/box. EX. T5. $950.00

SAVAGE, Anne. *Anglo-Saxon Chronicles.* Ils. dj. M. C1. $29.50

SAVAGE, Blake. *Rip Foster Rides the Gray Planet.* 1952. Whitman. sm 8vo. 250 p. EX. $7.50

SAVAGE, Christopher. *Mandarin Duck.* 1952. Black. 1st ed. dj. VG. $30.00

SAVAGE, E.A. *Story of Libraries & Book Collecting.* 1909. London. $30.00

SAVAGE, E.H. *Chronological History of Boston Watch & Police.* 1865. Boston. 2nd ed. 408 p. G. B2. $85.00

SAVAGE, H. & E.J. *Andre & Francois Andre Michaux.* 1986. VA U. Ils 1st ed. 435 p. dj. EX. M2. $30.00

SAVAGE, James. *Genealogical Dictionary of First Settlers of New England...* Baltimore. 4 vols. EX. T1. $65.00

SAVAGE, James. *History of New England.* 1853. Boston. 1st ed. 2 vols. xl. scarce. $55.00

SAVAGE-LANDOR, A.H. *Across Unknown S America.* c 1913. London. Ils. 2 vols. VG. M2. $95.00

SAVAGE-LANDOR, A.H. *Everywhere: Memoirs of an Explorer.* 1924. NY. Ils 1st Am ed. 2 vols. TEG. T5. $27.50

SAVANT, Jean. *Napoleon in His Time.* 1958. NY. dj. VG. $25.00

SAVINIO, Alberto. *Isadora Duncan.* 1979. Milan. Ricci. 1st ed. sgn Ricci. slipcase. EX. $200.00

SAVITCH, Jessica. *Anchorwoman.* 1982. NY. dj. VG. B2. $15.00

SAVONIUS, M. *Mushrooms & Fungi.* 1973. Octopus. Ils 1st ed. 4to. dj. EX. M2. $10.00

SAVORY, J. *George Lodge: Artist Naturalist.* 1986. Croom Helm. Ils. 118 p. dj. EX. M2. $45.00

SAVORY, T.H. *Spiders.* 1965. London. Muller. Ils 1st ed. 144 p. EX. M2. $13.00

SAWICKI, James. *Tank Battalions of the US Army.* 1983. np. Ils 1st ed. inscr. 427 p. dj. T5. $22.50

SAWVEL, F.B. *Anas of Thomas Jefferson.* 1903. NY. pls. VG. $12.50

SAWYER, C.W. *Our Rifles.* 1941. Boston. Ils. 412 p. VG. T5. $19.50

SAWYER, George. *S Institutions or Inquiry Into Origin & Prevalence Slavery.* 1859. Phil. 8vo. 393 p. $65.00

SAWYER & DARTON. *English Books, 1475-1900.* Ils. 8vo. 2 vols. VG. $80.00

SAXON, Peter. *Killing Bone.* 1970. Baker. dj. xl. P1. $5.00

SAXON, T.H. *Father MS.* 1965. Appleton Century. 427 p. dj. M2. $15.00

SAYER & BOTTING. *Nazi Gold.* 1984. NY. Congdon. dj. EX. $40.00

SAYERS, Dorothy. *Four Sacred Plays.* 1948. London. 1st ed. dj. $45.00

SAYERS, Dorothy. *World's Great Crime Stories.* 1939. VG. C1. $7.00

SAYRE, I.H. *Choosing an Enlarger for Graphic Arts.* 1966. Chicago. Photo TB Pub. 144 p. wraps. $12.50

SAYRE, I.H. *Photography & Platemaking for Photo-Lithography.* 1959. Chicago. Lithographic TB Pub. 454 p. $27.50

SBORDONI & FORESTIERO. *Butterflies of the World.* 1988. Crescent. Ils. 4to. 310 p. dj. M. M2. $35.00

SCACHERI & SCACHERI. *Fun of Photography.* 1938. Harcourt Brace. Ils. 374 p. $27.50

SCAGEL, R.F. *Evolutionary Survey of the Plant Kingdom.* 1965. London. Blackie. Ils. 658 p. dj. EX. M2. $30.00

SCAGNETTI, Jack. *Intimate Life of Rudolph Valentino.* 1975. 1st ed. dj. VG. $15.00

SCALIGERI, Josephi. *De Emendatione Temporum.* 1593. Scaligeri. tables. VG. $275.00

SCAMMELL, G.V. *World Encompassed: First European Maritime Empires.* 1981. CA U. Ils 1st ed. 538 p. dj. EX. M2. $13.00

SCARF, J.T. *History of Confederate States Navy From Its Organization...* 1887. Ils 1st ed. 824 p. EX. very scarce. J4. $135.00

SCARFE, Laurence. *Alphabets.* 1954. London. Batsford. 1st ed. dj. VG. $25.00

SCARISBRICK, J.J. *Henry VIII.* 1968. CA U. 1st ed. dj. J2. $15.00

SCHACHNER, Nathan. *Aaron Burr.* 1937. NY. Ils 1st ed. 563 p. G. T5. $25.00

SCHACHT. *My Own Particular Screwball.* 1955. NY. dj. VG. $12.00

SCHACK, William. *He Sat Among the Ashes: Biography of Louis Eilshemius.* 1939. Am Aritst Group. 1st ed. J2. $15.00

SCHACOCHIS, Bob. *Easy in the Islands.* 1985. NY. 1st ed. dj. EX. $20.00

SCHAEFFER, Emil. *Van Dyck: Des Meisters Gemalde.* 1909. Stuttgart/Leipzig. red cloth. D2. $75.00

SCHAEFFER, S.F. *Rhymes & Runes of the Toad.* 1975. Macmillan. Ils. 1st print. 71 p. dj. EX. M2. $5.00

SCHAFF, Morris. *Battle of the Wilderness.* 1910. maps. 345 p. K1. $45.00

SCHALDACH, William. *Carl Rungius: Big Game Painter.* 1945. Countryman Pr. 1/160. sgns. boxed. VG. $225.00

SCHALDACH, William. *Coverts & Casts: Field Sports.* 1946. Countryman Lib Pr. 2nd print. VG. $32.00

SCHALDACH, William. *Currents & Eddies.* 1944. NY. Ils 1st ed. 4to. $24.00

SCHALDACH, William. *Path to Enchantment: Artist in the Sonoran Desert.* 1963. Macmillan. Ils 1st ed. 226 p. dj. EX. M2. $40.00

SCHALDACH, William. *Upland Gunning.* 1946. NY. Country Pr. VG. $37.00

SCHALK, Emil. *Summary of the Art of War.* 1862. maps. 182 p. orig bdg. K1. $45.00

SCHALLER, G.B. *Giant Pandas of Worlong.* 1985. Chicago. Ils 1st ed. 289 p. dj. EX. M2. $25.00

SCHALLER, G.B. *Golden Shadows, Flying Hoofs.* 1973. Knopf. Ils 1st ed. 287 p. dj. EX. M2. $18.00

SCHALLER, G.B. *Mountain Gorilla: Ecology & Behavior.* 1976. Chicago. 35 photos. 429 p. EX. M2. $37.00

SCHALLER, G.B. *Mountain Monarchs: Wild Sheep & Goats of the Himalaya.* 1982. Chicago. 52 photos. 425 p. EX. M2. $17.00

SCHALLER, G.B. *Stones of Silence: Journeys in the Himalayas.* 1980. Viking. Ils 1st ed. 292 p. dj. EX. M2. $22.00

SCHALLER, G.B. *Year of the Gorilla.* 1964. Chicago. Ils. 260 p. dj. EX. M2. $18.00

SCHAPER, W.A. *Sectionalism & Representation in SC.* 1901. GPO. 227 p. $35.00

SCHAPIRO, E.I. *Wadsworth, Center to City.* 1938. Wadsworth. Ils. 203 p. wraps. T5. $12.50

SCHARF, J.T. *Chronicles of Baltimore.* 1874. Baltimore. 1st ed. 8vo. 756 p. VG. T1. $55.00

SCHAYER, Julia. *Tiger Lily.* 1883. Scribner. 1st ed. $12.00

SCHEFFER, T.H. *Mountain Beavers in the Pacific NW.* 1929. USDA. photos. M2. $3.00

SCHEFFER, V.B. *Little Calf.* 1970. Scribner. Ils. 140 p. dj. EX. M2. $5.00

SCHEFFER, V.B. *Year of the Seal.* 1970. Scribner. Ils. 205 p. dj. EX. M2. $5.00

SCHEIBER, H.N. *OH Canal Era: Case Study of Government & Economy, 1820-1861.* 1969. Athens. 1st ed. map. 430 p. xl. G. T5. $22.50

SCHEMMEL, W. *GA: Off the Beaten Path, Guide to Unique Places.* 1989. Globe. Ils. 140 p. M. M2. $7.00

SCHENDEL, Gordon. *Medicine in Mexico From Aztec Herbs to Belatrons.* 1968. TX U. 1st ed. dj. VG. J2. $22.50

SCHER, Bertha. *Joseph.* 1935. NY. $18.00

SCHER, Bertha. *Oneness of Life the I.* 1937. NY. $18.50

SCHERAGA & ROCHE. *Video Handbook.* 1949. NJ. Boyce. VG. $20.00

SCHERER, M.R. *Marvels of Ancient Rome.* 1955. NY. dj. J2. $20.00

SCHERMAN, K. *Spring on the Arctic Island.* 1956. Little Brown. Ils. 331 p. EX. M2. $9.00

SCHEVILL, Ferdinand. *Great Elector.* 1947. Chicago. 1st ed. dj. J2. $15.00

SCHIAVO. *Antonio Meucci: Inventor of Telephone.* 1958. NY. Vigo. EX. $15.00

SCHICKEL, Richard. *Disney Version.* 1968. Disney. 1st ed. 384 p. dj. VG. $12.00

SCHICKEL, Richard. *Disney Version.* 1968. Simon Schuster. not 1st ed. dj. VG. J2. $7.50

SCHIDER, Fritz. *Atlas of Anatomy for Aritsts.* 1947. NY. 1st Am ed. VG. $35.00

SCHIDROWITZ & DAWSON. *History of Rubber Industry.* 1952. Cambridge, Eng. Ils. 406 p. dj. VG. T5. $47.50

SCHIFF, Judith A. *Life & Letters of Charles A. Lindbergh: Commemorative View.* April, 1977. Yale. reprint. wraps. VG. T5. $4.50

SCHIFF, S.D. *Whispers, VI.* 1987. NY. dj. G. $10.00

SCHIFF. *Amorous Illustrations of Thomas Rowlandson.* 1969. NY. Ils Cytherea. dj. EX. $35.00

SCHILLER, Friedrich. *William Tell.* 1951. Zurich. Ils Charles Hug. slipcase. EX. $30.00

SCHILLER, Sepp. *Forgers, Dealers, Experts: Chapters in History of Art.* 1960. NY. Ils. EX. $25.00

SCHILLER. *Turandot.* 1918. Leipzig. Ils/sgn Goeller. G. $20.00

SCHILLINGS, C.G. *In Wildest Africa.* 1907. NY. Ils. 716 p. VG. B2. $37.50

SCHILLINGS, C.G. *With Flashlight & Rifle.* 1905. NY. Frans Zick. 1st Am ed. 421 p. $45.00

SCHINDLER, A. *Beethoven As I Knew Him.* 1966. NC U. dj. M. $52.00

SCHINDLER, Harold. *Orrin Porter Rockwell: Man of God, Son of Thunder.* 1966. UT U. 1st ed. J2. $20.00

SCHINDLER, Solomon. *Young W: Sequel to Edward Bellamy's Celebrated Novel...* 1894. Boston. Arena Pub. 1st ed. green bdg. $65.00

SCHINER, J.R. *Fauna Austriaca: Die Fliegen (Diptera).* 1862-1864. Wien. German text. 2 vols. VG. M2. $15.00

SCHLACKS, H.J. *Work of Henry John Schlacks, Ecclesiologist.* 1903. Chicago. Ils. 8vo. 79 p. $75.00

SCHLEE, S. *Edge of an Unfamiliar World: History of Oceanography.* 1973. Dutton. Ils 1st ed. 398 p. dj. EX. M2. $15.00

SCHLEGEL, A.W. *Gedichte.* 1800. Tubingen. German text. $240.00

SCHLEGEL & WULVERHORST. *World of Falconry.* 1979. Vendome. Ils. 179 p. dj. EX. M2. $70.00

SCHLEICHER, August. *Compendium der Vergleichenden Grammatik...* 1974. Hildesheim. Verlag. reprint of 1876 ed. M. $60.00

SCHLEICHER, Edythe Hembroff. *Emily Carr: Untold Story.* 1978. Seattle. Hancock House. 408 p. D2. $45.00

SCHLEY, Frank. *American Partidge & Pheasant Shooting.* 1877. Frederick, MD. Daughman. 1st ed. 8vo. 222 p. EX. M2. $150.00

SCHLUMBERGER. *Gold Coins of Europe Since 1800.* 1969. Sterling. dj. VG. $20.00

SCHMALENBACH, Fritz. *Die Malerei der Neuen Sachlichkeit.* 1973. Berlin. Mann. Ils. D2. $30.00

SCHMALENBACH, Werner. *Kurt Schwitters.* 1970. NY. Abrams. Ils. 420 p. 402 p. dj. D2. $250.00

SCHMECKEBIER, Laurence. *Handbook of Italian Renaissance Painting.* 1938. NY. Putnam. Orig ed. 362 p. D2. $30.00

SCHMECKEBIER, Laurence. *Modern Mexican Art.* 1939. MN U. J2. $35.00

SCHMIDLY, D. *TX Mammals E of the Balcones Fault Zone.* 1983. TX A&M U. Ils 1st ed. 400 p. EX. M2. $13.00

SCHMIDT, K.P. *American Alligator.* 1922. Field Mus. Ils. 15 p. M2. $3.00

SCHMIDT, K.P. *Homes & Habits of Wild Animals (N American Mammals).* 1934. Donohue. Ils Weber. 4to. 64 p. dj. EX. M2. $16.00

SCHMIDT, Otto. *Tyrolian Interiors.* 1919. Cleveland. Hansen. Ils. very scarce. D2. $225.00

SCHMIDT, W.S. *Doberman Pinscher in America.* 1940. Milwaukee. Ils 1st ed. 218 p. dj. VG. $30.00

SCHMIDT, Walter. *Stag at Eve.* 1931. NY. 4to. G. $20.00

SCHMIDT & GILBERT. *Big Game of N America: Ecology & Management.* 1980. Stackpole. Ils. 494 p. dj. EX. M2. $29.00

SCHMIDT. *Cobblestone Masonry.* 1966. Scottsville. 1/1000. VG. $70.00

SCHMOKEL, H. *Ur, Assur und Babylon.* 1955. Germany. German text. pls. VG. $14.00

SCHMUCKER, S.M. *History of Civil War in US.* 1865. rebound. VG. $45.00

SCHNECK, Jerome. *Hypnosis in Modern Medicine.* 1953. Charles Thomas. 1st ed. dj. VG. J2. $22.50

SCHNEEBAUM, T. *Keep the River on Your Right.* 1988. Grove. photos. 184 p. M. M2. $5.00

SCHNEEBAUM, T. *Where the Spirits Dwell: Odyssey in Jungles of New Guinea.* 1989. Grove. Ils. 221 p. M. M2. $7.00

SCHNEIDER, Bruno F. *John Rood's Sculpture.* 1958. Minneapolis. Ils. 112 p. D2. $50.00

SCHNEIDER, Estelle B. *King Arthur & the Knights of the Round Table.* 1954. Ils Barnum. 1st ed. juvenile. VG. C1. $7.50

SCHNEIDER, Lambert A. *Zur Sozialen Bedeutung der Archaischen Korenstatuen.* 1975. Hamburg. Ils. D2. $35.00

SCHNEIDER, Norris F. *Bibliography of Zanesville & Muskingham County, OH.* 1941. Zanesville. 23 p. wraps. VG. T5. $45.00

SCHNEIDER, Norris F. *Blennerhassett Island & the Burr Conspiracy.* 1950. Columbus. Ils. 36 p. wraps. VG. T5. $12.50

SCHNEIDER, Norris F. *Muskingham County Men & Women in WWII.* 1947. Zanesville. Ils. 511 p. fair. T5. $25.00

SCHNEIUR, Z. *Vilna.* 1923. Berlin. Hasefer. Ils Struck. 4to. EX. $250.00

SCHNITZLER, Arthur. *Hands Around.* 1929. NY. Schnitzler Soc. 1/1475. VG. $35.00

SCHOENER, Allan. *Portal to America: Lower E Side, 1870-1925.* 1967. Holt Rinehart. 1st ed. 256 p. dj. VG. $30.00

SCHOEPF, J.D. *Travels in the Confederation, 1783-1784.* 1911. Phil. 2 vols. $125.00

SCHOFFLER, Benedict. *Die Phototelegraphie und das Elektrische Fernsehen...* 1898. Leipzig. 27 p. printed wraps. $350.00

SCHOFIELD, W.A. *Chivalry in English Literature.* 1912. Harvard. sgn/inscr. VG. C1. $29.50

SCHOFIELD, William H. *Mythical Bards.* 1920. Harvard. 1st ed. VG. scarce. C1. $19.50

SCHOLTEN, C. *Munten van de Nederlandsche Gebeidsdeelen Overzee 1601-1948.* 1951. Amsterdam. Schulman. Dutch text. M. $20.00

SCHOLZ, Janos. *Drawings by 17th-C Italian Masters From Scholz Collection.* 1974. Stanford. 1/1200. 150 p. D2. $25.00

SCHOLZ, Janos. *16th-C Italian Drawings From Collection of Janos Scholz.* 1973-1974. NY. Ils. 144 p. D2. $25.00

SCHON, M.A. *Muscular System of the Red Howling Monkey.* 1968. US Nat Mus. Ils. 183 p. M2. $10.00

SCHONFIELD, Hugh. *New Hebrew Typography.* 1932. London. Ils. 4to. EX. $200.00

SCHOOLCRAFT, H.R. *American Indians: History, Condition & Prospects.* 1851. Rochester. 495 p. orig bdg. A3. $250.00

SCHOOLCRAFT, H.R. *Myth of Hiawatha.* 1856. Phil. 1st ed. G. B2. $80.00

SCHOONMAKER, W.J. *World of the Woodchuck.* 1966. Lippincott. Ils 1st ed. 146 p. dj. EX. M2. $14.00

SCHOONOVER, F.E. *Edge of the Wilderness: Portrait of Canadian N.* 1974. Methuen. sgn Cortlandt/Schoonover. dj. VG. $30.00

SCHRAG, Peter. *Decline of the Wasp.* 1971. Simon Schuster. 255 p. dj. M1. $6.50

SCHREINER, Olive. *So Here Then Are Dreams.* 1901. Roycroft. VG. $75.00

SCHREINER, Olive. *Trooper Peter Halket of Mashonaland.* 1897. London. 1st ed. $100.00

SCHREYVOGEL, Charles. *My Bunkie & Others.* 1909. Moffat Yard. Ils 1st ed. sgn. yellow bdg. VG. $750.00

SCHRINER, Olive. *S African Question.* 1899. Chicago. 1st ed. J2. $30.00

SCHROEDER, R.L. *Habitat Suitability Models: E Wild Turkey.* 1985. USFWS. 33 p. M2. $3.00

SCHRUMPF-PIERRON, Pierre. *Tobacco & Physical Efficiency.* 1927. NY. VG. $25.00

SCHUBERT, David. *Works & Days.* 1983. 1st book ed. stiff wraps. EX. C1. $6.50

SCHUCHERT & DUNBAR. *Stratigraphy of W Newfoundland.* 1934. Geol Soc Am. Ils. maps. inscr/sgn. EX. M2. $40.00

SCHUHMACHER, E. *Last Paradises: On Track of Rare Animals.* 1967. Doubleday. Ils. map. 315 p. dj. EX. M2. $20.00

SCHULBERG, B. *Swan Watch.* 1976. Delacorte. Ils. 147 p. dj. EX. M2. $9.00

SCHULBERG, Budd. *Sanctuary V.* 1969. NY. 1st ed. sgn. dj. VG. $35.00

SCHULER, G.S. *Black & Conservative.* 1966. Arlington House. 362 p. dj. $10.00

SCHULMAN, Jacques. *Nederlandsche Munten van 1795-1945.* 1946. Amsterdam. Schulman. VG. $10.00

SCHULTHESS, Emil. *Africa.* 1958. Simon Schuster. 1st ed. VG. $40.00

SCHULTZ, Charles. *You're in Love Charlie Brown.* 1968. World. Ils 1st ed. VG. B4. $18.00

SCHULTZ, Duane. *Hero of Bataan: Story of General Jonathan M. Wainwright.* 1981. NY. 1st ed. 479 p. dj. VG. T5. $16.50

SCHULTZ, G.D. *Lady From Savannah: Biography of Juliette Low.* 1958. 1st ed. sgn Low's niece. dj. fair. B2. $37.50

SCHULTZ, J.W. *My Life As an Indian.* 1907. Boston. Ils 1st ed. 8vo. VG. scarce. T1. $100.00

SCHULZ, Anne Markham. *Sculpture of Bernardo Rossellino & His Workshop.* 1977. Princeton. Ils. 176 p. dj. D2. $60.00

SCHULZ, G.T. *Sailing Round Cape Horn.* 1954. London. Ils. 4to. dj. VG. $35.00

SCHULZ & SIMMONS. *Offices in the Sky.* 1959. NY. 1st ed. dj. VG. $12.00

SCHULZE, W.H. *Walter H. Schulze: Peace Messenger.* 1925. private print. Ils. VG. $35.00

SCHURMACHER, E.C. *Nothing's Sacred on Sunday.* 1951. Crowell. dj. VG. P1. $20.25

SCHWAB, George. *Tribes of Liberian Hinterland.* 1947. Cambridge. Ils. wraps. G. T5. $47.50

SCHWARBERG, Gunther. *Murders at Bullenhuser Dam.* 1984. IN U. Ils 1st ed. EX. $12.00

SCHWARTZ, C.W. *Prairie Chicken in MO.* 1944. MO Conservation. 4to. dj. M2. $65.00

SCHWARTZ, C.W. & E.R. *Game Birds of HI.* 1949. HI Agric. photos. maps. 168 p. EX. M2. $20.00

SCHWARTZ, F. *Along AK's Great River.* 1983. AK NW. Ils. 4to. 95 p. M2. $8.00

SCHWARTZ, J.S. *Masterpieces of Manuscript Writing.* 1935. NY. reprint of 1741 London ed. 1/500. $25.00

SCHWARTZ, L.S. *Leaving Brooklyn.* 1989. Boston. 1st ed. sgn. dj. M. $15.00

SCHWARTZ & GARRIDO. *Cuban Lizards of Genus Sphaerodactylus.* 1985. Milwaukee. maps. 68 p. M2. $8.00

SCHWARTZ & HENDERSON. *W Indian Amphibians & Reptiles.* 1988. Milwaukee. maps. 264 p. EX. M2. $15.00

SCHWARZ, Arturo. *Complete Works of Marcel Duchamp.* 1970. NY. Abrams. 780 pls. 630 p. D2. $365.00

SCHWARZ, Heinrich. *David Octavius Hill: Master of Photography.* 1932. London. Harrap. 1st ed. 4to. VG. $85.00

SCHWARZ, Susan. *Alternatives.* 1st ed. pb. M. C1. $4.00

SCHWATKA, F. *Children of the Cold.* 1895. NY. Ils. EX. $25.00

SCHWATKA, F. *Summer in AK.* 1894. St. Louis. Ils. 418 p. VG. B2. $27.50

SCHWEIBERT, E. *Death of a River Keeper.* 1980. NY. 1st ed. dj. VG. B2. $22.50

SCHWEINFURTH, G. *Heart of Africa.* 1874. NY. Ils. map. 2 vols. G. $43.00

SCHWEITZER, Darrell. *Discovering Stephen King.* 1985. Starmont. EX. P1. $9.95

SCHWEITZER, Darrell. *Pathways to Elfland: Lord Dunsany.* 1989. Owlswick. 1st ed. dj. EX. P1. $25.00

SCHWERIN, Doris. *Diary of a Pigeon Watcher.* 1976. NY. Morrow. 1st ed. dj. EX. $20.00

SCHWITZKE, H. *Vier Fernsehspiele.* 1960. Stuttgart. 1st ed. 176 p. VG. $22.50

SCLATER, P.L. *Catalog of Collection of American Birds.* 1962. London. Trubner. 20 pls. 368 p. EX. M2. $250.00

SCOPPETTONE, S. *Suzuki Beane.* 1961. NY. 1st ed. dj. VG. B2. $27.50

SCORESBY. *Arctic Regions: Their Situation, Appearances, Climate...* nd. Phil. 192 p. fair. T5. $35.00

SCOTT, A.C. *Story of OK City.* 1939. OK City. Ils 1st ed. EX. $65.00

SCOTT, G. *Grouse Land & Fringe of the Moor.* 1937. London. photos. 197 p. dj. VG. $27.50

SCOTT, H.J. *Black School Superintendent: Messiah or Scapegoat.* 1980. Howard U. 262 p. dj. $8.50

SCOTT, J.A. *Butterflies of N America: Natural History & Field Guide.* 1986. Stanford. Ils. maps. 680 p. dj. M. M2. $45.00

SCOTT, J.D. *Alligator.* 1984. Putnam. Ils 1st ed. dj. EX. M2. $8.00

SCOTT, J.M. *Portrait of an Ice Cap.* 1955. Chatto Windus. 1st ed. dj. VG. J2. $15.00

SCOTT, J.P. *Animal Behavior.* 1958. Chicago. Ils. 281 p. M2. $6.00

SCOTT, J.R. *Princess Dehra.* 1908. Lippincott. 2nd ed. VG. $12.50

SCOTT, J.S. *Local Lads.* 1983. NY. 1st ed. dj. EX. $10.00

SCOTT, James. *Reports to Hague Conferences of 1899 & 1907.* 1917. Oxford. 940 p. VG. $40.00

SCOTT, Jeremy. *Mandrake Root.* 1946. Jarrolds. HrdCvr. VG. P1. $30.00

SCOTT, P. *Observations of Wildlife.* 1980. Cornell. Ils 1st ed. 112 p. dj. EX. M2. $15.00

SCOTT, P. *World Atlas of Birds.* 1974. Crescent. Ils. 4to. 272 p. dj. EX. M2. $22.00

SCOTT, P.P. *Lane, Colonel of Volunteers in Civil War, 11th OH Infantry.* 1930. private print. VG. $80.00

SCOTT, R.F. *Scott's Last Expedition.* 1913. Dodd Mead. Ils Wilson/Ponting. 2 vols. $115.00

SCOTT, R.F. *Scott's Last Expedition.* 1949. London. Murrary. Ils. 521 p. G. M2. $10.00

SCOTT, R.V. *Railroad Development Programs in the 20th C.* 1985. 231 p. $15.00

SCOTT, Robert. *Bohemian Flat.* nd. MN U. 1st ed. VG. J2. $20.00

SCOTT, W.H. *British Field Sports.* 1818. London. Sherwood Neeley Jones. 8vo. AEG. $480.00

SCOTT, Walter. *Anne of Geierstein.* 1829. Edinburgh. 1st ed. 3 vols. $75.00

SCOTT, Walter. *Antiquary.* 1816. London. 1st ed. 3 vols. rebound. VG. T5. $75.00

SCOTT, Walter. *Christmas in the Olden Time.* 1887. NY. J2. $20.00

SCOTT, Walter. *Ivanhoe.* Norwalk. Heritage. Ils Wilson. slipcase. EX. $15.00

SCOTT, Walter. *Lady of the Lake.* 1863. London. Bennett. VG. $110.00

SCOTT, Walter. *Monastery.* 1820. London. Longman. 1st ed. 3 vols. $120.00

SCOTT, Walter. *Poetical Works.* c 1900. VG. scarce. C1. $17.50

SCOTT, Walter. *Quentin Durward.* 1823. Edinburgh. 1st ed. 3 vols. VG. $90.00

SCOTT, Walter. *Quentin Durward.* 1940. NY. Ils Chambers. not 1st ed. VG. J2. $25.00

SCOTT, Walter. *Roxeby: A Poem.* 1812. Edinburgh. 2nd ed. 8vo. half leather. VG. T1. $45.00

SCOTT, Walter. *Waverly.* 1829. London. Ils. 12mo. 2 vols. EX. T1. $85.00

SCOTT. *Scott's Standard Postage Stamp Catalog.* 1936. 8vo. 1121 p. thumb index. cloth. EX. $8.00

SCOTT-GILES, C.W. *Romance of Heraldry.* 1957. London. dj. VG. $22.50

SCOTT-MAXWELL, Florida. *Measure of My Days.* 1975. Knopf. 12mo. dj. with sgn letter. $25.00

SCOVIL, E.R. *Little Prayers for Little Lips.* 1921. Altemus. Ils. VG. $20.00

SCRIBBINS, Jim. *Hiawatha Story.* 1970. 267 p. $30.00

SCRIPPS, J.L. *1860 Campaign Life of Lincoln Annotated.* 1931. Peoria. EX. $40.00

SCRIVEN, G.P. *Transmission of Military Information.* 1908. NY. Ils. tall 8vo. 152 p. $20.00

SCRUGGS, A.M. *Glory of Earth.* 1933. Oglethorpe U. 1st ed. sgn. 95 p. $27.50

SCUDDER, S.H. *Fossil Insects in American Tertiaries.* 1877. WA. 115 p. disbound. A3. $25.00

SCUDDER, S.H. *Fossil Insects of Green River Shales.* 1878. WA. 160 p. wraps. A3. $35.00

SCUDDER, S.H. *Tertiary Insects of N America.* 1890. US Geol Survey. Ils. 734 p. M2. $145.00

SCUDDER, S.H. *Tertiary Insects of N America.* 1890. WA. 28 pls. 734 p. VG. A3. $110.00

SCULL, Penrose. *Great Ships Around the World.* 1960. NY. 1st ed. 260 p. dj. G. T5. $27.50

SCULL. *Greek Mythology Systematized.* 1880. Porter Coates. G. $22.50

SCUVULLO, Francesco. *Photographs 1848-1984.* 1984. Harper. Ils 1st ed. folio. dj. $60.00

SEABROOK, W. *Jungle Ways.* 1931. Blue Ribbon. Ils. map. G. M2. $5.00

SEAGER, R. *Tyler Too.* 1963. McGraw. 1st ed. dj. M. $62.00

SEANATOR & KAMINER. *Health & Disease in Relation to Marriage & Married State.* c 1905. NY. 1257 p. $45.00

SEARE, Nicholas. *Rude Tales & Glorious.* 1983. 1st ed. dj. EX. C1. $10.00

SEARS, C.E. *Some American Primitives.* 1941. Boston. 1st ed. portraits. 291 p. T5. $25.00

SEARS, P.B. *Deserts on the March.* 1947. OK U. Revised 2nd ed. 178 p. dj. EX. M2. $10.00

SEARS, S.W. *American Heritage Century Collection of Civil War Art.* 1983. Heritage. Ils. 400 p. dj. EX. M2. $22.00

SEATON. *Yes, Lady Saheb.* 1925. NY. 1st ed. EX. $25.00

SEAWELL, M.E. *Fortunes of Fifi.* 1903. Bobbs Merrill. Ils Thulstrup. 1st ed. $12.00

SEAY, A. *Music in the Medieval World.* 1956. pb. VG. C1. $12.00

SEBOEK, Thomas. *Animal Communication.* 1973. IN U. 686 p. EX. $16.00

SECKEL, Dietrich. *Emakimono.* 1959. Pantheon. Trans Brownjohn. slipcase. EX. $120.00

SEDGEWICK, M.C. *Garden Month to Month.* 1907. Garden City. 1st ed. 4to. 516 p. EX. $30.00

SEDGWICK, A. *Proceedings of 4th International Congress of Zoology.* 1899. London. Cambridge. pls. 422 p. M2. $8.00

SEDGWICK, Noel. *Shooting Man's Years.* 1947. London. 2nd print. VG. $15.00

SEEBOHM, H. *Birds of Siberia.* 1901. London. Murray. Ils. fld map. VG. M2. $175.00

SEEBOHM, H. *Birds of the Japanese Empire.* 1890. London. Porter. Ils 1st ed. 386 p. rebound. EX. M2. $135.00

SEEGER, Alan. *Poems.* 1917. G. C1. $4.00

SEEHORN, M.E. *Reptiles & Amphibians of SE National Forests.* 1982. USFS. 85 p. EX. M2. $20.00

SEELEY, C.S. *Lost Canyon of the Toltecs.* 1893. Chicago. gilt cloth. EX. $20.00

SEELEY, L.B. *Fanny Burney & Her Friends.* 1890. London. Seeley. 9 pls. 331 p. EX. $55.00

SEELEY, L.B. *Mrs. Thrale, Afterwards Mrs. Piozzi.* 1891. Scribner Welford. 336 p. EX. $50.00

SEELEY, Levi. *New School Management.* 1903. Hinds Noble. 392 p. EX. $4.50

SEELYE, L.C. *Early History of Smith College, 1871-1910.* 1923. Boston. Ils. green cloth. EX. $30.00

SEFI, Alex. *Introduction to Advanced Philately.* 1926. London. 1/250. 8vo. VG. $100.00

SEGAL, Edith. *Take My Hand: Poems & Songs for Lovers & Rebels.* 1969. NY. Ils Kamen. 1st ed. dj. EX. $25.00

SEGAL, Erich. *Man, Woman & Child.* 1980. NY. 1st ed. dj. EX. $7.00

SEGER, J.H. *Early Days Among the Cheyenne & Arapahoe Indians.* 1934. Norman. 1st ed. inscr Vestal. dj. EX. $150.00

SEGER, J.H. *Early Days Among the Cheyenne & Arapahoe Indians.* 1956. Norman. Ils 2nd ed. dj. EX. $40.00

SEGURA, J.S. *Respuestas a las Objeciones mas Velgares Contra la Religion.* 1869. Orizaba. VG. $50.00

SEIDL, Anton. *Music of Modern World.* 1895. NY. Ils. pls. folio. 2 vols. VG. $85.00

SEIDMAN. *Labor Czars.* 1938. NY. VG. $25.00

SEITZ, D.C. *Joseph Pulitzer: His Life & Letters.* 1924. Simon Schuster. VG. $14.50

SEITZ, William. *Art of Assemblage.* 1961. NY. MOMA. Ils. sm 4to. 176 p. $37.50

SEKLER & CURTIS. *Le Corbusier at Work: Genesis of Carpenter Center...* 1978. Harvard. 1st ed. dj. VG. J2. $30.00

SELBY, Graham. *Knights of Dark Reknown.* VG. C1. $3.50

SELBY, Hubert. *Last Exit to Brooklyn.* 1964. NY. 1st ed. dj. EX. $45.00

SELDES, George. *7 Lively Arts.* 1924. NY. Ils. 398 p. index. VG. B2. $27.50

SELDIS, Henry. *Henry Moore in America.* 1973. NY. Praeger. Ils. 283 p. dj. D2. $25.00

SELEKMAN. *Employees` Representation in Coal Mines.* 1924. NY. Sage. 1st ed. dj. EX. $25.00

SELER, E. *Mexican & Central American Antiquities: Calendar Systems.* 1904. Bull. Ils. 682 p. EX. M2. $28.00

SELFRIDGE, T.O. *Reports of Explorations & Surveys...* 1874. WA. GPO. 14 pls. 17 fld maps. 4to. $65.00

SELIGMAN, G. *Most Notorious Victory, Man in Age of Automation.* 1966. NY. EX. $15.00

SELIGMAN, Germain. *Roger de la Fresnaye.* 1945. NY. Valentine. 1/775. D2. $125.00

SELL & WEYBRIGHT. *Buffalo Bill & the Wild W.* 1955. Oxford. 1st ed. dj. J2. $20.00

SELLARS. *Samuel Palmer.* 1974. St. Martin. 1st ed. dj. EX. $30.00

SELLERS, C.G. *S As American.* 1960. Chapel Hill. 216 p. dj. VG. $30.00

SELLERS, George. *Early Engineering: Reminiscences.* 1965. Smithsonian. 1st ed. VG. J2. $20.00

SELLERS, Hazel Crowson. *Old SC Churches.* 1941. Crowson. 1/1500. sgn. VG. T6. $130.00

SELLERS & TERRELL. *River of No Return.* 1973. Morrow. 279 p. dj. $10.00

SELLIN, Thorston. *Pioneering in Penology.* 1944. PA U. Ils. inscr. G. $30.00

SELOUS, F.C. *African Nature Notes.* 1908. London. Intro Roosevelt. 356 p. B2. $60.00

SELOUS, F.C. *Hunter's Wanderings in Africa.* 1907. London. 5th ed. fld map. TEG. EX. $65.00

SELOUS, F.C. *Recent Hunting Trips in British N America.* 1907. London. 65 photos. 400 p. $195.00

SELOUS, F.C. *Travel & Adventure in SE Africa.* 1893. London. 1st ed. fld map. $75.00

SELZER, Michael. *Deliverance Day: Last Hours at Dachau.* 1978. Phil. Ils 1st ed. dj. VG. $7.00

SEMMES, Raphael. *Service Afloat: Sumter & AL During War Between the States.* 1887. Baltimore. Ils. 883 p. VG. $85.00

SEMON, H.C.G. *Atlas of Commoner Skin Diseases With 103 Color Plates.* 1934. Baltimore. 1st ed. 4to. red buckram. EX. $80.00

SENDAK, Maurice. *Posters by Maurice Sendak.* 1986. NY. Ils 1st ed. 4to. EX. $9.00

SENDAK, Maurice. *Where the Wild Things Are.* 1963. Harper Row. Ils. VG. B4. $20.00

SENDREY. *Bibliography of Jewish Music.* 1969. NY. reprint. $45.00

SENET, A. *Man in Search of His Ancestors: Romance of Paleontology.* 1955. McGraw Hill. Ils. 274 p. dj. EX. M2. $10.00

SENIOR, Michael. *Tales of King Arthur.* Ils 1st pb ed. EX. C1. $11.50

SENIOR, Michael. *Tales of King Arthur.* 1981. NY. Schocken. Ils 1st ed. dj. M. C1. $19.50

SENN, N. *In the Heart of the Arctics.* 1907. Conkey. Ils. inscr. 336 p. G. M2. $25.00

SENN. *Nurse's Guide for Operating Room.* 1902. Chicago. Ils 8vo. 131 p. EX. P3. $25.00

SENNETT, G.B. *Ornithology on Lower Rio Grande of TX.* 1878. WA. 310 p. wraps loose. A3. $30.00

SEPKOSKI, J.J. *Compendium of Fossil Marine Families.* 1982. Milwaukee. 126 p. EX. M2. $19.00

SERE, F. *Select Examples of Ornaments of Middle Ages & Renaissance.* 1851. 28 pls. disbound. $50.00

SEREDY, Kate. *Chestry Oak.* 1948. Viking. 1st ed. dj. EX. $25.00

SERENA. *Lettergrams.* 1976. NY. $17.50

SERGEANT, B.W. *33rd Division Across No Man's Land.* 1919. Chicago. Ils 1st ed. cloth. B2. $40.00

SERGEANT, E.S. *Willa Cather.* 1953. Phil./NY. 1st ed. EX. $25.00

SERLING, R.J. *Ceiling Unlimited.* 1973. Wallsworth. Ils. 245 p. M. $20.00

SERLING, Rod. *Night Gallery.* 1971. Bantam. 1st ed. wraps. EX. $15.00

SERLING, Rod. *Stories From the Twilight Zone.* 1960. Bantam. 1st ed. wraps. EX. $20.00

SERVEN, J.E. *Colt Firearms From 1836.* 1981. PA. 401 p.d j. EX. $25.00

SERVENTY, V. & C. *Koala.* 1975. Dutton. Ils 1st ed. 80 p. dj. EX. M2. $10.00

SERVICE, Robert. *Ballads of a Bohemian.* 1921. NY. inscr. G. P3. $5.00

SERVICE, Robert. *Ploughman of the Moon.* 1945. NY. 3rd ed. dj. VG. B2. $30.00

SERVICE, Robert. *Rhymes of a Rolling Stone.* 1917. Dodd Mead. 8vo. gilt green cloth. G. $10.00

SERVICE, Robert. *Rhymes of Red Cross Man.* 1916. Toronto. $24.00

SERVICE, Robert. *Spell of the Yukon & Other Verses.* 1907. NY. 126 p. VG. T5. $12.50

SERVICE, Robert. *Why Not Grow Young.* 1928. NY. Ils 1st ed. 266 p. dj. VG. $25.00

SERVICE, W.S. *Owl.* 1969. Knopf. Ils 1st ed. dj. EX. M2. $10.00

SERVISS, G.P. *Edison's Conquest of Mars.* 1947. LA. 1st ed. dj. VG. scarce. $110.00

SERWER, Jacquelyn Days. *Gene Davis: Memorial Exhibition.* 1987. Smithsonian. photos. dj. D2. $50.00

SETH, Ronald. *Art of Spying.* 1957. Philosophical Lib. photos. G. M1. $15.00

SETON, Anya. *Avalon.* 1965. 1st ed. dj. VG. C1. $9.50

SETON, Anya. *Mistletoe & the Sword.* 1955. Garden City. Doubleday. 1st Am ed. dj. M. C1. $9.50

SETON, E.T. *Bannertail. Story of Gray Squirrel.* 1926. Scribner. Ils. 12mo. G. $6.00

SETON, E.T. *Book of Woodcraft.* 1917. Doubleday. VG. $25.00

SETON, E.T. *Collected Novels.* 1985. Castle. Ils 1st ed. 454 p. dj. EX. M2. $18.00

SETON, E.T. *Gospel of the Red Man.* 1936. Garden City. 1st ed. sgn. dj. VG. B2. $60.00

SETON, E.T. *Lives of Game Animals. Vol. 1, Part 1. Cats, Wolves, Foxes.* 1929. Doubleday. Ils. EX. M2. $30.00

SETON, E.T. *Lives of the Hunted.* 1901. Ils 1st ed. 1st imp. VG. $45.00

SETON, E.T. *Monarch of the Big Bear.* 1904. Ils 1st ed. 1st imp. gilt bdg. G. $25.00

SETON, E.T. *Trail of an Artist-Naturalist.* 1940. Scribner. Ils 1st ed. 412 p. dj. EX. M2. $35.00

SETON, E.T. *Trail of an Artist-Naturalist.* 1940. Scribner. 1st ed. G. $20.00

SETON, E.T. *Trail of Sand Hill Stag.* 1917. Scribner. Ils. 93 p. EX. $10.00

SETON, E.T. *Trail of Sandhill Stag.* 1899. Scribner. Ils 1st ed. 1st imp. fair. $25.00

SETON, E.T. *Trail of Sandhill Stag.* 1908. NY. Scribner. Ils. 12mo. EX. $40.00

SETON, E.T. *Wild Animals at Home.* 1913. Grosset Dunlap. Ils. reprint. 226 p. G. M2. $9.00

SETON, E.T. *Wild Animals I Have Known.* 1926. Scribner. later print. sgn. 298 p. dj. M2. $22.00

SETON, E.T. *Wolf in the Woods.* 1917. Doubleday. G. $8.00

SETON, Julia. *Fundamentals.* nd. London. $35.00

SETTLE, M.L. *All the Brave Promises.* 1966. NY. 1st ed. 176 p. G. T5. $27.50

SETTLE & SETTLE. *War Drums & Wagon Wheels.* 1966. Lincoln. 1st ed. dj. EX. $25.00

SEVAREID, Arnold. *Canoeing With the Cree.* 1935. Macmillan. 1st ed. G. J2. $22.50

SEVERIN, M.F. *Making a Bookplate.* 1949. Studio. 1st ed. dj. VG. J2. $25.00

SEVERIN, T. *African Adventure: 400 Years of Exploration.* 1973. Dutton. Ils 1st Am ed. 288 p. dj. EX. M2. $23.00

SEVERSON & MEDINA. *Deer & Elk Habitat Management in the SW.* 1983. Journal Range Management. 64 p. M2. $7.00

SEWALL, R. *Life of Emily Dickinson.* 1974. Farrar Straus. 2 vols. boxed. EX. $60.00

SEWALL, R.K. *Sketches of St. Augustine.* 1848. NY. 1st ed. 6 pls. VG. $100.00

SEWARD, W.H. *Life & Public Services of J.Q. Adams.* 1849. Auburn. 1st ed. VG. $75.00

SEWARD, W.H. *Seward's Travels Around the World.* 1873. NY. Ils 1st ed. 8vo. VG. $38.00

SEWELL, Anna. *Black Beauty.* 1946. Dodd Mead. Ils Beer. reprint of 1941. VG. B4. $18.00

SEWELL, M.E. *Franceska.* c 1902. Bowen Merrill. Ils Fisher. VG. $20.00

SEWELL, William. *History of Rise, Increase & Progress of Quakers.* c 1840s. Phil. 2 vols. new cloth. EX. M2. $65.00

SEWELL, William. *History of Rise, Increase & Progress of Quakers.* 1774. Burlington. 1st Am ed. folio. leather. $225.00

SEWTER, A.C. *Stained Glass of William Morris & His Circle.* 1974. Yale. 4to. VG. G2. $55.00

SEXTON, Anne. *Book of Folly.* 1972. Boston. 1st ed. dj. EX. $20.00

SEXTON, Anne. *Self-Portrait in Letters.* 1977. Boston. 1st ed. dj. EX. $15.00

SEXTON & BETTS. *American Theatres of Today.* 1927. NY. Architectural Book Pub. folio. VG. $135.00

SEXTUS, Carl. *Hypnotism: Guide to Science of How Subjects Are Influenced.* 1893. Boston. Ils 5th ed. 309 p. gilt blue bdg. $30.00

SEYMOUR, Maurice. *Ballet.* 1947. Chicago. Ils Seymour. dj. VG. $35.00

SEYMOUR, William. *Journal of S Expedition, 1780-1783.* 1896. Wilmington. 42 p. wraps. VG. $95.00

SEYMOUR. *Favorite Flowers.* 1949. Wise. Ils. VG. $10.00

SHAARA, Michael. *Broken Place.* 1981. McGraw Hill. 1st ed. dj. M. $10.00

SHACKLETON, E. *S.* 1920. Macmillan. VG. $50.00

SHACKLETON, Robert. *Book of Boston.* 1917. Phil. 2nd print. VG. $14.00

SHACKLETON, Robert. *Book of NY.* 1920. Phil. Ils Boyer. $30.00

SHACKLETON. *Auora Australis.* 1988. Auckland. 1/375. boxed. M. $300.00

SHADBOLT & RUHEN. *Isles of the S Pacific.* 1971. Nat Geog Soc. Ils. fld map. 211 p. dj. EX. M2. $9.00

SHAFFER, Burr. *Wonderful World of J. Wesley Smith.* 1971. NY. Scholastic Book Service. 4th print. $5.00

SHAFFER, G.D. *Ways of a Mud Dauber.* 1949. Stanford. Ils. 78 p. dj. EX. M2. $11.00

SHAFFER. *Wicker Man.* 1978. NY. dj. G. $5.00

SHAFTESBURY, Edmund. *Home-Training Courses in Metaphysics.* 1926. Ralston U. 5 vols. red/green bdg. VG. $35.00

SHAHN, Ben. *Love & Joy About Letters.* 1963. NY. rebound. slipcase. $85.00

SHAKELTON, E.H. *Heart of the Antarctic.* 1909. Lippincott. Ils. 2 vols. TEG. wraps. VG. $200.00

SHAKESPEARE, William. *As You Like It.* 1903. Roycroft. 4to. gray suede. EX. D1. $55.00

SHAKESPEARE, William. *As You Like It.* 1903. Roycroft. 4to. VG. D1. $35.00

SHAKESPEARE, William. *As You Like It.* 1930. London. Ils Austen. 1st ed. VG. J2. $30.00

SHAKESPEARE, William. *Complete Works of William Shakespeare.* nd. London. Swan Sonnenschein. 10 vols. $400.00

SHAKESPEARE, William. *Hamlet.* 1902. Roycroft. 4to. green suede/cloth. boxed. VG. D1. $50.00

SHAKESPEARE, William. *Hamlet.* 1905. Phil. Furness Variorum. 2 vols. TEG. $75.00

SHAKESPEARE, William. *Hey Nonny Yes: Passions & Conceits From Shakespeare.* 1947. London. Ils Ardizzone. 1st ed. dj. VG. $40.00

SHAKESPEARE, William. *King Lear.* Roycroft. brown/gray bdg. VG. D1. $40.00

SHAKESPEARE, William. *King Lear.* 1904. Roycroft. 4to. red suede. VG. D1. $50.00

SHAKESPEARE, William. *Life of King Henry IV.* 1951. Heritage. Ils Fritz Kredel. slipcase. VG. $22.50

SHAKESPEARE, William. *Nineteen Sonnets.* 1946. Golden Eagle. Ltd ed. EX. $40.00

SHAKESPEARE, William. *Plant Lore & Garden Craft of Shakespeare.* 1896. London. Ils Arnold. New ed. 8vo. TEG. $40.00

SHAKESPEARE, William. *Plays & Poems.* 1825. London. Wreath ed. 11 vols. G. $300.00

SHAKESPEARE, William. *Romeo & Juliet.* nd. Tuck. Ils Marchetti/Cortazzo. EX. $125.00

SHAKESPEARE, William. *Second Quarto.* 1885. London. facsimile. VG. $25.00

SHAKESPEARE, William. *Shakespeare's Heroines.* 1898. London. Bell. Ils. 26 pls. 341 p. VG. $40.00

SHAKESPEARE, William. *Shakespeare's Tragedies.* 1975. Franklin Lib. 640 p. AEG. M. $70.00

SHAKESPEARE, William. *Tempest.* nd. NY. Ils Rackham. J2. $55.00

SHAKESPEARE, William. *Tempest.* 1908. London. Ils Woodroffe. 4to. VG. $30.00

SHAKESPEARE, William. *Venus & Adonis.* 1930. Longman Green. Ils Kutcher. 12 pls. 4to. dj. VG. $35.00

SHAKESPEARE, William. *Works of William Shakespeare.* nd. NY. Virtue Yorston. 55 pls. 2 vols. J2. $100.00

SHAKESPEARE, William. *Works of William Shakespeare.* 1906. NY. Pickering Text. 21 vols. $600.00

SHALHOPE, R.E. *Sterling Price Portrait of S.* 1971. 311 p. dj. M. J4. $20.00

SHALHOPE, R. E. *Sterling Price, Portrait of a Southerner.* 1971. 1st ed. maps. EX. J4. $25.00

SHALLER, G.B. *Deer & Tiger: Study of Wildlife in India.* 1967. Chicago. Ils. 370 p. dj. EX. M2. $25.00

SHANAHAN, William. *Prussian Military Reforms, 1786-1813.* 1945. Columbia. 1st ed. 271 p. wraps. J2. $15.00

SHANKS, Edward. *Edgar Allan Poe.* 1937. Macmillan. 1st ed. dj. VG. D1. $15.00

SHANNON, Dell. *Destiny of Death.* 1984. NY. Morrow. 1st ed. dj. VG. $15.00

SHANNON, Dell. *Extra Kill.* 1962. Morrow. 1st ed. dj. EX. $15.00

SHANNON, K. *History of Isard Co., AR.* 1947. Little Rock. photos. 158 p. VG. M2. $40.00

SHANNON, M. *Boston Days of William Morris Hunt.* 1923. Boston. 41 pls. 8vo. TEG. boxed. EX. J2. $50.00

SHANOWER, Eric. *Enchanted Apples of Oz.* 1986. Chicago. Stated 1st print. 48 p. wraps. M. $20.00

SHAPIRO, David. *John Ashbery: An Introduction to Poetry.* 1979. Columbia U. 1st ed. dj. VG. $22.00

SHAPIRO, H.D. *Confiscation of Confederate Property in the S.* 1962. Ithaca. 58 p. printed wraps. xl. $27.50

SHAPIRO, Karl. *Adult Book Store.* 1976. NY. 1st Am ed. dj. VG. $22.00

SHAPIRO, Karl. *Edsel.* 1971. NY. Geis. 1st print. dj. EX. $25.00

SHAPIRO, Karl. *To Abolish Children.* 1968. Chicago. 1st ed. dj. VG. $25.00

SHAPIRO, S. *Our Changing Fisheries.* 1971. Nat Marine Fish Service. VG. M2. $12.00

SHAPIRO & MASON. *Fine Prints: Collecting, Buying & Selling.* 1976. Harper Row. Ils. 256 p. dj. D2. $24.50

SHAPLEY, H. *Treasury of Science.* 1958. Harper. Revised ed. 776 p. dj. EX. M2. $10.00

SHARKEY, John. *Celtic Mysteries: Ancient Religion.* 1987. reprint. M. C1. $14.00

SHARMAT. *Lancelot Closes at Five.* 1st ed. pb. C1. $3.50

SHARP, C.J. *Country Dance Book. Part 1.* 1909. London. wraps. VG. $10.00

SHARPE, P.B. *Complete Guide to Hand Loading.* 3rd ed. dj. VG. $36.00

SHARPE, R. *Handbook to Birds of Great Britain.* 1897-1897. Lloyd's Nat Hist. 4 vols. VG. M2. $90.00

SHARPE, Tom. *Great Pursuit.* 1977. London. 1st ed. dj. EX. $45.00

SHAVER, Richard. *Furniture Boys Like To Build.* 1940. NY. photos. plans. VG. $15.00

SHAW, Arnold. *Sinatra: 20th-C Romantic.* 1968. Holt Rinehart. 1st ed. 2nd print. dj. VG. $9.50

SHAW, Frank. *Deep Sea Chanties.* 1925. London. Ils Wilson. 4to. G. $18.00

SHAW, G. *General Zoology or Systematic Natural History.* 1800. London. Kearsley. 4 vols. calf bdg. M2. $235.00

SHAW, G.B. *Adventures of Black Girl in Search of God.* 1933. NY. Ils Farleigh. 1st ed. VG. $18.50

SHAW, G.B. *Adventures of Black Girl in Search of God.* 1933. NY. 1st ed. dj. G. $8.50

SHAW, G.B. *Apple Cart.* 1930. Constable. 1st ed. VG. J2. $20.00

SHAW, G.B. *Bernard Shaw Through the Camera.* 1948. London. 238 photos. 128 p. $55.00

SHAW, G.B. *Heartbreak House.* 1919. London. dj. EX. $60.00

SHAW, G.B. *Intelligent Woman's Guide to Socialism & Capitalism.* 1928. NY. 1st Am ed. dj. EX. scarce. $45.00

SHAW, G.B. *John Bull's Other Island & Major Barbara.* 1921. London. Constable. VG. $12.50

SHAW, G.B. *Major Critical Essays.* 1942. London. reprint. $24.00

SHAW, G.B. *On Going to Church.* 1896. Roycroft. 12mo. inscr Hubbard. VG. D1. $60.00

SHAW, G.B. *Quintessence of Ibsenism.* 1905. Brentano. TEG. VG. $15.00

SHAW, G.B. *Sixteen Self-Sketches.* 1949. NY. Ils. dj. VG. $12.00

SHAW, G.B. *St. Joan.* 1924. Constable. 1st ed. dj. boxed. VG. J2. $20.00

SHAW, G.B. *Tales. Told by Gladys Evan Morris.* 1929. London. Ils Trery. 1/200. VG. J2. $225.00

SHAW, G.B. *Two Plays for Puritans.* 1979. Norwalk. Heritage. quarto. slipcase. EX. $15.00

SHAW, Henry. *Dresses & Decorations of the Middle Ages.* 1858. London. Ils. 2 vols. VG. $395.00

SHAW, Henry. *Handbook of Medieval Alphabets & Devices.* 1856. London. VG. $225.00

SHAW, J.B. *Drawings of Domenico Tiepolo.* 1962. London. Faber. Ils. 101 p. dj. D2. $55.00

SHAW, J.B. *Drawings of Francesco Guardi.* 1951. Faber. VG. $35.00

SHAW, R.B. *Down Brakes.* 1961. 487 p. $25.00

SHAW, R.C. *Across the Plains in Forty-Nine.* 1948. Donnelley. Lakeside Classic. A3. $40.00

SHAW, Wilbur. *Gentleman Start Your Engines.* 1955. Coward McCann. 1st ed. VG. J2. $15.00

SHAW & POTAMKIN. *Our Lenin.* 1934. Internat Pub. Ils Siegel. VG. $45.00

SHAW & STEPHENS. *General Zoology or Systematic Natural History.* 1809-1826. Kearsley. 8 vols. EX. M2. $335.00

SHAY, Felix. *Elbert Hubbard of E Aurora.* 1926. NY. Wise. 1st ed. dj. EX. T6. $35.00

SHAY, Felix. *Elbert Hubbard of E Aurora.* 1926. Wise. Ils. 8vo. brown cloth. dj. VG. D1. $25.00

SHAY, J.M. *Out of Body Consciousness.* 1972. NY. $6.00

SHAZAR, Zalman. *Morning Stars.* 1967. Jewish Pub Soc. 8vo. gray cloth. dj. VG. $10.00

SHEA, J.G. *Discovery & Exploration of the MS Valley.* 1852. NY. 268 p. rebound. EX. $50.00

SHEA, J.G. *Discovery & Exploration of the MS Valley.* 1903. Albany. 2nd ed. xl. VG. J2. $35.00

SHEA, Nancy. *WAACS.* 1943. NY. 243 p. VG. T5. $19.50

SHEAHAN & UPTON. *Great Conflagration: Chicago, Its Past, Present & Future.* 1871. Chicago. 1st ed. 8vo. 458 p. scarce. G2. $32.00

SHECTER, L. *Once Upon the Polo Grounds.* 1970. Dial Pr. 1st ed. dj. VG. $7.00

SHEED. *3 Mobs: Labor, Church & Mafia.* 1974. NY. dj. $20.00

SHEEHAN, Fred. *Anzio: Epic of Bravery.* 1964. Norman. Ils 1st ed. sgn. 239 p. dj. G. T5. $22.50

SHEEHAN, P.P. *Abyss of Wonders.* 1953. Reading. 1st ed. dj. slipcase. $45.00

SHEELER, Charles. *Photographs.* 1987. Boston. 4to. 162 p. EX. $23.00

SHEER & RANKIN. *Rebels & Redcoats.* 1972. World. 572 p. dj. EX. M2. $18.00

SHEFFIELD, W.J. *Nilgai Antelope in TX.* 1983. TX A&M U. Ils. M. M2. $15.00

SHEFFY, L.F. *Life & Times of Timothy Dwight Hobart, 1855-1935.* 1950. Canyon, TX. Ils 1st ed. EX. $50.00

SHELDON, Charles. *Wilderness of Denali: Explorations of Hunter-Naturalist.* 1960. Scribner. 412 p. dj. EX. M2. $30.00

SHELDON, Charles. *Wilderness of N Pacific Coast Islands.* 1912. NY. 1st ed. $20.00

SHELDON, Charles. *Wilderness of Upper Yukon.* 1911. 1st ed. TEG. EX. $160.00

SHELDON, H.P. *Tranquility, Regained, Revisited.* 1945. W Hartford. boxed. VG. B2. $140.00

SHELDON, H.P. *Tranquility.* Derrydale. as issued. VG. B2. $140.00

SHELDON, R.L. *Scraps.* 1898. Akron. Werner. 218 p. cloth bdg. T5. $12.50

SHELDON, W.G. *Wilderness Home of the Giant Panda.* 1975. MA U. Ils. 196 p. dj. M. M2. $35.00

SHELDRICK, D. *Animal Kingdom: Story of Tsavo, Great African Game Park.* 1973. Bobbs Merrill. Ils 1st Am ed. dj. EX. M2. $15.00

SHELFORD, V.E. *Color & Color Pattern Mechanism of Tiger Beetles.* 1917. IL U. Ils. 134 p. EX. M2. $18.00

SHELLENBARGER, Samuel. *Token.* 1955. 2nd print. dj. VG. C1. $6.00

SHELLEY, E.M. *Hunting Big Game With Dogs in Africa.* 1924. Columbia. 1st ed. G. $65.00

SHELLEY, H.C. *John Undergill: Captain of New England & New Netherland.* 1932. NY. 1/500. pls. VG. $40.00

SHELLEY, M.W. *Frankenstein.* 1934. Ltd Ed Club. Ils Everett Henry. TEG. dj. EX. $80.00

SHELLEY, M.W. *Frankenstein.* 1983. NY. 1/500. sgn King/Wrightson. slipcase. EX. $180.00

SHELLEY, P.B. *Notebooks.* Edited by H. Buxton Forman. 1911. Boston. Bibliophile Soc. 3 vols. EX. $100.00

SHELLEY, P.B. *Sensitive Plant.* nd. Heinemann. orig gilt vellum. TEG. VG. J2. $250.00

SHELLEY, P.B. *Verse & Prose.* 1934. London. Curwen. 4 pls. $90.00

SHELTON, William. *History of Salmagundi Club As It Appeared in NY Herald...* 1927. private print. 1st ed. sgn. VG. J2. $12.50

SHEMEL & KRASILOVSKY. *This Business of Music.* 1964. Billboard Pub. 1st ed. dj. VG. $15.00

SHENTON, E.H. *Exploring the Ocean Depths: Story of Cousteau Diving Saucer.* 1968. NY. 2nd ed. 205 p. dj. EX. $15.00

SHENTON, J.P. *Reconstruction: Documentary History, 1856-1977.* 1963. NY. Putnam. 1st ed. dj. EX. $26.00

SHEPARD, Ernest. *Doom Pussy.* 1967. Book Club. dj. VG. $15.00

SHEPARD, Ernest. *Drawn From Life.* 1961. London. Methuen. 1st ed. dj. VG. $22.00

SHEPARD, Lucius. *Green Eyes.* 1986. London. 1st Eng ed. sgn. dj. EX. $100.00

SHEPARD, Lucius. *Jaguar Hunter.* 1987. Arkham House. 1st ed. dj. EX. $75.00

SHEPARD, Lucius. *Jaguar Hunter.* 1988. London. 1st ed. sgn. dj. EX. $65.00

SHEPARD, Odell. *Heart of Thoreau's Journals.* 1927. Houghton. 1/333. 8vo. red cloth. VG. G2. $45.00

SHEPARD, Odell. *Lore of the Unicorn.* 1930. Houghton. 1st ed. VG. J2. $30.00

SHEPARD, Odell. *Peddlar's Progress: Life of Bronson Alcott.* 1937. Little Brown. Deluxe Ltd 1st ed. sgn. boxed. J2. $45.00

SHEPARD, Sam. *Rolling Thunder Logbook.* 1977. Viking. dj. EX. $25.00

SHEPHARD, Esther. *Paul Bunyan.* c 1960s. Ils Rockwell Kent. dj. VG. C1. $7.00

SHEPHERD, G. *Silver Magnet: 30 Years in Mexican Silver Mine.* 1938. NY. Ils 1st ed. 302 p. dj. VG. B2. $27.50

SHEPHERD, J. *In God We Trust: All Others Cash.* 1966. NY. 1st ed. dj. VG. B2. $20.00

SHEPHERD, J. *Phantom of the Open Hearth.* 1978. Garden City. 1st ed. photos. 222 p. $27.50

SHEPHERD, M. *Road to Gandolfo.* 1975. NY. 1st ed. 3 djs. EX. $35.00

SHEPHERD, Mrs. E.R. *For Girls, a Special Physiology.* 1893. NY. Ils. 225 p. K1. $12.50

SHEPHERD & ELMES. *Metropolitan Improvements; or, London in 19th C.* 1978. NY. reprint of 1st ed. dj. J2. $15.00

SHEPHERD & JELLICO. *Gardens & Design.* 1927. London/NY. folio. $60.00

SHEPHERD. *Life of Robert E. Lee.* 1906. Neale. VG. $70.00

SHEPPARD, D.O. *Story of Barnesville, OH, 1808-1940.* 1942. Barnesville. inscr. 375 p. VG. T5. $35.00

SHEPPERD. *Pack & Paddock.* Derrydale. as issued. VG. B2. $90.00

SHEPPERSON, W.S. *Emigration & Disenchantment: Portraits of Englishmen...* 1965. OK U. 1st ed. 211 p. dj. EX. M2. $10.00

SHERATON, Thomas. *Complete Furniture Works.* 1946. NY. Towse Pub. lg folio. dj. VG. $150.00

SHERIDAN, P.H. *Outline Descriptions of Posts in Military Division of MO...* 1972. Old Army Pr. reprint of 1876 ed. 264 p. EX. M2. $15.00

SHERIDAN, P.H. *Personal Memoirs of P.H. Sheridan.* 1888. Webster. 2 vols. gilt green cloth. VG. $65.00

SHERIDAN, R.B. *School for Scandal.* nd. NY. Ils Hugh Thomson. J2. $50.00

SHERIDAN & ROSS. *Gargoyles & Grotesques: Paganism in Medieval Church.* 1975. Boston. NY Graphic Soc. Ils 127 p. dj. D2. $35.00

SHERIDAN. *Fall & Rise of Jimmy Hoffa.* 1972. NY. VG. $15.00

SHERLOCK, William. *Practical Discourse Concerning Death.* 1694. London. orig bdg. $350.00

SHERMAN, Allen. *Rape of the Ape.* 1st ed. dj. VG. $25.00

SHERMAN, J.W. *Talkative Table.* 1925. Boston. Ils Wireman. 1st ed. dj. EX. $20.00

SHERMAN, R.B. *Republican Party & Black America From McKinley to Hoover.* 1973. Charlottesville. 274 p. $22.50

SHERMAN, S.C. *Voice of the Whaleman.* 1965. Providence. dj. VG. $20.00

SHERMAN, W.T. *Memoirs.* 1875. NY. 1st ed. pocket map. 2 vols. VG. T5. $75.00

SHERMAN, W.T. *Personal Memoirs of General W.T. Sherman.* 1891. Webster. Ils. 2 vols. gilt green bdg. K1. $38.50

SHERMAN & KENT. *Children's Bible.* 1922. Scribner. Ils Taylor. 1st ed. VG. B4. $45.00

SHERRELL, Carl. *Raum.* 1977. Avon. 1st/only ed. pb. VG. C1. $5.00

SHERWOOD, I.R. *Memories of the War.* 1923. Toledo. 1st ed. presentation. $50.00

SHERWOOD, M. *Big Game in AK: History of Wildlife & People.* 1981. Yale. Ils. 200 p. dj. EX. M2. $30.00

SHERWOOD, M.B. *Pilgrim: William Brewster, a Biography.* 1982. VA. Ils 1st ed. sgn. dj. EX. T1. $22.00

SHERWOOD, Mrs. *Manners & Social Usages.* 1884. 495 p. K1. $9.50

SHERWOOD, R. *Roosevelt & Hopkins.* 1948. NY. 1st ed. EX. $15.00

SHERWOOD, R.E. *Petrified Forest: A Play.* 1935. Scribner. 1st ed. dj. EX. $15.00

SHIBER, Etta. *Paris Underground.* 1943. Scribner. 1st ed. dj. M1. $6.50

SHIELDS, G.O. *Big Game of N America.* 1890. Chicago. 1st ed. VG. $50.00

SHIELDS, J.W. Jr. *From Flintlock to M1.* 1954. NY. Ils 1st ed. 220 p. dj. VG. T5. $35.00

SHILO-COHEN. *Bezalel, 1906-1929.* 1983. Israel Mus. dj. EX. $200.00

SHINE, M.A. *NE Aborigines As They Appeared in the 18th C.* 1913. NE Acad Sc. 2 pls. 23 p. M2. $3.00

SHINGLETON, R.G. *John Taylor Wood: Sea Ghost of the Confederacy.* 1982. GA U. Ils. 242 p. dj. EX. M2. $20.00

SHINN, C.H. *Economic Study of Acacias.* 1913. USDA. 38 p. M2. $3.00

SHINN, C.H. *Mining Camps: Study in American Frontier Government.* 1885. NY. 1st ed. xl. $30.00

SHINN, E.H. *Memoirs of Dr. Erwin H. Shinn.* c 1964?. private print. presentation. M2. $10.00

SHINN, J.H. *Pioneers & Makers of AR.* reprint of 1908 ed. EX. M2. $30.00

SHINNO, Tat. *Flower Arrangements To Copy.* 1966. Doubleday. Ils 1st ed. 246 p. dj. EX. $25.00

SHIPHERD, Jacob. *History of Oberlin-Wellington Rescue.* 1859. Boston. tall 8vo. $125.00

SHIPPEN. *This Union Cause: Growth of Organized Labor in America.* 1958. dj. VG. $20.00

SHIRAS, George. *Hunting Wildlife With Camera & Flashlight.* 1935. Nat Geog Soc. 2 vols. EX. $32.50

SHIRER, W.L. *Berlin Diary, 1934-1941.* 1941. NY. 1st ed. VG. $15.00

SHIRER, W.L. *Berlin Diary, 1934-1941.* 1941. NY. 1st ed. 605 p. dj. M. $45.00

SHIRLEY, Glen. *Belle Starr & Her Times: Literature, Facts & Legends.* 1982. OK U. Ils 1st ed. sgn, 324 p. dj. M2. $25.00

SHIRLEY, Glen. *Buckskin & Spurs: Gallery of Frontier Rogues & Heroes.* 1958. Hastings. 1st ed. dj. EX. $15.00

SHIRLEY, Glen. *Heck Thomas: Frontier Marshal.* 1981. OK U. 1st print. 285 p. dj. EX. M2. $25.00

SHIRLEY, Glen. *Henry Starr: Last of the Real Badmen.* 1965. McKay. Ils 1st ed. 208 p. dj. EX. M2. $30.00

SHIRLEY, J.C. *Redwoods of Coast & Sierra.* 1938. CA U. Ils. map. 84 p. EX. M2. $4.00

SHISHKIN, K.B. *Floral Regions of the USSR. Vol. 19. Tubiflora.* 1974. Keter. Ils. fld maps. 556 p. EX. M2. $25.00

SHOEMAKER, M.M. *Great Siberian Railway.* 1903. NY. fld map. 243 p. fair. T5. $12.50

SHOENER. *Harlem on My Mind.* 1968. Random House. 1st ed. dj. VG. $45.00

SHOENFELD, A.H. *Joy Peddler.* 1927. NY. Penuel. 1/1285. sgn. $35.00

SHOJI & JOHNSON. *Japanese Principles of Design in Flower Arrangement.* 1950. Seattle. Ils. sgn Shoji. $35.00

SHOLOKHOV, Mikhail. *Virgin Soil Upturned.* c 1960. Moscow. 1st ed. 2 vols. dj. EX. $40.00

SHOR, E.N. *Fossils & Flies: Life of Samuel Wendell Williston.* 1971. OK U. Ils 1st ed. 285 p. dj. EX. M2. $22.00

SHORE, C. *With British Snipers.* 1948. Gerogetown, SC. Ils 1st ed. 351 p. dj. VG. B2. $60.00

SHORT, Anita. *Water Street Cemetery.* 1972. Greeneville. 16 p. wraps. VG. T5. $9.50

SHORT, C.B. *Ronald Reagan & the Public Lands.* 1989. TX A&M U. 1st ed. 178 p. M. M2. $8.00

SHORT, H.L. *Deer in AZ & NM: Ecology & Theory Explaining Population.* 1979. USFS. 25 p. M2. $3.00

SHORT, L.L. *Habits of Some Asian Woodpeckers (Aves, Picidae).* 1973. Am Mus Nat Hist. Ils. EX. M2. $25.00

SHORT, L.L. *Review of the Genera of Grouse.* 1967. Am Mus Nat Hist. 39 p. M2. $3.00

SHORT, Wayne. *Cheechakos.* 1964. Random House. Ils 1st ed. dj. EX. M2. $12.00

SHORT & STANLEY-BROWN. *Public Buildings: Survey of Architecture of Projects...* 1939. WA. J2. $125.00

SHORTT & CARTWRIGHT. *Treasury of Waterfowl.* 1957. Prentice Hall. Ils. folio. dj. EX. M2. $38.00

SHORTT & DOUGHTY. *Canada & Its Provinces.* 1914-1917. Edinburgh. 1/875. 23 vols. morocco. $1100.00

SHOSTAKOVICH, Dmitri. *Russian Symphony: Thoughts About Tchaikovsky.* 1947. Phil. 1st ed. dj. J2. $12.50

SHOTT, John. *Railroad Monopoly. Instrument of Banker Control...* 1950. WA. Public Affairs Inst. $10.00

SHUFELDT, R.W. *Scientific Taxidermy for Museums.* 1894. US Nat Mus. pls. wraps. EX. $25.00

SHULL, A.F. *Evolution.* 1936. McGraw Hill. Ils. 302 p. M2. $12.00

SHULMAN, Harry. *Slums of NY.* 1938. Boni. 1st ed. VG. J2. $20.00

SHULTHESS, E. *Africa.* 1959. 1st ed. dj. VG. $25.00

SHUMWAY & BROWER. *Oberliniana.* nd. Cleveland. 175 p. xl. G. T5. $22.50

SHUNAMI. *Bibliography of Jewish Bibliographys.* 1969. Jerusalem. EX. $30.00

SHURTLEFF, Harold. *Log Cabin Myth.* 1939. Harvard. 1st ed. J2. $40.00

SHURTLEFF, J.B. *Governmental Instructor.* 1847. NY. 189 p. orig bdg. K1. $9.50

SHURTLEFF, M. *Topographical & Historical Description of Boston.* 1871. Boston. fld map. $37.50

SHUTE, Henry. *Real Diary of a Real Boy.* 1904. Everett. $12.00

SHUTE, Nevil. *No Highway.* 1948. NY. 1st Am ed. dj. VG. $40.00

SHUTE, Nevil. *On the Beach.* 1957. Melbourne. Heinemann. red cloth. dj. EX. J2. $150.00

SHUTE, Nevil. *Round the Bend.* 1951. London. 1st ed. dj. VG. $40.00

SHUTE, Nevil. *Slide Rule.* 1954. Morrow. 1st ed. dj. VG. $30.00

SHUTE, Nevil. *Vinland the Good.* 1946. NY. 1st ed. dj. VG. B2. $27.50

SHUTES, M.H. *Lincoln & the Doctors.* 1933. Pioneer. 1/550. sgn. VG. $80.00

SIBLEY, Celestine. *Place Called Sweet Apple.* 1967. NY. dj. VG. $25.00

SIBLEY, Frank. *All by Wire.* 1905. Luce. G. $25.00

SIBLEY & WESTERMANN. *Liberia: Old & New, a Study of Social & Economic....*nd. London. Ils. 317 p. fair. T5. $22.50

SIBLIK, Jiri. *Drawings & Watercolors: Cezanne.* 1984. St. Paul. 3M Books. Ils. dj. D2. $95.00

SICKELS, Daniel. *Freemason's Monitor.* 1868. NY. Ils. AEG. leather. VG. $25.00

SIDGEWICK, J.B. *Heavens Above: Rationale of Astronomy.* 1950. NY. 1st Am ed. dj. VG. $12.00

SIDNEY, Margaret. *Five Little Peppers & How They Grew.* 1948. Grosset Dunlap. Ils Sharp. VG. B4. $20.00

SIDNEY, Margaret. *Five Little Peppers at Midway.* nd. Boston. VG. $7.00

SIDNEY, Margaret. *Five Little Peppers: Stories Polly Pepper Told.* 1899. Lee Shepard. Ils. G. $15.00

SIEFF, Jeanloup. *Jeanloup Sieff.* 1982. Prentice Hall. Ils. 63 p. printed wraps. $12.50

SIEGEL, Marcia. *Shapes of Change: Images of American Dance.* 1979. Houghton. 1st ed. dj. J2. $10.00

SIEGLER, H.R. *NH Nature Notes.* 1962. Equity. Ils. dj. EX. M2. $23.00

SIEGLER, Samuel. *Fertility in Women.* 1944. Phil. Lippincott. dj. VG. $20.00

SIEMEL, S. *Tigrero!* 1953. NY. photos. 266 p. VG. $10.00

SIENKIEWICZ. *Quo Vadis.* 1897. Boston. G. $13.00

SIEVERT, G.L. *Field Guide to Reptiles of OK.* c 1987. OK Wildlife Dept. 96 p. M2. $7.00

SIGAUD, L.A. *Air Power & Unification.* 1949. Harrisburg. 1st ed. 119 p. dj. G. T5. $27.50

SIGEL, G.A. *Germany's Army & Navy by Pen & Picture.* 1900. Akron. Werner. 41 pls. folio. J2. $350.00

SIGLER & MILLER. *Fishes of UT.* 1963. UT Fish/Game. Ils. 203 p. EX. M2. $13.00

SIGOURNEY, L.H. *Noble Deeds of American Women: Biographical Sketches...* 1851. Buffalo. Derby. 480 p. xl. poor. $45.00

SIKORSKY, I.I. *Story of Winged-S, an Autobiography.* 1942. NY. Ils. 275 p. G. T5. $45.00

SILL, E.R. *Hemione & Other Poems.* 1899. Boston/NY. 1st ed. 109 p. T5. $22.50

SILL, E.R. *Poems of Edward Roland Sill.* 1902. Cambridge. Riverside Pr. 1/500. 327 p. VG. T5. $65.00

SILL, E.R. *Poems.* 1887. Boston/NY. later ed. 112 p. cloth. VG. T5. $8.50

SILL, E.R. *Prose of Edward Roland Sill.* 1900. Boston/NY. later ed. 349 p. T5. $8.50

SILL, E.R. *What Happens at Death.* 1897. London. $15.00

SILLCOX, L.K. *Mastering Momentum.* 1955. 2nd ed. 242 p. $30.00

SILLMAN & GOODRICH. *World of Science, Art & Industry Illustrated.* 1854. NY. folio. VG. $200.00

SILLS, Beverly. *Bubbles.* 1976. Bobbs Merrill. 1st ed. 1st issue. dj. M. $48.00

SILLS, Beverly. *Bubbles.* 1976. Bobbs Merrill. 1st ed. 2nd print. dj. M. $30.00

SILLWELL, J.E. *Historical & Genealogical Miscellany Data...* 1970. Baltimore. 2nd print. 5 vols. EX. T1. $100.00

SILVER, Nathan. *Lost NY.* 1967. np. 2nd print. dj. EX. J2. $20.00

SILVERBERG, Robert. *Explorers of Space.* 1975. Nashville. 1st ed. dj. VG. $15.00

SIMAK, Clifford. *Fellowship of the Talisman.* nd. Book Club. C1. $4.00

SIMCA. *Owner's Complete Handbook of Repair & Maintence.* 1960. Los Angeles. pb. VG. $10.00

SIMENON. *Inspector Maigret & Killers.* 1954. NY. 1st ed. dj. VG. $20.00

SIMIC, Charles. *Nine Poems.* 1989. Exact Change. 1/300. sgn. folio. wraps. EX. $40.00

SIMIC, Charles. *Somewhere Among Us a Stone Is Taking Notes.* 1969. San Francisco. Hitchcock. sgn. $75.00

SIMIC, Charles. *What the Grass Says.* 1967. San Francisco. Kayak. 1/1000. wraps. EX. $55.00

SIMKINS, F.B. *S: Old & New, History 1820-1947.* 1947. NY. Ils 1st ed. sgn. dj. VG. $45.00

SIMMONS, H.E. *Concise Encyclopedia of the Civil War.* 1965. 221 p. dj. EX. J4. $5.00

SIMMONS, M.H. *Growing Acacias.* 1987. Kangaroo Pr. Ils 1st ed. EX. M2. $10.00

SIMMONS, Marc. *Turquoise Six-Guns. Story of Cerrillos, NM.* 1968. Galisteo Pr. Ils. VG. $15.00

SIMMS, E. *Natural History of British Birds.* 1983. London. Dent. Ils 1st ed. 367 p. dj. EX. M2. $12.00

SIMMS, F.W. *Practical Tunnelling.* 1860. London. EX. $14.00

SIMMS, J.M. *Story of My Life.* 1884. NY. Appleton. 1st ed. 471 p. $57.50

SIMMS, J.M. *Story of My Life.* 1886. NY. Appleton. 471 p. xl. $27.50

SIMMS, P.M. *Bible in America.* 1936. NY. 394 p. dj. VG. $45.00

SIMMS, W.G. *History of SC From Its First European Discovery to Present.* 1860. NY. Redfield. New Revised ed. 437 p. $85.00

SIMMS, W.G. *Tale of the Revolution.* 1882. NY. Armstrong. Ils Darley. xl. $20.00

SIMON, A.L. *Bottlescrew Days.* 1927. Small Maynard. 1st ed. EX. T5. $150.00

SIMON, Hilda. *Chameleons & Other Quick-Change Artists.* 1973. Dodd Mead. Ils. 157 p. dj. EX. M2. $13.00

SIMON, Hilda. *Date Palm: Bread of the Desert.* 1978. Dodd Mead. Ils 1st ed. dj. EX. M2. $20.00

SIMON, Hilda. *Snails of Land & Sea.* 1976. Vanguard. Ils. 143 p. dj. EX. M2. $10.00

SIMON, Hilda. *Splendor of Iridescence: Structural Colors in Animal World.* 1971. Dodd Mead. Ils. 4to. 268 p. dj. M2. $18.00

SIMON, Hilda. *Splendor of Iridescence: Structural Colors in Animal World.* 1971. Dodd Mead. 1st ed. dj. J2. $20.00

SIMON, R.L. *Big Fix.* 1974. London. 1st HrdCvr ed. sgn. VG. $45.00

SIMON, W. *Manual of Chemistry.* 1901. Ils. 613 p. VG. $5.00

SIMON & GEROUDET. *Last Survivors: Natural History of 48 Animals.* 1970. World. 44 color pls. 275 p. EX. M2. $20.00

SIMON. *Bibliotheca Bacchica.* 1972. London. Ils. dj. EX. $50.00

SIMONDS, William. *Henry Ford.* 1943. Bobbs Merrill. 1st ed. J2. $12.50

SIMPSON, E. *Maze.* 1975. NY. 1st ed. dj. EX. $25.00

SIMPSON, E.B. *Robert Louis Stevenson Originals.* 1913. NY. Ils 1st Am ed. 213 p. G. T5. $37.50

SIMPSON, Edward. *Yarnlets: Human Side of Navy.* 1934. 1st ed. VG. $15.00

SIMPSON, G.G. *Concession to Improbable: Unconventional Biography.* 1978. Yale. Ils. 291 p. dj. EX. M2. $22.00

SIMPSON, G.G. *Life of the Past: Introduction to Paleontology.* 1953. Yale. 198 p. EX. M2. $18.00

SIMPSON, G.G. *Penguins: Past & Present, Here & There.* 1976. Yale. Ils. map. 150 p. EX. M2. $9.00

SIMPSON, G.G. *Principles of Animal Taxonomy.* 1961. Columbia U. Ils. 247 p. EX. M2. $30.00

SIMPSON, G.G. *Tempo & Mode in Evolution.* 1949. Colombia U. Ils. 237 p. M2. $25.00

SIMPSON, G.L. *Cokers of Carolina, Social Biography of a Family.* 1956. Chapel Hill. 1st ed. map. 327 p. $37.50

SIMPSON, J.C. *Horse Portraiture.* 1868. NY. gilt bdg. VG. $40.00

SIMPSON, M.A. *Dying, Death & Grief: Critical Bibliography.* 1987. Pittsburgh. 259 p. VG. T5. $9.50

SIMPSON, Marc. *Winslow Homer: Paintings of the Civil War.* 1988. San Francisco. dj. EX. $35.00

SIMPSON, N.F. *Some Tall Tinkles.* 1968. London. 1st ed. 100 p. dj. VG. $25.00

SIMPSON & DAY. *Birds of Australia.* 1986. Tanager. 128 color pls. 352 p. dj. EX. M2. $55.00

SIMS, D.R. *Curiouser & Curiouser.* 1940. Simon Schuster. 1st ed. 204 p. dj. M1. $15.00

SIMS, George. *End of the Web.* 1976. NY. 1st ed. dj. EX. $10.00

SIMS, O.L. *Cowpokes, Nesters, & So Forth.* 1970. Austin. Ils 1st ed. dj. EX. $35.00

SIMS, O.L. *Gun Toters I Have Known.* 1967. Austin. Ils 1st ed. 1/750. sgn. EX. $50.00

SIMS, Patoy. *Klan.* 1978. photos. dj. M. J4. $18.50

SIMS. *Fighter Pilots: Comparison of RAF, USAAF & Luftwaffe.* 1967. London. 1st ed. $12.00

SINATRA, Nancy. *Frank Sinatra, My Father.* 1985. Doubleday. 1st ed. dj. M. $20.00

SINCLAIR, A. *Two Years on the AL.* 1895. Boston. Lee Shepard. Ils. G. R1. $250.00

SINCLAIR, Donald. *Bibliography: Civil War & NJ.* 1968. New Brunswick. Rutgers. Ltd ed. dj. M. $40.00

SINCLAIR, Jo. *Wasteland.* 1946. Harper. 3rd ed. 12mo. dj. G. $7.50

SINCLAIR, Upton. *American Outpost.* 1932. NY. sgn. G. $35.00

SINCLAIR, Upton. *American Outpost.* 1948. Girard. wraps. $15.00

SINCLAIR, Upton. *Autobiography.* 1962. 1st ed. dj. VG. $25.00

SINCLAIR, Upton. *Boston: A Novel.* 1928. NY. 1st ed. 2nd print. VG. $40.00

SINCLAIR, Upton. *Brass Check.* nd. Pasadena. 2nd ed. VG. $20.00

SINCLAIR, Upton. *Captain of Industry.* 1906. G. $30.00

SINCLAIR, Upton. *Goslings.* 1924. Pasadena. 1st ed. EX. $15.00

SINCLAIR, Upton. *I, Candidate for Governor.* 1934. LA. wraps. VG. $25.00

SINCLAIR, Upton. *Jungle.* 1965. Baltimore. Ils/sgn Martin. sgn Sinclair. dj. $100.00

SINCLAIR, Upton. *My Lifetime in Letters.* 1960. Columbia. dj. VG. $25.00

SINCLAIR, Upton. *No Parsaran!* 1937. Pasadena. pb. printed wraps. EX. $25.00

SINCLAIR, Upton. *Oil!* 1927. Grosset Dunlap. VG. $8.50

SINCLAIR, Upton. *Profits of Religion.* nd. Sinclair. sgn Frazer Hunt. $25.00

SINCLAIR, Upton. *Profits of Religion.* 1918. Pasadena. gilt brown cloth. VG. $10.00

SINCLAIR, Upton. *So Macht Man Dollars.* 1931. Berlin. Ils Heartfield. 1st German ed. dj. $175.00

SINCLAIR, Upton. *Upton Sinclair Anthology.* 1947. Culver City. dj. EX. $45.00

SINDEREN, Blake. *Mystic Genius.* 1949. Syracuse. Ils. dj. EX. $20.00

SINGER, Charles. *History of Biology.* 1950. Schuman. Ils. 579 p. EX. M2. $18.00

SINGER, Charles. *History of Technology.* 1954-1958. Oxford. 5 vols. djs. EX. $100.00

SINGER, I.B. *Gentleman From Cracow.* nd. Mirror. Ils/sgn Soyer. 1/2000. dj. EX. $115.00

SINGER, I.B. *Magician of Lublin.* Ltd Ed Club. slipcase. M. B3. $225.00

SINGER, I.B. *Pentitent.* 1983. Franklin Lib. 1st ed. sgn. AEG. full leather. $40.00

SINGER, I.B. *Shosha.* 1978. NY. 1st ed. dj. VG. $15.00

SINGER, I.B. *Two Stories.* Ltd Ed Club. slipcase. M. B3. $65.00

SINGER, Isidor. *Religion of Truth. Justice & Peace.* 1924. NY. Amos Soc. 1st ed. G. $5.00

SINGLETARY, O.A. *Negro Militia & Reconstruction.* 1957. Austin. 1st ed. dj. EX. $40.00

SINGLETON, Esther. *Story of the White House.* 1907. Ils. 2 vols. gilt blue bdg. K1. $18.50

SINGLETON, M.K. *H.L. Mencken & American Mercury Adventure.* 1962. Durham. 1st ed. green wraps. M. $20.00

SINGMASTER, Elsie. *Gettysburg Stories of Red Harvest & Aftermath.* 1913. Boston. Ils Steele/Chambers. dj. EX. $55.00

SINGULAR, Stephen. *Talked to Death: Life & Murder of Alan Berg.* nd. NY. M. $10.00

SINISTRARI, L.M. *Demoniality.* 1927. London. Ltd ed. 127 p. $125.00

SINSABAUGH, Chris. *Who, Me? Forty Years of Automobile History.* 1940. Detroit. 1st ed. inscr. 377 p. dj. G. T5. $65.00

SIRINGO, C.A. *Riata & Spurs.* 1927. Houghton. 1st ed. 1st issue. photos. $65.00

SIRINGO, C.A. *TX Cowboy; or, Fifteen Years on Hurricane Deck...* 1980. Time Life. reprint of 1885 ed. 316 p. EX. M2. $20.00

SITGREAVES, Lorenzo. *Report of Expedition Down Zuni & CO Rivers.* 1853. WA. Ils 1st ed. 198 p. $350.00

SITTS, P.E. *Glad Season.* 1967. Dutton. 240 p. dj. M1. $6.50

SITWELL, Edith. *Canticle of the Rose: Poems, 1917-1949.* 1949. NY. 1st ed. dj. EX. $35.00

SITWELL, Edith. *English Women.* 1932. Britain in Pictures. 1st ed. C1. $8.00

SITWELL, Edith. *Song of the Cold.* 1948. Vanguard. 1st ed. dj. $20.00

SITWELL, Hart. *Old Soggy No. 1.* 1954. NY. 1st ed. 249 p. dj. VG. B2. $47.50

SITWELL, N. *Wildlife '74: World of Conservation Yearbook.* 1974. Dansbury. Ils. 4to. 143 p. VG. M2. $11.00

SITWELL, Osbert. *Left Hand, Right Hand.* 1946. London. $8.00

SITWELL, Osbert. *Tales My Father Taught Me.* 1962. Hutchinson. 1st ed. dj. EX. $20.00

SITWELL, Sacheverell. *British Architects & Craftsmen: Survey of Taste, Design...* 1946. NY. dj. J2. $25.00

SITWELL, Sacheverell. *Conversation Pieces.* 1936. London. Ils. 8vo. 119 p. dj. EX. J2. $50.00

SITWELL, Sacheverell. *German Baroque Art.* 1928. NY. G. $20.00

SITWELL, Sacheverell. *Great Houses of Europe.* 1961. NY. dj. VG. J2. $20.00

SITWELL, Sacheverell. *Narrative Pictures.* 1937. London. 133 pls. 8vo. 122 p. dj. EX. J2. $50.00

SITWELL, Sacheverell. *S Baroque Art.* 1924. London. Ils. G. $25.00

SITWELL & PIPER. *On the Making of Gardens.* 1949. Dropmore. 1/1000. sgns. gilt green bdg. EX. $255.00

SIVANANDA, S.S. *Towering Satin of the Himalayas.* 1955. India. $18.00

SIWUNDHAL, Alice. *Autobiography of Princess Alice Siwundhal.* 1955. Mountain View. Ils. $8.50

SKEAVINGTON, George. *Modern System of Farriery.* nd. London. London Pub. 4to. morocco. J2. $175.00

SKELETON, J. *Plea for the Botanic Practice of Medicine.* 1853. London. Watson. 278 p. EX. M2. $90.00

SKELTON, C.L. *Riding W on the Pony Express.* 1942. Ils Paul Quin. 196 p. $12.00

SKELTON, John. *Ballade of the Scottysshe Kynge.* 1882. London. Elliot Stock. 96 p. VG. $45.00

SKELTON, MARSTON & PAINTER. *Vinland Map & the Tartar Relation.* 1965. New Haven. 289 p. dj. VG. T5. $19.50

SKELTON, R. *Decorative Printed Maps of 15th to 16th C.* 1952. London. 1st ed. $85.00

SKENE. *Treatise on Diseases in Women.* 1888. NY. Ils 1st ed. 9 pls. scarce. $75.00

SKIDMORE, H. *I Will Lift Up Mine Eyes.* 1936. Garden City. 1st ed. dj. EX. $40.00

SKIFF, F.W. *Adventures in Americana.* 1935. Portland. Ltd ed. sgn. VG. $40.00

SKINNER, B.F. *Walden Two.* 1948. NY. 1st ed. dj. EX. $30.00

SKINNER, J.S. *Dog & the Sportsman.* 1845. Phil. 1st ed. orig bdg. VG. rare. $250.00

SKINNER, M.P. *Bears in the Yellowstone.* 1925. Chicago. Ils 1st ed. VG. $20.00

SKINNER, M.P. *Birds of Yellowstone National Park.* 1925. Roosevelt Wildlife Bull. EX. M2. $10.00

SKINNER & SKINNER. *Child's Book of Country Stories.* 1935. Dial. Ils Smith. VG. $45.00

SKIPWITH, P. *Great Bird Illustrators & Their Art 1730-1930.* 1979. 65 color pls. 1st Am ed. 4to. dj. EX. M2. $45.00

SKOTTOWE, Augustine. *Life of Shakespeare.* 1824. London. 2 vols. scarce. $65.00

SKREBNESKI, Victor. *Five Beautiful Women.* 1987. Boston. 1st ed. sgn. dj. EX. $65.00

SKUTCH, A.F. *Bird Watcher's Adventures in Tropical America.* 1977. TX U. Ils Gardner, 327 p. dj. EX. M2. $20.00

SKUTCH, A.F. *Birds of Tropical America.* 1983. TX U. Ils 1st ed. 305 p. dj. EX. M2. $29.00

SKUTCH, A.F. *Life History of the Quetzal.* 1946. Smithsonian. later paper cover. M2. $5.00

SKUTCH, A.F. *Life of the Woodpecker.* 1985. Ibis. Ils. 4to. 136 p. dj. EX. M2. $45.00

SKUTCH, A.F. *Naturalist Amid Tropical Splendor.* 1987. IA U. Ils Gardner. 1st ed. 232 p. dj. M2. $25.00

SLACK, A. *Insect-Eating Plants & How To Grow Them.* 1988. WA U. 64 photos. 172 p. M. M2. $20.00

SLADE, Styne. *Darker Brother: Photography of James A. Warner.* 1974. NY. 1st ed. 1/8000. 4to. dj. EX. $24.00

SLATER, Michael. *Catalog of Suzannet-Charles Dickens` Collection.* 1975. London. dj. EX. $55.00

SLATKIN, Wendy. *Aristide Maillol in the 1890s.* 1982. Ann Arbor. Ils. 165 p. D2. $45.00

SLAUGHTER, F.C. *Flight From Natchez.* 1955. Doubleday. Book Club ed. 284 p. $7.50

SLAUGHTER, F.C. *Flight From Natchez.* 1955. Doubleday. 1st ed. 284 p. xl. $6.50

SLAUGHTER & WALTON. *About Bats: Chiropteran Symposium.* 1970. S Methodist U. Ils. 339 p. dj. EX. M2. $20.00

SLAUSON, H.W. *Everyman's Guide to Motor Efficiency.* 1927. Ils 393 p. VG. $10.00

SLESSER, M. *Red Peak.* 1964. NY. dj. VG. $15.00

SLESSOR, John. *Central Blue.* 1957. Praeger. Ils. 709 p. dj. $30.00

SLEZAK, Walter. *What Time's the Next Swan?* 1962. NY. 1st ed. sgn. dj. VG. $30.00

SLOAN, John. *Gist of Art.* 1939. NY. G. $20.00

SLOAN, John. *Gist of Art.* 1944. dj. VG. $10.00

SLOAN, John. *John Sloan's NY Scene: Diaries 1906-1913.* 1965. Harper Row. 1st ed. dj. VG. $35.00

SLOAN, R.E. *Rainbow Route.* 1975. Denver. Sundance. 1st ed. 2nd print. A3. $65.00

SLOANE, Eric. *American Barns & Covered Bridges.* c 1956. Funk Wagnall. dj. EX. $25.00

SLOANE, Eric. *American Yesterday.* c 1955. Funk Wagnall. dj. EX. $25.00

SLOANE, Eric. *Do's & Dont's of Yesterday.* 1972. Walker. 1st ed. 12mo. boxed. M. $17.50

SLOANE, Eric. *Eric Sloane's Weather Book.* 1974. NY. dj. EX. $25.00

SLOANE, Eric. *Folklore of American Weather.* 1963. NY. 1st ed. dj. VG. B2. $20.00

SLOANE, Eric. *Legacy.* 1979. NY. dj. EX. $25.00

SLOANE, Eric. *Little Red Schoolhouse.* 1972. NY. dj. VG. $18.00

SLOANE, Eric. *Seasons of America's Past.* 1958. NY. sgn. dj. EX. with sgn drawing. $85.00

SLOANE, Eric. *Spirits of `76.* 1973. NY. 1st ed. dj. VG. $15.00

SLOANE, Eric. *Vanishing Landscape.* c 1954. Funk Wagnall. dj. EX. $25.00

SLOANE, F.A. *Maverick in Mauve.* 1983. Garden City. 1st ed. inscr. dj. EX. $35.00

SLOANE, W.M. *Life of Napoleon Bonaparte.* 1909. NY. Ils. 4 vols. VG. $135.00

SLOANE, William. *Edge of Running Water.* 1945. Cleveland. reprint. inscr. 255 p. dj. G. T5. $12.50

SLOCUM, Joshua. *Sailing Alone Around the World.* 1985. Naval Inst. EX. $10.00

SLOCUM, R.B. *Biographical Dictionaries & Related Works.* 1986. Gale Research. 2nd ed. 2 vols. VG. T5. $45.00

SLOSSON, A.T. *Fishin` Jimmie.* 1898. NY. Ils Stephens. 3rd ed. 12mo. VG. $30.00

SLOSSON, A.T. *Heresy of Mehetabel Clark.* 1893. Harper. 1st ed. $12.00

SMAKOV, G. *Baryshnikov: From Russia to the W.* 1981. Farrar Straus. 1st ed. dj. EX. $50.00

SMALL, A. *Birds of CA.* 1974. Winchester. Ils. 310 p. dj. EX. M2. $30.00

SMALL, A.E. *Manual of Momoeopathic Practice.* 1857. Phil. 5th ed. VG. $55.00

SMALL, G.L. *Blue Whale.* 1971. Columbia U. Ils. 248 p. dj. EX. M2. $14.00

SMART, P. *International Butterfly Book.* 1975. Crowell. Ils. 4to. 275 p. dj. EX. M2. $30.00

SMEETON, D.D. *English Religion 1500-1540: Bibliography.* 1988. Mercer U. 115 p. VG. T5. $9.50

SMILES, Samuel. *Character, Conduct & Perserverance.* c 1860. 447 p. K1. $9.50

SMILEY, Jane. *Greenlanders.* 1988. NY. ARC. dj. $30.00

SMILEY, Jerome. *History of Denver With Outlines of Earlier History...* 1971. Unigraphic. reprint of 1901 ed. VG. A3. $90.00

SMIS, Richard. *Handbook to Library of British Museum.* 1854. London. morocco. $65.00

SMITH, A. *Jambo: African Balloon Safari.* 1963. Dutton. Ils 1st ed. 272 p. dj. EX. M2. $10.00

SMITH, A.H. *Field Guide to W Mushrooms.* 1975. MI U. color pls. 280 p. EX. M2. $10.00

SMITH, A.H. *How To Know the Gilled Mushrooms.* 1979. Brown. Ils. 334 p. EX. M2. $15.00

SMITH, A.H. *Mushroom Hunter's Field Guide.* 1969. MI U. Revised Enlarged ed. 264 p. EX. M2. $10.00

SMITH, A.J. *Men Against Mountains.* 1965. NY. Day. 1st ed. dj. VG. $16.00

SMITH, A.R.H. *Appreciation on Occasion of Her 80th Birthday...* 1956. Charleston. private print. 1/800. 59 p. $35.00

SMITH, A.R.H. *Dwelling Houses of Charleston...* 1917. Lippincott. Ils Simons. 1st ed. $135.00

SMITH, A.W. *New Theory of Evolution.* 1961. Abbey Pr. 8vo. gray cloth. G. $7.50

SMITH, Aaron. *Atrocities of Pirates.* 1929. Golden Cockerel. Ils Ravilious. VG. $75.00

SMITH, Abbie. *Bobtail Dixie.* 1902. Ils 4th ed. G. $14.00

SMITH, Adam. *Catalog of the Library of Adam Smith.* 1894. London. 1st ed. sgn Francis Wilson. $85.00

SMITH, Alexander. *Dreamthrop.* 1934. Oxford. VG. C1. $6.00

SMITH, Alexander. *General History of Lives & Robberies of Highwaymen.* nd. NY. Ils Hayward. dj. J2. $50.00

SMITH, Alolphe. *Street Life in London.* 1969. NY. Blom. reprint of 1877 ed. VG. $12.00

SMITH, Betty. *Tree Grows in Brooklyn.* 1943. Blakiston. 376 p. $35.00

SMITH, Bradley. *Japan: History in Art.* 1964. NY. 1st ed. 295 p. dj. VG. B2. $40.00

SMITH, C.A. *Edgar A. Poe: How To Know Him.* 1921. Garden City. 1st ed. brown cloth. dj. VG. D1. $20.00

SMITH, C.A. *Effects of Predation on Black-Tailed Deer Population Growth.* 1986. AK Fish/Game. 24 p. M2. $4.00

SMITH, C.A. *Lost Worlds.* 1944. Arkham House. 1st ed. dj. G. $45.00

SMITH, C.A. *O. Henry Biography.* 1916. Doubleday Page. Ils. 257 p. $45.00

SMITH, C.A. *Out of Space & Time.* 1942. Arkham House. 1st ed. EX. $55.00

SMITH, C.A. *Out of Space & Time.* 1942. Arkham House. 1st ed. inscr/sgn. dj. VG. $85.00

SMITH, C.G. *TNT & Other Nitros.* 1918. Van Nostrand. 8 vols. black cloth. G. $5.00

SMITH, C.H. *Natural History of the Human Species.* ca 1840s. 44 pls. 464 p. VG. M2. $20.00

SMITH, D. *Martyrs of the Oblong & the Little Nine.* 1948. Caldwell. EX. $40.00

SMITH, D.E.H. *Charlestonian's Recollections, 1846-1913.* 1950. Charleston. Carolina Art Assn. 1st ed. $27.50

SMITH, D.L. *Aucassin & Nicolete.* 1914. London. pls. 4to. slipcase. EX. $40.00

SMITH, D.V. *Chase & Civil War Politics.* 1931. Columbus. 181 p. VG. T5. $25.00

SMITH, Dave. *Onliness.* 1981. Baton Rouge. 1st ed. sgn. dj. EX. $20.00

SMITH, E. *Incidents of the US Christian Commission.* 1869. Phil. Ils. index. 512 p. scarce. K1. $27.50

SMITH, E.B. *Egyptian Architecture As Cultural Expression.* 1938. Ils 1st ed. 4to. 264 p. B1. $20.00

SMITH, E.C. *Borderland in the Civil War.* 1927. Macmillan. 1st ed. 412 p. EX. M2. $30.00

SMITH, E.W. *Aggrey of Africa.* 1929. NY. 1st ed. 8vo. dj. EX. T1. $35.00

SMITH, E.W. *Aggrey of Africa.* 1930. NY. Ils. 292 p. G. T5. $22.50

SMITH, E.W. *Further Adventures of the One-Eyed Poacher.* 1947. NY. Crown. 1/750. sgn. EX. $65.00

SMITH, E.W. *Life & Sport in Aiken.* Derrydale. as issued. VG. B2. $95.00

SMITH, E.W. *One-Eyed Poacher & ME Woods.* 1955. NY. 1st ed. dj. VG. B2. $20.00

SMITH, Elinor. *Aviatrix.* 1981. NY. 2nd print. 304 p. dj. T5. $35.00

SMITH, F.E. *Yazoo River.* 1988. MS U. Ils. 362 p. M. M2. $5.00

SMITH, F.H. *Armchair at the Inn.* 1912. Scribner. Ils Keller. 1st ed. VG. $12.00

SMITH, F.H. *Armchair at the Inn.* 1912. Scribner. 1st ed. 8vo. G. $7.50

SMITH, F.H. *Colonel Carter of Cartersville.* 1892. Boston. VG. $9.00

SMITH, F.H. *Day at Laguerre & Other Days.* 1892. Boston. 1/250. VG. P3. $95.00

SMITH, F.H. *Fortunes of Oliver Horn.* 1902. Scribner. Ils Walter Appleton Clark. 1st ed. $12.00

SMITH, F.H. *In Dickens' London.* 1914. Scribner. 1/50. sgn. gilt blue morocco. TEG. J2. $350.00

SMITH, F.H. *Kennedy Square.* 1911. Scribner. Ils Keller. 1st ed. $12.00

SMITH, F.H. *Outdoor Sketching.* 1915. Scribner. 1st ed. VG. $17.00

SMITH, F.H. *Peter.* 1908. Scribner. Ils Keller. 1st ed. $12.00

SMITH, F.H. *Under Dog.* 1903. NY. VG. $9.00

SMITH, G. *High Crimes & Misdemeanors: Impeachement & Trial of Johnson.* 1977. Morrow. Ils 1st ed. 320 p. dj. EX. M2. $11.00

SMITH, G.A. *Laurelled Chef d'Oeuvre d'Art From Paris Exhibition...* 1889. Phil. Gebbie. Ils. 2 vols. D2. $225.00

SMITH, G.M. *Windsinger.* 1976. Sierra Club. Ils. 175 p. EX. M2. $5.00

SMITH, G.T. *Birds of the SW Desert.* 1965. Doubleshoe. Ils. 68 p. EX. M2. $11.00

SMITH, G.W. *Battle of Seven Pines.* 1891. NY. 202 p. wraps. VG. $110.00

SMITH, G.W. *Confederate War Papers.* 1884. NY. 2nd ed. VG. $65.00

SMITH, Gibbs. *Joe Hill.* 1969. 4to. VG. $15.00

SMITH, H.A. *Great Chili Confrontration.* 1968. NY. 1st ed. dj. VG. B2. $22.50

SMITH, H.A. *Lo the Former Egyptian!* 1947. NY. Ils Hershfield. 1st ed. dj. EX. $35.00

SMITH, H.A. *Mr. Klein's Kampf.* 1939. NY. Ils Diamond. 1st ed. VG. $8.00

SMITH, H.G. *Arts of the Sailor.* 1953. Van Nostrand. 3rd ed. dj. VG. $15.00

SMITH, H.L. *Natural Philosophy for Use of Schools & Academies.* 1853. NY. 12mo. 358 p. black cloth. G. G2. $18.00

SMITH, H.M. *Fresh-Water Fishes of Siam or Thailand.* 1945. US Nat Mus. Ils. 622 p. EX. M2. $45.00

SMITH, H.V. & A.V. *How To Know the Non-Gilled Fleshy Fungi.* 1973. Brown. Ils. 402 p. EX. M2. $10.00

SMITH, Henry. *Virgin Land.* 1950. Harvard. 1st ed. J2. $15.00

SMITH, Horatio. *Festivals, Games & Amusements.* 1831. NY. Ils. maps. 355 p. K1. $18.50

SMITH, J.A. *Children's Illustrated Books.* 1958. London. Collins. Ils. dj. VG. $8.00

SMITH, J.F. *White Pillars.* 1941. NY. Bramhall. dj. EX. $25.00

SMITH, J.J. *Horticulturist & Journal of Rural Art & Rural Taste.* 1857. Phil. 17 pls. brown leather. $30.00

SMITH, J.R. *Springs & Wells of Manhattan & the Bronx at End of 19th C.* 1938. NY Hist Soc. photos. VG. $75.00

SMITH, J.V.C. *Natural History of Fishes of MA.* 1970. Freshet. Ils. 400 p. slipcase. EX. M2. $14.00

SMITH, J.W. *Child's Garden of Verses.* 1905. Scribner. 1st ed. VG. $65.00

SMITH, J.W. *Dickens' Children.* 1912. Scribner. 1st ed. VG. $45.00

SMITH, J.W. *Dickens' Children. Ten Drawings by Jessie Wilcox Smith.* 1912. NY. J2. $75.00

SMITH, J.W. *Heidi.* 1922. Phil. VG. E2. $40.00

SMITH, James. *Dictionary of Arts, Sciences & Manufactures...* 1856. Boston. Ils. 2 vols in 1. blue cloth. VG. T5. $95.00

SMITH, Jerome. *Trout & Angling: Part II of Fishes of MA.* 1929. Derrydale. 1/325. green bdg. $200.00

SMITH, Joe. *History of Harrison Co., IA.* 1888. Des Moines. 1st ed. J2. $60.00

SMITH, John. *General History of VA, New England & Summer Isles.* 1966. NY. facsimile of 1924 ed. boxed. VG. $42.50

SMITH, John. *True Travels, Adventures & Observations. Vol. I.* 1819. Richomond. VG. $150.00

SMITH, KLINE & FRENCH LAB. *Chlorpromazine & Mental Health.* 1955. Phil. Lea Febiger. 1st ed. EX. $40.00

SMITH, L. *Bob, a Dog.* 1988. Chapel Hill. Mud Puppy Pr. 1/26. sgn. slipcase. $175.00

SMITH, L.R. *Little Folks From Etiquette Town.* 1932. Whitman. Ils. VG. $20.00

SMITH, Lillian. *Killers of the Dream.* 1949. NY. 1st ed. dj. VG. $12.50

SMITH, Lillian. *Strange Fruit.* 1944. NY. Bookfind Club. 1st ed. dj. VG. $8.50

SMITH, M. *E Coast Marine Shells.* 1951. Edwards. Ils. 4to. 314 p. dj. EX. M2. $45.00

SMITH, M.A. *Reptilia & Amphibia. Vol. II: Sauria.* 1974. New Delhi. reprint of 1935 ed. 442 p. EX. M2. $45.00

SMITH, M.J. *Dodgers Bibliography From Brooklyn to Los Angeles.* 1988. Meckler. 153 p. VG. T5. $12.50

SMITH, M.L. *Historic Churches of the S.* 1952. Atlanta. Tupper Love. 1st ed. 125 p. $35.00

SMITH, Mrs. J.G. *Atla, Story of the Lost Island.* 1886. NY. 1st ed. inscr. 284 p. G. T5. $25.00

SMITH, N.A. *Boys & Girls of Bookland.* 1923. NY. Ils Smith. dj. VG. $30.00

SMITH, N.J. *Man, Fishes & the Amazon.* 1981. Columbia U. Review of 1st ed. 180 p. dj. M2. $19.00

SMITH, P.J. *On Strange Altars: Book of Enthusiasms.* 1924. NY. 1st ed. $25.00

SMITH, P.W. *Amphibians & Reptiles of IL.* 1961. IL Nat Hist Survey. Ils. 298 p. M2. $17.00

SMITH, R.I. *Intertidal Invertebrates of Central CA Coast.* 1970. CA U. Revised 2nd ed. 446 p. dj. EX. M2. $20.00

SMITH, R.K. *First Across!* 1973. Annapolis. Ils 279 p. dj. T5. $15.00

SMITH, R.L. *Ecology & Field Biology.* 1966. Harper Row. Ils. 686 p. G. M2. $8.00

SMITH, R.L. *Venomous Animals of AZ.* 1982. AZ U. Ils. 4to. 134 p. EX. M2. $20.00

SMITH, Reed. *Gullah.* 1926. Columbia, SC. 45 p. wraps. VG. $25.00

SMITH, S.A. *O. Henry Biography.* 1916. Garden City. 1st ed. G. $25.00

SMITH, S.B. *British Waders in Their Haunts.* 1950. London. Bell. Ils 1st ed. 162 p. dj. EX. M2. $19.00

SMITH, S.D. *Negro in Congress, 1870-1901.* 1940. Chapel Hill. 1st ed. dj. VG. $50.00

SMITH, Seba. *Life & Writings of Major Jack Downing.* 1833. Boston. Ils Johnston. 1st ed. VG. rare. $175.00

SMITH, Susy. *Life Is Forever.* 1974. NY. $15.00

SMITH, Thorne. *Biltmore Oswald.* 1918. NY. 1st ed. B2. $35.00

SMITH, W.A. *Train From Katanga.* 1965. NY. 1st ed. dj. VG. $45.00

SMITH, W.A. *When the Lion Feeds.* 1964. NY. 1st ed. dj. EX. $55.00

SMITH, W.C. *Everett Massacre: History of Class Struggle...* c 1917. Chicago. Pub Bureau. G. A3. $35.00

SMITH, W.F. *From Chattanooga to Petersburg Under Grant & Butler.* 1893. maps. plans. xl. K1. $24.50

SMITH, W.H. *History of State of IN From Earliest Explorations...* 1897. Indianapolis. Blair. 1st ed. 2 vols. xl. A3. $90.00

SMITH, W.H. *Life & Public Services of Arthur St. Clair.* 1882. Cincinnati. 1st ed. 2 vols. rebound. T5. $125.00

SMITH, W.L.G. *Life & Times of Lewis Cass.* 1856. NY. 1st ed. 781 p. G. T5. $55.00

SMITH, W.L.G. *Life at the S; or, Uncle Tom's Cabin As It Is...* 1852. Buffalo. Derby. Ils. rebound. VG. $65.00

SMITH, Wilbur. *Sparrow Falls.* 1977. London. 1st ed. dj. VG. B2. $45.00

SMITH, Wilbur. *When the Lion Feeds.* 1964. NY. 1st ed. dj. B2. $35.00

SMITH & ADDISON. *Bibliography of Parasites & Diseases of Ontario Wildlife.* 1982. Ontario. Nat Resources. 4to. 267 p. M2. $13.00

SMITH & DAVIS. *Select Letters of Major Jack Downing in the State of ME.* 1834. Phil. $45.00

SMITH & DEANE. *Journals of Rev. Thomas Smith & Rev. Samuel Deane...* 1849. Portland. Bailey. 8vo. orig bdg. J2. $75.00

SMITH & DOUGHTY. *Amazing Armadillo: Geography of a Folk Critter.* 1984. TX U. Ils 1st ed. 134 p. dj. EX. M2. $13.00

SMITH & HEEMSTRATA. *Smith's Sea Fishes.* 1986. S Africa. Ils 1st print. 1047 p. dj. M. M2. $110.00

SMITH & HENRY. *Short-Term Effect of Artificial Oases on Wildlife.* 1985. AZ U. 4to. 133 p. M2. $7.00

SMITH & HUMPHRIES. *Bibliography of Musical Works Published by John Walsh...* 1968. London. EX. $25.00

SMITH & PARMALEE. *Distributional Check List of Birds of IL.* 1955. IL Mus. 62 p. M2. $5.00

SMITH & TUCKER. *Photography in New Orleans. Early Years, 1840-1865.* 1982. Baton Rouge. 4to. 194 p. dj. $50.00

SMITH & WEBER. *Mushroom Hunter's Field Guide.* 1980. MI U. color pls. sgn. 316 p. EX. M2. $10.00

SMITHE, F.B. *Birds of Tikal.* 1966. Am Mus Nat Hist. 350 p. dj. M2. $30.00

SMITHERS, R.H.N. *Land Mammals of S Africa: Field Guide.* 1986. S Africa. Macmillan. Ils Abbott. 1st print. $23.00

SMITHSONIAN. *Fire of Life.* 1981. Smithsonian. 1st ed. 4to. 263 p. dj. EX. $5.00

SMITHSONIAN. *Magnificent Foragers.* 1978. color photos. 4to. dj. EX. M2. $12.00

SMOLEY, C.K. *Parallel Tables of Logarithms & Squares.* 1937. 193 p. EX. $2.00

SMOLLETT, Tobias. *Adventures of Roderick Random.* 1780. London. 10th ed. 2 vols. rebound. VG. $70.00

SMOLLETT, Tobias. *Expedition of Humphry Clinker. Vol. I.* 1813. Boston. 1st Am ed. $65.00

SMOUT, T.C. *Century of Scottish People, 1830-1950.* 1986. Yale. dj. EX. $15.00

SMYTH, C. Piazzi. *Great Pyramid: Its Secrets & Mysteries Revealed.* 1978. NY. Ils. 664 p. dj. EX. $12.50

SMYTH, D.M. *Hermit of the Saco.* 1901. Cambridge. 1st ed. pls. VG. $22.50

SMYTH, H.D. *For Military Purposes.* 1946. Princeton. 6th print. 308 p. wraps. VG. B1. $25.00

SMYTH, J.D. *Physiology of Cestodes.* 1969. Edinburgh. Oliver Boyd. 1st ed. 279 p. dj. M2. $15.00

SMYTH. *Teneriffe.* 1858. 1st ed. with stereographs. $450.00

SMYTHE, F.S. *Mountain Vision.* 1950. London. Hodder. 4th print. $37.50

SNELGROVE. *British Sporting & Animal Prints, 1658-1874.* 1981. London. Ils. 4to. 257 p. dj. EX. $75.00

SNELL, F.J. *King Arthur's Country.* 1926. London. 1st ed. VG. rare. C1. $39.50

SNELL, R.J. *Lost in the Air.* 1920. Chicago. 12mo. 271 p. VG. $15.00

SNELLER, A.G. *Vanished World.* 1964. Syracuse. Ils. 365 p. dj. EX. M2. $5.00

SNIDER, J.D. *I Love Books: Why, What, How & When We Should Read.* 1942. WA. $20.00

SNIDER. *Homer's Iliad: A Commentary.* 1922. St. Louis. Miner. G. $12.00

SNODGRASS, L.I. *Science & Practice of Photographic Printing.* 1931. NY. Falk. Ils 3rd ed. 337 p. $27.50

SNODGRASS, R.E. *Comparative Studies of Jaws of Mandibulate Arthropods.* 1950. Smithsonian. Ils. 85 p. M2. $10.00

SNODGRASS, R.E. *Crustacean Metamorphosis.* 1956. Smithsonian. Ils. 78 p. M2. $6.00

SNODGRASS, R.E. *Evolution of the Annelida: Onychophora & Arthropida.* 1938. Smithsonian. Ils. 159 p. VG. M2. $13.00

SNODGRASS, R.E. *Insect Metamorphosis.* 1954. Smithsonian. Ils. 124 p. M2. $8.00

SNODGRASS, W.D. *Heart's Needle.* 1959. NY. 1st ed. 1/1500. dj. EX. $175.00

SNODGRASS, W.D. *In W Review.* 1951. IA. $10.00

SNOW, Caleb H. *History of Boston...From Origins to Present Period.* 1928. Boston. Ils. maps. G. G2. $49.00

SNOW, E.R. *Famous Lighthouses of New England.* 1945. Boston. 1st ed. dj. VG. $20.00

SNOW, E.R. *Pilgrim Returns to Cape Cod.* 1946. Boston. 1st ed. dj. VG. $20.00

SNOW, E.R. *True Tales of Buried Treasure.* 1951. NY. Ils. sgn. dj. G. $18.00

SNOW, P. *Star Raft: China's Encounter With Africa.* 1988. Weindenfeld. Ils 1st Am ed. 250 p. dj. EX. M2. $10.00

SNOW, W.P. *S Generals: Their Lives & Campaigns.* 1866. NY. 18 portrait pls. 500 p. rebound. $35.00

SNOW & FROEHLICH. *Theory & Practice of Color.* 1920. NY. Prang. 3rd ed. 7 color charts. VG. $20.00

SNOW & MACHENNAN. *Songs of the Neukluk.* 1913. Council, AK. private print. presentation. 12mo. $52.50

SNOWDEN, W.H. *Some Old Historic Landmarks of VA & MD.* 1904. tall 8vo. wraps. VG. $25.00

SNOWDON, Tony. *Assignments.* 1972. Morrow. VG. $15.00

SNOWMAN, A. *Art of Carl Faberge.* 1952. Boston. 4to. cloth. dj. EX. J2. $100.00

SNYDER, Chris. *In th' Olde Dayes of Kyng Arthur (sic).* 1987. Ils Valentino. 1st ed. maps. stiff wraps. C1. $8.50

SNYDER, G. *In the Footsteps of Lewis & Clark.* 1970. Nat Geog Soc. Ils. 215 p. dj. EX. M2. $11.00

SNYDER, G. *Riprap.* 1959. Ashland, MA. 2nd ed. inscr. wraps. EX. $10.00

SOAMES, Mary. *Churchill Family Album.* 1985. Penguin. 1st ed. SftCvr. 4to. VG. D1. $25.00

SOBEL, Eli. *Tristan Romance in Meisterlieder of Hans Sachs.* 1963. CA U. German text. 60 p. dj. EX. C1. $17.00

SOBOL, D.J. *Civil War Sampler.* 1961. 1st ed. 202 p. EX. J4. $7.50

SOBY, James Thrall. *Prints of Paul Klee.* 1945. NY. Valentine. 1st ed. 1/1000. D2. $245.00

SOBY, James Thrall. *Romantic Painting in America.* 1943. MOMA. 1st ed. dj. $20.00

SOCIALIST LABOR PARTY. *Proceedings of 10th National Convention, June 2-6, 1900.* 1901. NY. VG. $50.00

SODERLUND, J.R. *Quakers & Slavery, a Divided Spirit.* 1985. Princeton. 1st ed. maps. tables. M. J4. $15.00

SOHRAB. *Broken Silence.* 1942. NY. 1st ed. sgn. dj. EX. $35.00

SOLBEAR. *Art of Projecting.* 1877. Boston. Ils 1st ed. 158 p. G. B1. $50.00

SOLEY, J.R. *Sailor Boys of '61.* 1888. Boston. Estes. Ils. VG. R1. $45.00

SOLOMON, Eric. *Faded Banner.* 1960. NY. 336 p. G. T5. $8.50

SOLOMON, Paul. *Excerpts From the Paul Solomon Tapes.* 1974. VA Beach. $18.50

SOLTYNSKI, Roman. *Glimpses of Polish Architecture.* c 1940. London. 4to. 56 p. wraps. $17.50

SOLZHENITSYN, A.I. *First Circle.* 1968. NY. 1st ed. 580 p. dj. G. T5. $17.50

SOLZHENITSYN, A.I. *For the Good of the Cause.* 1964. NY. 1st ed. dj. VG. $25.00

SOLZHENITSYN, A.I. *Gulag Archipelago, 1918-1956.* 1974. Harper Row. 1st ed. dj. VG. $13.00

SOLZHENITSYN, A.I. *One Day in the Life of Ivan Denisovich.* 1963. NY. Dutton. 1st ed. dj. VG. $18.00

SONDHEIM & LAPINE. *Sunday in the Park With George.* 1986. NY. Ltd ed. 1/250. sgns. slipcase. EX. $55.00

SONNECK, O.G.T. *Catalog of Opera Librettos Printed Before 1800.* 1914. Lib Congress. 2 vols. xl. A3. $90.00

SONNECK, O.G.T. *Orchestral Music Catalog.* 1912. Lib Congress. 663 p. xl. VG. A3. $50.00

SONNICHSEN, C.L. *Law W of the Pecos.* 1943. Macmillan. Ils 1st ed. 207 p. dj. VG. A3. $60.00

SONNICHSEN, C.L. *Roy Bean: Law W of the Pecos.* 1943. Devin Adair. photos. 207 p. dj. EX. M2. $10.00

SONNICHSEN & MORRISON. *Alias Billy the Kid: I Want To Die a Free Man.* 1955. NM U. photos. 136 p. VG. M2. $22.00

SONTAG, Alan. *Bridge Bum: My Life & Play.* 1977. Morrow. 1st ed. 1st print. dj. M. $35.00

SONTAG, Susan. *Benefactor.* 1963. NY. Farrar. 1st ed. dj. EX. $35.00

SONTAG, Susan. *Susan Sontag Reader.* 1982. NY. 1st ed. 1/350. sgn. slipcase. EX. $35.00

SOOTHILL, E. & R. *Wading Birds of the World.* 1982. Blanford. Ils 1st ed. 334 p. dj. EX. M2. $27.00

SOPER, M.F. *New Zealand Bird Portraits.* 1963. New Zealand. Ils 1st ed. EX. M2. $15.00

SOPHOCLES. *Antigone.* 1975. Haarlem. Ils Bennett. 1/2000. sgn. dj. EX. $45.00

SORELL, Walter. *Dance Has Many Faces.* 1951. Cleveland. VG. $20.00

SORELL, Walter. *Dance Through the Ages.* 1967. NY. 1st ed. dj. EX. $22.00

SORENSEN. *Kennedy.* 1965. NY. 1st ed. dj. EX. $7.50

SORIA, M.S. *Paintings of Francisco De Zurbaran.* 1953. London. Phaidon. red cloth. dj. EX. J2. $75.00

SORINE, D.S. *Stars of the Contemporary Ballet.* 1983. Dover. Ils. 4to. printed wraps. $10.00

SORINE, S. *Portraits: Avant-Propos par Andre Salmon.* 1929. Berlin. 36 color portraits. AEG. VG. J2. $500.00

SORLIER, Charles. *Chagall by Chagall.* 1982. Harrison House. Ils. 263 p. dj. D2. $75.00

SORLIER, Charles. *Chagall Lithographs V: 1974-1979.* 1984. NY. Ils. 4to. dj. EX. $75.00

SORLIER, Charles. *Chagall Lithographs VI: 1980-1985.* 1986. NY. 4to. dj. slipcase. EX. J2. $85.00

SORREL, W. *Journey Across Tibet.* 1988. Contemporary Books. dj. M. M2. $22.00

SORRENTINO, Gilbert. *Odd Number.* c 1985. CA. dj. EX. $20.00

SORSBY, A. *Clinical Genetics.* 1953. London. 603 p. VG. $48.00

SOULE, F. *Annals of San Francisco.* 1855. NY. Ils. 824 p. VG. $195.00

SOURIAU, Paul. *Aesthetics of Movement.* 1983. MA U. 1st ed. dj. J2. $12.50

SOUSA, J.P. *Fifth String.* 1902. Bobbs Merrill. VG. $10.00

SOUSA, J.P. *Marching Along.* 1st ed. dj. VG. B2. $35.00

SOUTH, R. *Moths of the British Isles.* 1980. London. Warne. Revised ed. 2 vols. dj. EX. M2. $45.00

SOUTHARD, C.Z. *Treatise on Trout for the Progressive Angler.* 1931. NY. 1st ed. VG. $50.00

SOUTHERN, Terry. *Red Dirt Marijuana & Other Stories.* 1st ed. dj. B7. $15.00

SOUTHWARD, E.C. *Pogonophora of the NW Atlantic: Nova Scotia to FL.* 1971. Smithsonian. Ils. 29 p. M2. $6.00

SOUTHWORTH, James. *Poetry of Thomas Hardy.* 1947. NY. 1st ed. G. $17.50

SOUTHWORTH & HAWES. *Spirit of Fact.* 1976. Boston. Godine. Ils. oblong 4to. 163 p. dj. $50.00

SOWERBY, J.E. *British Wild Flowers.* 1876. London. 89 pls. 8vo. 186 p. gilt green cloth. A3. $450.00

SOWERBY, R.R. *Sowerby of China: Arthur de Carle Sowerby.* 1956. England. Wilson. Ils. 58 p. dj. EX. M2. $20.00

SOWERBY & CRANE. *At Home.* c 1880s. Cincinnati. 8vo. $25.00

SOWLS, L.K. *Peccaries.* 1984. AZ U. Ils. maps. 251 p. dj. EX. M2. $25.00

SOWLS, L.K. *Prairie Ducks: Study of Behavior, Ecology & Management.* 1955. Stackpole. Ils 1st ed. 193 p. dj. EX. M2. $45.00

SPAETH, Sigmund. *Music & Dance in New England States.* 1953. Bu Musical Research. 1st ed. J2. $12.50

SPAIN, A.O. *Political Theory of John C. Calhoun.* 1951. NY. 306 p. dj. VG. $20.00

SPALDING, C.C. *Annals of City of KS Embracing Full Details of Trade...* 1950. Glenn. reprint of 1858 ed. EX. rare. M2. $10.00

SPANGENBERG, J. *Eviftein & Evangelien.* 1799. Berlin. Ils. thick quarto. G. $95.00

SPARACIO, D. *Frammenti Bio-Bibliografici, Scrittori, 600 al 1930.* 1931. Oderisi. xl. G1. $30.00

SPARK, Muriel. *Prime of Miss Jean Brodie.* 1961. London. Macmillan. presentation. sgn. EX. $40.00

SPARK, Muriel. *Prime of Miss Jean Brodie.* 1961. NY. 1st ed. dj. EX. $30.00

SPARK, Muriel. *Very Fine Clock.* 1969. London. Macmillan. Ils Gorey. dj. EX. $45.00

SPARK, Muriel. *Voices at Play.* 1961. London. 1st ed. dj. EX. $20.00

SPARKS, Jared. *Discovery of Animal Behavior.* 1982. Little Brown. Ils Am ed. 288 p. dj. EX. M2. $18.00

SPARKS, Jared. *Library of American Biography.* 1860. NY. 10 vols. VG. $40.00

SPARKS, Jared. *Life & Writings of George WA.* 1858. Boston. 12 vols. xl. VG. $75.00

SPARKS, Jared. *Life of Gouverneur Morris.* 1832. Boston. Gray Bowen. 3 vols. $75.00

SPARKS & SOPER. *Owls: Their Natural & Unnatural History.* 1970. Taplinger. Ils 1st ed. 206 p. dj. EX. M2. $20.00

SPAULDING, E.S. *Quails.* 1949. Macmillan. Ils Jaques. 1st print. dj. EX. M2. $65.00

SPAULDING, G.F. *On W Tour With WA Irving: Journal of Count De Pourtales.* 1968. OK U. Ils 1st ed. 90 p. EX. M2. $11.00

SPAULDING, Solomon. *Manuscript Found, Manuscript Story.* 1886. Salt Lake City. rebound. xl. G. T5. $35.00

SPAYDE, Jon. *Book of Flowers.* 1984. Exeter. Ils. pls. folio. dj. EX. $30.00

SPEAR, W.E. *N & S at Antietam & Gettysburg.* 1908. Boston. private print. 1st ed. G. $25.00

SPEARING, H.G. *Childhood of Art; or, Ascent of Man.* 1912. Kegan Paul. 1st ed. VG. J2. $30.00

SPEARMAN, F.H. *Strategy of Great Railroads.* 1914. 11 maps. 287 p. $35.00

SPEARS, Edward. *Assignment to Catastrophe.* 1954-1955. NY. 1st Am ed. 2 vols. djs. VG. T5. $47.50

SPEARS, J.R. *Capt. Nathaniel Brown Palmer: Old-Time Sailor of the Sea.* 1922. Macmillan. 252 p. dj. VG. $15.00

SPECK, Gordon. *Breeds & Half-Breeds.* 1969. Ils 1st ed. 15 maps. index. 361 p. K1. $9.50

SPEER, Albert. *Slave State.* 1981. London. 1st ed. dj. $10.00

SPEIDELL, John. *Geometrical Extraction; or, Compendious Collection Chiefe...* 1916. London. 1st ed. $275.00

SPEIRS, John. *Medieval English Poetry: Non-Chaucerian Tradition.* 1957. London. 1st ed. dj. M. C1. $20.00

SPELLMAN, Francis. *Prayers & Poems.* 1947. Scribner. sgn. 12mo. slipcase. VG. $35.00

SPELTZ, Alexander. *Styles of Ornament.* Grosset Dunlap. Ils. G. $25.00

SPENCE, Lewis. *Fairy Tradition in Britain.* 1948. Rider. dj. J2. $25.00

SPENCE, Lewis. *Magic Arts in Celtic Britain.* 198 p. VG. B1. $25.00

SPENCE, Lewis. *Mysteries of Britain.* nd. Rider. 3rd ed. J2. $17.50

SPENCER, Ambrose. *Narrative of Andersonville.* 1866. NY. 272 p. VG. $45.00

SPENCER, B.Z. *Tried & True; or, Love & Loyalty.* 1868. Springfield. 8vo. 394 p. G2. $12.00

SPENCER, D.A. *Photography of Today.* 1936. NY. reprint. 160 p. $20.00

SPENCER, Elizabeth. *Legacy.* Ltd 1st ed. sgn. M. B7. $50.00

SPENCER, Elizabeth. *Legacy.* 1988. Chapel Hill. Mud Puppy Pr. 1/26. sgn. boxed. M. $150.00

SPENCER, Elizabeth. *Legacy.* 1989. Chapel Hill. Mud Puppy Pr. 1/100. sgn. M. $50.00

SPENCER, H. *Works of Spencer.* Appleton. Westminster ed. 1/1000. 15 vols. $150.00

SPENCER, J.W. *From Corsicana to Appomattox.* 1984. TX Pr. Ils 1st ed. sgn. 199 p. dj. EX. M2. $25.00

SPENCER & BURROWS. *Early Day of Rock Island & Davenport.* 1942. Chicago. Lakeside Classic. 313 p. VG. T5. $30.00

SPENCER & BURROWS. *Early Day of Rock Island & Davenport.* 1942. Donnelley. Lakeside Classic. A3. $35.00

SPENCER & STEGMAIGER. *Agromyziadae of FL With Supplement on Species.* 1973. FL Dept Agric. Ils. 205 p. EX. M2. $17.00

SPENDER, Stephen. *Generous Days.* 1971. London. Faber. 1st ed. with sgn poem. EX. $250.00

SPENDER, Stephen. *Trial of a Judge.* 1938. London. Faber. 1st ed. inscr. dj. EX. $145.00

SPENDER & HOGARTH. *America Observed.* 1979. NY. Clarkson Potter. folio. EX. $45.00

SPENGLER, Oswald. *Decline of the W.* 1929. NY. 2 vols. $30.00

SPENGLER, Oswald. *Decline of the W.* 1988. Knopf. reprint. 2 vols. EX. $25.00

SPENGLER, Oswald. *Hour of Decision.* 1935. NY. $10.00

SPENSER, Edmund. *Wedding Songs.* 1923. Golden Cockerel. 1/320. 12mo. EX. $55.00

SPEWACK, Sam. *Skyscraper Murder.* 1928. Macauley. VG. $10.00

SPICE ISLAND. *Spice Island's Cookbook.* 1961. Menlo Park. 1st ed. dj. EX. $16.00

SPIELMAN, Jean. *Stoolpigeon & the Open Shop Movement.* 1923. Minneapolis. VG. $37.00

SPIELMANN, M.H. *Title Page of First Folio of Shakespeare's Plays...* 1924. London. 1st ed. 47 pls. $50.00

SPIESER, Robert. *Krankheiten Elektrischer Maschinen Transformatoren...* 1932. Berlin. Ils. inscr. G. $35.00

SPILLANE, Mickey. *Deep.* 1961. NY. 1st ed. dj. VG. $20.00

SPILLANE, Mickey. *Girl Hunters.* 1962. NY. Dutton. sgn. 12mo. VG. $22.00

SPILLER, B.L. *Firelight.* 1937. Derrydale. 1/950. EX. $180.00

SPILLER, B.L. *Grouse Feathers.* Derrydale. as issued. VG. B2. $115.00

SPILLER, B.L. *More Grouse Feathers.* 1938. Derrydale. 1/950. as issued. VG. B2. $160.00

SPILLER, B.L. *More Grouse Feathers.* 1972. Crown. 238 p. dj. EX. $20.00

SPILLER, B.L. *Thoroughbred.* 1936. Derrydale. 1/950. EX. $175.00

SPILLMAN, Ronald. *Complete Photo Book.* 1971. London. Fountain Pr. Ils. 191 p. dj. $35.00

SPINAGE, C.A. *Natural History of Antelopes.* 1986. London. Ils. 203 p. dj. EX. M2. $35.00

SPINDEN, Herbert J. *Ancient Civilizations of Mexico & Central America.* 1948. NY. Ils Revised ed. sgn. 271 p. VG. T5. $27.50

SPIVAK, J.L. *Honorable Spy: Exposing Japanese Military Intrigue in US.* 1939. NY. Modern Age Books. pb. EX. $20.00

SPIVEY, T.S. *Resurrection.* 1925. CA. $17.50

SPOONER, W.W. *Backwoodsmen; or, Tales of the Border.* 1883. Cincinnati. rebound. VG. $50.00

SPRAGUE, H.B. *Light & Shadows in Confederate Prisons.* 1915. NY. 1st ed. VG. $25.00

SPRAGUE, Marshall. *Gallery of Dudes.* 1967. Boston. Little Brown. Ils 1st ed. maps. dj. $10.00

SPRAGUE, Marshall. *Great Gates: Rocky Mountain Passes.* 1964. Boston. Little Brown. 1st ed. dj. EX. $16.00

SPRAGUE, Marshall. *Money Mountain: Story of Cripple Creek Gold.* 1953. Little Brown. photos. maps. 342 p. EX. M2. $11.00

SPRING, A.W. *Cheyenne & Black Hills Stage & Express Routes.* 1949. Glendale. 1st ed. VG. $85.00

SPRINGER, V.G. *Osteology & Classification of Fishes of Family Blenniidae.* 1968. US Nat Mus. Ils. 85 p. xl. EX. M2. $10.00

SPRINGIRTH, K.C. *Erie to Conneaut by Trolley.* 1968. Erie, PA. Ils. 103 p. mimeographed. VG. T5. $47.50

SPRINGMAN, Jack. *Beauty of Pebble Beach.* 1964. Phil. 1st ed. VG. B2. $75.00

SPRINGORM, Friedrich. *Ein Menschlich Land.* c 1950. Callwey. Ils. 119 p. dj. $37.50

SPRINGS, E.W. *Clothes Make the Man.* 1949. NY. Ils. 446 p. G. T5. $17.50

SPRINGS, E.W. *Rise & Fall of Carol Banks.* 1931. Garden City. 1st trade ed. 307 p. dj. G. T5. $25.00

SPROUSE, Deborah A. *Guide to Excavated Colonial & Revolutionary War Artifacts.* 1988. Ils. 4to. sgn. 131 p. M. K1. $19.50

SPRUNT, Alexander. *Carolina Low Country Impressions.* 1964. Devin Adaire. 1st ed. dj. VG. T6. $45.00

SPRUNT, Alexander. *FL Bird Life.* 1954. Coward McCann. Ils Jaques/Dick. 65 maps. EX. M2. $150.00

SPRUNT, Alexander. *N American Birds of Prey.* 1955. Harper. Ils 1st ed. 227 p. dj. EX. M2. $125.00

SPRUNT, Alexander. *SC Bird Life.* 1949. SC U. Ils Jaques/Peterson/Julien/others. $75.00

SPURR. *Paul Revere Album.* 1900. Boston. 4th ed. G. $30.00

SQUIRE, Charles. *Mythology of Ancient Britain & Ireland.* 1906. London. Constable. 1st ed. scarce. VG. C1. $17.00

SQUIRE, J.C. *Moon.* 1920. London. 1st ed. EX. $35.00

SQUIRES, W.H.T. *Through Three Centuries: Short History of VA.* 1929. Portsmouth. 1st ed. sgn/#d. 605 p. EX. M2. $80.00

SQUIRES, W.H.T. *Unleased at Long Last.* 1939. Printcraft. 1/495. sgn. xl. VG. R1. $30.00

ST. JOHN, Charles. *Wild Sports & Natural History of the Highlands.* 1919. Edinburgh. Ils Armour/Alexander. 472 p. $100.00

ST. JOHN, Nicole. *Guinevere's Gift.* 1977. Book Club. dj. VG. C1. $5.00

ST. JOHN, Perse. *Exile.* 1949. Pantheon. Bilingual ed. folio. EX. $25.00

STACKPOLE, E.J. *Chancellorsville: Lee's Greatest Battle.* 1958. Harrisburg. Ils 1st ed. 384 p. dj. VG. $20.00

STACKPOLE, E.J. *Sheridan in Shenandoah: Jubal Early's Nemesis.* 1961. Bonanza. reprint. 413 p. dj. EX. M2. $10.00

STACKPOLE PUBLISHING. *New Hunter's Encyclopedia.* 1966. 1131 p. VG. $12.50

STAENDER, V. *Adventures With Arctic Wildlife.* 1970. Caxton. Ils. 260 p. EX. M2. $13.00

STAENDER, V. & G. *Our Arctic Year.* 1984. AK NW. color photos. 149 p. EX. M2. $12.00

STAFF, Virgil. *D-Day on the W Pacific.* 1982. 223 p. $35.00

STAFFORD, Greg. *Gray Knight.* M. C1. $9.00

STAFFORD, Greg. *Pendragon Campaign.* Ils 76 p. stiff wraps. M. C1. $14.00

STAFFORD, Greg. *Prince Valiant: Storytelling Game.* 120 p. EX. C1. $11.00

STAFFORD, Greg. *Tournament of Dreams.* Pendragon Series. M. C1. $9.00

STAFFORD, Jean. *Catherine Wheel.* 1952. NY. 1st ed. dj. EX. $35.00

STAFFORD, Jean. *Mountain Lion.* 1947. NY. 1st ed. dj. VG. $20.00

STAFFORD, William. *Traveling Through the Dark.* 1962. NY. 1st ed. sgn. dj. VG. $50.00

STAFFORD-DEITSCH, J. *Shark: Photographer's Story.* 1987. Sierra Club. Ils 1st ed. 4to. 200 p. EX. M2. $19.00

STAHL, Norman. *Assault on Mavis A.* 1978. NY. 1st ed. dj. VG. $7.00

STALIN, Joseph. *Marxism & the National Question.* 1942. NY. dj. $25.00

STALLMAN, R.W. *Stephen Crane: Critical Bibliography.* 1972. IA State U. 1st ed. photos. dj. EX. $25.00

STAMETS & CHILTON. *Mushroom Cultivator: Practical Guide to Growing Mushrooms.* 1983. Agarikon. Ils. 415 p. EX. M2. $10.00

STAMPP, K.M. *Imperiled Union...* 1980. NY. Oxford. 1st ed. 320 p. dj. $25.00

STANARD, M.N. *Colonial VA: People & Customs.* 1917. Phil. Ltd 1st ed. 8vo. 376 p. VG. $85.00

STANARD, M.N. *Dreamer.* 1909. Richmond, VA. Bell. 1st ed. gilt green cloth. D1. $30.00

STANARD, M.N. *Poe Letters in the Valentine Museum.* 1925. Lippincott. 1st ed. 4to. black cloth. G. D1. $70.00

STANARD, M.N. *Story of VA's 1st C.* 1928. Phil. 1st ed. 27 pls. 331 p. VG. B1. $20.00

STANDING, Percy C. *Sir Lawrence Alma-Tadema, O.M., R.A.* 1905. London. Cassell. 40 pls. TEG. scarce. D2. $85.00

STANDISH, B.L. *Courtney of the Center Garden.* 1915. Barse Hopkins. 1st ed. VG. $25.00

STANDISH, Ronald. *Sapper.* 1953. London. Hodder Stoughton. 8th ed. dj. $8.50

STANDLEY, P.C. *Orchid Collecting in Central America.* 1925. Smithsonian. photos. later paper cover. M2. $3.00

STANEK, V.J. *Pictorial Encyclopedia of Animal Kingdom.* 1970. London. Hamlyn. Ils. 614 p. dj. EX. M2. $14.00

STANFORD, Ray. *Socorro Saucer in a Pentagon Pantry.* 1976. TX. $17.00

STANG, Joanne. *Shadows on the Sceptered Isle.* 1980. 1st ed. dj. EX. C1. $6.00

STANLEY, A.P. *Historical Memorials of Westminster Abbey.* 1887. NY. Ltd ed. 3 vols. $135.00

STANLEY, Edward. *Rock Cried Out.* 1949. NY. 1st ed. 311 p. dj. VG. T5. $12.50

STANLEY, F. *Santanta & the Kiowas.* 1968. Borger, TX. 1st ed. dj. EX. $40.00

STANLEY, H.M. *Darkest Africa.* 1891. NY. 2nd ed. 2 vols. $35.00

STANLEY, H.M. *My Kalulu, Prince, King & Slave: Story of Central Africa.* 1873. London. fair. $40.00

STANSBURY, Howard. *Exploration & Survey of Valley of Great Salt Lake of UT...* 1852. Phil. Lippincott Grambo. 486 p. VG. A3. $375.00

STANSBURY, Howard. *Exploration & Survey of Valley of Great Salt Lake of UT...* 1853. WA. Armstrong. with 2 maps in separate case. A3. $375.00

STANSBURY, Howard. *Survey of Cumberland River.* 1835. GPO. 12 maps. 2 fld maps. 24 p. VG. A3. $120.00

STANSBURY, Howard. *Survey of Kaskaskia & IL Rivers.* 1838. WA. fld map. 14 p. wraps. EX. $125.00

STANTON, M.O. *Encyclopedia of Face & Form Reading.* 1919. Davis. VG. $60.00

STANTON, W.C. *Clay & Spirit: USS Black W Pacific Cruise 1969.* 1969. San Francisco. photos. 4to. 71 p. G. T5. $32.50

STANTON, W.H. *Our Ancestors: The Stantons.* 1922. Phil. Ils. fld maps. 649 p. TEG. G. T5. $125.00

STANTON. *By Middle Seas.* 1927. photos. S2. $50.00

STANWELL-FLETCHER, T.C. *Tundra World.* 1952. Little Brown. Ils 1st ed. 266 p. VG. M2. $14.00

STAPLEDON, S.O. *Last & First Men: Story of Near & Far Future.* 1931. NY. 1st Am ed. dj. EX. $45.00

STAPLES, T.S. *Reconstruction in AR 1862-1874.* 1923. Columbia. 450 p. EX. M2. $35.00

STAR, John. *Lincoln & the Railroads.* 1927. NY. 1st ed. dj. VG. $20.00

STARCKE, Walter. *Ultimate Revolution.* 1969. NY. $12.50

STAROKADOMSKIY, L.M. *Charting the Russian N Sea Route.* 1976. Canada. McGill Queens U. 332 p. dj. EX. M2. $20.00

STARR, Frederick. *Truth About the Congo.* 1907. Forbes. photos. VG. $30.00

STARR, J.W. *Lincoln & the Railroads.* 1927. NY. 1st ed. 325 p. $35.00

STARR, L.M. *Bohemian Brigade: Civil War Newsmen in Action.* 1954. Knopf. Ils 1st ed. 367 p. dj. EX. M2. $20.00

STARRETT, Vincent. *Bookman's Holiday.* 1942. NY. 1st ed. dj. VG. $25.00

STARRETT, Vincent. *Books Alive.* 1940. NY. $20.00

STARRETT, Vincent. *Private Life of Sherlock Holmes.* 1961. London. dj. VG. $35.00

STARRETT, Vincent. *Private Life of Sherlock Holmes.* 1933. NY. Ils 1st ed. 8vo. blue cloth. dj. VG. T1. $50.00

STARRETT, Vincent. *Seaports in the Moon.* 1928. Garden City. 1st ed. VG. C1. $24.50

STARRETT, Vincent. *221B: Studies in Sherlock Holmes.* 1940. NY. Ils 1st ed. 8vo. red cloth. dj. VG. T1. $125.00

STARRETT & FRITZ. *Biological Investigation of Fishes of Lake Chautauqua, IL.* 1965. IL Nat Hist. Ils. 104 p. EX. M2. $15.00

STATLER, Oliver. *Modern Japanese Prints.* 1956. Rutland. 1st ed. dj. boxed. VG. B2. $90.00

STAUFER, Alvin F. *NY Central's Early Power. Vol. II, 1831-1916.* 1967. Carrollton, OH. Ils. 350 p. dj. VG. T5. $32.50

STAUFER, Alvin F. *Steam Power of the NY Central System. Vol. I, Modern Power.* 1961. np. Ils. 223 p. dj. VG. T5. $35.00

STAVIS. *Man Who Never Died: Joe Hill.* 1951. dj. VG. $25.00

STEAD, W.T. *Life Eternal.* 1933. London. $20.00

STEADMAN & ZOUSMER. *Galapagos: Discovery on Darwin's Island.* 1988. Smith. 51 color pls. 4to. 208 p. dj. M2. $25.00

STEANE, J.B. *Tennyson.* 1969. Arco. 1st ed. pb. VG. C1. $5.00

STEARN, Jess. *Adventures Into the Psychic.* 1969. NY. $18.50

STEARN, Jess. *Door to the Future.* 1963. NY. $20.00

STEARN, Jess. *Miracle Workers.* 1972. NY. $18.00

STEARNS, Charles. *Black Man of the S & the Rebels.* 1872. NY. 8 pls. 562 p. $70.00

STEBBINS, G. *Facts & Opinions Touching Origin...American Colonization.* 1853. Boston. 1st ed. inscr/sgn. VG. $100.00

STEBBINS, G.L. *Variation & the Evolution of Plants.* 1950. Columbia U. Ils. 634 p. EX. M2. $35.00

STEBBINS, R.C. *Field Guide to W Reptiles & Amphibians.* 1966. Houghton. Ils 1st print. maps. EX. M2. $22.00

STEDMAN, E.C. *Poets of America.* 1968. Scholarly Pr. reprint of 1898 ed. VG. D1. $12.00

STEED, Hal. *GA: Unfinished State.* 1942. NY. Ils. 344 p. VG. $30.00

STEEGMULLER, Francis. *Two Lives of James Jackson Jarves.* 1951. New Haven. Ils. 331 p. dj. G. T5. $17.50

STEEL, F.A. *English Fairy Tales.* 1920. Macmillan. J2. $25.00

STEEL, L.R. *Erma.* 1980. NY. sgn. dj. EX. $20.00

STEEL, R. *Sharks of the World.* 1986. Facts on File. Ils. 192 p. dj. EX. M2. $24.00

STEELE, F.L. *Timberline: Nature Guide to Mountains of NE.* 1982. Appalachian Mt Club. 285 p. M. M2. $13.00

STEELE, J.W. *Rand McNally & Co.'s New Guide to Pacific Santa Fe Route.* 1890. chicago. Ils. map. 211 p. A3. $60.00

STEELE, M.F. *American Campaigns.* 1943. WA. maps. 2 vols. G. T5. $65.00

STEELE, M.F. *American Campaigns.* 1947. 2 vols. VG. K1. $37.50

STEELE & FRENCH. *Indian Captive.* 1934. Woodstock. 1st ed. sgn French. 46 p. T5. $35.00

STEENHOF, K. *Management of Wintering Bald Eagles.* 1978. USFWS. photos. 59 p. M2. $5.00

STEER, John. *Concise History of Venetian Paintings.* 1970. NY. Praeger. Ils. 216 p. dj. D2. $20.00

STEFANSSON, Evelyn. *Here Is AK.* 1943. Scribner. 154 p. G. M1. $19.50

STEFANSSON, Evelyn. *Here Is AK.* 1956. Scribner. Revised ed. 178 p. dj. EX. M2. $10.00

STEFANSSON, V. *Adventure of Wrangel Island.* 1925. NY. Macmillan. Ils 1st ed. 8vo. 424 p. VG. $35.00

STEFANSSON, V. *Arctic Manual.* 1944. NY. presentation. VG. $40.00

STEFANSSON, V. *Discovery.* 1964. McGraw. 1st ed. dj. VG. $45.00

STEFANSSON, V. *Friendly Arctic: Story of Five Years in Polar Regions.* 1922. Macmillan. Ils 1st ed. fld map. 784 p. EX. M2. $55.00

STEFANSSON, V. *Great Adventures & Explorations From Earliest Times.* 1947. Dial. 788 p. dj. EX. M2. $10.00

STEFANSSON, V. *Greenland.* 1942. NY. 1st ed. EX. $45.00

STEFANSSON, V. *Not by Bread Alone.* 1946. NY. 1st ed. 339 p. dj. B2. $22.50

STEFANSSON, V. *Unsolved Mysteries of the Arctic.* 1938. NY. Ils/sgn Kent. 1st ed. 1/200. G. $85.00

STEGNER, Wallace. *Beyond the Hundreth Meridian: J.W. Powell & Opening the W.* 1954. Boston. Ils 1st ed. 438 p. dj. VG. A3. $60.00

STEGNER, Wallace. *Big Rock Candy Mountain.* 1943. NY. 1st ed. dj. VG. B2. $25.00

STEGNER, Wallace. *Big Rock Candy Mountain.* 1978. Franklin Lib. Ils Reid. Ltd ed. sgn. 8vo. EX. $60.00

STEGNER, Wallace. *On a Darkling Plain.* 1940. NY. 1st ed. dj. RS. B2. $45.00

STEICHEN, Edward. *Blue Ghost.* 1947. NY. Ils 1st ed. 149 p. T5. $125.00

STEICHEN, Edward. *Life in Photography.* 1963. Garden City. 1st ed. 1st state. dj. EX. $55.00

STEICHEN, Edward. *Power in the Pacific.* 1945. NY. dj. VG. $90.00

STEICHEN, Edward. *US Navy War Photographs.* 1946. NY. orig wraps. VG. $40.00

STEICHEN, Edward. *Victory Volume.* 1945. NY. 1st ed. VG. $30.00

STEIG, William. *All Embarrassed.* 1944. Duell Sloan. 1st ed. dj. VG. M1. $6.50

STEIG, William. *Rejected Lovers.* 1951. NY. 1st ed. EX. $15.00

STEIG, William. *Till Death Do Us Part.* 1947. Duell Sloan. 1st ed. dj. M1. $8.50

STEIG, William. *Zabajaba Jungle.* nd. NY. Farrar Straus. sgn. M. $12.50

STEIGNER, Henry. *Mysticism in Action.* 1941. LA. $12.50

STEIN, Fred. *German Portraits.* 1961. Stuttgart. VG. $25.00

STEIN, Gertrude. *Autobiography of Alice B. Toklas.* 1933. NY. Stated 1st ed. VG. $30.00

STEIN, Gertrude. *How To Write.* 1931. Paris. Plain ed. 1/1000. inscr. VG. $155.00

STEIN, Gertrude. *Lucy Church Amiably.* 1930. Paris. 1st ed. $115.00

STEIN, Gertrude. *Paris, France.* 1940. NY. 1st Am ed. dj. VG. B2. $40.00

STEIN, Gertrude. *Wars I Have Seen.* 1945. London. 1st ed. VG. $30.00

STEINBECK, John. *Acceptance Speech. Nobel Prize for Literature.* 1962. NY. Viking. 1/3200. 1st ed. wraps. scarce. $100.00

STEINBECK, John. *Acts of King Arthur & His Noble Knights.* 1977. 4th print. pb. VG. C1. $4.00

STEINBECK, John. *America & Americans.* 1966. Viking. 1st ed. dj. J2. $30.00

STEINBECK, John. *Bombs Away.* 1942. NY. Ils Swope. 1st ed. dj. EX. $35.00

STEINBECK, John. *Burning Bright.* 1950. Viking. 1st ed. 2nd bdg. dj. EX. $50.00

STEINBECK, John. *Cannery Row.* 1945. London. 1st ed. $30.00

STEINBECK, John. *Cannery Row.* 1945. NY. 1st ed. 2nd print. dj. EX. P3. $45.00

STEINBECK, John. *Cup of Gold.* 1936. Covici Friede. 2nd ed. blue cloth. dj. EX. J3. $80.00

STEINBECK, John. *E of Eden.* 1952. NY. 1st ed. dj. EX. P3. $95.00

STEINBECK, John. *Forgotten Village.* 1941. Viking. 1st ed. EX. $50.00

STEINBECK, John. *Grapes of Wrath.* 1939. London. 1st ed. dj. EX. scarce. $325.00

STEINBECK, John. *Grapes of Wrath.* 1940. Ltd Ed Club. Ils/sgn Benton. 1/1146. 2 vols. VG. $250.00

STEINBECK, John. *In Dubious Battle.* 1936. Modern Lib. 12mo. dj. VG. $30.00

STEINBECK, John. *Journal of a Novel.* 1969. NY. 1st ed. dj. EX. $45.00

STEINBECK, John. *La Coupe d'Or.* 1952. Paris. Gallimard. 1st ed. wraps. EX. $55.00

STEINBECK, John. *Log From Sea of Cortez.* 1951. NY. 1st ed. dj. VG. B2. $95.00

STEINBECK, John. *Log From Sea of Cortez.* 1951. NY. 1st ed. G. B2. $65.00

STEINBECK, John. *Mon Caniche, L'Amerique et Moi.* 1962. Paris. Del Duca. 1st ed. EX. $75.00

STEINBECK, John. *Moon Is Down.* 1942. NY. 1st ed. 1st issue. dj. VG. $55.00

STEINBECK, John. *Moon Is Down.* 1942. NY. 1st ed. 2nd issue. dj. EX. $45.00

STEINBECK, John. *Of Mice & Men.* 1937. NY. 1st ed. 2nd issue. dj. EX. P3. $40.00

STEINBECK, John. *Of Mice & Men.* 1947. World. dj. VG. $18.00

STEINBECK, John. *Of Mice & Men.* 1979. Heritage. Ils Martin. slipcase. M. C1. $22.50

STEINBECK, John. *Red Pony.* 1945. Covici Friede. Ltd 1st ed. boxed. $90.00

STEINBECK, John. *Red Pony.* 1945. Viking. Ils 1st ed. slipcase. EX. $35.00

STEINBECK, John. *Russian Journal, With Pictures by Robert Capa.* 1948. NY. Viking. 1st ed. 220 p. dj. M. $75.00

STEINBECK, John. *Short Novels of John Steinbeck.* 1953. Viking. dj. M. $20.00

STEINBECK, John. *Short Reign of Pippin IV.* 1957. London. 1st ed. VG. $40.00

STEINBECK, John. *Sweet Thursday.* 1954. NY. 1st ed. dj. EX. P3. $60.00

STEINBECK, John. *Sweet Thursday.* 1954. Viking. 1st ed. G. $20.00

STEINBECK, John. *To a God Unknown.* 1933. Robert Ballou. 1st ed. 1st issue. green cloth. $450.00

STEINBECK, John. *Tortilla Flat.* 1935. Covici Friede. 1st ed. 8vo. dj. $150.00

STEINBECK, John. *Tortilla Flat.* 1937. Modern Lib. dj. VG. $12.00

STEINBECK, John. *Tortilla Flat.* 1944. Lausanne. Ils 1st ed. wraps. EX. $45.00

STEINBECK, John. *Winter of Our Discontent.* 1961. London. Heinemann. 1st ed. dj. VG. $45.00

STEINBECK, John. *Winter of Our Discontent.* 1961. NY. 1st ed. dj. VG. B2. $50.00

STEINBECK, John. *Winter of Our Discontent.* 1961. NY. Viking. 2nd ed. dj. $12.50

STEINBRUNNER & PENZLER. *Encyclopedia of Mystery & Detection.* 1976. Book Club. 436 p. dj. EX. $35.00

STEINER, E.A. *On the Trail of the Immigrant.* 1906. NY. Ils. photos. green bdg. VG. $20.00

STEINER, George. *Portage to San Cristobal...* 1981. NY. 1st Am ed. dj. VG. $15.00

STEINER, J.F. *Treblinka.* 1967. NY. 1st ed. G. $4.00

STEINGRABER, Erich. *Antique Jewelry: Its History in Europe From 800 to 1900.* 1957. London. Thames Hudson. Ils. 191 p. D2. $45.00

STEINGRABER, Erich. *Royal Treasures.* 1968. Macmillan. photos. D2. $55.00

STEINMETZ, C.P. *Theory & Calculations of Electrical Apparatus.* 1917. NY. 1st ed. 4th imp. EX. $50.00

STENHOUSE, Mrs. T.B.H. *Expose of Polygamy in UT.* 1972. NY. Ils 2nd ed. 221 p. rebound. T5. $25.00

STENNETT, W.H. *History of Origin of Place Names Connected With Chicago...* 1908. Chicago. 1st ed. 202 p. stiff wraps. J2. $22.50

STEPHEN, Leslie. *Hours in a Library.* 1892. London. New ed. $20.00

STEPHEN, Leslie. *Hours in a Library. Second Series.* 1881. London. 2nd ed. $20.00

STEPHEN, Leslie. *Hours in a Library. Third Series.* 1879. London. 1st ed. $20.00

STEPHENS, A.H. *War Between the States.* 1868. Ils. 2 vols. VG. J4. $30.00

STEPHENS, H.B. *Jacques Cartier & His Four Voyages to Canada.* 1890. 8vo. $75.00

STEPHENS, J.L. *Incidents of Travel in Central America, Chiapas & Yucatan.* 1852. NY. Harper. Ils. 2 vols. VG. A3. $60.00

STEPHENS, J.L. *Incidents of Travel in Egypt, Arabia Petraea & Holy Land.* 1970. OK U. Ils 1st print. 473 p. dj. EX. M2. $20.00

STEPHENS, James. *Crock of Gold.* 1926. Macmillan. 1/525. pls. sgn. dj. EX. $125.00

STEPHENS, James. *Crock of Gold.* 1929. Ils MacKenzie. gilt green cloth. VG. C1. $12.50

STEPHENS, James. *Crock of Gold.* 1968. Ils MacKenzie. VG. C1. $8.00

STEPHENS, James. *Etched in Moonlight.* 1928. NY. 1st Am ed. sgn. slipcase. VG. T5. $150.00

STEPHENS, James. *Irish Fairy Tales.* 1920. London. Macmillan. Ils Rackham. 1st ed. EX. $95.00

STEPHENS, James. *Julia Elizabeth.* 1929. NY. 1/861. sgn. EX. P3. $60.00

STEPHENS, R.W. *Lone Wolf: Story of TX Ranger Captain M.T. Gonzaullas.* 1979. Dallas. 1/650. sgn. 8vo. tan cloth. EX. T1. $40.00

STEPHENSON, M.R. *Historical Sketch of Sinking Spring Presbyterian Church...* 1948. Wytheville. 1st ed. 104 p. wraps. VG. rare. $35.00

STEPHENSON, Nathaniel. *Abraham Lincoln & the Union.* 1921. Yale. index. 272 p. EX. K1. $9.50

STEPHENSON, Nathaniel. *Day of the Confederacy.* 1919. Yale. 214 p. K1. $9.50

STEPNIAK. *Russia Under the Tzars.* 1885. Scribner. VG. $25.00

STERLING, Charles. *La Nature Morte de l'Antiquite a Nos Jours.* 1952. Paris. Pierre Tisne. 147 p. dj. D2. $150.00

STERLING, D. *Story of Mosses, Ferns & Mushrooms.* 1955. Doubleday. Ils. 159 p. VG. M2. $10.00

STERLING, S.H. *Lady of King Arthur's Court.* 1907. Phil. VG. $15.00

STERLING, W.W. *Trails & Trials of TX Ranger.* 1959. np. private print. VG. scarce. $100.00

STERLING, W.W. *Trails & Trials of TX Ranger.* 1968. Norman. OK U Pr. Ils. VG. $35.00

STERN, Bert. *Last Sitting.* 1982. Morrow. 1st ed. dj. EX. $25.00

STERN, Harold P. *Birds, Beasts, Blossoms, & Bugs: Nature of Japan.* 1976. NY. Abrams. Ils. 196 p. stiff wraps. D2. $28.00

STERN, P.V.D. *Confederate Navy: Pictorial History.* 1962. Bonanza. reprint. 256 p. dj. EX. M2. $10.00

STERN, P.V.D. *Man Who Killed Lincoln.* 1939. 408 p. M. K1. $9.50

STERN, P.V.D. *Man Who Killed Lincoln.* 1939. Ils. 408 p. VG. J4. $5.00

STERN, P.V.D. *Man Who Killed Lincoln.* 1939. Literary Guild. Ils. 408 p. dj. EX. M2. $10.00

STERN, P.V.D. *Robert E. Lee: Man & Soldier.* 1963. Ils. 256 p. J4. $8.00

STERN, P.V.D. *Robert E. Lee: Man & Soldier.* 1963. NY. Ils 1st ed. 4to. 256 p. T5. $22.50

STERN, P.V.D. *Secret Missions of the Civil War.* 1959. Bonanza. reprint. 320 p. dj. EX. M2. $7.00

STERN, P.V.D. *When the Guns Roared.* 1965. 385 p. EX. J4. $10.00

STERNE, Laurence. *Life & Opinions of Tristram Shandy.* 1963. Norwalk. Heritage. Ils Cleland. slipcase. $15.00

STERNE, Laurence. *Sentimental Journey Through France & Italy.* 1910. London. Ils/sgn Hopkins. 1st ed. 1/500. $85.00

STERNE, Laurence. *Sentimental Journey Through France & Italy.* 1930. Three Sirens. Ils Mahlon Blaine. 192 p. VG. $12.00

STERNE, Margaret. *Passionate Eye: Life of William R. Valentiner.* 1960. Detroit. Wayne U. Ils. dj. D2. $30.00

STERNE & MARINO. *Psychotheology.* 1970. NY. $7.00

STEVENS, C.A. *Berden's US Sharpshooters in Army of the Potomac.* 1892. St. Paul. 8vo. 555 p. $150.00

STEVENS, C.W. *Fishing in ME Lakes.* 1884. Boston. Ils 1st ed. 217 p. G. B2. $42.50

STEVENS, Doris. *Jailed for Freedom.* 1920. NY. 1st ed. 388 p. VG. $20.00

STEVENS, F.W. *Beginnings of NY Central Railroad: A History.* 1926. NY. Ils 1st ed. 8vo. TEG. dj. EX. T1. $85.00

STEVENS, G.T. *Three Years in the 6th Corps.* 1984. Time Life. reprint of 1866 ed. AEG. M. M2. $40.00

STEVENS, Henry. *Catalog of My English Library.* 1853. London. 1/1000. presentation. sgn. 107 p. $30.00

STEVENS, James. *Dore Treasury: Collection of Best Engravings.* 1970. NY. Crown. Ils. 246 p. dj. D2. $40.00

STEVENS, P.H. *Search Out the Land: History of American Military Scouts.* 1969. Chicago. 1st ed. dj. M. $20.00

STEVENS, R. *Laggard.* 1975. Canada. Falconiforme. 310 p. EX. M2. $17.00

STEVENS, Shane. *Anvil Chorus.* 1985. NY. Delacorte. 1st ed. dj. M. $15.00

STEVENS, Shane. *Dead City.* 1973. NY. Holt. 1st ed. dj. EX. $15.00

STEVENS, Shane. *Go Down Dead.* 1966. Morrow. 1st ed. dj. EX. $20.00

STEVENS, T.W. *Lettering.* 1916. Prang. lg 8vo. G. $15.00

STEVENS, W.O. *Beyond the Sunset.* 1944. NY. $14.00

STEVENS, Wallace. *Auroras of Autumn.* 1950. NY. 1st ed. dj. EX. $85.00

STEVENS, Wallace. *Necessary Angel.* 1951. NY. 1st ed. dj. EX. $75.00

STEVENS. *Meet Mr. Grizzly: Saga of the Passing of the Grizzly.* 1950. London. G. $18.00

STEVENS. *NY Typographical Union No. 6: Study of Modern Trade Union...* 1913. sgn Rouse. VG. $40.00

STEVENSON, Elizabeth. *Lafcadio Hearn.* 1961. NY. 1st ed. 362 p. dj. EX. $15.00

STEVENSON, M.C. *Zuni Indians.* 1904. WA. Ils. 612 p. orig green bdg. A3. $175.00

STEVENSON, R.L. *Across the Plains.* 1904. NY. 317 p. K1. $14.50

STEVENSON, R.L. *Ballads.* 1890. Chatto Windus. 1st ed. VG. J2. $25.00

STEVENSON, R.L. *Black Arrows. Tale of the Two Roses.* 1916. Scribner. 1st ed. J2. $85.00

STEVENSON, R.L. *Child's Garden of Verse.* 1923. NY. Ils Smith. EX. $95.00

STEVENSON, R.L. *Complete Works.* 1906. Boston. 1/1000. TEG. 10 vols. VG. $75.00

STEVENSON, R.L. *Kidnapped.* 1886. London. Cassell. 1st ed. 2nd issue. $250.00

STEVENSON, R.L. *Kidnapped.* 1913. Scribner. Ils Wyeth. 1st ed. J2. $75.00

STEVENSON, R.L. *Kidnapped.* 1921. NY. Ils Rhead. not 1st ed. J2. $15.00

STEVENSON, R.L. *Lodging for the Night.* 1902. Roycroft. violet suede. VG. D1. $30.00

STEVENSON, R.L. *Lodging for the Night.* 1902. Roycroft. 8vo. dark red suede. VG. D1. $35.00

STEVENSON, R.L. *Lodging for the Night.* 1968. Mosher. 1/425. slipcase. VG. C1. $12.00

STEVENSON, R.L. *Master of Ballantrae.* 1889. London. Cassell. 1st ed. 332 p. $60.00

STEVENSON, R.L. *Memories & Portraits.* 1887. Chatto Windus. 1st ed. J2. $30.00

STEVENSON, R.L. *Mr. Baskerville & His Ward.* 1922. London. Chapman. slipcase. $20.00

STEVENSON, R.L. *Prayers Written at Vailima.* 1910. Chatto Windus. 8vo. TEG. EX. J2. $75.00

STEVENSON, R.L. *Prayers Written at Vailima.* 1928. London. Ils. 4to. dj. VG. $35.00

STEVENSON, R.L. *Silverado Squatters.* 1952. San Francisco. 1/900. M. $60.00

STEVENSON, R.L. *St. Ives.* 1897. NY. 1st ed. VG. $75.00

STEVENSON, R.L. *Strange Case of Dr. Jekyll & Mr. Hyde.* 1930. Dodd Mead. 1st ed. EX. $40.00

STEVENSON, R.L. *Travels With a Donkey in Cevennes.* nd. England. Nelson. 16mo. VG. $35.00

STEVENSON, R.L. *Travels With a Donkey in Cevennes.* 1931. NY. Ils Blampied. 1st ed. VG. J2. $25.00

STEVENSON, R.L. *Travels With a Donkey in Cevennes.* 1957. Ltd Ed Club. 1/1500. Ils/sgn Duvoisin. EX. C1. $24.50

STEVENSON, R.L. *Treasure Island.* 1939. Scribner. Ils Wyeth. B4. $35.00

STEVENSON, R.L. *Treasure Island.* 1947. Grosset Dunlap. Ils Price. 8vo. dj. EX. $7.50

STEVENSON, R.L. *Treasure of Franchard.* 1954. Rodale Pr. Ils Mutulay. slipcase. EX. C1. $14.00

STEVENSON, R.L. *Underwoods.* 1900. Mosher. 1st ed. 1/925. EX. $45.00

STEVENSON, R.L. *Virginibus Puerisque.* 1903. Roycroft. 8vo. red suede. orig box. M. D1. $75.00

STEVENSON, R.L. *Walt Whitman: An Essay.* 1900. Roycroft. Ils Gardner. 8vo. G. D1. $105.00

STEVENSON, R.L. *Walt Whitman: An Essay.* 1900. Roycroft. not Ltd ed. 8vo. VG. D1. $40.00

STEVENSON, R.L. *Will O' the Mill.* 1/100. sgn. dj. orig box. M. D1. $300.00

STEVENSON, R.L. *Will O' the Mill.* 1901. Roycroft. 1/350. sgn. red suede. 8vo. VG. D1. $75.00

STEVENSON, William G. *Thirteen Months in the Rebel Army.* 1862. 232 p. scarce. J4. $60.00

STEVENSON, William. *Man Called Intrepid.* 1976. NY/London. 1st ed. dj. M1. $6.50

STEVENSON PRESS. *Armadillo.* 1978. Ils. 49 p. M2. $4.00

STEVERS, Martin. *Steel Trails. The Epic of the Railroads.* 1933. NY. Milton Balch. Ils. $18.50

STEWARD, J.D. *Tabulation of Librarianship.* 1947. London. $30.00

STEWARD, R.J. *Book of Merlin: Insights From First Merlin Conference.* 1987. 1st ed. dj. M. C1. $24.00

STEWARD, William. *First Edition of Steward's Healing Art...* 1827. Saco, ME. Putnam Blake. B1. $100.00

STEWARD & KRIKORIAN. *Plants, Chemicals & Growth.* 1971. Academic Pr. 232 p. dj. EX. M2. $20.00

STEWART, A.F. *Paintings, Drawings & Prints in Collection of A.F. Stuart.* 1920. private print. 1/120. 4to. VG. $50.00

STEWART, D.O. *Perfect Behavior.* 1922. NY. 8vo. $10.00

STEWART, E.I. *Custer's Luck.* 1955. Norman. 1st ed. dj. VG. $65.00

STEWART, E.W. *Blazed Trail Stories.* 1904. McClure. 1st ed. VG. $12.00

STEWART, E.W. *Camp & Trail.* 1907. Outing Pub. 1st ed. VG. $15.00

STEWART, E.W. *Pass.* 1906. Outing Pub. 1st ed. G. $10.00

STEWART, E.W. *Road I Know.* 1942. Dutton. 1st ed. dj. VG. $12.00

STEWART, E.W. *Speaking for Myself.* 1943. Doubleday. 1st ed. dj. EX. $15.00

STEWART, E.W. *Stampede.* 1942. Doubleday. 1st ed. EX. $18.00

STEWART, F.M. *Mannings.* 1973. NY. 2nd print. 648 p. dj. T5. $17.50

STEWART, F.M. *Star Child.* 1974. Arbor House. 1st ed. EX. $10.00

STEWART, G.R. *Ordeal by Hunger.* 1960. Boston. New Enlarged ed. $15.00

STEWART, H.A. *Net of Fireflies.* 1966. Tuttle. 6th print. boxed. M. $26.00

STEWART, J.J. *Iron Trail to the Golden Spike.* 1969. Desert. 297 p. dj. EX. $6.50

STEWART, J.T. *Air Power: Decisive Force in Korea.* 1957. NY. Ils. 310 p. dj. VG. T5. $25.00

STEWART, Mary. *Crystal Cave.* 1970. London. 1st Eng ed. dj. T6. $40.00

STEWART, Mary. *Crystal Cave.* 1970. 1st Eng ed. dj. C1. $29.50

STEWART, Mary. *Last Enchantment.* 1st Am ed. 1st print. dj. M. C1. $7.50

STEWART, Mary. *Last Enchantment.* 1st Eng ed. dj. EX. C1. $10.00

STEWART, Mary. *Merlin Trilogy.* 1980. 1st ed. 1 vol. dj. EX. C1. $13.50

STEWART, Mary. *Touch Not the Cat.* 1976. NY. 1st ed. dj. EX. $9.50

STEWART, Mary. *Wicked Day.* 1983. 1st Am ed. dj. C1. $8.00

STEWART, Mother. *Memories of Crusade: Thrilling Account of Women of OH...* 1889. Columbus. 2nd ed. 535 p. VG. T5. $25.00

STEWART, R.J. *Book of Merlin: Insights From the Merlin Conference.* 1987. 1st ed. pb. VG. C1. $12.00

STEWART. *Index of VA Printed Genealogies.* 1930. Richmond. 265 p. EX. $35.00

STEWART. *Skull Fractures Roentgenologically Considered.* 1925. NY. Ils. 44 pls. 4to. 64 p. EX. P3. $59.00

STEYN, P. *Birds of Prey of S Africa: Their Identification & Histories.* 1983. Tanager. Ils. 309 p. dj. EX. M2. $40.00

STEYN, P. *Delight of Owls.* 1984. Tanager. Ils 1st ed. 159 p. dj. M. M2. $25.00

STEYN, P. *Eagle Days: Study of African Eagles at the Nest.* 1974. Sable. Ils. 158 p. dj. EX. M2. $25.00

STICK, David. *Aycock Brown's Outerbanks.* 1976. Norfolk, VA. 1st ed. 207 p. VG. $15.00

STICK, David. *Graveyard of the Atlantic: Shipwrecks of NC Coast.* 1952. Chapel Hill. Ils Frank Stick. 1st ed. sgn. T5. $17.50

STICK, David. *Outer Banks of NC.* 1958. Chapel Hill. 1st ed. 2nd print. 352 p. EX. $20.00

STICKNEY, J.L. *Life & Glorious Deeds of Admiral Dewey.* c 1899. np. Ils. 8vo. 434 p. G. G2. $14.00

STIDWORTHY, J. *Snakes of the World.* 1978. Grosset Dunlap. Revised ed. 160 p. EX. M2. $13.00

STIEGLITZ, Alfred. *America & Alfred Stieglitz.* 1934. Literary Guild. 1st ed. VG. $17.50

STIEGLITZ, Alfred. *GA O'Keeffe.* 1978. MOMA. 1st ed. boxed. EX. $75.00

STILES, H.R. *Bundling: Its Origin, Progress & Decline in America.* 1871. Albany. 1st ed. VG. $35.00

STILES, H.R. *On Bundling.* 1937. Peter Pauper. 1/1450. 8vo. VG. $20.00

STILL, J. *Run for Elbertas.* 1980. Lexington. Intro Cleanth Brooks. 1st ed. dj. $25.00

STILL, James. *On Troublesome Creek.* 1941. NY. 1st ed. VG. B2. $35.00

STILL, William. *Iron Afloat: Story of Confederate Armorclads.* 1971. Nashville. dj. VG. $20.00

STILLINGFLEET, E.D. *Origines Britannicae; or, Antiquities of British Churches.* 1685. London. 364 p. $300.00

STILLWELL, L. *Story of a Common Soldier: Army Life in Civil War 1861-1865.* 1983. Time Life. reprint of 1920 ed. AEG. M. M2. $40.00

STILLWELL, M.B. *Noah's Ark in Early Woodcuts & Modern Rhymes.* 1942. NY. Ils 1st ed. 1/300. $60.00

STILLWELL, Margaret. *Incunabula & Americana: 1450-1800.* 1961. NY. EX. $55.00

STILLWELL, N. *Bird Songs: Adventures & Techniques in Recording Songs.* 1964. Doubleday. Ils 1st ed. 194 p. dj. EX. M2. $10.00

STIMMER, Tobias. *Neue Kunstliche Figuren Biblischer.* 1576. Basle. Gwarin. 166 woodcuts. 4to. rare. J2. $900.00

STINE, G.F. *Airbrush in Photography.* 1920. Cleveland. Able Pub. Ils. 144 p. tall 8vo. $30.00

STIRLING, I. *Distribution & Abundance of Seals in E Beaufort Sea.* 1982. Canada. Wildlife Service. 23 p. M2. $3.00

STIRLING, I. *Ecology of the Polar Bear Along W Coast of Hudson Bay.* 1977. Canada. Wildlife Service. 64 p. M2. $5.00

STIRLING, I. *Population Ecology Studies of Polar Bear.* 1980. Canada. Wildlife Service. 33 p. M2. $4.00

STIRLING, William. *Cloister Life.* 1852. London. gilt brown morocco. VG. $95.00

STIRLING, William. *Some Apostles of Physiology...* 1902. London. Waterlow. Ltd ed. very scarce. $135.00

STIRLING & KILIAAN. *Population Ecology Studies of Polar Bear in N Labrador.* 1980. Canada. Wildlife Service. 21 p. M2. $3.00

STIRLING. *Book on Steam for Engineers.* 1906. NY. Consolidated Boiler Co. fair. $12.00

STIRLING-MAXWELL, William. *Annals of the Artists of Spain.* 1891. London. Nimmo. Ils 2nd ed. 4 vols. TEG. D2. $200.00

STOBART & DAVIS. *Rediscovery of America's Maritime Heritage.* 1865. Dutton. gilt white buckram. dj. EX. J2. $95.00

STOCK, Dennis. *CA Trip.* 1970. NY. Grossman. 1st ed. $25.00

STOCK, Dennis. *Jazz Street.* 1960. Doubleday. 1st ed. dj. VG. $45.00

STOCKTON, F.E. *Adventures of Captain Horn.* not 1st ed. G. C2. $9.00

STOCKTON, F.E. *Afield & Afloat.* Ils 1st ed. VG. C2. $20.00

STOCKTON, F.E. *Bicycle of Cathay.* Ils 1st ed. VG. C2. $14.00

STOCKTON, F.E. *Buccaneers & Pirates of Our Coast.* not 1st ed. VG. C2. $10.00

STOCKTON, F.E. *Captain's Toll Gate.* not 1st ed. VG. C2. $12.00

STOCKTON, F.E. *Casting Away of Mrs. Lecks & Mrs. Aleshine.* 1933. Ils Revised 1st ed. dj. VG. C2. $16.00

STOCKTON, F.E. *Fable & Fiction.* Rodale. Classics ed. boxed. VG. $10.00

STOCKTON, F.E. *Girl at Cobhurst.* Ils 1st ed. G. C2. $15.00

STOCKTON, F.E. *Queen's Museum & Other Fanciful Tales.* 1906. Scribner. Ils Richardson. 1st ed. VG. B4. $75.00

STOCKWELL, Elisha *Private Elisha Stockwell Jr. Sees the Civil War.* 1958. OK U. Ils 1st ed. 210 p. dj. EX. M2. $10.00

STODDARD, H.L. *Memoirs of a Naturalist.* 1969. OK U. Ils Sutton. 2nd print. dj. M2. $20.00

STODDARD, J.L. *Glimpses of World.* 1892. Chicago. portfolio. full leather. $35.00

STODDARD, J.L. *Portfolio of Photographs of Famous Scenes, Cities...* c 1895. Chicago. oblong folio. AEG. $22.00

STODDARD, J.L. *Scenic America: Beauties of W Hemisphere.* c 1895. Chicago. oblong folio. $27.00

STODDARD, T.T. *Anglin` Songs.* 1889. Eden. 324 p. VG. B1. $50.00

STODDARD. *New World of Islam.* 1921. Simon Schuster. map. 362 p. $25.00

STOKER, Bram. *Jewel of Seven Stars.* 1904. Harper. 1st Am ed. G. $40.00

STOKER, Bram. *Personal Reminiscences of Henry Irving.* 1908. NY. 8vo. 2 vols. TEG. EX. P3. $39.00

STOKES, D.W. *Guide to Behavior of Common Birds.* 1979. Little Brown. Ils 1st ed. 336 p. EX. M2. $9.00

STOKES, Winston. *Story of Hiawatha Adapted From Longfellow.* nd. NY. Stokes. Ils Kirk. 1st ed. J2. $25.00

STOKES. *Diseases of Heart & Aorta.* 1985. Birmingham. facsmile of 1853 ed. EX. P3. $45.00

STOLLER, R.J. *Splitting.* 1973. Quadragle. 1st ed. dj. EX. $25.00

STOLTZ & STOLTZ. *Norman Rockwell & the Saturday Evening Post: Later Years.* 1976. Four S Corp. Ils. 217 p. dj. D2. $65.00

STOME & STOME. *Open Elite? England, 1540-1880.* 1984. Oxford. dj. EX. $25.00

STONE, E.L. *Book Lover's Bouquet.* 1931. NY. Rudge. 1/525. EX. $35.00

STONE, Eugenia. *Page Boy of Camelot.* pb. scarce. juvenile. C1. $7.50

STONE, Eugenia. *Robin Hood's Arrow.* 1948. Ils Busoni. 1st ed. juvenile. dj. VG. C1. $17.50

STONE, Eugenia. *Squire for King Arthur.* c 1955. 3rd print. pictorial cloth. xl. C1. $12.50

STONE, George. *Glossary of Construction, Decoration & Use of Arms & Armor.* 1934. Portland. Southworth Pr. Ils. 694 p. $68.00

STONE, Harlan. *Law & Its Administration.* 1944. NY. 232 p. $35.00

STONE, Irving. *Immortal Wife.* 1944. NY. 1st ed. sgn. dj. VG. $15.00

STONE, Irving. *Men To Match My Mountains.* 1956. Doubleday. 1st ed. sgn. 8vo. M. $55.00

STONE, Irving. *Origin.* 1980. NY. 1st trade ed. dj. VG. $20.00

STONE, Irving. *Those Who Love.* 1965. Doubleday. inscr/sgn. VG. $15.00

STONE, J.F. *Canyon Country.* 1932. NY. 1st ed. presentation. sgn. VG. B2. $40.00

STONE, Robert. *Children of Light.* 1986. NY. AP. EX. $75.00

STONE, Robert. *Dog Soldiers.* 1974. Boston. 1st ed. dj. EX. $50.00

STONE, Robert. *Dog Soldiers.* 1974. Boston. 1st ed. inscr/sgn. dj. G. $40.00

STONE, Robert. *Flag for Sunrise.* 1981. NY. AP. M. $85.00

STONE, Robert. *Flag for Sunrise.* 1981. NY. 1st ed. dj. EX. $20.00

STONE, Robert. *Flag for Sunrise.* 1981. NY. 1st trade ed. sgn. dj. EX. $45.00

STONE, Robert. *Hall of Mirrors.* 1967. Boston. 1st ed. sgn. dj. EX. $100.00

STONE, W.I. *Life of Joseph Brant.* 1846. Cooperstown. pls. maps. 2 vols. $85.00

STONE & LOOMIS. *Millions for Defense: Pictorial History of America's Cup.* 1934. Derrydale. 1/175. 4to. blue cloth. EX. $175.00

STONE. *Bankside Costume Book for Children.* 1900. Saalfield. Ils. xl. VG. $9.00

STONE. *Passions of the Mind.* 1971. 1st ed. sgn. dj in plastic dj. VG. $50.00

STONEHILL, C.A. *Jewish Contribution to Civilization.* 1940. Cheltenham. Ltd ed. 198 p. G. $45.00

STONEHOUSE, G. *Green Leaves, New Chapters in Life of Charles Dickens.* 1931. London. 1st ed. wraps. xl. G. very scarce. $110.00

STONEY, S.G. *Plantations of Carolina Low Country...* 1938. Charleston. Carolina Art Assn. 1st ed. sgn. dj. $150.00

STONG, Phil. *Buckskin Breeches.* 1937. NY. 1st ed. sgn. 366 p. T5. $65.00

STONG, Phil. *Horses & Americans.* 1939. Stokes. Ils Wiese. Ltd ed. 1/250. sgn. VG. $45.00

STOPES, M. *Contraception.* 1932. London. Putnam. $48.00

STORER & TEVIS. *CA Grizzly.* 1978. NE U. photos. 335 p. EX. M2. $24.00

STOREY, David. *Restoration of Arnold Middleton.* 1967. London. 1st ed. dj. EX. $20.00

STORKE, E.G. *Domestic Animals.* 1859. NY. orig bdg. VG. scarce. $55.00

STORM, Theodore. *Oktoberlied.* 1945. LA. Ward Ritchie. 1/200. wraps. $45.00

STOUDT, J.J. *Consider the Lilies How They Grow... Vol. 2.* 1937. PA German Folklore Soc. fair. $50.00

STOUFFER, S.A. *American Soldier.* 1949. Princeton. 1st ed. 2 vols. djs. VG. T5. $75.00

STOUT, H.F. *Standt-Stoudt-Stout Family of OH & Their Ancestors...* 1935. np. 1/200. 325 p. T5. $47.50

STOUT, MATTHIESSEN & CLEM. *Shore Birds of N America.* 1967. Viking. EX. $140.00

STOUT, Rex. *Black Mountain.* 1955. London. 1st ed. dj. VG. $20.00

STOUT, Rex. *Black Orchids.* 1942. Farrar Rinehart. 1st ed. G. $45.00

STOUT, Rex. *Broken Vase.* 1941. Dell. 1st ed. pb. VG. $35.00

STOUT, Rex. *Doorbell Rang.* 1965. Viking. 1st ed. 2nd print. dj. EX. $35.00

STOUT, Rex. *Family Affair.* 1975. NY. 1st ed. dj. VG. $25.00

STOUT, Rex. *Golden Spiders.* 1953. Bantam. reprint. VG. $12.00

STOUT, Rex. *In the Best Families.* 1950. Viking. 1st ed. dj. EX. $45.00

STOUT, Rex. *In the Best of Fire.* 1960. NY. Review 1st ed. dj. VG. $45.00

STOUT, Rex. *League of Frightened Men.* 1935. Grosset Dunlap. G. $40.00

STOUT, Rex. *Please Pass the Guilt.* 1973. Viking. 1st ed. dj. EX. $10.00

STOUT, Rex. *Price of Murder.* 1936. Dell. 1st ed. pb. G. $35.00

STOUT, Rex. *Red Box.* 1937. NY. Farrar. 1st ed. VG. $60.00

STOUT, Rex. *Rubber Band.* 1936. Grosset Dunlap. G. $35.00

STOUT, Rex. *Second Confession.* 1949. Viking. 1st ed. VG. $80.00

STOUT, Rex. *Silent Speaker.* 1946. NY. 1st ed. dj. EX. $45.00

STOUT, Rex. *Some Buried Caesar.* 1941. Triangle. dj. VG. $15.00

STOUT, Rex. *Three Doors to Death.* 1950. NY. Viking. 1st ed. VG. $65.00

STOUT, Rex. *Too Many Cooks.* 1938. Am Magazine. dj. boxed. VG. $195.00

STOUT, Rex. *Too Many Cooks.* 1941. Triangle. dj. G. $7.50

STOUT, Rex. *Triple Jeopardy.* 1941. Bantam. reprint. VG. $12.00

STOUT, Rex. *Trouble in Triplicate.* 1949. Viking. 1st ed. VG. $80.00

STOVER, J.F. *American Railroads.* 1967. 30 p. $18.50

STOVER, J.F. *Iron Road to the W: American Railroads in the 1850s.* 1978. 266 p. $20.00

STOW & HOWES. *General Chronicle of England.* 1631. London. VG. $450.00

STOWE, C.E. *Life of Harriet Beecher.* 1890. Stowe. Ils Beman. 8vo. 530 p. VG. $25.00

STOWE, H.B. *Key to Uncle Tom's Cabin.* 1853. Boston. 1st ed. G. $75.00

STOWE, H.B. *Uncle Tom's Cabin.* 1853. Ils. 560 p. K1. $45.00

STOWE, H.B. *Uncle Tom's Cabin.* 1897. Winston. Ils. Dutch/Eng text. 200 p. G. B2. $65.00

STOWE, H.B. *Uncle Tom's Cabin.* 1938. NY. Ils Covarrubias. 4to. dj. EX. $170.00

STOWE & LYMAN. *Harriet Beecher Stowe.* 1911. Houghton. Ils 1st print. VG. $45.00

STRADER, W.A. *Fifty Years of Flight: Chronicle of Aviation Industry...* 1953. Cleveland. Eaton. Ils. 178 p. dj. VG. T5. $45.00

STRAHAN, Edward. *Art Gallery of the Exhibition...* 1877. Phil. Gebbie Barrie. Ils. AEG. D2. $135.00

STRAHAN, Edward. *Chefs-d'Oeuvre d'Art of International Exhibition, 1878.* c 1878. Phil. Ils. folio. D2. $175.00

STRAHORN, R.E. *To Rockies & Beyond; or, Summer on Union Pacific Railroad...* 1879. New W Pub. Revised Enlarged 2nd ed. wraps. $100.00

STRAKA, John. *Way It Was: Maple Heights, OH.* 1988. Maple Heights. Ils 1st ed. 128 p. dj. T5. $19.50

STRAKHOV, N.M. *Principles of Lithogenesis.* nd. 1st Eng ed. maps. 245 p. dj. EX. M2. $23.00

STRAND & NEWHALL. *Time in New England.* 1950. NY. pls. VG. $17.50

STRANG, Joanne. *Shadows on the Sceptered Isle.* 1980. 1st ed. dj. M. C1. $7.50

STRANGE, Michael. *Clare De Lune.* 1921. Putnam. VG. $4.00

STRATEMEYER, Edward. *Shorthand Tom the Reporter.* nd. Grosset. VG. P1. $15.00

STRATTON, J.L. *Pioneer Women: Voices From KS Frontier.* 1981. Simon Schuster. Ils 1st ed. 319 p. dj. EX. M2. $16.00

STRATTON, Porter. *Territorial Press of NM, 1834-1912.* 1969. NM U. 1st ed. dj. J2. $25.00

STRATTON, R.B. *Captivity of Oatman Girls.* 1860. NY. Carlton Porter. 290 p. scarce. A3. $180.00

STRATTON, Roy. *Decorated Corpse.* nd. Book Club. dj. VG. P1. $3.00

STRAUB, Peter. *Blue Rose.* 1985. Underwood. 1st ed. sgn. dj. boxed. EX. P1. $85.00

STRAUB, Peter. *Floating Dragon.* nd. Book Club. dj. VG. P1. $4.50

STRAUB, Peter. *Floating Dragon.* 1982. Underwood. 1st ed. sgn. dj. EX. P1. $100.00

STRAUB, Peter. *Floating Dragon.* 1983. Collins. 1st ed. sgn. dj. EX. P1. $35.00

STRAUB, Peter. *Floating Dragon.* 1983. Putnam. 1st ed. dj. VG. P1. $25.00

STRAUB, Peter. *General's Wife.* 1982. Donald Grant. 1st ed. sgn. no dj issued. EX. P1. $50.00

STRAUB, Peter. *Ghost Story.* 1979. Jonathan Cape. dj. EX. P1. $35.00

STRAUB, Peter. *Leeson Park & Belsize Square.* 1983. Underwood. 1st ed. sgn. dj. EX. P1. $45.00

STRAUB, Peter. *Marriages.* 1973. Coward McCann Geohegan. 1st ed. dj. $100.00

STRAUB, Peter. *Shadow Land.* 1980. Coward McCann. ARC. wraps. EX. $50.00

STRAUB, Peter. *Shadow Land.* 1980. Coward McCann. 1st ed. sgn. dj. EX. P1. $35.00

STRAUBEL, J.H. *Air Force Diary.* 1947. NY. 1st ed. 492 p. G. T5. $15.00

STRAUSS, Victor. *Printing Industry.* 1967. WA. Ils. 814 p. dj. EX. $75.00

STRAWSON, John. *Battle for the Ardennes.* 1972. NY. Ils 1st ed. 212 p. VG. T5. $17.50

STRAYER, Joseph. *Albigensian Crusades.* 1971. 1st ed. xl. VG. C1. $10.00

STRECHER, E.A. *Their Mother's Sons.* 1946. Lippincott. 12mo. VG. $10.00

STREET, G.S. *Books & Things: Collection of Stray Remarks.* 1905. London. 1st ed. $40.00

STREET, G.S. *Wise & the Wayward.* 1896. London. 1st ed. EX. $40.00

STREET, James. *Good-Bye My Lady.* 1941. Indianapolis. 1st ed. dj. VG. B2. $25.00

STREET, James. *In My Father's House.* 1941. NY. 1st ed. dj. VG. B2. $40.00

STREET, James. *Velvet Doublet.* nd. Book Club. dj. VG. P1. $3.00

STREET, N. *Pathway to Spiritual Healing.* 1865. London. $10.00

STREET, P. *Vanishing Animals: Preserving Nature's Rarities.* 1963. Dutton. Ils 1st ed. 232 p. dj. EX. M2. $10.00

STREET, P. *Wildlife Presevation.* 1971. Regnery. Ils. 141 p. dj. VG. M2. $6.00

STREETER, D.W. *Camels!* 1927. Putnam. Ils 1st ed. 277 p. dj. G. M2. $5.00

STREETER, F.B. *Ben Thompson: Man With a Gun.* 1957. Fell. Ils. 217 p. dj. EX. M2. $35.00

STREETER, T.W. *Celebrated Collection of Americana...Thomas W. Streeter.* 1966-1969. NY. 1st ed. 8 vols. glassine djs. $500.00

STRETE, Craig. *Death Chants.* 1988. Doubleday. 1st ed. dj. RS. EX. P1. $15.00

STRETE, Craig. *Dreams That Burn in the Night.* 1982. Doubleday. dj. EX. P1. $10.00

STRICKLAND, W.P. *Pioneers of the W.* 1856. NY. 1st ed. black leather solander case. J2. $275.00

STRIDBECK, Carl Gustaf. *Raphael Studies II: Raphael & Tradition.* 1963. Stockholm. Almqvist Wiksell. Ils. D2. $35.00

STRIEBER, Whitley. *Night Church.* nd. Book Club. dj. VG. P1. $4.50

STRIKER, Fran. *Clue of the Cypress Stump.* nd. Clover. G. P1. $6.00

STRIKER, Fran. *Hidden Stone Mystery.* nd. Grosset. VG. P1. $6.00

STRIKER, Fran. *Lone Ranger & Gold Robbery.* nd. NY. Grosset. dj. VG. $8.00

STRIKER, Fran. *Lone Ranger & the Mystery Ranch.* nd. Grosset. dj. xl. P1. $10.00

STRIKER, Fran. *Lone Ranger & the Outlaw Stronghold.* nd. Grosset. G. P1. $7.50

STRIKER, Fran. *Lone Ranger & Tonto.* nd. NY. Grosset. dj. VG. $8.00

STRIKER, Fran. *Lone Ranger at the Haunted Gulch.* nd. Grosset. dj. VG. P1. $10.00

STRIKER, Fran. *Lone Ranger at the Haunted Gulch.* nd. Grosset. VG. P1. $7.50

STRIKER, Fran. *Lone Ranger on Powderhorn Trail.* 1949. Grosset. 207 p. $7.50

STRIKER, Fran. *Lone Ranger Rides Again.* nd. Grosset. VG. P1. $8.50

STRIKER, Fran. *Lone Ranger Traps the Smugglers.* nd. Grosset. VG. P1. $7.50

STRIKER, Fran. *Sign of the Spiral.* nd. Grosset. VG. dj. P1. $12.50

STRIKER, Fran. *Telltale Scar.* nd. Grosset. G. P1. $6.00

STRIKER, Fran. *Telltale Scar.* 1947. Grosset. VG. P1. $9.00

STRINDBERG, August. *Lucky Pehr.* 1912. Cincinnati. 1st Am ed. VG. $30.00

STRINDBERG, August. *There Are Crimes & Crimes.* 1912. NY. 1st Am ed. VG. $35.00

STRINGER, Arthur. *City of Peril.* nd. Burt. VG. P1. $7.50

STRINGHAM, E. *Alexander Wilson: Founder of Scientific Ornithology.* 1958. private print. 29 p. M2. $5.00

STROHL, H.G. *Oesterreichisch-Ungarische Wappenrolle.* 1890. 12 color pls. VG. $75.00

STROMBERG, Gustaf. *Soul of the Universe.* 1948. Phil. $60.00

STRONG, Charles. *Art of Show Card Writing.* 1912. Detroit. School of Lettering. 3rd ed. VG. $30.00

STRONG, D.H. *Dreamers & Defenders: American Conservationists.* 1988. NE U. 295 p. M. M2. $8.00

STRONG, James. *New Harmony & Exposition of the Gospels...* 1852. NY. G. $42.50

STRONG, L.A.G. *Corporal Tune.* 1934. Gollancz. G. P1. $5.00

STRONG, Patience. *Quiet Corner Reflections.* 1951. Muller. 7th ed. G. P1. $5.00

STRONG, Patience. *Silver Linings.* 1940. John Miles. 2nd ed. dj. VG. P1. $10.00

STRONG, Phil. *Horses & Americans.* 1939. NY. Ils Wiese. 4to. tan cloth. VG. $45.00

STRONG, R.K. *Kingzett's Chemical Encyclopedia.* 1952. Van Nostrand. 8th ed. EX. $20.00

STRONG, R.P. *African Republic of Liberia & Belgian Congo.* 1930. Cambridge, MA. 2 vols. G. T5. $75.00

STROUD, John. *Soviet Transport Aircraft Since 1945.* 1968. NY. Ils. 318 p. VG. T5. $9.50

STROUD. *Inscribed Union Swords, 1861-1865.* nd. TX. Ils. sgn. 192 p. EX. $30.00

STROUSE, Jean. *Alice James, a Biography.* 1980. Houghton. 1st ed. dj. VG. $20.00

STROUT, R.L. *Maud.* 1939. Macmillan. VG. $40.00

STRUGATSKY, Arkady. *Ugly Swans.* 1979. Macmillan. 1st ed. dj. VG. P1. $15.00

STUART, Brian. *Mysterious Monsieur Moray.* 1950. Ward Lock. 1st ed. xl. VG. P1. $7.50

STUART, J. *History of Zulu Rebellion of 1906.* 1913. London. Ils. 5 maps. 6 plans. 581 p. B2. $85.00

STUART, Jesse. *Come Gentle Spring.* 1st ed. dj. VG. B7. $20.00

STUART, Jesse. *Man With a Bull-Tongued Plow.* 1934. NY. 1st ed. dj. VG. $250.00

STUART, Jesse. *Save Every Little Lamb.* 1956. McGraw Hill. sgn. 8vo. dj. EX. $80.00

STUART, Jesse. *Trees of Heaven.* 1940. NY. 1st ed. sgn. dj. EX. $125.00

STUCK, Hudson. *Ascent of Denali.* 1925. NY. Ils. fld map. 188 p. VG. B2. $45.00

STUCK, Hudson. *Ten Thousand Miles With a Dog Sled.* 1914. NY. Ils 1st ed. VG. $50.00

STUCKEY & KYLE. *Pecan Growing.* 1925. Macmillan. Ils 1st ed. 233 p. $27.50

STUDER, Jacob. *Birds of N America.* 1897. NY. 119 color pls. folio. VG. $275.00

STUDER, Jacob. *Popular Ornithology, Birds of N America.* 1977. Barrie. Imprint Soc. 1/500. folio. EX. $60.00

STUNTZ, D.E. *How To Identify Mushrooms to Genus IV.* 1977. Mad River. 94 p. M2. $5.00

STURGEON, Theodore. *Godbody.* 1986. Donald Fine. dj. VG. P1. $15.00

STURGEON, Theodore. *Golden Helix.* nd. Book Club. dj. EX. P1. $5.00

STURGEON, Theodore. *More Than Human.* nd. Book Club. dj. VG. P1. $4.50

STURGEON, Theodore. *More Than Human.* 1978. Ballantine. 1st ed. sgn. no dj issued. EX. P1. $35.00

STURGEON, Theodore. *Sturgeon Is Alive & Well.* nd. Book Club. dj. VG. P1. $4.50

STURGEON, Theodore. *Touch of Strange.* nd. Book Club. dj. VG. P1. $7.50

STURZAKER, D. & J. *Color & the Kabbalah.* 1975. NY. 1st ed. dj. VG. $25.00

STUTTON, Jeff. *Apollo At Go.* nd. Book Club. dj. xl. P1. $3.00

STYLES, Showell. *Tiger Patrol.* 1957. Collins. 1st ed. VG. P1. $10.00

STYRON, William. *Blankenship.* 1988. np. 1/126. sgn. dj. VG. $65.00

STYRON, William. *Confessions of Nat Turner.* 1967. NY. 1st ed. dj. EX. P3. $35.00

STYRON, William. *Lie Down in Darkness.* 1951. Indianapolis/NY. 1st ed. dj. EX. $90.00

STYRON, William. *Lie Down in Darkness.* 1983. Franklin Lib. 1st ed. sgn. AEG. full leather. $75.00

STYRON, William. *Quiet Dust.* 1982. NY. Ltd ed. 1/240. sgn. slipcase. $85.00

STYRON, William. *Quiet Dust.* 1982. Random House. 1st trade ed. dj. VG. $20.00

STYRON, William. *Set This House on Fire.* 1960. Random House. 1st ed. dj. EX. $55.00

STYRON, William. *Sophie's Choice.* 1979. Random House. 1st trade ed. dj. EX. $30.00

SUDELL, Richard. *Landscape & Garden. Vols. 1-5.* 1934-1938. London. 4to. EX. $175.00

SUDWORTH, Gwynedd. *Dragon & the Eagle.* 1980. London. 1st ed. dj. M. C1. $8.00

SUE, Eugene. *Wandering Jew.* 1844-1845. London. 1st ed. 3 vols. $90.00

SUE, Eugene. *Works of Eugene Sue.* nd. Boston. Nicolls. 1/1000. 11 vols. VG. $150.00

SUES, O.L. *Grigsby's Cowboys.* 1900. Salem, SD. Ils 1st ed. 359 p. scarce. T5. $175.00

SUETONIUS. *Lives of Twelve Caesars.* 1932. Verona. Ltd Ed Club. 4to. dj. EX. $90.00

SUGGS, R.C. *Lords of the Blue Pacific.* 1967. NY Graphic Soc. Ils. 151 p. dj. EX. M2. $4.00

SUGRUE, Thomas. *Stranger in the Earth.* 1948. NY. $40.00

SUHL, Yuri. *They Fought Back.* 1967. 327 p. xl. G. $12.00

SUKUL, D.R. *Yoga & Self-Culture.* 1943. NY. $9.00

SULLIVAN, James. *History of NY State, Vol. 3: French & Indian War to WWI.* nd. Lewis Hist Pub. $10.00

SULLIVAN, L.H. *Kindergarten Chats.* 1934. Scarab Fraternity Pr. 1st ed. B2. $275.00

SULLIVAN, Maurice. *Jedediah Smith, Trader & Trailbreaker.* 1936. NY. Pioneer Pr. Ils. 233 p. dj. VG. A3. $90.00

SULLIVAN. *Fabulous Wilson Mizner.* 1935. NY. Ils 1st ed. 324 p. dj. VG. B2. $22.50

SULLY, James. *Outlines of Psychology.* 1895. Appleton. 523 p. EX. $6.00

SULLY. *Memoirs Maximilian de Bethune, Duke of, Prime Minster...* 1763. London. 4th ed. 12mo. 6 vols. VG. $150.00

SULZBERGER, C.L. *Tooth Merchant.* 1973. Quadrangle. 1st ed. dj. VG. P1. $10.00

SULZBERGER, C.L. *WWII.* 1966. Am Heritage. VG. $14.00

SUMMERFIELD, Charles. *Rangers & Regulators of Tanaha; or, Life Among the Lawless.* 1856. NY. DeWitt. 1st ed. 397 p. orig bdg. A3. $140.00

SUMMERHAYES, Martha. *Vanished AZ.* 1939. Chicago. Lakeside Classic. 337 p. G. T5. $25.00

SUMMERHAYES, Martha. *Vanished AZ.* 1939. Donnelley. Lakeside Classic. A3. $45.00

SUMMERS, G. *Lure of the Falcon.* 1972. Simon Schuster. Ils 1st ed. 283 p. dj. EX. M2. $10.00

SUMMERS, G. *Owned by an Eagle.* 1977. Dutton. Review of 1st ed. 223 p. dj. M2. $18.00

SUMMERS, H.G. *On Strategy: Critical Analysis of Vietnam War.* 1982. Novato, CA. 1st ed. 224 p. dj. VG. T5. $12.50

SUMMERS, Montague. *Compendium Maleficarium by Brother Francesco Guazzo.* 1929. London. Rodker. VG. $110.00

SUMMERS, Montague. *Covent Garden Drollery.* 1927. London. 1/575. 12mo. VG. $45.00

SUMMERS, Montague. *Supernatural Omnibus.* 1961. Gollancz. 7th ed. dj. VG. P1. $22.50

SUMMERS, Montague. *Vampire: His Kith & Kin.* 1928. Kegan Paul. 1st Eng ed. EX. $60.00

SUMMERS, Richard. *Vigilante.* 1949. Duell Sloan. dj. G. P1. $7.50

SUMMERSON, John. *Architecture in Britain, 1530-1830.* 1954. Baltimore. 1st ed. VG. J2. $50.00

SUMNER, Charles. *Prophetic Voices Concerning America.* 1874. Boston. 12mo. 176 p. green cloth. xl. VG. G2. $11.00

SUMTER, Nathaniel. *Fifteen Letters...Introduction & Notations by M.V.S. White.* 1942. Columbia. private print. 1/500. 4to. 124 p. $75.00

SUNDBERG & RICHARDSON. *Mushrooms & Other Fungi of Land Between the Lakes.* 1980. S IL U. 92 color photos. 60 p. EX. M2. $5.00

SUNDELL, Nina. *Robert & Jane Meyerhoff Collection, 1958-1979.* 1980. Phoenix, MD. Ils. 76 p. D2. $17.00

SUNDER, J.E. *Bill Sublette: Mountain Man.* 1959. OK U. Ils 1st ed. 279 p. dj. EX. M2. $26.00

SUNDER, J.E. *Fur Trade on the Upper MO: 1840-1865.* 1965. OK U. Ils 1st ed. 295 p. dj. EX. M2. $37.00

SUNDER, J.E. *Joshua Pilcher: Fur Trader & Indian Agent.* 1968. OK U. Ils 1st ed. 203 p. dj. EX. M2. $22.00

SUNDERLAND, L.R. *Pathetism.* 1843. NY. 1st ed. 247 p. wraps. rare. $275.00

SUNOL. *TB Gregorian Chant.* 1930. Belgium. leather. VG. G1. $25.00

SURETTE, L.A. *By-Laws of Corinthian Lodge...* 1859. Concord. $75.00

SURFACE, Bill. *Roundup at the Double Diamond: American Cowboy Today.* 1974. Boston. 1st ed. dj. VG. $20.00

SURFACE, Frank. *Grain Trade During the World War.* 1928. Macmillan. 1st ed. J2. $12.50

SURIEU, R. *Sarv E naz Essai sur les Representations Erotiques...* 1967. Geneva. Ils. quarto. $75.00

SUSHEVER, A. *Vilna Ghetto, 1941-1944.* 1947. NY. Yiddish text. $75.00

SUTCLIFF, Rosemary. *Dawn Wind.* 1st Am ed. xl. VG. C1. $8.50

SUTCLIFF, Rosemary. *Eagle of the Ninth.* Puffin. pb. VG. scarce. C1. $6.00

SUTCLIFF, Rosemary. *Lantern Bearers.* 1979. Oxford. VG. C1. $11.50

SUTCLIFF, Rosemary. *Sword at Sunset.* Book Club. dj. VG. C1. $6.50

SUTCLIFF, Rosemary. *Tristan & Iseult.* 1974. London. Ils Ambrus. dj. EX. C1. $14.00

SUTCLIFFE, Alice. *Robert Fulton & the Clermont...* 1909. NY. 1st ed. 1/200. EX. $125.00

SUTERMIESTER. *Story of Papermaking.* 1954. Boston. 1st ed. EX. $25.00

SUTHERLAND, C.H.V. *Coinage in Roman Imperial Policy: 31 BC-AD 68.* 1951. London. Methuen. 1st ed. dj. EX. $36.00

SUTHERLAND, M.A. *Story of Corpus Christi.* 1916. Corpus Christi. VG. $85.00

SUTHERLAND, S.K. *Venomous Creatures of Australia.* 1981. Oxford U. Ils 1st ed. 128 p. M2. $28.00

SUTTON, A. & M. *Life of the Desert.* 1966. McGraw Hill. Ils. 4to. 232 p. VG. M2. $14.00

SUTTON, Francis. *Systematic Handbook of Volumetric Analysis.* 1911. 621 p. G. $4.00

SUTTON, G.M. *Bird Student: An Autobiography.* 1980. TX U. Ils 1st ed. 216 p. dj. EX. M2. $15.00

SUTTON, G.M. *Birds in the Wilderness: Adventures of an Ornithologist.* 1936. Macmillan. Ils 1st ed. 200 p. dj. EX. M2. $85.00

SUTTON, G.M. *Eskimo Year.* 1985. OK U. 1st print of 2nd ed. dj. EX. M2. $15.00

SUTTON, G.M. *Iceland Summer: Adventures of a Bird Painter.* 1974. OK U. Ils. 253 p. dj. EX. M2. $20.00

SUTTON, G.M. *Mexican Birds: First Impressions.* 1951. OK U. Ils 1st ed. 282 p. dj. EX. M2. $165.00

SUTTON, G.M. *Portraits of Mexican Birds: Fifty Selected Paintings.* 1975. OK U. 50 color pls. 113 p. EX. M2. $9.00

SUTTON, G.M. *To a Young Bird Artist.* 1979. OK U. Ils 1st ed. 147 p. dj. EX. M2. $15.00

SUTTON, H.E. *Genes, Enzymes & Inherited Diseases.* 1961. NY. 1st ed. EX. $50.00

SUTTON, Henry. *Vector.* 1970. Bernard Geis. 3rd ed. dj. VG. P1. $10.00

SUTTON, Horace. *Confessions of Grand Hotel: Waldorf-Astoria.* 1953. NY. 1st ed. sgn. $40.00

SUTTON, Jeff. *Atom Conspiracy.* 1963. Avalon. dj. EX. P1. $15.00

SUTTON, Jeff. *Atom Conspiracy.* 1963. Avalon. dj. xl. P1. $5.00

SUTTON, Margaret. *Haunted Attic.* nd. Grosset. VG. P1. $6.00

SUTTON, Margaret. *Magic Makers & the Golden Charm.* 1936. Grosset. Ils Pelagie Doane. G. $18.00

SUTTON, Margaret. *Mysterious Half Cat.* nd. Grosset Dunlap. VG. P1. $7.50

SUTTON, Margaret. *Mystic Ball.* nd. Grosset. dj. VG. P1. $10.00

SUTTON, Margaret. *Rainbow Riddle.* nd. Grosset. dj. VG. P1. $12.50

SUTTON, Margaret. *Secret of the Musical Tree.* nd. Grosset. VG. P1. $5.00

SUTTON, Margaret. *Seven Strange Clues.* 1932. Grosset. VG. P1. $15.00

SUTTON, Margaret. *Voice in the Suitcase.* 1935. Grosset. G. P1. $10.00

SUTTON, Margaret. *Warning on the Window.* nd. Grosset. VG. P1. $6.00

SUTTON, Margaret. *Whispered Watchword.* nd. Grosset. xl. rebound. VG. P1. $5.00

SUTULOV, A. *Copper Porphyries.* 1974. UT U. Ils. 200 p. dj. EX. M2. $18.00

SVININE, Paul. *Sketch of the Life of General Moreau.* 1814. NY. rebound. VG. T5. $25.00

SWAAN, W. *Gothic Cathedral.* 1969. NY. dj. $30.00

SWAAN, W. *Lost Cities of Asia: Ceylon, Burma, Cambodia.* 1966. Putnam. 1st Am ed. 103 pls. folio. dj. EX. $22.00

SWADOS, Harvey. *Story for Teddy & Others.* 1965. NY. 1st ed. dj. EX. $30.00

SWAIM, Don. *H.L. Mencken Murder Case.* 1988. St. Martin. 1st ed. dj. M. $10.00

SWAN, M. *Marches of El Dorado: British Guiana, Brazil & Venezuela.* 1958. Beacon. photos. maps. 304 p. dj. VG. M2. $11.00

SWAN, O.G. *Frontier Days.* 1928. Phil. 1st ed. 12 pls. 512 p. VG. T5. $35.00

SWANBERG, W.A. *First Blood, Story of Ft. Sumter.* 1957. 373 p. dj. $12.00

SWANK, W.G. *Mule Deer in AZ Chaparral.* 1958. AZ Fish/Game. photos. 109 p. EX. M2. $8.00

SWANNACK, J.D. *Big Juniper House of Mesa Verde.* 1969. Nat Park Service. EX. $25.00

SWANTON, J.R. *Myths & Tales of SE Indians.* 1929. Smithsonian. VG. $45.00

SWEDENBORG, Emanual. *Arcana Coelestia.* 1984. Standard ed. 39th print. 12 vols. VG. $85.00

SWEDENBORG, Emanuel. *Treatise Concerning Heaven & Its Wonders & Also Hell.* 1825. 8vo. 395 p. rebound gilt cloth. VG. T1. $125.00

SWEENEY, J.B. *Guide to Military Museums, Forts & Historical Sites in US.* 1981. NY. Ils 1st ed. 306 p. dj. VG. T5. $12.50

SWEENEY, J.B. *Pictorial History of Sea Monsters & Other Marine Life.* 1972. Bonanza. reprint. Ils. 4to. 314 p. dj. M2. $18.00

SWEENEY, J.J. *Marc Chagall.* 1946. MOMA. 1st ed. dj. G. $50.00

SWEENEY, W.C. *Military Intelligence: New Weapon of War.* 1924. NY. 1st ed. inscr. VG. $22.50

SWEENEY & SERT. *Antonio Gaudi.* 1960. NY. Praeger. Ils. 192 p. dj. D2. $55.00

SWEET & KNOX. *Sketches From TX Shiftings.* 1882. NY. 1st ed. 12mo. 228 p. G. G2. $37.00

SWEETING, C.G. *Combat Flying Clothing.* 1984. WA. Ils. 229 p. dj. EX. T5. $19.50

SWEETMAN, Luke. *Back Trailing on Open Range.* 1951. Caxton. 1st ed. sgn. EX. $50.00

SWEETSER, K.D. *Boys & Girls From Thackeray.* 1907. NY. Ils Williams. 1st ed. VG. $15.00

SWEETSER, M.F. *Guide to the White Mountains.* 1918. Houghton. fld map. 6 fld panoramas. G. M2. $10.00

SWEETSER, M.F. *King's Handbook of Boston Harbor.* c 1888. Boston. 3rd ed. VG. $20.00

SWEETSER, M.F. *Views of the White Mountains.* 1879. Franklin Pr. Ils. gilt green bdg. VG. $25.00

SWENGEL, F.M. *American Steam Locomotive. Vol. I, Evolution of Locomotive.* 1967. Davenport. Ils 1st ed. 269 p. dj. VG. T5. $35.00

SWIFT, H.H. *From the Eagle's Wing: Biography of John Muir.* 1962. NY. Ils Lynd Ward. 1st ed. dj. VG. T5. $19.50

SWIFT, Jonathan. *Gulliver's Travels.* 1913. NY. Ils Rhead. not 1st ed. J2. $15.00

SWIFT, Jonathan. *Gulliver's Travels.* 1947. Grosset Dunlap. Ils Watson. 8vo. dj. G. $7.50

SWIFT, Jonathan. *Gulliver's Travels.* 1979. Franklin Lib. Ils Morten. gilt bdg. M. C1. $19.50

SWIFT, Jonathan. *Miscellaneous Poems.* 1938. Golden Cockerel. 1/375. G. $75.00

SWIFT, L.F. *Yankee of the Yards: Biography of Gustavus Franklin Swift.* 1927. Chicago. 1st ed. sgn. dj. EX. $45.00

SWIGGETT, H. *Rebel Raider: Life of John Hunt Morgan.* 1937. Garden City. reprint. 341 p. VG. M2. $15.00

SWIGGETT, H. *War Out of Niagara: W. Butler & Tory Rangers.* 1963. VG. $17.50

SWINBURNE, A.C. *Springtide of Life.* 1908. Phil. Ils Rackham. orig bdg. EX. $175.00

SWINBURNE, A.C. *Springtide of Life.* 1928. Phil. Ils Rackham. VG. J2. $45.00

SWINBURNE, A.C. *Tristram of Lyonesse.* 1917. London. C1. $9.50

SWINEFORD, A.P. *History, Climate & Natural Resources.* 1898. Ils. photos. fld maps. 12mo. 256 p. EX. $35.00

SWINGLE, HORSTMAN & TOUSLEY. *Standard American Electrician.* 1913. Chicago. Special ed. AEG. black leather. $15.00

SWINNERTON, Frank. *London Bookman.* 1928. London. 1st ed. 240 p. G. T5. $15.00

SWINTON. *Swinton's Word Book of English Spelling, Oral & Written.* 1876. 12mo. 154 p. EX. $2.50

SWOPE, B.M.H. *History of Middle Spring Presbyterian Church...* 1900. Newville, PA. Ils. inscr. 227 p. fair. T5. $19.50

SWOPE, G.E. *History of Big Spring Presbyterian Church...* 1898. Newville, PA. 223 p. G. T5. $19.50

SYLVESTER, H.M. *Indian Wars of New England.* 1910. Boston. Clarke. 3 vols. xl. VG. $200.00

SYLVESTRE, Henri. *Marvels in Art of Fin de Siecle.* 1893. Phil. Gebbie. 100 pls. folio. 2 vols. J2. $150.00

SYMNS, A.M. *Dreams Which Come True: The Solution.* 1933. England. $27.50

SYMONDS, John Addington. *Wine, Women & Song.* 1925. London. 1st ed. dj. M. C1. $17.50

SYMONDS, R.W. *English Furniture From Charles II to George II.* 1929. NY. Internat Studio. 1/500. $250.00

SYMONS, Arthur. *Confessions: Study in Pathology.* 1930. Fountain Pr. 1/542. sgn. tall 8vo. EX. $75.00

SYMONS, Arthur. *Love's Cruelty.* 1924. NY. 1st ed. VG. C1. $5.00

SYMONS, Julian. *Criminal Acts.* nd. BOMC. dj. VG. P1. $10.00

SYMONS, Julian. *Julian Symons Omnibus.* 1967. Collins Crime Club. VG. P1. $15.00

SYMONS, Julian. *Man Whose Dreams Came True.* 1968. Harper Row. 1st ed. dj. VG. P1. $15.00

SYMONS, Julian. *Progress of a Crime.* nd. Book Club. VG. P1. $3.00

SYMONS, Julian. *Three Pipe Problems.* 1975. Collins Crime Club. 1st ed. P1. $20.00

SYMONS, Julian. *Verdict of 13.* 1979. Harper Row. 1st ed. dj. EX. P1. $10.00

SYNGE, J.M. *Deirdre of the Sorrows.* 1911. Dublin. 1st trade ed. gilt bdg. VG. C1. $10.00

SYNGE, J.M. *Dramatic Works of J.M. Synge.* 1915. Dublin. G. $35.00

SYNGE, J.M. *Playboy of the W World.* 1911. Boston. 1st Am ed. EX. $45.00

SYPHER, Wylie. *Enlightened England.* nd. Norton. 6th ed. dj. VG. P1. $10.00

SZABADI, Judit. *Jugendstil in Ungarn: Malerei, Graphik, Plastik.* 1982. Vienna/Munich. Ils. 150 p. dj. D2. $95.00

SZARKOWSKI, John. *Face of MN.* 1958. MN U. 1st ed. sgn. dj. EX. $75.00

SZARKOWSKI, John. *Photographer & the American Landscape.* 1966. NY. 2nd print. 48 p. printed wraps. $75.00

SZARKOWSKI, John. *Photographer's Eye.* 1966. NY. MOMA. Ils. 4to. 155 p. printed wraps. $95.00

SZMAGLEWSKA, Seweryna. *Smoke Over Birkenau.* 1947. NY. 1st ed. dj. G. $6.50

SZUKALSKI, Stanislaw. *Projects in Design: Sculpture & Architecture.* 1929. Chicago. Ils 1st ed. square 4to. scarce. T1. $75.00

SZULC, Tad. *Compulsive Spy.* 1974. Viking. 1st ed. dj. VG. M1. $9.50

SZYK, Arthur. *Anderson's Fairy Tales Illustrated by Arthur Szyk.* nd. Grosset. EX. $15.00

SZYK, Arthur. *Book of Ruth.* 1947. NY. $35.00

SZYK, Arthur. *New Order.* 1941. Putnam. 1st ed. dj. EX. $90.00

TABER, Gladys. *Another Path.* 1963. Phil. 1st ed. dj. VG. B2. $27.50

TABER, Gladys. *Book of Stillmeadow.* 1947. Phil. dj. G. $20.00

TABER, Gladys. *Book of Stillmeadow.* 1984. Harper Row. Ils. 273 p. dj. EX. M2. $12.00

TABER, Gladys. *Conversations With Amber.* 1978. Lippincott. 1st ed. dj. EX. $12.00

TABER, Gladys. *Country Chronicle.* 1974. Phil. 1st ed. dj. VG. B2. $17.50

TABER, Gladys. *Harvest at Stillmeadow.* 1940. Boston. 1st ed. VG. B2. $47.50

TABER, Gladys. *Harvest of Yesterdays.* 1976. Lippincott. 1st ed. dj. EX. $12.00

TABER, Gladys. *Harvest of Yesterdays.* 1976. Lippincott. 1st ed. sgn. dj. EX. $25.00

TABER, Gladys. *Mrs. Daffodil.* 1957. Phil. 1st ed. dj. VG. B2. $47.50

TABER, Gladys. *My Own Cape Cod.* c 1971. Lippincott. 2nd print. dj. EX. $15.00

TABER, Gladys. *One Dozen & One.* 1966. Lippincott. 1st ed. dj. $17.50

TABER, Gladys. *Stillmeadow & Sugarbridge.* 1953. Phil. 1st ed. dj. VG. B2. $25.00

TABER, Gladys. *Stillmeadow Calendar.* c 1967. Lippincott. 2nd print. dj. VG. $12.00

TABER, Gladys. *Stillmeadow Day Book.* 1955. Phil. 1st ed. dj. VG. B2. $25.00

TABER, Gladys. *Stillmeadow Sampler.* 1959. Phil. Lippincott. 282 p. dj. VG. $12.00

TABER, Gladys. *Stillmeadow Seasons.* 1959. Macrae Smith. Book Club. G. $20.00

TABORI, C. *My Occult Diary.* 1966. NY. $9.50

TACHDJIAN. *Pediatric Orthopedics.* 1972. 2 vols. VG. $90.00

TACK, Alfred. *Spy Who Wasn't Exchanged.* 1970. Mystery Book Guild. dj. VG. P1. $5.00

TAFT, Henry. *Japan & America: Journey & Political Survey.* 1932. Macmillan. 1st ed. J2. $12.50

TAFT, J. *Practical Treatise on Operative Dentistry.* 1868. Phil. 2nd ed. 8vo. 430 p. $80.00

TAFT, L. *History of American Sculpture.* 1903. NY. Ils. 4to. 544 p. TEG. gilt cloth. J2. $60.00

TAFT, Robert. *Photography & American Scene: Social History, 1839-1889.* 1938. 1st ed. VG. S2. $95.00

TAFT, Robert. *Photography & American Scene: Social History, 1839-1889.* 1942. NY. 2nd print. 546 p. VG. $35.00

TAFT, Robert. *Photography & American Scene: Social History, 1839-1889.* 1964. NY. reprint of 1938 ed. 546 p. wraps. $10.00

TAFT & BRYCE. *WA: Nation's Capital.* 1918. G. $22.50

TAGGARD, Genevieve. *Circumference.* 1929. NY. $22.50

TAGORE, Rabindranath. *Sheaves.* 1932. NY. 1st ed. dj. VG. $20.00

TAILLANDIER, Y. *Indelible Miro.* 1972. NY. 4to. cloth. VG. J2. $150.00

TAINE, H.A. *History of English Literature.* 1877. London. Trans Van Laun. New ed. 4 vols. $50.00

TAINE, John. *Crystal Horde.* 1952. Fantasy. 1st ed. dj. EX. P1. $30.00

TAINE, John. *Forbidden Garden.* 1947. Fantasy. 1st ed. VG. P1. $17.50

TAINE, John. *Forbidden Garden.* 1947. Reading. Fantasy. 1st trade ed. dj. EX. $35.00

TAINE, John. *Greatest Adventure.* 1929. NY. 1st ed. dj. G. scarce. $20.00

TAINE, John. *Seeds of Life.* 1951. Fantasy. 1st ed. dj. VG. P1. $35.00

TAINE, John. *Time Stream.* 1946. Providence. 1st ed. dj. VG. $60.00

TAIT, Katharine. *My Father, Bertrand Russell.* 1975. NY. 1st ed. dj. VG. $15.00

TAKEDA, Izumo. *Japanische Dramen.* c 1900. Leipzig. 1st ed. 4to. rare. $195.00

TALBOT, C.W. *Drawings From Clark Art Institute.* 1964. Yale. 1st ed. boxed. M. $200.00

TALBOT, Ethelbert. *My People of the Plains.* 1906. NY. 1st ed. photos. 264 p. TEG. T5. $25.00

TALBOT, G. *Butterflies.* 1978. India. reprint of 1947 ed. EX. M2. $65.00

TALBOT, T. *Soldier in the W: Letters of Theodore Talbot...* 1972. OK U. Ils 1st ed. 210 p. dj. EX. M2. $17.00

TALBOT & ROSENBERRY. *History of American Society University Women, 1881.* 1931. Boston. 1st ed. $15.00

TALESE, Gay. *Honor Thy Father.* nd. Book Club. dj. VG. P1. $3.00

TALIAFERRO, H.E. *Carolina Humor.* 1938. Richmond. Dietz Pr. presentation. sgn. dj. $55.00

TALLANT, Elizabeth. *In Constant Flight.* 1983. NY. 1st ed. dj. EX. $35.00

TALLANT, Elizabeth. *Museum Pieces.* 1985. NY. 1st ed. dj. EX. $30.00

TALLMADGE, T.E. *Story of Architecture in America.* 1927. NY. dj. J2. $20.00

TALLMADGE, T.E. *Story of Architecture in America.* 1927. NY. Ils 1st ed. 311 p. T5. $45.00

TALMAN, Frank. *Flying the Old Planes.* 1973. Doubleday. Ils. 4to. 255 p. dj. EX. $20.00

TANKERSLEY, A.B. *College Life at Old Ogelthorpe.* 1951. Athens. Ils 1st ed. 194 p. dj. EX. $15.00

TANNAHILL. *P's & Q's (Book on Art of Letter Arrangement).* 1923. Garden City. 1st ed. dj. G. $27.50

TANNARD, W.H. *History of 3rd Regiment, LA Infantry.* 1970. Dayton, OH. reprint of 1866 ed. 1/1000. T5. $32.50

TANNEN, Mary. *Wizard Children of Finn.* 1981. NY. 1st ed. juvenile. dj. VG. C1. $7.50

TANNENBAUM, S.A. *George Peele: Concise Bibliography.* 1940. NY. Ltd ed. 1/300. VG. $90.00

TANNER, C.T. *SW Indian Craft Art.* 1973. AR U. 4th ed. dj. M. $35.00

TANNER, H.S. *New Picture of Phil.; or, Stranger's Guide to the City...* 1844. NY. Ils. 12mo. 156 p. $250.00

TANNER, O. *Bears & Other Carnivores.* 1977. Time Life. color photos. 4to. 128 p. EX. M2. $11.00

TANNER, O. *Urban Wilds.* 1975. Time Life. color photos. map. 184 p. EX. M2. $5.00

TANNER, T.H. *Practical Treatise on Diseases of Infancy & Childhood.* 1861. Phil. 12mo. 464 p. G. G2. $33.00

TANSELLE. *Check List of Moby Dick: 1851-1976.* 1976. Chicago. 1st ed. VG. $10.00

TAPPAN, Eve M. *Stories of Legendary Heroes.* c 1907. gilt red cloth. VG. C1. $12.00

TAPPAN, Sarah. *Memoir of Mrs. Sarah Tappan.* 1834. NY. 150 p. fair. T5. $9.50

TAPPLY, W.G. *Death at Charity's Point.* 1984. Scribner. 1st ed. dj. VG. P1. $15.00

TAPPLY, W.G. *Follow the Sharks.* 1985. NY. Scribner. UCP. wraps. EX. $55.00

TAPPLY, W.G. *Follow the Sharks.* 1985. NY. 1st ed. dj. EX. $15.00

TARG, William. *Bibliophile in the Nursery.* 1957. Cleveland. 1st ed. dj. VG. B2. $50.00

TARG, William. *Carousel for Bibliophiles.* 1947. Duchnes. 1st ed. 8vo. dj. VG. G2. $55.00

TARG, William. *Ten Thousand Rare Books & Their Prices.* 1940. Targ Pub. EX. $30.00

TARKINGTON, Booth. *Image of Josephine.* 1945. Garden City. inscr. 12mo. EX. $95.00

TARKINGTON, Booth. *Monsieur Beaucaire.* 1900. McClure Phillips. sgn. 12mo. VG. $45.00

TARKINGTON, Booth. *Monsieur Beaucaire.* 1961. Heritage. Ils Cleland. 8vo. slipcase. EX. $15.00

TARKINGTON, Booth. *Penrod.* 1914. NY. Ils Grant. 1st ed. 2nd issue. $45.00

TARKINGTON, Booth. *Ramsey Milholland.* 1919. Doubleday. sgn. G. $30.00

TARKINGTON, Booth. *Rumbin Galleries.* 1937. Doubleday. 1st ed. inscr. 8vo. $55.00

TARKINGTON, Booth. *Seventeen.* 1916. Grosset Dunlap. dj. $25.00

TARKINGTON, Booth. *Women.* 1925. Doubleday. 1st ed. $18.00

TARR & MARTIN. *AK Glacier Studies.* 1914. Nat Geog Soc. Ils. maps. 498 p. VG. $135.00

TARVER, J. *Fur Animals, Alligator & the Fur Industry in LA.* 1987. LA Wildlife. photos. M2. $5.00

TATE, Allen. *Collected Essays.* 1959. Swallow. 1st ed. presentation. dj. J2. $65.00

TATE, Allen. *Collected Poems, 1919-1976.* 1977. Farrar. 1st ed. presentation. dj. J2. $35.00

TATE, Allen. *Forlorn Demon.* 1953. Regnery. 1st ed. dj. J2. $20.00

TATE, Allen. *Forlorn Demon.* 1953. Regnery. 1st ed. presentation. dj. J2. $45.00

TATE, Allen. *Jefferson Davis.* 1929. NY. 1st ed. 311 p. G. $30.00

TATE, Allen. *S Vanguard: John Peale Bishop Memorial Volume.* 1947. Prentice Hall. 1st ed. 331 p. $45.00

TATE, Allen. *Swimmers.* 1970. Scribner. 1st ed. presentation. dj. J2. $35.00

TATE, J. *Riven Goggeries.* 1979. NY. 1st ed. dj. EX. $20.00

TATE, James. *Constant Defender.* 1983. NY. UCP. wraps. VG. $40.00

TATE, Peter. *Faces in the Flames.* 1976. Doubleday. 1st ed. dj. VG. P1. $10.00

TATE, Peter. *Greencomber.* 1979. Doubleday. 1st ed. dj. EX. P1. $10.00

TATE, Peter. *Moon on the Iron Meadow.* 1974. Doubleday. 1st ed. dj. VG. P1. $10.00

TATHAM, Julie. *Cherry Ames, Dude Ranch Nurse.* nd. Grosset. VG. P1. $5.00

TATSCH & PRESCOTT. *Masonic Bookplates.* 1928. Cedar Rapids. 2nd print. 1/100. J2. $75.00

TATTERSALL, W.M. *Review of the Mysidacea of the US National Museum.* 1951. US Nat Mus. Ils. 292 p. M2. $5.00

TAUBMAN, Howard. *Making of the American Theatre.* 1965. Coward McCann. 1st ed. xl. EX. $8.00

TAULBOT, Ray. *Thoroughbred Horse Racing, Playing for Profit.* 1968. NY. Amer Pub. 17th print. 289 p. dj. VG. $20.00

TAUSSIG, C.W. *Rum: Romance & Rebellion.* 1928. NY. Ils Kappel. fair. $12.00

TAUSSIG, F. *Abortion, Spontaneous & Induced.* 1936. St. Louis. Ils 1st ed. 536 p. $65.00

TAVERNER, Eric. *Trout Fishing From All Angles.* 1929. Phil. Ils. dj. EX. $50.00

TAVERNER, P.A. *Birds of Canada.* 1934. Ottawa. color pls. 8vo. 445 p. VG. $40.00

TAVERNER, P.A. *Birds of E Canada.* 1922. Canada. Dept Mines. 2nd ed. 290 p. VG. M2. $12.00

TAVERNER, P.A. *Birds of Shoal Lake, Manitoba.* 1919. Ottawa. M2. $5.00

TAYLOR, A.B. *Introduction to Medieval Romance.* 1969. reprint of 1930 ed. M. C1. $22.00

TAYLOR, A.P. *Under HI Skies.* 1922. Honolulu. photos. VG. $50.00

TAYLOR, A.S. *On Poisons in Relation to Medical Jurisprudence & Medicine.* 1875. Lea. Ils. 788 p. EX. M2. $90.00

TAYLOR, A.Y. *Character Grams.* 1934. NY. $15.00

TAYLOR, Anna. *Gods Are Not Mocked.* 3rd print. dj. EX. C1. $6.00

TAYLOR, Bayard. *Egypt & Iceland in 1874.* 1874. NY. 16mo. VG. T1. $25.00

TAYLOR, Bayard. *Eldorado; or, Adventures in Path of Empire.* 1854. Putnam. 247 p. VG. A3. $70.00

TAYLOR, Bayard. *Eldorado; or, Adventures in Path of Empire...* 1949. Knopf. Ils 1st Borzoi ed. 375 p. EX. M2. $20.00

TAYLOR, Bayard. *Encyclopedia of Modern Travel.* 1856. Moore. Ils. maps. 956 p. VG. M2. $30.00

TAYLOR, Bayard. *Picturesque Europe.* 1875. NY. 3 vols. full leather. EX. B2. $375.00

TAYLOR, Benjamin. *Between the Gates.* 1878. Chicago. Ils. VG. $35.00

TAYLOR, Benjamin. *Storyology.* 1900. London. $25.00

TAYLOR, Bernard. *Godsend.* nd. Book Club. dj. VG. P1. $4.00

TAYLOR, Bob. *Life Pictures...Being Collection of Lectures & Addresses...* 1907. Nashville. Taylor Trotwood. 4to. 384 p. xl. $45.00

TAYLOR, Deems. *Walt Disney's Fantasia.* 1940. Simon Schuster. 2nd print. 158 p. D2. $150.00

TAYLOR, F.W. *Voyage 'Round the World in the US Frigate Columbia...* 1847. New Haven. 8vo. 2 vols in 1. VG. $150.00

TAYLOR, Frank. *Port & City of Phil.* 1912. Phil. Ils 1st ed. map. 8vo. EX. T1. $35.00

TAYLOR, G. *Account of the Genus Meconopsis.* 1934. New Flora Silva. 29 pls. 130 p. M2. $26.00

TAYLOR, I.T. *Cavalcade of Jackson Co.* 1938. San Antonio. 2nd ed. $50.00

TAYLOR, J. *Monsieur Tonson.* 1830. London. Ils Cruikshank. 2nd ed. wraps. G. $24.00

TAYLOR, J. *Pandoro: Last of Ivory Hunters.* 1955. NY. 1st ed. EX. $15.00

TAYLOR, J.A. *Being a Series of Agricultural Essays.* 1814. Columbia. 2nd ed. G. $70.00

TAYLOR, J.E. *Playtime Naturalist.* 1889. Appleton. Ils. 287 p. G. M2. $8.00

TAYLOR, J.W. *African Zoo in the Family.* 1965. Emerson. Ils. 185 p. dj. EX. M2. $13.00

TAYLOR, J.W. *History of State of OH: First Period 1650-1787.* 1854. Cincinnati. 1st ed. 557 p. fair. T5. $45.00

TAYLOR, John W.R. *Combat Aircraft of the World From 1909 to the Present.* 1969. NY. Ils. dj. VG. T5. $45.00

TAYLOR, John W.R. *Fire on the Beaches. N American Atlantic Coast in WWII.* 1958. NY. Ils 1st ed. 248 p. dj. VG. B2. $20.00

TAYLOR, John. *African Rifles & Cartridges.* 1948. Georgetown. 1st ed. dj. B2. $200.00

TAYLOR, John. *Big Game & Big Game Rifles.* 1958. London. dj. EX. $50.00

TAYLOR, Joseph. *Fast Life on the Modern Highway.* 1874. Ils. 220 p. gilt bdg. $35.00

TAYLOR, Joshua C. *Graphic Work of Umberto Boccioni.* 1961. Doubleday. Ils. D2. $65.00

TAYLOR, Keith. *Bard III: Wild Sea.* VG. C1. $3.00

TAYLOR, Keith. *Bard.* 1984. pb. VG. C1. $3.00

TAYLOR, N.W. *Life on a Whaler.* 1929. CT. 1st ed. 1/900. $48.00

TAYLOR, Norman. *Cinchona in Java: Story of Quinine.* 1945. NY. 1st ed. dj. VG. $17.50

TAYLOR, Peter. *Summons to Memphis.* 1986. NY. 1st ed. dj. EX. $35.00

TAYLOR, Phoebe Atwood. *Diplomatic Corpse.* nd. Norton. dj. xl. P1. $12.50

TAYLOR, Phoebe Atwood. *Going, Going, Gone.* nd. Norton. 1st ed. dj. EX. P1. $25.00

TAYLOR, Phoebe Atwood. *Going, Going, Gone.* 1944. Triangle. VG. P1. $20.00

TAYLOR, Phoebe Atwood. *Proof of the Pudding.* nd. Norton. dj. VG. P1. $12.50

TAYLOR, Phoebe Atwood. *Six Iron Spiders.* 1943. Triangle. 2nd ed. dj. VG. P1. $20.00

TAYLOR, Phoebe Atwood. *Spring Harrowing.* nd. Norton. dj. VG. P1. $25.00

TAYLOR, R. *By the Dawn's Early Light.* 1953. Holt. VG. M1. $6.50

TAYLOR, R.L. *Winston S. Churchill.* nd. BOMC. VG. P1. $5.00

TAYLOR, R.L. *Winston S. Churchill.* 1952. Doubleday. not 1st ed. blue cloth. VG. D1. $25.00

TAYLOR, R.L. *Winston S. Churchill.* 1952. Doubleday. 1st ed. blue cloth. dj. VG. D1. $35.00

TAYLOR, Samuel. *Angling in All Its Branches.* 1800. London. 298 p. rebound. $55.00

TAYLOR, Sharon. *Amazing Story of Lawlors in America.* 1982. np. 133 p. G. T5. $9.50

TAYLOR, T. *Mignificent Mitscher.* 1954. NY. 1st ed. dj. VG. B2. $47.50

TAYLOR, T.U. *Jesse Chisholm.* 1939. Bandera, TX. Ils 1st ed. sgn. EX. $40.00

TAYLOR, W.A. *Promising New Fruits.* 1908. USDA. 9 color pls. M2. $9.00

TAYLOR, W.C. *AK Ferns & Fern Allies.* 1984. Milwaukee Mus. Ils. 262 p. M. M2. $28.00

TAYLOR, W.H. *Four Years With General Lee.* 1878. 199 p. EX. J4. $50.00

TAYLOR, W.M. *Historical Sketch of Moravian Missions Among DE.* nd. np. reprint of 1891 ed. wraps. T5. $3.50

TAYLOR, W.R. *Marine Algae of NE Coast of N America.* 1937. MI U. 60 pls. 427 p. dj. EX. M2. $35.00

TAYLOR & ARLT. *Printing & Progress.* 1941. Berkeley. orig printed wraps. $25.00

TAYLOR & HARWELL. *Destruction & Reconstruction.* 1955. NY. 380 p. dj. VG. $20.00

TAYLOR & HYER. *Numerology: Its Facts & Secrets.* 1958. NY. $22.50

TAYLOR & NEU. *American Railroad Network, 1861-1890.* 1956. 113 p. $25.00

TEALE, E.W. *Days Without Time: Adventures of a Naturalist.* 1948. Dodd Mead. 144 photos. 283 p. EX. M2. $13.00

TEALE, E.W. *Dune Boy.* 1957. NY. dj. VG. B2. $17.50

TEALE, E.W. *Insect World of J. Henri Fabre.* 1949. Dodd Mead. 333 p. VG. M2. $11.00

TEALE, E.W. *Journey Into Summer.* 1960. Dodd Mead. photos. map. 366 p. dj. EX. M2. $9.00

TEALE, E.W. *N With the Spring.* 1957. Dodd Mead. Ils. 358 p. dj. EX. M2. $12.00

TEALE, E.W. *Wandering Through Winter.* 1965. Dodd Mead. photos. 370 p. dj. EX. M2. $11.00

TEASDALE, Sara. *Answering Voice: One Hundred Love Lyrics by Women.* 1917. Boston. 1st ed. 12mo. red leather. EX. $30.00

TEASDALE, Sara. *Collected Poems.* 1937. VG. C1. $7.50

TEASDALE, Sara. *Flame & Shadow.* 1925. NY. inscr/sgn. $50.00

TEASDALE, Sara. *Stars Tonight.* 1930. NY. Ltd ed. inscr/sgn. boxed. $85.00

TEASDALE, Sara. *Strange Victory.* 1933. NY. 1st ed. VG. $12.50

TEASDALE-BUCKELL, G.T. *Experts on Guns & Shooting.* 1900. London. EX. $130.00

TEBELL & JENNISON. *American Indian Wars.* 1960. NY. Harper. Ils 1st ed. fld map. dj. EX. $18.00

TEGG, Thomas. *Young Man's Book of Knowledge.* 1836. 1st Am ed. G. $25.00

TEILHET, Hildegarde Tolman. *Assassins.* nd. Book Club. dj. VG. P1. $4.00

TEITEBAUM, Gene. *Justice Louis D. Brandeis: Bibliography of Writings.* 1988. Rothman. 128 p. VG. T5. $9.50

TEIXIDOR, Felipe. *Ex Libis y Bibliotecas de Mexico.* 1931. Mexico. 1st ed. 550 p. stiff wraps. J2. $125.00

TELFAIR, R.C. *Cattle Egret: TX Focus & World View.* 1983. TX A&M U. photos. maps. 144 p. dj. M2. $17.00

TELFER, Dariel. *Caretakers.* 1959. Simon Schuster. 1st print. dj. VG. $8.50

TEMPLE, R. *Genus of China: 3,000 Years of Science.* 1986. Simon Schuster. Ils 1st ed. 254 p. dj. EX. M2. $20.00

TEMPLE, William F. *Martin Magnus on Mars.* 1956. Muller. 1st ed. dj. VG. P1. $17.50

TEMPLE, William F. *Shoot at the Moon.* nd. Book Club. dj. VG. P1. $2.75

TENEBRARUM, Hora. *Black Book of Poland.* 1942. Putnam. 1st ed. J2. $20.00

TENER, J.S. *Queen Elizabeth Islands Game Survey.* 1972. Canada. Wildlife Service. map. 50 p. M2. $5.00

TENN, William. *Children of Wonder.* nd. Book Club. dj. VG. P1. $7.50

TENNANT, A. *Snakes of TX.* 1984. TX Monthly. Ils 1st ed. 4to. 561 p. dj. EX. M2. $60.00

TENNYSON, Alfred Lord. *Elaine.* 1867. Cassell Petter. Ils Dore. gilt red cloth. AEG. J2. $150.00

TENNYSON, Alfred Lord. *Foresters: Robin Hood & Maid Marian.* 1892. NY. 1st Am ed. VG. C1. $12.00

TENNYSON, Alfred Lord. *Idylls of the King.* 1950. Ltd Ed Club. Ils Lynd Ward. boxed. EX. $75.00

TENNYSON, Alfred Lord. *In Memoriam.* 1933. London. Nonesuch. 1/2000. slipcase. EX. $75.00

TENNYSON, Alfred Lord. *Maud.* 1900. Roycroft. 1/100. Ils Lily Ess. VG. D1. $75.00

TENNYSON, Alfred Lord. *Prince.* 1884. Boston. MacDonald. full leather. $125.00

TENNYSON, Alfred Lord. *Princess.* 1911. Bobbs Merrill. Ils Christy. VG. J2. $35.00

TEPPER, Sheri. *Gate to Women's Country.* 1988. Doubleday. ARC. wraps. M. $15.00

TERHUNE, A.P. *Book of Sunnybank.* 1934. NY. Ils 1st ed. 273 p. VG. T5. $45.00

TERHUNE, A.P. *Critter & Other Dogs.* nd. Grosset Dunlap. dj. VG. P1. $10.00

TERHUNE, A.P. *Further Adventures of Lad.* nd. Grosset Dunlap. VG. P1. $7.50

TERHUNE, A.P. *Story of Damon & Pythias.* 1915. Grosset Dunlap. Movie ed. dj. VG. P1. $35.00

TERKEL, Studs. *Good War: Oral History of WWII.* 1984. Pantheon. 1st ed. 489 p. dj. EX. $18.00

TERRALL, Robert. *They Deal in Death.* 1943. Simon Schuster. 1st ed. dj. VG. P1. $15.00

TERRALL, Robert. *They Deal in Death.* 1944. Books Inc. VG. P1. $12.50

TERRASSE, Charles. *Paul Gauguin.* nd. Paris. Morance. loose as issued. D2. $55.00

TERRELL, J.U. *Furs by Astor.* 1964. Morrow. 400 p. dj. EX. M2. $17.00

TERRELL, J.U. *Reminiscences of Early Days of Ft. Worth.* 1906. Ft. Worth. 1st print. presentation. sgn. T5. $300.00

TERRELL, J.U. *Six Turnings: Major Changes in American W in 1806-1834.* 1968. Clark. 250 p. dj. EX. M2. $18.00

TERRELL, J.U. *War for the CO River.* 1965. Glendale. Clark. Ils. 2 vols. djs. VG. A3. $60.00

TERRES, J.K. *Songbirds in Your Garden.* 1968. Crowell. Expanded ed. 256 p. dj. EX. M2. $13.00

TERRY, Samuel. *How To Keep a Store.* 1887. Fowler Wells. 12th ed. G. $25.00

TERUKAZU. *Japanese Painting.* 1961. NY. Ils Skira. dj. EX. $50.00

TESIMOND, Oswald. *Gunpowder Plot: Narrative of Oswald Tesimond.* 1973. London. Folio Soc. boxed. EX. $35.00

TESNOHLIDEK, Rudolf. *Cunning Little Vixen.* 1985. NY. Ils Sendak. 1st ed. dj. M. $25.00

TESSIER, Thomas. *Shockwaves.* 1983. Severn House. 1st ed. dj. VG. P1. $25.00

TEUR. *Forgotten Children's Books.* 1898-1899. London. 1st ed. 510 p. VG. $50.00

TEVIS, Walter S. *Queen's Gambit.* nd. BOMC. dj. VG. P1. $5.00

TEVIS, Walter S. *Steps of the Sun.* 1983. Doubleday. 1st ed. dj. RS. EX. P1. $20.00

TEY, Josephine. *Four, Five & Six by Tey.* nd. BOMC. dj. VG. P1. $5.00

TEY, Josephine. *Franchise Affair.* 1950. Peter Davies. 2nd ed. G. P1. $5.00

TEY, Josephine. *Franchise Affair.* 1959. Peter Davis. 4th ed. dj. G. P1. $7.50

TEY, Josephine. *Shilling for Candles.* 1954. Macmillan. 2nd ed. VG. P1. $12.00

THACK, Charles C. Jr. *Creation of the Presidency: 1775-1789.* 1969. 2nd print. B7. $15.00

THACKERAY, W.M. *Essay on Genius of George Cruikshank.* 1884. London. $60.00

THACKERAY, W.M. *History of Pendennis.* 1850. London. 1st ed. 2 vols. VG. $50.00

THACKERAY, W.M. *History of Pendennis.* 1850. NY. Ils 1st Am ed. 2 vols. G. T5. $75.00

THACKERAY, W.M. *Orphan of Pimlico.* 1876. London. 1st ed. folio. EX. $175.00

THACKERAY, W.M. *Works of W.M. Thackeray.* 1903. NY. Kensington. 1/100. 32 vols. EX. $395.00

THANET, Octave. *Stories of a W Town.* 1893. NY. Ils Frost. 1st ed. 243 p. G. T5. $17.50

THAPAR, D.R. *Icons in Bronze: Introduction to Indian Metal Images.* 1961. Asia Pub House. 1st ed. J2. $20.00

THAPAR, V. *Tiger: Portrait of a Predator.* 1986. Facts on File. Ils 1st Am ed. 200 p. dj. EX. M2. $24.00

THARP, L.H. *Chaplain, NW Voyager.* 1946. London. Harrap. Ils. sgn. 12mo. VG. $30.00

THARP, L.H. *St. Gaudens & the Gilded Era.* 1969. Little Brown. 1st ed. dj. J2. $8.50

THAW. *Historical Sites in Burma.* 1972. Burma. gilt red leather. VG. $25.00

THAYER, E.H. *Wild Flowers of the Pacific Coast.* 1887. NY. 24 color pls. folio. $100.00

THAYER, Lee. *Dead Men's Shoes.* 1929. Sears. 1st ed. G. P1. $20.00

THAYER, Lee. *Hair's Breadth.* 1946. Dodd Mead. xl. P1. $6.00

THAYER, Tiffany. *Three Men.* nd. Grosset. VG. P1. $10.00

THAYER, Tiffany. *Three Sheet.* nd. Grosset. G. P1. $5.00

THEAKSTON, Michael. *British Angling Flies.* 1888. Ripon. Revised ed. 12mo. VG. $50.00

THEAL, G.M. *S Africa.* 1897. London. Ils. 12mo. 442 p. green bdg. xl. G2. $9.00

THENAULT, Georges. *Story of Lafayette Escadrille.* 1921. Boston. 1st Am ed. 172 p. scarce. T5. $125.00

THERBER, Helen. *Thurber & Co.* 1966. NY. 1st ed. VG. $35.00

THEROUX, Alexander. *Darconville's Cat.* 1981. NY. 1st ed. dj. VG. $50.00

THEROUX, Paul. *Black House.* 1974. Boston. 1st ed. dj. VG. $40.00

THEROUX, Paul. *Consul's File.* 1977. Boston. 1st ed. dj. VG. $20.00

THEROUX, Paul. *Family Arsenal.* nd. Houghton. 2nd ed. dj. VG. P1. $10.00

THEROUX, Paul. *Fang & the Indians.* 1963. Boston. 1st ed. dj. $35.00

THEROUX, Paul. *Girls at Play.* 1969. Boston. 1st ed. dj. $35.00

THEROUX, Paul. *Half Moon Street.* 1984. Boston. 1st ed. dj. EX. $15.00

THEROUX, Paul. *Jungle Lovers.* 1971. Boston. 1st ed. dj. $35.00

THEROUX, Paul. *Kingdom by the Sea.* 1983. Boston. 1st ed. sgn. dj. EX. $30.00

THEROUX, Paul. *London Snow.* 1979. London. Ils Lawrence. 1/450. sgns. dj. $65.00

THEROUX, Paul. *Mosquito Coast.* 1982. Boston. 1/350. sgn. boxed. EX. $75.00

THEROUX, Paul. *Mosquito Coast.* 1982. NY. 1st trade ed. dj. EX. $20.00

THEROUX, Paul. *Ozone.* 1986. Franklin Lib. 1st ed. sgn. AEG. full leather. $45.00

THEROUX, Paul. *Picture Palace.* 1978. London. 1st ed. VG. $20.00

THEROUX, Paul. *Turn of the Years.* 1982. London. Intro Pritchett. 1/150. sgns. M. $65.00

THEROUX, Paul. *Waldo.* 1967. Boston. 1st ed. dj. VG. $95.00

THEROUX, Paul. *Waldo.* 1967. London. 1st ed. dj. EX. $90.00

THEVENAZ, Paul. *Record of His Life & Art With Essay on Style by Artist.* 1922. private print. 1/1000. Art Deco bdg. $75.00

THIESSEN, Grant. *SF Collector Vol. 1.* 1980. Pandora. 1/140. HrdCvr. sgn/#d. EX. P1. $25.00

THIESSEN, Grant. *SF Collector Vol. 2.* 1981. Pandora. 1/250. HrdCvr. sgn/#d. EX. P1. $25.00

THIESSEN, Grant. *SF Collector Vol. 3.* 1981. Pandora. 1/250. HrdCvr. sgn/#d. EX. P1. $25.00

THIMM, C. *Complete Bibliography of Fencing & Duelling.* 1896. London. pls. 4to. $110.00

THIND, B.S. *Jesus: The Christ in the Light of Spiriutal Science. Vol. 1.* nd. CA. $8.50

THIND, B.S. *Radiant Road to Reality.* 1947. LA. $12.00

THIND, B.S. *Wisdom & the Wheel Book III.* nd. St. Louis. $20.00

THIRKELL, Angela. *Miss Bunting.* 1945. London. 1st ed. $23.00

THOMAS, A.G. *Great Books & Book Collectors.* 1975. NY. 4to. dj. EX. $32.00

THOMAS, Arthur. *In Days of Brigham Young.* 1914. VG. $8.00

THOMAS, Augustus. *Print of My Remembrance.* 1922. Scribner. Ils. VG. $35.00

THOMAS, B.P. *Abraham Lincoln.* 1965. Knopf. 8th print. dj. EX. $12.00

THOMAS, Bob. *Walt Disney: Art of Animation, Story of Disney Studio...* 1958. Golden Pr. Ils. photos. dj. D2. $95.00

THOMAS, C. *Introduction to Study of N American Archaeology.* 1903. Clarke. Ils. 391 p. VG. M2. $27.00

THOMAS, C. *Leftover Life To Kill.* 1957. London. 1st ed. dj. EX. $40.00

THOMAS, Craig. *Winter Hawk.* 1987. Collins. 1st ed. dj. EX. P1. $20.00

THOMAS, Cyrus. *Zoology & Potany, Part 1: Synopsis of Acrididae of N Am.* 1873. WA. 262 p. wraps. A3. $120.00

THOMAS, D.G. *US Silencer Patents 1888-1972.* 1973. Paladin. 1st ed. 2 vols. VG. $25.00

THOMAS, D.M. *White Hotel.* 1981. Viking. dj. EX. $12.50

THOMAS, Dylan. *Collected Poems, 1934-1952.* 1952. London. Ltd 1st ed. dj. EX. $125.00

THOMAS, Dylan. *Collected Poems.* 1953. New Directions. 1st ed. 1st state. dj. VG. $95.00

THOMAS, Dylan. *Doctor & the Devils.* 1953. London. 1st ed. 138 p. dj. G. T5. $25.00

THOMAS, Dylan. *Letters to Vernon Watkins.* 1957. London. 1st ed. dj. EX. $45.00

THOMAS, Dylan. *New Poems.* 1943. New Directions. 1st ed. wraps. dj. EX. $85.00

THOMAS, Dylan. *Notebooks of Dylan Thomas.* 1967. New Directions. 1st ed. dj. EX. $40.00

THOMAS, Dylan. *Portrait of the Artist As a Young Dog.* 1940. New Directions. 1st Am ed. dj. VG. scarce. $100.00

THOMAS, Dylan. *Quite Early One Morning.* 1954. London. 1st ed. 1st print. $75.00

THOMAS, Dylan. *Quite Early One Morning.* 1954. London. 2nd ed. dj. VG. $30.00

THOMAS, Dylan. *Under Milk Wood.* 1952. New Directions. 1st ed. dj. EX. $40.00

THOMAS, Dylan. *Under Milk Wood.* 1954. New Directions. red cloth. dj. VG. $35.00

THOMAS, E.M. *Confederacy As A Revolutionary Experience.* 1971. Prentice Hall. 150 p. dj. EX. M2. $8.00

THOMAS, E.M. *Confederate Nation: 1861-1865.* 1979. Harper Row. 1st ed. 384 p. dj. VG. $15.00

THOMAS, E.M. *Confederate Nation: 1861-1865.* 1979. NY. Ils. 384 p. K1. $9.50

THOMAS, E.M. *Harmless People.* 1959. Knopf. Ils 1st ed. 266 p. dj. EX. M2. $14.00

THOMAS, E.M. *Mary at the Farm & Book of Recipes.* 1915. Norristown. 1st ed. VG. $25.00

THOMAS, G.C. *Practical Book of Outdoor Rose Growing.* 1920. Phil. 5th ed. VG. $45.00

THOMAS, Gabriel. *Historical & Geographical Account of Province...PA & NJ.* 1848. NY. facsimile. fld map. VG. $35.00

THOMAS, H.C. *Red Ryder & Adventure at Chimney Rock.* 1946. Whitman. dj. VG. P1. $17.50

THOMAS, Isaiah. *Dictionary of the Bible.* 1798. Worcester. 1st Am ed. 8vo. leather. VG. $85.00

THOMAS, Isaiah. *History of Printing in America.* 1970. Barre. Imprint Soc. 1st ed. slipcase. M. $150.00

THOMAS, J.F. *Beyond Normal Cognition.* 1937. Boston. $50.00

THOMAS, J.J. *Fruit Culturist.* 1846. NY. VG. P3. $85.00

THOMAS, Leslie. *Orange Wednesday.* 1967. Delacorte. dj. VG. P1. $17.50

THOMAS, Lillian Beynon. *New Secret.* 1946. Thomas Allen. VG. P1. $5.00

THOMAS, Louis. *Good Children Don't Kill.* 1968. Dodd Mead. 1st ed. dj. EX. P1. $10.00

THOMAS, Lowell. *Beyond Khyber Pass.* 1925. Century. G. $10.00

THOMAS, Lowell. *European Skyways.* 1927. Boston. Ils 1st ed. 524 p. VG. T5. $22.50

THOMAS, Lowell. *First World Flight.* 1927. Boston. 4th print. sgn Erik Nelson. VG. $50.00

THOMAS, Lowell. *Tall Tales.* 1931. Funk Wagnall. 3rd print. sgn. G. $18.50

THOMAS, Ross. *Briarpatch.* nd. Book Club. dj. VG. P1. $4.50

THOMAS, Ross. *Briarpatch.* 1984. Simon Schuster. 1st ed. dj. EX. P1. $15.95

THOMAS, Ross. *Cast a Yellow Shadow.* 1967. Morrow. 1st ed. dj. VG. P1. $30.00

THOMAS, Ross. *Chinaman's Chance.* 1978. Simon Schuster. 1st ed. dj. xl. P1. $12.50

THOMAS, Ross. *Cold War Swap.* 1966. Morrow. 2nd ed. dj. VG. P1. $15.00

THOMAS, Ross. *If You Can't Be Good.* 1973. Morrow. 1st ed. dj. xl. P1. $10.00

THOMAS, Ross. *Missionary Stew.* nd. Morrow. 2nd ed. dj. EX. P1. $10.00

THOMAS, Ross. *Money Harvest.* 1975. Morrow. 1st ed. dj. VG. P1. $17.50

THOMAS, Ross. *Out on the Rim.* 1987. Mysterious Pr. dj. EX. P1. $17.95

THOMAS, Ross. *Porkchoppers.* 1972. Morrow. dj. P1. $7.50

THOMAS, Rowan. *Born in Battle.* 1944. 1st ed. EX. $18.00

THOMAS, Sewell. *Silhouettes of Charles Thomas.* 1959. Caxton. 1/2000. sgn. $15.00

THOMAS & HYMAN. *Life & Times of Lincoln's Secretary of War.* 1962. NY. 1st ed. 642 p. dj. VG. T5. $27.50

THOMASON, J.F. *Foundations of Public Schools of SC.* 1925. Columbia. State Co. 237 p. xl. $10.00

THOMASON, J.W. *Adventures of General Marbot.* 1935. Scribner. A ed. lg 8vo. VG. $20.00

THOMASON, J.W. *Lone Star Preachers.* 1941. Ils. 296 p. dj. EX. J4. $20.00

THOMASON, John. *Salt Winds & Gobi Dust.* 1934. NY. 1st ed. dj. VG. B2. $37.50

THOMES, Robert. *War With the S: History of Great American Rebellion.* 1872-1877. 4to. 3 vols. EAG. VG. J2. $150.00

THOMMEN, G. *Is This Your Day?* 1964. NY. $16.00

THOMPSON, A.W. *They Were Open Range Days.* 1946. Denver. World. 1/500. 194 p. dj. very scarce. A3. $90.00

THOMPSON, Ames. *Strange Adventure Stories for Boys.* 1935. Cupples Leon. dj. VG. P1. $15.00

THOMPSON, D.A. *Reef Fishes of the Sea of Cortez.* 1987. AZ U. 32 color pls. 302 p. M. M2. $20.00

THOMPSON, D.P. *Green Mountain Boys: Historic Tale of Settlement of VT.* 1848. Boston. Revised 2nd ed. VG. $35.00

THOMPSON, Dorothy. *I Saw Hitler!* 1932. NY. Ils 1st ed. dj. VG. T5. $22.50

THOMPSON, Estelle. *Hunter in the Dark.* nd. Book Club. dj. VG. P1. $4.00

THOMPSON, Francis. *Hound of Heaven.* c 1920. London. Birdsall bdg. G. $25.00

THOMPSON, Francis. *New Poems.* 1897. Westminster. 1st ed. VG. G2. $200.00

THOMPSON, Francis. *Poems.* 1893. London. Ils Housman. 1st ed. VG. G2. $200.00

THOMPSON, Francis. *Shelley.* 1909. London. 1st ed. VG. G2. $160.00

THOMPSON, Francis. *Sister Songs.* 1895. London. Ils Housman. 1st ed. VG. G2. $200.00

THOMPSON, H.S. *Fear & Loathing in Las Vegas.* 1971. NY. 1st ed. dj. EX. $35.00

THOMPSON, Ignatius. *Patriots Monitor for VT.* 1810. Randolph, VT. Wright. 208 p. VG. A3. $45.00

THOMPSON, J.H. *History of County of Highland in State of OH...* 1878. Hillsboro, OH. 1st ed. 132 p. VG. T5. $95.00

THOMPSON, J.W. *Ancient Libraries.* 1940. Berkeley. Ils. dj. $22.50

THOMPSON, Jim. *Now & On Earth.* 1986. Macmillan. dj. M. P1. $40.00

THOMPSON, Joseph. *Singular & Surprising Adventures of Joseph Thompson.* 1865. Halifax. 1st ed. 24mo. gilt brown cloth. T1. $85.00

THOMPSON, Joyce. *Conscience Place.* 1984. Doubleday. 1st ed. dj. RS. EX. P1. $17.50

THOMPSON, Kay. *Eloise in Moscow.* 1959. NY. 1st print. dj. C4. $45.00

THOMPSON, Kay. *Eloise in Moscow.* 1959. Simon Schuster. Ils Knight. 1st ed. dj. B4. $65.00

THOMPSON, Kay. *Eloise.* 1955. NY. 1st ed. dj. VG. J2. $50.00

THOMPSON, L. *Meiville's Quarrel With God.* 1952. Princeton. 1st ed. dj. VG. B2. $40.00

THOMPSON, M. *Birds From N Borneo.* 1966. KS U. EX. M2. $4.00

THOMPSON, Morton. *Joe, the Wounded Tennis Player.* 1946. Sun Dial. dj. G. P1. $6.00

THOMPSON, R.H. *Modern Yucatecan Maya Pottery Making.* 1958. Am Archaeol Soc. 157 p. EX. M2. $18.00

THOMPSON, R.P. *Giant Horse of Oz.* 1928. Reilly Lee. 1st ed. dj. G. $200.00

THOMPSON, R.P. *Grampa in Oz.* c 1930s. reprint of 1924. 271 p. G. $22.50

THOMPSON, R.P. *Jack Pumpkinhead of Oz.* c 1930s. reprint of 1929. 256 p. G. $25.00

THOMPSON, R.P. *Jack Pumpkinhead of Oz.* 1929. Reilly Lee. 1st ed. dj. $200.00

THOMPSON, R.P. *Wishing Horse of Oz.* 1935. Reilly Lee. Ils Neill. 1st ed. green bdg. VG. $175.00

THOMPSON, R.W. *Churchill & Morton.* 1976. London. Hodder. 1st ed. dj. VG. D1. $35.00

THOMPSON, S. *Folktale.* 1946. 1st ed. VG. C1. $12.50

THOMPSON, Slason. *Railway Library, 1910. 2nd Series.* 1911. Chicago. Gunthorp Warren. xl. $17.50

THOMPSON, Vance. *Green Ray.* nd. Burt. VG. P1. $6.00

THOMPSON, Vance. *Pointed Tower.* nd. Burt. VG. P1. $6.00

THOMPSON, Vance. *Scarlet Iris.* nd. Burt. VG. P1. $6.00

THOMPSON, Virginia. *Between the Acts.* 1941. NY. 1st ed. dj. VG. $45.00

THOMPSON, W.H. *Assignment: Churchill.* 1955. Farrar Straus. 1st ed. gray cloth. dj. VG. D1. $30.00

THOMPSON, W.I. *Islands Out of Time.* 1985. Dial/Doubleday. 1st ed. dj. RS. EX. P1. $17.50

THOMPSON & ELY. *Birds in KS. Vol. I.* 1989. KS U. 404 p. M. M2. $25.00

THOMPSON & GOLDIN. *Hospital: Social & Architectural History.* 1975. Yale. Ils. 4to. 349 p. dj. EX. M2. $25.00

THOMPSON. *How To Train in Archery.* 1879. NY. 1st ed. EX. $22.00

THOMSON, Basil. *Mystery of French Milliner.* 1937. Crime Club. xl. P1. $10.00

THOMSON, Basil. *P.C. Richardson's First Case.* nd. Burt. VG. P1. $7.50

THOMSON, Basil. *Story of Scotland Yard.* 1936. NY. Ils. photos. dj. fair. $12.00

THOMSON, C.W. *Depths of the Sea: Account of...Dredging Cruises...* 1870. NY/London. Ils 1st ed. 8vo. $50.00

THOMSON, G.M. *Search for the NW Passage.* 1975. Macmillan. 1st ed. map. 288 p. EX. M2. $17.00

THOMSON, H. Douglas. *Great Book of Thrillers.* 1935. Odhams. VG. P1. $25.00

THOMSON, H. Douglas. *Great Book of Thrillers.* 1937. Odhams. G. P1. $20.00

THOMSON, H. Douglas. *Mystery Book.* 1934. Collins. Ils. 1079 p. VG. P1. $35.00

THOMSON, Hugh. *Our Village.* 1893. London. Ils 1st ed. gilt calf. $45.00

THOMSON, Ignatius. *Patriot's Monitor for NH.* 1810. Randolph, VT. Wright. 204 p. orig bdg. A3. $40.00

THOMSON, James. *Poetical Works of James Thomson.* 1777. Edinburg. 32mo. 2 vols in 1. VG. $67.00

THOMSON, James. *Seasons.* 1927. London. Nonesuch. 1/1500. 4to. VG. $80.00

THOMSON, June. *Case Closed.* 1977. Doubleday. 1st ed. dj. xl. P1. $5.00

THOMSON, Malcolm. *Churchill: His Life & Times*. 1965. Odham. Special Memorial ed. red cloth. D1. $25.00

THOMSON, Malcolm. *Life & Times of Winston S. Churchill*. nd. (1947?) Odham. blue cloth. dj. VG. D1. $20.00

THOMSON, S.R. *Kate Greenaway: Catalog of Greenaway Collection...* 1977. Wayne State. 1st ed. dj. M. $40.00

THOMSON, Virgil. *Musical Scene*. 1945. NY. 1st ed. sgn. $35.00

THOMSON, Virgil. *Virgil Thomson*. 1967. Knopf. dj. VG. $42.00

THOMSON, W.G. *Tapestry Weaving in England From Earliest Times...* nd. London. Ils. 4to. disbound. $50.00

THONE, F.E. *Trees & Flowers of Yellowstone National Park*. 1923. Haynes. Ils. 70 p. EX. M2. $5.00

THORBURN, Lois & Don. *No Tumult No Shouting*. 1945. NY. 1st ed. photos. 148 p. dj. T5. $47.50

THOREAU, H.D. *Cape Cod*. 1865. Boston. purple cloth. VG. $250.00

THOREAU, H.D. *Essay on Friendship*. 1903. Roycroft. 1st ed. VG. $175.00

THOREAU, H.D. *First Days of Winter, Winter at Walden, Winter's Dominion...* 1962-1966. Riverside. Ltd ed. 4 vols. J2. $75.00

THOREAU, H.D. *Men of Concord*. 1936. Boston. Ils Wyeth. dj. boxed. VG. B2. $115.00

THOREAU, H.D. *Men of Concord*. 1936. Houghton. Ils Wyeth. 1st ed. G. J2. $35.00

THOREAU, H.D. *Sir Walter Raleigh*. 1905. Bibliophile Soc. 1/489. boxed. J2. $75.00

THOREAU, H.D. *Thoreau on Birds*. 1964. McGraw Hill. 1st ed. dj. J2. $20.00

THOREAU, H.D. *Walden*. 1889. Boston. 12mo. 2 vols. gilt blue cloth. T1. $50.00

THOREAU, H.D. *Walden*. 1906. London. Art Nouveau bdg. $45.00

THOREAU, H.D. *Walden*. 1946. Houghton. Ils/Intro Teale. 1st ed. dj. J2. $22.50

THOREAU, H.D. *Walden; or, Life in the Woods*. 1927. Houghton. Ils Daglish. 1/500. 8vo. VG. $50.00

THOREAU, H.D. *Walden; or, Life in the Woods*. 1936. Merrymount. Ils/sgn Steichen. 8vo. slipcase. $250.00

THOREAU, H.D. *Week on the Concord & Merrimack Rivers*. 1975. Heritage. sm quarto. slipcase. EX. $15.00

THOREAU, H.D. *Week on the Concord & Merrimack Rivers*. 1975. Ltd Ed Club. slipcase. M. $100.00

THORIN, Duane. *Ride to Panmunjom*. 1956. Chicago. 1st ed. 303 p. dj. T5. $9.50

THORINGTON, J. *Glittering Mountains of Canada*. 1925. Phil. EX. $45.00

THORN, Ronald Scott. *Twin Serpents*. nd. Book Club. dj. VG. P1. $3.00

THORNBURG, Newton. *Black Angus*. 1978. Little Brown. 1st ed. dj. G. P1. $15.00

THORNBURY, Walter. *Life of J.M.W. Turner*. 1897. Chatto Windus. Revised New ed. J2. $20.00

THORNDIKE, Joseph. *Very Rich*. 1976. Crown. Ils. 352 p. dj. D2. $30.00

THORNDIKE, Joseph. *Very Rich*. 1976. Heritage. Ils. folio. dj. EX. $35.00

THORNE, Diana. *Your Dogs & Mine*. 1935. NY. Ils. 115 p. dj. G. T5. $17.50

THORNE, Guy. *Ravenscroft Affair*. nd. Grosset. dj. VG. P1. $12.50

THORNE, Guy. *Vintage of Vice*. 1927. Benman. dj. G. P1. $7.50

THORNE, Guy. *When It Was Dark*. 1905. Wm. Briggs. VG. P1. $7.50

THORNE. *Lazy Bear Lane*. 1921. Ils Smith. 1st ed. VG. E2. $20.00

THORNTON, J.W. *Landing at Cape Ann; or, Charter of First Permanent Colony*. 1854. Boston. map. fld charter. fair. $25.00

THORNTON, Mary Taylor. *When Pan Pipes*. nd. Wm. Briggs. VG. P1. $7.50

THORNTON, Richard. *Recognition of Robert Frost*. 1937. NY. 1st ed. dj. EX. $65.00

THORP, R.W. *Doc Carver, Spirit Gun of the W.* 1957. Glendale. 1st ed. dj. VG. B2. $37.50

THORP, Roderick. *Detective*. nd. Book Club. dj. VG. P1. $4.50

THORP, Roderick. *Detective*. 1966. Dial. 1st ed. dj. VG. P1. $7.50

THORP, Roderick. *Nothing Lasts Forever*. 1979. Norton. dj. EX. P1. $10.00

THORP, Willard. *S Reader*. 1955. NY. Knopf. 1st ed. dj. EX. $22.00

THORPE, Leslie. *Textbook on Aviation*. 1930. San Francisco. 4to. 4 vols. wraps. T5. $65.00

THORSMARK, Thora. *Children of Lapland*. 1936. Chicago. Ils. square 8vo. VG. $12.00

THORWALD, Jurgen. *Century of the Surgeon*. 1957. Pantheon. dj. VG. $17.50

THORWALD, Jurgen. *Science & Secrets of Early Medicine*. 1963. NY. 1st Am ed. EX. $45.00

THRALL, H.S. *Pictorial History of TX*. 1879. St. Louis. 2nd ed. 861 p. $125.00

THRESHER, R.E. *Reef Fish: Behavior & Ecology on Reef & in Aquarium*. 1980. Palmetto. Ils 1st Am ed. 171 p. dj. EX. M2. $18.00

THRIFT, Minton. *Memoir of Rev. Jesse With Extracts From His Journals*. 1823. NY. Bangs Mason. VG. $150.00

THROOP, A.J. *Mound Builders of IL*. 1928. E St. Louis. wraps. M. $20.00

THROWER, Rayner. *Pirate Picture*. 1980. London. Phillmore. reprint. T6. $15.00

THURBER, Francis. *From Plantation to Cup*. 1883. Am Grocery Pub. 3rd ed. 416 p. VG. B1. $35.00

THURBER, James. *Beast in Me & Other Animals*. 1948. Harcourt. ARC. 1st ed. dj. RS. VG. $70.00

THURBER, James. *Fables for Our Times*. 1940. NY. 4to. dj. VG. $37.50

THURBER, James. *Many Moons*. 1943. NY. 1st ed. dj. VG. B2. $25.00

THURBER, James. *Men, Women & Dogs*. 1943. NY. 1st ed. dj. VG. B2. $40.00

THURBER, James. *Middle-Aged Man on Flying Trapeze*. 1st ed. 8vo. VG. $30.00

THURBER, James. *My World & Welcome to It*. 1942. NY. 8vo. VG. $25.00

THURBER, James. *Thurber & Co.* 1966. Harper Row. 1st ed. dj. VG. M1. $17.50

THURBER, James. *Thurber Album*. 1952. NY. 1st ed. dj. $25.00

THURBER, James. *Thurber Country*. 1953. NY. 8vo. dj. $20.00

THURBER, James. *White Deer*. 1945. Harcourt Brace. 1st ed. dj. VG. M1. $30.00

THURBER, James. *Wonderful O.* nd. Simon Schuster. 2nd ed. dj. xl. P1. $10.00

THURBER, James. *Years With Ross*. 1959. Boston. dj. VG. $15.00

THURMAN, Howard. *With Head & Heart*. 1979. NY. dj. EX. $7.50

THURSTON, C.B. *Jingle of a Jap*. nd. Boston. VG. $35.00

THURSTON, Robert. *Alicia II.* 1978. Putnam. 1st ed. dj. EX. P1. $10.00

THWAITES, R.G. *Father Marquette.* 1911. Appleton. Ils 244 p. G. M2. $8.00

TIBBLES, T.H. *Buckskin & Blanket Days: Memoirs of Friend of Indians.* 1985. Chicago. Lakeside Classic. 466 p. EX. T5. $17.50

TICHENOR. *Rhymes of the Revolution.* 1914. St. Louis. stiff wraps. scarce. $40.00

TIDD, William. *Practice of Court of King's Bench Court of Common Pleas.* 1807. NY. 2nd ed. 1 vol only. fair. $15.00

TIECK, W.A. *Riverdale, Kingsbridge, Spuyten Duyvil.* 1968. Revell. 1st ed. glassine dj. EX. $50.00

TIEDMANN, A.R. *Symposium on Biology of Atriplex & Related Chenopods.* 1984. USFS. Ils. 4to. 309 p. M2. $13.00

TIETZE, H. *Tizian Gemalde und Zeichnungen.* 1936. Vienna. 328 pls. 8vo. 365 p. dj. EX. J2. $75.00

TIETZE-CONRAT, E. *Dwarfs & Jesters in Art.* 1957. Phaidon. 1st ed. dj. J2. $25.00

TIFFANY & COMPANY. *Tiffany Table Settings.* 1960. NY. 1st ed. 4to. dj. VG. $15.00

TILDEN, J.H. *Stuffed Club. Vol. 3.* 1902-1903. Denver. 518 p. VG. B1. $25.00

TILDEN, W.T. *My Story.* 1948. Hellman. Stated Pre-Pub print. dj. EX. $55.00

TILGHMAN, Z.A. *Outlaw Days.* 1962. OK City. Ils 1st ed. wraps. EX. $40.00

TILGHMAN, Z.A. *Quanah: Eagle of Comanches.* 1938. OK City. Ils 1st ed. dj. EX. $45.00

TIME LIFE. *Elephants & Other Land Giants.* 1977. color photos. 4to. 128 p. EX. M2. $11.00

TIME LIFE. *Giants & Ogres.* VG. C1. $11.50

TIME LIFE. *Magical Beasts.* VG. C1. $11.00

TIME LIFE. *Missing Link: Emergence of Man.* 1972. Ils. 160 p. VG. M2. $3.00

TIME LIFE. *Time Life Collectors' Library of Civil War.* Time Life. 14 vols. $115.00

TIME LIFE. *Time Life Collectors' Library of Viet Nam War.* Time Life. 14 vols. $35.00

TIME LIFE. *Unforgettable Winston S. Churchill: Giant of the Century.* 1965. Time. Ils. SftCvr. VG. D1. $25.00

TIMLIN, Mabel. *Keynesian Economics.* 1942. Toronto U. 1st ed. J2. $15.00

TIMME, W. *Lectures on Endocrinology.* 1924. NY. Hoeber. Ils 1st ed. 123 p. VG. $35.00

TIMMEN, F. *Blow for the Landing.* 1973. Caldwell. Ils 1st ed. dj. VG. B2. $22.50

TIMPSON, T. *Memoirs of Mrs. Elizabeth Fry.* 1847. NY. 12mo. 330 p. brown cloth. fair. G2. $24.00

TIMS, Margaret. *Jane Addams of Hull House.* 1961. George Allen. 1st ed. VG. J2. $12.50

TINCKER, M.A. *Two Coronets.* 1889. Houghton Mifflin. 1st ed. $12.00

TINDALLY, G.B. *Pursuit of S History: Addresses of S Historical Association.* 1964. Baton Rouge. 1st ed. dj. EX. $18.00

TINKCOM. *Republicans & Federalists in PA, 1790-1801.* 1950. Harrisburg. VG. $15.00

TINKER, B. *Mexican Wilderness & Wildlife.* 1978. TX U. Ils. 131 p. dj. EX. M2. $10.00

TINKLE, Lon. *American Original: Life of J. Frank Dobie.* 1978. Boston. 1st ed. sgn. 264 p. dj. T5. $9.50

TINSLEY, R. *All About Small Game Hunting in America.* 1976. Winchester. Ils. dj. EX. $12.00

TIPPING, H.A. *Grinling Gibbons & the Woodwork of His Age, 1648-1720.* 1914. London. dj. VG. J2. $250.00

TIPPING, H.A. *Story of Montacute & Its House.* 1933. London. 1st ed. VG. J2. $20.00

TISSOT, S.A. *Essay on Diseases.* 1769. London. 2nd ed. VG. $110.00

TITLER, D.M. *Day the Red Baron Died.* 1970. NY. dj. EX. $18.50

TITMARSH, M.A. *Mrs. Perkin's Ball.* 1848. Chapman Hall. 21 pls. AEG. G. $35.00

TITUS, Eve. *Basil & the Lost Colony.* 1964. 1st ed. sgn. dj. VG. $50.00

TOBRINER, Stephen. *Genesis of Noto.* 1982. Berkeley. dj. EX. P3. $50.00

TODD, C.B. *General History of Burr Family.* 1902. NY. 4th ed. VG. $45.00

TODD, Fritz. *Soldiers of the American Army, 1775-1954.* 1954. Chicago. Ils Kredel. Revised ed. dj. T5. $37.50

TODD, John. *Early Settlement & Growth of W IA...* 1906. Des Moines. 203 p. VG. A3. $60.00

TODD, John. *Sunset Land; or, Great Pacific Slope.* 1873. Boston. fair. $20.00

TODD & BOWDEN. *Tauchnitz International Editions in English, 1841-1955...* 1989. NY. 1047 p. plastic dj. EX. $75.00

TOKAY, Elbert. *Human Body & How It Works.* 1949. Perma P43. VG. P1. $5.00

TOKIOKA, T. *Pacific Tunicata of the US Natural Museum.* 1967. US Nat Mus. Ils 247 p. xl. M2. $15.00

TOKLAS, A.B. *Alice B. Toklas Cookbook.* 1954. NY. Harper. Ils Francis Rose. 1st Am ed. EX. $25.00

TOLAND, John. *No Man's Land, 1918, Last Year of the Great War.* 1980. NY. 1st ed. 651 p. dj. VG. T5. $17.50

TOLKIEN, J.R.R. *Book of Lost Tales.* nd. Book Club. dj. VG. P1. $4.50

TOLKIEN, J.R.R. *Father Christmas Letters.* 1976. Houghton. dj. VG. $25.00

TOLKIEN, J.R.R. *Hobbit.* 1938. Boston. 1st Am ed. dj. VG. B2. $135.00

TOLKIEN, J.R.R. *Letters of J.R.R. Tolkien.* 1981. Houghton. 1st Am ed. dj. EX. P1. $20.00

TOLKIEN, J.R.R. *Return of the King.* nd. Houghton. 15th print. VG. P1. $10.00

TOLKIEN, J.R.R. *Return of the King.* 1966. Houghton. 2nd ed. dj. VG. $15.00

TOLKIEN, J.R.R. *Silmarillion.* 1977. Allen Unwin. 1st ed. dj. EX. P1. $25.00

TOLKIEN, J.R.R. *Silmarillion.* 1977. Houghton. 1st ed. dj. VG. P1. $12.50

TOLKIEN, J.R.R. *Silmarillion.* 1977. 1st ed. 1st state. dj. C1. $9.50

TOLKIEN, J.R.R. *Smith of Wooton Major & Farmer Giles of Ham.* c 1976 Book Club. Ils Baynes. dj. EX. C1. $5.00

TOLKIEN, J.R.R. *Smith of Wooton Major.* 1967. Houghton. 1st ed. dj. EX. P1. $50.00

TOLKIEN, J.R.R. *Smith of Wooton Major.* 1967. Houghton. 1st ed. VG. P1. $30.00

TOLKIEN, J.R.R. *Tree & Leaf.* 1965. Boston. 1st Am ed. dj. EX. $35.00

TOLLER, Ernst. *Das Schwalbenbuch.* 1923. Potsdam. Kiepenheuer. 1st ed. wraps. EX. $100.00

TOLSTOY, Alexandra. *Tragedy of Tolstoy.* 1933. New Haven. 1st ed. sgn. VG. $35.00

TOLSTOY, Leo. *Anna Karenina.* 1886. NY. Crowell. 1st ed. $150.00

TOLSTOY, Leo. *Anna Karenina.* 1933. Moscow. Ltd Ed Club. 2 vols. VG. $35.00

TOLSTOY, Leo. *Anna Karenina.* 1939. Random House. 2 vols. $50.00

TOLSTOY, Leo. *Anna Karenina.* 1944. Doubleday. Ils/sgn Eichenberg. 8vo. slipcase. $125.00

TOLSTOY, Leo. *War & Peace.* nd. Modern Lib Giant. dj. G. $5.00

TOLSTOY, Leo. *War & Peace.* 1886. 1st Eng ed. xl. VG. $400.00

TOLSTOY, Nikolai. *Coming of the King.* 1st pb ed. M. C1. $6.00

TOLSTOY & CLAY. *Ocean Acoustics.* 1966. McGraw Hill. G. $20.00

TOMES, Robert. *Champagne Country.* 1867. NY. Hurd Houghton. 8vo. inscr. J2. $250.00

TOMES, Robert. *Panama in 1855: Account of Panama Railroad.* 1855. Harper. $40.00

TOMLIN, E.W. *Great Philosophers of the E World.* 1952. London. Skeffington. 1st ed. dj. VG. $11.00

TOMLIN, E.W. *Simone Weil.* 1954. Yale. 1st ed. dj. VG. $12.50

TOMLINSON, H.M. *All of Our Yesterdays.* 1930. London. Heinemann. sgn. slipcase. EX. $50.00

TOMLINSON, H.M. *Waiting for Daylight.* 1922. London. 1st ed. inscr. dj. EX. $75.00

TOMPKINS, Calvin. *Merchants & Masterpieces: Story of Metropolitan Museum...* 1970. NY. Dutton. Ils 383 p. xl. D2. $30.00

TOMPKINS, D.A. *History of Mecklenburg Country & City of Charlotte.* 1903. 2 vols. VG. $40.00

TOMPKINS, Stuart. *Russian Intelligentsia.* 1957. OK U. 1st ed. dj. J2. $15.00

TOMPKINS, Stuart. *Russian Mind.* 1953. OK U. 1st ed. dj. J2. $15.00

TOMPKINS, Walker A. *Roy Rogers & Ghost of Mystery Rancho.* nd. Whitman. dj. VG. P1. $15.00

TOMPKINS & BIRD. *Secret Life of Plants.* 1972. Harper. 402 p. dj. EX. M2. $18.00

TONGE, Thomas. *All About Co. for Home-Seekers, Tourists, Investors...* 1913. Denver. Smith Brooks. Ils. wraps. VG. A3. $40.00

TOOBIN, Jerome. *Agitato.* 1975. NY. Viking. inscr/sgn. EX. $22.00

TOOKER, R. *Day of the Brown Horde.* 1929. NY. 1st ed. dj. VG. $75.00

TOOLEY, R.V. *English Books With Color Plates, 1790-1860.* 1935. London. 1st ed. dj. EX. $85.00

TOOLEY, R.V. *English Books With Color Plates, 1790-1860.* 1987. London. pls. dj. EX. $40.00

TOOLEY, R.V. *Landmarks of Map Making.* 1968. Amsterdam. Elsevier. Ils. 276 p. dj. VG. B2. $70.00

TOOLEY, R.V. *Maps & Map Makers.* 1978. NY. Crown. Ils. cream cloth. dj. VG. $20.00

TOOMI. *Eesti-Rahvatantsud (Estonian Folk Dances).* 1953. Tallinn. color pls. 4to. G. G1. $25.00

TOOMY, Thomas. *O'Toomeys of Croom & Their Descendants.* 1920. St. Louis. VG. B1. $15.00

TOPOLSKI, Feliks. *Topolski's Legal London.* 1961. London. Ils 1st ed. 76 p. dj. VG. T1. $85.00

TOPONCE, A. *Reminiscences of Alexander Toponce.* 1971. OK U. New ed. 1st print. 221 p. dj. M2. $10.00

TORDAY, R. *On the Trail of the Bushongo.* 1969. Negro U. reprint of 1925 ed. 286 p. EX. M2. $24.00

TORDOFF, H.R. *Check List of Birds of KS.* 1956. KS U. M2. $3.00

TORMAY, Cecile. *Outlaw's Diary.* 1924. NY. photos. 233 p. VG. T5. $17.50

TORME, Mel. *Wynner.* 1978. NY. Stein Day. sgn. 347 p. dj. VG. M1. $9.50

TORRE, C. *Cyclophorid Operculate Land Mollusks of America.* 1942. US Nat Mus. 42 pls. 306 p. EX. M2. $43.00

TORRE, Mario. *Carlos Merida en Sus 90 Anos.* 1/3500. sgn. dj. VG. $50.00

TORRES, David. *Studies on Clarin: Annotated Bibliography.* Scarecrow. 204 p. VG. T5. $8.50

TORREY, John. *Flora of State of NY.* 1843. Albany. 162 pls. 2 vols. VG. $625.00

TORRIANI, Aimee. *Jester's Prayer.* 1942. St. Meinhard, IN. VG. C1. $10.00

TORROELLA, Rafael Santos. *Hartung: Olis I Aiguades Damunt Cartre 1973-1977.* nd. (1976?) Poligrafa. Ils. D2. $40.00

TORRY, E.N. *Round My Library Fire: Book About Books.* 1947. London. 1st ed. $25.00

TOTH, Karl. *Woman & Rocco in France.* 1931. Phil. Ils. dj. EX. $30.00

TOTTON, A.K. *Synopsis of the Siphonophora.* 1965. British Mus. 40 pls. 230 p. dj. EX. M2. $75.00

TOULMIN, Harry. *Digest of Laws of State of AL.* 1823. Cahawba. 1st ed. 1066 p. VG. very scarce. $295.00

TOULOUSE-LAUTREC & JOYANT. *Art of Cuisine.* 1966. Holt Rinehart. 1st ed. dj. EX. $35.00

TOULOUSE-LAUTREC. *One Hundred Unpublished Drawings.* nd. Boston. Book & Art Shop. 1/1500. boxed. EX. $85.00

TOUSEY, S. *Medical Electricity, Roentgen Rays & Radium.* 1916. Ils. 1219 p. $85.00

TOVEY, Charles. *Wit, Wisdom & Morals Distilled From Bacchus.* 1878. London. 1st ed. sgn. VG. $85.00

TOWBRIDGE, J.T. *Tour of the Battlefields.* 1866. 590 p. orig bdg. K1. $37.50

TOWNE & WENTWORTH. *Cattle & Men.* 1955. Norman. Ils 1st ed. dj. EX. $40.00

TOWNER, Wesley. *Elegant Auctioneers.* 1970. Hill Wang. Ils. 632 p. dj. D2. $45.00

TOWNSEND, G.A. *Life, Crime & Capture of John Wilkes Booth.* NY. 1/1000. facsimile of 1865 ed. M. J4. $10.00

TOWNSEND, G.A. *Rustics in Rebellion.* 1950. dj. VG. J4. $12.50

TOWNSEND, Gilbert. *Carpentry & Joinery.* 1913. Ils. 258 p. EX. $5.00

TOWNSEND, J.F. *Francis Peyre Porcher, M.D.* March, 1939. presentation. sgn. 12 p. $65.00

TOWNSEND, J.R. *Written for Children...* 1975. Lippincott. Ils. 368 p. dj. VG. $10.00

TOWNSEND, L.T. *History of 16th Regiment, NH Volunteers.* 1897. WA. 1st ed. $45.00

TOWNSEND, W.H. *Lincoln & the Bluegrass.* 1955. KY U. dj. EX. $25.00

TOYNBEE, Philip. *Prothalamium: Cycle of the Holy Grail.* 1970. reprint of 1947 ed. M. C1. $9.50

TRACEY, H. *African Dances Witwatersrand Gold Mines.* 1952. Johannesburg. 1st ed. 4to. EX. G1. $25.00

TRACHTMAN, P. *Gunfighters.* 1974. Time Life. Ils 1st ed. 4to. 238 p. EX. M2. $17.00

TRACY, Don. *Big Blackout.* nd. Book Club. dj. G. P1. $3.00

TRACY, Don. *Criss-Cross.* 1948. Triangle. dj. G. P1. $12.50

TRACY, Joseph. *History of American Missions to Heathen...* 1840. Worcester. Spooner Howland. 1st ed. 726 p. EX. $50.00

TRACY, Louis. *American Emperor.* 1918. Putnam. gilt-lettered bdg. VG. P1. $75.00

TRACY, Louis. *Lastingham Murder.* 1929. Clode. VG. P1. $18.25

TRACY, Louis. *Man With the 6th Sense.* nd. Hodder. G. P1. $18.25

TRACY, Louis. *Mysterious Disappearance.* nd. Grosset. VG. P1. $7.50

TRAEGER, J. *Philipp Otto Funge und sein Werk.* 1975. Munich. Ils. 4to. 556 p. dj. EX. J2. $175.00

TRAILL, C.P. *Backwoods of Canada: Letters From Wife of Emigrant Officer.* 1836. London. Ils 2nd ed. 351 p. xl. VG. T5. $65.00

TRAIN, Arthur. *His Children's Children.* 1923. Scribner. VG. P1. $7.50

TRAIN, Arthur. *Mr. Tutt Finds a Way.* 1945. Scribner. 1st ed. G. P1. $12.50

TRAIN, Arthur. *True Stories of Crime.* 1922. Scribner. VG. P1. $8.00

TRAIN, Arthur. *Yankee Lawyer.* 1946. Scribner. Lib bdg. xl. VG. P1. $6.00

TRAORE, Bakary. *Le Theatre Negro: Africain et ses Fonctions Sociales...* 1958. Paris. Presence Africaine. 159 p. wraps. $37.50

TRAPHAGEN, E. *Costume Design & Illustrations.* 1918. NY. VG. $35.00

TRAPIER, E. *Ribera.* 1952. NY. Ils. 8vo. EX. J2. $100.00

TRAPROCK, W.E. *My N Exposure: Kawa at the Pole.* 1922. NY. Putnam. Ils Owens. 245 p. $12.50

TRASK, J.J. *Stonington Houses: Panorama of New England Architecture...* 1976. NY. inscr/sgn. orig printed wraps. J2. $15.00

TRATMAN, E.E.R. *Railway Track & Track Work.* 1909. Ils 3rd ed. 520 p. $42.00

TRAUBEL, Helen. *Metropolitan Opera Murders.* nd. Book Club. dj. xl. P1. $4.00

TRAVEN, B. *Creation of Sun & Moon.* 1971. London. Ils 1st ed. dj. EX. $35.00

TRAVER, Robert. *Anatomy of Murder.* 1958. St. martin. dj. VG. $15.00

TRAVERS, Hugh. *Madame Aubry Dines With Death.* 1967. Harper Row. 1st ed. dj. VG. P1. $10.00

TRAVERS, P.L. *Mary Poppins in the Kitchen.* 1st ed. 2nd print. dj. VG. $12.50

TRAVERS, P.L. *Mary Poppins Opens the Door.* 1943. Reynal Hitchcock. 1st ed. dj. VG. $20.00

TRAVERS, P.L. *Mary Poppins.* 1934. Reynal Hitchcock. 1st ed. dj. VG. $22.00

TRAVIS, Gerry. *Big Bite.* 1957. Mystery House. 1st ed. dj. EX. P1. $9.00

TRAVIS, W. *Shark for Sale.* 1961. Rand McNally. Ils 1st Am ed. 181 p. dj. EX. M2. $15.00

TRAXEL, David. *American Saga: Life & Times of Rockwell Kent.* 1980. Harper. 1st ed. dj. VG. $18.00

TREADGOLD, Donald. *Great Siberian Migration.* 1957. Princeton. 1st ed. dj. J2. $15.00

TREAT, Lawrence. *B As in Banshee.* 1940. NY. AP. 1st ed. 295 p. blue wraps. VG. T1. $75.00

TREAT, Lawrence. *B As in Banshee.* 1940. NY. ARC. 1st ed. color wraps. VG. $50.00

TREAT, Lawrence. *H As in Hunted.* nd. Collier. VG. P1. $10.00

TREAT, Lawrence. *H As in Hunted.* nd. Collier. xl. G. P1. $5.00

TREAT, Lawrence. *O As in Omen.* Duell Sloan. 2nd ed. VG. P1. $10.00

TREAT, Lawrence. *Q As in Quicksand.* 1947. Duell Sloan. 1st ed. xl. rebound. P1. $6.00

TREDGOLD, Thomas. *Elementary Principles of Carpentry.* 1820. London. folio. VG. $100.00

TREDWELL. *Monograph on Privately Printed Books.* 1881. Brooklyn. 4to. 161 p. wraps. VG. B1. $20.00

TREECE, Henry. *Dark Island.* 1st Eng ed. dj. VG. C1. $14.00

TREECE, Henry. *Eagle King.* 1965. 1st Am ed. dj. EX. C1. $10.00

TREECE, Henry. *Electra.* 1972. pb. VG. C1. $4.50

TREECE, Henry. *Great Captains.* 1956. NY. 1st ed. dj. VG. C1. $24.50

TREECE, Henry. *Green Man.* 1966. NY. 1st Am ed. dj. EX. scarce. C1. $29.50

TREECE, Henry. *Green Man.* 1968. not 1st ed. pb. G. C1. $3.50

TREECE, Henry. *Green Man.* 1968. 1st ed. pb. VG. C1. $7.00

TREECE, Henry. *Horned Helmet.* Puffin. pb. VG. C1. $5.00

TREECE, Henry. *Invaders.* 1972. dj. EX. C1. $7.50

TREECE, Henry. *Jason.* 1961. London. 1st Eng ed. VG. C1. $7.00

TREECE, Henry. *Man With a Sword.* 1979. Oxford. 1st ed. VG. C1. $7.50

TREECE, Henry. *Oedipus.* 1964. Bodley Head. 1st ed. xl. G. P1. $5.00

TREECE, Henry. *Ride Into Danger.* 1959. Criterion. xl. VG. P1. $5.00

TREFETHEN, J.B. *Wild Sheep of Modern N America.* 1975. Boone/Crockett Club. photos. 302 p. EX. M2. $13.00

TREMAYNE, Peter. *Fires of Lan-Kern.* 1980. St. Martin. dj. EX. P1. $15.00

TREMAYNE, Peter. *Irish Masters of Fantasy.* 1979. Wolfhound. 1st ed. dj. VG. P1. $17.50

TRENCH, B.L.P. *Eternal Subject.* 1973. London. $18.50

TRENKER, Luis. *Berge und Heimat...* 1939. Berlin. 258 photos. 4to. 138 p. $150.00

TRENKER, Luis. *Mein Berge, das Bergbuch...* 1935. Berlin. 188 photos. sm 4to. 148 p. $100.00

TRENT, L. *Trail of the Trents.* 1954. Boston. dj. EX. $10.00

TRENT. *R.L. Stevenson's Workshop.* 1921. Biblio Soc. 1st ed. 1/450. slipcase. EX. $70.00

TREVANIAN. *Loo Sanction.* 1973. NY. Crown. 1st ed. dj. EX. $10.00

TREVANIAN. *Summer of Katya.* 1983. Granada. 1st ed. dj. VG. P1. $17.50

TREVARTHEN, H.P. *World D: Being a Brief Account of Founding of Helioxenon.* 1935. Sheed World. dj. G. $150.00

TREVELYAN, G.O. *Early History of Charles James Fox.* 1880. London. Longman Green. sgn Fox. 8vo. VG. $125.00

TREVER, Albert. *History of Greek Economic Thought.* 1916. Chicago U. 1st ed. wraps. G. J2. $12.50

TREVOR, Elleston. *Night Stop.* 1975. Doubleday. 1st ed. dj. xl. P1. $5.00

TREXLER, H.A. *Confederate Ironclad VA.* 1938. Chicago. EX. $75.00

TREXLER, H.A. *Slavery in MO 1804-1865.* 1914. Johns Hopkins. 259 p. EX. M2. $45.00

TRICE & SIMON. *Thirty-Fourth US Naval Construction Battalion.* 1946. San Francisco. photos. G. T5. $125.00

TRIDON, Andre. *Psychoanalysis & Love.* 1949. Perma P50. VG. P1. $5.00

TRILLEN, Calvin. *Education in GA.* 1964. NY. 1st ed. dj. EX. $30.00

TRILLING, L. *Liberal Imagination.* 1950. NY. Viking. 1st ed. dj. VG. $15.00

TRIMBLE, S. *Words From Land: Encounters With Natural History Writing.* 1988. Smith. 303 p. dj. M. M2. $17.00

TRIMPEY, A.K. *My First Love: Story of Becky & Other Dolls.* 1946. Buraboo, WI. Ils 1st ed. sgn. 59 p. fair. T5. $12.50

TRIMPEY, A.K. *Story of My Dolls.* 1935. Racine. 1st ed. sgn. dj. VG. $40.00

TRIPLETT, F. *Conquering the Wilderness.* 1895. Chicago. fair. $30.00

TRIPP, Miles. *Some Predators Are Male.* 1985. St. Martin. 1st ed. dj. EX. P1. $12.95

TRISTRAM & JAMES. *Wall Paintings in Croughton Church, Northamptonshire.* 1927. Oxford. reprint. VG. J2. $45.00

TRIVAS, N. *Paintings of Frans Hals.* 1941. London. 159 pls. 4to. 231 p. EX. J2. $50.00

TROLLOPE, A. *Small House at Allington.* London. 1st ed. 1st issue. 2 vols. EX. T5. $350.00

TROLLOPE, Anthony. *Ralph the Heir.* 1871. Harper. VG. J3. $250.00

TROLLOPE, Frances. *Domestic Manners of Americans.* Imprint Soc. reprint. boxed. EX. $17.50

TROTSKY, Leon. *Bolsheviki & World Peace.* 1918. NY. 1st ed. VG. $50.00

TROTSKY, Leon. *Case of Leon Trotsky.* 1937. London. 1st ed. 617 p. VG. B2. $45.00

TROTSKY, Leon. *History of Russian Revolution.* 1932. Simon Schuster. 1st ed. 3 vols. VG. $75.00

TROTSKY, Leon. *My Life.* 1930. Scribner. 1st A print. VG. $50.00

TROTTA, Geri. *Veronica Died Monday.* 1952. Dodd Mead. 1st ed. xl. P1. $5.00

TROUGHTON, E. *Furred Animals of Australia.* 1954. Sydney. Revised ed. 376 p. dj. EX. M2. $40.00

TROW, M.J. *Supreme Adventure of Inspector Lestrade.* 1985. Stein Day. dj. VG. P1. $20.00

TROWBRIDGE, C. *Crow Island Journal.* 1970. NY. Ils 1st ed. 144 p. dj. EX. $7.50

TROWBRIDGE, J.T. *Picture of the Desolated States & Work of Restoration...* 1868. 736 p. VG. J4. $32.50

TROY, Jack. *Leading a Bulldog's Life.* 1948. Atlanta. 1st ed. 172 p. dj. VG. $15.00

TRUBY, J.D. *Silencers, Snipers & Assassins.* 1972. Palden Pr. 1st ed. dj. G. $28.00

TRUDEAU. *Rap Master Ronnie.* Lord John. sgn. EX. $70.00

TRUE, F.W. *Revision of the American Moles.* 1896. Smithsonian. Ils. 111 p. M2. $5.00

TRUESDALE, Dr. Jackson. *Scraps of History.* nd. (1940?) np. 150 p. stiff wraps. G. T5. $22.50

TRUETT, R.B. *Trade & Travel Around S Appalachians Before 1830.* 1935. Chapel Hill. 1st ed. dj. EX. $60.00

TRUMAN, Harry S. *Memoirs: Years of Decisions, Years of Trials & Hope.* 1955-1956. KS City Ltd ed. 2 vols. sgn. T5. $195.00

TRUMAN, Margaret. *Harry S. Truman.* 1973. Morrow. Ils. 602 p. EX. $6.00

TRUSS, Seldon. *In Secret Places.* 1958. Crime Club. 1st ed. xl. P1. $5.00

TRUSS, Seldon. *Technique for Treachery.* 1963. Crime Club. 1st ed. dj. xl. P1. $5.00

TRUSS, Seldon. *Turmoil at Brede.* 1931. Mystery League. 1st ed. VG. P1. $10.00

TRYCKARE, Tre. *Lore of Flight.* 1970. Gothenburgh. Ils. 430 p. dj. VG. T5. $12.50

TSE-TUNG, Mao. *Selected Military Writings.* 1963. Peking. 1st ed. dj. boxed. M. $24.00

TSOU, Tang. *America's Failure in China, 1941-1950.* 1963. Chicago U. 1st ed. dj. J2. $15.00

TUBB, E.C. *Alien Seed.* 1976. Arthur Barker. dj. xl. P1. $5.00

TUBB, E.C. *Alien Seed.* 1976. Arthur Barker. 1st ed. dj. VG. P1. $12.50

TUBB, E.C. *Scatter of Stardust.* 1976. Dobson. 1st ed. dj. EX. P1. $15.00

TUBBY, G.O. *Psychics & Mediums.* 1935. Boston. $25.00

TUCHMAN, Barbara. *Stilwell & the American Experience in China, 1911-1945.* 1971. NY. Ils 1st ed. 621 p. dj. VG. T5. $27.50

TUCHMAN, Barbara. *Zimmerman Telegram.* 1958. NY. 1st ed. dj. B2. $30.00

TUCK, Davis. *Complete English Setter.* 1951. Denlinger. 1st ed. glassine dj. VG. B2. $35.00

TUCK, G.S. *Field Guide to Sea Brids of Britain & the World.* 1980. London. 48 color pls. 313 maps. 292 p. M2. $18.00

TUCK, H.C. *Four Years at the U of GA: 1877-1881.* 1938. Athens. Ils 1st ed. 251 p. VG. $25.00

TUCKER, B.R. *Lost Lenore.* 1929. Liberty Pr. 1st ed. purple cloth. EX. D1. $8.00

TUCKER, C.F. *Apocryka.* 1918. Oxford. Brooke ed. 456 p. G. B1. $25.00

TUCKER, G.W. *Lee & the Gettysburg Campaign.* c 1933. Richmond. EX. $25.00

TUCKER, Glenn. *Tucumseh: Vision of Glory.* 1956. Indianapolis. 1st ed. maps. 399 p. T5. $47.50

TUCKER, Jean. *Read the Answer in the Stars.* 1925. NY. $10.00

TUCKER, S.G. *Dissertation on Slavery: With Proposal for Abolition...* 1861. NY. reprint. 8vo. 104 p. VG. $60.00

TUCKER, Sophie. *Some of These Days.* 1945. NY. 1st ed. inscr/sgn. $45.00

TUCKER, Wilson. *Bomb.* 1955. Rinehart. 1st ed. xl. rebound. P1. $7.50

TUCKER, Wilson. *Dove.* 1948. Rinehart. 1st ed. dj. VG. P1. $50.00

TUCKER, Wilson. *Ice & Iron.* nd. Book Club. dj. EX. P1. $3.00

TUCKER, Wilson. *Lincoln Hunters.* nd. Book Club. dj. VG. P1. $4.50

TUCKER, Wilson. *Long Loud Silence.* nd. Book Club. dj. VG. P1. $7.50

TUCKER, Wilson. *Procession of the Damned.* 1965. Crime Club. 1st ed. dj. VG. P1. $25.00

TUCKER, Wilson. *Red Herring.* 1951. Rinehart. 1st ed. dj. xl. P1. $25.00

TUCKER, Wilson. *Stalking Man.* 1950. Cassell. xl. P1. $20.00

TUCKER, Wilson. *This Witch.* 1971. Doubleday. 1st ed. dj. xl. P1. $7.50

TUCKERMAN, H.T. *America & Her Commentators.* 1864. NY. 1st ed. xl. G. $15.00

TUDOR, E.G. *Chagall at the Met.* 1971. NY. dj. slipcase. EX. $75.00

TUDOR, Tasha. *Betty Crocker's Kitchen Gardens.* 1971. Universal. M. $25.00

TUDOR, Tasha. *Mother Goose.* 1944. Walck. VG. B4. $30.00

TUDOR, Tasha. *New England Buttry Shelf Cookbook.* 1970. NY. 1st ed. dj. VG. B2. $50.00

TUDOR, Tasha. *Selected & Illustrated Mother Goose.* 1944. Walck. VG. B4. $30.00

TUER, A. *Bartolozzi & His Works.* 1881. London. 13 pls. 4to. 2 vols. VG. G2. $110.00

TUER, A. *Old London Cries.* 1885. London. 1st ed. 12mo. slipcase. VG. G2. $70.00

TUER, A. *Pages & Pictures From Forgotten Children's Books.* 1898-1899. London. 1st trade ed. TEG. T5. $125.00

TUER, A. *Stories From Old-Fashioned Children's Books.* c 1899. London. 1st ed. $85.00

TUKE, John. *General View of Agriculture of N Riding of Yorkshire.* 1800. London. Macmillan. 14 pls. map. 355 p. A3. $150.00

TULKITSUV, Z. *Dos Shtetl.* 1946. Warsaw-Lodz. $30.00

TUNIS, Edwin. *Colonial Craftsmen & Beginnings of American Industry.* 1965. Crowell. Ils. dj. D2. $35.00

TUNIS, Edwin. *Wheels: Pictorial History.* 1955. Cleveland. Ils 1st ed. 96 p. dj. VG. T5. $12.50

TUNNEY, Christopher. *Biographical Dictionary of WWII.* 1972. NY. Ils 1st ed. 216 p. dj. EX. T5. $12.50

TUNNICLIFFE, C.F. *Tunnicliffe's Birds: Measured Drawings.* 1984. Little Brown. Ils 1st Am ed. folio. dj. EX. M2. $45.00

TUPPER, Harmon. *To the Great Ocean.* 1965. Boston. Ils 1st ed. 536 p. dj. G. T5. $25.00

TURBAK, G. *America's Great Cats.* 1986. Northland. Ils 1st ed. 77 p. M. M2. $10.00

TURBAK, G. *Twilight Hunters: Wolves, Coyotes & Foxes.* 1987. Northland. Ils 1st ed. 102 p. M. M2. $12.00

TURBOTT, E.G. *Buller's Birds of New Zealand.* 1982. New Zealand. Ils Keulmans. dj. slipcase. M. M2. $85.00

TURKLE, Briton. *Magic of Millicant Musgrave.* 1967. NY. 1st ed. presentation. sgn. dj. EX. $30.00

TURKLE, Briton. *Mooncoin Castle.* 1970. 1st ed. xl. VG. C1. $6.00

TURNBULL, A.S. *King's Orchard.* 1963. Boston. 1st print. dj. VG. $9.50

TURNBULL, Andrew. *Scott Fitzgerald.* 1962. NY. 1st ed. dj. EX. $25.00

TURNBULL, Andrew. *Scott Fitzgerald.* 1962. Scribner. 2nd print. dj. VG. T6. $10.00

TURNBULL, C.M. *Mountain People.* 1972. Simon Schuster. Ils. 309 p. dj. EX. M2. $13.00

TURNBULL, Stephen. *Book of the Samurai: Warrior Class of Japan.* 1982. NY. Ils. dj. M. $20.00

TURNER, C.L. *Crayfishes of OH.* 1926. OH Biol Survey. 2 pls. maps. M2. $10.00

TURNER, C.W. *Chessie's Road.* 1956. Richmond. Ils 1st ed. 286 p. dj. VG. T5. $32.50

TURNER, D. *Vampire Bat: Field Study in Behavior & Ecology.* 1975. John Hopkins. 15 photos. 145 p. dj. EX. M2. $10.00

TURNER, D.T. *Black American Literature.* 1970. Columbus. Merrill. 610 p. dj. $27.50

TURNER, F.B. *Reptiles & Amphibians of Yellowstone National Park.* 1955. Yellowstone Lib. Ils 40 p. M2. $10.00

TURNER, F.J. *Character & Influence of Indian Trade in WI.* 1977. OK U. 1st ed. 92 p. dj. EX. M2. $16.00

TURNER, F.J. *Frontier in American History.* 1931. NY. VG. $15.00

TURNER, Frederick. *Double Shadow.* 1978. Berkley Putnam. 1st ed. dj. EX. P1. $12.50

TURNER, G.E. *Victory Rode the Rails.* 1953. 1st ed. 419 p. $37.50

TURNER, J.F. *Magnificent Bald Eagle.* 1971. Random House. photos. 81 p. dj. EX. M2. $8.00

TURNER, James. *Fourth Ghost Book.* 1965. Barrie Rockliff. dj. VG. P1. $17.50

TURNER, K.C. *Red Men Calling on Great White Father.* 1951. Norman. Ils 1st ed. dj. EX. $35.00

TURNER, Marie. *In the Land of Breathitt.* 1941. Am Guide Series. 1st ed. dj. J2. $20.00

TURNER, Roy. *King of the Lordless Country.* 1971. London. 1st ed. dj. VG. C1. $6.00

TURNER, William Price. *Circle of Squares.* 1969. Walker. dj. VG. P1. $10.00

TURNOR, Reginald. *Smaller English House, 1500-1939.* 1952. London. cloth. EX. J2. $25.00

TUROW, Scott. *Presumed Innocent.* 1988. NY. ARC. VG. $30.00

TURRELL, Charles. *Miniatures.* 1913. London. Lane. 1/100. sgn. AEG. EX. J2. $100.00

TURTON, Godfrey. *Devil's Churchyard.* 1970. Doubleday. 1st ed. dj. EX. P1. $10.00

TUSHNET, Leonard. *Uses of Adversity.* 1966. NY. 1st ed. dj. G. $6.00

TUTHILL, Mrs. L.C. *Mirror of Life.* 1848. Phil. Ils. brown leather. $17.00

TVARDOVSKY, Alexander. *Tyorkin & the Stovemakers.* 1974. Trans Anthony Rudolf. dj. VG. $12.00

TWAIN, Mark. *$1,000,000 Bank Note.* 1893. Webster. VG. $80.00

TWAIN, Mark. *Adventures of Huckleberry Finn.* 1933. Ltd Ed Club. J2. $50.00

TWAIN, Mark. *Adventures of Tom Sawyer.* 1936. NY. Ils Rockwell. dj. G. $20.00

TWAIN, Mark. *American Claimant.* 1892. NY. Ils 1st ed. 8vo. EX. T1. $95.00

TWAIN, Mark. *American Claimant.* 1896. Webster. 1st ed. G. J2. $60.00

TWAIN, Mark. *Autobiography & First Romance.* 1871. NY. 1st ed. 1st issue. $150.00

TWAIN, Mark. *Autobiography & First Romance.* 1871. NY. Sheldon. 1st ed. 2nd issue. purple bdg. $60.00

TWAIN, Mark. *Captain Stromfield's Visit to Heaven.* 1909. NY. 1st ed. VG. $35.00

TWAIN, Mark. *Christian Science.* 1907. Harper. 1st ed. 8vo. red cloth. VG. G2. $60.00

TWAIN, Mark. *Conversation at the Time of the Tudors.* nd. NY. Stuart. gilt red cloth. VG. $12.00

TWAIN, Mark. *CT Yankee in King Arthur's Court.* nd. Book League. dj. EX. P1. $10.00

TWAIN, Mark. *CT Yankee in King Arthur's Court.* nd. Grosset. dj. VG. P1. $7.50

TWAIN, Mark. *CT Yankee in King Arthur's Court.* nd. Musson. VG. P1. $7.50

TWAIN, Mark. *CT Yankee in King Arthur's Court.* 1889. NY. gilt olive cloth. EX. $125.00

TWAIN, Mark. *CT Yankee in King Arthur's Court.* 1890. Webster. decorated bdg. G. P1. $75.00

TWAIN, Mark. *Double-Barrelled Detective Story.* April, 1902. Harper. Ils 1st ed. TEG. $95.00

TWAIN, Mark. *Editorial Wild Oats.* 1905. NY. 1st ed. scarce. $60.00

TWAIN, Mark. *English As She Is Taught.* 1900. Boston. Mutual Book. green bdg. EX. $45.00

TWAIN, Mark. *Extract From Captain Stromfield's Visit to Heaven.* 1909. NY. red cloth. EX. P3. $30.00

TWAIN, Mark. *Extracts From Adam's Diary.* 1904. NY. Ils 1st Separate ed. 89 p. G. T5. $55.00

TWAIN, Mark. *Following the Equator.* 1897. Hartford. Ils 1st ed. 1st issue. 8vo. VG. T1. $45.00

TWAIN, Mark. *Huckleberry Finn.* 1968. Ils Rockwell. boxed. EX. $25.00

TWAIN, Mark. *Innocents Abroad.* 1869. Hartford. Ils 1st ed. mixed state. VG. $145.00

TWAIN, Mark. *Innocents Abroad.* 1869. Hartford. 1st ed. 3rd issue. gilt black bdg. $125.00

TWAIN, Mark. *Life on the MS.* 1883. Boston. Osgood. 1st Am ed. 1st issue. VG. $200.00

TWAIN, Mark. *Life on the MS.* 1883. London. Ils 1st ed. 1st state. VG. $195.00

TWAIN, Mark. *Mark Twain's Autobiography.* 1924. NY. 1st ed. 2 vols. djs. VG. B2. $60.00

TWAIN, Mark. *Mark Twain's Library of Humor, Men & Things.* Feb., 1906. NY/London. Harper. 1st ed. VG. $75.00

TWAIN, Mark. *Merry Tales.* 1892. NY. 1st ed. VG. $65.00

TWAIN, Mark. *More Tramps Abroad.* 1898. Chato Windus. TEG. EX. $50.00

TWAIN, Mark. *Mysterious Stranger.* 1916. Harper. Ils Wyeth. VG. B2. $60.00

TWAIN, Mark. *Personal Recollections of Joan of Arc.* 1896. NY. 1st ed. 1st state. VG. G1. $95.00

TWAIN, Mark. *Plymouth Rock & Pilgrims & Other Salutory Platform Opinions.* 1984. Harper Row. 1st ed. dj. EX. $25.00

TWAIN, Mark. *Prince & the Pauper.* 1882. Boston. Osgood. 1st Am ed. 1st issue. $175.00

TWAIN, Mark. *Prince & the Pauper.* 1887. Webster. gilt green bdg. EX. $100.00

TWAIN, Mark. *Quaker City Holy Land Excursion.* 1986. Omaha. Buttonmaker Pr. 1/150. $60.00

TWAIN, Mark. *Treasury of Mark Twain.* 1967. Hallmark. dj. VG. P1. $7.50

TWAIN, Mark. *Twain Short Stories.* c 1923. Collier. 12mo. gilt leather. VG. $25.00

TWAIN, Mark. *War Prayer.* 1968. Ils Groth. dj. EX. $5.00

TWAIN, Mark. *1601: Conversation As It Was by Social Fireside.* nd. 80 p. dj. slipcase. EX. $65.00

TWAIN, S.L. *Curious Republic of Condour.* 1919. NY. 1st ed. EX. $65.00

TWISS, Travers. *OR Territory.* 1846. NY. Appleton. 1st Am ed. G. scarce. J3. $110.00

TYAS, Robert. *Beautiful Birds: First Series.* nd. London. Ils Andrews. gilt blue bdg. $150.00

TYCE, Richard. *Edward Albee: A Bibliography.* Scarecrow Pr. 212 p. VG. T5. $9.50

TYLER, Anne. *Accidental Tourist.* 1985. NY. 1st ed. dj. EX. $35.00

TYLER, Anne. *Accidental Tourist.* 1985. NY. 1st ed. dj. EX. with sgn leaf. $60.00

TYLER, Anne. *Celestial Navigation.* 1974. Knopf. $55.00

TYLER, Anne. *Dinner at Homesick Restaurant.* 1982. Knopf. 1st ed. dj. $25.00

TYLER, Anne. *Earthly Possessions.* 1977. Knopf. 1st ed. dj. $45.00

TYLER, Anne. *Morgan's Passing.* 1980. Knopf. 1st ed. dj. EX. $50.00

TYLER, Anne. *Slipping Down Life.* 1970. Knopf. 1st ed. dj. $40.00

TYLER, F. *Man Who Made Music.* 1947. Harrap. xl. P1. $5.00

TYLER, G.C. *Whatever Goes Up.* 1934. Bobbs Merrill. Ils. G. $12.00

TYLER, G.W. *History of Bell Co.* 1936. San Antonio. 1st ed. 425 p. VG. B1. $65.00

TYLER, J.J. *Early Freemasonry of Geauga, Ashtabula & Lake Co.* 1942. np. 2 parts. wraps. VG. T5. $17.50

TYLER, J.J. *Pioneer Presbyterian Work Among OH Indians.* nd. Warren, OH. 48 p. map. wraps. VG. T5. $19.50

TYLER, M.W. *Recollections of Civil War.* 1912. NY. 1st ed. dj. EX. $40.00

TYLER, P.F. *Historical View of Progress of Discovery on N Coasts of Am.* 1843. NY. Harper. Ils. fld map. 360 p. VG. A3. $90.00

TYLER, Royall. *Chestnut Tree.* 1931. VT. Driftwood Pr. Ltd ed. $40.00

TYMN & SCHLOBIN. *Year's Scholarship in SF, 1972-1975.* nd. Kent State. HrdCvr. P1. $15.00

TYMN & SCHLOBIN. *Year's Scholarship in SF, 1976-1979.* nd. Kent State. HrdCvr. P1. $15.00

TYNAN, Kathleen. *Agatha.* 1978. Ballantine. dj. EX. P1. $8.00

TYNDALL, John. *Forms of Water in Clouds & Rivers, Ice & Glaciers.* 1872. NY. Ils. fair. $25.00

TYNDALL, John. *Fragments of Science for Unscientific People.* 1894. NY. 2 vols. $30.00

TYREE, Marion Cabell. *Housekeeping in Old VA.* nd. Favorite. reprint of 1879 ed. P1. $10.00

TYRELL, G.N.M. *Science & Psychical Phenomena.* 1938. London. $60.00

TYRON, Thomas. *Harvest Home.* 1973. NY. Knopf. 400 p. black cloth. VG. $10.00

TYRRELL, R. & E. *Hummingbirds: Their Life & Behavior.* 1985. Crown. Ils. 256 p. dj. EX. M2. $30.00

TYSON, C.B. *Poconos.* 1929. Innes. Ils. 193 p. VG. $25.00

U

UBBELOHDE, C. *CO Reader.* 1973. Pruett. map. 342 p. EX. M2. $10.00

UDEN, Grant. *Knight & Merchant.* 1966. 1st ed. xl. VG. C1. $7.50

UHER & PAVLIK. *Dialogue of Forms.* 1977. St. Martin. VG. $35.00

UHNAK, Dorothy. *False Witness.* 1981. Simon Schuster. 1st ed. dj. EX. P1. $10.00

UHNAK, Dorothy. *Investigation.* nd. Book Club. dj. VG. P1. $4.00

UHNAK, Dorothy. *Law & Order.* nd. Book Club. dj. VG. P1. $4.00

UKERS, William. *Romance of Tea.* 1936. NY. Ils 1st ed. 276 p. dj. VG. B2. $40.00

ULLMAN, Alan. *Sorry, Wrong Number.* 1948. Random House. 1st ed. dj. VG. $17.50

ULLMAN, J.M. *Neon Haystack.* nd. Book Club. dj. VG. P1. $3.00

ULLMAN, J.N. *Judge Takes the Stand.* 1933. NY. Knopf. 1st ed. sgn. 8vo. EX. $20.00

ULLMAN, J.R. *Kingdom of Adventure: Everest.* 1947. Sloane. photos. maps. 411 p. dj. VG. M2. $10.00

ULLMAN, J.R. *White Tower.* 1945. Lippincott. 479 p. $4.00

ULLMAN, S. *Valentino As I Knew Him.* 1926. NY. Ils 1st ed. 8vo. VG. $25.00

ULMANN, Doris. *Appalachian Photographs.* 1971. Penland, NC. Jargon. 1st ed. square 4to. dj. EX. $30.00

ULMANN, Doris. *Darkness & the Light.* 1974. Millerton. Aperture. 1st ed. 4to. dj. EX. $30.00

ULMANN & ZIMMERMAN. *Working With Dreams.* 1979. NY. $15.00

ULPH, Owen. *Leather Throne.* 1984. Salt Lake City. 1/100. sgn. dj. maroon slipcase. M. $95.00

UNDE, W. *Vincent Van Gogh.* nd. London. 120 pls. 4to. dj. EX. J2. $50.00

UNDERHILL, R. *Indians of the Pacific NW.* 1945. US Dept Interior. 232 p. EX. $6.00

UNDERWOOD, J.C. *Monument to Confederate Dead at Chicago.* 1896. Souvenir ed. 285 p. EX. scarce. J4. $40.00

UNDERWOOD, John. *Stinsons.* 1969. Ils. 4to. 80 p. dj. EX. $20.00

UNDERWOOD, Leon. *Siamese Cat.* 1928. NY. Brentano. 1/2500. dj. J2. $25.00

UNDERWOOD, Michael. *Crooked Wood.* 1978. Macmillan. 1st ed. dj. xl. P1. $5.00

UNDERWOOD, Michael. *Double Jeopardy.* 1981. St. Martin. dj. EX. P1. $15.00

UNDERWOOD, Michael. *Lawful Pursuit.* 1958. Crime Club. 1st ed. dj. G. P1. $8.00

UNDERWOOD, Michael. *Smooth Justice.* 1979. Macmillan. 1st ed. dj. xl. P1. $5.00

UNDERWOOD, Michael. *Unprofessional Spy.* 1964. McDonald. 1st ed. dj. xl. P1. $5.00

UNDERWOOD & MILLER. *Bare Bones: Conversations on Terror With Stephen King.* 1988. NY. 1st ed. dj. EX. $25.00

UNDERWOOD & MILLER. *Fear Itself.* 1982. San Francisco. 1st ed. 1/5000. red/black bdg. dj. $35.00

UNDERWOOD & MILLER. *Fear Itself.* 1984. Plume 25527. VG. P1. $10.00

UNDSET, Sigrid. *Bridal Wreath.* 1928. not 1st ed. dj. VG. C1. $7.50

UNDSET, Sigrid. *Faithful Wife.* 1937. NY. 1st Am ed. dj. EX. $20.00

UNDSET, Sigrid. *Kristin Labransdatter.* 1946. Knopf. 1st ed. 3 vols. $35.00

UNDSET, Sigrid. *Madame Dorthea.* 1940. NY. 1st Am ed. dj. EX. $20.00

UNGER, Frederick. *Roosevelt's African Trip.* 1909. Hoey. VG. $15.00

UNTERMEYER, Louis. *Book of Noble Thoughts.* 1946. Am Artist Group. 1st ed. J2. $17.50

UNTERMEYER, Louis. *Burning Bush.* 1928. NY. 1st ed. 2nd print. with sgn postcard. $30.00

UNTERMEYER, Louis. *Modern British Poetry.* 1925. Harcourt Brace. 8vo. black cloth. G. $7.50

UNTERMEYER, Louis. *Wonderful Adventures of Paul Bunyan.* 1973. Heritage. sm quarto. slipcase. EX. $15.00

UNWIN, Stanley. *Truth About Publishing.* 1946. London. Ils. pls. dj. $15.00

UPDIKE, D.B. *Printing Types, History & Form.* 1937. 2nd ed. 2 vols. $65.00

UPDIKE, H. *History of Episcopal Church in Narragansett.* 1847. VG. $30.00

UPDIKE, John. *Bech Is Back.* 1982. 1st ed. 1/500. sgn. dj. boxed. M. $65.00

UPDIKE, John. *Buchanan Dying.* 1974. Knopf. 1st ed. EX. $20.00

UPDIKE, John. *Coup.* 1978. Knopf. 1st ed. dj. EX. $20.00

UPDIKE, John. *Coup.* 1979. London. 1st ed. dj. $20.00

UPDIKE, John. *Couples.* 1968. Knopf. 1st ed. dj. VG. $30.00

UPDIKE, John. *From Journal of a Leper.* 1978. Northridge. Lord John. 1st ed. 1/300. sgn. EX. $60.00

UPDIKE, John. *Hawthorne's Creed.* 1981. Targ. Ltd ed. 1/250. sgn. EX. $60.00

UPDIKE, John. *Just Looking: Essays on Art.* 1989. NY. 1st ed. 1/250. sgn. boxed. M. $150.00

UPDIKE, John. *Marry Me.* 1976. NY. 1st trade ed. dj. VG. $18.00

UPDIKE, John. *Midpoint & Other Poems.* 1969. Knopf. 1st trade ed. dj. EX. $35.00

UPDIKE, John. *Month of Sundays.* 1975. NY. 1st ed. dj. M. $15.00

UPDIKE, John. *Month of Sundays.* 1975. NY. 1st ed. sgn. dj. EX. $30.00

UPDIKE, John. *Museums & Women & Other Stories.* 1972. NY. 1st ed. 1/350. sgn. dj. slipcase. EX. $125.00

UPDIKE, John. *Of the Farm.* 1965. NY. 1st ed. dj. EX. $45.00

UPDIKE, John. *Picked-Up Pieces.* 1975. Knopf. 1st Am ed. dj. EX. $20.00

UPDIKE, John. *Poorhouse Fair.* 1959. NY. 1st Am ed. dj. VG. $65.00

UPDIKE, John. *Problems.* 1979. NY. 1/350. sgn/#d. slipcase. VG. $100.00

UPDIKE, John. *Rabbit Is Rich.* 1981. NY. 1st ed. dj. VG. $15.00

UPDIKE, John. *Rabbit Is Rich.* 1981. NY. 1st ed. sgn. dj. EX. $45.00

UPDIKE, John. *Rabbit Redux.* 1971. Knopf. 1st ed. plastic dj. M. $55.00

UPDIKE, John. *Rabbit Redux.* 1971. NY. 1st Am ed. dj. VG. $20.00

UPDIKE, John. *Rabbit Run.* 1960. NY. Knopf. Stated 1st ed. dj. VG. $65.00

UPDIKE, John. *Rabbit Run.* 1961. NY. 1st ed. dj. xl. VG. $25.00

UPDIKE, John. *Roger's Version.* 1986. Franklin Soc. 1st ed. leather. EX. $45.00

UPDIKE, John. *Same Door.* 1959. NY. dj. EX. $65.00

UPDIKE, John. *Self-Consciousness.* 1989. NY. 1st ed. 1/250. sgn. dj. boxed. M. $150.00

UPDIKE, John. *Talk From the Fifties.* 1979. Lord John. 1/300. sgn/#d. EX. $75.00

UPDIKE, John. *Telephone Poles.* 1963. NY. 1st ed. dj. EX. $25.00

UPFIELD, A.W. *Author Bites the Dust.* 1967. Angus Robertson. dj. xl. P1. $10.00

UPFIELD, A.W. *Bachelors of Broken Hill.* 1950. Crime Club. 1st ed. VG. P1. $10.00

UPFIELD, A.W. *Bone Is Pointed.* 1966. Agnus Robertson. dj. xl. P1. $10.00

UPFIELD, A.W. *Bony & the Mouse.* 1966. Heinemann. 5th print. xl. VG. P1. $7.50

UPFIELD, A.W. *Bushranger of the Skies.* 1963. Angus Robertson. xl. VG. P1. $7.50

UPFIELD, A.W. *Death of a Swagman.* 1945. Crime Club. 1st ed. dj. xl. P1. $15.00

UPFIELD, A.W. *Death of a Swagman.* 1962. Angus Robertson. dj. xl. P1. $12.50

UPFIELD, A.W. *Devil's Steps.* 1965. Angus Robertson. xl. VG. P1. $10.00

UPFIELD, A.W. *Gripped by Drought.* 1990. Macmillan. dj. EX. P1. $30.00

UPFIELD, A.W. *Lure of the Bush.* 1965. Doubleday. 1st Am ed. dj. EX. $35.00

UPFIELD, A.W. *Man of Two Tribes.* 1956. Crime Club. 1st ed. dj. VG. P1. $20.00

UPFIELD, A.W. *Mr. Jelly's Business.* 1964. Angus Robertson. xl. P1. $10.00

UPFIELD, A.W. *Murchison Murders.* 1987. Dennis McMillan. 1st ed. dj. P1. $15.00

UPFIELD, A.W. *New Shoe.* CA U. 2nd ed. EX. P1. $10.00

UPFIELD, A.W. *New Shoe.* Mystery Lib. 2nd ed. EX. P1. $10.00

UPFIELD, A.W. *New Shoe.* nd. CA U. 3rd ed. dj. VG. P1. $15.00

UPFIELD, A.W. *Royal Abduction.* 1984. Dennis McMillan. dj. EX. P1. $25.00

UPFIELD, A.W. *Widows of Broome.* nd. Book Club. dj. xl. P1. $3.50

UPFIELD, A.W. *Widows of Broome.* nd. Book Club. VG. P1. $4.00

UPFIELD, A.W. *Winds of Evil.* 1961. Angus Robertson. dj. VG. P1. $20.00

UPHAM, C. *Life, Explorations & Public Services of John C. Fremont.* 1856. Boston. Ils. 12mo. 366 p. VG. G2. $30.00

UPHAM, C. *Salem Witchcraft in Outline.* 1891. Salem. Ils 1st ed. 12mo. VG. T1. $45.00

UPHOFF & UPHOFF. *New Psychic Frontiers.* 1975. England. $19.00

UPHOFF. *Kohler on Strike: 30 Years of Conflict.* 1966. dj. VG. $20.00

UPSON, W.H. *Piano Movers.* 1927. St. Charles. 1st ed. VG. B2. $30.00

UPTON, Anthony. *Finland, 1939-1940.* 1979. Newark. 1st Am ed. dj. EX. $15.00

UPTON, Anthony. *Rockdale.* 1978. NY. 1st ed. dj. EX. $30.00

UPTON, H.T. *History of W Reserve.* 1910. Chicago. 1st ed. 3 vols. rebound. VG. T5. $195.00

UPTON, Richard. *Ft. Custer on Big Horn, 1877-1898.* 1973. Glendale. Clark. presentation. VG. A3. $50.00

UPTON, Robert. *Golden Fleecing.* 1979. St. Martin. 1st ed. dj. EX. P1. $10.00

URBAN, E.K. *Birds From Coahuila, Mexico.* 1959. KS U. EX. M2. $5.00

URBAN, J.W. *Battlefield & Prison Pen.* c 1882. np. Ils. 12mo. 486 p. G. G2. $29.00

URBINO. *Arms, Arts & Literature of Italy: 1440-1630.* 1909. Laone. Revised ed. TEG. 3 vols. VG. $45.00

URIS, L.M. *Angry Hills.* 1955. NY. 1st print. dj. EX. $30.00

URNITZ, Harry. *Invasion of Privacy.* 1956. Perman. pb. P1. $10.00

URQUHART, Fred. *Winston S. Churchill.* 1955. London. Cassell. black cloth. dj. VG. D1. $35.00

URWIN & FAGAN. *Custer & His Times.* 1987. np. Ils. 305 p. wraps. VG. T5. $12.50

US GOVERNMENT PRINTING OFFICE. *Nazi Conspiracy & Aggression.* 9 vols. $75.00

US MARINE CORPS. *Recruit Depot Yearbook. Third Battalion, Platoon 324.* 1957. San Diego. 84 p. EX. $5.00

US NAVY. *Bluejackets' Manual of US Navy.* 1918. Military Pub. 6th ed. 821 p. M1. $9.50

US NAVY. *Bluejackets` Manual of US Navy.* 1973. sm 8vo. 644 p. EX. $2.00

US NAVY. *Civil War Naval Chronology 1861-1865.* 1971. WA. Ils. 1090 p. M2. $35.00

US NAVY. *Machinist's Mate 3 & 2.* 1972. 4to. 432 p. EX. $3.00

US NAVY. *Principles of Naval Engineering.* 1970. 4to. 659 p. EX. $4.00

US RUBBER CO. *Keds. Facts for Salesman.* 1920. G. $25.00

USDA. *Farmers in a Changing World. Yearbook of 1940.* 1940. VG. $9.00

USIN, M.J. *Guide to Fishes of Temperate Atlantic Coast.* 1977. Dutton. Ils 1st ed. 262 p. dj. EX. M2. $15.00

UTLEY, R.M. *Frontier Regulars: US Army & Indians, 1866-1891.* Book Club. photos. map. 466 p. dj. G. T5. $12.50

UTLEY, R.M. *Frontier Regulars: US Army & Indians, 1866-1891.* 1973. Macmillan. 14 maps. 466 p. VG. M2. $18.00

UTLEY, R.M. *Life in Custer's Calvary: Life & Letters...* 1977. Yale. photos. 302 p. dj. EX. M2. $33.00

UTLEY & WASHBURN. *History of the Indian Wars.* 1977. Am Heritage. Ils. 4to. 352 p. dj. EX. M2. $19.00

UTTERBACK, W.I. *Naiades of MO.* 1916. Notre Dame. 28 pls. 200 p. rebound. EX. M2. $25.00

UTTLEY, Alison. *Traveler in Time.* 1958. Faber. dj. xl. P1. $7.50

UZANNE, Octave. *Book Hunter in Paris.* 1893. London. Ils. $60.00

VACHELL, H.A. *Hill.* 1906. Dodd Mead. 1st ed. $12.00

VACHSS, Andrew. *Blue Belle.* 1988. Knopf. 1st ed. dj. EX. P1. $17.50

VACHSS, Andrew. *Flood.* 1985. NY. 1st ed. dj. EX. $15.00

VACHSS, Andrew. *Strega.* 1987. NY. 1st ed. dj. EX. $15.00

VAETH, J.G. *Graf Zeppelin: Adventures of Aerial Globetrotter.* 1958. NY. Ils 1st ed. 235 p. dj. VG. T5. $55.00

VAIL, R.W.G. *Voice of the Old Frontier.* 1949. PA U. 1st ed. J2. $40.00

VAILLANT, G.C. *Aztecs of Mexico.* 1941. NY. 1st ed. VG. $15.00

VAIZEY, M. *Artist As a Photographer.* 1982. Holt Rinehart. 1st ed. dj. EX. $15.00

VALE, C. *Spirit of St. Louis.* nd. Doran. 1st ed. dj. VG. $15.00

VALE, R.B. *Wings, Fur & Shot.* 1936. Harrisburg. 1st ed. VG. B2. $35.00

VALE, Richard X. *Tom Beatty Ace of the Service.* 1934. Whitman. VG. P1. $25.00

VALENTI, Angelo. *Solome.* 1945. Heritage. slipcase. VG. $15.00

VALENTI, Angelo. *Song of Songs Which Is Solomon's.* nd. Heritage. full leather. slipcase. VG. $45.00

VALENTINE, J.M. *MS Sandhill Crane Recovery Plan.* 1984. USFWS. 60 p. M2. $7.00

VALENTINE, Tom. *Psychic Surgery.* nd. Book Club. dj. VG. P1. $3.00

VALENTINE & SONS. *Bonnie Scotland.* c 1910. Dundee. oblong 4to. G. $35.00

VALENTINER, W. *Henry Goldman Collection.* 1922. NY. 32 pls. folio. TEG. EX. J2. $275.00

VALENTINO, Rudolph. *Day Dreams.* 1923. NY. 1st ed. G. $15.00

VALENTINO, Rudolph. *Intimate Journal of Rudolph Valentino.* 1931. William Fargo. dj. EX. $25.00

VALENTINO, Rudolph. *My Private Diary.* 1929. Occult Pub. G. $7.00

VALENZUELA, Luisa. *Lizard's Trail.* 1983. Farrar Straus. Trans Rabassa. 1st print. dj. EX. $8.00

VALERY, M.P. *Etat de la Vertu.* 1935. Paris. 1/230. wraps. VG. $105.00

VALERY, M.P. *Mer Marines Marins.* 1930. Paris. Ils. 4to. wraps. $100.00

VALIN, Jonathan. *Day of Wrath.* 1982. NY. 1st ed. dj. $15.00

VALIN, Jonathan. *Dead Letter.* 1981. Dodd Mead. 1st ed. dj. VG. P1. $10.00

VALIN, Jonathan. *Life's Work.* nd. Book Club. dj. EX. P1. $4.50

VALIN, Jonathan. *Life's Work.* 1986. Delacorte. 1st ed. dj. M. $10.00

VALIN, Jonathan. *Natural Causes.* 1983. Congdon Weed. 1st ed. dj. xl. P1. $6.00

VALIN, Jonathan. *Natural Causes.* 1983. NY. 1st ed. dj. EX. $15.00

VALLEJO, Boris. *Fantastic Art of Boris Vallejo.* 1978. Del Rey. EX. P1. $20.00

VALLERY-RADOT, Rene. *Life of Pasteur.* 1908. NY. inscr. 8vo. 484 p. $25.00

VALLERY-RADOT, Rene. *Life of Pasteur.* 1919. London. reprint. 484 p. rebound. $15.00

VALTIN, Jan. *Out of the Night.* 1942. Garden City. $8.00

VAMBERY, Arminius. *Arminius Vambery: His Life & Adventures.* 1884. London. 14 pls. 370 p. VG. $65.00

VAN ASH & ROHMER. *Master of Villainy.* 1972. Bowling Green. dj. xl. P1. $17.50

VAN ASTEN, Gail. *Blind Knight.* Ace. 1st ed. pb. EX. C1. $4.00

VAN ATTA, Winfred. *Shock Treatment.* nd. Book Club. dj. VG. P1. $3.00

VAN AUKEN, K.L. *Signalman & His Work.* 1921. Brotherhood RR Signalman. 8vo. EX. $2.50

VAN BRUNT, J. *CA Missions: Painted & Described.* 1932. 24 pls. dj. G. $47.00

VAN DE WATER, Frederic F. *Plunder.* 1933. Canadian Crime Club. dj. VG. P1. $15.00

VAN DE WATER, Frederic F. *Plunder.* 1933. Crime Club. 1st ed. xl. VG. P1. $7.50

VAN DE WATER, Frederic F. *Still Waters.* 1929. Crime Club. 1st ed. xl. G. P1. $6.00

VAN DE WETERING, Janwillem. *ME Massacre.* nd. Book Club. dj. VG. P1. $5.00

VAN DE WETERING, Janwillem. *Mind Murders.* nd. Book Club. dj. VG. P1. $4.50

VAN DER POST, Laurens. *Face Beside the Fire.* 1953. London. Hogarth. 1st ed. VG. $35.00

VAN DER WEYDE, E.W. *Life & Works of Thomas Paine.* 1925. Nat Hist Soc. 8 vols. $35.00

VAN DER WEYDE, E.W. *Life & Works of Thomas Paine.* 1925. New Rochelle. 10 vols. djs. VG. $110.00

VAN DEUSEN, G.G. *William Henry Seward: Lincoln's Secretary of State...* 1967. 666 p. dj. EX. $15.00

VAN DEVIER, R.B. *Son of MI: Short Biography of Byron A. Dunn.* 1949. Akron. Ils. 27 p. wraps. T5. $12.50

VAN DINE, S.S. *Bishop Murder Case.* nd. Collier. VG. P1. $10.00

VAN DINE, S.S. *Bishop Murder Case.* nd. Grosset. VG. P1. $10.00

VAN DINE, S.S. *Bishop Murder Case.* 1929. Scribner. G. P1. $6.00

VAN DINE, S.S. *Bishop Murder Case.* 1929. Scribner. 1st ed. VG. P1. $20.00

VAN DINE, S.S. *Canary Murder Case.* nd. Collier. VG. P1. $10.00

VAN DINE, S.S. *Canary Murder Case.* nd. Grosset. G. P1. $6.00

VAN DINE, S.S. *Canary Murder Case.* 1927. Scribner. VG. $18.00

VAN DINE, S.S. *Garden Murder Case.* 1935. Scribner. 1st ed. VG. P1. $35.00

VAN DINE, S.S. *Greene Murder Case.* 1928. Scribner. G. P1. $10.00

VAN DINE, S.S. *Greene Murder Case.* 1928. Scribner. 1st ed. VG. P1. $25.00

VAN DINE, S.S. *Kennel Murder Case.* 1933. Scribner. 1st ed. G. $15.00

VAN DINE, S.S. *Kidnap Murder Case.* 1936. Scribner. 1st ed. dj. VG. $45.00

VAN DINE, S.S. *Scarab Murder Case.* 1930. Scribner. 1st ed. dj. VG. $25.00

VAN DINE, S.S. *Scarab Murder Case.* 1945. Tower. G. P1. $7.50

VAN DINE, S.S. *World's Great Detective Stories.* nd. Blue Ribbon. P1. $20.00

VAN DOREN, Carl. *Benjamin Franklin: Phil., London & Paris.* 1938. NY. Viking. 1/625. sgn. 8vo. 3 vols. $175.00

VAN DOREN, Carl. *James Branch Cabell.* 1925. NY. dj. VG. $30.00

VAN DOREN, Carl. *Secret History of the American Revolution.* 1941. NY. 1st ed. sgn. dj. $40.00

VAN DOREN, Mark. *Country Year.* 1946. NY. Sloan. 1st ed. sgn. 131 p. G. M1. $17.50

VAN DYKE, Henry. *Ruling Passion.* 1901. NY. 1st ed. VG. $20.00

VAN DYKE, Henry. *Travel Diary of an Angler.* 1929. Derrydale. 1/750. 8vo. blue bdg. EX. $125.00

VAN DYKE, Henry. *Unknown Quantity.* 1912. Scribner. Ils 1st ed. EX. $12.00

VAN DYKE, J.C. *Rembrandt Drawings & Etchings With Critical Reassignments...* 1927. NY/London. 4to. VG. $25.00

VAN DYKE, T.S. *Flirtation Camp; or, Rifle, Rod & Gun in CA.* 1881. NY. Fords Howard Hulbert. $40.00

VAN DYNE, Edith. *Aunt Jane's Nieces in Red Cross.* nd. Reilly Lee. dj. VG. P1. $10.00

VAN FLEET, Clark. *Steelhead to a Fly.* 1954. Boston. 1st ed. dj. VG. B2. $25.00

VAN GOGH, Vincent. *Letters to an Artist From Van Gogh to A.R. Van Rappard.* 1936. NY. 20 pls. 229 p. slipcase. EX. J2. $100.00

VAN GULIK, Robert. *Given Day.* 1984. Dennis McMillan. dj. EX. P1. $40.00

VAN GULIK, Robert. *Judge Dee at Work.* 1967. London. 1st ed. dj. EX. $15.00

VAN GULIK, Robert. *Lacquer Screen.* 1969. Scribner. 1st ed. dj. VG. P1. $50.00

VAN GULIK, Robert. *Necklace & Calabash.* 1967. Heinemann. 1st ed. dj. xl. P1. $10.00

VAN HOESEN & WALTER. *Bibliography: An Introductory Manual.* 1928. NY. Ils 1st ed. $35.00

VAN LHIN, Erik. *Battle on Mercury.* 1958. Winston. 2nd ed. dj. VG. P1. $25.00

VAN LOON, Hendrik. *History With a Match Being Account of Earliest Navigators...* 1917. NY. McKay. Ils. 127 p. VG. $50.00

VAN LOON, Hendrik. *Man the Miracle Worker.* 1928. Liveright. 1st ed. inscr. 8vo. VG. $55.00

VAN LOON, Hendrik. *Simon Bolivar.* 1943. NY. 1st ed. G. $12.00

VAN LUSTBADER, Eric. *Dai-San.* 1978. Doubleday. 1st ed. dj. EX. P1. $22.50

VAN LUSTBADER, Eric. *Sirens.* 1981. Evans. 1st ed. dj. VG. P1. $15.00

VAN MATER. *Veterinary Opthalmology.* 1897. NY. Ils 1st ed. EX. $25.00

VAN MELVIN. *Big Heart.* 1957. San Francisco. 4to. VG. $45.00

VAN METRE, T.W. *Trains, Tracks & Travel.* 1927. . 2nd ed. 236 p. $27.50

VAN MUELE, Martin. *Satirical Drawings.* 1970. Cytheria Pr. 1st ed. dj. EX. $35.00

VAN ORMAN, W.T. *Wizard of the Winds.* 1978. St. Cloud, MN. Ils 1st ed. 278 p. dj. VG. T5. $12.50

VAN OVER, R. *Unifinished Man.* 1972. NY. $19.00

VAN PATTEN, Nathan. *Newly Discovered Issue of Scott's Vision of Don Roderick.* 1937. London. sgn. $10.00

VAN PELT, D. *Leslie's History of Greater NY.* 1898. NY. Arkell. 3 vols. VG. $145.00

VAN RENSSELAER, Florence. *Livingston Family in America & Its Scottish Origins.* 1949. NY. William Bird. 413 p. wraps. VG. $45.00

VAN SCHAICK, George. *Son of Otter.* 1915. Boston. 12mo. 345 p. VG. $15.00

VAN SCYOC, S.J. *Cloud Cry.* 1977. Berkley. dj. EX. P1. $10.00

VAN SCYOC, S.J. *Star Mother.* nd. Book Club. dj. VG. P1. $4.50

VAN SCYOC, S.J. *Star Mother.* 1976. Berkley Putnam. 1st ed. dj. xl. P1. $7.50

VAN THAL, Herbert. *Great Ghost Stories.* 1962. Arthur Barker. 2nd ed. VG. P1. $12.50

VAN UTK. *Story of American Fox Hunting.* Derrydale. as issued. VG. B2. $115.00

VAN VECHTEN, Carl. *Nigger Heaven.* 1951. Avon. EX. $40.00

VAN VECHTEN, Carl. *Portraits.* 1978. Bobbs Merrill. 1st ed. dj. EX. $20.00

VAN VECHTEN, Carl. *Tiger in the House.* 1940. NY. Ils. 367 p. VG. $35.00

VAN VOGT, A.E. *Empire of the Atom.* nd. Book Club. dj. VG. P1. $5.00

VAN VOGT, A.E. *Masters of Time.* 1940. Fantasy. 1st ed. dj. VG. P1. $75.00

VAN VOGT, A.E. *Masters of Time.* 1940. Reading. Fantasy. 1st trade ed. $45.00

VAN VOGT, A.E. *Mind Cage.* nd. Book Club. dj. VG. P1. $3.00

VAN VOGT, A.E. *Mixed Men.* nd. Book Club. dj. VG. P1. $6.00

VAN VOGT, A.E. *Quest for the Future.* nd. Book Club. dj. VG. P1. $4.50

VAN VOGT, A.E. *Rogue Ship.* nd. Book Club. dj. VG. P1. $3.00

VAN VOGT, A.E. *Rogue Ship.* 1965. Doubleday. 1st ed. dj. VG. P1. $25.00

VAN VOGT, A.E. *Slan.* 1946. Arkham House. 1st book ed. EX. $80.00

VAN VOGT, A.E. *Slan.* 1951. Simon Schuster. dj. G. P1. $20.00

VAN VOGT, A.E. *Triad.* nd. Book Club. dj. VG. P1. $7.50

VAN VOGT, A.E. *Van Vogt Omnibus.* 1971. Sidgwick Jackson. 1st ed. dj. P1. $12.50

VAN VOGT, A.E. *Weapon Makers.* 1952. Greenberg. dj. VG. P1. $25.00

VAN VOGT, A.E. *Weapon Shops of Isher.* 1951. Greenberg. dj. VG. P1. $45.00

VAN VOGT, A.E. *World of Null-A.* 1950. Grosset Dunlap. dj. VG. P1. $35.00

VAN WYCK, Frederick. *Select Patents of NY Towns.* 1938. Boston. 1st ed. 1/125. 180 p. G. T5. $25.00

VAN WYCK, William. *Sinister Shepard.* 1934. Primavera Pr. 1/1000. 85 p. G. T5. $22.50

VANBRUGH, John. *Complete Works.* 1927. London. Nonesuch. Review ed. 1/3000. EX. $125.00

VANCE, E.G. *Black Beauty.* 1949. Random House. 64 p. EX. $17.50

VANCE, Jack. *Cugel's Saga.* 1983. Timescape. 1st ed. dj. EX. P1. $17.50

VANCE, Jack. *Dirdir.* 1980. Underwood. 1st ed. sgn. no dj issued. EX. P1. $30.00

VANCE, Jack. *Moon Moth.* 1975. Dobson. dj. EX. P1. $22.50

VANCE, Jack. *Pnume.* 1975. Dobson. dj. EX. P1. $22.50

VANCE, Jack. *Vandals of the Void.* 1953. Winston. 1st ed. VG. P1. $35.00

VANCE, L.J. *Alias the Lone Wolf.* nd. Grosset. G. P1. $5.00

VANCE, L.J. *Brass Bowl.* nd. Burt. G. P1. $6.00

VANCE, L.J. *Dead Ride Hard.* 1926. Copp Clarke. 1st ed. VG. P1. $17.50

VANCE, L.J. *Fortune Hunter.* nd. Grosset. G. P1. $5.00

VANCE, L.J. *Lone Wolf.* 1914. Little Brown. 1st ed. VG. P1. $25.00

VANCE, L.J. *Red Masquerade.* 1921. Doubleday Page. VG. P1. $17.50

VANCE, L.J. *Romance of Terrence O'Rourke.* 1907. Bobbs Merrill. P1. $8.00

VANCE, L.J. *White Fire.* nd. Grosset. P1. $7.50

VANCE, L.J. *Woman in the Shadow.* 1930. Lippincott. 2nd ed. G. P1. $15.00

VANCE, R.B. *All These People.* 1945. Chapel Hill. Ils 1st ed. 503 p. dj. VG. $25.00

VANDERCOOK, John W. *Murder in Haiti.* nd. Book Club. dj. VG. P1. $3.00

VANDERCOOK, John W. *Murder in Trinidad.* 1941. Triangle. 2nd ed. G. P1. $5.00

VANDIVER, F.E. *Idea of the S: Pursuit of a Central Theme.* 1964. Chicago. 82 p. dj. EX. $25.00

VANDOYER. *Beauties de la Provence.* 1926. Paris. 1st ed. 1/60. orig wraps. $48.00

VANSTORY, Burnette. *GA's Land of the Golden Isles.* 1956. Athens. 1st ed. sgn. 202 p. G. $15.00

VARGA. *Waldo Peirce.* 1941. NY. Hyperion Harper. Ils. VG. $25.00

VARGAS & AUSTIN. *Vargas.* 1978. Harmong. 4th ed. dj. EX. $20.00

VARLEY, John. *Demon.* nd. Book Club. dj. VG. P1. $4.50

VARLEY, John. *Ophiuchi Hotline.* nd. Book Club. dj. VG. P1. $3.50

VARNA, Andrew. *Gift of Time: Autobiography of International Smuggler.* 1956. NY. 1st ed. black cloth. dj. EX. $30.00

VARNER, J. & J.J. *Dogs of Conquest.* 1983. OK U. Ils. 238 p. dj. EX. M2. $18.00

VARON, D. *Architectural Composition.* 1923. NY. 40 pls. presentation. sgn. $27.00

VARON, D. *Indication in Architectural Design.* 1916. NY. pls. 4to. $20.00

VASARELY, Victor. *Vasarely.* 1965. Griffon. pls. dj. D2. $125.00

VASARI, Giorgio. *Lives of the Most Eminent Painters, Sculptors, Architects.* 1850-1851. London. Bohn. 4 vols. D2. $55.00

VASQUEZ, Antonio de Espinosa. *Compendium & Descriptions of the W Indies.* 1942. Smithsonian. 862 p. EX. M2. $75.00

VASSOS, John. *Gray's Elegy.* 1931. Dutton. 1st ed. dj. VG. $30.00

VATHER. *Arabian Tale.* 1945. Ltd Ed Club. boxed. EX. $40.00

VATTEL, M.D. *Law of Nations.* 1820. Northampton. xl. VG. $40.00

VAUGHAN, Herbert. *Welsh Bookplates in Collection of Sir Evan Jones.* 1920. London. Ltd 1st ed. 1/150. sgn/#d. J2. $100.00

VAUGHAN, T.W. *Eocene & Lower Oligocene Coral Faunas of US.* 1900. US Geol Survey. 24 pls. 4to. 205 p. EX. M2. $90.00

VAUGHAN, T.W. *Recent Madreporaria of HI Islands & Laysan.* 1907. US Nat Mus. 96 pls. 4to. 427 p. EX. M2. $85.00

VAUGHAN. *New Album of London Photographs.* c 1896. London. Vaughan. Ils. oblong 8vo. $25.00

VAUGHN, J.W. *Battle of Platte Bridge.* 1965. Norman. dj. EX. $12.00

VAUGHN, J.W. *Indian Fights: New Facts on Seven Encounters.* 1966. Norman. dj. EX. $22.00

VAUGHN, V.C. *Infection & Immunity.* 1915. Chicago. 1st ed. 2 vols. VG. $110.00

VAUPELL. *Den Dansk-Norske Haers Historie.* 1872. Copenhagen. Ils Lund. maps. 2 vols. VG. $300.00

VAVRA. *Equus.* 1977. NY. 1st ed. 4to. dj. EX. $32.50

VECCHIO, Walter. *Fashion Makers, a Photographic Record.* 1968. NY. Crown. Ils. sm folio. 277 p. dj. $35.00

VEDDER, E.B. *Beriberi.* 1913. NY. William Wood. 1st ed. VG. $120.00

VEDDER, E.B. *Chiropractic Physiology.* 1921. 4th ed. VG. $35.00

VEECK, Bill. *Thirty Tons a Day.* 1972. NY. Viking. dj. EX. $20.00

VEECK & LINN. *Veeck-As in Wreck.* 1962. Putnam. Book Club ed. dj. with sgn card. $30.00

VENNING, Michael. *Murder Through the Looking Glass.* 1943. Coward McCann. 1st ed. dj. VG. P1. $30.00

VERDON, Rene. *White House Chef Cookbook.* nd. Cookbook. dj. VG. P1. $5.00

VERE, B.D. *King Arthur: His Symbolic Story in Verse.* 1930. Tintagel. 1st/only ed. VG. C1. $29.00

VERGA, Giovanni. *House by the Medlar Tree.* 1953. NY. Grove. 2nd ed. 8vo. 247 p. dj. VG. $15.00

VERGA, Giovanni. *Little Novels of Sicily.* 1953. NY. Grove. 1st ed. 8vo. 226 p. dj. EX. $15.00

VERLAINE, Paul. *Jadis et Naguere.* 1936. Paris. Ils Bernard Naudin. leather. $60.00

VERLAINE, Paul. *Sagesse.* 1913. Paris. 1/947. TEG. VG. $150.00

VERNE, Jules. *Adventures in Land of Behemoth.* 1875. Boston. VG. C2. $25.00

VERNE, Jules. *Around the World in Eighty Days.* nd. Collins. leather bdg. boxed. VG. P1. $25.00

VERNE, Jules. *English at the N Pole.* nd. Collins. leather bdg. boxed. VG. P1. $25.00

VERNE, Jules. *From the Clouds to the Mountains.* 1874. Boston. 1st Am ed. VG. $40.00

VERNE, Jules. *From the Earth to the Moon.* 1874. NY. Ils 1st Am ed. 323 p. xl. G. T5. $45.00

VERNE, Jules. *Journey to Center of Earth.* c 1875. Boston. G. C2. $15.00

VERNE, Jules. *Meridiana; or, Adventures of Three Englishmen...* 1875. NY. 1st ed. VG. C2. $35.00

VERNE, Jules. *Michael Strogoff.* nd. Hurst. VG. P1. $7.50

VERNE, Jules. *Michael Strogoff.* 1927. NY. Ils Wyeth. 9 pls. VG. $25.00

VERNE, Jules. *Mysterious Island.* 1920. Scribner. Ils Wyeth. VG. B4. $65.00

VERNE, Jules. *Omnibus of Jules Verne.* nd. Lippincott. VG. P1. $7.50

VERNE, Jules. *Round the Moon.* 1963. Arco. 2nd ed. dj. xl. P1. $6.00

VERNE, Jules. *School of Crusoes.* 1966. Arco. 1st ed. dj. EX. P1. $10.00

VERNE, Jules. *Yesterday & Tomorrow.* 1965. Arco. 1st ed. dj. xl. P1. $5.00

VERNE, Jules. *20,000 Leagues Under the Sea.* 1932. Winston. Ils Fische. 8vo. G. $7.50

VERNER, E.O. *Mellowed by Time.* 1953. Columbia. 3rd print. sgn. dj. EX. T6. $25.00

VERNER, E.O. *Stonewall Ladies.* 1963. Charleston. Tradd. tall 8vo. 144 p. $27.50

VERNON, A. *History & Romance of the Horse.* 1946. Dover. Ils. 525 p. VG. M2. $17.00

VERRILL, A. Hyatt. *Boys' Book of Buccaneers.* 1927. Dodd Mead. G. P1. $12.00

VERRILL, A. Hyatt. *Bridge of Light.* 1950. Fantasy. 1st ed. dj. VG. P1. $40.00

VERRILL, A. Hyatt. *Carib Gold.* nd. Childrens Pr. dj. VG. P1. $15.00

VERRILL, A. Hyatt. *Strange Fish & Their Stories.* 1948. Page. 2 color pls. 220 p. EX. M2. $11.00

VERRILL, H.H. *Real Story of the Whaler.* 1916. NY. 1st ed. VG. $45.00

VERTES, M. *Variations.* 1961. Greenwich. 4to. dj. EX. J2. $75.00

VERVOORT, W. *Free-Living Copepoda From Ifaluk Atoll in Caroline Islands.* 1964. US Nat Mus. Ils. 431 p. EX. M2. $25.00

VESCE, Thomas. *Marvels of Rigomer.* 1988. Garland. 1st ed. no dj issued. M. C1. $54.00

VESEY-FITZGERALD, B. *Worlds of Ants, Bees & Wasps.* 1969. Pelham. Ils 1st ed. 117 p. dj. VG. M2. $7.00

VESTAL, Stanley. *Jim Bridger: Mountain Man.* 1946. Morrow. Ils. maps. 333 p. dj. VG. $20.00

VESTAL, Stanley. *Kit Carson.* 1928. Boston. ARC. G. $20.00

VESTAL, Stanley. *Kit Carson.* 1928. Houghton. VG. $10.00

VESTAL, Stanley. *Missionary.* 1945. NY. 1st ed. dj. VG. B2. $20.00

VESTAL, Stanley. *MO.* 1945. Farrar Rinehart. 1st ed. dj. M2. $15.00

VESTAL, Stanley. *Old Santa Fe Trail.* 1939. Houghton. Ils. dj. $30.00

VESTAL, Stanley. *Queen of the Cowtowns.* 1952. Harper. Ils 1st ed. 285 p. dj. EX. M2. $35.00

VESTAL, Stanley. *Sitting Bull: Champion of the Sioux.* 1965. OK U. map. 346 p. VG. M2. $18.00

VESTAL, Stanley. *Warpath & Council Fire.* 1948. NY. Ils 1st ed. 338 p. dj. VG. B2. $37.50

VESTEL, S. *Big Foot Wallace.* 1942. Boston. 1st ed. 299 p. VG. B2. $35.00

VETERANS OF FOREIGN WARS. *Pictorial History of the Korean War.* 1951. np. MacArthur Reports. Ils. 394 p. T5. $17.50

VETH. *Dutch Bookplates.* 1950. NY. Golden Griffin. 1/500. EX. $40.00

VIAL, James. *Evolutionary Biology of the Anturans.* 1973. MO U. Ils. maps. 470 p. dj. EX. M2. $25.00

VICAR. *Company Owns the Tools.* 1942. dj. VG. $30.00

VICENZA, Basilica Palladiana. *Catalogo Della Mostra Francesco Maffei.* 1956. Venezia. Ils. dj. D2. $25.00

VICKERS, John. *Old Vic in Photographs.* 1947. London. Saturn. Ils. photos. VG. $8.50

VICKERS, Roy. *Department of Dead Ends.* 1973. Hutchinson. dj. VG. P1. $12.50

VICKERS, Roy. *Double Image.* nd. Detective Book Club. dj. VG. P1. $4.00

VICKERS, Roy. *Sole Survivor.* 1951. Doubleday Book Club. VG. P1. $7.50

VICTOR, O.J. *History of the S Rebellion.* 1861-1864. fld map by Colton. 4 vols. K1. $95.00

VICTOR, O.J. *Life, Times & Services of Anthony Wayne.* 1861. NY. 95 p. wraps. VG. T5. $22.50

VICTOR, Thomas. *Making of a Dance. Baryshnikov & Fracci in Medea.* 1976. NY. Holt. 1st ed. photos. 4to. $27.50

VIDA, J.A. *Las Caides del Toro Durante La Lidia.* 1977. Madrid. Ils. EX. $40.00

VIDAL, Gore. *Best Television Plays.* 1956. NY. 1st ed. 250 p. wraps. $17.50

VIDAL, Gore. *City & the Pillar.* 1948. Dutton. 1st ed. dj. VG. $25.00

VIDAL, Gore. *Duluth.* 1983. NY. 1st ed. dj. VG. $10.00

VIDAL, Gore. *Myra Breckinridge.* 1968. Boston. 1st ed. dj. VG. $25.00

VIDAL, Gore. *Reflections From Sinking Ship.* 1969. Little Brown. 1st ed. dj. VG. $25.00

VIDAL, Gore. *Season of Comfort.* 1949. Dutton. 1st ed. dj. $35.00

VIDAL, Gore. *Thirsty Evil: Seven Short Stories.* 1956. NY. 1st ed. dj. EX. $30.00

VIDAL, Gore. *Two Sisters.* 1970. Boston. 1st ed. dj. VG. $20.00

VIDAL, Gore. *Views From a Window.* 1980. NJ. 1st Am ed. dj. VG. $25.00

VIDAL, Gore. *Visit to a Small Planet.* 1956. Boston. Little Brown. 1st ed. dj. EX. $30.00

VIDAL, Gore. *Visit to a Small Planet.* 1960. NY. 1st Am ed. dj. VG. $10.00

VIDAL, Gore. *1876: A Novel.* 1976. NY. Ltd ed. 1/300. sgn. 364 p. slipcase. T5. $50.00

VIDAL, Gore. *1876: A Novel.* 1976. Random House. 1st Am ed. dj. VG. $15.00

VIENOT, Pierre. *Etudes Psychor morphologiques de Visages sous la Direction...* 1947. Paris. Calliope. Ils. $75.00

VIERECK, George Sylvester. *Nude in the Mirror.* 1953. Woodford. 1st ed. dj. VG. P1. $20.00

VIERECK, Peter. *Dream & Responsibility.* 1953. WA U. inscr. 12mo. dj. EX. $25.00

VIETZEN, R.C. *Ancient Man in N OH.* 1941. Lorain, OH. Ils 1st ed. 165 p. VG. T5. $35.00

VIETZEN, R.C. *Indians of Lake Erie Basin or Lost Nations.* 1965. Wahoo, NE. Ils. inscr. 370 p. dj. VG. T5. $35.00

VIETZEN, R.C. *Shakin' the Bushes: From Paleo to Historic Indians.* 1976. Elyria, OH. Ils 1st ed. 278 p. dj. EX. T5. $25.00

VILAS, C.N. & N.R. *FL Marine Shells.* 1945. Aberdeen. 12 color pls. 150 p. dj. G. M2. $7.00

VILFROY, Daniel. *War in the W: Battle of France, May-June, 1940.* 1942. Harrisburg. maps. 163 p. VG. T5. $35.00

VILIMKOVA, Milada. *Egyptian Jewelry.* 1969. London. Hamlyn. Ils. dj. D2. $75.00

VILLA, J. *Venomous Snakes of Nicaragua.* 1984. Milwaukee. photos. map. 42 p. EX. M2. $8.00

VILLEE & DETHIER. *Biological Principals & Processes.* 1971. Saunders. Ils. 1009 p. M2. $18.00

VILLIARD, P. *Moths & How To Rear Them.* 1969. Funk Wagnall. photos. 242 p. dj. EX. M2. $18.00

VILLIARD, P. *Raising Small Animals for Fun & Profit.* 1973. Winchester. photos. 160 p. dj. EX. M2. $11.00

VILLIERS, Alan. *Cruise of the Concord.* 1957. NY. Ils 1st ed. dj. VG. $35.00

VILLIERS, Alan. *Falmouth for Orders.* 1974. NY. tall 8vo. $35.00

VILLIERS, Alan. *Men, Ships & the Sea.* 1973. Nat Geog Soc. Ils. 436 p. dj. EX. M2. $10.00

VILLIERS, Alan. *Wild Ocean.* 1957. Nat Geog Soc. 326 p. VG. $9.00

VILLON, Francois. *Complete Works Translated by J.U. Nicolson.* 1928. Covici Friede. Ils King. 2 vols. djs. VG. J2. $40.00

VILLON, Francois. *Complete Works. Vol. I & II.* 1928. Ils King. Trans/sgn Nicolson. 1/960. djs. VG. $30.00

VILLON, Francois. *Lyrical Poems.* Ltd Ed Club. slipcase. M. B3. $50.00

VINCENT, Harry. *Sea Fish of Trinidad.* 1910. private print. Ils 1st ed. maps. 97 p. EX. $27.50

VINCENT, L.H. *American Literary Masters.* 1906. Houghton. 1st Am ed. 12mo. VG. $20.00

VINCENT, L.H. *Bibliotaph & Other People.* 1898. Boston. 1st ed. 233 p. G. T5. $25.00

VINCENT, W. *Commerce & Navigation of Ancients in India Ocean.* 1807. London. 2 vols. VG. $250.00

VINE, Barbara. *Dark-Adapted Eye.* 1986. Viking. 1st ed. dj. VG. P1. $15.00

VINEY, Charles. *Sherlock Holmes in London.* 1989. Houghton. photos. dj. EX. P1. $24.95

VINGE, Joan D. *Fireship.* nd. Book Club. dj. VG. P1. $4.00

VINGE, Joan D. *World's End.* nd. Book Club. dj. EX. P1. $4.50

VINGE, Vernor. *Across Realtime.* nd. Book Club. dj. VG. P1. $7.50

VINGE, Vernor. *Witling.* 1976. Dobson. 1st ed. dj. EX. P1. $35.00

VINING, E.G. *Return to Japan.* 1960. Lippincott. dj. EX. $7.50

VINING, E.G. *VA Exiles.* nd. Book Club. dj. EX. P1. $3.00

VINOGRAD, Y. *Rare Hebrew Books.* 1987. Jerusalem. Ltd ed. 1/320. $250.00

VINTON, Iris. *We Were There With Jean Lafitte at New Orleans...* 1957. NY. Grosset. Ils Glaubke. 182 p. juvenile. $6.50

VIRGIL. *Aenies. Translated Into Blank Verse by Joseph Trapp.* 1718. London. 2 vols. $200.00

VIRGIL. *Bucolica, Georgica, et Aeneis.* 1745. Dublin. EX. $125.00

VIRGINIA STATE LIBRARY. *More Confederate Imprints.* 1957. 2 vols. VG. very scarce. J4. $50.00

VIRION, Charles. *French Country Cookbook.* nd. Book Club. dj. VG. P1. $5.00

VISCOTT, David. *How To Live With Another Person.* 1975. Arbor House. dj. VG. $8.50

VISHNIAC, R. *Building Blocks of Life.* 1971. Scribner. inscr. dj. VG. $25.00

VISWANATHAN. *Earth Ruth Truth.* 1948. India. $8.50

VITT, D.H. *Mosses, Lichens & Ferns of NW N America.* 1988. WA U. Ils 1st ed. 296 p. M. M2. $19.00

VIVIAN, Francis. *Dead Opposite the Church.* 1959. Jenkins. 1st ed. VG. P1. $10.00

VLEKKE, Bernard. *Nusantara: History of E Indian Archipelago.* 1943. Harvard. J2. $20.00

VOGEL, Amos. *Film As a Subversive Art.* 1974. NY. Ils. pb. VG. $25.00

VOGEL, H. *La Photographie et la Chimie de la Lumiere...* 1876. Paris. Ils. 270 p. $150.00

VOGEL, Z. *Reptile Life.* nd. London. Spring. Ils. 4to. 80 p. VG. M2. $19.00

VOGT, Paul. *Best of Christian Rohlfs.* 1964. Atlantis Books. Trans Rosenwald. Ils. dj. D2. $35.00

VOGT, R.C. *Natural History of Amphibians & Reptiles of WI.* 1981. Milwaukee. 266 color photos. 208 p. dj. M2. $20.00

VOLLMER & PARKER. *Crime, Crooks & Cops.* 1937. Funk Wagnall. VG. P1. $15.00

VOLTAIRE. *Canadide.* 1929. Literary Guild. Ils Kent. VG. B4. $55.00

VOLTAIRE. *Candide.* 1930. Three Sirens. Ils Blaine. 144 p. VG. $12.00

VOLTAIRE. *Odalisque.* 1928. Voltaire Soc. 1st ed. leather. $75.00

VOLTAIRE. *Zadig & Other Romances.* 1926. Dodd Mead. Ils. orange cloth. VG. $20.00

VON BAYROS, Franz. *Amorous Drawings of Marquis Von Bayros.* 1968. NY. Cythera. 4to. 239 p. EX. $30.00

VON BULOW. *Mein Bericht zur Marneschlacht.* 1919. Berlin. pocket maps. 85 p. wraps. fair. T5. $37.50

VON CLES-REDEN. *Buried People.* 1956. Scribner. 1st Am ed. pls. dj. VG. $12.50

VON DER GABELENTZ, Hanns C. *Conrad Felixmuller: Ein Beitrag zur Frage der Tafelmalerei.* 1946. 2nd ed. D2. $55.00

VON DER PORTEN, Edward P. *German Navy in WWII.* 1969. NY. Ils. 274 p. dj. VG. T5. $8.50

VON DODERER & WINSTON. *Demons.* 1961. NY. 1st Am ed. 2 vols. djs. EX. $45.00

VON FALKE, Jacob. *Art in the House.* 1879. Boston. Prang. Ils. 4to. AEG. $150.00

VON FALKE, Otto. *Majolika: Handbucher der Koniglichenn Museen Zu Berlin.* 1907. Berlin. G. $25.00

VON FREEDEN, Max H. *Balthasar Neumann: Leben & Werk.* 1953. Munich/Berlin. Ils. dj. D2. $40.00

VON FRIEDEN, L. *Mushrooms of the World.* 1969. Bobbs Merrill. 186 color pls. 439 p. dj. EX. M2. $12.00

VON FRISCH, K. *Bees: Their Vision, Chemical Senses & Language.* 1953. Cornell. Ils. 119 p. EX. M2. $17.00

VON FRISCH, K. *Dancing Bees: Account of Life & Senses of Honey Bee.* 1955. Harcourt Brace. Ils 1st Am ed. 183 p. dj. G. M2. $7.00

VON GUDEN, Kenneth. *Flights of Fancy.* 1989. McFarland. 1st ed. EX. P1. $25.95

VON HAGEN, V.W. *Ancient Sun Kingdoms of Americas.* 1961. Cleveland. World. 1st Am ed. dj. EX. $25.00

VON HAGEN, V.W. *Desert Kingdoms of Peru.* 1965. NY Graphic Soc. Ils 1st Am ed. 191 p. dj. EX. M2. $20.00

VON HAGEN, V.W. *Frederick Catherwood Archt.* 1950. NY. Oxford U. Intro Huxley. 177 p. dj. VG. $20.00

VON HAGEN, V.W. *John Lloyd Stephens & Lost Cities of Central America.* 1947. OK U. Ils 1st ed. map. 324 p. VG. M2. $15.00

VON HAGEN, V.W. *S America: Green World of Naturalists.* 1951. Eyre Spottiswoode. Ils. dj. EX. M2. $27.00

VON HARDESTY. *Red Phoenix: Rise of Soviet Air Power, 1941-1945.* 1982. Smithsonian. Ils 1st ed. 4to. 288 p. M. T5. $24.95

VON HOFFMAN, C. *Jungle Gods.* 1929. Burt. Ils. 286 p. VG. M2. $8.00

VON HOLST, H. *Constitutional History of US: 1750-1861.* 1879-1904. 8 vols. gilt green bdg. VG. B7. $75.00

VON HOLST, Niels. *Creators, Collectors & Connoisseurs.* 1967. Putnam. 32 pls. 400 p. dj. D2. $75.00

VON HUMBOLDT, Alexander. *Cosmos: Sketch of Physical Description of Universe.* 1850. 5 vols. TB. EX. $72.50

VON HUTTEN, Baroness. *Pam.* nd. Readers Lib. dj. G. P1. $15.00

VON HUTTEN, Baroness. *What Became of Pam.* nd. Readers Lib. dj. VG. P1. $15.00

VON KLENNER, K.E. *Greater Revelation.* 1925. NY. $8.50

VON KRAFT-EBING, R. *Psychopathia Sexualis With Especial Reference...* 1892. Phil. VG. $30.00

VON LANG, Jochen. *Eichmann Interrogated*. 1983. NY. 1st ed. dj. $7.00

VON LARISCH, R. *Uber Leserlichkeit von Ornamentalescriften*. 1904. Wien. 1st ed. wraps. VG. $125.00

VON LOGA, Valerian. *Francisco de Goya*. nd. Leipzig. Ils. D2. $65.00

VON MELLENTHIN, F.W. *Panzer Battles: Study of Employment of Armor in WWII*. 1956. Norman. Ils. fld maps. 383 p. G. T5. $45.00

VON MEYER, E. *History of Chemistry From Earliest Times*. 1906. Macmillan. 691 p. G. M2. $10.00

VON MONTS, H.G. *De Joden in Nederland*. nd. np. Ils. 8vo. printed wraps. $300.00

VON NEUMANN & GOLDSTINE. *Preliminary Electronic Computing Instrument...* 1947. 2nd ed. G. $550.00

VON NIEMAYER. *Clinical Lectures on Pulmanory Consumption*. 1870. London. 1st ed. xl. VG. $75.00

VON PAPEN, Franz. *Memoirs*. 1952. London. Deutsch. sgn. 8vo. xl. VG. $85.00

VON RHAU, Henry. *Tale of the Nineties*. 1930. NY. private print. Ils Peers. $35.00

VON SALIS & RIKLE. *Years in Switzerland*. 1966. CA U. Ils. wraps. VG. $7.50

VON SCHRENK-NOTZIG, A. *Therapeutic Suggestion in Psychopathia Sexualis*. 1895. Phil. EX. $20.00

VON SCHROTTER, Hermann. *Tagebuch Einer Jagdreise an den Oberen Nil*. 1926. Berlin. Kittler. Ils. fld map. $150.00

VON SYDOW, Eckardt. *Die Deutsche Expressionistische Kultur und Malerei*. 1920. Berlin. Verlag. Ils. D2. $65.00

VON TRAPP, Maria. *Von Trapp Family: Stowe, VT*. nd. Boston. Bromley. sgn. 24 p. VG. M1. $8.50

VONNEGUT, Kurt. *Bluebeard*. 1987. Delacorte. Ltd ed. 1/500. sgn. slipcase. $60.00

VONNEGUT, Kurt. *Bluebeard*. 1987. Delacorte. 1st trade ed. M. $10.00

VONNEGUT, Kurt. *Breakfast of Champions*. 1973. Delacorte. 5th ed. dj. EX. P1. $10.00

VONNEGUT, Kurt. *Dead-Eye Dick*. 1983. London. 1st ed. dj. VG. $25.00

VONNEGUT, Kurt. *God Bless You, Mr. Rosewater; or, Pearls Before Swine*. 1965. NY. 1st ed. dj. M. $125.00

VONNEGUT, Kurt. *Jailbird*. 1979. Delacorte. 1st ed. dj. G. P1. $7.50

VONNEGUT, Kurt. *Jailbird*. 1979. NY. 1st ed. dj. VG. $22.00

VONNEGUT, Kurt. *Mother Night*. 1963. Fawcett. 1st pb ed. $30.00

VONNEGUT, Kurt. *Mother Night*. 1966. Harper. 1st HrdCvr ed. VG. $70.00

VONNEGUT, Kurt. *Nothing Is Lost Save Honor*. 1984. 1st ed. 1/300. sgn. EX. $65.00

VONNEGUT, Kurt. *Palm Sunday*. 1981. Delacorte. 1st ed. dj. EX. P1. $20.00

VONNEGUT, Kurt. *Player Piano*. nd. Book Club. dj. VG. P1. $4.50

VONNEGUT, Kurt. *Slaughterhouse Five*. 1969. 5th print. dj. G. $10.00

VONNEGUT, Kurt. *Slaughterhouse Five; or, Children's Crusade...* 1978. Franklin Lib. Ltd ed. sgn. 8vo. EX. $60.00

VONNEGUT, Kurt. *Wampeters, Foma & Granfalloons*. 1974. NY. 1st Am ed. dj. VG. $30.00

VONNEGUT, Kurt. *Welcome to the Monkey House: Collection of Short Stories...* 1968. NY. 1st ed. 298 p. dj. EX. T5. $125.00

VOORHEES, M.B. *Korean Tales*. 1952. NY. 1st ed. 209 p. G. T5. $22.50

VOORHIS, H.V.B. *E Star: Evolution From a Rite to an Orger*. 1954. NY. Ils. 237 p. VG. T5. $25.00

VOOUS, K.H. *Owls of N Hemisphere*. 1988. MIT Pr. Ils Cameron. 4to. 320 p. dj. M2. $48.00

VORIS, A.C. *Memorial Address*. 1878. Akron. 16 p. wraps. VG. T5. $4.50

VORONOFF, Serge. *Sources of Life*. 1943. Boston. Humphries. 1st Am ed. dj. VG. $20.00

VORRES, I. *Last Grand Duchess*. 1965. NY. 1st ed. dj. VG. B2. $35.00

VORZIMMER, P.J. *Charles Darwin & Years of Controversey: 1859-1882*. 1970. Temple U. 300 p. dj. EX. M2. $25.00

VOSS, Richard. *Monk & the Hangman's Daughter*. nd. Norwalk. Heritage. quarto. slipcase. EX. $15.00

VOYCE, Arthur. *Moscow-Kremlin History of Architecture & Treasures*. nd. CA U. dj. VG. $20.00

VOZNESENSKY. *Selected Poems*. nd. np. 1st ed. inscr. wraps. EX. $15.00

VUKELICH, George. *Fisherman's Beach*. 1962. NY. 1st ed. dj. EX. $10.00

VYDRA, Josef. *Folk Painting on Glass*. nd. Artia. dj. J2. $25.00

W

WA-SHA-QUON-ASIN (GRAY OWL). *Tales of an Empty Cabin.* 1936. London. Dickson. 2nd print. sgn. 335 p. M1. $35.00

WACK, H.W. *Story of the Congo Free State.* 1905. NY. Ils 1st ed. maps. inscr/sgn. VG. $65.00

WADDELL, Joseph. *Annals of Augusta Co., VA, 1726-1871.* 1902. Staunton. Revised 2nd ed. 545 p. VG. $95.00

WADDELL, L.A. *British Edda.* 1930. London. rare. C1. $59.00

WADE, Henry. *Duke of York's Steps.* 1929. Constable. 1st ed. G. P1. $12.50

WADE, Henry. *Heir Presumptive.* 1953. Macmillan. 1st ed. dj. VG. P1. $20.00

WADE, Henry. *Litmore Snatch.* 1957. Macmillan. 1st ed. dj. VG. P1. $22.50

WADE, J.D. *Augustus Baldwin Longstreet.* 1924. NY. 1st ed. 392 p. xl. G. $25.00

WADE, Jonathan. *Back To Life.* 1961. Pantheon. dj. EX. P1. $5.00

WADE-GERY, H.T. *Terpisichore & Other Poems.* 1922. Golden Cockerel. 1/350. 12mo. EX. $50.00

WADELTON, Maggie Owen. *Sarah Mandrake.* 1946. Bobbs Merrill. 1st ed. G. P1. $5.00

WAGEKNECHT, Edward. *Six Novels of the Supernatural.* 1944. Viking. 1st ed. VG. P1. $35.00

WAGEMANN, C.E. *Covered Bridges of New England.* 1932. Rutland. 1/500. sgn. J2. $75.00

WAGENKNECHT, Edward. *Fireside Book of Ghost Stories.* 1947. Bobbs Merrill. VG. P1. $22.50

WAGER, V.A. *Frogs of S Africa.* 1986. S Africa. Revised ed. 183 p. EX. M2. $28.00

WAGER, Walter. *Blue Murder.* 1981. Arbor House. 1st ed. dj. VG. P1. $15.00

WAGER, Walter. *Otto's Boy.* 1985. Macmillan. 1st ed. dj. EX. P1. $16.00

WAGER, Walter. *Sledgehammer.* nd. Book Club. dj. VG. P1. $3.00

WAGER, Walter. *Telefon.* nd. Book Club. dj. EX. P1. $3.00

WAGGONER, M.S. *Long Haul W: Great Canal Era, 1817-1850.* 1958. Ils. 320 p. dj. $15.00

WAGNER, Alfred. *Die Parfumerie Industrie, Nachschlagebuch fur den Parfumeur.* nd. (1928?) Halle (Saale) Ils. 596 p. G. T5. $37.50

WAGNER, CAMP & BECKER. *Plains & Rockies: Critical Bibliography of Exploration...* 1982. San Francisco. Howell. 745 p. M. A3. $140.00

WAGNER, E.F. *Foundation to Flute Playing.* 1918. NY. Fischer. pb. VG. $12.00

WAGNER, F.H. *Wildlife of Deserts.* 1984. Abrams. Ils. 231 p. dj. EX. M2. $22.00

WAGNER, Jane. *Search for Intelligent Life in the Universe.* 1986. NY. 1st ed. dj. EX. $15.00

WAGNER, Karl Edward. *In a Lonely Place.* 1983. Scream Pr. 1st ed. sgn/#d. dj. boxed. EX. P1. $50.00

WAGNER, Richard. *Letters of Richard Wagner, the Burrell Collection.* 1950. Macmillan. 1st ed. dj. J2. $15.00

WAGNER, Richard. *Ring of the Nibelung.* 1939. NY. Ils Rackham. 4to. dj. VG. T1. $100.00

WAGNER, Richard. *Tannhauser.* 1911. NY. Ils Pogany. 4to. VG. $100.00

WAGNER & ALDON. *Manual of Saltbushes in NM.* 1978. USFS. Ils. maps. 50 p. M2. $5.00

WAGNER & KELLEY. *US Army & Navy.* 1899. Akron. Werner. 43 pls. gilt cloth. AEG. xl. J2. $450.00

WAHL, A.H. *Handsome, But Dead.* 1942. Howell Soskin. dj. EX. $10.00

WAINWRIGHT, J.M. *General Wainwright's Story.* 1946. NY. 1st ed. 314 p. T5. $22.50

WAINWRIGHT, John. *Acquittal.* 1976. Macmillan. 1st ed. dj. xl. P1. $5.00

WAINWRIGHT, John. *Dominoes.* 1980. Macmillan. 1st ed. dj. VG. P1. $15.00

WAINWRIGHT, John. *Pool of Tears.* 1977. Macmillan. 1st ed. dj. xl. P1. $5.00

WAINWRIGHT, John. *Who Goes Next?* 1976. St. Martin. 1st ed. dj. VG. P1. $15.00

WAITE, A.E. *Complete Manual of Occult Divination.* 1972. NY U Books. 2 vols. EX. $45.00

WAITE, A.E. *Hidden Church of the Holy Grail.* 1909. London. 1st ed. 714 p. rebound. VG. $75.00

WAITE, A.E. *Hidden Church of the Holy Grail.* 1989. Yogi Pub. 1st ed. gilt leatherette. M. C1. $34.50

WAITE, A.E. *Mormon Prophet & His Harem.* 1866. Cambridge. 1st ed. G. $80.00

WAITE, A.E. *Pictorial Key to the Tarot.* 1983. pb. M. C1. $6.50

WAKEFIELD, Dan. *Selling Out.* 1985. Little Brown. 1st ed. dj. EX. $17.00

WAKEFIELD, Dan. *Under the Apple Tree.* 1982. Delacorte. 1st ed. dj. EX. $15.00

WAKEFIELD, H.R. *Clock Strikes Twelve.* 1946. Arkham House. 1st ed. dj. VG. P1. $35.00

WAKEFIELD, H.R. *Hearken to the Evidence.* 1934. Doubleday Doran. VG. P1. $15.00

WAKEFIELD, H.R. *Strayers From Sheol.* 1961. Arkham House. 1st ed. dj. VG. P1. $25.00

WAKEFIELD, Tom. *Love Siege.* 1979. London. 1st ed. dj. M. $10.00

WAKELEY, J.B. *Lost Chapters Recovered From Early History Methodism.* 1858. NY. Ils 1st ed. 295 p. G. $35.00

WAKEMAN, Goeffrey. *Victorian Book Illustration.* 1973. Newton Abbot. 1st ed. dj. EX. $55.00

WAKOSKI, Diane. *Collected Greed, Parts 1-13.* 1984. Black Sparrow. 1/200. sgn. EX. $35.00

WAKOSKI, Diane. *Saturn's Ring.* 1982. NY. Targ. 1/250. sgn. glassine dj. EX. $40.00

WAKOSKI, Diane. *Waiting for the King of Spain.* 1976. Black Sparrow. 1/250. sgn. EX. $35.00

WAKSMAN, S.A. *Soil Microbiology.* 1963. Wiley. Ils. 356 p. EX. M2. $16.00

WALCOTT, C.D. *Fossil Medusae.* 1898. US Geol Survey. Ils. 4to. 201 p. VG. M2. $135.00

WALCOTT. *Poems of the Caribbean.* Ltd Ed Club. slipcase. M. B3. $45.00

WALDEN, H.T. *Big Stony.* Derrydale. as issued. VG. B2. $115.00

WALDEN, H.T. *Big Stony.* 1940. Derrydale. 1/350. 12mo. dj. EX. $180.00

WALDEN, H.T. *Familiar Fresh-Water Fishes of America.* 1964. Harper. Ils 1st ed. P1. $15.00

WALDEN, H.T. *Last Pool.* 1972. Crown. reprint. dj. EX. $7.50

WALDEN, Herwarth. *Einblick in Kunst: Expressionismus, Futurismus, Kubismus.* 1924. Berlin. Verlag. Ils. Franz Marc. 176 p. D2. $185.00

WALDEN, J.B. *Long Whip.* 1936. NY. Ils 1st ed. dj. EX. $10.00

WALDMAN, Milton. *Americana, the Literature of American History.* 1925. NY. VG. $25.00

WALDO, Myra. *Pancake Cookbook.* 1963. 146 p. pb. EX. $2.00

WALDO, Myra. *Pleasures of Wine.* nd. Gramercy. dj. VG. P1. $6.00

WALDO, S.P. *Life & Character of Stephen Decatur.* 1822. Middletown. Revised 2nd ed. orig calf. T5. $95.00

WALDO. *Grenfell, Knight Errant of the N.* 1924. Phil. Ils 1st ed. VG. $20.00

WALDORF, J.T. *Kid on the Comstock: Reminiscences of VA City Childhood.* 1970. Am W. Ils. 198 p. dj. EX. M2. $15.00

WALDRON, W.H. *Elements of Trench Warfare: Bayonet & Training.* 1917. NY. Ils. 225 p. G. T5. $12.50

WALDRON & WHIGHAM. *Lightrunner.* 1983. Donning. Ltd 1st ed. sgn/#d. boxed. EX. P1. $30.00

WALDROP, Howard. *Dozen Tough Jobs.* 1989. Ziesing. 1st ed. dj. EX. P1. $16.00

WALDROP, Howard. *Howard Who?* 1986. Doubleday. 1st ed. dj. VG. P1. $12.95

WALDROP, Howard. *Them Bones.* 1989. Ziesing. dj. EX. P1. $20.00

WALEY, Arthur. *Introduction to Study of Chinese Painting.* 1923. London. Ils. VG. $95.00

WALEY, Arthur. *Opium War Through Chinese Eyes.* 1958. London. 1st ed. dj. EX. $22.00

WALFORD, L.A. *Marine Game Fishes of the Pacific Coast.* 1974. Smithsonian. Ils. 4to. 206 p. EX. M2. $16.00

WALKER, Alexander. *Intermarriage: or, Mode in Which, & Causes Why, Beauty...* 1839. NY. Ils. poor. $20.00

WALKER, Alexander. *Woman Physiologically Considered As to Mind, Morals...* 1845. NY. disbound. poor. $20.00

WALKER, Alice. *Color Purple.* 1982. Harcourt Brace. 1st ed. dj. EX. scarce. T6. $300.00

WALKER, Alice. *Color Purple.* 1986. London. Womans. 1st Eng HrdCvr ed. dj. M. T6. $90.00

WALKER, B.S. *Great Divide.* 1973. Time Life. color photos. maps. 184 p. EX. M2. $5.00

WALKER, David. *Lord's Pink Ocean.* 1972. Collins. 1st ed. dj. VG. P1. $10.00

WALKER, David. *Lord's Pink Ocean.* 1972. Houghton. 1st ed. dj. EX. P1. $10.00

WALKER, E.P. *Mammals of the World.* 1975. Johns Hopkins. 3rd ed. 2 vols. slipcase. EX. M2. $40.00

WALKER, E.S. *Treetops Hotel.* 1964. Hale. photos. 190 p. dj. EX. M2. $10.00

WALKER, H.J. *Jesse James, the Outlaw.* 1961. Des Moines. Ils 1st ed. dj. EX. T5. $35.00

WALKER, H.P. *Wagonmasters: High Plains Freighting to 1880.* 1966. Norman. Ils. dj. EX. $25.00

WALKER, Hugh. *TN Tales.* 1970. Nashville. Auora Pub. inscr. 8vo. EX. $22.00

WALKER, J. *Johnstown Horror.* 1889. Ils. 520 p. G. $15.00

WALKER, J.M. *Life of Capt. Joseph Fry, Cuban Martyr.* 1875. Hartford. green bdg. $65.00

WALKER, Marian. *Flowering Bulbs for Winter Windows.* 1965. NJ. Ils. 8vo. 107 p. yellow bdg. $15.00

WALKER, R.S. *Torchlights to Cherokees: Brainerd Mission.* 1931. Macmillan. Ils 1st ed. 340 p. dj. VG. A3. $60.00

WALKER, T. *Life in the AK Bush.* 1979. AK NW. Ils. 135 p. M. M2. $8.00

WALKER, T. *Red Salmon, Brown Bear: Story of AK Lake.* 1971. World. Ils 1st print. 226 p. dj. EX. M2. $10.00

WALKER, T.J. *Whale Primer With Special Attention to CA Gray Whale.* 1962. Cabrillo Hist Assn. 58 p. M2. $8.00

WALKER, W.R. *Architectural Portfolio.* 1895. Providence. Ils. 4to. $150.00

WALKER, Walter. *Two Dude Defense.* 1985. NY. Harper. 1st ed. dj. EX. $15.00

WALL, Alexander. *Books on Architecture Printed in America, 1775-1830.* 1925. Cambridge. wraps. $10.00

WALL, J.F. *Henry Watterson: Reconstructed Rebel.* 1956. NY. 362 p. dj. VG. $20.00

WALL, O.A. *Sex & Sex Worship.* 1922. St. Louis. Ils. 608 p. EX. $75.00

WALLACE, Anthony. *Rockdale.* 1978. NY. Revised 1st ed. dj. EX. $30.00

WALLACE, D.R. *Idle Weeds: Life of a Sandstone Ridge.* 1980. Sierra Club. Ils 1st ed. 183 p. dj. EX. M2. $12.00

WALLACE, Edgar. *Again the Ringer.* 1952. Hodder Stoughton. 12th print. P1. $7.50

WALLACE, Edgar. *Again the Three Just Men.* nd. Burt. dj. VG. P1. $10.00

WALLACE, Edgar. *Again the Three Just Men.* 1933. Garden City. Doubleday. $10.00

WALLACE, Edgar. *Avenger.* nd. Leisure Lib. dj. VG. P1. $17.50

WALLACE, Edgar. *Black Abbot.* nd. Burt. VG. P1. $10.00

WALLACE, Edgar. *Black.* 1930. Crime Club. G. P1. $10.00

WALLACE, Edgar. *Bones in London.* 1972. Hutchinson. dj. VG. P1. $15.00

WALLACE, Edgar. *Bones.* nd. Ward Lock. dj. VG. P1. $17.50

WALLACE, Edgar. *Bones.* nd. Ward Lock. dj. xl. P1. $7.50

WALLACE, Edgar. *Bosambo of the River.* nd. Ward Lock. VG. P1. $20.00

WALLACE, Edgar. *Crimson Circle.* nd. Book Club. dj. VG. P1. $4.50

WALLACE, Edgar. *Crimson Circle.* nd. Burt. VG. P1. $7.50

WALLACE, Edgar. *Daffodil Mystery.* nd. Ward Lock Ryerson. dj. VG. P1. $25.00

WALLACE, Edgar. *Dark Eyes of London.* nd. Ward Lock. xl. G. P1. $6.00

WALLACE, Edgar. *Day of Uniting.* 1930. Mystery League. 1st ed. dj. VG. P1. $25.00

WALLACE, Edgar. *Devil Man.* 1933. Collins Crime Club. 5th print. P1. $8.00

WALLACE, Edgar. *Door With Seven Locks.* nd. Hodder Stoughton. G. P1. $5.00

WALLACE, Edgar. *Double.* nd. Grosset. VG. P1. $7.50

WALLACE, Edgar. *Double.* 1928. Garden City. Doubleday. $7.50

WALLACE, Edgar. *Edgar Wallace Reader of Mystery.* 1943. Tower. VG. P1. $15.00

WALLACE, Edgar. *Face in the Night.* nd. Burt. dj. VG. P1. $12.50

WALLACE, Edgar. *Flying Squad.* nd. Hodder Stoughton. VG. P1. $12.50

WALLACE, Edgar. *Flying Squad.* nd. Burt. VG. P1. $7.50

WALLACE, Edgar. *Flying Squad.* nd. Crime Club. 1st ed. VG. P1. $17.50

WALLACE, Edgar. *Four Just Men.* 1905. Tallis Pr. 1st ed. xl. P1. $75.00

WALLACE, Edgar. *Fourth Plague.* 1930. Garden City. $12.50

WALLACE, Edgar. *Frightened Lady.* 1932. Hodder Stoughton. G. P1. $10.00

WALLACE, Edgar. *Frightened Lady.* 1933. Musson. 1st ed. G. P1. $10.00

WALLACE, Edgar. *Frightened Lady.* 1949. Hodder Stoughton. 7th ed. dj. P1. $10.00

WALLACE, Edgar. *Governor of Chi-Foo.* 1933. World. 1st ed. dj. VG. P1. $60.00

WALLACE, Edgar. *Green Ribbon.* nd. Hutchinson. 35th ed. G. P1. $6.00

WALLACE, Edgar. *Green Ribbon.* 1931. Doubleday Doran. G. P1. $6.00

WALLACE, Edgar. *Hairy Arm.* 1938. Triangle. VG. P1. $12.00

WALLACE, Edgar. *Hand of Power.* 1930. Mystery League. 1st ed. VG. P1. $15.00

WALLACE, Edgar. *Jack O'Judgment.* nd. Ward Lock. dj. VG. P1. $17.50

WALLACE, Edgar. *Just Men of Cordova.* 1930. Doubleday Doran. xl. G. P1. $6.00

WALLACE, Edgar. *Keepers of the King's Peace.* nd. Ward Lock. VG. P1. $20.00

WALLACE, Edgar. *King by Night.* 1928. John Long. VG. P1. $15.00

WALLACE, Edgar. *Lieutenant Bones.* nd. Ward Lock. VG. P1. $20.00

WALLACE, Edgar. *Lieutenant Bones.* 1972. Tom Stacey. dj. EX. P1. $12.50

WALLACE, Edgar. *Lone House Mystery.* nd. Collins. P1. $17.50

WALLACE, Edgar. *Man at the Carlton.* nd. Burt. VG. P1. $8.00

WALLACE, Edgar. *Man at the Carlton.* 1931. Musson. 1st Canadian HrdCvr ed. VG. P1. $10.00

WALLACE, Edgar. *Man From Morocco.* 1926. John Long. G. P1. $10.00

WALLACE, Edgar. *Man Who Knew.* nd. Newnes. G. P1. $7.50

WALLACE, Edgar. *Man Who Knew.* nd. Panther. xl. G. P1. $7.00

WALLACE, Edgar. *Melody of Death.* nd. Readers Lib. dj. VG. P1. $20.00

WALLACE, Edgar. *Melody of Death.* nd. Burt. dj. VG. P1. $12.00

WALLACE, Edgar. *Mr. Commissioner Sanders.* 1930. Doubleday. dj. VG. P1. $35.00

WALLACE, Edgar. *Northing Tramp.* 1931. Doubleday. VG. P1. $12.00

WALLACE, Edgar. *On the Spot.* 1955. John Long. dj. xl. P1. $10.00

WALLACE, Edgar. *People on the River.* nd. Ward Lock. VG. P1. $20.00

WALLACE, Edgar. *Ringer.* 1952. Hodder Stoughton. dj. VG. P1. $15.00

WALLACE, Edgar. *Sanders of the River.* nd. Ward Lock. dj. xl. P1. $12.00

WALLACE, Edgar. *Sanders of the River.* 1972. Tom Stacey. dj. EX. P1. $12.50

WALLACE, Edgar. *Sanders of the River.* nd. Ward Lock. VG. P1. $20.00

WALLACE, Edgar. *Sandi the King-Maker.* nd. Ward Lock. VG. P1. $20.00

WALLACE, Edgar. *Scotland Yard Book.* nd. Burt. dj. VG. P1. $25.00

WALLACE, Edgar. *Scotland Yard Book.* 1932. Crime Club. 1st ed. dj. VG. $25.00

WALLACE, Edgar. *Secret House.* nd. Ward Lock. VG. P1. $12.50

WALLACE, Edgar. *Sinister Man.* nd. Burt. VG. P1. $7.50

WALLACE, Edgar. *Sinister Man.* 1938. Triangle. VG. P1. $7.50

WALLACE, Edgar. *Sinister Man.* 1951. Hodder Stoughton. VG. P1. $7.50

WALLACE, Edgar. *Square Emerald.* 1932. Musson Hodder Stoughton. xl. P1. $7.50

WALLACE, Edgar. *Squeaker.* nd. Burt. VG. P1. $7.50

WALLACE, Edgar. *Squealer.* 1931. Doubleday. VG. P1. $10.00

WALLACE, Edgar. *Steward.* 1932. Collins. 1st ed. VG. P1. $30.00

WALLACE, Edgar. *Strange Countess.* 1950. Hodder Stoughton. 28th print. P1. $10.00

WALLACE, Edgar. *Terrible People.* 1929. Doubleday. G. P1. $6.00

WALLACE, Edgar. *Terror Keep.* nd. Hodder Stoughton. VG. P1. $7.50

WALLACE, Edgar. *Terror Keep.* 1928. Doubleday. VG. P1. $10.00

WALLACE, Edgar. *Traitor's Gate.* nd. Burt. VG. P1. $7.50

WALLACE, Edgar. *Traitor's Gate.* 1927. Doubleday Page. 1st ed. G. P1. $10.00

WALLACE, Edgar. *Twister.* 1970. John Long. G. P1. $7.50

WALLACE, Edgar. *When the Gangs Came to London.* nd. Burt. dj. VG. P1. $10.00

WALLACE, Edgar. *White Face.* nd. Crime Club. VG. P1. $10.00

WALLACE, Edgar. *White Face.* 1932. Doubleday Doran. G. P1. $7.50

WALLACE, Edgar. *White Face.* 1932. Musson Hodder Stoughton. VG. P1. $15.00

WALLACE, G.B. *Way to Game Abundance: Explanation of Game Cycles.* 1949. Scribner. 1st ed. dj. VG. $15.00

WALLACE, Henry. *New Frontiers.* 1934. Reynal Hitchcock. 1st ed. dj. VG. $30.00

WALLACE, I. *Birds of Prey of Britain & Europe.* 1983. Oxford U. 34 color pls. map. 88 p. dj. M2. $18.00

WALLACE, Ian. *Deathstar Voyage.* 1969. Putnam. 1st ed. dj. xl. P1. $7.50

WALLACE, Ian. *Deathstar Voyage.* 1972. Dobson. 1st ed. dj. EX. P1. $12.50

WALLACE, Ian. *Pan Sagittarius.* 1973. Putnam. dj. EX. P1. $15.00

WALLACE, Ian. *Purloined Prince.* 1971. McCall. 1st ed. dj. VG. P1. $25.00

WALLACE, Irving. *Miracle.* 1984. NY. 1st ed. dj. VG. $7.00

WALLACE, J.B. *History of Kershaw Lodge No. 29 Ancient Free Masons.* 1933. Camden. $9.00

WALLACE, Lew. *Ben Hur.* 1901. Players ed. photos. TEG. $40.00

WALLACE, Lew. *Ben Hur.* 1960. Ltd Ed Club. Ils/sgn Mugnaini. slipcase. EX. $40.00

WALLACE, Lew. *Fair God.* 1899. Boston. Ils Pape. 1st ed. 2 vols. $60.00

WALLACE, Lew. *Famous Paintings of the World.* 1894. NY. Fine Art Pub. pls. D2. $150.00

WALLACE, Lew. *Life of General Benjamin Harrison.* 1888. Phil. Ils 1st ed. 578 p. rebound. VG. T5. $27.50

WALLACE, Lew. *Prince of India.* 1893. NY. 1st ed. EX. $35.00

WALLACE, R. *Grand Canyon.* 1972. Time Life. color photos. map. 184 p. EX. M2. $8.00

WALLACE, R. *HI.* 1973. Time Life. color photos. 184 p. EX. M2. $8.00

WALLACE, Susan. *Land of the Pueblos.* 1890. Ils. 285 p. EX. K1. $21.00

WALLACE, Willard. *Traitorous Hero.* 1954. NY. 1st ed. dj. VG. $15.00

WALLACE & HOEBEL. *Comanches: Lords of S Plains.* 1969. OK U. Ils. 381 p. dj. M2. $19.00

WALLACE & WALLACE. *Ginevra: A Christmas Story.* 1887. VG. $85.00

WALLACK, L.R. *Anatomy of Firearms.* 1965. NY. Ils. dj. EX. $15.00

WALLER, M.E. *Daughter of the Rich.* 1927. Boston. Ils. juvenile. VG. $25.00

WALLER. *Monumental Brasses From 13th to 16th C.* 1864. 62 pls. morocco. VG. $225.00

WALLEY, Dean. *Little Book of Proverbs.* 1968. Hallmark. dj. VG. P1. $5.00

WALLING, R.A.J. *Corpse by Any Other Name.* 1943. Morrow. xl. P1. $7.50

WALLING, R.A.J. *Corpse With the Eerie Eye.* nd. Book Inc. G. P1. $5.00

WALLING, R.A.J. *Corpse With the Eerie Eye.* nd. Collier. VG. P1. $7.50

WALLING, R.A.J. *Corpse With the Floating Foot.* 1936. Morrow. 1st ed. dj. EX. $35.00

WALLING, R.A.J. *Corpse Without a Clue.* 1944. Doubleday Book Club. VG. P1. $15.00

WALLING, William. *World I Left Behind Me.* 1979. St. Martin. 1st ed. P1. $10.00

WALLIS, Dave. *Only Lovers Left Alive.* 1964. Dutton. 1st ed. dj. VG. P1. $12.50

WALLIS & WALLIS. *Micmac Indians of E Canada.* 1955. MN U. 1st ed. presentation. sgn. 8vo. VG. T1. $35.00

WALLIS-TAYLOR, A.J. *Motor Cars; or, Power Carriages for Common Roads.* 1897. London. Crosby Lockwood. 1st ed. G. J3. $75.00

WALLMANN, Jeffrey M. *Judas Cross.* 1974. Random House. 1st ed. dj. xl. P1. $5.00

WALLMO, O.C. *Mule & Black-Tailed Deer in N America.* 1981. NE U. photos. 605 p. dj. EX. M2. $35.00

WALLOP, Douglas. *Year Yankees Lost Pennant.* nd. BOMC. dj. VG. P1. $3.00

WALPOLE, Horace. *Apple Trees.* 1932. Golden Cockerel. Ils Lamb. $50.00

WALPOLE, Hugh. *Book of Crisis.* c 1940?. London. $20.00

WALPOLE, Hugh. *Jeremy & Hamlet.* 1923. NY. 1st Am ed. sgn. 305 p. VG. T5. $12.50

WALPOLE, Hugh. *Jeremy.* 1919. Doran. Ils Shepard. 1st ed. dj. $30.00

WALPOLE, Hugh. *Killer & the Slain.* 1942. Macmillan. 2nd ed. G. P1. $6.00

WALPOLE, Hugh. *Mr. Huffam.* 1938. private print. 1/200. VG. P1. $30.00

WALPOLE, Hugh. *Portrait of a Man With Red Hair.* nd. Daily Express. dj. VG. P1. $10.00

WALPOLE, Hugh. *Portrait of a Man With Red Hair.* 1925. NY. 1/250. sgn. 323 p. dj. slipcase. EX. T5. $35.00

WALPOLE, Hugh. *Portrait of a Man With Red Hair.* 1926. Doran. 1st ed. dj. VG. $20.00

WALSH, E.H. *Monk of Gethsemane.* 1893. Brooklyn. Ils. 471 p. xl. $20.00

WALSH, John. *Poe the Detective.* 1968. Rutgers. 1st ed. black cloth. dj. EX. D1. $30.00

WALSH, Maurice. *Key Above the Door.* 1929. Chambers. 14th print. G. P1. $10.00

WALSH, Maurice. *Small Dark Man.* 1929. Chambers. 1st ed. VG. P1. $20.00

WALSH, R.J. *Making of Buffalo Bill.* 1928. Indianapolis. Ils 1st ed. VG. $25.00

WALSH, Thomas. *Dangerous Passenger.* 1959. Doubleday. VG. P1. $7.50

WALSH, Thomas. *Dark Window.* 1956. Little Brown. 1st ed. dj. xl. P1. $5.00

WALSH, Thomas. *Face of the Enemy.* 1967. Doubleday Book Club. VG. P1. $7.50

WALSH, Thomas. *Night Watch.* nd. Book Club. dj. G. P1. $3.50

WALSH, Thomas. *Prison Ship & Other Poems.* 1909. Boston. 1st ed. inscr/sgn. $30.00

WALSH, Thomas. *Tenth Point.* 1964. Simon Schuster. 1st ed. dj. VG. P1. $15.00

WALSH, Thomas. *Tenth Point.* 1965. Doubleday Book Club. VG. P1. $8.00

WALSO, S.P. *Tour of James Monroe, President of US, N & E US in 1817...* 1820. Hartford. 12mo. 348 p. G. G2. $56.00

WALTARI, Mika. *Egyptian.* 1949. NY. 1st ed. dj. EX. $17.00

WALTER, Elizabeth. *In the Mist.* 1979. Arkham House. 1st ed. dj. EX. P1. $15.00

WALTER, Elizabeth. *Sin Eater.* 1967. Harvill. dj. VG. P1. $20.00

WALTER, H. *Eleonora's Falcon: Adaptions to Prey & Habitat.* 1979. Chicago U. Ils 1st ed. maps. 410 p. dj. M. M2. $25.00

WALTER, W.W. *Great Understander.* 1983. Walter Trust. reprint of 1931 ed. 315 p. EX. M2. $18.00

WALTERS, Frank. *CO.* 1946. NY. 1st ed. Rivers of Am Series. 400 p. EX. A3. $35.00

WALTON, Alan Hull. *Open Grave.* 1969. Neville Spearman. dj. VG. $12.50

WALTON, B.J. *Development of Techniques for Raptor Management.* 1977. CA Fish/Game. M2. $5.00

WALTON, Bryce. *Sons of the Ocean Deeps.* 1952. Winston. 1st ed. VG. P1. $15.00

WALTON, Evangeline. *Sword Is Forged.* 1983. 1st Am ed. VG. C1. $6.50

WALTON, Evangeline. *Witch House.* 1945. Arkham House. 1st ed. dj. EX. P1. $40.00

WALTON, George. *Fearless & Free: Seminole Indian War, 1835-1842.* 1977. Bobbs Merrill. dj. M. $28.00

WALTON, George. *Sentinel of the Plains.* 1973. Prentice Hall. Ils 1st ed. 210 p. dj. EX. M2. $17.00

WALTON, Izaak. *Compleat Angler.* nd. Phil. Ils Rackham. VG. J2. $65.00

WALTON, Izaak. *Compleat Angler.* 1888. London. 1/250. sgn. 2 vols. with sgn letter. S2. $2500.00

WALTON, Izaak. *Compleat Angler.* 1924. London. 2nd ed. AEG. EX. $300.00

WALTON, Izaak. *Compleat Angler.* 1924. London. Major. 2nd ed. 416 p. VG. $100.00

WALTON, Izaak. *Compleat Angler.* 1926. London. cloth bdg. M. $35.00

WALTON, Izaak. *Compleat Angler.* 1927. London. Butterworth. Ils Daglish. $80.00

WALTON, Izaak. *Lives of John Donne, H. Wotton...* 1817. York. 3rd ed. 2 vols. $95.00

WALTON, Paul H. *Dali & Miro.* 1967. NY. Tudor. Ils. dj. D2. $25.00

WALTON, R.K. *Bird Finding in New England.* 1988. Godine. Ils 1st ed. 328 p. M. M2. $15.00

WALTON, Thomas. *Present-Day Shipbuilding.* 1907. London. Ils. 8vo. 224 p. xl. VG. $35.00

WALTON, W.I. *Osteopathic Diagnosis & Technique Procedures.* 1972. CO Springs. 547 p. gilt maroon cloth. EX. $30.00

WALTON, W.M. *Life & Adventures of Ben Thompson.* 1956. Steck. facsimile of 1884 ed. 1/2500. M2. $35.00

WALWORTH. *Kateri Tekakwitha.* 1926. Albany. green cloth. VG. $15.00

WAMBAUGH, Joseph. *Choir Boys.* nd. Book Club. dj. VG. P1. $4.00

WAMBAUGH, Joseph. *Echoes in the Darkness.* 1987. Morrow. 1st ed. dj. EX. $7.50

WAMBAUGH, Joseph. *Glitter Dome.* 1981. NY. 1st ed. dj. EX. $25.00

WANDREI, Donald. *Eye & the Finger.* 1944. Arkham House. 1st ed. sgn. EX. $120.00

WANDREI, Donald. *Poems for Midnight.* 1964. Arkham House. 1st ed. dj. EX. P1. $100.00

WANDREI, Donald. *Strange Harvest.* 1965. Arkham House. 1st ed. dj. EX. P1. $35.00

WANDREI, Donald. *Web of Easter Island.* 1948. Arkham House. 1st ed. dj. EX. P1. $45.00

WANGERIN, Walter. *Book of Sorrows.* 1985. Harper Row. 1st ed. dj. EX. P1. $15.95

WANGERIN, Walter. *Book of the Dun Cow.* 1978. Harper Row. 2nd ed. dj. VG. P1. $10.00

WANGERIN, Walter. *Book of the Dun Cow.* 1980. Allen Lane. dj. EX. P1. $25.00

WARBURG, Frederic. *Occupation for Gentlemen.* 1959. London. Ils 1st ed. dj. M. $36.00

WARBURG, James P. *Hell Bent for Election.* 1936. Doubleday. VG. P1. $3.00

WARCH & FANTON. *John Brown.* 1973. Prentice Hall. 1st ed. 184 p. dj. EX. M2. $5.00

WARD, Andrew. *Souvenir History of General U.S. Grant & His Tomb.* 1907. NY. 22 p. wraps. VG. T5. $17.50

WARD, Artemus. *Encyclopedia of Food.* 1923. NY. J2. $85.00

WARD, Artemus. *Grocers' Handbook & Directory for 1886.* 1886. Phil. Ils. fair. $25.00

WARD, C.W. *American Carnation.* 1903. NY. EX. $50.00

WARD, Christopher. *Dutch & Swedes in DE, 1609-1664.* 1930. PA U. 1st ed. 2nd print. EX. $25.00

WARD, Christopher. *Sir Galahad & Other Rhymes.* 1936. 1st ed. dj. VG. C1. $14.50

WARD, H.P. *Follett-Dewey, Fassett-Safford Ancestory of M.D. Follett...* 1896. np. Ils. 281 p. fair. T5. $45.00

WARD, J.A. *Railroads & the Character of America, 1820-1887.* 1986. Ils. 200 p. $16.50

WARD, Julian. *Compass Points To Fear.* nd. Hodder Stoughton. xl. VG. P1. $5.00

WARD, Lynd. *Biggest Bear.* 1960. Boston. dj. J2. $25.00

WARD, Lynd. *God's Man: Novel in Woodcuts.* 1929. NY. 2nd print. VG. $25.00

WARD, Lynd. *God's Man: Novel in Woodcuts.* 1930. NY. 4th print. J2. $22.50

WARD, Lynd. *Madman's Drum.* 1930. NY. 1st ed. dj. G. $60.00

WARD, Lynd. *Madman's Drum.* 1930. NY. Cape. 1st ed. 8vo. EX. $85.00

WARD, Lynd. *Many Mansions.* 1947. NY. 1st ed. dj. VG. $16.50

WARD, Lynd. *Wild Pilgrimage.* 1932. NY. $45.00

WARD, Lynd. *Writings of Thomas Jefferson.* 1967. Lunenberg. 1/1500. sgn. 4to. slipcase. M. $100.00

WARD, Mrs. Humphrey. *Marcella.* 1894. NY. 2 vols. G. $40.00

WARD, Mrs. Humphrey. *Telescope Teachings.* 1859. London. Ils 1st ed. 12mo. 207 p. rebound. $35.00

WARD, P.D. *Natural History of Nautilus.* 1987. Allen Unwin. Ils 1st ed. 267 p. dj. EX. M2. $25.00

WARD, Rowland. *Records of Big Game Containing Account of Distribution...* 1896. London. VG. $375.00

WARD, Thomas. *England's Reformation: A Poem.* 1825. Phil. Cummiskey. 8vo. full leather. M1. $20.00

WARD & DRUMMOND. *I Can't. Can & Can't Series.* 1888. Ils. G. $18.00

WARD & MC NEER. *Prince Bantam.* 1929. Children Book Club. Ils. G. $28.00

WARD. *American Activities in Central Pacific, 1790-1870.* 1966. Gregg Pr. Ils. 8vo. 8 vols. slipcase. EX. $100.00

WARDE, Beatrice. *Bookmaking & Kindred Amenities: Being Collection of Essays.* 1942. New Brunswick. 1st ed. 1/1500. dj. $40.00

WARDHAUGH, A.A. *Owls of Britain & Europe.* 1983. England. Ils 1st ed. 128 p. dj. EX. M2. $17.00

WARDMORE, George. *Trip to AK.* 1884. Boston. $80.00

WARE, Francis. *First-Hand Bits of Stable Lore.* 1903. Boston. VG. $20.00

WARE, Louis. *George Foster Peabody.* 1951. Athens. 1st ed. 227 p. VG. $10.00

WARE & PENDERGAST. *Cigar Store Figures in American Folk Art.* 1953. Lightner. M1. $22.50

WARHOL, Andy. *A.* 1968. NY. 1st Am ed. sgn. dj. EX. $100.00

WARHOL, Andy. *Raid the Icebox I With Andy Warhol...* 1970. Providence. Ils. 103 p. printed wraps. $75.00

WARING, George. *Elements of Agriculture.* 1870. NY. Tribune. Revised ed. 254 p. VG. $12.50

WARING, Guy. *My Pioneer Past.* 1936. Boston. 256 p. $30.00

WARING, Janet. *Early American Wall Stencils.* 1937. NY. Ils. photos. pls. dj. G. T5. $25.00

WARING, S. *Wild Garland.* 1827. London. 12 colored pls. $125.00

WARMOTH, Henry Clay. *War, Politics & Reconstruction; or, Stormy Days in LA.* 1930. NY. 285 p. K1. $21.50

WARNER, C.D. *In the Levant.* 1882. Boston. VG. $15.00

WARNER, C.D. *One Horseback in VA, NC & TN.* 1888. Boston. 1st ed. $20.00

WARNER, George. *Catalog of Manuscripts & Monuments of Alleyn's College...* 1881. London. VG. $35.00

WARNER, J.A. *Life & Art of the N American Indian.* 1975. NY. Crescent. Ils. folio. 168 p. dj. $75.00

WARNER, John. *Reference Library Methods.* 1928. London. pls. $35.00

WARNER, Langdon. *Craft of the Japanese Sculptor.* 1936. Ils Warde. 1st ed. 85 pls. 55 p. VG. B1. $45.00

WARNER, Mignon. *Death in Time.* 1982. Crime Club. 1st ed. dj. EX. P1. $10.00

WARNER, Mignon. *Death in Time.* 1982. Crime Club. 1st ed. dj. xl. P1. $5.00

WARNER, Mignon. *Girl Who Was Clairvoyant.* 1982. Crime Club. 1st ed. dj. VG. P1. $12.50

WARNER, S.T. *Kingdoms of Elfin.* 1977. Viking. 1st ed. dj. VG. P1. $17.50

WARNER, W.R. *Oriental Objects of Art Collected by W.R. Warner.* 1921. 50 pls. VG. $125.00

WARREN, Bill. *Middle of the Country.* 1970. NY. Ils. 160 p. wraps. T5. $5.50

WARREN, J.C. *Columnae Adiposae: Newly-Described Structure of Cutis Vera.* 1882. Cambridge. Riverside. Ils. 36 p. wraps. EX. $45.00

WARREN, Joseph. *Revenge.* nd. Grosset. Movie ed. VG. P1. $20.00

WARREN, Louis. *Lincoln's Parentage & Childhood.* 1926. NY. Ils 1st ed. 392 p. dj. VG. B2. $40.00

WARREN, R. *TX Refugee: Story of Field & Camp Life, Civil War.* 1889. Phil. VG. $17.00

WARREN, R.P. *All the King's Men.* 1953. Modern Lib. 1st ed. dj. VG. $15.00

WARREN, R.P. *Audubon: A Vision.* Ltd ed. sgn. dj. boxed. B7. $115.00

WARREN, R.P. *Band of Angels.* 1955. NY. 1st ed. 375 p. dj. VG. T5. $15.00

WARREN, R.P. *Being Here: Poetry 1977-1980.* 1980. NY. 1st trade ed. dj. EX. $25.00

WARREN, R.P. *Being Here: Poetry 1977-1980.* 1980. Random House. 1st ed. sgn. dj. EX. $40.00

WARREN, R.P. *Cave.* 1959. Random House. 1st ed. sgn. dj. VG. $55.00

WARREN, R.P. *Chief Joseph of Nez Perce Who Call Themselves Nimipus...* 1983. Random House. 1/250. sgn. gilt maroon bdg. boxed. $100.00

WARREN, R.P. *Circus in the Attic.* 1943. NY. 1st ed. dj. VG. B2. $70.00

WARREN, R.P. *Flood.* 1964. Random House. Book Club ed. $4.50

WARREN, R.P. *Flood.* 1964. Random House. 1st trade ed. dj. M. $25.00

WARREN, R.P. *Jefferson Davis Gets His Citizenship Back.* 1980. KY. 1st ed. dj. M. $25.00

WARREN, R.P. *Place To Come To.* 1977. NY. 1st ed. dj. EX. B2. $25.00

WARREN, R.P. *Rumor Verified.* 1981. NY. 1st ed. sgn. dj. EX. $75.00

WARREN, R.P. *Selected Poems, 1923-1975.* 1976. Franklin Lib. Ils Dillon. Ltd 1st ed. 294 p. $55.00

WARREN, R.P. *Who Speaks for the Negro?* 1965. Random House. 1st ed. sgn. dj. EX. $55.00

WARREN, R.P. *Wilderness: Tale of the Civil War.* 1961. Random House. 1st print. dj. EX. $50.00

WARREN, R.P. *World Enough & Time.* 1950. Random House. 1st ed. dj. $40.00

WARREN, W.L. *King John.* 1978. CA U. lg pb. VG. C1. $6.00

WARREN & BENSON. *Only Four Escaped.* 1959. 1st Am ed. $15.00

WARWICH, P.B. *Storage Battery.* 1896. Ils Bubier. 1st ed. VG. $14.00

WARWICK, Sidney. *Silver Basilisk.* nd. Hodder Stoughton. dj. G. P1. $10.00

WASHBURN, Bradford. *Bradford on Mt. WA.* 1928. NY. Ils. 123 p. G. T5. $9.50

WASHBURN, D.K. *Hopi Kachina: Spirit of Life.* 1980. CA Acad Sc. Ils. square 4to. 158 p. EX. M2. $25.00

WASHBURN, F.L. *Diptera of MN.* 1906. MN U. Ils. 164 p. G. M2. $10.00

WASHBURN, Mark. *Armageddon Game.* 1977. Putnam. 1st ed. dj. VG. P1. $8.00

WASHBURNE, H.C. & A. *Land of the Good Shadows: Life Story of Anauta.* 1940. NY. John Day. Ils. 329 p. M1. $10.00

WASHBURNE, Heluiz. *Little Elephant Catches Cold.* c 1937. Chicago. 1st ed. 8vo. VG. $15.00

WASHINGTON, B.T. *Character Building.* 1902. NY. Doubleday. 1st ed. 291 p. VG. $40.00

WASHINGTON, B.T. *Tuskegee & Its People: Their Ideals & Achievements.* 1905. NY. 1st ed. EX. $75.00

WASHINGTON, B.T. *Up From Slavery.* 1901. NY. 1st ed. TEG. gilt buckram. EX. $55.00

WASHINGTON, B.T. *Working With the Hands.* 1904. Doubleday. Ils Johnston. 1st ed. VG. $75.00

WASHINGTON, George. *Official Letters to American Congress.* 1796. Boston. 2 vols. leather. G. $125.00

WASSERMAN, J.L. *Metamorphoses in 19th-C Sculpture.* 1975. Fogg Art Mus. 4to. dj. EX. $22.50

WASSING, Rene. *African Art.* 1968. Abrams. Ils 1st ed. dj. EX. $50.00

WASSON, R. *Hall Carbine Affair: Essay in Historiography.* 1971. Danbury. 3rd print. 1/26. slipcase. $150.00

WATANA, Onoto. *Japanese Nightingale.* 1902. NY. 1st ed. 3 pls. VG. $35.00

WATERHOUSE, N.E. *Comprehensive Catalog of Postage Stamps of the USA.* 1916. London. Godden. VG. $12.00

WATERMAN, T.T. *Dwellings of Colonial America.* 1950. NC U. photos. slipcase. EX. $45.00

WATERMAN, T.T. *Mansions of VA.* 1945. Chapel Hill. 2nd ed. boxed. EX. $22.00

WATERMAN. *History of Angling.* 1981. Tulsa. Ils. dj. EX. $15.00

WATERS, Frank. *Midas of the Rockies.* 1949. Sage. Ils. 347 p. EX. $20.00

WATERS, Thomas. *Recollections of a Policeman.* 1852. NY. Pirated 1st ed. rare. $350.00

WATKING, L.E. *Spin & Marty.* 1956. Whitman. G. P1. $4.50

WATKINS, J.L. *100 Greatest Advertisements: Who Wrote Them & What They Did.* 1949. NY. Moore. Intro Rubicam. 4to. EX. $50.00

WATKINS, Leslie. *Unexploded Man.* 1968. Morrow. 1st ed. dj. EX. $15.00

WATKINS, M.G. *Gleanings From Natural History of the Ancients.* 1885. Elliot Stock. 1st ed. G. J2. $25.00

WATKINS, Vernon. *Breaking of the Wave.* 1979. Suffolk. Ipswich. 1st ed. dj. wraps. EX. $15.00

WATKINS, Vernon. *Unity of the Stream.* 1978. Redding Ridge. 1st ed. dj. VG. C1. $17.00

WATKINS, William Jon. *Litany of Sh'Reev.* 1976. Doubleday. 1st ed. dj. EX. P1. $10.00

WATKINS. *CA: An Illustrated History.* 1972. Ils. 541 p. dj. K1. $21.00

WATKINSON, Valerie. *Sped Arrow.* 1964. Scribner. 1st ed. dj. xl. P1. $5.00

WATNEY, John. *Mervyn Peake.* 1976. St. Martin. 1st ed. dj. VG. $20.00

WATSON, Alexander. *American Home Garden.* 1859. NY. Ils. 531 p. $40.00

WATSON, Andrew. *Manuscripts of Henry Savile of Banke.* 1969. London. Ils. EX. $18.00

WATSON, B.F. *Addresses, Reviews & Episodes Concerning 6th MA Regiment.* 1901. 142 p. AEG. VG. J4. $35.00

WATSON, Colin. *Just What the Doctor Ordered.* nd. Book Club. dj. VG. P1. $4.00

WATSON, Colin. *Snobbery With Violence.* 1979. London. Revised ed. dj. EX. $30.00

WATSON, E.W. *Twenty Painters & How They Work.* 1950. NY. Ils 1st ed. dj. VG. B2. $32.50

WATSON, Elkanah. *Man & Times of the Revolution.* 1861. NY. 2nd ed. G. $17.50

WATSON, Ernest. *Outdoor Sketching.* 1946. NY. Ils 1st ed. 4to. dj. EX. T1. $25.00

WATSON, Forbes. *Allen Tucker.* 1932. Whitney Mus. Ils. dj. D2. $35.00

WATSON, H.O. *Chanco: US Army Homing Pigeon.* 1938. NY. Ils. photos. G. $15.00

WATSON, Ian. *Queenmagic, Kingmagic.* 1986. St. Martin. 1st ed. dj. VG. P1. $14.95

WATSON, P. *Sea Shepherd: My Fight for Whales & Seals.* 1982. Norton. Ils 1st ed. 258 p. dj. EX. M2. $5.00

WATSON, P.F. *Artificial Breeding of Non-Domestic Animals.* 1978. Academic Pr. Ils. 376 p. dj. EX. M2. $15.00

WATSON, Richard. *Life of Rev. John Wesley.* 1831. NY. 1st Am Official ed. VG. $20.00

WATSON, Sydney. *In the Twinkling of an Eye.* nd. Nicholson. VG. P1. $7.50

WATSON, Sydney. *Mark of the Beast.* nd. Nicholson. VG. P1. $7.50

WATSON, Sydney. *Mark of the Beast.* 1933. Revell. dj. EX. P1. $8.00

WATSON, Sydney. *Scarlet & Purple.* nd. Nicholson. dj. VG. P1. $8.00

WATSON, Sydney. *Scarlet & Purple.* 1933. Revell. dj. VG. P1. $8.00

WATSON, T.L. *Building & Ornamental Stones of NC.* 1906. Raleigh. Ils. maps. diagrams. 283 p. $125.00

WATSON, Virginia. *Princess Pocahontas.* 1916. Penn. Ils Wharton. VG. $35.00

WATSON, William. *Style in Arts of China.* 1974. London. Ils. wraps. $10.00

WATSON & DORMAN. *Directory of All Business & Professional Men of Wooster...* 1897. Conneaut, OH. maps. index. 91 p. with map. T5. $45.00

WATSON & REES. *Mystery of the Downs.* nd. Grosset. VG. P1. $7.50

WATSON. *With Cortez the Conqueror.* Ils Schoonover. dj. VG. E2. $18.00

WATTERSON, Henry. *History of Spanish-American War.* 1898. NY. photos. pls. 662 p. VG. T5. $35.00

WATTERSON, Henry. *Marse Henry: Autobiography.* 1919. NY. 2 vols. VG. $30.00

WATTJES & WARNERS. *Amsterdams Bouwkunst en Stadsschoon, 1306-1942.* 1948. Amsterdam. 4to. Dutch text. dj. VG. $25.00

WATTS, Alan. *Watercourse Way.* 1975. Pantheon. Ils 1st ed. dj. EX. $45.00

WATTS, Isaac. *Horae Lyricae Poems.* 1792. Phil. Aitken. 12mo. full leather. G. $55.00

WATTS, Isaac. *Psalms of David.* 1808. Sutton, MA. 400 p. full leather. K1. $12.00

WATTS, Isaac. *Short View of Whole Scripture History...* 1797. Carlisle, PA. $100.00

WATTS, M.S. *Ultimate.* 1962. CA. $17.50

WATTS, M.S. *You Are the Splendor.* 1963. NY. $17.50

WAUCHOPE, Robert. *Handbook of Middle-American Indians.* 1964-1971. Austin. 1st ed. 11 vols. djs. B2. $275.00

WAUER, R.H. *Birds of Big Bend National Park.* 1973. TX U. Ils. map. 223 p. EX. M2. $9.00

WAUER & CARTER. *Birds of Zion National Park & Vicinity.* 1965. Zion Nat Park. Ils. 92 p. VG. M2. $8.00

WAUGH, Alec. *Hot Countries.* 1930. Farrar Rinehart. Ils Ward. $15.00

WAUGH, Arthur. *Georgian Stories.* 1927. 1st ed. G. $75.00

WAUGH, Auberon. *Consider the Lilies.* 1968. Little Brown. 1st Am ed. dj. EX. $25.00

WAUGH, Evelyn. *Basis Seal Rides Again.* 1963. Little Brown. Ltd ed. 1/1000. sgn. VG. $130.00

WAUGH, Evelyn. *Handful of Dust.* 1945. New Directions. New Classics Lib. 12mo. dj. EX. $25.00

WAUGH, Evelyn. *Helena.* 1950. Boston. 1st ed. dj. EX. P3. $20.00

WAUGH, Evelyn. *Helena.* 1950. Chapman Hall. 1st Eng ed. dj. EX. $47.50

WAUGH, Evelyn. *Little Learning.* 1964. Boston. 1st Am ed. dj. VG. $20.00

WAUGH, Evelyn. *Little Learning.* 1964. London. 1st ed. dj. EX. $40.00

WAUGH, Evelyn. *Loved Ones.* 1948. Boston. 1st Am ed. sgn. dj. EX. $25.00

WAUGH, Evelyn. *Men at Arms.* 1952. London. Chapman Hall. presentation. dj. EX. $65.00

WAUGH, Evelyn. *Monsignor Ronald Knox.* 1959. 1st Am ed. EX. $15.00

WAUGH, Evelyn. *Ordeal of Gilbert Pinfold.* 1957. London. 1st ed. dj. EX. $35.00

WAUGH, Evelyn. *Scott-King's Modern Europe.* 1947. London. dj. EX. $40.00

WAUGH, Evelyn. *Tourist in Africa.* 1st ed. dj. VG. $25.00

WAUGH, F.A. *Outdoor Theatres: Design, Construction & Use...* 1917. Boston. Badger. Ils. photos. VG. $12.00

WAUGH, F.A. *TB of Landscape Gardening.* 1922. NY. xl. VG. P3. $25.00

WAUGH, Hillary. *Con Game.* nd. Book Club. dj. VG. P1. $4.00

WAUGH, Hillary. *Eighth Mrs. Bluebeard.* nd. Book Club. dj. VG. P1. $4.00

WAUGH, Hillary. *End of a Party.* 1965. Crime Club. 1st ed. dj. xl. P1. $7.50

WAUGH, Hillary. *Girl on the Run.* 1965. Crime Club. 1st ed. dj. xl. P1. $7.50

WAUGH, Hillary. *Last Seen Wearing.* 1978. CA U. EX. P1. $10.00

WAUGH, Hillary. *Late Mrs. D.* nd. Book Club. dj. xl. P1. $4.00

WAUGH, Hillary. *Merchants of Menace.* nd. Book Club. dj. VG. P1. $5.00

WAUGH, Hillary. *Pure Poison.* 1966. Crime Club. 1st ed. dj. xl. P1. $5.00

WAUGH, Hillary. *Rich Man, Dead Man.* 1956. Crime Club. 1st ed. dj. VG. P1. $15.00

WAUGH & GREENBERG. *Arbor House Celebrity Book of Horror.* c 1981. Arbor House. dj. EX. P1. $30.00

WAUGH & GREENBERG. *Cults!* 1983. Beaufort. 1st ed. dj. EX. P1. $25.00

WAUGH & GREENBERG. *13 Short Horror Novels.* 1987. Bonanza. 1st ed. dj. EX. P1. $15.00

WAY, D. *Spear Fisherman's Handbook.* 1981. London. Hale. Ils 1st ed. 160 p. dj. EX. M2. $13.00

WAY, Frederick Jr. *Pilotin' Comes Natural.* 1943. NY. Ils Cosgrove. 271 p. dj. G. T5. $19.50

WAY, William. *History of the New England Society of Charleston.* 1920. Charleston. 1st ed. gilt cloth. EX. T6. $40.00

WAY. *Allegheny.* 1942. NY. 1st ed. dj. EX. B2. $25.00

WAYLAND, J.W. *History of Shenandoah Co., VA.* 1927. Strasburg. 1st ed. EX. scare. $65.00

WAYLAND, J.W. *Stonewall Jackson's Way.* 1940. photos. maps. 244 p. dj. scarce. J4. $25.00

WAYNE, John. *America, Why I Love Her.* 1977. Ils 1st ed. dj. EX. $25.00

WAYNE, Joseph. *By Gun & Spur.* 1952. Dutton. 1st ed. VG. P1. $10.00

WAYNE, Pilar. *My Life With the Duke.* 1987. McGraw. dj. EX. $15.00

WAYRE, P. *River People.* 1976. Taplinger. Ils 1st Am ed. 189 p. dj. EX. M2. $25.00

WEATHERLY, A.E. *First Hundred Years of Historic Guilford, 1771-1871.* 1971. Ils. 207 p. dj. M. J4. $32.50

WEATHERLY, F.E. *For Old Acquaintance: Autograph Album.* c 1890. London. Ils. 24 p. EX. $35.00

WEATHERS, W.W. *Birds of S CA's Deep Canyons.* 1983. CA U. Ils 1st ed. 266 p. dj. EX. M2. $27.00

WEAVER, E. *Notes on Military Explosives.* 1906. Wiley. 382 p. VG. $30.00

WEAVER, G.S. *Lives & Graves of Our Presidents.* 1883. Ils. 530 p. EX. $12.50

WEAVER, Gordon. *Give Him a Stone.* 1975. NY. Crown. 1st ed. dj. EX. $15.00

WEAVER, J.B. *Call to Action.* 1892. IA Printing. 445 p. EX. $8.00

WEAVER, John. *Secret Memoirs: Historical & Gallant.* 1709. London. full leather. EX. $40.00

WEAVER, Lawrence. *Small Country Houses: Their Repair & Enlargement.* 1914. London. VG. J2. $45.00

WEAVER, M.P. *Aztecs, Maya & Their Predecessors: Archaeology.* 1972. Seminar Pr. Ils. 4to. 347 p. EX. M2. $28.00

WEAVER, Richard. *S Tradition at Bay.* 1968. Book Club. 422 p. dj. J4. $8.50

WEAVER, Tom. *Interviews SF Horror Movie Makers.* 1988. McFarland. 1st ed. EX. P1. $29.95

WEBB, A.P. *Bibliography of Works of Thomas Hardy.* 1916. London. VG. $40.00

WEBB, A.S. *Peninsula.* 1881. NY. 1st ed. 219 p. G. T5. $30.00

WEBB, Charles. *Love, Roger.* 1969. Boston. Houghton Mifflin. dj. EX. $15.00

WEBB, Jack. *Big Sin.* nd. Rinehart. 2nd ed. dj. G. P1. $15.00

WEBB, Jack. *Delicate Darling.* 1959. Rinehart. 1st ed. dj. xl. P1. $5.00

WEBB, Lance. *Discovering Love.* 1959. Nashville. $8.00

WEBB, Mary. *Chinese Lion.* 1937. London. 1/350. slipcase. $75.00

WEBB, P. *Comin' 'Round the Mountain.* 1938. NY. 1st ed. inscr. VG. C4. $35.00

WEBB, Sharon. *Earthchild.* 1982. Atheneum Argo. 1st ed. dj. VG. P1. $15.00

WEBB, W.E. *Buffalo Land: Authentic Account of Discoveries...* 1872. Phil. Hubbard. Ils. 503 p. VG. A3. $80.00

WEBB, W.P. *Handbook of TX.* 1952. Austin. Lakeside Pr. 2 vols. djs. EX. $60.00

WEBB, W.P. *History As High Adventure.* 1969. Austin. Pemberton Pr. 1st ed. dj. EX. T6. $35.00

WEBB, W.P. *TX Rangers.* 1935. Ils. 584 p. red cloth. dj. VG. $45.00

WEBB, Willard. *Crucial Moments of the Civil War.* 1961. 356 p. dj. EX. J4. $8.50

WEBB & JONES. *Annotated Check List of NE Bats.* 1952. KS U. M2. $3.00

WEBBER, A.R. *Early History of Elyria & Her People.* 1930. Elyria. Ils. inscr. 326 p. EX. T5. $42.50

WEBBER, B. *James Orrock: RI Painter, Connoisseur, Collector.* 1903. London. 149 pls. 2 vols. gilt cloth. J2. $200.00

WEBBER, E. *Escape to Utopia: Communal Movement in America.* 1959. NY. Ils 1st ed. 444 p. dj. VG. B2. $17.50

WEBBER, Georgiana. *Anyone for Orchids?* 1978. Schiffer Ltd. dj. EX. $10.00

WEBBER, Malcolm. *Medicine Show.* 1941. Caldwell. Ils Harting. 1st ed. 265 p. dj. T5. $19.50

WEBER, Bruce. *Bruce Weber.* 1983. Twelvetrees Pr. 1st ed. inscr. dj. EX. $55.00

WEBER, C.J. *Hardy Music at Colby.* 1945. Waterville, ME. 1/200. dj. EX. $20.00

WEBER, C.J. *Thomas Hardy in ME.* 1942. Southworth Anthoensen. 1/425. VG. $30.00

WEBER, J.C. *Die Alpen Pflanzen.* 1872. Munchen. Kaizer. 400 pls. 4 vols. VG. $750.00

WEBER, Rubin. *Grave-Maker's House.* nd. Book Club. dj. VG. P1. $3.00

WEBER, W.A. *Homes & Habits of Wild Animals.* 1934. Donahue. 1st ed. dj. G. $30.00

WEBER & SMITH. *Field Guide to S Mushrooms.* 1985. MI U. Ils 1st ed. sgn Weber. 280 p. M2. $5.00

WEBSTER, D.B. *Suicide Special.* 1958. Harrisburg. 1st ed. dj. VG. B2. $35.00

WEBSTER, D.K. *Myth & Man-Eater: Story of the Shark.* 1963. Norton. Ils 1st Am ed. 223 p. VG. M2. $9.00

WEBSTER, Daniel. *Address to Citizens of Pittsburgh, July 9, 1833.* 1833. Boston. 1st ed. 32 p. EX. $55.00

WEBSTER, Daniel. *Letters of Daniel Webster.* Oct., 1902. McClure. TEG. EX. $27.00

WEBSTER, Daniel. *Private Correspondence of Daniel Webster.* 1857. Boston. 2 vols. B7. $75.00

WEBSTER, Daniel. *Remarks of Mr. Webster on Different Occasions...* 1834. WA. 1st ed. disbound pamphlet. $17.50

WEBSTER, F.A.M. *Lord of the Leopards.* nd. Hutchinson. dj. VG. P1. $25.00

WEBSTER, F.A.M. *Slapstick.* 1978. Dell 18009. G. P1. $2.00

WEBSTER, F.A.M. *Slapstick.* 1980. Dell 18009. 3rd ed. VG. P1. $2.50

WEBSTER, H.K. *Quartz Eye.* 1928. Indianapolis. $25.00

WEBSTER, H.T. *Who Dealt This Mess?* 1948. Doubleday. 1st ed. dj. VG. $17.50

WEBSTER, Hutton. *Magic: Sociological Study.* 1948. Stanford. 1st ed. J2. $25.00

WEBSTER, J.D. *Survey of Gulf Coast at Mouth of Rio Grande.* 1850. GPO. maps. wraps. EX. $75.00

WEBSTER, John. *Dutchess of Malfi.* 1945. London. 1/100. VG. $18.00

WEBSTER, Noah. *American Selection of Lessons in Reading & Speaking.* 1805. Hudson Goodwin. 16th ed. 536 p. leather. $55.00

WEBSTER, Noah. *Legacy From Tenerife.* 1984. Doubleday. 1st ed. dj. EX. P1. $12.50

WEBSTER, Noah. *Webster's Dictionary: American Dictionary English Language.* 1850. Springfield. Merriman. 1452 p. G. $125.00

WEBSTER, Noah. *Webster's New Counting House Edition Dictionary.* 1874. Ils. 632 p. VG. $45.00

WEBSTER, Noah. *Webster's New International Dictionary of English Language.* 1949. Springfield. Unabridged 2nd ed. 4to. 3570 p. VG. $100.00

WEBSTER, Noah. *Webster's New International Dictionary of English Language.* 1957. $95.00

WEBSTER, Noah. *Webster's New International Dictionary of English Language.* 1961. 3rd ed. $44.00

WEBSTER, Noah. *3rd International Dictionary of English Language Unabridged.* 1981. Chicago. Britannica. 3 vols. EX. $60.00

WECHSBERG. *Blue Trout & Black Truffles.* 1966. NY. EX. $10.00

WECHSBURG, J. *Glory of the Violin.* 1973. NY. 1st ed. dj. VG. B2. $27.50

WEDGEWOOD. *Revised Statutes of MA.* 1844. Boston. 116 p. K1. $6.00

WEED, C.M. *Butterflies Worth Knowing.* 1919. Doubleday Page. Ils. 286 p. rebound. M2. $14.00

WEED, W.H. *Geology & Ore Deposits of Butte District, MT.* 1912. US Geol Survey. HrdCvr. 25 maps. 262 p. EX. $12.50

WEEDEN, Howard. *Bandanna Ballads.* 1901. NY. Intro Harris. 91 p. B2. $47.50

WEEGEE. *Naked City.* 1945. NY. G. S2. $35.00

WEEGEE. *Naked Holywood.* 1953. NY. dj. EX. P3. $60.00

WEEGEE. *Weege's People.* dj. EX. S2. $65.00

WEEKS, Edward. *Moisie Salmon Club.* 1971. Barre Pub. 1/1500. sgn. boxed. M. $85.00

WEEKS, Morris. *Beer & Brewing in America.* 1949. US Brewers Foundation. EX. P1. $6.00

WEEKS, R.K. *Convict B 14.* 1920. Brentano. VG. P1. $20.00

WEEKS & TREGANOWAN. *Rugs & Carpets of Europe & the W World.* 1969. Phil. Ils 1st ed. 4to. 251 p. dj. VG. $25.00

WEEMS, J.E. *Men Without Countries.* 1969. Houghton. Ils 1st ed. 272 p. dj. EX. M2. $10.00

WEES, Frances Shelley. *Country of the Strangers.* 1960. Doubleday. 1st Review ed. dj. VG. P1. $20.00

WEES, Frances Shelley. *M'Lord I Am Not Guilty.* nd. Book Club. dj. VG. P1. $4.00

WEGMANN, Edward. *Design & Construction of Dams.* 1903. NY. Ils. 4to. 254 p. T5. $95.00

WEID & GREBNER. *Eclectic Series, German Second Reader.* 1886. 143 p. TB. EX. $5.00

WEIDHORN, Manfred. *Sword & Pen: Survey of Writings of Sir Winston Churchill.* 1974. NM U. 1st ed. dj. EX. $25.00

WEIDLER, A. *Contributions Toward Medical Psychology.* 1953. NY. 2 vols. $57.00

WEIGALL, Arthur. *Glory of the Pharaohs.* 1923. Putnam. Ils 1st ed. G. $20.00

WEIGLEY, Russell. *American Way of War.* 1973. NY. 1st ed. dj. VG. $25.00

WEIK, Jesse. *Real Lincoln: Portrait.* 1922. Houghton. G. $30.00

WEIL, Simone. *Notebooks.* 1956. London. 2 vols. djs. VG. $40.00

WEILER, Clemens. *Alexej Jawlensky: Kopfe, Gesichte, Meditationen.* 1970. Verlag. Ils. dj. D2. $150.00

WEINER, A.S. *Blood Groups & Blood Transfusion.* nd. Thomas. 1st ed. VG. $55.00

WEINGARTEN, A. *Sky Is Falling.* 1977. NY. Ils 1st ed. 260 p. dj. VG. B2. $17.50

WEINSTEIN, Howard. *Covenant of the Crown.* nd. Book Club. dj. VG. P1. $5.00

WEINSTEIN & BOOTH. *Collection, Use & Care of Historical Photographs.* 1982. Nashville. 3rd print. 224 p. dj. EX. $12.00

WEIRAUCH, Anna Elisabet. *Scorpion.* 1932. Greenberg. VG. P1. $10.00

WEISGARD, L. *Cinderella.* 1938. NY. dj. VG. $30.00

WEISHUHN, L.L. *Annotated Bibliography of TX White-Tailed Deer Reasearch.* 1979. TX Parks/Wildlife. 82 p. EX. M2. $7.00

WEISS, David. *Sacred & Profane.* 1968. NY. 1st ed. dj. VG. B2. $20.00

WEISS, Richard. *World Without Frontiers.* 1940. Sydney. $12.50

WEITENKAMPF, Frank. *Illustrated Book.* 1938. Cambridge. Ils. 314 p. dj. VG. $35.00

WEITZMAN, D. *Underfoot.* 1976. Scribner. 1st ed. VG. $20.00

WEITZMANN, Kurt. *Ancient Book Illumination.* 1959. Harvard. 1st ed. dj. J2. $25.00

WELCH, Jack. *History of Hancock Co., VA & WV.* 1963. Wheeling. Ils 1st ed. 202 p. G. T5. $22.50

WELCH, James. *Riding the Earth Boy 40.* 1976. NY. Harper. 1st ed. dj. EX. $20.00

WELCH, Spencer Glascow. *Confederate Surgeon's Letters to His Wife.* 1954. reprint of 1911 ed. M. J4. $32.50

WELCH. *Bibliography of American Children's Books Prior to 1821.* 1972. $65.00

WELCHMAN, Gordon. *Hut Six Story. Breaking the Enigma Code.* 1982. NY. dj. EX. $20.00

WELD, E.F. *Ransomed Bride: A Tale.* 1946. NY. 1st ed. $50.00

WELD, Isaac. *Travels Through States of N Ameria & Provinces...Canada...* 1800. 3rd ed. pls. maps. plans. 8vo. 3 vols. VG. $425.00

WELK & MC GEEHAN. *Wunnerful, Wunnerful!* 1971. Prentice Hall. 294 p. dj. VG. M1. $9.50

WELKER, R.H. *Birds & Men: American Birds in Science, Art, Literature.* 1966. Atheneum. Ils. 230 p. EX. M2. $5.00

WELLARD, J. *Man in a Helmet.* 1947. London. Ils 1st ed. dj. VG. $25.00

WELLBY, M.S. *Twixt Sirdar & Menelik.* 1901. NY. 1st ed. inscr. 401 p. VG. $50.00

WELLER, M.C. *Island Waterfowl.* 1980. IA U. Ils 1st ed. 121 p. dj. EX. M2. $17.00

WELLES, Gideon. *Diary of Gideon Welles.* 1911. Boston. 1st ed. 3 vols. $65.00

WELLES, R.E. & F.B. *Bighorn of Death Valley.* 1961. Nat Park Service. Ils. 242 p. M2. $11.00

WELLINGTON, A.M. *Economic Theory of Location of Railways*. 1899. 6th ed. 980 p. $55.00

WELLMAN, Manly Wade. *After Dark*. nd. Book Club. dj. EX. P1. $4.50

WELLMAN, Manly Wade. *Cahena*. 1986. Doubleday. 1st ed. dj. EX. P1. $15.00

WELLMAN, Manly Wade. *Lonely Vigils*. 1981. Carcosa. 1st ed. sgn. dj. EX. P1. $125.00

WELLMAN, Manly Wade. *Sleuth Patrol*. 1947. NY. 1st ed. dj. EX. $20.00

WELLMAN, Manly Wade. *Unknown Lands*. 1956. Holiday House. xl. G. P1. $10.00

WELLMAN, Manly Wade. *Valley So Low*. 1987. Doubleday. 1st ed. dj. RS. EX. P1. $17.50

WELLMAN, Manly Wade. *What Dreams May Come*. 1983. Doubleday. 1st ed. dj. EX. $8.50

WELLMAN, Manly Wade. *Worse Things Waiting*. 1973. Carcosa. 1st ed. sgn. dj. EX. P1. $150.00

WELLMAN, P.I. *Iron Mistress*. 1951. Doubleday. Book Club ed. dj. VG. $10.00

WELLMAN, P.I. *Span of Evil*. 1946. NY. 1st ed. dj. VG. $22.50

WELLMAN, P.I. *Trampling Herd*. 1939. NY. 1st ed. inscr. EX. $35.00

WELLS, Carolyn. *Affair at Flower Acres*. nd. Doubleday Doran. VG. P1. $15.00

WELLS, Carolyn. *All at Sea*. 1927. Lippincott. G. P1. $15.00

WELLS, Carolyn. *Broken O*. nd. Burt. VG. P1. $7.50

WELLS, Carolyn. *Bronze Hand*. nd. Burt. G. P1. $6.00

WELLS, Carolyn. *Deep Lake Mystery*. 1929. Collier. G. P1. $7.50

WELLS, Carolyn. *Importance of Being Murdered*. 1939. Lippincott. xl. P1. $7.50

WELLS, Carolyn. *Importance of Being Murdered*. 1939. Phil. 1st ed. dj. VG. T1. $30.00

WELLS, Carolyn. *In the Tiger's Cage*. nd. Burt. VG. P1. $7.50

WELLS, Carolyn. *Missing Link*. 1939. Triangle. dj. VG. P1. $10.00

WELLS, Carolyn. *Missing Link*. 1939. Triangle. G. P1. $6.00

WELLS, Carolyn. *Money Musk*. 1936. Lippincott. G. P1. $10.00

WELLS, Carolyn. *Skeleton at the Feast*. nd. Burt. G. P1. $5.00

WELLS, Carolyn. *Sleeping Dogs*. nd. Collier. G. P1. $7.50

WELLS, Dean Faulkner. *Great American Writers' Cookbook*. 1981. Oxford, MS. Yoknapatawpha. 1st ed. sgn. VG. T6. $30.00

WELLS, H.G. *Autocracy of Mr. Parham*. 1930. Doubleday. 1st ed. dj. G. P1. $45.00

WELLS, H.G. *Bealby*. 1915. Macmillan. VG. P1. $25.00

WELLS, H.G. *Christian Albertina's Father*. 1925. London. later print. sgn. dj. EX. $90.00

WELLS, H.G. *Collector's Book of SF by H.G. Wells*. 1978. Castle. dj. EX. P1. $10.00

WELLS, H.G. *Complete SF Treasury of H.G. Wells*. 1978. Avenel. dj. EX. P1. $10.00

WELLS, H.G. *Croquet Player*. 1937. Viking. dj. VG. P1. $12.50

WELLS, H.G. *Door in the Wall*. 1922. Ltd ed. 1/600. very scarce. S2. $600.00

WELLS, H.G. *Food of the Gods*. nd. (c 1909) Nelsons. sgn. VG. P1. $350.00

WELLS, H. G. *Food of the Gods*. 1923. Collins. G. P1. $15.00

WELLS, H.G. *History of Mr. Polly*. nd. Collins. leather bdg. boxed. VG. P1. $25.00

WELLS, H.G. *History of Mr. Polly*. 1957. Folio Soc. Ils Ribbons. 1st ed. slipcase. C1. $14.00

WELLS, H.G. *In the Days of the Comet*. nd. Collins. G. P1. $7.00

WELLS, H.G. *In the Days of the Comet*. 1906. NY. Century. 1st ed. VG. $125.00

WELLS, H.G. *Invisible Man*. nd. Nelson. G. P1. $5.00

WELLS, H.G. *Meanwhile, a Picture of a Lady*. 1927. London. 1st ed. VG. $50.00

WELLS, H.G. *Men Like Gods*. 1923. London. 1st ed. 2nd bdg. dj. EX. $100.00

WELLS, H.G. *Mr. Blettsworthy on Rampole Island*. 1928. Ernest Benn. 1st Eng ed. dj. VG. P1. $20.00

WELLS, H.G. *Mr. Britling Sees It Through*. 1916. Macmillan. 5th print. VG. P1. $10.00

WELLS, H.G. *Mr. Britling Sees It Through*. 1916. Macmillan. 8th print. G. P1. $5.50

WELLS, H.G. *New Worlds for Old*. 1908. London. 1st ed. VG. $40.00

WELLS, H.G. *Outline of History*. 1929. Garden City. 1 vol ed. G. $12.50

WELLS, H.G. *Passionate Friends*. 1913. Harper. 1st ed. VG. P1. $40.00

WELLS, H.G. *Salvaging of Civilization*. 1921. Cassell. VG. P1. $20.00

WELLS, H.G. *Science of Life*. 1931. NY. 1/750. sgn. 4 vols. $75.00

WELLS, H.G. *Science of Life*. 1931. NY. 4 vols. VG. $30.00

WELLS, H.G. *Science of Life*. 1934. Garden City. Ils. 1514 p. VG. $15.00

WELLS, H.G. *Secret Places of the Heart*. London. 1st ed. dj. EX. $125.00

WELLS, H.G. *Secret Places of the Heart*. 1922. Macmillan. VG. P1. $30.00

WELLS, H.G. *Seven Famous Novels by H.G. Wells*. 1934. Knopf. 1st ed. VG. P1. $15.00

WELLS, H.G. *Shape of Things To Come*. 1933. Hutchinson. VG. P1. $60.00

WELLS, H.G. *Soul of a Bishop*. 1917. Macmillan. 1st ed. VG. P1. $15.00

WELLS, H.G. *Tales of Space & Time*. 1899. Doubleday McClure. 1st ed. EX. $100.00

WELLS, H.G. *Tales of the Unexpected*. nd. Collins. VG. P1. $10.00

WELLS, H.G. *Tales of Wonder*. nd. Collins. G. P1. $9.00

WELLS, H.G. *Things To Come: Film by H.G. Wells*. 1935. Macmillan. Movie ed. VG. P1. $75.00

WELLS, H.G. *Time Machine*. 1931. Random House. Ils Dwiggins. 1st ed. EX. $20.00

WELLS, H.G. *Tono Bungay*. nd. Collins. leather bdg. boxed. VG. P1. $25.00

WELLS, H.G. *Tono Bungay*. 1934. Collins. 12th print. VG. P1. $7.00

WELLS, H.G. *Tono Bungay*. 1949. Collins. dj. VG. P1. $10.00

WELLS, H.G. *Valley of Spiders*. nd. Novel Lib. dj. VG. P1. $25.00

WELLS, H.G. *War in the Air*. George Bell. Ils 4th ed. G. P1. $30.00

WELLS, H.G. *War of the Worlds*. 1954. Whitman. VG. P1. $7.50

WELLS, H.G. *War That Will End War*. 1914. Duffield. 1st ed. VG. P1. $35.00

WELLS, H.G. *War That Will End War*. 1914. NY. G. $12.00

WELLS, H.G. *Wife of Sir Isaac Harman*. 1914. Macmillan. 1st ed. G. P1. $7.50

WELLS, H.G. *Works*. 1924-1926. Atlantic ed. 1/1050. sgn. 20 vols. $175.00

WELLS, H.G. *World of W. Clissold*. 1926. NY. 1st ed. 2 vols. djs. VG. $20.00

WELLS, H.G. *World Set Free*. 1914. NY. Dutton. 1st Am ed. dj. EX. $40.00

WELLS, Helen. *Cherry Ames, Senior Nurse*. nd. Grosset. VG. P1. $5.00

WELLS, Helen. *Vicki Finds the Answer*. nd. Grosset. VG. P1. $4.00

WELLS, Horace. *Discovery of Nitrous Oxide Gas*. 1852. Hartford. wraps. G. $85.00

WELLS, J.M. *Chisholm Massacre*. 1878. WA. 12mo. 331 p. G. G2. $42.00

WELLS, L.E. *Brand of Evil*. 1971. Berkley X2071. 2nd ed. pb. P1. $3.00

WELLS, R.B.D. *New Illustrated Handbook of Phrenology*. 1899. London. Vickers. sgn. gilt bdg. M1. $45.00

WELLS, R.F. *With Ceasar's Legions*. 1923. Boston. Ils Frank Merrill. VG. C1. $9.50

WELLS, Stuart. *SF & Heroic Fantasy Author Index*. 1978. Purple Unicorn. EX. P1. $10.00

WELLS, Tobias. *Dinky Died*. 1970. Doubleday. 1st ed. dj. EX. P1. $12.50

WELLS, Tobias. *How To Kill a Man*. 1972. Crime Club. 1st ed. dj. xl. P1. $5.00

WELLS, Tobias. *Young Can Die Protesting*. 1969. Crime Club. 1st ed. dj. xl. P1. $5.00

WELLS, W. *Life & Public Services of Samuel Adams*. 1865. 1st ed. 3 vols. G. $110.00

WELLS & HOOPER. *Modern Cabinet Work*. 1910. London/NY. Ils. 4to. 384 p. VG. C4. $75.00

WELLS. *Manners, Culture & Dress*. 1890. 502 p. K1. $13.50

WELLS-GOSLING, N. *Flying Squirrels: Gliders in the Dark*. 1985. Smithsonian. Ils. 128 p. maps. EX. M2. $24.00

WELSH, Herbert. *Report of Visit to Navajo, Pueblo & Hualapais Indians...* 1885. Phil. Indian Rights Assn. wraps. xl. A3. $120.00

WELTY, Earl. *76 Bonanza: Life & Times of Union Oil Co.* 1966. CA. 1st ed. 4to. 352 p. dj. EX. $23.00

WELTY, Eudora. *Acrobats in the Park*. 1980. CA. Deluxe ed. 1/100. sgn. EX. $125.00

WELTY, Eudora. *Acrobats in the Park*. 1980. Lord John. 1/100. sgn/#d. special bdg. M. $150.00

WELTY, Eudora. *Bride of Innisfallen*. 1955. NY. Harcourt. 1st ed. sgn. dj. VG. $30.00

WELTY, Eudora. *Bye-Bye Brevoort: A Skit*. 1980. Jackson. New Stage/Palaemon. 1/400. sgn. EX. $95.00

WELTY, Eudora. *Curtain of Green & Other Stories*. 1979. Harcourt Brace. 1st Harvest ed. sgn. pb. wraps. $25.00

WELTY, Eudora. *Delta Wedding*. 1946. NY. Review 1st ed. VG. $40.00

WELTY, Eudora. *Eye of the Story*. 1978. NY. 1st trade ed. dj. EX. $25.00

WELTY, Eudora. *Fairy Tale of the Natchez Trace*. 1975. Jackson. MS Hist Soc. 1st ed. 1/1000. EX. $65.00

WELTY, Eudora. *Golden Apples*. 1949. Harcourt. 1st ed. dj. EX. $45.00

WELTY, Eudora. *Losing Battles*. 1970. NY. 1st ed. dj. EX. $55.00

WELTY, Eudora. *Losing Battles*. 1970. NY. 1st ed. dj. VG. $35.00

WELTY, Eudora. *Optimist's Daughter*. 1st ed. dj. VG. B7. $40.00

WELTY, Eudora. *Ponder Heart*. 1954. London. 1st ed. dj. VG. $85.00

WELTY, Eudora. *Rober Bridegroom*. 1942. Doubleday. 1st ed. EX. $25.00

WELTY, Eudora. *Rober Bridegroom*. 1978. Harvest. 1st ed. dj. $25.00

WELTY, Eudora. *Short Stories*. 1950. NY. Ltd 1st ed. 1/1500. wraps. $75.00

WELTY, Eudora. *Three Papers on Fiction*. 1962. Northampton. wraps. $65.00

WELTY, Eudora. *Wide Net*. 1945. London. Bodley Head. 1st ed. VG. $75.00

WELTY, J.C. *Life of Birds*. 1979. Saunders. photos. map. 623 p. VG. M2. $12.00

WELZL, Jan. *Thirty Years in Golden N.* 1932. Macmillan. VG. P1. $12.50

WELZL, Jan. *Thirty Years in Golden N.* 1932. Macmillan. 1st ed. fld map. 336 p. G. M2. $9.00

WEMMER, C.M. *Biology & Management of Cervidae*. 1987. Smithsonian. Ils 577 p. M. M2. $40.00

WENDELL, Barrett. *Rankell's Remains*. 1887. Boston. EX. $15.00

WENDT, E.C. *Asiatic Cholera*. 1885. NY. Wood. 1st ed. VG. $25.00

WENDT, H. *In Search of Adam*. 1956. Houghton. Ils 1st ed. 540 p. VG. M2. $7.00

WENDT, H. *Sex Life of Animals*. 1965. Simon Schuster. Ils. 383 p. EX. M2. $6.00

WENIGER, D. *Cacti of TX & Neighboring States*. 1984. TX U. Ils 1st ed. 356 p. dj. EX. M2. $16.00

WENTWORTH, G.A. *Elements of Algebra*. 1886. Ginn. 510 p. TB. G. $3.00

WENTWORTH, G.A. *New School of Algebra*. 1900. Ginn. 407 p. EX. $6.00

WENTWORTH, G.A. *Plane & Solid Geometry*. 1900. Ginn. 473 p. EX. $5.00

WENTWORTH, G.A. *Shorter Course in Algebra*. 1894. Ginn. 250 p. EX. $3.00

WENTWORTH, Patricia. *Alington Inheritance*. nd. Book Club. dj. VG. P1. $4.00

WENTWORTH, Patricia. *Gazebo*. nd. Book Club. dj. VG. P1. $6.00

WENTWORTH, Patricia. *Gazebo*. nd. Book Club. xl. P1. $3.00

WENTWORTH, Patricia. *Gazebo*. 1958. London. Hodder. 1st ed. dj. VG. $30.00

WENTWORTH, Patricia. *Pilgrim's Rest*. 1948. Hodder Stoughton. 1st ed. G. P1. $15.00

WERFEL, Franz. *Der Abituriententag. Die Geschichte Einer Jugenschuld*. 1928. Bern. Zsolnays. 1st ed. red cloth. EX. $50.00

WERLER, J.E. *Poisonous Snakes of TX*. 1978. TX Parks/Wildlife. Ils. 53 p. M2. $7.00

WERNER, A. *Butterflies & Moths*. 1956. Random House. 36 pls. 4to. 175 p. dj. EX. M2. $45.00

WERNER, E.E. *Erinnerungen aus Meinem Leben*. 1897. Akron. photos. 259 p. AEG. VG. T5. $75.00

WERNER, Herman. *On the W Frontier With the US Cavalry*. 1934. np. 1st ed. sgn. 98 p. wraps. T5. $37.50

WERNER, Jane. *Walt Disney's Living Desert*. 1954. NY. Ils 1st ed. 8vo. $25.00

WERNER, M.R. *Tammany Hall*. 1929. Doubleday. Ils 1st ed. 586 p. $12.00

WERTENBACKER, C.C. *Invasion!* 1944. London/NY. Appleton. 1st ed. 8vo. VG. $25.00

WERTENBAKER, T.J. *VA Under the Stuarts, 1607-1688*. 1914. Princeton. 271 p. $45.00

WERTHAM, Frederic. *Seduction of the Innocent*. 1954. Ils 1st ed. xl. G. $40.00

WESCHER, Paul. *Time in Waste Basket: Poems, Collages, Parables & Dreams*. 1950. Big Sur. Ils. D2. $25.00

WESLEY & HOMER. *Wesley Offering; or, Wesley & His Times*. 1852. Auburn. Derby Miller. 12mo. G. $15.00

WESLEY. *Extract of Journal: Travel in GA & His Return to London*. 1755. London. fair. $110.00

WEST, Geoffrey. *Charles Darwin: A Portrait*. 1938. Yale. 1st ed. J2. $25.00

WEST, H.F. *Nature Writers: Guide to Richer Reading*. 1939. Stephen Daye. 1st ed. dj. J2. $22.50

WEST, Jerry. *Happy Hollister Series*. 1950s. Doubleday. 20 vols. djs. VG. $90.00

WEST, Jessamyn. *Cress Delahanty*. 1954. London. 1st ed. dj. VG. $40.00

WEST, Michael. *Clairdelune & Other Troubadour Romances*. c 1924. Harrap. Ils Evelyn Paul. 1st ed. VG. C1. $59.00

WEST, Nathanael. *Day of the Locust*. 1951. London. 1st ed. dj. EX. $45.00

WEST, R. *Black Lamb & Gray Falcon*. 1941. NY. 2nd print. 2 vols. djs. EX. $40.00

WEST, R.S. *Gideon Welles: Lincoln's Navy Department*. 1943. Bobbs Merrill. Ils 1st ed. 379 p. dj. EX. M2. $20.00

WEST, R.S. *Lincoln's Scapegoat General: Life of B.F. Butler, 1818-1893*. 1965. 1st ed. 462 p. VG. $12.50

WEST, Steven. *Psycho-Calisthentics*. 1975. NY. $15.00

WEST, Tom. *Bushwhack Basin*. 1956. W Novel Classic. VG. P1. $12.50

WEST, Tom. *Gunsmoke Gold*. 1952. Dutton. 1st ed. dj. VG. P1. $7.50

WEST, Wallace. *Memory Bank*. 1961. Avalon. dj. VG. P1. $15.00

WEST, Wallace. *Time Lockers*. 1964. Avalon. dj. xl. P1. $5.00

WEST, Wallace. *Time Lockers*. 1964. Avalon. 1st ed. dj. VG. $8.50

WEST & MACLEAN. *Dark Wing*. 1979. Atheneum. 1st ed. dj. EX. P1. $15.00

WEST. *World Is Made of Glass*. 1983. NY. Morrow. 1st ed. 322 p. dj. VG. $13.00

WESTBROOK, Mary. *History of HI Islands*. 1924. 1st ed. inscr. VG. $20.00

WESTCOTE, Rodman. *Fancies & Phantasies*. 1926. NY. $5.00

WESTERMAN, Percy F. *Captain Cain*. 1945. Musson. dj. VG. P1. $10.00

WESTERMAN, Percy F. *Desolation Island*. nd. Blackie. 4 pl. VG. P1. $9.25

WESTERMAN, Percy F. *New Percy F. Westerman Omnibus Book*. nd. Blackie. VG. P1. $15.00

WESTERMEIER, C.P. *Who Rush to Glory: Cowboy Volunteers of 1898*. 1958. Caxton. Ils. 272 p. EX. M2. $15.00

WESTING, Frederick. *Erie Power: Steam & Diesel Locomotives, 1840-1970*. 1970. Medina, OH. Ils. 447 p. dj. VG. T5. $37.50

WESTING, Frederick. *Locomotives That Baldwin Built*. 1966. Bonanza. Ils. 192 p. pb. $14.00

WESTING, Frederick. *Locomotives That Baldwin Built*. 1966. NY. dj. EX. $25.00

WESTLAKE, Donald E. *Bank Shot*. nd. Book Club. dj. VG. P1. $4.00

WESTLAKE, Donald E. *Brothers' Keepers*. 1975. Evans. dj. xl. P1. $7.50

WESTLAKE, Donald E. *Busy Body*. nd. Book Club. dj. VG. P1. $4.00

WESTLAKE, Donald E. *Busy Body*. 1966. Boardman. dj. VG. P1. $25.00

WESTLAKE, Donald E. *Cops & Robbers*. nd. Book Club. dj. VG. P1. $4.50

WESTLAKE, Donald E. *Curious Facts Preceeding My Execution*. 1968. NY. dj. VG. $30.00

WESTLAKE, Donald E. *Enough*. 1977. Evans. 1st ed. dj. xl. P1. $7.50

WESTLAKE, Donald E. *Fugitive Pigeon*. nd. Book Club. VG. P1. $4.00

WESTLAKE, Donald E. *God Save the Mark*. nd. Book Club. dj. xl. P1. $3.00

WESTLAKE, Donald E. *High Adventure*. 1985. NY. 1st ed. sgn. dj. EX. $20.00

WESTLAKE, Donald E. *Killy*. 1963. Random House. 1st ed. VG. P1. $30.00

WESTLAKE, Donald E. *Levine*. 1984. Mysterious Pr. 1st ed. dj. VG. P1. $12.50

WESTLAKE, Donald E. *Likely Story*. 1984. Penzler. 1st ed. dj. xl. P1. $6.00

WESTLAKE, Donald E. *Somebody Owes Me Money*. nd. Book Club. dj. VG. P1. $5.00

WESTLAKE, Donald E. *Under an English Heaven*. Simon Schuster. 2nd ed. dj. EX. P1. $12.50

WESTLEY, G.D. *Planning the Location of Urban-Suburban Rail Lines*. 1978. 161 p. $14.00

WESTMACOTT, Mary. *Giants' Bread*. 1930. Doubleday. 1st Am ed. VG. $50.00

WESTON, Carolyn. *Rouse the Demon*. Random House. 2nd ed. dj. VG. P1. $7.50

WESTON, Edward. *Daybook. Vol. 1: Mexico*. 1961. Eastman House Monograph II. $85.00

WESTON, Edward. *His Life & Photographs*. 1979. NY. Revised ed. oblong folio. dj. $75.00

WESTON, Edward. *Nudes*. 1977. Review ed. dj. EX. S2. $150.00

WESTON, Edward. *Nudes*. 1977. NY. Millerton. 1st trade ed. dj. EX. $95.00

WESTON, Garnett. *Hidden Portal*. nd. Collier. VG. P1. $10.00

WESTON, Garnett. *Murder in Haste*. 1935. Stokes. G. P1. $8.00

WESTON, Jessie L. *Arthurian Romances Unrepresented in Malory, No. III*. 1910. London. Nutt. Ils 2nd imp. VG. scarce. C1. $24.00

WESTON, Jessie L. *Chief Middle-English Poets*. 1914. 1st ed. VG. C1. $9.50

WESTON, Jessie L. *From Ritual to Romance*. 1941. NY. HrdCvr ed. VG. C1. $39.00

WESTON, Jessie L. *Quest of the Holy Grail*. 1913. London. Bell. 1st ed. VG. C1. $75.00

WESTON, Jessie L. *Romance, Vision & Satire*. 1912. Boston/NY. 1st ed. red cloth. C1. $21.50

WESTON, Jessie L. *Romance Cycle of Charlemagne & His Peers*. 1905. London. 2nd ed. VG. rare. C1. $19.50

WESTON, Peter. *Andromeda 2*. 1977. Dobson. 1st ed. dj. EX. P1. $12.50

WESTON, T.A. *Practical Carnation Culture*. 1931. NY. Ils 1st ed. EX. $15.00

WESTON & WESTON. *CA & the W.* 1940. Duell Sloan. 1st ed. VG. $70.00

WESTON & WESTON. *CA & the W.* 1940. Duell Sloan. 1st ed. 4to. 127 p. dj. M. $150.00

WESTON & WESTON. *Camera Pictures of Malta.* nd. Middlesbrough, England. fair. $30.00

WESTWOOD, J.O. *Butterflies of Great Britain With Their Transformations.* 1887. London. Routledge. Ils. pls. 140 p. EX. M2. $465.00

WETANSON, Burt. *Hunters.* 1978. Doubleday. 1st ed. dj. EX. P1. $10.00

WETHERELL, John. *Adventures of John Wetherll.* 1953. Doubleday. 1st ed. dj. VG. $30.00

WETJEN, Albert. *Youth Walks on the Highway.* 1930. Heron Pr. Ils Maxwell. 1/750. slipcase. EX. $45.00

WETMORE, A. *Birds of the Republic of Panama. Part 1.* 1965. Smithsonian. Ils. 484 p. EX. M2. $30.00

WETMORE, A. *Birds of the Republic of Panama. Part 2.* 1965. Smithsonian. Ils. 606 p. EX. M2. $30.00

WETMORE, A. *Last of Great Scouts (Buffalo Bill).* 1899. Chicago. Ils Remington/ Deming. G. $35.00

WETMORE, H.C. *Last of the Great Scouts: Life of Col. William F. Cody...* 1899. Duluth. Ils 2nd ed. VG. $50.00

WETMORE & GREY. *Last of the Great Scouts.* 1918. Grosset Dunlap. 333 p. EX. $10.00

WETZEL, F.D. *Epistle to White Christmas.* 1948. Phil. Christian Education Pr. 96 p. dj. $6.50

WETZEL, George T. *Gothic Horror & Other Weird Tales.* 1978. Weirdbook. 1/250. HrdCvr ed. P1. $35.00

WEULESSEE, G. *Le Japan d'Aujourd.* 1905. Paris. 12mo. 364 p. VG. B1. $40.00

WEVERKA, Robert. *One Minute to Eternity.* 1968. Morrow. dj. VG. P1. $7.50

WEY, Francis. *Rome.* nd. London. New ed. 72 pls. J2. $15.00

WEYER, E.M. *Strangest Creatures on Earth.* 1953. Sheridan. 255 p. VG. M2. $3.00

WEYGAND, Maxime. *Historie de l'Armie Francaise.* 1938. np. (Paris) 1/500. 4to. VG. $100.00

WEYGANDT, Cornelius. *White Hills.* 1934. NY. Ils 1st ed. 399 p. G. T5. $35.00

WEYGOLDT, P. *Biology of Pseudoscorpions.* 1969. Harvard. Ils. 145 p. xl. M2. $10.00

WHALEN, M.J. *Amateur Gunsmithing.* 1924. WA. 1st ed. VG. $20.00

WHALEN, Phillip. *You Didn't Even Try.* 1967. Coyote. wraps. VG. $12.50

WHALEY, Barton. *Code Word Barbarossa.* 1963. MIT Pr. dj. VG. M1. $17.50

WHALLEY, J.I. *Cobwebs To Catch Flies.* 1975. CA U. Ils. 163 p. dj. VG. $15.00

WHAN, M.D. *Edge of Taos Desert.* 1937. NY. Ils 1st ed. dj. VG. B2. $30.00

WHARTON, David. *AK Gold Rush.* 1972. Bloomington. dj. EX. $15.00

WHARTON, Edith. *Book of the Homeless.* 1916. 1st trade ed. pls. EX. $60.00

WHARTON, Edith. *Children.* 1928. NY. 1st ed. 1st print. dj. M. $50.00

WHARTON, Edith. *Children.* 1928. NY. Appleton. 1st ed. VG. $10.00

WHARTON, Edith. *Descent of Man.* 1904. NY. 1st ed. EX. $75.00

WHARTON, Edith. *Ethan Frome.* 1922. NY. Scribner. VG. $20.00

WHARTON, Edith. *Gods Arrive.* 1932. NY. 1st ed. dj. EX. P3. $75.00

WHARTON, Edith. *Human Nature.* 1933. NY. 1st ed. dj. EX. $25.00

WHARTON, Edith. *In Morocco.* 1920. Scribner. G. $35.00

WHARTON, Edith. *Italian Backgrounds.* 1905. NY. 1st ed. EX. $25.00

WHARTON, Edith. *Italian Villas & Their Gardens.* 1904. NY. Century. Ils Parrish. 1st ed. VG. J2. $200.00

WHARTON, Edith. *Old NY. The Spark.* 1924. NY/London. 1st ed. early state. dj. EX. $20.00

WHARTON, Edith. *Son at the Front.* 1923. NY. 1st ed. 1st issue. dj. VG. scarce. $130.00

WHARTON, Edith. *Tales of Men & Ghosts.* 1914. Scribner. EX. P1. $30.00

WHARTON, William. *Birdy.* 1979. NY/London. 1st ed. dj. EX. $30.00

WHARTON, William. *Dad.* 1981. London. 1st ed. dj. EX. $20.00

WHARTON, William. *Midnight Clear.* 1982. NY. 1st Am ed. dj. VG. $20.00

WHARTON & CODMAN. *Decoration of Houses.* 1902. Scribner. VG. $50.00

WHEAT, C.I. *Shirley Letters From CA Mines 1851-1852.* 1970. NY. Knopf. Ils. 216 p. VG. A3. $25.00

WHEAT, C.I. *Trailing the Forty-Niners Through Death Valley.* 1939. San Francisco. Ils. map. 37 p. wraps. A3. $60.00

WHEAT, Marvin. *Travels on W Slopes of Mexican Cordilla.* 1857. San Francisco. EX. B1. $300.00

WHEATLEY, Dennis. *Bill for the Use of a Body.* 1964. Hutchinson. 1st ed. dj. VG. P1. $15.00

WHEATLEY, Dennis. *Codeword Golden Fleece.* 1947. Universal Books. VG. P1. $3.00

WHEATLEY, Dennis. *Codeword Golden Fleece.* 1952. Hutchinson. 3rd ed. G. P1. $7.50

WHEATLEY, Dennis. *Curtain of Fear.* nd. Book Club. dj. G. P1. $2.75

WHEATLEY, Dennis. *Curtain of Fear.* 1953. Hutchinson. 1st ed. dj. VG. P1. $30.00

WHEATLEY, Dennis. *Dark Secret of Josephine.* 1955. Hutchinson. VG. P1. $15.00

WHEATLEY, Dennis. *Eunuch of Stamboul.* 1935. Boston. AP. dj. VG. $50.00

WHEATLEY, Dennis. *Haunting of Toby Jugg.* 1951. Hutchinson. 3rd ed. dj. G. P1. $25.00

WHEATLEY, Dennis. *Ka of Gifford Hillary.* nd. Book Club. dj. VG. P1. $4.25

WHEATLEY, Dennis. *Man Who Missed the War.* 1946. Book Club. dj. VG. P1. $7.50

WHEATLEY, Dennis. *Man Who Missed the War.* 1953. Hutchinson. 3rd ed. VG. P1. $12.00

WHEATLEY, Dennis. *Murder Off Miami.* nd. Hutchinson. reprint. P1. $20.00

WHEATLEY, Dennis. *Rape of Venice.* London. 1st ed. dj. EX. $20.00

WHEATLEY, Dennis. *Rising Storm.* nd. Hutchinson. G. P1. $12.50

WHEATLEY, Dennis. *Secret War.* 1954. Hutchinson. 8th print. dj. VG. P1. $10.00

WHEATLEY, Dennis. *Star of Ill-Omen.* 1952. Hutchinson. 1st ed. dj. VG. P1. $40.00

WHEATLEY, Dennis. *Strange Conflict.* 1950. Hutchinson. dj. G. P1. $12.50

WHEATLEY, Dennis. *Strange Conflict.* 1952. Hutchinson. dj. VG. P1. $25.00

WHEATLEY, Dennis. *Strange Story of Linda Lee.* nd. Book Club. dj. VG. P1. $5.00

WHEATLEY, Dennis. *Such Power Is Dangerous.* 1965. Hutchinson. 10th print. dj. xl. P1. $5.00

WHEATLEY, Dennis. *They Found Atlantis.* 1954. Hutchinson. 7th print. VG. P1. $10.00

WHEATLEY, Dennis. *To the Devil: A Daughter.* 1953. Hutchinson. 2nd ed. dj. VG. P1. $30.00

WHEATLEY, Dennis. *Total War.* 1942. London. 1st ed. inscr/sgn. wraps. $30.00

WHEATLEY, Dennis. *Vendetta in Spain.* 1961. Book Club. VG. P1. $5.00

WHEATLEY, Dennis. *Vendetta in Spain.* 1961. Hutchinson. dj. VG. P1. $20.00

WHEATLEY, H.B. *How To Form a Library.* 1886. London. $15.00

WHEATLEY, H.B. *Literary Blunders.* 1905. London. $20.00

WHEATLEY, H.B. *Prices of Books: Inquiry Into Changes in Price of Books...* 1898. London. 1st ed. $45.00

WHEATLEY & DELAMOTTE. *Art Work in Gold & Silver Medieval Practical-Art Handbooks.* 1882. NY. disbound. $35.00

WHEELER, G.C. *Mono-Alu Folklore.* 1926. London. Routledge. 396 p. VG. $35.00

WHEELER, G.M. *Preliminary Report Concerning Explorations & Surveys NV, AZ.* 1872. WA. GPO. fld map. EX. very scarce. A3. $180.00

WHEELER, L.P. *Josiah Wheeler Gibbs: History of a Great Mind.* 1962. Yale U. Ils. 270 p. dj. EX. M2. $12.00

WHEELER, Lucinda. *Brief Sketch of Christian Experience.* 1892. Clarks Corners. 12mo. G. $12.50

WHEELER, Monroe. *Britain at War.* 1941. NY. Ils. 97 p. dj. xl. T5. $22.50

WHEELER, R. *Sherman's March.* 1978. Crowell. Ils 1st ed. 241 p. dj. EX. M2. $10.00

WHEELER, W.M. *Ants.* 1926. NY. Ils. 663 p. dj. $35.00

WHEELER, W.M. *Ants.* 1960. Columbia U. Ils. 663 p. EX. M2. $35.00

WHEELER & WHEELER. *Mount Independence: Hubbardton 1776 Military Road.* 1968. Benson, VT. Ils. maps. inscr. 357 p. VG. T5. $12.50

WHEELER. *Year 'Round: Perennial Miscellany for Fox Hunters.* 1968. WA. slipcase. EX. $17.00

WHEELWRIGHT, Mary. *Navajo Creation Myth: Story of Emergence.* 1942. Santa Fe. Ltd ed. 1/1000. xl. A3. $80.00

WHELEN, Townsend. *Hunting Rifle.* 1940. Harrisburg. 1st ed. dj. VG. $35.00

WHELEN, Townsend. *Telescopic Rifle Sights.* 1944. Plantersville. Ils 2nd ed. $15.00

WHERRY, E.T. *S Fern Guide: SE & Midland US.* 1964. Doubleday. Ils 1st ed. 349 p. dj. EX. M2. $15.00

WHERRY, E.T. *Wild Flower Guide: NE & Midland US.* 1954. Doubleday. Ils. 202 p. G. M2. $7.00

WHETSTONE, Cindy. *Oral History of Vietnam.* 1989. Massillon, OH. Ils 1st ed. spiral bdg. M. T5. $8.50

WHINNEY, Margaret. *Christopher Wren.* 1971. Praeger. Ils. 216 p. dj. D2. $30.00

WHINNEY & GUNNIS. *Collection of Models by John Flaxman R.A.* 1967. Athlone. Ils. dj. D2. $40.00

WHINNEY & MILLAR. *English Art 1625-1714.* 1957. Oxford. Clarendon. Orig ed. dj. D2. $85.00

WHIPPLE, John. *Discourse Delivered Before Municipal Authorities...1838.* 1838. Providence. Knowles Vose. 30 p. EX. $55.00

WHIPPLE, Wayne. *Story Life of Lincoln.* 1908. Winston. G. $30.00

WHIPPLE, Wayne. *Story of the American Flag.* 1910. Phil. Ils. 8vo. 162 p. EX. $40.00

WHISTLER, J.M. *Eden Versus Whistler: Baronet & Butterfly, Valentine...* 1899. NY. Russell. 1/125. 4to. rebound. EX. $350.00

WHISTLER, J.M. *Gentle Art of Making Enemies.* 1890. London. Heinemann. gilt bdg. VG. $85.00

WHISTLER, Laurence. *Engraved Glass of Laurence Whistler.* 1952. Cupid Pr. 1/500. sgn. dj. VG. $65.00

WHISTLER, Rex. *New Forget-Me-Not.* 1929. London. Cobden Saunderson. 1/360. sgn. VG. $105.00

WHISTLER, Rex. *Story of Mr. Korah by Christabel Aberconway.* 1954. London. Ils. dj. EX. $20.00

WHITAKER, Arthur. *Spanish-American Frontier: 1783-1795...* 1927. Houghton. 1st ed. VG. J2. $20.00

WHITAKER, C.H. *Rameses to Rockefeller: Story of Architecture.* 1934. NY. 1st ed. J2. $15.00

WHITAKER, Herman. *W Winds: CA Book of Fiction Written by CA Authors...* 1914. San Francisco. Elder. presentation. 219 p. G. A3. $45.00

WHITAKER, J.V. *Art Treasures of England.* 1876. Phil. Gebbie Barrie. Ils. folio. $100.00

WHITAKER, R. *Common Indian Snakes: A Field Guide.* 1978. India. Macmillan. photos. 154 p. G. M2. $12.00

WHITBY & DONBROOK. *Synthetic Rubber.* 1954. Am Chem Soc. 1st ed. 4to. EX. $20.00

WHITCHER, W.F. *History of Town of Haverhill.* 1919. NH. VG. $20.00

WHITE, A. *Seven Tickets to Singapore.* 1939. Houghton. 1st ed. dj. G. P1. $25.00

WHITE, A.D. *Autobiography.* 1907. Century. later print. dj. VG. $18.00

WHITE, A.T. *First Men in the Works.* 1953. 5th print. 178 p. dj. juvenile. $9.00

WHITE, Alain. *History of Town: Litchfield, CT, 1720-1920.* 1930. Ils 1st ed. 360 p. VG. $30.00

WHITE, B. *Book of Daniel Drew.* 1911. reprint. 423 p. $10.50

WHITE, Benjamin. *Silver: Its History & Romance.* 1917. London/NY/Toronto. Ils. G. $35.00

WHITE, Christopher. *Rubens & His World.* 1968. Viking. Studio Book. Ils. 144 p. D2. $25.00

WHITE, Clarcence C. *Forty Negro Spirituals.* 1927. Phil. 1st ed. 4to. VG. T1. $35.00

WHITE, Colin. *Edmund Dulac.* 1976. NY. Scribner. 1st ed. dj. VG. $25.00

WHITE, E. *American Orchid Culture.* 1939. NY. Ils 256 p. G. $26.00

WHITE, E.B. *Fox of Peapack & Other Poems.* 1938. NY. 1st ed. VG. $35.00

WHITE, E.B. *Here Is NY.* 1949. NY. 1st ed. dj. EX. $20.00

WHITE, E.B. *Poems & Sketches of E.B. White.* 1981. NY. 1st ed. dj. EX. $25.00

WHITE, E.B. *Points of My Compass.* 1962. Harper. 1st ed. dj. $35.00

WHITE, E.B. *Second Tree From the Corner.* 1954. Harper. 1st ed. $45.00

WHITE, E.B. *Stuart Little*. 1945. Harper. Ils Williams. 1st ed. dj. EX. $50.00

WHITE, E.B. *Subtreasury of American Humor*. nd. Coward McCann. P1. $10.00

WHITE, E.B. *Subtreasury of American Humor*. nd. BOMC. dj. VG. P1. $7.50

WHITE, E.B. *Wild Flag*. 1946. Boston. 1st ed. dj. VG. $30.00

WHITE, E.G. *Great Controversy Between Christ & Satan*. 1888. Oakland. G. $15.00

WHITE, E.L. *Step in the Dark*. 1946. Books Inc. VG. P1. $7.50

WHITE, E.O. *Coming of Theodora*. 1895. Houghton Mifflin. 1st ed. $12.00

WHITE, E.O. *William Orne White: Record of Ninety Years*. 1917. Boston. 1st ed. sgn. 283 p. VG. T5. $25.00

WHITE, Frederick. *Spickle Fisherman*. Derrydale. as issued. VG. B2. $95.00

WHITE, Frederick. *Spickle Fisherman*. Derrydale. 1/775. EX. $150.00

WHITE, Gilbert. *Natural History of Selborne*. c 1845. London. New ed. $70.00

WHITE, Gilbert. *Natural History of Selborne*. 1890. London. VG. $45.00

WHITE, Gilbert. *Natural History of Selborne*. 1903. London/Paris/NY/Melbourne. 1st ed. $125.00

WHITE, Gilbert. *Natural History of Selbourne*. 1924. London. Ils 1st ed. 248 p. VG. M2. $25.00

WHITE, Gilbert. *Natural History of Selbourne*. 1929. London. Ils Daglish. dj. VG. J2. $40.00

WHITE, Gilbert. *Thirty Years in Tropical Australia*. 1919. 1st ed. J2. $20.00

WHITE, H.C. *Abraham Baldwin*. 1926. Athens. 1st ed. 196 p. VG. $45.00

WHITE, Homer. *Norwich Cadets*. 1873. 136 p. K1. $27.50

WHITE, J.H. *Cincinnati Locomotive Builders, 1845-1868*. 1965. Ils. 167 p. $25.00

WHITE, J.M. *Land God Made in Anger: Reflections on SW Africa*. 1969. Rand McNally. Ils 1st Am ed. 308 p. dj. EX. M2. $16.00

WHITE, J.M. *World Elsewhere*. 1975. Crowell. Ils 1st ed. maps. 320 p. dj. M2. $10.00

WHITE, Jane. *Comet*. 1976. Harper Row. 1st ed. dj. EX. P1. $10.00

WHITE, L.J. *Politics on the SW Frontier: AR Territory 1819-1836*. 1964. Memphis U. Ils. 219 p. dj. EX. M2. $20.00

WHITE, Leslie Turner. *Magnus the Magnificent*. nd. Book Club. dj. VG. P1. $3.00

WHITE, Lionel. *Time of Terror*. 1960. Dutton. 1st ed. G. P1. $7.50

WHITE, Mark. *Building the St. Pierre Dory*. 1978. Camden. 1st ed. 4to. dj. EX. $20.00

WHITE, Nathan William. *From Fedala to Berchtesgaden*. 1947. np. Ils 1st ed. maps. xl. T5. $125.00

WHITE, P.D. *Heart Disease in General Practice*. 1937. Profession Circle ed. VG. $15.00

WHITE, Patrick. *Tree of Man*. 1955. NY. 1st ed. dj. VG. $20.00

WHITE, Paul. *Jungle Doctor Stings a Scorpion*. 1963. Grand Rapids. Ils. 121 p. VG. $15.00

WHITE, Robb. *Run Masked*. 1938. NY. 1st ed. dj. VG. B2. $27.50

WHITE, S.E. *African Campfires*. 1913. Doubleday Page. 1st ed. 378 p. VG. $22.50

WHITE, S.E. *Camp & Trail*. 1907. Outing Pub. Ils 1st ed. G. $40.00

WHITE, S.E. *Conjuror's House*. 1903. McClure Phillips. 1st ed. VG. P1. $25.00

WHITE, S.E. *Gold*. 1913. Ils. 437 p. K1. $16.50

WHITE, S.E. *Leopard Woman*. 1916. Garden City. Ils 1st ed. 313 p. G. T5. $9.50

WHITE, S.E. *Mountains*. 1904. NY. 1st ed. VG. B2. $20.00

WHITE, S.E. *Mystery*. 1907. McClure Phillips. 1st ed. VG. P1. $20.00

WHITE, T.H. *Book of Beasts*. 1954. London. Ils 1st ed. dj. EX. $95.00

WHITE, T.H. *Book of Merlyn*. 1977. TX U. 1st ed. dj. VG. P1. $17.50

WHITE, T.H. *Farewell Victoria*. 1969. Jonathan Cape. 2nd ed. dj. xl. P1. $6.00

WHITE, T.H. *Ill-Made Knight*. 1940. NY. 1st ed. gilt bdg. EX. C1. $44.00

WHITE, T.H. *Once & Future King*. nd. Book Club. dj. VG. P1. $6.00

WHITE, T.H. *Sword in the Stone*. nd. BOMC. dj. VG. P1. $6.00

WHITE, T.H. *Sword in the Stone*. 1939. NY. Book Club. VG. C1. $4.00

WHITE, T.H. *Sword in the Stone*. 1959. London. dj. G. xl. C1. $2.50

WHITE, T.H. *Sword in the Stone*. 1964. Time Reading Program. VG. C1. $5.00

WHITE, Teri. *Bleeding Heart*. 1984. NY. 1st ed. dj. EX. $10.00

WHITE, W.A. *Calvin Coolidge: Man Who Is President*. 1925. Macmillan. 1st print. VG. scarce. $50.00

WHITE, W.A. *Court of Boyville*. 1899. NY. 1st ed. $65.00

WHITE, W.A. *In the Heart of a Fool*. 1918. NY. 1st ed. VG. $14.00

WHITE, W.A. *Martial Adventures of Henry & Me*. 1918. Macmillan. 338 p. M1. $9.50

WHITE, W.A. *Masks in a Pageant*. 1938. NY. 1st ed. inscr. VG. $15.00

WHITE, W.L. *Back Down the Ridge*. 1953. NY. 1st ed. presentation. sgn. dj. B2. $25.00

WHITE, W.L. *Queens Die Proudly*. 1943. NY. 1st ed. blue bdg. EX. $15.00

WHITE, W.P. *Buster*. 1925. 384 p. $12.00

WHITE, W.S. *Professional: Lyndon B. Johnson*. 1964. Boston. 4th print. inscr/sgn. 273 p. T5. $195.00

WHITE & IVEY. *Old Folks Concert, an Original Drama...* 1905. Johnston, SC. Bailey. Ils. 11 p. printed wraps. $22.50

WHITE & PLEASANTS. *War of 4,000 Years*. 1846. Phil. Griffith Simon. 295 p. G. $30.00

WHITEFIELD, Edwin. *Homes of Our Forefathers in ME, NH & VT*. 1886. Reading, MA. 1st ed. 36 pls. $125.00

WHITEFIELD, Edwin. *Homes of Our Forefathers*. 1880. Boston. 3rd ed. 33 pls. square 8vo. $125.00

WHITEHEAD, D. *FBI Story*. 1956. Random House. 368 p. dj. EX. $10.00

WHITEHEAD, David. *London Then, London Now: London Scene Changes...* 1969. London. Watson. 1st ed. 4to. 192 p. dj. $37.50

WHITEHEAD, G.K. *Deer of the World*. 1972. Viking. Ils. 194 p. dj. EX. M2. $28.00

WHITEHEAD, Henry S. *W India Lights*. 1946. Arkham House. dj. G. P1. $35.00

WHITEHEAD, Henry S. *W India Lights.* 1946. Arkham House. 1st ed. dj. EX. P1. $45.00

WHITEHEAD, L. *New House That Jack Built.* 1865. NY. Beadle. Ils 1st ed. 29 p. wraps. $100.00

WHITEHEAD AIRCRAFT COMPANY. *Commerce After War: Look at Past & Future of Air Travel.* 1917. Middlesex. Ils. 158 p. wraps. $90.00

WHITEHOUSE, A. *Hero Without Honor.* 1972. NY. 1st ed. 322 p. dj. VG. T5. $15.00

WHITEHOUSE, A. *Years of the Sky Kings.* 1959. NY. Ils 1st ed. 336 p. dj. VG. T5. $12.50

WHITEHOUSE, E. *TX Flowers in Natural Color.* 1948. private print. 2nd ed. 212 p. dj. EX. scarce. M2. $45.00

WHITELEY, Derek Pepys. *George du Maurier: His Life & Work.* 1947. NY. Pellegrini. Ils. 122 p. dj. D2. $38.50

WHITELOCK, L.C. *Mad Madonna.* 1895. Knight. 1st ed. $12.00

WHITELY, Opal. *Story of Opal.* 1921. Boston. 3rd ed. sgn. with photo. VG. B2. $40.00

WHITFORD, Frank. *Expressionsim.* 1970. London/NY. Ils. 189 p. dj. D2. $45.00

WHITFORD, W.C. *CO Volunteers in Civil War: NM Campaign in 1862.* 1906. Denver. 1st ed. M. $100.00

WHITING, Lilian. *Paris the Beautiful.* 1908. Boston. Little Brown. VG. $17.50

WHITLEY, C.J. *Open Secret, Intuition & Reality.* 1912. London. Rider. 12mo. blue cloth. G. $7.50

WHITLOCK, Brand. *Forty Years of It.* 1914. Appleton. 1st ed. inscr/sgn. VG. $28.00

WHITLOCK, Brand. *Lafayette.* 1929. NY. Ils 1st ed. 2 vols. VG. T1. $25.00

WHITLOCK, Brand. *Turn of the Balance.* 1907. Bobbs Merrill. Ils Hambridger. 8vo. $7.50

WHITLOCK, V.H. *Cowboy Life on the Llano Estacado.* 1970. Norman. Ils 1st ed. dj. EX. $35.00

WHITMAN, Alfred. *Charles Turner, A.R.A.* 1907. London. 1/50. VG. $75.00

WHITMAN, S.E. *Troopers: Informal History of Plains Cavalry, 1865-1890.* 1962. Hastings House. dj. EX. $18.00

WHITMAN, S.H. *Edgar A. Poe & His Critics.* 1860. Rudd Carlton. 1st ed. 12mo. russet cloth. VG. D1. $80.00

WHITMAN, Walt. *Complete Prose Works.* 1907. Boston. 1st ed. 527 p. gilt green cloth. VG. T1. $50.00

WHITMAN, Walt. *In Reminiscences of Abraham Lincoln.* 1886. NY. 1st ed. G. $30.00

WHITMAN, Walt. *Leaves of Grass.* nd. NY. Heritage. reprint. dj. J2. $15.00

WHITMAN, Walt. *Leaves of Grass.* 1891-1892. Phil. green cloth. EX. T5. $200.00

WHITMAN, Walt. *Leaves of Grass.* 1940. NY. Doubleday. Ils Daniel. 1st ed. slipcase. EX. $20.00

WHITMAN, Walt. *Leaves of Grass.* 1942. Ltd ed. Ils Edward Weston. 2 vols. VG. S2. $500.00

WHITMAN, Walt. *Leaves of Grass.* 1959. Viking. Intro Cowley. 1st ed. dj. EX. $15.00

WHITMAN, Walt. *Leaves of Grass.* 1966. Eakins. facsimile of 1st ed. slipcase. EX. $42.00

WHITMAN, Walt. *Leaves of Grass.* 1968. Peter Pauper. Ils Gorton. 1st ed. dj. VG. $7.50

WHITMAN, Walt. *Leaves of Grass.* 1976. Paddington Pr. reprint of 1942 Ltd Ed Club. dj. $65.00

WHITMAN, Walt. *Out of the Cradle-Endlessly Rocking.* 1926. NY. June House. 1/180. G. T5. $25.00

WHITMAN, Walt. *Pictures: An Unpublished Poem.* 1927. NY. 1st ed. 1/700. $55.00

WHITMAN, Walt. *Salut au Mond!* 1930. Random House. Ils/sgn Pressig. Review ed. G2. $125.00

WHITMAN, Walt. *Song of Myself.* 1904. Roycroft. 8vo. red suede. VG. D1. $40.00

WHITMAN, Walt. *Specimen Days & Collections.* 1882. Phil. Rees Welsh. 1st ed. 1st issue. VG. $225.00

WHITMAN, Walt. *Specimen Days in America.* nd. London. Scotts Lib. G. $20.00

WHITMAN, Walt. *There Was a Child Went Forth.* 1968. Ils Tyler. 1/200. 4to. dj. EX. G2. $150.00

WHITMAN, Walt. *Wound Dresser.* 1949. Bodley Pr. dj. VG. P1. $15.00

WHITMAN, Walt. *Writings of Walt Whitman.* Camden. 1/500. 10 vols. TEG. djs. EX. $450.00

WHITMORE, W.H. *Elements of Heraldry.* 1968. Rutland. Ils. 106 p. G. T5. $6.50

WHITNEY, H. *Hunting With the Eskimos.* 1910. London. 1st ed. EX. $80.00

WHITNEY, H. *King Bear of Kodiak Island.* 1912. Chicago. Ils 1st ed. EX. $10.00

WHITNEY, H.C. *Life on the Circuit With Lincoln.* 1940. Caldwell. dj. EX. $75.00

WHITNEY, Phyllis A. *Columbella.* nd. BOMC. dj. VG. P1. $3.50

WHITNEY, Phyllis A. *Hunter's Green.* nd. BOMC. dj. VG. P1. $3.50

WHITNEY, Phyllis A. *Listen for the Whisperer.* nd. BOMC. dj. VG. P1. $4.00

WHITNEY, Phyllis A. *Poinciana.* nd. BOMC. dj. VG. P1. $3.50

WHITNEY, Phyllis A. *Winter People.* nd. BOMC. dj. VG. P1. $3.50

WHITNEY, Richard. *Report of President, May 1, 1930.* 1931. NY Stock Exchange. presentation. $45.00

WHITNEY, T.R. *Defense of the American Policy...Interference of the Papacy.* 1856. NY. 1st ed. VG. $25.00

WHITON, J.M. *Six Weeks` Preparation for Reading Caesar.* 1883. 75 p. TB. VG. $4.00

WHITTAKER, J. *We Thought We Heard the Angels Sing.* 1943. Dutton. 1st ed. dj. EX. $40.00

WHITTELSEY & SONNECK. *Catalog of First Editions of Stephen C. Foster.* 1915. Lib Congress. 69 p. A3. $35.00

WHITTEMORE. *Fulfillment Prophecies of Steamboat & Railroad.* 1909. np. Ils. 80 p. VG. C4. $35.00

WHITTEN, Leslie H. *Progeny of the Adder.* 1966. Hodder Stoughton. 1st ed. P1. $20.00

WHITTEN, T. *Gibbons of Siberut.* 1982. London. Dent. Ils 1st ed. 207 p. dj. EX. M2. $17.00

WHITTIER, J.G. *PA Pilgrim.* 1872. Boston. 1st ed. 12mo. green cloth. VG. $30.00

WHITTIER, J.G. *Snow Bound.* 1866. 1st ed. 1st state. G. J2. $60.00

WHITTINGTON, Harry. *Treachery Trail.* 1968. Whitman. VG. P1. $7.50

WHITTINGTON, Harry. *Vengeance Valley.* 1946. Phoenix. dj. VG. P1. $10.00

WHITTLE, T. *Plant Hunters: Account of Careers & Methods.* 1970. Chilton. Ils 1st ed. 281 p. dj. EX. M2. $26.00

WHITTLESEY, C.W. *Crossing & Re-Crossing CT River.* 1938. Ils 1st ed. xl. G. R1. $15.00

WHITTLESEY, Charles. *Fugitive Essays.* 1852. Hudson, OH. 1st ed. 397 p. scarce. T5. $225.00

WHITTLESEY. *Memorials of the Whittlesey Farm.* 1955. np. tables. 125 p. VG. C4. $65.00

WHITTON, F.E. *Wolfe & N America.* 1929. Little Brown. 1st ed. J2. $15.00

WHONE, Herbert. *Hidden Face of Music.* 1974. London. with sgn card. EX. $18.00

WHYMPER, E. *Scrambles Amongst the Alps in Years 1860-1869.* 1872. Phil. Ils. $45.00

WIBBERLEY, Leonard. *Adventures of an Elephant Boy.* 1968. Morrow. dj. xl. P1. $6.00

WIBBERLEY, Leonard. *Centurion.* 1966. Morrow. dj. xl. P1. $5.00

WIBBERLEY, Leonard. *Epics of Everest.* 1966. Farrar Straus. 5th print. dj. xl. P1. $5.00

WIBBERLEY, Leonard. *Last Stand of Father Felix.* 1974. Morrow. 1st ed. P1. $12.00

WIBBERLEY, Leonard. *Mouse on the Moon.* 1962. Morrow. 1st ed. dj. VG. $12.50

WIBBERLEY, Leonard. *Mouse That Saved the W.* 1981. Morrow. 1st ed. dj. M. $10.00

WIBBERLEY, Leonard. *Quest of Excalibur.* 1959. NY. Putnam. 1st ed. xl. scarce. C1. $16.50

WIBBERLEY, Leonard. *Sea Captain From Salem.* 1966. Farrar Straus. 6th print. dj. xl. P1. $5.00

WIBBERLEY, Leonard. *Something To Read.* 1967. Ives Washburn. 1st ed. dj. G. P1. $10.00

WICKENDEN, J. *Claim in the Hills.* 1957. Rinehart. 275 p. dj. EX. M2. $7.00

WICKER. *Unto This Hour.* 1984. Viking. 1st ed. EX. $9.00

WICKERSHAM, James. *Old Yukon.* 1938. WA Law Book Co. 1st ed. 514 p. M1. $25.00

WICKHAM, Gertrude. *Memorial to Pioneer Women of W Reserve.* 1896-1897. np. 1st ed. 4 parts in wraps. VG. T5. $125.00

WICKS, Mark. *To Mars Via the Moon: Astronomical Fantasy Story.* 1911. Phil. Ils. G. $25.00

WICKSON, E. *CA Fruits.* 1891. 2nd ed. photos. ads. G. $30.00

WICKWARE, Francis Sill. *Dangerous Ground.* nd. Literary Guild. dj. VG. P1. $7.00

WICKWARE, Francis Sill. *Dangerous Ground.* nd. Doubleday. VG. P1. $7.50

WIDDEMER, Margaret. *Dark Cavalier.* dj. VG. C1. $7.00

WIDEMAN, J.E. *Brothers & Keepers.* 1984. Holt Rinehart. 4th ed. 243 p. dj. M1. $8.00

WIDEMAN, J.E. *Reuben.* 1987. NY. Holt. 1st ed. dj. M. $10.00

WIENER, Lionel. *Articulated Locomotives.* 1970. reprint of 1930 ed. 632 p. $30.00

WIENER, Otto. *Farbenphotographie und Verwandte Naturwissenschaftliche...* 1908. Leipzig. Vogel. 28 p. sm 4to. printed wraps. $17.50

WIENERS, John. *Asylum Poems.* 1969. Angel Hair. 1/200. inscr. EX. $50.00

WIENERS, John. *Playboy.* 1972. Good Gay Poets. sgn. EX. $50.00

WIENERS, John. *Selected Poems, 1958-1984.* 1986. Black Sparrow. 1/226. sgn Wieners/Foye/Ginsberg. $50.00

WIENERS, John. *Unhired.* 1968. Perishable Pr. 1/250. wraps. EX. $25.00

WIENERS, John. *Upstairs.* 1967. Gallery Upstairs. 1/100. sgn. EX. $30.00

WIENERS, John. *Youth.* 1970. Phoenix. 1/100. wraps. EX. $35.00

WIENERS, John. *Youth.* 1970. Phoenix. 1/26. sgn/lettered. wraps. EX. $60.00

WIGGIN, K.D. *Arabian Nights.* 1942. NY. $45.00

WIGGIN, K.D. *Old Peabody Pew: Christmas Romance of Country Church.* 1907. Boston. Ils Stephens. 1st ed. dj. G. $12.00

WIGGIN, K.D. *Penelope's Irish Experiences.* 1901. Houghton. 1st ed. green bdg. $20.00

WIGGIN, K.D. *Penelope's Progress.* 1898. Houghton. VG. $10.00

WIGGIN, K.D. *Rebecca of Sunnybrook Farm.* nd. Grosset. VG. P1. $15.00

WIGGIN, K.D. *Rebecca of Sunnybrook Farm.* 1903. Boston. 1st ed. 327 p. G. T5. $25.00

WIGGIN, K.D. *Timothy's Quest: Story for Anybody, Young or Old...* 1918. Houghton. presentation. sgn. 210 p. VG. $45.00

WIGGINTON, Eliot. *Foxfire Book 2.* 1973. Foxfire Books. $12.00

WIGGLESWORTH, Michael. *Day of Doom.* 1867. NY. reprint of 1715 ed. VG. $15.00

WIGGLESWORTH, V.B. *Control & Growth of Form: Study of Epidermal Cell of Insect.* 1959. Cornell U. Ils. 140 p. EX. M2. $10.00

WIGGLESWORTH, V.B. *Physiology of Insect Metamorphosis.* 1954. Cambridge U. Ils. 152 p. dj. EX. M2. $13.00

WIGGLESWORTH, V.B. *Principles of Insect Physiology.* 1965. London. Ils. 741 p. dj. EX. M2. $25.00

WIJNBEEK, D. *De Nachtwacht: Historie van een Meesterwerk.* 1944. Amsterdam. 1/50. pls. 210 p. $35.00

WILBER & SCHOENHOLTZ. *Silver Wings.* 1948. Appleton Century. Ils Caniff. P1. $20.00

WILBOR, John. *Wilbores in America.* 1907. St. Paul. 21 p. poor. B1. $40.00

WILBUR, D.N. *Iran: Past & Present.* 1948. Princeton. 1st ed. presentation. dj. VG. $15.00

WILBUR, Richard. *Elizabeth Bishop: Memorial Tribute.* nd. np. 1st ed. 1/174. sgn/#d. $40.00

WILBUR, Richard. *Pedestrian Flight.* 1981. Palaemon. 1/110. sgn. M. $45.00

WILBUR, Richard. *Things of This World.* 1956 or 1957. not 1st but early ed. dj. C1. $5.00

WILBUR & YONGE. *Physiology of Mollusca.* 1964. Academic Pr. Ils. 2 vols. djs. EX. M2. $55.00

WILCOX, Collin. *Aftershock.* nd. Book Club. VG. P1. $2.50

WILCOX, Collin. *Doctor, Lawyer.* nd. Book Club. dj. VG. P1. $4.00

WILCOX, Collin. *Long Way Down.* nd. Book Club. dj. VG. P1. $4.00

WILCOX, R.T. *Mode in Furs.* 1951. NY. Ils 1st ed. 257 p. VG. B2. $57.50

WILCOX. *Evolutions of Line, As Practiced by Austrian Infantry...* 1860. NY. 1st ed. 8 fld pls. EX. $55.00

WILD, P. *Pioneer Conservationists of W America.* 1979. Mountain Pr. Ils. 246 p. dj. EX. M2. $16.00

WILD, P. *Saguaro Forest.* 1986. Northland. Ils 1st ed. 64 p. EX. M2. $10.00

WILD BIRD SOCIETY OF JAPAN. *Field Guide to the Birds of Japan.* 1985. Japan. Ils. maps. 336 p. EX. M2. $22.00

WILDASH, P. *Birds of S Viet Nam.* 1968. Tuttle. 25 color pls. 234 p. dj. EX. M2. $25.00

WILDE, Oscar. *Ballad of Reading Gaol.* 1898. London. Leonard Smithers. 1/800. EX. $500.00

WILDE, Oscar. *Ballad of Reading Gaol.* 1902. Boston. Ltd ed. 1/550. dj. $65.00

WILDE, Oscar. *Ballad of Reading Gaol.* 1924. London. Ils Masereel. $250.00

WILDE, Oscar. *Ballad of Reading Gaol.* 1928. NY. Ils Lynd Ward. J2. $60.00

WILDE, Oscar. *Ballad of Reading Gaol.* 1930. NY. Ils John Vassos. J2. $40.00

WILDE, Oscar. *Birthday of the Infanta.* 1929. NY. Ils Bianco. 1st ed. VG. J2. $15.00

WILDE, Oscar. *Critic in Pall Mall.* 1919. London. Methuen. 1st ed. gilt bdg. dj. EX. $45.00

WILDE, Oscar. *Der Junge Koenig.* 1919. Potsdam. sm 4to. VG. $35.00

WILDE, Oscar. *For Love of a King.* 1922. London. Ltd 1st ed. $75.00

WILDE, Oscar. *House of Pomegranates.* 1891. London. Ils Ricketts/Shannon. 1st ed. B4. $375.00

WILDE, Oscar. *Ideal Husband.* 1899. London. Leonard Smithers. gilt bdg. EX. $150.00

WILDE, Oscar. *Picture of Dorian Gray.* 1913. London. Simpkin Marshall. 1st ed. 8vo. $60.00

WILDE, Oscar. *Picture of Dorian Gray.* 1930. Liveright. Ils Majeska. Ltd 1st ed. EX. $75.00

WILDE, Oscar. *Picture of Dorian Gray.* 1931. Three Sirens. Ils Trugo. 120 p. VG. $12.00

WILDE, Oscar. *Picture of Dorian Gray.* 1944. Tower. dj. xl. P1. $10.00

WILDE, Oscar. *Picture of Dorian Gray.* 1957. NY. Ils Lucille Corcos. slipcase. EX. $25.00

WILDE, Oscar. *Picture of Dorian Gray.* 1957. NY. Ltd Ed Club. 1/1500. boxed. M. $50.00

WILDE, Oscar. *Poems.* 1881. Boston. 1st ed. VG. $115.00

WILDE, Oscar. *Poems.* 1927. NY. Ils Bosschere. 1/2000. VG. J2. $30.00

WILDE, Oscar. *Portrait of Mr. W.H.* 1921. NY. Mitchell Kennerley. 1/1000. EX. $55.00

WILDE, Oscar. *Remarkable Rocket.* 1974. Johnson. Ils Coleman. wraps. $22.00

WILDE, Oscar. *Salome.* 1911. Portland. Mosher. 1st ed. 1/500. 12mo. $52.50

WILDE, Oscar. *Salome.* 1920. London. Ils Beardsley. 1st ed. $85.00

WILDE, Oscar. *Salome.* 1927. Grabhorn. Ltd ed. 1/195. boxed. $90.00

WILDE, Oscar. *Salome.* 1927. NY. Ils Vassos. Ltd ed. 1/500. $45.00

WILDE, Oscar. *Salome.* 1938. Ltd Ed Club. Ils Beardsley. 2 vols. dj. EX. $225.00

WILDE, Oscar. *Salome.* 1973. Heritage. Ils Angelo. quarto. slipcase. EX. $15.00

WILDE, Oscar. *Satyricon Petronius Arbiter.* private print. 1/1200. red cloth. VG. $30.00

WILDE, Oscar. *Sixteen Letters From Oscar Wilde.* 1930. London. Faber. 1/550. TEG. gilt bdg. dj. EX. $65.00

WILDE, Oscar. *Soul of Man Under Socialism.* 1910. Boston. 1st ed. VG. $40.00

WILDE, Oscar. *Wilde & the Nineties: Essay & Exhibition.* 1966. Princeton. wraps. $15.00

WILDE & BORSTEN. *Loving Gentleman.* 1976. Simon Schuster. Ils 1st ed. 334 p. dj. $27.50

WILDENSTEIN, Georges. *Chardin.* 1969. Greenwich. NY Graphic Soc. 2nd ed. 276 p. D2. $475.00

WILDENSTEIN, Georges. *Ingres.* 1954. London/NY. Phaidon/Garden City. 120 pls. D2. $220.00

WILDER, Cherry. *Luck of Brin's Five.* 1977. Atheneum. 1st ed. dj. EX. P1. $20.00

WILDER, Cherry. *Nearest Fire.* 1980. Atheneum. 1st ed. dj. EX. P1. $20.00

WILDER, Cherry. *Tapestry Warriors.* 1983. Atheneum Argo. 1st ed. dj. EX. P1. $15.00

WILDER, F.L. *Sporting Prints.* 1974. Viking. Ils. 4to. 224 p. EX. $25.00

WILDER, I. *Morphology of Amphibian Metamorphosis.* 1925. Smith College. Ils. 161 p. EX. M2. $13.00

WILDER, L.I. *These Happy Golden Years.* 1943. Harper. Ils Sewell/Boyle. 1st ed. dj. $15.00

WILDER, Robert. *Fruit of the Poppy.* nd. Book Club. dj. VG. P1. $3.00

WILDER, Thornton. *Angel That Troubled the Waters.* 1928. NY. Coward. 1st ed. 1/775. sgn. 8vo. dj. EX. $75.00

WILDER, Thornton. *Bridge of San Luis Rey.* 1928. Longman. not 1st ed. navy cloth. EX. $20.00

WILDER, Thornton. *Bridge of San Luis Rey.* 1928. NY. Boni. 13th print. VG. $25.00

WILDER, Thornton. *Bridge of San Luis Rey.* 1929. NY. Boni. Ltd ed. 1/100. sgns. VG. $150.00

WILDER, Thornton. *Heaven My Destination.* 1935. NY. 1st ed. dj. VG. B2. $15.00

WILDER, Thornton. *Ides of March.* 1948. NY. 1st ed. dj. EX. P3. $25.00

WILDER, Thornton. *Our Town.* 1958. Longman. 3rd ed. VG. P1. $6.00

WILDER, Thornton. *Skin of Our Teeth.* 1942. Harper. 1st ed. dj. with sgn card. $65.00

WILDER, Thornton. *Theophilus N.* 1973. Harper. 1st ed. dj. EX. $25.00

WILDER, Thornton. *Theophilus N.* 1973. Harper. 1st ed. inscr/sgn. dj. EX. $47.50

WILDER, Thornton. *Woman of Andros.* 1930. NY. Boni. 3rd print. VG. $60.00

WILDWOOD, W. *Frank Forester's Fugitive Sporting Sketches.* 1879. Westfield, WI. 8vo. red bdg. EX. $165.00

WILEY, B.I. *Embattled Confederates: Illustrated History of Civil War.* 1964. Bonanza. reprint. 290 p. dj. EX. M2. $10.00

WILEY, B.I. *Letters of Warren Akin: Confederate Congressman.* 1959. Athens. 151 p. dj. VG. $25.00

WILEY, F.A. *Ernest Thompson Seton's America.* 1954. Devin Adair. Ils 1st ed. 413 p. VG. M2. $9.00

WILEY & MILHOLLEN *They Who Fought Here.* 1959. reprint. 273 p. dj. M. J4. $12.50

WILEY & MILHOLLEN. *They Who Fought Here.* 1959. Bonanza. reprint. 4to. 273 p. dj. EX. M2. $10.00

WILFORD, J.N. *Riddle of the Dinosaur.* 1985. Knopf. Ils 1st ed. 304 p. dj. EX. M2. $20.00

WILHELM, James. *Romance of Arthur I.* 1984. stiff paper covers. M. C1. $12.50

WILHELM, James. *Romance of Arthur III.* 1988. Garland. 1st ed. pb. M. C1. $12.00

WILHELM, John. *Wilhelm's Guide to All Mexico.* 1978. McGraw Hill. 5th ed. 21 maps. index. P1. $9.00

WILHELM, Kate. *Abyss.* 1971. Doubleday. 1st ed. dj. xl. P1. $7.50

WILHELM, Kate. *Clewiston Test.* 1976. Farrar Straus. 3rd ed. dj. EX. P1. $9.25

WILHELM, Kate. *Downstairs Room.* 1968. Doubleday. 1st ed. dj. xl. P1. $7.50

WILHELM, Kate. *Infinity Box.* 1975. Harper Row. 1st ed. dj. VG. P1. $17.50

WILHELM, Kate. *Juniper Time.* 1979. Harper Row. dj. EX. P1. $20.00

WILHELM, Kate. *Killer Thing.* nd. Book Club. dj. VG. P1. $4.00

WILHELM, Kate. *Let the Fire Fall.* 1969. Garden City. 1st ed. dj. EX. $25.00

WILHELM, Kate. *Let the Fire Fall.* 1969. Jenkins. dj. G. P1. $15.00

WILHELM, Kate. *Mile-Long Spaceship.* 1980. Gregg Pr. no dj issued. P1. $10.00

WILHELM, Kate. *Somerset Dreams.* 1978. Harper Row. 1st ed. dj. EX. P1. $20.00

WILHELM, Kate. *Where Late the Sweet Birds Sang.* 1977. Harper Row. 3rd ed. dj. EX. P1. $12.50

WILHELM, P. *Travels in N America 1823-1824.* 1973. OK U. Ils 1st ed. maps. 456 p. dj. M2. $35.00

WILK, Max. *Kissinger Noodles.* 1976. Norton. 1st ed. dj. VG. P1. $12.50

WILK, Max. *My Masterpiece.* 1970. Norton. 1st ed. dj. xl. P1. $7.50

WILKIE, D. *Gentians.* 1950. London. Country Life. Revised ed. dj. M2. $11.00

WILKIE, Wendell. *One World.* 1943. Simon Schuster. 8vo. with sgn letter. VG. $15.00

WILKINS, Cary. *Treasury of Fantasy.* 1981. Avenel. 1st ed. dj. EX. P1. $12.50

WILKINS, H.T. *Modern Buried Treasure Hunters.* c 1934. NY. Ils. dj. $12.00

WILKINS, H.T. *Panorama of Treasure Hunting Romantic Adventures...* 1940. NY. Ils. VG. $12.00

WILKINS, H.T. *Pirate Treasure.* 1937. NY. Ils. VG. $12.00

WILKINS, Thurman. *Clarence King: A Biography.* 1958. NY. Macmillan. Ils. 441 p. dj. xl. A3. $30.00

WILKINS, W. *Dickens in Cartoon & Caricature.* 1924. Boston. Bibliophile Soc. 1/440. 60 pls. VG. $40.00

WILKINS & SHERMAN. *Thoughts Through Space.* 1942. NY. $60.00

WILKINS-FREEMAN, Mary E. *Collected Ghost Stories.* 1974. Arkham House. 1st ed. dj. EX. P1. $15.00

WILKINSON, Albert E. *Handy Book of Gardening.* 1950. Perma P63. VG. P1. $5.00

WILKINSON, J. *Shah-Namah of Firdausi.* 1931. Oxford. Ils. 4to. dj. EX. J2. $75.00

WILKINSON, M. *Greenwood, Sebastion Co., AR: 110 Years a County Seat.* 1961. Farmers Bank. photos. 48 p. EX. M2. $4.00

WILKINSON, S. *Moss on the N Side.* 1966. Boston. 1st ed. dj. EX. $50.00

WILKINSON. *Strabismus Etiology & Treatment.* 1927. St. Louis. 1st ed. VG. $35.00

WILL, James. *Cowboys N & S.* 1925. NY. 2nd ed. VG. B2. $45.00

WILLANS, Geoffrey. *Down With Skool!* 1953. Parrish. 1st ed. dj. VG. P1. $10.00

WILLARD, D. *History of Greenfield, MA.* 1838. Phil. 1st ed. $37.50

WILLARD, D.E. *Story of the Prairies.* 1902. Chicago. G. $25.00

WILLARD, Daniel. *MT: Geological Story.* 1935. Lancaster. Ils 1st ed. 8vo. dj. G. T1. $30.00

WILLARD, T.A. *Bride of Rain God: Princess of Chichen-itza...* 1930. Cleveland. Ils Harold Miles. 11 pls. $30.00

WILLARD, T.A. *City of Sacred Well.* 1926. NY. VG. $15.00

WILLEFORD, Charles. *Cockfighter Journal.* 1989. Santa Barbara. 1st ed. 1/300. sgn. M. $50.00

WILLEFORD, Charles. *Kiss Your Ass Good-Bye.* 1987. Dennis McMillan. 1st ed. dj. P1. $40.00

WILLEFORD, Charles. *Miami Blues.* 1984. NY. St. Martin. 1st ed. dj. VG. $25.00

WILLEFORD, Charles. *Proletarian Laughter.* 1948. Yonkers. 1/1000. wraps. EX. $75.00

WILLEFORD, Charles. *Sideswipe.* 1987. St. Martin. 1st ed. dj. M. $20.00

WILLEFORD, Charles. *Something About a Soldier.* 1986. NY. 1st ed. dj. EX. $10.00

WILLETS, Gilson. *Our Boys in Camp.* 1898. NY. Neely. oblong 8vo. printed wraps. $50.00

WILLEY, G.R. *Prehistoric Maya Settlements in Belize Valley.* 1965. Peabody Mus. Ils. fld map. slipcase. EX. M2. $95.00

WILLIAM, Charles. *King God Didn't Save.* 1st ed. dj. VG. B2. $17.50

WILLIAM PRINCE OF SWEDEN. *Wild African Animals I Have Known.* 1923. London. Lane. Ils 1st ed. 4to. 315 p. VG. M2. $45.00

WILLIAMS, A. *Airpower.* 1940. NY. 1st ed. 433 p. G. T5. $22.50

WILLIAMS, A.B. *Hampton & His Red Shirts.* 1935. Charleston. 1st ed. dj. xl. VG. B2. $45.00

WILLIAMS, A.B. *Shrimps, Lobsters & Crabs of Atlantic Coast.* 1984. Smithsonian. Ils. 568 p. EX. M2. $45.00

WILLIAMS, A.C. *Dictionary of Trout Flies & Flies for Sea Trout & Grayling.* 1949. London. Ils 1st ed. dj. VG. $50.00

WILLIAMS, A.C. *Trout Flies: Discussion & Dictionary.* 1932. London. pls. gilt green morocco. $85.00

WILLIAMS, A.S. *Demon of the Orient: Our Opium Smokers As They Are...* 1883. NY. 12mo. G. $25.00

WILLIAMS, Alan. *Snake Water.* 1966. Odhams. dj. xl. P1. $10.00

WILLIAMS, Ariadna. *Hosts of Darkness.* 1921. Constable. 1st ed. G. P1. $5.00

WILLIAMS, C.R.A. *Biography of Revolutionary Heroes...* 1839. Providence. Williams. 12mo. 312 p. rebound. EX. $40.00

WILLIAMS, Charles. *All Hallow's Eve.* 1981. reprint. pb. VG. C1. $4.00

WILLIAMS, Charles. *Dead Calm.* nd. Book Club. dj. VG. P1. $3.00

WILLIAMS, Charles. *Dead Calm.* 1963. Viking. 1st ed. dj. xl. P1. $5.00

WILLIAMS, Charles. *Descent Into Hell.* 1949. Pelligrini Cudahy. VG. P1. $25.00

WILLIAMS, Charles. *Descent Into Hell.* 1983. pb. M. C1. $5.00

WILLIAMS, Charles. *Greater Trumps.* 1978. pb. VG. C1. $9.00

WILLIAMS, Charles. *Man on a Leash.* nd. Book Club. dj. VG. P1. $3.00

WILLIAMS, Charles. *Principles of Medicine.* 1853. Blanchard Lee. 476 p. full leather. K1. $23.50

WILLIAMS, Charles. *War in Heaven.* c 1970s. pb. VG. C1. $7.00

WILLIAMS, Charles. *War in Heaven.* 1985. pb. M. C1. $9.50

WILLIAMS, Charles. *Witchcraft.* 1941. London. 1st ed. EX. $40.00

WILLIAMS, David. *Copper, Gold & Treasure.* 1982. St. Martin. 1st ed. dj. VG. P1. $10.00

WILLIAMS, David. *Murder in Advent.* 1985. St. Martin. 1st ed. dj. EX. P1. $14.95

WILLIAMS, David. *Treasure by Degrees.* 1977. St. Martin. 1st ed. dj. VG. P1. $15.00

WILLIAMS, E.B. *One Man's Freedom.* 1962. Atheneum. dj. EX. $25.00

WILLIAMS, Emlyn. *Headlong.* 1983. NY. 1st ed. dj. EX. $35.00

WILLIAMS, Eric. *Wooden Horse.* 1949. NY. 1st ed. 255 p. T5. $15.00

WILLIAMS, Franklin. *Index of Dedications & Commendatory Verses in English Books.* 1962. London. Ils. 4to. dj. VG. $40.00

WILLIAMS, G.A. *Madoc: Making of a Myth.* 1979. 1st Eng ed. dj. M. C1. $17.00

WILLIAMS, G.C. *Adaptation & Natural Selection: Critique of Thought.* 1966. Princeton. 307 p. EX. M2. $17.00

WILLIAMS, G.F. *Bullet & Shell.* 1882. Ils Forbes. 1st ed. 454 p. K1. $28.50

WILLIAMS, G.H. *Life on a Locomotive.* 1971. 219 p. $17.50

WILLIAMS, G.M. *Siege of Trencher's Farm.* 1969. Secker Warburg. dj. xl. P1. $5.00

WILLIAMS, Glyndwr. *Documents Relating to Anson's Voyage Around the World...* 1967. Navy Records Soc. 1st ed. J2. $25.00

WILLIAMS, H.L. *History of Craighead Co., AR.* 1930. Parke Harper. Ils. 648 p. EX. M2. $45.00

WILLIAMS, Harry. *TX Trails: Legends of Great SW.* 1932. San Antonio. sgn. VG. $45.00

WILLIAMS, Henri. *Rochefort: Prince of Gutter Press.* 1956. EX. $15.00

WILLIAMS, J.A. *Love.* 1988. Babcock Koontz. 1/40. sgns. M. $125.00

WILLIAMS, J.A. *Love.* 1988. Babcock Koontz. 1st ed. 1/200. sgn. wraps. $45.00

WILLIAMS, J.G. *Field Guide to Birds of E & Central Africa.* 1969. Collins. Ils. 288 p. dj. G. M2. $15.00

WILLIAMS, J.H. *Elephant Bill.* 1950. Doubleday. Ils 1st ed. map. 250 p. dj. VG. M2. $10.00

WILLIAMS, J.H. *Guardians of the Columbia, Mt. Hood, Mt. Adams...* 1912. Tacoma. Williams. tall 8vo. 144 p. $35.00

WILLIAMS, J.H. *Mountain That Was God.* 1911. Tacoma. Williams. 2nd ed. 142 p. $35.00

WILLIAMS, J.R. *Bull of the Woods & Out Our Way.* 1952. Scribner. VG. $45.00

WILLIAMS, J.R. *Cowboys Out Our Way.* 1951. Scribner. VG. $55.00

WILLIAMS, J.R. *Out Our Way.* 1943. NY. 1st ed. dj. B2. $65.00

WILLIAMS, J.W. *Big Ranch Country.* 1954. Wichita Falls. Ils 1st ed. dj. EX. $40.00

WILLIAMS, Jay. *Sword of King Arthur.* 1968. Ils Glanzman. 1st ed. 2nd print. xl. C1. $9.50

WILLIAMS, John. *Click Song.* 1982. NY. 1st ed. sgn. dj. EX. $25.00

WILLIAMS, John. *Man Who Cried I Am.* 1967. NY. sgn. dj. EX. $30.00

WILLIAMS, John. *Redeemed Captive Returning to Zion.* 1853. Northampton. 2 pls. 192 p. G. $45.00

WILLIAMS, Joseph. *Tour of OR in 1841-1842.* 1921. NY. reprint. 1/250. xl. VG. $45.00

WILLIAMS, Joy. *Changeling.* 1978. Doubleday. 1st ed. dj. VG. P1. $7.50

WILLIAMS, Joy. *State of Grace.* 1973. NY. 1st ed. EX. $25.00

WILLIAMS, L. *Samba & the Monkey Mind.* 1965. Norton. Ils 1st ed. 146 p. dj. EX. M2. $10.00

WILLIAMS, L.E. *FL Snail Kite Recovery Plan.* 1986. USFWS. 48 p. M2. $6.00

WILLIAMS, M.C. *Early Mackinac: Fairy Island.* 1898. St. Louis. Ils. pb. fair. $18.00

WILLIAMS, Margaret. *Complete Works of the Pearl Poet.* 1967. 1st ed. dj. VG. C1. $8.00

WILLIAMS, Margaret. *Glee-Wood: Passages From Middle-English Literature.* 549 p. xl. VG. C1. $9.00

WILLIAMS, Mrs. *Biography of Revolutionary Heroes, W. Barton & S. Olney.* 1839. Providence. Ils 1st ed. 8vo. G. $45.00

WILLIAMS, O.E. *Bench & Bar of WA Co., AR, 1828-1861.* 1961. WA Co Hist Soc. Ils. 4to. 34 p. EX. M2. $7.00

WILLIAMS, Paul. *Only Apparently Real.* 1986. Arbor House. EX. P1. $7.95

WILLIAMS, S. *Footprints of Elephant Bill.* 1962. McKay. Ils 1st Am ed. 234 p. dj. EX. M2. $12.00

WILLIAMS, S.C. *Dawn of TN Valley & TN History.* 1937. Johnson City. 1st ed. inscr/sgn. VG. scarce. $150.00

WILLIAMS, S.C. *TN During the Revolutionary War.* 1944. Nashville. 1st ed. inscr/sgn. EX. $85.00

WILLIAMS, S.T. *Tour in Scotland & Other Manuscript Notes by WA Irving.* 1927. New Haven. 1/525. 146 p. TEG. xl. VG. $25.00

WILLIAMS, S.W. *Middle Kingdom (Chinese Empire).* 1848. Wiley Putnam. 2 vols. VG. $350.00

WILLIAMS, Stephen. *Narrative of Captivity of Stephen Williams.* 1889. Deerfield. printed wraps. G. $25.00

WILLIAMS, T.B. *Soul of the Red Man.* 1938. np. Ils 1st ed. inscr. EX. $25.00

WILLIAMS, T.H. *Americans at War: Development of American Military System.* 1960. LA U. 1st ed. 138 p. dj. VG. T5. $19.50

WILLIAMS, T.H. *McClellan, Sherman & Grant.* 1962. Rutgers. 1st ed. dj. VG. $9.00

WILLIAMS, Tenessee. *Suddenly Last Summer.* 1958. New Directions. 1st ed. dj. VG. $70.00

WILLIAMS, Tennessee. *Baby Doll.* 1956. NY. 1st ed. dj. VG. B2. $35.00

WILLIAMS, Tennessee. *Battle of Angels.* 1945. Murray. 1st ed. wraps. EX. $300.00

WILLIAMS, Tennessee. *Cat on a Hot Tin Roof.* 1955. New Directions. 1st ed. dj. EX. $65.00

WILLIAMS, Tennessee. *Collected Stories.* 1985. NY. Ils Warhol bdg. dj. EX. $12.00

WILLIAMS, Tennessee. *Glass Menagerie.* 1945. Random House. 1st ed. $75.00

WILLIAMS, Tennessee. *Moise & the World of Reason.* 1975. NY. 1st ed. dj. G. $20.00

WILLIAMS, Tennessee. *Moise & the World of Reason.* 1975. NY. 1st ed. sgn. dj. M. $100.00

WILLIAMS, Tennessee. *Period of Adjustment.* 1960. New Directions. 1st ed. dj. EX. $45.00

WILLIAMS, Tennessee. *Period of Adjustment: Serious Comedy.* 1961. London. Secker Warburg. 1st ed. dj. EX. $60.00

WILLIAMS, Tennessee. *Roman Spring of Mrs. Stone.* 1950. New Directions. 1st ed. dj. G. $15.00

WILLIAMS, Tennessee. *Rose Tattoo.* 1951. New Directions. 1st ed. 1st bdg. dj. M. $75.00

WILLIAMS, Tennessee. *Small Craft Warnings.* 1973. Secker Warburg. 1st Eng ed. dj. EX. $35.00

WILLIAMS, Tennessee. *Streetcar Named Desire.* London. 1st ed. dj. VG. $50.00

WILLIAMS, Tennessee. *Streetcar Named Desire.* Ltd Ed Club. slipcase. M. B3. $60.00

WILLIAMS, Tennessee. *Streetcar Named Desire.* 1947. London. 1st ed. dj. EX. P3. $70.00

WILLIAMS, Tennessee. *Summer & Smoke.* 1948. New Directions. dj. VG. $30.00

WILLIAMS, Tennessee. *Sweet Bird of Youth.* 1959. New Directions. 1st ed. dj. $50.00

WILLIAMS, Tennessee. *Sweet Bird of Youth.* 1961. London. 1st ed. dj. EX. $50.00

WILLIAMS, Tennessee. *TN Williams' Collected Stories.* 1985. New Directions. Intro Vidal. Warhol bdg. dj. EX. $30.00

WILLIAMS, Tennessee. *TN Williams' Letters to Donald Windham.* 1976. Verona. 1st ed. 1/500. wraps. slipcase. $100.00

WILLIAMS, Tennessee. *TN Williams' Letters to Donald Windham.* 1977. NY. 1st trade ed. dj. EX. $25.00

WILLIAMS, Tennessee. *Wagon Full of Cotton.* 1949. Lehmann. dj. VG. $40.00

WILLIAMS, Valentine. *Mr. Ramosi.* nd. Hodder Stoughton. G. P1. $7.50

WILLIAMS, Valentine. *Mr. Ramosi.* nd. Grosset. xl. P1. $5.00

WILLIAMS, Valentine. *Mystery of the Gold Box.* nd. Collier. VG. P1. $10.00

WILLIAMS, Valentine. *Red Mass.* nd. Hodder Stoughton. VG. P1. $15.00

WILLIAMS, W.C. *Build-Up.* 1952. NY. 1st ed. dj. EX. $55.00

WILLIAMS, W.C. *Paterson, Book Five.* 1958. New Directions. dj. EX. $100.00

WILLIAMS, W.C. *Yes, Mrs. Williams.* 1959. McDowell. 1st ed. dj. J2. $25.00

WILLIAMS, W.D. *Make Light of It: Collected Stories.* 1949. NY. 1st ed. 1st print. dj. VG. $20.00

WILLIAMS, W.G. *Days of Darkness: Gettysburg Civilians.* 1987. 254 p. dj. EX. J4. $15.00

WILLIAMS, W.J. *Hardwired.* 1986. Tower. 1st ed. dj. EX. P1. $15.95

WILLIAMS & WILLIAMS. *Great Houses of America.* 1966. NY. 1st ed. dj. EX. J2. $22.50

WILLIAMS. *Bibliography of Writings of Lewis Carroll.* 1924. London. 1st ed. dj. VG. $85.00

WILLIAMS. *Happy End.* Derrydale. as issued. VG. B2. $95.00

WILLIAMS-ELLIS, Amabel & Owen. *Out of This World 4.* 1964. Blackie. dj. VG. P1. $13.75

WILLIAMSON, Audrey. *Mystery of the Princes.* 1978. 1st ed. lg pb. M. C1. $9.50

WILLIAMSON, G. *Daniel Gardner.* 1921. London. Ils. 4to. dj. VG. J2. $100.00

WILLIAMSON, H. *Illustrated Tarka the Otter: His Joyful Water.* 1986. Webb Bower. Ils. 207 p. dj. M. M2. $20.00

WILLIAMSON, H.D. *Year of the Kangaroo.* 1977. Scribner. Ils 1st ed. maps. 187 p. dj. M2. $9.00

WILLIAMSON, H.E. *Winchester: Gun That Won the W.* 1963. Barnes. Ils. 4to. 494 p. dj. EX. $18.50

WILLIAMSON, H.F. *Winchester: Gun That Won the W.* 1952. 1st ed. dj. G. $70.00

WILLIAMSON, Hugh Ross. *Catherine de Medici.* 1973. Viking. Studio Book. Ils 288 p. dj. D2. $35.00

WILLIAMSON, Hugh Ross. *Lorenzo the Magnificent.* 1974. NY. Putnam. Ils 288 p. dj. D2. $35.00

WILLIAMSON, J.L.P. *English-Dakota Dictionary.* 1902. NY. VG. $75.00

WILLIAMSON, J.N. *How To Write Horror.* 1987. Writers Digest. P1. $15.95

WILLIAMSON, J.N. *Masques.* 1984. Maclay. 1st ed. sgn. dj. EX. P1. $25.00

WILLIAMSON, Jack. *Brother to Demons Brother, Brother to Gods.* 1979. Bobbs Merrill. 1st ed. dj. EX. P1. $17.50

WILLIAMSON, Jack. *Cometeers.* 1950. Fantasy. 1st ed. dj. G. P1. $25.00

WILLIAMSON, Jack. *Dragon's Island.* 1951. Simon Schuster. 1st ed. VG. P1. $22.50

WILLIAMSON, Jack. *Early Williamson.* 1975. Doubleday. 1st ed. dj. VG. P1. $20.00

WILLIAMSON, Jack. *Humanoid Touch.* nd. Book Club. dj. EX. P1. $4.00

WILLIAMSON, Jack. *Humanoid Touch.* 1980. Phantasia. 1st ed. 1/500. sgn. dj. EX. P1. $45.00

WILLIAMSON, Jack. *Legion of Time.* 1952. Fantasy. 1st ed. dj. EX. $40.00

WILLIAMSON, Jack. *Legion of Time.* 1952. Fantasy. 1st ed. dj. VG. P1. $25.00

WILLIAMSON, Jack. *Power of Blackness.* 1976. Berkley Putnam. 1st ed. dj. xl. P1. $5.00

WILLIAMSON, M.L. *Life of General Thomas J. Jackson.* 1899. Ils. 248 p. juvenile. G. J4. $15.00

WILLIAMSON, Moncrieff. *Death in Picture.* 1982. Toronto. Musson. 1st ed. inscr/sgn. dj. EX. $25.00

WILLIAMSON, Moncrieff. *Robert Harris: Unconventional Biography.* 1970. Toronto. McClelland Stewart. slipcase. D2. $45.00

WILLIAMSON, R.S. *Report of a Reconnaissance in CA.* 1856. WA. G. $100.00

WILLIAMSON, R.S. *Report of Explorations in CA, Vol V: US Pacific Railroad...* 1856. WA. Nicholson. Ils. 400 p. A3. $350.00

WILLIAMSON. *Age of Drake.* 1938. London. Black. VG. $17.50

WILLINGHAM, Calder. *End As a Man.* 1947. Vanguard. 1st ed. 2nd issue. dj. EX. $20.00

WILLINGHAM, Calder. *Rambling Rose.* 1972. NY. Delacorte. EX. $27.50

WILLIS, John. *Dance World 1967.* 1967. NY. Crown. Ils. sm 4to. 224 p. dj. $27.50

WILLIS, John. *Screen World Annual 1973. Vol. 24.* 1st ed. dj. EX. $30.00

WILLIS, Lionel. *Coastal Trade.* 1975. London. Intro Greenhill. pls. slipcase. M. $80.00

WILLIS, N.P. *American Scenery; or, Land, Lake & River Illustrations...* 1852. London. Virtue. 77 pls. sm folio. AEG. VG. J2. $500.00

WILLIS & COYNE. *Scenery & Antiquities of Ireland.* 1841. London. Virtue. 118 pls. folio. diced calf. J2. $250.00

WILLISON, George F. *Saints & Strangers.* nd. BOMC. dj. VG. P1. $4.00

WILLOCK, C. *Enormous Zoo: Profile of the Uganda National Parks.* 1965. Harcourt Brace. Ils 1st Am ed. dj. EX. M2. $17.00

WILLOUGHBY, C.A. *Shanghai Conspiracy.* 1952. Dutton. VG. M1. $10.00

WILLOUGHBY, M.F. *Rum War at Sea.* 1964. WA. GPO. EX. $12.00

WILLOUGHBY, W.C. *Soul of Bantu: Story of Magico-Religious Practices...* 1928. Doubleday. 1st ed. sgn. 8vo. with sgn letter. $65.00

WILLOUGHBY, W.C. *Soul of the Bantu: Magico-Religious Practices & Beliefs.* 1928. Garden City. G. $25.00

WILLOUGHBY, W.C. *Soul of the Bantu: Nature, Worship & Taboo.* 1932. Hartford. G. $25.00

WILLS, Cecil M. *Chamois Murder.* 1935. Unicorn Pr. 1st ed. sgn. dj. VG. P1. $25.00

WILLS, Garry. *Nixon Agonistes.* 1970. NY. Houghton. 8vo. dj. VG. $15.00

WILLS, Geoffrey. *Practical Guide to Antique Collecting.* nd. Gramercy. dj. VG. P1. $7.50

WILLSHIRE, William Hughes. *Introduction to Study & Collection of Ancient Prints.* 1877. London. Ellis White. 2 vols. D2. $250.00

WILLSON, Beckles. *John Slidell & Confederates in Paris, 1862-1865.* 1970. 296 p. EX. J4. $15.00

WILLSON, R.T. *First Hundred Years of Cuyahoga Co.: 1853-1953.* 1953. Cleveland. Ils. photos. 55 p. T5. $15.00

WILMERDING, John. *American Art.* 1976. Middlesex. Penguin. 1st ed. 4to. 322 p. $85.00

WILMERDING, John. *Fritz Hugh Lane.* 1971. Praeger. Ils. dj. D2. $50.00

WILMERDING, John. *History of American Marine Painting.* 1968. Boston. Ils 1st ed. 379 p. dj. EX. $75.00

WILSON, Adrian. *Spice Islands Cookbook.* 1962. Menlo Park. Ils 2nd ed. EX. $15.00

WILSON, Angus. *Anglo-Saxon Attitudes.* 1956. London. 1st ed. dj. VG. $20.00

WILSON, Angus. *As If by Magic.* nd. NY. Viking. 1st ed. dj. VG. $24.00

WILSON, Angus. *Late Call.* 1964. London. Secker Warburg. 1st ed. dj. EX. $20.00

WILSON, Angus. *Middle Age of Mrs. Eliot.* 1958. London. Secker Warburg. 1st ed. dj. EX. $22.00

WILSON, Angus. *Old Men at the Zoo.* 1961. London. Secker Warburg. 1st ed. dj. VG. $22.00

WILSON, Angus. *Setting the World on Fire.* 1980. NY. Viking. 1st ed. dj. EX. $16.00

WILSON, C.M. *Backwoods America.* 1934. Chapel Hill. Ils Wooten. 1st ed. dj. EX. $55.00

WILSON, Colin. *Mind Parasites.* 1967. 1st ed. dj. VG. B2. $22.50

WILSON, Colin. *Outsider.* 1956. Boston. 1st ed. dj. VG. B2. $15.00

WILSON, Colin. *Ritual in the Dark.* 1960. London. 1st ed. dj. VG. $50.00

WILSON, Colin. *Schoolgirl Murder Case.* 1975. Hart Davis. 2nd ed. dj. EX. P1. $15.00

WILSON, Colin. *Statue of Man.* 1959. 1st ed. VG. $5.00

WILSON, Colin. *Voyage to a Beginning.* 1969. NY. 1st ed. dj. VG. B2. $20.00

WILSON, Craig. *Index to Samuel A. Lane's Fifty Years & Over in Akron...* 1987. Akron. 192 p. wraps. M. T5. $15.95

WILSON, E. *Axel's Castle.* 1931. NY. 1st ed. VG. $20.00

WILSON, E. *Memoirs of Hecate Co.* 1946. Garden City. 1st ed. dj. VG. $35.00

WILSON, E. *Minado: Tale of Quebec Wilderness.* nd. NY. Appleton Century Crafts. 191 p. M1. $7.50

WILSON, E. *Patriotic Gore.* 1962. NY. 1st ed. dj. EX. $35.00

WILSON, E.E. *Slipstream: Autobiography of Air Craftsman.* 1950. NY. Review 1st ed. 328 p. dj. G. T5. $25.00

WILSON, E.H. *America's Greatest Garden.* 1925. Boston. Ils 2nd ed. 123 p. VG. $30.00

WILSON, E.H. *Aristocrats of the Garden.* 1926. Boston. Ils. 1st print. TEG. dj. VG. $45.00

WILSON, E.L. *Wilson's Photographics: Series of Lessons...* 1881. NY. Ils. pls. $45.00

WILSON, E.O. *Insect Societies.* 1974. Harvard. Ils. 548 p. dj. EX. M2. $25.00

WILSON, Earl. *Show Business Nobody Knows.* nd. Book Club. VG. P1. $3.00

WILSON, Edith. *My Memoir.* 1939. Indianapolis. Ils 1st ed. VG. $10.00

WILSON, Edmund. *Patriotic Gore: Studies in Literature of Civil War.* 1962. NY. Oxford. 1st ed. 816 p. $45.00

WILSON, Edmund. *Piece of My Mind.* 1956. 1st ed. sgn. dj. VG. B2. $15.00

WILSON, Edmund. *Triple Thinkers.* 1938. NY. dj. EX. $20.00

WILSON, Erasmus. *Students' Book of Cutaneous Medicine & Diseases of Skin.* 1865. London. 1st ed. 517 p. green cloth. EX. $70.00

WILSON, Erica. *Needle Play.* 1975. Scribner. Ils. 189 p. dj. $12.50

WILSON, F.P. *Black Wind.* 1988. NY. ARC. wraps. M. $15.00

WILSON, F.P. *Enemy of the State.* 1980. Doubleday. 1st ed. dj. xl. P1. $7.50

WILSON, F.P. *Keep.* 1981. NY. 1st ed. dj. EX. $20.00

WILSON, F.P. *Soft & Others.* 1989. NY. UCP. wraps. M. $15.00

WILSON, F.P. *Sword of the Lictor.* 1981. Timescape. 1st ed. dj. EX. $12.00

WILSON, G.R. *Ariman's World.* 1957. Random House. Ils. dj. M1. $10.00

WILSON, Gahan. *Eddy Deco's Last Caper.* 1987. Time Books. 1st ed. sgn. 213 p. VG. M1. $30.00

WILSON, H.M. *Great Valley Patriots: WV in Struggle for Liberty.* 1976. Staunton. dj. EX. $25.00

WILSON, H.V. *African Violet & Gesneriad Questions Answered by 20 Experts.* 1966. Princeton. Ils 1st ed. dj. EX. $20.00

WILSON, H.V. *Observations on Gemmule & Egg Development of Marine Sponges.* 1894. Ginn. pls. rebound. VG. M2. $25.00

WILSON, H.W. *Battleships in Action. Vol. II.* nd. London. Sampson Low. Ils. 8vo. VG. $60.00

WILSON, Hazel. *Herbert's Space Trip.* 1965. Knopf. VG. P1. $15.00

WILSON, Helen. *African Violets.* 1966. Van Nostrand. VG. $12.50

WILSON, J.F. *Master Key.* nd. Grosset. Movie ed. VG. P1. $20.00

WILSON, J.H. *Nell Gwyn.* 1952. Pellegrini Cudahy. VG. $17.00

WILSON, J.M. *Tales of the Borders & Scotland.* c 1880. London. 12mo. 4 vols. EX. $75.00

WILSON, J.M. *Wilson's Tales of the Borders.* 1947. Ettrick Pr. 2nd ed. VG. P1. $15.00

WILSON, J.P. *Easy Introduction to Knowledge of Hebrew Language...* 1912. Phil. 1st ed. $125.00

WILSON, K.A. *Owl Studies at Ann Arbor, MI.* 1938. Auk. no cover. M2. $3.00

WILSON, LeGrand J. *Confederate Soldier.* Forword Wiley. 213 p. dj. EX. J4. $25.00

WILSON, Louis. *U of NC: 1900-1930.* 1957. Chapel Hill. 1st ed. 633 p. dj. VG. $30.00

WILSON, P. *Australia's Butterflies.* 1987. Kangaroo. Ils 1st ed. 64 p. M. M2. $15.00

WILSON, R.A. *Gertrude Stein: A Bibliography.* 1974. NY. sgn. VG. $22.00

WILSON, R.D. *Jim Crow Joins Up.* 1944. NY. VG. $15.00

WILSON, R.L. *Book of Colt Engravings.* 1982. 2nd ed. G. $190.00

WILSON, R.R. *Lincoln in Caricature.* 1945. NY. Elmira. Ltd ed. sgn/#d. VG. $65.00

WILSON, Steve. *Dealer's Move.* 1978. Macmillan. 1st ed. dj. EX. P1. $15.00

WILSON & BONAPARTE. *American Ornithology: Natural History Birds of US.* c 1878. London. Cassell Potter Galpin. 3 vols. M2. $350.00

WILSON. *Manual of Dental Prosthetics.* 1917. Phil. Ils 3rd ed. 8vo. VG. $30.00

WILSTACH, F.J. *Wild Bill Hickok: Prince of the Pistoleers.* 1926. Doubleday. lacks 1 photo. G. $7.50

WILSTACH, F.J. *Wild Bill Hickok: Prince of the Pistoleers.* 1926. NY. Ils 1st ed. 304 p. VG. T5. $45.00

WILSTACH, Paul. *Hudson River Landings.* 1933. Indianapolis. 1st ed. VG. $25.00

WILSTACH, Paul. *Potomac Landings.* 1932. Indianapolis. Ils 378 p. VG. $15.00

WILSTACH, Paul. *Richard Mansfield: Man & Actor.* 1908. Scribner. $10.00

WILTSE, C.M. *John C. Calhoun, Nationalist, 1782-1828.* 1944. Bobbs Merrill. 1st ed. 477 p. $5.00

WIMBERLY, Lowry Charles. *Folklore in English & Scottish Ballads.* 1965. Dover. pb. VG. C1. $9.00

WINCHELL, Alexander. *Preadamites: Existence of Man Before Adam, a Study...* 1880. Chicago. Ils 8vo. VG. T1. $50.00

WINCHESTER, Alice. *Versatile Yankee: Art of Jonathan Fisher, 1768-1847.* 1973. Pine Pr. dj. J2. $20.00

WINCHESTER, E. *Course of Lectures on Prophecies.* 1800. Walpole. 1st Am ed. 2 vols. G. $95.00

WINCKEL, F.W. *Technik U. Aufgaben des Fernsehens.* 1930. Berlin. Ils. 74 p. wraps. $15.00

WIND, H.W. *World of P.G. Wodehouse.* 1972. Praeger. dj. VG. P1. $20.00

WINDHAM, Donald. *Tanaquil.* 1977. Holt. 1st ed. dj. EX. $20.00

WINEPAHL, Robert. *Gold Rush Voyage on the Bark Orion: From Boston...* 1978. Clark. 1st ed. dj. J2. $20.00

WINFIELD, Arthur M. *Rover Boys on Treasure Isle.* nd. Whitman. VG. P1. $6.00

WINGFIELD. *History of Caroline Co.* 1924. Richmond. 1/1000. B1. $75.00

WINKLER, F. *Die Zeichnungen Albrecht Durers.* 1936. Berlin. Ils 24 pls. 4to. 194 p. VG. J2. $150.00

WINKLER, Mrs. A.V. *Confederate Capitol & Hood's TX Brigade.* 1894. 312 p. EX. extremely scarce. J4. $195.00

WINKWORTH, Catherine. *Christian Singers of Germany.* 1869. London. Ils. 340 p. AEG. EX. $60.00

WINSHIP, A.E. *Jukes-Edwards.* 1900. Harrisburg. 12mo. 88 p. dj. VG. $10.00

WINSLOW, D.G. *Essentials of Design.* 1924. NY. Ils. 255 p. $10.00

WINSON, T. *Peripheral Vascular Disease.* 1959. Springfield. 845 p. $45.00

WINSOR, Justin. *Narrative & Critical History of America.* 1889. Houghton. 16 vols. VG. $225.00

WINSOR, Kathleen. *Lovers.* 1952. London. 1st ed. dj. EX. $15.00

WINSTON, R.W. *Robert E. Lee: A Biography.* 1934. Grosset Dunlap. Ils. maps. 428 p. VG. M2. $12.00

WINSTON. *Fighting Squadron.* 1946. 1st ed. dj. $25.00

WINTER, D.E. *Prime Evil.* 1988. NH. 1st ed. sgn King/Cady/Barker/10 others. R1. $600.00

WINTER, D.E. *Stephen King: Art of Darkness.* 1984. New Am Lib. 1st print. gray/black bdg. dj. EX. $35.00

WINTER, Ella. *Not To Yield.* 1963. Harcourt Brace. 1st ed. dj. EX. $23.00

WINTER, Ella. *Red Virtue.* 1933. Harcourt. 1st ed. inscr/sgn. dj. VG. $17.50

WINTER, G. *Country Camera, 1844-1914.* 1971. London. Ils. 4to. 120 p. $42.50

WINTER, George. *Journals & Indian Paintings of George Winter 1837-1839.* 1948. Indianapolis. IN Hist Soc. 1st ed. VG. M1. $125.00

WINTER, Milo. *Bible Storybook.* 1925. Rand McNally. Ils. VG. $17.50

WINTER, Milo. *Three Musketeers.* Windermere. G. E2. $15.00

WINTER, N.O. *FL: Land of Enchantment.* 1918. Page. Ils 1st ed. 380 p. EX. M2. $15.00

WINTERBOTHAM, Russ. *Joyce of the Secret Squadron.* nd. Whitman. dj. VG. P1. $20.00

WINTERS, Erastus. *In the 50th OH, Serving Uncle Sam.* 1905. E Walnut Hill. 1st ed. 188 p. wraps. G. T5. $225.00

WINTERS, Jonathan. *Mouse Breath: Conformity & Other Social Illustrations.* 1965. Bobbs Merrill. dj. EX. $20.00

WINTERS, L.L. *True Hard Scrabble.* 1974. Phil. sgn. cloth. dj. $15.00

WINTHROP, John. *History of New England.* 1853. Boston. 2 vols. VG. $100.00

WINTHROP, John. *History of New England.* 1908. Scribner. 2 vols. VG. $35.00

WINTHROP, Theodore. *Canoe & Saddle: Adventures Among NW Rivers & Forests...* 1863. Ticknor Fields. 375 p. A3. $60.00

WINTNER, A. *Spektratheorie.* 1929. Leipzig. 1st ed. G. $75.00

WINWAR, Frances. *Haunted Palace.* 1959. Harper. 1st ed. turquoise cloth. dj. D1. $18.00

WINWARD, Walter. *Fives Wild.* 1976. Atheneum. 1st ed. dj. VG. P1. $15.00

WIRT, L. *AK Adventures.* 1937. NY. Ils. photos. fair. $12.00

WIRT, Mildred A. *Ghost Beyond the Gate.* 1943. Cupples Leon. VG. P1. $10.00

WIRT, William. *Life of Patrick Henry.* 1919. Phil. Webster. 3rd ed. orig tree calf. G. $35.00

WISBESKI, D. *Okee: Story of an Otter in the House.* 1964. Farrar Straus. Ils 1st print. 246 p. dj. EX. M2. $20.00

WISE, John. *Churches' Quarrel Exposed.* 1715. Boston. Boone. 1st ed. 116 p. orig bdg. EX. $500.00

WISE & COMPANY. *New Garden Encyclopedia.* 1941. Ils. 1348 p. EX. $5.00

WISE & ROSS. *Espionage Establishment.* 1967. Random House. 1st print. dj. VG. M1. $5.00

WISE & ROSS. *Invisible Government.* 1964. Random House. dj. VG. M1. $6.50

WISH, Harvey. *Reconstruction in S, 1865-1877: Firsthand Accounts.* 1965. NY. Farrar. 1st ed. dj. VG. $18.00

WISH, Harvey. *Society & Thought in Early America.* 1950. Longman Green. Ils 1st ed. 612 p. EX. M2. $22.00

WISHENGRAD, H. *Eternal Light.* 1947. NY. 1st ed. 412 p. VG. $27.50

WISHNER, L. *Chipmunks: Secrets of Their Solitary Lives.* 1982. Smithsonian. Ils 1st ed. 144 p. dj. M. M2. $14.00

WISNER, B. *How To Catch Salt-Water Fish.* 1955. Essy. Ils. 247 p. dj. VG. $7.50

WISTAR, Isaac Jones. *Autobiography of I.J. Wistar: Half a Century in War & Peace.* 1937. Phil. Ils 2nd ed. 4to. 528 p. dj. VG. T5. $95.00

WISTER, Owen. *Journey in Search of Christmas.* 1904. NY. Ils Remington. 1st ed. VG. G2. $40.00

WISTER, Owen. *Lin McLean.* nd. Burt. G. P1. $6.00

WISTER, Owen. *Neighbors Henceforth.* 1922. Macmillan. 1st ed. $12.00

WISTER, Owen. *Pentacost of Calamity.* 1915. Macmillan. 1st ed. 8th print. VG. scarce. $95.00

WISTER, Owen. *Roosevelt: Story of a Friendship.* 1930. NY. 1st ed. VG. $27.50

WISTER, Owen. *Virginian.* 1904. NY. 1st pb ed. VG. $45.00

WISTRAND, A. *Handboki Rattsmedicinen.* 1853. Stockholm. 2 vols. leather. $65.00

WITH, Karl. *Marc Chagall.* 1923. Leipzig. Ils. D2. $50.00

WITHER, George. *Speculum Speculativum; or, Considering Glass...* 1660. London. 1st ed. 1st issue. rebound. VG. G2. $95.00

WITHERBY, H.F. *Light From the Land of the Sphinx.* 1896. London. Witherby. $75.00

WITHERING, William. *Account of Foxglove & Some of Its Medical Uses.* nd. London. Broomsleigh. 1/250. J2. $50.00

WITHERS, Percy. *Buried Life. Personal Recollections of A.E. Housman.* 1940. London. 1st ed. dj. VG. $30.00

WITHEY, L. *Voyages of Discovery: Captain Cook & Exploration of Pacific.* 1987. Morrow. Review of 1st ed. 512 p. dj. M2. $20.00

WITHINGTON, Antoinette. *Golden Cloak.* 1953. Honolulu. Ils. 312 p. dj. VG. $20.00

WITNEY & JOHNSON. *Railway Country: Across Canada by Train.* 1985. . 200 p. $35.00

WITTER, Dean. *Meanderings of a Fisherman.* nd. private print. Ils. 4to. EX. $20.00

WITTER, Herman R. *Canton.* 1922. Canton. Ils. 4to. T5. $35.00

WITTKE, Carl. *History of the State of OH.* 1941-1944. Columbus. 6 vols. G. T5. $125.00

WITTKOWER, Rudolf. *Art & Architecture in Italy 1600-1750.* 1965. Baltimore. Penguin. Revised 2nd ed. dj. D2. $55.00

WITTKOWER, Rudolf. *Gian Lorenzo Berini: Sculptor of Roman Baroque.* 1966. London. Ils. 4to. dj. J2. $75.00

WITTKOWER, Rudolf. *Gian Lorenzo Berini: Sculptor of Roman Baroque.* 1966. London. Phaidon. 2nd ed. 286 p. dj. D2. $75.00

WITWER, H.C. *Fighting Back.* nd. Grosset. Movie ed. VG. P1. $17.50

WITWER, H.C. *Leather Pushers.* nd. Grosset. Movie ed. VG. P1. $17.50

WODEHOUSE, P.G. *Adventures of Sally.* nd. Jenkins. 7th print. EX. P1. $35.00

WODEHOUSE, P.G. *Aunts Aren't Gentlemen.* 1975. Barrie Jenkins. 2nd ed. dj. EX. P1. $22.50

WODEHOUSE, P.G. *Author! Author!* 1962. NY. 1st ed. dj. EX. $25.00

WODEHOUSE, P.G. *Bachelors Anonymous.* 1973. Barrie Jenkins. 1st ed. dj. EX. P1. $25.00

WODEHOUSE, P.G. *Bachelors Anonymous.* 1974. Simon Schuster. 1st ed. dj. EX. P1. $25.00

WODEHOUSE, P.G. *Barny in Wonderland.* 1978. London. dj. EX. $27.00

WODEHOUSE, P.G. *Bertie Wooster Sees It Through.* 1955. NY. 1st ed. dj. EX. $25.00

WODEHOUSE, P.G. *Big Money.* nd. Jenkins. dj. VG. P1. $65.00

WODEHOUSE, P.G. *Bill the Conqueror.* nd. Goodchild. 1st Canadian ed. G. P1. $35.00

WODEHOUSE, P.G. *Bill the Conqueror.* 1925. Methuen. 3rd ed. G. P1. $25.00

WODEHOUSE, P.G. *Bill the Conqueror.* 1934. Methuen. 15th print. VG. P1. $30.00

WODEHOUSE, P.G. *Blandings Castle.* 1935. Jenkins. 1st ed. G. P1. $50.00

WODEHOUSE, P.G. *Brinkley Manor.* 1939. Triangle. 5th ed. dj. VG. P1. $35.00

WODEHOUSE, P.G. *Butler Did It.* 1957. Simon Schuster. dj. xl. fair. P1. $12.50

WODEHOUSE, P.G. *Carry on Jeeves.* nd. Jenkins. 3rd ed. VG. P1. $25.00

WODEHOUSE, P.G. *Century of Humor.* 1934. Hutchinson. VG. P1. $50.00

WODEHOUSE, P.G. *Clicking of Cuthbert.* nd. Jenkins. VG. P1. $30.00

WODEHOUSE, P.G. *Code of the Woosters.* nd. Jenkins. 6th print. VG. P1. $25.00

WODEHOUSE, P.G. *Code of the Woosters.* 1939. Dial. VG. P1. $30.00

WODEHOUSE, P.G. *Damsel in Distress.* 1975. Barrie Jenkins. dj. VG. P1. $20.00

WODEHOUSE, P.G. *Five Complete Novels.* 1983. Avenel. 1st ed. dj. EX. P1. $15.00

WODEHOUSE, P.G. *Full Moon.* nd. London. Jenkins. dj. VG. $55.00

WODEHOUSE, P.G. *Full Moon.* 1947. Doubleday. 1st ed. VG. P1. $40.00

WODEHOUSE, P.G. *Girl on the Boat.* nd. Jenkins. VG. P1. $30.00

WODEHOUSE, P.G. *Gold Bat.* 1974. Souvenir Pr. dj. EX. P1. $15.00

WODEHOUSE, P.G. *He Rather Enjoyed It.* 1925. NY. 1st ed. dj. VG. scarce. $75.00

WODEHOUSE, P.G. *Head of Kay's.* 1922. Black. 4th ed. VG. P1. $40.00

WODEHOUSE, P.G. *Heavy Weather.* nd. Jenkins. 5th ed. VG. P1. $25.00

WODEHOUSE, P.G. *Heavy Weather.* 1933. McClelland. 1st Canadian ed. G. P1. $35.00

WODEHOUSE, P.G. *Heavy Weather.* 1933. McClelland. 1st Canadian ed. VG. P1. $60.00

WODEHOUSE, P.G. *Hot Water.* nd. Jenkins. dj. G. P1. $40.00

WODEHOUSE, P.G. *Hot Water.* 1932. McClelland. 1st Canadian ed. VG. P1. $50.00

WODEHOUSE, P.G. *If I Were You.* nd. Jenkins. 9th ed. dj. G. P1. $40.00

WODEHOUSE, P.G. *If I Were You.* 1931. Jenkins. 2nd ed. G. P1. $35.00

WODEHOUSE, P.G. *Indiscretions of Archie.* 1921. Doran. G. P1. $35.00

WODEHOUSE, P.G. *Jeeves & the Tie That Binds.* 1971. Simon Schuster. 1st ed. dj. EX. P1. $25.00

WODEHOUSE, P.G. *Jeeves in the Offing.* 1960. Jenkins. 1st ed. dj. VG. P1. $30.00

WODEHOUSE, P.G. *Jill the Reckless.* nd. Jenkins. 9th print. VG. P1. $30.00

WODEHOUSE, P.G. *Laughing Gas.* 1936. McClelland. 1st Canadian ed. VG. P1. $50.00

WODEHOUSE, P.G. *Leave It to Psmith.* nd. Jenkins. 13th print. dj. G. P1. $40.00

WODEHOUSE, P.G. *Lord Emsworth & Others.* 1956. Jenkins. VG. P1. $20.00

WODEHOUSE, P.G. *Luck of the Bodkins.* 1935. McClelland. 1st Canadian ed. dj. VG. P1. $75.00

WODEHOUSE, P.G. *Luck of the Bodkins.* 1975. Barrie Jenkins. dj. EX. P1. $25.00

WODEHOUSE, P.G. *Man Upstairs.* 1924. Methuen. 9th print. VG. P1. $40.00

WODEHOUSE, P.G. *Man With Two Left Feet.* 1932. Methuen. 12th print. dj. VG. P1. $50.00

WODEHOUSE, P.G. *Mating Season.* 1949. Didier. 1st ed. VG. P1. $40.00

WODEHOUSE, P.G. *Meet Mr. Mulliner.* nd. Burt. dj. VG. P1. $60.00

WODEHOUSE, P.G. *Mike at Wrykyn.* 1953. Meredith. 1st ed. dj. VG. P1. $60.00

WODEHOUSE, P.G. *Money for Nothing.* nd. Jenkins. 2nd ed. VG. P1. $35.00

WODEHOUSE, P.G. *Most of P.G. Wodehouse.* 1960. Simon Schuster. 1st ed. dj. VG. P1. $30.00

WODEHOUSE, P.G. *Much Obliged, Jeeves.* 1971. Barrie Jenkins. 2nd ed. dj. EX. P1. $25.00

WODEHOUSE, P.G. *Mulliner Omnibus.* 1935. Jenkins. 1st ed. G. P1. $35.00

WODEHOUSE, P.G. *Not George WA.* 1980. Continuum. dj. EX. P1. $12.50

WODEHOUSE, P.G. *Nothing But Wodehouse.* 1946. Doubleday. dj. VG. P1. $35.00

WODEHOUSE, P.G. *Pearls, Girls & Monty Bodkin.* 1972. Barrie Jenkins. 1st ed. dj. EX. P1. $30.00

WODEHOUSE, P.G. *Pelican at Blandings.* 1969. Jenkins. 1st ed. dj. EX. P1. $35.00

WODEHOUSE, P.G. *Perfect's Uncle.* 1972. Souvenir Pr. dj. EX. P1. $15.00

WODEHOUSE, P.G. *Picadilly Jim.* nd. Jenkins. Popular ed. dj. G. P1. $40.00

WODEHOUSE, P.G. *Piccadilly Jim.* nd. Jenkins. 14th print. VG. P1. $25.00

WODEHOUSE, P.G. *Plot That Thickened.* 1973. NY. 1st ed. dj. EX. $18.00

WODEHOUSE, P.G. *Pothunters.* 1972. Souvenir Pr. dj. EX. P1. $12.50

WODEHOUSE, P.G. *Prince & Betty.* 1912. NY. Ils Grefe. 1st Am ed. VG. T5. $195.00

WODEHOUSE, P.G. *Prince & Betty.* 1912. Watts. Popular ed. VG. P1. $250.00

WODEHOUSE, P.G. *Quick Service.* 1941. Longman Green. 1st Canadian ed. VG. P1. $40.00

WODEHOUSE, P.G. *Right Ho, Jeeves.* 1934. McClelland. 1st Canadian ed. VG. P1. $60.00

WODEHOUSE, P.G. *Service With a Smile.* 1962. Jenkins. 1st ed. dj. VG. P1. $40.00

WODEHOUSE, P.G. *Small Bachelor.* 1936. Methuen. 10th ed. VG. P1. $30.00

WODEHOUSE, P.G. *Something Fresh.* 1924. Methuen. 9th ed. VG. P1. $35.00

WODEHOUSE, P.G. *Something Fresh.* 1931. Methuen. 13th print. G. P1. $25.00

WODEHOUSE, P.G. *Summer Lightning.* nd. Jenkins. 7th print. dj. VG. P1. $45.00

WODEHOUSE, P.G. *Summer Moonshine.* nd. Jenkins. 2nd ed. G. P1. $25.00

WODEHOUSE, P.G. *Summer Moonshine.* 1937. Doubleday Doran. 1st ed. VG. P1. $50.00

WODEHOUSE, P.G. *Sunset at Blandings.* 1977. Simon Schuster. Ils Ionicus. 1st Am ed. VG. $10.00

WODEHOUSE, P.G. *Tales of St. Austin's.* 1972. Souvenir Pr. dj. EX. P1. $15.00

WODEHOUSE, P.G. *Thank You, Jeeves.* nd. Jenkins. VG. P1. $25.00

WODEHOUSE, P.G. *Thank You, Jeeves.* nd. Triangle. VG. P1. $17.50

WODEHOUSE, P.G. *The Butler Did It.* 1957. Simon Schuster. 1st ed. dj. $30.00

WODEHOUSE, P.G. *Ukridge.* 1924. Jenkins. 1st ed. G. P1. $50.00

WODEHOUSE, P.G. *Uncle Dynamite.* 1948. NY. Didier. dj. VG. scarce. $50.00

WODEHOUSE, P.G. *Uncle Fred in the Springtime.* 1939. McClelland. 1st Canadian ed. dj. VG. P1. $75.00

WODEHOUSE, P.G. *Uneasy Money.* 1931. Methuen. 15th print. VG. P1. $35.00

WODEHOUSE, P.G. *Very Good, Jeeves.* 1930. McClelland. 1st Canadian ed. VG. P1. $60.00

WODEHOUSE, P.G. *Very Good, Jeeves.* 1930. NY. 1st Am ed. 340 p. G. T5. $35.00

WODEHOUSE, P.G. *Weekend Wodehouse.* 1940. Garden City. G. P1. $35.00

WODEHOUSE, P.G. *White Feather.* 1972. Souvenir Pr. dj. EX. P1. $12.50

WODEHOUSE, P.G. *Wodehouse Nuggets.* 1983. Hutchinson. 1st ed. dj. EX. P1. $17.50

WODEHOUSE, P.G. *Wodehouse on Crime.* 1981. Ellery Queen Mystery Club. dj. P1. $20.00

WODEHOUSE, P.G. *Wodehouse on Golf.* 1940. Doubleday. 1st ed. dj. xl. P1. $35.00

WODEHOUSE, P.G. *World of Jeeves.* 1976. Barrie Jenkins. 4th ed. dj. VG. P1. $25.00

WODEHOUSE, P.G. *World of Mr. Mulliner.* 1972. Barrie Jenkins. 1st ed. dj. VG. P1. $25.00

WODEHOUSE, P.G. *Young Men in Spats.* 1936. Jenkins. 1st ed. xl. G. P1. $40.00

WODEHOUSE, P.G. *Young Men in Spats.* 1936. McClelland. 1st Canadian ed. VG. P1. $50.00

WODEHOUSE & BOLTON. *Bring on the Girls.* 1953. Simon Schuster. 1st ed. G. P1. $40.00

WOIWODE, Larry. *Beyond the Bedroom Wall.* 1975. NY. 1st ed. dj. EX. $15.00

WOIWODE, Larry. *Poppa John.* 1981. NY. 1st ed. dj. EX. $10.00

WOLANIN, Barbara A. *Arthur B. Carles: Painting With Color.* 1983. Phil. Ils. 176 p. D2. $30.00

WOLDMAN. *Lincoln & the Russians.* 1952. Cleveland. 1st ed. VG. $20.00

WOLF, E.R. *Sons of the Shaking Earth.* 1959. Chicago U. Ils. map. 303 p. dj. EX. M2. $13.00

WOLF, Gary K. *Generation Removed.* 1977. Doubleday. 1st ed. dj. EX. $10.00

WOLF, Gary K. *Killerbowl.* 1975. Doubleday. 1st ed. dj. EX. P1. $10.00

WOLF, Gary K. *Resurrectionist.* 1979. Doubleday. 1st ed. dj. EX. P1. $10.00

WOLF, Gary K. *Who Censored Roger Rabbit?* 1981. St. Martin. 1st ed. dj. xl. P1. $10.00

WOLF, Howard & Ralph. *Rubber: Story of Glory & Greed.* 1936. NY. 1st ed. 533 p. G. T5. $19.50

WOLF, Howard. *Tin Roof Anthology.* 1952. Phil. wraps. EX. T5. $8.50

WOLF, Leonard. *Annotated Dracula.* 1975. 1st ed. facsimile of 1897 ed. VG. C1. $19.50

WOLF, R.F. *Indian Rubber Man: Story of Charles Goodyear.* 1939. Caldwell. 291 p. VG. T5. $15.00

WOLF, Reinhart. *NY in Photographien.* 1980. Hamburg. sm folio. stiff wraps. EX. $75.00

WOLF, Thomas. *Mannerhouse.* 1st ed. inscr. dj. EX. B7. $35.00

WOLF & FLEMING. *Rosenbach: Biography.* 1960. Cleveland. 1st ed. dj. EX. $60.00

WOLFE, Alfred. *In AK Waters.* 1942. Caxton. Ils. sgn. dj. VG. very scarce. A3. $65.00

WOLFE, Bertram. *Fabulous Life of Diego Rivera.* 1963. Stein. 1st ed. dj. J2. $15.00

WOLFE, Bertram. *Ideology in Power: Reflections on Russian Revolution.* 1969. 1st ed. dj. J2. $12.50

WOLFE, Gene. *Citadel of the Autarch.* nd. Book Club. dj. VG. P1. $4.50

WOLFE, Gene. *Citadel of the Autarch.* 1983. Timescape. 1st ed. dj. EX. P1. $50.00

WOLFE, Gene. *Claw of the Conciliator.* 1981. Timescape. 1st ed. dj. EX. P1. $50.00

WOLFE, Gene. *Fifth Head of Cerberus.* 1972. Scribner. 1st ed. dj. EX. P1. $35.00

WOLFE, Gene. *Free Live Free.* 1985. Tower. 1st ed. dj. EX. P1. $16.95

WOLFE, Gene. *Peace.* 1975. Harper Row. 1st ed. dj. EX. P1. $35.00

WOLFE, Gene. *Urth of the New Sun.* 1987. Ultramarine. Ltd ed. 1/150. sgn. dj. M. $150.00

WOLFE, Thomas. *Bonfire of Vanities.* 1987. NY. 1st ed. dj. EX. $55.00

WOLFE, Thomas. *Candy Kolored Tangerine Flake Streamline Baby.* 1965. Farrar. 2nd ed. sgn. dj. VG. $30.00

WOLFE, Thomas. *Daily Log of Great Parks Trip, June 20-July 2, 1938.* 1951. Pittsburgh. 1st ed. dj. VG. T5. $32.50

WOLFE, Thomas. *Death to Morning.* 1935. NY. dj. EX. $120.00

WOLFE, Thomas. *Electric Kool-Aid Acid Test.* 1968. NY. 1st ed. dj. EX. $30.00

WOLFE, Thomas. *From Death to Morning.* 1935. Scribner. 1st ed. VG. $60.00

WOLFE, Thomas. *Hills Beyond.* 1941. NY. 1st ed. dj. EX. $85.00

WOLFE, Thomas. *In Our Time.* 1980. NY. 1st ed. dj. VG. $12.50

WOLFE, Thomas. *Look Homeward Angel.* 1974. NY. Scribner. 1st ed. G. $30.00

WOLFE, Thomas. *Look Homeward Angel.* 1977. Franklin Mint. Ils Reingold. Ltd ed. EX. $37.50

WOLFE, Thomas. *Mannerhouse.* 1948. NY. Ltd 1st ed. 1/500. dj. boxed. $115.00

WOLFE, Thomas. *Mauve Gloves & Madmen.* 1976. Clutter Vine. 1st ed. 243 p. dj. VG. $17.50

WOLFE, Thomas. *Of Time & the River.* 1935. NY. 1st ed. dj. $60.00

WOLFE, Thomas. *Portable Thomas Wolfe.* 1946. NY. Viking. 1st ed. dj. EX. $10.00

WOLFE, Thomas. *Pump House Gang.* 1968. NY. 1st ed. dj. EX. $30.00

WOLFE, Thomas. *Purple Decades.* 1982. NY. UCP. wraps. EX. $40.00

WOLFE, Thomas. *Radical Chic & Mau-Mauing the Flak Catchers.* 1st ed. sgn. dj. EX. B7. $35.00

WOLFE, Thomas. *Right Stuff.* 1979. NY. 1st ed. dj. EX. $65.00

WOLFE, Thomas. *Selected Great Stories.* 1945. Avon. 1st ed. wraps. VG. $25.00

WOLFE, Thomas. *Short Stories.* 1947. Penguin. 1st ed. EX. $25.00

WOLFE, Thomas. *Stone, Leaf, Door.* 1st ed. dj. VG. B7. $40.00

WOLFE, Thomas. *Three Decades of Criticism.* 1973. NY. NY U. 2nd print. 304 p. $20.00

WOLFE, Thomas. *Web & Rock.* 1939. NY/London. 1st ed. dj. $65.00

WOLFE, Thomas. *Years of Wandering in Many Lands & Cities.* 1949. NY. 1st ed. 1/600. slipcase. EX. $150.00

WOLFE, Thomas. *You Can't Go Home Again.* 1940. NY. 1st ed. VG. $40.00

WOLFERT, Ira. *American Guerrilla in the Phillippines.* 1945. NY. dj. fair. $12.00

WOLFF, L. *Electrocardiography.* 1950. Saunders. 1st ed. VG. $30.00

WOLFF, Leon. *Low Level Mission: Story of Ploesti Raids.* 1957. NY. Ils 1st ed. 240 p. dj. VG. T5. $32.50

WOLFF, Paul. *Kleine Itall Ienfahat.* 1938. Berlin. dj. VG. S2. $75.00

WOLFF, Paul. *Meine Erfahrungen mit der Leica...* 1934. Frankfurt. 192 photos. sm folio. $85.00

WOLFF, Paul. *Meine Erfahrungen mit der Leica...* 1939. Frankfurt. Revised ed. 161 pls. sgn. 242 p. $125.00

WOLFF, Paul. *My First Ten Years With the Leica.* c 1935. VG. $24.00

WOLFF, Tobias. *Back in the World.* 1985. Boston. 1st ed. sgn. EX. $30.00

WOLFF, W. *Island of Death.* 1973. Hacker. 20 pls. 228 p. EX. M2. $15.00

WOLFFE, Jabez. *Swimming.* nd. Foulsham. VG. P1. $4.00

WOLFHEIM, J.H. *Primates of World: Distribution, Abundance & Conservation.* 1983. WA U. Ils 1st ed. 831 p. M. M2. $55.00

WOLITZER, Hilma. *In the Flesh.* 1977. Morrow. 1st ed. dj. EX. $20.00

WOLLE, M.S. *Bonanza Trail.* 1952. NY. 1st ed. dj. VG. $22.50

WOLLE, M.S. *Stampede to Timberline: Ghost Towns & Mining Camps of CO.* 1952. private print. Ils. 544 p. dj. EX. M2. $18.00

WOLLHEIM, Donald A. *Mike Mars at Cape Canaveral.* 1961. Doubleday. 1st ed. sgn. dj. VG. P1. $25.00

WOLLHEIM, Donald A. *Mike Mars Astronaut.* 1961. Doubleday. 1st ed. dj. VG. P1. $12.00

WOLLHEIM, Donald A. *Mike Mars in Orbit.* 1961. Doubleday. 1st ed. dj. VG. P1. $12.00

WOLLHEIM, Donald A. *Mike Mars in Orbit.* 1961. Doubleday. 1st ed. sgn. dj. VG. P1. $25.00

WOLLHEIM, Donald A. *Portable Novels of Science.* 1945. Viking. 1st ed. VG. P1. $35.00

WOLLHEIM, Donald A. *Secret of the Martian Moons.* 1958. Winston. 3rd ed. dj. VG. P1. $7.50

WOLLHEIM, Donald A. *Universe Makers.* nd. Harper Row. VG. P1. $10.00

WOLLHEIM, Donald A. *1977 Annual World's Best SF.* nd. Book Club. dj. VG. P1. $4.50

WOLSELEY, G.J.W. *American Civil War: English View.* 1964. VA U. 230 p. dj. EX. $10.00

WOMACK, John. *Zapata & the Mexican Revoltion.* 1969. NY. 1st ed. dj. EX. $25.00

WONG, Jeanyee. *Buddha: Life & Teachings.* c 1950s. Peter Pauper. slipcase. M. C1. $14.00

WOOD, C. *Safari S America.* 1973. Taplinger. Ils 1st Am ed. 224 p. dj. EX. M2. $14.00

WOOD, Casey. *Grassus de Oculis.* 1929. Stanford. facsimile of 1747 ed. boxed. B2. $50.00

WOOD, Casey. *Introduction to Literature of Vertebrate Zoology.* 1974. reprint. 643 p. VG. $95.00

WOOD, Casey. *Memorandum Book of 10th-C Oculist.* 1936. Chicago. 1st ed. 232 p. VG. B2. $95.00

WOOD, Clement. *Eagle Sonnets.* 1942. NY. 1st ed. dj. VG. B2. $27.50

WOOD, E.O. *Historic Mackinac.* 1918. NY. 2 vols. EX. $150.00

WOOD, Eric. *Boy's Book of Pioneers.* nd. Funk Wagnall. 4 pls. G. $25.00

WOOD, Ernest. *Glorious Presence.* 1951. NY. $75.00

WOOD, Ernest. *Great Systems of Yoga.* 1954. NY. 168 p. dj. EX. $15.00

WOOD, J.G. *Homes Without Hands Being Description of Animals...* 1866. NY. Harper. 651 p. orig bdg. VG. A3. $50.00

WOOD, J.G. *Nature's Teachings: Human Invention Anticipated by Nature.* 1885. Ils 1st ed. gilt green bdg. VG. $35.00

WOOD, K. *Birds & Animals of the Rockies.* c 1950s. Larson. Ils. 157 p. EX. M2. $7.00

WOOD, Michael. *In Search of the Dark Ages.* 1987. 1st pb ed. VG. C1. $11.00

WOOD, Michael. *In Search of the Trojan War.* c 1985. NY. color pls. dj. VG. $12.50

WOOD, Mrs. Henry. *E Lynne.* nd. Unabridged ed. EX. $57.50

WOOD, R. *Ruins of Palmyra.* 1753. 1st ed. 57 pls. VG. $1400.00

WOOD, R.G. *Stephen Harriman Long: Army Engineer, Explorer, Inventor.* 1966. Clark. Ils. 282 p. EX. M2. $28.00

WOOD, R.K. *Tourist's Russia.* 1912. NY. Ils. 253 p. red cloth. EX. $45.00

WOOD, Robin. *Hitchcock's Films.* 1969. Castle. Enlarged 2nd ed. dj. J2. $7.50

WOOD, Stanley. *Over the Range to the Golden Gate: Complete Tourist Guide...* 1908. Chicago. Donnelley. 342 p. A3. $30.00

WOOD, Sumner. *Taverns & Turnpikes of Blanford.* 1903. Springfield. Ils. fld map. VG. C4. $65.00

WOOD, T.M. *George du Maurier: Satirist of the Victorians.* 1913. NY. VG. J2. $50.00

WOOD, Ted. *Fool's Gold.* 1986. NY. 1st ed. dj. EX. $15.00

WOOD, W. *Index Entomologicus: Complete Illustrated Catalog.* 1839. London. Wood. 54 hand-colored pls. 266 p. EX. M2. $875.00

WOOD, Wallace. *Odkin, Son of Odkin.* 1981. Wallace Wood. 1st ed. dj. EX. P1. $25.00

WOOD, Wallace. *Wizard King.* 1978. Wallace Wood. 1st ed. sgn. dj. EX. P1. $45.00

WOOD, Warren. *Tragedy of Deserted Isle.* 1909. Boston. presentation. VG. $10.00

WOOD, William. *Fight for Canada: Sketch From History of Great Imperial War.* 1906. Boston. Ils. map. 8vo. green cloth. VG. T1. $40.00

WOOD & GEASLAND. *Twins.* nd. Book Club. dj. VG. P1. $4.00

WOOD & GEASLAND. *Twins.* 1977. NY. 1st ed. dj. EX. $35.00

WOOD & TINKER. *Fifty Years of Bird Migration at Ann Arbor, MI.* 1934. MI Mus. 56 p. later paper cover. M2. $4.00

WOODALL, Ronald. *Magnificent Derelicts.* 1977. WA U. 1st ed. dj. EX. $25.00

WOODBURNE. *Essentials of Human Anatomy.* 1958. 2nd print. 4to. 620 p. VG. $20.00

WOODBURY, Augustus. *Major General Ambrose E. Burnside & the 9th Army Corps.* 1867. Providence. Ils 1st ed. 554 p. K1. $65.00

WOODBURY, George. *Story of Stanley Steamer.* 1950. NY. facsimile of 1916 catalog. T5. $17.50

WOODFIN, M.H. *Another Secret Diary of William Byrd of Westover.* 1942. Richmond. 1st ed. 490 p. dj. VG. B2. $30.00

WOODFORD, Jack. *Evangelical Cockroach.* 1929. NY. Carrier. 1st ed. dj. EX. $15.00

WOODFORD, Jack. *Sinful Daughter.* 1951. Arco. 1st ed. dj. VG. P1. $12.50

WOODFORD, Jack. *Two Can Play.* 1952. Signature Pr. dj. VG. P1. $12.50

WOODFORD, M. *Manual of Falconry.* 1972. London. Black. Ils 2nd ed. 194 p. dj. EX. M2. $30.00

WOODHAM-SMITH, C. *Queen Victoria.* 1972. Knopf. EX. $24.00

WOODHOUSE. *TB of Naval Aeronautics.* 1917. NY. Ils. sm folio. VG. C4. $185.00

WOODIN, A. *Home Is the Desert.* 1965. Macmillan. Ils. 247 p. dj. VG. $10.00

WOODIWISS, John C. *Some New Ghost Stories.* 1931. Simpkin Marshall. 1st ed. VG. P1. $90.00

WOODLEY, T.F. *Thaddeus Stevens.* 1934. Telegraph Pr. Ils. 664 p. G. M2. $20.00

WOODROW, Mrs. Wilson. *Moonhill Mystery.* 1930. Macauley. VG. P1. $10.00

WOODRUFF, H.S. *Mis' Beauty.* 1911. NY. Doran. Ils Jacobs. 1st ed. 163 p. $35.00

WOODRUFF, R.E. *Making of a Railroad Officer.* 1925. 245 p. xl. $25.00

WOODRUFF, W.E. *Wilderness to Statehood.* 1961. Times Echo Pr. 217 p. EX. M2. $25.00

WOODRUFF, W.E. *With the Light Guns in '61-'65.* 1903. Eagle Pr. facsimile reprint. 115 p. EX. M2. $35.00

WOODS, C.E. *Electric Automobile: Its Construction, Care & Operation.* 1900. Chicago. Ils 1st ed. G. T1. $65.00

WOODS, D.B. *Sixteen Months in Gold Diggings.* 1851. NY. 1st ed. inscr. 199 p. EX. $175.00

WOODS, John. *Two Years' Residence on English Prairie of IL.* 1968. Donnelley. Lakeside Classic. A3. $35.00

WOODS, R.L. *Treasury of the Familiar.* 1945. 7th ed. 751 p. dj. VG. $10.00

WOODS, Sara. *Enter a Gentlewoman.* 1982. Macmillan. 1st ed. dj. xl. P1. $5.00

WOODS, Sara. *Knives Have Edges.* 1968. Collins Crime Club. 1st ed. VG. P1. $5.00

WOODS, Sara. *Knives Have Edges.* 1968. Holt Rinehart. 1st ed. dj. VG. P1. $15.00

WOODS, Sara. *Tarry & Be Hanged.* nd. Book Club. dj. VG. P1. $4.50

WOODS, Sara. *Tarry & Be Hanged.* 1971. Holt Rinehart. 1st ed. dj. EX. P1. $15.00

WOODS, Sara. *This Fatal Writ.* nd. Book Club. dj. VG. P1. $4.50

WOODS, Sara. *Though I Know She Lies.* nd. Book Club. dj. G. P1. $4.50

WOODS, Sara. *Villains by Necessity.* 1982. St. Martin. 1st ed. dj. VG. P1. $12.50

WOODS, Sara. *Yet She Must Die.* nd. Book Club. dj. VG. P1. $4.50

WOODS, Stuart. *Under the Lake.* nd. Book Club. dj. VG. P1. $4.50

WOODWARD, C.V. *Tom Watson.* 1973. Savannah. dj. VG. $15.00

WOODWARD, W.E. *Meet General Grant.* 1928. Ils. 512 p. J4. $8.50

WOODWARD, W.E. *Meet General Grant.* 1946. Liveright. Ils. 524 p. EX. M2. $10.00

WOODWARD & O'CONNOR. *Peter Pan Picture Book.* 1907. London. J2. $80.00

WOODWORTH, Francis C. *Stories About Birds With Pictures To Match.* 1851. Boston. Ils. 336 p. K1. $18.50

WOOLCOT, Alexander. *Woolcot Reader.* 1935. NY. 1/1500. B2. $35.00

WOOLEY, Persia. *Child of N Spring.* 1989. 1st ed. pb. M. C1. $5.00

WOOLEY, Persia. *Child of the Spring.* 1987. NY. 1st ed. dj. M. C1. $12.00

WOOLF, B.S. *How To See Ceylon.* 1929. Colombo. 4th ed. map. $25.00

WOOLF, James D. *How To Use Imagination To Make Money.* 1950. Perma P68. VG. P1. $5.00

WOOLF, Leonard. *Calendar of Consolation.* 1968. Funk Wagnall. 1st Am ed. dj. EX. $25.00

WOOLF, Virginia. *Common Reader.* 1925. NY. 1st ed. EX. $52.50

WOOLF, Virginia. *Years.* 1937. London. Hogarth. 1st ed. 8vo. dj. $185.00

WOOLF, Virginia. *Flush: A Biography.* 1933. NY. 1st ed. dj. EX. $15.00

WOOLF, Virginia. *Hours in Library.* 1957. NY. 1st ed. glassine dj. $45.00

WOOLF, Virginia. *Room of One's Own.* 1929. NY/London. Ltd ed. 1/492. 159 p. M. $65.00

WOOLF, Virginia. *Waves.* 1931. Harcourt Brace. 1st Am ed. dj. EX. $135.00

WOOLF, Virginia. *Waves.* 1931. London. Hogarth. VG. $90.00

WOOLF, Virginia. *Writer's Diary.* 1954. NY. 1st Am ed. EX. $35.00

WOOLLCOTT, Alexander. *Portable Woollcott.* 1946. Viking. VG. P1. $7.50

WOOLLCOTT, Alexander. *Woollcott Reader.* 1935. NY. 1st ed. 1/1500. sgn. boxed. $50.00

WOOLLCOTT, Alexander. *Woollcott's Second Reader.* 1937. NY. Viking. Ltd 1st ed. 1/1500. sgn. TEG. VG. $75.00

WOOLLEY, Leonard. *Abraham: Recent Discoveries & Hebrew Origins.* 1936. NY. 1st ed. EX. $25.00

WOOLLEY, Roger. *Modern Trout Fly Dressing.* 1932. London. 1st ed. 12mo. VG. $35.00

WOOLMAN, John. *Journals & Essays.* 1922. NY. 1st ed. pls. G. $10.00

WOOLRICH, Cornell. *Hotel Room.* 1958. Random House. 1st ed. dj. VG. P1. $75.00

WOOLRICH, Cornell. *Into the Night.* 1987. NY. sgn Lawrence Block. dj. EX. $20.00

WORCESTER, G.R.G. *Junks & Sampans of the Yangtze.* 1971. Naval Pr. dj. G. $50.00

WORCESTER, J.E. *Elements of History: Ancient & Modern.* 1839. Boston. fld map. charts. 403 p. fair. T5. $35.00

WORCESTER, Samuel. *Primer of English Language for Use of Families & Schools.* 1842. Hallowell, ME. 12mo. printed wraps. $25.00

WORDSWORTH, William. *Guide Through the District of Lakes in N of England.* 1835. London. 5th ed. 12mo. 139 p. $50.00

WORDSWORTH, William. *Prelude.* 1850. Moxon. 1st ed. Riviere bdg. J2. $150.00

WORGAN, George. *Art of Modeling Flowers in Wax.* 1869. Phil. 2nd ed. 12mo. gilt cloth. VG. T1. $85.00

WORK, B.G. *Songs of Henry Clay Work.* nd. (1910?) NY. folio. G. G1. $25.00

WORK, John. *American Negro Songs: Comprehensive Collection...* c 1940. Howell. 1st ed. VG. $75.00

WORLEY, T.R. *Early History of Des Arc & Its People.* 1957. White River Journal. 82 p. M2. $5.00

WORMINGTON & LISTER. *Archeological Investigations on Uncompahgre Plateau.* 1956. Denver. Ils. 138 p. wraps. A3. $35.00

WORMSER, Richard. *Kidnapped Circus.* 1968. Morrow. 1st ed. dj. xl. P1. $5.00

WORMSER, Richard. *Lonesome Quarter.* nd. Sears Readers Club. VG. P1. $4.50

WORSHAM, J.H. *One of Jackson's Foot Cavalry.* 1982. Time Life. facsimile of 1912 ed. AEG. M. M2. $40.00

WORTH, C.B. *Mosquito Safari: Naturalist in S Africa.* 1971. Simon Schuster. Ils 1st ed. 316 p. dj. EX. M2. $12.00

WORTH, C.B. *Natualist in Trinidad.* 1967. Lippincott. Ils 1st ed. maps. 291 p. dj. M2. $16.00

WORTLEY, E.S. *Travels in the US...During 1849 & 1850.* 1851. Harper. 1st Am ed. 463 p. VG. A3. $90.00

WORTMAN, Denis. *Divine Processional.* 1903. NY. $12.50

WORTS, George F. *Five Who Vanished.* 1945. McBride. 2nd ed. VG. P1. $20.00

WORVILL, Roy. *Exploring Space.* 1964. Willis Hepworth. VG. P1. $3.00

WOUK, Herman. *Inside, Outside.* 1985. Little Brown. 1st ed. dj. EX. $20.00

WOUK, Herman. *Winds of War.* 1971. Little Brown. 8vo. dj. M. $40.00

WPA WRITER'S PROGRAM. *Almanac for Bostonians, 1939.* 1938. NYC. Ils. 120 p. fair. T5. $25.00

WPA WRITER'S PROGRAM. *American Guide to ID.* 1937. Caxton. Ils 1st ed. 431 p. dj. VG. B2. $250.00

WPA WRITER'S PROGRAM. *Copper Camp: Richest Hill on Earth.* 1943. NY. 1st ed. dj. VG. B2. $27.50

WPA WRITER'S PROGRAM. *Guide to FL.* 1939. NY. Ils. fld map. 600 p. dj. VG. $30.00

WPA WRITER'S PROGRAM. *Guide to IL.* 1983. Pantheon. 1st ed. pb. M. $8.80

WPA WRITER'S PROGRAM. *Hands That Built NH.* 1940. VT. Daye Pr. Ils. photos. dj. VG. $21.00

WPA WRITER'S PROGRAM. *In the Land of Beathitt.* 1941. Northport. 1st ed. photos. dj. $35.00

WPA WRITER'S PROGRAM. *NE: Guide to the Corn Husker State.* 1939. NY. 1st ed. pocket map. dj. VG. $45.00

WPA WRITER'S PROGRAM. *NJ: Guide to Its Present & Past.* 1939. NY. 1st ed. pocket map. dj. VG. $35.00

WPA WRITER'S PROGRAM. *Palmetto Pioneers.* SC. Dept Education. 81 p. $12.50

WPA WRITER'S PROGRAM. *San Antonio.* 1941. Am Guide Series. 1st ed. VG. B2. $35.00

WPA WRITER'S PROGRAM. *Urban Workers on Relief.* 1936. GPO. 2 vols. wraps. VG. $24.00

WPA WRITER'S PROGRAM. *Warren Co.* 1942. Glens Falls. Am Guide Series. 1st ed. dj. EX. $45.00

WRAIGHT, Robert. *Art Game.* 1966. Simon Schuster. Ils 224 p. dj. D2. $25.00

WRANGLE, Nikolaus Baron. *Die Meisterwerke der Gemalde-Galerie in der Ermitage...* 1918. Munich. Ils D2. $35.00

WRAXALL, N. *Tour Through Some of N Parts of Europe...* 1776. London. 3rd ed. G. $125.00

WREDE, S. *Modern Poster.* 1988. Boston. MOMA. Ils 1st ed. 4to. 263 p. EX. $25.00

WREN, M.K. *Nothing's Certain but Death.* 1978. Crime Club. dj. VG. P1. $10.00

WREN, M.K. *Oh, Bury Me Not.* 1976. Crime Club. 1st ed. dj. xl. P1. $5.00

WREN, M.K. *Seasons of Death.* 1984. Firecrest. dj. VG. P1. $15.00

WREN, P.C. *Beau Geste.* c 1926. Grosset Dunlap. G. $30.00

WREN, P.C. *Beau Geste.* 1952. Murray. 48th print. dj. xl. P1. $7.50

WREN, P.C. *Beau Ideal.* 1952. Murray. 9th print. dj. VG. P1. $17.50

WREN, P.C. *Beau Sabreur.* nd. Grosset. Movie ed. VG. P1. $15.00

WREN, P.C. *Beau Sabreur.* 1953. Murray. 8th print. dj. VG. P1. $17.50

WREN, P.C. *Sowing Glory.* 1931. Longman Green. 1st ed. xl. G. P1. $7.50

WREN, P.C. *Uniform of Glory.* 1956. Gryphon. 3rd ed. dj. VG. P1. $17.50

WREN, P.C. *Wages of Virtue.* 1949. Murray. 26th ed. dj. VG. P1. $17.50

WREN & MC KAY. *Second Baffle Book.* 1929. Crime Club. 1st ed. VG. P1. $20.00

WRIGHT, A.H. *Life Histories of Frogs of Okefinokee Swamp, GA.* 1932. Macmillan. Ils 1st ed. sgn. 497 p. xl. M2. $135.00

WRIGHT, A.M.R. *Old Ironsides.* nd. Grosset. Movie ed. G. P1. $12.50

WRIGHT, A.T. *Islandia.* 1942. NY. 1st ed. dj. VG. B2. $42.50

WRIGHT, A.T. *Islandia.* 1958. NY. 2nd ed. dj. VG. B2. $22.50

WRIGHT, B.A. *House Divided.* 1947. Boston. 1st ed. sgn. VG. $45.00

WRIGHT, B.C. *1st Cavalry Division in WWII.* 1947. Tokyo. Ils. presentation. 4to. 245 p. C4. $95.00

WRIGHT, B.F. *Real Mother Goose.* 1926. Rand McNally. Ils. 4to. $25.00

WRIGHT, B.L. *Diary of a Member of First Pack Train To Leave Ft. Smith...* 1969. Palo Duro Pr. 60 p. EX. M2. $3.00

WRIGHT, B.S. *Black Duck Spring.* 1966. Dutton. Ils 1st ed. 191 p. dj. EX. M2. $20.00

WRIGHT, C.E. *Manufacture of Optical Glass & of Optical Systems.* 1921. WA. Ils. 309 p. G. T5. $35.00

WRIGHT, C.R. *Diary of Humfrey Wanley, 1715-1726.* 1966. London. 2 vols. djs. VG. $40.00

WRIGHT, Cedric. *Words of the Earth.* 1960. San Francisco. dj. EX. P3. $50.00

WRIGHT, Charles. *OH Regimental History.* 1887. 143 p. EX. K1. $65.00

WRIGHT, E.W. *Lewis & Dryden's Marine History of Pacific NW.* 1895. Portland. 1st ed. full leather. $325.00

WRIGHT, Elizabeth. *Life of Joseph Wright.* 1932. Oxford. 1st ed. 2 vols. J2. $50.00

WRIGHT, Eric. *Body Surrounded by Water.* 1987. Collins Crime Club. 1st ed. P1. $15.00

WRIGHT, Eric. *Night the Gods Smiled.* 1983. Scribner. 1st ed. dj. EX. P1. $15.00

WRIGHT, Eric. *Question of Murder.* 1988. Scribner. 1st ed. dj. EX. P1. $15.95

WRIGHT, F.L. *American Architecture.* 1955. Horizon. 1st ed. EX. $50.00

WRIGHT, F.L. *Architecture: Man in Possession of His Earth.* 1962. NY. 1st ed. dj. EX. $40.00

WRIGHT, F.L. *Autobiography.* 1932. Longman Green. 1st ed. sgn Sandburg. G. B2. $950.00

WRIGHT, F.L. *Autobiography.* 1933. NY. Ils 2nd print. photos. 395 p. T5. $55.00

WRIGHT, F.L. *Autobiography.* 1977. NY. dj. VG. J2. $17.50

WRIGHT, F.L. *Drawings of F.L. Wright.* 1962. NY. 1st ed. dj. EX. $125.00

WRIGHT, F.L. *Future of Architecture.* 1935. NY. 1st ed. dj. EX. $75.00

WRIGHT, F.L. *Future of Architecture.* 1965. Horizon. 1st ed. dj. VG. $45.00

WRIGHT, F.L. *Genius & the Mobocracy.* 1949. Duell Sloan. 1st ed. dj. VG. $60.00

WRIGHT, F.L. *Genius & the Mobocracy.* 1949. NY. Stated 1st ed. white cloth. dj. EX. $75.00

WRIGHT, F.L. *Japanese Prints.* 1967. NY. sgn. slipcase. EX. $90.00

WRIGHT, F.L. *Living City.* 1958. NY. 1st ed. dj. $65.00

WRIGHT, F.L. *Natural House.* 1954. NY. Ils 1st ed. 223 p. VG. T5. $125.00

WRIGHT, F.L. *On Architecture.* 1941. Duell Sloan. 1st ed. VG. $84.00

WRIGHT, F.L. *Testament.* 1957. NY. dj. J2. $30.00

WRIGHT, F.L. *Writings & Buildings.* 1960. Horizon. 1st ed. VG. $30.00

WRIGHT, G.F. *Asiatic Russia.* 1902. NY. McClure. Ils 1st ed. 2 vols. VG. $50.00

WRIGHT, G.F. *Ice Age in N America.* 1891. NY. 3rd ed. xl. $22.50

WRIGHT, G.F. *See OH First: Guide to Best Routes...* 1915. Oberlin. 85 p. wraps. fair. T5. $12.50

WRIGHT, Grahame. *Jog Rummage.* 1974. Random House. 1st ed. dj. EX. P1. $10.00

WRIGHT, H.B. *Cinderella.* nd. NY. Burt. green cloth. dj. EX. $18.00

WRIGHT, H.B. *Eyes of the World.* 1914. Book Supply. VG. P1. $10.00

WRIGHT, H.B. *Helen of the Old House.* 1921. Appleton. 1st ed. EX. $15.00

WRIGHT, H.B. *Long Ago Told.* 1919. NY. 1st ed. leather. VG. B2. $300.00

WRIGHT, H.B. *Ma Cinderella.* 1932. NY. 1st ed. VG. B2. $100.00

WRIGHT, H.B. *Man Who Went Away.* 1942. NY. 1st ed. G. B2. $75.00

WRIGHT, H.B. *Mine With the Iron Door.* 1923. Appleton. 1st ed. EX. $16.00

WRIGHT, H.B. *Printer of Udells.* 1903. Chicago. 1st ed. VG. B2. $50.00

WRIGHT, H.B. *Re-Creation of Brian Kent.* 1919. Book Supply. 1st ed. EX. $15.00

WRIGHT, H.B. *Shepherd of the Hills.* nd. NY. Burt. maroon cloth. VG. $10.00

WRIGHT, H.B. *Shepherd of the Hills.* 1907. Burt. VG. $10.00

WRIGHT, H.B. *Son of His Father.* 1925. Appleton. 1st ed. EX. $15.00

WRIGHT, H.B. *Their Yesterdays.* 1912. Book Supply. 1st ed. $14.00

WRIGHT, H.B. *Their Yesterdays.* 1912. Chicago. 1st ed. dj. $30.00

WRIGHT, H.B. *When a Man's a Man.* 1916. Book Supply. 1st ed. EX. $15.00

WRIGHT, H.B. *When a Man's a Man.* 1916. Book Supply. 1st ed. G. P1. $7.50

WRIGHT, J.F. *Saskatchewan: History of a Province.* 1955. McClelland. Ils. maps. 292 p. dj. EX. M2. $10.00

WRIGHT, J.L. *My Father Who Is on Earth.* 1946. NY. 1st ed. dj. VG. B2. $50.00

WRIGHT, J.V. *Dr. Wright's Book of Nutritional Therapy.* 1979. Penn. $12.50

WRIGHT, James. *To a Blossoming Pear Tree.* 1977. NY. 1st ed. dj. M. $15.00

WRIGHT, June. *Devil's Caress.* 1952. Hutchinson. 1st ed. VG. P1. $20.00

WRIGHT, Louis. *Gold, Glory & the Gospel.* 1970. NY. 1st ed. dj. EX. $15.00

WRIGHT, M.J. *Leslie's Official History of Spanish-American War.* 1899. WA. Ils. folio. $112.00

WRIGHT, M.T. *Charioteers.* 1912. Appleton. 1st ed. $12.00

WRIGHT, R.V. *Material Handling Encyclopedia.* 1921. Simmons Boardman. Ils. 4to. $75.00

WRIGHT, Richard. *Black Boy.* 1945. Harper. 8vo. blue cloth. EX. $35.00

WRIGHT, Richard. *Native Son.* 1940. Harper. 1st ed. 359 p. dj. $35.00

WRIGHT, Richard. *Native Son.* 1940. NY. 5th ed. dj. EX. $25.00

WRIGHT, Richard. *12 Million Black Voices.* 1942. NY. Viking. 2nd print. 4to. dj. VG. $55.00

WRIGHT, S.F. *Deluge.* 1928. Cosmopolitan. 1st ed. VG. P1. $25.00

WRIGHT, S.F. *Elfwin.* 1930. Longman. 1st ed. dj. VG. P1. $40.00

WRIGHT, S.F. *Island of Captain Sparrow.* nd. Grosset Dunlap. VG. P1. $15.00

WRIGHT, S.F. *Throne of Saturn.* 1949. Arkham House. 1st ed. dj. VG. P1. $30.00

WRIGHT, S.F. *World Below.* 1949. Chicago. dj. EX. $35.00

WRIGHT, S.F. *World Below.* 1949. Shasta. dj. VG. P1. $25.00

WRIGHT, Stuart. *Historical Sketch of Person Co., NC.* 1974. 232 p. sgn. gilt bdg. M. J4. $20.00

WRIGHT, Thomas. *History of Caricature & Grotesque in Literature & Art.* 1875. Chatto Windus. J2. $25.00

WRIGHT, Thomas. *History of Scotland From the Earliest Period.* c 1875. Glasgow. 3 vols. rebound. VG. T5. $145.00

WRIGHT, W. *Heiress.* 1978. WA. 1st ed. dj. VG. B2. $25.00

WRIGHT, W.H. *Black Bear.* 1910. Scribner. 1st ed. VG. $65.00

WRIGHT, W.H. *Grizzly Bear.* 1909. Scribner. 1st ed. G. $70.00

WRIGHT, W.H. *Grizzly Bear.* 1910. Scribner. photos. 274 p. EX. M2. $85.00

WRIGHT & COUES. *Citizen Bird.* 1897. London. Ils Fuertes. 1st ed. VG. $130.00

WRIGHT & FRY. *Puritans in S Seas.* 1936. NY. Ils 1st ed. dj. $36.00

WRIGHT & SUMMERS. *Systemic Pathology.* 1966. London. 2 vols. EX. $87.00

WRIGHT. *Horatio Greenough, First American Sculptor.* 1963. Phil. $45.00

WRIGHTSON, Patricia. *Down to Earth.* 1965. Harcourt Brace. 1st ed. Lib bdg. xl. P1. $5.00

WRIGHTSON, Patricia. *Down to Earth.* 1965. Hutchinson. dj. xl. P1. $7.50

WU & MURPHY. *SF From China.* 1989. Praeger. 1st ed. Lib bdg. xl. P1. $5.00

WUERTH. *Catalog of Etchings of Joseph Pennell.* 1928. Boston. 1/465. with sgn etching. VG. $475.00

WULFF, Lee. *Atlantic Salmon.* 1958. NY. 1st trade ed. 4to. dj. VG. $50.00

WULFFEN, Erich. *Woman As a Sexual Criminal.* 1934. NY. Am Ethno Pr. 1st Am ed. EX. $60.00

WYCKOFF, Capwell. *Mystery at Lake Retreat.* nd. Saalfield. dj. VG. P1. $7.50

WYCKOFF, P.A. *Lone Star Martin of TX Rangers.* 1939. Whitman. Big Little Book. P1. $10.00

WYCKOFF, P.A. *Wings of the USA.* 1940. Whitman. Better Little Book. VG. P1. $15.00

WYDOSKI & WHITNEY. *Inland Fishes of WA (state).* 1979. WA U. 76 color photos. 220 p. dj. M. M2. $25.00

WYETH, Andrew. *Helga Pictures.* 1987. NY. Abrams. Ils. 4to. 208 p. EX. $17.00

WYETH, Andrew. *Wyeth at Kuerners.* 1976. Boston. Ils. oblong folio. dj. G. $50.00

WYETH, Andrew. *Wyeth at Kuerners.* 1976. Boston. 1st print. folio. dj. EX. T5. $250.00

WYETH, J. *Devil Forrest.* 1959. NY. 1st ed. 604 p. dj. VG. B2. $45.00

WYETH, J.A. *General Robert E. Lee Commemorative Address...* 1906. NY. NY S Soc. 22 p. printed wraps. $35.00

WYETH, N.C. *Black Arrow.* 1917. Scribner. Ils. G. $35.00

WYETH, N.C. *Boy's King Arthur.* 1926. Scribner. Ils. VG. $40.00

WYETH, N.C. *Kidnapped.* 1927. Scribner. Ils. VG. $40.00

WYETH, N.C. *Marauders of the Sea.* 1935. NY. Ils Hurd. 1st ed. J2. $45.00

WYKOFF, Capnell. *Mercer Boys' Mystery Case.* 1918. World. G. $7.50

WYLD, George. *Theosophy.* 1894. London. $150.00

WYLD, L.D. *Low Bridge! Folklore & the Erie Canal.* 1962. Ils. 212 p. $22.50

WYLIE, Elinor. *Black Armour.* 1923. Doran. 77 p. glassine wraps. G. $15.00

WYLIE, Elinor. *Venetian Glass Nephew.* 1925. NY. Doran. 1/250. sgn. $45.00

WYLIE, I. *Cuckoo.* 1981. Universe. photos. 176 p. dj. EX. M2. $14.00

WYLIE, Philip. *Corpses at Indian Stones.* 1943. Farrar Rinehart. xl. P1. $7.50

WYLIE, Philip. *Corpses at Indian Stones.* 1943. Farrar Rinehart. 1st ed. G. P1. $20.00

WYLIE, Philip. *Denizens of the Deep.* 1953. NY. Ils Dower. 222 p. VG. $15.00

WYLIE, Philip. *Essay on Morals.* 1947. NY. 1st ed. dj. VG. B2. $15.00

WYLIE, Philip. *Three To Be Read.* 1951. NY. 1st ed. dj. VG. B2. $20.00

WYLIE & BALMER. *When Worlds Collide.* nd. Lippincott. dj. VG. P1. $35.00

WYMAN, L.P. *Blind Man's Inlet.* nd. Saalfield. VG. P1. $5.00

WYND, Oswald. *Death of the Red Flower.* 1965. Cassell. 1st ed. dj. xl. P1. $6.00

WYND, Oswald. *Ginger Tree.* nd. Book Club. dj. EX. P1. $4.50

WYND, Oswald. *Ginger Tree.* 1977. Collins. 1st ed. dj. xl. P1. $5.00

WYND, Oswald. *Hawser Pirates.* 1970. Cassell. 1st ed. dj. xl. P1. $6.00

WYND, Oswald. *40 Days*. 1972. Collins. 1st ed. dj. EX. P1. $15.00

WYNDHAM, John. *Chocky*. nd. Book Club. 1st Am HrdCvr ed. dj. VG. P1. $3.00

WYNDHAM, John. *Day of the Triffids*. nd. Book Club. dj. VG. P1. $4.50

WYNDHAM, John. *Midwich Cuckoos*. 1969. Walker. dj. xl. P1. $7.50

WYNDHAM, John. *Village of the Damned*. 1960. Ball. EX. $20.00

WYNDHAM-LEWIS & LEE. *Stuffed Owl: Anthology of Bad Verse*. 1930. Ils Beerbohm. Expanded 2nd ed. dj. VG. C1. $7.50

WYNNE, Anthony. *Green Knife*. 1939. Caxton. VG. P1. $12.50

X

XANTUS, Janos. *Letter From N America & Travels in S CA.* 1975. Detroit. Trans Schoenman. 2 vols. djs. VG. $17.50

XANTUS, Janos. *Travels in S CA.* 1976. Wayne U. Trans Schoenman. 212 p. dj. EX. M2. $20.00

XIBERTA, B.M. *Scriptoribus Saeculi XIV Ordine Carmelitarum.* 1931. Louvain. xl. G1. $30.00

XIYANG, T. *Living Treasures: Odyssey Through China's Nature Preserves.* 1987. Bantam. Ils 1st ed. 196 p. dj. EX. M2. $24.00

Y

oYAGGY, L.W. *Museum of Antiquity.* 1881. Ils. VG. $195.00

YAGGY & HAINES. *Museum of Antiquity: Description of Ancient Life...* 1884. Alexandria, VA. Grant. Ils. pls. 944 p. D2. $125.00

YALE UNIVERSITY PRESS. *Introductory Meteorology.* 1918. CT. 1st ed. dj. VG. $15.00

YAMAGUTI, S. *Parasitic Copepods & Branchiura of Fishes.* 1963. Interscience. 333 pls. 1104 p. dj. EX. M2. $65.00

YANG, M.C. *Chinese Village: Taitou in Shantung Province.* 1945. Columbia U. dj. EX. $17.50

YANGEY, B. *My Life With Elvis.* 1977. NY. 1st ed. dj. VG. B2. $22.50

YARBRO, C.Q. *False Dawn.* nd. Book Club. dj. EX. P1. $4.00

YARBRO, C.Q. *False Dawn.* 1978. Doubleday. 1st ed. dj. EX. P1. $17.50

YARBRO, C.Q. *Hotel Transylvania.* nd. Book Club. dj. VG. P1. $3.50

YARBRO, C.Q. *Hyacinths.* 1983. Doubleday. 1st ed. dj. VG. P1. $15.00

YARBRO, C.Q. *Palace.* nd. Book Club. dj. VG. P1. $4.00

YARDLEY, H.O. *Education of Poker Player.* 1957. Simon Schuster. 2nd ed. 129 p. dj. EX. $20.00

YARDLEY, P.T. *Milestones & Milestones.* 1981. Ils. 330 p. $18.50

YASHIRO, Yukio. *Botticelli, Sandro & the Florentine Renaissance.* 1929. London. Medici Soc. Ils. G. $50.00

YATES, Dornford. *As Berry & I Were Saying.* 1953. Ward Lock. 4th ed. dj. G. P1. $12.50

YATES, Dornford. *Berry & Co.* 1976. Ward Lock. dj. EX. P1. $15.00

YATES, Dornford. *Blind Corner.* 1927. Hodder Stoughton. 3rd ed. VG. P1. $20.00

YATES, Dornford. *Eye for a Tooth.* 1944. Putnam. 1st ed. dj. VG. P1. $22.50

YATES, Dornford. *Jonah & Co.* nd. Ward Lock. VG. P1. $17.50

YATES, Dornford. *Laughing Bacchante.* 1949. Putnam. 1st ed. dj. VG. P1. $20.00

YATES, Dorothy. *Lady From VT: Dorothy Canfield Fisher's Life & World.* 1971. Brattleboro. wraps. EX. $8.00

YATES, Elizabeth. *On That Night.* 1969. NY. 1st ed. dj. EX. $8.50

YATES, Helen Eva. *How To Travel for Fun.* 1950. Perma P83. VG. P1. $5.00

YATES, Margaret Tayler. *Murder by the Yard.* 1943. Macmillan. 3rd ed. dj. G. P1. $10.00

YATES, R.F. *Antique Fakes & Their Detection.* 1950. NY. Gramercy. Ils. 229 p. dj. D2. $18.00

YATES, R.F. *How To Improve Your Model Railroad.* 1952. 8vo. 110 p. VG. $5.00

YATES, Richard. *Young Hearts Crying.* 1984. Delacorte. 1st ed. dj. EX. $17.00

YAVNO, Max. *Photography of Max Yavno.* 1981. CA U. 1st ed. sgn. dj. EX. $65.00

YEATES, G.K. *Bird Photography.* 1946. London. Faber. Ils. 120 p. $20.00

YEATS, J.B. *Treasure of the Garden.* nd. London. Elkin Mathews. 1st ed. 4to. $160.00

YEATS, W.B. *Autobiographies.* 1955. London. 1st ed. dj. VG. $25.00

YEATS, W.B. *Autobiography.* 1938. NY. Ils 1st ed. 479 p. dj. VG. B2. $32.50

YEATS, W.B. *Bounty of Sweden.* 1925. Dublin. Caula Pr. Ltd ed. 1/400. $150.00

YEATS, W.B. *Collected Poems of W.B. Yeats.* 1979. Franklin. 1st ed. gilt bdg. EX. T6. $20.00

YEATS, W.B. *Cutting of an Agate.* 1919. London. 1st ed. EX. $45.00

YEATS, W.B. *Dramatis Personae.* 1936. Macmillan. Ils 1st Am ed. 8vo. dj. VG. G2. $40.00

YEATS, W.B. *Early Poems & Stories.* 1925. London. 1st ed. dj. EX. $85.00

YEATS, W.B. *Full Moon in March.* 1935. London. 1st ed. dj. $110.00

YEATS, W.B. *Green Helmet & Other Poems.* 1912. NY. 1st Am ed. 12mo. EX. $65.00

YEATS, W.B. *If I Were Four & Twenty.* 1940. Cuala Pr. 1/450. orig glassine dj. T6. $140.00

YEATS, W.B. *King of the Great Clock Tower.* 1934. Dublin. Cuala Pr. Ltd ed. 1/400. $150.00

YEATS, W.B. *Lyrical Poems.* 1908. NY. Macmillan. AEG. Knowlton bdg. VG. $300.00

YEATS, W.B. *Poems.* 1908. London. 5th Eng ed. VG. $100.00

YEATS, W.B. *Poems.* 1957. Variorum ed. 1/825. sgn. boxed. $400.00

YEATS, W.B. *Reveries Over Childhood & Youth & Trembling of the Veil.* 1927. NY. 1/250. sgn. 447 p. slipcase. EX. T5. $395.00

YEATS, W.B. *Selection From Poetry.* 1913. Leipzig. 1st ed. wraps. VG. $70.00

YEATS, W.B. *Three Things.* 1929. London. 1st ed. wraps. G. $30.00

YEATS, W.B. *Where There Is Nothing.* 1903. London. 1st ed. 12mo. $60.00

YEE, Chiang. *Silent Traveler in San Francisco.* 1964. NY. Norton. 1st ed. dj. VG. $12.00

YEGOROVA, K. *Leningrad: House of Peter I, Summer Gardens & Palace...* 1975. Leningrad. dj. slipcase. EX. J2. $30.00

YEOMAN, R.S. *Catalog of Modern World Coins.* 1964. Whitman. 6th ed. VG. P1. $7.50

YEOMAN, R.S. *Guide Book of US Coins.* 1966. Whitman. EX. $6.00

YEOMAN, R.S. *Guide Book of US Coins.* 1976. Whitman. EX. $5.00

YEOMAN, R.S. *Guide Book of US Coins.* 1981. Whitman. EX. $2.00

YEOWELL. *Who's Who in Arabian Horses.* 1988. Premier ed. 1/1500. 8vo. padded leather. EX. $40.00

YERBURY, F.R. *Georgian Details of Domestic Architecture.* 1926. Boston/NY. pls. VG. $50.00

YERBY, Frank. *Garfield Honor.* nd. Book Club. dj. VG. P1. $3.00

YERBY, Frank. *Vixens, a Novel.* 1947. NY. Dial. 347 p. $4.50

YESLAH. *Tenderfoot in S CA.* 1908. Little Ives. sgn. dj. G. $45.00

YEVTUSHENKO, Yevgeny. *From Desire to Desire.* 1976. Doubleday. 1st Am ed. dj. EX. $15.00

YEVTUSHENKO, Yevgeny. *Wild Berries.* 1984. 1st ed. dj. RS. EX. $25.00

YGLESIAS, Rafael. *Game Player.* c 1978. Doubleday. dj. G. $15.00

YING, Jianzhe. *Icones of Medicinal Fungi From China.* 1987. Beijing. Science Pr. Ils. 575 p. $70.00

YIZKOR. *In Remembrance of Fallen Jewish Watchmen & Workers...Isreal.* 1917. NY. Palestine Committee. EX. $200.00

YLLA. *Animals.* dj. EX. S2. $30.00

YNTEMA, Sharon. *More Than 100 Women SF Writers.* 1988. Crossing Pr. HrdCvr. P1. $30.00

YODER, Robert M. *Saturday Evening Post Carnival of Humor.* nd. Prentice Hall. dj. VG. P1. $20.00

YOGENDRA, Shri Vijayadev. *Is Your Sickness Real?* 1978. Macmillan. 1st ed. dj. EX. P1. $10.00

YOLEN, Jane. *Cards of Grief.* c 1984. Book Club. dj. EX. C1. $3.50

YOLEN, Jane. *Dove Isabeau.* 1989. Harcourt Brace Jovanovich. P1. $13.95

YOLEN, Jane. *Imaginary Lands.* 1986. 1st ed. dj. M. C1. $24.00

YOLEN, Jane. *Magic Three of Solatia.* 1974. Crowell. 1st ed. dj. EX. P1. $20.00

YOLEN, Jane. *Owl Moon.* 1987. Ils Schoenherr. 1st ed. juvenile. dj. M. C1. $7.50

YOLEN, Jane. *Tales of Wonder.* 1983. 1st Am ed. dj. EX. C1. $15.00

YOLEN, Jane. *Tales of Wonder.* 1983. Schocken. 1st ed. dj. EX. P1. $14.95

YOLEN, Jane. *Zoo 2000.* nd. Seabury. 2nd ed. dj. VG. P1. $15.00

YONGE, S.H. *Site of Old James Towne, 1607-1698.* 1907. Richmond. Ils. fld maps. 151 p. G. $25.00

YORK, Andrew. *Captivator.* 1974. Crime Club. VG. P1. $10.00

YORK, Andrew. *Eliminator.* Lippincott. 2nd ed. dj. EX. P1. $8.00

YORK, Andrew. *Predator.* 1968. Lippincott. 1st ed. dj. EX. P1. $10.00

YORK, Andrew. *Tallant for Disaster.* 1978. Crime Club. 1st ed. dj. VG. P1. $12.00

YORK, Andrew. *Tallant for Disaster.* 1978. Hutchinson. 1st ed. dj. xl. P1. $5.00

YORK, Andrew. *Tallant for Trouble.* 1977. Hutchinson. 1st ed. dj. xl. P1. $5.00

YORK, Jeremy. *Hide & Kill.* 1960. Scribner. 1st ed. dj. VG. P1. $7.50

YORK, Jeremy. *So Soon To Die.* 1956. Scribner. 1st ed. dj. G. P1. $7.50

YORKE, Curtis. *Enchanted!* nd. Leisure Lib. dj. VG. P1. $13.75

YORKE, F.R.S. *Modern House.* 1935. London. 4to. gray cloth. VG. $25.00

YORKE, Lane. *Zelda: A Worksheet.* 1983. NY. Paris Review. only ed. wraps. T6. $10.00

YORKE, Malcolm. *Eric Gill.* 1981. London. Constable. 1st ed. dj. VG. $20.00

YORKE, Margaret. *Come-On.* 1978. Harper Row. 1st ed. dj. VG. P1. $15.00

YORKE, Margaret. *Hand of Death.* 1981. St. Martin. 1st ed. dj. EX. P1. $12.95

YOSHIDA, Shigeru. *Yoshida Memoirs.* 1962. Boston. 1st Am ed. dj. VG. $25.00

YOUD, Samuel. *Messages of Love.* 1961. Simon Schuster. 1st ed. VG. P1. $10.00

YOUD, Samuel. *Opportunist.* 1955. Harper. 1st ed. dj. xl. P1. $10.00

YOUNG, Agatha. *Women & the Crisis: Women of N in Civil War.* 1959. McDowell Obolensky. 1st ed. dj. VG. $18.00

YOUNG, Alexander. *Chronicles of the Pilgrim Fathers of Colony of Plymouth...* 1844. Boston. 8vo. black cloth. G. T1. $35.00

YOUNG, Art. *On My Way.* 1928. Liveright. 1/1000. VG. B2. $50.00

YOUNG, Chic. *Blondie & Dogwood in Hot Water.* 1946. Better Little Book. VG. P1. $17.50

YOUNG, Egerton. *Battle of the Bears.* 1907. Boston. Ils 1st ed. $15.00

YOUNG, Egerton. *Hector, My Dog.* 1905. Boston. Ils 1st ed. G. $20.00

YOUNG, Egerton. *My Dogs in the N Land.* 1902. NY. Ils 4th ed. EX. $20.00

YOUNG, Egerton. *Stories From Indian Wigwams & N Campfires.* 1897. London. Kelly. Ils. 294 p. VG. A3. $40.00

YOUNG, F.B. *Century of Boys' Stories.* nd. Hutchinson. 1024 p. VG. P1. $30.00

YOUNG, F.B. *Christmas Box.* nd. London. 1st ed. dj. VG. J2. $12.50

YOUNG, F.B. *Portrait of a Village.* 1938. NY. Ils 1st Am ed. 179 p. dj. VG. T5. $27.50

YOUNG, F.M. *Man Meets Grissly.* 1980. Houghton. 1st ed. 298 p. dj. EX. M2. $19.00

YOUNG, G.F. *E & W Through Fifteen Centuries. Vol. II.* 1916. 1st ed. map. G. C1. $12.00

YOUNG, Gordon. *Devil's Passport.* 1942. Triangle. dj. VG. P1. $10.00

YOUNG, J.B. *Battle of Gettysburg.* 1913. NY. Ils 1st ed. 463 p. $30.00

YOUNG, J.B. *What a Boy Saw in the Army.* 1894. NY. Ils Beard. 1st ed. VG. R1. $125.00

YOUNG, J.C. *Liberia Rediscovered.* 1934. Garden City. Ils 1st ed. 212 p. VG. T5. $17.50

YOUNG, J.C. *Marse Robert: Knight of the Confederacy.* 1931. Grosset Dunlap. reprint. map. 356 p. VG. M2. $6.00

YOUNG, J.R. *Around the World With General Grant.* 1879. NY. Am News Co. 2 vols. VG. $35.00

YOUNG, James. *Toadstool Millionaires.* 1961. Princeton. dj. VG. $25.00

YOUNG, M.E. *Redskins, Ruffleshirts & Rednecks: Indian Allotments in AL.* 1961. Norman. Ils 1st ed. dj. EX. $45.00

YOUNG, N.C. *Old Economy-Ambridge Sesqui-Centennial Historical Booklet.* 1974. np. 191 p. wraps. G. T5. $12.50

YOUNG, Norwood. *Growth of Napoleon.* 1910. London. Murray. Ils. 418 p. VG. $15.00

YOUNG, Perry. *Mistick Krewe.* 1931. New Orleans. Carnival. Ils 1st ed. G. $35.00

YOUNG, Robert. *Cosmic Knights.* 1985. Signet. 1st pb ed. EX. C1. $4.00

YOUNG, S. *Immortal Shadows.* 1948. NY. 1st ed. inscr. dj. EX. $50.00

YOUNG, S.H. *AK Days With John Muir.* 1915. NY. 1st ed. dj. VG. B2. $27.50

YOUNG, S.P. *Bobcat in N America: History, Life Habits, Economic Status.* 1978. NE U. Ils. 193 p. EX. M2. $7.00

YOUNG, S.P. *Last of the Loners.* 1970. Macmillan. Ils 1st ed. 316 p. M2. $18.00

YOUNG, Stark. *Pavilion.* 1951. Scribner. 1st ed. dj. EX. $20.00

YOUNG, Stark. *So Red the Rose.* 1934. NY. Scribner. red cloth. $25.00

YOUNG, Stark. *Theatre Practice.* 1926. NY. 1st ed. dj. VG. B2. $30.00

YOUNG, Vash. *Fortune To Share.* 1932. Bobbs Merrill. 11th print. dj. VG. P1. $10.00

YOUNG, Vernon. *Cinema Borealis: Ingmar Bergman & Swedish Ethos.* 1971. NY. 1st print. dj. EX. $18.00

YOUNG, Waldemar. *Birds of Rhiannon: A Grove Play.* 1930. San Francisco. Bohemian Club. 1/1500. 96 p. C1. $44.50

YOUNG & GOLDMAN. *Puma: Mysterious American Cat.* 1946. Am Wildlife Inst. 1st ed. EX. M2. $95.00

YOUNG & GOLDMAN. *Wolves of N America.* 1944. Am Wildlife Inst. 1st ed. dj. M2. $95.00

YOUNG & LANG. *Woodstock Festival Remembered.* 1979. Random House. Ils. photos. 64 p. M. $12.50

YOUNG & MAZET. *Shark! Shark! Thirty-Year Odyssey of Pioneer Shark Hunter.* 1933. Gotham. Ils 1st ed. 287 p. M2. $48.00

YOUNG LORDS PARTY & ABRAMSON. *Pa-lan-te Young Lords Party.* 1971. McGraw Hill. 1st ed. 159 p. paper wraps. M1. $9.50

YOUNGBLOOD & FULLER. *Expanded Cinema.* 1970. London. 1st ed. 432 p. dj. VG. $37.50

YOUNGHUSBAND, Francis. *Coming Country.* 1928. Murray. 1st ed. dj. $20.00

YOUNT, John. *Hardcastle.* 1980. NY. Marek. 1st ed. sgn. M. $25.00

YOURCENAR, Marguerite. *Coup de Grace.* 1957. NY. 1st Am ed. dj. VG. $22.00

YOUSSOUPOFF, Prince Felix. *Lost Splendor.* 1954. NY. 1st ed. dj. VG. B2. $40.00

YOUSSOUPOFF, Prince Felix. *Rasputin.* 1927. NY. 246 p. VG. $45.00

YRIARTE, Charles. *Figaro: Salon 1892.* 1892. Paris. Goupil. Ils. 121 p. D2. $115.00

YUDOVIN & MALKIN. *Yiddisher Folks Ormanment.* 1970. Tel Aviv. facsimile of 1920 ed. wraps. $150.00

YUKON FISH & WILDLIFE. *Wolf Population Research & Management Studies.* 1986. 76 p. paper cover. M2. $15.00

YUTANG, Lin. *Juniper Loa.* 1963. World. 1st ed. dj. VG. P1. $10.00

YUTANG, Lin. *Moment in Peking.* 1939. NY. $75.00

YUTANG, Lin. *Versillion Gate.* 1953. NY. $45.00

YUTANG, Lin. *With Love & Irony.* 1940. NY. $75.00

ZAEHRINGER. *Solid Propellant Rockets.* 1958. 2nd Stage Rocket Co. 1st print. B1. $35.00

ZAGAT, Arthur Leo. *Seven Out of Time.* 1949. Fantasy. 1st ed. dj. VG. P1. $30.00

ZAHARIAS, B.D. *This Life I've Lived.* 1955. NY. 1st ed. dj. VG. B2. $22.50

ZAHL, P.A. *Flamingo Hunt.* 1952. Bobbs Merrill. 1st ed. dj. EX. M2. $10.00

ZAHM, A.F. *Aerial Navigation.* 1911. NY. Appleton. Ils 1st ed. 496 p. VG. $45.00

ZAHM, J.A. *Quest of Eldorado.* 1917. NY. Ils 1st ed. maps. 261 p. G. $30.00

ZAHORSKI, K.J. *Peter Beagle.* 1988. Starmont Reader Guide. EX. P1. $9.95

ZANELLI. *Reggimento, Piemonte, Reale Cavalleria.* 1892. Italy. Ils. 4to. VG. $75.00

ZANGWILL, Israel. *Children of the Ghetto.* 1892. Phil. 2 vols. EX. $150.00

ZANGWILL, Israel. *Mantle of Elijah.* 1900. London. 1st ed. dj. EX. $65.00

ZATURENSKA, Marya. *Christina Rossetti: Portrait With Background.* 1949. NY. 1st print. gilt blue cloth. dj. T1. $35.00

ZCHOKKE. *History of Switzerland.* 1855. Francis. Trans Shaw. 1st ed. 405 p. VG. $20.00

ZEBROWSKI, George. *Macrolife.* 1979. Harper Row. 1st ed. dj. EX. P1. $10.00

ZEBROWSKI, George. *Sunspacer.* 1978. Harper Row. 1st ed. dj. EX. P1. $15.00

ZECKENDORF, W. *Zeckendorf.* 1970. NY. 1st ed. dj. EX. B2. $30.00

ZECKENDORF, W. *Zeckendorf.* 1970. NY. 1st ed. dj. G. $12.00

ZEIGER, Henry A. *Spy Who Can in With the Gold.* 1966. Duell. 1st ed. dj. VG. P1. $17.50

ZEISBERGER, David. *Diary of David Zeisberger: Moravian Missionary.* 1885. Cincinnati. Clarke. 1st ed. 2 vols. G. T5. $250.00

ZEITLIN & WOODBRIDGE. *Life & Letters of Stuart P. Sherman.* 1929. NY. 1st ed. sgn. 2 vols. VG. $50.00

ZELAZNY, Roger. *Blood of Amber.* 1986. Arbor House. 1st ed. dj. EX. P1. $14.95

ZELAZNY, Roger. *Changeling.* nd. Book Club. dj. EX. P1. $4.00

ZELAZNY, Roger. *Courts of Chaos.* 1978. Doubleday. 1st ed. dj. EX. P1. $35.00

ZELAZNY, Roger. *Doorways in the Sand.* nd. Book Club. dj. VG. P1. $4.00

ZELAZNY, Roger. *Doorways in the Sand.* 1977. Allen. 1st ed. dj. EX. P1. $20.00

ZELAZNY, Roger. *Eye of the Cat.* 1982. Timescape. 1st ed. dj. VG. P1. $20.00

ZELAZNY, Roger. *Guns of Avalon.* SF Book Club. 1st ed. 2 vols. VG. C1. $6.00

ZELAZNY, Roger. *Hand of Oberon.* 1976. Doubleday. 1st ed. dj. EX. P1. $40.00

ZELAZNY, Roger. *Illustrated Roger Zelazny.* 1978. Baronet. 1st ed. sgn. no dj issued. EX. P1. $60.00

ZELAZNY, Roger. *Jack of Shadows.* nd. Book Club. dj. VG. P1. $4.50

ZELAZNY, Roger. *Jack of Shadows.* 1971. Walker. 1st ed. dj. xl. P1. $7.50

ZELAZNY, Roger. *Last Defender of Camelot.* Book Club. dj. VG. C1. $5.00

ZELAZNY, Roger. *Lord of Light.* nd. Book Club. dj. VG. P1. $4.50

ZELAZNY, Roger. *Madwand.* nd. Book Club. dj. EX. P1. $4.00

ZELAZNY, Roger. *Madwand.* 1981. Phantasia. 1/750. sgn. dj. slipcase. EX. P1. $60.00

ZELAZNY, Roger. *Roadmarks.* 1979. Del Rey. 1st ed. dj. EX. P1. $25.00

ZELAZNY, Roger. *Sign of Chaos.* 1987. Arbor House. 1st ed. dj. EX. P1. $15.95

ZELAZNY, Roger. *Unicorn Variations.* nd. Book Club. dj. EX. P1. $5.00

ZELAZNY, Roger. *Unicorn Variations.* 1983. Timescape. 1st ed. dj. EX. $30.00

ZEMPEL & VERKLER. *First Editions: Guide to Identification.* 1989. Peoria. Expanded 2nd ed. 307 p. dj. T5. $28.00

ZERN, Ed. *How To Tell Fish From Fishermen.* 1947. Appleton Century. Ils. VG. $7.50

ZERN, Ed. *To Hell With Fishing.* 1945. Ils Webster. 1st ed. dj. EX. $12.00

ZERNER, Henri. *School of Fontainebleau: Etchings & Engravings.* 1969. NY. Abrams. Trans Baron. Ils. 316 p. D2. $225.00

ZETLIN, Mihail. *Decembrists.* 1958. Free Pr Glencoe. 1st ed. J2. $15.00

ZEUNER, Frederick. *History of Domesticated Animals.* 1963. Harper. J2. $30.00

ZHIMING, D. *Dinosaurs From China.* 1988. British Mus. color photos. 114 p. M. M2. $20.00

ZIEMKE, Earl F. *German N Theater of Operations, 1940-1945.* 1959. WA. Ils. 10 fld maps. 342 p. G. T5. $37.50

ZIESLER & HOFER. *Safari: E African Diaries of Wildlife Photographer.* 1984. Facts on File. 133 color photos. 197 p. dj. M2. $25.00

ZIFF, Paul. *J.M. Hanson.* 1962. Ithaca. Cornell U. Ils. D2. $30.00

ZIGROSSER, Carl. *Prints & Their Creators: World History.* 1974. NY. Crown. Revised 2nd ed. 136 p. dj. D2. $75.00

ZIGROSSER, Carl. *Six Centuries of Fine Prints.* 1939. NY. Garden City. Ils. 406 p. D2. $50.00

ZILBOORG, Gregory. *History of Medical Psychology.* 1941. NY. Norton. 1st ed. 606 p. dj. VG. $25.00

ZIMEN, E. *Wolf: His Place in the Natural World.* 1981. Souvenir. 42 color photos. 373 p. dj. EX. M2. $18.00

ZIMEN, E. *Wolf: Species in Danger.* 1981. Delacorte. Ils 1st Am ed. 373 p. dj. EX. M2. $24.00

ZIMILES & ZIMILES. *Early American Mills.* 1973. NY. 1st ed. 4to. 290 p. dj. EX. G1. $27.00

ZIMMER, J.T. *Birds of Thomas County (NE) Forest Reserve.* 1913. NE Ornith Union. later cover. M2. $4.00

ZIMMERMAN, C.L. *White Eagle.* 1941. Harrisburg. VG. $50.00

ZIMROTH, P.L. *Perversions of Justice.* 1974. Viking. 1st ed. dj. VG. $16.00

ZINSSER, Hans. *Rats, Lice & History.* 1935. NY. $12.50

ZINSSER, W.K. *Search & Research: Collections & Uses.* 1961. NY. $35.00

ZINSSER. *TB of Bacteriology.* 1922. NY. Ils 5th ed. 8vo. 1193 p. VG. $40.00

ZOCHERT, Donald. *Man of Glass.* 1981. Holt Rinehart. 1st ed. dj. VG. P1. $12.50

ZOLA, Emile. *Nana.* 1950. Perma Giants. VG. P1. $12.50

ZOLA, Emile. *Nana.* 1976. Norwalk. Heritage. quarto. slipcase. EX. $15.00

ZOLOTOW, Maurice. *Billy Wilder in Hollywood.* 1977. NY. dj. EX. $15.00

ZOLOTOW, Maurice. *Shooting Star.* 1974. NY. 1st ed. VG. B2. $22.50

ZUCCOTTI, Susan. *Italians & the Holocaust.* 1987. NY. 1st ed. dj. EX. $7.50

ZUCKERMAN, George. *Last Flapper.* 1969. Little Brown. 1st ed. dj. EX. T6. $20.00

ZUCKERMAN, L. *Great Zoos of the World: Their Origin & Significance.* 1980. Weidenfeld. Ils. 231 p. dj. EX. M2. $18.00

ZUCKERMAN, S. *Social Life of Monkeys & Apes.* 1981. London. reprint of 1932 ed. dj. EX. M2. $18.00

ZUKOFSKY, Louis. *A.* 1977. CA U. 1st ed. dj. J2. $15.00

ZUKOFSKY, Louis. *Little.* 1970. Grossman. 1st ed. dj. J2. $17.50

ZUKOFSKY, Louis. *Prepositions: Collected Critical Essays.* 1967. Horizon. 1st ed. dj. J2. $12.50

ZUSI, R.L. *Structural Adaptations of Head & Neck in the Black Skimmer.* 1962. Nuttall Ornith Club. 101 p. M2. $10.00

ZWEIG, Stefan. *Amok. Novelellan Einer Leidenschaft.* 1922. Leipzig. 1st ed. inscr/sgn. 295 p. EX. $175.00

ZWEITE, Armin. *Alexej Jawlensky.* 1983. Munich. Prestel. Ils. 360 p. D2. $125.00

ZWETSCH, James Carlton. *Handy Guide to First Aid.* 1937. Whitman. VG. P1. $5.00

ZWINGER, A. *Desert Country Near the Sea: Natural History of Baja, CA.* 1983. Harper Row. Ils 1st ed. 399 p. dj. EX. M2. $20.00

Bookbuyers

In this section of the book we have listed buyers of books and related material. When you correspond with these dealers, be sure to enclose a self-addressed stamped envelope if you want a reply. Do not send lists of books for appraisal. If you wish to sell your books, quote the price you want or send a list and ask if there are any they might be interested in and the price they would be willing to pay. If you want the list back, be sure to send a S.A.S.E. large enough for the listing to be returned. When you list your books, do so by author, full title, publisher and place, date, edition, and condition, noting any defects on cover or contents.

African-American Literature & History
Gordon & Gordon Booksellers
P.O. Box 128
W Park, NY 12493

Alcoholics Anonymous
1939-1954
Paul Melzer Fine Books
P.O. Box 1143
Redlands, CA 92373
714-792-7299

American Fiction
20th Century.
Mason's Rare & Used Books
115 S Main St.
Chambersburg, PA 17201
717-261-0541

Americana
Art Source International
1237 Pearl St.
Boulder, CO 80302
303-444-4080

The Bookseller Inc.
521 W Exchange St.
Akron, OH 44302
216-762-3101

Gordon Totty
Scarce Paper Americana
347 Shady Lake Parkway
Baton Rouge, La 70810
504-766-8625

John L. Heflin Jr.
5708 Brentwood Trace
Brentwood, TN 37027
615-373-2917

Ellen Roth
47 Truman Dr.
Marlboro, NJ 07746

Bernard Rogers, Bookseller
P.O. Box 149
Winterville, GA 30683-0149
404-742-8047

Bookmine
1015 2nd St.
Old Sacramento, CA 95814

Jim Hodgson Books
908 S Manlius St.
Fayetteville, NY 13066

Susan Heller/Pages for Sages
P.O. Box 22219
Beachwood, OH 44122

The Book Inn
6401 University
Lubbock, TX 79413
806-793-0342

Homebiz Books & More
2919 Mistwood Forest Dr.
Chester, VA 23831-7043

Fritz T. Brown Books
5 Claremont Pl.
Cranford, NJ 07016

K.C. Owings
P.O. Box 19
N Abington, MA 02351
617-857-1655

Animation Art
Cohen Books & Collectibles
P.O. Box 810310
Boca Raton, FL 33481

Antiques & Collectibles
Homebiz Books & More
2919 Mistwood Forest Dr.
Chester, VA 23831-7043

Archery
Melvin Marcher, Bookseller
6204 N Vermont
Oklahoma City, OK 73112

Art
Heritage Book Shop, Inc.
8540 Melrose Ave.
Los Angeles, CA 90069
213-659-3674

Significant Books
3053 Madison Rd.
Cincinnati, OH 45209

Fine & applied art books & catalogs
Hours by appointment.
Davis & Schorr Art Books
P.O. Box 56054
Sherman Oaks, CA 91413-1054
818-787-1322

Atlases & Maps
Bernard Rogers, Bookseller
P.O. Box 149
Winterville, GA 30683-0149
404-742-8047

Gordon Totty
Scarce Paper Americana
347 Shady Lake Parkway
Baton Rouge, LA 70810
504-766-8625

Art Source International
1237 Pearl St.
Boulder, CO 80302
303-444-4080

Autographs
Letters, manuscripts, documents.
Paul Melzer Fine Books
P.O. Box 1143
Redlands, CA 92373
714-792-7299

K.C. Owings
P.O. Box 19
N Abington, MA 02351
617-857-1655

Heritage Book Shop, Inc.
8540 Melrose Ave.
Los Angeles, CA 90069
213-659-3674

Aviation
The Bookseller, Inc.
521 W Exchange St.
Akron, OH 44302

Baseball
Mason's Rare & Used Books
115 S Main St.
Chambersburg, PA 17201
717-261-0541

Biographies
Ellen Roth
47 Truman Dr.
Marlboro, NJ 07746

Black American Fiction & Poetry
Mason's Rare & Used Books
115 S Main St.
Chambersburg, PA 17201
717-261-0541

Black Hills
Allen J. Petersen, Books
809-20 St. S
Fargo, ND 58103

Book Search Service
Avonlea Books
P.O. Box 74, Main Station
White Plains, NY 10602
914-946-5923

Ellen Roth
47 Truman Dr.
Marlboro, NJ 07746

Bookmine
1015 2nd St.
Old Sacramento, CA 95814

Fritz T. Brown Books
5 Claremont Pl.
Cranford, NJ 07016

Books About Books
Camelot Books
P.O. Box 2883
Vista, CA 92083
619-940-9472

Susan Heller/Pages for Sages
P.O. Box 22219
Beachwood, OH 44122

Bottles
Homebiz Books & More
2919 Mistwood Forest Dr.
Chester, VA 23831-7043

Boys Series
Harland H. Eastman
P.O. Box 276, 66 Main St.
Springvale, ME 04083

California
Old, Unusual.
Paul Melzer Fine Books
P.O. Box 1143
Redlands, CA 92373
714-792-7299

Marc Chagall
Fine illustrated.
Paul Melzer Fine Books
P.O. Box 1143
Redlands, CA 92373
741-792-7299

Children's Illustrated
Bookmine
1015 2nd St.
Old Sacramento, CA 95814

Book Treasures
P.O. Box 121
E Norwich, NY 11732

Agatha Christie
Dale Weber Books
5740 Livernois
Rochester, MI 48064

Sir W.S. Churchill
Dale Weber Books
5740 Livernois
Rochester, MI 48064

Civil War
Burke's Bookstore, Inc.
1719 Poplar Ave.
Memphis, TN 38104

Mason's Rare & Used Books
115 S Main St.
Chambersburg, PA 17201
717-261-0541

John L. Heflin Jr.
5708 Brentwood Trace
Brentwood, TN 37027
615-373-2917

K.C. Owings
P.O. Box 19
N Abington, MA 02351
617-857-1655

Gordon Totty
Scarce Paper Americana
347 Shady Lake Parkway
Baton Rouge, LA 70810
504-766-8625

Homebiz Books & More
2919 Mistwood Forest Dr.
Chester, VA 23831-7043

Collector Paperbacks
Pandora's Books Ltd.
P.O. Box BB-54
Neche, ND 48265

Cook Books
Significant Books
3053 Madison Rd.
Cincinnati, OH 45209

Country Living
The Abstract
4850 W Mooresville Rd.
Indianapolis, IN 46241

Dakota Territory
Allen J. Petersen, Books
809-20 St. S.
Fargo, ND 58103

Detective Fiction
The Book Baron
1236 S Magnolia Ave.
Anaheim, Ca 92804
714-527-7022

Disney
Pre-1950.
Cohen Books & Collectibles
P.O. Box 810310
Boca Raton, FL 33481

Documents
Gordon Totty
Scarce Paper Americana
347 Shady Lake Parkway
Baton Rouge, LA 70810

Early Travel, Exploration & Voyages
Heritage Book Shop, Inc.
8540 Melrose Ave.
Los Angeles, CA 90069
213-659-3675

Jim Hodgson Books
908 S Manlius St.
Fayetteville, NY 13066

Art Source International
1237 Pearl St.
Boulder, CO 80302
303-444-4080

Older material.
Paul Melzer Fine Books
P.O. Box 11437
Redlands, CA 92373
714-792-7299

Fine Bindings
Heritage Book Shop, Inc.
8540 Melrose Ave.
Los Angeles, CA 90069
213-659-3674

Susan Heller/Pages for Sages
P.O. Box 22219
Beachwood, OH 44122

James Cummins, Bookseller
Country Annex, Box 232
Pottersville, NJ 07979

Firearms & Edged Weapons
Melvin Marcher, Bookseller
6204 N Vermont
Oklahoma City, OK 73112

First Editions
Burke's Bookstore, Inc.
1719 Poplar Ave.
Memphis, TN 38104

Susan Heller/Pages for Sages
P.O. Box 22219
Beachwood, OH 44122

Bookmine
1015 2nd St.
Old Sacramento, CA 95814

Heritage Book Shop, Inc.
8540 Melrose Ave.
Los Angeles, CA 90069
213-659-3674

This Side of Paradise
P.O. Box 31994
Charleston, SC 29417

Ellen Roth
47 Truman Dr.
Marlboro, NJ 07746

Bernard Rogers, Bookseller
P.O. Box 149
Winterville, GA 30683-0149
404-742-8047

James Cummins, Bookseller
Country Annex, Box 232
Pottersville, NJ 07979

Fishing
Jim Hodgson Books
908 S Manlius St.
Fayetteville, NY 13066

Melvin Marcher, Bookseller
6204 N Vermont
Oklahoma City, OK 73112

Fore-Edged Painted Books
This Side of Paradise
P.O. Box 31994
Charleston, SC 294170

Gambling & Gaming
Gambler's Book Club
630 S Eleventh St.
Las Vegas, NV 89101
702-382-7555

Genealogy & Local History
Fritz T. Brown Books
5 Claremont Pl.
Cranford, NJ 07016

Geology
Art Source International
1237 Pearl St.
Boulder, CO 80302
303-444-4080

General Antiquarian
Bookmine
1015 2nd St.
Old Sacramento, CA 95814

General Out-of-Print
Bicentennial Book Shop
820 S Westnedge Ave.
Kalamazoo, MI 49008
616-345-5987

Ellen Roth
47 Truman Dr.
Marlboro, NJ 07746

James Cummins, Bookseller
Country Annex, Box 232
Pottersville, NJ 07979

The Book Inn
6410 University
Lubbock, TX 79413

The Abstract
4850 W Mooresville Rd.
Indianapolis, IN 46241

Gene Vinik Books
2213 E Copper St.
Tucson, AZ 85719

Tuttle Antiquarian Books, Inc.
P.O. Box 541
Rutland, VT 05701

Significant Books
3053 Madison Rd.
Cincinnati, OH 45209

Glass
Homebiz Books & More
2919 Mistwood Forest Dr.
Chester, VA 23831-7043

Golf
Mason's Rare & Used Books
115 S Main St.
Chambersburg, PA 17201

Guidebooks
Art Source International
1237 Pearl St.
Boulder, CO 80302
303-444-4080

History
Regional & local.
Significant Books
3053 Madison Rd.
Cincinnati, OH 45209

Horticulture
Abstract
4850 W Mooresville Rd.
Indianapolis, IN 46241

Horror
Pandora's Books Ltd.
P.O. Box BB-54
Neche, ND 58265

Hunting
Jim Hodgson Books
908 S Manlius St.
Fayetteville, NY 13066

Melvin Marcher, Bookseller
6204 N Vermont
Oklahoma City, OK 73112

Illustrated Books
Bernard Rogers, Bookseller
P.O. Box 149
Winterville, GA 30683-0149
404-742-8047

Book Treasures
P.O. Box 121
E Norwich, NY 11732

Susan Heller/Pages for Sages
P.O. Box 22219
Beachwood, OH 44122

James Cummins, Bookseller
Country Annex, Box 232
Pottersville, NJ 07979

Indians & Indian Wars
Art Source International
1237 Pearl St.
Boulder, CO 80302
303-444-4080

James Joyce
Paul Melzer Fine Books
P.O. Box 1143
Redlands, CA 92373
714-792-7299

Juvenile
Harland H. Eastman
P.O. Box 276, 66 Main St.
Springvale, ME 04083

Gordon & Gordon Booksellers
P.O. Box 128
W Park, NY 12493

Susan Heller/Pages for Sages
P.O. Box 22219
Beachwood, OH 44122

Ellen Roth
47 Truman Dr.
Marlboro, NJ 07746

King Arthur
Camelot Books
P.O. Box 2883
Vista, CA 92083
619-940-9472

Stephen King
Dale Weber Books
5740 Livernois
Rochester, MI 48064

Literature
Susan Heller/Pages for Sages
P.O. Box 22219
Beachwood, OH 44122

This Side of Paradise
P.O. Box 31994
Charleston, SC 29417

James Cummins, Bookseller
Country Annex, Box 232
Pottersville, NJ 07979

Maine
*Authors, non-fiction, local, county &
state history.*
Harland H. Eastman
P.O. Box 276, 66 Main St.
Springvale, ME 04083

Manuscripts
Heritage Book Shop, Inc.
8540 Melrose Ave.
Los Angeles, CA 90069
213-659-3674

Mathematics
Significant Books
3053 Madison Rd.
Cincinnati, OH 45209

Medical
Significant Books
3053 Madison Rd.
Cincinnati, OH 45209

Bookmine
1015 2nd St.
Old Sacramento, CA 95814

Medieval
Camelot Books
P.O. Box 2883
Vista, CA 92083
619-940-9472

Merlin
Camelot Books
P.O. Box 2883
Vista, CA 92083
619-940-9472

Militaria
The Bookseller, Inc.
521 W Exchange St.
Akron, OH 44302

Gordon Totty
Scarce Paper Americana
347 Shady Lake Parkway
Baton Rouge, LA 70810
504-766-8625

Significant Books
3053 Madison Rd.
Cincinnati, OH 45209

Mississippi
Choctaw Books
406 Manship St.
Jackson, MS 39212

L.M. Montgomery
Avonlea Books
P.O. Box 74, Main Station
White Plains, NY 10602
914-946-5923

Mystery
Pandora's Books Ltd.
P.O. Box BB-54
Neche, ND 48265

Camelot Books
P.O. Box 2883
Vista, CA 92083
619-940-9472

Natural History
Melvin Marcher, Bookseller
6204 N Vermont
Oklahoma City, OK 73112

The Abstract
4850 W Mooresville Rd.
Indianapolis, IN 46241

Newspapers
Gordon Totty
Scarce Paper Americana
347 Shady Lake Parkway
Baton Rouge, LA 70810
504-766-8625

North Dakota
Allen J. Petersen, Books
809-20 St. S
Fargo, ND 48103

Occult
Significant Books
3053 Madison Rd.
Cincinnati, OH 45209

Ohio
The Bookseller, Inc.
521 W Exchange St.
Akron, OH 44302

Pennsylvania
Mason's Rare & Used Books
115 S Main St.
Chambersburg, PA 17201
717-261-0541

Photography
Significant Books
3053 Madison Rd.
Cincinnati, OH 45209

Susan Heller/Pages for Sages
P.O. Box 22219
Beachwood, OH 44122

Edgar Allan Poe
Dale Weber Books
5740 Livernois
Rochester, MI 48064

Press Books
Heritage Book Shop, Inc.
8540 Melrose Ave.
Los Angeles, CA 90069
213-659-3674

Susan Heller/Pages for Sages
P.O. Box 22219
Beachwood, OH 44122

Pulp Magazines
Pandora's Books Ltd.
P.O. Box BB-54
Neche, ND 58265

Railroads & Railroadiana
Mason's Rare & Used Books
115 S Main St.
Chambersburg, PA 17201

Rare & Unusual Books
Gene Vinik Books
2213 E Copper St.
Tucson, AZ 85719

Paul Melzer Fine Books
P.O. Box 1143
Redlands, Ca 92373; 714-792-7299

James Cummins, Bookseller
Country Annex, Box 232
Pottersville, NJ 07979

Heritage Book Shop, Inc.
8540 Melrose Ave.
Los Angeles, CA 90069
213-659-3674

Susan Heller/Pages for Sages
P.O. Box 22219
Beachwood, OH 44122

Revolutionary War
K.C. Owings
P.O. Box 19
N Abington, MA 02351
617-857-1655

Roycroft Press
Dale Weber Books
5740 Livernois
Rochester, MI 48064

Science
Art Source International
1237 Pearl St.
Boulder, CO 80302
303-444-4080

Significant Books
3053 Madison Rd.
Cincinnati, OH 45209

Science Fiction
The Book Baron
1236 S Magnolia Ave.
Anaheim, CA 92804
714-527-7022

Pandora's Books Ltd.
P.O. Box BB-54
Neche, ND 58265

Signed Editions
Susan Heller/Pages for Sages
P.O. Box 22219
Beachwood, OH 44122

Sports
James Cummins, Bookseller
Country Annex, Box 232
Pottersville, NJ 07979

Significant Books
3053 Madison Rd.
Cincinnati, OH 45209

The South
Bernard Rogers, Bookseller
P.O. Box 149
Winterville, GA 30683-0149
404-742-8047

Burke's Bookstore, Inc.
1719 Poplar Ave.
Memphis, TN 38104

This Side of Paradise
P.O. Box 31994
Charleston, SC 29417

History & literature.
Choctaw Books
406 Manship St.
Jackson, MS 39212

South Carolina
This Side of Paradise
P.O. Box 31994
Charleston, SC 29417

Transportation
Bookmine
1015 2nd St.
Old Sacramento, CA 95814

The Bookseller Inc.
521 W Exchange St.
Akron, OH 44302
216-762-3101

Treasure Hunting
Homebiz Books & More
2919 Mistwood Forest Dr.
Chester, VA 23831-7043

Virginia
'A Likely Story!'
738 W 22nd St. #6
Norfolk, VA 23517

Western Americana
Allen J. Petersen, Books
809-20 St. S
Fargo, ND 58103

The Book Baron
1236 S Magnolia Ave.
Anaheim, CA 92804
714-527-7022

Pandora's Books Ltd.
P.O. Box BB-54
Neche, ND 58265

Westerns
The Book Baron
1236 S Magnolia Ave.
Anaheim, CA 92804
714-527-7022

Pandora's Books Ltd.
P.O. Box BB-54
Neche, ND 58265

Woman Authors
British Stamp Exchange
12 Fairlawn Ave.
N Weymouth, MA 02191

World Wars I & II
The Bookseller Inc.
521 W Exchange St.
Akron, OH 44302
216-762-3101

Also all other wars.
British Stamp Exchange
12 Fairlawn Ave.
N Weymouth, MA 02191

Booksellers

This section of the book lists names and addresses of used book dealers who have contributed the retail listings contained in this edition of *Huxford's Old Book Value Guide*. The code (A1, S7, etc.) located before the price in some of our listings refers to the dealer offering that particular book for sale. Given below are the dealer names and their codes.

A1
'A Likely Story!'
738 W 22nd St. #6
Norfolk, VA 23517

A2
Allen J. Peterson, Books
809-20 St. S
Fargo, ND 58103

A3
Art Source International
1237 Pearl St.
Boulder, CO 80302
303-444-4080

A4
Artis Books
P.O. Box 822
Alpena, MI 49707-0822

A5
Avonlea Books
P.O. Box 74, Main Station
White Plains, NY 10602
914-946-5923

B1
Bernard Rogers, Bookseller
P.O. Box 149
Winterville, GA 30683-0149
404-742-8047

B2
Bicentennial Book Shop
820 S Westnedge Ave.
Kalamazoo, MI 49008
616-345-5987

B3
Book Baron
1236 S Magnolia Ave.
Anaheim, CA 92804
714-527-7022

B4
Book Treasures
P.O. Box 121
E Norwich, NY 11732

B5
Bookmine
1015 2nd St.
Old Sacramento, CA 94814

B6
British Stamp Exchange
12 Fairlawn Ave.
N Weymouth, MA 02191

B7
Burke's Bookstore, Inc.
1719 Poplar Ave.
Memphis, TN 38104

C1
Camelot Books
P.O. Box 2883
Vista, CA 92083
619-940-9472

C2
Choctaw Books
406 Manship St.
Jackson, MS 39212

C3
Cohen Books & Collectibles
P.O. Box 81030
Boca Raton, FL 33481

C4
Cover to Cover
P.O. Box 687
Chapel Hill, NC 27514

D1
Dale Weber Books
5740 Livernois
Rochester, MI 48064
313-651-3177

D2
Davis & Schorr Art Books
P.O. Box 56054
Sherman Oaks, CA 91413-1054
818-787-1322

E1
Elder's Book Store
2115 Elliston Pl.
Nashville, TN 37205

E2
Ellen Roth
47 Truman Dr.
Marlboro, NJ 07746

F1
Fritz T. Brown Books
5 Claremont Pl.
Cranford, NJ 07016

G1
Gene Vinik Books
2213 E Copper St.
Tucson, AZ 85719

G2
Gordon & Gordon Booksellers
P.O. Box 128
W Park, NY 12493

G3
Gordon Totty
Scarce Paper Americana
347 Shady Lake Parkway
Baton Rouge, LA 70810
504-766-8625

G4
Gambler's Book Club
630 S 11th St.
Las Vegas, NV 89101
701-382-7555

H1
Harland H. Eastman
P.O. Box 276, 66 Main St.
Springvale, ME 04083

H2
Heritage Book Shop, Inc.
8540 Melrose Ave.
Los Angeles, CA 90069
213-659-3674

H3
Homebiz Books & More
2919 Mistood Forest Dr.
Chester, VA 23831-7043

J1
J. Arthur Robinson, Bookseller
56413 29 Palms Hwy.
Yucca Valley, CA 92284

J2
James Cummins, Bookseller
Country Annex, Box 232
Pottersville, NJ 07979

J3
Jim Hodgson Books
908 S Manlius St.
Fayetteville, NY 13066

J4
John L. Heflin Jr.
5708 Brentwood Trace
Brentwood, TN 37027
615-373-2917

K1
K.C. Owings
P.O. Box 19
N Abington, MA 02351
617-857-1655

M1
Mason's Rare & Used Books
115 S Main St.
Chambersburg, PA 17701
717-261-0541

M2
Melvin Marcher, Bookseller
6204 N Vermont
Oklahoma City, OK 73112

P1
Pandora's Books Ltd.
P.O. Box BB-54
Neche, ND 58265

P2
Parnassus Books
218 N 9th St.
Boise, ID 83702

P3
Paul Melzer Fine Books
P.O. Box 1143
Redlands, CA 92373
714-792-7299

R1
Ron's Reading Room
235 Wilbar Dr.
Stratford, CT 06497

S1
Significant Books
3053 Madison Rd.
Cincinnati, OH 45209

S2
Susan Heller/Pages for Sages
P.O. Box 22219
Beachwood, OH 44122

T1
Terry Harper, Bookseller
P.O. Box 37
Bristol, VT 05443-0037

T2
The Abstract
4850 W Mooresville Rd.
Indianapolis, IN 46241

T3
The Book Inn
6401 University
Lubbock, TX 79413
806-793-0342

T4
The Book Stop III
1440 E Charleston Blvd.
Las Vegas, NV 89104

T5
The Bookseller, Inc.
521 W Exchange St.
Akron, OH 44302

T6
This Side of Paradise
P.O. Box 31994
Charleston, SC 29417

T7
Tuttle Antiquarian Books, Inc.
P.O. Box 541
Rutland, VT 04701

V1
Volume I Books
407 Augusta St.
Greenville, SC 29601

Schroeder's Antiques
Price Guide

Schroeder's Antiques Price Guide has become THE household name in the antiques & collectibles field. Our team of editors work year around with more than 200 contributors to bring you our #1 best-selling book on antiques & collectibles.

With more than 50,000 items identified & priced, *Schroeder's* is a must for the collector & dealer alike. If it merits the interest of today's collector, you'll find it in *Schroeder's.* Each subject is represented with histories and background information. In addition, hundreds of sharp original photos are used each year to illustrate not only the rare and unusual, but the everyday "fun-type" collectibles as well -- not postage stamp pictures, but large close-up shots that show important details clearly.

Our editors compile a new book each year. Never do we merely change prices. Accuracy is our primary aim. Prices are gathered over the entire year previous to publication, from ads and personal contacts. Then each category is thoroughly checked to spot inconsistencies, listings that may not be entirely reflective of actual market dealings, and lines too vague to be of merit. Only the best of the lot remains for publication. You'll find *Schroeder's Antiques Price Guide* the one to buy for factual information and quality.

No dealer, collector or investor can afford not to own this book. It is available from your favorite bookseller or antiques dealer at the low price of $12.95. If you are unable to find this price guide in your area, it's available from Collector Books, P.O. Box 3009, Paducah, KY 42001 at $12.95 plus $2.00 for postage and handling.

8½ x 11", 608 Pages   **$12.95**

COLLECTOR BOOKS
A Division of Schroeder Publishing Co., Inc.